Map

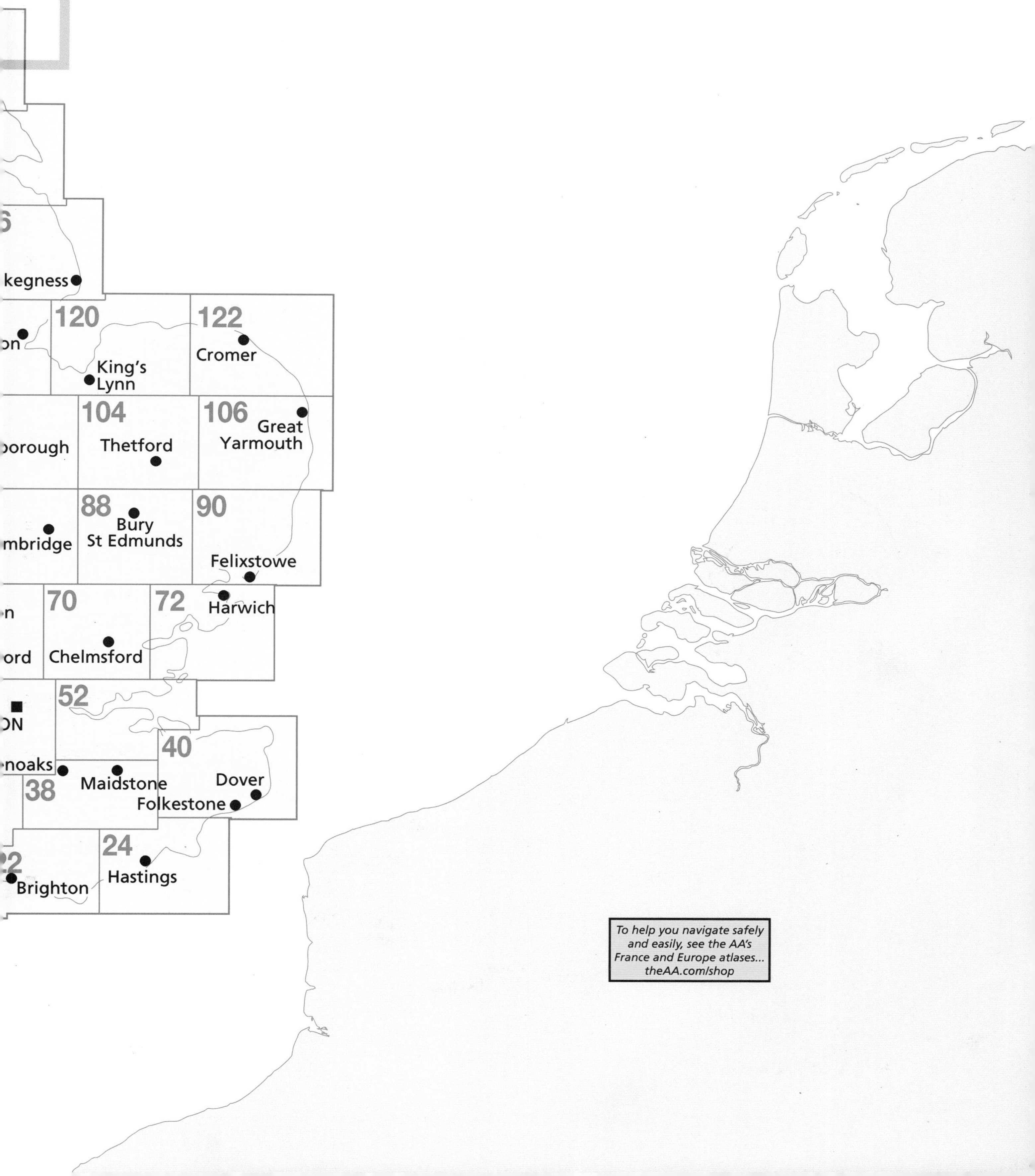

6

kegness

120

on

King's
Lynn

122

Cromer

104

borough

Thetford

106

Great
Yarmouth

88

mbridge

Bury
St Edmunds

90

Felixstowe

70

n

Chelmsford

72

Harwich

52

ON

40

noaks

Maidstone

Dover

38

Folkestone

22

24

Brighton

Hastings

*To help you navigate safely
and easily, see the AA's
France and Europe atlases...
theAA.com/shop*

EASY READ
BRITAIN

Atlas contents

Map pages south	**inside front cover**
Route planner	*II–VII*
Atlas symbols	*VIII–1*
Road maps 1:148,000 scale	**2–283**
Channel Islands 1:100,000 scale	9
Isle of Man 1:200,000 scale	154
Orkney Islands 1:450,000 scale	275
Shetland Islands 1:450,000 scale	281
Western Isles 1:480,000 scale	282–283
Restricted junctions	**284–285**
Index to place names	**286–368**
County, administrative area map	286–287
Map pages north	**inside back cover**

18th edition June 2017

© AA Media Limited 2017
Original edition printed 2000.

Cartography: All cartography in this atlas edited, designed and produced by the Mapping Services Department of AA Publishing (A05506).

This atlas contains Ordnance Survey data © Crown copyright and database right 2017.

Publisher's notes: Published by AA Publishing (a trading name of AA Media Limited, whose registered office is Fanum House, Basing View, Basingstoke, Hampshire RG21 4EA, UK. Registered number 06112600).

ISBN: 978 0 7495 7857 2

A CIP catalogue record for this book is available from The British Library.

Disclaimer: The contents of this atlas are believed to be correct at the time of the latest revision, it will not contain any subsequent amended, new or temporary information including diversions and traffic control or enforcement systems. The publishers cannot be held responsible or liable for any loss or damage occasioned to any person acting or refraining from action as a result of any use or reliance on material in this atlas, nor for any errors, omissions or changes in such material. This does not affect your statutory rights.

The publishers would welcome information to correct any errors or omissions and to keep this atlas up to date. Please write to the Atlas Editor, AA Publishing, The Automobile Association, Fanum House, Basing View, Basingstoke, Hampshire RG21 4EA, UK.
E-mail: *roadatlasfeedback@theaa.com*

Acknowledgements: AA Publishing would like to thank the following for their assistance in producing this atlas: Crematoria data provided by Cremation Society of Great Britain. Cadw, English Heritage, Forestry Commission, Historic Scotland, Johnsons, National Trust and National Trust for Scotland, RSPB, The Wildlife Trust, Scottish Natural Heritage, Natural England, The Countryside Council for Wales. Award winning beaches from 'Blue Flag' and 'Keep Scotland Beautiful' (summer 2016 data): for latest information visit *www.blueflag.org* and *www.keepscotlandbeautiful.org*

Printer: Printed in Romania by G. Canale & C. S.p.A.

Scale 1:148,000
or 2.34 miles to 1 inch

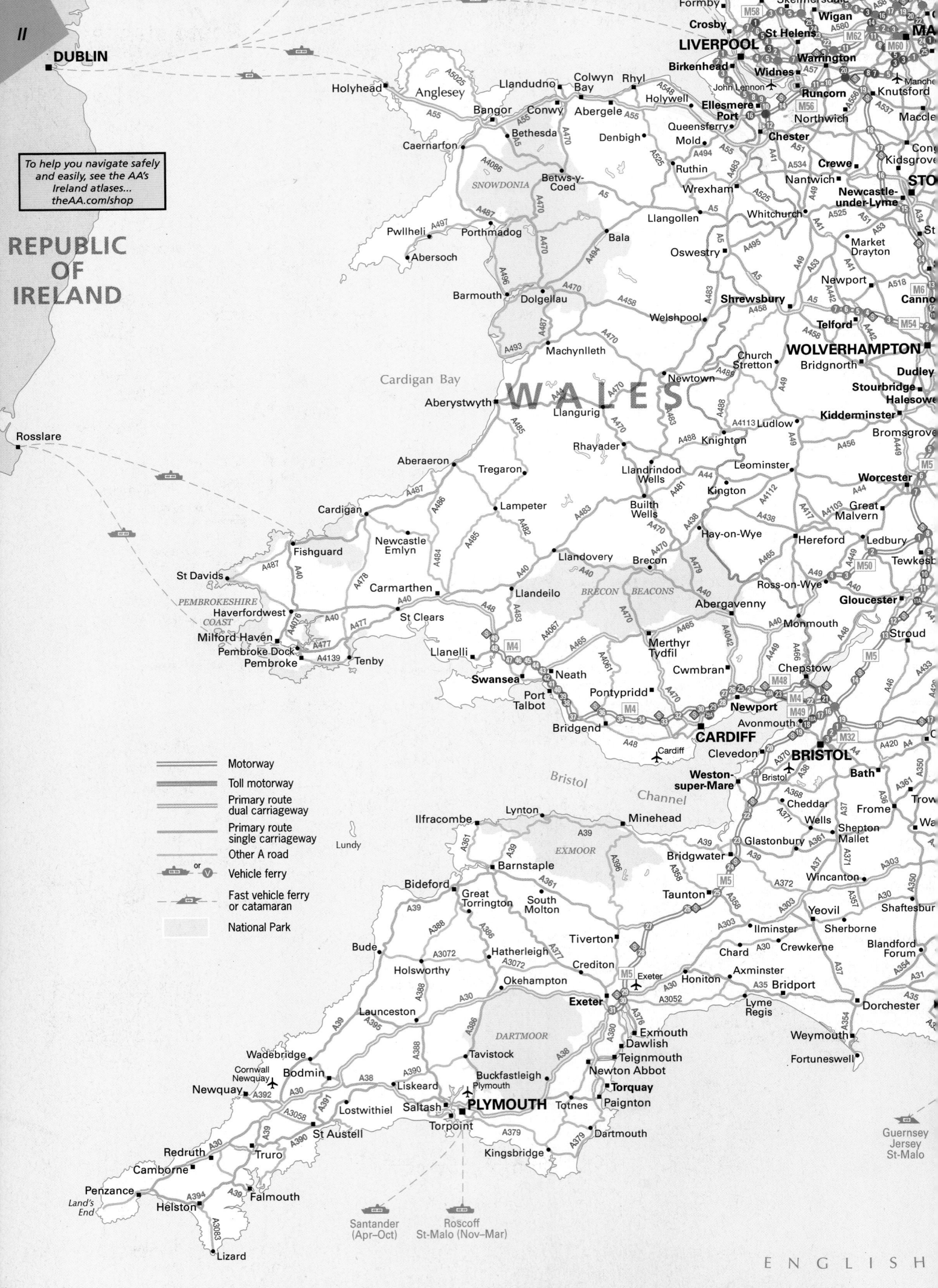

DUBLIN

Holyhead

Anglesey
A5025

A55 Bangor
Bethesda
Caernarfon

A4086

SNOWDONIA

Llandudno
Colwyn Bay
Conwy
Abergele
A55

Rhyl
Holywell

Denbigh

Betws-y-Coed

A470

A5

Llangollen

Oswestry

REPUBLIC
OF
IRELAND

To help you navigate safely
and easily, see the AA's
Ireland atlases...
theAA.com/shop

Pwllheli
Abersoch

A497

Porthmadog

A496

Barmouth

A487

A493

Dolgellau

Machynlleth

A470

A487

A458 Welshpool

Bala

Newtown

A470

Cardigan Bay

Aberystwyth

Llangurig

A485

Rhayader

A470

Knighton

Llandrindod
Wells

Tregaron

A487

Aberaeron

A482

Lampeter

A483

Builth
Wells

A470

Hay-on-Wye

Cardigan

A486

A484

A485

Llandovery

Brecon

A40

A479

Newcastle
Emlyn

Fishguard

A487

A40

St Davids

A478

Carmarthen

A48

Llandeilo

A463

BRECON BEACONS

A465

Abergavenny

PEMBROKESHIRE
COAST

Haverfordwest

A40

St Clears

A4067

A470

A40

Monmouth

A4042

Milford Haven
Pembroke Dock
Pembroke

A477

A4139

Tenby

Llanelli

A465

Merthyr
Tydfil

Cwmbran

Chepstow

Swansea

Neath

A4061

M4

Port
Talbot

Pontypridd

A470

Newport

Avonmouth

Bridgend

A48

CARDIFF

Cardiff

Clevedon

Rosslare

Lundy

Ilfracombe

Lynton

Minehead

Weston-
super-Mare

Bristol

Bristol

Channel

Cheddar

A371

Wells

A361

EXMOOR

A39

A396

A39

Bridgwater

A38

Shepton
Mallet

A361 Barnstaple

Glastonbury

Bideford

Great
Torrington

South
Molton

A361

A372

Taunton

M5

Wincanton

Bude

A388

A386

A39

Holsworthy

A3072

Hatherleigh

A377

Tiverton

Crediton

A30

Honiton

Chard

Crewkerne

Yeovil

Ilminster

Sherborne

Shaftesbur

Blandford
Forum

A3072

A386

Okehampton

M5

Exeter

A3052

Axminster

A35 Bridport

Launceston

A388

A30

Exeter

A376

A380

DARTMOOR

Exmouth

Dawlish

Lyme
Regis

Dorchester

Wadebridge

A30

Bodmin

A38

Tavistock

Buckfastleigh

Teignmouth
Newton Abbot

Weymouth

Fortuneswell

Cornwall
Newquay

Newquay

A392

Liskeard

Plymouth

Torquay
Paignton

Lostwithiel

Saltash

PLYMOUTH

Totnes

St Austell

Torpoint

A379

Redruth

Truro

A390

A39

Kingsbridge

A379

Dartmouth

Guernsey
Jersey
St-Malo

Camborne

Penzance

A394

Falmouth

Land's
End

Helston

A3083

Lizard

Santander
(Apr–Oct)

Roscoff
St-Malo (Nov–Mar)

ENGLISH

Motorway
Toll motorway
Primary route
dual carriageway
Primary route
single carriageway
Other A road
or V Vehicle ferry
Fast vehicle ferry
or catamaran
National Park

Ormskirk
Formby
Skelmersdale
Bolton
Crosby
Wigan
M58
St Helens
LIVERPOOL
Birkenhead
Widnes
Warrington
Runcorn
Manche
Knutsford
John Lennon
Ellesmere
Port
Northwich
Maccle
Queensferry
Chester
Mold
A51
Crewe
Ruthin
A534
Nantwich
Kidsgrove
Wrexham
A525
Whitchurch
Market
Drayton
STO
St
Newport
A41
M6
Shrewsbury
Canno
Church
Stretton
Telford
M54
WOLVERHAMPTON
Bridgnorth
Dudley
Stourbridge
Halesowe
Ludlow
Kidderminster
Leominster
Bromsgrove
Worcester
Kington
Great
Malvern
M5
Hereford
Ledbury
Ross-on-Wye
M50
Tewkesb
Gloucester
Stroud
M5
M48
M4
M49
BRISTOL
Bath
M32
Trow
A350
Frome
Wa

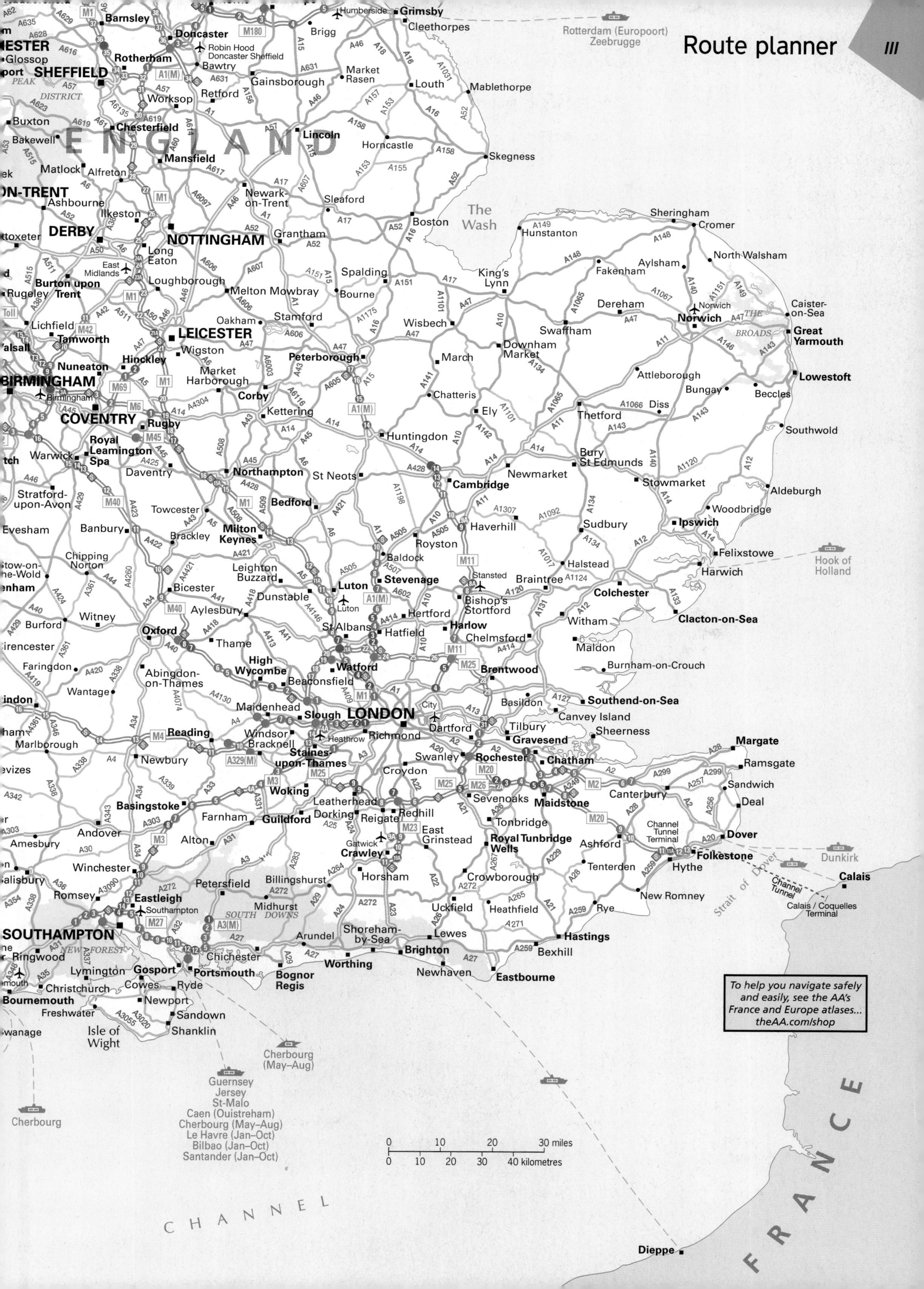
ENGLAND
Barnsley
Doncaster
Robin Hood Doncaster Sheffield
Grimsby
Humberside
Cleethorpes
Rotterdam (Europoort)
Zeebrugge
Brigg
Rotherham
SHEFFIELD
Glossop
Bawtry
Gainsborough
Market Rasen
Louth
Mablethorpe
PEAK DISTRICT
Retford
Worksop
Buxton
Chesterfield
Bakewell
Lincoln
Horncastle
Skegness
Mansfield
Matlock
Alfreton
Newark-on-Trent
Sleaford
Ashbourne
Ilkeston
DERBY
NOTTINGHAM
Grantham
Boston
The Wash
Hunstanton
Sheringham
Cromer
Long Eaton
East Midlands
Burton upon Trent
Rugeley
Loughborough
Melton Mowbray
Spalding
Bourne
King's Lynn
Fakenham
Aylsham
North Walsham
Lichfield
Tamworth
Oakham
Stamford
Wisbech
Swaffham
Dereham
Norwich
THE BROADS
Caister-on-Sea
Great Yarmouth
LEICESTER
Wigston
Walsall
Nuneaton
Hinckley
Market Harborough
Peterborough
March
Downham Market
Attleborough
Lowestoft
BIRMINGHAM
Birmingham
Corby
Chatteris
Bungay
Beccles
COVENTRY
Rugby
Kettering
Ely
Thetford
Diss
Southwold
Royal Leamington Spa
Warwick
Huntingdon
Bury St Edmunds
Daventry
Northampton
St Neots
Cambridge
Newmarket
Stowmarket
Aldeburgh
Stratford-upon-Avon
Bedford
Towcester
Woodbridge
Evesham
Banbury
Milton Keynes
Brackley
Haverhill
Sudbury
Ipswich
Felixstowe
Royston
Baldock
Chipping Norton
Halstead
Harwich
Hook of Holland
Stow-on-the-Wold
Leighton Buzzard
Stevenage
Stansted
Braintree
Bicester
Luton
Dunstable
Bishop's Stortford
Colchester
Witney
Aylesbury
Hertford
Witham
Clacton-on-Sea
Burford
Oxford
St Albans
Hatfield
Harlow
Chelmsford
Maldon
Cirencester
Thame
High Wycombe
Watford
Brentwood
Burnham-on-Crouch
Faringdon
Abingdon-on-Thames
Beaconsfield
Wantage
Swindon
Maidenhead
Slough
LONDON
City
Basildon
Southend-on-Sea
Canvey Island
Reading
Windsor
Bracknell
Heathrow
Richmond
Dartford
Tilbury
Gravesend
Sheerness
Marlborough
Newbury
Staines-upon-Thames
Swanley
Rochester
Chatham
Margate
Ramsgate
Devizes
Croydon
Woking
Sevenoaks
Maidstone
Canterbury
Sandwich
Deal
Basingstoke
Farnham
Guildford
Leatherhead
Dorking
Reigate
Redhill
Tonbridge
Andover
Amesbury
Alton
East Grinstead
Gatwick
Crawley
Royal Tunbridge Wells
Ashford
Channel Tunnel Terminal
Dover
Folkestone
Hythe
Dunkirk
Winchester
Salisbury
Horsham
Crowborough
Tenterden
Calais
Channel Tunnel
Calais / Coquelles Terminal
Strait of Dover
Romsey
Petersfield
Billingshurst
Eastleigh
Southampton
Midhurst
SOUTH DOWNS
Uckfield
Heathfield
New Romney
Rye
SOUTHAMPTON
Arundel
Shoreham-by-Sea
Lewes
Hastings
Bexhill
NEW FOREST
Ringwood
Chichester
Brighton
Worthing
Newhaven
Eastbourne
Lymington
Gosport
Portsmouth
Bognor Regis
Christchurch
Cowes
Ryde
Bournemouth
Newport
Freshwater
Sandown
Shanklin
Swanage
Isle of Wight
Cherbourg (May–Aug)
Guernsey
Jersey
St-Malo
Caen (Ouistreham)
Cherbourg (May–Aug)
Le Havre (Jan–Oct)
Bilbao (Jan–Oct)
Santander (Jan–Oct)
Cherbourg
CHANNEL
FRANCE
Dieppe
0 10 20 30 miles
0 10 20 30 40 kilometres
To help you navigate safely and easily, see the AA's France and Europe atlases... theAA.com/shop

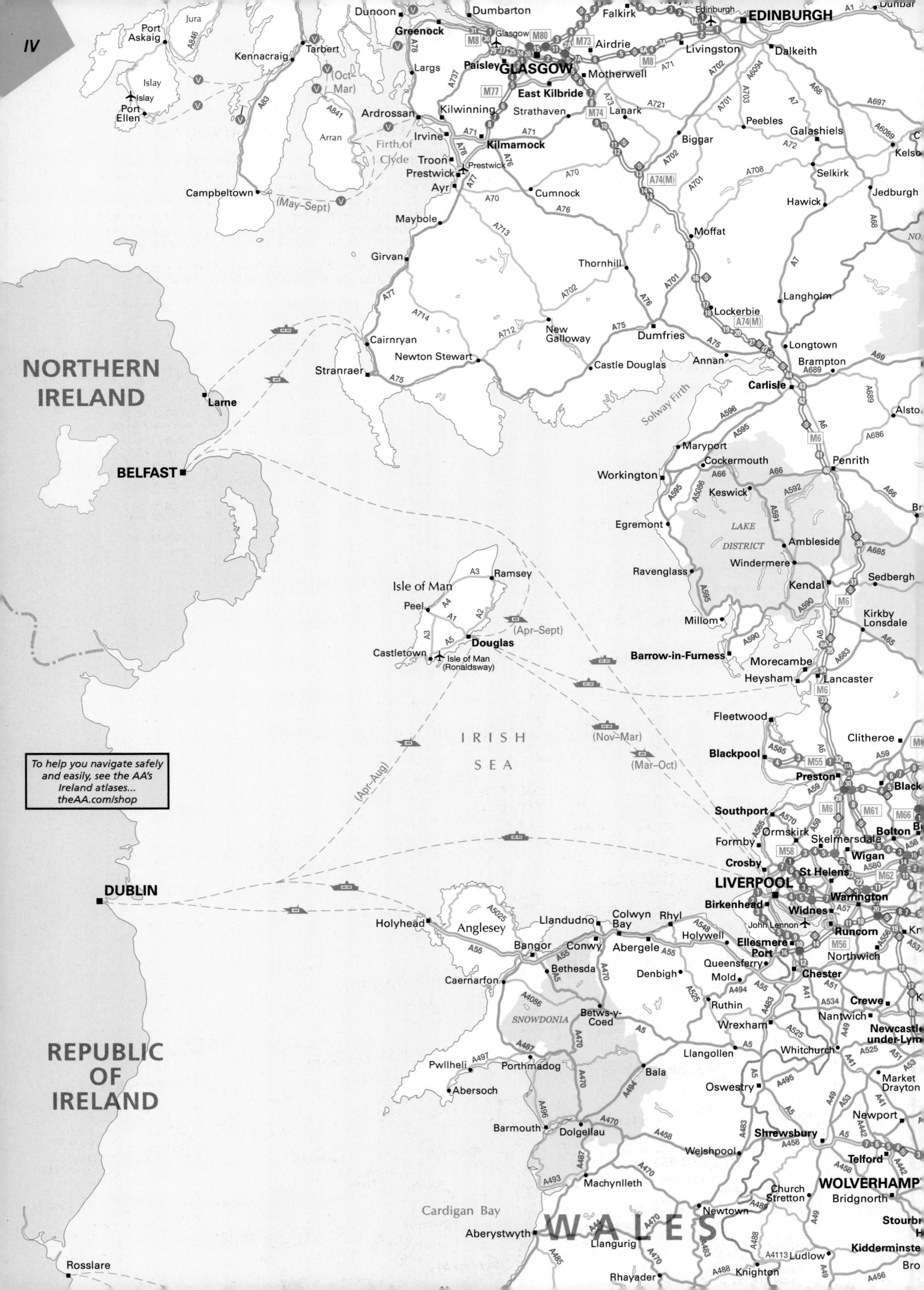

IV

NORTHERN IRELAND

REPUBLIC OF IRELAND

WALES

SNOWDONIA

Cardigan Bay

IRISH SEA

Firth of Clyde

Solway Firth

LAKE DISTRICT

To help you navigate safely and easily, see the AA's Ireland atlases...
theAA.com/shop

EDINBURGH
GLASGOW
Paisley
East Kilbride
Greenock
Dumbarton
Dunoon
Falkirk
Airdrie
Motherwell
Livingston
Dalkeith
Peebles
Galashiels
Kelso
Selkirk
Jedburgh
Hawick
Biggar
Lanark
Strathaven
Kilmarnock
Kilwinning
Irvine
Troon
Prestwick
Ayr
Cumnock
Moffat
Langholm
Thornhill
Lockerbie
New Galloway
Dumfries
Annan
Longtown
Brampton
Carlisle
Alsto
Maybole
Girvan
Newton Stewart
Castle Douglas
Penrith
Maryport
Cockermouth
Workington
Keswick
Egremont
Ambleside
Windermere
Ravenglass
Kendal
Sedbergh
Millom
Kirkby Lonsdale
Barrow-in-Furness
Morecambe
Heysham
Lancaster
Fleetwood
Clitheroe
Blackpool
Preston
Black
Southport
Ormskirk
Skelmersdale
Bolton
Formby
Wigan
Crosby
St Helens
LIVERPOOL
Birkenhead
Widnes
Warrington
Runcorn
Kr
Ellesmere Port
Northwich
Chester
Crewe
Nantwich
Newcastle-under-Lym
Market Drayton
Newport
Shrewsbury
Telford
WOLVERHAMP
Bridgnorth
Stourbr
Kidderminste
Bro
Welshpool
Machynlleth
Newtown
Church Stretton
Ludlow
Knighton
Rhayader
Llangurig
Aberystwyth
Llangollen
Whitchurch
Oswestry
Bala
Dolgellau
Barmouth
Betws-y-Coed
Ruthin
Mold
Denbigh
Queensferry
Holywell
Abergele
Conwy
Bangor
Bethesda
Caernarfon
Pwllheli
Porthmadog
Abersoch
Llandudno
Colwyn Bay
Rhyl
Holyhead
Anglesey
Dublin

Port Askaig
Jura
Dunbar
Kennacraig
Tarbert
Islay
Port Ellen
Islay
Largs
Campbeltown
Arran
Ardrossan
Rosslare

Isle of Man
Ramsey
Peel
Douglas
Castletown
Isle of Man (Ronaldsway)

Larne
BELFAST
Stranraer
Cairnryan

DUBLIN

(Oct–Mar)
(May–Sept)
(Apr–Sept)
(Nov–Mar)
(Mar–Oct)
(Apr–Aug)

EMERGENCY DIVERSION ROUTES

In an emergency it may be necessary to close a section of motorway or other main road to traffic, so a temporary sign may advise drivers to follow a diversion route. To help drivers navigate the route, black symbols on yellowpatches may be permanently displayed on existing direction signs, including motorway signs. Symbols may also be used on separate signs with yellow backgrounds.

For further information see *theaa.com/motoring_advice/ general-advice/emergency-diversion-routes.html*

Motorway
Toll motorway
Primary route dual carriageway
Primary route single carriageway
Other A road
Vehicle ferry
Fast vehicle ferry or catamaran
National Park

Eyemouth
Berwick-upon-Tweed
Wooler
Alnwick
Amble
Otterburn
Morpeth
Ashington
Corbridge
Newcastle
North Shields
Tynemouth
South Shields
Amsterdam (IJmuiden)
Gateshead
NEWCASTLE UPON TYNE
SUNDERLAND
Consett
Chester-le-Street
Durham
Hartlepool
Bishop Auckland
Stockton-on-Tees
Middlesbrough
Barnard Castle
Darlington
Guisborough
Whitby
Richmond
Durham Tees Valley
NORTH YORK MOORS
Northallerton
Leyburn
Scarborough
YORKSHIRE DALES
Thirsk
Pickering
Filey
Helmsley
Ripon
Easingwold
Malton
Bridlington
Harrogate
Driffield
Otley
Wetherby
York
Leeds Bradford
Market Weighton
BRADFORD
LEEDS
Selby
Beverley
Keighley
Halifax
Goole
KINGSTON UPON HULL
Withernsea
Huddersfield
Wakefield
Pontefract
Barnsley
Thorne
Scunthorpe
Immingham
Oldham
Doncaster
Humberside
Grimsby
MANCHESTER
Robin Hood Doncaster Sheffield
Bawtry
Cleethorpes
Rotterdam (Europoort) Zeebrugge
Glossop
Rotherham
Brigg
Stockport
SHEFFIELD
Gainsborough
Market Rasen
Louth
Mablethorpe
PEAK DISTRICT
Worksop
Retford
Buxton
Chesterfield
Lincoln
Horncastle
Skegness
Bakewell
Mansfield
Leek
Matlock
Alfreton
STOKE-ON-TRENT
Ashbourne
Ilkeston
Newark-on-Trent
Sleaford
Boston
The Wash
Sheringham
Cromer
Hunstanton
North Walsham
DERBY
NOTTINGHAM
Grantham
King's Lynn
Aylsham
Uttoxeter
Long Eaton
East Midlands
Loughborough
Spalding
Bourne
Fakenham
Dereham
Norwich
Caister-on-Sea
Stafford
Burton upon Trent
Melton Mowbray
Swaffham
THE BROADS
Rugeley
Lichfield
Oakham
Stamford
Wisbech
Downham Market
Great Yarmouth
Walsall
Tamworth
LEICESTER
Wigston
March
Attleborough
Lowestoft
BIRMINGHAM
Hinckley
Market Harborough
Peterborough
Corby
Chatteris
Bungay
Beccles
Nuneaton
Kettering
Ely
Thetford
Diss
Southwold
COVENTRY
Rugby
Huntingdon
Royal Leamington
Warwick
Bury

Western Isles

Outer Hebrides

Port Nis
(Port of Ness)

Steornabhagh
(Stornoway)
Stornoway

Isle of
Lewis

The Minch

Taransay

Tairbeart
(Tarbert)

Harris

Sound of Harris

Uibhist a Tuath
(North Uist)

Loch nam Madadh
(Lochmaddy)

Beinn na Faoghla
(Benbecula)
Benbecula

Uibhist a Deas
(South Uist)

Loch Baghasdail
(Lochboisdale)

Sound of Barra

Barra

Barraigh
(Barra)

(Apr–Oct)
Weds

Inner Hebrides

Rùm

Eigg

Coll

Tiree

Fionnphort

Colonsay

Dunvegan

Portree

Uig

Isle
of
Skye

Raasay

Kyle of
Lochalsh

Armadale

Mallaig

Tobermory

Lochaline

Craignure

Isle of Mull

Oban

Gairloch

Kinlochewe

Achnasheen

Scourie

Ullapool

Altnaharra

Tongue

Scrabster
Thur

Melvich

Lairg

Bonar
Bridge

Tain

Helms

Alness

Dingwall

Cromarty

Nairn

Forres

Inverness
Inverness

Moray Firth

Grantown-
on-Spey

A940

A938

A95

Drumnadrochit

Invermoriston

Invergarry

Newtonmore

Kingussie

Aviemore

CAIRNGORM

Brae

SCOTLAN

Fort William

Ballachulish

Pitlochry

Aberfeldy

Blairgow

Killin

Tyndrum

Lochearnhead

Crianlarich

Crieff

Auchterarder

LOCH LOMOND
AND THE
TROSSACHS

Callander

Inveraray

Lochgilphead

Dunblane

Alloa

Stirling

Dunfermline

Rosyth

Falkirk

Helensburgh

Dunoon

Dumbarton

Greenock

Glasgow

Airdrie

Liv

Paisley GLASGOW

Motherwell

Largs

East Kilbride

Lanark

Port
Askaig

Jura

Tarbert

Kennacraig

(Oct–
Mar)

Islay

Port
Ellen

Arran

(May–Sept)

Campbeltown

Kilwinning

Strathaven

Kilmarnock

Ardrossan

Irvine

Troon
Prestwick

Prestwick

Ayr

Maybole

Cumnock

Bigg

Firth
of
Clyde

Motorway

Toll motorway

Primary route
dual carriageway

Primary route
single carriageway

Other A road

or   Vehicle ferry

Fast vehicle ferry
or catamaran

National Park

0   10   20   30 miles

0   10   20   30   40 kilometres

Orkney Islands

Papa Westray
North Ronaldsay
Westray
Rousay
Eday
Sanday
Stronsay
A966
Mainland
Shapinsay
Stromness
Kirkwall
Kirkwall
Lerwick
A964
A960
Hoy
A961
St Margaret's Hope
Aberdeen
South Ronaldsay
Scrabster
Gills

Shetland Islands

Unst
A968
Yell
Fetlar
A970
Out Skerries
Scatsta
Vidlin
Papa Stour
Whalsay
A971
A970
Mainland
Tingwall
Foula
Scalloway
Lerwick
Bressay
A970
Sumburgh
Fair Isle
Kirkwall Aberdeen

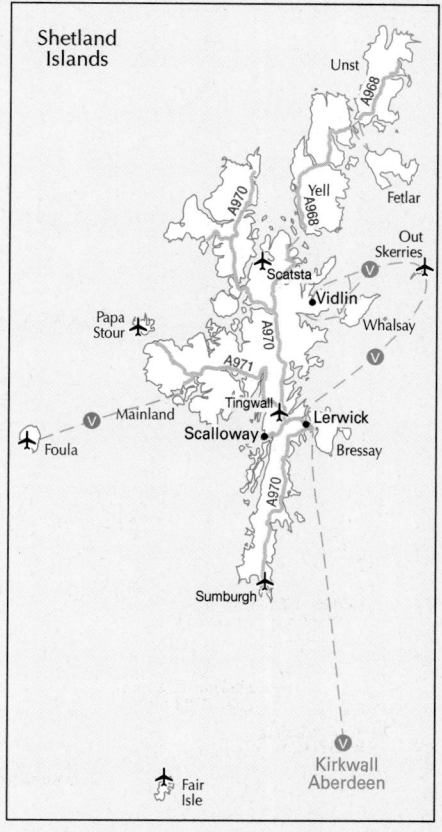

Kirkwall
Orkney Islands
St Margaret's Hope
Gills
John o' Groats
A836
Wick John o' Groats
A882
Wick
A99
Lerwick

Cullen
Banff
Fraserburgh
A98
A98
A90
gin
Keith
Turriff
A952
Peterhead
A941
A96
A95
A947
A90
Aberlour
Huntly
Oldmeldrum
Ellon
Inverurie
A90
Aberdeen
mintoul
A96
Aberdeen
A93
Ballater
Banchory
A90
Stonehaven
A92
A90
Brechin
Montrose
Forfar
A94
A90
upar Angus
A92
Arbroath
Dundee
Carnoustie
NORTH SEA
A90
A92
Newport-on-Tay
A91
St Andrews
A91
Cupar
A915 A917
Glenrothes
Kirkcaldy
Firth of Forth
A1
Dunbar
EDINBURGH
Dalkeith
Eyemouth
A6094
A703
A7
A68
A697
Berwick-upon-Tweed
Peebles
A4698
Galashiels
Coldstream
A1
A72
Kelso
Wooler
A708
Selkirk
Jedburgh
A697
Hawick
Alnwick
A68
NORTHUMBERLAND
A1
A1068
Amble

FERRY OPERATORS

Hebrides and west coast Scotland
calmac.co.uk
skyeferry.co.uk
western-ferries.co.uk

Orkney and Shetland
northlinkferries.co.uk
pentlandferries.co.uk
orkneyferries.co.uk
shetland.gov.uk/ferries

Isle of Man
steam-packet.com

Ireland
irishferries.com
poferries.com
stenaline.co.uk

North Sea (Scandinavia and Benelux)
dfdsseaways.co.uk
poferries.com

Isle of Wight
wightlink.co.uk
redfunnel.co.uk

Channel Islands
condorferries.co.uk

France and Belgium
brittany-ferries.co.uk
condorferries.co.uk
eurotunnel.com
dfdsseaways.co.uk
poferries.com

Northern Spain
brittany-ferries.co.uk

Motoring information

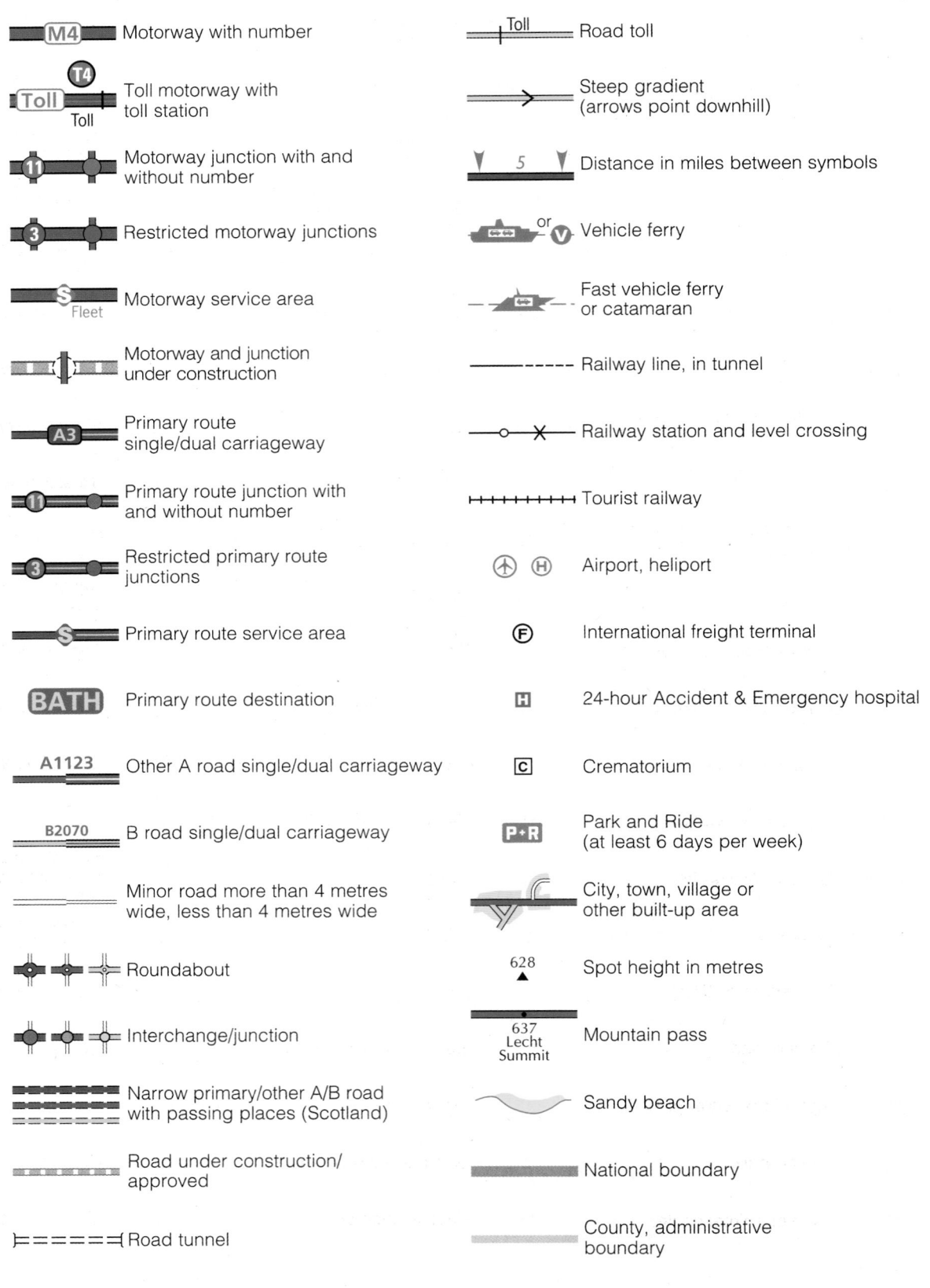

Motorway with number

Toll motorway with toll station

Motorway junction with and without number

Restricted motorway junctions

Motorway service area

Motorway and junction under construction

Primary route single/dual carriageway

Primary route junction with and without number

Restricted primary route junctions

Primary route service area

Primary route destination

Other A road single/dual carriageway

B road single/dual carriageway

Minor road more than 4 metres wide, less than 4 metres wide

Roundabout

Interchange/junction

Narrow primary/other A/B road with passing places (Scotland)

Road under construction/ approved

Road tunnel

Road toll

Steep gradient (arrows point downhill)

Distance in miles between symbols

Vehicle ferry

Fast vehicle ferry or catamaran

Railway line, in tunnel

Railway station and level crossing

Tourist railway

Airport, heliport

International freight terminal

24-hour Accident & Emergency hospital

Crematorium

Park and Ride (at least 6 days per week)

City, town, village or other built-up area

Spot height in metres

Mountain pass

Sandy beach

National boundary

County, administrative boundary

Touring information
To avoid disappointment, check opening times before visiting

Scenic route	Zoological or wildlife collection	County cricket ground
Tourist Information Centre	Bird collection, aquarium	Rugby Union national stadium
Tourist Information Centre (seasonal)	RSPB site	International athletics stadium
Visitor or heritage centre	National Nature Reserve (England, Scotland, Wales)	Horse racing
Picnic site	Local nature reserve	Show jumping/equestrian circuit
Caravan site (AA inspected)	Wildlife Trust reserve	Motor-racing circuit
Camping site (AA inspected)	Forest drive	Air show venue
Caravan & camping site (AA inspected)	National trail	Ski slope (natural)
Abbey, cathedral or priory	Waterfall	Ski slope (artificial)
Ruined abbey, cathedral or priory	Viewpoint	National Trust property
Castle	Hill-fort	National Trust for Scotland property
Historic house or building	Roman antiquity	English Heritage site
Museum or art gallery	Prehistoric monument	Historic Scotland site
Industrial interest	Battle site with year	Cadw (Welsh heritage) site
Aqueduct or viaduct	Steam railway centre	Other place of interest
Garden, Arboretum	Cave	Boxed symbols indicate attractions within urban areas
Vineyard	Windmill	World Heritage Site (UNESCO)
Brewery or distillery	Monument	National Park
Country park	Beach (award winning)	National Scenic Area (Scotland)
Agricultural showground	Lighthouse	Forest Park
Theme park	Golf course (AA listed)	Heritage coast
Farm or animal centre	Football stadium	Major shopping centre

Land's End & the Lizard

G **H** **J** **K**

Whiteworks
ROYAL HILL
worthy
Pou gate
Goodstone

12
R Meavy
B3212
Venford Reservoir
Holne
River Dart
Rew
13
Hele
Ashburton
We gwel
East
1

Walkhampton
Burrator Reservoir
Michelcombe
Hembury Castle
Woodland
Denbury

Dousland
Yelverton
Sheepstor
516
RYDERS HILL
Scorriton
Buckfast
Thornecroft
Forder Green
Torbrya
Devon Distillo

Meavy
DARTMOOR
480
Buckfastleigh
Butterfly Farm & Otter Sanctuary
Landscove
Woolston
Broadhem
2

Clearbrook
NATIONAL
Upper Plym Valley
Deancombe
Pennywell Farm
West Combe
Staverton
mbe
Devon Railway

Goodameavy
Dewerstone
Brisworthy
471
SHELL TOP
PARK
Dean Prior
Dean
Dartir
Week
Shinnersbridge
Littleher

Shaugh Prior
Harbourneford
Didworthy
A38
Rattery
A385
Cott
Berry Pomer

Bickleigh
Wotter
Lee Moor
R Erme
Aish
Lutton
Hillside
Mill Cross
Long Cause
Totnes Castle
Totn
3

Lutton
Dartmoor Zoological Park
Cornwood
Harford
South Brent
Brent Mill
Tigley
Blakemore
Belsford
Sharpham

YMOUTH
P R
Hemerdon
Sparkwell
BUTTERDON HILL
Cheston
Wrangaton
Avonwick
Harberton
East Leigh
Luscombe
3

B3417
Venton
Bittaford
B3213
Diptford
Harbertonford
Bow
Yetson
Washbourne

Plympton
Ivybridge
Woodland
Ugborough
North Huish
Curtisknowle
Allaleigh
4

R Plym
Lee Mill
Penquit
A3121
Ludbrook
Lupridge
Moreleigh
Halwell
A3121

Elburton
Keaton
Ermington
Brownston
California Cross
Woodford
Blackaw

stock
Brixton
Yealmbridge
Westlake
Worston
River Erme
Modbury
East Leigh
Hendham
B3196
Hutcherleigh
Millcombe
Abbotsleigh
East
5

Spriddlestone
Yealmpton
Torr
Dunstone
Ford
A379
Woolston
Woodleigh

addiscombe
Knighton
Luson
Holbeton
B3186
Ashford
Loddiswell
East Allington
Cole's Cross
stone

West ibury
Newton Ferrers
Bridgend
Battisborough Cross
St Ann's Chapel
9
Aveton Gifford
Ledstone
Goveton
Harleston

nbury
Noss Mayo
Mothecombe
Kingston
B3392
Bridge End
Churchstow
Buckland-Tout-Saints
Start
Sherford
Frittiscom

ara int
Netton
Stoke Point
Erme Mouth
Ringmore
Bigbury
A381
Dodbrooke
East Charleton
Chillington
6

Beacon Point
Challaborough
Buckland
Kingsbridge
Kernborough
A379
Frogmore
Stok

Bigbury-on-Sea
Burgh Island
Bantham
Upton
South Milton
West Alvington
Kingsbridge Estuary
Woolston
Lincombe
South Pool
Ford

Thurlestone
Sutton
West Charleton
A379

Bigbury Bay
South Huish
Galmpton
Malborough
Batson
Salcombe
Chivelstone
Kellaton

Hope
Bolt Tail
Bolberry
Collaton
Soar
Rew
Combe
East Portlemouth
South Allington
Bickerto
7

Overbeck's House
Rickham
Prawle Point
East Prawle
8

South Devon Heritage Coast
Bolt Head

G **H** **J** **K** **L** **M**

8

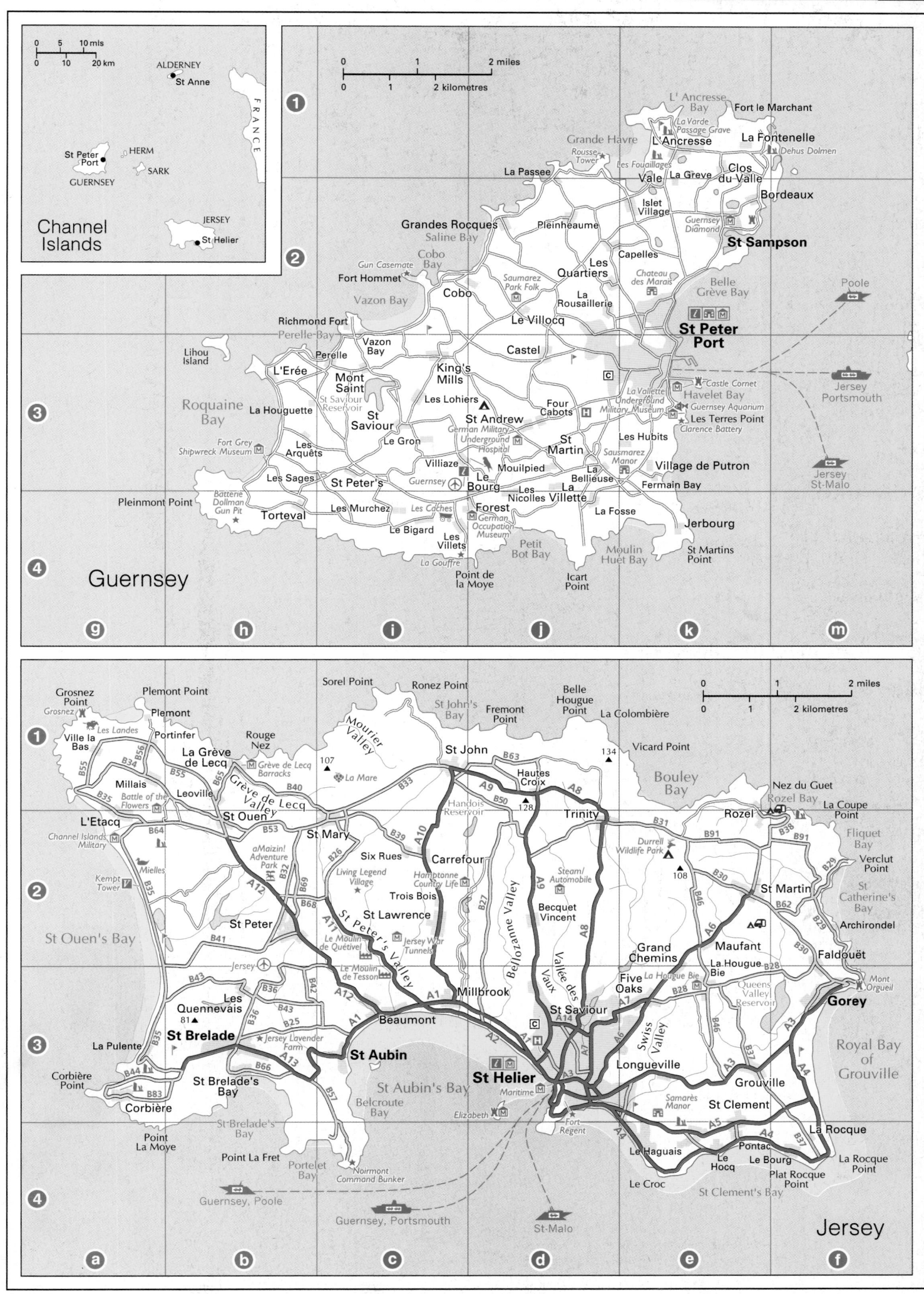

Channel Islands

ALDERNEY
• St Anne

FRANCE

St Peter Port •
HERM
SARK
GUERNSEY

JERSEY
• St Helier

Guernsey

0   5   10 mls
0   10   20 km

0   1   2 miles
0   1   2 kilometres

L' Ancresse Bay
Fort le Marchant
La Varde Passage Grave
L'Ancresse
La Fontenelle
Dehus Dolmen
Grande Havre
Rousse Tower
Les Fouaillages
La Grève
Clos du Valle
La Passee
Vale
Bordeaux
Islet Village
Guernsey Diamond
St Sampson
Grandes Rocques
Pleinheaume
Les Quartiers
Capelles
Saline Bay
Cobo Bay
Saumarez Park Folk
La Rousaillerie
Chateau des Marais
Belle Grève Bay
Gun Casemate
Fort Hommet
Cobo
Le Villocq
St Peter Port
Poole
Vazon Bay
Castel
Richmond Fort
Perelle Bay
Vazon Bay
King's Mills
Lihou Island
Perelle
Les Lohiers
Four Cabots
La Vallette Underground Military Museum
Castle Cornet
Havelet Bay
Guernsey Aquarium
Jersey Portsmouth
L'Erée
Mont Saint
Roquaine Bay
La Hougette
St Saviour Reservoir
St Saviour
Le Gron
St Andrew
German Military Underground Hospital
St Martin
Les Hubits
Sausmarez Manor
Les Terres Point
Clarence Battery
Fort Grey Shipwreck Museum
Les Arquêts
Villiaze
Mouilpied
La Bellieuse
Village de Putron
Jersey St-Malo
Les Sages
St Peter's
Guernsey
Le Bourg
Les Nicolles
La Villette
Fermain Bay
Pleinmont Point
Batterie Dollman Gun Pit
Les Murchez
Les Caches
Forest
La Fosse
Torteval
Le Bigard
German Occupation Museum
Jerbourg
Les Villets
Petit Bot Bay
Moulin Huet Bay
St Martins Point
La Gouffre
Point de la Moye
Icart Point

Jersey

0   1   2 miles
0   1   2 kilometres

Grosnez Point
Grosnez
Les Landes
Plemont Point
Plemont
Portinfer
Sorel Point
Ronez Point
St John's Bay
Fremont Point
Belle Hougue Point
La Colombière
Bouley Bay
Nez du Guet
Ville la Bas
B55   B56   B34
Rouge Nez
Mourier Valley
107
La Mare
St John
B63
Vicard Point
134
Rozel Bay
La Coupe Point
Millais
Battle of the Flowers
B55   B35
Grève de Lecq Valley
Grève de Lecq Barracks
Hautes Croix
A9   B50   A8
Trinity
B31
Rozel
Fliquet Bay
L'Etacq
Channel Islands Military
B64
Leoville
B40
St Ouen
Handois Reservoir
128
Durrell Wildlife Park
B91
B38   B91
Verclut Point
B29
Kempt Tower
Mielles
B53
St Mary
B39   A10
Six Rues
Carrefour
B27
Steam/Automobile
108
B46
St Martin
St Catherine's Bay
Archirondel
St Ouen's Bay
B35
aMaizin! Adventure Park
B26
Living Legend Village
Hamptonne Country Life
Bellozanne Valley
A9
Becquet Vincent
A8
B30
B62
Faldouët
B32   B69
St Peter
Trois Bois
St Lawrence
Vallée des Vaux
Grand Chemins
Maufant
Mont Orgueil
B41   A11
Jersey
Le Moulin de Quétivel
Jersey War Tunnels
A8
Five Oaks
La Hougue Bie
B28
Queens Valley Reservoir
Les Quennevais
81
B43   B68
Le Moulin de Tesson
A1
B28
Gorey
B36   A12
St Brelade
B36   B25   B42
Millbrook
Beaumont
St Saviour
A14
Swiss Valley
A3
Royal Bay of Grouville
La Pulente
B44
B43   A13
St Aubin
St Helier
A3
Longueville
Grouville
A4
Corbière Point
B66   B57
St Brelade's Bay
St Aubin's Bay
Maritime
A3
A2
A7
Grouville
B37
A4
Corbière
B83
Belcroute Bay
Elizabeth
Fort Regent
A5
St Clement
La Rocque
Point La Moye
St-Brelade's Bay
A4
Pontac
B31
La Rocque Point
Point La Fret
Portelet Bay
Noirmont Command Bunker
Le Haguais
Le Bourg
Plat Rocque Point
Guernsey, Poole
Le Hocq
Le Croc
St Clement's Bay
Guernsey, Portsmouth
St-Malo

A B C D E F

Isles of Scilly

White Island

ST MARTIN'S

King Charles's

Old Grimsby

BRYHER

Cromwell's

49 St Martin's Head

38

Higher Town

42

Pool

New Grimsby

Lizard Point

Old Blockhouse

Great Ganilly

Eastern Isles

Isles of Scilly Heritage Coast

Crow Bar

Great Arthur

Samson

Tresco Abbey

TRESCO

Innisidgen Tomb

Crow Sound

North West Channel

Bant's Carn Burial

Harry's Walls

A3110

ST MARY'S

Higher & Lower Moors

Deep Point

Hugh Town

Garrison Walls

Porth Hellick Downs Tombs

Isles of Scilly (St Mary's)

Old Town

Broad Sound

Annet

St Mary's Sound

Peninnis Head

Middle Town

Gugh

ST AGNES

Horse Point

Smith Sound

Western Rocks

```
0        1         2 miles
0    1        2 kilometres
```

a b c d

Pentire Point - Widemouth Heritage Coast

Witchcraft

Boscastle

Trevalga

Castle

TINTAGEL HEAD

Trethevey

Tintagel

Bossiney

Old Post Office

Penhallic Point

Tregatta

Treknow

Trewarmett

Trebarwith

Penpethy

Treligga

Rockhead

South West Coast Path

Delabole

Pengelly

Trevia

Westdowns

Valley Truckle

Lanteglos

Port Isaac Bay

Helstone

Rumps Point

Kelland Head

Varley Head

Port-Gaverne

Trewalder

Port Quin Bay

Port Quin

Port Isaac

St Teath

Knightsmill

Treveighan

Pentire Point

New Polzeath

Trewetha

Michaelst

Padstow Bay

Bee Centre

Plain Street

Treburgett

Treharrock

Hayle Bay

Long Cross

Trelights

Pendoggett

Stepper Point

Polzeath

Tregellist

St Endellion

Trelill

Trenewth

A39

Trevose Head Heritage Coast

Gunver Head

Hawker's Cove

Trebetherick

B3314

St Minver

Trequite

St Tudy

St

TREVOSE HEAD

Mother Ivey's Bay

Crugmeer

Prideaux Place

Trevanger Pityme

Trewethern

St Kew

Lank

Dinas Head

Trevose

Harlyn Bay

Rock

Splatt

Hendra

St Kew Highway

Wenfordbridge

Penpon

Constantine Bay

Harlyn

Trevone Treator

Stoptide

Padstow

Chapel Amble

St Mabyn

Blisland

Treyarnon

Towan

Windmill

Dinas

Tregonce

Tredethy

Trehemborne

St Merryn

Shop

Trevorrick

Tregunna

Trevanson

Bodieve

Hellandbridge

Porthcothan

St Issey

Edmonton

Royal Cornwall

Egloshayle

Croanford

Penrose

Little Petherick

Trenance

Wadebridge

Treneague

Sladesbridge

Pencarrow House

Park Head

Treburrick

Rumford

Tredinnick

Hay

Burlawn

Colquite

Helland

Bedruthan Steps

Engollan

St Ervan

4

Whitecross

St Breock

Polbrock

Lane End

Washaway

Carne

Downhill

Trelow

St Jidgey

St Breock Downs Monolith

5

Brocton

Dunmere

Nine Maidens

```
0     1    2    3    4       5 miles
0   1   2   3   4   5   6   7   8 kilometres
```

A B C D E F

1 2 3 4 5 6 7 8

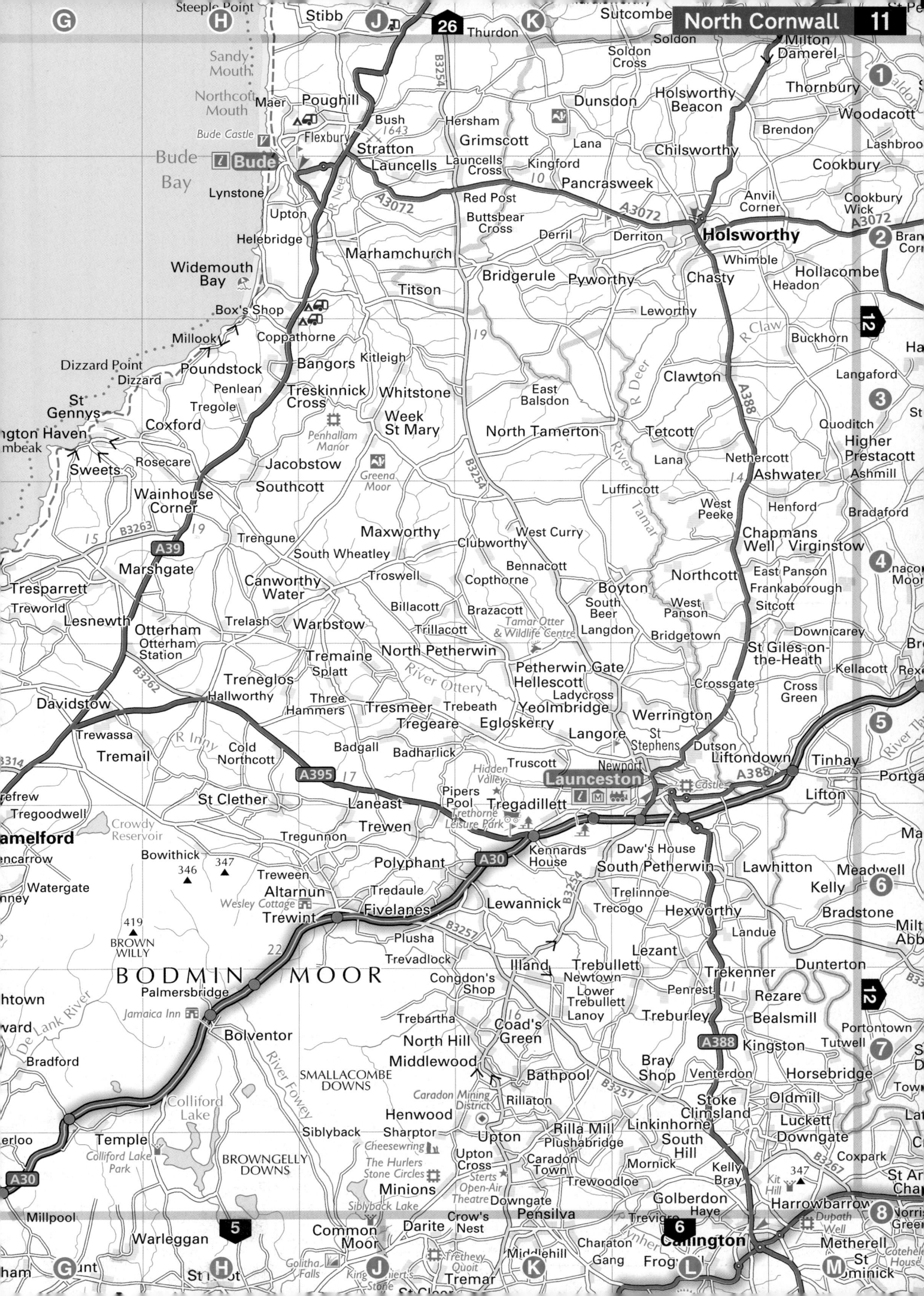

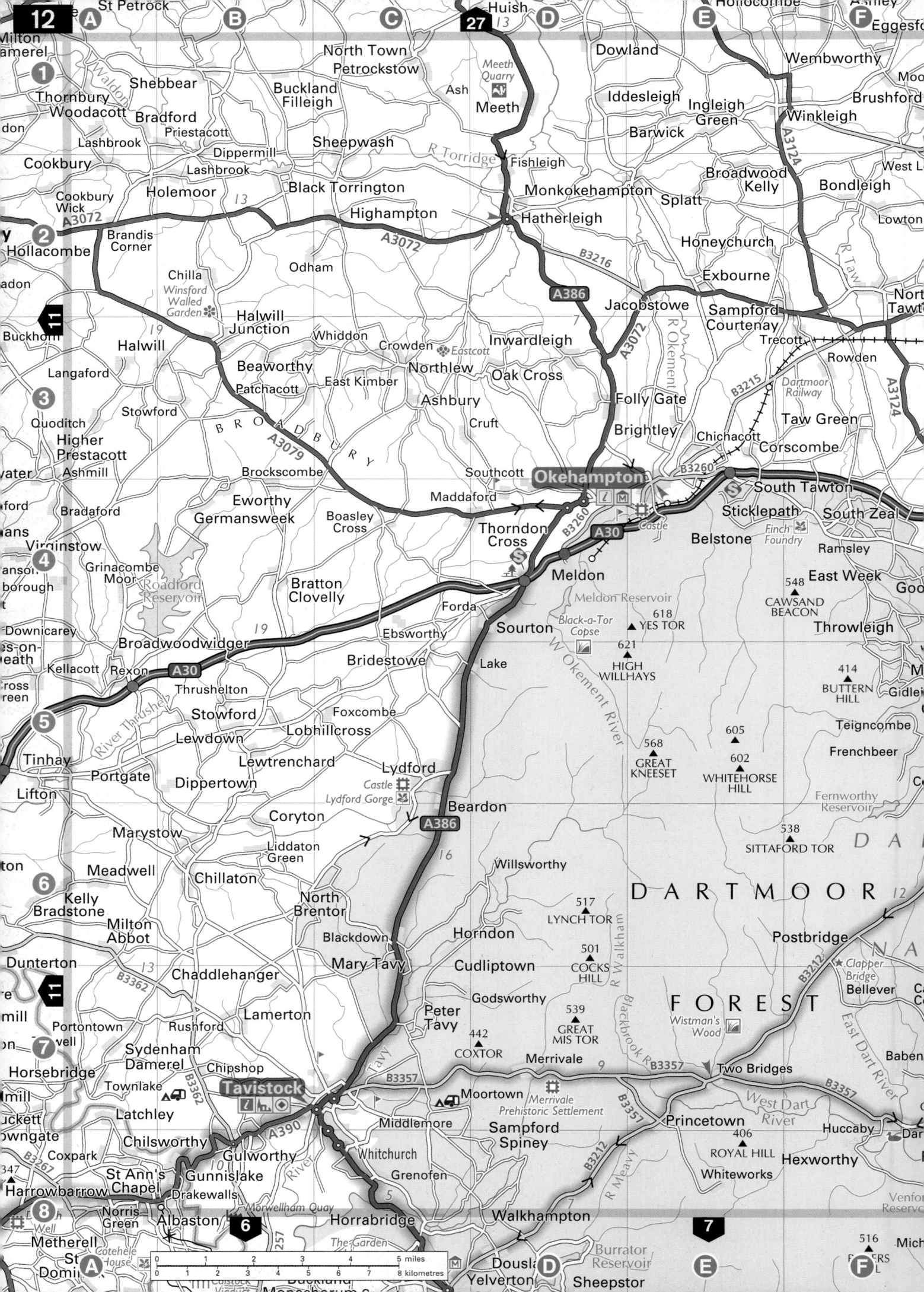

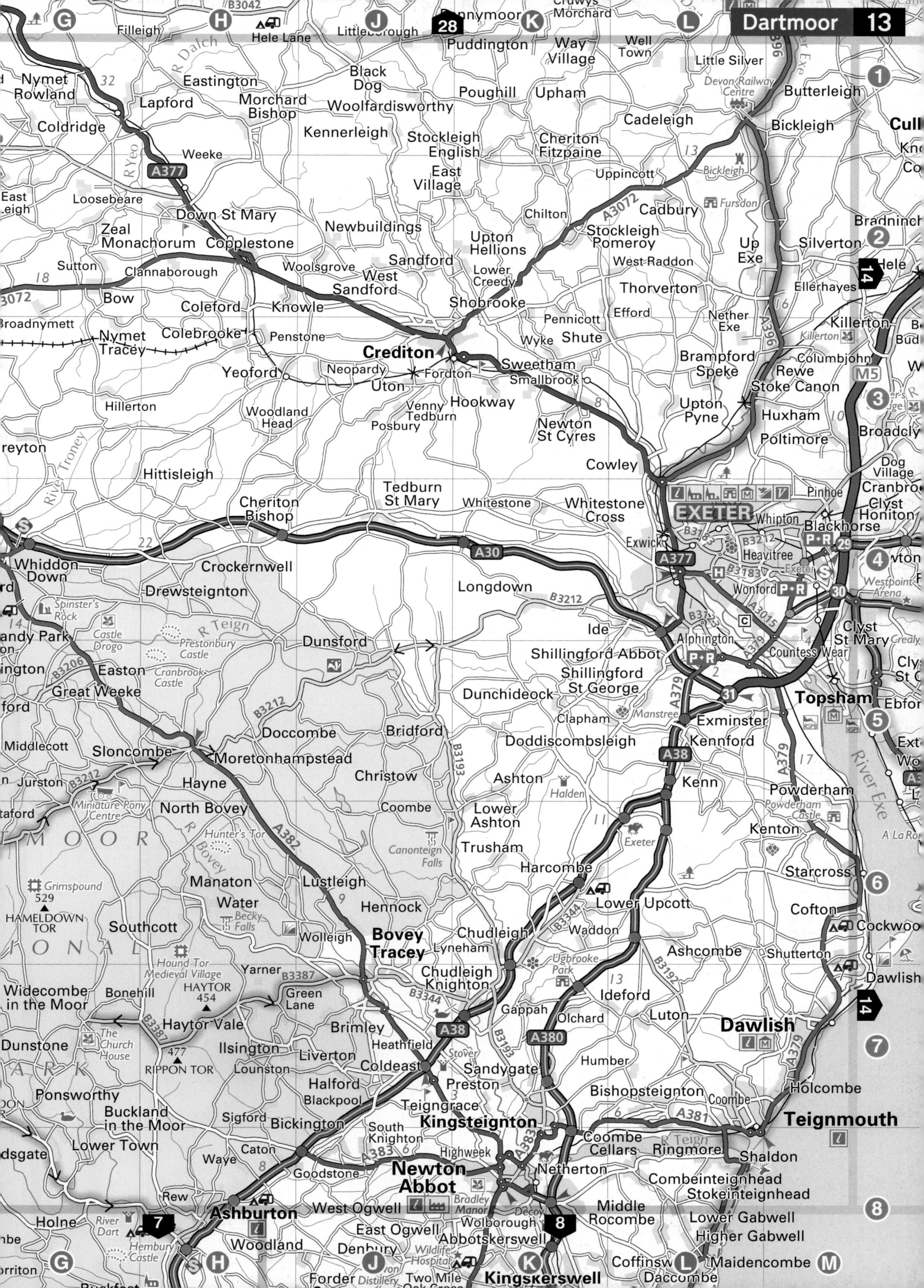

L Y M E B A Y

Jurassic Coast
(Dorset & East Devon Coast)

Jurassic Coast
(Dorset & East Devon Coast)

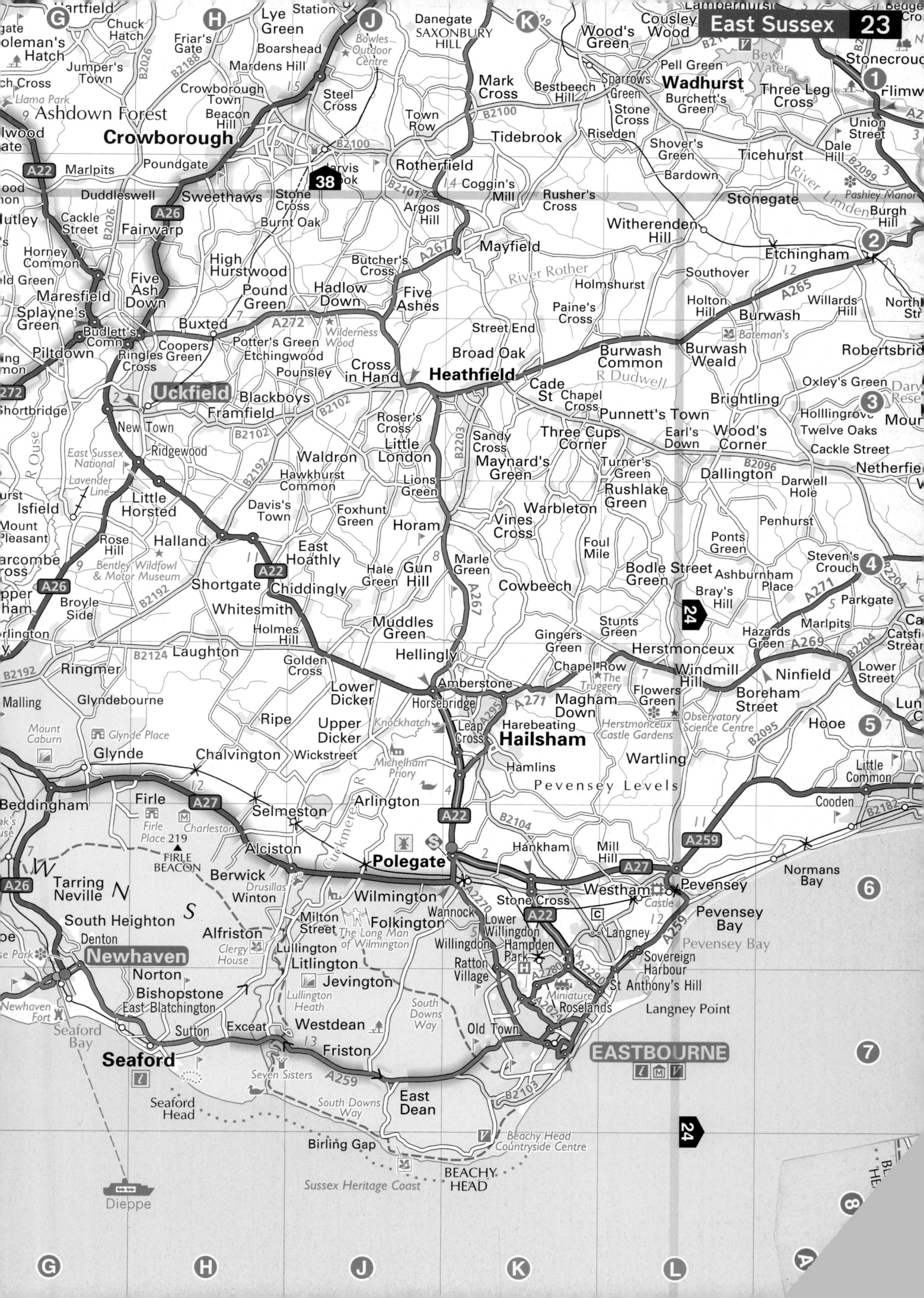

A B C D E F

1

2

North West
Point

*Lundy
Heritage Coast*   ☒ LUNDY

▲ 142

*Marine
Reserve* ☒   *Marisco* ☒
Shutter Point   ✗ Surf Point

3

4

B A R N S T A P L E

O R

5

B I D E F O R D   B A Y

HARTLAND POINT   *Shipload
Bay*

Titchberry   Brownsham

Damehole
Point   *Hartland Abbey
& Gardens*

Stoke   ⌂   ☒ *Hartlan
Hartland   Heritage C

Hartland Quay   B3248   Velly   ☒ Clovelly

☒   Hartland   4   Buck's
Spekes Mill   Higher Mills
Mouth   Clovelly   *Ho
                                                              Cre

6   Milford   *Docton Mill
                   Gardens*   Philham   *Milky Way*   Buck's
          ✿   Cross
Elmscott   Edistone   Woolfardisworthy   🏛   A39

Hardisworthy   Tosberry   Cranford   Park

South   Parkham
Hole   Ash

Welcombe   Meddon   Ashmansworth

Mead   Darracott   East
7   *Gooseham   Woolley   Putford
                        Mill*
Gooseham   Eastcott   *16*   East   *Gnome   West
                                        Youlstone   Dinworthy   Reserve* ★ Putfor
Morwenstow   H
Higher Sharpnose Point   West Youlstone   Colscott

*South West   Shop   A39   Bradworthy
Coast Path*   Woodford   *Bi

Lower Sharpnose Point   Kimworthy   Sutcombe

Steeple Point   Kilkhampton   *Tamar
8   Lakes*   Alfardisworthy   Sutcombe
          Stibb   ⛺🚂   Sutcombemill

                   Thurdon   Soldon   *River*
A   0 1 2 3 4 5 miles   D 11   E Soldon   F   Da
          0 1 2 3 4 5 6 7 8 kilometres   Cross
          Mouth   B3254

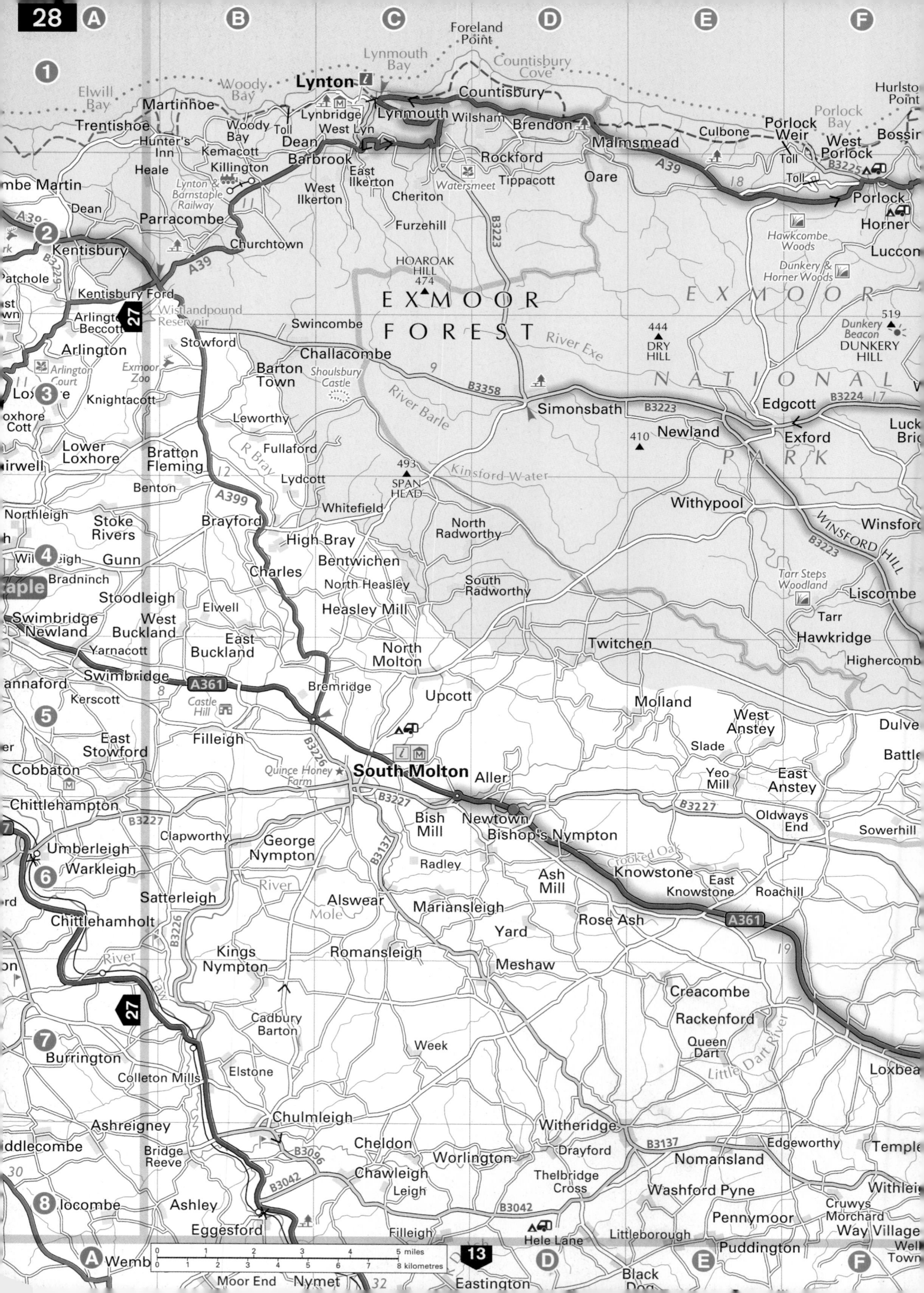

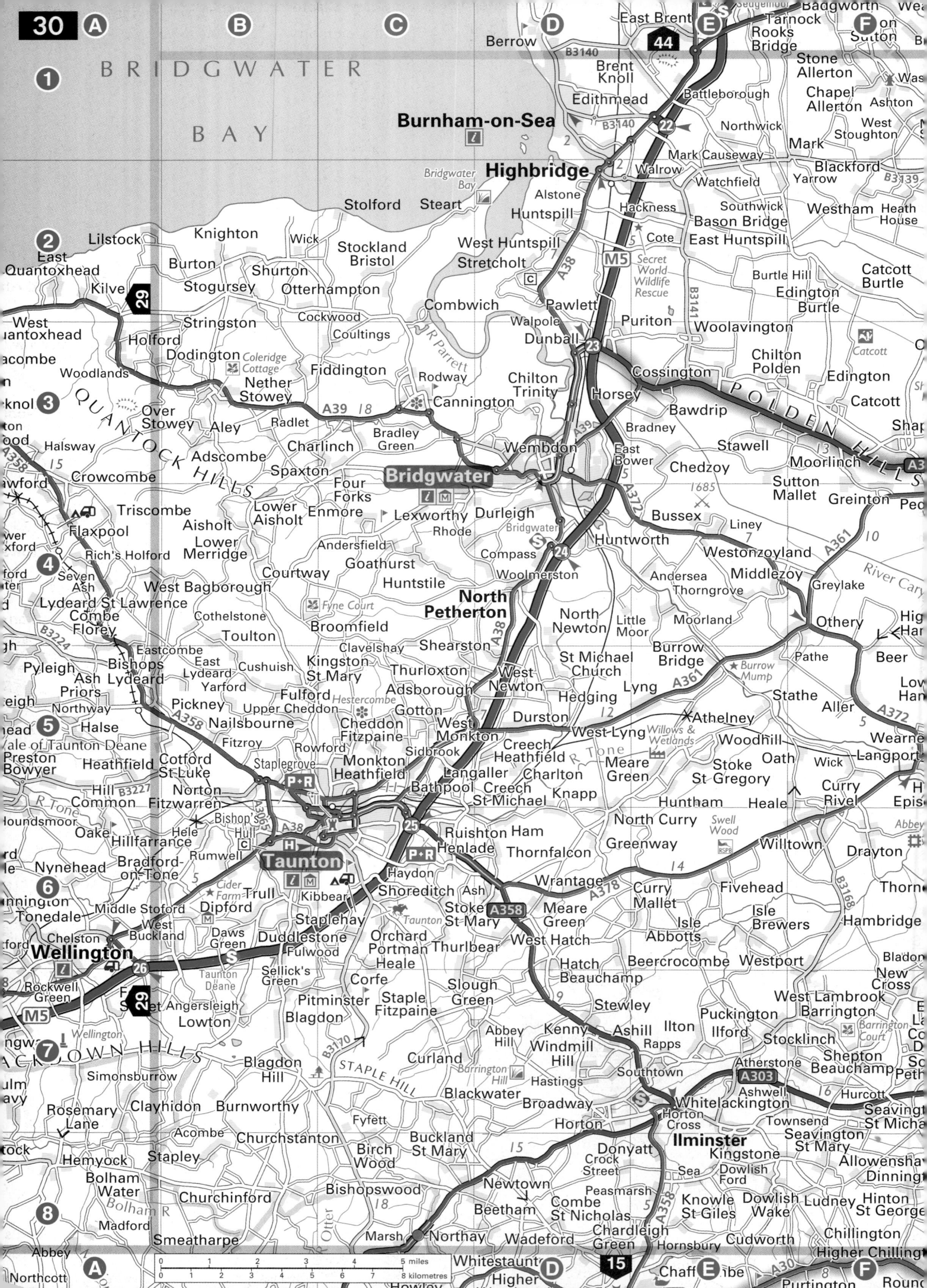

G H J 45 K B3135 Chewton Mendip Easton Clapton

Draycott Priddy East Water B3114 Bathway Chilcompton Stratton-on-the-Fosse Kilmersdon A362

Clewer Old Ditch Ebbor Gorge Green Ore Emborough Gurney Slade Downside Holcombe Highbury Newbury Upper Vobster Bu Di

Cocklake Rodney Stoke A371 Westbury-sub-Mendip Wookey Hole B3135 B3139 Binegar Downside Nettlebridge Ham A37 A367 Coleford Vobster Whatley Mells Little

Wedmore Latcham Theale Easton Lower Milton Walcombe West Horrington A37 Ashwick Oakhill Stoke St Michael East End Leigh upon Mendip Downhead Chantry Castle Little Elm

Bagley B3139 Panborough Henton Wookey Burcott Mill Dulcote Dinder West Horrington East Horrington Darshill Shepton Mallet Dean Leighton Cloford Trudoxh A361 A362

Westhay Moor Bleadney Yarley Worth Coxley Wick Wells Croscombe A371 Charlton Doulting Cranmore East Cranmore Higher Alham 32 est Town Wanstrow

Westhay Lower Godney Upper Godney Polsham Coxley Worminster North Town West Compton Pilton East Compton Royal Bath & West Chesterblade Prestleigh Stoney Stratton Westcombe Milton Clevedon Batcombe SEAT HILL North Brewham Upton Nobl

Meare Fish House Stileway Northload Bridge Brindham Glastonbury Tor Havyatt A361 Street on the Fosse Pylle Evercreech B3081 West End Bruton Dovecote South Brewham King Alfred's Tower Hardw

Meare Stileway Glastonbury Northover Asney Walton Edgarley West Pennard Woodland Street Coxbridge West Bradley East Pennard Hembridge Wraxall Ditcheat Lamyatt Cole Redlynch Shepton Montague Charlton Bl Musgrove Stoney Stoke Barr Pensely

Street Butleigh Wootton West Town Tilham Street Parbrook Huxham Green Stone A37 Alhampton Hornblotton Green Clanville Wyke Champflower Ansford Pitcombe Castle Cary Bratton Seymour Wincanton Bayford

Compton Dundon Butleigh Baltonsborough Gosling Street Catsham Four Foot Southwood West Lydford East Lydford Alford Lovington B3152 Galhampton Yarlington Woolston A371 Wi nto

Dundon BRADLEY HILL Stembridge Tower Mill Littleton Barton St David Silver Street Kingweston B3153 Keinton Mandeville Lydford-on-Fosse Wheathill Foddington Babcary North Barrow South Barrow Brookhampton A303 Lattiford 5

Somerton Pitney Midney Charlton Mackrell Charlton Adam Haynes International Motor Sparkford Little Weston North Cadbury Blackford Holton Compton Pauncefoot Maperton North Cheriton

Upton B3153 South Hill Catsgore B3151 Kingsdon Downhead West Camel Queen Camel South Cadbury South Cheriton Horsington Abbas Comb

Long Sutton chelney Knole Little Load A372 Podimore Wales Camel Sutton Montis Charlton Horethorne Stowell North Cheriton

ibsbury Long Sutton Long Load B3165 B3151 Northover RNAS Yeovilton Fleet Air Arm Bridgehampton Chilton Cantelo Marston Magna Corton Denham B3145 Templecombe 6

uchelney Ham Ilchester Yeovilton Limington Ashington Rimpton Milborne Wick Charlton Horethorne Yenston

sbury Milton scopi Stapleton Coat nbridge A303 A37 Witcombe Ash Tintinhull Garden Draycott West Mudford Adber Sandford Orcas Manor House Milborne Port Hens ge Ash Henst Ma

Martock Hurst Priory Treasurer's House Chilthorne Domer Tintinhull Yeovil Marsh Mudford Sock Mudford Up Mudford Trent Nether Compton Poyntington Oborne 32 A30

Bower Hinton Stoke sub Hamdon Montacute A3088 Odcombe Yeovil Over Compton Stallen Goathill Sherborne Old Castle Haydon Purse Caundle 7

Norton sub Hamdon Ham Hill Montacute House Preston Plucknett A30 Sherborne Sherborne Castle & Gardens Stalbridge Weston Stourton Caundle

Wigborough Little Norton Chiselborough Brympton West Coker Barwick Bradford Abbas North Wootton Bishop's Caundle A3030

East Chinnock Burton Stoford Thornford Folke Lydlin A357

Middle Chinnock Hardington Moor East Coker Beer Hackett Lillington Longburton Caundle Marsh Holwell

rriott R Parrett Hardington Mandeville Haselbury Plucknett Sutton Bingham Ryme Intrinseca Yetminster Knighton Boys Hill Crouch Hill Pleck Packers King's Kin 8

Crewkerne G 15 H ington Marsh Closwo J A37 Hamlet K 16 L M East Pulham Hazelbu
A356 North Perrott B3 Sandhills Holnest B31

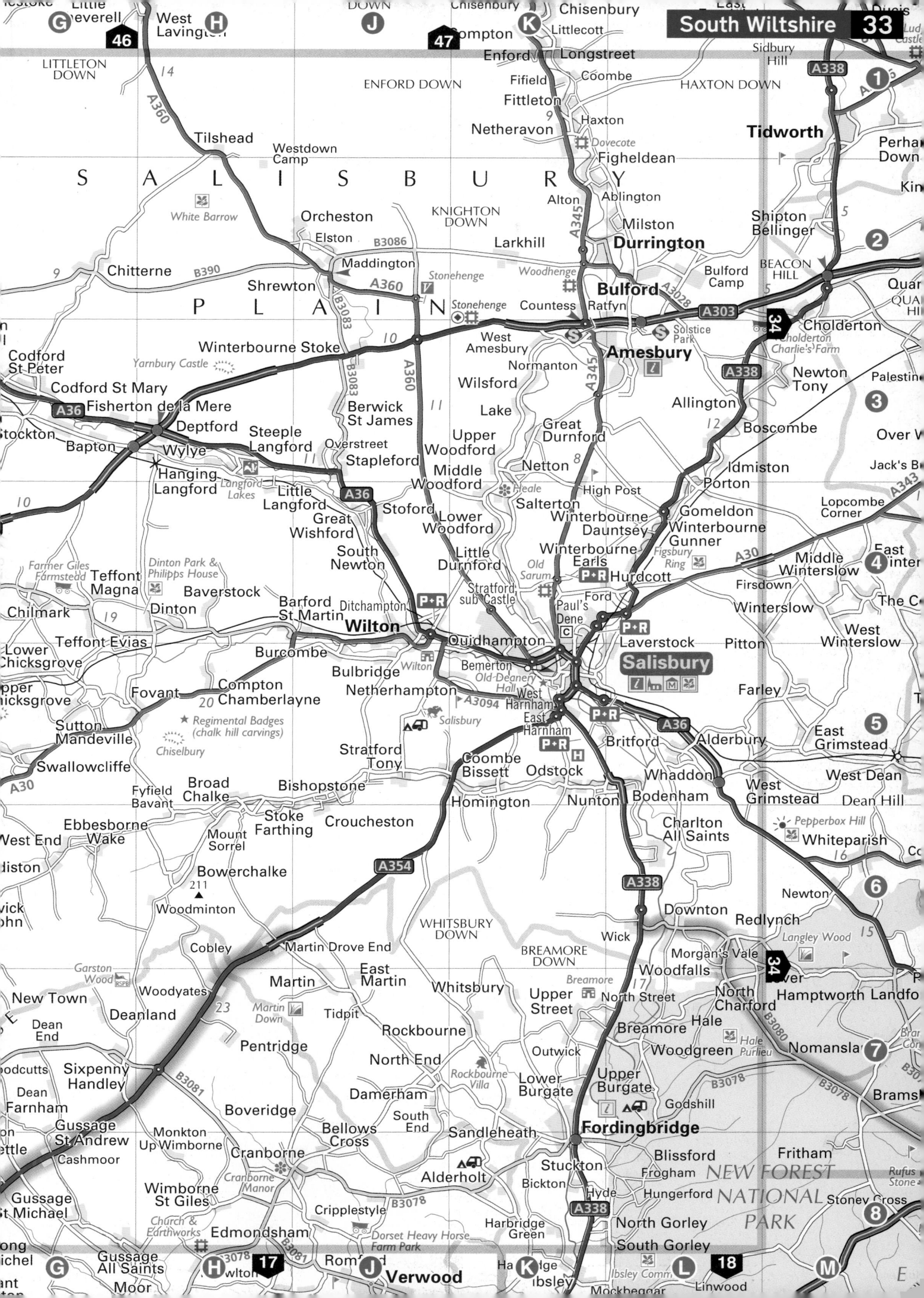

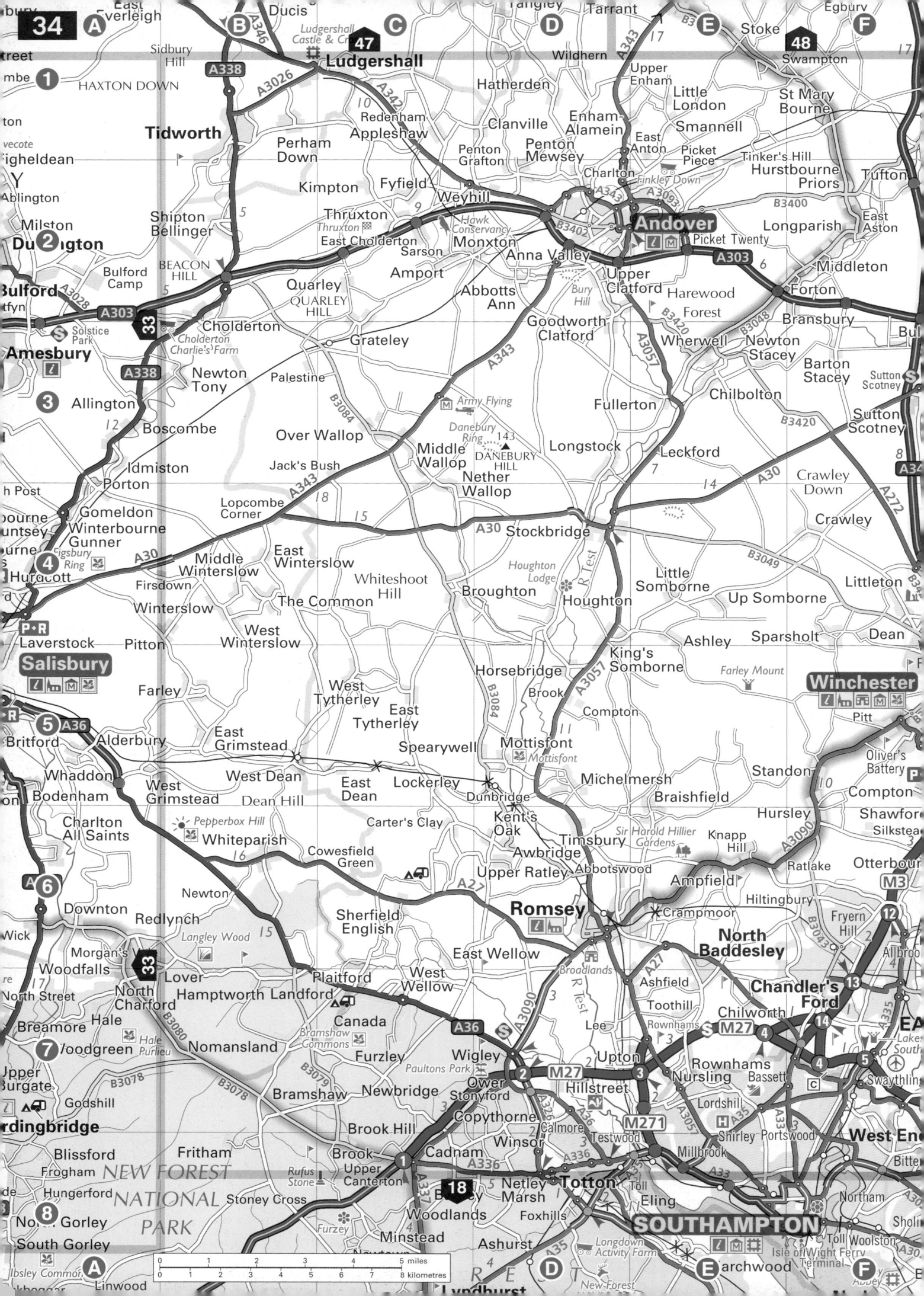

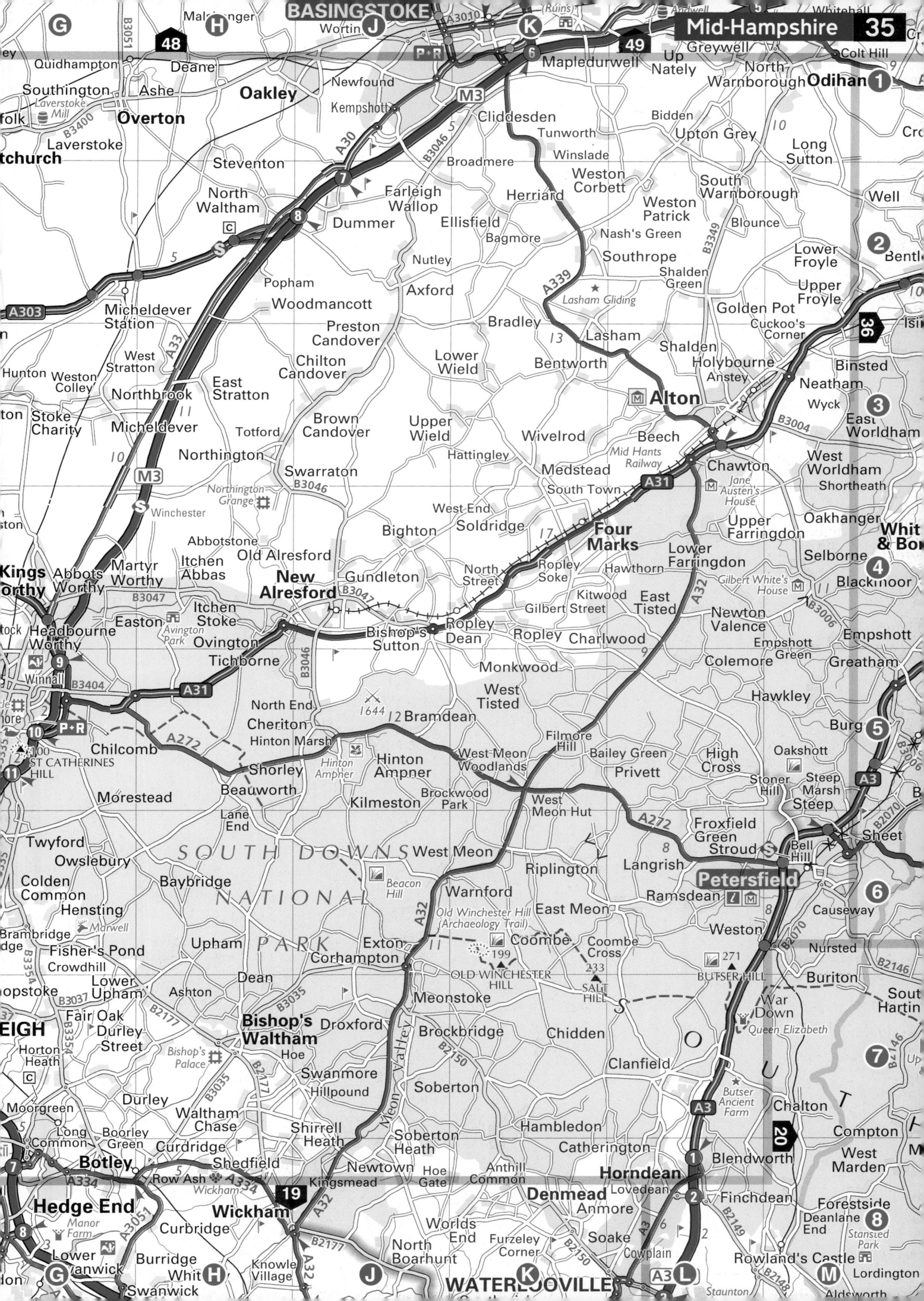

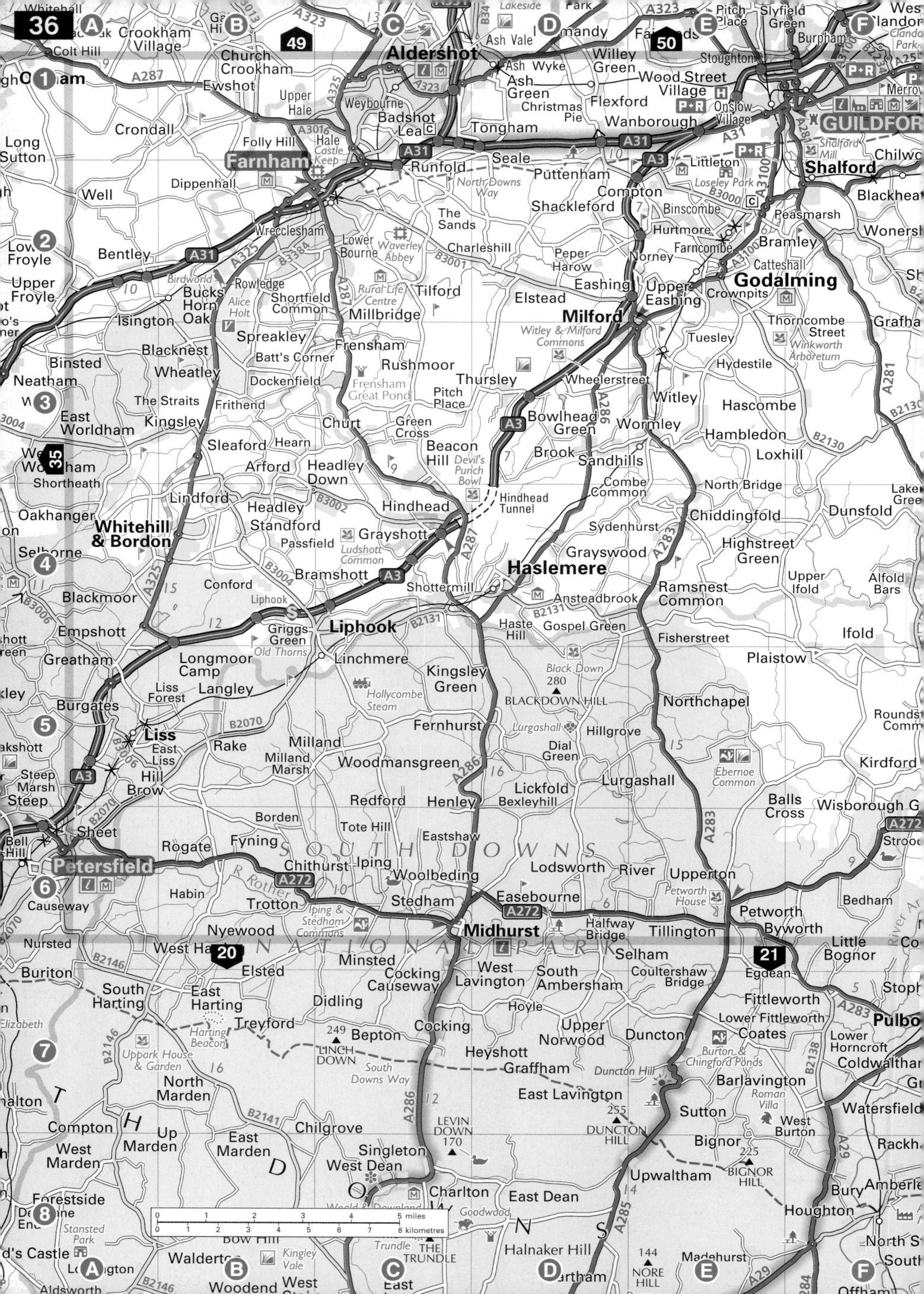

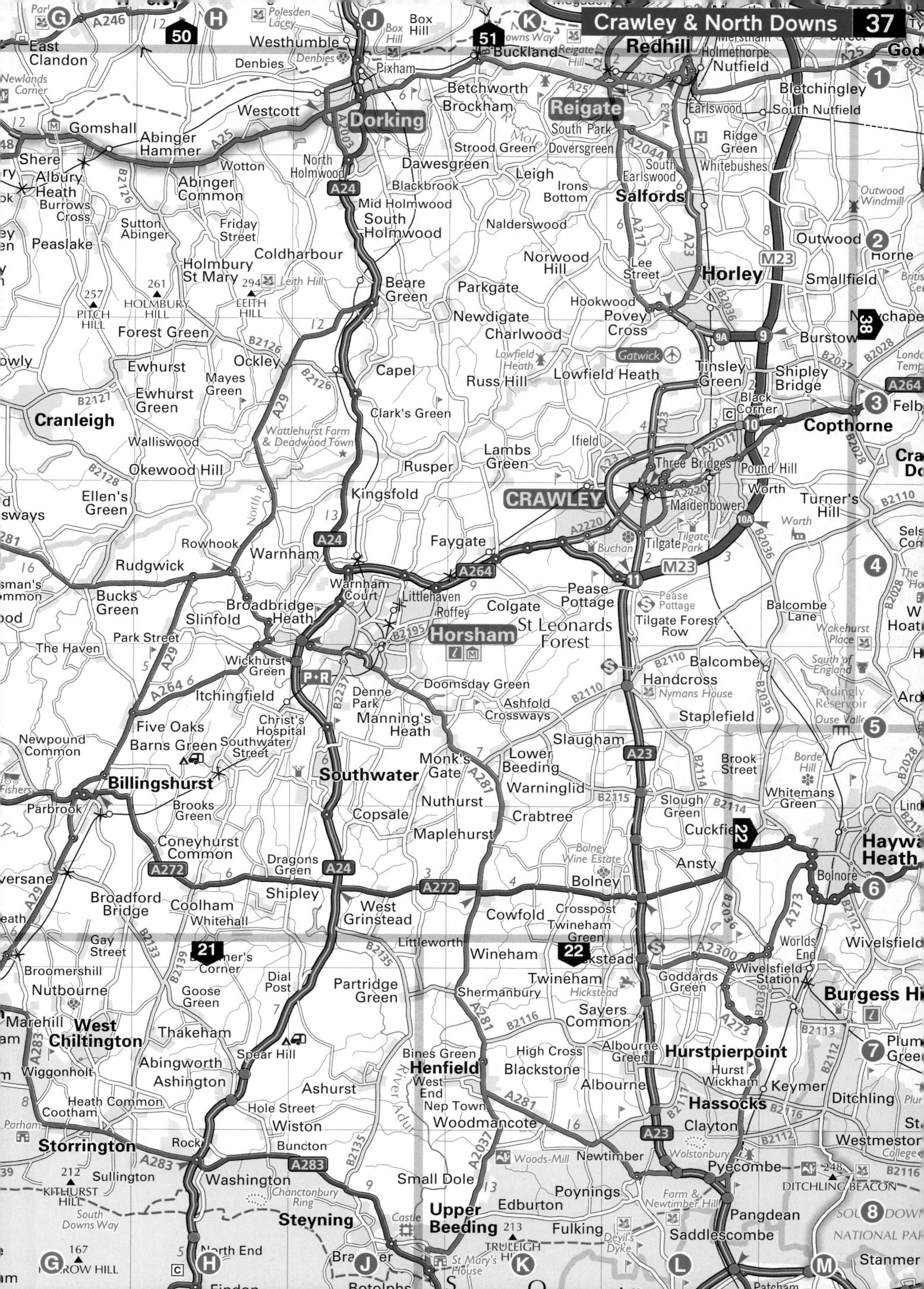

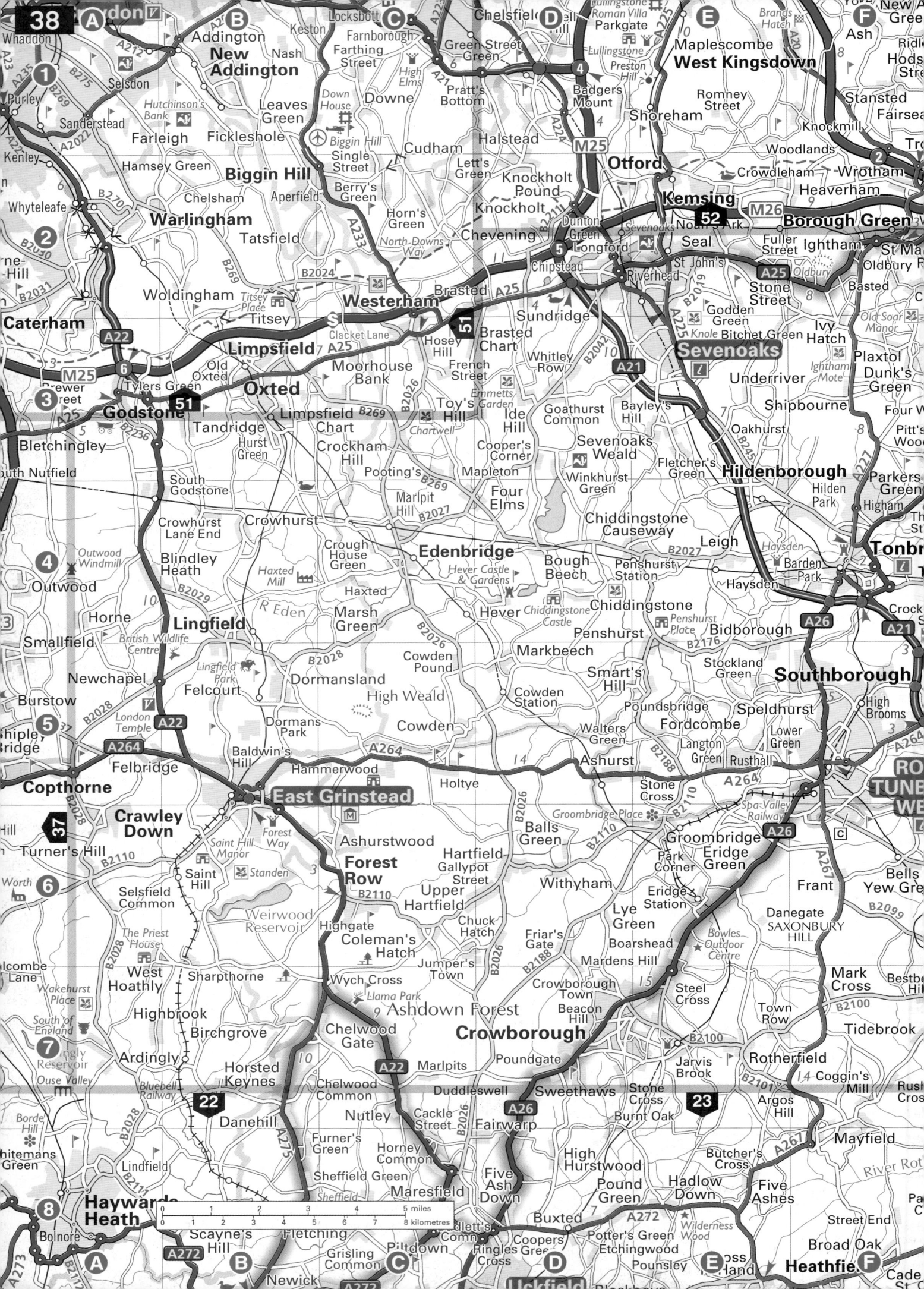

MAIDSTONE

Snodland · Aylesford · Ditton · West Malling · Addington · Leybourne · West Peckham · Nettlestead · Mereworth · Wateringbury · Teston · East Barming · Barming Heath · Kings Hill · East Malling · Larkfield · Allington · Sandling · Boxley · Detling · Thurnham · Bearsted · Hollingbourne · Broad Street · Harrietsham · Lenham · Sandway · Lenham Heath · Egerton · Boughton Malherbe · Ulcombe · Sutton Valence · East Sutton · Chart Sutton · Boughton Monchelsea · Langley Green · Coxheath · Linton · Hunton · Benover · Chainhurst · Yalding · Laddingford · Collier Street · Marden · Marden Thorn · Staplehurst · Headcorn · Smarden · Biddenden · Frittenden · Sissinghurst · Cranbrook · Goudhurst · Lamberhurst · Horsmonden · Brenchley · Matfield · Paddock Wood · Hawkhurst · Tenterden · Rolvenden · Benenden · Sandhurst · Newenden · Northiam · Bodiam · Robertsbridge · Ticehurst · Wadhurst · Burwash · Flimwell · Hurst Green · Etchingham · Stonegate

River Beult · River Teise · River Medway · River Rother · River Limden

M20 · M2 · A20 · A21 · A26 · A228 · A229 · A249 · A262 · A268 · A274 · A2 · A265

Kent & East Sussex Railway · Bedgebury National Pinetum · Scotney Castle · Sissinghurst Castle · Bodiam Castle · Leeds Castle · Bewl Water · Hop Farm Family Park · Great Dixter House & Gardens · Pashley Manor · Bateman's · Finchcocks · Iden Croft Herbs · Chapel Down Winery · The C M Booth Collection of Historic Vehicles · Kent Event Centre

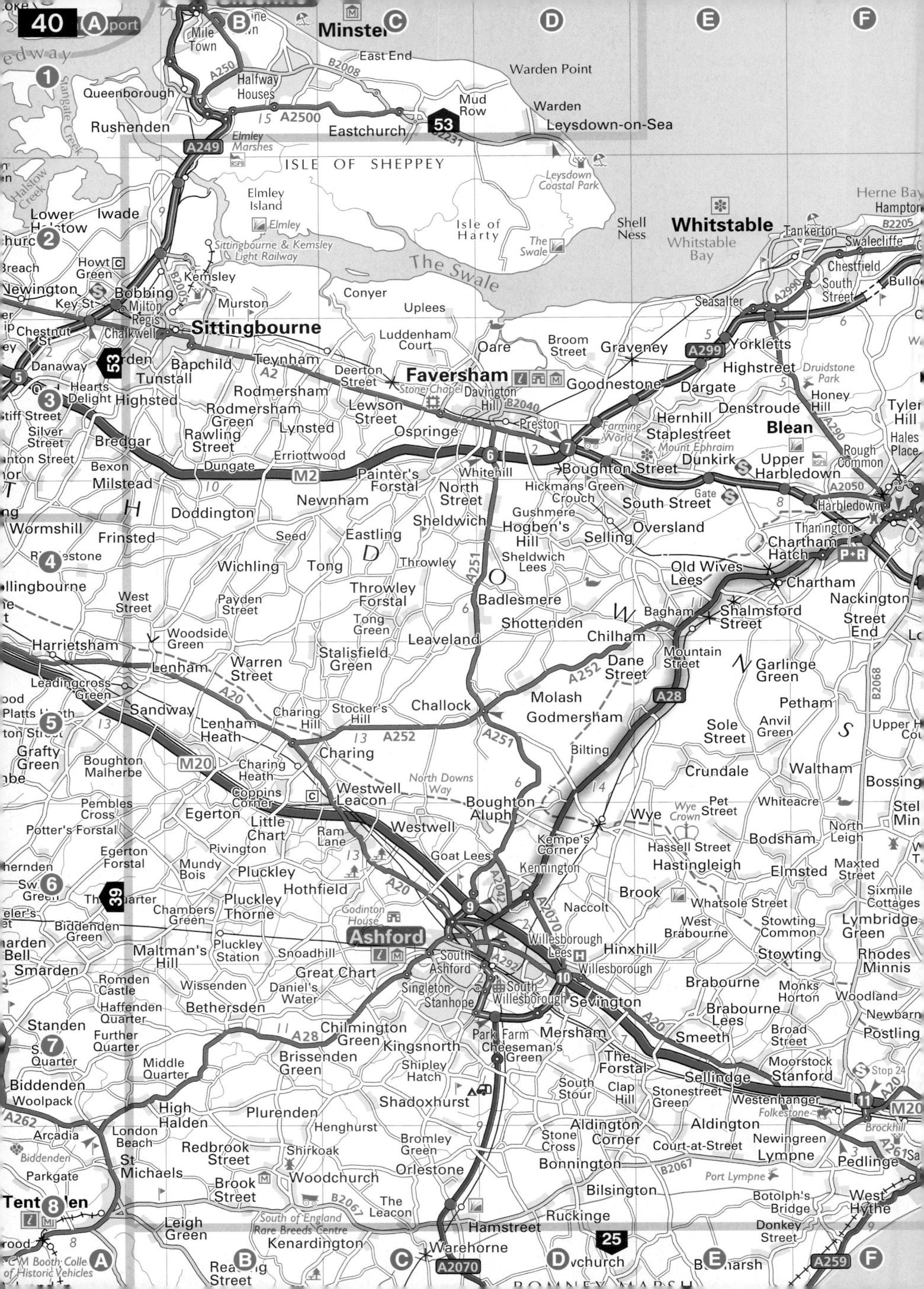

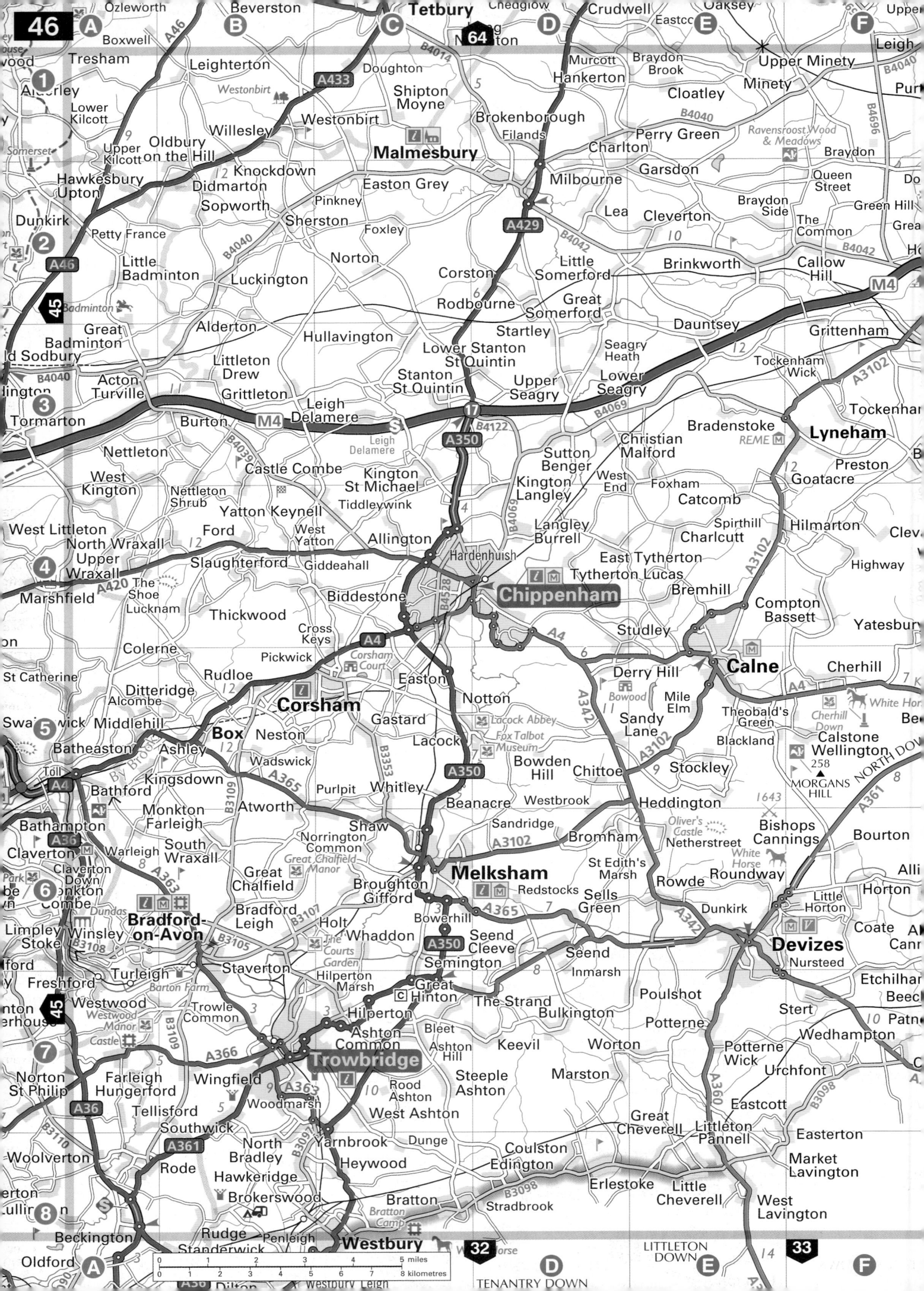

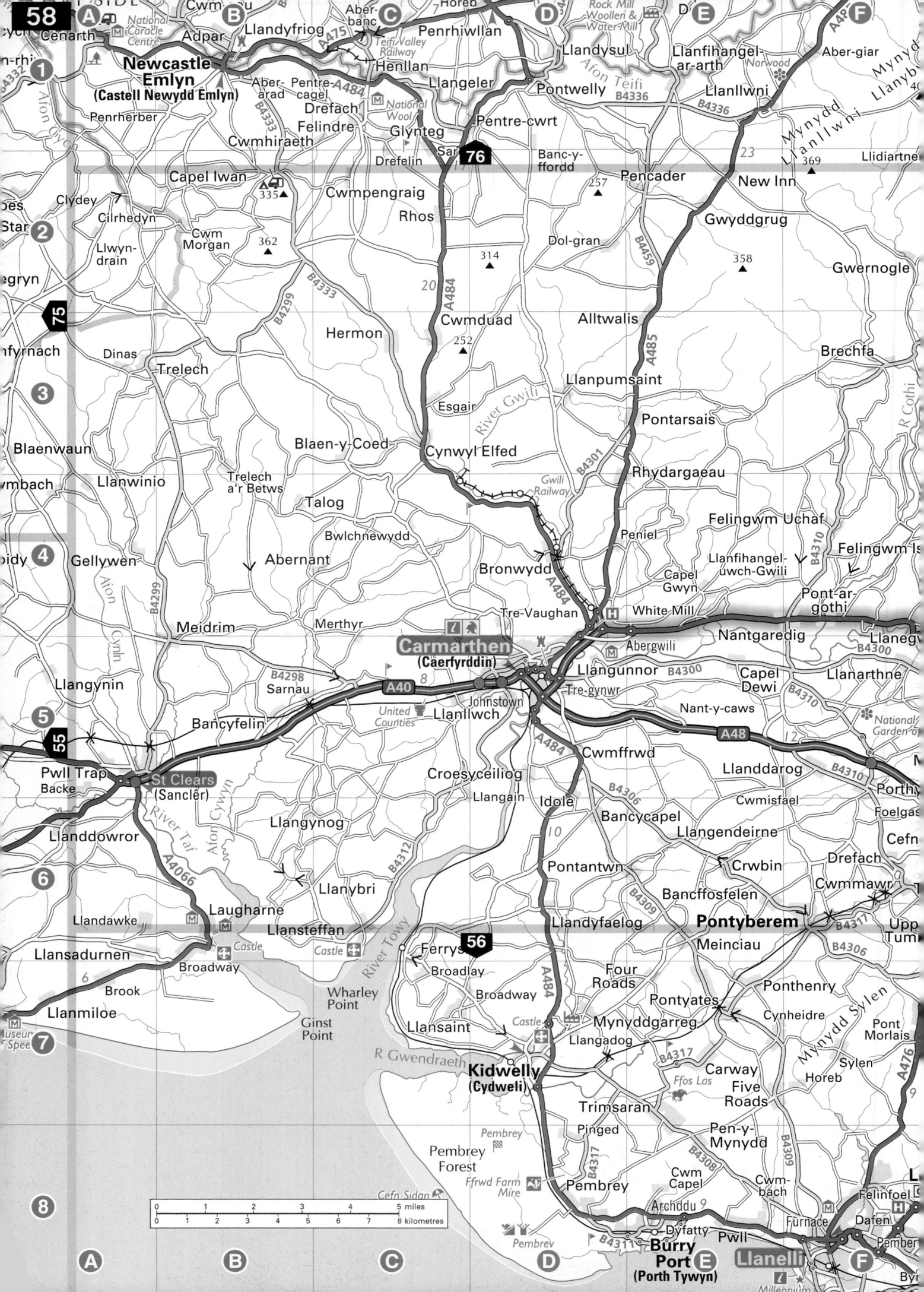

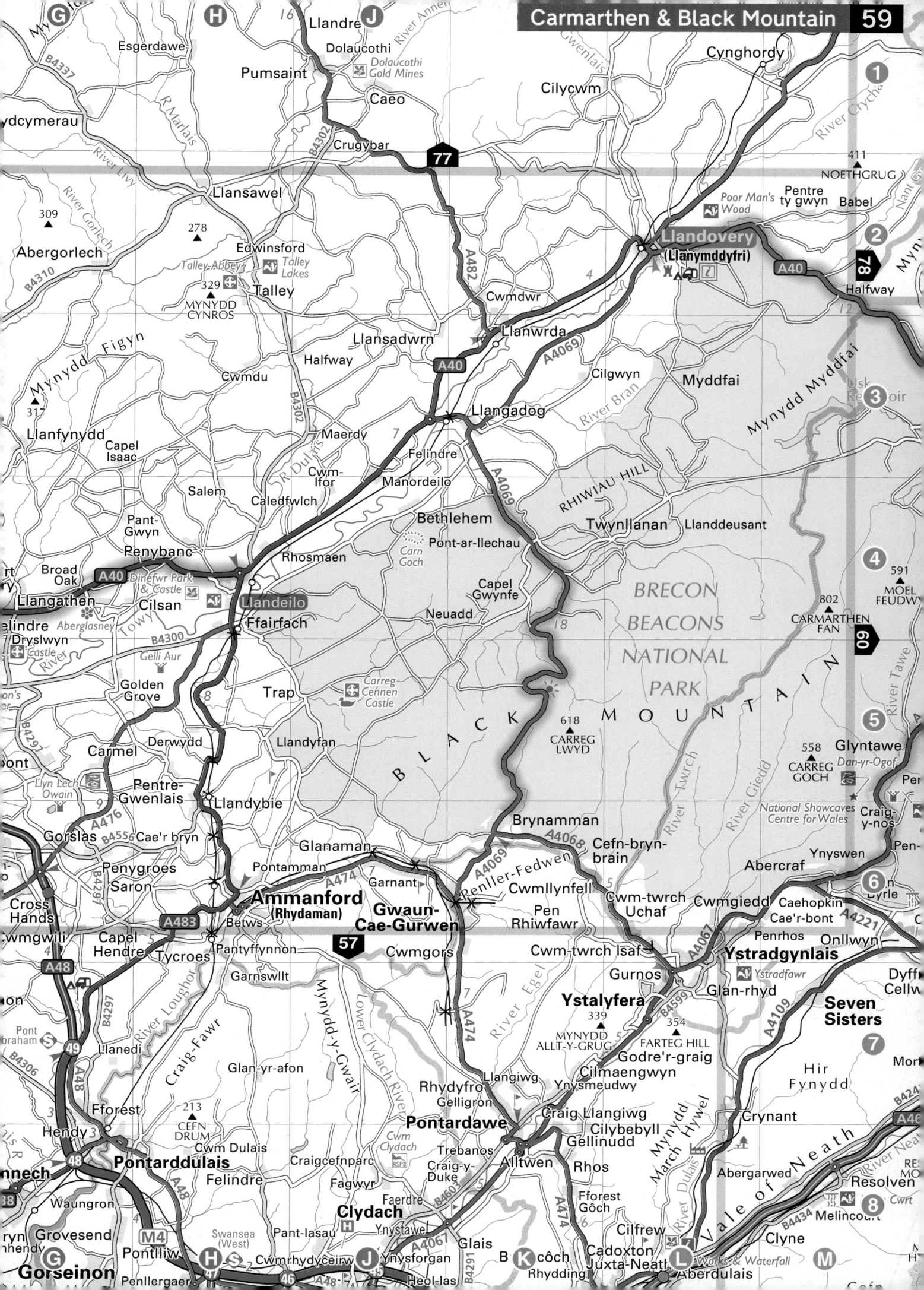

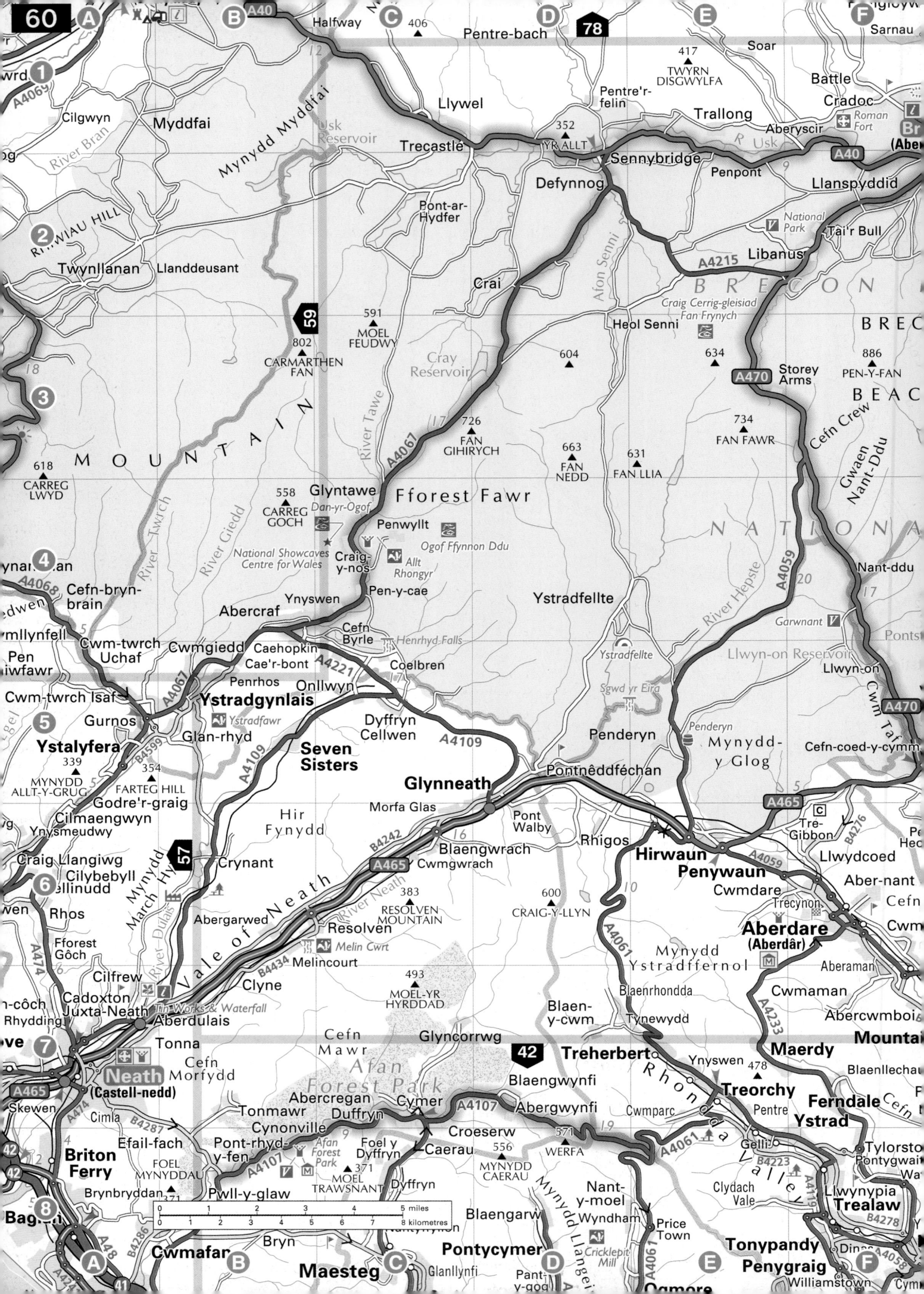

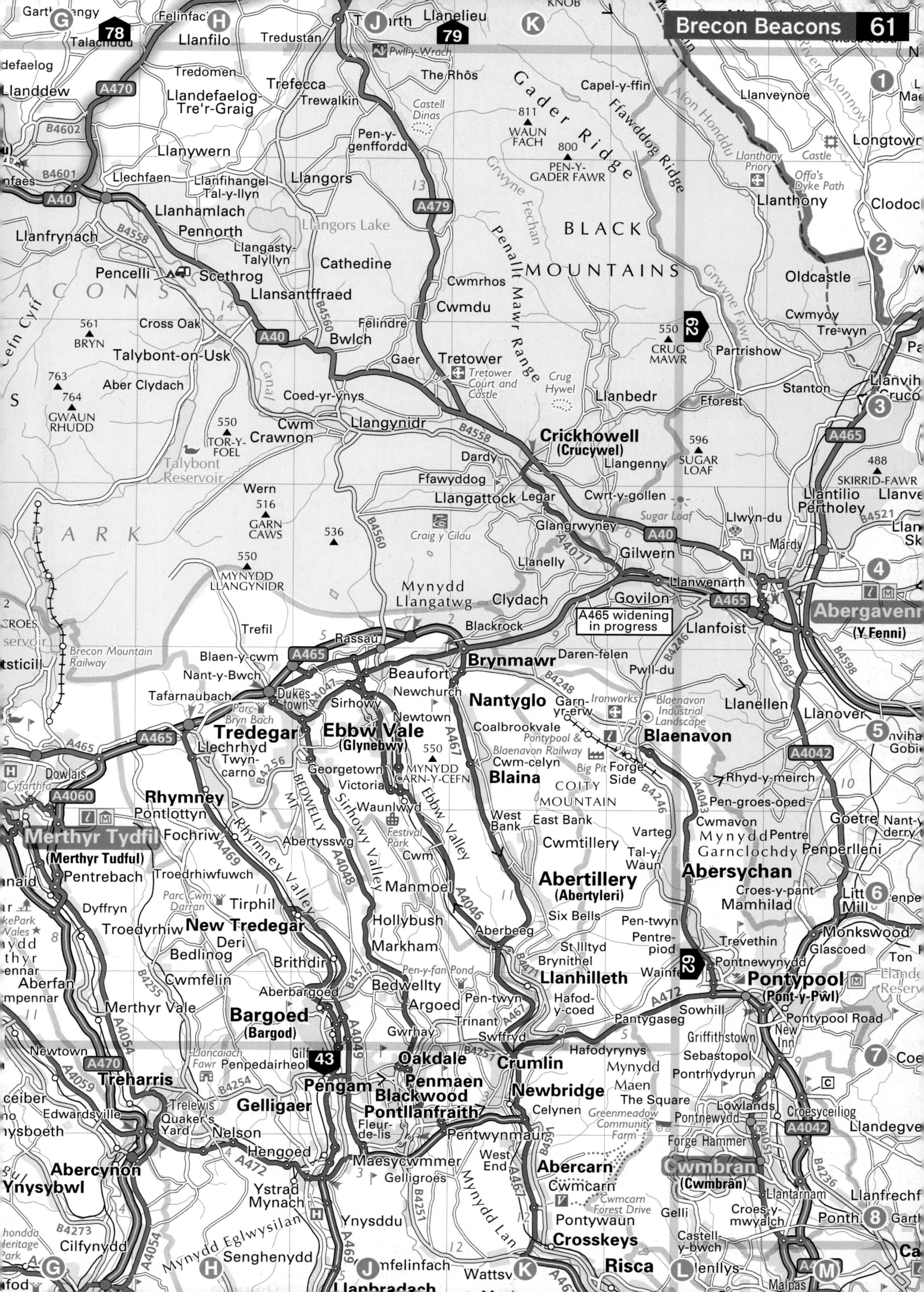

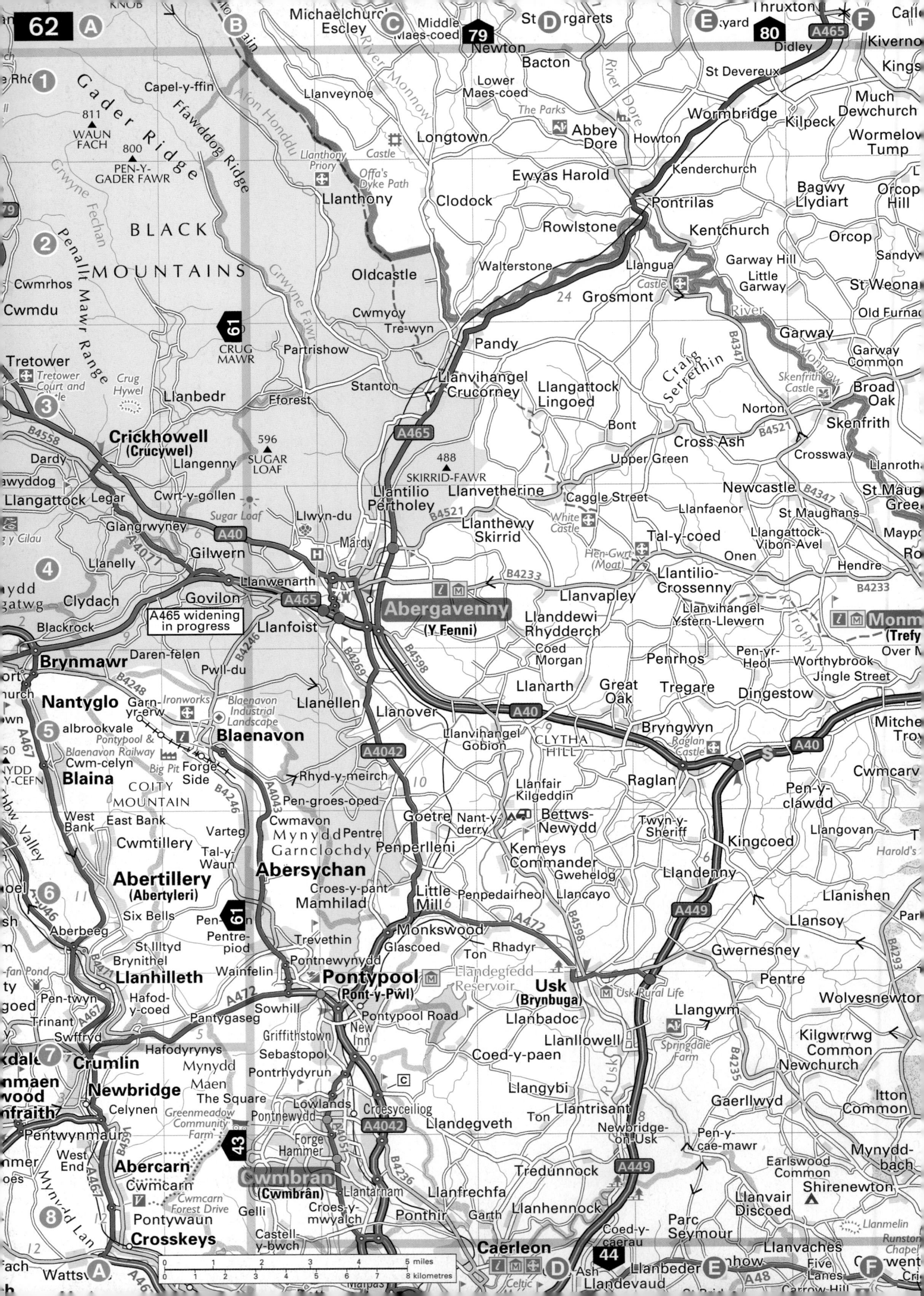

Aconbury
Newtown
Little Dewchurch
Ballingham
Fownhope
Peartree Green
Lower Buckenhill
Sollers Hope
Much Marcle
Donnington
Bromsberrow Heath
Playley Green
Pendock
Lowbands

Little Birch
Much Birch
Carey
Brockhampton
Ladyridge
Stocking
Lyne Down
Dymock
St Mary's Church
Kempley Green
Redmarley D'Abitot
Poolhill
Brand Green
Corse
Upleadon

Hoarwithy
Pen-allt
Fawley Chapel
How Caple
Perrystone Hill
Kempley
Four Oaks
Three Choirs
Brand Green
Corse

Llandinabo
King's Caple
Foy
Wye Valley
Upton Bishop
Shaw Common
Blackwellsend Green

Harewood End
Sellack
Baysham
Strangford
Brampton Abbotts
Hole-in-the-Wall
Crow Hill
Upton Crews
Gorsley
Newent
Hartpury

Michaelchurch
Netherton
Bridstow
Phocle Green
Rudhall
Ross-on-Wye
Linton
Linton Hill
Gorsley Common
Kilcot
Malswick
Kent's Green
Highleadon

St Owens Cross
Peterstow
Wilton
Ashfield
Weston under Penyard
Ryeford
Bromsash
Aston Crews
Little Gorsley
Clifford's Mesne
Taynton
Rudford
Maisemore
Highnam

Tretire
Three Ashes
Glewstone
Tudorville
Hom Green
Pontshill
Lea
Aston Ingham
Glasshouse
Dursley Cross
May Hill
Glasshouse Hill
Huntley
Highnam
Bulley

Llangarron
Pencraig
Goodrich Castle
Coughton
Howle Hill
East Dean
Hope Mansell
Boxbush
Longhope
Birdwood
Churcham
GLOUC

Ruxton Green
Walford
Kerne Bridge
Crooked End
Mitcheldean
Dick Whittington Farm Park
Little London
Oakle Street
Minsterworth
Elmore Back

Llangrove
Marstow
Old Forge
Welsh Bicknor
Ruardean
Drybrook
Abenhall
Blaisdon
Northwood Green
Chaxhill
Elmore

Welsh Newton
Whitchurch
Crocker's Ash
Great Doward
Symonds Yat (East)
Lower Lydbrook
Ruardean Woodside
Ruardean Hill
Brierley
Nailbridge
Flaxley
Westbury on Severn
Stantway
Bollow
Farleys End
Quedgele

Dixton
Ganarew
Little Doward
Symonds Yat (West)
English Bicknor
Worrall Hill
Upper Lydbrook
Broadmoor
Elton
Littledean
Westbury Court Garden
Longney
Hardwicke
Epney

Castle
The Kymin
Wyesham
Hillersland
Christchurch
Berry Hill
Edge End
Cinderford
Forest of Dean
Ruspidge
Newnham on Severn
Ruddle
The Dean
Broadoak
Boxbush
Rodley
Milton End

Staunton
Mile End
Broadwell
Beechenhurst Lodge
Upper Soudley
Lower Soudley
Brain's Green
Arlingham
Fretherne
Saul
Upper Framilode
Moreton Valence
Whitminster

Whitecliffe
Coleford
Milkwall
Clearwell Meend
Parkend
Yorkley
Blakeney
Awre
Frampton-on-Severn
Northington

Penallt
Redbrook
Newland
Perrygrove Railway
Highbury Puzzlewood Wood
Clearwell Caves
Ellwood
Marsh Lane
Whitecroft
Nibley
Purton
Etloe
River Severn
Claypits
Alkerton
Eastington
Cambridge
Stonehou

Pen-twyn
Tre-gagle
Clearwell
Stowe
Dean Forest Railway
Allaston
Purton
Slimbridge Wetland Centre
Shepherds Patch
Slimbridge
Middle Street

Whitebrook
Maryland
Ceciliford
Lower Meend
St Briavels Castle
St Briavels
Bream
Lydney
Sharpness
Hinton
Moorend
Frocester

Llandogo
Broadstone
Catbrook
Coldharbour
Hewelsfield
Aylburton
Newtown
Halmore
Gossington
Coaley
Lower Cam
Far Green

Tintern Parva
Chapel Hill
Brockweir
Woolaston Common
Park Hill
Alvington
Smallbrook
Sharpness
Breadstone
Berkeley Heath
Slimbridge
Stinchcombe
Cam
Ashmead Green

Tintern Abbey
Wye Valley
Netherend
Woolaston
Hook Street
Berkeley
Ham
Dr Jenner's
Berkeley
Newport
Uley
Woodmancote

Boughspring
Lancaut
High Woolaston
Stroat
Wibdon
Bevington
Nupdown
Woodford
Stone
Lower Wick
Nibley Green
Pitt Court
Millend

Woodcroft
National Diving Centre
Shepperdine
Hystfield
Woodford Stone
Lower Stone
North Nibley
Bournstream
Coombe

Tidenham
Tutshill
Sedbury
Oldbury-on-Severn
Oldbury Naite
Hill
Falfield
Whitfield
Michaelwood
Wotton-under-Edge

Chepstow (Cas-gwent)
Bulwarks Camp
Beachley
Pullens Green
Cowhill
Rockhampton
Lower Morton
Tortworth
Charfield
Kingswood
Tresham

Mathern
Littleton-on-Severn
Milbury Heath
Cromhall
Bibstow
Townwell
Alderley

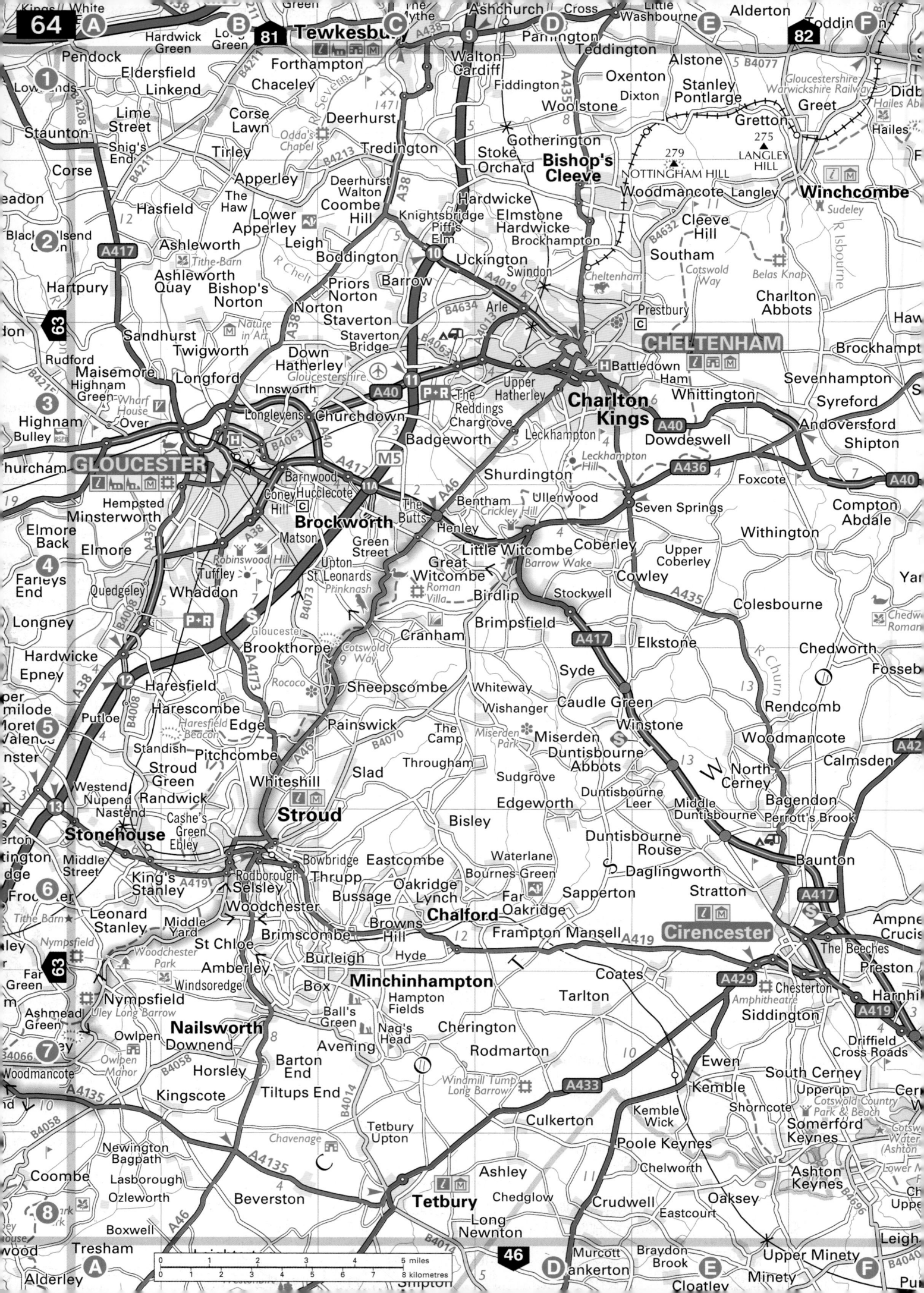

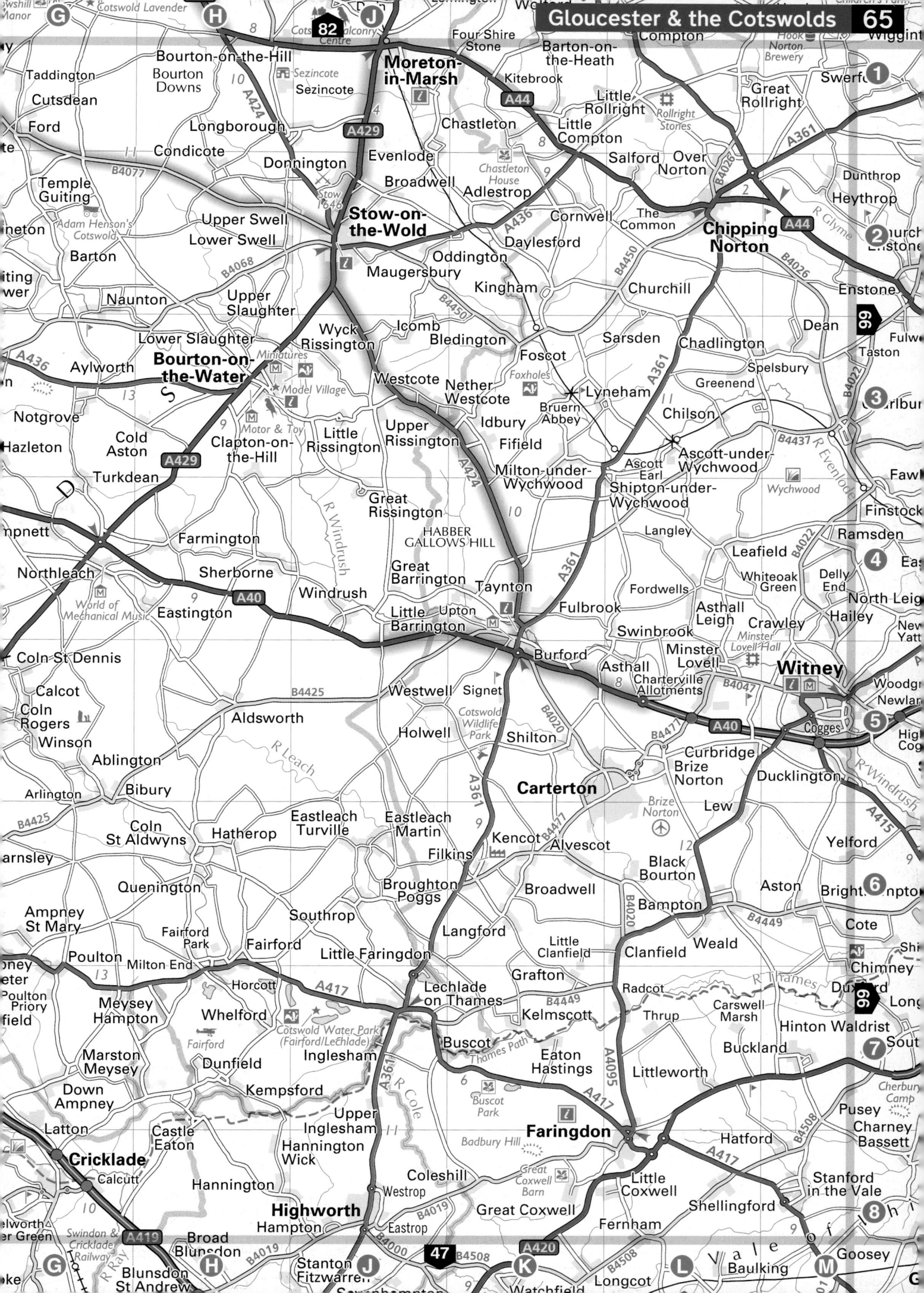

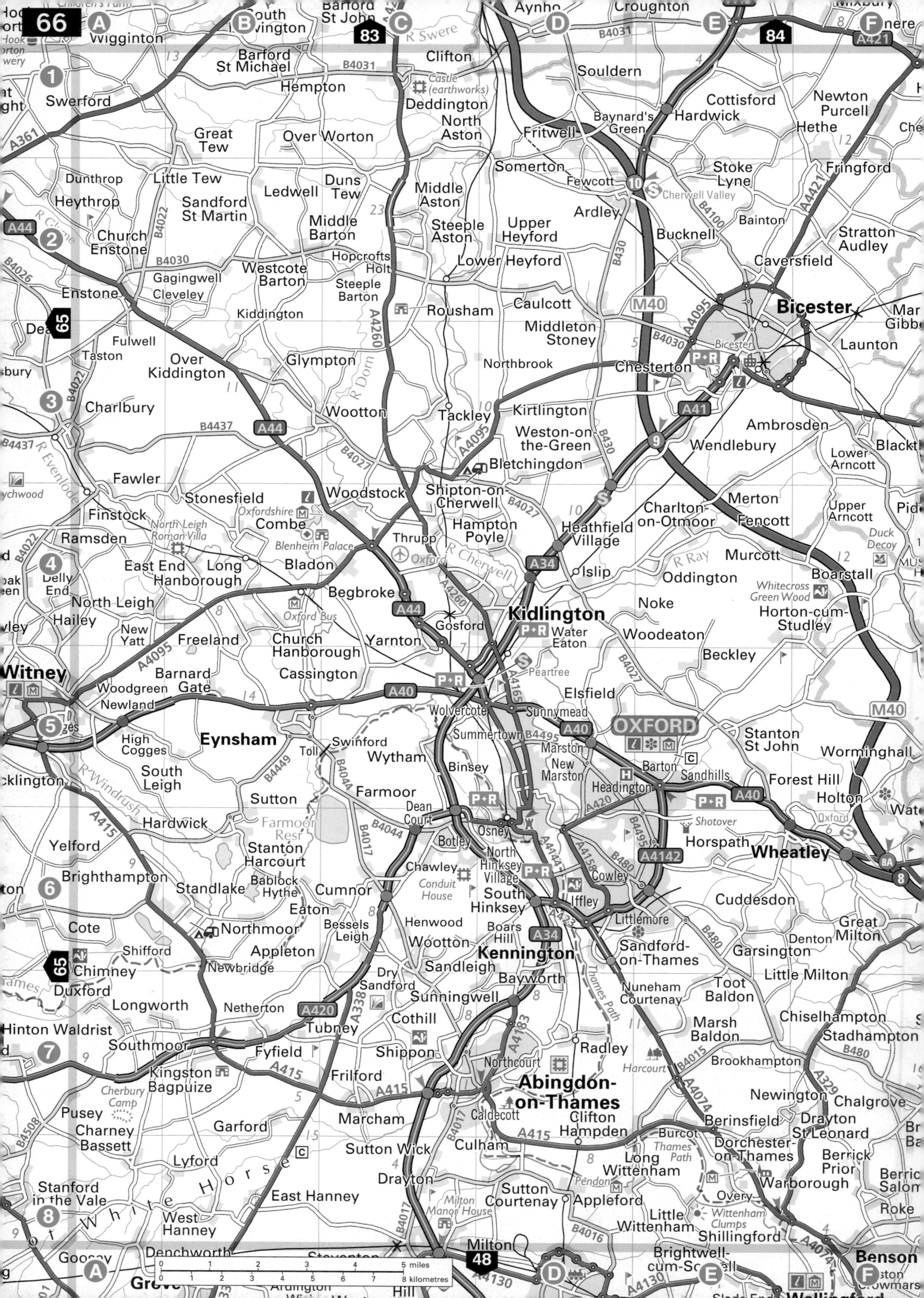

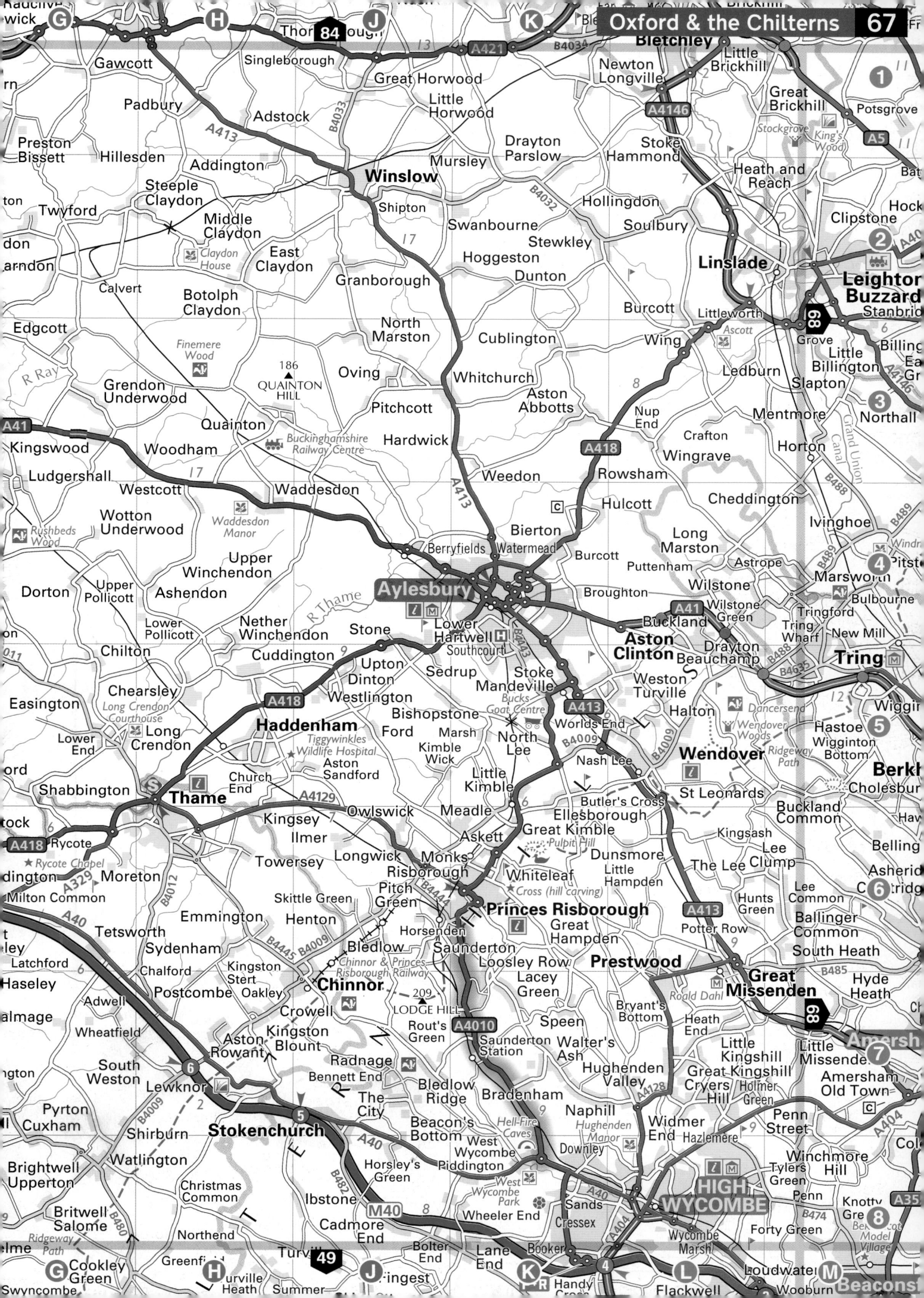

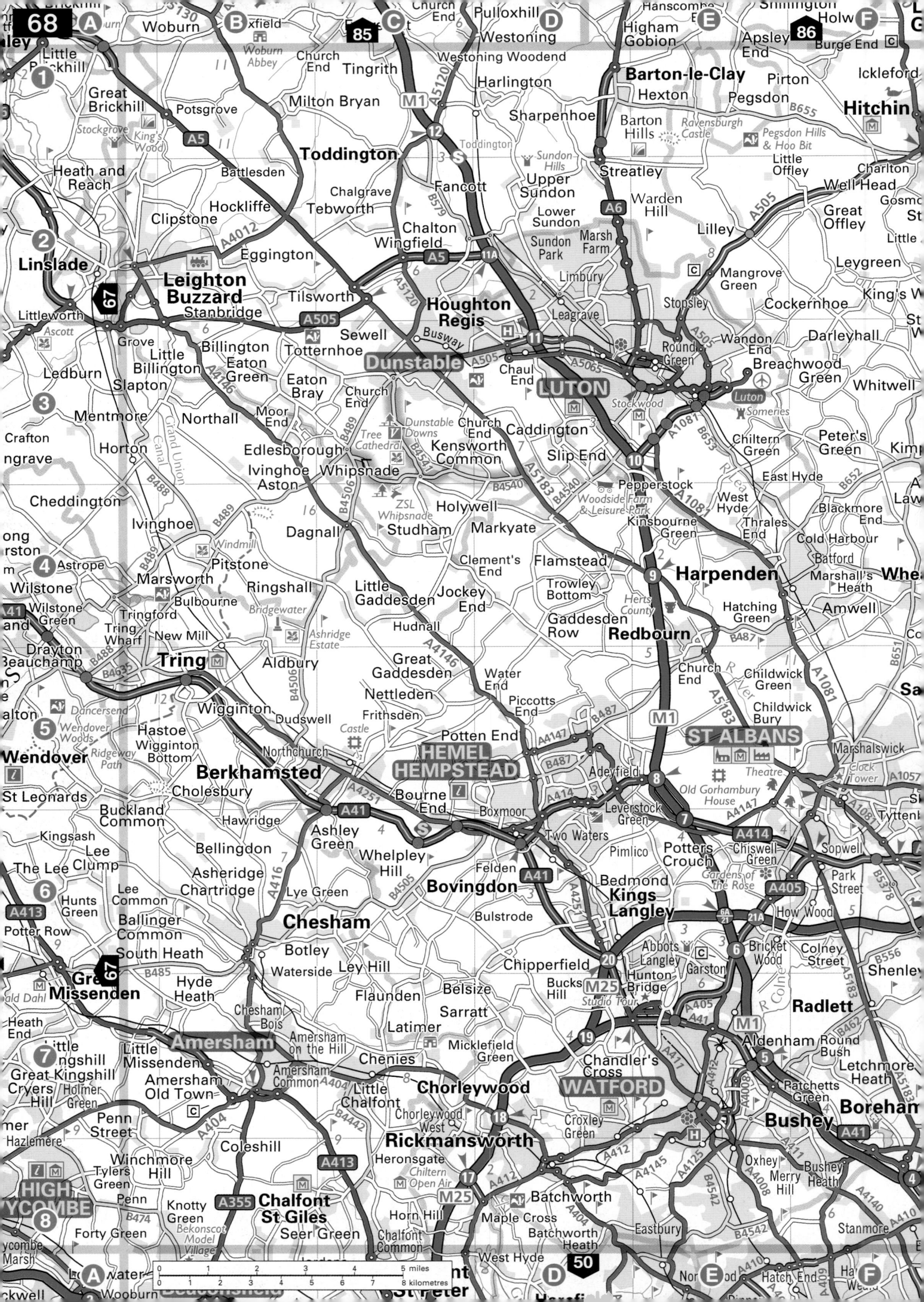

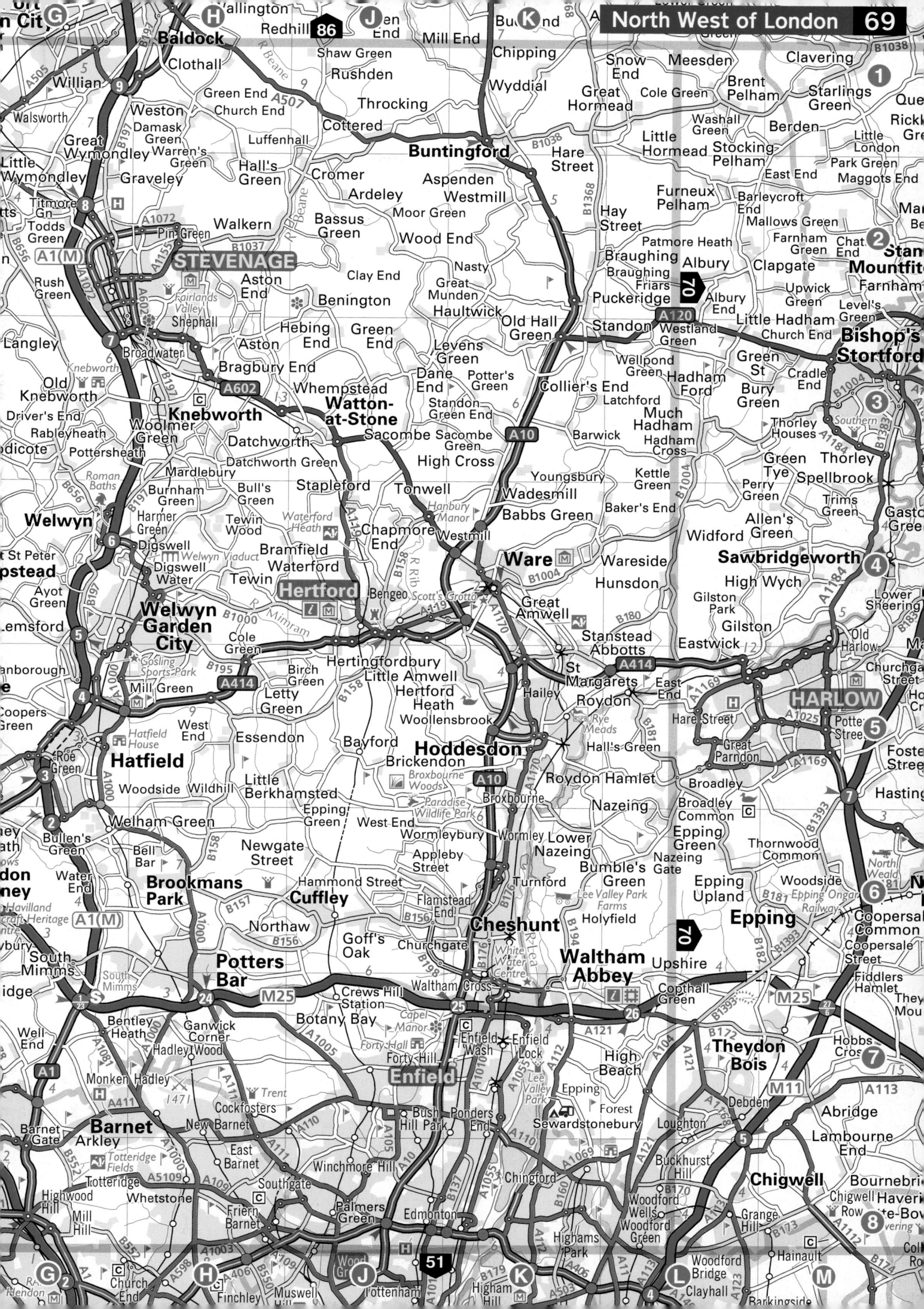

70

A and **B** **C** **D** **E** **F**

Mill End
Chipping
Wyddial

Anstey
Lower Green
Snow End
Meesden
Roas Green
Stickling Green
Clavering
Wicken Bonhunt
Rickling
Widdington
Debden End
Thaxted

Great Hormead
Cole Green
Brent Pelham
Starlings Green
Quendon
Rickling Green
Prior's Hall Barn
Hamperden End
Cutler's Green
Sibley's Green
Monk Street
Bardfield End Green

ntingford
Aspenden
Westmill Green
Washall Green
Little Hormead
Stocking Pelham
Berden
Little London
Park Green
Maggots End
Ugley
Manuden
Ugley Green
Woodend Green
Broxted
Tilty
Great Easton
Lindse

d Er
Nasty
Hare Street
Hay Street
Furneux Pelham
Barleycroft End
Mallows Green
Farnham Green
Chatter End
Stansted Mountfitchet
Bentfield Green
Pledgdon Green
Elsenham
Fuller's End
Gaunt's End
Brick End
Molehill Green
Great Easton
Little Easton

Great Munden
Haultwick
Patmore Heath
Braughing
Albury
Braughing Friars
Clapgate
Upwick Green
Farnham
Level's Green
Burton End
Tye Green
Bamber's Green
Great Dunmow
Chur

Levens Green
Old Hall Green
Puckeridge
Standon
Westland Green
Albury End
Little Hadham
Church End
Bishop's Stortford
Birchanger
Stansted
A120
Smith's Green
Takeley

ane
Stand
Green End
Potter's Green
Collier's End
Latchford
Westmill Green
Hadham Ford
Green St
Cradle End
Bury Green
B1004
Southern
A1060
A120
Takeley St
Brewers End
Little Canfield

Sacombe Green
High Cross
A10
Barwick
Much Hadham
Hadham Cross
Thorley Houses
Thorley
Great Hallingbury
Birchanger Green
Hatfield Forest
Hope End Green

well
Hanbury Manor
Youngsbury
Wadesmill
Babbs Green
Baker's End
Kettle Green
Green Tye
Spellbrook
Perry Green
Little Hallingbury
Wright's Green
Hatfield Broad Oak
Taverners Green
Great Canfield
High Roding
Bishop's Green

Westmill
Ware
Wareside
Hunsdon
Widford
Allen's Green
Trims Green
Gaston Green
Broad Street
Aythorpe Roding
Keeres Green
THE RODING
High Ea

Sawbridgeworth
High Wych
Gilston Park
Gilston
Lower Sheering
Sheering
M11
Hatfield Heath
Ardley End
White Roding
A1060
Roundbush Green
Leaden Roding
Margaret Roding
Clatterfor End
High Ea

Great Amwell
Stanstead Abbotts
Eastwick
Old Harlow
Churchgate Street
Matching Tye
Matching
Newman's End
Manwood Green
Abbess Roding
Nether Street
Pepper's Green
Farn End
Go East

ry well
ford heath
St Margarets
Hailey
Roydon
East End
A1169
HARLOW
A1025
Hobbs Cross
Carters Green
Matching Green
Beauchamp Roding
Birds Green
Shellow Bowells
Boyt Cros

Hoddesdon
lens
Rye Meads
Hall's Green
Great Parndon
Hare Street
A1169
Potter Street
Threshers Bush
High Laver
Little Laver
Norwood End
Miller's Green
Radley Green
Cooksmill Green

A10
A170
Roydon Hamlet
Broadley
Broadley Common
Foster Street
Magdalen Laver
Fyfield
Willingale
Radley Green

xbourne ods
Nazeing
Epping Green
Nazeing Gate
Thornwood Common
Hastingwood
A414
Tyler's Green
Bobbingworth
Shelley
Moreton
Norton Mandeville
Norton Heath
Highwood

rmleybury
Wormley
Lower Nazeing
Bumble's Green
Holyfield
Woodside
Bovinger
North Weald Bassett
Greensted
Wooden Church
High Ongar
Chipping Ongar
Blackmore
Mill Green

Cheshunt
Turnford
Lee Valley Park Farms
Epping Upland
B181
Epping Ongar Railway
Coopersale Common
Toot Hill
Marden Ash
Paslow Wood Common
Stondon Massey
Fryerning
Heybridge

A194
Waltham Abbey
Upshire
Copthall Green
Epping
Coopersale Street
Fiddlers Hamlet
Theydon Mount
Stanford Rivers
Stondon Massey
Hook End
Wyatt's Green

ltham Cross
Enfield
Enfield Lock
High Beach
M25
Hobbs Cross
Theydon Bois
Stapleford Tawney
Nuclear Bunker
Hare Street
Doddinghurst
Fox Hatch
BRENTWOOD

ield
Lee Valley Park
Epping Forest
Sewardstonebury
Loughton
Debden
Abridge
Lambourne End
Passingford Bridge
Kelvedon Hatch
Navestock
Navestock Side
Crow Green
Pilgrims Hatch
Shenfield
Hutto

High Beach
Chingford
Buckhurst Hill
Chigwell
Bournebridge
Sabine's Green
Wattons Green
Stapleford Abbotts
South Weald
Coxtie Green
Mountnessing
Ingra

nton
Woodford Wells
Woodford Green
Grange Hill
Havering atte-Bower
Havering
Noak Hill
Harold Hill
Brook Street
Littl Wars

Highams Park
Highams Hill
Woodford
Hainault
Collier Row
Gidea
Harold
Great
Thornton

Scale
0 1 2 3 4 5 miles
0 1 2 3 4 5 6 7 8 kilometres

52

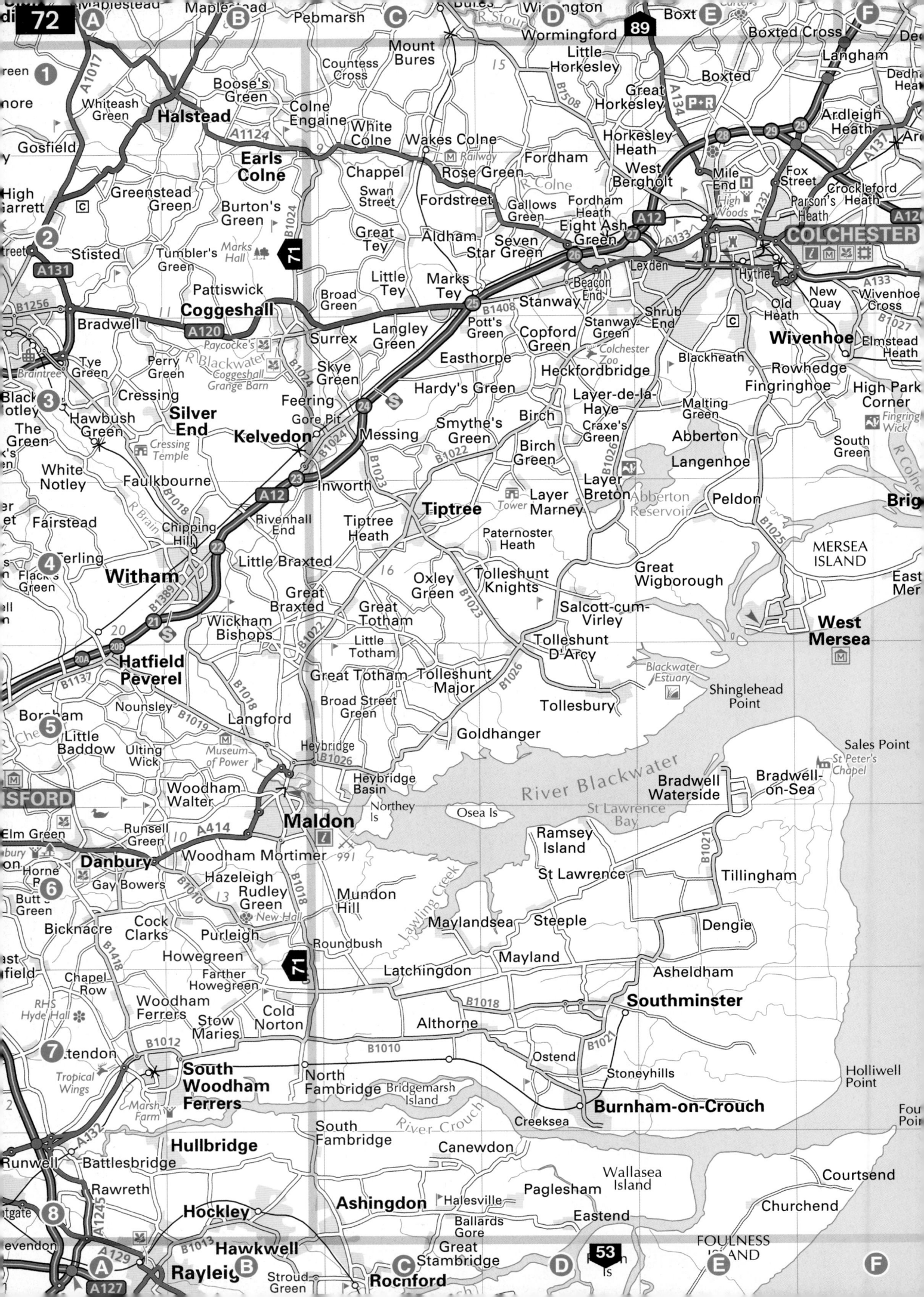

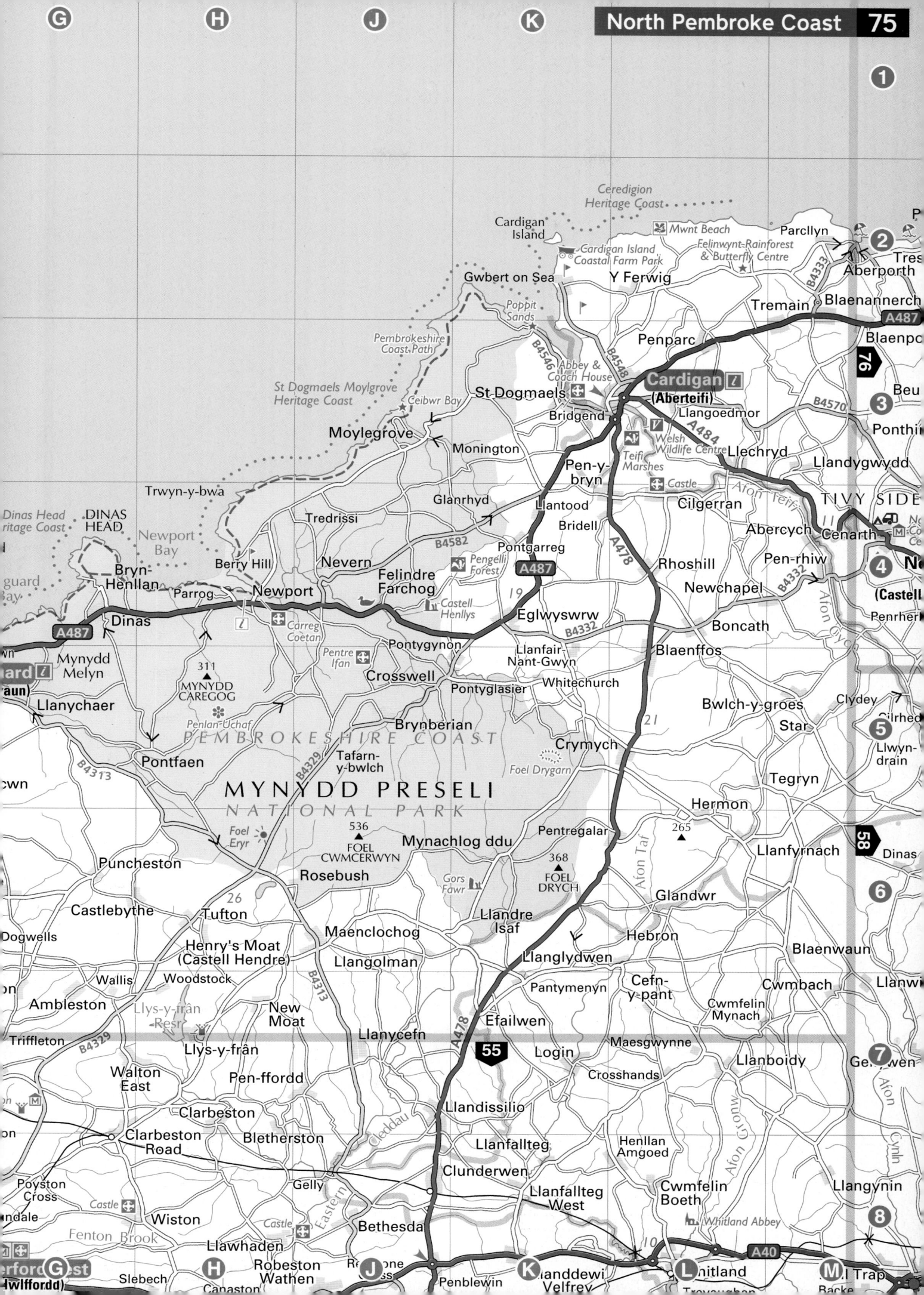

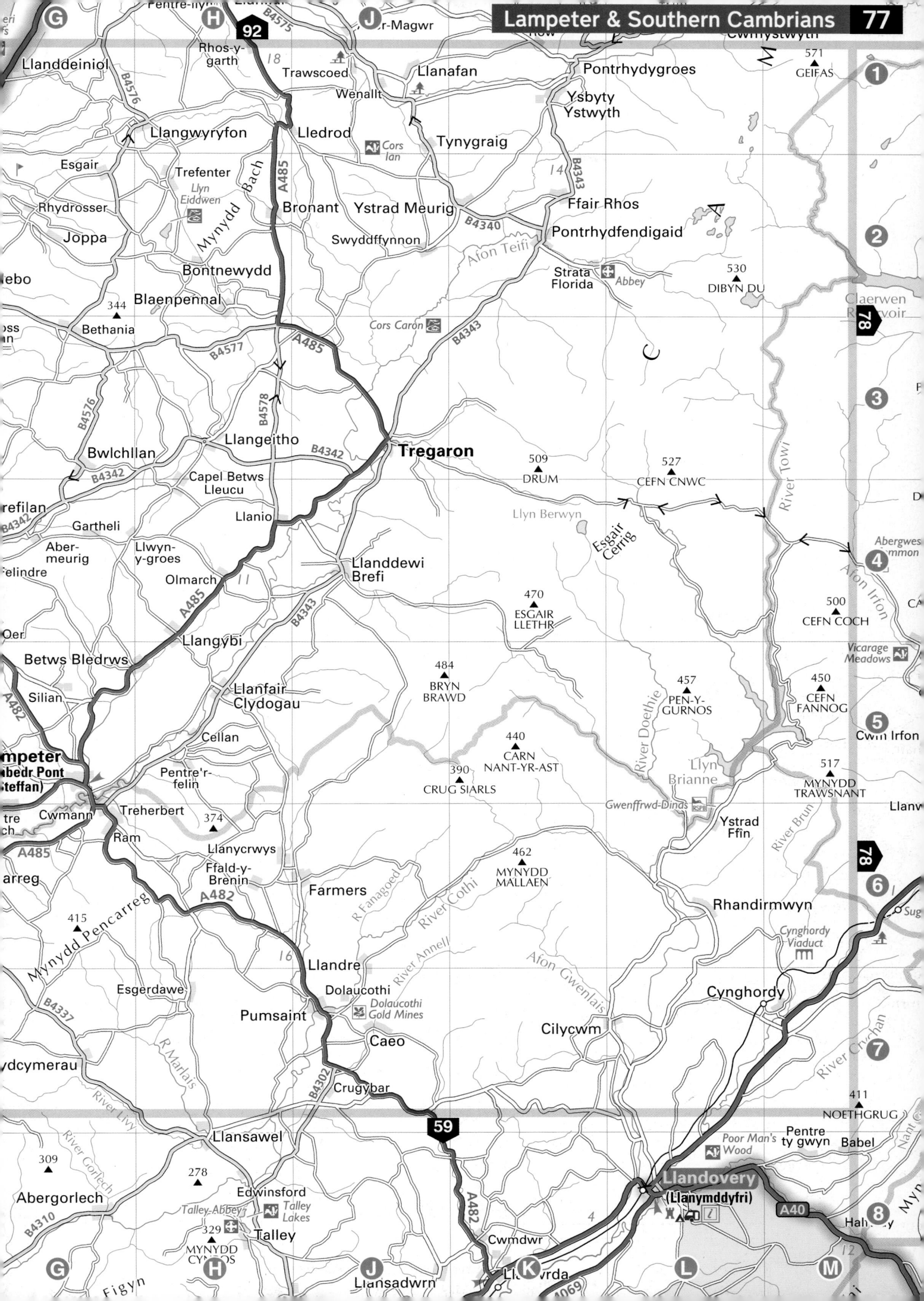

G H J

Pentre-llyn 92 B4575 r-Magwr Now Cwmystwyth
Rhos-y-garth B4575 571 GEIFAS
18 Trawscoed Llanafan Pontrhydygroes
Wenallt Ysbyty Ystwyth
Llanddeiniol Llangwyryfon Lledrod Cors Ian Tynygraig B4343 Ffair Rhos
B4576 Trefenter Llyn Eiddwen Bronant Ystrad Meurig B4340 Pontrhydfendigaid
Esgair Swyddffynnon Afon Teifi Strata Florida Abbey 530 DIBYN DU
Rhydrosser Mynydd Bach 530
Joppa Bontnewydd Claerwen Reservoir
Nebo 78
Blaenpennal 344 Cors Carôn B4343 1
Bethania 509 DRUM 527 CEFN CNWC River Towy 2
B4577 A485 3
B4578 Llangeitho B4342 Tregaron Llyn Berwyn Esgair Cerrig Abergwesyn Common
Bwlchllan B4578 Capel Betws Lleucu 4
B4342 Llanio 470 ESGAIR LLETHR Afon Irfon 500 CEFN COCH
refilan Gartheli Aber-meurig Llwyn-y-groes 484 BRYN BRAWD 457 PEN-Y-GURNOS 450 CEFN FANNOG Vicarage Meadows
Felindre Olmarch 11 Llanddewi Brefi River Doethie 5
Oer A485 B4343 440 CARN NANT-YR-AST 517 MYNYDD TRAWSNANT
Betws Bledrws Llangybi 390 CRUG SIARLS Llyn Brianne Cwm Irfon
Silian Llanfair Clydogau Gwenffrwd-Dinas RSPB Ystrad Ffin River Bran
A482 Cellan Llanv
mpeter Pentre'r-felin 462 MYNYDD MALLAEN 6 78
bedr Pont teffan) Cwmann 374 Rhandirmwyn
Treherbert R Fanagoed River Cothi Cynghordy Viaduct
tre ch A485 Ram Llanycrwys Cynghordy
arreg Ffald-y-Brenin A482 Farmers Afon Gwenlais 7
415 Mynydd Pencarreg Llandre River Annell Cilycwm 411 NOETHGRUG
Esgerdawe Dolaucothi Pentre ty gwyn
B4337 16 Pumsaint Dolaucothi Gold Mines Poor Man's Wood Babel
ydcymerau Caeo River Crychan
River Livy Crugybar 59 Llandovery 8
309 R Marlais A482 (Llanymddyfri) A40
Abergorlech 278 Llansawel Cwmdwr Hal y
B4310 River Gorlech Edwinsford 4
329 Talley Abbey Talley Lakes Talley
MYNYDD CYNROS A482
G H J K L M
Llansadwrn rda A069 12 Figyn

59

92

78

78

A40

A485

A482

A40

B4302

1069

16

14

18

11

4

12

A343 B4340 B4343 B4342 B4578 B4577 B4576 B4337 B4310

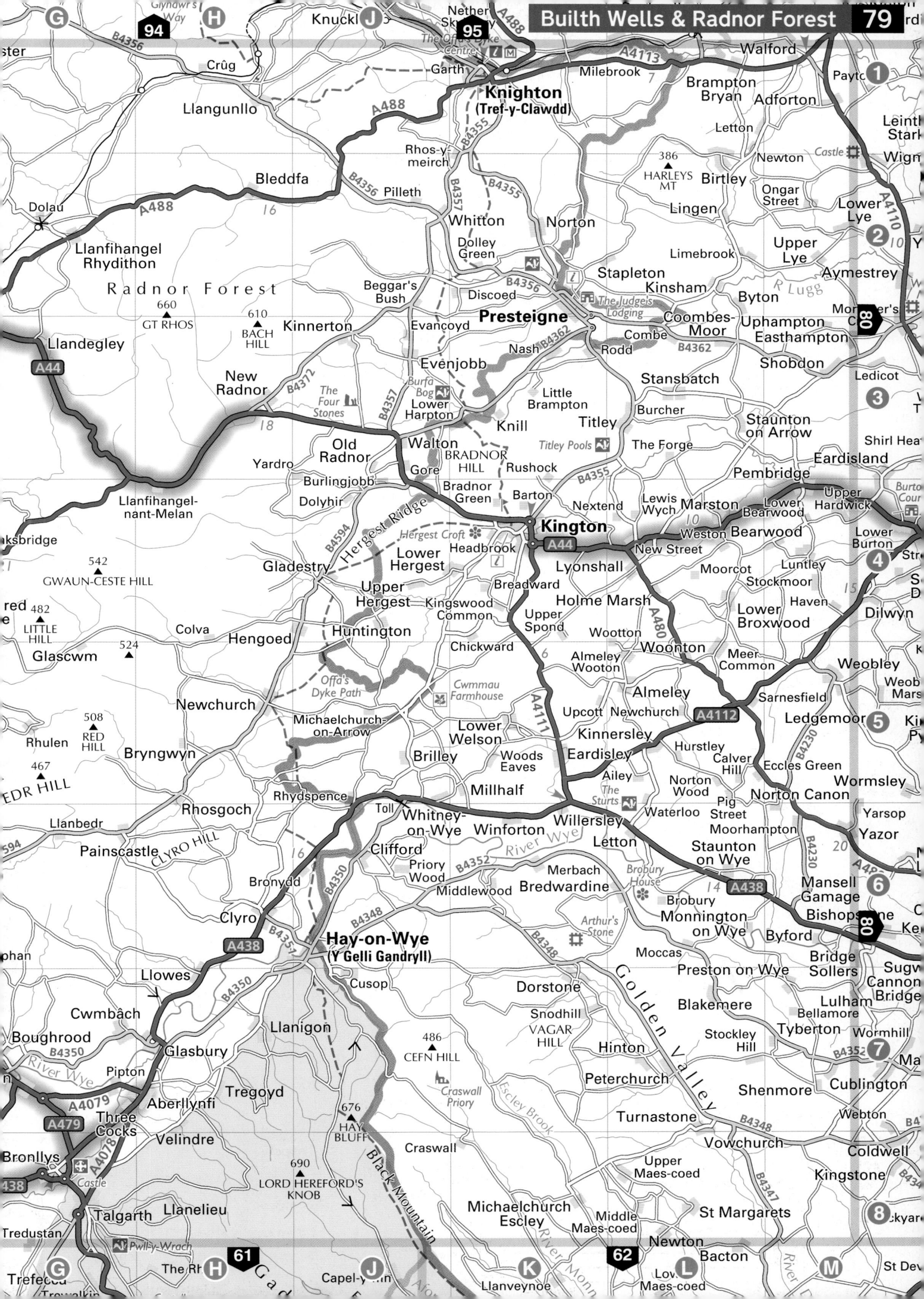

Burrington
Pipe Aston
Elton
Overton
Ashford Carbonell
Whitton
Whitton
Greete
Nash
Bickley
Milson
Neen Sollars
Mamb
Bay

Paytoe
Leinthall Starkes
Richards Castle
Ashford Bowdler
Middleton
Little Hereford
Bleathwood
Boraston
Knighton on Teme
A456
Comm

Castle
Wigmore
Oreleton Common
Comberton
Woofferton
Brimfield Cross
Burford
Berrington
Callows Grave
Tenbury Wells
Rochford
Upper Rochford
Hanley Orl
Sta
on

Lower Lye
Leinthall Earls
Ashley Moor
Wyson
Orleton
Brimfield
Stony Cross
Berrington Green
St Michaels
Kyrewood
Hanley Child
Stoc

Aymestrey
Yatton
Croft Ambrey
Bircher
Middleton on the Hill
Miles Hope
Kyre Park
Bank Street
Stoke Bliss
Sweet Green
Broadheath
Upper Sapey

Croft Castle
Water Mill
Yarpole
Moreton Eye
Ashton
Leysters
Kyre Green
Wolferlow

Lucton
Bicton
Luston
Berrington Hall
The Hundred
Woonton
Grafton
Bockleton
Collington

Lugg
Mortimer's Cross
Lugg Green
Aston
Whyle
Grantsfield
Hatfield
Thornbury
Old Church
Tedstone Wafer

Ledicot
Kingsland
West Town
Cobnash
The Broad
Kimbolton
Stockton
Pudleston
Grendon Green
Edwyn Ralph
Bredenbury
Edvin Loach
Sandy Cross

Shirl Heath
Lawton
Cholstrey
Ebnall
Leominster
Steen's Bridge
Docklow
A44
Bromyard Downs

Eardisland
Monkland
Baron's Cross
Stretford
Humber
Marston Stannett
Bromyard

Upper Hardwick
Wall End
Newtown
Ivington
Stoke Prior
Risbury
Bredenbury

Lower Burton
Stretford
Ivington Green
Brierley
Wharton
Marlbrook
Risbury
Hegdon Hill
Munderfield Row
Stanford Bishop

Sollers Dilwyn
Aulden
Upper Hill
Newton
Bowley Town
Pencombe
Little Cowarne
Stoke Cross
Munderfield Stocks

Dilwyn
Birley
Hope under Dinmore
Bodenham
Bowley
England's Gate
Ullingswick
Stoke Lacy
Bishop's Frome

Weobley
Knapton Green
Bush Bank
Westhope
Bodenham Moor
Maund Bryan
Pool Head
Stoke Lacy
Panks Bridge

Weobley Marsh
King's Pyon
Highway
Urdimarsh
The Vauld
Upper Town
A417
Moreton Jeffries
Much Cowarne
Five Bridges

Ledgemoor
Canon Pyon
Wellington
Walker's Green
Felton
Burley Gate
Lower Egleton
Castle Frome

Wormsley
Auberrow
Marden
Preston Wynne
Hillhampton
Ocle Pychard
Newtown
Upper Egleton
Stretton Grandison

Yarsop
Yazor
Tillington Common
Wellington Marsh
Franklands Gate
Sutton St Nicholas
Withington
Westhide
Monkhide
Canon Frome

Mansell Lacy
Tillington
Portway
Sutton Marsh
Withington Marsh
A4103
Yarkhill
Lower Town

Brinsop
Moreton on Lugg
Nunnington
Shucknall
Swinmore Common

Garnage
Bishopstone
Credenhill
Burghill
Upper Lyde
A49
Pipe and Lyde
White Stone
Weston Beggard
Ashperton

Kenchester
Stretton Sugwas
A4103
Holmer
Shelwick
Hagley
Stoke Edith
Tarrington
Trumpet

Sugwas Pool
Swainshill
Huntington
Westfields
Lugwardine
Perton
A417
Munsley

Bridge Sollers
Cannon Bridge
King's Acre
A438
Bartestree
Dormington
Clouds
Stoke Edith
A438

Lulham
Upper Breinton
Breinton
Tupsley
Hampton Bishop
Durlow Common
Putley Green
Aylton
Waller's Green

Bellamore
Wormhill
Eaton Bishop
Ruckhall
Hereford
Clehonger
Belmont
Warham
Blackmarstone
Lower Bullingham
Rotherwas Chapel
Checkley
Putley

Madley
Clehonger
Grafton
Dinedor
Mordiford
Woolhope
Rushall

Webton
Goose Pool
Bullinghope
Portway
Dinedor Hill
Twyford Common
Holme Lacy
Kynaston
Little Marcl

Coldwell
Cobhall Common
Allensmore
Callow
Aconbury
Newtown
Fownhope
Lower Buckenhill
Sollers Hope
Hellens Manor

Kingstone
Hungerstone
Haywood
Little
Peartree Green
Westons Cider
Much Marc
Dym

Thruxton
Cockyard
A465
Kivernoll
Didley
Ballin
Ladyridge
Stocking
Lyne Down
B4024

97

G H Ribbesford J A449 Callow Hill Lye Head Hoobrook K tow Brock B ington Catshi Staple Hill Apes Dale
Pond nk Gorst Hill Summerfield Wilden Shenstone Chaddesley Corbett Dodford Woodcote Park Gate Lickey End Lint
mon Bliss Gate Upper Milton Torton Charlton Cakebole Rushock Woodcote Green Sidemoor Burcot Blackwe
ws op Rock Heightington Stourport-on-Severn Hartlebury Purshull Green A448 Stoke Heath Aston Fields Finstall Bro Gre A449
Greenway Areley Kings Titton Waresley Elmley Lovett Green Cooksey Green Bromsgrove Rock Hill Tardebigge Tutnall A44
Dunley Astley Cross Chadwick Lincomb Norchard Acton Dunhampton Bryan's Green Elmbridge Upton Warren M5 Stoke Prior Stoke Pound Banks Green Foxly
Pensax Abberley Abberley Common The Burf Crossway Green Cutnall Green Broad Alley Stoke Wharf Woodgate
Menithwood Redmarley Noutard's Green Comhampton Sytchampton Dunhampton Hampton Lovett Avoncroft Webbs of Wychbold Harbours Hill Lower Bentley 82
diston Teme Great Witley Frog Pool Northampton Doverdale Oldfield Rashwood Wychbold Astwood Sharpway Gate Hanbury Mount Pleasant
apey mon Stanford Bridge WOODBURY HILL 276 Shrawley Uphampton Holt Fleet Ombersley Hadley Droitwich Spa A38 Gallows Green Hadzor Hanbury Hall Woolmere Green Har Gre
Shelsley Walsh Witley Court Sankyn's Green Holt Heath Holt Sinton Salwarpe B4090 Goosehill Green Mere Green Bradley Green Littlewo
Clifton upon Teme Shelsley Beauchamp Ockeridge Hill Side Oakall Green Grimley Sinton Chatley Ladywood Dunhampstead Phepson Broughton Green Bradley
Martley Wichenford Sinton Green Sinton Moseley Hawford Hawford Dovecote Fernhill Heath Martin Hussingtree Oddingley Himbleton Earls Common Stock Green
stone mere Berrow Green Shoulton Hallow Heath Northwick Hindlip Tibberton Sale Green Huddington Stock Wood
Horsham Wants Green Hallow WORCESTER Rainbow Hill Warndon Crowle Green Broughton Hackett The Bourne Dormston
tbourne Knightwick Collins Green Lower Broadheath Broad Green Upper Broadheath Elgar Newtown Trotshill Crowle A422 Grafton Flyford Flyford Flavell Go
Bringsty Common Lulsley Broadwas Ravenhills Green Leigh Court Barn Henwick Rushwick St Johns A44 Cherry Orchard Whittington Spetchley Spetchley Park Churchill Sneachill Upton Snodsbury North Piddle Abberton
Alfrick Brockamin Bransford Upper Wick Lower Wick A4538 Norton White Ladies Aston Naunton Beauchamp
Suckley Alfrick Pound Smith End Green Leigh Sinton A4103 Bowling Green Powick A4440 Pole Elm Littleworth Peopleton Bishampton
np Longley Green Storridge Stifford's Bridge Lower Howsell Callow End Kempsey Hatfield Green Street Stoulton Hawbridge Drakes Broughton Pinvin Throckmor
Greenhill Greenhill Upper Howsell Deblin's Green Newland Draycott Napleton Pirton Stonehall Wadborough Upper Moor Lower Moor
ony Cross Cradley West Malvern Mathon Malvern Link Madresfield Kerswell Green Ramsden Pershore Wyre Piddle Fladbury Cha
dgeway Cross Ham Green Great Malvern Guarlford Clifton Rhydd Birch Green Besford Defford Pensham Wick Cropthorne Charlton
ll Storeyard Green South End Lower Wyche Hanley Swan Hanley Castle High Green Croome Birlingham Little Comberton
ow en Colwall Upper Wyche Three Counties Severn Stoke Kinnersley Earl's Croome Dunstall Common Woodmancote Great Comberton Brickleham
Loxter Malvern Wells Gilbert's End Holly Green Baughton Eckington Elmley Castle Netherto
ington ow Wellington Heath Herefordshire Beacon 340 Little Malvern Hook Bank Tiltridge Upton-upon-Severn Strensham (northbound) The Grove Strensham Bredon Hill 82
A449 Chandlers Cross Upper Welland Welland Ryall Naunton Upper Strensham Strensham (southbound) Bredon's Norton Ashto under Hill 7
Newtown Eastnor 286 Hollybush Castlemorton Common Longdon Heath Newbridge Green Uckinghall Queenhill Hill End Lower Westmancote Overbury Grafton
A417 Parkway Camer's Green Rye Street Longdon Ripple Twyning Green Bredon's Hardwick Kinsham Conderton Beckford
A216 Bromsberrow Kings Green White End Sledge Green Berrow Puckrup Shuthonger Church End Bredon Silk Mill A46 Grea Washbo
Broom's Green Hardwick Green Long Green Bushley Green Bushley The Mythe Ashchurch Aston-on-Carrant Aston Cross Little Washbourn
Bromsberrow Heath Pendock M50 Tewkesbury 64 Forthampton Walton Cardiff Pamington Teddington Alstone 8
G H J Playley Green Eldersfie Linken K Chaceley L A438 M Oxen Stanley Pontlarge
Redmarley Lowbands Forthampton A435 Dixton

1 2 3 4 5 6 7 8

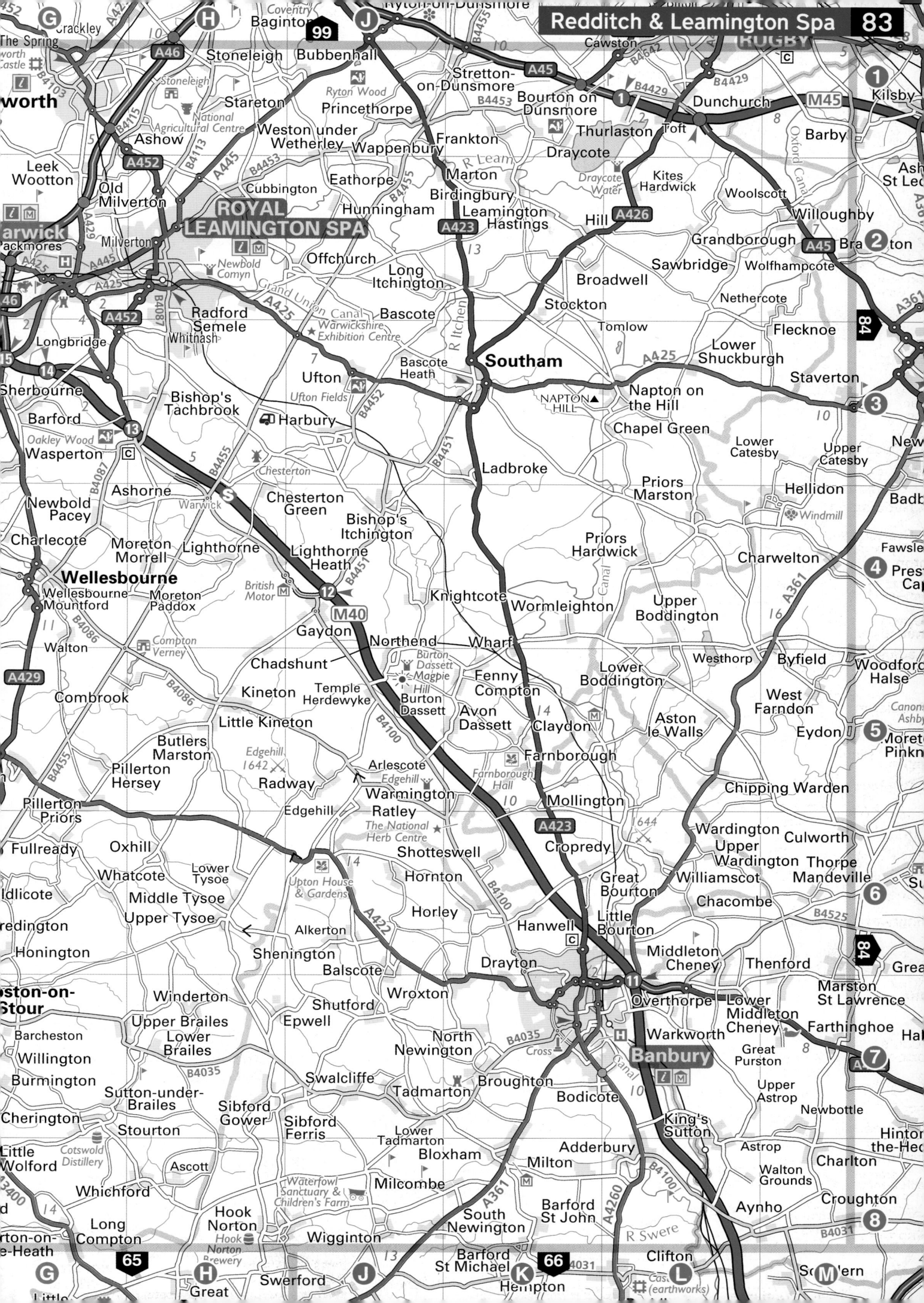

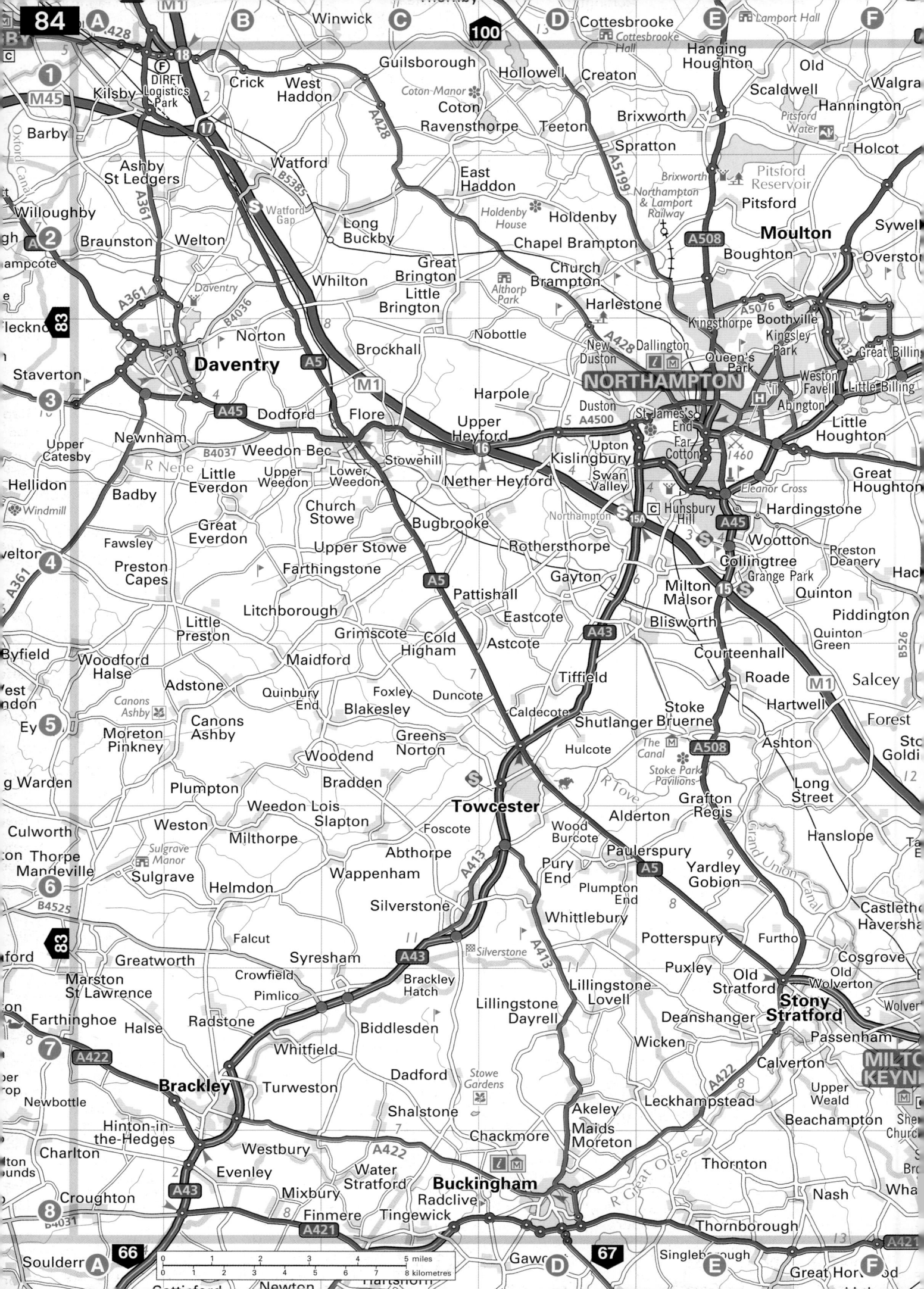

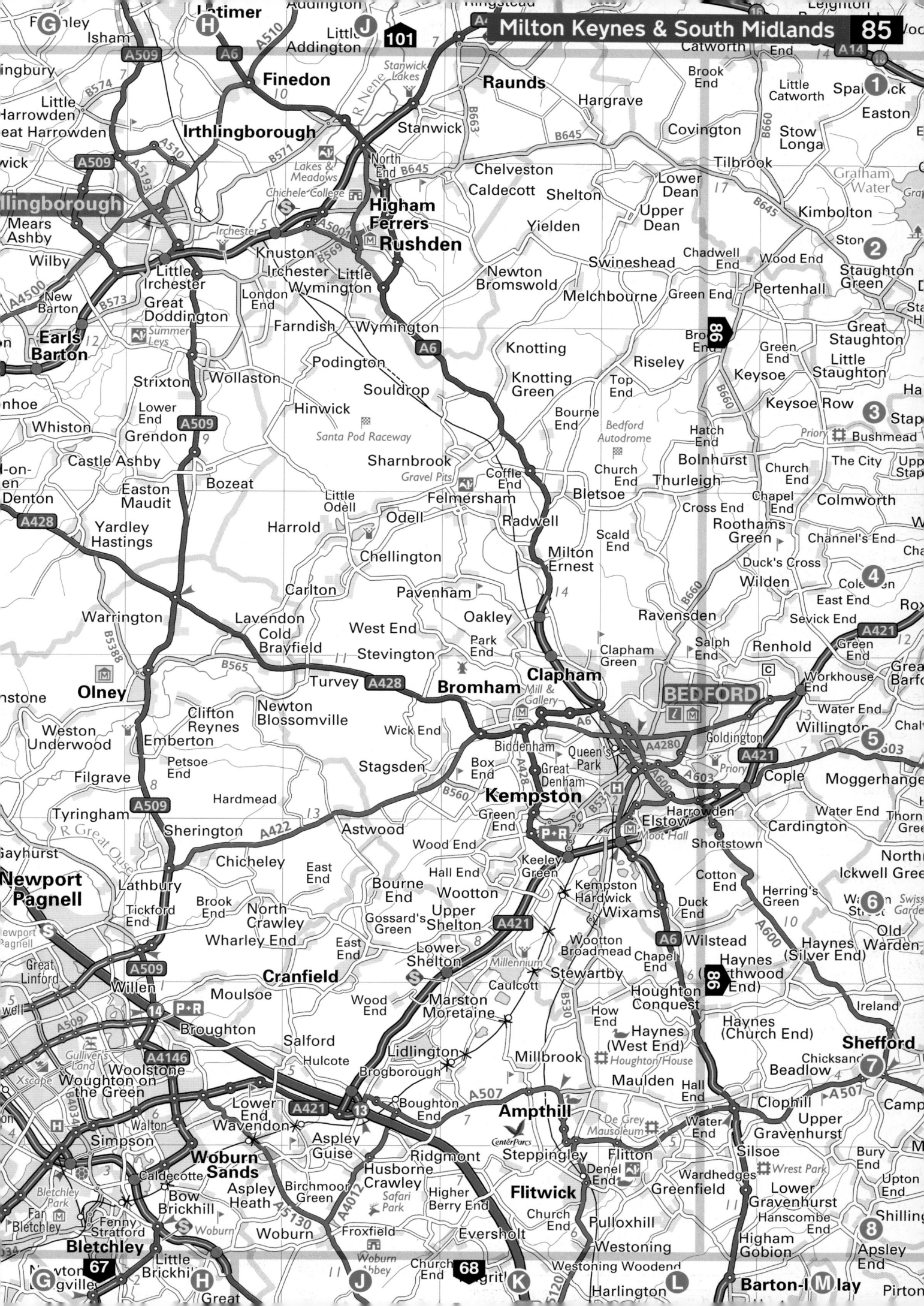

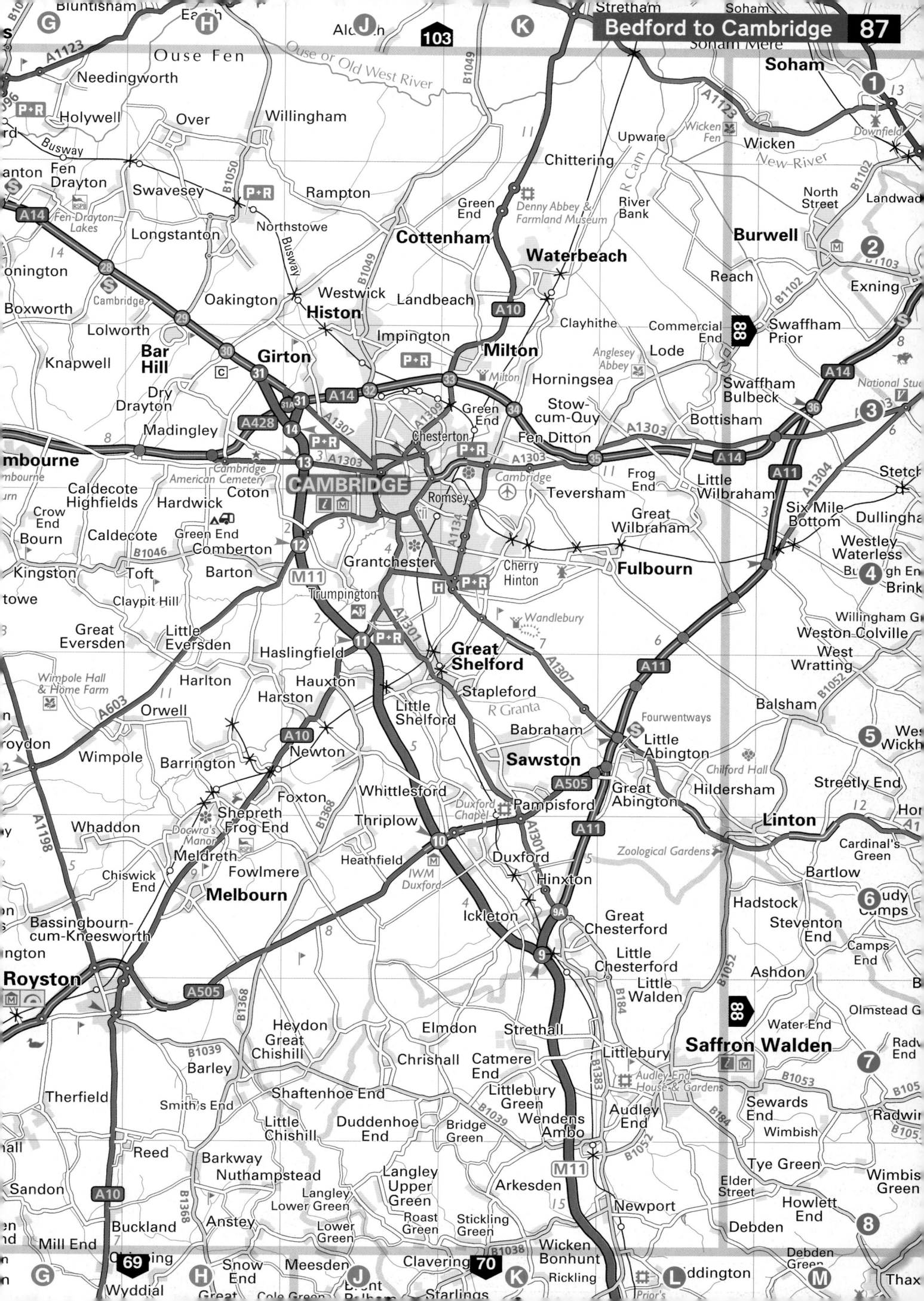

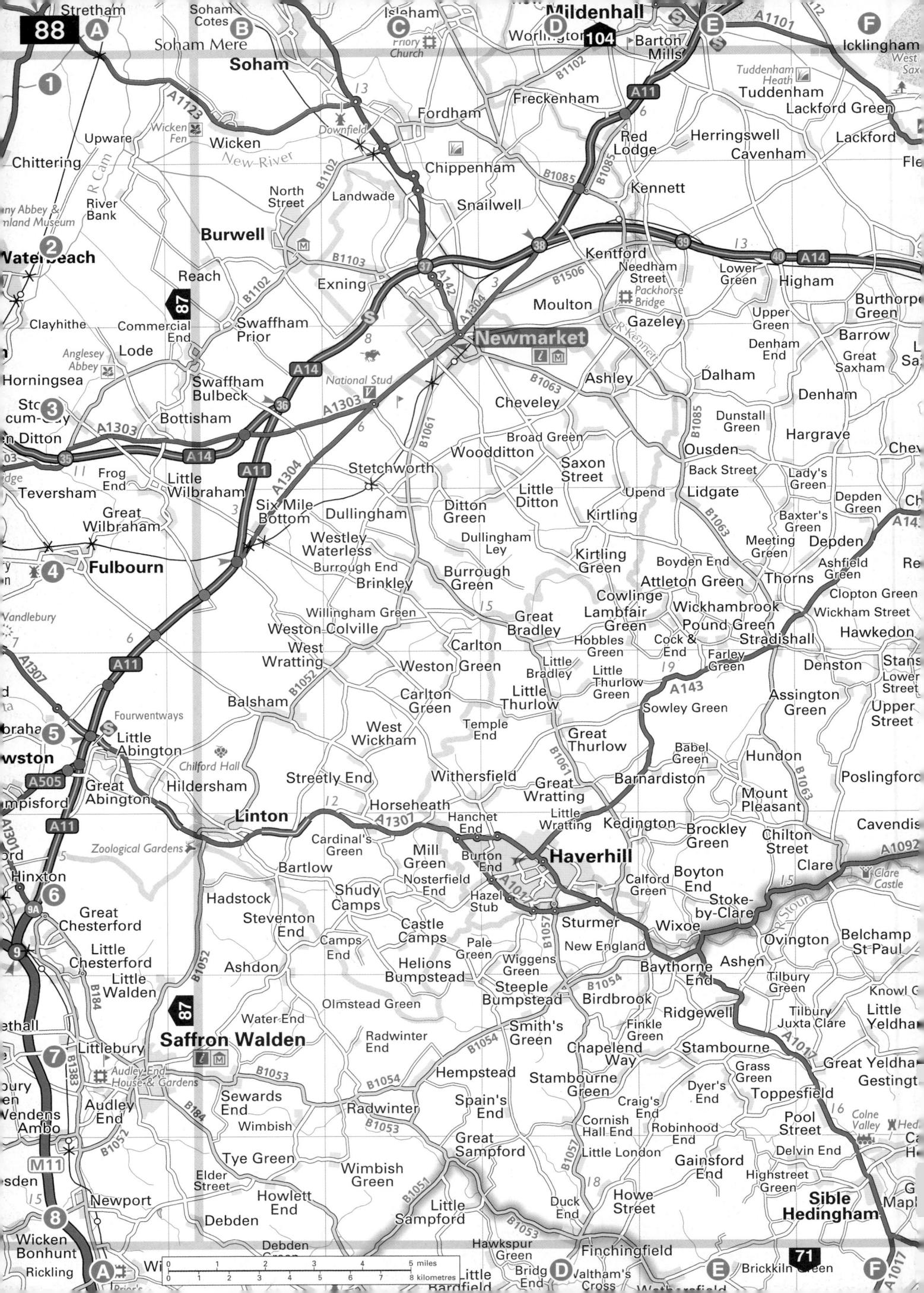

G   H   Bardw   J   105   Stanton   K   Wattisfield

Ixworth Thorpe
Bangrove
Upthorpe   Allwood Green   Mill Street   Thornham Parv
1
Troston
Walsham le Willows   Cranmer Green   Gislingham   Thornham Magna
Ampton   Great Livermere
Brockley   A143   West Street   Crowland   Badwell Green   Westhorpe   Finningham   Wickham Street
West Stow   Ingham   Langham   Four Ashes   Wyverstone Street   Wickham Skeith   Wickham Green
Culford   Timworth   Ixworth   Badwell Ash   Long Thurlow   Wyverstone   Cotton   Brockford Street
2
Timworth Green   Conyer's Green   Upper Town   Hunston   Stowlangtoft   Great Ashfield   Earl's Green   Bacton   Mendlesham
Fornham St Martin   Grimstone End   Stanton Street   Hunston Green   Bacton Green   Cow Green   Ford's Green   Mendlesham Green
A1101   R Lark   6   Great Barton   Pakenham   Norton Little Green   Haughley Green   Canhams Green   Brown Street
Fornham All Saints   B1106   Cattishall   Thurston   Great Green   Norton   Elmswell   Base Green   Wetherden   Gipping   Middlewood Green
A143   Battlies Green   Thurston Planch   Tostock   Broadgrass Gn   Dagworth   Haughley   Old Newton   Saxham Street   le Stonham
42   43   Bury St Edmunds   44   45   Beyton Gn   46   Beyton   16   47   A14   49   A1308   Stowupland   3
Blackthorpe   Kingshall Street   Woolpit   Harleston   Stowmarket   Forward Green   Earl Stonham
Horringer   Rushbrooke   Rougham   Hessett   Drinkstone Green   Woolpit Green   Clopton Green   Onehouse   Combs Ford   Creeting St Mary
High Green   Sicklesmere   Little Welnetham   Bradfield St George   Drinkstone   Borley Green   Buxhall Fen Street   Great Finborough   Combs   4
Nowton   Bradfield Combust   Maypole Green   Rattlesden   Buxhall   Mill Green   Needham Market
Hawstead   Great Welnetham   Bradfield St Clare   Gedding   Poystreet Green   Moats Tye   Battisford   Needham Lake
Whepstead   Hawstead Green   Bush Green   Bradfield Woods   Felsham   Brettenham   Battisford Tye   B1078   Barking
Mickley Green   Hoggards Green   Oldhall Green   Great Green   Hightown Green   Charles Tye   Ringshall   Lower Street
Gulling Green   Melon Green   Stanningfield   Cross Green   Thorpe Green   Cooks Green   Cross Green   Bird Street   Barking Tye   Baylham
Harrow Green   Windsor Green   Lawshall Green   Cockfield   Thorpe Morieux   Wattisham   Ringshall Stocks   Upper Street   5
Lawshall   Shimpling Street   A1141   Preston St Mary   Hitcham Causeway   Hitcham Street   Hitcham   Nedging Tye   Great Bricett   Offton
Audley End   A134   Alpheton   Kettlebaston   Bildeston   Greenstreet Green   Naughton   Somersham   Little Blakenham
Hartest   Giffords Hall   Guildhall   Lavenham   Brent Eleigh   Monks Eleigh   B1078   Nedging   Flowton
Shimpling   Little Hall   Swingleton Green   Chelsworth   Ash Street   Whatfield   Elmsett   Bramford
Boxted   Bridge Street   B1071   B1115   Semer   Elmsett
Stanstead   Melford Hall   Little Waldingfield   Milden   Lindsey Tye   Stone Street   Aldham   Sproughton
Glemsford   B1065   B1066   Kentwell Hall & Gardens   Acton   Rose Green   Lindsey   A1071   Wolves Wood   Burstall   6
Pentlow   Long Melford   Great Waldingfield   St James's Chapel   Kersey Tye   Duke Street   Hintlesham
Foxearth   A134   3   Liston   Newman's Green   B1115   Wicker Street Green   Kersey   Coram Street   Hadleigh   Chattisham   Washbrook
Borley   Newton   Edwardstone   Groton   Horners Green   Kersey Upland   90   Coles Green   Copdock
Belchamp Walter   Borley Green   A134   Chilton   Cornard Tye   Boxford   Calais Street   Hadleigh Heath   Layham   B1070
Sudbury   Ballingdon   Great Cornard   Little Cornard   A1071   12   Hagmore Green   Stone Street   Whitestreet Green   Bower House Tye   Polstead Heath   Great Wenham   Little Wenham
Buttock End   Bulmer   Middleton   Assington   A134   Leavenheath   Polstead   Shelley   Raydon   Capel St Mary   7
Bulmer Tye   Great Henny   Workhouse Green   Rose Green   Stone Street   Lower Raydon   A12   Bentley
Wickham St Paul   Henny Street   Twinstead   B1508   Dorking Tye   Honey Tye   R Box   Stoke-by-Nayland   Higham Stratford St Mary   Holton St Mary   East Bergholt
A131   Alphamstone   Lamarsh   Nayland   15   Thorington Street   B1068   B1070   East End
Lucking Street   Cross End   B1068   B1087   Boxted Cross   B1029
Little Maplestead   Pebmarsh   Mount Bures   Wissington   Wormingford   R Stour   Boxted   Dedham   Flatford Mill & Bridge Cottage   Mistley
8
Boose's   G   H   Countess Cross   J   Horkesley   72   K   Boxted   L   Langham   Mar   Manningtree   Dedham   M

A   B   C   D   106   E   F

Stanton   Wattisfield   andle Street   Yaxley   Eye   Denham Green   Wootten Green   Rus Gre   Wilby

Upthorpe   Allwood Green   Thornham Parva   Braiseworth   Redlingfield Green   Horham   Athelington Street   Coal Street   Crown Corner

West Street   Walsham le Willows   Cranmer Green   Mill Street   Thornham Magna   Stoke Ash   Standwell Green   Occold   Redlingfield   Dublin   Southolt   Stanway Green   Crown Corner

angham   Badwell Ash   Four Ashes   Crowland   Finningham   Wickham Street   Wickham Green   Thorndon   Bedingfield   Kenton   Bedfield   Saxte   Little Gr

Hunston   Long Thurlow   Badwell Green   Westhorpe   Wickham Skeith   Thwaite   Rishangles   Hestley Green   Bedingfield Green   Monk Soham   Bedfield Little Green   Post Mill

Stowlangtoft   Great Ashfield   Wyverstone Street   Cotton   Brockford Street   Wetheringsett   Blacksmith's Green   Aspall   Debenham   Ashfield cum Thorpe

Stanton Street   Hunston Green   Earl's Green   Bacton   Wyverstone   Ford's Green   Brockford Green   Park Green   Fen Street   Winston

Norton Little Green   Bacton Green   Cow Green   Canhams Green   Mendlesham   Aspall   Wetherup Street   Mickfield   Cretingham   Brande

Norton   Elmswell   Haughley Green   Ward Green   Brown Street   Mendlesham Green   Middlewood Green   Stonham Aspal   Mid Suffolk   Suffolk Owl Sanctuary   Pettaugh   Framsden   Monewden

Woolpit   Broadgrass Gn   Base Green   Old Newton   Saxham Street   Little Stonham   Crowfield Green   Helmingham Hall   Otley Green   Charsfield

Haughley   Dagworth   Gipping   Earl Stonham   Crowfield   Helmingham   Gosbeck   Otley   Clopton Corner   Dallingho

Woolpit Green   Borley Green   Harleston   Stowupland   Forward Green   Creeting St Mary   Ashbocking   Deb

Rattlesden   Clopton Green   Onehouse   Stowmarket   Combs Ford   Coddenham   Hemingstone   Swilland   Burgh

Buxhall Fen Street   Buxhall   Great Finborough   Combs   Barking   Lower Street   Bells Cross   Grundisburgh   Bredf

Poystreet Green   Mill Green   Hightown Green   Moats Tye   Needham Market   Needham Lake   Barking Tye   Baylham   Barham   Henley   Witnesham   Hasketon

Brettenham   Battisford Tye   Battisford   Ringshall   Upper Street   Great Blakenham   Claydon   Akenham   Tuddenham   Boot Street   Great Bealings

Cross Green   Bird Street   Charles Tye   Ringshall Stocks   Little Blakenham   Culpho   Littley Bealings   Playford

Cooks Green   Wattisham   Nedging Tye   Great Bricett   Offton   Somersham   Whitton   Castle Hill   Westerfield   Rushmere St Andrew   Kesgrave

am Causeway   Hitcham   Greenstreet Green   Naughton   Flowton   Bramford   IPSWICH   Mar Hea

cham Street   Bildeston   Nedging   Ash Street   Whatfield   Elmsett   Sproughton   Chantry

Monks Eleigh   Chelsworth   Semer   Aldham   Burstall   Washbrook   Coles Green   Belstead   Orwell Bridge   Nacton

Lindsey Tye   Lindsey   Stone Street   Wolves Wood   Hintlesham   Duke Street   Copdock   Wherstead   Freston   Woolverstone   Levington

Rose Green   St James's Chapel   Coram Street   Hadleigh   Chattisham   Jimmy's Farm   Tattingstone White Horse   Pin Mill

Kersey Tye   Kersey   Hadleigh Heath   Layham   Great Wenham   Little Wenham   Tattingstone   Chelmondiston

Wicker Street Green   Kersey Upland   Bower House Tye   Polstead Heath   Raydon   Capel St Mary   Bentley   Freston   Holbrook   Lower Holbrook   Shotley Street

Horners Green   Calais Street   Whitestreet Green   Shelley   Lower Raydon   Holton St Mary   Copdock   East End   Upper Street   Stutton   Erwarton   Shot

Polstead   Higham   Stratford St Mary   East Bergholt   Brantham   Holbrook   Alton Water   Harkstead   Shotley Gate

Stoke-by-Nayland   Thorington Street   Boxted Cross   Dedham   Cattawade   Holbrook Bay   River Orwell   International Ferry Terminal

Boxted   angham   Dedham Heath   Mistley   Mistley Towers   River Stour   Wrabness   Stour Estuary   Parkeston Quay   Parkeston

Finningtree   New Mistley   73   F

A   B   C   D   E   F

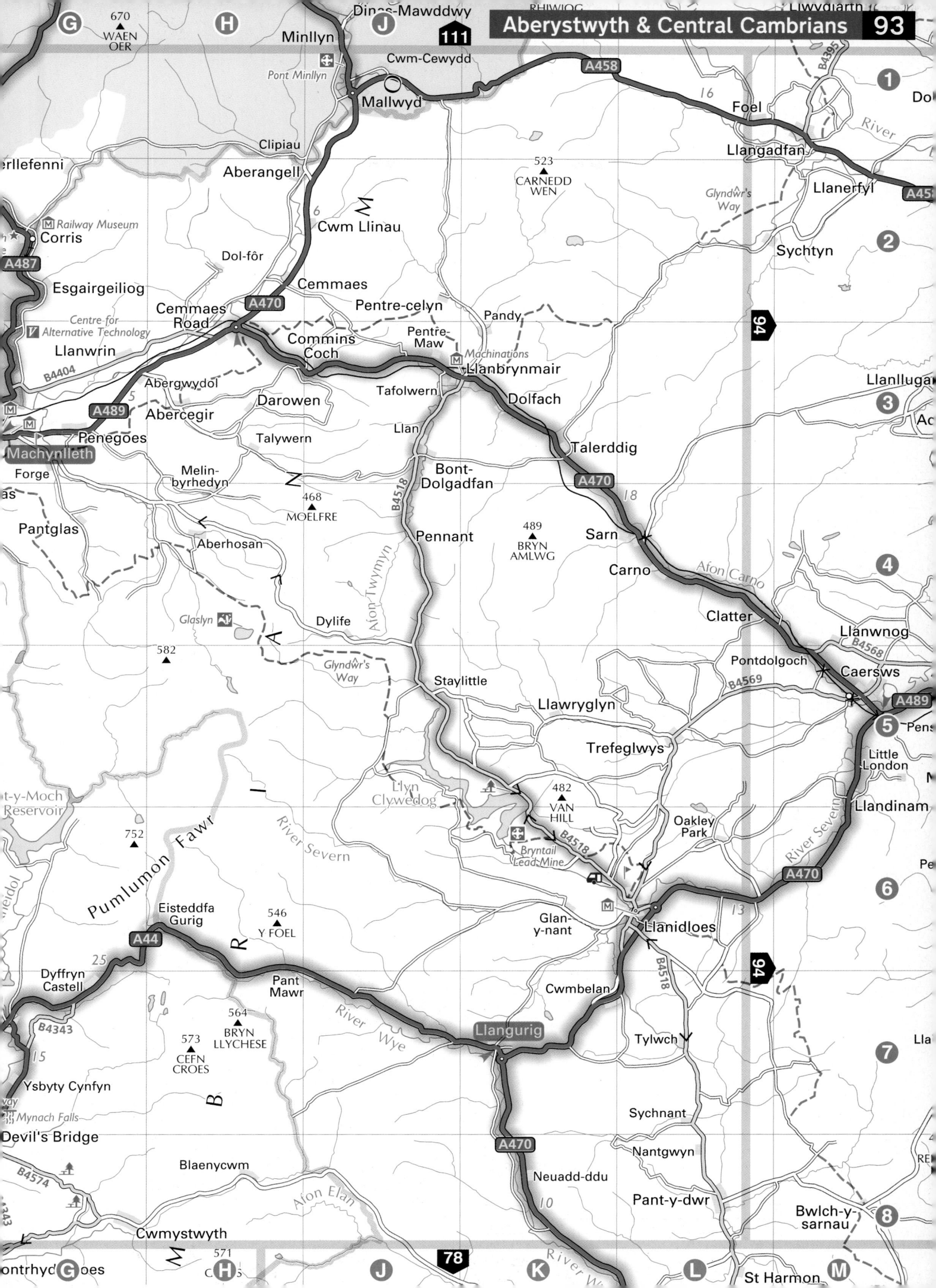

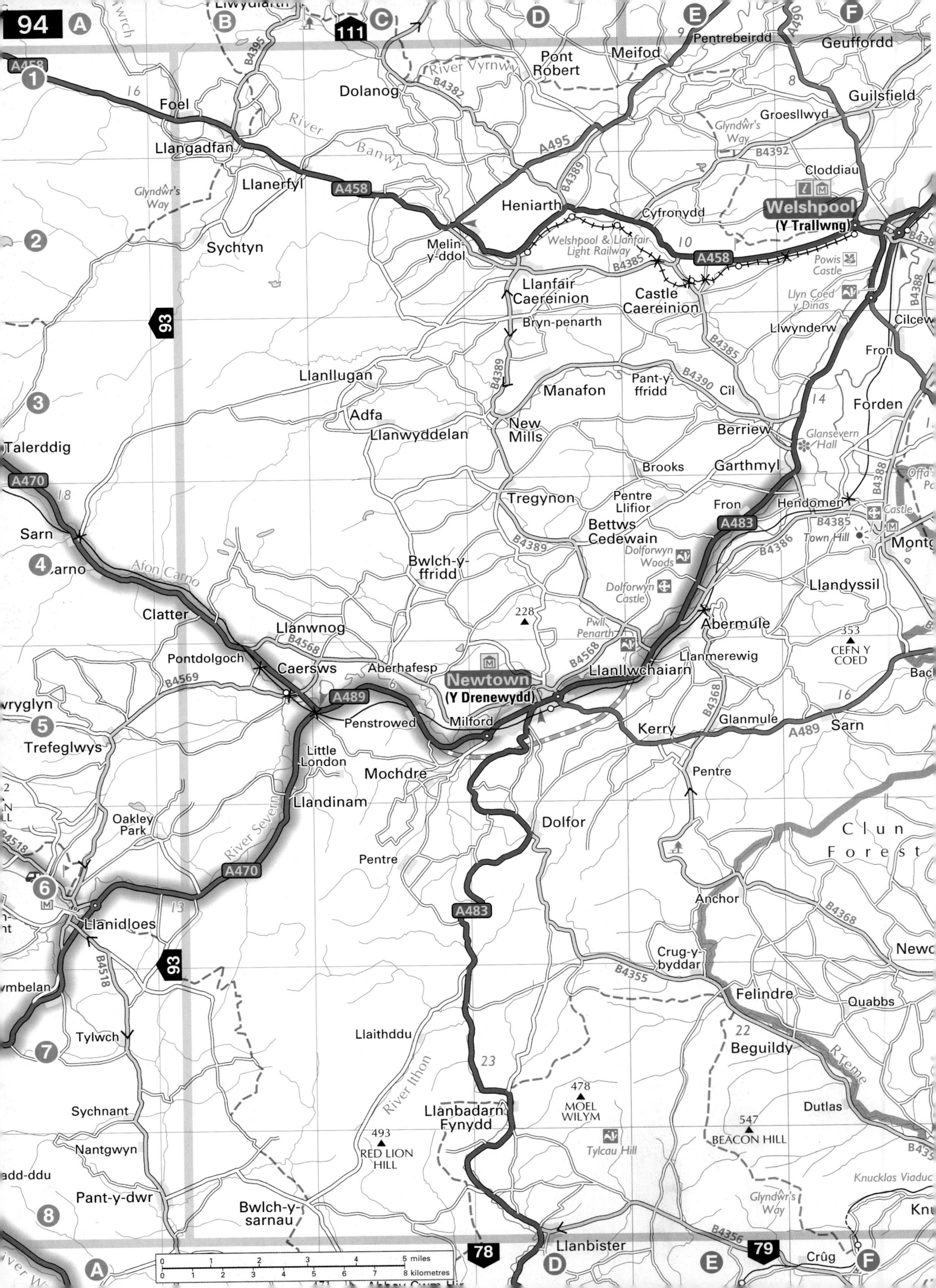

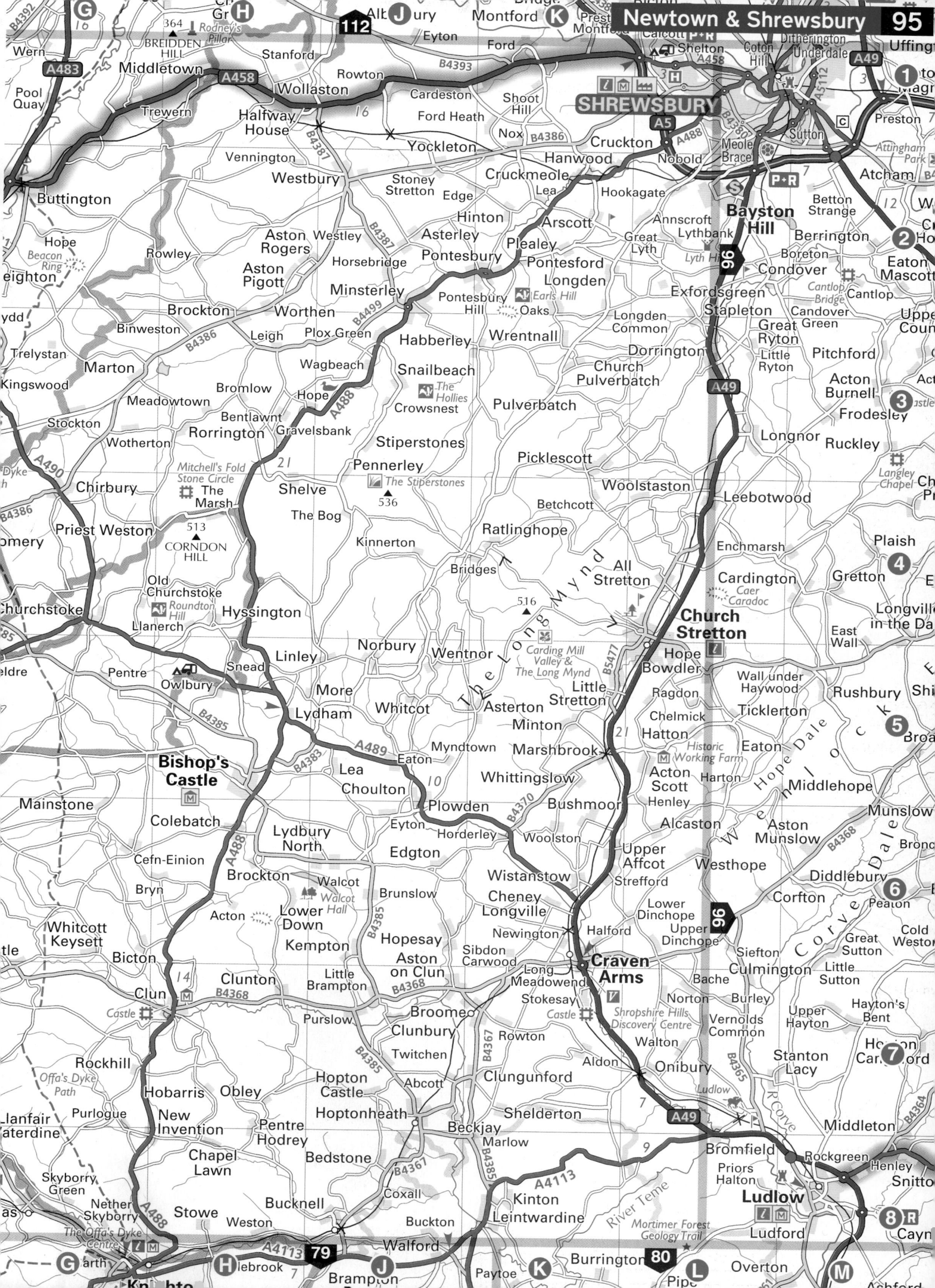

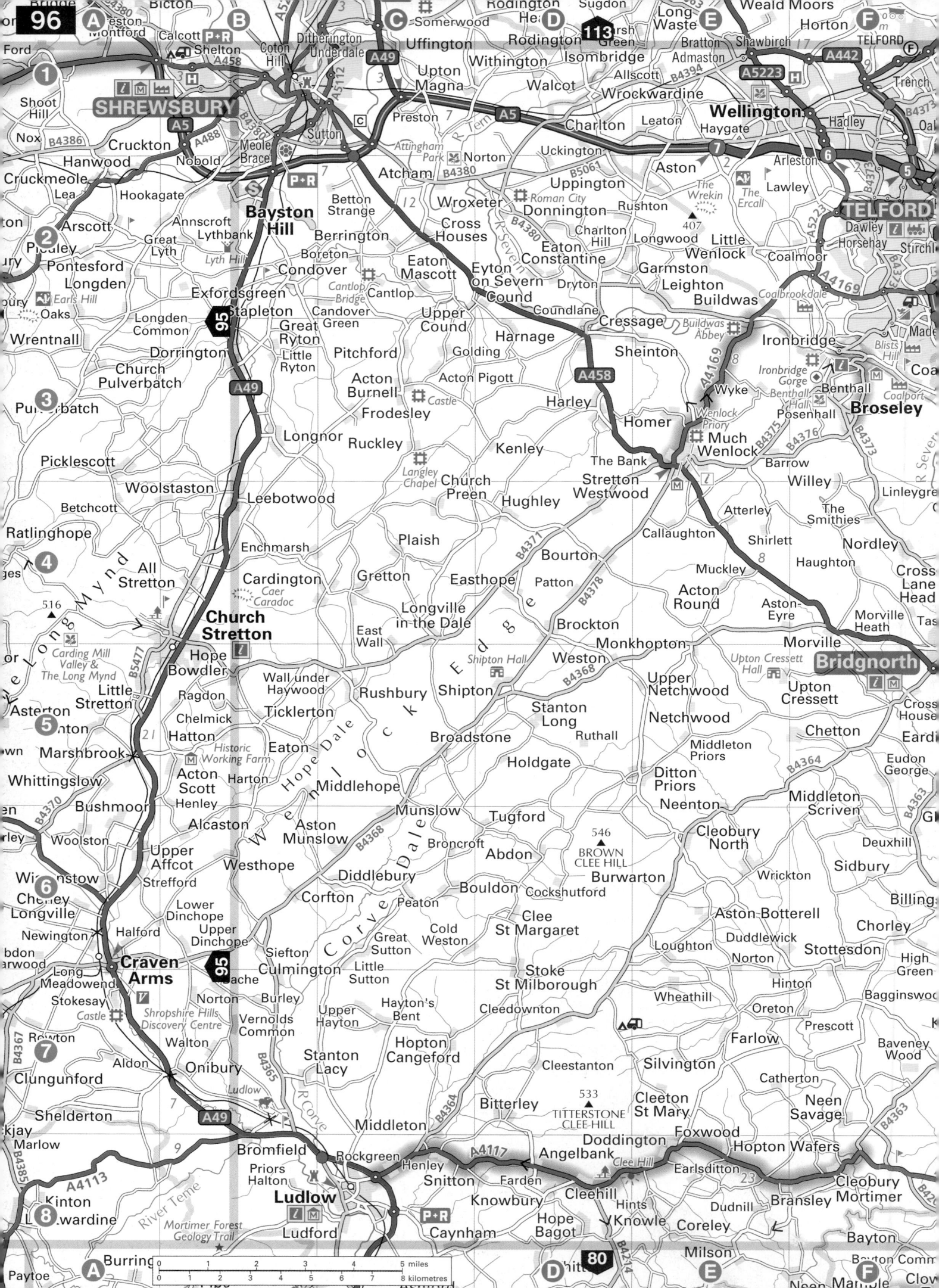

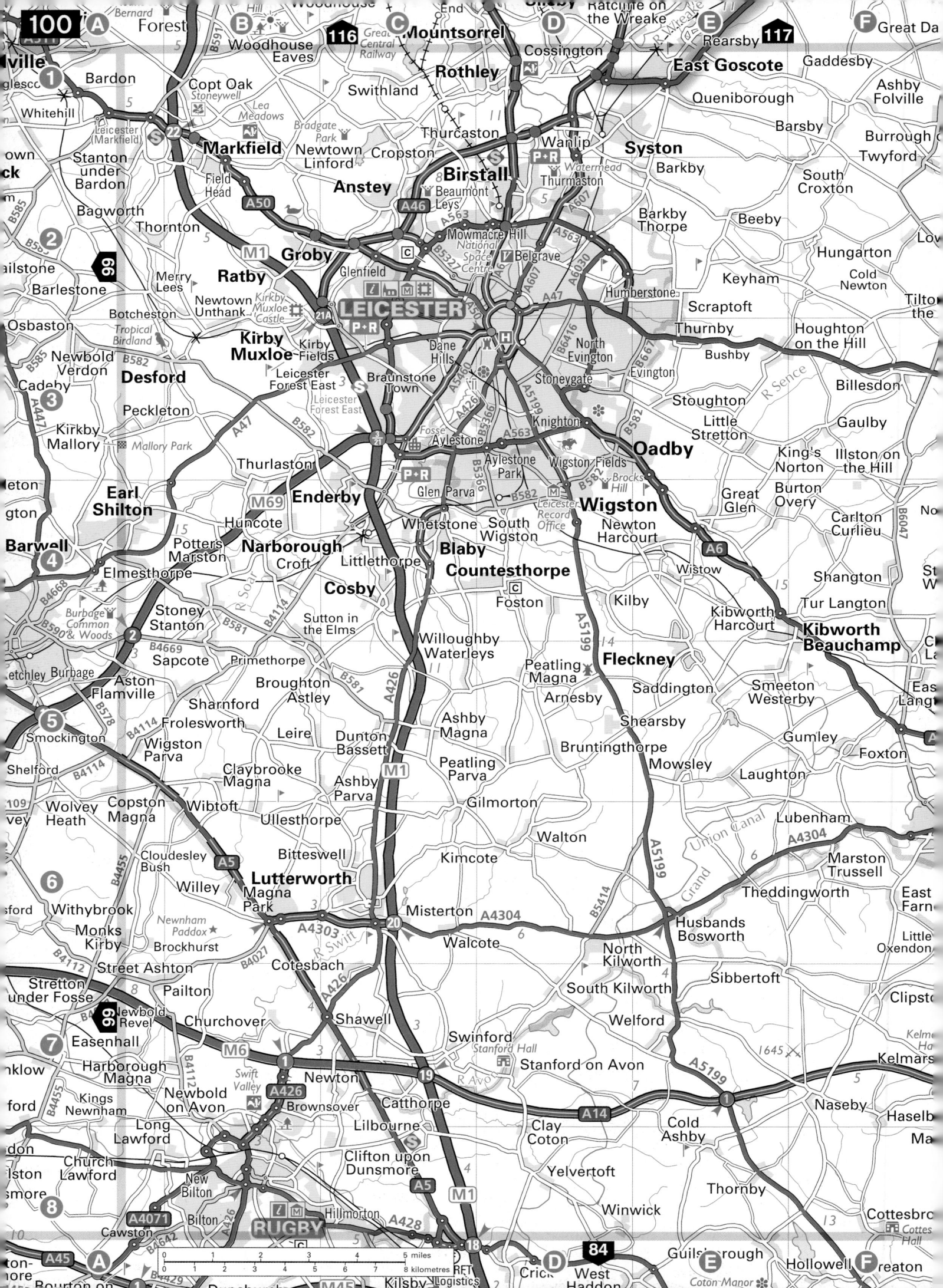

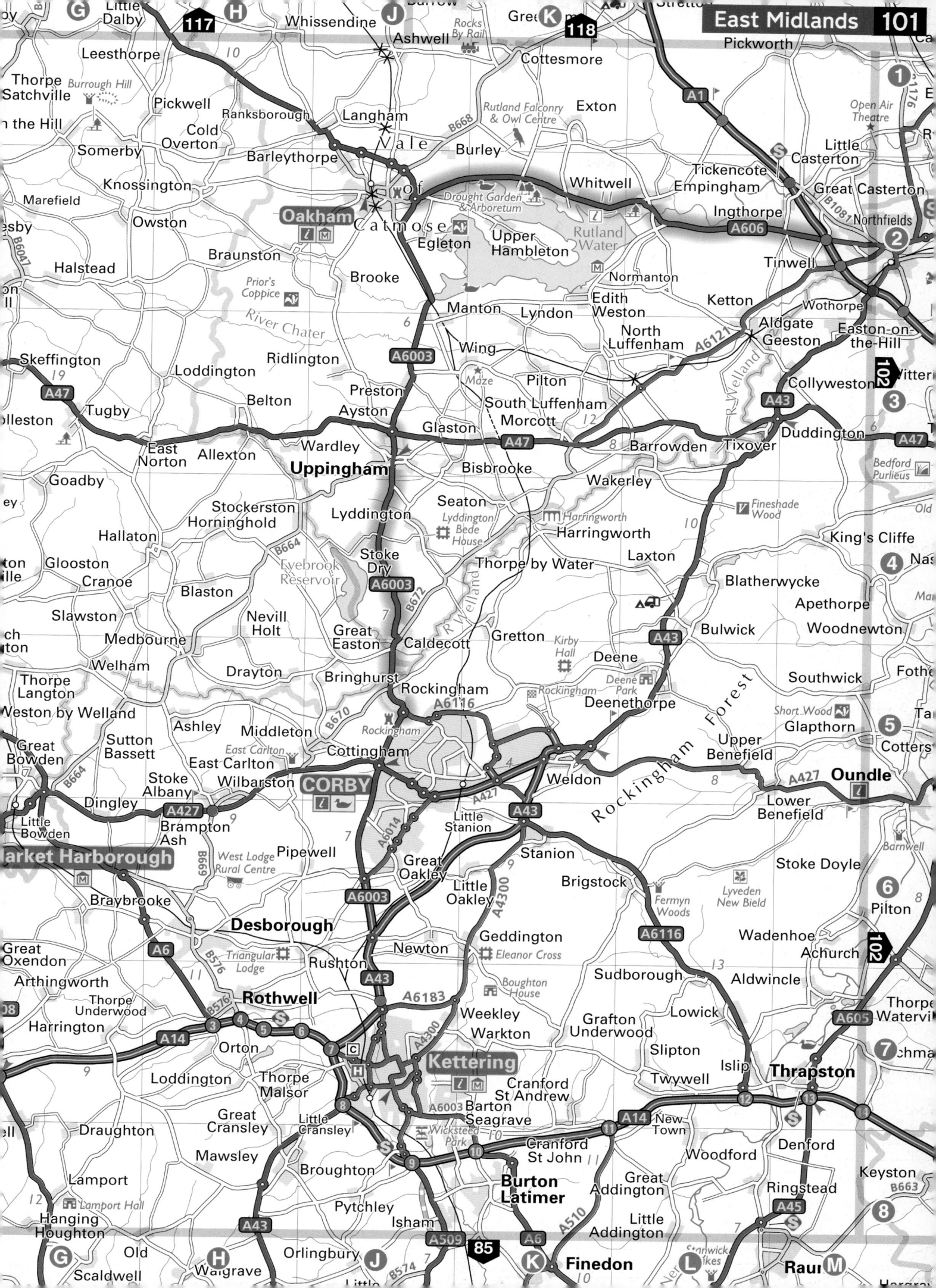

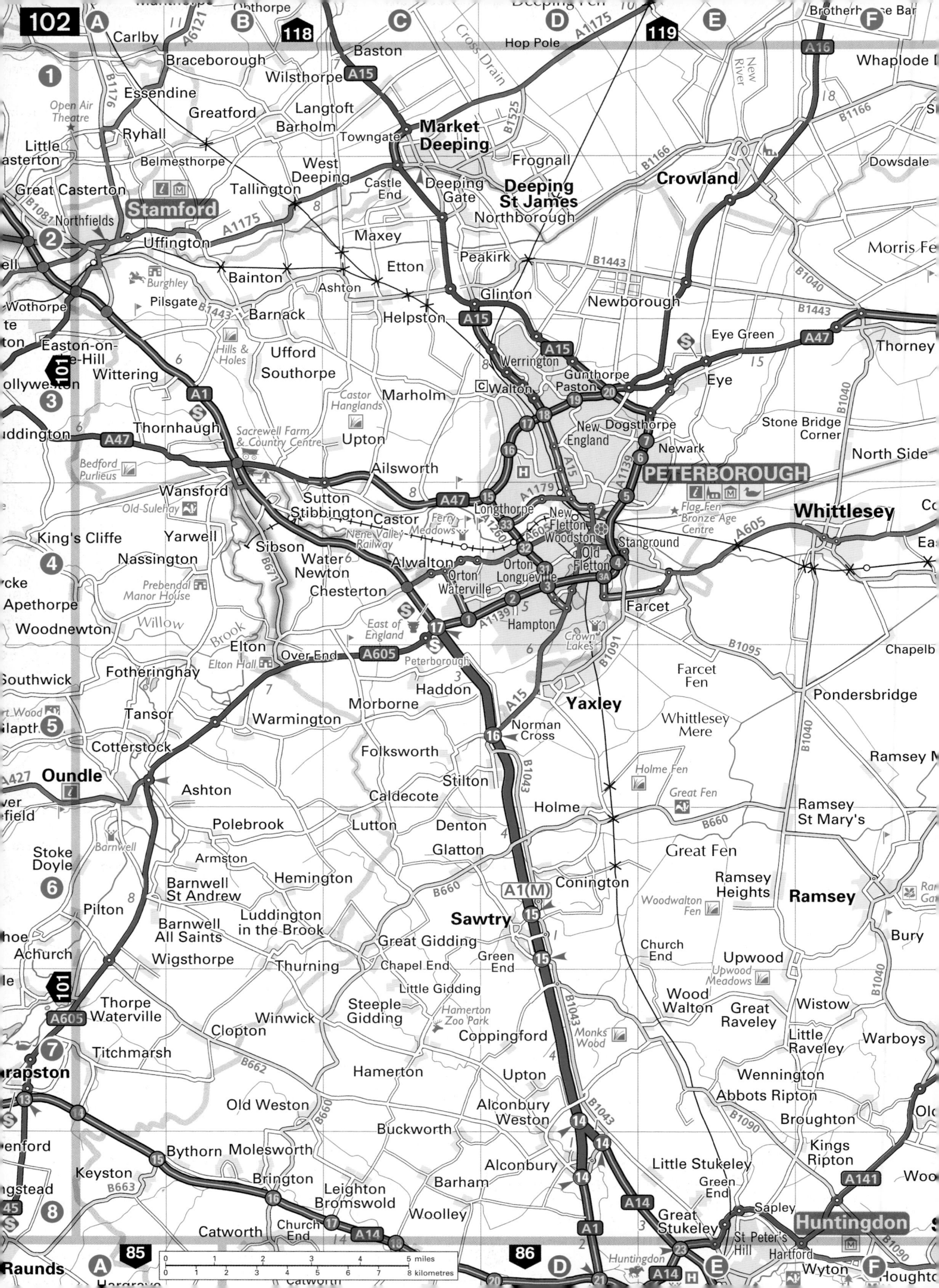

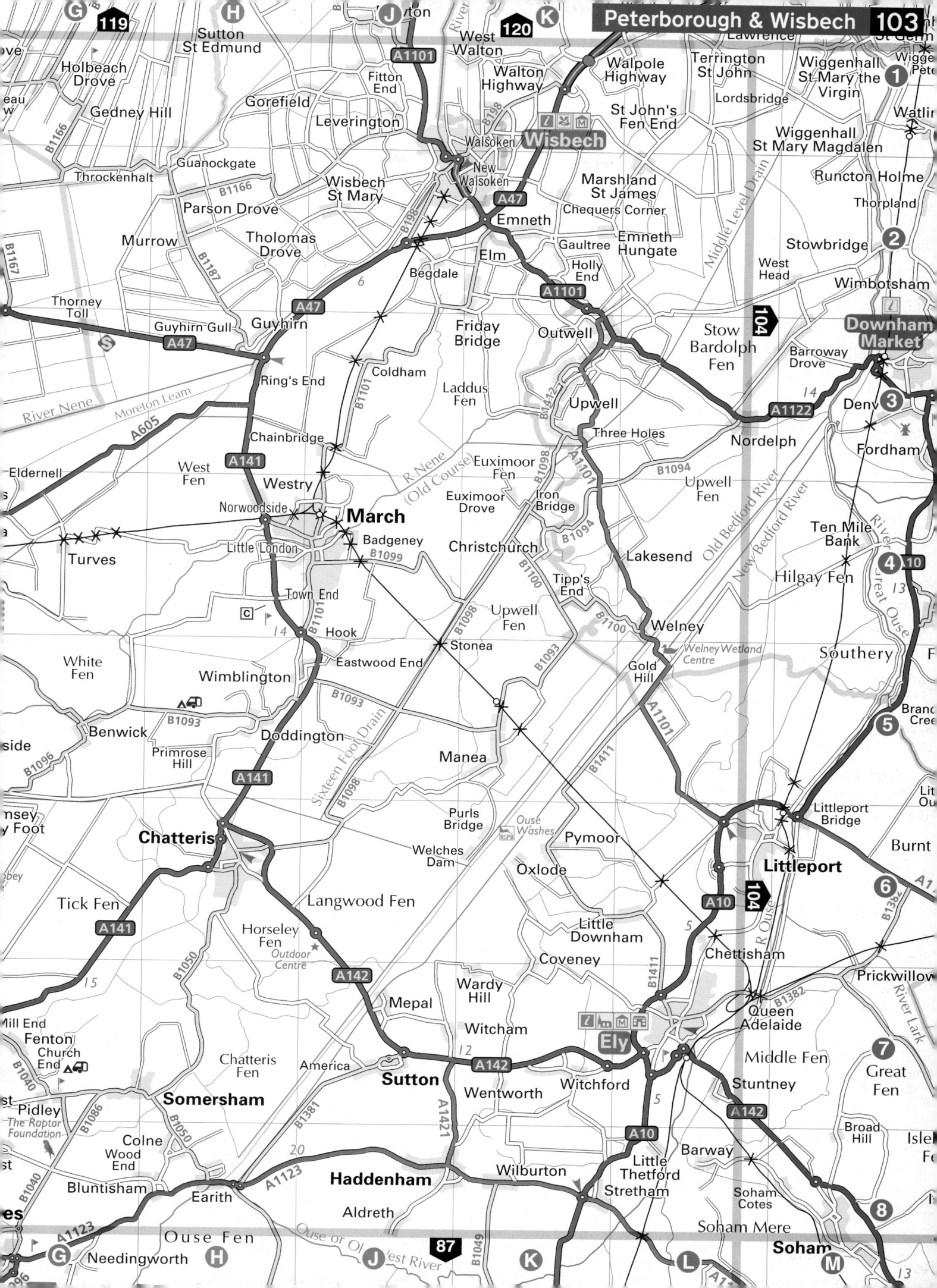

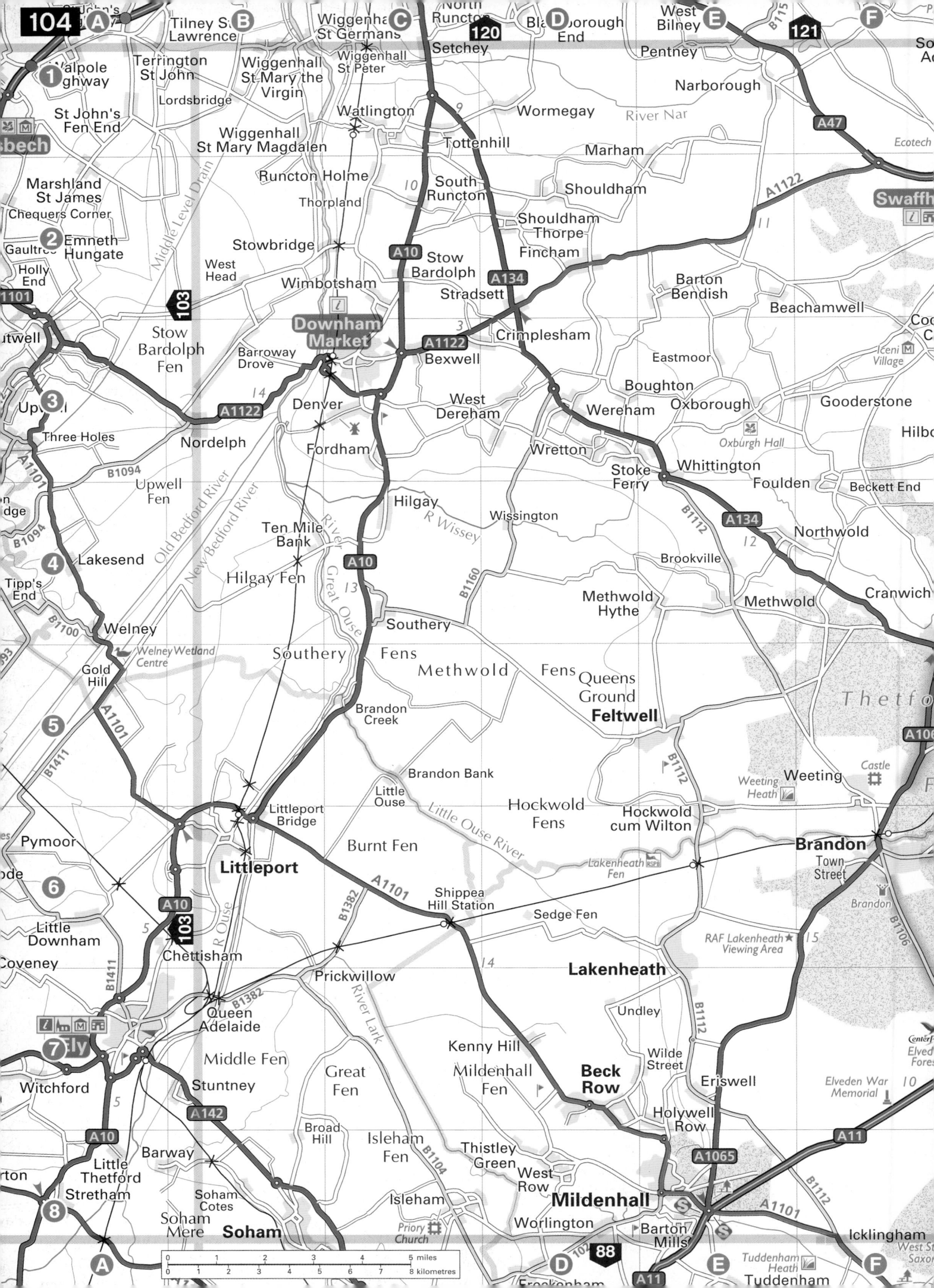

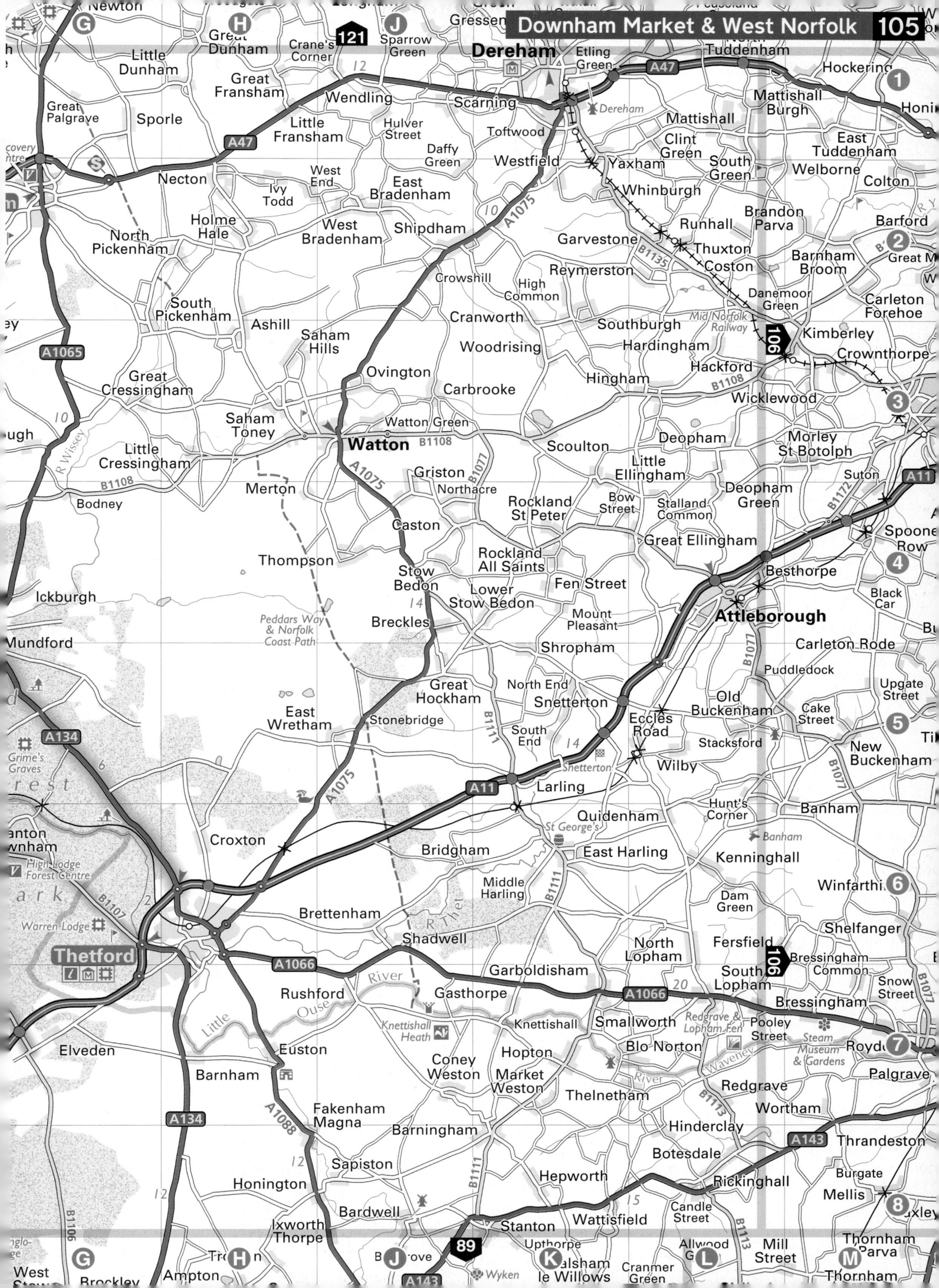

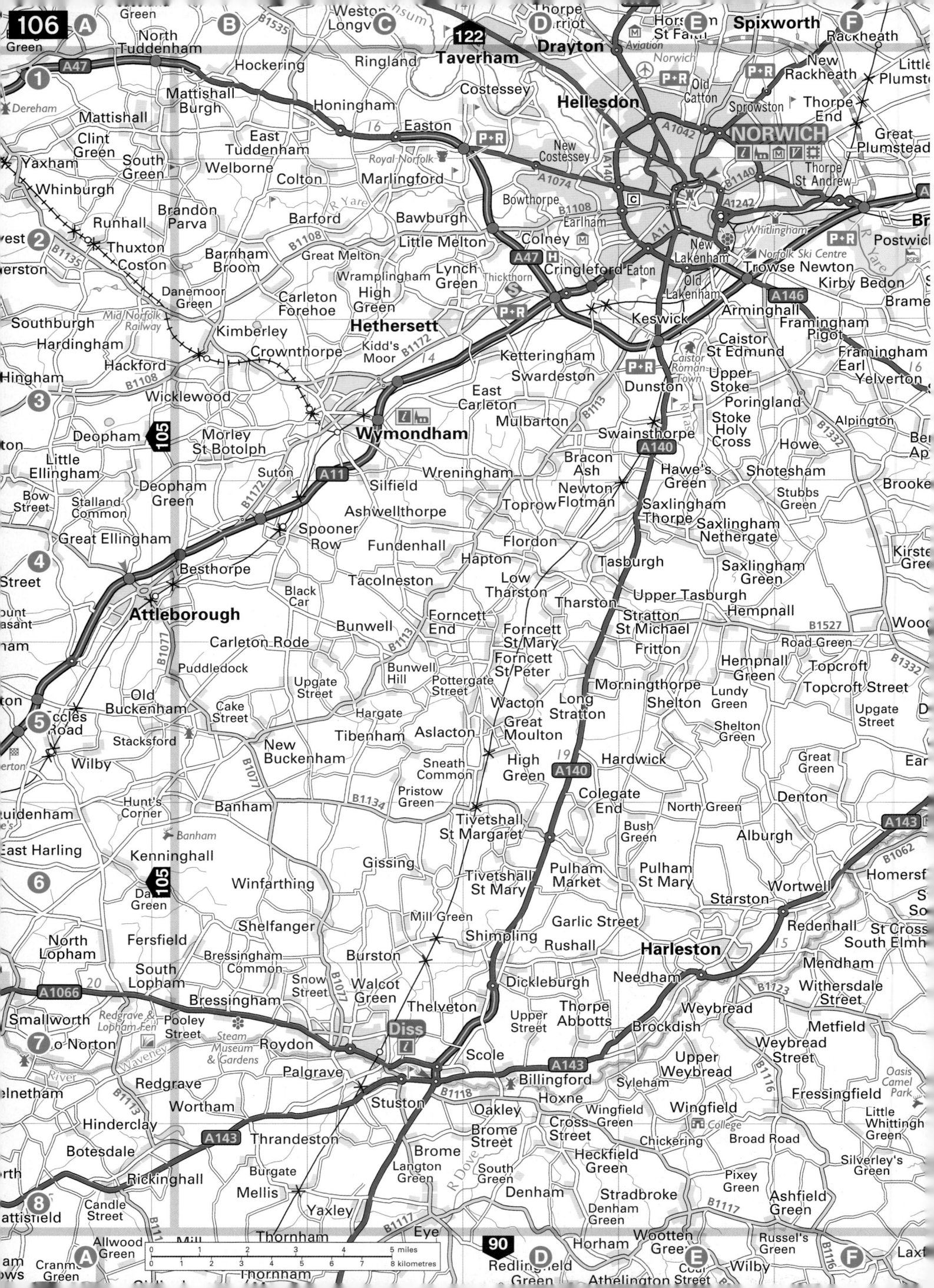

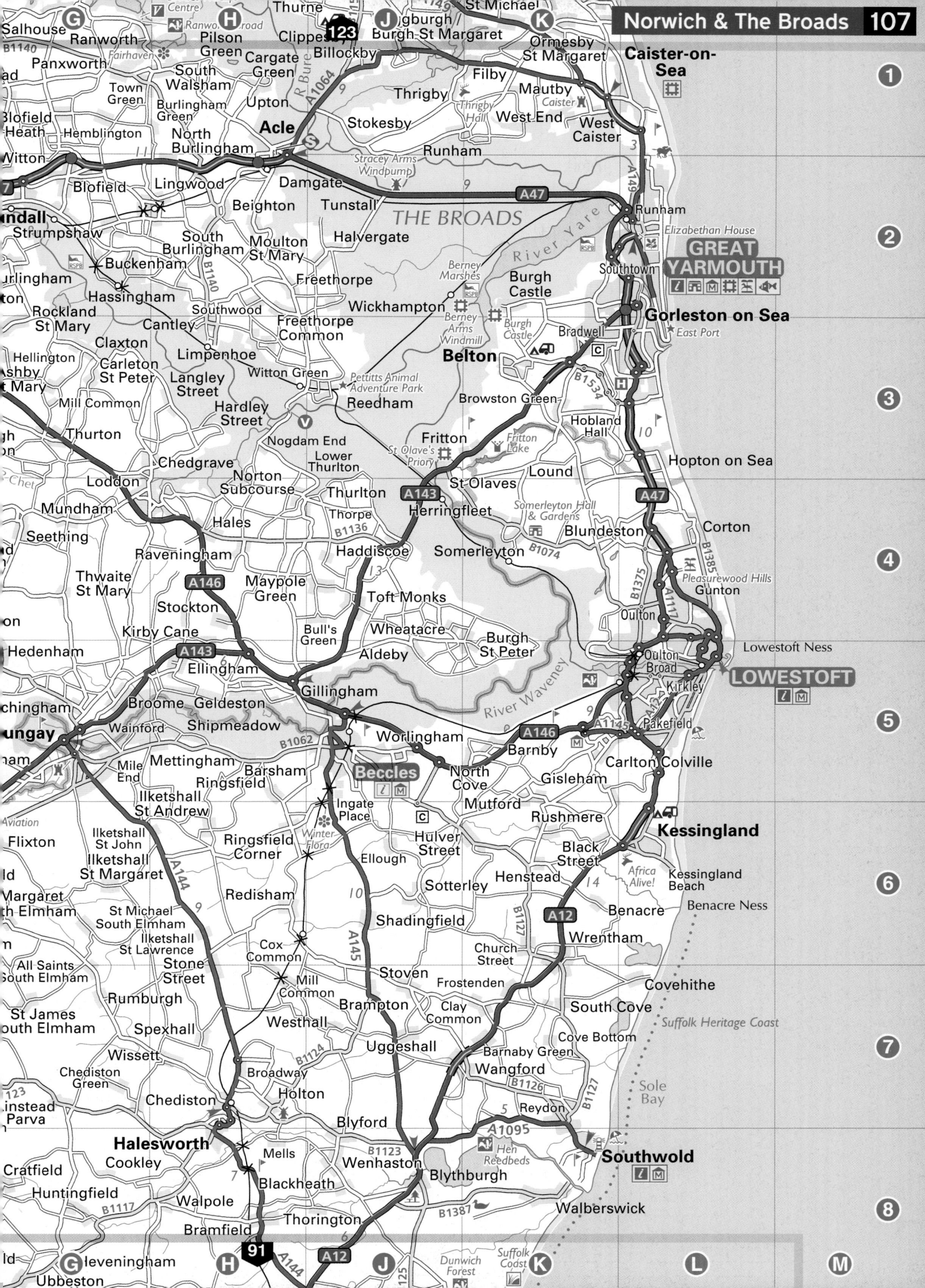

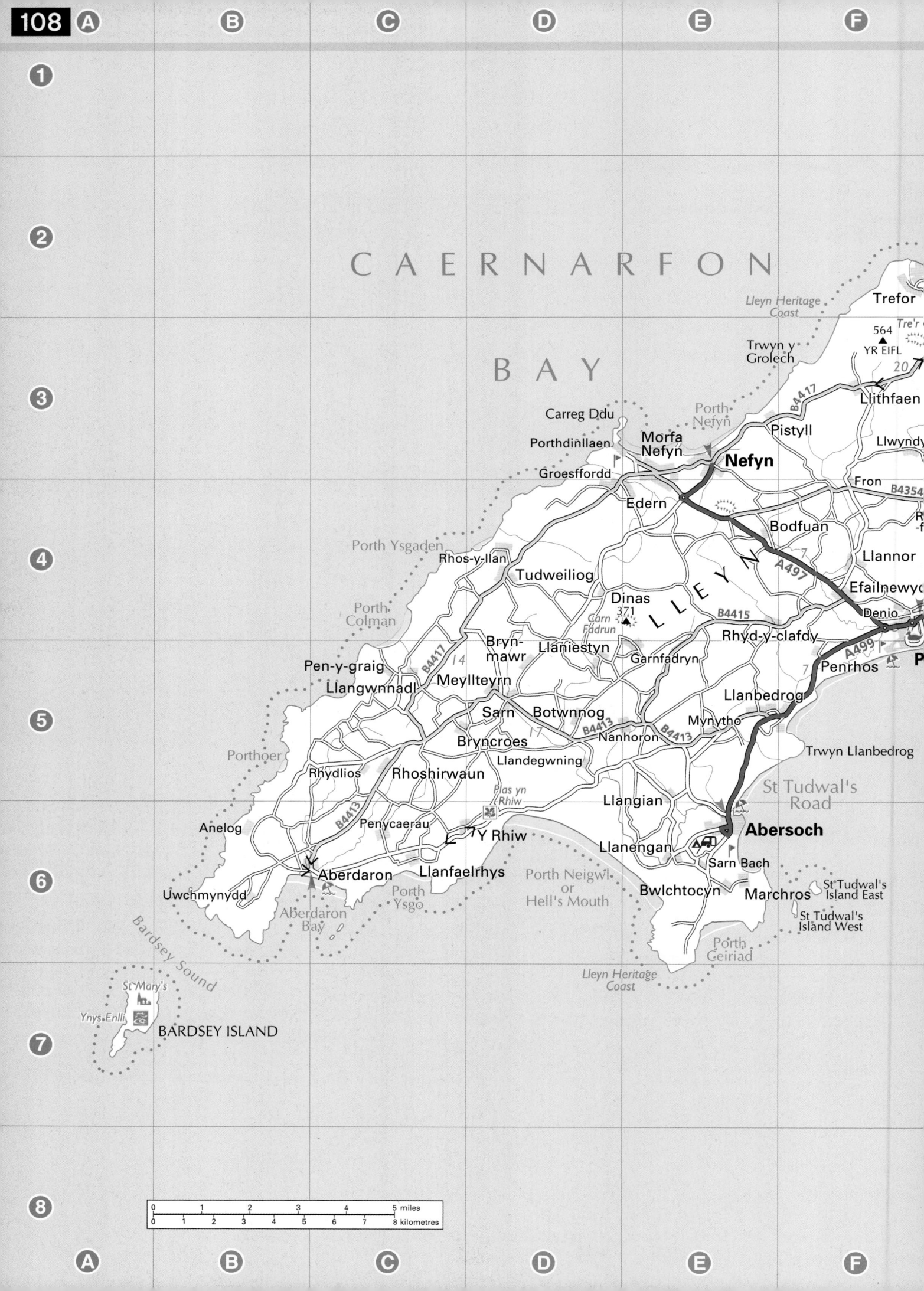

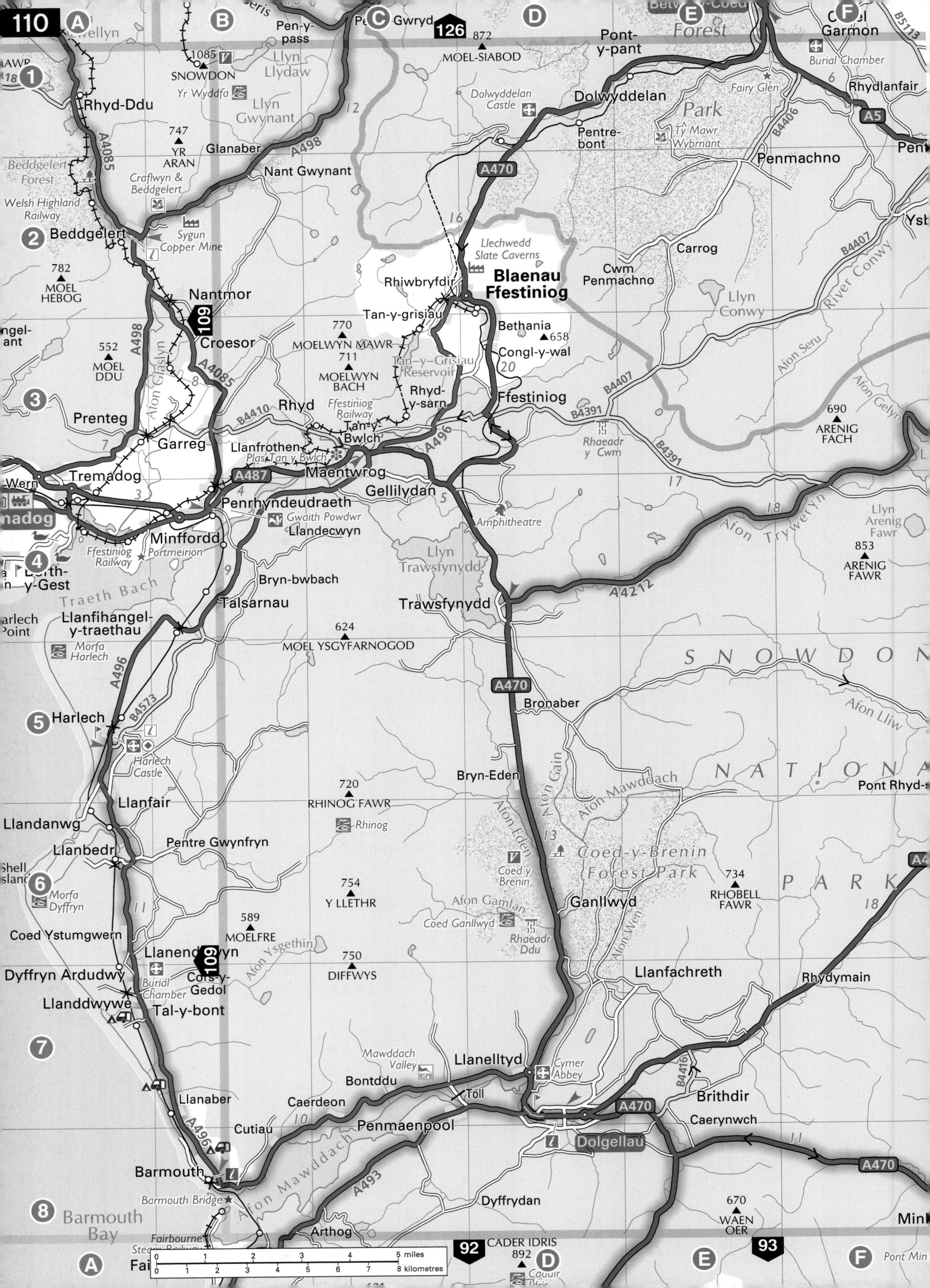

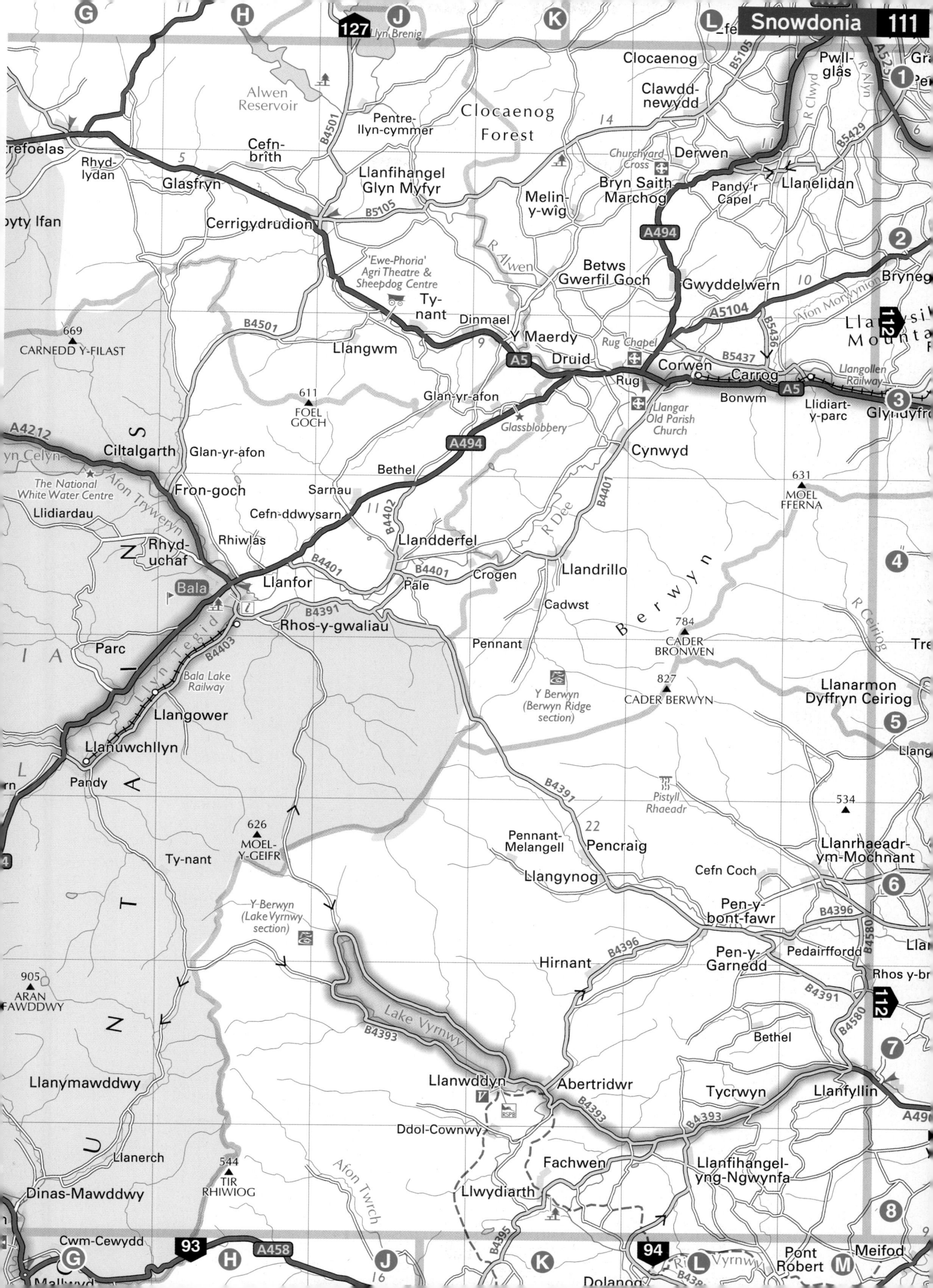

Crewe Green

Harthill · Peckforton · Radmore Green · Rease Heath · Wistaston · Wells Green · Gresty Green

Clutton · 129 · Broxton · Barnhill · Irwardsley · Bulkeley · Ridley Green · Brindley · Burland · A51 · Willaston · Shavington · Weston

534 · Barton · Fuller's Moor · Gallantry Bank · Croxton Green · 534 · Faddiley · Stoneley Green · Gradeley Green · Acton · Nantwich · Butt Green · Haymoor Green · Hough

A41 · Watermill · Bickerton · Cholmondeley Castle · A49 · Chorley · Ravensmoor · Stapeley · Hack Green · Chorlton · Wybunbury · A51 · Walgherton

Castletown · Stretton · Edge Green · Duckington · Hampton Green · Hetherson Green · Bickley Moss · Norbury Common · Wrenbury · Secret Bunker · Sound · Broomhill Green · Hatherton · Hunsterson · Checkle

Tilston · Horton Green · Hampton Heath · Bickley · Norbury · Gaunton's Bank · Pinsley Green · A530 · Aston · Newhall · Hankelow · Audlem · Bridgemere · Check Green

Shocklach · Chorlton Lane · Malpas · No Man's Heath · Bickley Hall Farm · Marbury · Marley Green · Dodd's Green · Royal's Green · Lightwood Green · Coxbank · Kinsey Heath · Woore · 114

ddington Heath · Upper Threapwood · Oldcastle Heath · Bradley Common · Marley Green · Hollyhurst · Wirswall · Burleydam · A525 · Adderley · Dorrington · Knighton · Bearstone

Tallarn Green · Higher Wych · Bell o' th' Hill · Grindley Brook · Whitchurch · Broughall · Catteralslane · Wilkesley · Shropshire Union Canal · Norton in Hales · Betton · Muckle

eman's Green · Eglwys Cross · The Chequer · Redbrook · A525 · Ash Magna · Ightfield · Calverhall · A525 · Woore

anmer · Bronington · Alkington · Ash Parva · Longslow · Sandylane · A53

A495 · Arowry · Tilstock · Prees Heath · Prees Higher Heath · Sandford · Moreton Say · Longford · Almington · Blore · Hookg

Fenn's, Whixall & Bettisfield Mosses · Platt Lane · Steel Heath · A49 · A41 · Darliston · Bletchley · Ternhill · Market Drayton · Hales

hampton · Bettisfield · Welsh End · Hollinwood · Prees · Prees Lower Heath · Fauls · Marchamley Wood · Lostford · Sutton · The Fouralls · Woodseaves · Chipr

Balmer Heath · Whixall · Coton · Quina Brook · Prees Green · Marchamley · Old Colehurst Manor · Cheswardine

Lyneal · Northwood · Paddolgreen · Newtown · Ryebank · Lowe · Hawkstone · Wollerton · Hodnet · Stoke Heath · Wistanswick · Lockleywood · Lipley

English Frankton · Wolverley · Horton · Creamore Bank · Weston-under-Redcastle · Marchamley · Stoke upon Tern · Heathcote · Millgreen · Goldstone · Great Soudl

Brownheath · Loppington · Noneley · Aston · Wixhill · Hodnet Hall · Howle · Hungryhatton · Little Soudley

ckshutt · Wem · Commonwood · Barkers Green · Lee Brockhurst · Moston · Bury Walls · Booley · High Hatton · Ollerton · Child's Ercall · Stanford Bridge · Hinstock · Ellerton

Weston llingfields · Sleap · Preston Brockhurst · Besford · Stanton upon Hine Heath · Peplow · Eaton upon Tern · Sambrook

Burlton · Myddle · Alderton · Clive · A53 · High Hatton · Pickst · Pu

Eyton · Newton on the Hill · Yorton Heath · Grinshill · Moreton Corbet · Ellerdine Heath · Great Bolas · Stanford Bridge · Chetwynd

Harmer Hill · A49 · Moretonmill · A442 · Eaton upon Tern · Edgmond sh · B5062

church · Old Woods · Merrington · Shawbury · Edgebolton · Cold Hatton · Meeson · Tibberton · Edgmond

alford · Preston Gubbals · Hadnall · Little Wytheford · Rowton · Cold Hatton Heath · Cherrington · Adeney · Longford

ton · Bomere Heath · Astley · Bings · Great Wytheford · Walton · Moortown · Waters Upton · B5062 · Church Aston

Walford Heath · Leaton · Albrighton · Poynton Green · High Ercall · Cotwall · Crudgington · Kynnersley · A518

Fitz · Battlefield · Poynton · Tern · Eyton upon the Weald Moors

Rosehill · Harlescott · Haughton · B5062 · Roden · Longdon upon Tern · Sugdon · Sleapford · Eyton upon the Weald Moors · Horton · TELFORD · nning

Bicton · A528 · Haughmond Abbey · Rodington Heath · Marsh Green · Long Waste · Muxton · Lilyhur

ston tford · Calcott · Shelton · Ditherington · Coton Hill · Underdale · A49 · Uffington · Rodington · Withingto · 96 · ombridge · Bratton · Shawbirch · A442 · Donnington · Granville Donninghto

A458 · Upton Magna · Walcot · Wrockwardine · Admaston · A5223 · Trench

96

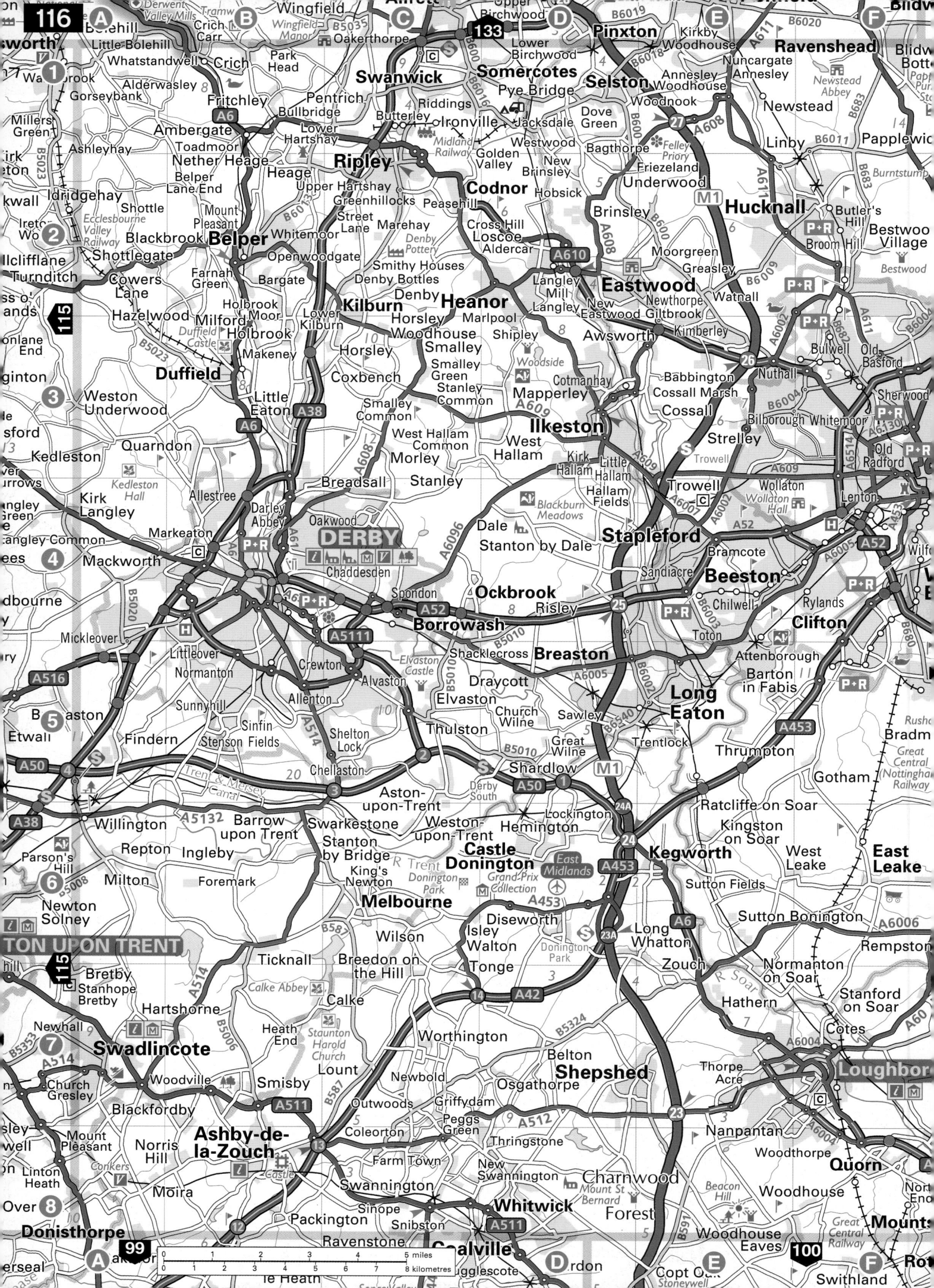

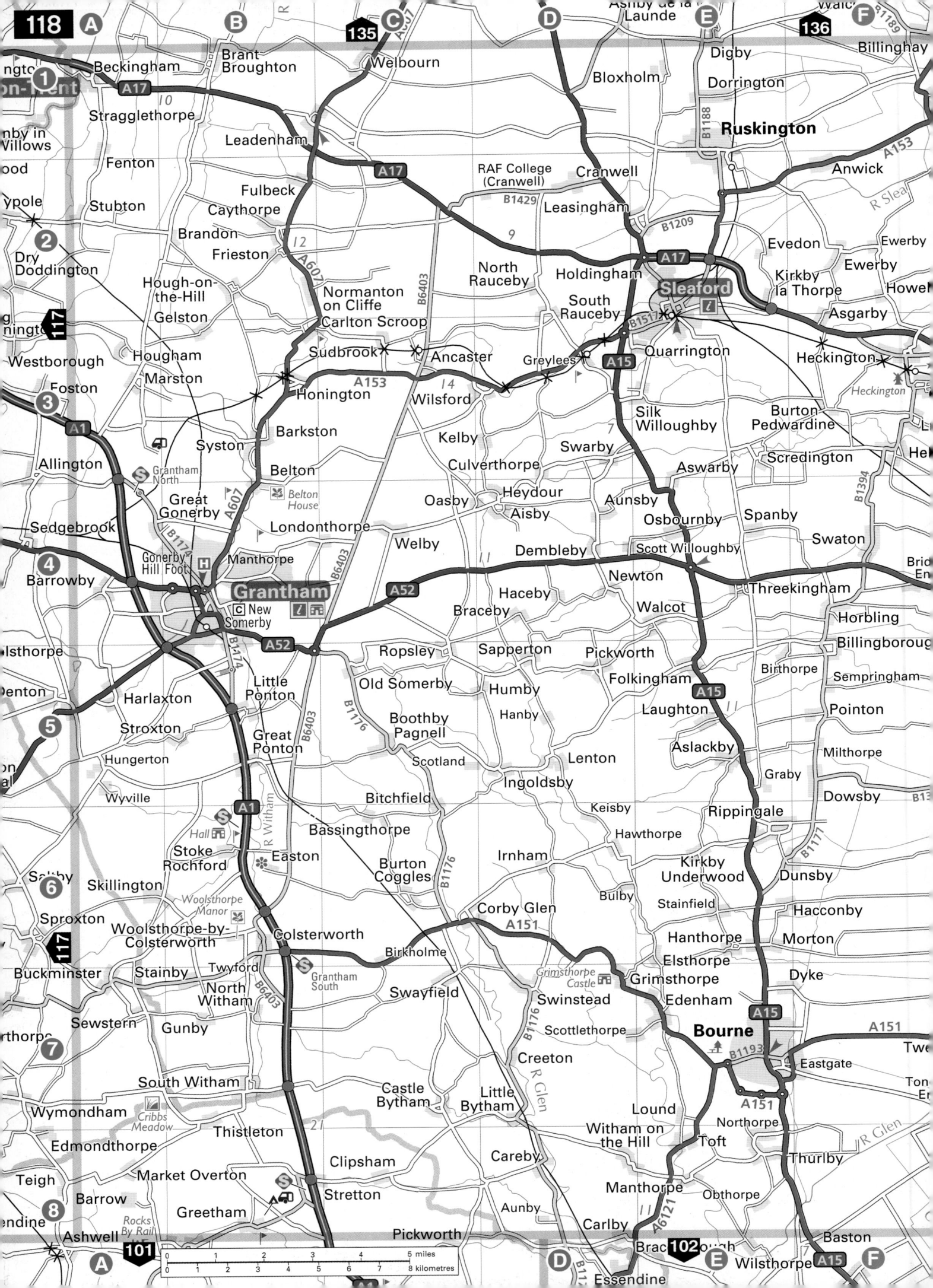

B
D
E
F

Friskney
Friskney Eaudike

Wrangle
Common 1

Wrangle
Lowgate
Wrangle

Hurn's End 2

casgate

gton
End

◄119

3

THE WASH

4

5

Dawsmere
Gedney
Drove End
B1359

ach
thew

6 utton

◄119

napelgate
Little London
★Butterfly & Falconry Park

Wingland

The Wash

Long Sutton

Sutton
Bridge

Walpole
Cross Keys

**Terrington
St Clement**

Little
London

West
Lynn

7

osses

Tydd
Gote

Tydd
St Mary

Walpole
St Andrew

Hay Green

Clenchwarton

A17

11

Tilney
All Saints

South
Lynn

Four
Gotes

Walpole
St Peter

Tilney High End

A47

B1165

Tydd
St Giles

8 wton

Ingleborough

St John's
Highway

Tilney St
Lawrence

Saddlebow

West
Winch

Wiggenhall
St Germans

A11 103

Fitton

West
Walton

Wiggenhall
St Mary the
Virgin

A

103

Holme Dunes
Holme nex
the Sea

Old
Hunstanton

i ⌷

Hunstanton

Ringstead

A149

Norfolk
Lavender

Heacham

Sedgeford

Snettisham

Park
Southgate

Shernbo

RSPB Snettisham
Ingoldisthorpe

12

B1440

Pe
& C

Dersingham

Doddshill

Dersingham
Bog

Wolferton

Sandringha
West New

Babingley River

A149

B1439

Castle Rising

North
Wootton

Castle

A148
Roydon

Congham

A1078

South Wootton

A148

A149

Roydon
Common

Pott
Row

B1153

Gaywood

H

4

C

Fairstead

Bawsey

Bawsey

B1145

Gayton

King's Lynn

i ⌷ M

Brow-of-
the-Hill

Ashwicker

A47

A10

North
Runcton

Fair Green

Middleton

East
Winch

West
Bilney

Blackborough
End

Setchey

104 F

Pentney

D 104 D

E 104 E

0 1 2 3 4 5 miles
0 1 2 3 4 5 6 7 8 kilometres

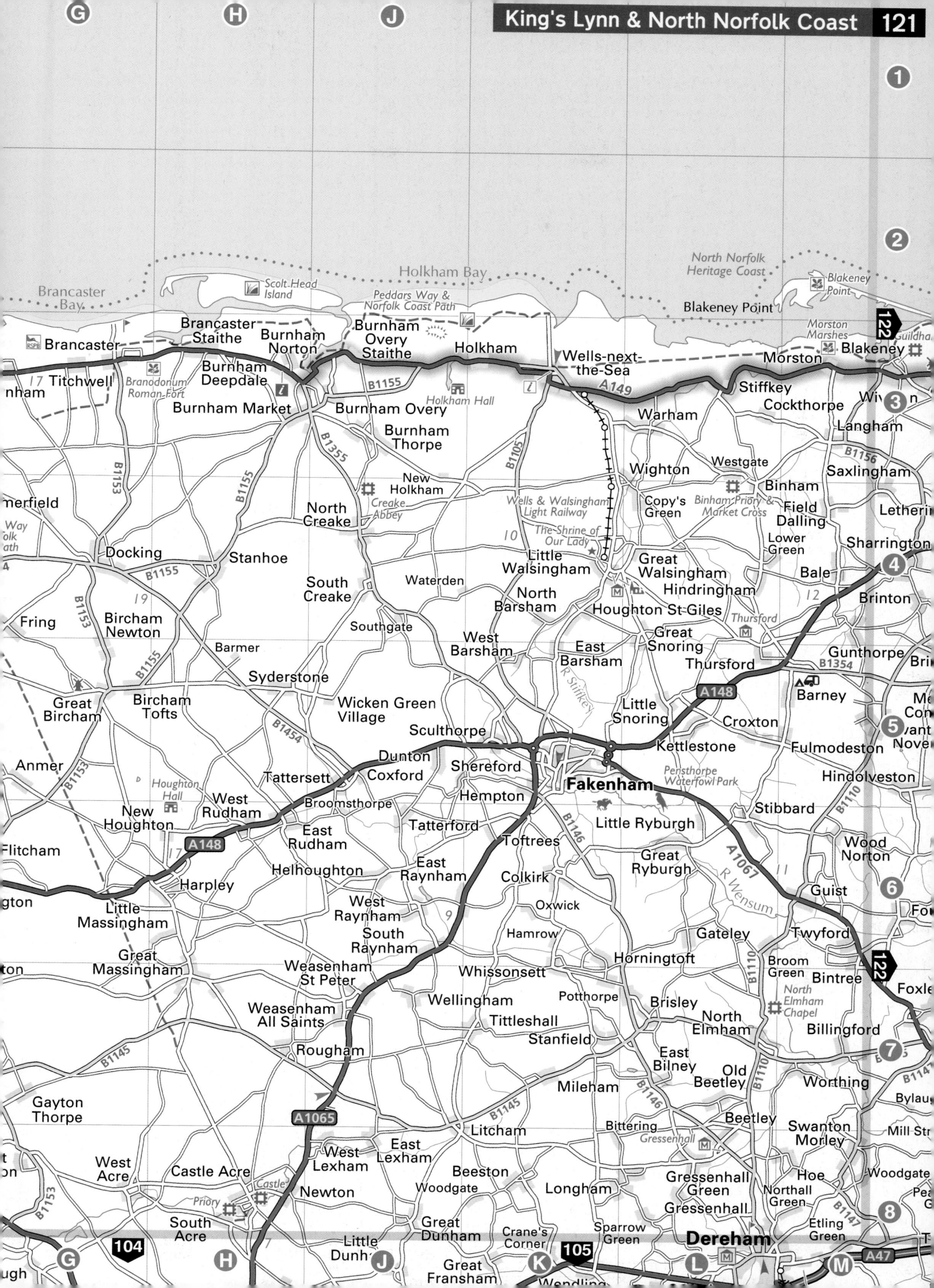

G H J

1
2
3
4
5
6
7
8

Brancaster Bay

Scolt Head Island

Holkham Bay

North Norfolk Heritage Coast

Blakeney Point

Peddars Way & Norfolk Coast Path

Blakeney Point

Morston Marshes

122

Brancaster

Brancaster Staithe

Burnham Norton

Burnham Overy Staithe

Holkham

Wells-next-the-Sea

Morston

Blakeney

Guildha

RSPB

17 Titchwell

nham

Branodunum Roman Fort

Burnham Deepdale

A149

Stiffkey

Cockthorpe

Wiv n

Burnham Market

B1155

Burnham Overy

Warham

Langham

B1156

Saxlingham

Holkham Hall

Wighton

Westgate

Binham

Letheri

nerfield

Burnham Thorpe

Copy's Green

Binham Priory & Market Cross

Field Dalling

Way olk ath

New Holkham

B1105

Wells & Walsingham Light Railway

Lower Green

Sharrington

North Creake

Creake Abbey

10

The Shrine of Our Lady

Little Walsingham

Great Walsingham

Hindringham

Bale

Brinton

Docking

Stanhoe

B1155

South Creake

Waterden

North Barsham

Houghton St Giles

Great Snoring

Thursford

12

Gunthorpe

Bri

Fring

B1153

Bircham Newton

Barmer

Southgate

West Barsham

East Barsham

Great Snoring

Thursford

A148

B1354

Barney

M Con ant Nove

Great Bircham

Bircham Tofts

Syderstone

Wicken Green Village

Little Snoring

Croxton

Fulmodeston

Hindolveston

Anmer

B1153

Houghton Hall

Sculthorpe

Kettlestone

Stibbard

B1110

New Houghton

West Rudham

Tattersett

Dunton Coxford

Shereford

Fakenham

Pensthorpe Waterfowl Park

Wood Norton

A148

Broomsthorpe

Hempton

B1146

Little Ryburgh

A1067

R Wensum

Flitcham

East Rudham

Tatterford

Toftrees

Great Ryburgh

Guist

Harpley

Helhoughton

East Raynham

Colkirk

11

Twyford

122

Little Massingham

West Raynham

Oxwick

Gateley

Broom Green

Bintree

Foxle

Great Massingham

South Raynham

Hamrow

Horningtoft

North Elmham Chapel

B1110

Gayton Thorpe

Weasenham St Peter

Whissonsett

Potthorpe

Brisley

North Elmham

Billingford

B 5

ton

Weasenham All Saints

Wellingham

Tittleshall

Stanfield

East Bilney

Old Beetley

Worthing

B1147

Rougham

Litcham

Mileham

Beetley

B1146

Swanton Morley

Bylau

West Acre

Castle Acre

Priory

Castle

Newton

West Lexham

East Lexham

Beeston Woodgate

Longham

Bittering

Gressenhall

Gressenhall Green

Hoe

Northall Green

Woodgate

Pea

Mill Str

B1147

8

ugh

B1153

South Acre

104

Little Dunh

Great Dunham

Crane's Corner

Sparrow Green

105

Dereham

A47

Flitcham

A1065

Great Fransham

Wendling

G H J K L M

104 105

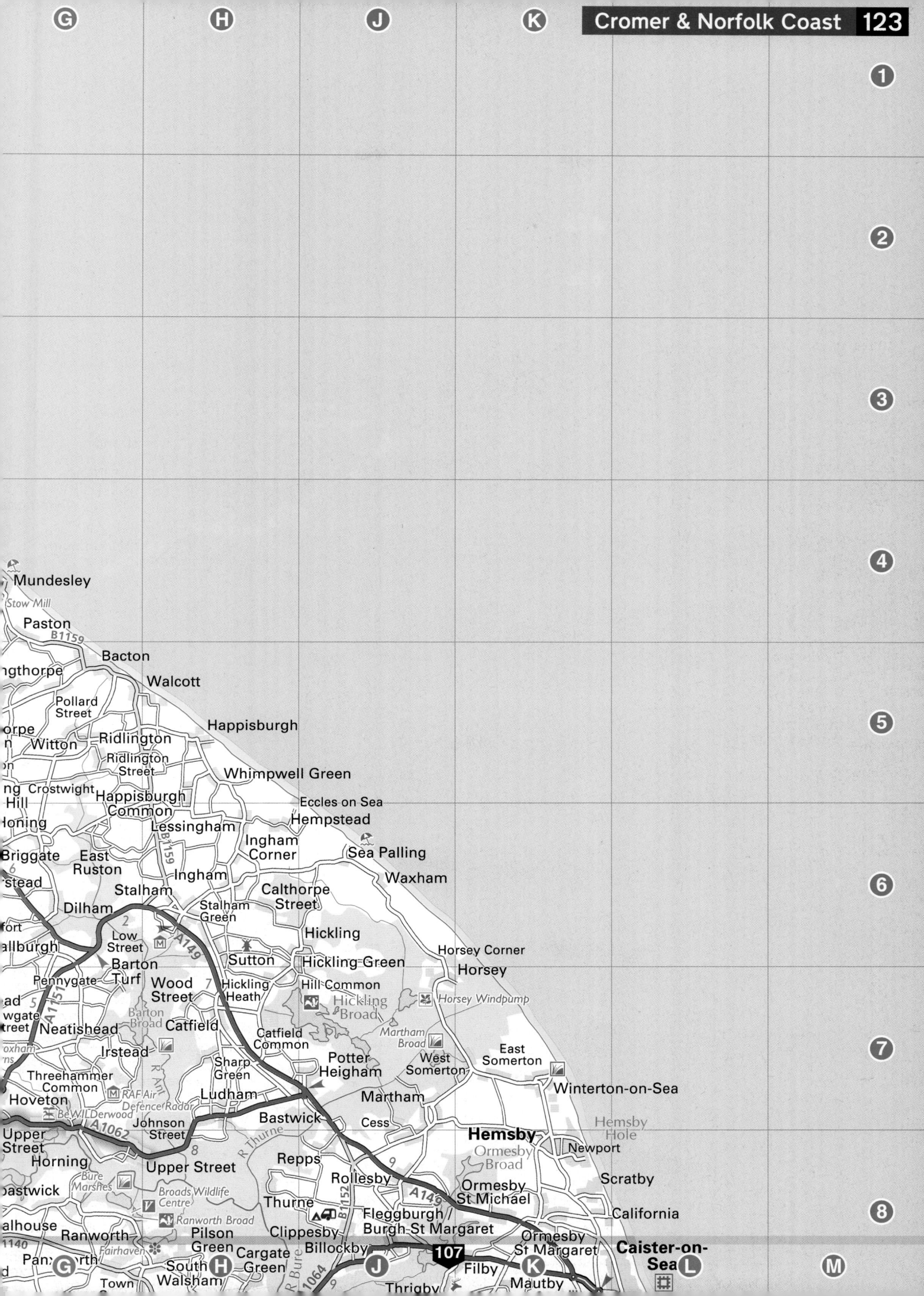

G H J K

1
2
3
4
5
6
7
8

Mundesley
Stow Mill
Paston
B1159
Bacton
ngthorpe
Pollard
Street
Walcott
horpe
Witton
Ridlington
Happisburgh
Ridlington
Street
Crostwight
Whimpwell Green
Hill
ng
Happisburgh
Common
Eccles on Sea
Honing
Lessingham
Hempstead
Briggate
East
Ruston
Ingham
Corner
Sea Palling
stead
Ingham
Waxham
Dilham
Stalham
Calthorpe
Street
Stalham
Green
Hickling
fort
Low
Street
Sutton
Hickling Green
Horsey Corner
allburgh
Barton
Turf
Hill Common
Horsey
Pennygate
Wood
Street
Hickling
Heath
Horsey Windpump
ad
Barton
Broad
Catfield
Hickling
Broad
wgate
treet
Neatishead
Catfield
Common
Martham
Broad
East
Somerton
oxham
ns
Irstead
R Ant
Sharp
Green
Potter
Heigham
West
Somerton
Threehammer
Common
RAF Air
Defence Radar
Ludham
Winterton-on-Sea
Hoveton
BeWILDerwood
Johnson
Street
Bastwick
Martham
Cess
Hemsby
Hole
Upper
Street
A1062
Repps
Horning
Upper Street
R Thurne
Rollesby
A149
Hemsby
Ormesby
Broad
Newport
Scratby
astwick
Bure
Marshes
Thurne
B1152
Ormesby
St Michael
California
Broads Wildlife
Centre
Ranworth Broad
Fleggburgh
Burgh St Margaret
alhouse
A1140
Ranworth
Pilson
Green
Clippesby
Billockby
Ormesby
St Margaret
Caister-on-
Sea
Pan orth
Fairhaven
Cargate
Green
107
Filby
South
Walsham
Town
R Bure
1064
Thrigby
Mautby

G H J K L M

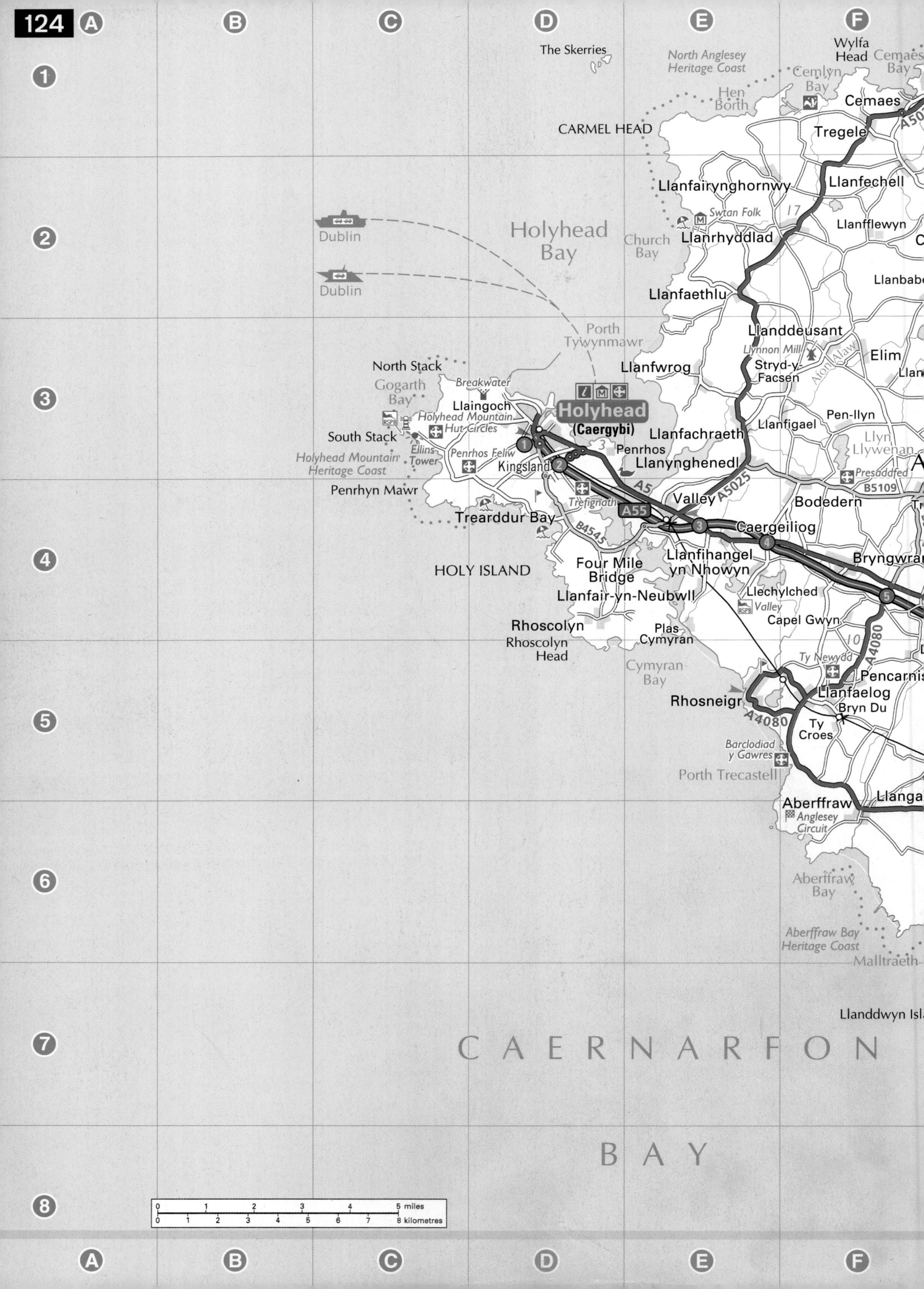

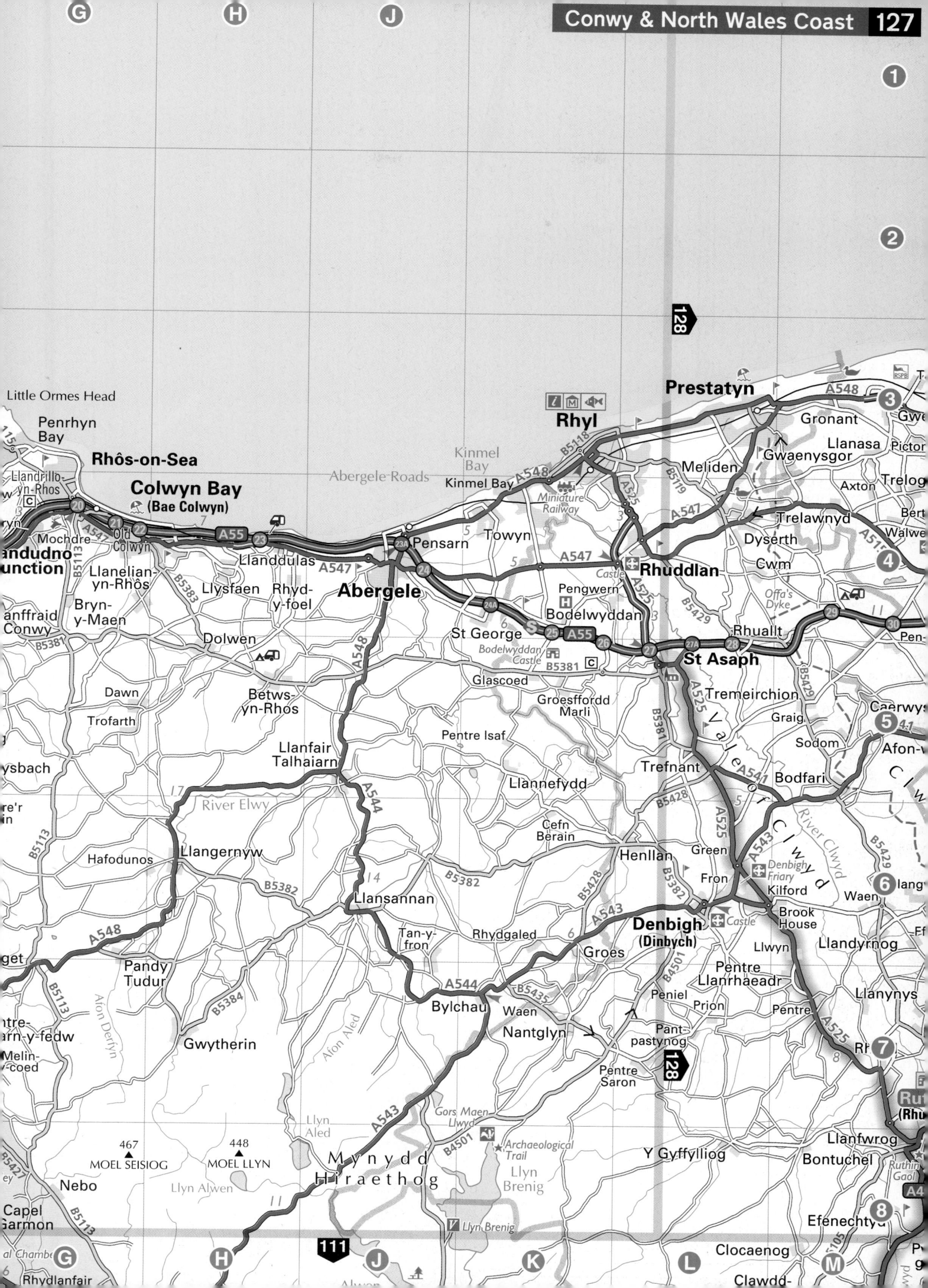

G H J

1

2

128

Little Ormes Head

Penrhyn Bay

Prestatyn

Rhyl

Rhôs-on-Sea

3

Kinmel Bay

Gronant

Llanasa

Gwe

Pictor

Colwyn Bay
(Bae Colwyn)

Llandrillo-yn-Rhos

C

20

Abergele-Roads

Kinmel Bay

Gwaenysgor

Meliden

Axton

Trelog

andudno unction

Mochdre

21 22

Old Colwyn

7

A55

23

A547

23A Pensarn

Towyn

5

A547

Trelawnyd

Dyserth

Bert

Walwe

A55

Llanelian-yn-Rhos

Llanddulas

A547

Miniature Railway

A547

Rhuddlan

Cwm

A515

4

anffraid Conwy

B5381

Bryn-y-Maen

Llysfaen

Rhyd-y-foel

Abergele

24

5

Castle

Pengwern

A525

Offa's Dyke

B5381

ysbach

Dolwen

24A

St George

6

Bodelwyddan

B5429

Rhuallt

29

30

Pen

e'r in

Betws-yn-Rhos

25

A55

26

27

27A

28

St Asaph

A525

B5429

Caerwys

5

A544

Bodelwyddan Castle

B5381

C

Glascoed

Groesffordd Marli

Tremeirchion

Graig

Afon

B5113

Pentre Isaf

Trefnant

A541

Bodfari

Sodom

River Elwy

Llannefydd

B5428

A525

5

Clw

Hafodunos

Llangernyw

Cefn Berain

Henllan

Green Fron

A543

Denbigh Friary

6

lang

B5382

Llansannan

Tan-y-fron

Rhydgaled

6

Groes

Denbigh
(Dinbych)

Castle

Brook House

Kilford

Llwyn

Llandyrnog

Waen

Ff

A548

Pandy Tudur

B5384

A544

B5435

Bylchau

Waen

Nantglyn

Peniel

Prion

Pant-pastynog

Pentre Llanrhaeadr

Pentre

Llanynys

A525

Rh

7

tre arn-y-fedw

Afon Derfyn

Gwytherin

Pentre Saron

128

Melin-coed

A543

Gors Maen Llwyd

Archaeological Trail

Llanfwrog

Capel armon

467 MOEL SEISIOG

448 MOEL LLYN

Llyn Aled

B4501

Llyn Brenig

Y Gyffylliog

Bontuchel

Ruthin Gaol

A4

Nebo

Llyn Alwen

Mynydd Hiraethog

11

Efenechtyd

8

al Chamber

B5113

Llyn Brenig

Clocaenog

Clawdd

Rhydlanfair

111

G H J K L M

Alwen

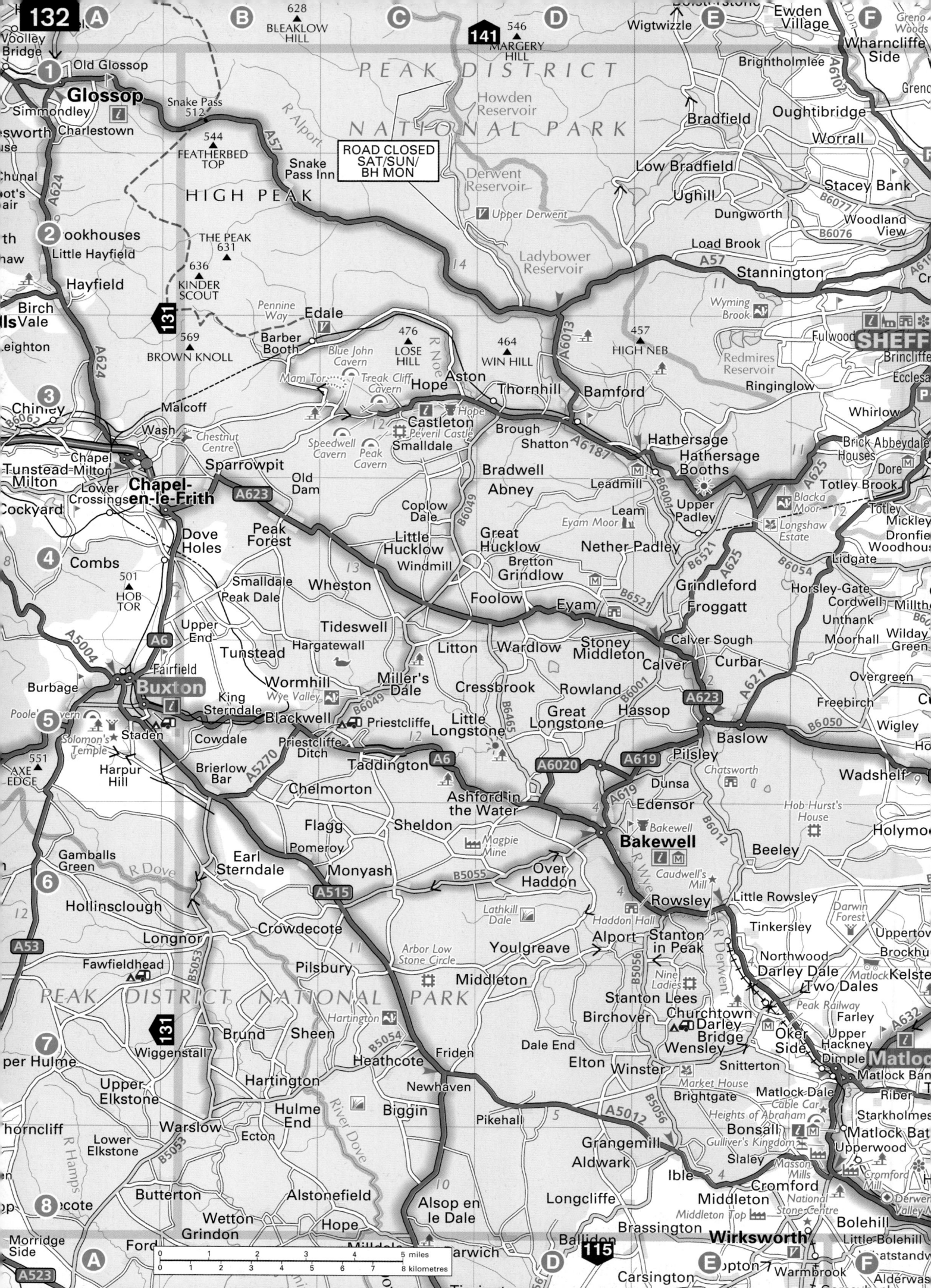

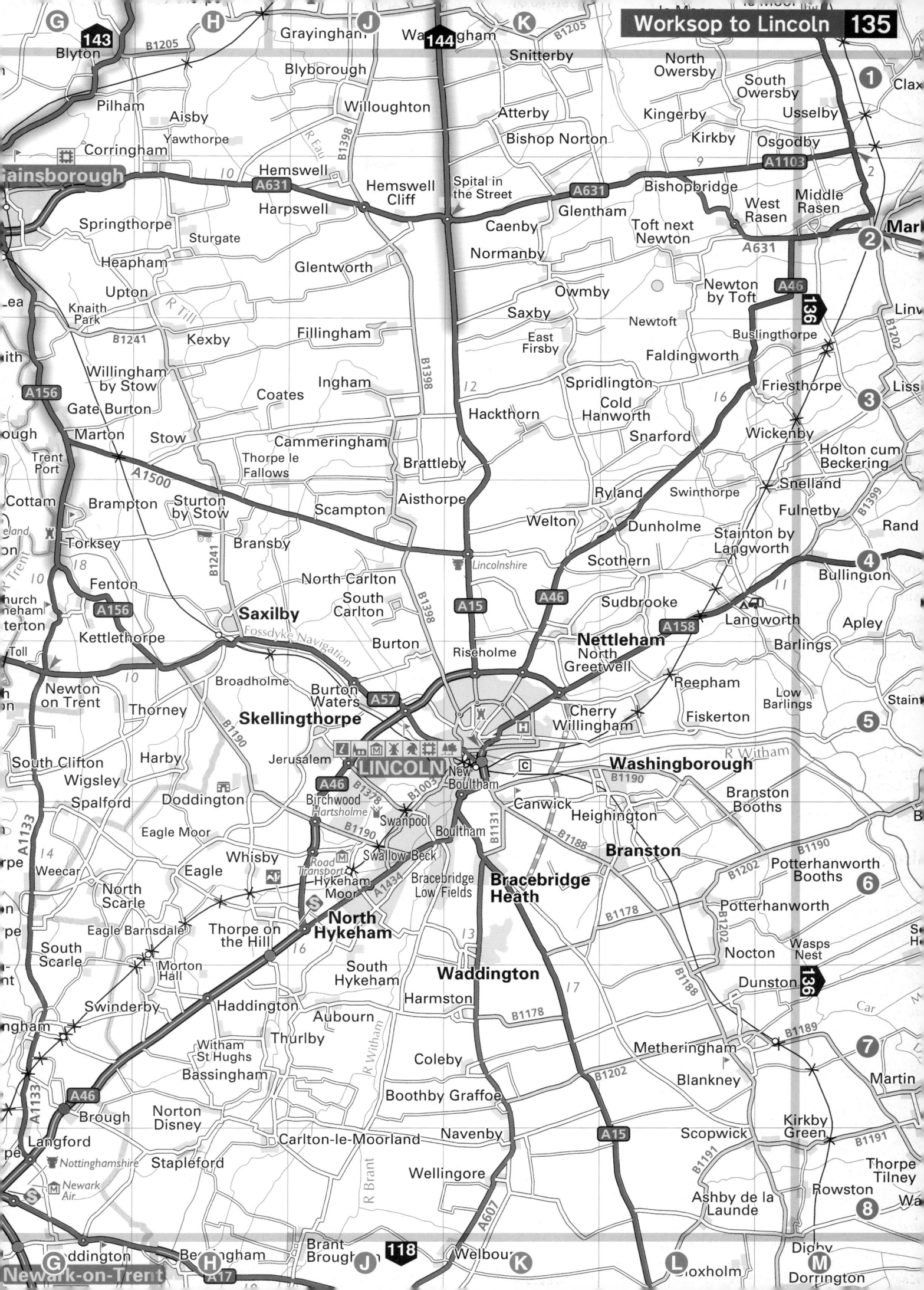

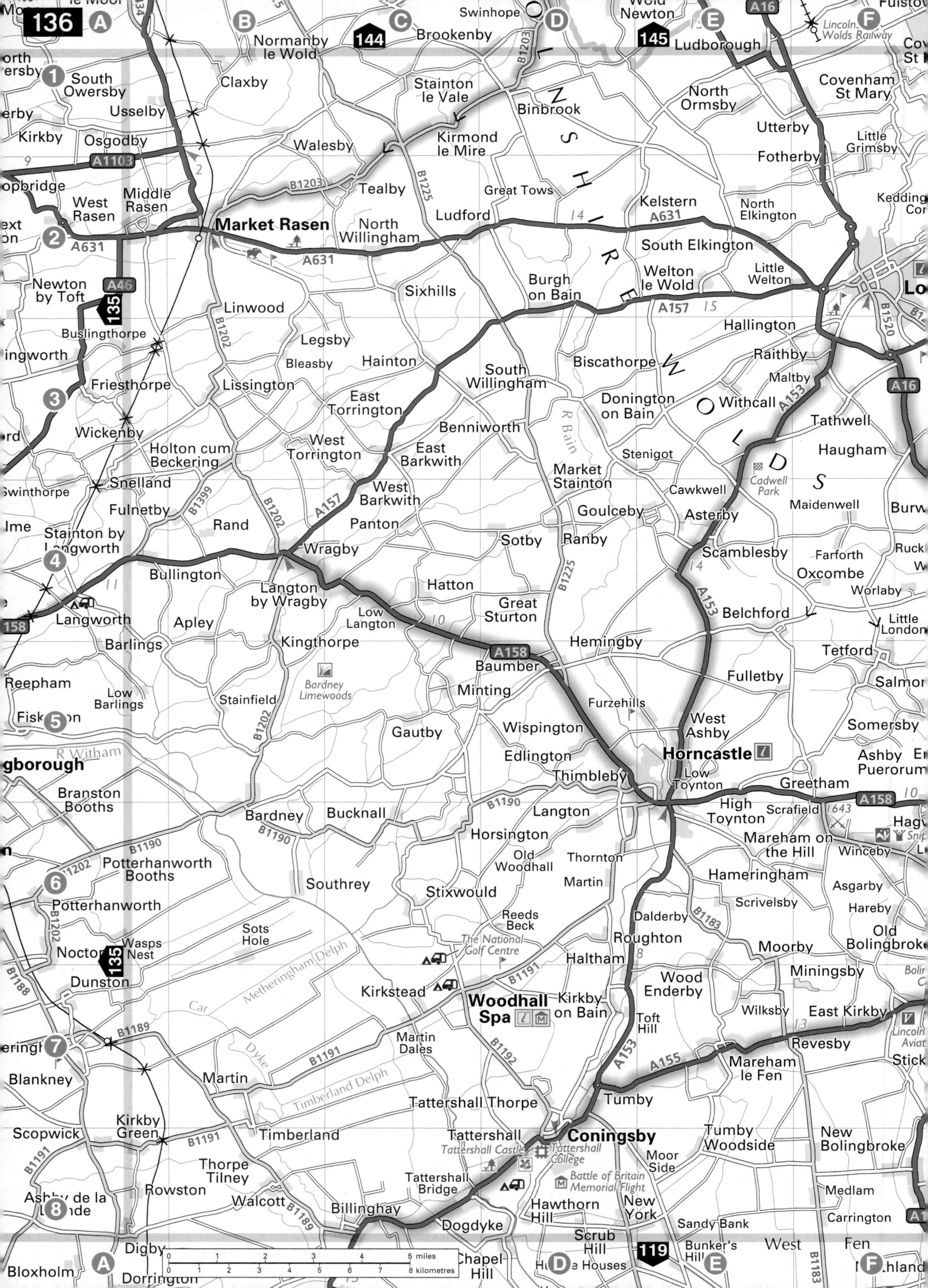

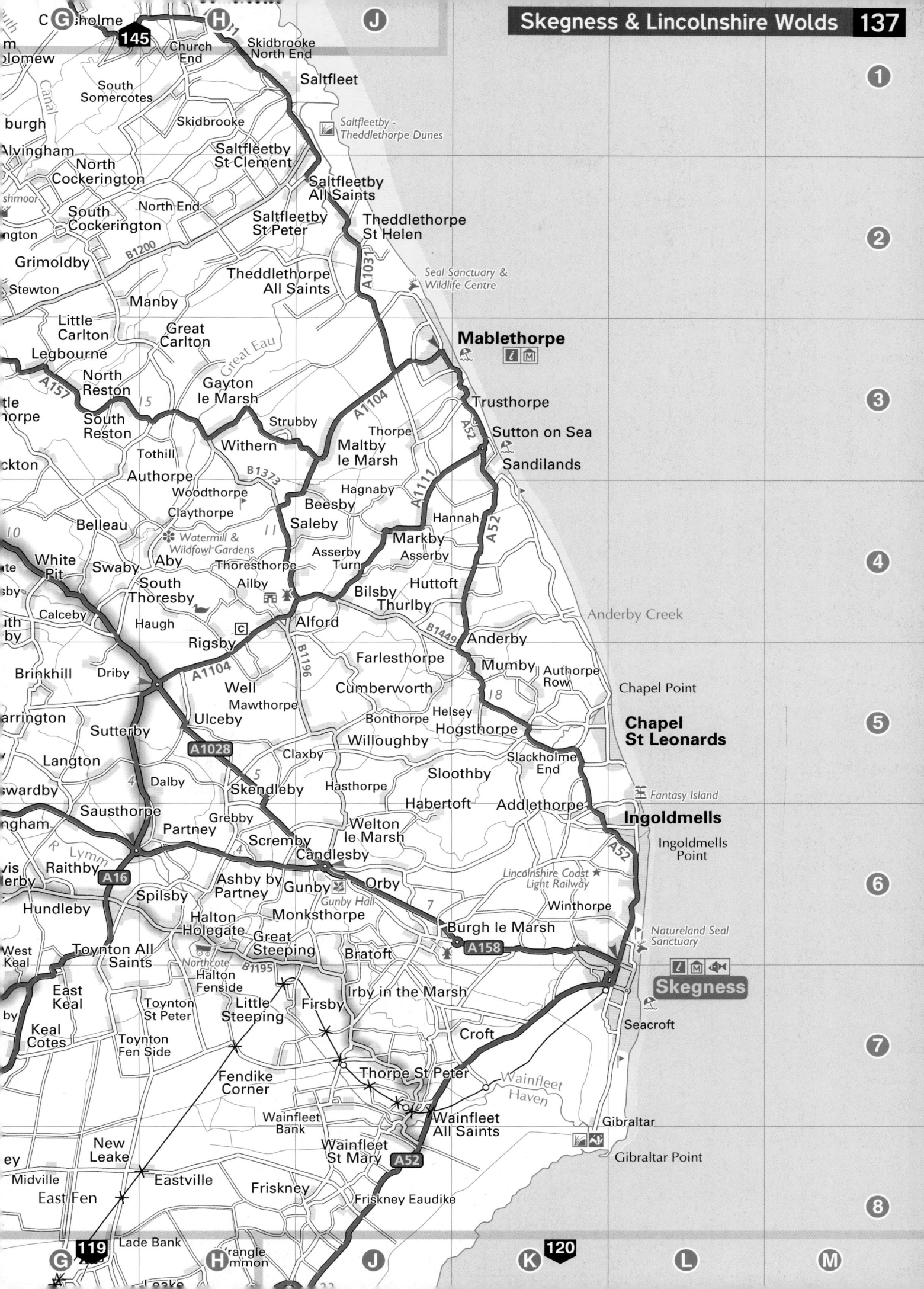

C G holme
145
Church
End
Skidbrooke
North End
Saltfleet

South
Somercotes
Skidbrooke
Saltfleetby - Theddlethorpe Dunes
Saltfleetby
St Clement

North End
Saltfleetby
All Saints

North
Cockerington
South
Cockerington

Saltfleetby
St Peter
Theddlethorpe
St Helen

Grimoldby
B1200

Theddlethorpe
All Saints
A1031
Seal Sanctuary &
Wildlife Centre

Stewton
Manby

Little
Carlton
Great
Carlton

Legbourne
North
Reston
Gayton
le Marsh
Mablethorpe
i M

A157
15
Strubby
Thorpe
Trusthorpe

South
Reston
Withern
Maltby
le Marsh
A52
Sutton on Sea

Tothill
A1104
Sandilands

Authorpe
Woodthorpe
Hagnaby
A1111

Claythorpe
Beesby
Hannah

Belleau
Watermill &
Wildfowl Gardens
Saleby

White
Pit
Swaby
Aby
Thoresthorpe
Markby
Asserby

South
Thoresby
Ailby
Asserby
Turn
Huttoft
Anderby Creek

Calceby
Haugh
Bilsby
Thurlby

Alford
B1449
Anderby

Brinkhill
Driby
Rigsby
C
Farlesthorpe
Mumby
Authorpe
Row
Chapel Point

arrington
A1104
Well
Cumberworth
18

Sutterby
B1196
Mawthorpe
Ulceby
Helsey
**Chapel
St Leonards**

Langton
A1028
Bonthorpe
Hogsthorpe

swardby
Dalby
Claxby
Willoughby
Slackholme
End

R Lymn
4
Skendleby
Hasthorpe
Sloothby

Sausthorpe
Grebby
Welton
le Marsh
Habertoft
Addlethorpe
Fantasy Island

Raithby
Partney
Scremby
Ingoldmells

erby
A16
Candlesby
Ingoldmells
Point

Spilsby
Ashby by
Partney
Gunby
Orby
A52

Hundleby
Monksthorpe
Gunby Hall
7
Winthorpe
Lincolnshire Coast
Light Railway

Halton
Holegate
Great
Steeping
Burgh le Marsh
A158

West
Keal
Toynton All
Saints
Bratoft
Natureland Seal
Sanctuary

East
Keal
Northcote
Halton
Fenside
B1195
Irby in the Marsh
Skegness
i M

Keal
Cotes
Toynton
St Peter
Little
Steeping
Firsby
Croft
Seacroft

Toynton
Fen Side
Wainfleet
Haven

Fendike
Corner
Thorpe St Peter
Gibraltar

New
Leake
Wainfleet
Bank
Wainfleet
All Saints
Gibraltar Point

Midville
Wainfleet
St Mary
A52

East Fen
Eastville
Friskney
Friskney Eaudike

119
Lade Bank
rangle
mmon
120

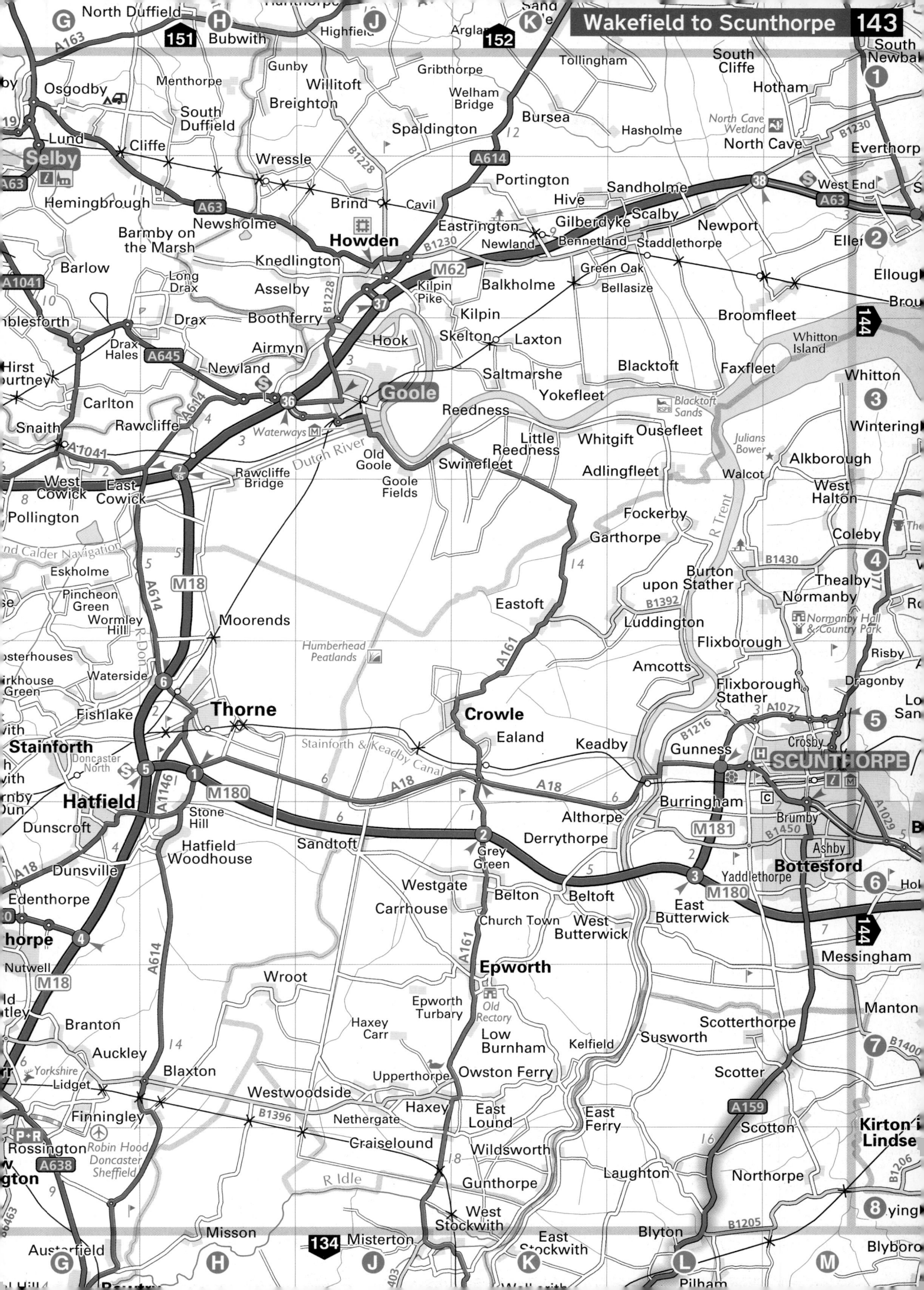

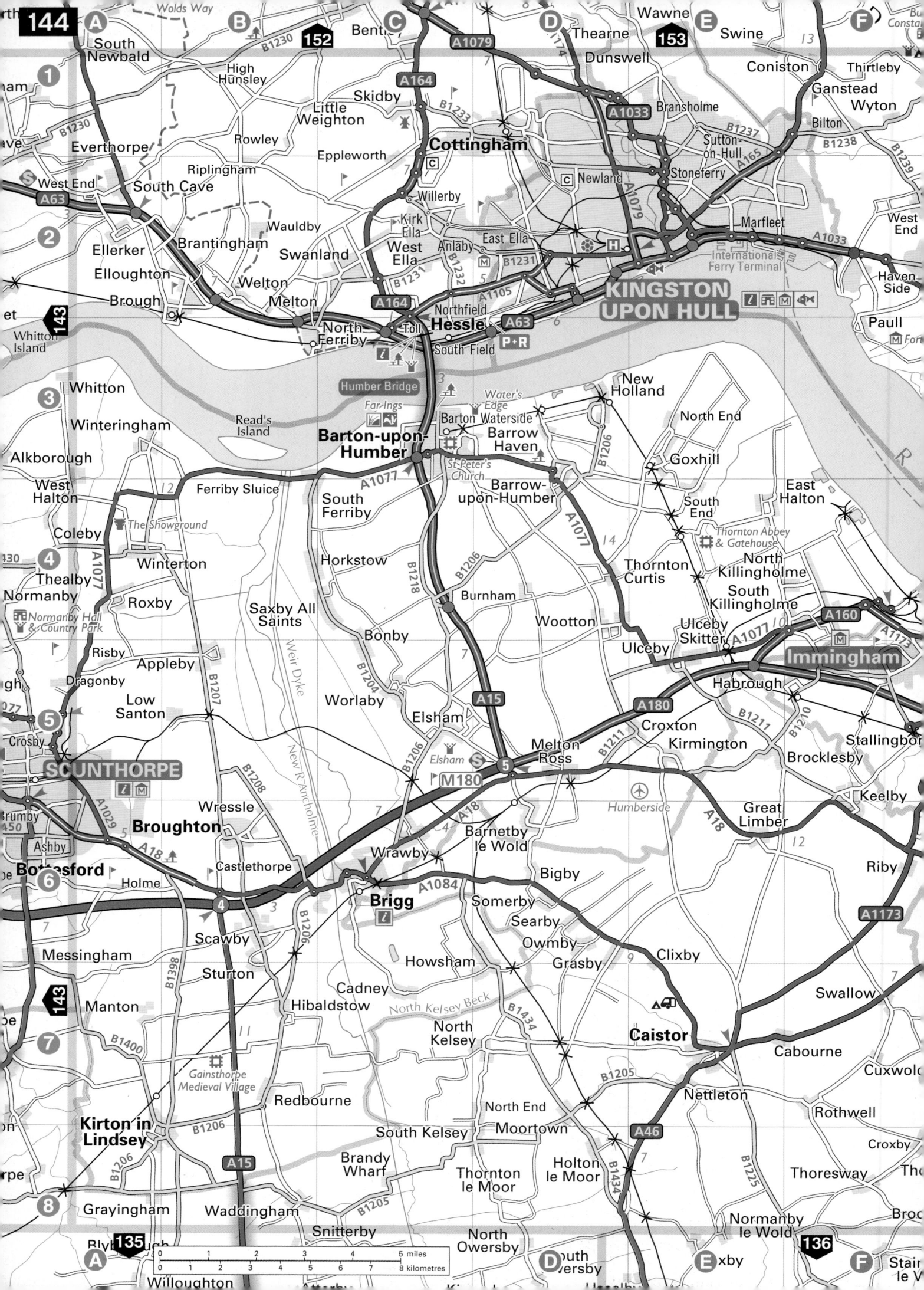

G   B1238   B1242   H   J   1

Flinto   153   Garton
   Grimston
   Fitling
broatley   Humbleton   Hilston
   Owstwick   Tunstall   2
elley   Danthorpe   North
Elstronwick   End   Waxholme
East End   Burton   Roos   Rimswell   B1242
eston   Pidsea   West   Owthorne
   End   B1362   Withernsea   i
edon   B1362   East End   M
   Burstwick   Halsham   Hollym
Thorngumbald   A1033   3
Ryehill   16   Keyingham   Holmpton
   Ottringham   Winestead   4   Out
   A1033   Newton
   Patrington
   Patrington   Welwick
   Haven   Weeton   B1445   Easington
   Sunk   Skeffling   South End   4
   Island   Spurn
   Heritage Coast
nmingham
ock   Kilnsea   V

   Spurn Point
A180   GRIMSBY   M V   5
B1210   S7
ealing   West Marsh   Spurn Heritage Coast
   Great   B136   Little   Old   SPURN HEAD
   Coates   Coates   Clee   A180
Aylesby   Nunsthorpe   C   Cleethorpes   i
   A46   A16   Thrunscoe   The Jungle   Rotterdam (Europoort)
Irby upon   6   Bradley   Scartho   A1098   Cleethorpes   Cleethorpes Coast   Zeebrugge
Humber   A46   H   B1203   Light Railway
   Laceby   Humberston
Waltham   B1219
   Barnoldby   New Waltham
   le Beck   Brigsley   Holton   Tetney
Beelsby   Ashby cum   le Clay   Marshes   RSPB   7
   Hatcliffe   Fenby   North   A1031
   A18   Waithe   End   Tetney
West   Grainsby   Tetney   Lock
Ravendale   East   North   North
   Ravendale   Thoresby   Cotes
by   B1201   Churchthorpe   West   Marshchapel   Donna
nhope   17   29   End   Eskham   Nook
   Wold   North   Grainthorpe
by   Newton   15   Fulstow   Louth   Conisholme   North   A1031
B1203   A16   Lincolnshire   Covenham   Somercotes
   Ludborough   Wolds Railway   St Bartholomew   Church   Skidbrooke
G   136   J   K   End   North End   8
   North   Covenham   South   L   Saltf'   M
   Ormsby   St Mary   Somercotes

A   B   C   D   E   F

1

155

156

Haverigg Point

Sandscale Haws

North Walney

South Lakes Safari Zoo

Askam in Furness

Marton   **Swarthmoor**   nal Foot

Lindal in Furness

Conishead Prior

Great Urswick

Little Urswick   Brow End

Bardsea

Dalton-in-Furness

Scales

Baycliff

BARROW-IN-FURNESS

Hawcoat   Newton

Furness Abbey   *Bow Bridge*

Stainton with Adgarley

Watermill

Aldingham

North Scale

Dendron   **Gleaston**

2

Vickerstown   Barrow Island

Roose

Leece

Newbiggin

ISLE OF WALNEY

Biggar

Roa Island

Rampside

Roosebeck

3

Sheep Island

Piel Castle   Foulney Island

Piel Island

Hilpsford Point   *South Walney*   Piel Bar

4

Douglas

5

6

i M **Fleetwood**

Rossall Point

i **Cleveleys**

Thor

7

Little Bispham   Nor   Churc

Norbreck

Bispham

North Shore   Warbreck   Nc

Hoohill

8

| 0 | 1 | 2 | 3 | 4 | 5 miles |
| 0 | 1 | 2 | 3 | 4 | 5 | 6 | 7 | 8 kilometres |

i M **BLACKPOOL**

138

A   B   C   D   E   F

South

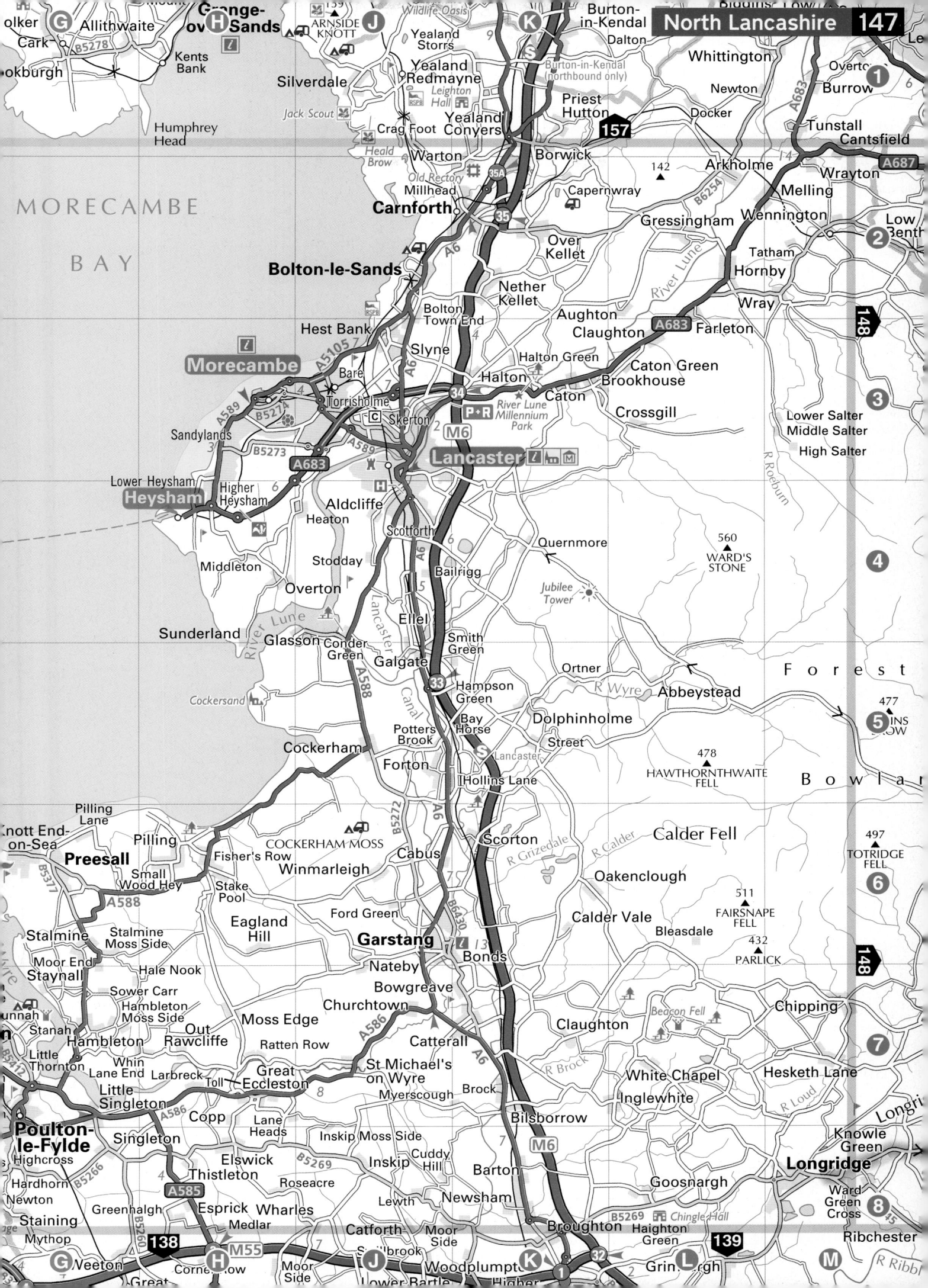

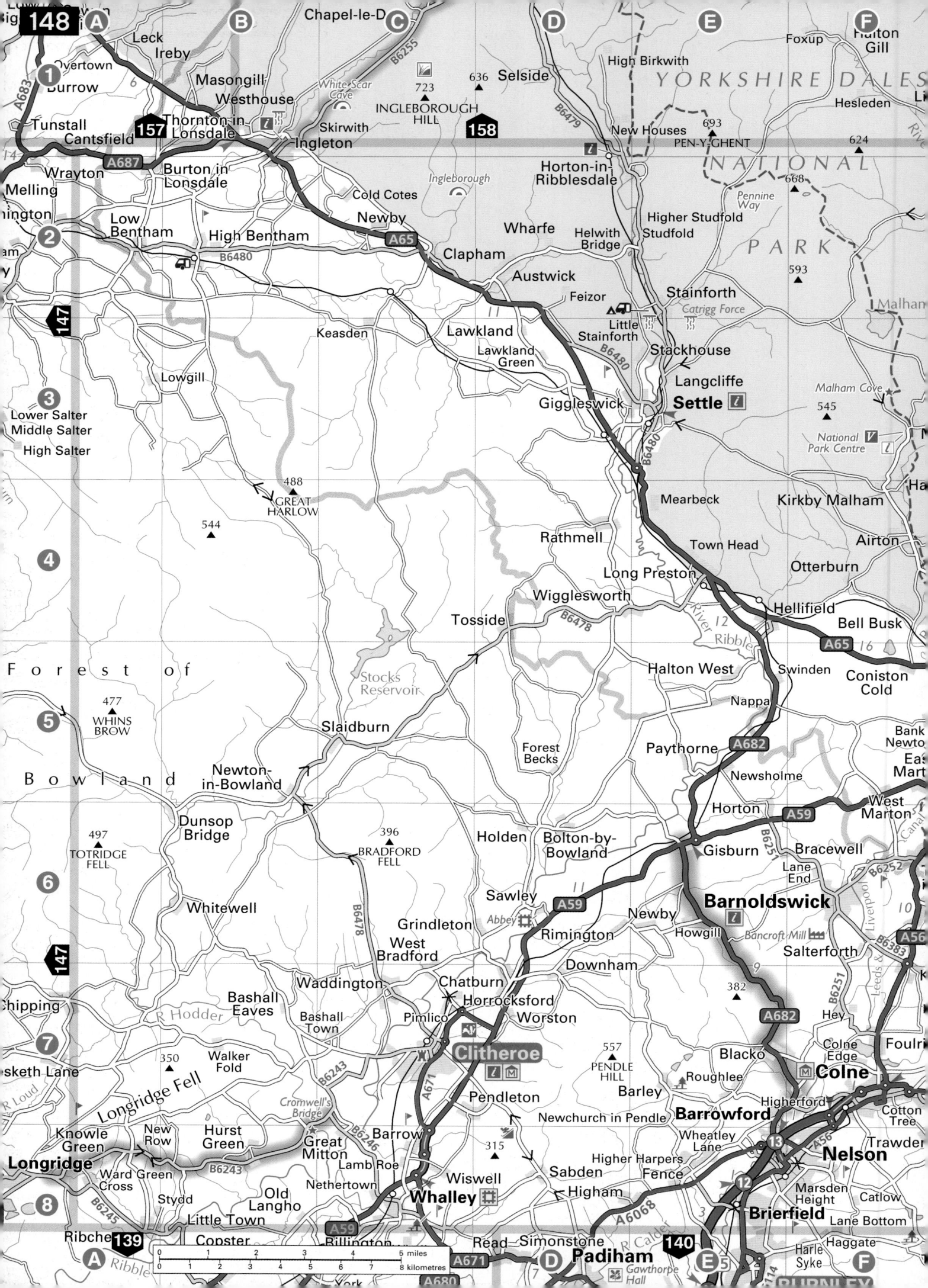

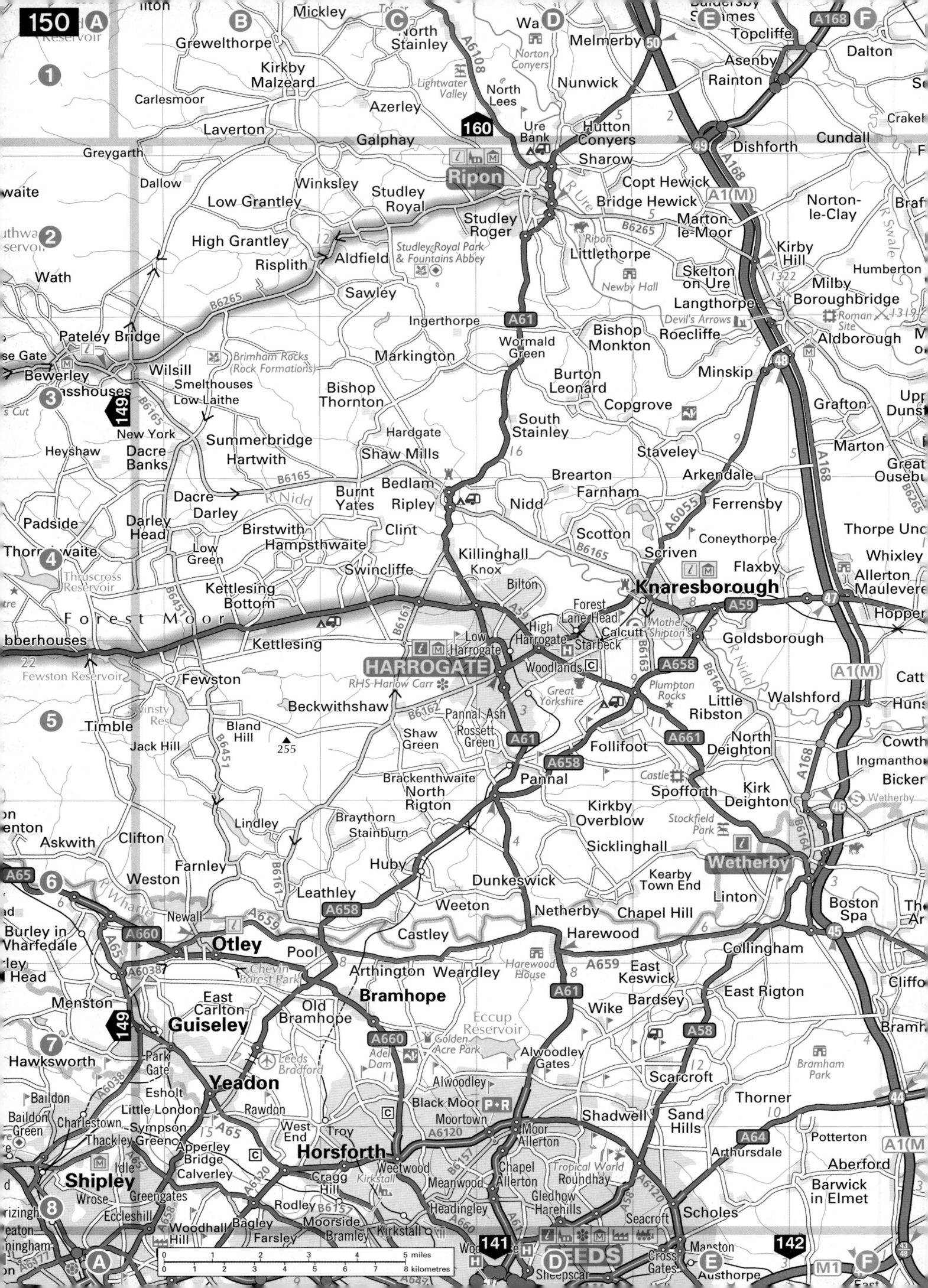

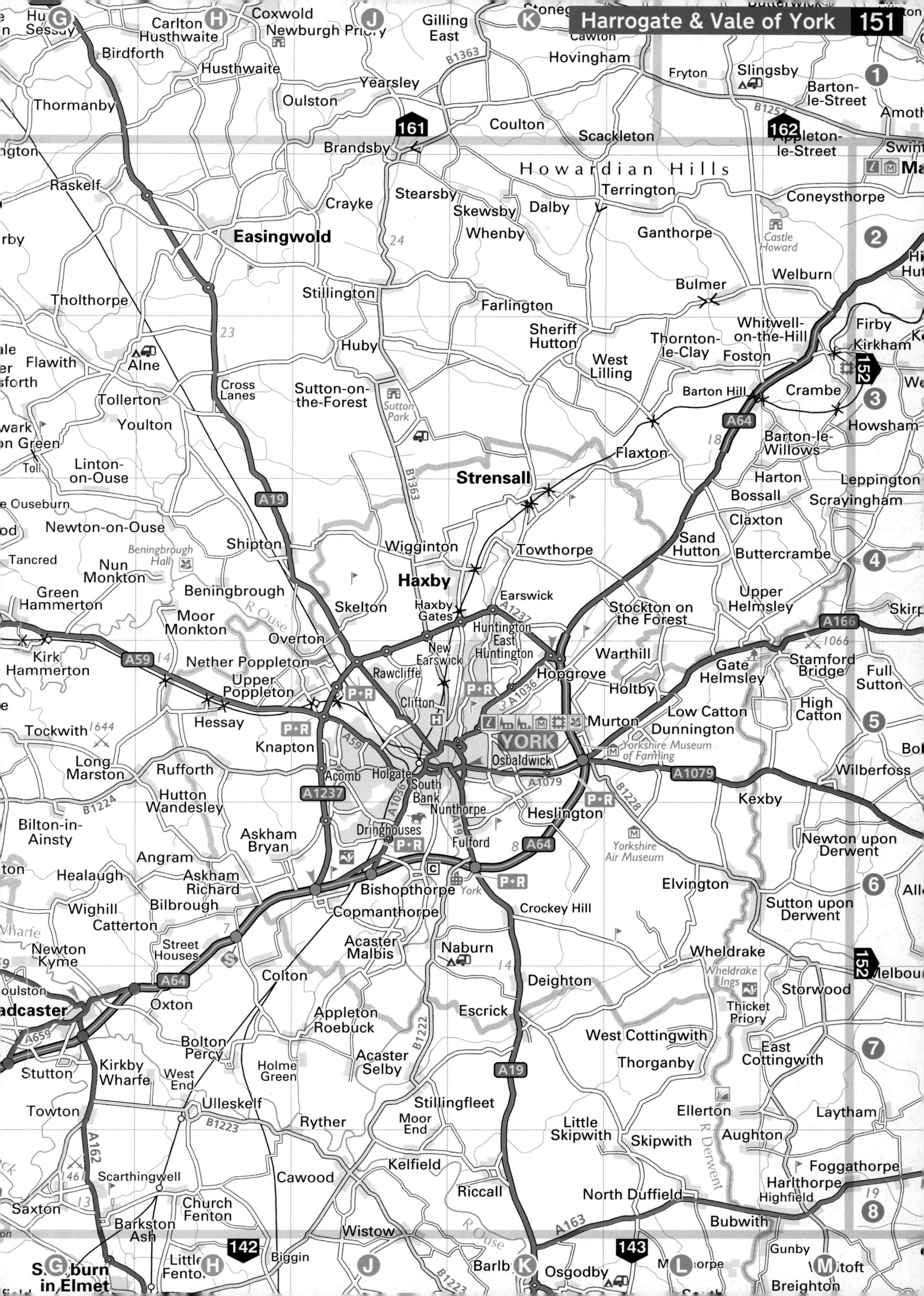

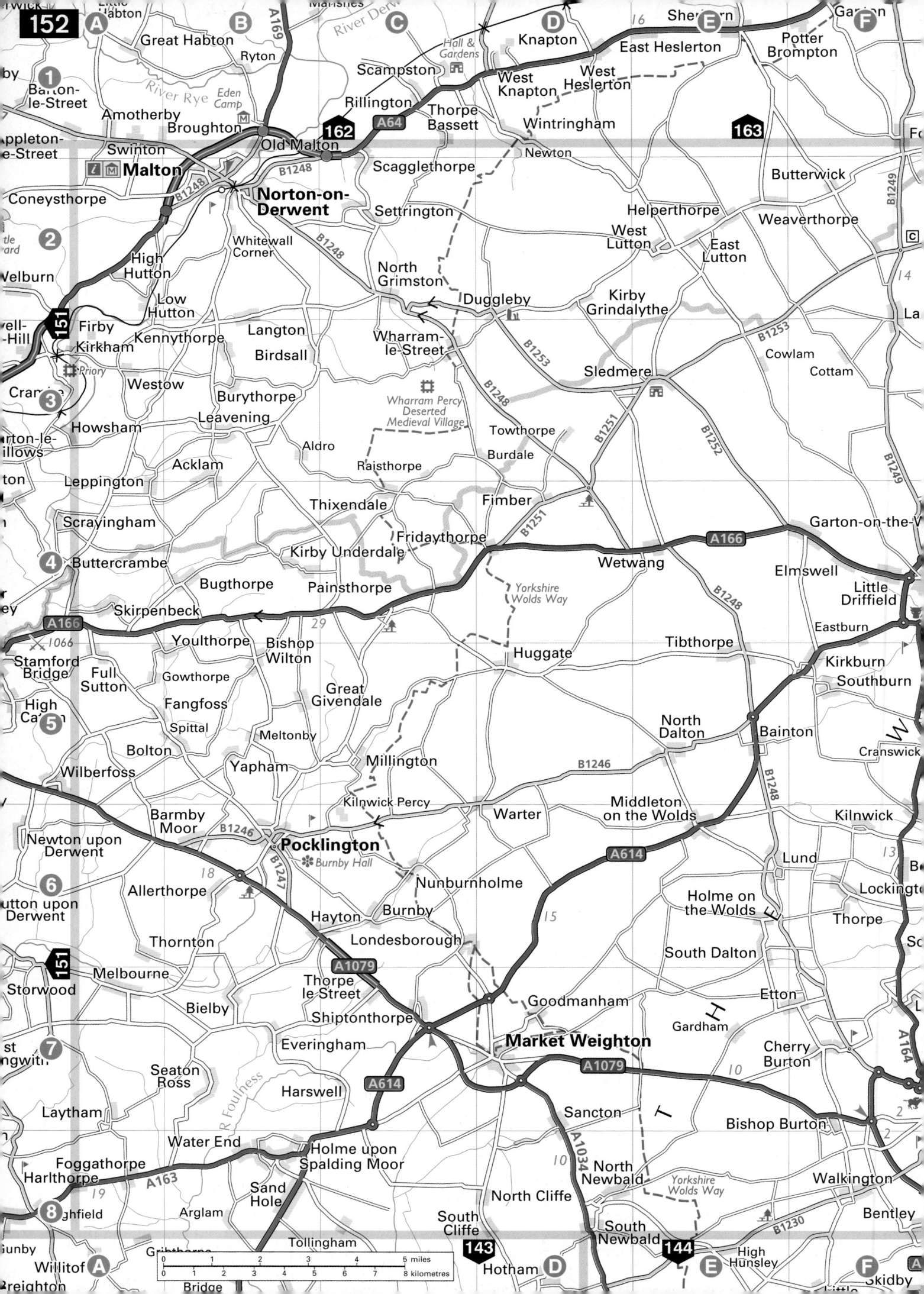

POINT OF AYRE

Rue Point

Point Cranstal

The Lhen
Cranstal

Bride

A10

Ayres

Shellag Point

Jurby Head
Andreas

Jurby
Sandygate

Regaby

St Jude's
Ballachurry
Fort

The Cronk
The Grove

Ramsey
Bay

Close
Sulby
Sulby R.
Ramsey
(Rhumsaa)

Sartfield
Churchtown
Manx Electric Railway

Ballaugh
Cronk
Sumark
Glen
Auldyn
Port e Vullen

Orrisdale
Curraghs
Ancient Crosses

Orrisdale Head
Dreemskerry
Maughold

ISLE OF
561
NORTH
BARRULE
Maughold
Head

Kirk Michael
Ravensdale
MAN
Ballajora

Block
Eary
Corrany
Ballafayle

Cooildarry
Castbal yn Ard

488
Sulby
620
SNAEFELL
462
Glen
Mona

Barregarrow
Reservoir
SLIEAU LHEAN

Knocksharry
The Bungalow
Laxey
Dhoon
Bay

Peel Castle
B10
Snaefell
Mountain
Railway
Great
Laxey
Wheel

St Patrick's Isle
Cronk-y-Voddy
545
BEINN-Y-PHOTT
ELLAN
Ballalheannagh
King Orry's Grave

Peel
(Purt ny-hInshey)
487
COLDEN
Millennium
Way
TT Circuit
Old
Laxey

Contrary Head
Corrins
Folly
VANNIN
Laxey
Bay

Patrick
479
SLIEAU RUY
Creg ny Baa
Baldrine

St John's
Greeba
Cloven Stones

Glen Maye
Baldwin
Clay Head

Lower
Foxdale
Crosby
Glen
Vine
Strang
Onchan
(Kiondroghad)
Groudle Glen
Railway

Niarbyl
Dalby
Foxdale
Eairy
Union Mills
Norse
Houses
Cronkbourne
Onchan Head

Niarbyl Bay
Round
Table
Braaid
Belfast
(Apr-Sept)

Dalby
Mountain
483
SOUTH
BARRULE
DOUGLAS
(DOOLISH)

437
CRONK NY
ARREY LAA
Closeclark
Brough
Fort
St Marks
Douglas
Head
Heysham
(Mar-Oct)

Fleshwick
Bay
Ballamodha
Millennium
Way
Ballakelly
Port Soderick
(Apr-Aug)
(Nov-Mar)
Liverpool

Ballakilpheric
Grenaby
Santon
Isle of Man
Steam Railway
Santon Head
Birkenhead

Milners Tower
Colby
Ballabeg
Rushen
Abbey
Cronk ny
Merriu
Dublin

Bradda Head
Ballafesson
Silverdale Glen
Ballasalla

Port Erin
Howe
Meayll
Circle
Castletown
Derbyhaven
Isle of Man (Ronaldsway)

Calf of
Man
Cregneash
Port
St Mary
Hango
Hill
Derby Fort

Spanish
Head
Scarlett
Point
Close ny
Chollagh
Scarlett
Castletown
Bay
Herring Tower

Caigher
Point
Dreswick Point

Manx Heritage site

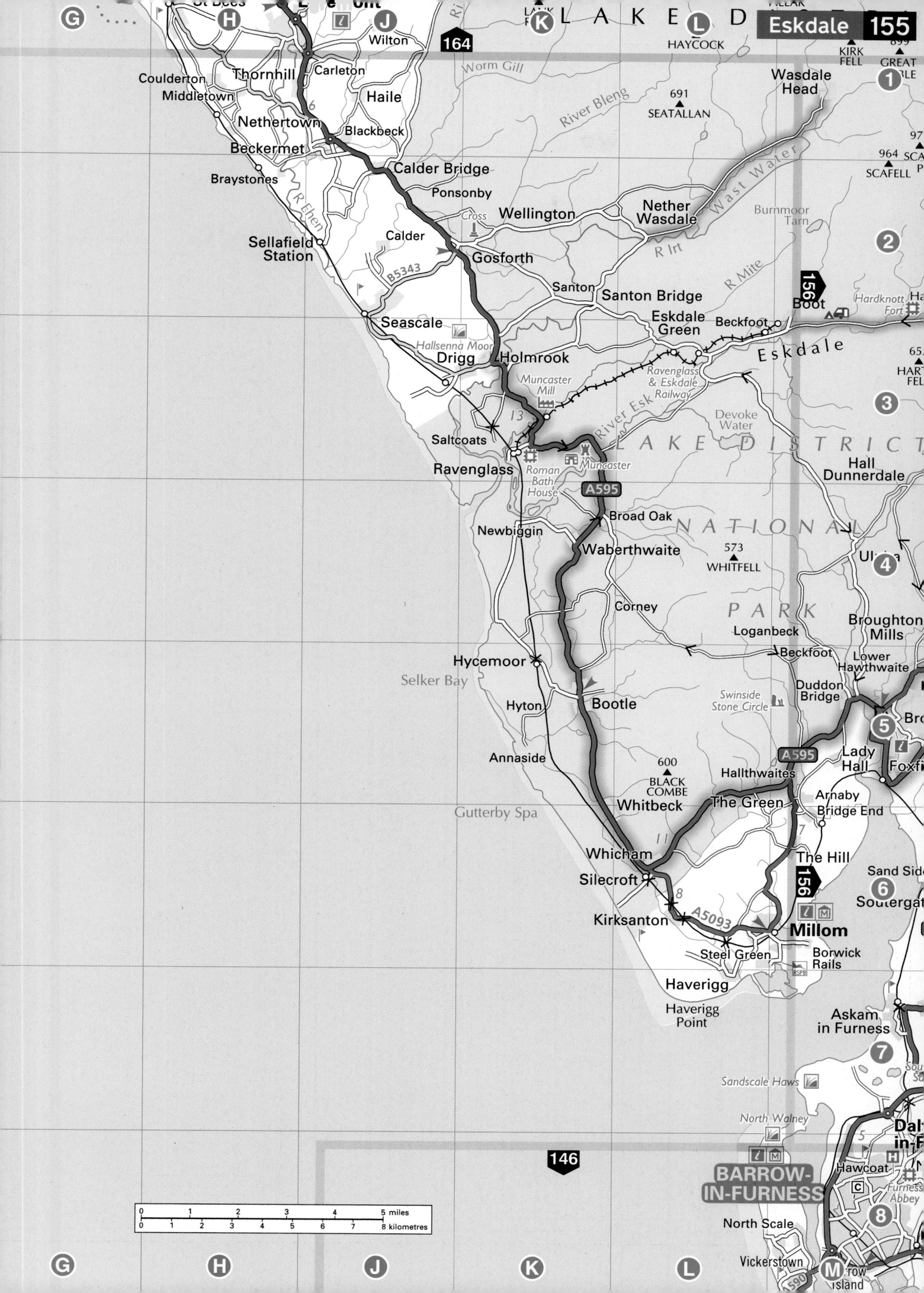

G · · · · H J K **L** A K E D L

164

Eskdale 155

St Bees
Wilton
Thornhill Carleton LADY FELL K LAKED HAYCOCK L
Coulderton Middletown Haile
Nethertown Blackbeck
Beckermet Calder Bridge
Braystones Ponsonby
R Ehen Calder Wellington Nether Wasdale
Sellafield Station B5343 Gosforth
Cross Santon Santon Bridge
Seascale Eskdale Green Beckfoot Boot
Hallsenna Moor Drigg Holmrook
Muncaster Mill Ravenglass & Eskdale Railway ESKDALE
Saltcoats River Esk LAKE DISTRICT
Ravenglass Roman Bath House Muncaster Devoke Water Hall Dunnerdale
A595 Broad Oak NATIONAL
Newbiggin Waberthwaite 573 WHITFELL Ulpha
Corney PARK
Loganbeck Broughton Mills
Hycemoor Beckfoot Lower Hawthwaite
Selker Bay Hyton Bootle Swinside Stone Circle Duddon Bridge
Annaside A595 Lady Hall Foxfi
600 BLACK COMBE Hallthwaites Arnaby Bridge End
Gutterby Spa Whitbeck The Green
Whicham Sand Side
Silecroft The Hill Soutergat
Kirksanton A5093 156 Millom
Steel Green Borwick Rails
Haverigg Askam in Furness
Haverigg Point

146

Sandscale Haws
North Walney Dal -in-F
BARROW- Hawcoat
IN-FURNESS Furness Abbey
North Scale
0 1 2 3 4 5 miles
0 1 2 3 4 5 6 7 8 kilometres
Vickerstown row Island

G H J K L M

Wasdale Head
KIRK FELL GREAT BLE 899
97
SCA 964 SCAFELL P
691 SEATALLAN
Burnmoor Tarn
West Water
R Irt
R Mite
Hardknott Fort
65.
HAR FEL
156

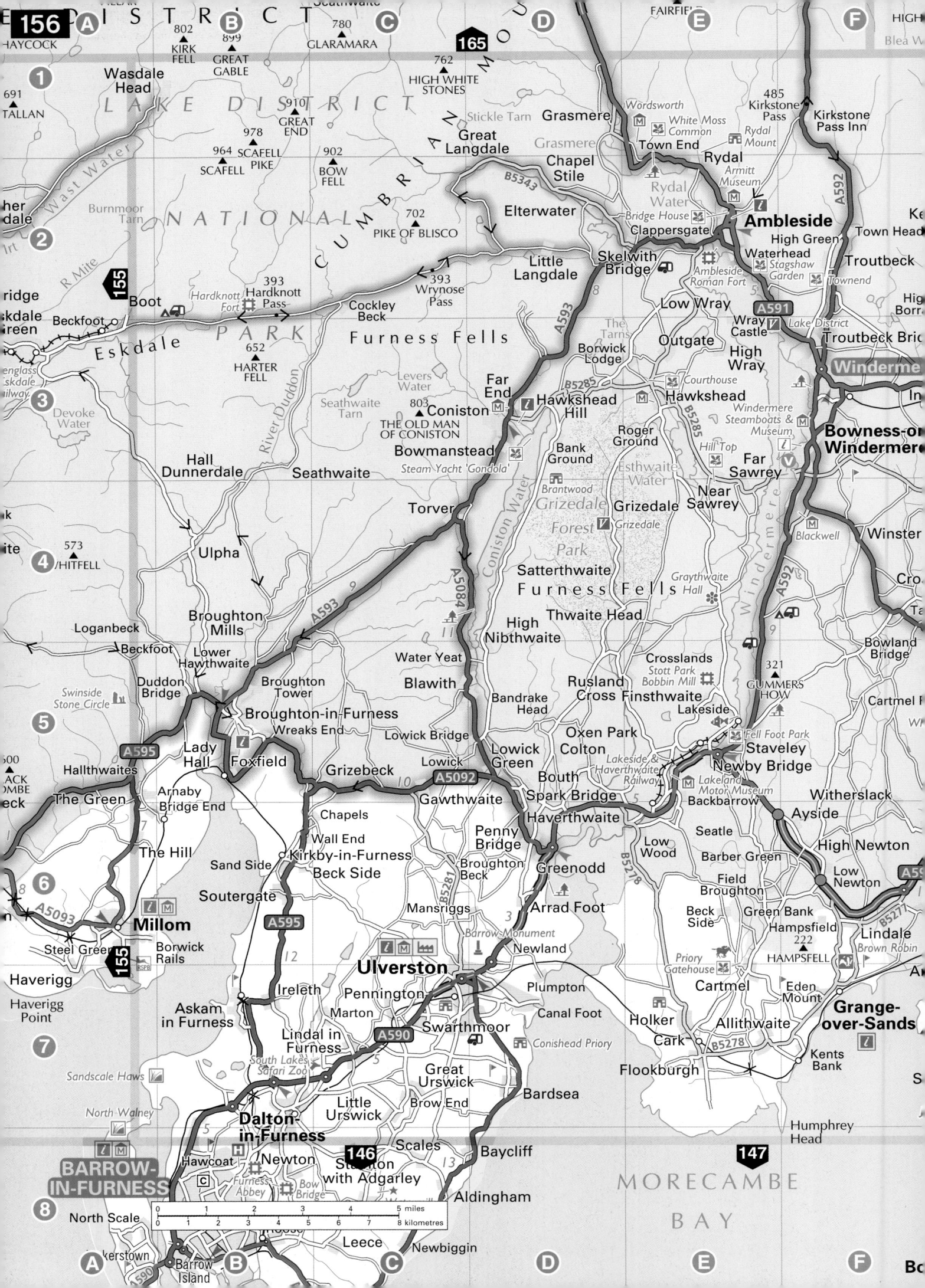

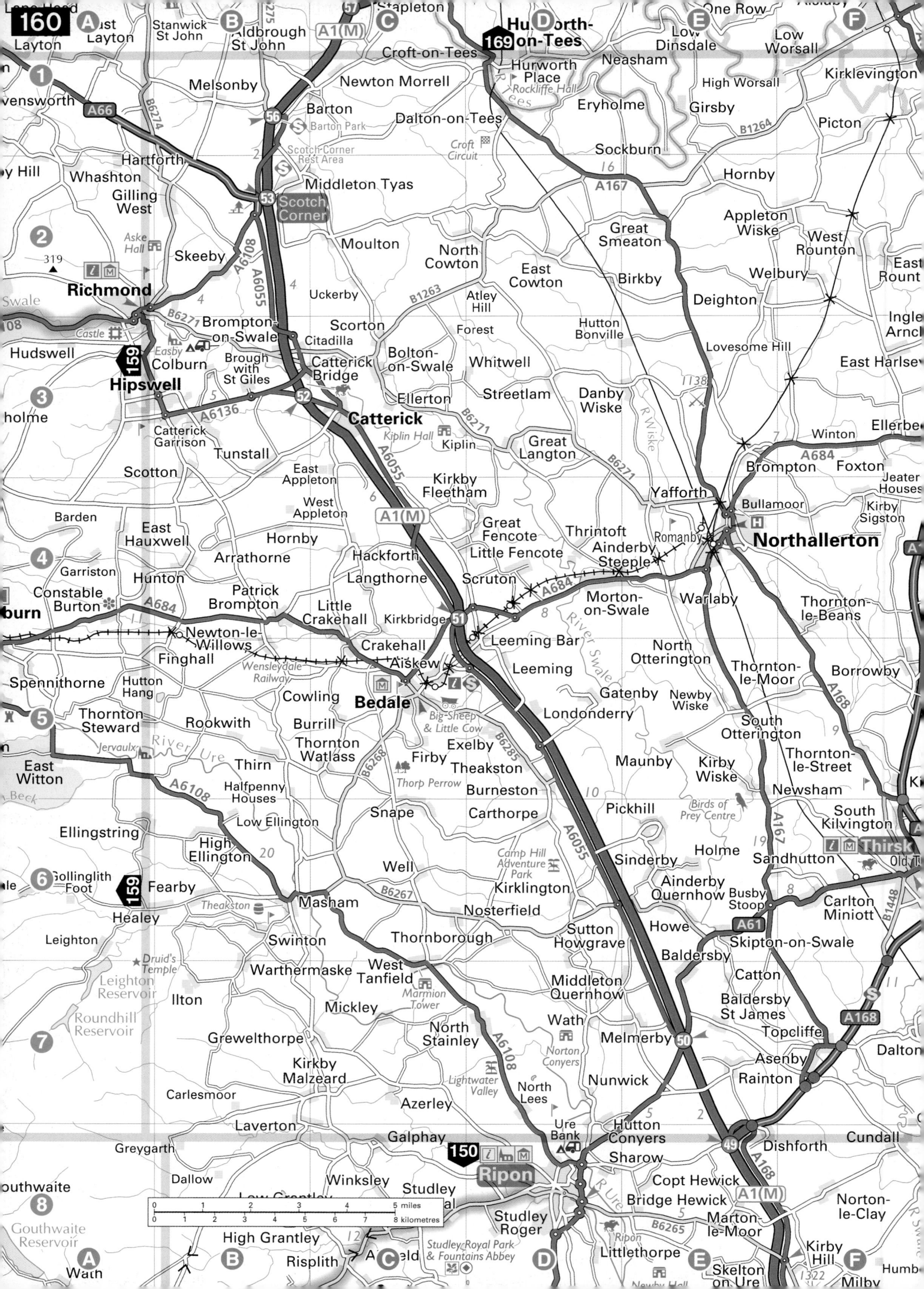

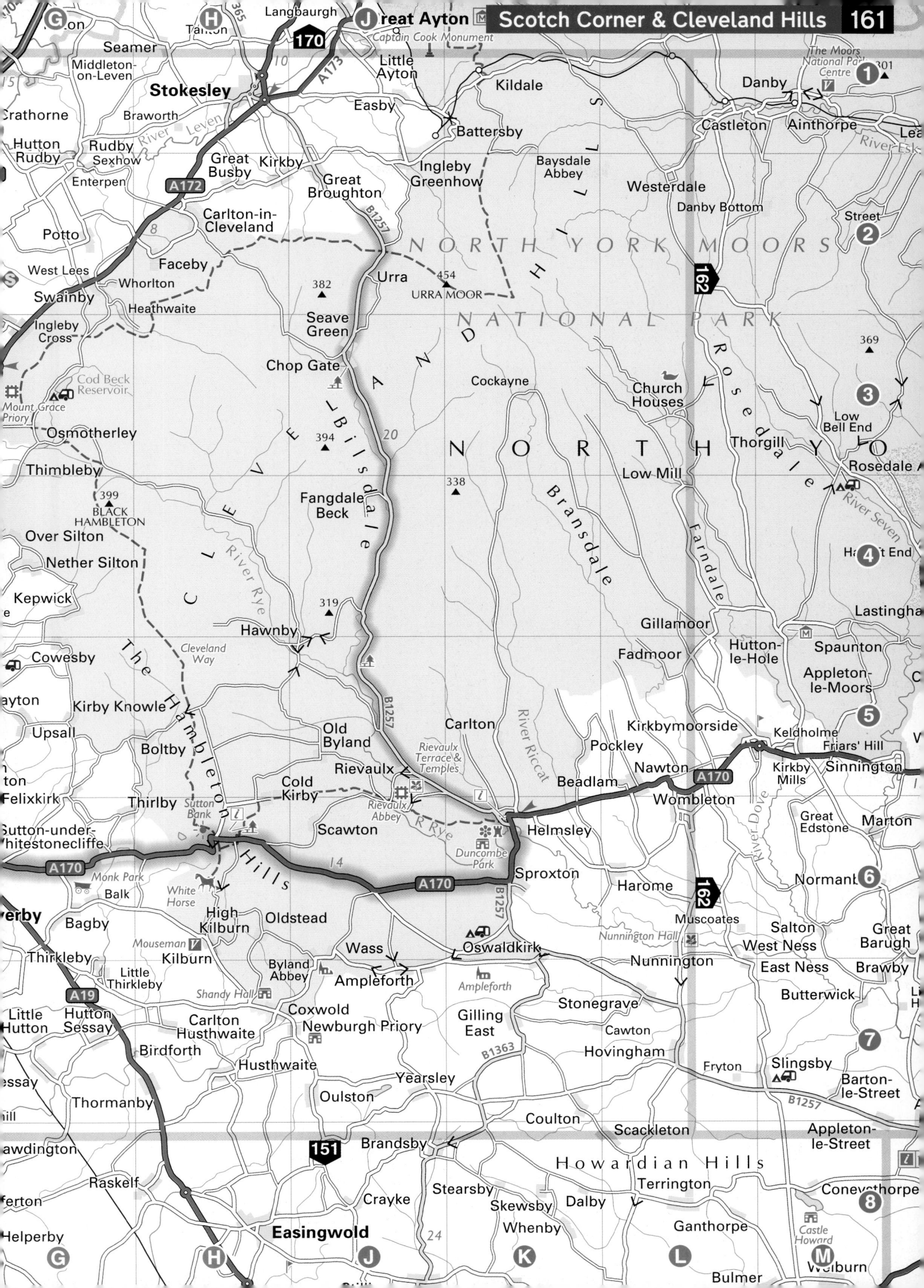

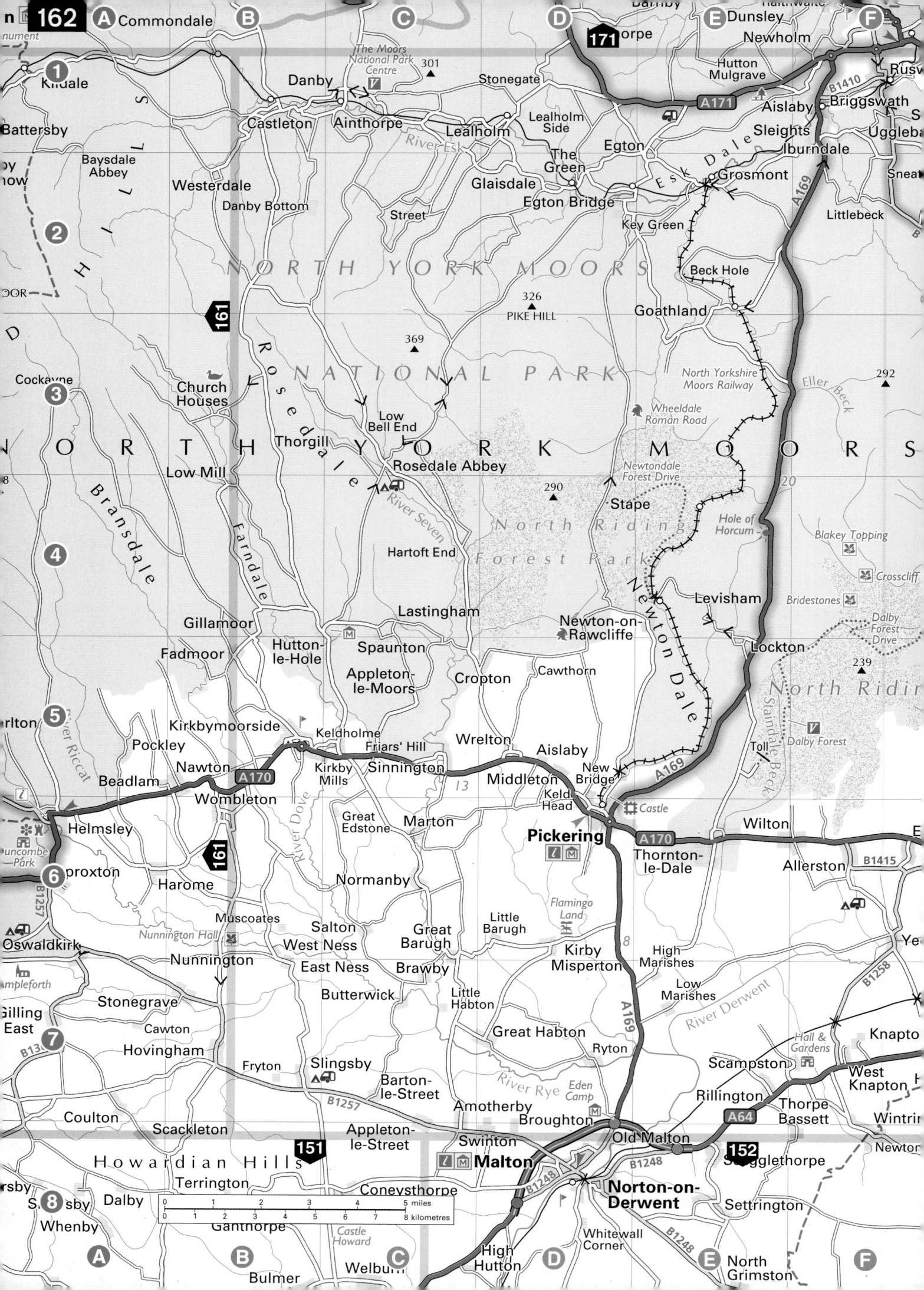

A B C 176 D E F

1

Kingsid
Wolsty
Beckfoot
Pelutho Highlaws
Newtown
Holme St Cuthbert
Tarns
Mealrigg

2
Mawbray Salta
Dubmill Point
Edderside New
Cowper
Westnewton Yo

Allonby
Allonby
Bay
Aspatria
Hayton
A596
Prospect
Oughtersid
Allerby
Arkleby

3
Crosscanonby
Parsonby
Crosby Crosby
Villa Bullgill
Gilcrux
Fort
River Ellen
Greengill
Maryport
Dearham
Townhead
Ellenborough
Risehow
Tallentire
A594
Fothergill
Woodside
Bridekirk
Broughton Redm
Flimby Moor

4
St Helens Standingstone Dovenby A595
Siddick High Great Little Broughton
Seaton Great Broughton Papcastle Jennings
Camerton
North Side Clifton A66 Cocker
Bridgefoot Brigham

5
Workington Stainburn 8 Greysouthen
Moss A596 Little Eaglesfield
Bay Mossbay 9 Clifton
Westfield 4 Deanscales Low Lorto
Salterbeck Winscales Dean Mosser Mains
High Branthwaite Pardshaw Thackthw
Harrington Ullock
Harrington A597 Mockerkin
Grayson Green C Waterend
Distington A5086

6
Common End Gilgarran Loweswater
Pica 572
Lowca Howgate Kidburngill Lamplugh Loweswa
Parton Low Brownrigg 16
A595 Moresby Asby L A K E
Moresby Arlecdon Crumm
Parks Rowrah Kirkland Wate
Whitehaven High Scale Force
Kells Hensingham Leys Ennerdale 615
Saltom Frizington Bridge 636
Bay B5295 B5294 Winder
Mirehouse Cleator River Ehen Ennerdale N A T I O
Sandwith Moor Moor Water
Sandwith Row River Calder 533
Newtown LANK L A K E
St Bees Head Rottington Cleator RIGG 798
RSPB Bigrigg HAYCO
St Bees Head 691
Heritage Coast St Bees Egremont SEATALLAN

8
0 1 2 3 4 5 miles
0 1 2 3 4 5 6 7 8 kilometres
Wilton
Could on Carleton 155 Worm Gill
Thornhill River Bleng
Mi letown Haile

A B C D E F

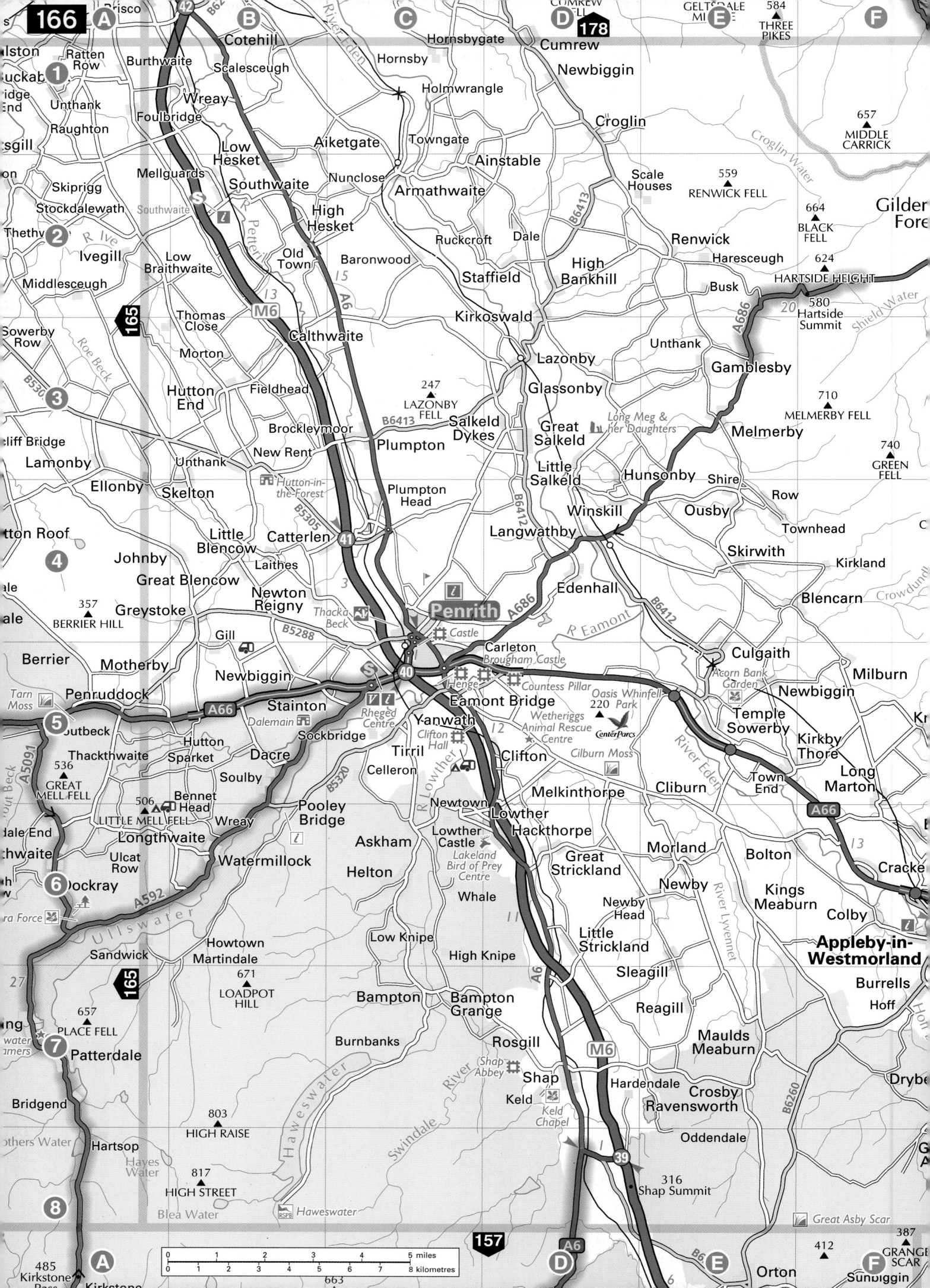

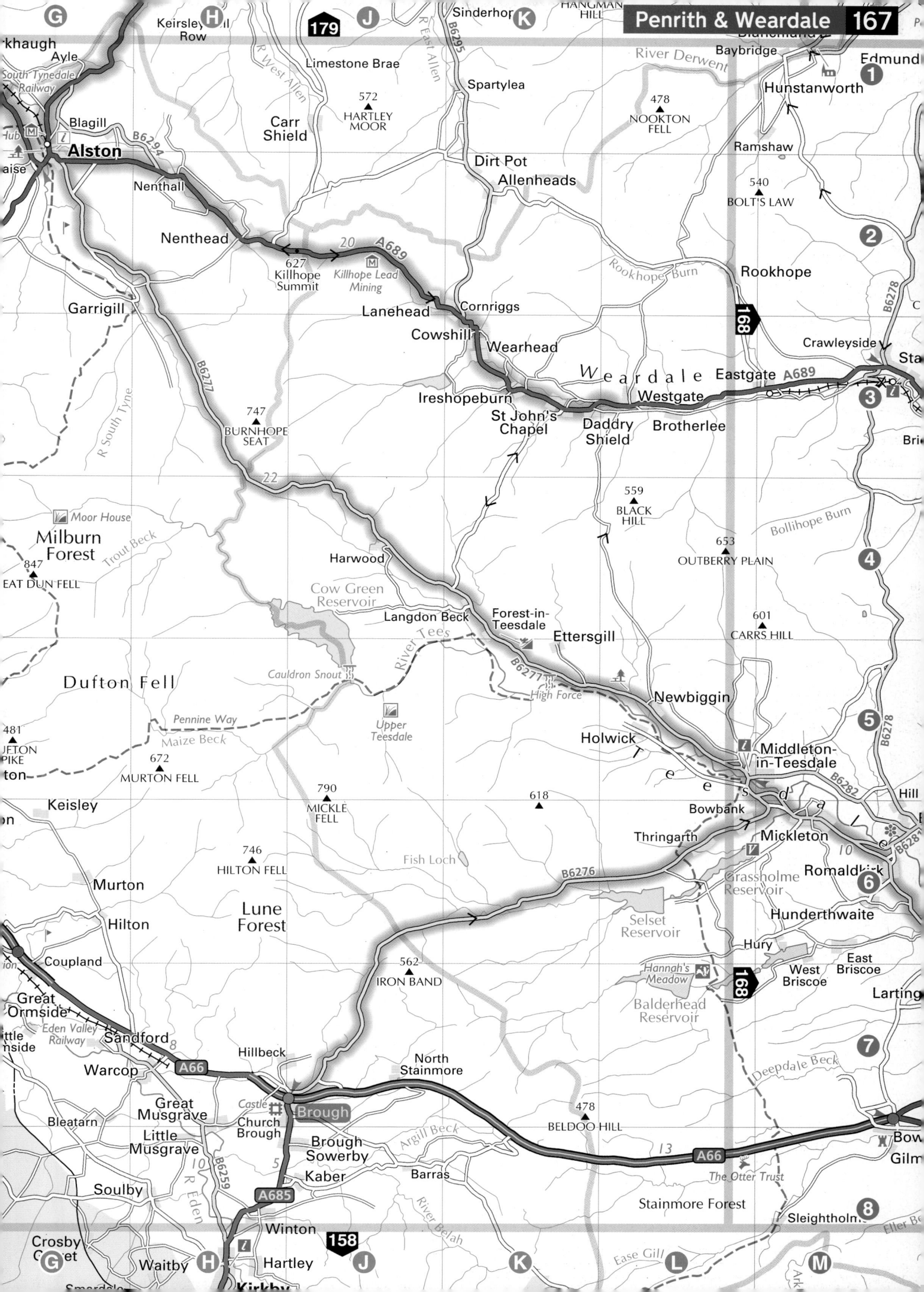

G   H   179   J   Sinderhor   K   HANGMAN HILL

Keirsley Hill Row

khaugh
Ayle
Limestone Brae
R West Allen
R East Allen
B6295
Blanchland
Baybridge
Edmund
South Tynedale Railway
Hub M
Blagill
Alston
Nenthall
Carr Shield
572 ▲ HARTLEY MOOR
Spartylea
478 ▲ NOOKTON FELL
Hunstanworth
Ramshaw
1
aise
Nenthead
B6294
Dirt Pot
Allenheads
540 ▲ BOLT'S LAW
2
Garrigill
627 Killhope Summit
M Killhope Lead Mining
20   A689
Lanehead
Cornriggs
Cowshill
Wearhead
Rookhope Burn
Rookhope
B6278
B6277
Ireshopeburn
Weardale Eastgate A689
Westgate
Crawleyside
168
Sta
3
Bri
St John's Chapel
Daddry Shield
Brotherlee
747 ▲ BURNHOPE SEAT
R South Tyne
22
559 ▲ BLACK HILL
653 ▲ OUTBERRY PLAIN
Bollihope Burn
4
Moor House
Milburn Forest
847 ▲ EAT DUN FELL
Trout Beck
Harwood
Cow Green Reservoir
Langdon Beck
River Tees
Forest-in-Teesdale
Ettersgill
601 ▲ CARRS HILL
Dufton Fell
Cauldron Snout
B6277
High Force
Newbiggin
5
B6278
481 ▲ UFTON PIKE
Pennine Way
Maize Beck
672 ▲ MURTON FELL
Upper Teesdale
Holwick
T e e s
Middleton-in-Teesdale
B6282
Hill
ton
Keisley
790 ▲ MICKLE FELL
618 ▲
Bowbank
d a l e
B628
Murton
746 ▲ HILTON FELL
Fish Loch
Thringarth
B6276
Mickleton
10
Romaldkirk
6
Hilton
Lune Forest
562 ▲ IRON BAND
Grassholme Reservoir
Selset Reservoir
Hunderthwaite
Hury
Great Ormside
Eden Valley Railway
Sandford
8
Coupland
Hillbeck
North Stainmore
Hannah's Meadow
168
West Briscoe
East Briscoe
Larting
7
ion
ttle nside
Warcop
A66
Great Musgrave
Castle
Church Brough
Brough
Brough Sowerby
Balderhead Reservoir
478 ▲ BELDOO HILL
Deepdale Beck
Bleatarn
Little Musgrave
B6259
Kaber
Barras
Argill Beck
13   A66
The Otter Trust
Bow
Gilm
Soulby
10
5
A685
Winton
158
River Belah
Stainmore Forest
Sleighthol
8
Crosby
i
Waitby
Hartley
River Eden
G   H   J   K   Ease Gill   L   Eller Gill   M
Smardale
Kirkby

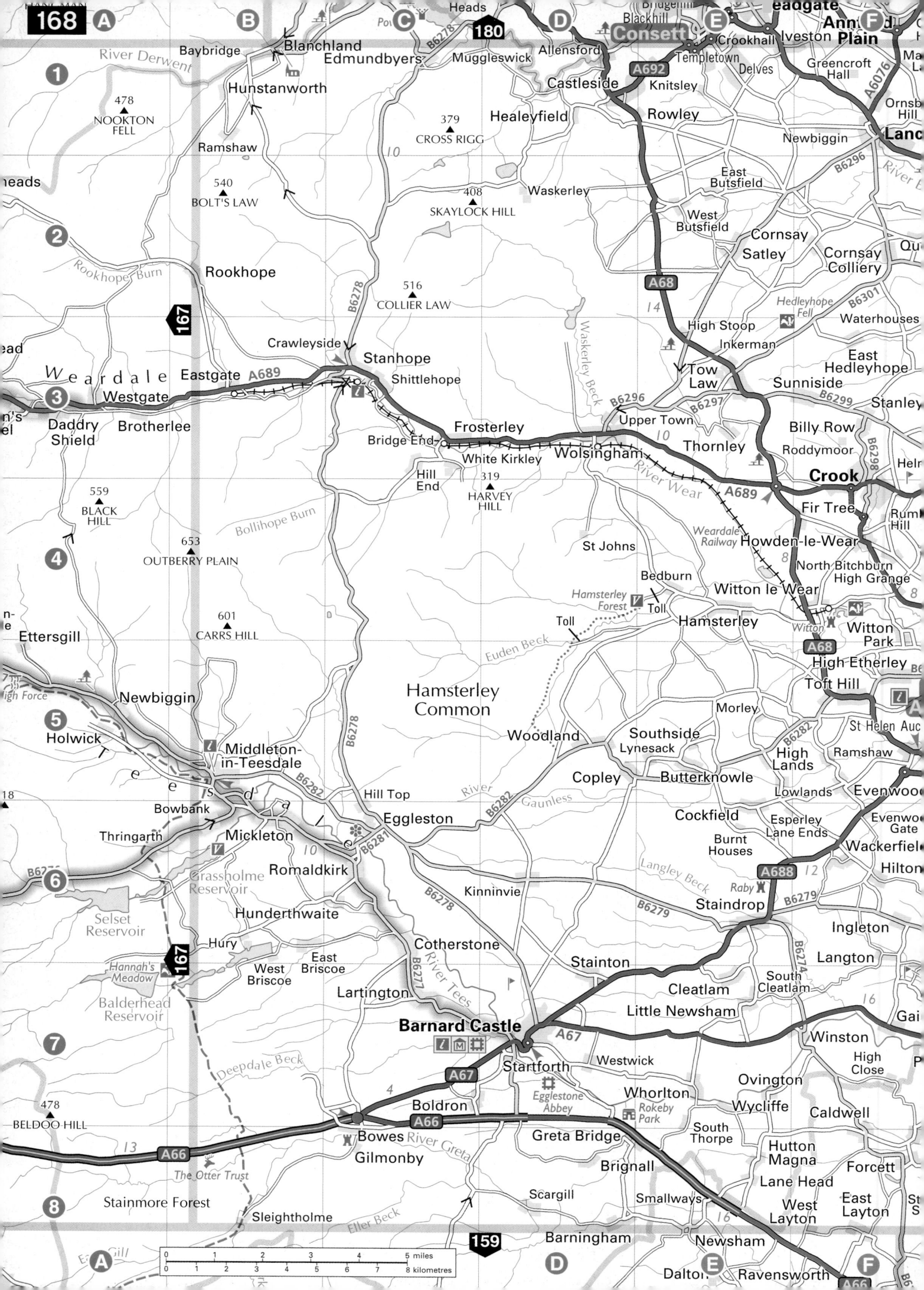

1

2

3

4

5

6

Smugglers
ew Brotton
Carlin
How
Skinningrove   Hummersea Scar
Upton   Boulby
ilton
Loftus   Staithes
Dalehouse   Captain Cook & Staithes
Easington   Heritage Centre
ilton   16   Port Mulgrave
horpe   Liverton   North Yorkshire and
             Mines   Hinderwell   Cleveland Heritage Coast
iverton   Roxby   Newton   Runswick
             Handale   Mulgrave   Runswick   Bay
                        Borrowby   Kettleness
                                    Ellerby   Goldsborough   Overdale
                                                                                   Wyke
rsholm   Scaling   B1266   A174   Lythe
             Gerrick   Sandsend
                        Scaling   Mickleby   Sandsend   Sandsend
                        Dam   West   East   Wyke
                    22   Barnby Barnby   **Whitby**
                                                                 Raithwaite
                                    Ugthorpe   Dunsley   Saltwick
                                                      Newholm   Bay
anby   The Moors
         National Park   162   Abbey
         Centre 301   Hutton   Ruswarp
G   H   Stone H e   Mulgrave J   A171   K   10   St L acre   M
                                                Aislaby Briggswath   Sneaton   High Hawsker

7

8

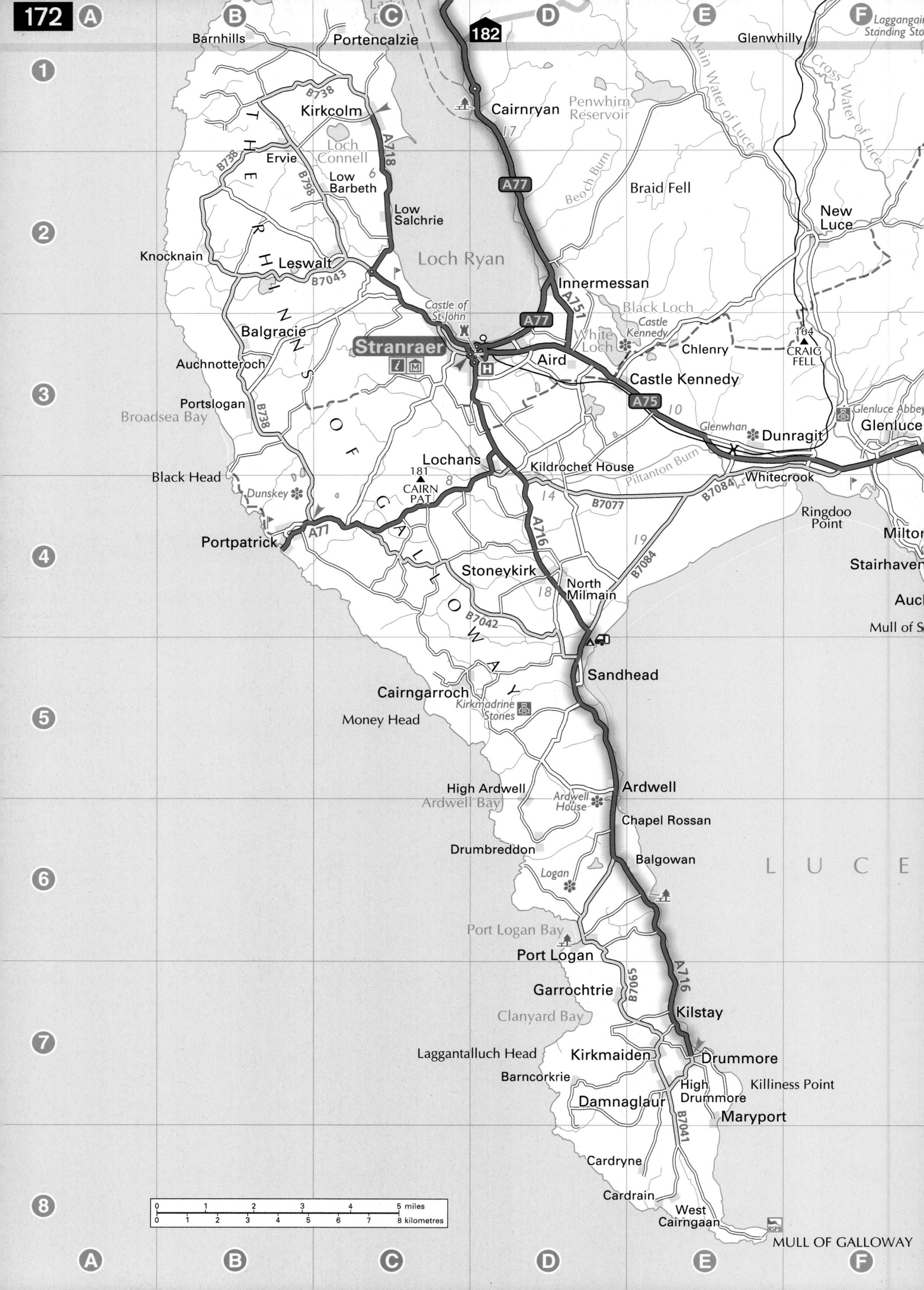

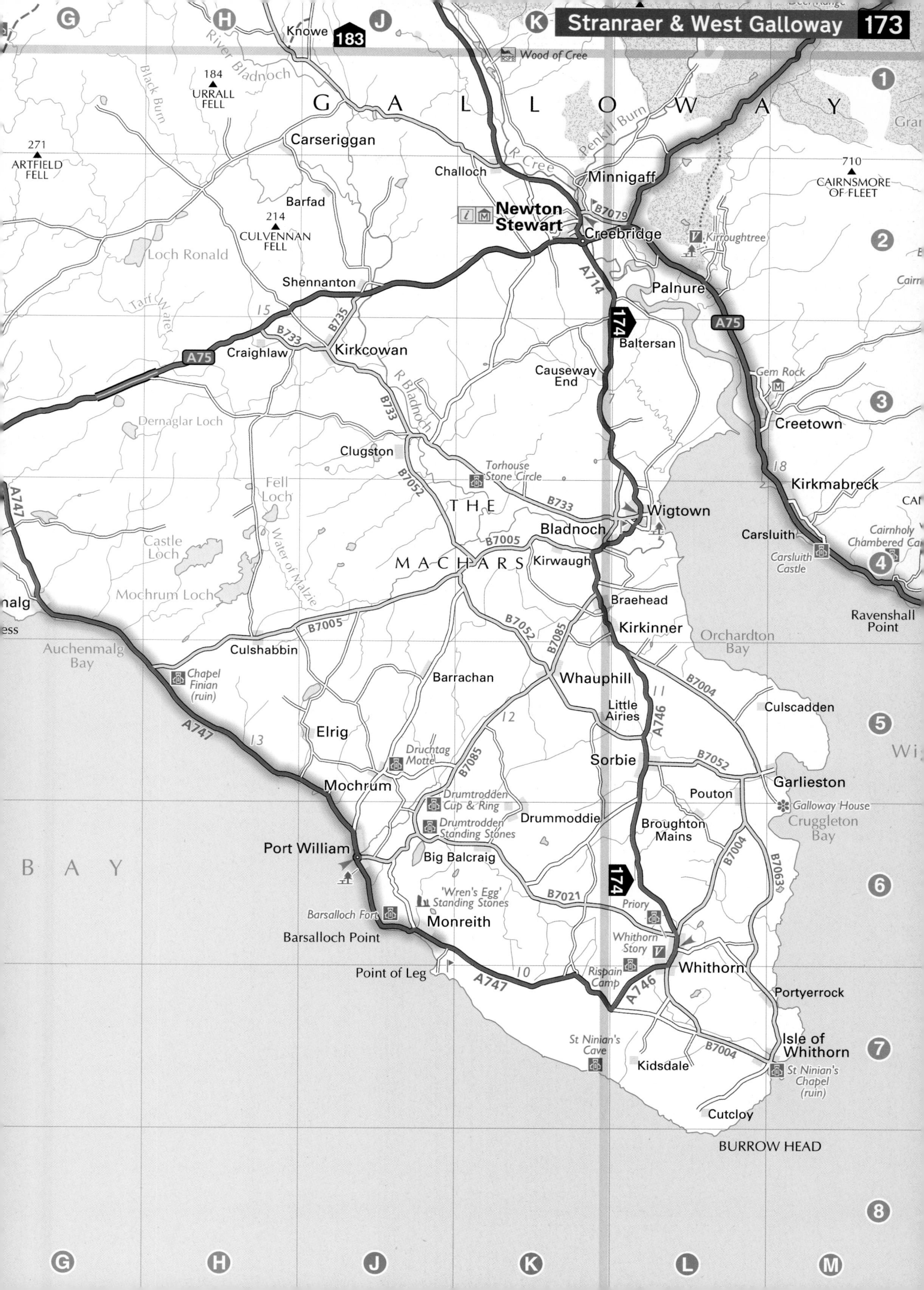

G   H   J   K

1
2
3
4
5
6
7
8

Knowe **183**

Wood of Cree
RSPB

R Cree

River Bladnoch

G A L L O W A Y

Gra

271
▲
ARTFIELD
FELL

184
▲
URRALL
FELL

710
▲
CAIRNSMORE
OF FLEET

Carseriggan

Challoch
Minnigaff

Barfad

214
▲
CULVENNAN
FELL

Loch Ronald

Black Burn

**Newton
Stewart**

B7079

Creebridge

Kirroughtree

Cairn

Palnure

A75

Shennanton

174
Baltersan

Gem Rock
M

Tarf Water
15
B735
B733

A75
Craighlaw

Kirkcowan

Causeway
End

Creetown

18

Dernaglar Loch

B733

R Bladnoch

Clugston

Torhouse
Stone Circle

Kirkmabreck

A747

Fell
Loch

B7052

Wigtown

2

Castle
Loch

THE

B733

Bladnoch

Carsluith

Cairnholy
Chambered Ca

nalg
ess

Mochrum Loch

Water of Malzie

B7005

MACHARS

Kirwaugh

Carsluith
Castle

CA

Auchenmalg
Bay

B7005

Culshabbin

B7052

Braehead

Ravenshall
Point

Chapel
Finian
(ruin)

Barrachan

B7085

Kirkinner

Orchardton
Bay

13

A747

Elrig

Druchtag
Motte

12

B7085

Whauphill

Little
Aíries

11

B7004

A746

Culscadden

Mochrum

Drumtrodden
Cup & Ring

Drumtrodden
Standing Stones

Drummoddie

Sorbie

B7052

Pouton

Garlieston

Galloway House

B7004

Port William

Big Balcraig

B7021

Broughton
Mains

Cruggleton
Bay

B7063

B A Y

'Wren's Egg'
Standing Stones

174

Priory

Barsalloch Fort

Monreith

Barsalloch Point

Whithorn
Story V

Point of Leg

A747
10

Rispain
Camp

A746

Whithorn

Portyerrock

St Ninian's
Cave

B7004

Isle of
Whithorn

Kidsdale

St Ninian's
Chapel
(ruin)

Cutcloy

BURROW HEAD

Wi

G   H   J   K   L   M

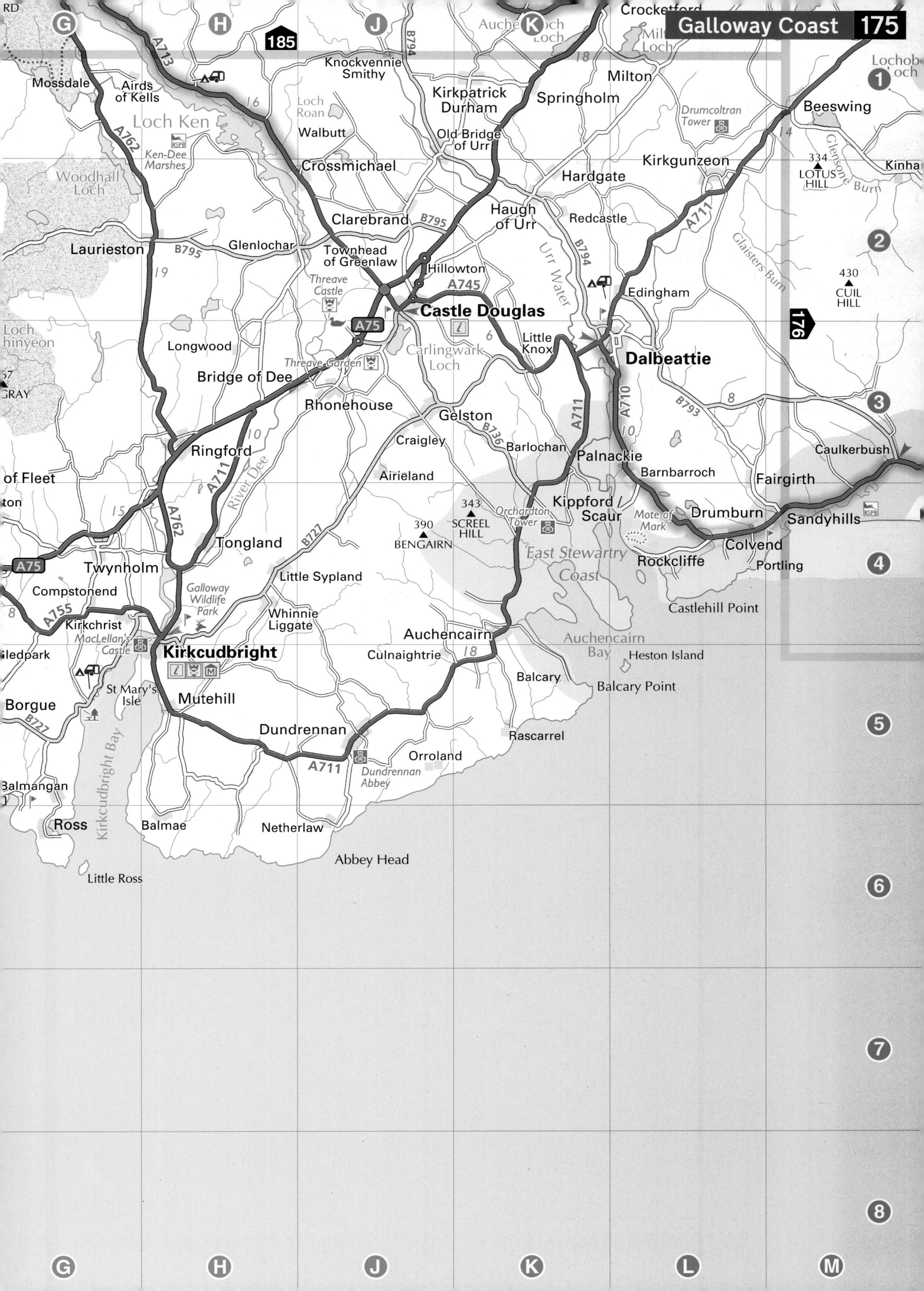

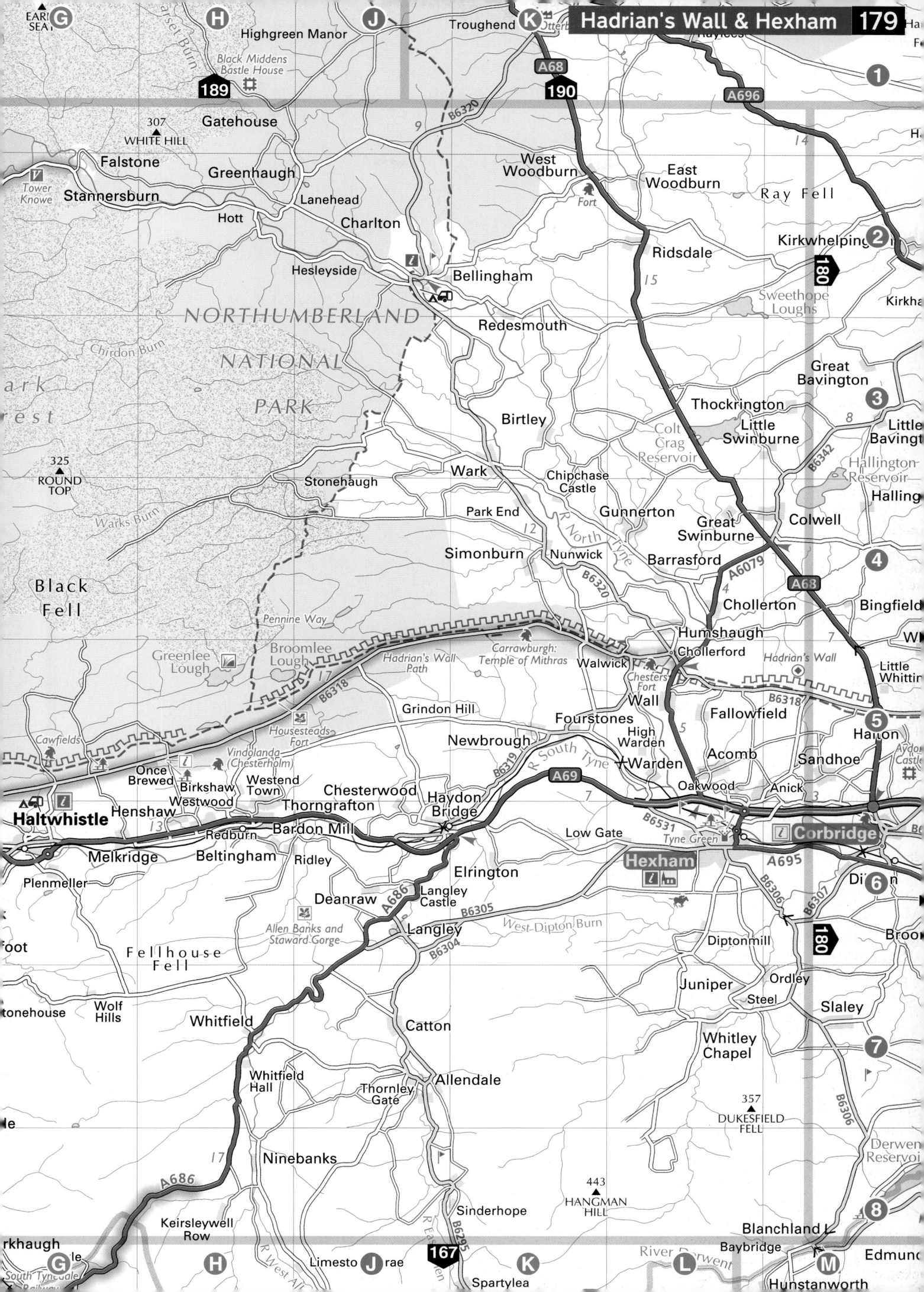

G Ellington
Linton Lynemouth
am 1068

H

J

K

1

A189 Wood 191 Beacon Point
QE2
hington A197 M Woodhorn Demesne
Hirst H
North **Newbiggin-by-**
Seaton **the-Sea**
Wansbeck B1334
Riverside
eepwash Stakeford North Seaton Colliery
West Sleekburn

2

and Guide Bomarsund
ate Post A1147
on East Cambois
dlington Sleekburn North Blyth
68 B1331 A193 C Cowpen
Bebside **Blyth**
East B1505 A189 Newsham
Hartford New
A192 Delaval

3

Shankhouse A1061
lington New A193
East Hartley Seaton
Cramlington Seaton Sluice
B1326 A190 Seaton Hartley
aton 2 S H Seghill Hall C
rn **Seaton** St Mary's
Annitsford **Delaval**

4

Dudley Holywell B1325
Vide Burradon A192 B1325 9
pen Camperdown A1148 C
Killingworth Earsdon **Whitley** i
A1056 Backworth Monkseaton **Bay**
A189 Shiremoor Cullercoats
Forest Hall A191 Murton H
A191 A193
Longbenton New C **Tynemouth**
Rising York i Tynemouth Priory
Jesmond Sun A19 4 & Castle
A1058 **North** 4
Shields **SOUTH**
Wallsend Willington **SHIELDS**
Heaton Int. Ferry i M
Toll Terminal
Walker **Jarrow** Tyne Tunnel A183 Westoe
Byker B1313 A185 Harton Marsden
Felling **Hebburn** A1300 H Bay
A184 Monkton C Marsden Souter Lighthouse
Wardley A194 & The Leas
GATESHEAD Boldon B1298 Cleadon Souter Point
C 3 Colliery A183
i A184 2 West **Whitburn**
H B1288 Boldon B1299
Low 2 East A1018
Fell A194(M) Boldon A184 Whitburn
Bowes Railway Bay
& Museum Hylton Fulwell Seaburn
Springwell Castle Southwick Roker
el-of 1 Usworth A19 Castletown Monkwearmouth
orth C A195 Wetland i M
Birtley 65 Centre
th Portobello A1231 South C **SUNDERLAND**
WASHINGTON Hylton A183 H B1522
Washington Pennywell Hendon
Urpeth S Offerton
Ouston 64 A195 A183 High Newport Grangetown
Perkinsville Fatfield Penshaw 2 A690 New Tunstall
Penshaw Monument Herrington Silksworth Ryhope Durham
River Wear B1286 Heritage Coast
lton 63 Shiney Row New Herrington A1018
Pelton A183 Philadelphia 6
ll Fell Houghton Bournmoor Newbottle A19 3 B1287
Chester- Gate High **Houghton-**
le-Street B1284 Dubmire **le-Sprir**
Great 169 Colliery B1404 Seaton **Seaham**

G

H

J

K

L

M

1
2
3
4
5

Amsterdam
(IJmuiden)

6
7
8

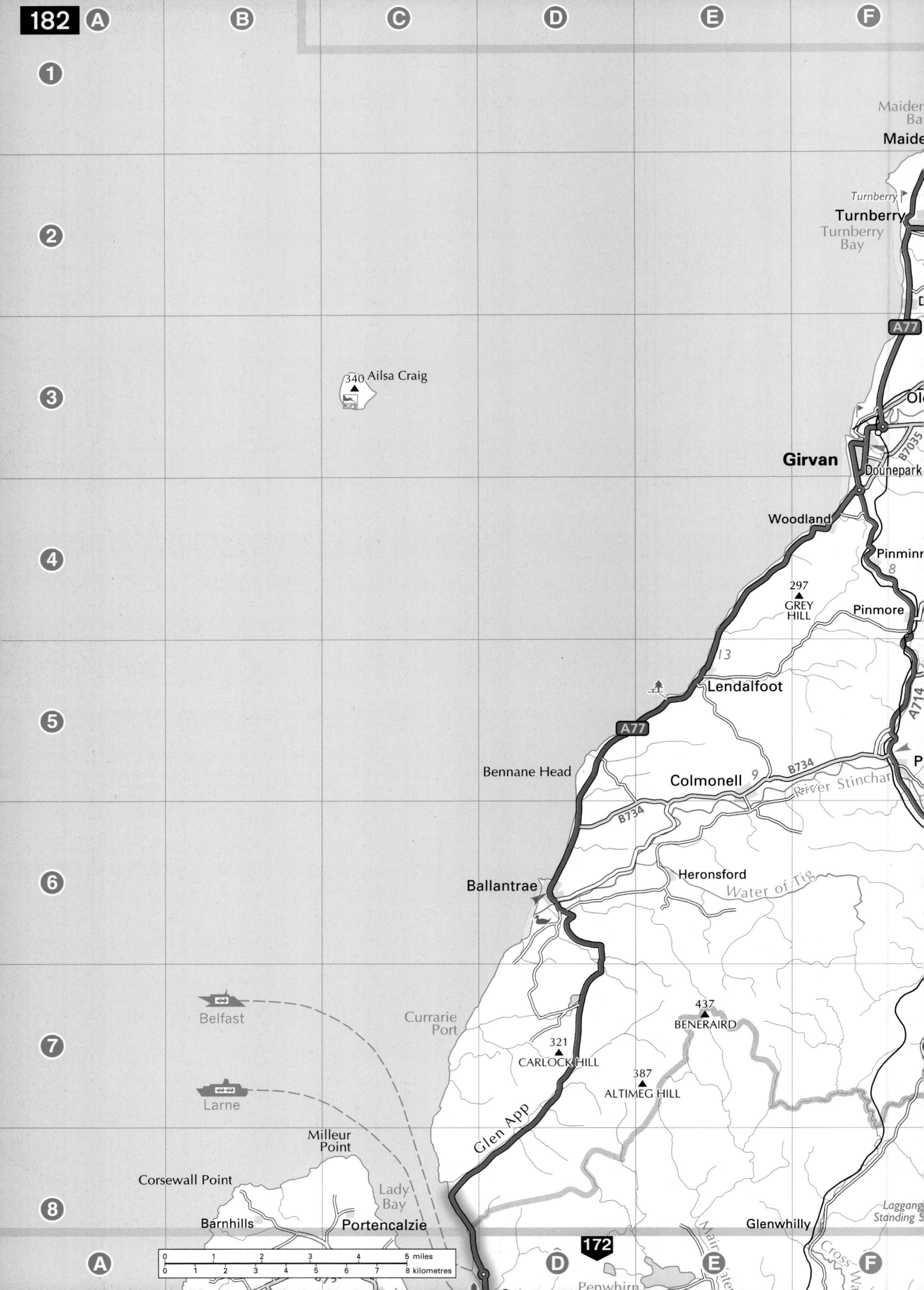

A   B   C   D   E   F

1

2

Maiden
Bay
Maide

Turnberry
Turnberry
Turnberry
Bay

A77

3

340 Ailsa Craig
▲
RSPB

Ol

Girvan

Dounepark

B7035

Woodland

4

Pinminr
8

297
▲
GREY
HILL

Pinmore

A714

13

Lendalfoot

5

A77

Bennane Head

Colmonell   9   B734

B734

River Stinchar

P

6

Heronsford   Water of Tig

Ballantrae

437
▲
BENERAIRD

7

Belfast

Currarie
Port

321
▲
CARLOCK HILL

387
▲
ALTIMEG HILL

Larne

Milleur
Point

Glen App

8

Corsewall Point

Lady
Bay

Laggan
Standing S

Portencalzie

Glenwhilly

Barnhills

A   **172**   D   E   F

0 1 2 3 4 5 miles
0 1 2 3 4 5 6 7 8 kilometres

Penwhirn

Cross Wa

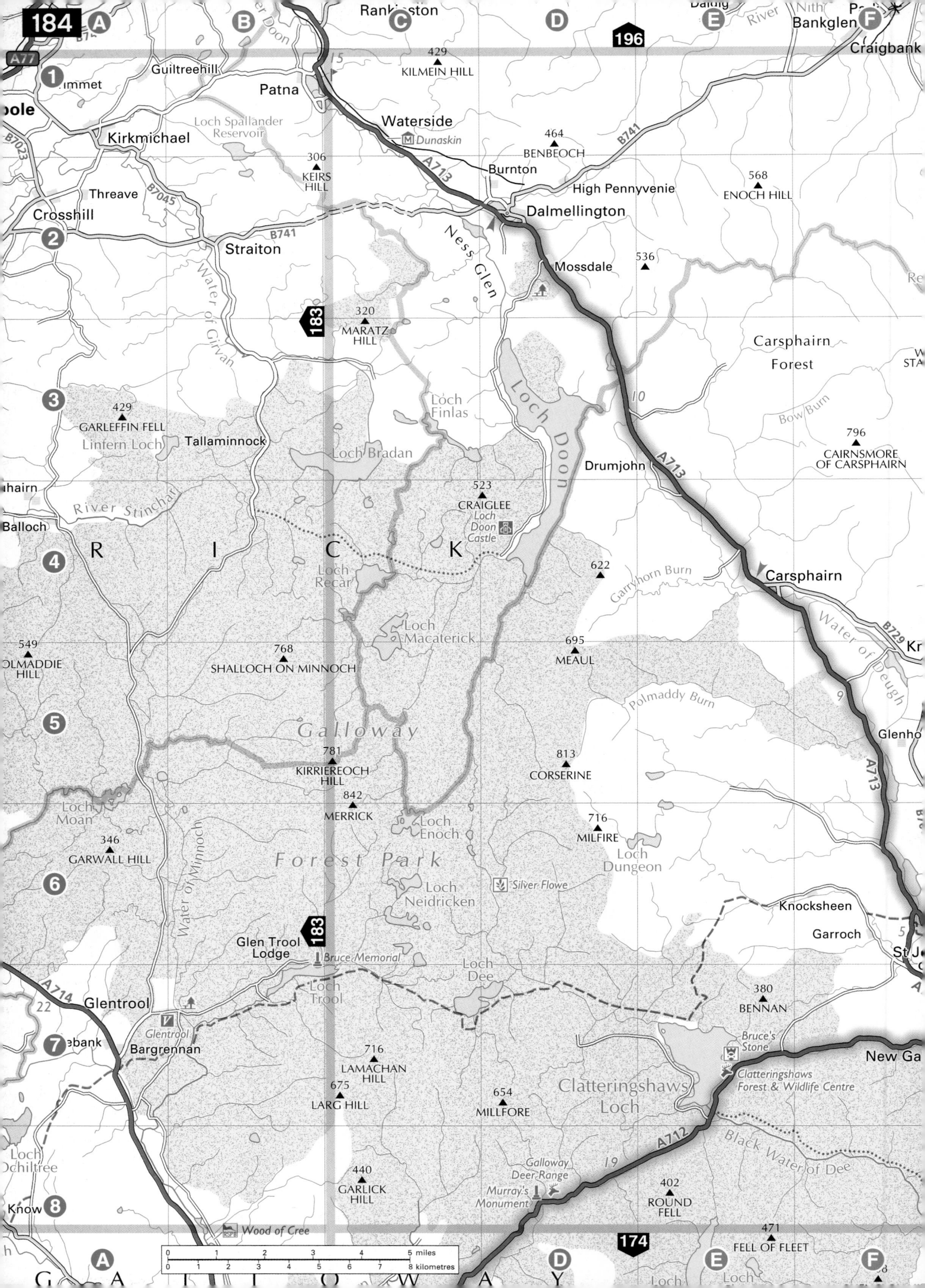

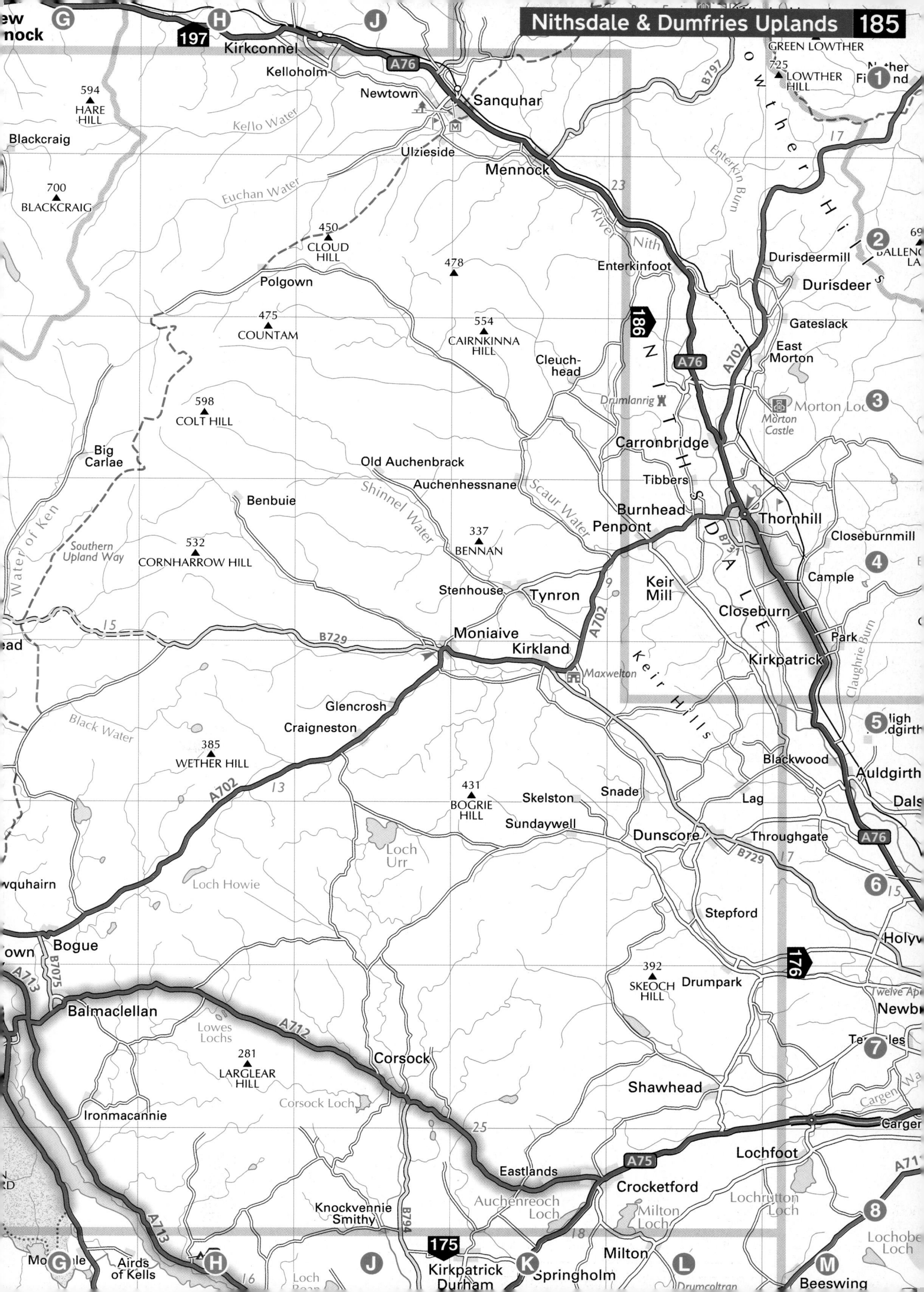

G H J

197
Kirkconnel
A76
Kelloholm
Newtown
Sanquhar
GREEN LOWTHER
725 ▲
LOWTHER HILL
Nether Fin nd
1

594 ▲
HARE HILL
Blackcraig
Ulzieside
Mennock
B797
2
BALLENC LA
69

700 ▲
BLACKCRAIG
Kello Water
River Nith
23
Durisdeermill
Durisdeer

Euchan Water
Enterkin Burn

450 ▲
CLOUD HILL
Polgown
478 ▲
Enterkinfoot
186
A76
A702
Gateslack
East Morton
3

475 ▲
COUNTAM
554 ▲
CAIRNKINNA HILL
Cleuch-head
Drumlanrig
Morton Loch
Morton Castle

598 ▲
COLT HILL
Carronbridge
Tibbers

Big Carlae
Old Auchenbrack
Auchenhessnane
Shinnel Water
Scaur Water
Burnhead
Penpont
Thornhill
Closeburnmill
4

Benbuie
337 ▲
BENNAN
Keir Mill
Cample

Southern Upland Way
532 ▲
CORNHARROW HILL
Stenhouse
Tynron
9
Closeburn
B731
5
igh dgirth

Water of Ken
15
B729
Moniaive
Kirkland
A702
Maxwelton
Keir Hills
Park
Kirkpatrick

Black Water
Glencrosh
Craigneston
385 ▲
WETHER HILL
A702
13
431 ▲
BOGRIE HILL
Skelston
Snade
Blackwood
Lag
Auldgirth
Dals

Loch Howie
Loch Urr
Sundaywell
Dunscore
Throughgate
B729
17
A76
6
15

Bogue
Stepford
Holyw

A713
B7075
392 ▲
SKEOCH HILL
Drumpark
176
Twelve Ap

Balmaclellan
A712
Lowes Lochs
281 ▲
LARGLEAR HILL
Corsock
Shawhead
Newb
7
Te es
Cargen W

Ironmacannie
Corsock Loch
25
A75
Lochfoot
Carger
A71

D
Knockvennie Smithy
B794
Eastlands
Crocketford
Auchenreoch Loch
Milton Loch
Lochrutton Loch
8

G
Mo le
Airds of Kells
A713
H
16
175
J
Kirkpatrick Durham
K
Springholm
Milton
L
Drumcoltran
Beeswing
M
Lochobe Loch

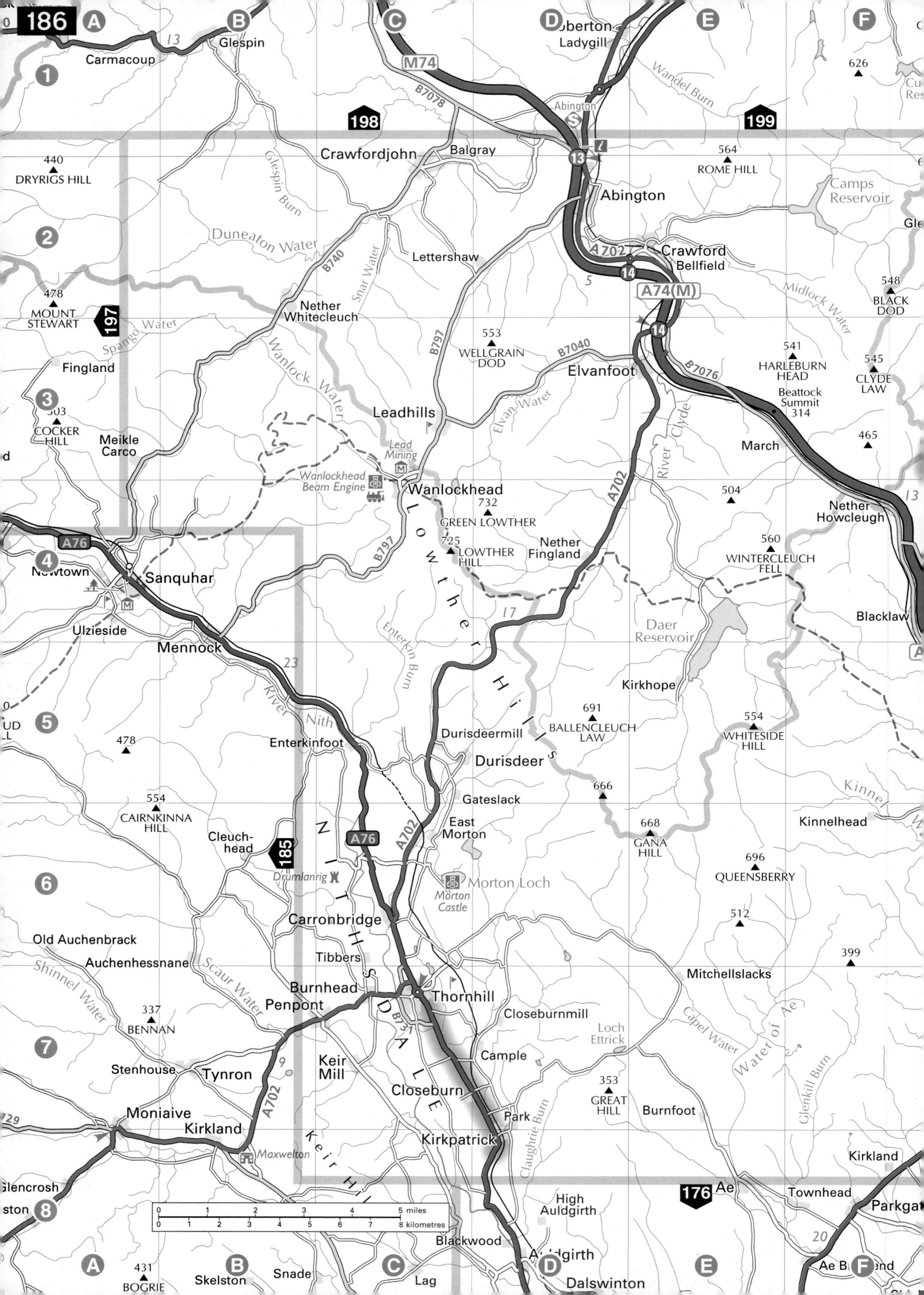

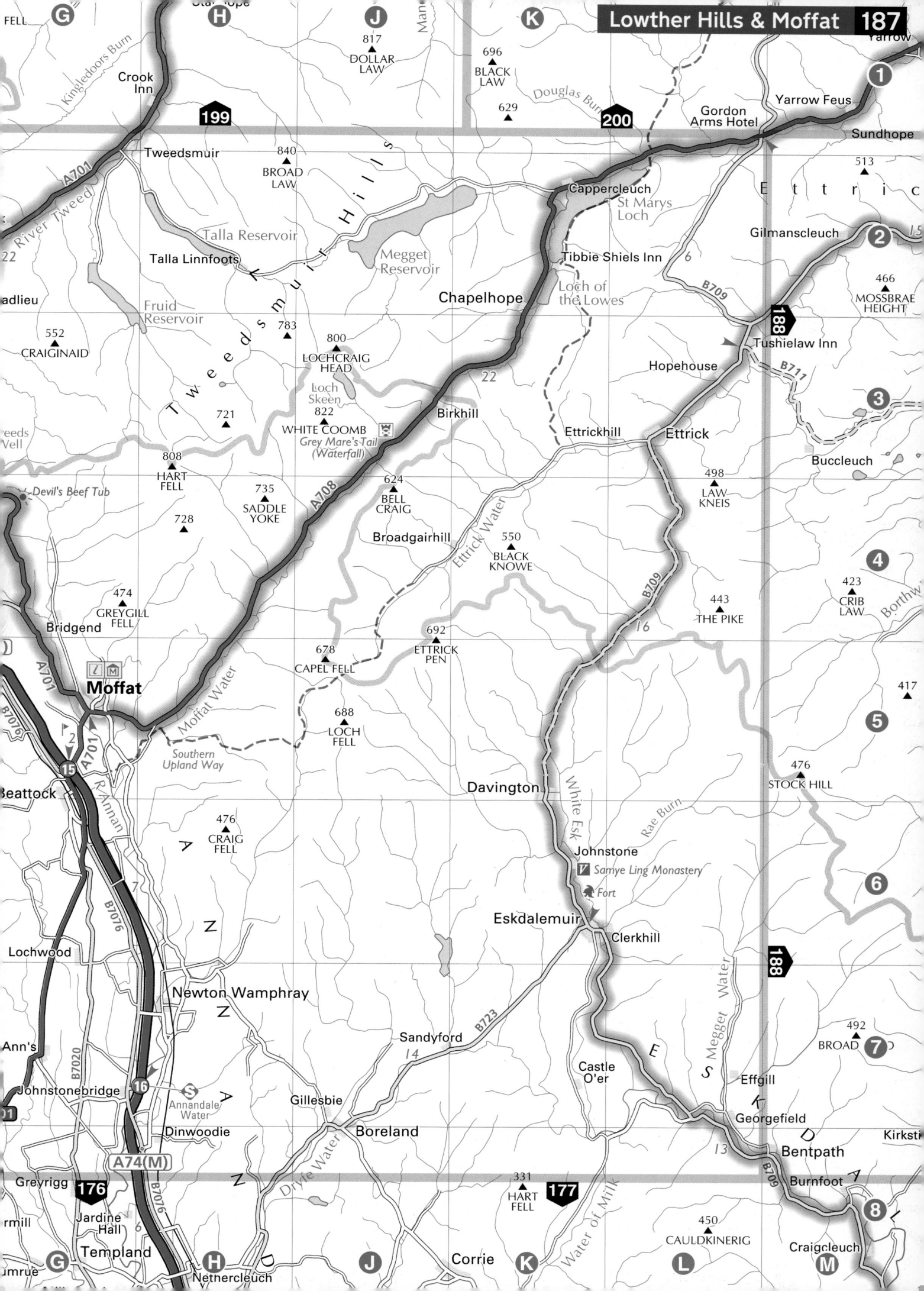

G   H   J   K   1

Yarrow

817
DOLLAR
LAW ▲

696
BLACK ▲
LAW

629 ▲

Douglas Burn

199

200

Yarrow Feus

Gordon
Arms Hotel

Sundhope

Crook
Inn

FELL

Kingledoors Burn

Cappercleuch

513 ▲

Ettric

Tweedsmuir

840
BROAD ▲
LAW

St Marys
Loch

Gilmanscleuch

2

15

River Tweed

22

Talla Reservoir

Talla Linnfoots

Megget
Reservoir

Tibbie Shiels Inn

6

B709

466 ▲
MOSSBRAE
HEIGHT

adlieu

Chapelhope

Loch of
the Lowes

188

Fruid
Reservoir

783 ▲

800
LOCHCRAIG ▲
HEAD

Hopehouse

B717

Tushielaw Inn

3

552 ▲
CRAIGINAID

Loch
Skeen

Birkhill

Ettrickhill

Ettrick

Buccleuch

eeds
Vell

721 ▲

822
WHITE COOMB ▲
Grey Mare's Tail
(Waterfall)

498 ▲
LAW
KNEIS

808 ▲
HART
FELL

Devil's Beef Tub

735 ▲
SADDLE
YOKE

624
BELL ▲
CRAIG

Ettrick Water

4

728 ▲

A708

Broadgairhill

550
BLACK ▲
KNOWE

423 ▲
CRIB
LAW

Borthw

443 ▲
THE PIKE

B709

16

474 ▲
GREYGILL
FELL

692
ETTRICK ▲
PEN

417 ▲

Bridgend

678
CAPEL FELL ▲

5

i   M

Moffat

688
LOCH ▲
FELL

476
STOCK HILL ▲

A701

Moffat Water

Southern
Upland Way

2

15

Davington

White Esk

Rae Burn

Beattock

476 ▲
CRAIG
FELL

R. Annan

A
N
Z
A

Johnstone

Samye Ling Monastery

188

Fort

6

Lochwood

Eskdalemuir

Clerkhill

B7076

Newton Wamphray

Z
Z
A

E
S

B723

492 ▲
BROAD

7

Ann's

B7020

16

Sandyford

14

Castle
O'er

Effgill

Johnstonebridge

S

Gillesbie

Georgefield

K
D

Dinwoodie

Annandale
Water

Boreland

Dryfe Water

Kirksti

A74(M)

13

B709

Bentpath

176

Greyrigg

Z

331
HART ▲
FELL

177

Burnfoot

8

mill

Jardine
Hall

B7076

6

Water of Milk

450 ▲
CAULDKINERIG

L
D
A

Craigcleuch

Templand

Nethercleuch

Corrie

Craigcleuch

mrue

G   H   J   K   L   M

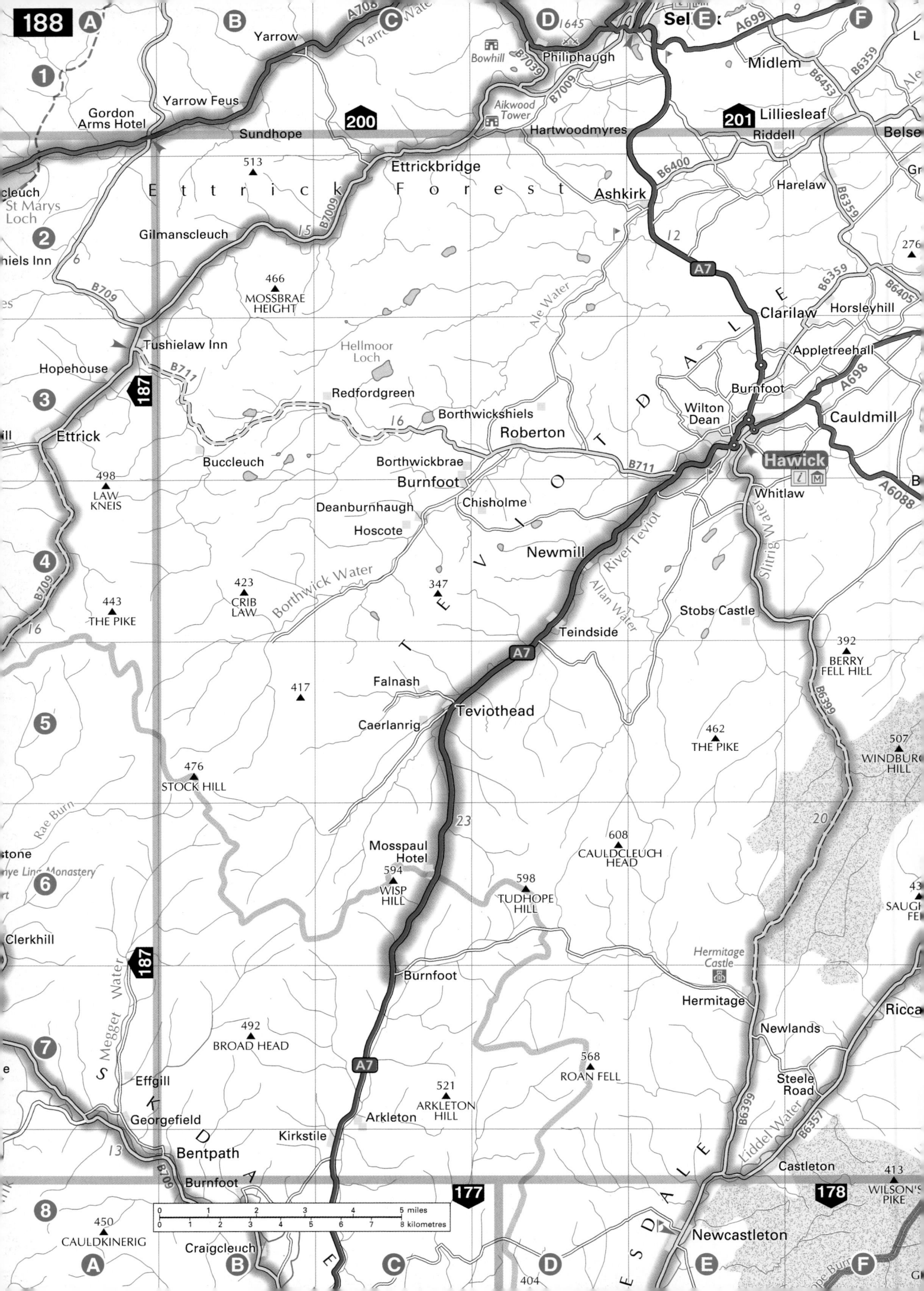

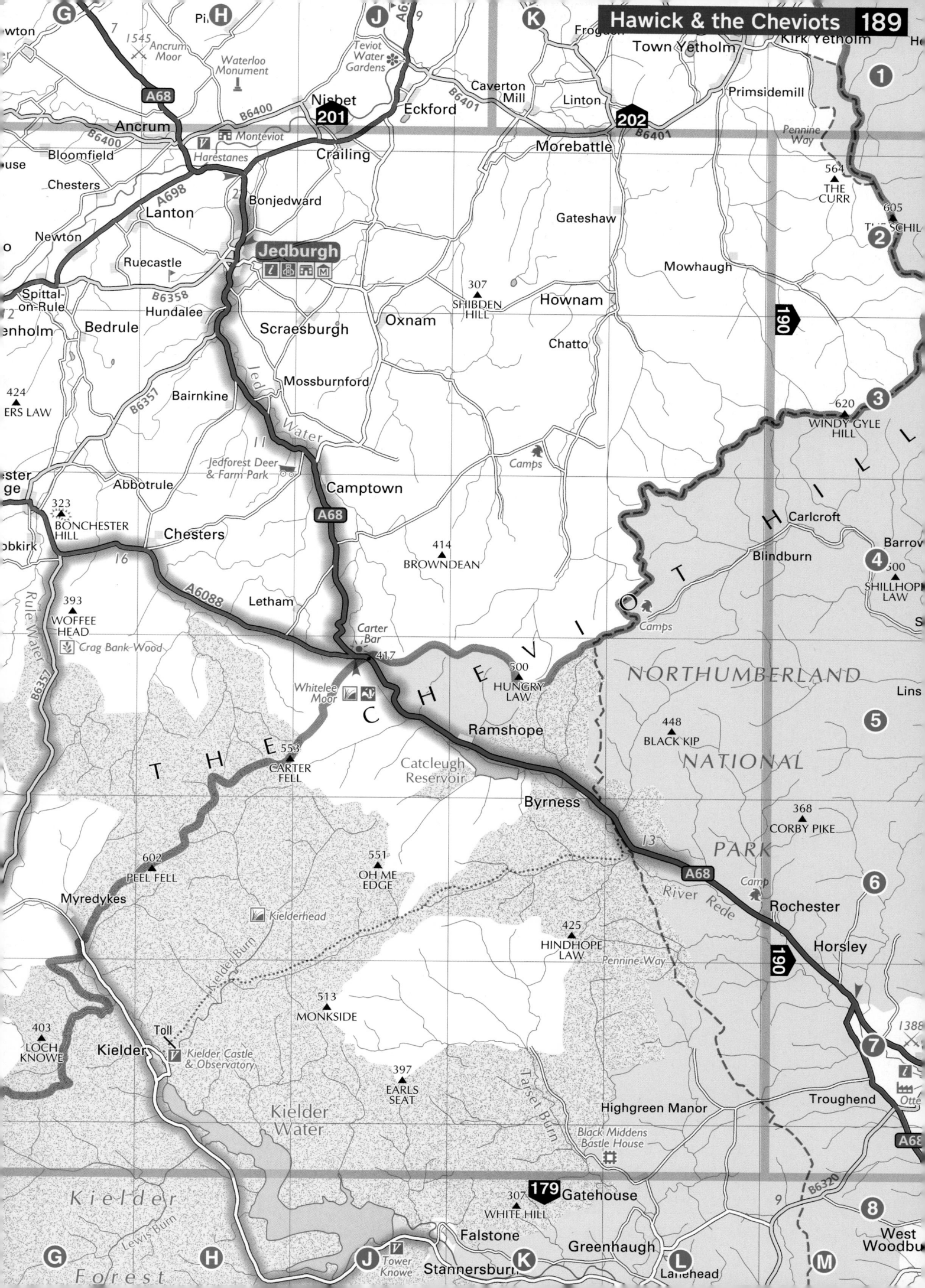

G H Pi J A6 9 K Frogde Town Yetholm Kirk Yetholm He

1545 Ancrum Moor Waterloo Monument Teviot Water Gardens Caverton Mill Linton Primsidemill

Pennine Way

A68 B6400 Nisbet 201 Eckford B6401 202 Morebattle 564 THE CURR

Ancrum Monteviot Crailing B6400 Gateshaw Mowhaugh 605 THE SCHIL 2

Bloomfield Harestanes Bonjedward

Chesters Lanton 2 Hownam 190

Newton Ruecastle Jedburgh i Chatto

Spittal- on-Rule B6358 Hundalee Scraesburgh Oxnam 307 SHIBDEN HILL Carlcroft

enholm Bedrule Mossburnford Camps Blindburn Barrov 4

424 ERS LAW B6357 Bairnkine Jedforest Deer & Farm Park Camptown T 620 WINDY GYLE HILL 3 500 SHILLHOP LAW

ster ge Abbotrule A68 I O Camps

323 BONCHESTER HILL Chesters BROWNDEAN 414 T NORTHUMBERLAND Lins

bkirk 16 A6088 Letham Carter Bar 417 H 500 HUNGRY LAW 448 BLACK KIP 5

393 WOFFEE HEAD Crag Bank Wood A68 Whitelee Moor C E Ramshope NATIONAL

Rule Water B6357 THE 553 CARTER FELL Catcleugh Reservoir Byrness PARK 368 CORBY PIKE

602 PEEL FELL 551 OH ME EDGE A68 13 Camp River Rede Rochester 6

Myredykes Kielderhead Kielder Burn Horsley

403 LOCH KNOWE Kielder Toll Kielder Castle & Observatory 513 MONKSIDE 425 HINDHOPE LAW Pennine Way 190 1388 7 i

397 EARLS SEAT Highgreen Manor Troughend

Kielder Water Black Middens Bastle House A68

179 307 Gatehouse 9 8

Kielder Forest WHITE HILL Falstone Greenhaugh West Woodbu

G H J Tower Knowe Stannersburn K Lanehead L M

A B C D E F

205

Muasdale

Glenacardoch
Point

Belloch

Barr Water

Bri

Glenbarr

MacAlister Clan

454
BEINN AN TUIRC

Torri

Cleongart

319

408
BORD
MOR

N

Sadde

Bellochantuy Bay

Bellochantuy

194

Loch

396
SGREADAN
HILL

Ugadale

Tangy Loch

Glen Lussa

Peninver

Ardnacro
Bay

Kilkenzie

A83

Kilmichael

B842

Machrihanish
Bay

Campbeltown

Campbeltown

i

B842

Machrihanish

B842

Campbeltown
Loch

Island Dav

6

B843

Stewarton

Kilkerran

Drumlemble

Kildalloig

Earadale Point

352
BEINN GHUILEAN

Achinhoan

385
THE
STATE

10

446
CNOC
MOY

Conie Glen

Glen Kerran

Ru S

Dalsmeran

Glen Breakevie

B842

Strone Glen

Cattadale

Polliwilline Bay

BEINN NA LICE

Carskey

Southend

Macharioch

428

MULL
OF
KINTYRE

Dunaverty

Carskey Bay

Sanda Sound

Sheep Island

Borgadalemore Point

Sanda Island

A B C D E F

G **H** Balliekine **J** BEINN NUIS **K** Glen Rosa

Carradale

B879

Carradale House

Waterfoot

Carradale Point

Iorsa Water

Merkland Point

Brodick Castle, Garden & Country Park

1

Brodick Bay

Strathwhillan

Brodick

Corriegills

A R R A N

Auchagallon Stone Circle

Machrie

Machrie Bay

512

A'CHRUACH

4

Clauchlands Point

2

Tormore

Machrie Moor Stone Circles

B880

503

Margnaheglish

A841

Lamlash

Moss Farm Road Stone Circle

Balmichael

BEINN BHREAC

Lamlash Bay

Holy Island

addell Bay

Torbeg

Shiskine

Balmichael

Cordon

Drumadoon Point

Blackwaterfoot

Auchencairn

Kingscross

Knockenkelly

Drumadoon Bay

Kilpatrick

Glen Scorrodale

Carn Ban

Whiting Bay

Whiting Bay

3

Kilpatrick Dun

194 Brown Head

Glen Ashdale

Largymore

V

Corriecravie

Largybeg

Sliddery

Dippen

Dippen Head

Torr a' Chaisteal Fort

Kilmory Water

Kilmory

Bennan

Kildonan

(May-Sept, Sat only)

4

Lagg

Torrylin Cairn

195

Bennan Head

Pladda

5

6

7

340 Ailsa Craig

RSPB

8

G **H** **J** **K** **L** **M**

G H J K

Garroch Head

Ga...ty

207

Little
Cumbrae
Island

Fairlie ...

K

Hunterston
Power Station

12

Drakemyre

Dalry

A737

Blackshaw

Munnoch

B780

Portencross
Farland Head

B7048

B781

B780

Dalgarven
Mill

CUN

Seamill

B7047

West
Kilbride

B780

B714

Dalgarven

7

A78

B77

Sannox

A78

A78

Kilwinning

A738

A738

7

B71

Corrie

Ardrossan

Horse Isle

Stevenston

Saltcoats

196

Ardeer

B779

B780

Irvine

Maritime

Full

6

Merkland Point

Brodick Castle, Garden
& Country Park

Brodick
Bay

FIRTH

V

Irvine

Bay

Strathwhillan

OF

Corriegills

CLYDE

4

A841

Clauchlands Point

Bara

H

Margnaheglish

Lamlash
Bay

V

ash

Holy Island

Troon

Cordon

Auchencairn

Kingscross

4

Knockenkelly

Lady Isle

5

Whiting
Bay

Whiting Bay

(May-Sept, Sat only)

(May-Sept)

P

en Ashdale

Largymore

V

Largybeg

Dippen

Dippen Head

6

Ayr

Bay

Kildonan

196

adda

i M A

Heads
of Ayr

Doonfo

Burns Cott

Heads of Ayr

A719

7

All

Fisherton

Rob

Bi

Dunure

Culroy

Drumshang

Croy Brae
(Electric Brae)

Knoweside

8

Culzean
Bay

Culzean Castle
& Country ...

182

L

Pennyglen

M

Mayb

G H J K Whitefaulas

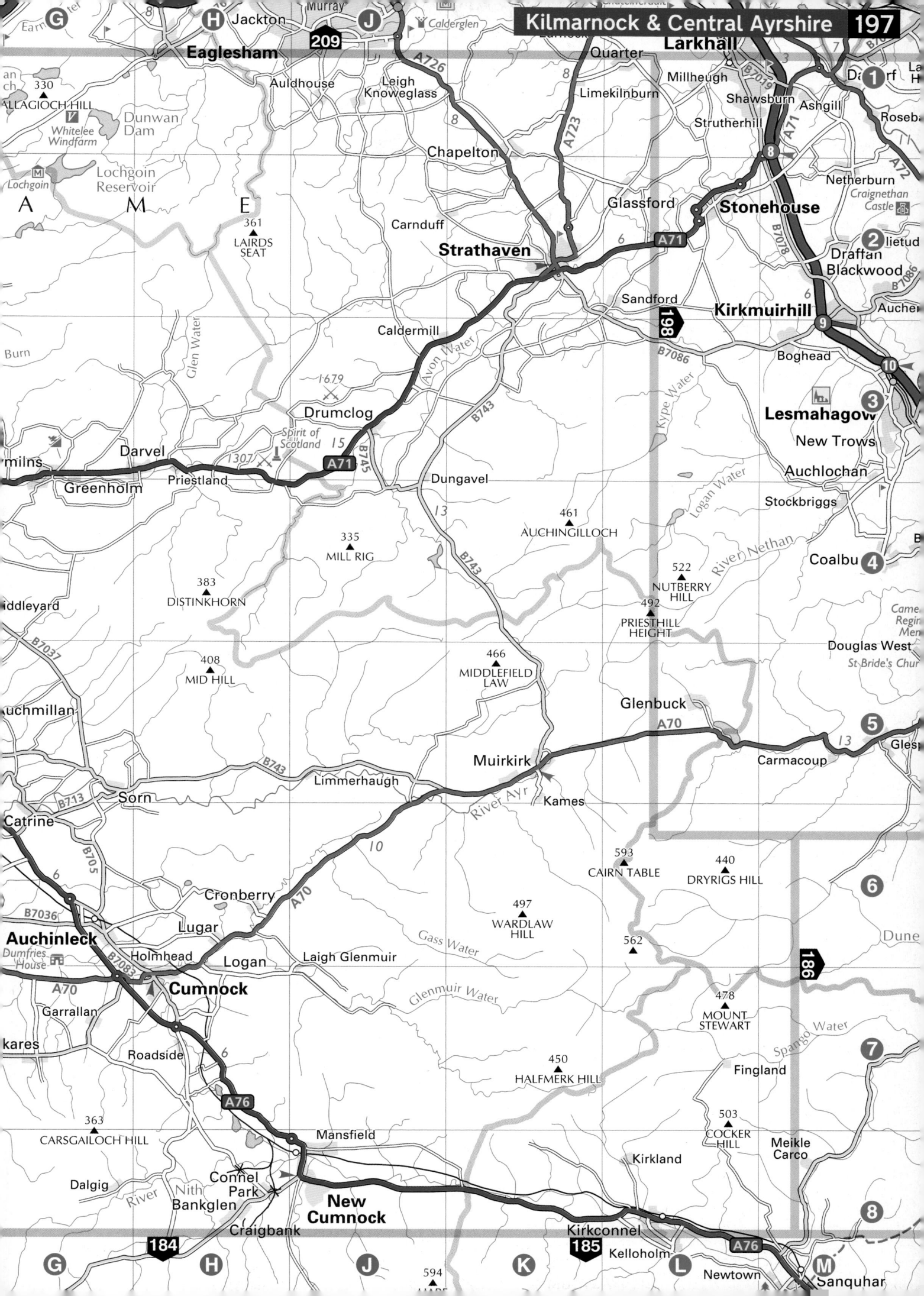

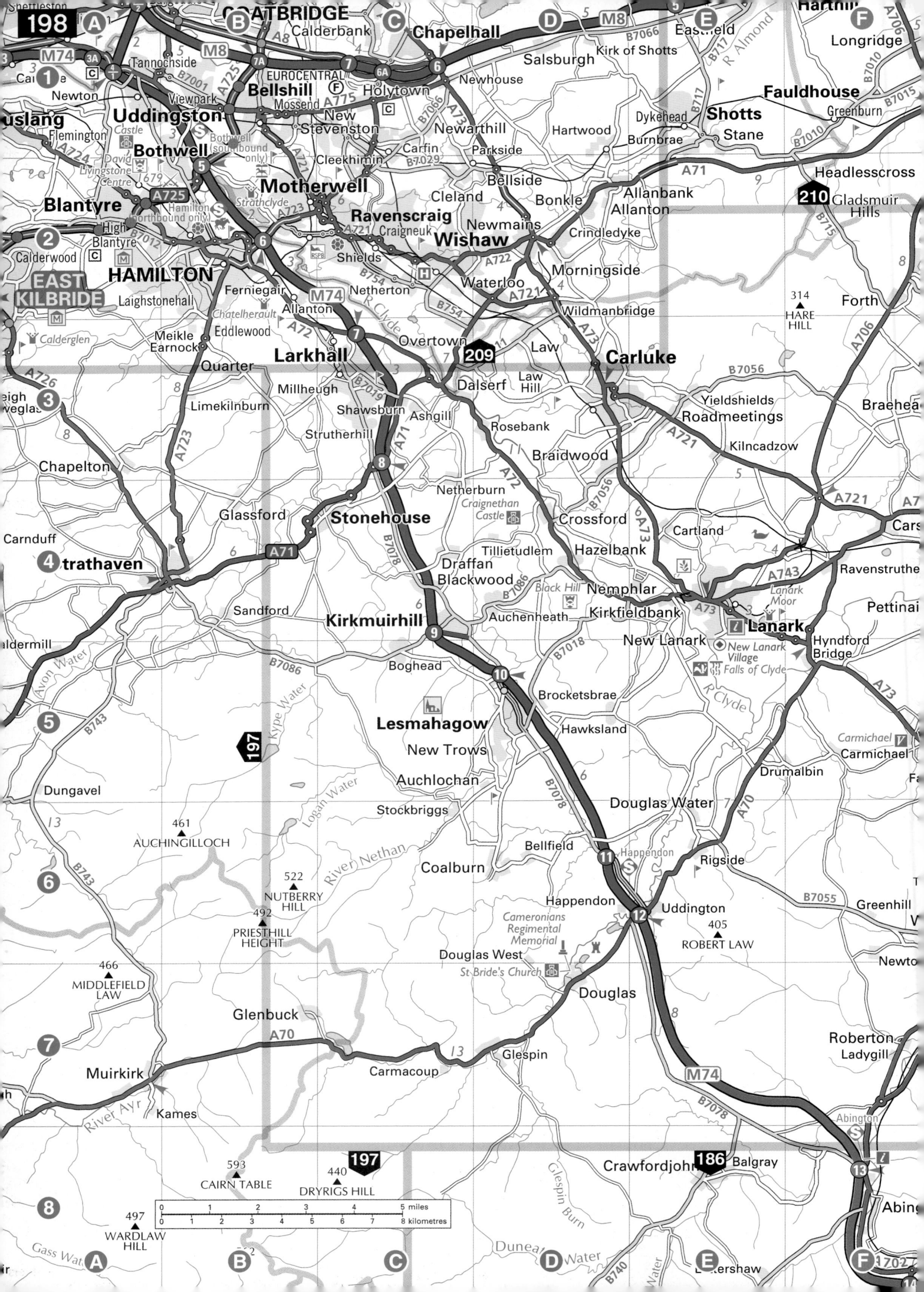

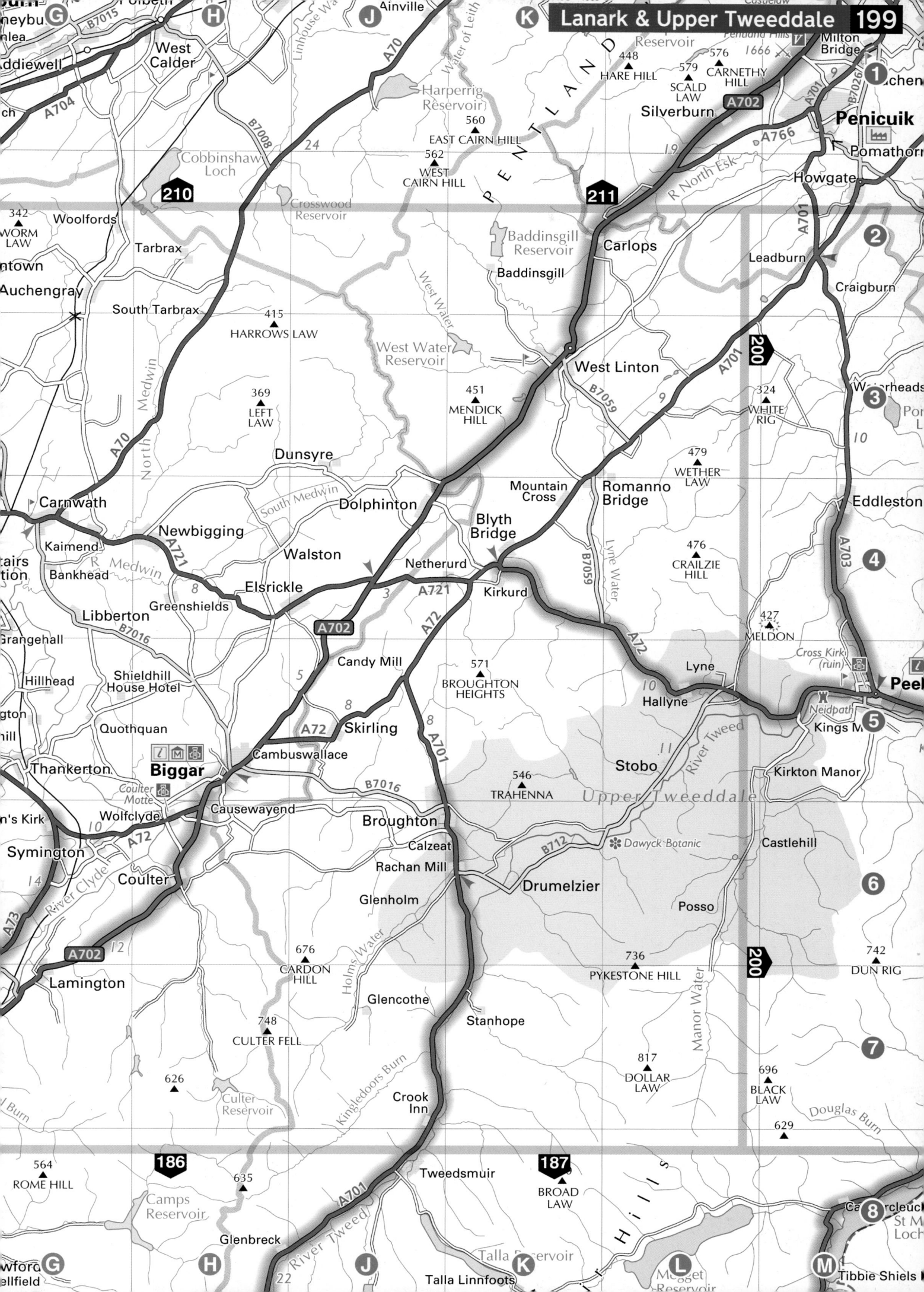

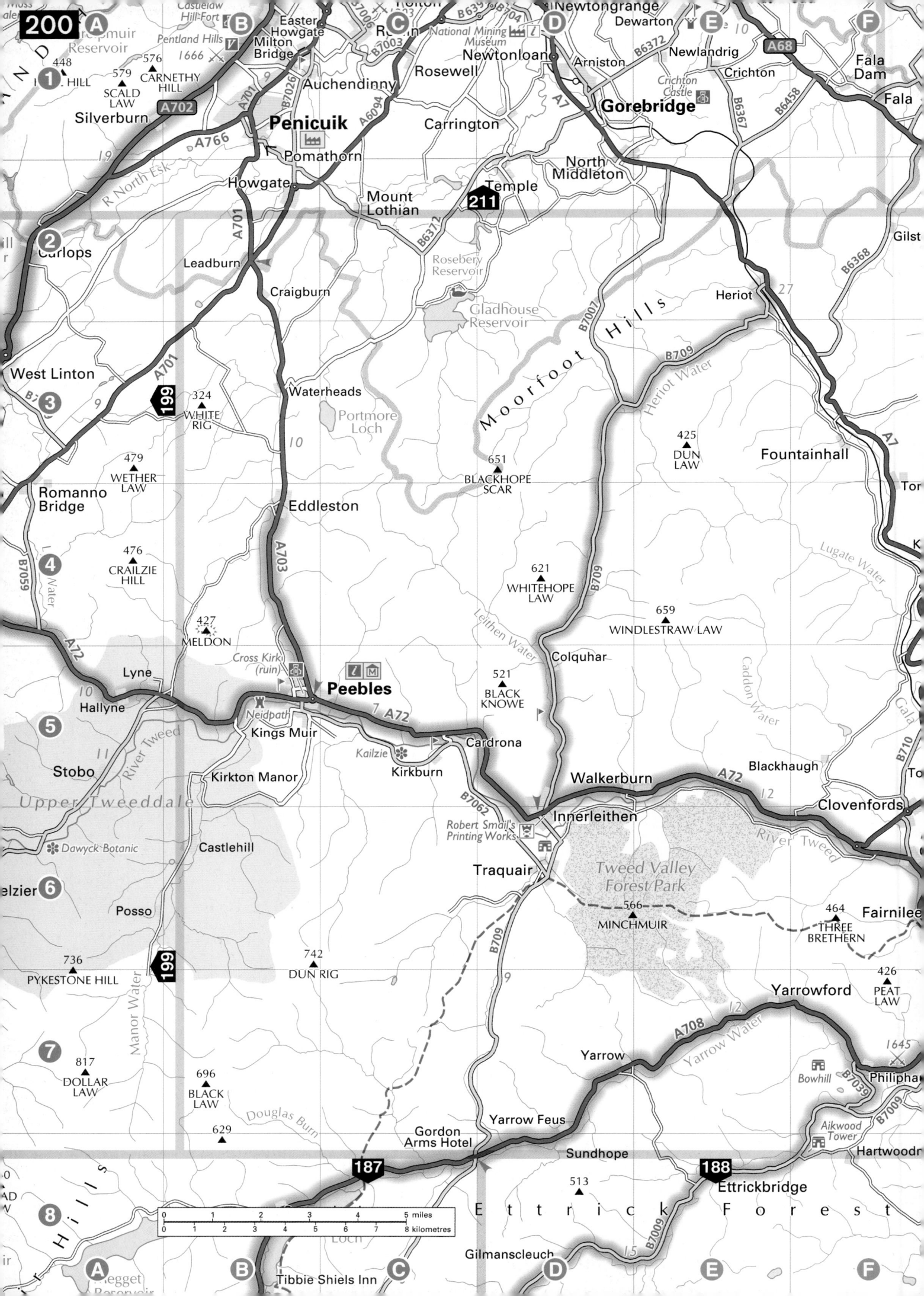

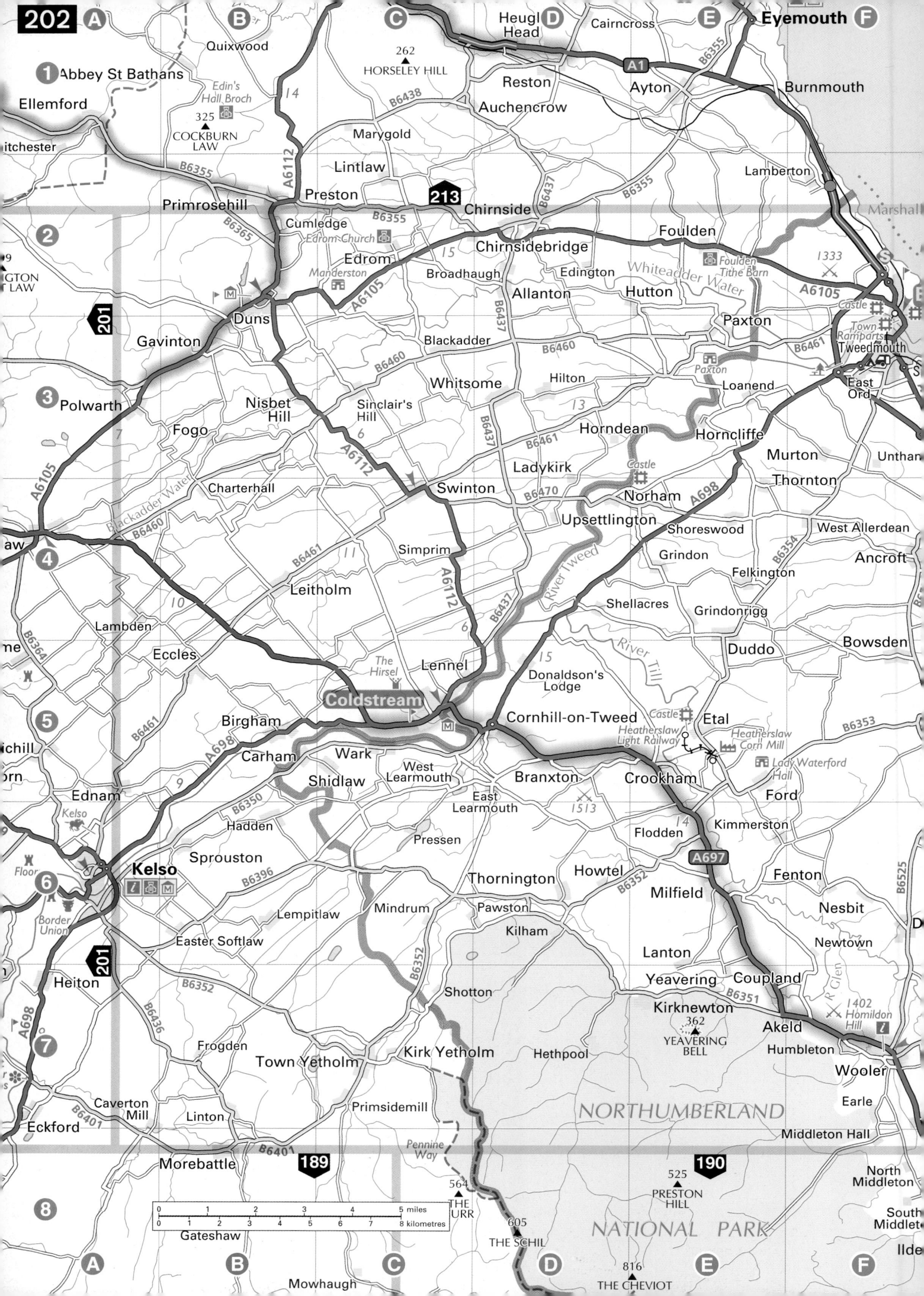

1

2

ows Bay

orthumberland
tage Coast

ick-upon-Tweed

3

Huds
Head

merston

Cheswick

CAUSEWAY
FLOODED
AT HIGH TIDE

4

Goswick

Haggerston

15

Beal

HOLY ISLAND

Fenham

Holy
Island

Lindisfarne
Castle

B6353

Lindisfarne
Priory

Castle Point

West
Kyloe

Guile Point

Lowick

Fenwick

5

Longstone

Buckton

Smeafield

Elwick

FARNE
ISLANDS

Detchant

Ross

Staple
Sound

Holburn

St Cuthbert's
Cave

Low
Middleton

Easington

Budle
Bay

Bamburgh

Inner
Sound

North Northumberland
Heritage Coast

Middleton

B1342

Hetton
Steads

Belford

Waren
Mill

Budle

Bamburgh

6

North
Hazelrigg

Outchester

Spindlestone

Burton

New
Shoreston

B6349

South
Hazelrigg

9

Bradford

Seahouses

gton

Warenton

Bellshill

Lucker

Elford

North Sunderland

East
Horton

B6348

Adderstone

B1341

Beadnell

Chatton

Warenford

Newham

Swinhoe

7

Head

Chillingham
Wild Cattle
Park

Ros Castle

Chathill

Tughall

B1340

Beadnell
Bay

Newtown

Newstead

Ellingham

Preston

urn
wer

190

Hepburn

Preston
Pele Tower

191

Brunton

Newton-by-the-Sea

Embleton &
Newton Links

14

Christon
Bank

Embleton

8

267

CATERAN
HILL

Brownieside

Doxford

North
Charlton

Fallodon

Embleton
Bay

Old Bewick

West
Ditchburn

South
Charlton

B347

Dunstan
Steads

Dunstanburgh
Castle

B6346

Harehope

J

K

L

Dunstan

M

G | H | J | K

214

215

206

194

192

udha' a' Ghil G

Sween

Danna Island **1**

Ellary

St Cormac's Chapel

Kilmory Knap Chapel

Kilmory **2**

Point of Knap

Kilmory Bay

506 ▲ SCRINADLE

398 ▲ BEINN TARSUINN

Jura Forest

784 ▲ BEINN AN OIR

Paps of Jura

734 ▲

Loch a Chnuic Bhric

Jura

24

Knockrome Ardfernal

J U R A

Lo Caolisr

C henga **3**

Coulaghai

Kilberry Sculptured Stones

Kilberry

Kilberry Head

Keppoch Point

213 ▲ CRUACH A

Tiretigan

Loch Stornoway **4**

560 ▲ GLASS BHEINN

Feolin Ferry V

Keils

529 ▲ DUBHA BHEINN

Craighouse

Small Isles

342 ▲ BRAT BHEINN

Rudha na Gaillich

Cabrach

Islay

Am Fraoch Eilean

Brosdale Island

Rudha na Tràille

McArthur's Head

29

R NAM EANN

Port Askaig - Kennacraig V

Ronan Poin **5**

Arc

Rudha Liath

Ardtalla

Claggain Bay

EIGEIR

Kinerarach

Tarbert

Sound of Gigha

Kintour

Kildalton Cross

Ardmore Point

GIGHA

Rhunahaorine Point **6**

Port Ellen - Kennacraig

Eilean a' Chuirn

Ardminish

V

Rhunahaorine

Achamore

38

Rudha na Gainmhich

Cara

Tayinloan V

7

A83

Muasdale **8**

Glenacardoch Point

Belloch

Barr Water

Gl barr L

MacAlister Clan M

G | H | J | K

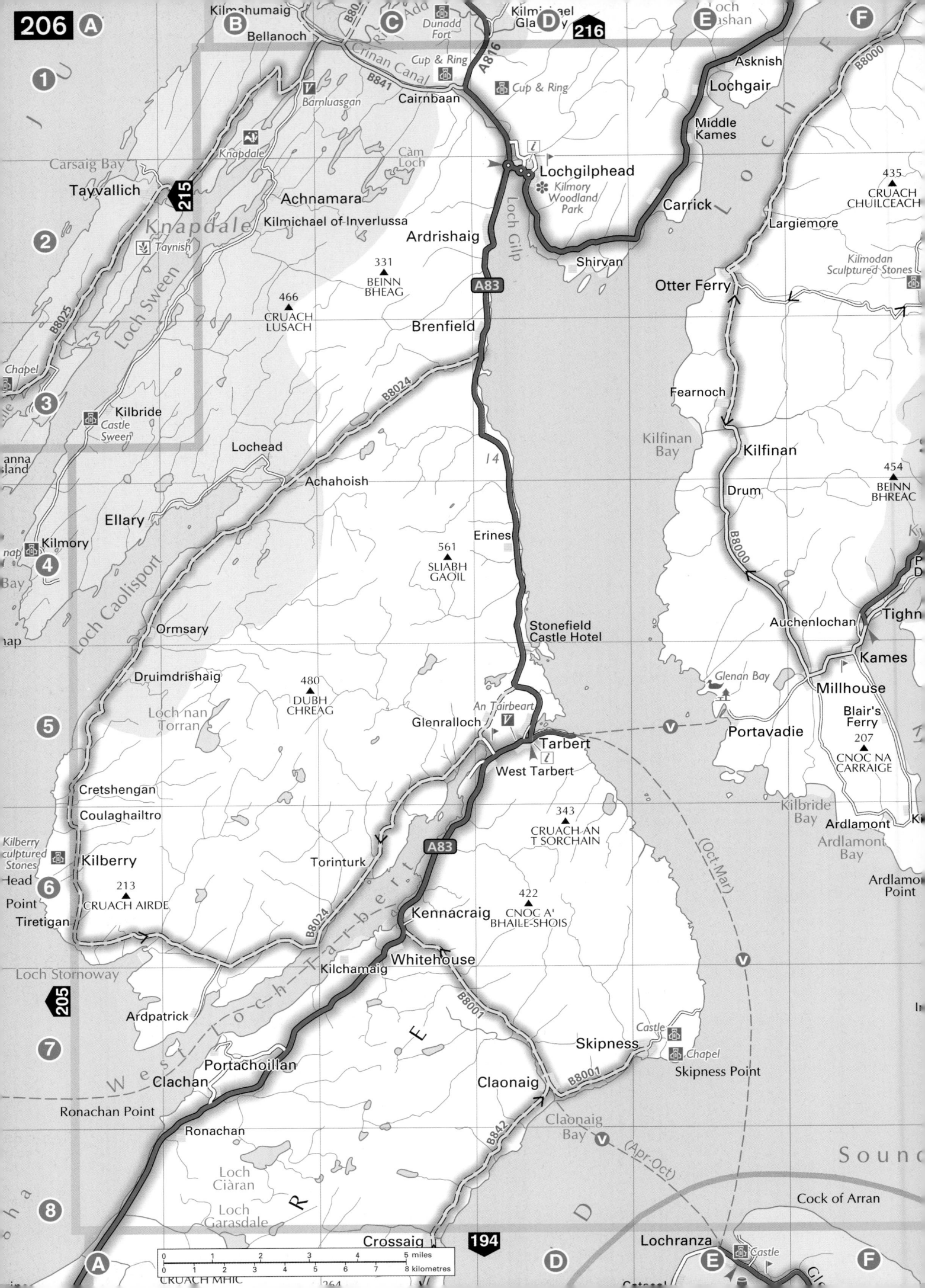

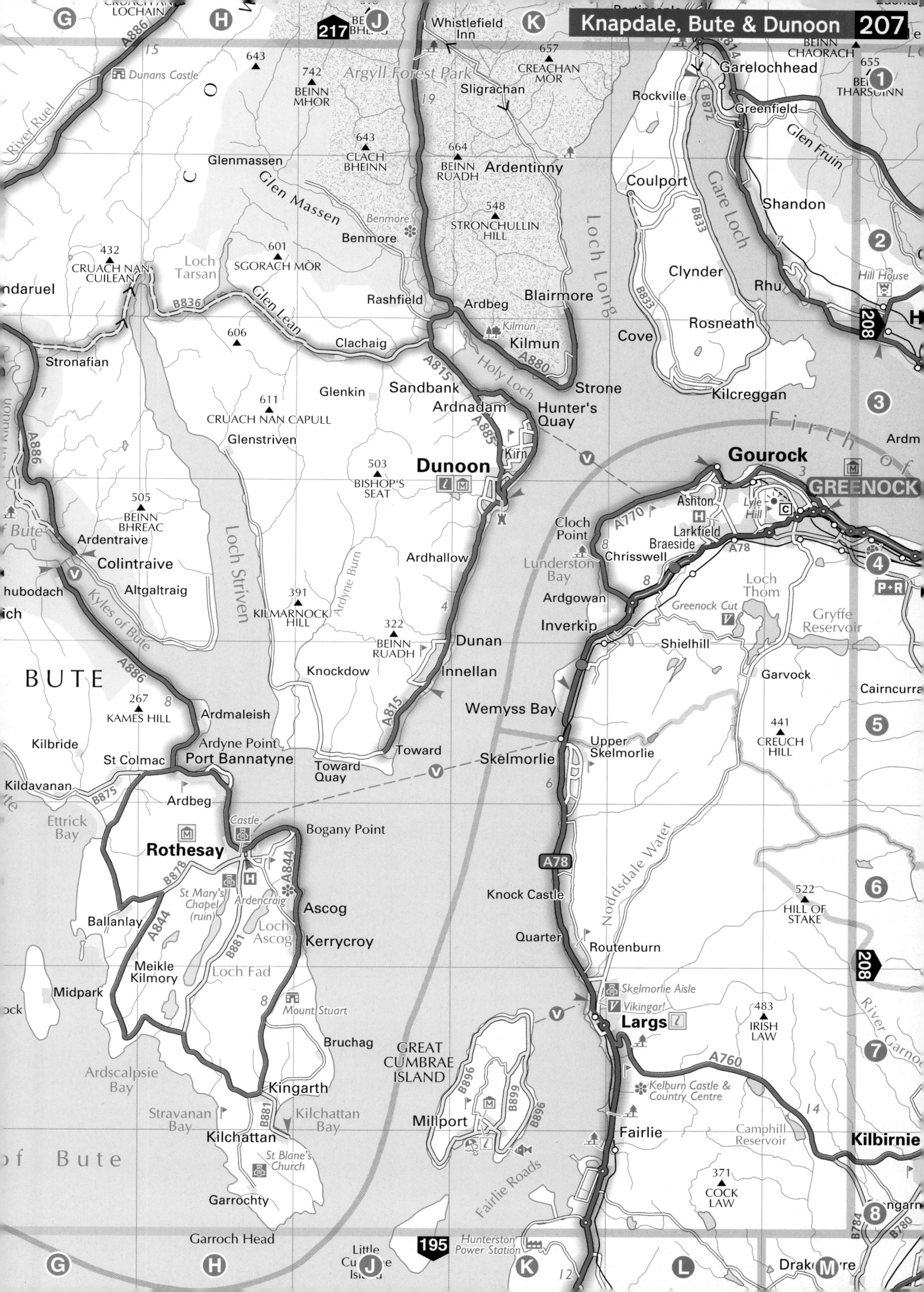

G **H** **J** **217** **K**

GREENOCK

Gourock

Dunoon

Rothesay

BUTE

Largs

Kilbirnie

GREAT CUMBRAE ISLAND

Millport

1
2
3
4
5
6
7
8

208

CROACH'AN LOCHAIN
A886
Dunans Castle
643
742 BEINN MHOR
Argyll Forest Park
BE BHE
Whistlefield Inn
657 CREACHAN MOR
Sligrachan
BEINN CHAORACH
655 BEI THARSUINN
Garelochhead

Glenmassen
643 CLACH BHEINN
664 BEINN RUADH
Ardentinny
Rockville
Greenfield
Glen Fruin
A814

River Ruel
Glen Massen
548 STRONCHULLIN HILL
Coulport
Shandon
B833
B872

432 CRUACH NAN CUILEAN
Loch Tarsan
601 SGORACH MÒR
Benmore
Rashfield
Ardbeg
Kilmun
A880
Strone
Clynder
Rhu
Hill House
B833

ndaruel
Stronafian
B836
Glen Lean
606
Clachaig
A815
Holy Loch
Hunter's Quay
Cove
Kilcreggan
Rosneath

505 BEINN BHREAC
Glenkin
Sandbank
Ardnadam
A885
Kirn
Firth of
Ardm

Ardentraive
503 BISHOP'S SEAT
Dunoon
Cloch Point
Ashton
Lyle Hill
GREENOCK

Colintraive
CRUACH NAN CAPULL 611
Glenstriven
Ardhallow
Lunderston Bay
A770
Larkfield
Braeside
Chrisswell
A78

hubodach
Altgaltraig
Loch Striven
391 KILMARNOCK HILL
Ardgowan
Inverkip
Greenock Cut
Loch Thom
Gryffe Reservoir
4
P+R

Kyles of Bute
A886
322 BEINN RUADH
Dunan
Shielhill
Garvock
Cairncurra

BUTE
267 KAMES HILL
Ardmaleish
Knockdow
Innellan
A815
Wemyss Bay
441 CREUCH HILL
5

Kilbride
St Colmac
Ardyne Point
Port Bannatyne
Toward
Upper Skelmorlie
Skelmorlie

Kildavanan
B875
Ardbeg
Toward Quay

Ettrick Bay
Castle
Bogany Point
A78
Knock Castle
522 HILL OF STAKE
6

Rothesay
B878
St Mary's Chapel (ruin)
Ardencraig
Ascog
Noddsdale Water
Quarter
Routenburn

Ballanlay
A844
Loch Ascog
Kerrycroy
7

Meikle Kilmory
Loch Fad
B881
Mount Stuart
Skelmorlie Aisle
Vikingar!
Largs
483 IRISH LAW
A760
River Garnoc
14

Midpark
Bruchag
GREAT CUMBRAE ISLAND
B896
Kelburn Castle & Country Centre
Fairlie
Camphill Reservoir
Kilbirnie

Ardscalpsie Bay
Kingarth
B881
Kilchattan Bay
B899
B896
Millport
B784
B780

Stravanan Bay
Kilchattan
St Blane's Church
371 COCK LAW
ngarn
8

of Bute
Garrochty
Garroch Head
Little Cu Isla
195
Hunterston Power Station
J **K** **L** Drak M re

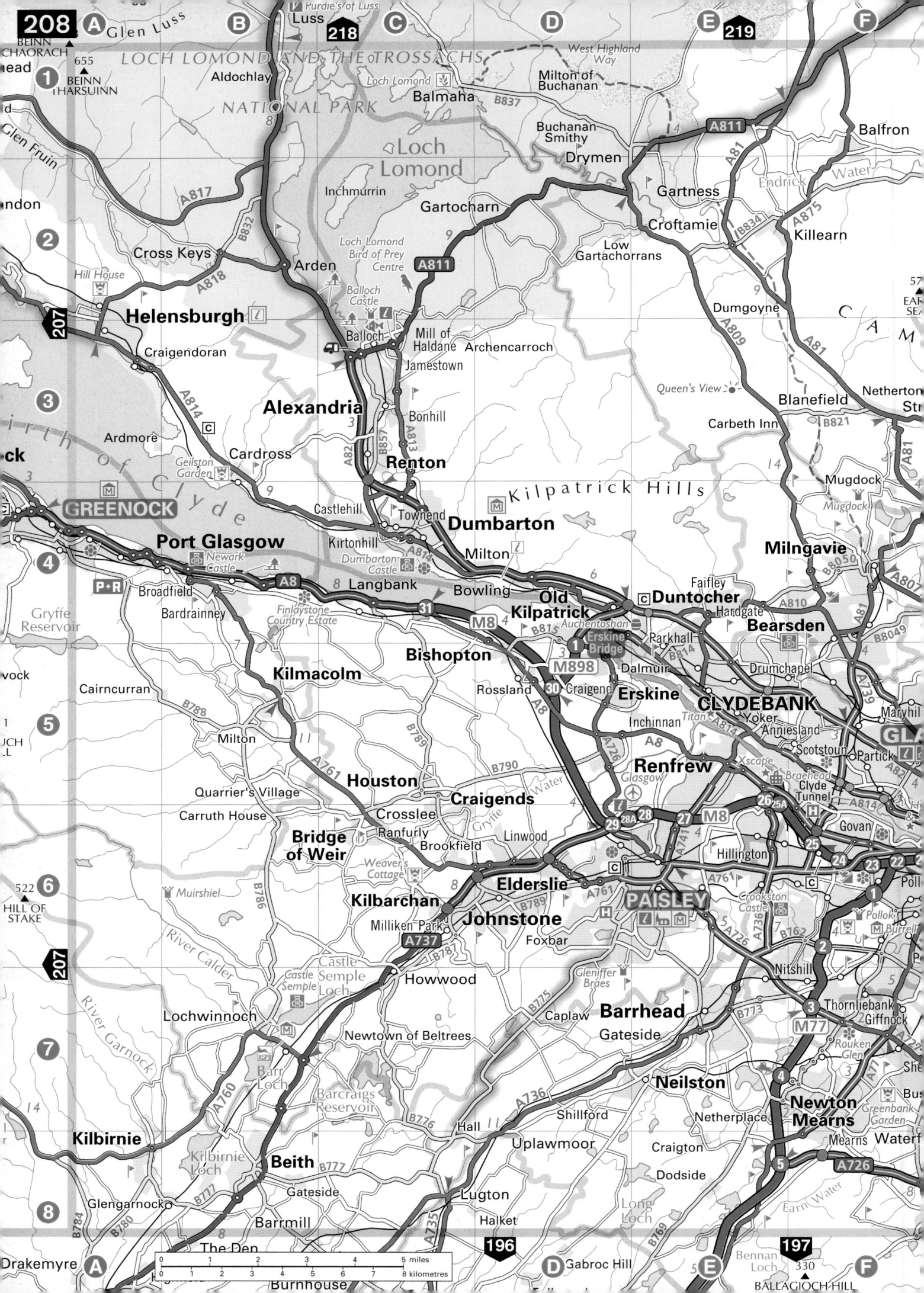

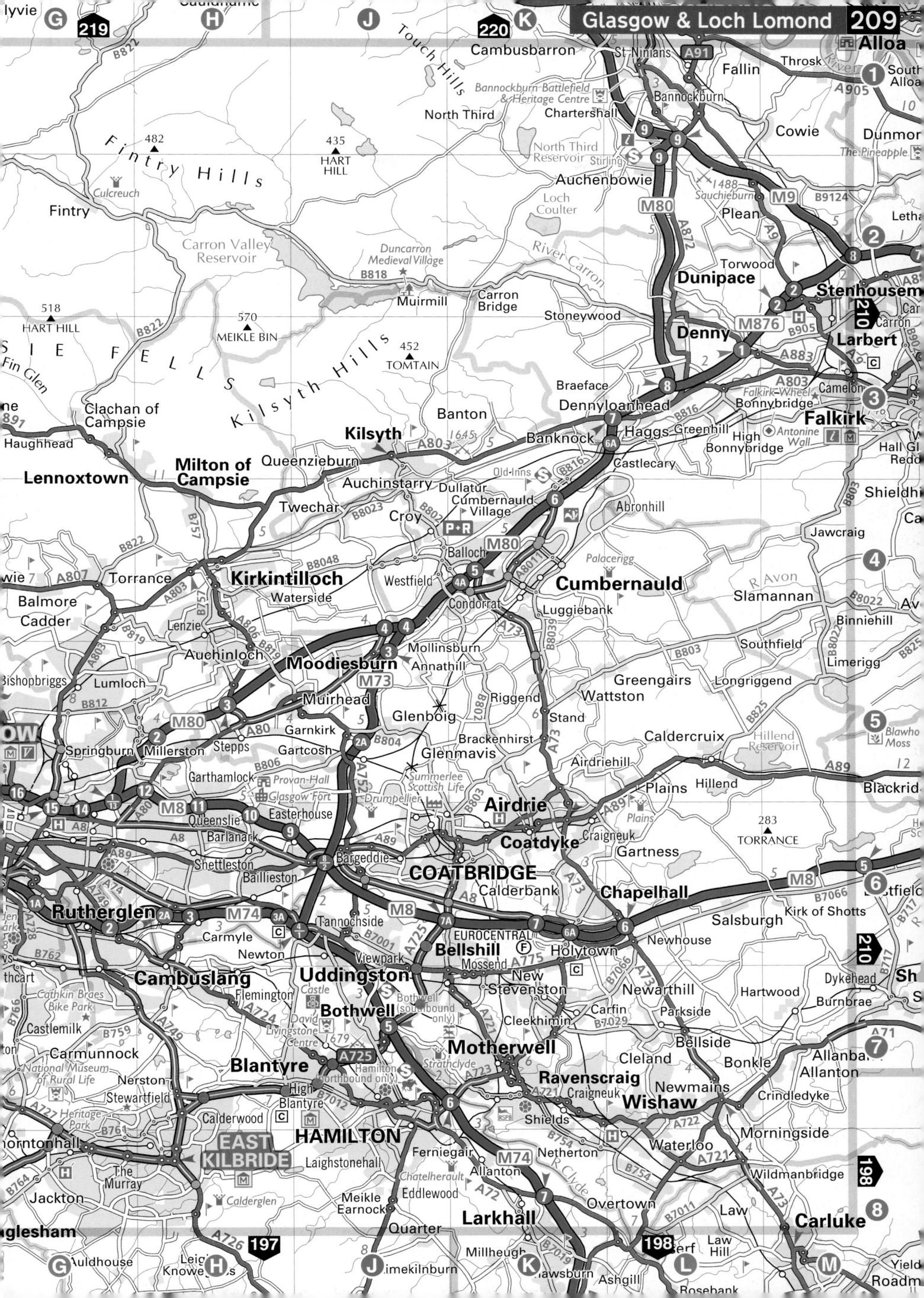

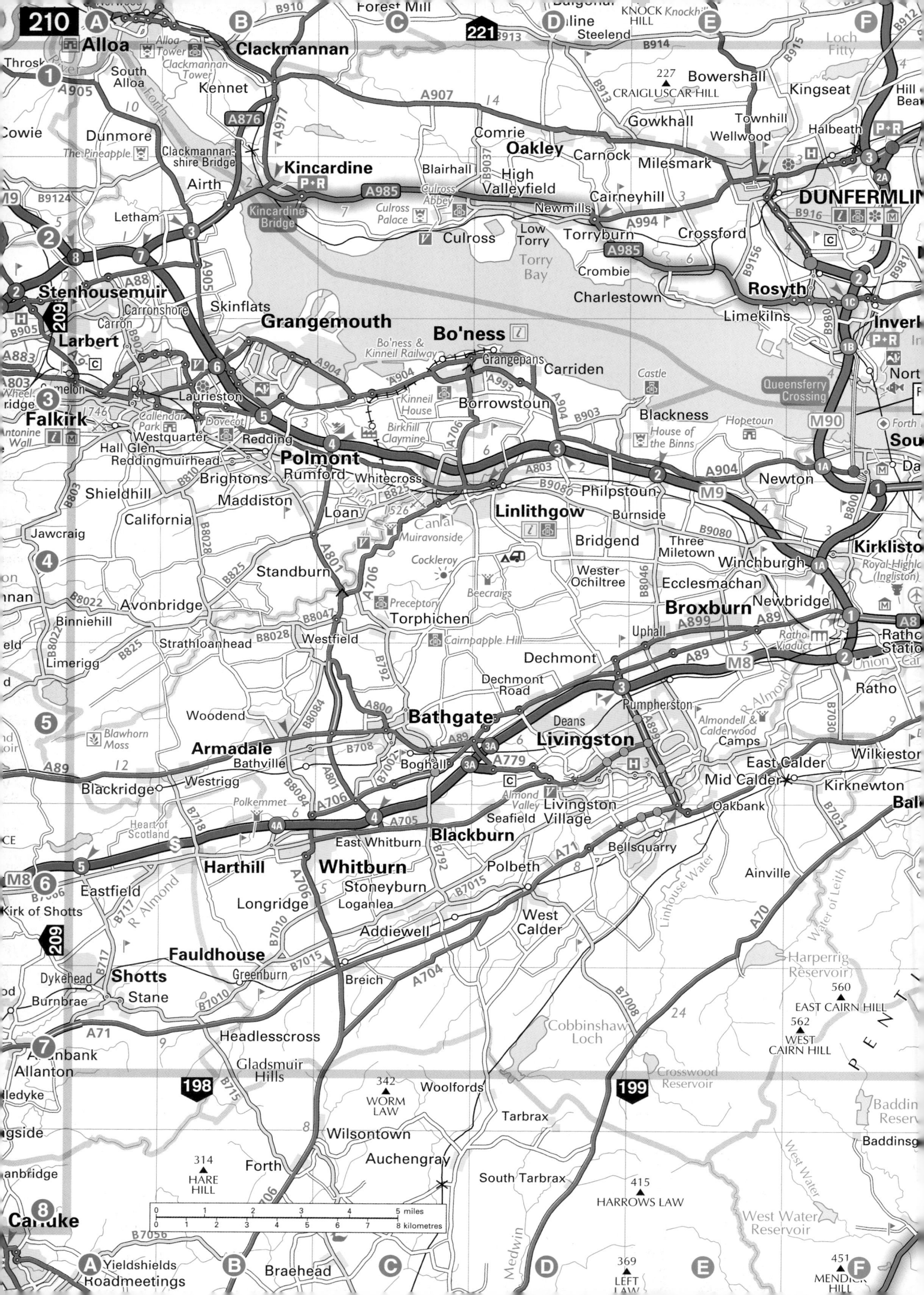

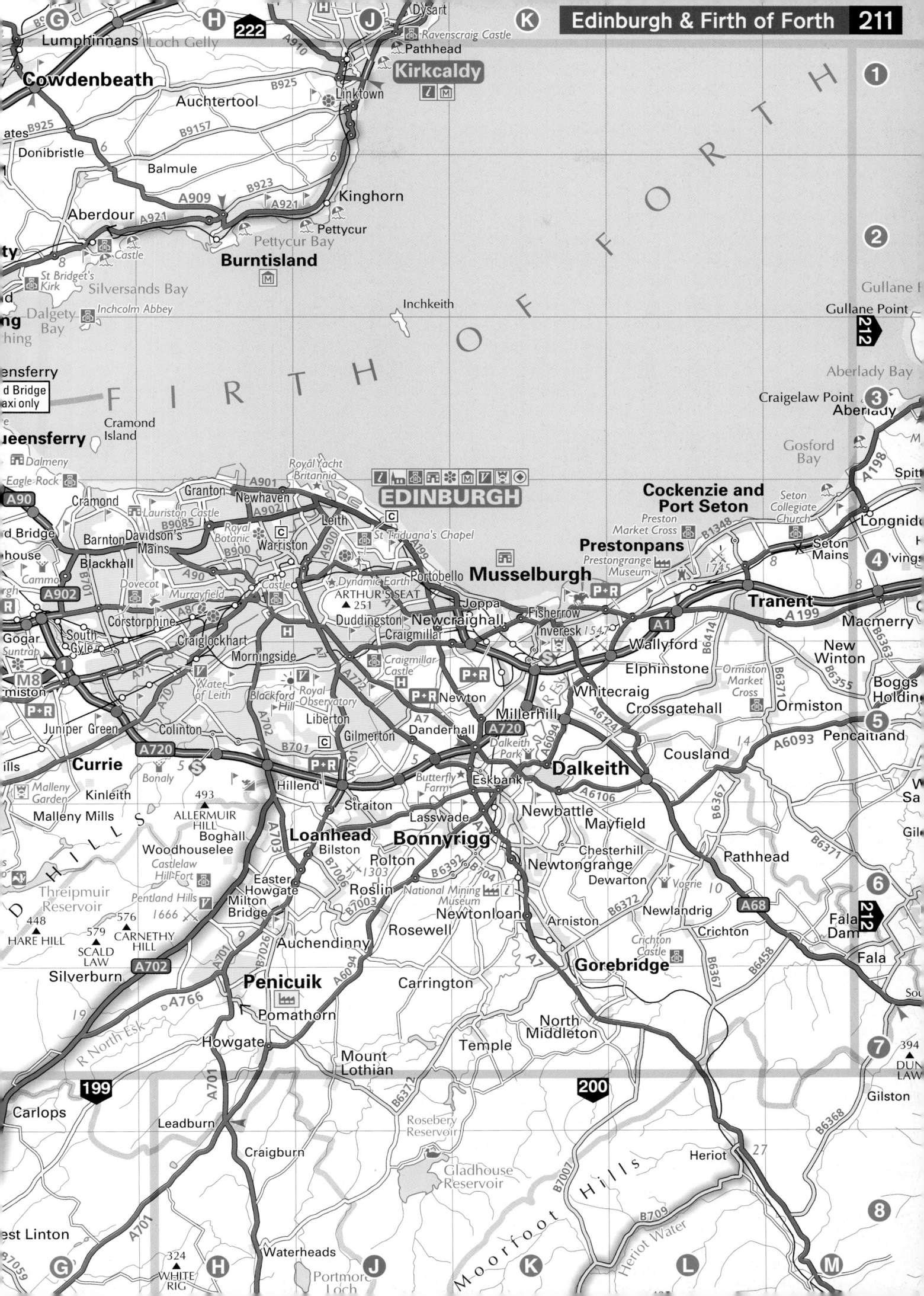

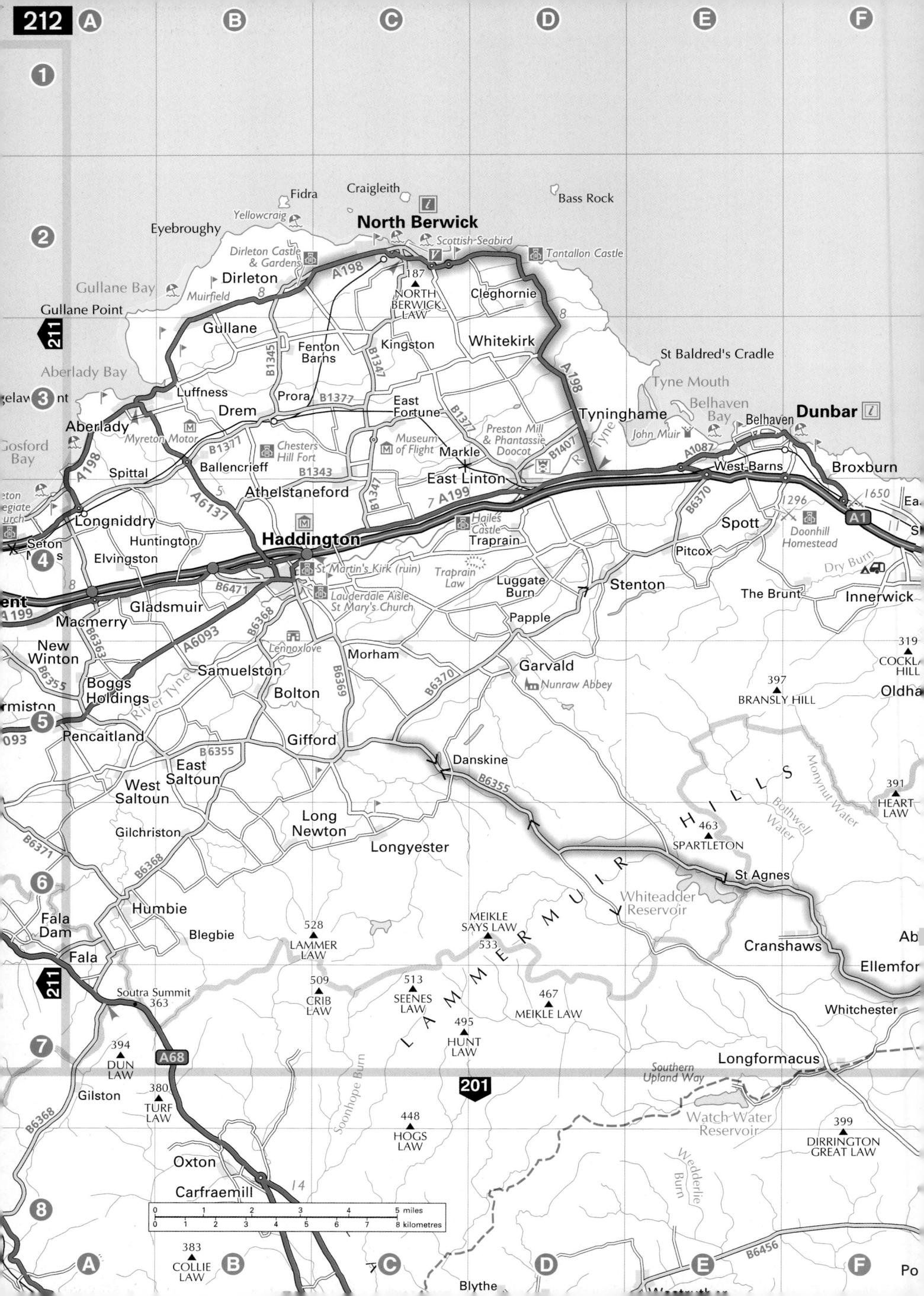

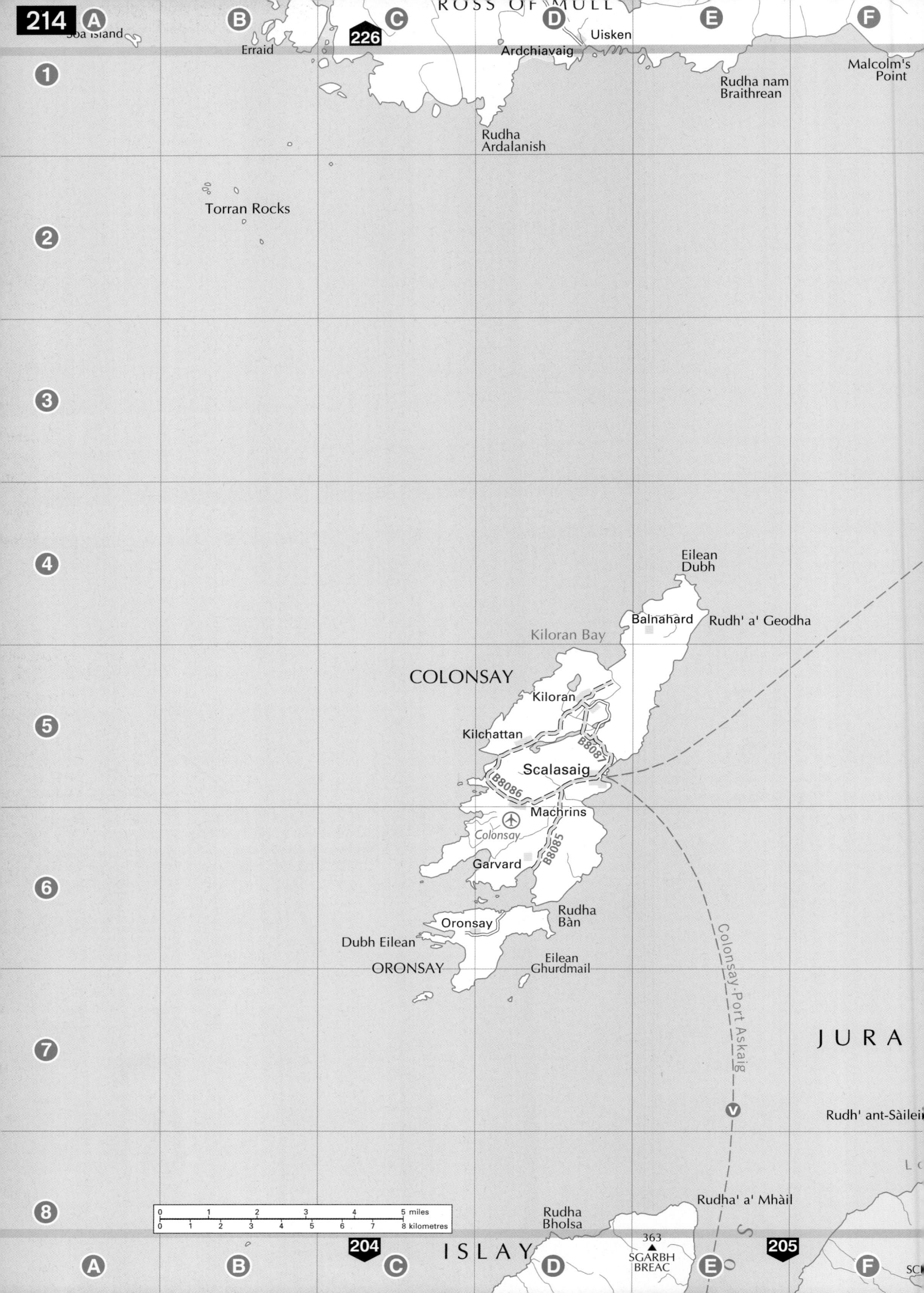

ROSS OF MULL

Soa Island

Erraid

Uisken

Ardchiavaig

1

Rudha nam
Braithrean

Malcolm's
Point

Rudha
Ardalanish

Torran Rocks

2

3

4

Eilean
Dubh

Balnahard   Rudh' a' Geodha

Kiloran Bay

COLONSAY

Kiloran

5

Kilchattan

B8087

Scalasaig

B8086

Machrins

Colonsay

B8085

Garvard

6

Rudha
Bàn

Oronsay

Dubh Eilean

Eilean
Ghurdmail

ORONSAY

7

Colonsay-Port Askaig

JURA

V

Rudh' ant-Sàilei

Rudha' a' Mhàil

8

0   1   2   3   4   5 miles
0   1   2   3   4   5   6   7   8 kilometres

Rudha
Bholsa

ISLAY

SGARBH
BREAC

SC

G H J K

227

1

Insh
Island
Clachan-Seil
SEIL
Ellenabeich   Easdale
Easdale
Balvicar

B844   B8003

2

V

Cuan

Seil Sound

Cullipool

Torsa

Degnish

LUING

Loch Melfort

A81

Arduaine

216

GARVELLACHS

Garbh Eileach

Eilean
Dubh Mòr

Monastery & Beehive Cells
Eileach
an Naoimh

LUNGA

Scarba, Lunga
and the
Garvellachs

SCARBA

Toberonochy

Shuna Sound

SHUNA

Shuna
Point

3

Cra
Haven

Craigdhu

Ardfern

Kint

12

En Mhic

En Rig

Car

4

448
▲
CRUACH SCARBA

Aird

Craignish Point

Island
Macaskin

Slockavulli
Temple Wood
Stone Circles
Ri Cruin Ca
Poltalloc

5

Gulf of Corryvreckan

Glengarrisdale
Bay

295
▲
CRUACH NA
SEILCHEIG

Loch Crinan

Crinan

Kilmahumaig

Bellanoch

B8025

Crinan
Rive

Glendebadel Bay

364
▲
BEN
GARRISDALE

Lealt Burn

Loch of Jura

B841

Bárnlu

6

Corpach Bay

466
▲
BEINN
BHREAC

Lussa River

Glen Grundale

Knapdale

Carsaig Bay

Tayvallich

Achnamara

Kilmichael of Inverluss

n-Bay

453
▲
RAINBERG MÒR

A846

Ardlussa

Lussa Point
Lussagiven

Loch
gh Mòr

Loch Sween

B8025

Taynish

206

7

331
▲
BEINN
BHEAC

466
▲
CRUACH
LUSACH

8

Keills Chapel

arbert

Kilbride
Castle
Sween

Lochead

205

G H J

Loch na Cille
Danna
Island

K

L

M chahoish

398

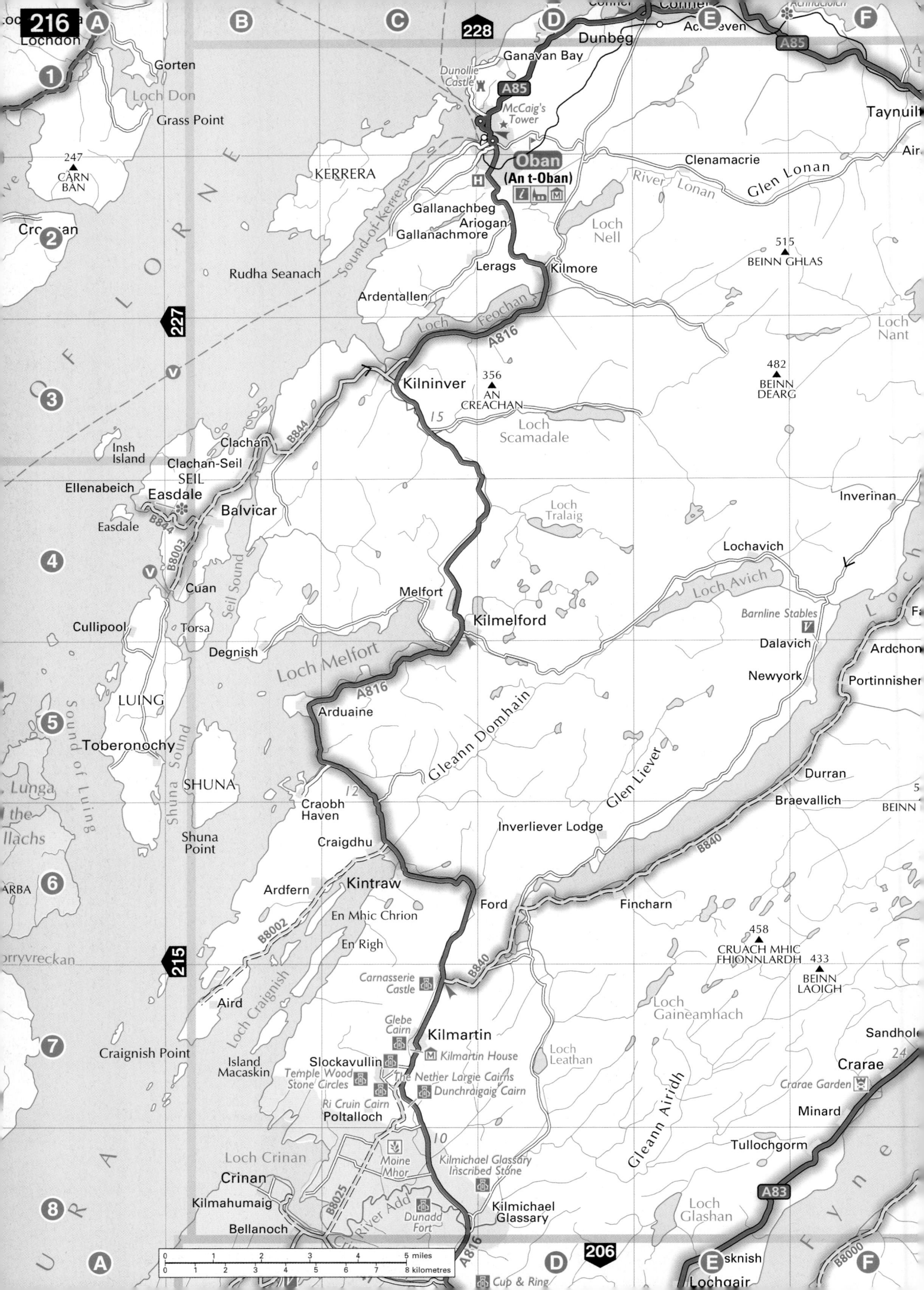

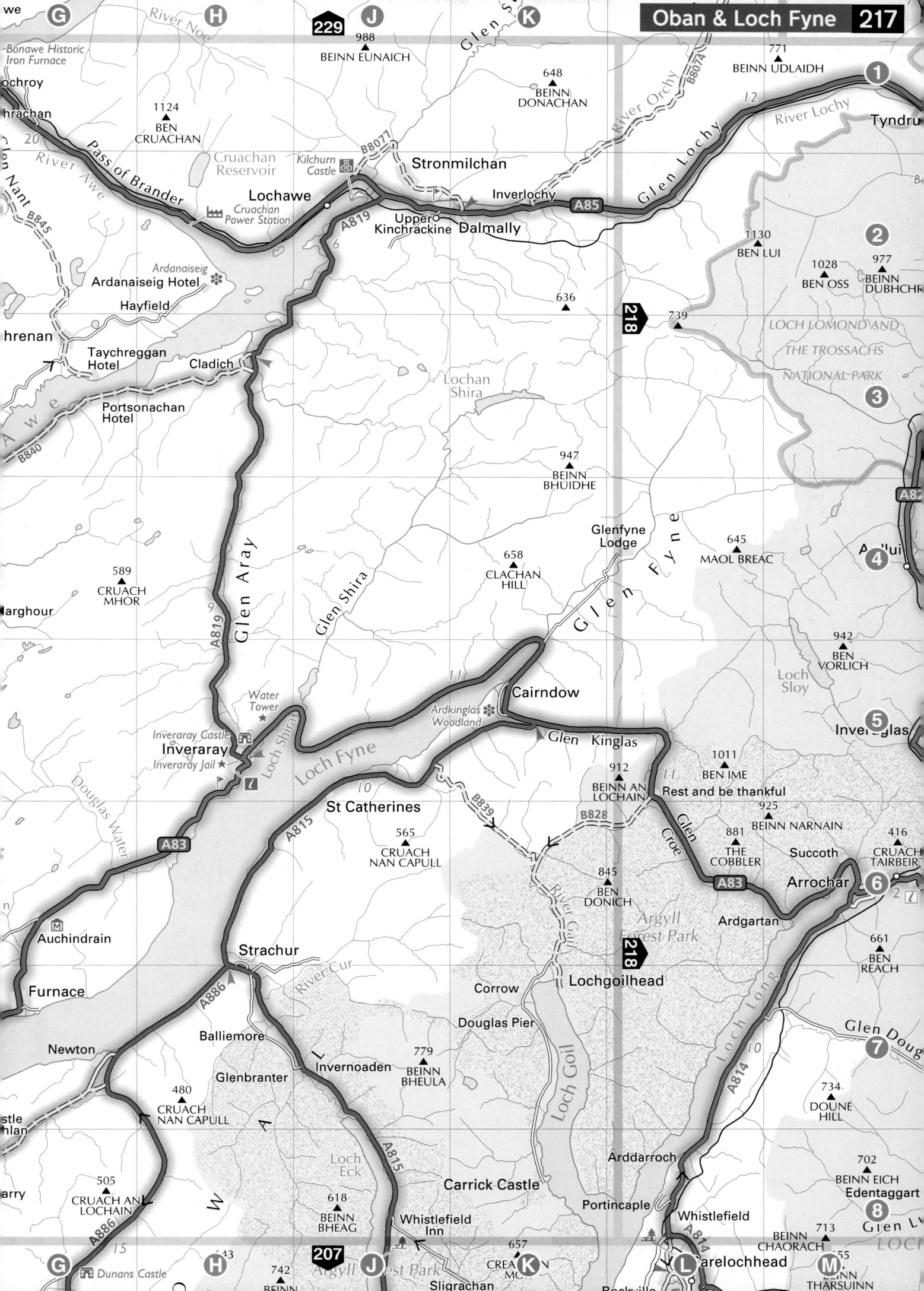

G H 229 J K

Bonawe Historic Iron Furnace
ochroy
hrachan
Glen S
Glen Lochy
B8074
River Orchy
River Lochy
771
BEINN UDLAIDH
Tyndru
1
988
BEINN EUNAICH
1124
BEN CRUACHAN
648
BEINN DONACHAN
River Awe
Pass of Brander
20
Glen Nant B845
River Awe
Cruachan Reservoir
Kilchurn Castle
B8077
Stronmilchan
B8077
Inverlochy
A85
Glen Lochy
12
Lochawe
Cruachan Power Station
Upper Kinchrackine
Dalmally
A819
6
2
1130
BEN LUI
1028
BEN OSS
977
BEINN DUBHCHR
Ardanaiseig
Ardanaiseig Hotel
Hayfield
636
218
739
LOCH LOMOND AND
THE TROSSACHS
hrenan
Taychreggan Hotel
Cladich
A
W
e
B840
Portsonachan Hotel
Lochan Shira
NATIONAL PARK
3
A82
947
BEINN BHUIDHE
Glen Aray
A819
9
Glen Shira
Glenfyne Lodge
Glen Fyne
658
CLACHAN HILL
645
MAOL BREAC
A lui
4
589
CRUACH MHOR
arghour
Water Tower
Glen Shira
11
Cairndow
Ardkinglas Woodland
Glen Fyne
942
BEN VORLICH
Loch Sloy
5
Inver glas
Inveraray Castle
Loch Shira
INVERARAY
Inveraray Jail
i
Loch Fyne
Glen Kinglas
1011
BEN IME
Rest and be thankful
925
BEINN NARNAIN
Douglas Water
A83
A815
St Catherines
10
B839
912
BEINN AN LOCHAIN
B828
Glen Croe
881
THE COBBLER
Succoth
416
CRUACH TAIRBEIR
6
2
i
565
CRUACH NAN CAPULL
845
BEN DONICH
A83
Ardgartan
Arrochar
Auchindrain
River Gail
Argyll Forest Park
218
661
BEN REACH
n
Furnace
Strachur
A886
River Cur
Corrow
Douglas Pier
Lochgoilhead
Glen Doug
7
Newton
Balliemore
A815
L
Invernoaden
779
BEINN BHEULA
A814
10
Loch Long
734
DOUNE HILL
Glenbranter
480
CRUACH NAN CAPULL
A
W
Loch Goil
Arddarroch
702
BEINN EICH
Edentaggart
8
stle
hlan
505
CRUACH AN LOCHAIN
A886
Loch Eck
618
BEINN BHEAG
A815
Carrick Castle
Portincaple
Whistlefield
A814
713
BEINN CHAORACH
arry
15
Dunans Castle
Argyll est Park
742
BEIN
207
J est Park
Sligrachan
657
CREA MO
arelochhead
TH
TARSUINN
G H J K L M

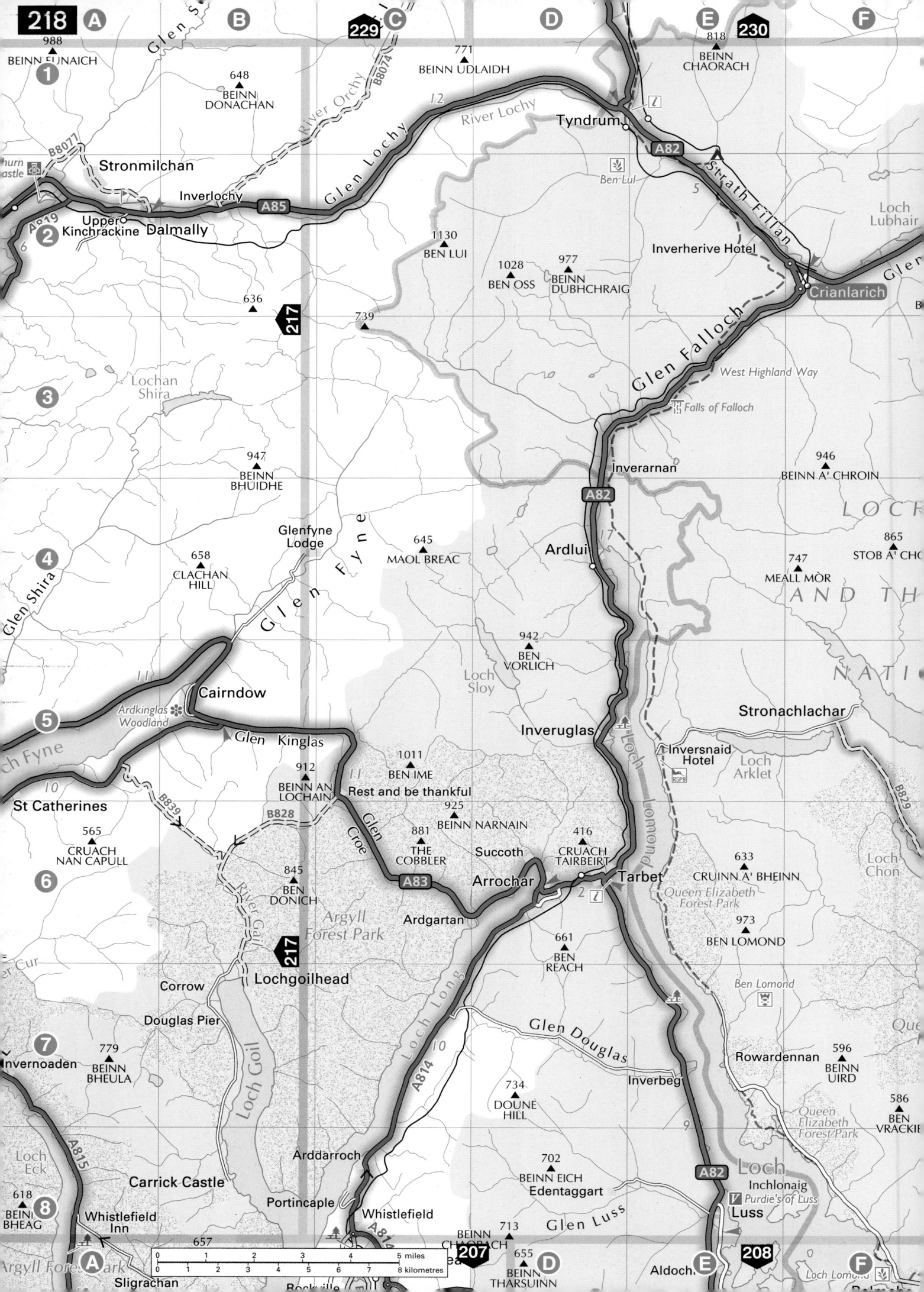

G   230   H   J   Finlarig   231   A

937
HEATHAICH

879
CREAG
UCHDAG

1

Killin
Falls of Dochart
Breadalbane
Folklore Centre

682
RUADH MHEALL

Loch
Lednock

B

R

E

A

D

Auchlyne

A85

River Dochart

Dochart

A85

Glen Ogle

5

Glen Beich

671
SRON
MHOR

Inve

Loch E

2

Glen

778
MEALL AN
FHIODHAIN

Dalveich

St Fillans

220

A85

Lochearnhead

Loch Earn

River Earn

A84

Ardvorlich

Balquhidder

Auchtubh

Glen Vorlich

3

Craigruie

Kingshouse
Hotel

985
BEN VORLICH

Glen

Loch Voil

975
STUC A' CHROIN

Ballimore

Strathyre

Dalchruin

OMOND

Loch
Doine

Loch

TROSSACHS

818
BENVANE

Strathyre
Forest

14

Ardchullarie
More

630
MEALL
ODHAR

4

671
MEALL
CALA

Queen Elizabeth
Forest Park

Loch
Lubnaig

AL PARK

876
BEN LEDI

Kilmahog
Woollen Mill

5

n Katrine

SS Sir
Walter Scott

Glen Finglas
Reservoir

Falls of Leny

Callander
(Calasraid)

The
Trossachs

Brig o'Turk

10

Kilmahog

Coilantogle

A821

Upper
Drumbane

Trossachs Pier

729
BEN
VENUE

Loch
Achray

Lendrick

Loch Venachar

Rob Roy
& Trossachs

A84

700
BEINN
BHREAC

Queen Elizabeth
Forest Park

A821

Loch
Drunkie

Menteith Hills

427
BEINN
DEARG

A81

6

Drumvaich

B8032

Burn of
Cambus

6

Altskeith
Hotel

7

Toll

Ruskie

220

Buchany

ochard

Loch Ard

Milton

Queen Elizabeth
Forest Park

4   A81

Port of
Menteith

Goodie Water

Thornhill

Deanston

Doun

B822

B826

Doune Castle

Meldrum

izabeth
Park

Duchray Water

Aberfoyle

Scottish
Wool Centre

Inchmahome
Priory

Lake of
Menteith

Flanders Moss

A873

B8031

6

7

air Dr

208
ELRIG

Cunninghame Graham
Memorial

Dykehead

River

B822

Gartmore

A81

B8034

Forth

19

B8075

Dalmary

B835

A811

Arnprior

Kippen

Gargunnock

A811

West Highland
Way

209

Buchlyvie

B822

Cauldhame

8

G   Milton
Buchanan   H   J   K   B822   L   M   Touch Hills

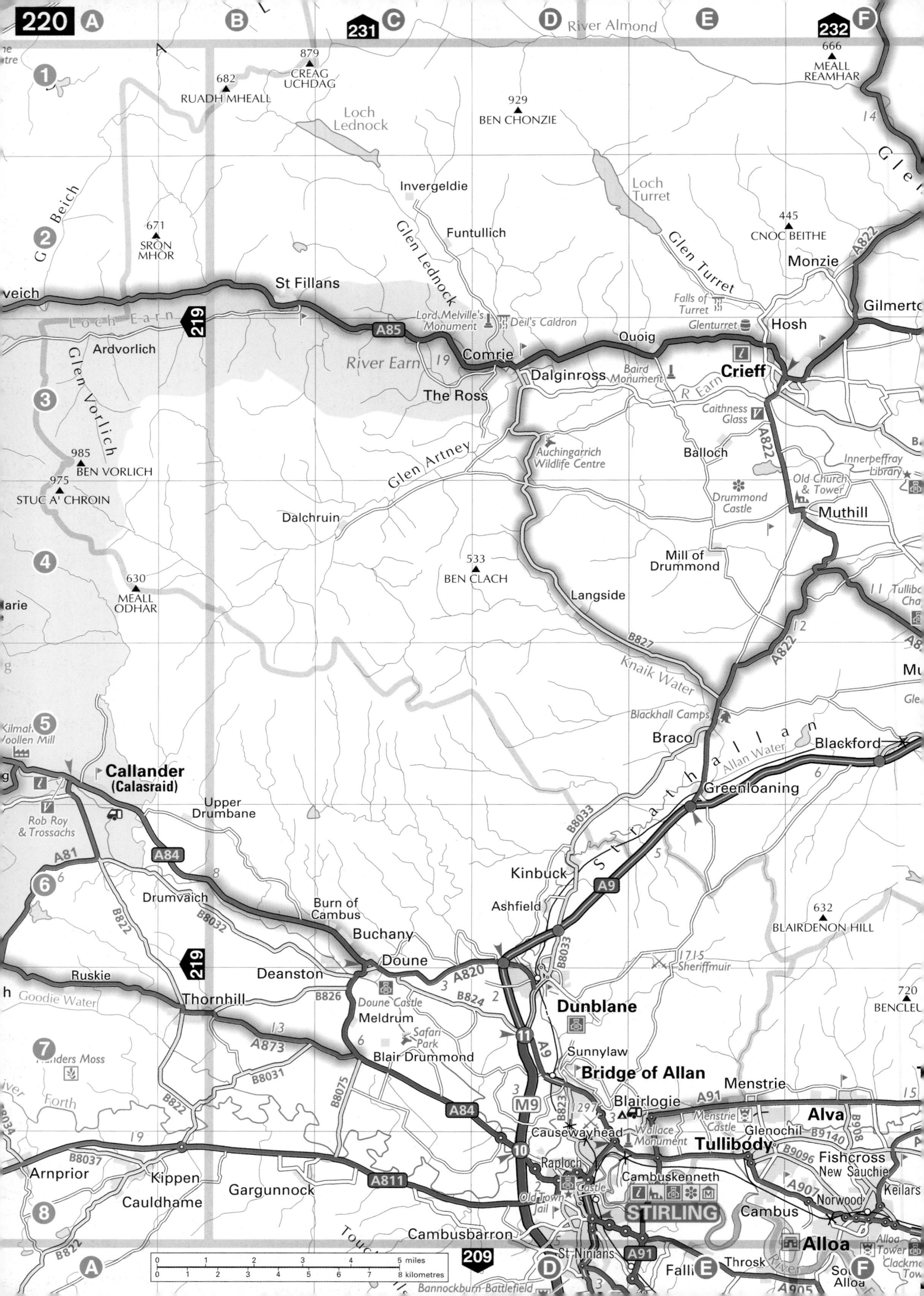

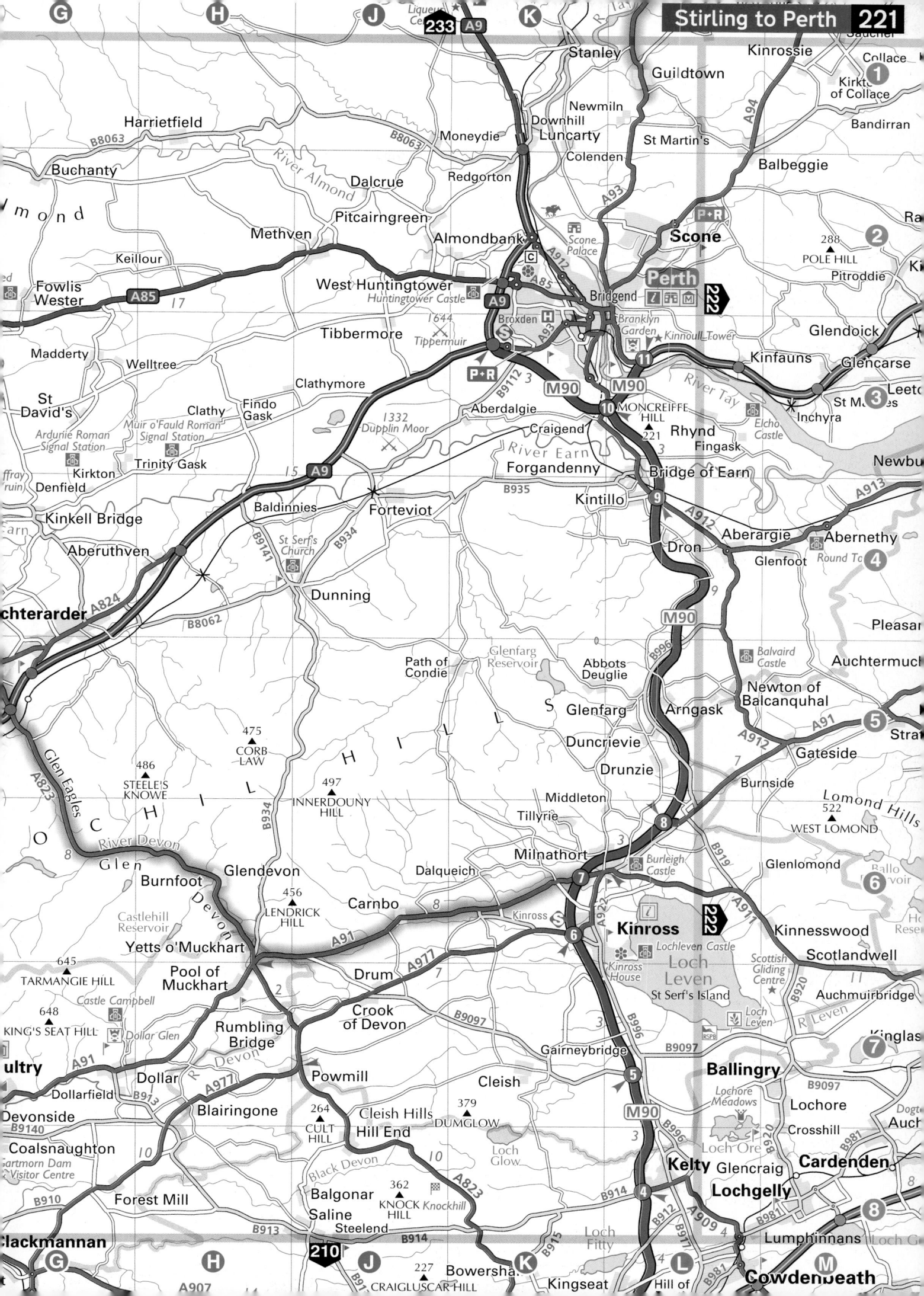

G   H   J   233 A9   K   1

Stanley
Kinrossie
Collace
Guildtown
Kirkton
of Collace
Bandirran
Harrietfield
Moneydie
Newmiln
Downhill
Luncarty
St Martin's
Balbeggie
Buchanty
B8063
B8063
Redgorton
Colenden
A94
2
Keillour
Dalcrue
288
POLE HILL
Methven
Pitcairngreen
Pitroddie
Fowlis
Wester
A85 17
West Huntingtower
Almondbank
A912
Scone
Palace
Scone
P+R
Perth
222
Huntingtower Castle
C
A9
Bridgend
Branklyn
Garden
Glendoick
Madderty
Welltree
Tibbermore
1644
A85
Broxden
A93
Kinnoull Tower
Kinfauns
Glencarse
Tippermuir
River Tay
3
St David's
Clathymore
P+R
B9112 3
M90
Aberdalgie
M90
Inchyra
Leeto
Ardunie Roman
Signal Station
Clathy
Findo Gask
1332
Dupplin Moor
Craigend
10
MONCREIFFE
HILL
Rhynd
Fingask
Elcho
Castle
Newbu
Muir o'Fauld Roman
Signal Station
Trinity Gask
A9 15
River Earn
221
A913
fray
ruin
Kirkton
Denfield
Baldinnies
Forteviot
Forgandenny
Bridge of Earn
9
Aberargie
Abernethy
4
Kinkell Bridge
B9141
St Serf's
Church
B934
B935
Kintillo
Dron
Glenfoot
Round To
Earn
Aberuthven
Dunning
9
chterarder
A824
B8062
Path of
Condie
Glenfarg
Reservoir
Abbots
Deuglie
M90
B996
Balvaird
Castle
Auchtermuc
Pleasar
475
CORB
LAW
S
Glenfarg
Arngask
Newton of
Balcanquhal
5
A91
486
STEELE'S
KNOWE
H
Duncrievie
A912
Gateside
Strat
Glen Eagles
A823
River Devon
B934
497
INNERDOUNY
HILL
I
Drunzie
Middleton
Tillyrie
Burnside
7
522
WEST LOMOND
Lomond Hills
6
Glen
Devon
L
Dalqueich
8
Milnathort
3
B919
Glenlomond
Ballo
voir
Burnfoot
Glendevon
456
LENDRICK
HILL
L
Carnbo
A91
8
Kinross
7
Burleigh
Castle
Kinnesswood
Scotlandwell
Castlehill
Reservoir
Yetts o'Muckhart
6
Kinross
S
Kinross
222
A911
Auchmuirbridge
ultry
A91
Pool of
Muckhart
Drum
A977
7
Kinross
House
Loch
Leven
St Serf's Island
Scottish
Gliding
Centre
B920
645
TARMANGIE HILL
Castle Campbell
2
Crook
of Devon
B9097
Loch
Leven
RSPB
11
648
KING'S SEAT HILL
Dollar Glen
Rumbling
Bridge
Gairneybridge
B9097
7
Kinglas
Dollar
Powmill
Cleish
5
M90
Ballingry
Dollarfield
Blairingone
264
CULT
HILL
Cleish Hills
Hill End
379
DUMGLOW
3
Lochore
Meadows
Lochore
B9097
Crosshill
Auch
Coalsnaughton
Forest Mill
10
Black Devon
10
A823
Loch
Glow
B996
B920
Kelty
Glencraig
Cardenden
Saline
Steelend
362
KNOCK
HILL
Knockhill
B914
Loch
Ore
Lochgelly
8
B910
B913
227
B914
Loch
Fitty
B912
A909
Lumphinnans
Loch Ge
lackmannan
A907
210
CRAIGLUSCAR HILL
Bowersha
Kingseat
Hill of
Cowdenbeath

G   H   210 J   K   L   M

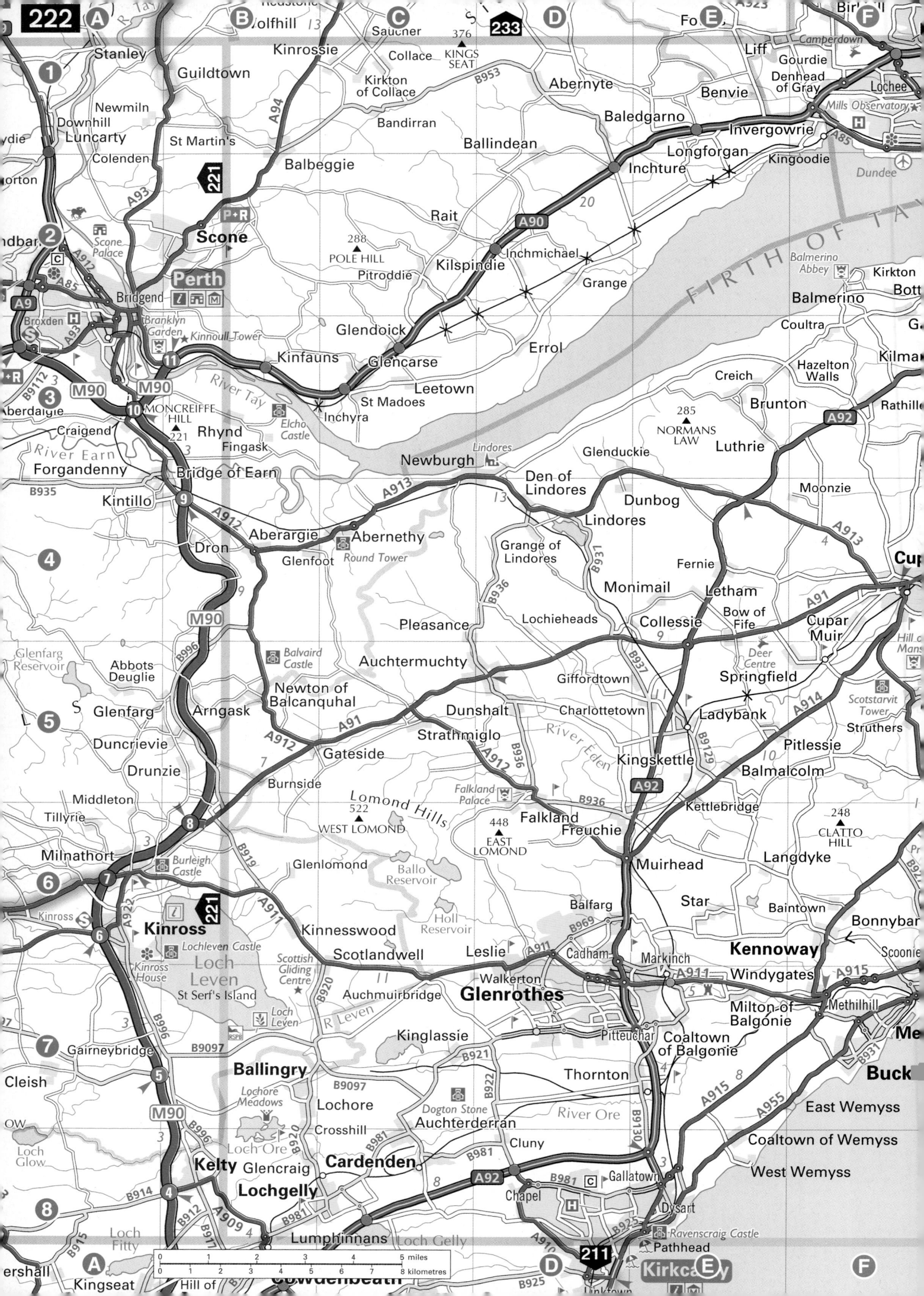

Grish
Clabhach
Ballyh
Hogh Bay
Totronal
Bagh a Chaisteil
(Castlebay)
Feall
Bay
Coll
Ach
Arileod
Uig
(Apr-Oct, Weds only)
RSPB
Calgary Point
Crossapol
Bay
Rudha
Fàsach
Loch Breachacha
Gunna
Caoles
Rudha Dubh
B8069
Rudha Port
Bhiosd
Clachan
Mor
Balephetrish
Bay
Ruaig
Loch
Bhasapoll
B8068
Haugh
Bay
Ballevullin
Cornoigmore
Kenovay
Gott
Bay
Kilkenneth
B8068
Tiree
Scarinish
Moss
Heylipoll
B8065
Middleton
B8065
Crossapol
TIREE
Barrapoll
Hynish Bay
Loch a
Phuill
B8067
Balemartine
Mannel
Rinn
Thorbhais
Balephuil
Bay
Hynish

0   1   2   3   4   5 miles
0   1   2   3   4   5   6   7   8 kilometres

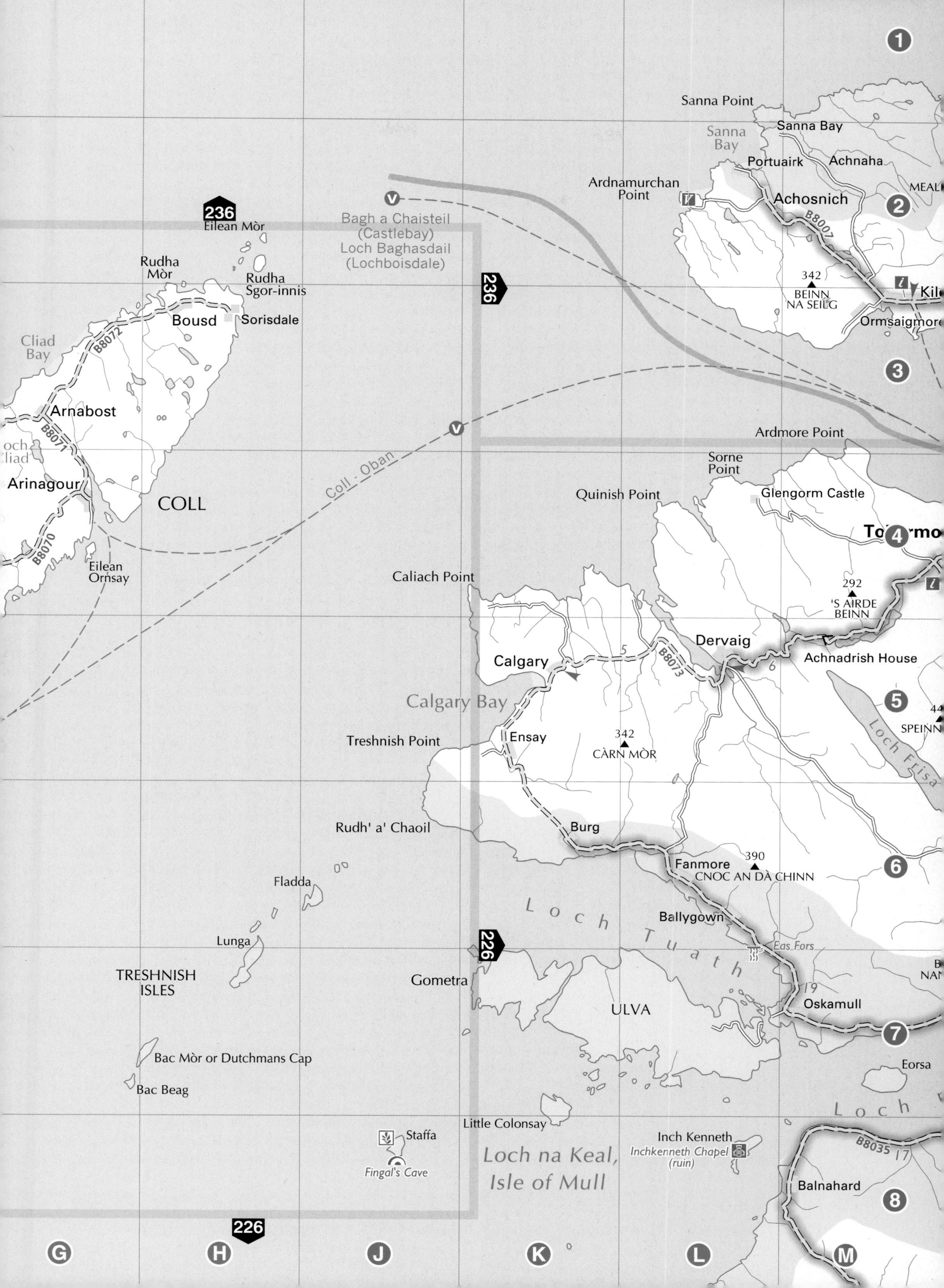

1

Sanna Point

Sanna Bay

Sanna Bay

Ardnamurchan Point

Portuairk   Achnaha

Achosnich

2

B8007

MEAL

342
BEINN
NA SEILG

i

Kil

Ormsaigmore

3

Ardmore Point

236
Eilean Mòr

Bagh a Chaisteil
(Castlebay)
Loch Baghasdail
(Lochboisdale)

236

V

V

Coll - Oban

Rudha Mòr

Rudha Sgor-innis

Bousd   Sorisdale

Cliad Bay

B8072

och liad

Arnabost

B8071

Arinagour

COLL

B8070

Eilean Ornsay

Sorne Point

Quinish Point

Glengorm Castle

To rmo
4

292
'S AIRDE BEINN

i

Caliach Point

Dervaig

B8073

Achnadrish House

5

Calgary

Loch Frisa

SPEINN

44

Calgary Bay

Treshnish Point

Ensay

342
CÀRN MÒR

Rudh' a' Chaoil

Burg

Fanmore
CNOC AN DÀ CHINN

390

6

Ballygown

Eas Fors

Loch Tuath

Fladda

Lunga

TRESHNISH ISLES

Gometra

226

ULVA

Oskamull

19

7

B
NAN

Bac Mòr or Dutchmans Cap

Eorsa

Bac Beag

Little Colonsay

Staffa

Fingal's Cave

**Loch na Keal,
Isle of Mull**

Inch Kenneth
Inchkenneth Chapel
(ruin)

Balnahard

B8035   17

Loch

8

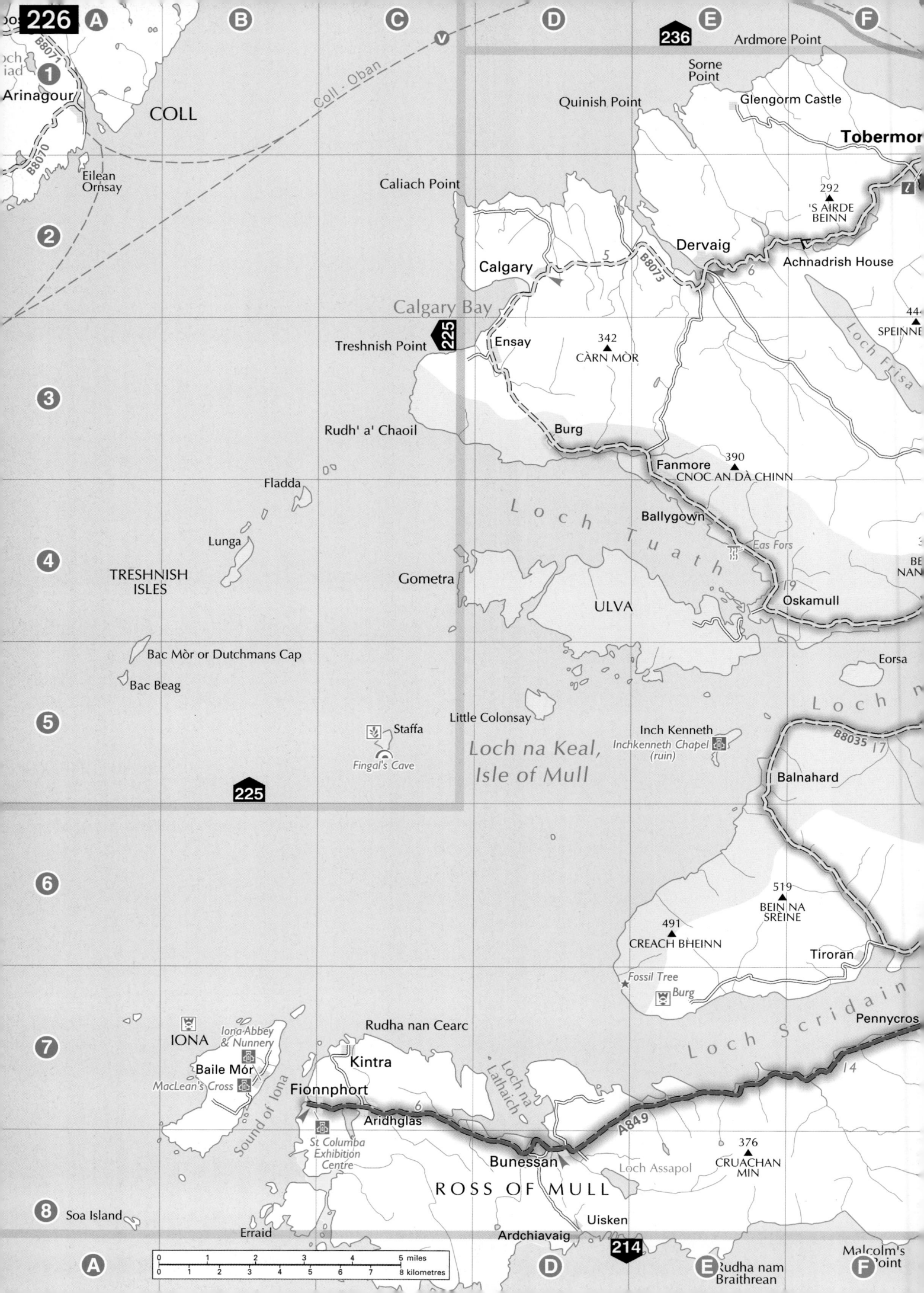

G   H   J   237   K   L

1
Liddesdale
A884
Lochuisge
20

571
BEINN
LADAIN
522
MEALL A' CHOISE
738
BEINN MHEADHOIN
2
Oronsay
Carna

Auliston
Point
Loch
Teacuis
Glen Dubh
228

Calve
Island
Drimnin
437
BEINN
BHUIDHE
550
SÌTHEAN NA RAPLAICH
Loch
Arienas
Acharn
Gleann Geal

Claggan
339
MEALL DAMH
3
Larachbeg
A848
B849
A884
Rannoch River
Achranich
Loch Téarnait

Fuinary
Loch
Aline

en Aros
Sound of Mull
Lochaline
464
GLAIS
BHEINN
514
AN
SLEAGHOCH
4
Aros
Glenaros House
Salen
A849
Fishnish
Point
Fishnish Pier
v

Killiechronan
B8035
2
Glen Forsa
11
Scallastle Bay
Rudha an
Ridire
Bernera
Island
Kilchera

Gruline
408
BEINN
NAN LUS
Altcreich
H
i
L
Macquarie
Mausoleum
ISLE
Loch Bà
636
BEINN
MHEADHON
Craignure
v
5

591
BEINN A' GHRÀIG
OF
766
DUN DA
GHAOITHE
Duart Bay
Duart
Point
Duart
Torosay

966
BEN
MORE
704
CRUACHAN
DEARG
MULL
17
A849
Lochdonhead
Lochdon
Gorten

Strathcoil
Loch Don
Grass Point
6
Glen More
247
CARN
BÀN
KERRERA

of
och
A849
698
BEN CREACH
Loch Spelve
Croggan
216

Loch
Fuaran
717
BEN
BUIE
Rudha Seanach
7

Pennyghael
503
BEINN NA
CROISE
Lochbuie
Loch
Uisg
337
MAOL
BÀN
Ar

Leidle Water
Carsaig
Rudha
Dubh
Loch Buie
377
DRUIM
FADA
Colonsay - Oban
v
Clachan
B844
8

6
NN
GACH
FIRTH   OF   LORN
Insh
Island
Clachan-Seil
SEIL
Ellenabeich
Easdale
Balvicar

G   H   J   215   K   L   M

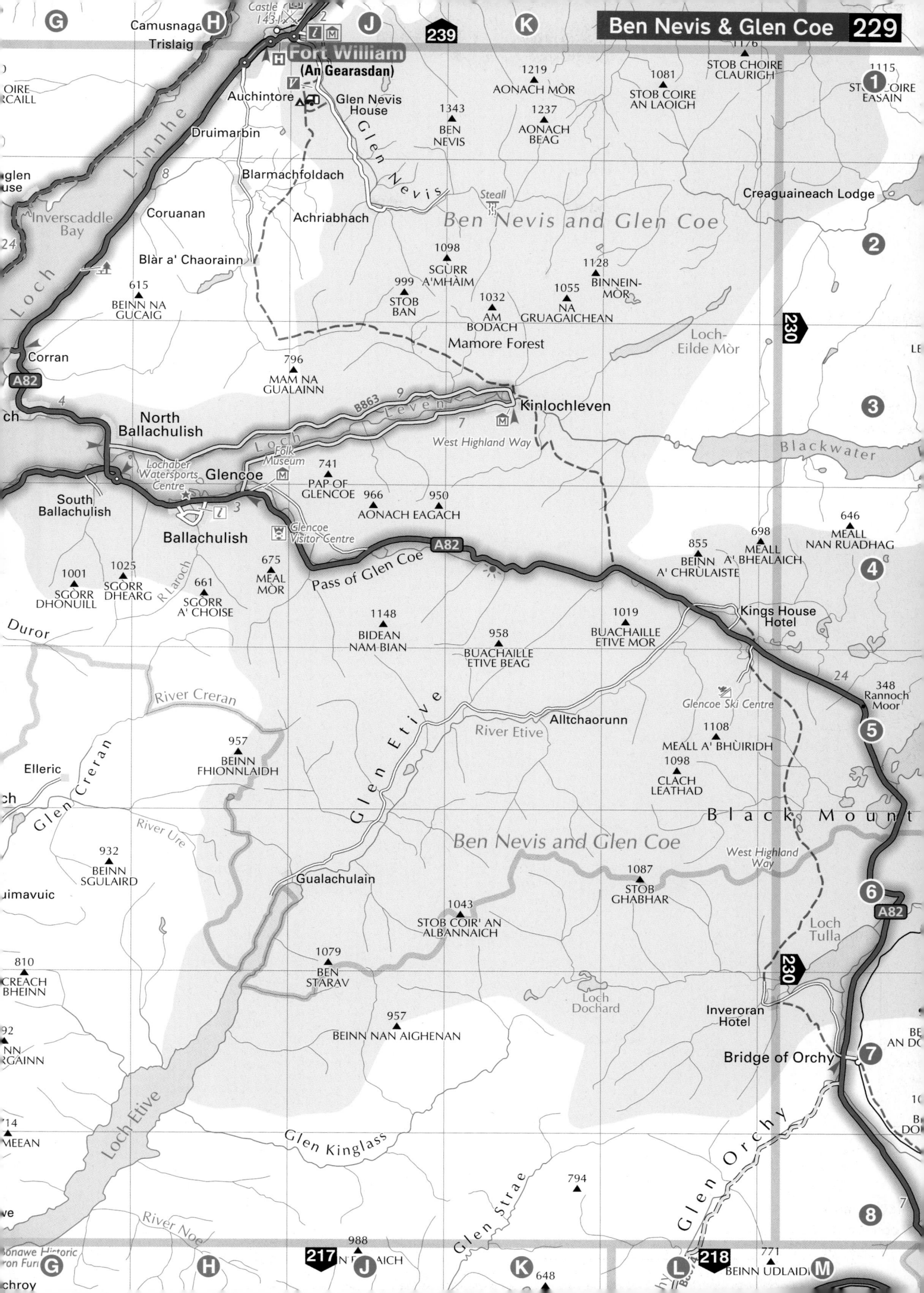

G
H
J
239
K
1

Camusnaga
Trislaig
Castle 143·1
Fort William
(An Gearasdan)
Auchintore
Glen Nevis
House
Druimarbin
1176
STOB CHOIRE
CLAURIGH
1115
ST COIRE
EASAIN

AONACH MÒR 1219
1081
STOB COIRE
AN LAOIGH

1343
BEN
NEVIS
1237
AONACH
BEAG

Blarmachfoldach

Loch Linnhe

Inverscaddle
Bay

Coruanan

Achriabhach

Steall

Ben Nevis and Glen Coe

2

Blàr a' Chaorainn

1098
SGÙRR
A'MHÀIM

1128
BINNEIN-
MÒR

Creaguaineach Lodge

615
BEINN NA
GUCAIG

999
STOB
BAN

1032
AM
BODACH

1055
NA
GRUAGAICHEAN

Corran

796
MAM NA
GUALAINN

Mamore Forest

Loch-
Eilde Mòr

230

3

A82

B863
9
Leven
7

Kinlochleven

North
Ballachulish

Loch

West Highland Way

Blackwater

Lochaber
Watersports
Centre

Folk
Museum

741

Glencoe

PAP OF
GLENCOE

966
AONACH EAGACH
950

646
MEALL
NAN RUADHAG

South
Ballachulish

3

Glencoe
Visitor Centre

698
MEALL
A' BHEALAICH

4

Ballachulish

855
BEINN
A' CHRÙLAISTE

1001
SGÒRR
DHONUILL

1025
SGÒRR
DHEARG

661
SGÒRR
A' CHOISE

675
MEAL
MÒR

Pass of Glen Coe

A82

Kings House
Hotel

Duror

1148
BIDEAN
NAM BIAN

958
BUACHAILLE
ETIVE BEAG

1019
BUACHAILLE
ETIVE MOR

24

348
Rannoch
Moor

R Laroch

Glencoe Ski Centre

5

River Creran

Glen Etive

River Etive

Alltchaorunn

1108
MEALL A' BHÙIRIDH

Elleric

957
BEINN
FHIONNLAIDH

1098
CLACH
LEATHAD

Black Mount

Glen Creran

River Ure

Ben Nevis and Glen Coe

West Highland Way

932
BEINN
SGULAIRD

Gualachulain

1087
STOB
GHABHAR

6

A82

uimavuic

1043
STOB COIR' AN
ALBANNAICH

Loch
Tulla

810
CREACH
BHEINN

1079
BEN
STARAV

230

92
NN
RGAINN

Loch
Dochard

Inveroran
Hotel

957
BEINN NAN AIGHENAN

Bridge of Orchy

7

Loch Etive

Glen Kinglass

BE
AN DO

14
MEEAN

River Noe

Glen Strae

794

Glen Orchy

8

Bonawe Historic
ron Furn

988
N F AICH

217

G
H
J
648

K
771
BEINN UDLAIDH
218
L
M

chroy

G H J 241 K

1

1008
BEINN
UDLAMAIN
991
SGAIRNEACH
MHOR

Dalnaspidal

Loch Garry

Loch
Con

Dalnacardoch

Glen Garry

A9

491
CRAIG
BHAGAILTEACH

2

Cl
Donnachaidh

Calvine Bruar

Struan

Pitagowan
Old Struan
232
Blai

Loch
Errochty

841
BEINN
MHOLACH

Trinafour

B847

Glen Errochty

Tay Forest Park

3

511
TORR
DUBH

892
BEINN
A' CHUALLAICH

Tressait B8019

Queen's
View

Tay
Forest Park

lichonan

Loch Rannoch

Kinloch
Rannoch

Drumchastle

Dunalastair

B846

R Tummel

Tummel
Bridge

Loch Tummel

Frenich

Foss

Loch Tumm

Daloist

Tay Forest Park

4

Inverhadden

Tempar

Dunalastair
Water

Carie

Camghouran

Tay Forest Park

Loch Rannoch and Glen Lyon

1081
SCHIEHALLION

Glengoulandie
Deer Park

Tay Forest
Park

780
MEALL
TAIRNEACHAN

780
FARRAGON
HILL

Loch
Glassie

745
MEALL A' MHUIC

824
BEINN
DEARG

1027
CARN
GORM

1042
CARN
MAIRG

B846

5

Menzies

We

Camserney

Dull

Dewars

Coshieville

Keltneyburn

G

en Lyon

Bridge of Balgie

River Lyon

River Tay

Fortingall

Tay
Forest
Park

River Tay

Croftmoraig
Stone Circle

6

780
MEALL
LUAIDHE

924
MEALL A' CHOIRE
LEITH

1116
MEALL
GARBH

1000
MEALL
GREIGH

Fearnan

Acharn

Kenmore

A827

232

E

IGHREAG

1214
BEN LAWERS

Lochan na
Làirige

Leckbuie

713
BEINN
BHREAC

The Crannog
Centre

Glen Quaich

MEAL

7

Ben Lawers

Lawers

A827
25

Loch Tay

River Quaich

A

864
SRON A' CHAOINEIDH

N

802
MEALL NAM
FUARAN

Milton
Morenish

Morenish

Ardeonaig

B

River Almond

8

Moirlanich
Longhouse

Finlarig

Killin

Breadalbane
Folklore Centre

Dochar

L

A

Y

D

682

879
CREAG
UCHDAG

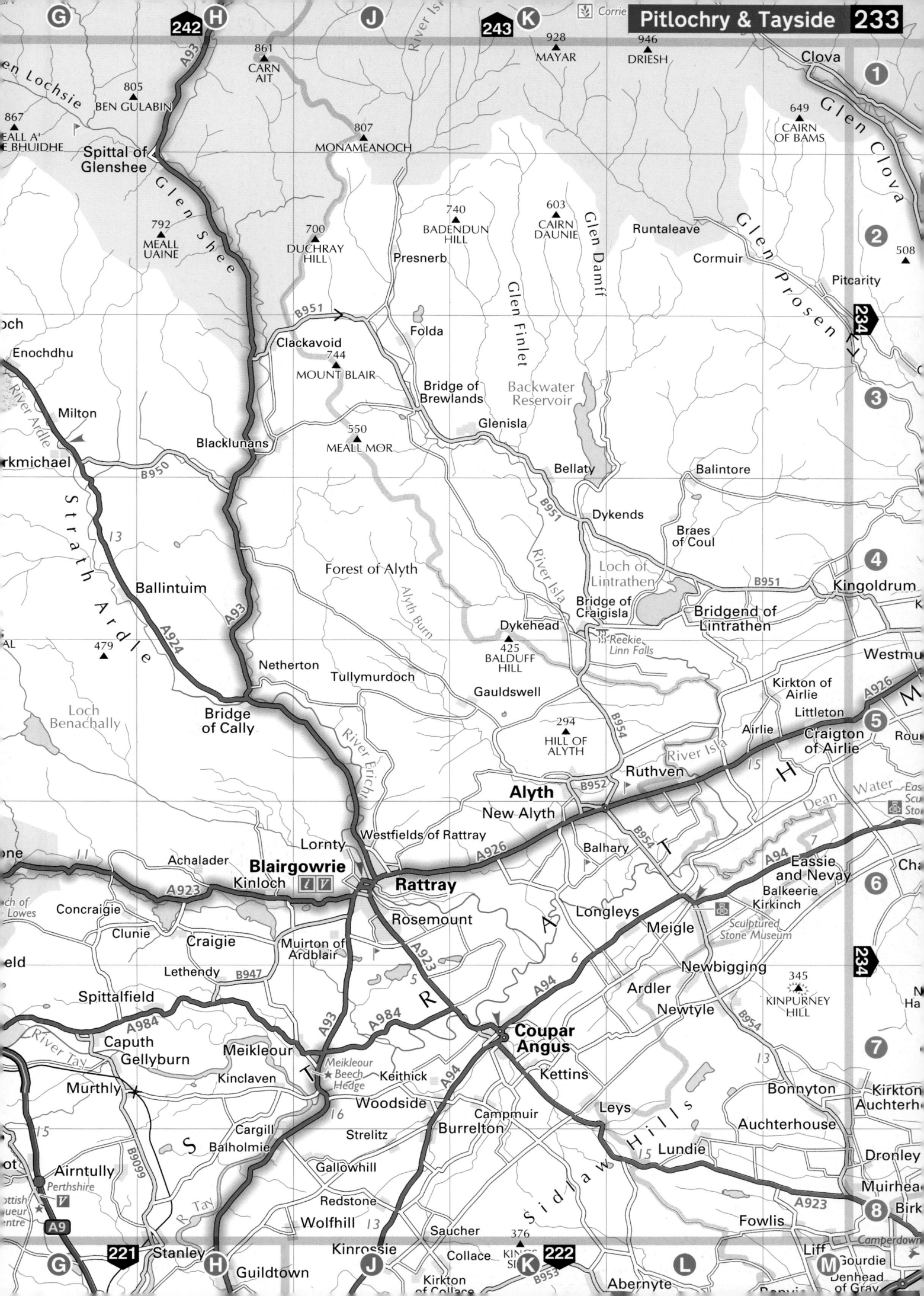

🌿 *Corrie*

G   242 H   J   243 K

River Isl

1

928
▲ MAYAR
946
▲ DRIESH
Clova

Glen Clova

861
▲ CARN
AIT

805
▲ BEN GULABIN

Glen Lochsie

867
▲ EALL A'
E BHUIDHE

Spittal of
Glenshee

807
▲ MONAMEANOCH

649
▲ CAIRN
OF BAMS

2

Runtaleave

Cormuir

508
▲

Pitcarity

234

792
▲ MEALL
UAINE

700
▲ DUCHRAY
HILL

740
▲ BADENDUN
HILL

603
▲ CAIRN
DAUNIE

Glen Damff

Glen Prosen

3

och
Enochdhu

Glen Shee

Milton

River Ardle

kmichael

B951

Clackavoid
744
▲ MOUNT BLAIR

Folda

Presnerb

Bridge of
Brewlands

Glen Finlet

Backwater
Reservoir

Glenisla

Balintore

4

Blacklunans

B950

550
▲ MEALL MOR

Bellaty

River Isla

Dykends

Braes
of Coul

B951

Loch of
Lintrathen

Kingoldrum

Strath Ardle

13

Ballintuim

A93

A924

Forest of Alyth

Alyth Burn

Bridge of
Craigisla

Bridgend of
Lintrathen

B951

Westmu

5

479
▲

Loch
Benachally

Netherton

Tullymurdoch

Dykehead
425
▲ BALDUFF
HILL

Gauldswell

Reekie
Linn Falls

Kirkton of
Airlie

Littleton

Airlie

Craigton
of Airlie

A926

Rou

Bridge
of Cally

294
▲ HILL OF
ALYTH

B954

River Isla

15

H

Water

Eas
Scu
Sto

Dean

one

11

Achalader

Kinloch

River Ericht

Blairgowrie

i V

Lornty

Westfields of Rattray

Alyth

New Alyth

B952

Ruthven

A94

Eassie
and Nevay

7

6

Balkeerie
Kirkinch

6

Concraigie

Clunie

Craigie

Muirton of
Ardblair

A923

Rattray

Rosemount

A926

Balhary

B954

Longleys

Meigle

Sculptured
Stone Museum

Newbigging

345
▲

ch of
Lowes

Lethendy

B947

5

A93

A923

A984

A

R

A94

Ardler

Newtyle

B954

KINPURNEY
HILL

234

eld

Spittalfield

A984

Caputh
Gellyburn

Meikleour

Kinclaven

Meikleour
★ Beech
Hedge

Keithick

A94

T

R

6

**Coupar
Angus**

Kettins

Leys

Lundie

Bonnyton

Kirkton
Auchterh

7

River Tay

Murthly

Cargill

Balholmie

Woodside

Strelitz

Campmuir

Burrelton

Sidlaw Hills

15

Auchterhouse

Dronley

15

16

S

Airntully

Perthshire
V

Scottish
queur
entre
★

A9

B9099

Stanley

221 G

Guildtown

H

Gallowhill

Redstone

Wolfhill 13

Kinrossie

J

Saucher

Collace

376
▲

KINGS
SI

222 K

B953

Kirkton
of Collace

Abernyte

L

Fowlis

Liff

Gourdie
Denhead
of Gray

A923

8

Birk

Camperdown

Muirhea

M

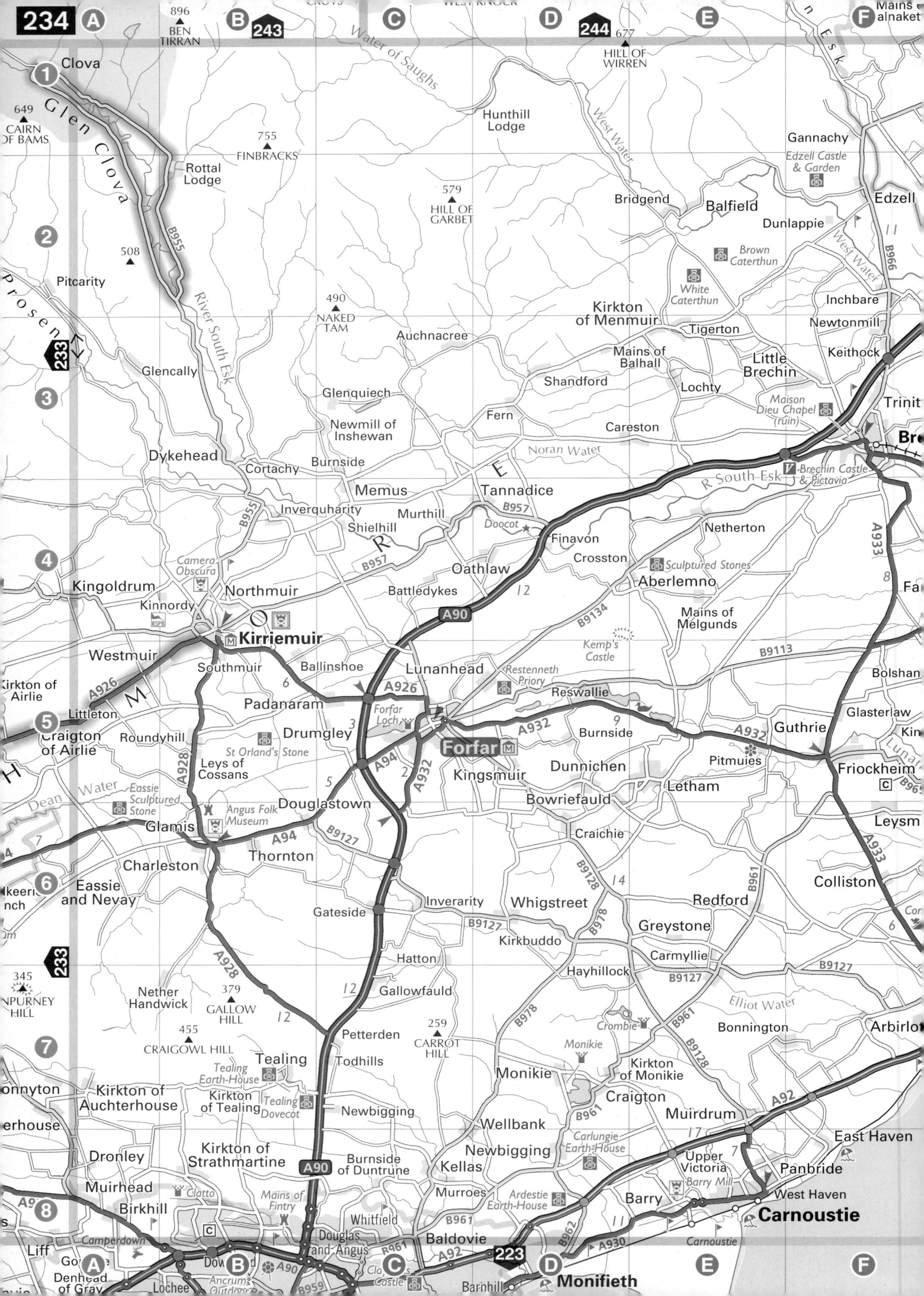

A Bhrideanach

570
▲
ORVAL

MOR

Ru na Roinne

246

Kinloch
Loch
Scresort

RÙM

810
▲
ASKIVAL

Harris
Bay

763
▲
SGÙRR NAN
GILLEAN

The Small Isles

Rudha nam
Meirleach

Sound of Rùm

Bay of
Laig

Cleadale

Rudha an
Fhasaidh

Laig

299
▲
AN
CRUACHAN

EIGG

Kildonn

393
▲
AN SGÙRR

Sandavore

Sound of Eigg

Eilean
Chathastail

Eilean
nan Each

MUCK

Port Mor

Sanna Point

Sanna Bay

Sanna
Bay

Portuairk

Achnaha

MEALL

Ardnamurchan
Point

Achosnich

B8007

V

Bagh a Chaisteil
(Castlebay)
Loch Baghasdail
(Lochboisdale)

342
▲
BEINN
NA SEILG

Kilc

Eilean Mòr

Rudha
Mòr

Rudha
Sgor-innis

Bousd

Sorisdale

COLL

225

Ormsaigmore

Cliad
Bay

B8072

Coll · Oban

V

ost

B8071

0   1   2   3   4   5 miles
0 1 2 3 4 5 6 7 8 kilometres

Ardmore Point

Arinagour

Sorne
P

226

Quinish Point

Glengorm Castle

KNOYD

Inverie Bay

1

Rudha Raonuill

BEINN

2

lesm

Loch Nevis

Tarbet

Swordland

238

Loch Morar

Lettermorar

Meoble

3

MEITH

River Meoble

G

Point of Sleat

H

Ard Thurinish

247

J

V

K anda

Courteachan

Mallaig (Malaig)

V

Mallaigvaig

547

CÀRN A'GHOBHAIR

437

SGURR BHUIDHE

Loch an Nostaire

Glasnacardoch Bay

B8008

Beoraidbeg

Morar

Bracora

Bracorina

Glenancross

A830

503

CÀRN A' MHÀDAIDH-RUAIDH

Bunacaimb

Eilean Ighe

Back of Keppoch

600

SIDHEAN MOR

Arisaig

Loch nan Ceall

10

Prince Charlie's Cairn

Kinlochnanuagh

Luinga Mhòr

Rudh' Arisaig

103

CRUACH DOIRE

Druimindarroch

Arisaig House

Loch nan Uamh

Polnish

Ardnish

Lochailort

Inverailort

Loch Eilt

4

Sound of Arisaig

Rudha Choalais

Loch Ailort

A861

877

ROIS-BHEINN

712

Smearisary

Glenuig

21

664

BEINN GAIRE

5

Eilean Shona

Loch Moidart

Tioram

Seven Men of Moidart

Kinlochmoidart

Brunery

Glen Forsian

Glen Moidart

MOIDART

Loch S

6

Loch

Glen Hurich

Rudha Aird Druimnich

Ockle Point

Morar, Moidart and Ardnamurchan

239

BEINN BHREAC

Ardmolich

Dalnabreck

Dalelia

228

Polloch

Loch Doilo

Lilmory

Ockle

Ardtoe

Shielfoot

Mingarrypark

356

BEINN BHREAC

Kentra

B8044

Blain

Branault

Arevegaig

ARDNAMURCHAN

Acharacle

Claish Moss

SUNAR

846

BEINN RESIPOL

7

Loch Mudle

437

Salen

A861

Resipole

12

527

BEN HIANT

19

Glenbeg

512

BEN LAGA

B8007

Loch

Sunart

Glencripesdale

Anaheilt

Ardslignish

Glenborrodale

Laga

RSPB

339

GEÀRR CHREAG

Camasine

Woodend

Ardnastang

8

Oronsay

Carna

Auliston Point

227

Liddesdale

Camasachoirce

A884

M

G

H

J

K

L

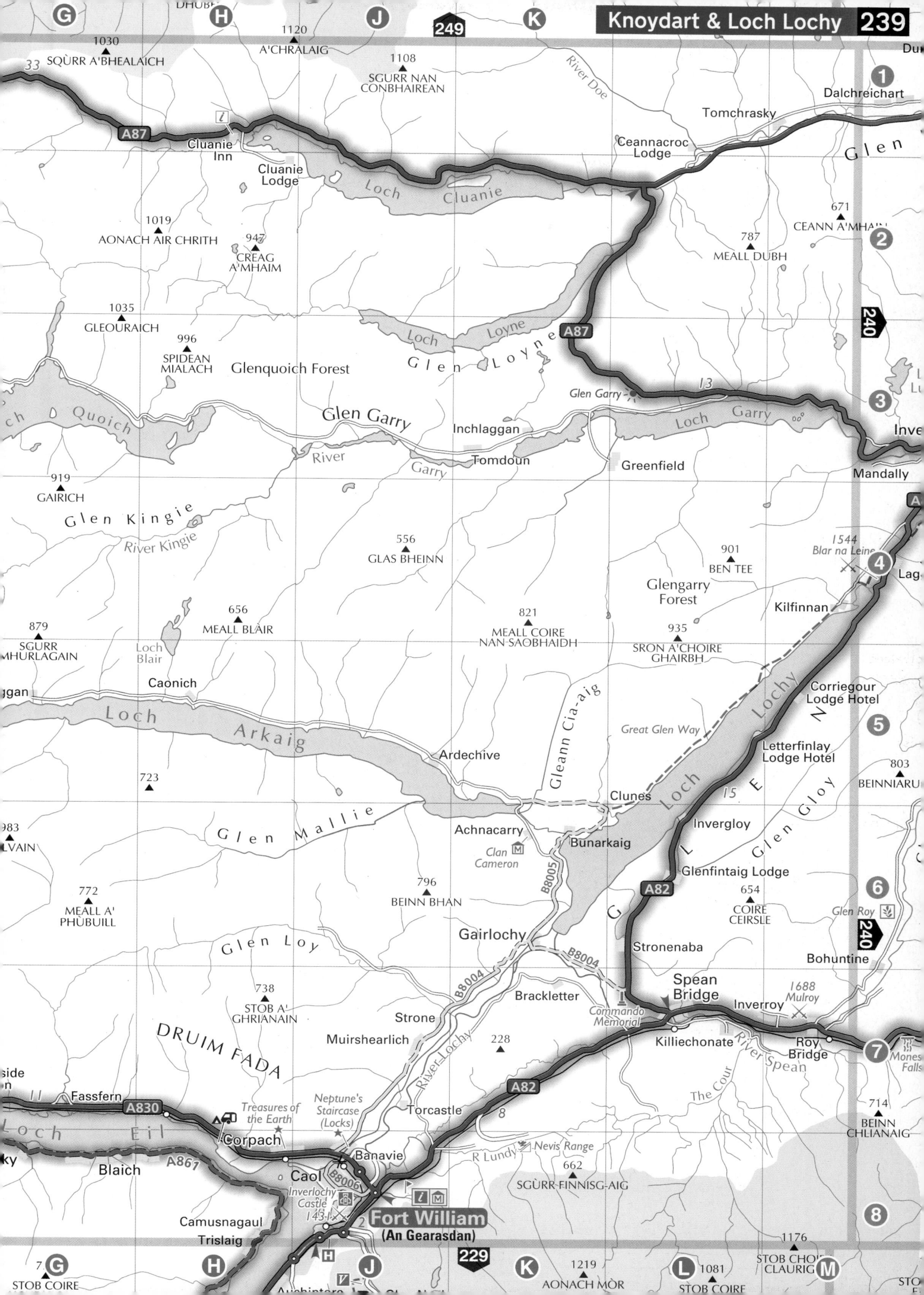

G H J 249 K

1030 SQÙRR A'BHEALAICH
33
A87
Cluanie Inn
Cluanie Lodge

DHUBE
1120 A'CHRALAIG
1108 SGURR NAN CONBHAIREAN

River Doe

Dalchreichart
Tomchrasky
Ceannacroc Lodge
Glen
1

Loch Cluanie

671 CEANN A'MHAIN
2
787 MEALL DUBH
240

1019 AONACH AIR CHRITH
947 CREAG A'MHAIM

1035 GLEOURAICH
996 SPIDEAN MIALACH
Glenquoich Forest

Loch Loyne
A87
Glen Loyne
13
Glen Garry
Loch Garry
3
Inve

ch D Quoich
Glen Garry
Inchlaggan
Tomdoun
Greenfield
Mandally
A

River Garry

919 GAIRICH
Glen Kingie
River Kingie

556 GLAS BHEINN

901 BEN TEE
935 SRON A'CHOIRE GHAIRBH
Glengarry Forest

1544 Blar na Leine
4
Lag

656 MEALL BLAIR
821 MEALL COIRE NAN-SAOBHAIDH
Kilfinnan

879 SGURR MHURLAGAIN
Loch Blair
Caonich

Corriegour Lodge Hotel
5
803 BEINNIARU

ggan
Loch Arkaig
Ardechive
Gleann Cia-aig
Great Glen Way
Loch Lochy
N
Letterfinlay Lodge Hotel

983 LVAIN
723
Clunes
15
E

Glen Mallie
Achnacarry
Clan Cameron
Bunarkaig
Invergloy
Glen Gloy
6
654 COIRE CEIRSLE
Glen Roy
240

772 MEALL A' PHÙBUILL
796 BEINN BHAN
B8005
Glenfintaig Lodge

Gairlochy
G
Stronenaba
1688 Mulroy
Bohuntine

Glen Loy
738 STOB A' GHRIANAIN
Brackletter
B8004
Spean Bridge
Inverroy
Roy Bridge
7
Mones Falls

DRUIM FADA
Strone
Muirshearlich
River Lochy
228
Commando Memorial
Killiechonate
River Spean
714 BEINN CHLIANAIG

side
n
Fassfern
A830
Treasures of the Earth
Neptune's Staircase (Locks)
Torcastle
8
A82
The Cour

Loch Eil
A861
Corpach
Banavie
R Lundy
Nevis Range
662 SGÙRR-FINNISG-AIG

ky
Blaich
Camusnagaul
Trislaig
Caol
B8006
Inverlochy Castle
143
Fort William (An Gearasdan)
229

7 G STOB COIRE
H
J
Auchintore
K AONACH MÒR 1219
L STOB COIRE 1081
M STOB CHOIR CLAURIG 1176
8

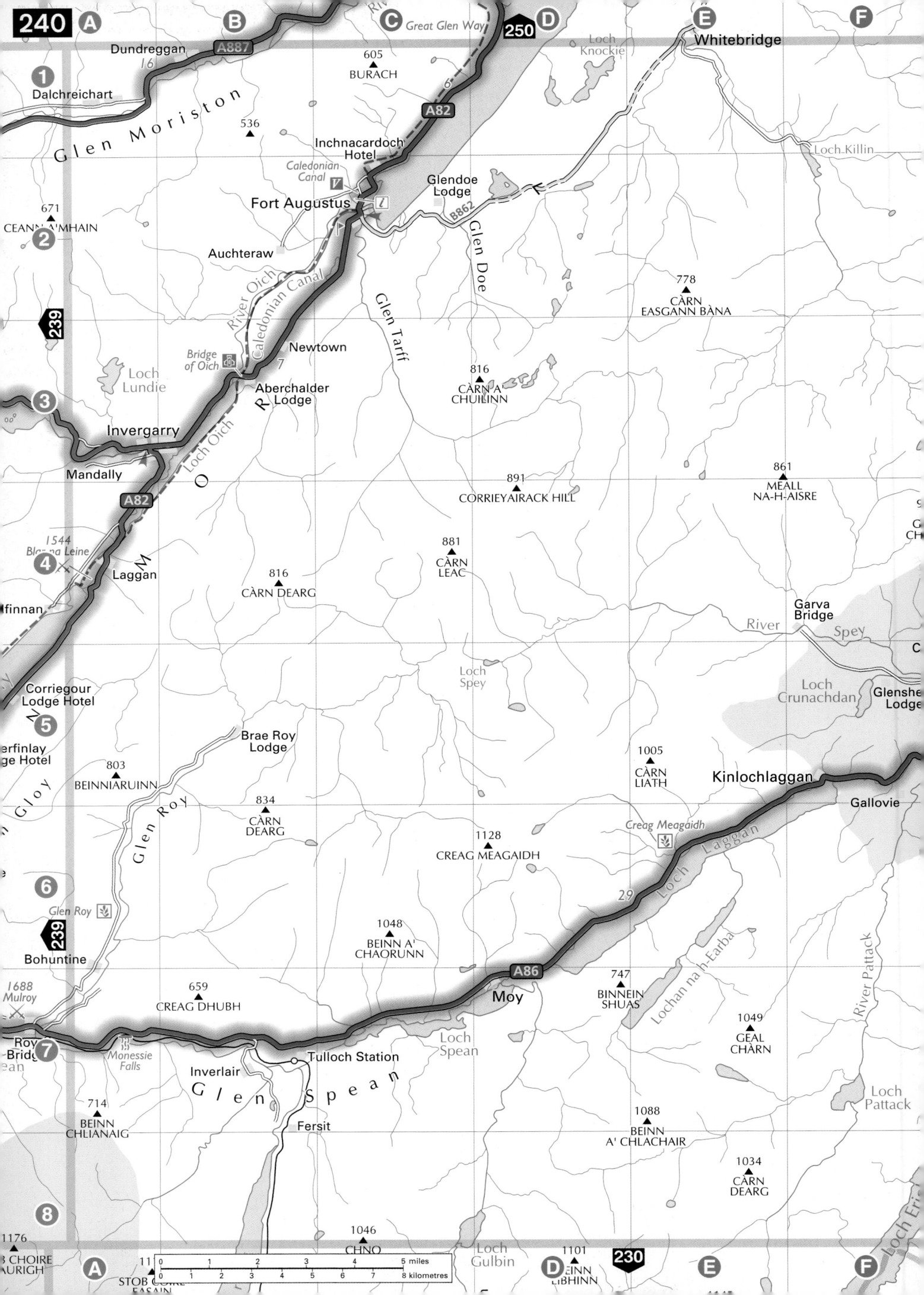

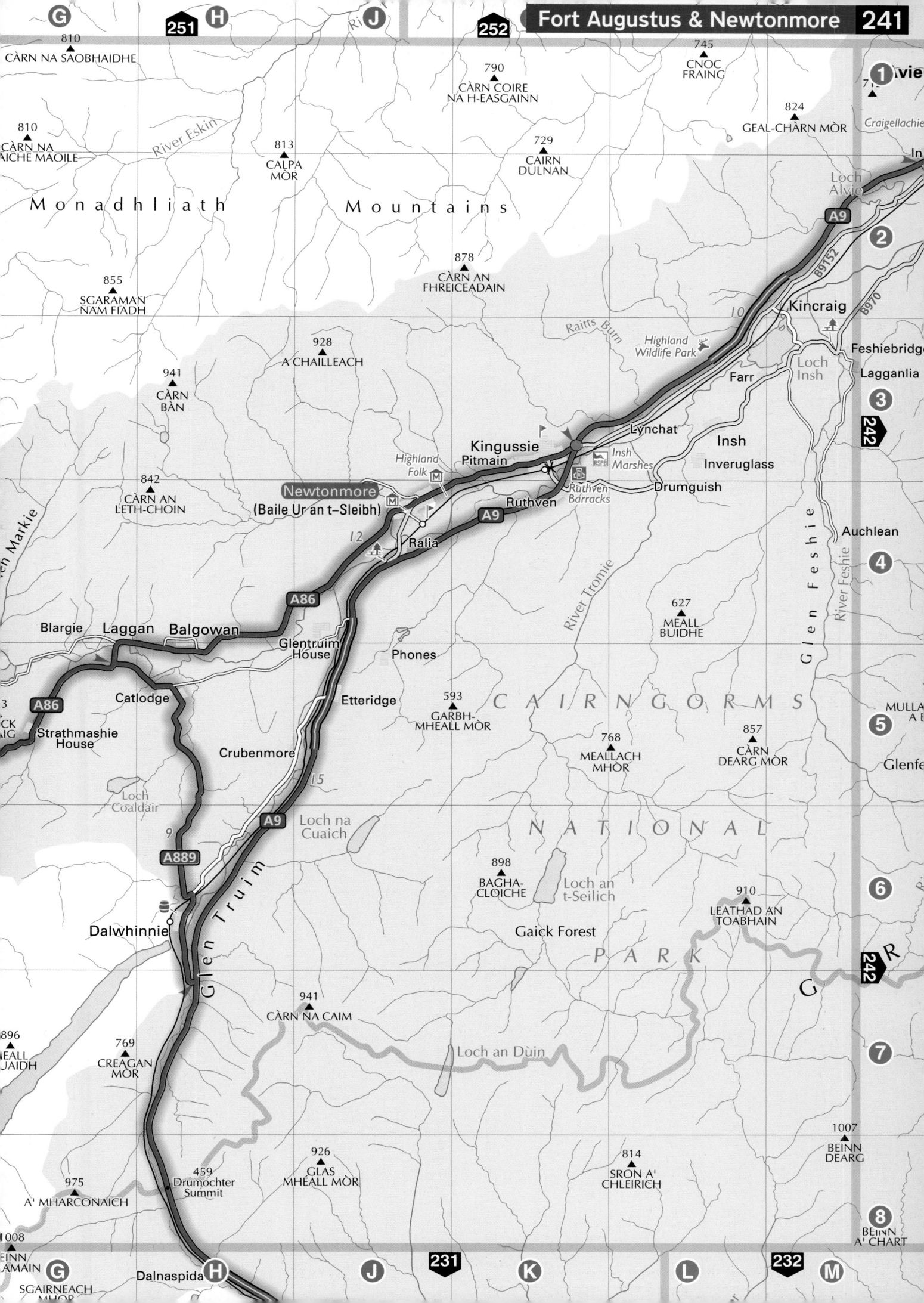

G | 251 | H | J | 252

810
▲
CÀRN NA SAOBHAIDHE

810
▲
CÀRN NA
AICHE MAOILE

River Eskin

813
▲
CALPA
MÒR

M o n a d h l i a t h   M o u n t a i n s

790
▲
CÀRN COIRE
NA H-EASGAINN

745
▲
CNOC
FRAING

1 ▲ vie

824
▲
GEAL-CHÀRN MÒR

Craigellachie

855
▲
SGARAMAN
NAM FIADH

729
▲
CAIRN
DULNAN

Loch Alvie

A9

2

878
▲
CÀRN AN
FHREICEADAIN

B9152

941
▲
CÀRN
BÀN

928
▲
A CHAILLEACH

Raitts Burn

Highland
Wildlife Park

10

B970

Kincraig

Feshiebridg

842
▲
CÀRN AN
LETH-CHOIN

*Highland
Folk* M

Kingussie
Pitmain

Lynchat

*Loch
Insh*

Farr

Insh

Lagganlia

3

242

Inveruglass

Newtonmore
(Baile Ur an t-Sleibh) M

A9

Ruthven

Ruthven
Barracks

RSPB

Insh
Marshes

Drumguish

Auchlean

4

Glen Markie

Ralia

River Tromie

627
▲
MEALL
BUIDHE

Glen Feshie

River Feshie

A86

Blargie   Laggan   Balgowan

Glentruim
House

Phones

C A I R N G O R M S

MULLA
A B

5

A86
CK
IG

Strathmashie
House

Catlodge

Etteridge

593
▲
GARBH-
MHEALL MÒR

768
▲
MEALLACH
MHOR

857
▲
CÀRN
DEARG MÒR

Glenfe

Crubenmore

15

N A T I O N A L

*Loch
Coaldair*

A9

*Loch na
Cuaich*

898
▲
BAGHA-
CLOICHE

*Loch an
t-Seilich*

910
▲
LEATHAD AN
TOABHAIN

6

A889

9

Gaick Forest

P A R K

242

R

896
▲
EALL
JAIDH

Dalwhinnie

Glen Truim

G

941
▲
CÀRN NA CAIM

Loch an Dùin

7

769
▲
CREAGAN
MOR

1007
▲
BEINN
DEARG

975
▲
A' MHARCONAICH

459
▲
Drumochter
Summit

926
▲
GLAS
MHÉALL MÒR

814
▲
SRON A'
CHLEIRICH

1008
▲
EINN
AMAIN

G

H

Dalnaspida

J | 231 | K | L | 232 | M

8
BEINN
A' CHART

SGAIRNEACH
MHOR

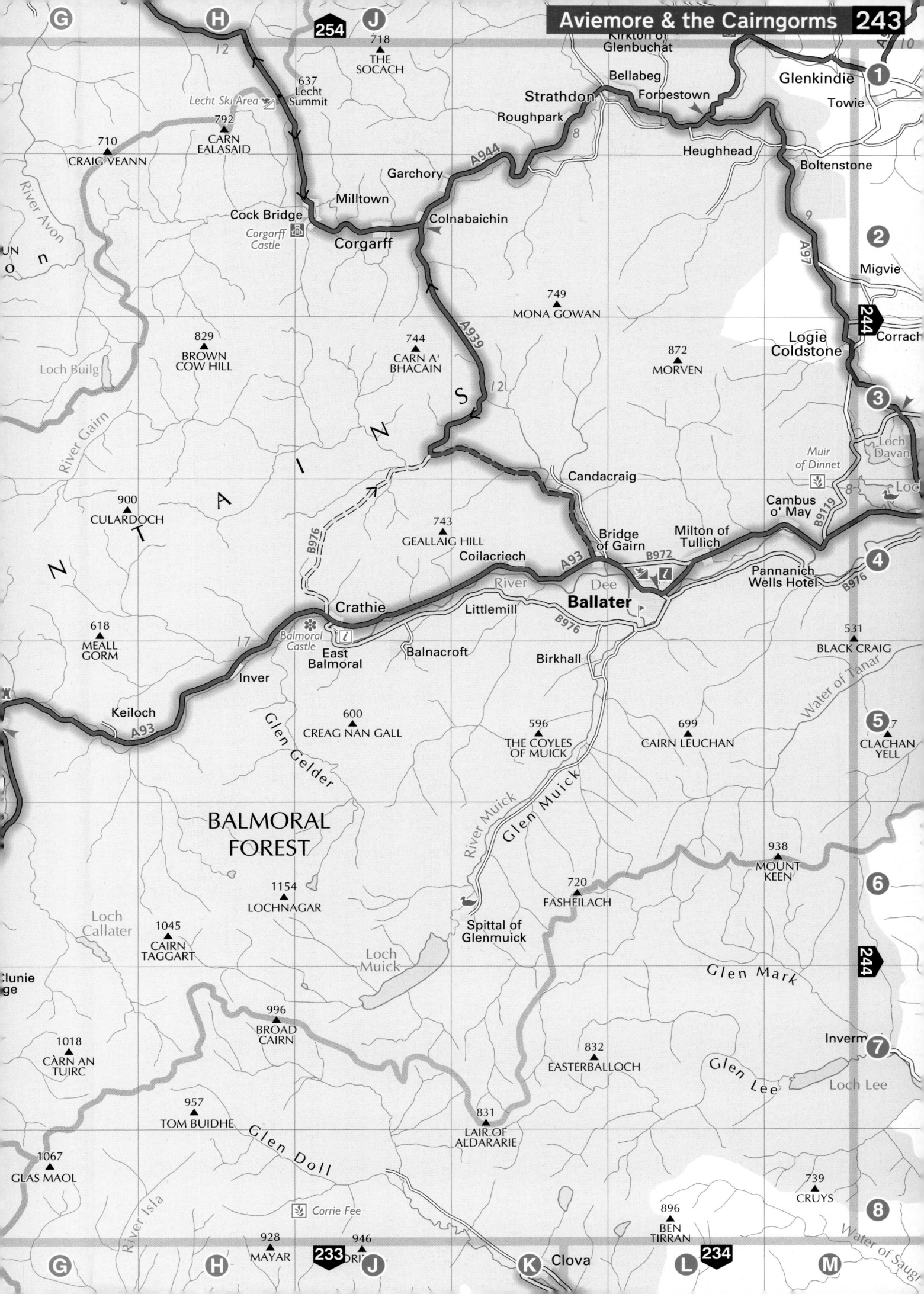

G **H** 254 **J**

12

718
▲ THE
SOCACH

637 Lecht
Summit

Lecht Ski Area

Loch Buig

792
▲ CARN
EALASAID

710
▲
CRAIG VEANN

Milltown

Cock Bridge

Corgarff Castle

Corgarff

Colnabaichin

Kirkton of
Glenbuchat

Bellabeg
Strathdon   Forbestown
Roughpark

A944   Heughhead

Garchory

749
▲ MONA GOWAN

Glenkindie **1**
Towie

Boltenstone

A97   9

2
Migvie

244
Corrach

829
▲ BROWN
COW HILL

744
▲ CARN A'
BHACAIN

A939

12

River Avon

Loch Buig

872
▲ MORVEN

Logie
Coldstone

3
Loch
Davan

*Muir
of Dinnet*

900
▲
CULARDOCH

B976

743
▲
GEALLAIG HILL

Candacraig

Coilacriech

Cambus
o' May

B9119   8   Loc

Bridge
of Gairn

Milton of
Tullich

B972

4

River Gairn

A93

River Dee

Ballater

Pannanich
Wells Hotel

B976

618
▲ MEALL
GORM

Crathie

Littlemill

B976

531
▲
BLACK CRAIG

Balmoral Castle

East
Balmoral

Balnacroft

Birkhall

Water of Tanar

Inver

600
▲
CREAG NAN GALL

596
▲ THE COYLES
OF MUICK

699
▲
CAIRN LEUCHAN

5
.7
CLACHAN
YELL

Keiloch
A93

17

Glen Gelder

**BALMORAL
FOREST**

1154
▲
LOCHNAGAR

River Muick

Glen Muick

720
▲
FASHEILACH

938
▲
MOUNT
KEEN

6

*Loch
Callater*

1045
▲
CAIRN
TAGGART

Spittal of
Glenmuick

*Loch
Muick*

244
Glen Mark

Clunie
ge

996
▲
BROAD
CAIRN

832
▲
EASTERBALLOCH

Inverm **7**

Glen Lee

Loch Lee

1018
▲
CÀRN AN
TUIRC

957
▲
TOM BUIDHE

831
▲
LAIR OF
ALDARARIE

Glen Doll

1067
▲
GLAS MAOL

River Isla

Corrie Fee

739
▲
CRUYS

8

896
▲
BEN
TIRRAN

Water of Saugh

G 928
▲
MAYAR **H** 233 946
DRI **J** Clova **K** **L** 234 **M**

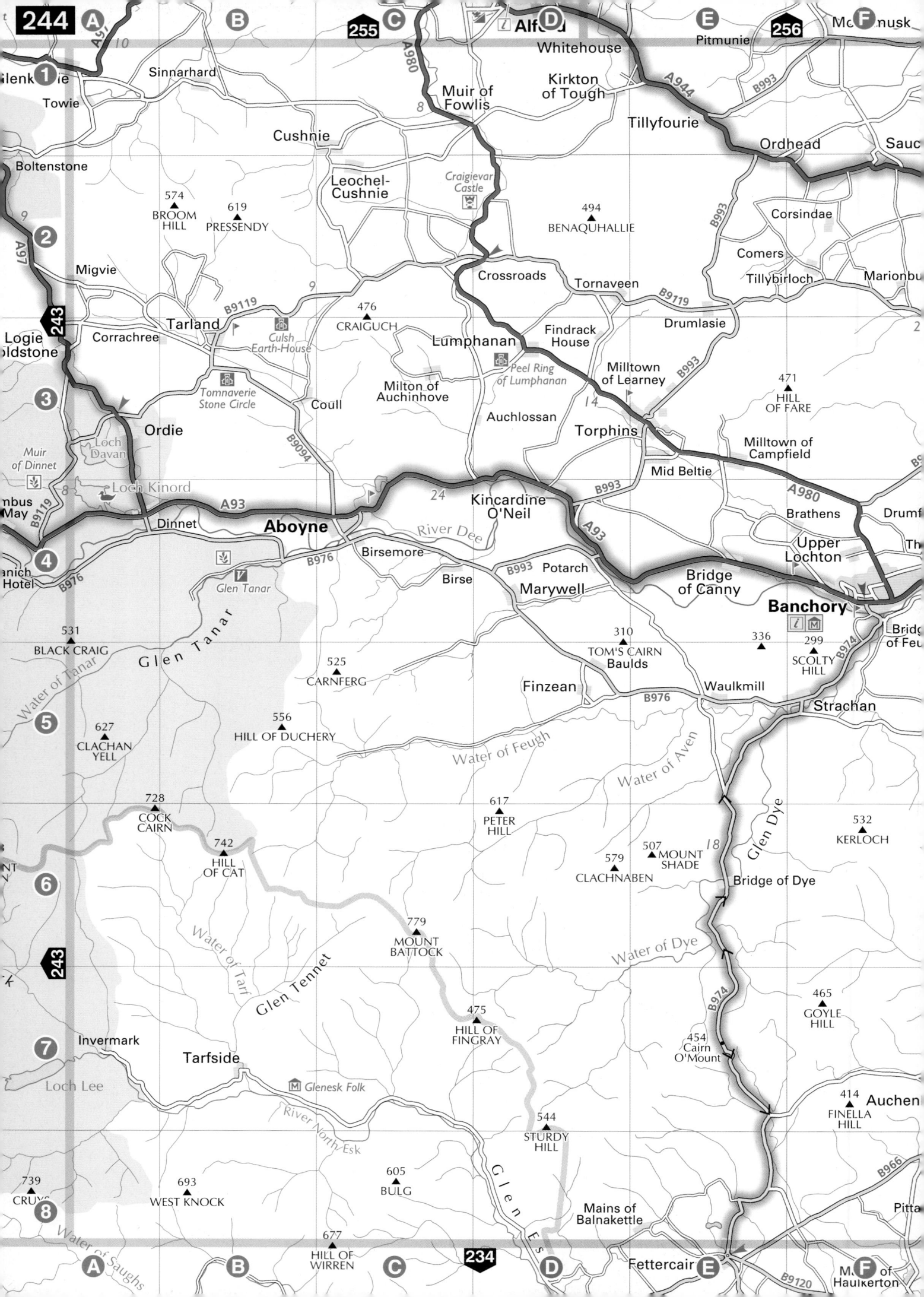

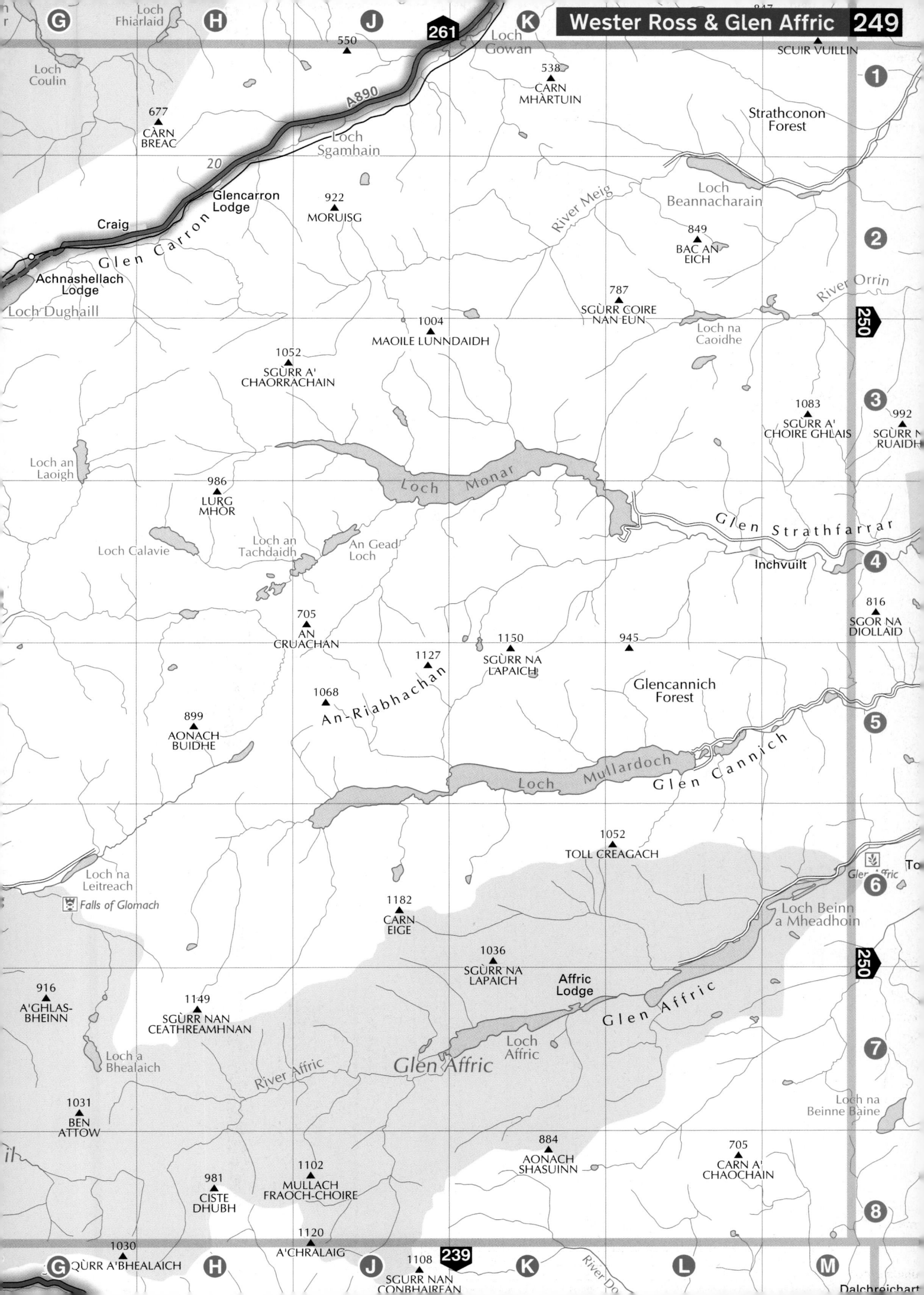

G H J **261** K

550

Loch Fhiarlaid

Loch Gowan

SCUIR VUILLIN

1

Loch Coulin

538
CARN MHÀRTUIN

Strathconon Forest

A890

677
CÀRN BREAC

20

Loch Sgamhain

Loch Beannacharain

Glencarron Lodge

922
MORUISG

849
BAC AN EICH

2

Craig

Glen Carron

River Meig

River Orrin

Achnashellach Lodge

787
SGÙRR COIRE NAN EUN

Loch na Caoidhe

250

Loch Dughaill

1004
MAOILE LUNNDAIDH

1083
SGÙRR A' CHOIRE GHLAIS

992
SGÙRR N RUAIDH

3

1052
SGÙRR A' CHAORRACHAIN

Loch an Laoigh

Loch Monar

Glen Strathfarrar

986
LURG MHOR

Inchvuilt

4

Loch Calavie

Loch an Tachdaidh

An Gead Loch

816
SGOR NA DIOLLAID

705
AN CRUACHAN

1150
SGÙRR NA LAPAICH

945

1127

Glencannich Forest

1068

An-Riabhachan

5

899
AONACH BUIDHE

Loch Mullardoch

Glen Cannich

1052
TOLL CREAGACH

6

Loch na Leitreach

Glen Affric

Falls of Glomach

Loch Beinn a Mheadhoin

1182
CARN EIGE

250

1036
SGÙRR NA LAPAICH

Affric Lodge

Glen Affric

916
A'GHLAS-BHEINN

1149
SGÙRR NAN CEATHREAMHNAN

Loch Affric

Glen Affric

7

Loch a Bhealaich

River Affric

Loch na Beinne Baine

1031
BEN ATTOW

884
AONACH SHASUINN

705
CARN A' CHAOCHAIN

981
CISTE DHUBH

1102
MULLACH FRAOCH-CHOIRE

8

1030
SGÙRR A'BHEALAICH

1120
A'CHRALAIG

239

1108
SGURR NAN CONBHAIRFAN

River D

Dalchreichart

G H J K L M

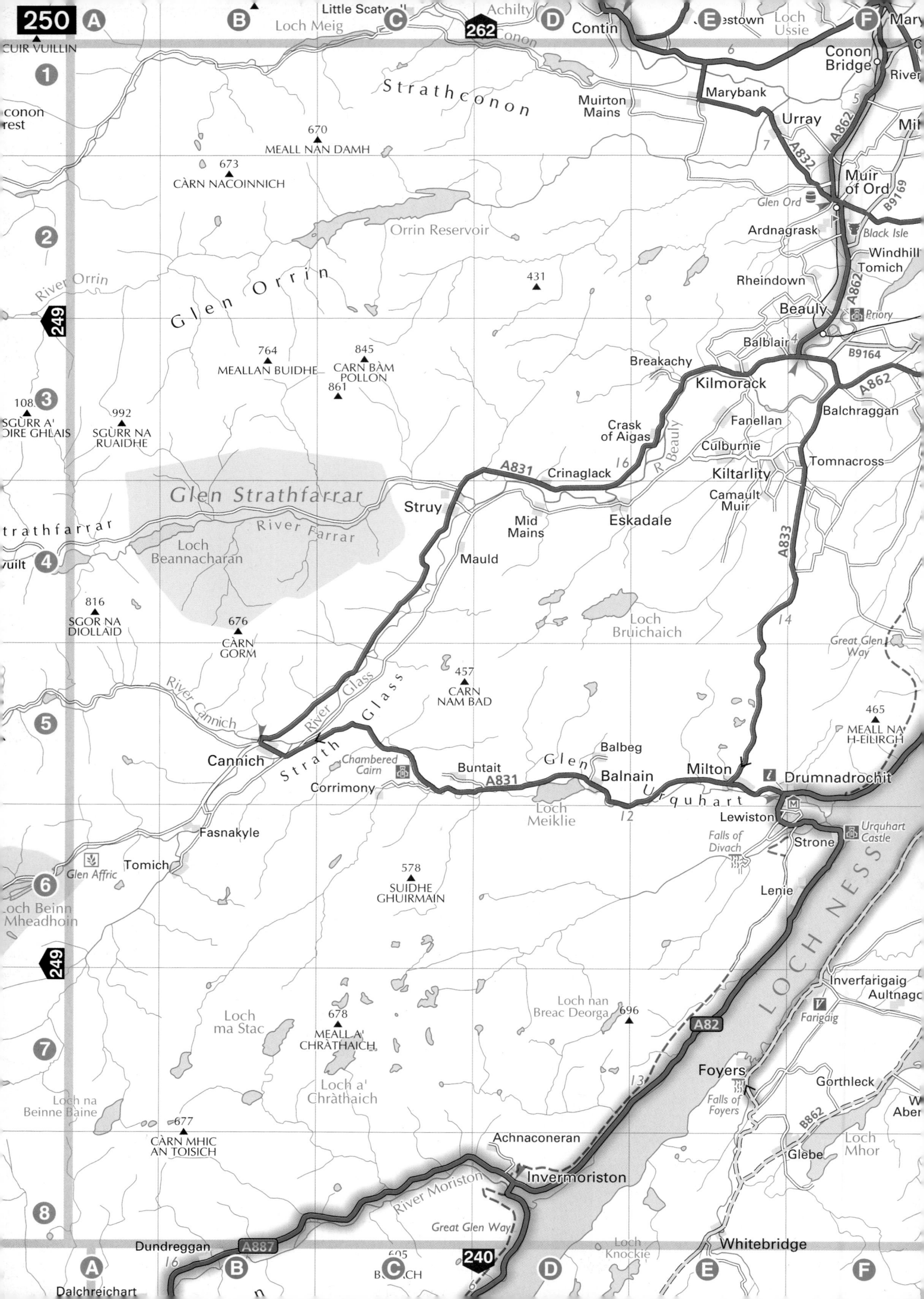

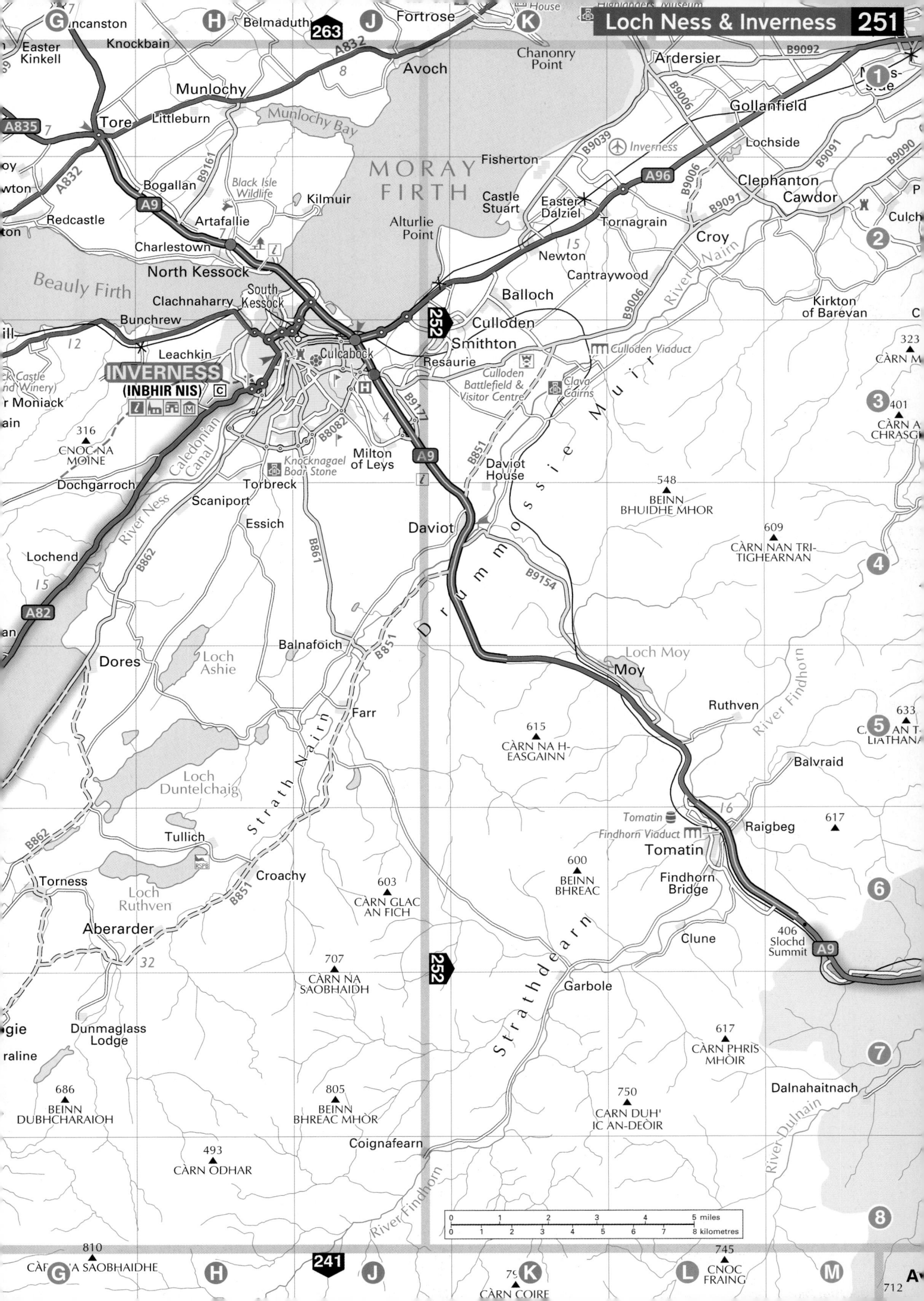

G | H | 263 A832 | J | Fortrose | K | House | Highlanders Museum

ncanston | Belmaduthy | Avoch

Easter Kinkell | Knockbain | Chanonry Point | Ardersier | B9092 | 1

Munlochy | Munlochy Bay | B9006 | Gollanfield | Nss-de

A835 | Tore | Littleburn | Fisherton | B9039 | Inverness | Lochside | B9091 | B9090

Bogallan | Black Isle Wildlife | Kilmuir | MORAY FIRTH | Castle Stuart | Easter Dalziel | A96 | B9006 | Clephanton | Cawdor | Culch | 2

Redcastle | Artafallie | Alturlie Point | Newton | Tornagrain | B9091 | Croy | Kirkton of Barevan | C

Charlestown | North Kessock | 7 | Cantraywood | River Nairn | 3 | 323 | CÀRN M

r Moniack | Clachnaharry | South Kessock | Balloch | B9006 | 401 | CÀRN A CHRASG

INVERNESS (INBHIR NIS) | Culcabock | 252 | Culloden | Smithton | Culloden Viaduct

Leachkin | Resaurie | Culloden Battlefield & Visitor Centre | Clava Cairns | Drummossie Muir | 548 | BEINN BHUIDHE MHOR | 4

316 | CNOC·NA MOINE | Milton of Leys | B9177 | B851 | Daviot House | 609 | CÀRN NAN TRI-TIGHEARNAN

Dochgarroch | B8082 | Knocknagael Boar Stone | A9 | 4 | Daviot

Torbreck | Scaniport | Essich | B861 | B9154 | Loch Moy | 633 | C AN T-LIATHANA | 5

Lochend | River Ness | 15 | Balnafoich | Moy | Ruthven | Balvraid

A82 | Loch Ashie | B851 | Farr | 615 | CÀRN NA H-EASGAINN | River Findhorn

Dores | Loch Duntelchaig | Strath Nairn | 16 | Tomatin | 617 | Raigbeg | 6

Tullich | RSPB | Croachy | Tomatin | Findhorn Viaduct | Findhorn Bridge

B862 | Loch Ruthven | 603 | CÀRN GLAC AN FICH | 600 | BEINN BHREAC | Clune | 406 Slochd Summit | A9

Torness | Aberarder | 32 | 707 | CÀRN NA SAOBHAIDH | 252 | Garbole | Strathdearn | 7

gie | Dunmaglass Lodge | 617 | CÀRN PHRIS MHOIR

raline | 805 | BEINN BHREAC MHÒR | 750 | CARN DUH' IC AN-DEÒIR | Dalnahaitnach

686 | BEINN DUBHCHARAIOH | 493 | CÀRN ODHAR | Coignafearn | River Dulnain | 8

810 | CÀ 'A SAOBHAIDHE | G | H | 241 | J | 79 | K | CÀRN COIRE | 745 | CNOC FRAING | L | M | 712 | A

0 1 2 3 4 5 miles
0 1 2 3 4 5 6 7 8 kilometres

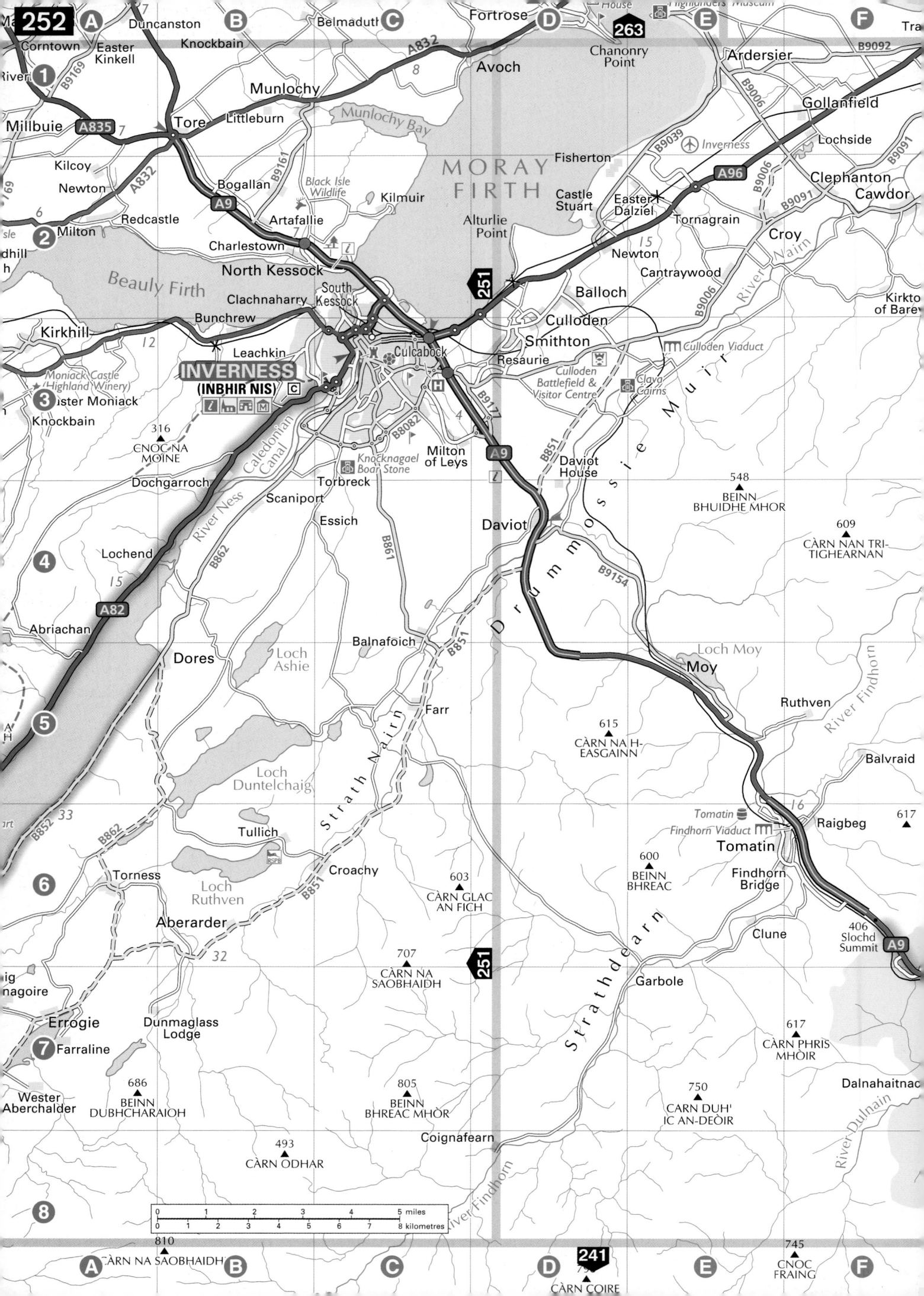

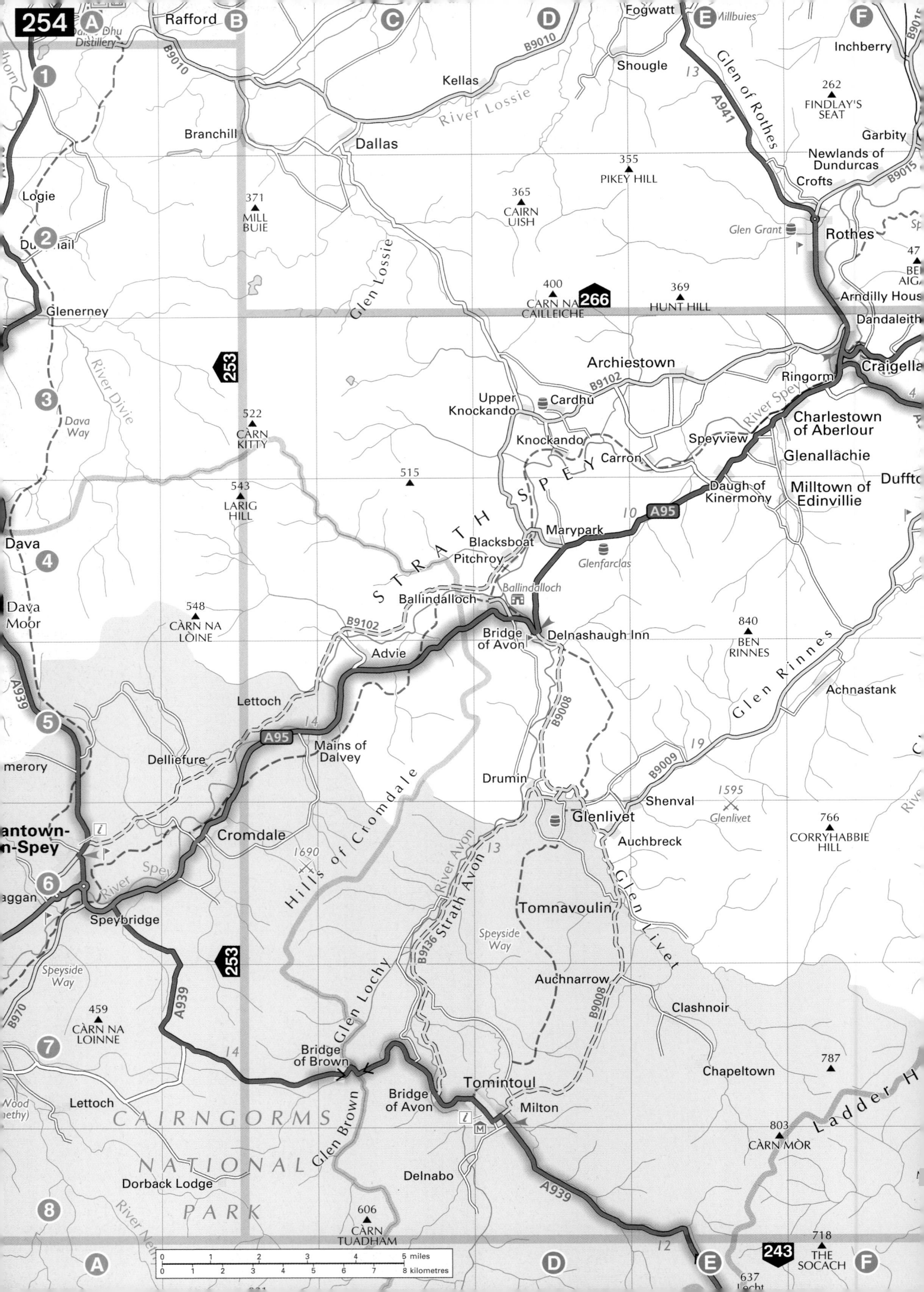

C quish
A96
WHITEASH HILL
MILLSTONE HILL
LURG HILL
G
H
J
K

250
THIEF'S HILL
Forgie
Grange Crossroads
Berryhillock
429
KNOCK HILL
20
Glenbarry
271
WETHER HILL
Lootcherbrae
1

Sound Muir
Aultmore
Forgieside
Bracobrae
Knock
Drumnagorrach

Newmill
B9017
Davoch of Grange
Farmtown
Bridge of Marnoch

Rumbach
Strath Isla
A95

Upper Mulben
Strathisla
River Isla
Rothiemay
2

uchroisk
Fife Keith
Keith
365
MEIKLE BALLOCH
Inverkeit

B9103
Mulben
Rosarie

Deanshaugh
Tauchers
Keith & Dufftown Railway
B9014
Bogniebrae

A95
12
338
HILL OF TOWIE
A96
267
Ruthven
Forgue

372
KNOCKAN
B9115
11
Cairnie
3
256

ggieknockater
Drummuir
B9022
River Deveron

nfiddich
B9014
Balvenie Castle
Milltown of Auchindoun
A920
14
Nordic Ski Centre
Castle
Affleck
Drumblade

Kirktown Mortlach
Auchindoun Castle
Haugh of Glass
Huntly
Brideswell
4

A941
Bridgend
Kirkstile
Strath Bogie
A96
Thomastown

503
525
Culdrain
5
Hillhead
Bainshol

440
CRANSMILL HILL
Kirkney
Gartly
419
WICHACH HILL
466
HILL OF FOUDLAN
Glens of Foudlar
5

564
TAP O' NOTH
A97
Leith Hall
Largie

Bridgend
18
Mains of Lesmoir
Picardy Symbol Stone

571
ROUND HILL
Cabrach
Belhinnie
Rhynie
Cottown
Kennethmont
B9002
Dunnideer
Insch

Aldivalloch
Aldunie
A941
Clatt
Duncanstone

B9002
A97
Leslie
6
256

629
HILL OF THREE STONES
722
THE BUCK
St Mary's Kirk (Ruin)
5
484
MIRE OF MIDGATES
Lethenty
B992

enyon
Lumsden
CORREEN HILLS
7

632
CREAG AN EUNAN
475
BRUX HILL

Rinmore
Mossat
A944
Tullynessle
Keig

Belnacraig
Kildrummy Castle
Kildrummy
6
Scotsmill
Montgarrie

Kirkton of Glenbuchat
Glenbuchat Castle
Milltown
Bridge of Alford
Haughton House
Alford Valley Railway
8

243
A97
10
Alford

G
H
J
Sinnarhard
K
244
L
Whitehouse

Bellabeg
Glenkindie
Muir of
M Kirkton

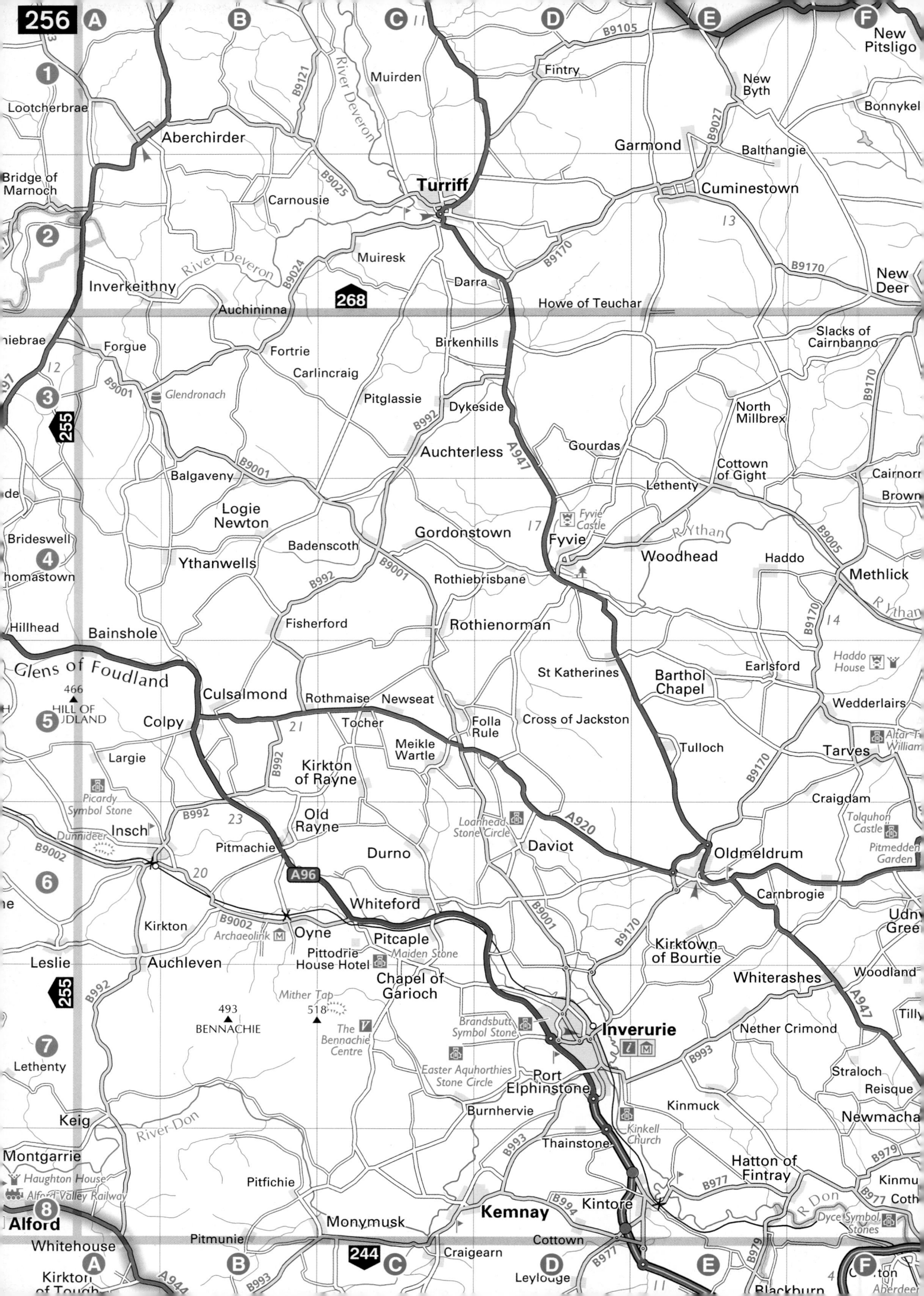

G H J K

1

2

3

4

5

6

7

8

Strichen
New Leeds
Leys
Crimond
Blackhill
18
Denhead
Backfolds
Kirktown
St Fergus
A90
Fetterangus
Rora
A952
B9093
Maud
B9106
Deer Abbey
Dunshillock
Mintlaw
Longside
Inverugie
Buchanhaven
Peterhead
A981 A950
B9029
Old Deer
Aden
Aberdeenshire Farming
269
A950
Peterhead
Peterhead Bay
B9029
Blackhill of Clackriach
Stuartfield
Inverquhomery
Hillhead of Cocklaw
Burnhaven
B9028
Drymuir
Bulwark
Millbreck
Nether Kinmundy
Blackhill
Stirling
Buchan Ness
Boddam
Nethermuir
Clola
Lendrum Terrace
B9030
Kinnadie
Auchnagatt
12
Kinknockie
Longhaven
A90
Inkhorn
Coldwells
Ardallie
Hatton
Auchiries
Bullers of Buchan
A948
A952
North Haven
Arthrath
Muirtack
14
21
Slains
Bogbrae
Cruden Bay
Ythanbank
Birness
Chapel Hill
Bay of Cruden
Auchedly
Whinnyfold
The Skares
Kinharrachie
Artrochie
20
Ellon
P+R
B9005
Esslemont
Kirkton of Logie Buchan
Kirktown of Slains
A920
10
Collieston
itmedden
Logierieve
6
Forvie
Housieside
B9000
A90
B9000
Udny Station
Newburgh
Cultercullen
Foveran
A975
5
Delfrigs
Causeyend
B979
Balmedie
Whitecairns
Belhelvie
B999
B977
Balmedie
A90
Potterton
A90
245
Blackdog
G H J K L M

0 1 2 3 4 5 miles
0 1 2 3 4 5 6 7 8 kilometres

River Ugie

A   B   C   D   E   F

1

2

3

4

5

6

7

8

A   B   C   D   E   F

The Little Minch

Fladda-chùain

Rudha Hun

Dur

Tairbeart
(Tarbert)

Lùb Score

Borneskitaig

Kilmuir

Kilvax

Balgown

Lini

Loch nam Madadh
(Lochmaddy)

Totscore

Waternish Point

Idrigill

Ascrib
Islands

Uig Bay

(U

283
BEN
GEARY

Geary

Loch Snizort

Earlish

Trumpan

Ardmore
Point

Gillen

Hallin

16

A87

DUNVEGAN
HEAD

Isay   Mingay

Stein   Lusta

214
BEN
DIUBAIG

Greshornish
House
Hotel

Loch Snizort

King

Loch Dunvegan

Loch
Bay

Claigan

Bay

22

Treaslane

Loch Greshornish

Loch Pooltiel

Boreraig

Uig

327
BEINN
BHREAC

B886

Flashader

A850

Feriniquarrie

Totaig

Upperglen

Edinbane

Bernisdale

Oisgill Bay

Glendale

Milovaig

Lephin

B884

Colbost

Dunvegan

ISLE OF

Sk

Waterstein

Toy

Colbost Croft

Skinidin

Giant Angus MacAskill

A864

265
BEN
AKETIL

271
CRUACHAN BEINN
A' CHEARCAILL

Neist
Point

Kilmuir

Lonmore

SKYE

Moonen Bay

Roskhill

Duirnish

469
HEALAVAL
MORE

Ramasaig

Orbost

Roag

Caroy River

Hoe Rape

Vatten

A863

Glen Ose

488
HEALAVAL
BHEAG

Harlosh

Ose

Hoe Point

368

Harlosh
Island

Harlosh
Point

Colbost
Point

Dun
Beag

Bracadale

0   1   2   3   4   5 miles

0   1   2   3   4   5   6   7   8 kilometres

Tarner
Island

Coille

G H J K L

1
2
260
3
4

Rudha na Fearn

Òb Chuaig

5 uaig

Callakille

Lonbain

6

248

7

Applecross Bay

Milton

Camu

Aird Dhu'

8

an Troдday

North Duntulm

Kilmaluag

useum nd Life

Flodigarry

Eilean Flodigarry

Poldorais

Staffin Bay

Staffin Island

542
MEAL NA SUIREAMACH

Digg

Brogaig

Stenscholl

Staffin

464
BIODA BUIDHE

Trotternish

Kilt Rock

Ellishader

Maligar

Marishader

Valtos

Rudha nam Brathairean

611
BEINN EDRA

Garros

Culnaknock

Lealt

River Conon

Tote

608
CREAG A' LAIN

A855

Loch a' Bhràige

RONA

einlich

hisdal

451
BEINN A' SGA

719
Old Man of Storr

THE STORR

River Romesdal

nesdal

vre

River Haulton

Kensaleyre

Loch Leathan

Eilean Tigh

16

Loch Fada

Eilean Fladday

B8036

Carbost

Borve

Manish Point

Loch Arnish

Torran

Arnish

Drumuie

A855

312

Glengrasco

Torvaig

Brochel

SOUND OF RAASAY

INNER SOUND

Portree

Seafield

417
BEINN NA GRÈINE

Penifiler

412
BEN TIANAVAIG

RAASAY

Glenmore

Glenvarragill

G Mugeary A87 H

Camastianav

J

Tianavaig Bay

247 DÙN CAAN

Oskaig

444

K

Rudha na' Leac

L

M

Toscaig

A B C D E F

1

2

3

4

5

259

6

7

8

Rudha Reidh

Foura

Cove

Stattic Point

Rudha Beag

Mellon
Udrigle

GRUINARD
ISLAND

Bad

296
AN
CUAIDH

Melvaig

Aultgrishin

293
CNOC
BREAC

North Erradale

Big Sand

Longa
Island

Loch
Gairloch

Port
Henderson

Badachro

Opinan

South Erradale

Redpoint

Red
Point

Rudha
na Fearn

Fearnmore

Fearnbeg

Arrina

Cuaig

Callakille

B8021

B8057

Mellon
Charles

Ormiscaig

Aultbea

ISLE
OF EWE

Loch Ewe

Inverasdale

Naast

Inverewe
Garden

Poolewe

Londubh

Strath

Smithstown

Lonemore

Auchtercairn

Heritage

Gairloch

Eilean
Horrisdale

B8056

A832

Charlestown

421
MEALL AN
DOIREIN

Loch Bad
an Sgalaig

Loch Ghaineamhach

Loch a
Ghodhainn

619
BEINN BHREAC

875
BAOSBHEINN

Loch a'
Bhealaich

985
BEINN
ALLIGIN

Loch
Torridon

Craig River

Lower
Diabaig

Loch Diabaig

Alligin Shuas

Inveralligin

Kenmore

Ardheslaig

Torridon
House

Upper Loch Torridon

Ob
Chuaig

Rudha Beag

Laide

Gruinard
Bay

Gruinard

Little Gruinard River

Loch
Fada

347
CREA
MHEAL

681
BEINN A'
CHAISGEIN BE

250
MEALL NA MEINE

Wester

791
BEINN
AIRIDH CHARR

Fionn
Loch

Loch

Loch na
A-Oidhche

855
BEINN
AN EÒIN

724

BE

Lettere
Fore

Letterewe

Loch Maree
Hotel

Talladale

A832

Maree

19

914
BEINN DEARG

1009
RUADH-
STAC MÒR

97

1024
LIATHACH

1053

Glen Torridon

BEINN

Torridon

Countryside Centre

Annat

Shieldaig

248

SGU
DU

7

A   B   C   D   E   F

0   1   2   3   4   5 miles
0   1   2   3   4   5   6   7   8 kilometres

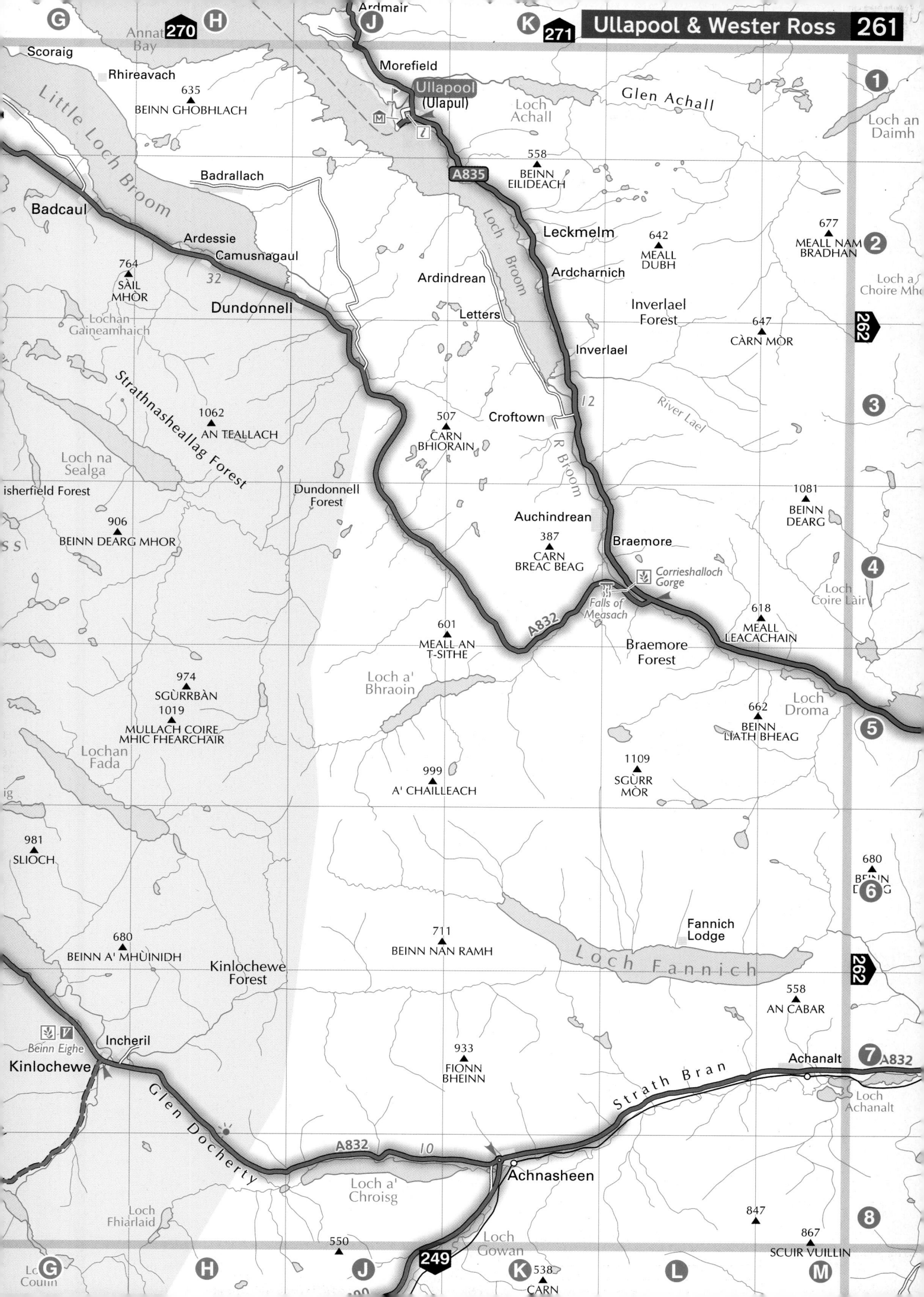

Scoraig

Annat Bay

Ardmair

Morefield

Ullapool (Ulapul)

Loch Achall

Glen Achall

Loch an Daimh

1

Rhireavach

635 ▲ BEINN GHOBHLACH

A835

558 ▲ BEINN EILIDEACH

Leckmelm

642 ▲ MEALL DUBH

677 ▲ MEALL NAM BRADHAN

2

Badrallach

Loch a Choire Mho

262

Badcaul

Ardessie

Camusnagaul

764 ▲ SÀIL MHÒR

32

Ardindrean

Letters

Ardcharnich

Inverlael Forest

647 ▲ CÀRN MÒR

Dundonnell

Lochan Gaineamhaich

Inverlael

12

3

isherfield Forest

Loch na Sealga

Strathnasheallag Forest

1062 ▲ AN TEALLACH

Dundonnell Forest

507 ▲ CARN BHIORAIN

Croftown

R. Broom

River Lael

1081 ▲ BEINN DEARG

ss

906 ▲ BEINN DEARG MHOR

Auchindrean

Braemore

387 ▲ CARN BREAC BEAG

Corrieshalloch Gorge

618 ▲ MEALL LEACACHAIN

Loch Coire Làir

4

Falls of Measach

A832

601 ▲ MEALL AN T-SITHE

Braemore Forest

Loch Droma

974 ▲ SGÙRRBÀN

1019 ▲ MULLACH COIRE MHIC FHEARCHAIR

Loch a' Bhraoin

662 ▲ BEINN LIATH BHEAG

5

Lochan Fada

1109 ▲ SGÙRR MÒR

ig

999 ▲ A' CHAILLEACH

981 ▲ SLIOCH

680 ▲ BEINN DE G

6

Fannich Lodge

680 ▲ BEINN A' MHÙINIDH

Kinlochewe Forest

711 ▲ BEINN NAN RAMH

Loch Fannich

262

558 ▲ AN CABAR

Beinn Eighe

Incheril

933 ▲ FIONN BHEINN

Strath Bran

Achanalt

7 A832

Kinlochewe

Glen Docherty

Loch a' Chroisg

A832

10

Achnasheen

Loch Achanalt

847 ▲

867 ▲ SCUIR VUILLIN

8

Loch Fhiarlaid

550 ▲

249

Loch Gowan

Lo Coulin

G   H   J   K   538 ▲ CARN   L   M

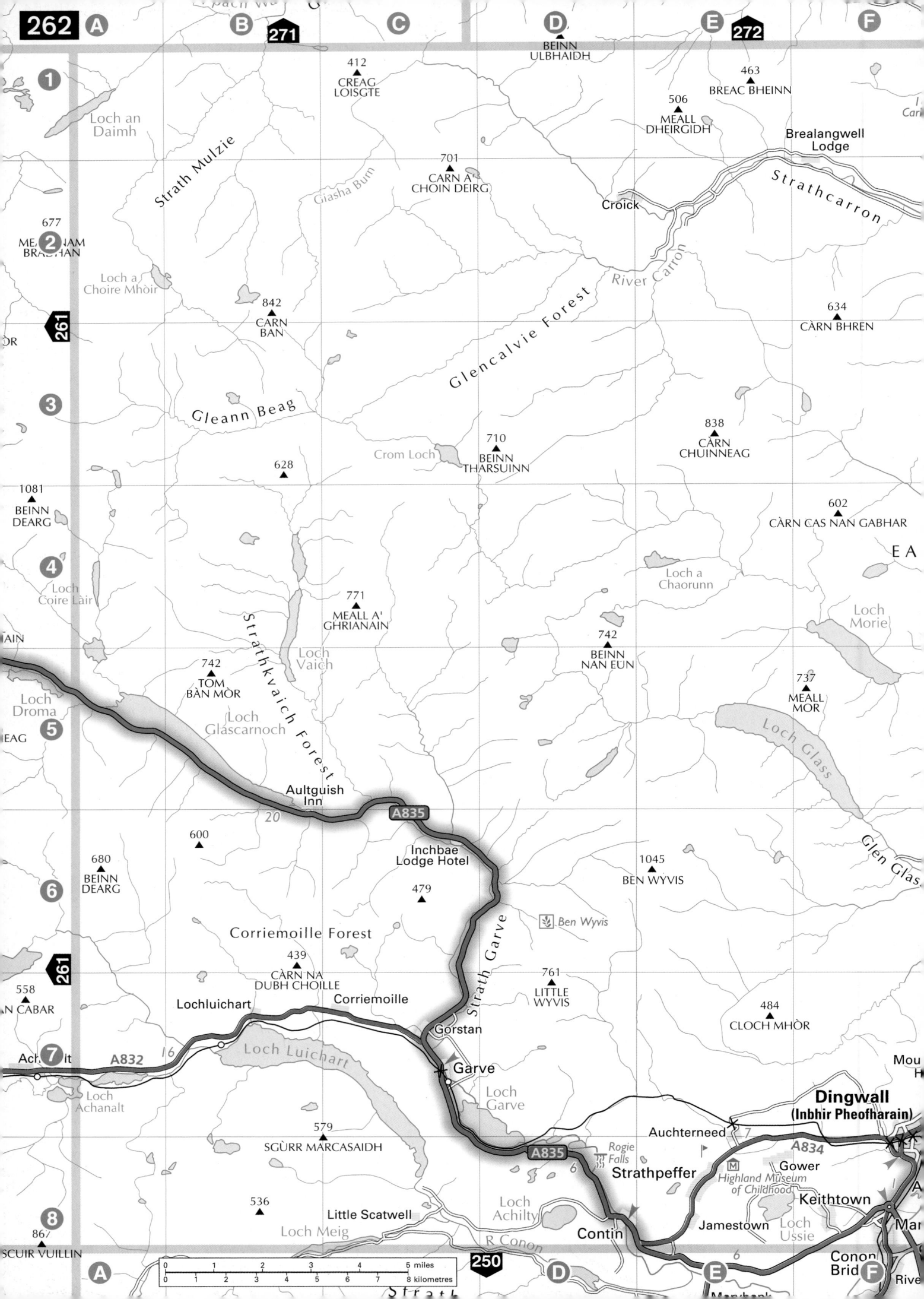

A B C 273 D E F

1

Cambusavie
Platform
Badninish
Skelbo
Skelbo Street
Loch
Fleet
Achvaich
Fourpenny
Rearquhar
Birichin
Embo
Astle
Embo Street
Evelix
Pitgrudy
ngda 2
Clashmore
A949
Camore
Royal Dornoch
Whiteface
A9
Dornoch
Historylinks
och Firth
Cuthill
263
Dornoch
Point
Dornoch Firth
Ferrytown
Cambuscurrie
Bay
Ardmore
Dornoch
Firth Bridge
Innis Mhor
Brucefield
Tarbat Ness
Wilkhaven
ton 3
Ferry
Point
Dornoch Firth
Portmahomack
A836
Glenmorangie
Morangie
Inver
Rockfield
B9165
284
Tain
(Baile Dhubhthaich)
Arboll
MORANGIE
FOREST
Toulvaddie
Lochslin
379
Loch
Eye
Rhynie
4
OC AN
BHAIL
Newfield
B9165
Hill of
Fearn
Balmuchy
Hilton of Cadboll
Chapel (ruin)
Fearn
Tullich
Ballchraggan
B9166
Hilton
Kildary
Arabella
Balintore
Milton
Shandwick
Shandwick Bay
5
Delny
Kilmuir
Ankerville
B9175
Barbaraville
Pitcalnie
Nigg Bay
Nigg
nagarron 8
Balintraid
Saltburn
Nigg
Ferry
B817
6
Invergordon
Cromarty
Hugh Miller's Cottage
Cromarty
Bay
Newton
Udale
Bay
B9163
263
Navity
air
RSPB
Allerton
Jemimaville
Upper Eathie
7
A832
MORAY FIRTH
B9160
10
Culbin
Forest
E
Kintessac
Raddery
Fairy Glen
RSPB
Whiteness Head
Brodie
Castle
Rosemarkie
Groam
House
Fort-George & The
Highlanders' Museum
Nairn
(Inbhir Nàrann)
Culbin
Sands
D
Cathedral
Fo 8 se
RSPB
A96
Brodie
Chanonry
Boath
Doocot
A96
Avoch A
0   1   2   3   4   5 miles
0   1   2   3   4   5   6   7   8 kilometres
252
Mossside
D
Tradespark
Household
E 253
F
Whitemie
1645

1
2
3
4
5

Branderburgh
△🚐 Stotfield
B9040
Lossiemouth

Burghead
Well
Hopeman   Burnside
Burghead   B9012   Duffus
Cummingston   St Peter's Kirk
B9013   & Parish Cross
Roseisle   Loch
B9012   Duffus   Spynie
Burghead Bay   Castle   6
College of   Spynie
Roseisle   Palace   Stonewells
Kir
Lochill   on
Findhorn   Quarrywood   Viewfield
Hempriggs   B9089   Bishopmill   Elgin   Calcots
oin   Innesmill
ds   Findhorn   Newton
Bay   Kinloss   Coltfield   A96   H   Urquhart
Kincorth   Glen Moray   New Elgin   Lhanbryde   7
House   Alves   12   The
Grange Hall   Kilbuiack   Lochs
Sueno's Stone   Muir of   Linkwood   9
erow   Miltonduff   A96
Forres   Mosstodlo
Califer   Pluscarden   Clackmarras   Crof
Dallas Dhu   Rafford   Barnhill   Longmorn   B9103   of Dipp
Distillery   Fogwatt   Millbuies   Orbl   ton
B9010   8
G   253   H   B9010   J   Shougle   L   Inchberry
Kellas   Glen of   B9015
262   M

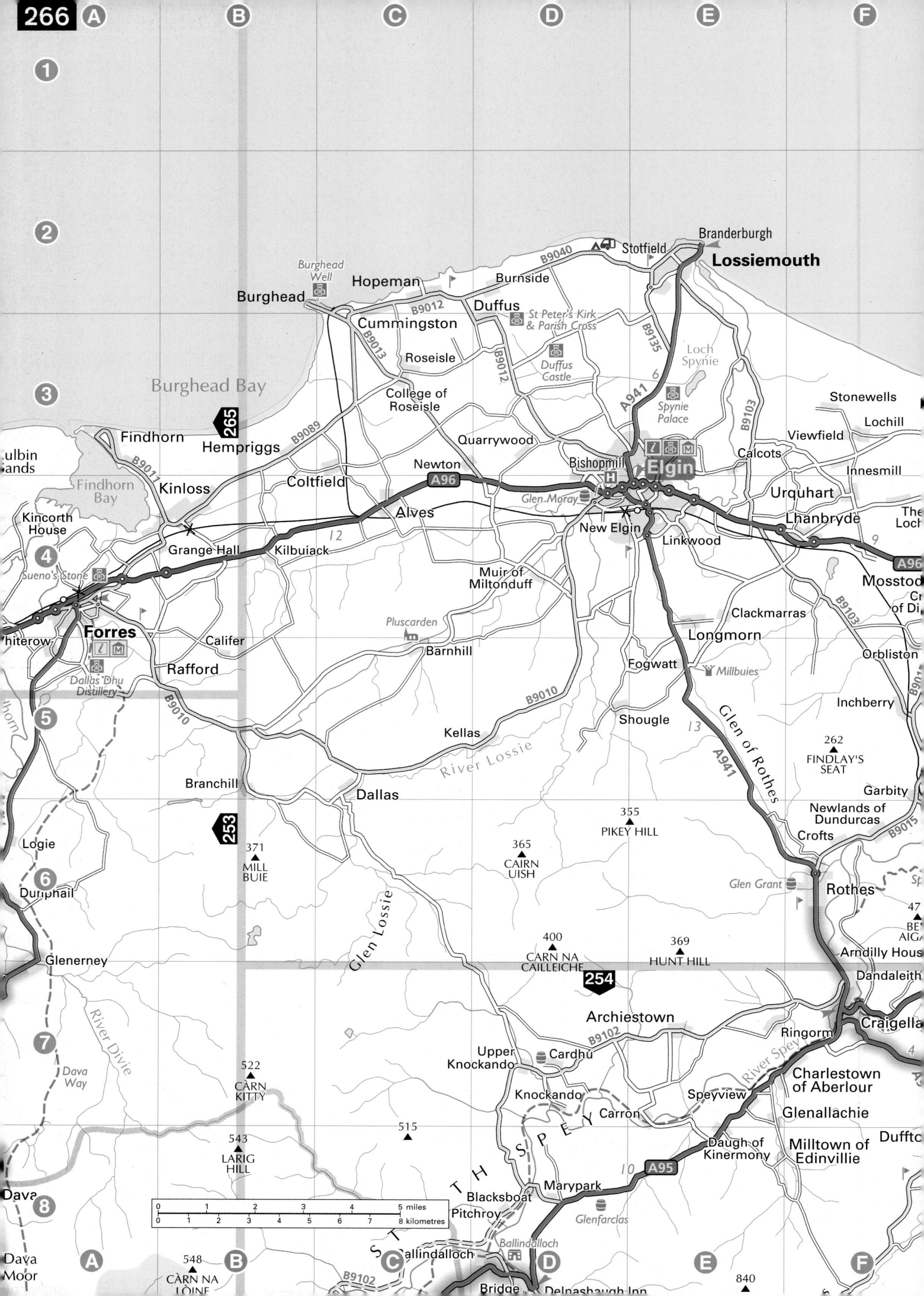

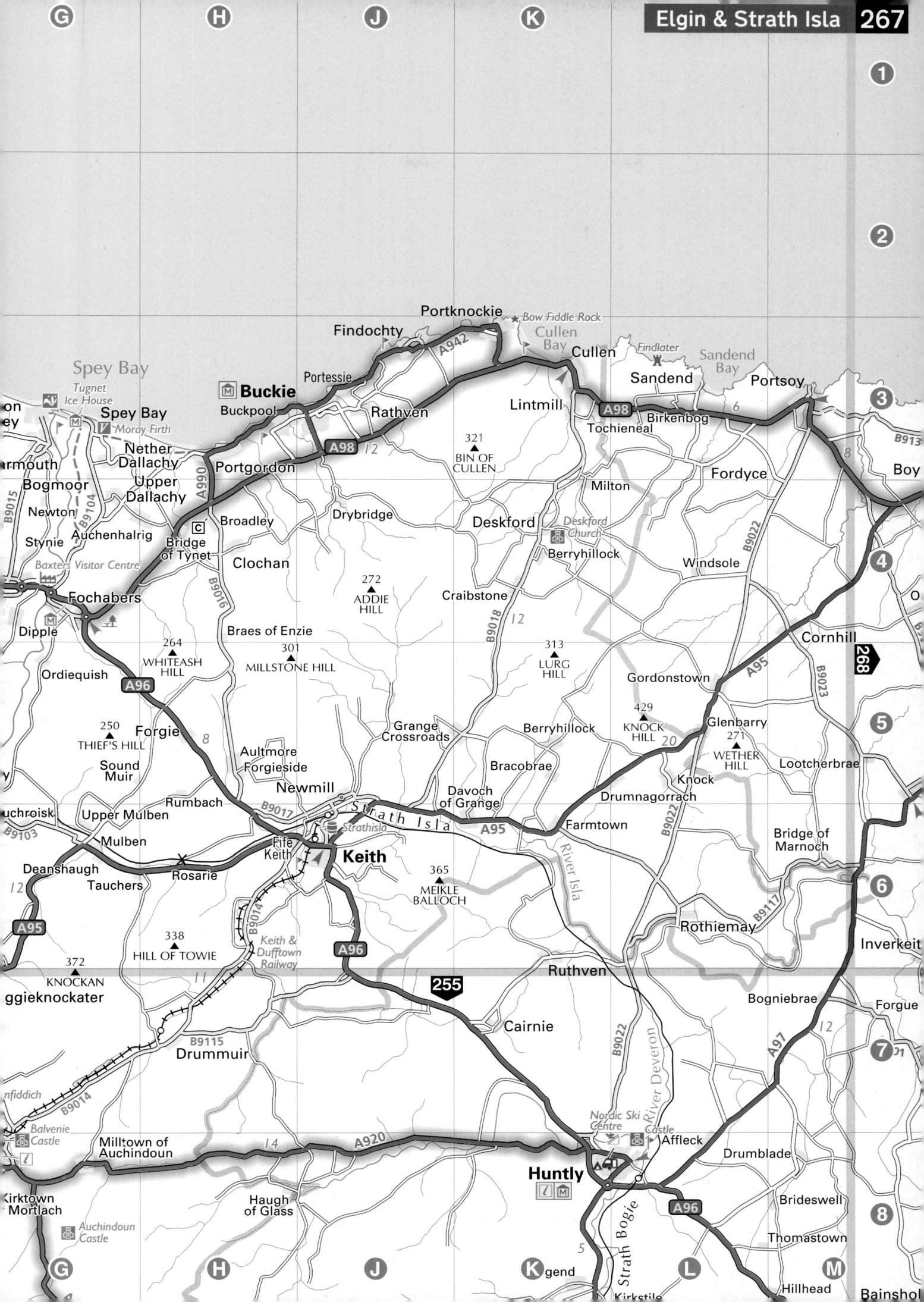

G **H** **J** **K**

1

2

Rosehearty

Castle Lighthouse
& Museum
Sandhaven
Kinnaird
Head

Fraserburgh *i*

3

Pittulie

Peathill

Craigiefold

Percyhorner

Coburby

B9031

Kirktown

Pitblae

Mid Ardlaw

A90

Fraserburgh
Bay

Maggie's
Hoosie

Cairnbulg

Inverallochy

Whitelinks Bay

yndlie

B9032

Memsie

Rathen

St Combs

B9033

A98

Memsie
Cairn

A981

Newburgh

Lonmay

Crofts
of Savoch

4

234
WAUGHTON
HILL

12

Rattray Head

B9093

Strichen

New
Leeds

A952

12

Crimond

Loch of
Strathbeg

RSPB

Blackhill

18

5

B9093

Leys

Denhead

Backfolds

Kirktown

Fetterangus

Rora

St Fergus

A981

A950

6

Deer
Abbey

Dunshillock

A90

River Ugie

6

Maud

B9106

Old
Deer

Aden

Mintlaw

Longside

Inverugie

Buchanhaven

Peterhead M

B9029

B9029

Aberdeenshire
Farming

A950

Peterhead

B9028

Blackhill of
Clackriach

Drymuir

Bulwark

Stuartfield

257

Inverquhomery

9

Hillhead
of Cocklaw

A1982

Peterhead
Bay

Burnhaven

7

Nethermuir

Millbreck

Nether
Kinmundy

Buchan
Ness

B9030

Kinnadie

Clola

Blackhill

Stirling

Boddam

Auchnagatt

12

Kinknockie

Lendrum
Terrace

Inkhorn

Coldwells

Ardallie

Longhaven

8

A948

A952

Hatton

A90

Auchiries

Bullers
of Buchan

North Haven

Arthrat

Muirtack

14

21

Slains

Cruden Bay

G **H** **J** **K** **L** **M**

Ⓐ   Ⓑ   Ⓒ   Ⓓ   Ⓔ   Ⓕ Rud
Mh

①

Eddrachil
Bay

OLDANY
ISLAND

Point of Stoer

Culkein
Drumbeg

Old Man
of Stoer

Culkein

Clashnessie
Bay

Oldany

Drumbeg

Achnacarnin

②

Clashmore

Clashnessie

Loch
Poll

Nedd

Stoer

③

Clachtoll

B869

Loch
Beannach

Bay of Clachtoll

Rhicarn

Achmelvich
Bay

A837

Achmelvich

Baddidarrach

🅻

Soyea Island

Loch Inver

Lochinver

Strathan

A s s y n

④

Inverkirkaig

Eilean Mòr

River Kirkaig

Fionn
Loch   su

Rhu
Coigach

Enard Bay

⑤

Rubha Mòr

Reiff

Achnahaird

Loch
Siónasca

Eilean Mullagrach

Altandhu

Loch
Osgaig

Isle Ristol

Polbain

612
STAC POLLAIDH

⑥

Glas-leac Mòr

SUMMER ISLES

Badentarbet

Achiltibuie

769
CUL BEA

Tanera
Beg

Badentarbat
Bay

Polglass

Loch
Lurgainn

Ⓥ

Steornabhagh
(Stornoway)

Tanera
Mòr

🅰🅥 Ben Mor
Coigach

C O I G A C H

Glas-leac Beag

Horse
Island

Horse
Sound

652
**BEN MORE
COIGACH**

⑦

Eilean Dubh

Achduart

Priest
Island

Culnacraig

Strathcanaire

Greenstone
Point

Leac Dhonn

Isle
Martin

Strath

⑧

Cailleach Head

A835

Rudha Beag

Ardmair

Ⓐ
llon
urigle

Scoraig

Annat
Bay

Mo Ⓕ ld

Ⓓ hireavach

Ⓔ

Ⓕ Ullapo

0   1   2   3   4   5 miles
0   1   2   3   4   5   6   7   8 kilometres

635

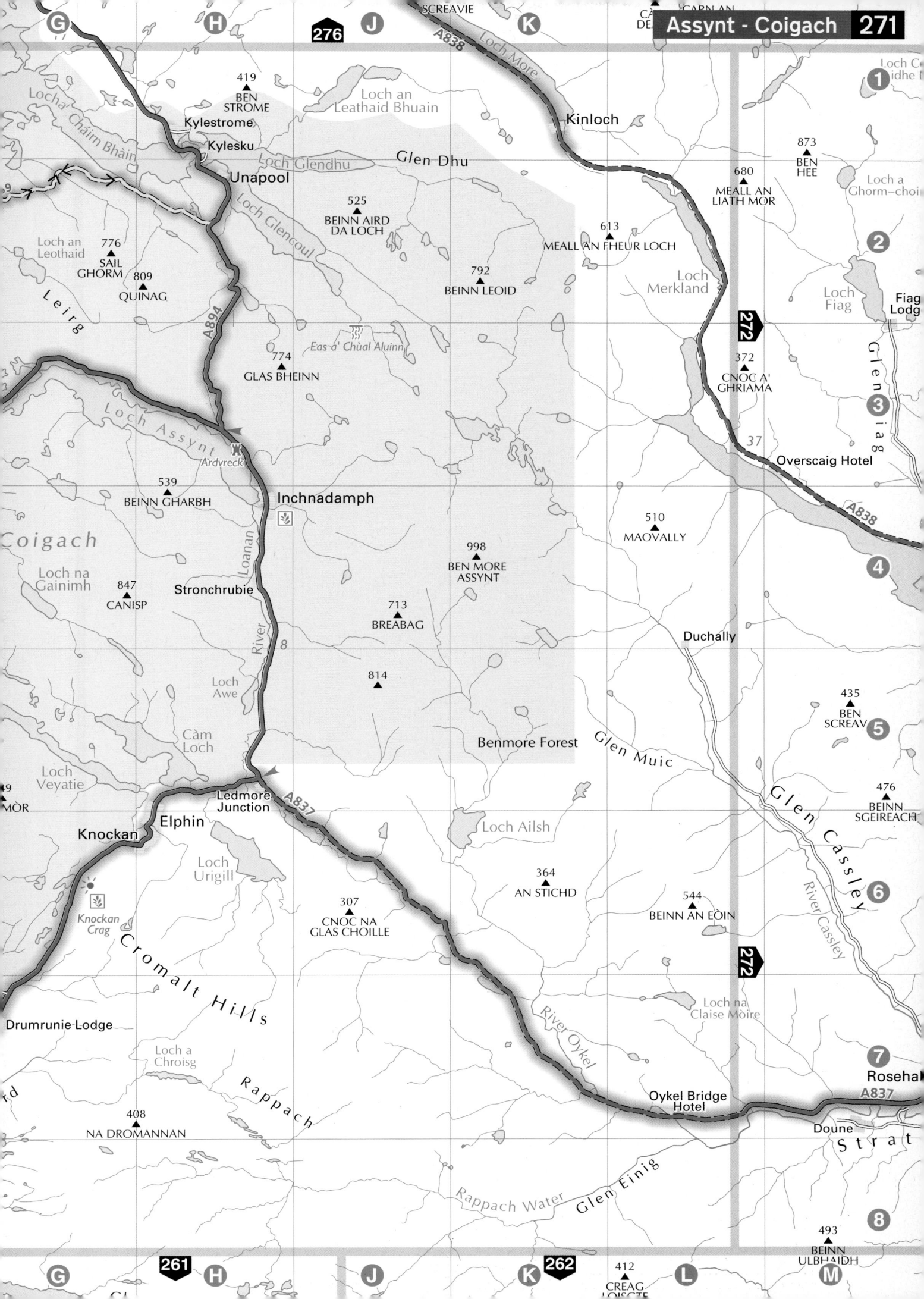

G   H   276   J   K   A838   SCREAVIE   CÀRN AN   CÀRN AN
DE...

Loch C
...idhe-choi   1

Loch More   Kinloch   873
BEN
HEE

419
BEN
STROME   Loch an
Leathaid Bhuain   680
MEALL AN
LIATH MOR   Loch a
Ghorm-choi

Kylestrome   525
BEINN AIRD
DA LOCH   613
MEALL AN FHEUR LOCH   2

Kylesku   Glen Dhu

Unapool   Loch Glendhu   Loch Fiag   Fiag
Lodg

Locha Chàirn Bhàin   792
BEINN LEOID   Loch
Merkland

776
SAIL
GHORM   809
QUINAG   774
GLAS BHEINN   Eas-a' Chùal Aluinn   272   372
CNOC A'
GHRIAMA   3

Leirg   Loch Assynt   Glen...lag

37   Overscaig Hotel

A838

Ardvreck   510
MAOVALLY   4

539
BEINN GHARBH   Inchnadamph   998
BEN MORE
ASSYNT

Coigach   Duchally

847
CANISP   Stronchrubie   713
BREABAG   435
BEN
SCREAV   5

Loch na
Gainimh   River   8   814

Loch
Awe   Benmore Forest   Glen Muic   476
BEINN
SGEIREACH

Loch
Veyatie   Càm
Loch   Loch Ailsh   Glen Cassley

9   MÒR   Ledmore
Junction   A837   River Cassley   6

Knockan   Elphin   364
AN STICHD   544
BEINN AN EÒIN

Loch
Urigill   307
CNOC NA
GLAS CHOILLE   272

Knockan
Crag   Loch na
Claise Mòire

Cromalt Hills   Rappach   River Oykel   7

Drumrunie Lodge   Rosehal

Loch a
Chroisg   Oykel Bridge
Hotel   A837

rd   408
NA DROMANNAN   Doune

Strat

Glen Einig

Rappach Water   493
BEINN
ULBHAIDH

G   261   H   262   J   K   L   412
CREAG   M

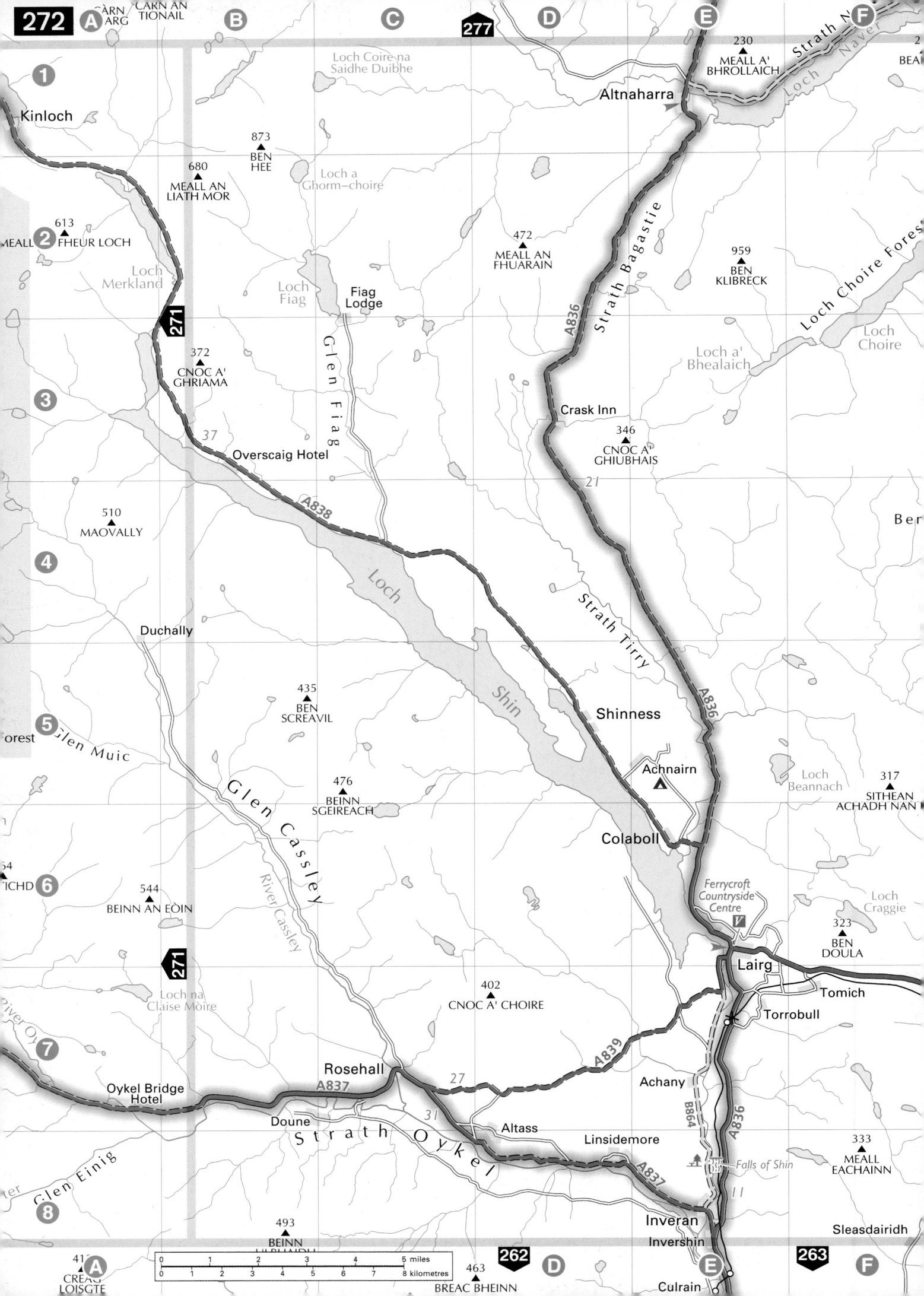

G H J K

278 BEN GRIAM

Loch an
Ruathair

A897

1

440 ▲

KNOCKFIN
HEIGHTS

432 ▲

Loch
Rimsdale

Loch
nan Clàr

Loch
Badanlòch

Loch
Arichlinie

B871

Kinbrace

River Helmsdale

2

437 ▲

CNOC COIRE
NA FEÀRNA

Kinbrace Burn

Loch an
Altan Fheàrna

Loch
Truderscaig

202 ▲
CNOC DAIL-
CHAIRN

Strath Free

274

518 ▲
CNOC A
EIREANNA

694 ▲
CREAG N-
IOLAIRE

434 ▲
CNOC AN LIATH-
BHAID MHÒIR

Borrobol Forest

Loch
Ascaig

Suisgill Burn

3

713 ▲
CREAG
MHÒR

Gorm–loch
Mòr

364 ▲
CNOC NA
BREUN-CHOILLE

388 ▲
CREAG NAM FIÀDH

Learable Hill
Cairns, Stone Row
& Stone Circles

17

Kildonan Lodge

ine Forest

Strath Skinsdale

Strath of Kildonan

Kildonan 416
BEINN
DUBHAIN

4

A897

as-
Mòr

337 ▲
CNOC NA H-
INNSE MOIRE

River Helms

Tor

IAN
MOR

2

421 ▲
CNOC NAN CRÙBAG MÒR

624 ▲
BEINN
DHORAIN

Glen Loth

BEIN
MÈI

5

Black Water

River Brora

Balnacoil
Lodge

539 ▲
COL-
BHEINN

Lothm

Lothbeg

6

293 ▲
CNOC
LEAMHNACHD

Strath Brora

River Brora

Loch
Brora

21

Dalreavoch
Lodge

Loch
Horn

520 ▲
BEN
HORN

274

Dalchalm

Brora

7

14

Rogart

Golspie Burn

378 ▲
CAGAR
FEOSAIG

Backies

Carn Liath

Doll

A9

313 ▲
CREAGAN
GLAS

446 ▲
BEN LUNDIE

383 ▲
BEN BHRAGGIE

Rhives

Dunrobin Castle

Golspie

8

349 ▲
BEINN
DO___ILL

263 G H

Torboll

Cambusavie
Platform

264 K

Loch
Fleet

Skelbo

J

Badninish

L M

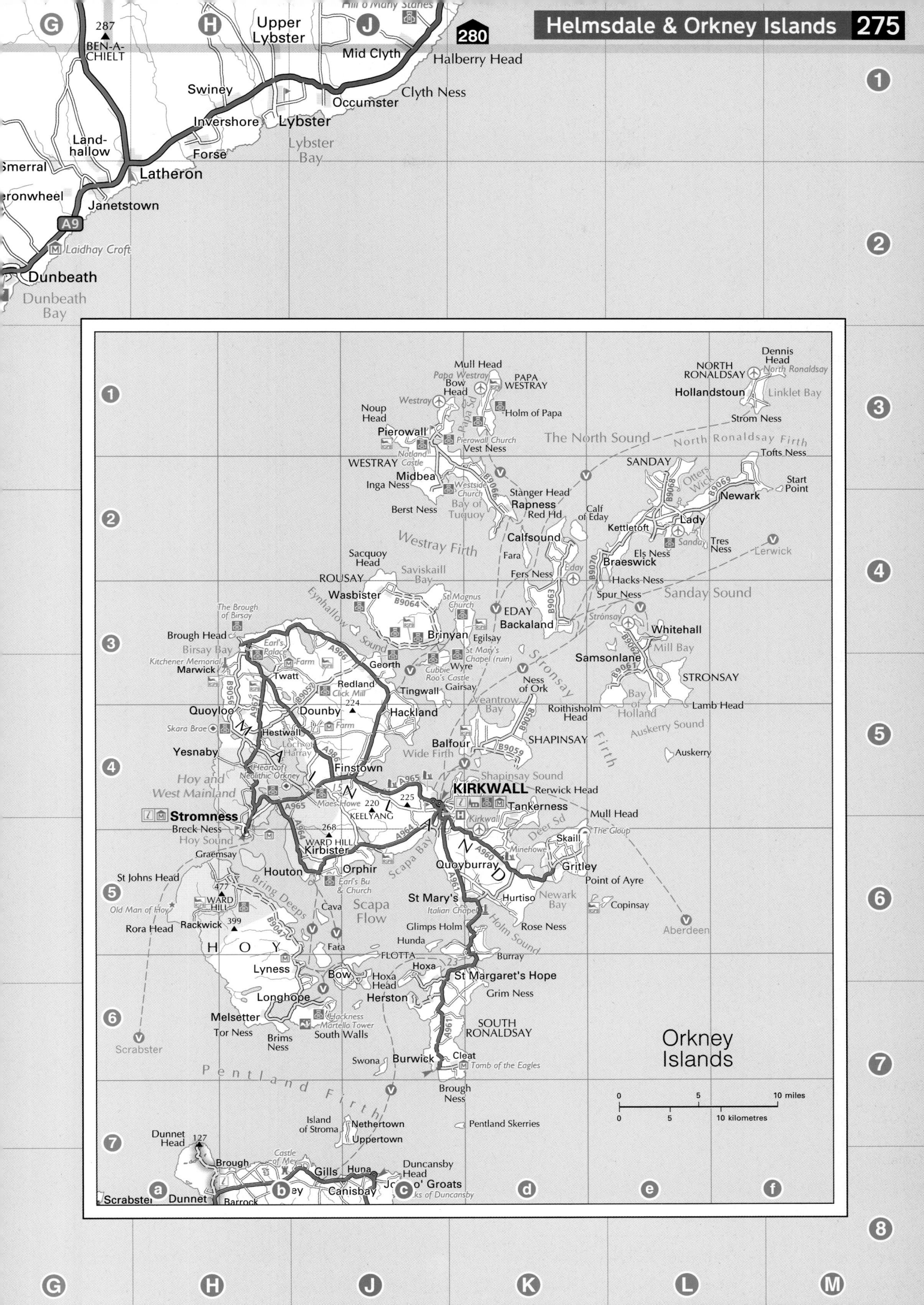

Orkney
Islands

1

2

CAPE WRATH

Kearvaig
Bay

Cléit
Dhubh

Faraid
Head

371
▲
SGRIBHIS-
BHEINN

297
▲
CNOC A
GHIUBHAIS

300
▲
MAOVALLY

Balnakeil
Bay

THE PARPH

457
▲
FASHVEN

Balnakeil ⓘ

Durness

Sangomor

3

Sandwood
Bay

Loch Àirigh
ná Beinne

Keolda

Sandwood
Loch

485
▲
CREAG
RIABACH

Rudh' an Fhir Leithe

468
▲
BEINN
DEARG MHÒR

464
▲
MEALL
NA MÒINE

331
▲
GHLAS-
BHEINN

Kyle of Durness

A838

4

Sheigra

489
▲
MEALL
NA CRÀ

Balchreick

Blairmore

Strath Shinary

521
▲
FARVEALL

19

Oldshoremore

355
▲
AN
SOCACH

Kinlochbervie

773
▲
BEINN
SPIONNAIDH

Loch Clash

Badcall

B801

801
▲
CRANSTACKIE

5

Loch Inchard

Achriesgill

Strath Dionard

River Dionard

Strath Beag

Rhiconich

Loch-na-
Claise Càrnaich

Rudha Ruadh

908
▲
FOINAVEN

Skerricha

Fanagmore

6

Tarbet

Loch Laxford

A838

North-west Sutherland

Loch na Tuadh

Foindle

HANDA
ISLAND

7

River Laxford

786
▲
ARKLE

Laxford
Bridge

Scourie
Bay

A894

Loch
Stack

729
▲
SÀBHAL BEAG

7

Scourie More

Scourie

721
▲
BEN STACK

Badcall

386
▲
BEN
AUSKAIRD

Strath Stack

333
▲
BEN
SCREAVIE

800
▲

796
▲
CÀRN
DEARG

757
▲
CARN A
TIONA

Badcall Ba

Loch a'
Mhuilinn

Achfary

8

Rudh' a'
Mhucard

17

A838

Loch M

| 0 | 1 | 2 | 3 | 4 | 5 miles |
| 0 | 1 | 2 | 3 | 4 | 5 | 6 | 7 | 8 kilometres |

ANY Eddrachillis Loc BEN Loch an

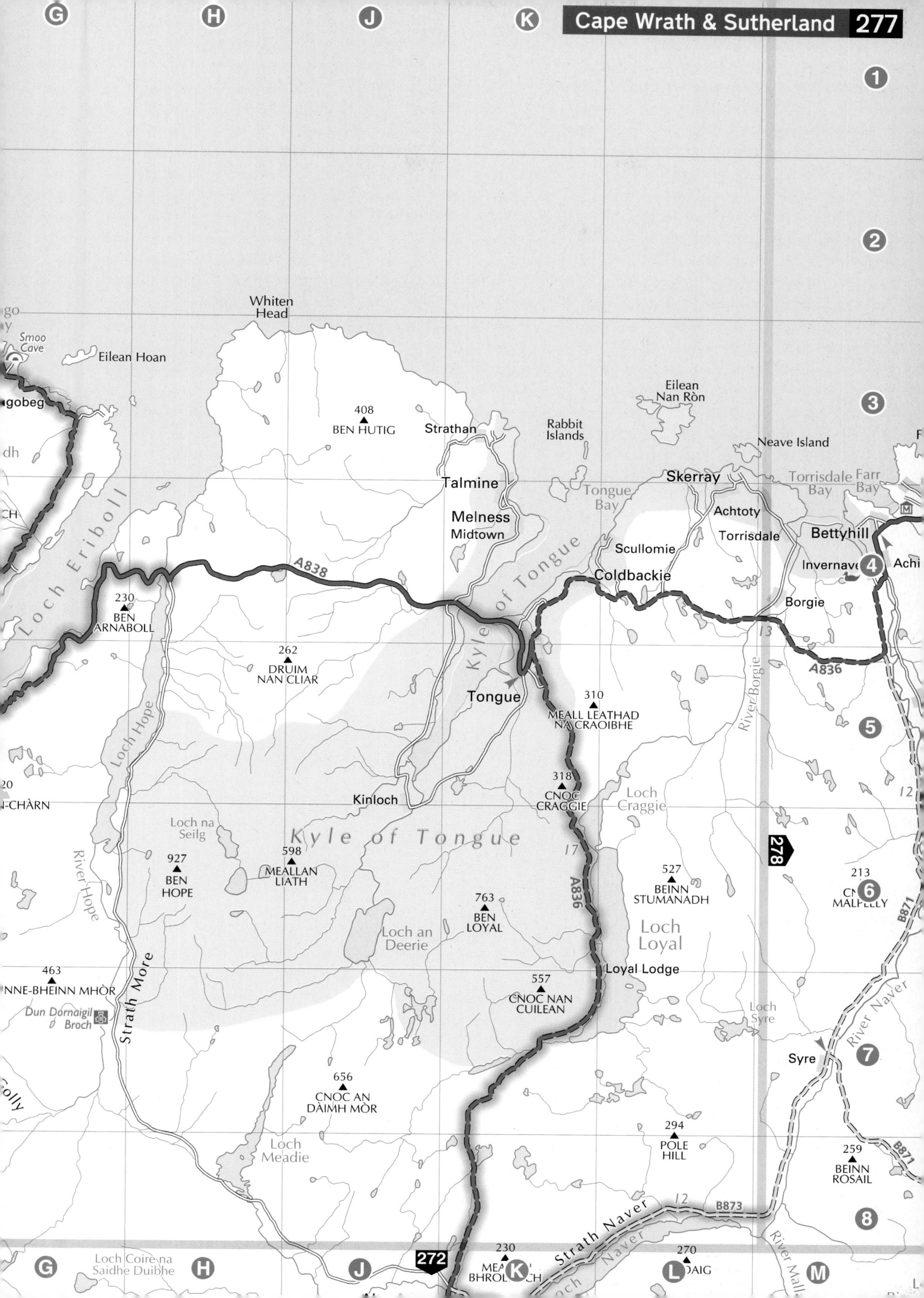

G   H   J   K

1
2
3
4
5
6
7
8

Smoo Cave
Eilean Hoan
gobeg
dh
CH

Loch Eriboll

230
BEN ARNABOLL

Strath More

Loch Hope

River Hope

20
-CHÀRN

NNE-BHEINN MHÒR   463

Dun Dornaigil Broch

olly

Whiten Head

408
BEN HUTIG

Strathan

Talmine

Melness
Midtown

A838

262
DRUIM NAN CLIAR

Loch na Seilg

927
BEN HOPE

598
MEALLAN LIATH

Kinloch

Loch an Deerie

763
BEN LOYAL

656
CNOC AN DÀIMH MÒR

Loch Meadie

Kyle of Tongue

Tongue

Tongue Bay

Rabbit Islands

Eilean Nan Ròn

Skerray

Scullomie

Coldbackie

Kyle of Tongue

310
MEALL LEATHAD NA CRAOIBHE

318
CNOC CRAGGIE

Loch Craggie

17

A836

527
BEIN STUMANADH

Loch Loyal

Loyal Lodge

557
CNOC NAN CUILEAN

294
POLE HILL

Neave Island

Achtoty

Torrisdale

Torrisdale Bay

Farr Bay

Bettyhill

Invernave

Achi

Borgie

River Borgie

A836

13

12

278

213
CN MALFELLY

6

Loch Syre

Syre

River Naver

Strath Naver

259
BEINN ROSAIL

B871

B873

12

Loch Coire na Saidhe Duibhe

272

230
MEA BHROL CH

LOAIG   270

Loch Naver

River Mall

G   H   J   K   L   M

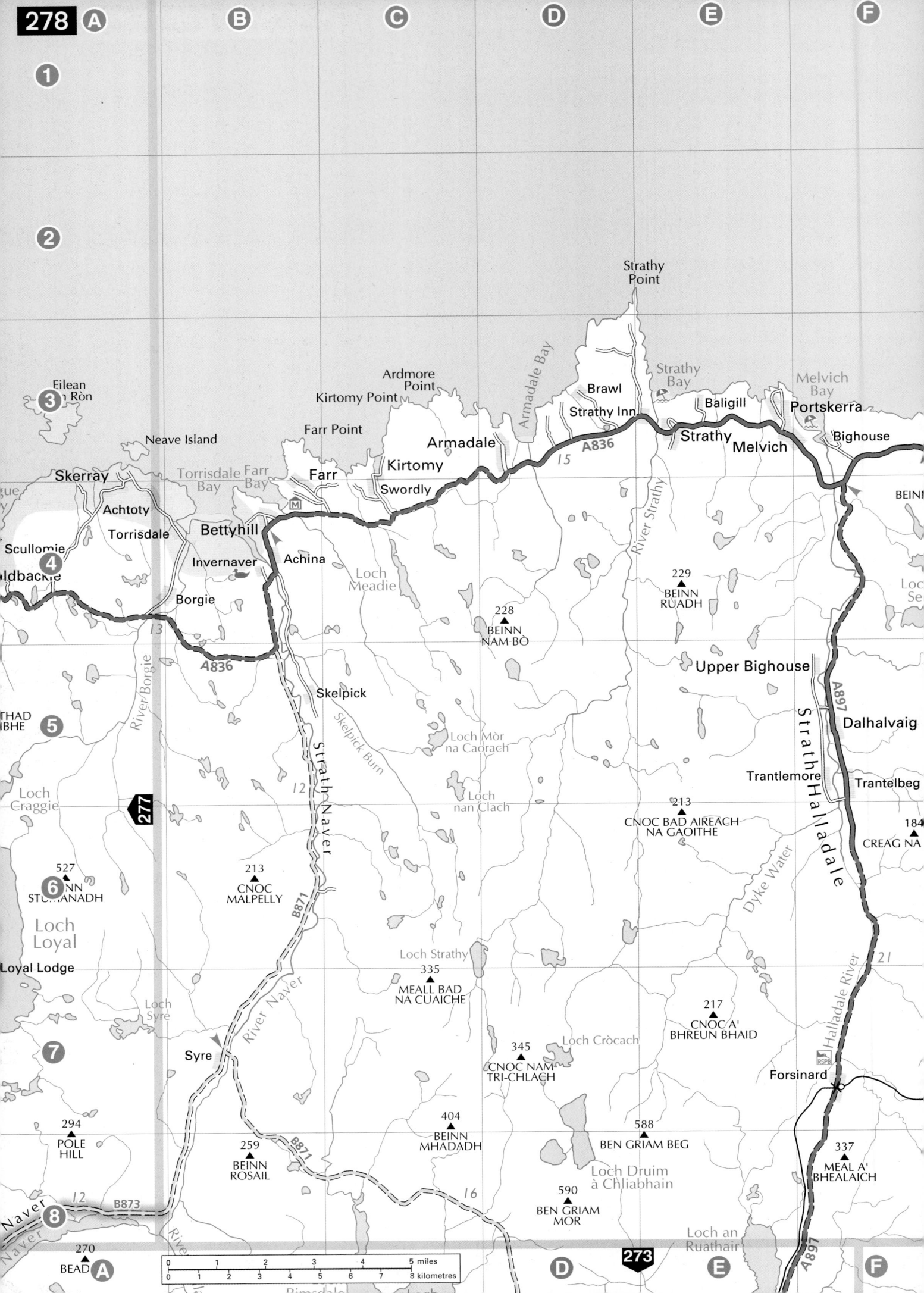

G   H   J   K

1

DUNNET HEAD 127

Stromness V

Briga Head

PENT

121 Brough

DUNNET HILL St John's Loch

Brims Ness   Holborn Head

Clarden Head

West Dunnet B855

2 Dunnet

St Mary's Chapel (ruin)

Scrabster A9 Thurso Bay

Crosskirk A836

Dunnet Bay

Castlehill

Thurso 5 Murkle

A836 Castletown

16 Bridge of Forss

Skiall Lythmore

B874 280

Gr

Sandside Bay Upper Dounreay

Achreamie Glengolly A9 Weydale

Olrig House B876

Tai **3**

Isauld Cnoc Freiceadain Long Cairns

Hilliclay

Reay Achvarasdal Shebster

Forss Water Westfield

Sordale

Bower

242 BEINN RATHA

Loch Calder

B874 Roadside Knockdee

Loch Scarmclate **4** Halcro

Broubster

Clayock Gillock

290 BEIN NAM BAD MHÒR

Shurrery

B870 Halkirk Georgemas Junction Station

A882 21 Loch Watten

243 CNOC AN DARAIN BHÀIN

Shurrery Lodge

Loch Scye

Harpsdale 176 SPITTAL HILL

B870 **5** Watten

160 BRAIGH FÉITH HEMIGAL

Dorrery Scotscalder Station

Loch Shurrery

Olgrinmore River Thurso Spittal

75 OC GALL

Loch Tuim Ghlais

Loch Caluim

132 DRUIM A' CHRACAIRNIE

Mybster Loch of Toftingall

6

203 CNOC PREAS A'MHADAIDH

200 CNOC BEUL NA FAIRE

Westerdale 23 280

136 BEINN CHÀITEAG

Strath Beg

Altnabreac Station

Loch More

Loch Ruard A9

Achavanich Loch Stemster

7 BALLH HIL

Rumsdale Water

Strathmore Water

Loch an Thulachan

Loch Sand

248 STEMSTER HILL

Clutt Water Dalnawillan Lodge

226 COIRE NA BEINN

Loch Rangag

G Lodge

348 BEN ALISKY

274

287 BEN-A-CHIELT

8

U Ly

G   H   J   K   L   M Swiney

CNOCAN CONACHREAC

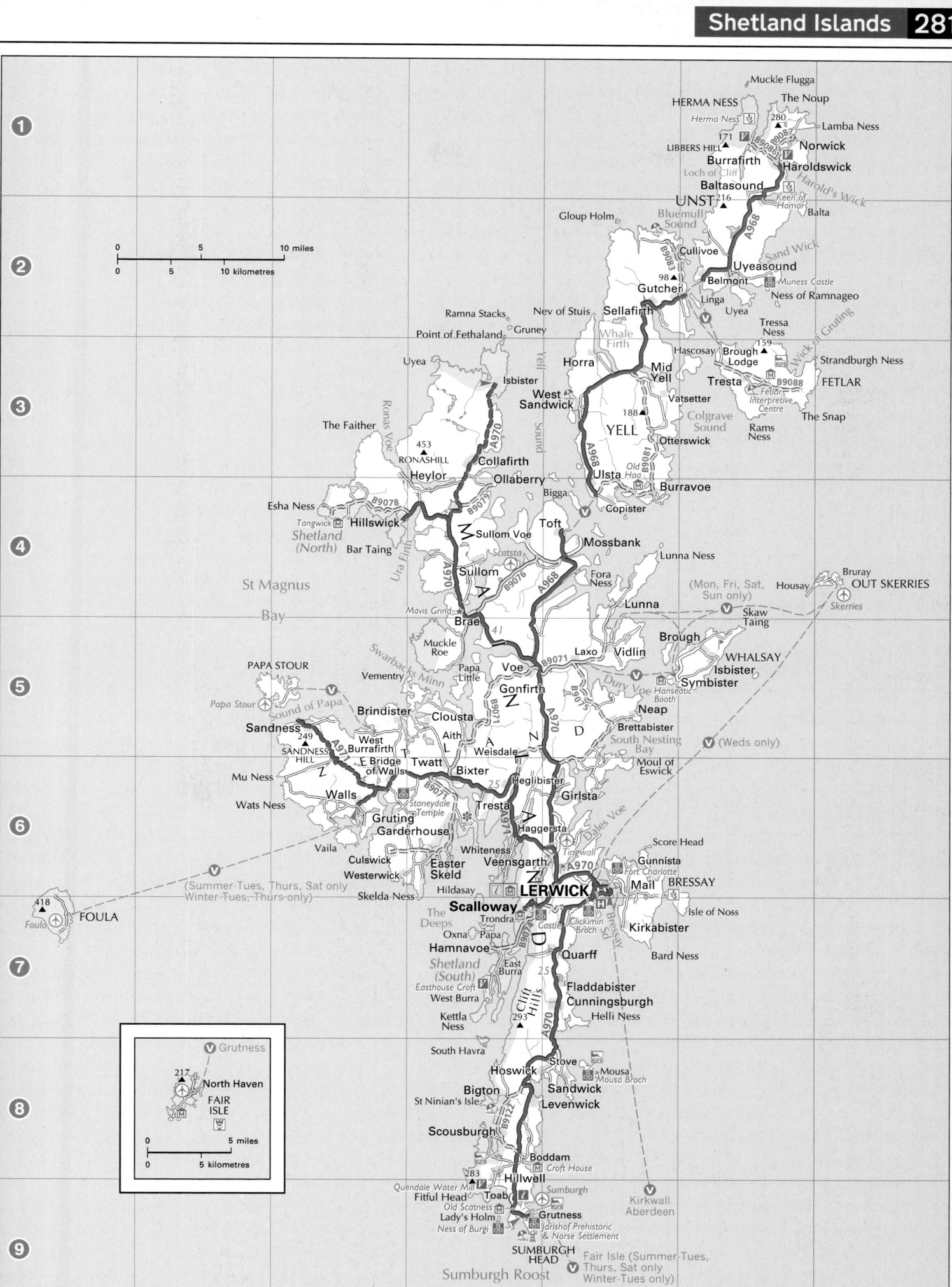

0   5   10 miles
0   5   10 kilometres

Muckle Flugga
HERMA NESS   The Noup
Herma Ness   280   Lamba Ness
LIBBERS HILL   171   Norwick
Burrafirth   Haroldswick
Loch of Cliff   Baltasound
UNST   216   Balta
Gloup Holm   Keen of Hamar
Bluemull Sound   Sand Wick
B9083   Cullivoe   Uyeasound
Ramna Stacks   Nev of Stuis   98   Belmont   Muness Castle
Point of Fethaland   Gruney   Gutcher   Linga   Ness of Ramnageo
Sellafirth   Uyea
Whale   Tressa Ness   Wick of Gruting
Uyea   Horra   Firth   Hascosay   Brough   159   Strandburgh Ness
Isbister   West   Mid   Lodge
Sandwick   Yell   Tresta   B9088   FETLAR
The Faither   Vatsetter   Fetlar Interpretive Centre   The Snap
453   YELL   188   Rams Ness
RONASHILL   Collafirth   Otterswick
Heylor   Ollaberry   Old Haa
Bigga   Ulsta   Burravoe
Esha Ness   B9078   Copister
Tangwick   Hillswick   Toft   Lunna Ness
Shetland   Bar Taing   Sullom Voe   Mossbank   Bruray   Housay
(North)   Scatsta   Fora Ness   OUT SKERRIES
St Magnus   Sullom   Lunna   (Mon, Fri, Sat, Sun only)   Skaw Taing   Skerries
Bay   A970   B9076   A968   Brough
Mavis Grind   Laxo   Vidlin   WHALSAY
PAPA STOUR   Brae   B9071   Isbister
41   Voe   Symbister
Muckle Roe   Gonfirth   Dury Voe   Neap   Hanseatic Booth
Papa Little   Brettabister
Vementry   South Nesting Bay   (Weds only)
Papa Stour   Brindister   Clousta   Moul of Eswick
Sound of Papa   Aith
Sandness   West Burrafirth   Weisdale   Score Head
249   Twatt   Bixter   Heglibister   Gunnista   Fort Charlotte
SANDNESS HILL   Bridge   Girlsta   BRESSAY
Mu Ness   of Walls   Tresta   Mail
Wats Ness   Walls   Staneydale Temple   Haggersta   Isle of Noss
Gruting   Tingwall
Garderhouse   Whiteness   A971   Bard Ness
Vaila   Veensgarth   A970
Culswick   Easter   LERWICK   Kirkabister
FOULA   418   Westerwick   Skeld   Hildasay   Clickimin Broch
Foula   Skelda Ness   Scalloway   Castle
The Deeps   Trondra
(Summer-Tues, Thurs, Sat only   Oxna   Papa   Quarff
Winter-Tues, Thurs only)   Hamnavoe   East   Fladdabister
Shetland   Burra   Cunningsburgh   Helli Ness
(South)   West Burra   293
Easthouse Croft   Cliff Hills   A970
Kettla Ness
South Havra   Stove
Hoswick   Mousa
Bigton   Sandwick   Mousa Broch
St Ninian's Isle   Levenwick
Scousburgh   B9122
Boddam
Croft House
Quendale Water Mill   283   Hillwell   Sumburgh
Fitful Head   Toab   Kirkwall
Old Scatness   Aberdeen
Lady's Holm   Grutness
Ness of Burgi   Jarlshof Prehistoric & Norse Settlement
SUMBURGH HEAD   Fair Isle (Summer-Tues, Thurs, Sat only   Winter-Tues only)
Sumburgh Roost

Grutness
217   North Haven
FAIR ISLE
0   5 miles
0   5 kilometres

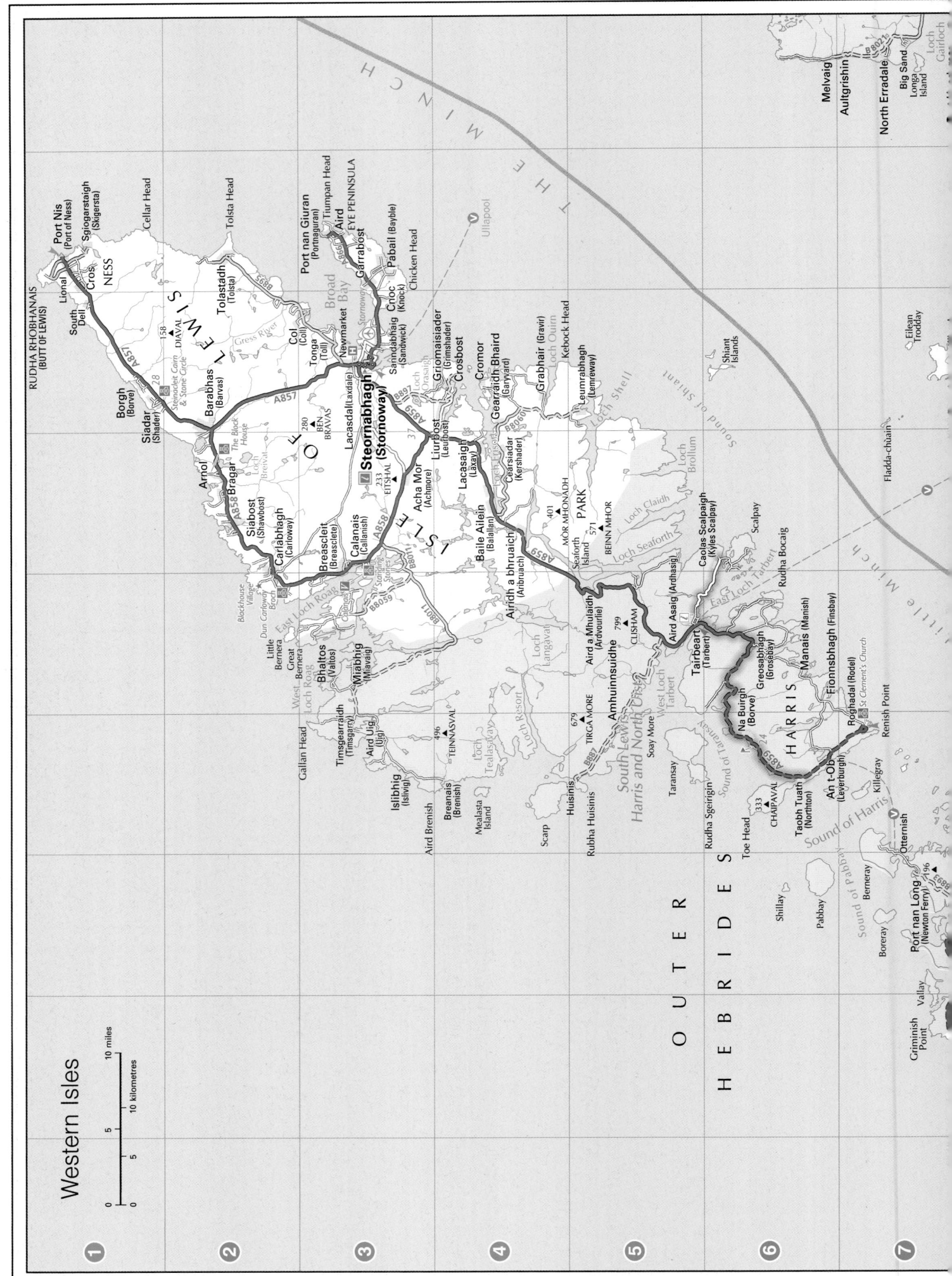

Western Isles

THE MINCH

LEWIS

ISLE OF LEWIS

PARK

South Lewis, Harris and North Uist

HARRIS

OUTER HEBRIDES

Little Minch

Sound of Shiant

Sound of Taransay

Sound of Pabbay

Sound of Harris

10 miles
10 kilometres

Rudha Rhobhanais (Butt of Lewis)
Port Nis (Port of Ness)
Sgiogarstaigh (Skigersta)
Cellar Head
Lìonal
Cros
South Dell
NESS
Tolastadh (Tolsta)
Tolsta Head
Siadar (Shader)
Borgh (Borve)
Barabhas (Barvas)
Steinaclet Cairn & Stone Circle
The Block House
Arnol
Bràgar
158
DIABAL
Loch Breivat
BEN BRAVAS
280
A857
Col (Coll)
Gress River
Tonga (Tolt)
Newmarket
Broad Bay
Stornoway
Tìumpan Head
EYE PENINSULA
Aird
Port nan Giùran (Portnaguran)
Garrabost
Pabail (Bayble)
Chicken Head
Cnoc (Knock)
Sanndabhaig (Sandwick)
Steòrnabhagh (Stornoway)
Lacasdail (Laxdale)
Loch Orasaigh
Griomaisiader (Grimshader)
Crosbost
Cromor
Grabhair (Gravir)
Loch Oirm
Gearraidh Bhaird (Garyard)
Kebock Head
Grabhair
Leumrabhagh (Lemreway)
Loch Shell
Shiant Islands
Eilean Trodday
Fladda-chùain
Liurbost (Leurbost)
Acha Mòr (Achmore)
233 EITSHAL
Lacasaigh (Laxay)
Cearsiadar (Kershader)
MOR MHONADH
401
BEINN MHOR
571
Loch Claidh
Loch Seaforth
Caolas Scalpaigh (Kyles Scalpay)
Scalpay
Rudha Bocaig
Loch Brollum
Seaforth Island
Calanais (Callanish)
Breascleit (Breasclete)
Càrlabhagh (Carloway)
Siabost (Shawbost)
Blackhouse Village
Dun Carloway Broch
Baile Ailein (Balallan)
Àiridh a bhruaich (Aribruaich)
Aird a Mhulaidh (Ardvourlie)
CLISHAM
799
Aird Asaig (Ardhasig)
East Loch Tarbert
Tairbeart (Tarbert)
West Loch Tarbert
Manais (Manish)
Fìonnsbhagh (Finsbay)
Greosabhagh (Grosebay)
Na Buirgh (Borve)
Roghadal (Rodel)
St Clement's Church
Renish Point
An t-Ob (Leverburgh)
Taobh Tuath (Northton)
CHAIPAVAL
333
Toe Head
Rudha Sgeirigin
Killegray
Ensay
Berneray
Otternish
Port nan Long (Newton Ferry)
796
Griminish Point
Vallay
Boreray
Pabbay
Shillay
Berneray
Melvaig
Aultgrishin
North Erradale
Big Sand
Longa Island
Loch Gairloch
Ullapool
Little Bernera
Great Bernera
Bhaltos (Valtos)
Miabhig (Miavaig)
Aird Uig (Uig)
Loch Roag
East Loch Roag
West Loch Roag
Gallan Head
Timsgearraidh (Timsgarry)
496 TEINNASVAL
Loch Tealasavay
TIRGA MORE
679
Loch Langavat
Loch Resort
Amhuinnsuidhe
Soay More
Taransay
Islibhig (Islivig)
Breanais (Brenish)
Mealasta Island
Huisinis
Rubha Huisinis
Scarp
Aird Brenish
A857
28
A858
A859
A858
B8011
B8059
B8060
A865
B897
B8001
A8021
A855
A832
A896
E899
688
37

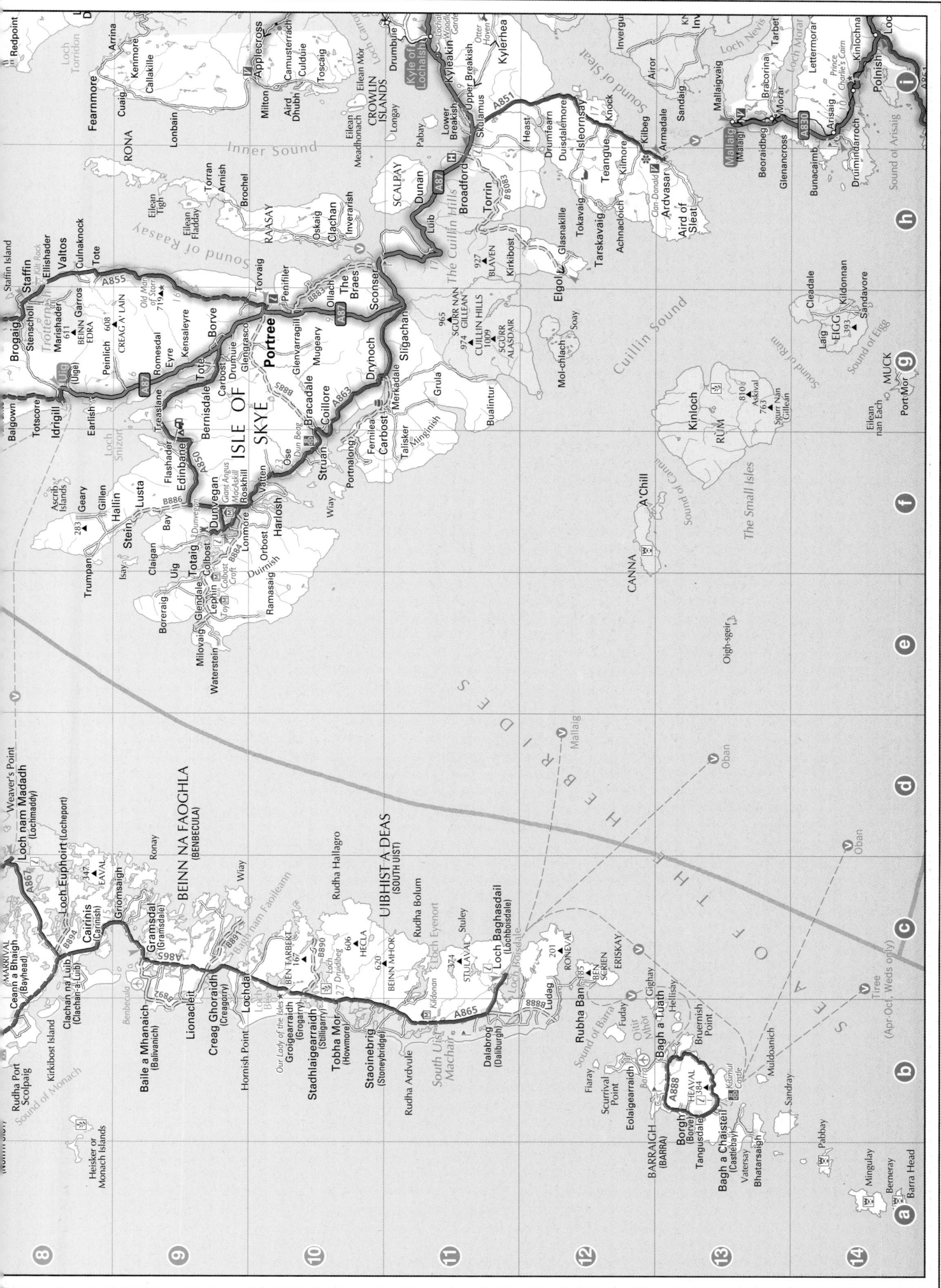

Motorway and Primary Route junctions which have access or exit restrictions are shown on the map pages thus:

M1 London - Leeds

Junction	Northbound	Southbound
2	Access only from A1 (northbound)	Exit only to A1 (southbound)
4	Access only from A41 (northbound)	Exit only to A41 (southbound)
6A	Access only from M25 (no link from A405)	Exit only to M25 (no link from A405)
7	Access only from A414	Exit only to A414
17	Exit only to M45	Access only from M45
19	Exit only to M6 (northbound)	Exit only to A14 (southbound)
21A	Exit only, no access	Access only, no exit
23A	Access only from A42	No restriction
24A	Access only, no exit	Exit only, no access
35A	Exit only, no access	Access only, no exit
43	Exit only to M621	Access only from M621
48	Exit only to A1(M) (northbound)	Access only from A1(M) (southbound)

M2 Rochester - Faversham

Junction	Westbound	Eastbound
1	No exit to A2 (eastbound)	No access from A2 (westbound)

M3 Sunbury - Southampton

Junction	Northeastbound	Southwestbound
8	Access only from A303, no exit	Exit only to A303, no access
10	Exit only, no access	Access only, no exit
14	Access from M27 only, no exit	No access to M27 (westbound)

M4 London - South Wales

Junction	Westbound	Eastbound
1	Access only from A4 (westbound)	Exit only to A4 (eastbound)
2	Access only from A4 (westbound)	Access only from A4 (eastbound)
21	Exit only to M48	Access only from M48
23	Access only from M48	Exit only to M48
25	Exit only, no access	Access only, no exit
25A	Exit only, no access	Access only, no exit
29	Exit only to A48(M)	Access only from A48(M)
38	Exit only, no access	No restriction
39	Access only, no exit	No access or exit
42	Exit only to A483	Access only from A483

M5 Birmingham - Exeter

Junction	Northeastbound	Southwestbound
10	Access only, no exit	Exit only, no access
11A	Access only from A417 (westbound)	Exit only to A417 (eastbound)
18A	Exit only to M49	Access only from M49
18	Exit only, no access	Access only, no exit

M6 Toll Motorway

Junction	Northwestbound	Southeastbound
T1	Access only, no exit	No access or exit
T2	No access or exit	Exit only, no access
T5	Access only, no exit	Exit only to A5148 (northbound), no access
T7	Exit only, no access	Access only, no exit
T8	Exit only, no access	Access only, no exit

M6 Rugby - Carlisle

Junction	Northbound	Southbound
3A	Exit only to M6 Toll	Access only from M6 Toll
4	Exit only to M42 (southbound) & A446	Exit only to A446
4A	Access only from M42 (southbound)	Exit only to M42
5	Exit only, no access	Access only, no exit
10A	Exit only to M54	Access only from M54
11A	Access only from M6 Toll	Exit only to M6 Toll
with M56 (jct 20A)	No restriction	Access only from M56 (eastbound)
20	Exit only to M56 (westbound)	Access only from M56 (eastbound)
24	Access only, no exit	Exit only, no access
25	Exit only, no access	Access only, no exit

30	Access only from M61	Exit only to M61
31A	Exit only, no access	Access only, no exit
45	Exit only, no access	Access only, no exit

M8 Edinburgh - Bishopton

Junction	Westbound	Eastbound
6	Exit only, no access	Access only, no exit
6A	Access only, no exit	Exit only, no access
7	Access only, no exit	Exit only, no access
7A	Exit only, no access	Access only from A725 (northbound), no exit
8	No access from M73 (southbound) or from A8 (eastbound) & A89	No exit to M73 (northbound) or to A8 (westbound) & A89
9	Access only, no exit	Exit only, no access
13	Access only from M80 (southbound)	Exit only to M80 (northbound)
14	Access only, no exit	Exit only, no access
16	Exit only to A804	Access only from A879
17	Exit only to A82	No restriction
18	Access only from A82 (eastbound)	Exit only to A814
19	No access from A814 (westbound)	Exit only to A814 (westbound)
20	Exit only, no access	Access only, no exit
21	Access only, no exit	Exit only to A8
22	Exit only to M77 (southbound)	Access only from M77 (northbound)
23	Exit only to B768	Access only from B768
25	No access or exit from or to A8	No access or exit from or to A8
25A	Exit only, no access	Access only, no exit
28	Exit only, no access	Access only, no exit
28A	Exit only to A737	Access only from A737

M9 Edinburgh - Dunblane

Junction	Northwestbound	Southeastbound
2	Access only, no exit	Exit only, no access
3	Exit only, no access	Access only, no exit
6	Access only, no exit	Exit only to A905
8	Exit only to M876 (southwestbound)	Access only from M876 (northeastbound)

M11 London - Cambridge

Junction	Northbound	Southbound
4	Access only from A406 (eastbound)	Exit only to A406
5	Exit only, no access	Access only, no exit
8A	Exit only, no access	No direct access, use jct 8
9	Exit only to A11	Access only from A11
13	Exit only, no access	Access only, no exit
14	Exit only, no access	Access only, no exit

M20 Swanley - Folkestone

Junction	Northwestbound	Southeastbound
2	Staggered junction; follow signs - access only	Staggered junction; follow signs - exit only
3	Exit only to M26 (westbound)	Access only from M26 (eastbound)
5	Access only from A20	For access follow signs - exit only to A20
6	No restriction	For exit follow signs
11A	Access only, no exit	Exit only, no access

M23 Hooley - Crawley

Junction	Northbound	Southbound
7	Exit only to A23 (northbound)	Access only from A23 (southbound)
10A	Access only, no exit	Exit only, no access

M25 London Orbital Motorway

Junction	Clockwise	Anticlockwise
1B	No direct access, use slip road to jct 2 Exit only	Access only, no exit
5	No exit to M26 (eastbound)	No access from M26
19	Exit only, no access	Access only, no exit
21	Access only from M1 (southbound) Exit only to M1 (northbound)	Access only from M1 (southbound) Exit only to M1 (northbound)
31	No exit (use slip road via jct 30), access only	No access (use slip road via jct 30), exit only

M26 Sevenoaks - Wrotham

Junction	Westbound	Eastbound
with M25 (jct 5)	Exit only to clockwise M25 (westbound)	Access only from anticlockwise M25 (eastbound)
with M20 (jct 3)	Access only from M20 (northwestbound)	Exit only to M20 (southeastbound)

M27 Cadnam - Portsmouth

Junction	Westbound	Eastbound
4	Staggered junction; follow signs - access only from M3 (southbound). Exit only to M3 (northbound)	Staggered junction; follow signs - access only from M3 (southbound). Exit only to M3 (northbound)
10	Exit only, no access	Access only, no exit
12	Staggered junction; follow signs - exit only to M275 (southbound)	Staggered junction; follow signs - access only from M275 (northbound)

M40 London - Birmingham

Junction	Northwestbound	Southeastbound
3	Exit only, no access	Access only, no exit
7	Exit only, no access	Access only, no exit
8	Exit only to M40/A40	Access only from M40/A40
13	Exit only, no access	Access only, no exit
14	Access only, no exit	Exit only, no access
16	Access only, no exit	Exit only, no access

M42 Bromsgrove - Measham

Junction	Northeastbound	Southwestbound
1	Access only, no exit	Exit only, no access
7	Exit only to M6 (northwestbound)	Access only from M6 (northwestbound)
7A	Exit only to M6 (southeastbound)	No access or exit
8	Access only from M6 (southeastbound)	Exit only to M6 (northwestbound)

M45 Coventry - M1

Junction	Westbound	Eastbound
Dunchurch (unnumbered)	Access only from A45	Exit only, no access
with M1 (jct 17)	Access only from M1 (northbound)	Exit only to M1 (southbound)

M48 Chepstow

Junction	Westbound	Eastbound
21	Access only from M4 (westbound)	Exit only to M4 (eastbound)
23	No exit to M4 (eastbound)	No access from M4 (westbound)

M53 Mersey Tunnel - Chester

Junction	Northbound	Southbound
11	Access only from M56 (westbound) Exit only to M56 (eastbound)	Access only from M56 (westbound) Exit only to M56 (eastbound)

M54 Telford - Birmingham

Junction	Westbound	Eastbound
with M6 (jct 10A)	Access only from M6 (northbound)	Exit only to M6 (southbound)

M56 Chester - Manchester

Junction	Westbound	Eastbound
1	Access only from M60 (westbound)	Exit only to M60 (eastbound) & A34 (northbound)
2	Exit only, no access	Access only, no exit
3	Access only, no exit	Exit only, no access
4	Exit only, no access	Access only, no exit
7	Exit only, no access	No restriction
8	Access only, no exit	No access or exit
9	No exit to M6 (southbound)	No access from M6 (northbound)
15	Exit only to M53	Access only from M53
16	No access or exit	No restriction

M57 Liverpool Outer Ring Road

Junction	Northwestbound	Southeastbound
3	Access only, no exit	Exit only, no access
5	Access only from A580 (westbound)	Exit only, no access

M58 Liverpool - Wigan

Junction	Westbound	Eastbound
1	Exit only, no access	Access only, no exit

M60 Manchester Orbital

Junction	Clockwise	Anticlockwise
2	Access only, no exit	Exit only, no access
3	No access from M56	Access only from A34 (northbound)
4	Access only from A34 (northbound). Exit only to M56	Access only from M56 (eastbound). Exit only to A34 (southbound)
5	Access and exit only from and to A5103 (northbound)	Access and exit only from and to A5103 (southbound)
7	No direct access, use slip road to jct 8. Exit only to A56	Access only from A56. No exit, use jct 8
14	Access from A580 (eastbound)	Exit only to A580 (westbound)
16	Access only, no exit	Exit only, no access
20	Exit only, no access	Access only, no exit
22	No restriction	Exit only, no access
25	Exit only, no access	No restriction
26	No restriction	Exit only, no access
27	Access only, no exit	Exit only, no access

M61 Manchester - Preston

Junction	Northwestbound	Southeastbound
3	No access or exit	Exit only, no access
with M6 (jct 30)	Exit only to M6 (northbound)	Access only from M6 (southbound)

M62 Liverpool - Kingston upon Hull

Junction	Westbound	Eastbound
23	Access only, no exit	Exit only, no access
32A	No access to A1(M) (southbound)	No restriction

M65 Preston - Colne

Junction	Northeastbound	Southwestbound
9	Exit only, no access	Access only, no exit
11	Access only, no exit	Exit only, no access

M66 Bury

Junction	Northbound	Southbound
with A56	Exit only to A56 (northbound)	Access only from A56 (southbound)
1	Exit only, no access	Access only, no exit

M67 Hyde Bypass

Junction	Westbound	Eastbound
1	Access only, no exit	Exit only, no access
2	Access only, no exit	Exit only, no access
3	Exit only, no access	No restriction

M69 Coventry - Leicester

Junction	Northbound	Southbound
2	Access only, no exit	Exit only, no access

M73 East of Glasgow

Junction	Northbound	Southbound
1	No exit to A74 & A721	No exit to A74 & A721
2	No access from or exit to A89. No access from M8 (eastbound)	No access from or exit to A89. No exit to M8 (westbound)

M74 and A74(M) Glasgow - Gretna

Junction	Northbound	Southbound
3	Exit only, no access	Access only, no exit
3A	Access only, no exit	Exit only, no access
4	No access from A74 & A721	Access only, no exit to A74 & A721
7	Exit only, no access	Exit only, no access
9	No access or exit	Exit only, no access
10	No restriction	Access only, no exit

M77 Glasgow - Kilmarnock

Junction	Northbound	Southbound
with M8 (jct 22)	No exit to M8 (westbound)	No access from M8 (eastbound)
4	Access only, no exit	Exit only, no access
6	Access only, no exit	Exit only, no access
7	Access only, no exit	No restriction
8	Exit only, no access	Exit only, no access

M80 Glasgow - Stirling

Junction	Northbound	Southbound
4A	Exit only, no access	Access only, no exit
6A	Access only, no exit	Exit only, no access
8	Exit only to M876 (northeastbound)	Access only from M876 (southwestbound)

M90 Edinburgh - Perth

Junction	Northbound	Southbound
1	No exit, access only	Exit only to A90 (eastbound)
2A	Exit only to A92 (eastbound)	Access only from A92 (westbound)
7	Access only, no exit	Exit only, no access
8	Exit only, no access	Access only, no exit
10	No access from A912. No exit to A912 (southbound)	No access from A912 (northbound) No exit to A912

M180 Doncaster - Grimsby

Junction	Westbound	Eastbound
1	Access only, no exit	Exit only, no access

M606 Bradford Spur

Junction	Northbound	Southbound
2	Exit only, no access	No restriction

M621 Leeds - M1

Junction	Clockwise	Anticlockwise
2A	Access only, no exit	Exit only, no access
4	No exit or access	No restriction
5	Access only, no exit	Exit only, no access
6	Exit only, no access	Access only, no exit
with M1 (jct 43)	Exit only to M1 (southbound)	Access only from M1 (northbound)

M876 Bonnybridge - Kincardine Bridge

Junction	Northeastbound	Southwestbound
with M80 (jct 5)	Access only from M80 (northeastbound)	Exit only to M80 (southwestbound)
with M9 (jct 8)	Exit only to M9 (eastbound)	Access only from M9 (westbound)

A1(M) South Mimms - Baldock

Junction	Northbound	Southbound
2	Exit only, no access	Access only, no exit
3	No restriction	Exit only, no access
5	Access only, no exit	No access or exit

A1(M) Pontefract - Bedale

Junction	Northbound	Southbound
41	No access to M62 (eastbound)	No restriction
43	Access only from M1 (northbound)	Exit only to M1 (southbound)

A1(M) Scotch Corner - Newcastle upon Tyne

Junction	Northbound	Southbound
57	Exit only to A66(M) (eastbound)	Access only from A66(M) (westbound)
65	No access Exit only to A194(M) & A1 (northbound)	No exit Access only from A194(M) & A1 (southbound)

A3(M) Horndean - Havant

Junction	Northbound	Southbound
1	Access only from A3	Exit only to A3
4	Exit only, no access	Access only, no exit

A38(M) Birmingham, Victoria Road (Park Circus)

Junction	Northbound	Southbound
with B4132	No exit	No access

A48(M) Cardiff Spur

Junction	Westbound	Eastbound
29	Access only from M4 (westbound)	Exit only to M4 (eastbound)
29A	Exit only to A48 (westbound)	Access only from A48 (eastbound)

A57(M) Manchester, Brook Street (A34)

Junction	Westbound	Eastbound
with A34	No exit	No access

A58(M) Leeds, Park Lane and Westgate

Junction	Northbound	Southbound
with A58	No restriction	No access

A64(M) Leeds, Clay Pit Lane (A58)

Junction	Westbound	Eastbound
with A58	No exit (to Clay Pit Lane)	No access (from Clay Pit Lane)

A66(M) Darlington Spur

Junction	Westbound	Eastbound
with A1(M) (jct 57)	Exit only to A1(M) (southbound)	Access only from A1(M) (northbound)

A74(M) Gretna - Abington

Junction	Northbound	Southbound
18	Exit only, no access	No exit

A194(M) Newcastle upon Tyne

Junction	Northbound	Southbound
with A1(M) (jct 65)	Access only from A1(M) (northbound)	Exit only to A1(M) (southbound)

A12 M25 - Ipswich

Junction	Northeastbound	Southwestbound
13	Access only, no exit	No restriction
14	Exit only, no access	Access only, no exit
20A	Exit only, no access	Access only, no exit
20B	Access only, no exit	Exit only, no access
21	No restriction	Access only, no exit
23	Access only, no exit	Exit only, no access
24	Access only, no exit	Exit only, no access
27	Exit only, no access	Access only, no exit
Dedham & Stratford St Mary (unnumbered)	Exit only	Access only

A14 M1 - Felixstowe

Junction	Westbound	Eastbound
with M1/M6 (jct19)	Exit only to M6 and M1 (northbound)	Access only from M6 and M1 (southbound)
4	Exit only, no access	Access only, no exit
31	Exit only to M11 (for London)	Access only, no exit
31A	Exit only to A14 (northbound)	Access only, no exit
34	Access only, no exit	Exit only, no access
36	Exit only to A11, access only from A1303	Access only from A11
38	Access only from A11	Exit only to A11
39	Exit only, no access	Access only, no exit
61	Access only, no exit	Exit only, no access

A55 Holyhead - Chester

Junction	Westbound	Eastbound
8A	Exit only, no access	Access only, no exit
23A	Access only, no exit	Exit only, no access
24A	Exit only, no access	No access or exit
27A	No restriction	No access or exit
33A	Exit only, no access	No access or exit
33B	Access only, no exit	Exit only, no access
36A	Exit only to A5104	Access only from A5104

This index lists places appearing in the main-map section of the atlas in alphabetical order. The reference following each name gives the atlas page number and grid reference of the square in which the place appears. The map shows counties, unitary authorities and administrative areas, together with a list of the abbreviated name forms used in the index.

Scotland

Abers	**Aberdeenshire**
Ag & B	**Argyll and Bute**
Angus	**Angus**
Border	**Scottish Borders**
C Aber	**City of Aberdeen**
C Dund	**City of Dundee**
C Edin	**City of Edinburgh**
C Glas	**City of Glasgow**
Clacks	**Clackmannanshire (1)**
D & G	**Dumfries & Galloway**
E Ayrs	**East Ayrshire**
E Duns	**East Dunbartonshire (2)**
E Loth	**East Lothian**
E Rens	**East Renfrewshire (3)**
Falk	**Falkirk**
Fife	**Fife**
Highld	**Highland**
Inver	**Inverclyde (4)**
Mdloth	**Midlothian (5)**
Moray	**Moray**
N Ayrs	**North Ayrshire**
N Lans	**North Lanarkshire (6)**
Ork	**Orkney Islands**
P & K	**Perth & Kinross**
Rens	**Renfrewshire (7)**
S Ayrs	**South Ayrshire**
S Lans	**South Lanarkshire**
Shet	**Shetland Islands**
Stirlg	**Stirling**
W Duns	**West Dunbartonshire (8)**
W Isls	**Western Isles (Na h-Eileanan an Iar)**
W Loth	**West Lothian**

Wales

Blae G	**Blaenau Gwent (9)**
Brdgnd	**Bridgend (10)**
Caerph	**Caerphilly (11)**
Cardif	**Cardiff**
Carmth	**Carmarthenshire**
Cerdgn	**Ceredigion**
Conwy	**Conwy**
Denbgs	**Denbighshire**
Flints	**Flintshire**
Gwynd	**Gwynedd**
IoA	**Isle of Anglesey**
Mons	**Monmouthshire**
Myr Td	**Merthyr Tydfil (12)**
Neath	**Neath Port Talbot (13)**
Newpt	**Newport (14)**
Pembks	**Pembrokeshire**
Powys	**Powys**
Rhondd	**Rhondda Cynon Taff (15)**
Swans	**Swansea**
Torfn	**Torfaen (16)**
V Glam	**Vale of Glamorgan (17)**
Wrexhm	**Wrexham**

Channel Islands & Isle of Man

Guern	**Guernsey**
Jersey	**Jersey**
IoM	**Isle of Man**

England

BaNES	**Bath & N E Somerset (18)**
Barns	**Barnsley (19)**
Bed	**Bedford**
Birm	**Birmingham**
Bl w D	**Blackburn with Darwen (20)**
Bmouth	**Bournemouth**
Bolton	**Bolton (21)**
Bpool	**Blackpool**
Br & H	**Brighton & Hove (22)**
Br For	**Bracknell Forest (23)**
Bristl	**City of Bristol**
Bucks	**Buckinghamshire**
Bury	**Bury (24)**
C Beds	**Central Bedfordshire**
C Brad	**City of Bradford**
C Derb	**City of Derby**
C KuH	**City of Kingston upon Hull**
C Leic	**City of Leicester**
C Nott	**City of Nottingham**
C Pete	**City of Peterborough**
C Plym	**City of Plymouth**
C Port	**City of Portsmouth**
C Sotn	**City of Southampton**
C Stke	**City of Stoke-on-Trent**
C York	**City of York**
Calder	**Calderdale (25)**
Cambs	**Cambridgeshire**
Ches E	**Cheshire East**
Ches W	**Cheshire West and Chester**
Cnwll	**Cornwall**
Covtry	**Coventry**
Cumb	**Cumbria**
Darltn	**Darlington (26)**
Derbys	**Derbyshire**
Devon	**Devon**
Donc	**Doncaster (27)**
Dorset	**Dorset**
Dudley	**Dudley (28)**
Dur	**Durham**
E R Yk	**East Riding of Yorkshire**
E Susx	**East Sussex**
Essex	**Essex**
Gatesd	**Gateshead (29)**
Gloucs	**Gloucestershire**
Gt Lon	**Greater London**
Halton	**Halton (30)**
Hants	**Hampshire**
Hartpl	**Hartlepool (31)**
Herefs	**Herefordshire**
Herts	**Hertfordshire**
IoS	**Isles of Scilly**
IoW	**Isle of Wight**
Kent	**Kent**
Kirk	**Kirklees (32)**
Knows	**Knowsley (33)**
Lancs	**Lancashire**
Leeds	**Leeds**
Leics	**Leicestershire**
Lincs	**Lincolnshire**
Lpool	**Liverpool**
Luton	**Luton**
M Keyn	**Milton Keynes**
Manch	**Manchester**
Medway	**Medway**
Middsb	**Middlesbrough**
N Linc	**North Lincolnshire**
N Som	**North Somerset (34)**
N Tyne	**North Tyneside (35)**
N u Ty	**Newcastle upon Tyne**
N York	**North Yorkshire**
NE Lin	**North East Lincolnshire**
Nhants	**Northamptonshire**
Norfk	**Norfolk**
Notts	**Nottinghamshire**
Nthumb	**Northumberland**
Oldham	**Oldham (36)**
Oxon	**Oxfordshire**
Poole	**Poole**
R & Cl	**Redcar & Cleveland**
Readg	**Reading**
Rochdl	**Rochdale (37)**
Rothm	**Rotherham (38)**
Rutlnd	**Rutland**
S Glos	**South Gloucestershire (39)**
S on T	**Stockton-on-Tees (40)**
S Tyne	**South Tyneside (41)**
Salfd	**Salford (42)**
Sandw	**Sandwell (43)**
Sefton	**Sefton (44)**
Sheff	**Sheffield**
Shrops	**Shropshire**
Slough	**Slough (45)**
Solhll	**Solihull (46)**
Somset	**Somerset**
St Hel	**St Helens (47)**
Staffs	**Staffordshire**
Sthend	**Southend-on-Sea**
Stockp	**Stockport (48)**
Suffk	**Suffolk**
Sundld	**Sunderland**
Surrey	**Surrey**
Swindn	**Swindon**
Tamesd	**Tameside (49)**
Thurr	**Thurrock (50)**
Torbay	**Torbay**
Traffd	**Trafford (51)**
W & M	**Windsor and Maidenhead (52)**
W Berk	**West Berkshire**
W Susx	**West Sussex**
Wakefd	**Wakefield (53)**
Warrtn	**Warrington (54)**
Warwks	**Warwickshire**
Wigan	**Wigan (55)**
Wilts	**Wiltshire**
Wirral	**Wirral (56)**
Wokham	**Wokingham (57)**
Wolves	**Wolverhampton (58)**
Worcs	**Worcestershire**
Wrekin	**Telford & Wrekin (59)**
Wsall	**Walsall (60)**

ORKNEY ISLANDS

SHETLAND ISLANDS

WESTERN ISLES (Na h-Eileanan an Iar)

HIGHLAND

MORAY

S C O T L A N D

Aberdeen

ABERDEENSHIRE

ANGUS

PERTH & KINROSS

Dundee

ARGYLL AND BUTE

STIRLING

FIFE

1

8
2
4 Glasgow
7
3
FALK
6
W LOTH
Edinburgh
E LOTH
5

NORTH AYRSHIRE

S LANS

SCOTTISH BORDERS

E AYRS

S AYRS

DUMFRIES & GALLOWAY

NORTHUMBERLAND

Newcastle upon Tyne
35
29 41
Sunderland

CUMBRIA

DURHAM
31
26 40 R & CL
Middlesbrough

IoM

NORTH YORKSHIRE

Blackpool

LANCASHIRE

Bradford
York
Leeds
EAST RIDING OF YORKSHIRE
Kingston upon Hull

20
55
25
21 24 37
44 47 36 32
Liverpool 33 42 49 53
56 54 51 Manchester 19 N LINC
30 48 38 NE LIN
Sheffield
27

IoA

CONWY

FLINTS
CHES W
CHES E

DERBYS

LINCOLNSHIRE

DENBGS

WREXHAM

Stoke-on-Trent

NOTTS

GWYNEDD

Derby
Nottingham

STAFFS

59

LEICS

RUTLAND

Peterborough

NORFOLK

SHROPSHIRE

58 60
28 43 Birmingham
46 Coventry

NHANTS

CAMBS

POWYS

WORCS

WARWKS

Milton Keynes

SUFFOLK

CERDGN

HEREFS

W A L E S

E N G L A N D

BED
BEDS Luton

PEMBKS

CARMTH

12 9
13 15 16
10 11 MONS
17 14

GLOUCS

OXON

BUCKS

HERTS

ESSEX

Swansea

Cardiff

Bristol 39
34
18

Swindon

Reading
52 45
W BERK
57 23

GREATER LONDON

Southend-on-Sea
50

MEDWAY

WILTSHIRE

SURREY

KENT

SOMERSET

HAMPSHIRE

W SUSX

E SUSX
22

DEVON

DORSET

Bournemouth
Poole
IoW
Southampton
Portsmouth

CORNWALL

Plymouth
Torbay

CHANNEL ISLANDS

Guernsey

Jersey

IoS

A

Abbas Combe Somset ... 32 B6
Abberley Worcs ... 81 H2
Abberley Common Worcs ... 81 G2
Abberton Essex ... 72 E3
Abberton Worcs ... 82 A4
Abberwick Nthumb ... 191 G3
Abbess Roding Essex ... 70 E5
Abbey Devon ... 29 L8
Abbey-Cwm-Hir Powys ... 78 E1
Abbeydale Sheff ... 132 F3
Abbey Dore Herefs ... 62 D1
Abbey Green Staffs ... 131 J8
Abbey Hill Somset ... 30 D7
Abbey St Bathans Border ... 213 G6
Abbeystead Lancs ... 147 L5
Abbey Town Cumb ... 177 G8
Abbey Valley Crematorium
  Derbys ... 116 C1
Abbey Village Lancs ... 139 J3
Abbey Wood Gt Lon ... 52 A3
Abbotrule Border ... 189 G4
Abbots Bickington Devon ... 27 G8
Abbots Bromley Staffs ... 115 H6
Abbotsbury Dorset ... 16 A5
Abbot's Chair Derbys ... 131 K2
Abbots Deuglie P & K ... 221 K5
Abbotsham Devon ... 27 G5
Abbotskerswell Devon ... 8 C1
Abbots Langley Herts ... 68 E6
Abbotsleigh Devon ... 8 B5
Abbots Leigh N Som ... 45 G4
Abbotsley Cambs ... 86 E4
Abbots Morton Worcs ... 82 B4
Abbots Ripton Cambs ... 102 E7
Abbot's Salford Warwks ... 82 C5
Abbotstone Hants ... 35 H4
Abbotswood Hants ... 34 D6
Abbots Worthy Hants ... 35 G4
Abbotts Ann Hants ... 34 D2
Abbott Street Dorset ... 17 J3
Abcott Shrops ... 95 J7
Abdon Shrops ... 96 D6
Abenhall Gloucs ... 63 K4
Aberaeron Cerdgn ... 76 E3
Aberaman Rhondd ... 60 F7
Aberangell Gwynd ... 93 J2
Aber-arad Carmth ... 76 B7
Aberarder Highld ... 251 H6
Aberargie P & K ... 222 B4
Aberarth Cerdgn ... 76 E3
Aberavon Neath ... 57 K7
Aber-banc Cerdgn ... 76 C7
Aberbargoed Caerph ... 61 J7
Aberbeeg Blae G ... 61 K6
Abercanaid Myr Td ... 61 G6
Abercarn Caerph ... 43 K3
Abercastle Pembks ... 74 D5
Abercegir Powys ... 93 H3
Aberchalder Lodge Highld ... 240 B3
Aberchirder Abers ... 268 A5
Aber Clydach Powys ... 61 H3
Abercraf Powys ... 59 M6
Abercregan Neath ... 42 C2
Abercwmboi Rhondd ... 60 F7
Abercych Pembks ... 75 M4
Abercynon Rhondd ... 43 G3
Aberdalgie P & K ... 221 K3
Aberdare Rhondd ... 60 F6
Aberdaron Gwynd ... 108 C6
Aberdeen C Aber ... 245 L2
Aberdeen Crematorium
  C Aber ... 245 K2
Aberdesach Gwynd ... 109 G1
Aberdour Fife ... 211 G2
Aberdulais Neath ... 57 L5
Aberdyfi Gwynd ... 92 D4
Aberedw Powys ... 78 F6
Abereiddy Pembks ... 74 C6
Abererch Gwynd ... 109 G4
Aberfan Myr Td ... 61 G7
Aberfeldy P & K ... 232 C5
Aberffraw IoA ... 124 F6
Aberffrwd Cerdgn ... 92 E7
Aberford Leeds ... 150 F8
Aberfoyle Stirlg ... 219 H7
Abergarw Brdgnd ... 42 D5
Abergarwed Neath ... 60 B6
Abergavenny Mons ... 62 C4
Abergele Conwy ... 127 J4
Aber-giar Carmth ... 76 F7
Abergorlech Carmth ... 59 G2
Abergwesyn Powys ... 78 A4
Abergwili Carmth ... 58 D5
Abergwydol Powys ... 93 G3
Abergwynfi Neath ... 42 D3
Abergwyngregyn Gwynd ... 126 C5

Abergynolwyn Gwynd ... 92 E2
Aberhafesp Powys ... 94 C5
Aberhosan Powys ... 93 H4
Aberkenfig Brdgnd ... 42 D5
Aberlady E Loth ... 212 A3
Aberlemno Angus ... 234 E4
Aberllefenni Gwynd ... 93 G2
Aberllynfi Powys ... 79 H7
Aberlour, Charlestown of
  Moray ... 254 E3
Aber-Magwr Cerdgn ... 92 E8
Aber-meurig Cerdgn ... 77 G4
Abermorddu Flints ... 129 G8
Abermule Powys ... 94 E4
Abernant Carmth ... 58 C4
Aber-nant Rhondd ... 60 F6
Abernethy P & K ... 222 C4
Abernyte P & K ... 222 D1
Aberporth Cerdgn ... 76 A5
Abersoch Gwynd ... 108 E6
Abersychan Torfn ... 62 B6
Aberthin V Glam ... 42 F6
Abertillery Blae G ... 61 K6
Abertridwr Caerph ... 43 H4
Abertridwr Powys ... 111 K7
Abertysswg Caerph ... 61 H6
Aberuthven P & K ... 221 H4
Aberyscir Powys ... 60 F1
Aberystwyth Cerdgn ... 92 C7
Aberystwyth Crematorium
  Cerdgn ... 92 D6
Abingdon-on-Thames Oxon ... 66 C7
Abinger Common Surrey ... 37 H2
Abinger Hammer Surrey ... 37 G2
Abington Nhants ... 84 F3
Abington S Lans ... 186 D2
Abington Pigotts Cambs ... 86 F6
Abingworth W Susx ... 21 J3
Ab Kettleby Leics ... 117 J7
Ab Lench Worcs ... 82 B5
Ablington Gloucs ... 65 G5
Ablington Wilts ... 33 K2
Abney Derbys ... 132 D4
Above Church Staffs ... 115 G2
Aboyne Abers ... 244 C4
Abram Wigan ... 139 J7
Abriachan Highld ... 250 F4
Abridge Essex ... 70 C7
Abronhill N Lans ... 209 L4
Abson S Glos ... 45 L4
Abthorpe Nhants ... 84 C6
Aby Lincs ... 137 H4
Acaster Malbis C York ... 151 J6
Acaster Selby N York ... 151 J7
Accrington Lancs ... 139 M2
Accrington Crematorium
  Lancs ... 140 A2
Acha Ag & B ... 224 F4
Achahoish Ag & B ... 206 B3
Achalader P & K ... 233 H6
Achaleven Ag & B ... 228 E8
Acha Mor W Isls ... 282 f3
Achanalt Highld ... 261 M7
Achandunie Highld ... 263 H5
Achany Highld ... 272 E7
Acharacle Highld ... 237 K7
Acharn Highld ... 227 K2
Acharn P & K ... 231 L6
Achavanich Highld ... 279 L7
Achduart Highld ... 270 D7
Achfary Highld ... 276 D8
A'Chill Highld ... 246 C7
Achiltibuie Highld ... 270 D6
Achina Highld ... 278 B4
Achinhoan Ag & B ... 192 F5
Achintee Highld ... 248 F3
Achintraid Highld ... 248 D4
Achmelvich Highld ... 270 E3
Achmore Highld ... 248 D5
Achmore W Isls ... 282 f3
Achnacarnin Highld ... 270 D2
Achnacarry Highld ... 239 K6
Achnacloich Highld ... 247 J6
Achnaconeran Highld ... 250 D8
Achnacroish Ag & B ... 228 C7
Achnadrish House Ag & B ... 226 F2
Achnafauld P & K ... 232 C8
Achnagarron Highld ... 263 J6
Achnaha Highld ... 236 F6
Achnahaird Highld ... 270 D5
Achnahannet Highld ... 253 J6
Achnairn Highld ... 272 E5
Achnalea Highld ... 228 C3
Achnamara Ag & B ... 206 B2
Achnasheen Highld ... 261 K8
Achnashellach Lodge Highld ... 249 G2
Achnastank Moray ... 254 F5
Achosnich Highld ... 236 E7
Achranich Highld ... 227 K3

Achreamie Highld ... 279 H3
Achriabhach Highld ... 229 J2
Achriesgill Highld ... 276 D5
Achtoty Highld ... 277 M4
Achurch Nhants ... 102 A6
Achvaich Highld ... 263 J1
Achvarasdal Highld ... 279 H3
Ackergill Highld ... 280 E5
Acklam Middsb ... 170 C7
Acklam N York ... 152 B5
Ackleton Shrops ... 97 H4
Acklington Nthumb ... 191 J6
Ackton Wakefd ... 142 C3
Ackworth Moor Top Wakefd ... 142 C4
Acle Norfk ... 107 H1
Acock's Green Birm ... 98 E6
Acol Kent ... 41 J2
Acomb C York ... 151 J5
Acomb Nthumb ... 179 L5
Acombe Somset ... 30 B8
Aconbury Herefs ... 80 C8
Acre Lancs ... 140 B3
Acrefair Wrexhm ... 112 D3
Acton Ches E ... 113 K1
Acton Dorset ... 17 J7
Acton Gt Lon ... 51 G3
Acton Shrops ... 95 H6
Acton Staffs ... 114 C3
Acton Suffk ... 89 H6
Acton Worcs ... 81 J2
Acton Beauchamp Herefs ... 80 F5
Acton Bridge Ches W ... 130 B4
Acton Burnell Shrops ... 96 C3
Acton Green Herefs ... 81 G5
Acton Park Wrexhm ... 112 E1
Acton Pigott Shrops ... 96 C3
Acton Round Shrops ... 96 E4
Acton Scott Shrops ... 95 L5
Acton Trussell Staffs ... 114 E7
Acton Turville S Glos ... 46 A3
Adbaston Staffs ... 114 B6
Adber Dorset ... 31 K6
Adbolton Notts ... 117 G4
Adderbury Oxon ... 83 L8
Adderley Shrops ... 113 L3
Adderstone Nthumb ... 203 J7
Addiewell W Loth ... 210 C6
Addingham C Brad ... 149 K6
Addington Bucks ... 67 H2
Addington Gt Lon ... 51 K6
Addington Kent ... 52 E7
Addiscombe Gt Lon ... 51 J5
Addlestone Surrey ... 50 D6
Addlestonemoor Surrey ... 50 D6
Addlethorpe Lincs ... 137 K6
Adeney Wrekin ... 113 M7
Adeyfield Herts ... 68 D5
Adfa Powys ... 94 C3
Adforton Herefs ... 79 M1
Adisham Kent ... 41 H4
Adlestrop Gloucs ... 65 K2
Adlingfleet E R Yk ... 143 L3
Adlington Ches E ... 131 H4
Adlington Lancs ... 139 J5
Admaston Staffs ... 115 G7
Admaston Wrekin ... 96 E1
Admington Warwks ... 82 E6
Adpar Cerdgn ... 76 B7
Adsborough Somset ... 30 D5
Adscombe Somset ... 30 B3
Adstock Bucks ... 67 H1
Adstone Nhants ... 84 B5
Adswood Stockp ... 131 H2
Adversane W Susx ... 37 G6
Advie Highld ... 254 C5
Adwalton Leeds ... 141 K2
Adwell Oxon ... 67 G7
Adwick le Street Donc ... 142 E6
Adwick upon Dearne Donc ... 142 D7
Ae D & G ... 176 C1
Ae Bridgend D & G ... 176 D2
Affetside Bury ... 139 M5
Affleck Abers ... 255 L4
Affpuddle Dorset ... 16 F4
Affric Lodge Highld ... 249 K7
Afon-wen Flints ... 128 D5
Afton Devon ... 8 C2
Afton IoW ... 18 E6
Agecroft Crematorium Salfd ... 140 B7
Agglethorpe N York ... 159 K5
Aigburth Lpool ... 129 J2
Aike E R Yk ... 153 G6
Aiketgate Cumb ... 166 B1
Aikhead Cumb ... 165 H1
Aikton Cumb ... 177 J8
Ailby Lincs ... 137 H4
Ailey Herefs ... 79 L5
Ailsworth C Pete ... 102 C4
Ainderby Quernhow N York ... 160 E6

Ainderby Steeple N York ... 160 E4
Aingers Green Essex ... 73 G3
Ainsdale Sefton ... 138 C5
Ainsdale-on-Sea Sefton ... 138 C5
Ainstable Cumb ... 166 C2
Ainsworth Bury ... 139 M5
Ainthorpe N York ... 162 C1
Aintree Sefton ... 138 D8
Ainville W Loth ... 210 F6
Aird Ag & B ... 216 B7
Aird D & G ... 172 B3
Aird W Isls ... 282 h3
Aird a Mhulaidh W Isls ... 282 e5
Aird Asaig W Isls ... 282 e5
Aird Dhubh Highld ... 248 A4
Airdeny Ag & B ... 216 F1
Aird of Kinloch Ag & B ... 227 G6
Aird of Sleat Highld ... 247 J8
Airdrie N Lans ... 209 K6
Airdriehill N Lans ... 209 K5
Airds of Kells D & G ... 175 G1
Aird Uig W Isls ... 282 d3
Airidh a bhruaich W Isls ... 282 f4
Airieland D & G ... 175 J3
Airlie Angus ... 233 M5
Airmyn E R Yk ... 143 J3
Airntully P & K ... 233 G8
Airor Highld ... 247 M7
Airth Falk ... 210 B2
Airton N York ... 148 F4
Aisby Lincs ... 118 D4
Aisby Lincs ... 135 H1
Aisgill Cumb ... 158 D3
Aish Devon ... 7 K3
Aish Devon ... 8 C3
Aisholt Somset ... 30 B4
Aiskew N York ... 160 C5
Aislaby N York ... 162 D5
Aislaby N York ... 162 F1
Aislaby S on T ... 169 L8
Aisthorpe Lincs ... 135 J4
Aith Shet ... 281 d5
Akeld Nthumb ... 202 E7
Akeley Bucks ... 84 D7
Akenham Suffk ... 90 D5
Albaston Cnwll ... 12 A8
Alberbury Shrops ... 112 E8
Albourne W Susx ... 22 C4
Albourne Green W Susx ... 22 C4
Albrighton Shrops ... 97 H3
Albrighton Shrops ... 113 H7
Alburgh Norfk ... 106 F6
Albury Herts ... 70 B2
Albury Oxon ... 67 G6
Albury Surrey ... 37 G2
Albury End Herts ... 70 B2
Albury Heath Surrey ... 37 G2
Alby Hill Norfk ... 122 D5
Alcaig Highld ... 263 G8
Alcaston Shrops ... 95 L6
Alcester Warwks ... 82 C4
Alcester Lane End Birm ... 98 D7
Alciston E Susx ... 23 H6
Alcombe Somset ... 29 H2
Alcombe Wilts ... 46 A5
Alconbury Cambs ... 102 D8
Alconbury Weston Cambs ... 102 D7
Aldborough N York ... 150 F3
Aldborough Norfk ... 122 D5
Aldbourne Wilts ... 47 K4
Aldbrough E R Yk ... 153 L8
Aldbrough St John N York ... 169 G8
Aldbury Herts ... 68 B4
Aldcliffe Lancs ... 147 J4
Aldclune P & K ... 232 D3
Aldeburgh Suffk ... 91 K4
Aldeby Norfk ... 107 J5
Aldenham Herts ... 68 F7
Alderbury Wilts ... 33 L5
Aldercar Derbys ... 116 D2
Alderford Norfk ... 122 C7
Alderholt Dorset ... 33 K8
Alderley Gloucs ... 45 M1
Alderley Edge Ches E ... 131 G4
Aldermans Green Covtry ... 99 K6
Aldermaston W Berk ... 48 E6
Alderminster Warwks ... 82 F5
Alder Moor Staffs ... 115 L6
Aldersey Green Ches W ... 129 K8
Aldershot Hants ... 36 C1
Alderton Gloucs ... 82 B8
Alderton Nhants ... 84 E6
Alderton Shrops ... 113 H6
Alderton Suffk ... 91 H7
Alderton Wilts ... 46 B2
Alderwasley Derbys ... 116 A1
Aldfield N York ... 150 C2
Aldford Ches W ... 129 K7
Aldgate Rutlnd ... 101 L3

Aldham Essex 72 D2
Aldham Suffk 90 B6
Aldingbourne W Susx 20 F5
Aldingham Cumb 146 E2
Aldington Kent 40 E8
Aldington Worcs 82 C6
Aldington Corner Kent 40 E7
Aldivalloch Moray 255 G6
Aldochlay Ag & B 208 B1
Aldon Shrops 95 K7
Aldoth Cumb 164 F1
Aldreth Cambs 103 J8
Aldridge Wsall 98 D3
Aldringham Suffk 91 K3
Aldro N York 152 B3
Aldsworth Gloucs 65 H5
Aldsworth W Susx 20 C5
Aldunie Moray 255 G6
Aldwark Derbys 132 E8
Aldwark N York 151 G3
Aldwick W Susx 20 E7
Aldwincle Nhants 101 M7
Aldworth W Berk 48 E3
Alexandria W Duns 208 C3
Aley Somset 30 B3
Alfardisworthy Devon 26 E8
Alfington Devon 14 D3
Alfold Surrey 36 F4
Alfold Bars W Susx 36 F4
Alfold Crossways Surrey 36 F4
Alford Abers 255 M8
Alford Lincs 137 H4
Alford Somset 31 K4
Alford Crematorium Lincs 137 H4
Alfreton Derbys 133 H8
Alfrick Worcs 81 H4
Alfrick Pound Worcs 81 G5
Alfriston E Susx 23 H6
Algarkirk Lincs 119 J3
Alhampton Somset 31 K4
Alkborough N Linc 143 M3
Alkerton Gloucs 63 M6
Alkerton Oxon 83 J6
Alkham Kent 41 H6
Alkington Shrops 113 H4
Alkmonton Derbys 115 K4
Allaleigh Devon 8 B4
Allanaquoich Abers 242 F5
Allanbank N Lans 209 M7
Allanton Border 202 D2
Allanton N Lans 209 M7
Allanton S Lans 209 K8
Allaston Gloucs 63 J6
Allbrook Hants 34 F6
All Cannings Wilts 46 F6
Allendale Nthumb 179 J7
Allen End Warwks 98 F4
Allenheads Nthumb 167 K2
Allensford Dur 168 D1
Allen's Green Herts 70 C4
Allensmore Herefs 80 B8
Allenton C Derb 116 B5
Aller Devon 28 D5
Aller Somset 30 F5
Allerby Cumb 164 E3
Allercombe Devon 14 B4
Allerford Somset 28 F2
Allerston N York 162 F6
Allerthorpe E R Yk 152 B6
Allerton C Brad 141 H1
Allerton Highld 263 K6
Allerton Lpool 129 J2
Allerton Bywater Leeds 142 C2
Allerton Mauleverer N York 150 F4
Allesley Covtry 99 J7
Allestree C Derb 116 B4
Allet Common Cnwll 4 C5
Allexton Leics 101 H3
Allgreave Ches E 131 J6
Allhallows Medway 53 H3
Allhallows-on-Sea Medway 53 H3
Alligin Shuas Highld 260 D8
Allimore Green Staffs 114 D7
Allington Dorset 15 K4
Allington Kent 53 G7
Allington Lincs 117 M3
Allington Wilts 33 L3
Allington Wilts 46 C4
Allington Wilts 46 F6
Allithwaite Cumb 156 E7
Alloa Clacks 220 F8
Allonby Cumb 164 E2
Allostock Ches W 130 E5
Alloway S Ayrs 196 C7
Allowenshay Somset 30 F8
All Saints South Elmham Suffk 107 G7
Allscott Shrops 97 G4
Allscott Wrekin 96 E1
All Stretton Shrops 95 L4

Alltami Flints 129 G6
Alltchaorunn Highld 229 K5
Alltmawr Powys 78 F6
Alltwalis Carmth 58 E3
Alltwen Neath 57 K4
Alltyblaca Cerdgn 76 F6
Allweston Dorset 31 L8
Allwood Green Suffk 90 B1
Almeley Herefs 79 L5
Almeley Wooton Herefs 79 L5
Almer Dorset 17 H3
Almholme Donc 142 F6
Almington Staffs 113 M4
Almodington W Susx 20 D7
Almondbank P & K 221 J2
Almondbury Kirk 141 J5
Almondsbury S Glos 45 J2
Alne N York 151 G3
Alness Highld 263 H6
Alnham Nthumb 190 E4
Alnmouth Nthumb 191 J4
Alnwick Nthumb 191 H3
Alperton Gt Lon 50 F2
Alphamstone Essex 89 H8
Alpheton Suffk 89 H5
Alphington Devon 13 L4
Alpington Norfk 106 F3
Alport Derbys 132 D6
Alpraham Ches E 130 B7
Alresford Essex 72 F3
Alrewas Staffs 115 K8
Alsager Ches E 130 F8
Alsagers Bank Staffs 114 C2
Alsop en le Dale Derbys 132 C8
Alston Cumb 167 G2
Alston Devon 15 G2
Alstone Gloucs 82 A8
Alstone Somset 30 D2
Alstonefield Staffs 132 C8
Alston Sutton Somset 44 E8
Alswear Devon 28 C6
Alt Oldham 140 E7
Altandhu Highld 270 C5
Altarnun Cnwll 11 J6
Altass Highld 272 D8
Altcreich Ag & B 227 K5
Altgaltraig Ag & B 207 G4
Altham Lancs 140 A1
Althorne Essex 72 D7
Althorpe N Linc 143 L6
Altnabreac Station Highld 279 H7
Altnaharra Highld 272 E1
Altofts Wakefd 142 B3
Alton Derbys 133 G6
Alton Hants 35 L3
Alton Staffs 115 H3
Alton Wilts 33 K4
Alton Barnes Wilts 47 G6
Alton Pancras Dorset 16 D2
Alton Priors Wilts 47 G6
Altrincham Traffd 130 E2
Altrincham Crematorium Traffd 130 E2
Altskeith Hotel Stirlg 219 G6
Alva Clacks 220 F7
Alvanley Ches W 129 L5
Alvaston C Derb 116 C5
Alvechurch Worcs 82 B1
Alvecote Warwks 99 H3
Alvediston Wilts 33 G6
Alveley Shrops 97 G6
Alverdiscott Devon 27 J4
Alverstoke Hants 19 K4
Alverstone IoW 19 K6
Alverthorpe Wakefd 141 M3
Alverton Notts 117 L3
Alves Moray 266 C4
Alvescot Oxon 65 K6
Alveston S Glos 45 J1
Alveston Warwks 82 F4
Alvingham Lincs 137 G2
Alvington Gloucs 63 J7
Alwalton C Pete 102 C4
Alwinton Nthumb 190 C5
Alwoodley Leeds 150 C7
Alwoodley Gates Leeds 150 D7
Alyth P & K 233 L5
Ambergate Derbys 116 B1
Amber Hill Lincs 119 H2
Amberley Gloucs 64 B6
Amberley W Susx 21 H4
Amber Row Derbys 133 G8
Amberstone E Susx 23 K5
Amble Nthumb 191 K5
Amblecote Dudley 97 K6
Ambler Thorn C Brad 141 H2
Ambleside Cumb 156 E2
Ambleston Pembks 75 G7
Ambrosden Oxon 66 F3

Amcotts N Linc 143 L5
America Cambs 103 J7
Amersham Bucks 68 B7
Amersham Common Bucks 68 B7
Amersham Old Town Bucks 68 B7
Amersham on the Hill Bucks 68 B7
Amerton Staffs 114 F6
Amesbury Wilts 33 K3
Amhuinnsuidhe W Isls 282 d5
Amington Staffs 99 G3
Amisfield D & G 176 D2
Amlwch IoA 125 H1
Ammanford Carmth 59 H6
Amotherby N York 162 C7
Ampfield Hants 34 E6
Ampleforth N York 161 J7
Ampney Crucis Gloucs 64 F6
Ampney St Mary Gloucs 65 G6
Ampney St Peter Gloucs 65 G6
Amport Hants 34 C2
Ampthill C Beds 85 K7
Ampton Suffk 89 H1
Amroth Pembks 55 K5
Amulree P & K 232 D8
Amwell Herts 68 F4
Anaheilt Highld 228 C3
Ancaster Lincs 118 C3
Anchor Shrops 94 E6
Ancroft Nthumb 202 F4
Ancrum Border 189 H1
Ancton W Susx 21 G6
Anderby Lincs 137 K6
Andersea Somset 30 E4
Andersfield Somset 30 C4
Anderson Dorset 17 G3
Anderton Ches W 130 C4
Anderton Cnwll 6 E4
Andover Hants 34 D2
Andoversford Gloucs 64 F3
Andreas IoM 154 f2
Anelog Gwynd 108 B6
Anerley Gt Lon 51 J5
Anfield Lpool 129 J1
Anfield Crematorium Lpool 129 J1
Angarrack Cnwll 2 F3
Angarrick Cnwll 3 K4
Angelbank Shrops 96 D8
Angersleigh Somset 30 B7
Angerton Cumb 177 H7
Angle Pembks 54 D6
Anglesey IoA 125 G3
Angmering W Susx 21 H6
Angram N York 151 H6
Angram N York 158 F3
Angrouse Cnwll 3 H7
Anick Nthumb 179 L5
Ankerville Highld 264 C5
Ankle Hill Leics 117 K7
Anlaby E R Yk 144 C2
Anmer Norfk 121 G5
Anmore Hants 19 L1
Annan D & G 177 G5
Annaside Cumb 155 K5
Annat Highld 248 E1
Annathill N Lans 209 J5
Anna Valley Hants 34 D2
Annbank S Ayrs 196 E6
Annesley Notts 116 E1
Annesley Woodhouse Notts 116 E1
Annfield Plain Dur 180 E8
Anniesland C Glas 208 F5
Annitsford N Tyne 181 G4
Annscroft Shrops 95 L2
Ansdell Lancs 138 D2
Ansford Somset 31 L4
Ansley Warwks 99 J5
Anslow Staffs 115 L6
Anslow Gate Staffs 115 K6
Anslow Lees Staffs 115 K6
Ansteadbrook Surrey 36 E4
Anstey Hants 35 L3
Anstey Herts 87 H8
Anstey Leics 100 E2
Anstruther Fife 223 K6
Ansty W Susx 37 L6
Ansty Warwks 99 L6
Ansty Wilts 33 G5
Ansty Cross Dorset 16 E2
Anthill Common Hants 19 L1
Anthonys Surrey 50 C6
Anthorn Cumb 177 G7
Antingham Norfk 122 E5
An t-Ob W Isls 282 d6
Anton's Gowt Lincs 119 J2
Antony Cnwll 6 D4
Antrobus Ches W 130 C4
Anvil Corner Devon 11 M2
Anvil Green Kent 40 E5
Anwick Lincs 118 F2

Anwoth D & G 174 F4
Aperfield Gt Lon 51 L7
Apes Dale Worcs 82 A1
Apethorpe Nhants 102 A4
Apeton Staffs 114 D7
Apley Lincs 136 B5
Apperknowle Derbys 133 H4
Apperley Gloucs 64 B2
Apperley Bridge C Brad 150 B8
Apperley Dene Nthumb 180 C7
Appersett N York 158 E4
Appin Ag & B 228 E6
Appleby N Linc 144 B5
Appleby-in-Westmorland Cumb 166 F6
Appleby Magna Leics 99 J2
Appleby Parva Leics 99 J2
Appleby Street Herts 69 J6
Applecross Highld 248 A3
Appledore Devon 27 H5
Appledore Devon 29 K7
Appledore Kent 25 H2
Appledore Heath Kent 25 H1
Appleford Oxon 66 D8
Applegarth Town D & G 176 F2
Applehaigh Wakefd 142 A5
Appleshaw Hants 34 C1
Applethwaite Cumb 165 J3
Appleton Halton 129 M2
Appleton Oxon 66 C6
Appleton Warrtn 130 B3
Appleton-le-Moors N York 162 C5
Appleton-le-Street N York 162 C7
Appleton Roebuck N York 151 J7
Appleton Thorn Warrtn 130 C3
Appleton Wiske N York 160 F2
Appletreehall Border 188 F3
Appletreewick N York 149 J4
Appley Somset 29 K6
Appley Bridge Lancs 139 G6
Apse Heath IoW 19 J7
Apsley End C Beds 86 C8
Apuldram W Susx 20 D6
Arabella Highld 264 C5
Arbirlot Angus 234 F7
Arboll Highld 264 D3
Arborfield Wokham 49 H5
Arborfield Cross Wokham 49 J5
Arbourthorne Sheff 133 G3
Arbroath Angus 235 G7
Arbuthnott Abers 245 H8
Arcadia Kent 39 L6
Archddu Carmth 56 E4
Archdeacon Newton Darltn 169 H7
Archencarroch W Duns 208 C3
Archiestown Moray 254 E3
Archirondel Jersey 9 f2
Arclid Green Ches E 130 F7
Ardallie Abers 257 J4
Ardanaiseig Hotel Ag & B 217 H2
Ardaneaskan Highld 248 D4
Ardarroch Highld 248 D4
Ardbeg Ag & B 204 F7
Ardbeg Ag & B 207 H5
Ardbeg Ag & B 207 K2
Ardcharnich Highld 261 K2
Ardchiavaig Ag & B 214 D1
Ardchonnel Ag & B 216 F5
Ardchullarie More Stirlg 219 K4
Arddarroch Ag & B 218 C8
Arddleen Powys 112 C8
Ardechive Highld 239 J5
Ardeer N Ayrs 196 B3
Ardeley Herts 69 J2
Ardelve Highld 248 D6
Arden Ag & B 208 B2
Ardens Grafton Warwks 82 D4
Ardentallen Ag & B 216 C2
Ardentinny Ag & B 207 K2
Ardentraive Ag & B 207 G4
Ardeonaig Stirlg 231 J8
Ardersier Highld 252 E1
Ardessie Highld 261 H2
Ardfern Ag & B 216 C6
Ardfernal Ag & B 205 J2
Ardgartan Ag & B 218 D6
Ardgay Highld 263 G2
Ardgour Highld 229 G3
Ardgowan Inver 207 L4
Ardhallow Ag & B 207 K4
Ardhasig W Isls 282 e5
Ardheslaig Highld 260 C8
Ardindrean Highld 261 K2
Ardingly W Susx 38 A7
Ardington Oxon 48 B1
Ardington Wick Oxon 48 B1
Ardlamont Ag & B 206 F6
Ardleigh Essex 72 F1
Ardleigh Heath Essex 72 F1

Ardler P & K.................... 233 L7
Ardley Oxon 66 D2
Ardley End Essex 70 D4
Ardlui Ag & B 218 D4
Ardlussa Ag & B 215 J6
Ardmair Highld 270 F8
Ardmaleish Ag & B 207 H5
Ardminish Ag & B 205 L6
Ardmolich Highld 237 K6
Ardmore Ag & B 208 A3
Ardmore Highld 263 J3
Ardnadam Ag & B 207 K3
Ardnagrask Highld 250 F2
Ardnarff Highld 248 E4
Ardnastang Highld 228 B3
Ardpatrick Ag & B 206 B7
Ardrishaig Ag & B 206 D2
Ardross Highld 263 H5
Ardrossan N Ayrs 195 L3
Ardsley Barns 142 B6
Ardsley East Leeds 141 M3
Ardslignish Highld 237 H8
Ardtalla Ag & B 205 G5
Ardtoe Highld 237 J6
Arduaine Ag & B 216 B5
Ardullie Highld 263 G7
Ardvasar Highld 247 K7
Ardvorlich P & K 219 K3
Ardvourlie W Isls 282 e5
Ardwell D & G 172 D5
Ardwick Manch 140 C8
Areley Kings Worcs 81 H1
Arevegaig Highld 237 J7
Arford Hants 36 B3
Arglam E R Yk 152 B8
Argoed Caerph 61 J7
Argoed Shrops 112 E7
Argoed Mill Powys 78 D3
Argos Hill E Susx 23 J2
Aribruach W Isls 282 f4
Aridhglas Ag & B 226 C7
Arileod Ag & B 224 F4
Arinagour Ag & B 225 G4
Ariogan Ag & B 216 D2
Arisaig Highld 237 J3
Arisaig House Highld 237 K4
Arkendale N York 150 E4
Arkesden Essex 87 K8
Arkholme Lancs 147 L2
Arkleby Cumb 164 F3
Arkleton D & G 188 C7
Arkle Town N York 159 H2
Arkley Gt Lon 69 G7
Arksey Donc 142 F6
Arkwright Town Derbys ... 133 H5
Arle Gloucs 64 D2
Arlecdon Cumb 164 D7
Arlescote Warwks 83 J4
Arlesey C Beds 86 D7
Arleston Wrekin 96 F1
Arley Ches E 130 C3
Arley Warwks 99 H5
Arlingham Gloucs 63 L5
Arlington Devon 27 L3
Arlington E Susx 23 J5
Arlington Gloucs 65 G5
Arlington Beccott Devon .. 27 L3
Armadale Highld 247 K7
Armadale Highld 278 D3
Armadale W Loth 210 B5
Armaside Cumb 164 F5
Armathwaite Cumb 166 C2
Arminghall Norfk 106 E3
Armitage Staffs 115 H8
Armitage Bridge Kirk 141 H5
Armley Leeds 141 L1
Armscote Warwks 82 F6
Armshead Staffs 114 E2
Armston Nhants 102 B6
Armthorpe Donc 143 G6
Arnabost Ag & B 225 G3
Arnaby Cumb 156 A5
Arncliffe N York 149 G2
Arncliffe Cote N York 149 G2
Arncroach Fife 223 J6
Arndilly House Moray 266 F6
Arne Dorset 17 J5
Arnesby Leics 100 D5
Arngask P & K 221 L5
Arnisdale Highld 238 D2
Arnish Highld 259 K7
Arniston Mdloth 211 K6
Arnol W Isls 282 f2
Arnold E R Yk 153 H7
Arnold Notts 117 G2
Arnprior Stirlg 219 K8
Arnside Cumb 157 G7
Aros Ag & B 227 G3
Arowry Wrexhm 113 G4

Arrad Foot Cumb 156 D6
Arram E R Yk 153 G7
Arran N Ayrs 194 E4
Arrathorne N York 160 B4
Arreton IoW 19 J6
Arrina Highld 260 B8
Arrington Cambs 87 G5
Arrochar Ag & B 218 D6
Arrow Warwks 82 C4
Arrowfield Top Worcs 98 C8
Arscott Shrops 95 K4
Artafallie Highld 251 H2
Arthington Leeds 150 C6
Arthingworth Nhants 101 G7
Arthog Gwynd 110 C8
Arthrath Abers 257 H4
Arthursdale Leeds 150 E8
Artrochie Abers 257 J5
Arundel W Susx 21 G5
Asby Cumb 164 E6
Ascog Ag & B 207 J6
Ascot W & M 50 A5
Ascott Warwks 83 H8
Ascott Earl Oxon 65 L3
Ascott-under-Wychwood
   Oxon 65 L3
Asenby N York 160 F7
Asfordby Leics 117 J7
Asfordby Hill Leics 117 J7
Asgarby Lincs 118 F3
Asgarby Lincs 136 F6
Ash Devon 8 C5
Ash Devon 12 C1
Ash Dorset 32 E8
Ash Kent 41 J4
Ash Kent 52 D6
Ash Somset 30 D5
Ash Somset 31 G6
Ash Surrey 36 D1
Ashampstead W Berk 48 E4
Ashampstead Green W Berk .. 48 E3
Ashbocking Suffk 90 E4
Ashbourne Derbys 115 K2
Ashbrittle Somset 29 J6
Ashburnham Place E Susx .. 24 C4
Ashburton Devon 13 H8
Ashbury Devon 12 C3
Ashbury Oxon 47 K2
Ashby N Linc 143 M6
Ashby by Partney Lincs ... 137 H6
Ashby cum Fenby NE Lin .. 145 H1
Ashby de la Launde Lincs .. 135 L8
Ashby-de-la-Zouch Leics .. 116 B8
Ashby Folville Leics 100 F1
Ashby Magna Leics 100 C5
Ashby Parva Leics 100 C5
Ashby Puerorum Lincs 136 F5
Ashby St Ledgers Nhants .. 84 B2
Ashby St Mary Norfk 107 G3
Ashchurch Gloucs 81 L8
Ashcombe Devon 13 L6
Ashcombe N Som 44 C6
Ashcott Somset 31 G3
Ashdon Essex 88 B6
Ashe Hants 35 H1
Asheldham Essex 72 E6
Ashen Essex 88 E6
Ashendon Bucks 67 H4
Asheridge Bucks 68 B6
Ashfield Hants 34 E7
Ashfield Herefs 63 H2
Ashfield Stirlg 220 D6
Ashfield cum Thorpe Suffk .. 90 F2
Ashfield Green Suffk 88 F4
Ashfield Green Suffk 106 F8
Ashfold Crossways W Susx .. 37 K5
Ashford Devon 7 K5
Ashford Devon 27 J4
Ashford Kent 40 D6
Ashford Surrey 50 D4
Ashford Bowdler Shrops .. 80 C1
Ashford Carbonell Shrops .. 80 C1
Ashford Hill Hants 48 E6
Ashford in the Water Derbys .. 132 D5
Ashgill S Lans 198 C3
Ash Green Surrey 36 D1
Ash Green Warwks 99 J6
Ashill Devon 29 K8
Ashill Norfk 105 H3
Ashill Somset 30 D7
Ashingdon Essex 72 C8
Ashington Nthumb 181 G1
Ashington Poole 17 K3
Ashington Somset 31 J6
Ashington W Susx 21 K4
Ashkirk Border 188 E2
Ashlett Hants 19 G3
Ashleworth Gloucs 64 A2
Ashleworth Quay Gloucs .. 64 B2

Ashley Cambs 88 D3
Ashley Ches E 130 F3
Ashley Devon 28 B8
Ashley Dorset 18 A3
Ashley Gloucs 64 D8
Ashley Hants 18 C4
Ashley Hants 34 E4
Ashley Kent 41 J5
Ashley Nhants 101 H5
Ashley Staffs 114 B4
Ashley Wilts 46 B5
Ashley Green Bucks 68 B6
Ashleyhay Derbys 115 M1
Ashley Heath Dorset 17 M2
Ashley Moor Herefs 80 B2
Ash Magna Shrops 113 J4
Ashmansworth Hants 48 B7
Ashmansworthy Devon 26 C7
Ashmead Green Gloucs 63 M7
Ashmill Devon 11 M3
Ash Mill Devon 28 D6
Ashmore Dorset 32 F7
Ashmore Green W Berk ... 48 D5
Ashorne Warwks 83 G4
Ashover Derbys 133 G7
Ashover Hay Derbys 133 G7
Ashow Warwks 83 H1
Ash Parva Shrops 113 J4
Ashperton Herefs 80 E7
Ashprington Devon 8 B3
Ash Priors Somset 29 L5
Ashreigney Devon 27 L8
Ash Street Suffk 89 K6
Ashtead Surrey 50 F7
Ash Thomas Devon 29 H8
Ashton C Pete 102 B2
Ashton Ches W 129 L6
Ashton Cnwll 2 F5
Ashton Devon 13 K5
Ashton Hants 35 H1
Ashton Herefs 80 C2
Ashton Inver 207 L4
Ashton Nhants 84 E5
Ashton Nhants 102 B5
Ashton Somset 30 F1
Ashton Common Wilts 46 C7
Ashton Hill Wilts 46 C7
Ashton-in-Makerfield Wigan .. 139 H7
Ashton Keynes Wilts 64 F8
Ashton under Hill Worcs .. 82 A7
Ashton-under-Lyne Tamesd .. 140 E7
Ashton upon Mersey Traffd .. 130 F1
Ashurst Hants 18 E2
Ashurst Kent 38 D5
Ashurst Lancs 138 F6
Ashurst W Susx 21 L4
Ashurstwood W Susx 38 B6
Ash Vale Surrey 49 L8
Ashwater Devon 11 M4
Ashwell Herts 86 F7
Ashwell Rutlnd 101 J1
Ashwell Somset 30 E7
Ashwell End Herts 86 E7
Ashwellthorpe Norfk 106 C4
Ashwick Somset 31 K1
Ashwicken Norfk 120 F7
Ashwood Staffs 97 K5
Askam in Furness Cumb .. 156 B7
Askern Donc 142 F5
Askerswell Dorset 15 M4
Askett Bucks 67 K6
Askham Cumb 166 C6
Askham Notts 134 E5
Askham Bryan C York 151 H6
Askham Richard C York 151 H6
Asknish Ag & B 206 E1
Askrigg N York 159 G4
Askwith N York 149 L6
Aslackby Lincs 118 E5
Aslacton Norfk 106 D5
Aslockton Notts 117 K3
Asney Somset 31 G3
Aspall Suffk 90 E2
Aspatria Cumb 164 F2
Aspenden Herts 69 K2
Aspenshaw Derbys 131 K2
Asperton Lincs 119 J4
Aspley Staffs 114 C5
Aspley Guise C Beds 85 J8
Aspley Heath C Beds 85 H8
Aspley Heath Warwks 82 C1
Aspull Wigan 139 J8
Aspull Common Wigan 139 J8
Asselby E R Yk 143 H2
Asserby Lincs 137 J4
Asserby Turn Lincs 137 J4
Assington Suffk 89 J7
Assington Green Suffk 88 F5
Astbury Ches E 131 G7

Astcote Nhants 84 D4
Asterby Lincs 136 E4
Asterley Shrops 95 J2
Asterton Shrops 95 K5
Asthall Oxon 65 L5
Asthall Leigh Oxon 65 L4
Astle Highld 263 K2
Astley Shrops 113 H6
Astley Warwks 99 J5
Astley Wigan 139 L7
Astley Worcs 81 H2
Astley Abbots Shrops 96 E4
Astley Bridge Bolton 139 L5
Astley Cross Worcs 81 J1
Astley Green Wigan 139 L7
Aston Birm 98 D5
Aston Ches E 113 K2
Aston Ches W 130 A4
Aston Derbys 132 C4
Aston Flints 129 G6
Aston Herefs 80 B3
Aston Herts 69 H3
Aston Oxon 65 M6
Aston Rothm 133 J3
Aston Shrops 97 H5
Aston Shrops 113 H6
Aston Staffs 114 B3
Aston Staffs 114 D6
Aston Wokham 49 J2
Aston Wrekin 96 C2
Aston Abbotts Bucks 67 K3
Aston Botterell Shrops 96 E6
Aston-by-Stone Staffs 114 C6
Aston Cantlow Warwks 82 D3
Aston Clinton Bucks 67 L4
Aston Crews Herefs 63 K3
Aston Cross Gloucs 81 L8
Aston End Herts 69 H2
Aston-Eyre Shrops 96 E4
Aston Fields Worcs 81 M2
Aston Flamville Leics 100 A5
Aston Heath Ches W 130 A4
Aston Ingham Herefs 63 K3
Aston juxta Mondrum Ches E .. 130 C8
Aston le Walls Nhants 83 L4
Aston Magna Gloucs 82 E8
Aston Munslow Shrops 96 C6
Aston-on-Carrant Gloucs .. 81 L8
Aston on Clun Shrops 95 J7
Aston Pigott Shrops 95 H2
Aston Rogers Shrops 95 H2
Aston Rowant Oxon 67 H7
Aston Sandford Bucks 67 J5
Aston Somerville Worcs ... 82 B7
Aston-sub-Edge Gloucs ... 82 D7
Aston Tirrold Oxon 48 E3
Aston-upon-Trent Derbys .. 116 C5
Aston Upthorpe Oxon 48 E2
Astrop Nhants 83 L7
Astrope Herts 67 L4
Astwick C Beds 86 E7
Astwith Derbys 133 J6
Astwood M Keyn 85 L2
Astwood Worcs 81 L2
Astwood Bank Worcs 82 B3
Aswarby Lincs 118 E4
Aswardby Lincs 137 G5
Atcham Shrops 96 C2
Atch Lench Worcs 82 B5
Athelhampton Dorset 16 E4
Athelington Suffk 90 F1
Athelney Somset 30 E5
Athelstaneford E Loth 212 C4
Atherfield Green IoW 19 H7
Atherington Devon 27 L6
Atherington W Susx 21 G6
Atherstone Somset 30 F7
Atherstone Warwks 99 J4
Atherstone on Stour Warwks .. 82 F5
Atherton Wigan 139 K7
Atley Hill N York 160 D2
Atlow Derbys 115 L2
Attadale Highld 248 E4
Attenborough Notts 116 E5
Atterby Lincs 135 L2
Attercliffe Sheff 133 G2
Atterley Shrops 96 E4
Atterton Leics 99 K4
Attleborough Norfk 105 L4
Attleborough Warwks 99 K5
Attlebridge Norfk 122 C8
Attleton Green Suffk 88 E4
Atwick E R Yk 153 K5
Atworth Wilts 46 B6
Auberrow Herefs 80 C6
Aubourn Lincs 135 J7
Auchbreck Moray 254 D6
Auchedly Abers 257 G5
Auchenblae Abers 244 F7

Auchenbowie Stirlg 209 L2
Auchencairn D & G 175 K4
Auchencairn D & G 176 C2
Auchencairn N Ayrs 195 G5
Auchencrow Border 213 J7
Auchendinny Mdloth 211 H6
Auchengray S Lans 199 G2
Auchenhalrig Moray 267 H4
Auchenheath S Lans 198 D4
Auchenhessnane D & G 185 K4
Auchenlochan Ag & B 206 F4
Auchenmade N Ayrs 196 C2
Auchenmalg D & G 173 G4
Auchentiber N Ayrs 196 D2
Auchindrain Ag & B 217 G6
Auchindrean Highld 261 K4
Auchininna Abers 268 B6
Auchinleck E Ayrs 197 G6
Auchinloch N Lans 209 H5
Auchinstarry N Lans 209 J4
Auchintore Highld 229 H1
Auchiries Abers 257 K4
Auchlean Highld 241 M4
Auchlee Abers 245 K4
Auchleven Abers 256 A6
Auchlochan S Lans 198 D5
Auchlossan Abers 244 D3
Auchlyne Stirlg 219 H1
Auchmillan E Ayrs 197 G5
Auchmithie Angus 235 G6
Auchmuirbridge Fife 222 C7
Auchnacree Angus 234 C3
Auchnagatt Abers 257 G3
Auchnarrow Moray 254 D7
Auchnotteroch D & G 172 B3
Auchroisk Moray 267 G6
Auchterarder P & K 221 G4
Auchteraw Highld 240 B2
Auchterblair Highld 253 H7
Auchtercairn Highld 260 C4
Auchterderran Fife 222 C8
Auchterhouse Angus 233 M7
Auchterless Abers 256 C3
Auchtermuchty Fife 222 D5
Auchterneed Highld 262 E7
Auchtertool Fife 211 H1
Auchtertyre Highld 248 D6
Auchtubh Stirlg 219 J3
Auckengill Highld 280 E3
Auckley Donc 143 G7
Audenshaw Tamesd 140 D8
Audlem Ches E 113 L3
Audley Staffs 114 C2
Audley End Essex 87 L1
Audley End Essex 89 G7
Audley End Suffk 89 G4
Audmore Staffs 114 C7
Audnam Dudley 97 K6
Aughertree Cumb 165 H3
Aughton E R Yk 151 L8
Aughton Lancs 138 E6
Aughton Lancs 147 L2
Aughton Rothm 133 J2
Aughton Wilts 47 K7
Aughton Park Lancs 138 E6
Auldearn Highld 253 H1
Aulden Herefs 80 B4
Auldgirth D & G 176 B2
Auldhouse S Lans 197 J1
Ault a' chruinn Highld 248 F7
Aultbea Highld 260 D2
Aultgrishin Highld 260 B3
Aultguish Inn Highld 262 B6
Ault Hucknall Derbys 133 J6
Aultmore Moray 267 H5
Aultnagoire Highld 250 F7
Aultnamain Inn Highld 263 J4
Aunby Lincs 118 D8
Aunk Devon 14 B3
Aunsby Lincs 118 D4
Aust S Glos 45 H1
Austendike Lincs 119 J7
Austerfield Donc 134 D1
Austerlands Oldham 140 E6
Austhorpe Leeds 142 B1
Austonley Kirk 141 H6
Austrey Warwks 99 J2
Austwick N York 148 D3
Authorpe Lincs 137 G3
Authorpe Row Lincs 137 K5
Avebury Wilts 47 G5
Avebury Trusloe Wilts 47 G5
Aveley Thurr 52 C3
Avening Gloucs 64 C7
Averham Notts 117 K1
Aveton Gifford Devon 7 K5
Aviemore Highld 242 B1
Avington W Berk 48 A5
Avoch Highld 251 J1

Avon Hants 18 A4
Avonbridge Falk 210 B4
Avon Dassett Warwks 83 K5
Avonmouth Bristl 45 G3
Avonwick Devon 7 K3
Awbridge Hants 34 D6
Awkley S Glos 45 H1
Awliscombe Devon 14 D2
Awre Gloucs 63 L5
Awsworth Notts 116 K3
Axborough Worcs 97 J7
Axbridge Somset 44 E8
Axford Hants 35 J2
Axford Wilts 47 K5
Axmansford Hants 48 E6
Axminster Devon 15 G3
Axmouth Devon 14 F4
Axton Flints 128 D4
Aycliffe Dur 169 H6
Aydon Nthumb 180 B5
Aylburton Gloucs 63 J6
Ayle Nthumb 167 G1
Aylesbeare Devon 14 B4
Aylesbury Bucks 67 K4
Aylesbury Crematorium Bucks 67 K4
Aylesby NE Lin 145 G6
Aylesford Kent 52 F7
Aylesham Kent 41 H5
Aylestone C Leic 100 C3
Aylestone Park C Leic 100 D3
Aylmerton Norfk 122 D4
Aylsham Norfk 122 D6
Aylton Herefs 80 F7
Aylworth Gloucs 65 G3
Aymestrey Herefs 80 A2
Aynho Nhants 83 L8
Ayot Green Herts 69 G4
Ayot St Lawrence Herts 69 G4
Ayot St Peter Herts 69 G4
Ayr S Ayrs 196 C6
Aysgarth N York 159 H5
Ayshford Devon 29 J7
Ayside Cumb 156 F6
Ayston Rutlnd 101 J3
Aythorpe Roding Essex 70 E4
Ayton Border 213 K6
Azerley N York 160 C7

B

Babbacombe Torbay 8 D2
Babbington Notts 116 E3
Babbinswood Shrops 112 E5
Babbs Green Herts 69 K4
Babcary Somset 31 J5
Babel Carmth 59 M2
Babel Green Suffk 88 E5
Babell Flints 128 E5
Babeny Devon 12 F7
Bablock Hythe Oxon 66 B6
Babraham Cambs 87 K5
Babworth Notts 134 D3
Bachau IoA 125 H3
Bache Shrops 95 L7
Bacheldre Powys 94 F5
Bachelor's Bump E Susx 24 F5
Backaland Ork 275 d3
Backbarrow Cumb 156 E5
Backe Carmth 58 A5
Backfolds Abers 269 J5
Backford Ches W 129 J5
Backford Cross Ches W 129 J5
Backies Highld 273 K7
Back of Keppoch Highld 237 J3
Back o' th' Brook Staffs 115 H1
Back Street Suffk 88 E3
Backwell N Som 44 F5
Backworth N Tyne 181 H4
Bacon's End Solhll 98 F6
Baconsthorpe Norfk 122 C4
Bacton Herefs 62 D1
Bacton Norfk 123 G5
Bacton Suffk 90 C2
Bacton Green Suffk 90 B2
Bacup Lancs 140 C3
Badachro Highld 260 C5
Badbury Swindn 47 J3
Badby Nhants 84 A3
Badcall Highld 276 B7
Badcall Highld 276 C5
Badcaul Highld 261 G2
Baddeley Edge C Stke 114 E1
Baddeley Green C Stke 114 E1
Baddesley Clinton Warwks 82 F1
Baddesley Ensor Warwks 99 H4
Baddidarrach Highld 270 E3
Baddinsgill Border 199 K2

Badenscoth Abers 256 C4
Badentarbet Highld 270 D6
Badenyon Abers 255 G2
Badgall Cnwll 11 J5
Badgeney Cambs 103 J4
Badger Shrops 97 H3
Badger's Cross Cnwll 2 E3
Badgers Mount Kent 52 B6
Badgeworth Gloucs 64 C3
Badgworth Somset 44 E8
Badharlick Cnwll 11 J5
Badicaul Highld 248 B6
Badingham Suffk 91 G2
Badlesmere Kent 40 D4
Badlieu Border 187 G2
Badlipster Highld 280 B6
Badluarach Highld 261 G1
Badninish Highld 263 K1
Badrallach Highld 261 H2
Badsey Worcs 82 C6
Badshot Lea Surrey 36 C1
Badsworth Wakefd 142 D5
Badwell Ash Suffk 89 K2
Badwell Green Suffk 89 K2
Bagber Dorset 32 C8
Bagby N York 161 G6
Bag Enderby Lincs 136 F5
Bagendon Gloucs 64 E5
Bagginswood Shrops 96 F7
Baggrow Cumb 165 G2
Bagh a Chaisteil W Isls 283 b13
Bagham Kent 40 E4
Bagh a Tuath W Isls 283 b13
Bagillt Flints 128 F4
Baginton Warwks 99 K8
Baglan Neath 57 K6
Bagley Leeds 141 K1
Bagley Shrops 112 F6
Bagley Somset 31 G2
Bagmore Hants 35 K2
Bagnall Staffs 114 E1
Bagnor W Berk 48 C5
Bagshot Surrey 49 M6
Bagshot Wilts 47 L6
Bagstone S Glos 45 K2
Bagthorpe Notts 116 D1
Bagworth Leics 99 M2
Bagwy Llydiart Herefs 62 F2
Baildon C Brad 149 L7
Baildon Green C Brad 149 L7
Baile Ailein W Isls 282 f4
Baile a Mhanaich W Isls 283 c9
Baile Mór Ag & B 226 B7
Bailey Green Hants 35 K5
Baileyhead Cumb 178 C3
Bailiff Bridge Calder 141 J3
Baillieston C Glas 209 H6
Bailrigg Lancs 147 J4
Bainbridge N York 159 G4
Bainshole Abers 256 A5
Bainton C Pete 102 B2
Bainton E R Yk 152 E5
Bainton Oxon 66 E2
Baintown Fife 222 F6
Bairnkine Border 189 H3
Baker's End Herts 69 L4
Baker Street Thurr 52 D3
Bakewell Derbys 132 D6
Bala Gwynd 111 H4
Balallan W Isls 282 f4
Balbeg Highld 250 D5
Balbeggie P & K 222 B1
Balblair Highld 250 E3
Balblair Highld 263 J6
Balby Donc 142 E7
Balcary D & G 175 K5
Balchraggan Highld 250 E3
Balchreick Highld 276 B4
Balcombe W Susx 37 M5
Balcombe Lane W Susx 37 M4
Balcomie Links Fife 223 L5
Baldersby N York 160 E7
Baldersby St James N York 160 E7
Balderstone Lancs 139 J1
Balderstone Rochdl 140 D5
Balderton Notts 117 L1
Baldhu Cnwll 4 C6
Baldinnie Fife 223 G4
Baldinnies P & K 221 J4
Baldock Herts 86 E8
Baldovie C Dund 234 C4
Baldrine IoM 154 f5
Baldslow E Susx 24 E4
Baldwin IoM 154 e6
Baldwinholme Cumb 177 K8
Baldwin's Gate Staffs 114 B3
Baldwin's Hill W Susx 38 B5
Bale Norfk 121 M4
Baledgarno P & K 222 D1

Balemartine Ag & B 224 C7
Balerno C Edin 211 G5
Balfarg Fife 222 D6
Balfield Angus 234 E2
Balfour Ork 275 d4
Balfron Stirlg 208 F1
Balgaveny Abers 256 B4
Balgonar Fife 221 J8
Balgowan D & G 172 E6
Balgowan Highld 241 H4
Balgown Highld 258 F6
Balgracie D & G 172 B3
Balgray S Lans 186 C2
Balham Gt Lon 51 H4
Balhary P & K 233 L6
Balholmie P & K 233 H8
Baligill Highld 278 E3
Balintore Angus 233 L4
Balintore Highld 264 D5
Balintraid Highld 263 K5
Balivanich W Isls 283 c9
Balk N York 161 G6
Balkeerie Angus 233 M6
Balkholme E R Yk 143 K2
Ballabeg IoM 154 c7
Ballachulish Highld 229 H4
Ballafesson IoM 154 b7
Ballajora IoM 154 g4
Ballakilpheric IoM 154 b7
Ballamodha IoM 154 c7
Ballanlay Ag & B 207 G6
Ballantrae S Ayrs 182 D6
Ballards Gore Essex 72 C8
Ballards Green Warwks 99 H5
Ballasalla IoM 154 C7
Ballater Abers 243 L4
Ballaugh IoM 154 d3
Ballchraggan Highld 263 K5
Ballencrieff E Loth 212 B3
Ballevullin Ag & B 224 B6
Ball Green C Stke 114 D1
Ball Haye Green Staffs 131 K8
Ball Hill Hants 48 B6
Ballidon Derbys 115 K1
Balliekine N Ayrs 194 D3
Balliemore Ag & B 217 H7
Balligmorrie S Ayrs 183 G5
Ballimore Stirlg 219 H4
Ballindalloch Moray 254 D4
Ballindean P & K 222 D2
Ballingdon Suffk 89 H7
Ballinger Common Bucks 67 M6
Ballingham Herefs 63 H1
Ballingry Fife 222 B7
Ballinluig P & K 232 E5
Ballinshoe Angus 234 B5
Ballintuim P & K 233 G4
Balloch Highld 252 D2
Balloch N Lans 209 K4
Balloch P & K 220 E3
Balloch S Ayrs 183 J4
Balloch W Duns 208 C3
Balls Cross W Susx 36 E5
Balls Green E Susx 38 D6
Ball's Green Gloucs 64 B7
Ballygown Ag & B 226 E4
Ballygrant Ag & B 204 F3
Ballyhaugh Ag & B 224 F4
Balmacara Highld 248 C6
Balmaclellan D & G 185 G7
Balmae D & G 175 H6
Balmaha Stirlg 208 C1
Balmalcolm Fife 222 E5
Balmangan D & G 175 G5
Balmedie Abers 257 H8
Balmer Heath Shrops 113 G4
Balmerino Fife 222 F2
Balmerlawn Hants 18 D3
Balmichael N Ayrs 194 E5
Balmore E Duns 209 G4
Balmuchy Highld 264 D4
Balmule Fife 211 H2
Balmullo Fife 223 G3
Balnacoil Lodge Highld 273 J5
Balnacra Highld 248 F3
Balnacroft Abers 243 J5
Balnafoich Highld 251 J4
Balnaguard P & K 232 D5
Balnahard Ag & B 214 E4
Balnahard Ag & B 226 E5
Balnain Highld 250 D5
Balnakeil Highld 276 F3
Balne N York 142 F4
Balquharn P & K 232 F8
Balquhidder Stirlg 219 H3
Balsall Common Solhll 99 G8
Balsall Heath Birm 98 D6
Balsall Street Solhll 99 G8
Balscote Oxon 83 J6

Balsham Cambs ... 88 B5
Baltasound Shet ... 281 f1
Balterley Staffs ... 114 B2
Balterley Green Staffs ... 114 B2
Balterley Heath Staffs ... 114 B2
Baltersan D & G ... 174 C3
Balthangie Abers ... 268 E6
Baltonsborough Somset ... 31 J4
Balvicar Ag & B ... 216 B4
Balvraid Highld ... 248 D8
Balvraid Highld ... 252 F5
Balwest Cnwll ... 2 F5
Bamber Bridge Lancs ... 139 H3
Bamber's Green Essex ... 70 E3
Bamburgh Nthumb ... 203 K6
Bamford Derbys ... 132 D3
Bamford Rochdl ... 140 C5
Bampton Cumb ... 166 C7
Bampton Devon ... 29 G6
Bampton Oxon ... 65 L6
Bampton Grange Cumb ... 166 C7
Banavie Highld ... 239 J8
Banbury Oxon ... 83 K7
Banbury Crematorium Oxon ... 83 K6
Bancffosfelen Carmth ... 58 E6
Banchory Abers ... 244 F4
Banchory-Devenick Abers ... 245 K3
Bancycapel Carmth ... 58 D6
Bancyfelin Carmth ... 58 B5
Banc-y-ffordd Carmth ... 76 D7
Bandirran P & K ... 222 C1
Bandrake Head Cumb ... 156 D5
Banff Abers ... 268 C3
Bangor Gwynd ... 125 K5
Bangor Crematorium Gwynd ... 125 L5
Bangor-on-Dee Wrexhm ... 112 F2
Bangors Cnwll ... 11 H3
Bangor's Green Lancs ... 138 D6
Bangrove Suffk ... 89 J1
Banham Norfk ... 106 B6
Bank Hants ... 18 D2
Bankend D & G ... 176 D5
Bankfoot P & K ... 233 G8
Bankglen E Ayrs ... 197 H8
Bank Ground Cumb ... 156 D3
Bankhead C Aber ... 245 K2
Bankhead S Lans ... 199 G4
Bank Newton N York ... 148 F5
Banknock Falk ... 209 K3
Banks Cumb ... 178 D6
Banks Lancs ... 138 E4
Banks Green Worcs ... 82 A2
Bankshill D & G ... 177 G3
Bank Street Worcs ... 80 E3
Bank Top Calder ... 141 H3
Bank Top Lancs ... 139 G6
Banningham Norfk ... 122 E5
Bannister Green Essex ... 71 G3
Bannockburn Stirlg ... 209 L1
Banstead Surrey ... 51 H7
Bantham Devon ... 7 K6
Banton N Lans ... 209 K3
Banwell N Som ... 44 E7
Bapchild Kent ... 40 B3
Bapton Wilts ... 33 G3
Barabhas W Isls ... 282 g2
Barassie S Ayrs ... 196 C4
Barbaraville Highld ... 263 K5
Barber Booth Derbys ... 132 B3
Barber Green Cumb ... 156 F6
Barbieston S Ayrs ... 196 E7
Barbon Cumb ... 157 K6
Barbridge Ches E ... 130 B8
Barbrook Devon ... 28 C2
Barby Nhants ... 84 A1
Barcaldine Ag & B ... 228 F7
Barcheston Warwks ... 83 G7
Barclose Cumb ... 178 B6
Barcombe E Susx ... 22 F4
Barcombe Cross E Susx ... 23 G4
Barcroft C Brad ... 149 J8
Barden N York ... 159 L4
Barden Park Kent ... 38 F4
Bardfield End Green Essex ... 70 F1
Bardfield Saling Essex ... 71 G2
Bardney Lincs ... 136 B6
Bardon Leics ... 99 M1
Bardon Mill Nthumb ... 179 H6
Bardowie E Duns ... 209 G4
Bardrainney Inver ... 208 B4
Bardsea Cumb ... 156 D7
Bardsey Leeds ... 150 E7
Bardsey Island Gwynd ... 108 A7
Bardsley Oldham ... 140 D7
Bardwell Suffk ... 105 J8
Bare Lancs ... 147 J3
Bareppa Cnwll ... 3 K5
Barfad D & G ... 173 J2

Barford Norfk ... 106 C2
Barford Warwks ... 83 G3
Barford St John Oxon ... 83 K8
Barford St Martin Wilts ... 33 J4
Barford St Michael Oxon ... 83 K8
Barfrestone Kent ... 41 H5
Bargate Derbys ... 116 B2
Bargeddie N Lans ... 209 J6
Bargoed Caerph ... 61 J7
Bargrennan D & G ... 183 J7
Barham Cambs ... 102 C8
Barham Kent ... 41 G5
Barham Suffk ... 90 D5
Barham Crematorium Kent ... 41 H5
Bar Hill Cambs ... 87 H3
Barholm Lincs ... 102 B1
Barkby Leics ... 100 E2
Barkby Thorpe Leics ... 100 E2
Barkers Green Shrops ... 113 H6
Barkestone-le-Vale Leics ... 117 K4
Barkham Wokham ... 49 J5
Barking Gt Lon ... 51 L2
Barking Suffk ... 90 C4
Barkingside Gt Lon ... 51 L1
Barking Tye Suffk ... 90 C5
Barkisland Calder ... 141 G4
Barkla Shop Cnwll ... 4 B5
Barkston Lincs ... 118 B3
Barkston Ash N York ... 151 G8
Barkway Herts ... 87 H8
Barlanark C Glas ... 209 H6
Barlaston Staffs ... 114 D4
Barlavington W Susx ... 21 G4
Barlborough Derbys ... 133 J4
Barlby N York ... 143 G1
Barlestone Leics ... 99 L2
Barley Herts ... 87 H7
Barley Lancs ... 148 E7
Barleycroft End Herts ... 70 B2
Barley Hole Rothm ... 142 B8
Barleythorpe Rutlnd ... 101 J2
Barling Essex ... 53 K1
Barlings Lincs ... 135 M5
Barlochan D & G ... 175 K3
Barlow Derbys ... 133 G5
Barlow Gatesd ... 180 E6
Barlow N York ... 143 G2
Barmby Moor E R Yk ... 152 B6
Barmby on the Marsh E R Yk ... 143 H2
Barmer Norfk ... 121 H5
Barming Heath Kent ... 39 J2
Barmollack Ag & B ... 194 C2
Barmouth Gwynd ... 109 L8
Barmpton Darltn ... 169 J7
Barmston E R Yk ... 153 J4
Barnaby Green Suffk ... 107 K7
Barnacarry Ag & B ... 216 F8
Barnack C Pete ... 102 B2
Barnacle Warwks ... 99 K6
Barnard Castle Dur ... 168 D7
Barnard Gate Oxon ... 66 B5
Barnardiston Suffk ... 88 E5
Barnbarroch D & G ... 175 L3
Barnburgh Donc ... 142 D7
Barnby Suffk ... 107 K5
Barnby Dun Donc ... 142 F6
Barnby in the Willows Notts ... 117 M1
Barnby Moor Notts ... 134 D3
Barncorkrie D & G ... 172 D7
Barnehurst Gt Lon ... 52 B4
Barnes Gt Lon ... 51 G4
Barnes Street Kent ... 39 G4
Barnet Gt Lon ... 69 H7
Barnetby le Wold N Linc ... 144 D6
Barnet Gate Gt Lon ... 69 G8
Barney Norfk ... 121 M5
Barnham Suffk ... 105 H7
Barnham W Susx ... 20 F6
Barnham Broom Norfk ... 106 B2
Barnhead Angus ... 235 G2
Barnhill C Dund ... 223 H1
Barnhill Ches W ... 113 H1
Barnhill Moray ... 266 C5
Barnhills D & G ... 182 B8
Barningham Dur ... 168 D8
Barningham Suffk ... 105 K8
Barnoldby le Beck NE Lin ... 145 G7
Barnoldswick Lancs ... 148 F6
Barnsdale Bar Donc ... 142 D5
Barns Green W Susx ... 37 H5
Barnsley Barns ... 142 A6
Barnsley Gloucs ... 65 G6
Barnsley Crematorium Barns ... 142 B6
Barnsole Kent ... 41 J4
Barnstaple Devon ... 27 K4
Barnston Essex ... 70 F3
Barnston Wirral ... 129 G3
Barnstone Notts ... 117 J4
Barnt Green Worcs ... 98 C8

Barnton C Edin ... 211 G4
Barnton Ches W ... 130 C5
Barnwell All Saints Nhants ... 102 A6
Barnwell St Andrew Nhants ... 102 A6
Barnwood Gloucs ... 64 B3
Baron's Cross Herefs ... 80 B4
Baronwood Cumb ... 166 C2
Barr S Ayrs ... 183 H4
Barra W Isls ... 283 b13
Barrachan D & G ... 173 J5
Barraigh W Isls ... 283 b13
Barrapoll Ag & B ... 224 B6
Barras Cumb ... 167 J8
Barrasford Nthumb ... 179 L4
Barregarrow IoM ... 154 d4
Barrets Green Ches E ... 130 B7
Barrhead E Rens ... 208 E7
Barrhill S Ayrs ... 183 G6
Barrington Cambs ... 87 H5
Barrington Somset ... 30 F7
Barripper Cnwll ... 3 G3
Barrmill N Ayrs ... 196 D1
Barrock Highld ... 280 C2
Barrow Gloucs ... 64 C2
Barrow Lancs ... 148 C8
Barrow Rutlnd ... 118 A8
Barrow Shrops ... 96 E3
Barrow Somset ... 32 B4
Barrow Suffk ... 88 F3
Barroway Drove Norfk ... 104 B3
Barrow Bridge Bolton ... 139 K5
Barrow Burn Nthumb ... 190 B4
Barrowby Lincs ... 118 A4
Barrowden Rutlnd ... 101 L3
Barrowford Lancs ... 148 E7
Barrow Gurney N Som ... 45 G5
Barrow Haven N Linc ... 144 D3
Barrow Hill Derbys ... 133 H4
Barrow-in-Furness Cumb ... 146 D2
Barrow Island Cumb ... 146 D2
Barrow Nook Lancs ... 138 F7
Barrow's Green Ches E ... 130 D8
Barrow Street Wilts ... 32 D5
Barrow-upon-Humber N Linc ... 144 D4
Barrow upon Soar Leics ... 116 F8
Barrow upon Trent Derbys ... 116 B6
Barrow Vale BaNES ... 45 J7
Barry Angus ... 234 E8
Barry V Glam ... 43 H7
Barry Island V Glam ... 43 H8
Barsby Leics ... 100 F1
Barsham Suffk ... 107 H5
Barston Solhll ... 99 G7
Bartestree Herefs ... 80 D7
Barthol Chapel Abers ... 256 E5
Bartholomew Green Essex ... 71 H3
Barthomley Ches E ... 114 B1
Bartley Hants ... 18 D1
Bartley Green Birm ... 98 C7
Bartlow Cambs ... 88 B6
Barton Cambs ... 87 H4
Barton Ches W ... 113 G1
Barton Gloucs ... 65 G2
Barton Herefs ... 79 K4
Barton Lancs ... 138 D6
Barton Lancs ... 147 K8
Barton N York ... 160 C1
Barton Oxon ... 66 E5
Barton Torbay ... 8 D2
Barton Warwks ... 82 D5
Barton Bendish Norfk ... 104 E2
Barton End Gloucs ... 64 B7
Barton Green Staffs ... 115 K7
Barton Hartshorn Bucks ... 66 F1
Barton Hill N York ... 151 L3
Barton in Fabis Notts ... 116 E5
Barton in the Beans Leics ... 99 L2
Barton-le-Clay C Beds ... 68 D1
Barton-le-Street N York ... 162 C7
Barton-le-Willows N York ... 151 M3
Barton Mills Suffk ... 104 E8
Barton-on-Sea Hants ... 18 C5
Barton-on-the-Heath Warwks ... 83 G8
Barton St David Somset ... 31 J4
Barton Seagrave Nhants ... 101 J7
Barton Stacey Hants ... 34 F3
Barton Town Devon ... 28 B3
Barton Turf Norfk ... 123 G7
Barton-under-Needwood
     Staffs ... 115 K7
Barton-upon-Humber N Linc ... 144 C3
Barton upon Irwell Salfd ... 140 A8
Barton Waterside N Linc ... 144 C3
Barugh Barns ... 141 M6
Barugh Green Barns ... 141 M6
Barvas W Isls ... 282 g2
Barway Cambs ... 103 L8
Barwell Leics ... 99 L4
Barwick Devon ... 12 E1

Barwick Herts ... 69 K3
Barwick Somset ... 31 J8
Barwick in Elmet Leeds ... 150 F8
Baschurch Shrops ... 112 F7
Bascote Warwks ... 83 J3
Bascote Heath Warwks ... 83 J3
Base Green Suffk ... 89 L3
Basford Green Staffs ... 114 F1
Bashall Eaves Lancs ... 148 B7
Bashall Town Lancs ... 148 C7
Bashley Hants ... 18 C4
Basildon Essex ... 52 F1
Basildon & District
     Crematorium Essex ... 53 G2
Basingstoke Hants ... 48 F8
Basingstoke Crematorium
     Hants ... 35 H2
Baslow Derbys ... 132 E5
Bason Bridge Somset ... 30 E2
Bassaleg Newpt ... 44 B2
Bassendean Border ... 201 K4
Bassenthwaite Cumb ... 165 H4
Bassett C Sotn ... 34 F7
Bassingbourn-cum-
     Kneesworth Cambs ... 87 G6
Bassingfield Notts ... 117 G4
Bassingham Lincs ... 135 H7
Bassingthorpe Lincs ... 118 C6
Bassus Green Herts ... 69 J3
Basted Kent ... 38 F2
Baston Lincs ... 102 C1
Bastwick Norfk ... 123 J8
Batch Somset ... 44 C7
Batchworth Herts ... 68 D8
Batchworth Heath Herts ... 68 D8
Batcombe Dorset ... 16 B2
Batcombe Somset ... 31 M3
Bate Heath Ches E ... 130 D4
Batford Herts ... 68 F4
Bath BaNES ... 45 L6
Bathampton BaNES ... 45 M5
Bathealton Somset ... 29 K6
Batheaston BaNES ... 45 M5
Bathford BaNES ... 46 A5
Bathgate W Loth ... 210 C5
Bathley Notts ... 134 F7
Bathpool Cnwll ... 11 K7
Bathpool Somset ... 30 C5
Bath Side Essex ... 73 K1
Bathville W Loth ... 210 B5
Bathway Somset ... 45 H8
Batley Kirk ... 141 K3
Batsford Gloucs ... 82 E8
Batson Devon ... 7 L7
Battersby N York ... 161 K1
Battersea Gt Lon ... 51 H4
Battisborough Cross Devon ... 7 H5
Battisford Suffk ... 90 C4
Battisford Tye Suffk ... 89 L4
Battle E Susx ... 24 D4
Battle Powys ... 60 F1
Battleborough Somset ... 30 E1
Battledown Gloucs ... 64 D3
Battledykes Angus ... 234 C4
Battlefield Shrops ... 113 H8
Battlesbridge Essex ... 71 J8
Battlesden C Beds ... 68 B2
Battleton Somset ... 29 G5
Battlies Green Suffk ... 89 H2
Battram Leics ... 99 L2
Battramsley Cross Hants ... 18 E4
Batt's Corner Hants ... 36 B3
Baughton Worcs ... 81 K6
Baughurst Hants ... 48 E7
Baulds Abers ... 244 D5
Baulking Oxon ... 47 L1
Baumber Lincs ... 136 D5
Baunton Gloucs ... 64 E6
Baveney Wood Shrops ... 96 F7
Baverstock Wilts ... 33 H4
Bawburgh Norfk ... 106 D2
Bawdeswell Norfk ... 122 A7
Bawdrip Somset ... 30 E3
Bawdsey Suffk ... 91 H7
Bawsey Norfk ... 120 E7
Bawtry Donc ... 134 C1
Baxenden Lancs ... 140 A4
Baxterley Warwks ... 99 H4
Baxter's Green Suffk ... 88 E4
Bay Highld ... 258 D6
Bayble W Isls ... 282 h3
Baybridge Hants ... 35 H6
Baybridge Nthumb ... 168 B1
Baycliff Cumb ... 146 F2
Baydon Wilts ... 47 L3
Bayford Herts ... 69 J5
Bayford Somset ... 32 B5
Bayhead W Isls ... 283 b8
Bay Horse Lancs ... 147 K5

Bayley's Hill Kent 38 D3
Baylham Suffk 90 C5
Baynard's Green Oxon 66 E1
Baysdale Abbey N York 161 K1
Baysham Herefs 63 H2
Bayston Hill Shrops 96 B2
Baythorne End Essex 88 E6
Bayton Worcs 96 F8
Bayton Common Worcs 81 G1
Bayworth Oxon 66 D6
Beach S Glos 45 L5
Beachampton Bucks 84 E7
Beachamwell Norfk 104 E2
Beachley Gloucs 45 H1
Beacon Devon 14 E2
Beacon End Essex 72 D2
Beacon Hill E Susx 38 D7
Beacon Hill Kent 39 K6
Beacon Hill Notts 117 L1
Beacon Hill Surrey 36 C3
Beacon's Bottom Bucks 67 J8
Beaconsfield Bucks 50 B1
Beadlam N York 161 L5
Beadlow C Beds 86 C7
Beadnell Nthumb 203 L7
Beaford Devon 27 K7
Beal N York 142 E3
Beal Nthumb 203 H4
Bealbury Cnwll 6 D2
Bealsmill Cnwll 11 L7
Beam Hill Staffs 115 L6
Beamhurst Staffs 115 H4
Beaminster Dorset 15 L2
Beamish Dur 180 F8
Beamsley N York 149 K5
Bean Kent 52 C4
Beanacre Wilts 46 C5
Beanley Nthumb 190 F3
Beardon Devon 12 C5
Beardwood Bl w D 139 K2
Beare Devon 14 A2
Beare Green Surrey 37 J2
Bearley Warwks 82 E3
Bearley Cross Warwks 82 E3
Bearpark Dur 169 G2
Bearsden E Duns 208 F4
Bearsted Kent 39 K2
Bearstone Shrops 114 A4
Bearwood Birm 98 C6
Bearwood Herefs 79 M4
Bearwood Poole 17 L3
Beattock D & G 187 G6
Beauchamp Roding Essex 70 E5
Beauchief Sheff 132 F3
Beaudesert Warwks 82 E2
Beaufort Blae G 61 J5
Beaulieu Hants 18 F3
Beaulieu Road Station Hants 18 E2
Beauly Highld 250 F2
Beaumaris IoA 126 B4
Beaumont Cumb 177 K7
Beaumont Essex 73 H2
Beaumont Jersey 9 c3
Beaumont Hill Darltn 169 J7
Beaumont Leys C Leic 100 C2
Beausale Warwks 82 F1
Beauworth Hants 35 J5
Beaworthy Devon 12 B3
Beazley End Essex 71 H1
Bebington Wirral 129 H3
Bebside Nthumb 181 G3
Beccles Suffk 107 J5
Becconsall Lancs 138 F3
Beckbury Shrops 97 H3
Beckenham Gt Lon 51 K5
Beckenham Crematorium
Gt Lon 51 K5
Beckermet Cumb 155 J1
Beckett End Norfk 104 F4
Beckfoot Cumb 155 L3
Beckfoot Cumb 156 B5
Beck Foot Cumb 157 K3
Beckfoot Cumb 164 E1
Beckford Worcs 82 A8
Beckhampton Wilts 47 G5
Beck Hole N York 162 E2
Beckingham Lincs 118 A1
Beckingham Notts 134 F2
Beckington Somset 46 A8
Beckjay Shrops 95 J7
Beckley E Susx 24 F3
Beckley Hants 18 C4
Beckley Oxon 66 E5
Beck Row Suffk 104 D7
Becks C Brad 149 J6
Beck Side Cumb 156 B6
Beck Side Cumb 156 E6
Beckton Gt Lon 51 L3
Beckwithshaw N York 150 C5

Becontree Gt Lon 52 A2
Becquet Vincent Jersey 9 d2
Bedale N York 160 C5
Bedburn Dur 168 E4
Bedchester Dorset 32 E7
Beddau Rhondd 43 G4
Beddgelert Gwynd 109 L2
Beddingham E Susx 23 G5
Beddington Gt Lon 51 J6
Beddington Corner Gt Lon 51 J5
Bedfield Suffk 90 F2
Bedfield Little Green Suffk 90 F2
Bedford Bed 85 L5
Bedford Crematorium Bed 86 B5
Bedgebury Cross Kent 39 H6
Bedham W Susx 36 F6
Bedhampton Hants 20 A5
Bedingfield Suffk 90 E2
Bedingfield Green Suffk 90 E2
Bedlam N York 150 C3
Bedlington Nthumb 181 G3
Bedlinog Myr Td 61 H6
Bedminster Bristl 45 H5
Bedminster Down Bristl 45 H5
Bedmond Herts 68 C6
Bednall Staffs 114 F7
Bedrule Border 189 G3
Bedstone Shrops 95 J8
Bedwas Caerph 43 J4
Bedwellty Caerph 61 J7
Bedworth Warwks 99 K6
Bedworth Woodlands Warwks 99 K6
Beeby Leics 100 E2
Beech Hants 35 L3
Beech Staffs 114 D4
Beech Hill W Berk 49 G6
Beechingstoke Wilts 47 G7
Beedon W Berk 48 C3
Beedon Hill W Berk 48 C3
Beeford E R Yk 153 H5
Beeley Derbys 132 E6
Beelsby NE Lin 145 G7
Beenham W Berk 48 E5
Beenham's Heath W & M 49 K4
Beeny Cnwll 11 G4
Beer Devon 14 F5
Beer Somset 30 F4
Beercrocombe Somset 30 D6
Beer Hackett Dorset 31 K8
Beesands Devon 8 B6
Beesby Lincs 137 J4
Beeson Devon 8 B6
Beeston C Beds 86 D5
Beeston Ches W 129 M7
Beeston Leeds 141 L2
Beeston Norfk 121 K8
Beeston Notts 116 E4
Beeston Regis Norfk 122 D3
Beeswing D & G 176 A5
Beetham Cumb 157 H6
Beetham Somset 30 D8
Beetley Norfk 121 L8
Began Cardif 43 K5
Begbroke Oxon 66 C4
Begdale Cambs 103 J2
Begelly Pembks 55 J5
Beggarington Hill Leeds 141 L3
Beggar's Bush Powys 79 J2
Beguildy Powys 94 F7
Beighton Norfk 107 H2
Beighton Sheff 133 J3
Beinn Na Faoghla W Isls 283 c9
Beith N Ayrs 208 B8
Bekesbourne Kent 41 G4
Bekesbourne Hill Kent 41 G4
Belaugh Norfk 122 F7
Belbroughton Worcs 97 L7
Belchalwell Dorset 16 F1
Belchalwell Street Dorset 16 F1
Belchamp Otten Essex 88 F6
Belchamp St Paul Essex 88 F6
Belchamp Walter Essex 89 G7
Belchford Lincs 136 E5
Belford Nthumb 203 H6
Belgrave C Leic 100 D2
Belhaven E Loth 212 E3
Belhelvie Abers 257 H8
Belhinnie Abers 255 J6
Bellabeg Abers 243 K1
Bellamore Herefs 79 M7
Bellanoch Ag & B 216 B8
Bellasize E R Yk 143 K2
Bellaty Angus 233 K3
Bell Bar Herts 69 H3
Bell Busk N York 148 F4
Belleau Lincs 137 G4
Bell End Worcs 97 L7
Bellerby N York 159 K4
Bellever Devon 12 F7

Belle Vue Cumb 177 L7
Belle Vue Wakefd 142 A4
Bellfield S Lans 186 E2
Bellfield S Lans 198 D6
Bell Heath Worcs 97 L7
Bell Hill Hants 35 M6
Bellingdon Bucks 68 B6
Bellingham Nthumb 179 J2
Belloch Ag & B 192 D1
Bellochantuy Ag & B 192 D2
Bell o' th' Hill Ches W 113 H2
Bellows Cross Dorset 33 J8
Bells Cross Suffk 90 D5
Bellshill N Lans 209 J7
Bellshill Nthumb 203 J7
Bellside N Lans 209 L7
Bellsquarry W Loth 210 D6
Bells Yew Green E Susx 38 F6
Belluton BaNES 45 J6
Belmaduthy Highld 263 H8
Belmesthorpe Rutlnd 102 A2
Belmont Bl w D 139 K4
Belmont Gt Lon 51 H6
Belmont S Ayrs 196 C7
Belmont Shet 281 f2
Belnacraig Abers 255 H8
Belowda Cnwll 4 F3
Belper Derbys 116 B2
Belper Lane End Derbys 116 B2
Belph Derbys 133 L4
Belsay Nthumb 180 D3
Belses Border 201 J8
Belsford Devon 7 L3
Belsize Herts 68 D7
Belstead Suffk 90 D7
Belstone Devon 13 G5
Belthorn Lancs 139 L3
Beltinge Kent 41 G2
Beltingham Nthumb 179 H6
Beltoft N Linc 143 K7
Belton Leics 116 D7
Belton Lincs 118 B3
Belton N Linc 143 K6
Belton Norfk 107 K8
Belton Rutlnd 101 H3
Beltring Kent 39 H4
Belvedere Gt Lon 52 B3
Belvoir Leics 117 L5
Bembridge IoW 19 L6
Bemerton Wilts 33 K5
Bempton E R Yk 153 K2
Benacre Suffk 107 K6
Benbecula W Isls 283 c9
Benbuie D & G 185 H4
Benderloch Ag & B 228 D7
Benenden Kent 39 K6
Benfieldside Dur 180 D8
Bengates Norfk 122 F6
Bengeo Herts 69 J4
Bengeworth Worcs 82 B6
Benhall Green Suffk 91 J3
Benhall Street Suffk 91 H3
Benholm Abers 235 K2
Beningbrough N York 151 H4
Benington Herts 69 J2
Benington Lincs 119 L2
Benington Sea End Lincs 119 L2
Benllech IoA 125 J3
Benmore Ag & B 207 J2
Bennacott Cnwll 11 K4
Bennan N Ayrs 193 K4
Bennet Head Cumb 166 B6
Bennetland E R Yk 143 L2
Bennett End Bucks 67 J7
Benniworth Lincs 136 D3
Benover Kent 39 H4
Ben Rhydding C Brad 149 L6
Benslie N Ayrs 196 C2
Benson Oxon 66 F8
Bentfield Green Essex 70 D2
Benthall Shrops 96 F3
Bentham Gloucs 64 C4
Benthoul C Aber 245 H3
Bentlawnt Shrops 95 H3
Bentley Donc 142 E6
Bentley E R Yk 152 F8
Bentley Hants 36 A2
Bentley Suffk 90 D7
Bentley Warwks 99 H4
Bentley Crematorium Essex 70 E7
Bentley Heath Herts 69 H1
Bentley Heath Solhll 98 F8
Benton Devon 28 B4
Bentwichen Devon 28 C4
Bentworth Hants 35 K3
Benvie Angus 222 E1
Benville Dorset 15 M2
Benwick Cambs 103 G5

Beoley Worcs 82 C1
Beoraidbeg Highld 237 K2
Bepton W Susx 20 D3
Berden Essex 70 C1
Berea Pembks 74 C6
Bere Alston Devon 6 E2
Bere Ferrers Devon 6 E2
Berepper Cnwll 3 G6
Bere Regis Dorset 17 G4
Bergh Apton Norfk 106 F3
Berhill Somset 31 G4
Berinsfield Oxon 66 E7
Berkeley Gloucs 63 K7
Berkeley Heath Gloucs 63 K7
Berkeley Road Gloucs 63 L7
Berkhamsted Herts 68 C5
Berkley Somset 32 D1
Berkswell Solhll 99 H7
Bermondsey Gt Lon 51 J3
Bermuda Warwks 99 K5
Bernera Highld 248 C7
Bernisdale Highld 258 F6
Berrick Prior Oxon 66 F8
Berrick Salome Oxon 66 F8
Berriedale Highld 274 F3
Berrier Cumb 165 L5
Berriew Powys 94 E3
Berrington Nthumb 202 F4
Berrington Shrops 96 C2
Berrington Worcs 80 D2
Berrington Green Worcs 80 D2
Berrow Somset 44 C8
Berrow Worcs 81 H8
Berrow Green Worcs 81 H3
Berry Brow Kirk 141 H5
Berry Cross Devon 27 H7
Berry Down Cross Devon 27 K2
Berryfields Bucks 67 J4
Berry Hill Gloucs 63 H4
Berry Hill Pembks 75 H4
Berryhillock Moray 267 K4
Berryhillock Moray 267 K5
Berrynarbor Devon 27 K2
Berry Pomeroy Devon 8 B3
Berry's Green Gt Lon 51 L7
Bersham Wrexhm 112 D2
Bersted W Susx 20 F6
Berthengam Flints 128 D4
Berwick E Susx 23 H6
Berwick Bassett Wilts 47 G4
Berwick Hill Nthumb 180 E4
Berwick St James Wilts 33 J3
Berwick St John Wilts 32 F6
Berwick St Leonard Wilts 32 F4
Berwick-upon-Tweed Nthumb 202 F2
Bescaby Leics 117 L6
Bescar Lancs 138 E5
Besford Shrops 113 J6
Besford Worcs 81 J5
Bessacarr Donc 142 F7
Bessels Leigh Oxon 66 C6
Besses o' th' Barn Bury 140 B6
Bessingby E R Yk 153 J3
Bessingham Norfk 122 D4
Bestbeech Hill E Susx 38 F7
Besthorpe Norfk 106 B4
Besthorpe Notts 135 G6
Bestwood Village Notts 116 F2
Beswick E R Yk 152 F6
Betchcott Shrops 95 K4
Betchworth Surrey 37 K1
Bethania Cerdgn 77 G3
Bethania Gwynd 110 D3
Bethel Gwynd 111 J4
Bethel Gwynd 125 J6
Bethel IoA 125 G5
Bethel Powys 111 L7
Bethersden Kent 40 B7
Bethesda Gwynd 126 C6
Bethesda Pembks 55 J3
Bethlehem Carmth 59 J4
Bethnal Green Gt Lon 51 K2
Betley Staffs 114 B2
Betsham Kent 52 D4
Betteshanger Kent 41 J5
Bettiscombe Dorset 15 J3
Bettisfield Wrexhm 113 G4
Betton Shrops 113 M2
Betton Strange Shrops 96 C2
Bettws Newpt 44 C1
Bettws Cedewain Powys 94 D4
Bettws Evan Cerdgn 76 B5
Bettws-Newydd Mons 62 D6
Bettyhill Highld 278 B4
Betws Brdgnd 42 D4
Betws Carmth 59 H6
Betws Bledrws Cerdgn 77 H5
Betws Garmon Gwynd 125 K8
Betws Gwerfil Goch Denbgs 111 K2

Betws-y-Coed Conwy 126 F8
Betws-yn-Rhos Conwy 127 H5
Beulah Cerdgn 76 B6
Beulah Powys 78 C5
Bevendean Br & H 22 E6
Bevercotes Notts 134 D5
Beverley E R Yk 153 G7
Beverston Gloucs 64 B8
Bevington Gloucs 63 K7
Bewaldeth Cumb 165 H4
Bewcastle Cumb 178 D4
Bewdley Worcs 97 H8
Bewerley N York 149 L3
Bewholme E R Yk 153 J6
Bewlbridge Kent 39 H6
Bexhill E Susx 24 D5
Bexley Gt Lon 52 B4
Bexleyheath Gt Lon 52 A4
Bexleyhill W Susx 36 D6
Bexon Kent 53 J7
Bexwell Norfk 104 C3
Beyton Suffk 89 J3
Beyton Green Suffk 89 J3
Bhaltos W Isls 282 e3
Bhatarsaigh W Isls 283 b13
Bibstone S Glos 45 K1
Bibury Gloucs 65 G5
Bicester Oxon 66 E3
Bickenhill Solhll 99 G7
Bicker Lincs 119 H4
Bicker Bar Lincs 119 H4
Bicker Gauntlet Lincs 119 H4
Bickershaw Wigan 139 J7
Bickerstaffe Lancs 138 F7
Bickerton Ches E 113 H1
Bickerton Devon 8 B7
Bickerton N York 151 G5
Bickerton Nthumb 190 E6
Bickford Staffs 114 D8
Bickington Devon 13 J8
Bickington Devon 27 J4
Bickleigh Devon 7 G2
Bickleigh Devon 13 M1
Bickleton Devon 27 J5
Bickley Ches W 113 J2
Bickley Gt Lon 51 L5
Bickley N York 163 G4
Bickley Worcs 80 E1
Bickley Moss Ches W 113 J2
Bicknacre Essex 71 J6
Bicknoller Somset 29 K3
Bicknor Kent 53 J7
Bickton Hants 33 K8
Bicton Herefs 80 B2
Bicton Shrops 95 G6
Bicton Shrops 113 G8
Bidborough Kent 38 E5
Bidden Hants 35 L1
Biddenden Kent 39 L5
Biddenden Green Kent 39 M5
Biddenham Bed 85 K5
Biddestone Wilts 46 B4
Biddisham Somset 44 D8
Biddlesden Bucks 84 C7
Biddlestone Nthumb 190 D4
Biddulph Staffs 131 H7
Biddulph Moor Staffs 131 H8
Bideford Devon 27 H5
Bidford-on-Avon Warwks 82 D5
Bidston Wirral 129 G2
Bielby E R Yk 152 B7
Bieldside C Aber 245 K3
Bierley IoW 19 H8
Bierton Bucks 67 K4
Big Balcraig D & G 173 K6
Bigbury Devon 7 K5
Bigbury-on-Sea Devon 7 J6
Bigby Lincs 144 D6
Big Carlae D & G 185 G3
Biggar Cumb 146 D3
Biggar S Lans 199 H5
Biggin Derbys 115 L2
Biggin Derbys 132 C7
Biggin N York 142 E1
Biggin Hill Gt Lon 51 L7
Biggleswade C Beds 86 D6
Bigholms D & G 177 K3
Bighouse Highld 278 D3
Bighton Hants 35 J4
Biglands Cumb 177 H8
Bignor W Susx 21 G4
Bigrigg Cumb 164 D8
Big Sand Highld 260 B4
Bigton Shet 281 d8
Bilborough C Nott 116 E3
Bilbrook Somset 29 J3
Bilbrook Staffs 97 K3
Bilbrough N York 151 H6
Bilbster Highld 280 C5

Bildershaw Dur 169 G6
Bildeston Suffk 89 K5
Billacott Cnwll 11 J4
Billericay Essex 71 G8
Billesdon Leics 100 F3
Billesley Warwks 82 D4
Billingborough Lincs 118 F5
Billinge St Hel 139 G7
Billingford Norfk 106 D7
Billingford Norfk 121 M7
Billingham S on T 170 B6
Billinghay Lincs 136 C8
Billingley Barns 142 C6
Billingshurst W Susx 37 G5
Billingsley Shrops 97 G6
Billington C Beds 68 B3
Billington Lancs 148 C8
Billington Staffs 114 D7
Billockby Norfk 107 J1
Billy Row Dur 168 F3
Bilsborrow Lancs 147 K7
Bilsby Lincs 137 J4
Bilsham W Susx 21 G6
Bilsington Kent 40 D8
Bilsthorpe Notts 134 C7
Bilsthorpe Moor Notts 134 C7
Bilston Mdloth 211 J6
Bilston Wolves 98 B4
Bilstone Leics 99 K2
Bilting Kent 40 D5
Bilton E R Yk 144 F1
Bilton N York 150 D4
Bilton Nthumb 191 J4
Bilton Warwks 100 B8
Bilton Banks Nthumb 191 J4
Bilton-in-Ainsty N York 151 G6
Binbrook Lincs 136 D1
Binchester Blocks Dur 169 G4
Bincombe Dorset 16 D5
Binegar Somset 31 K1
Bines Green W Susx 21 L3
Binfield Br For 49 K4
Binfield Heath Oxon 49 H3
Bingfield Nthumb 180 A4
Bingham Notts 117 J3
Bingham's Melcombe Dorset 16 E2
Bingley C Brad 149 K7
Bings Shrops 113 J7
Binham Norfk 121 L4
Binley Covtry 99 K7
Binley Hants 48 B8
Binley Woods Warwks 99 L7
Binnegar Dorset 17 G5
Binniehill Falk 209 M4
Binscombe Surrey 36 E2
Binsey Oxon 66 C5
Binstead IoW 19 K5
Binsted Hants 36 A3
Binsted W Susx 21 G5
Binton Warwks 82 D4
Bintree Norfk 121 M7
Binweston Shrops 95 H3
Birch Essex 72 D3
Birch Rochdl 140 C6
Bircham Newton Norfk 121 G5
Bircham Tofts Norfk 121 G5
Birchanger Essex 70 D3
Birch Cross Staffs 115 J5
Birchencliffe Kirk 141 H4
Bircher Herefs 80 B2
Birchfield Birm 98 D5
Birch Green Essex 72 D3
Birch Green Herts 69 J5
Birch Green Worcs 81 K6
Birchgrove Cardif 43 J5
Birchgrove Swans 57 K5
Birchgrove W Susx 38 B7
Birch Heath Ches W 130 A7
Birch Hill Ches W 129 M5
Birchington Kent 41 J2
Birchington-on-Sea Kent 41 J2
Birchley Heath Warwks 99 H4
Birchmoor Warwks 99 H3
Birchmoor Green C Beds 85 J2
Birchover Derbys 132 E7
Birch Vale Derbys 131 K2
Birchwood Lincs 135 J6
Birch Wood Somset 30 C4
Birchwood Warrtn 130 C2
Bircotes Notts 134 C2
Birdbrook Essex 88 E7
Birdforth N York 161 D7
Birdham W Susx 20 D6
Birdingbury Warwks 83 K2
Birdlip Gloucs 64 D4
Birdoswald Cumb 178 D5
Birdsall N York 152 B3
Birds Edge Kirk 141 K6
Birds Green Essex 70 E5

Birdsgreen Shrops 97 H6
Birdsmoorgate Dorset 15 J3
Bird Street Suffk 89 K5
Birdwell Barns 142 A7
Birdwood Gloucs 63 L3
Birgham Border 202 B5
Birichin Highld 263 K2
Birkacre Lancs 139 H5
Birkby N York 160 D2
Birkdale Sefton 138 C5
Birkenbog Abers 267 L3
Birkenhead Wirral 129 H2
Birkenhead (Queensway)
  Tunnel Lpool 129 H2
Birkenhills Abers 256 D3
Birkenshaw Kirk 141 K2
Birkhall Abers 243 K5
Birkhill Angus 234 A8
Birkhill D & G 187 J3
Birkholme Lincs 118 C6
Birkin N York 142 E2
Birks Leeds 141 L2
Birkshaw Nthumb 179 H5
Birley Herefs 80 B4
Birley Carr Sheff 133 G1
Birling Kent 52 E6
Birling Nthumb 191 K5
Birling Gap E Susx 23 J8
Birlingham Worcs 81 K6
Birmingham Birm 98 D6
Birnam P & K 232 F7
Birness Abers 257 H5
Birse Abers 244 C4
Birsemore Abers 244 C4
Birstall Kirk 141 K3
Birstall Leics 100 D2
Birstwith N York 150 B4
Birthorpe Lincs 118 E5
Birtley Gatesd 181 G7
Birtley Herefs 79 L2
Birtley Nthumb 179 K3
Birtley Crematorium Gatesd 181 G7
Birts Street Worcs 81 H7
Bisbrooke Rutlnd 101 J3
Biscathorpe Lincs 136 D3
Biscovey Cnwll 5 H4
Bisham W & M 49 K2
Bishampton Worcs 82 A5
Bish Mill Devon 28 C6
Bishop Auckland Dur 169 G5
Bishopbridge Lincs 135 L2
Bishopbriggs E Duns 209 G5
Bishop Burton E R Yk 152 F7
Bishop Middleham Dur 169 J4
Bishopmill Moray 266 E3
Bishop Monkton N York 150 D3
Bishop Norton Lincs 135 K1
Bishopsbourne Kent 41 G5
Bishops Cannings Wilts 46 F6
Bishop's Castle Shrops 95 H5
Bishop's Caundle Dorset 32 B8
Bishop's Cleeve Gloucs 64 D2
Bishop's Frome Herefs 80 F5
Bishops Gate Surrey 50 B5
Bishop's Green Essex 70 F3
Bishop's Green Hants 48 D6
Bishop's Hull Somset 30 B6
Bishop's Itchington Warwks 83 J4
Bishops Lydeard Somset 29 M5
Bishop's Norton Gloucs 64 C2
Bishop's Nympton Devon 28 D6
Bishop's Offley Staffs 114 B5
Bishop's Stortford Herts 70 C3
Bishop's Sutton Hants 35 J4
Bishop's Tachbrook Warwks 83 H3
Bishop's Tawton Devon 27 K5
Bishopsteignton Devon 13 L7
Bishopstoke Hants 34 F7
Bishopston Swans 57 G7
Bishopstone Bucks 67 J5
Bishopstone E Susx 23 G7
Bishopstone Herefs 80 A6
Bishopstone Kent 41 G2
Bishopstone Swindn 47 K2
Bishopstone Wilts 33 J5
Bishopstrow Wilts 32 E2
Bishop Sutton BaNES 45 H7
Bishop's Waltham Hants 35 H7
Bishopswood Somset 30 C8
Bishop's Wood Staffs 97 J2
Bishopsworth Bristl 45 H5
Bishop Thornton N York 150 C3
Bishopthorpe C York 151 J6
Bishopton Darltn 169 K6
Bishopton Rens 208 D5
Bishopton Warwks 82 E4
Bishop Wilton E R Yk 152 B5
Bishton Newpt 44 D2
Bishton Staffs 115 G7

Bisley Gloucs 64 C6
Bisley Surrey 50 B7
Bisley Camp Surrey 50 B7
Bispham Bpool 146 F7
Bispham Green Lancs 138 F5
Bissoe Cnwll 3 K3
Bisterne Hants 18 A3
Bitchet Green Kent 38 E3
Bitchfield Lincs 118 C6
Bittadon Devon 27 K3
Bittaford Devon 7 K5
Bittering Norfk 121 K8
Bitterley Shrops 96 D7
Bitterne C Sotn 34 F8
Bitteswell Leics 100 C4
Bitton S Glos 45 K5
Bix Oxon 49 H2
Bixter Shet 281 d6
Blaby Leics 100 C4
Blackadder Border 202 C3
Blackawton Devon 8 B4
Blackbeck Cumb 155 J1
Blackborough Devon 14 C1
Blackborough End Norfk 120 E8
Black Bourton Oxon 65 L6
Blackboys E Susx 23 J3
Blackbrook Derbys 116 B2
Blackbrook St Hel 139 G8
Blackbrook Staffs 114 B4
Blackbrook Surrey 37 J2
Blackburn Abers 245 J1
Blackburn Bl w D 139 K2
Blackburn Rothm 133 H3
Blackburn W Loth 210 C6
Black Callerton N u Ty 180 E5
Black Car Norfk 106 B4
Black Corner W Susx 37 L3
Blackcraig E Ayrs 185 G1
Black Crofts Ag & B 228 E8
Black Cross Cnwll 4 D5
Blackden Heath Ches E 130 F5
Blackdog Abers 245 L1
Black Dog Devon 13 J1
Blackdown Devon 12 C6
Blackdown Dorset 15 J2
Blackdyke Cumb 176 F8
Blacker Barns 142 A5
Blacker Hill Barns 142 B7
Blackfen Gt Lon 51 M4
Blackfield Hants 19 G3
Blackford Cumb 177 K6
Blackford P & K 220 F5
Blackford Somset 30 F2
Blackford Somset 31 L5
Blackfordby Leics 116 B7
Blackgang IoW 19 H8
Blackhall C Edin 211 G4
Blackhall Dur 170 B3
Blackhall Colliery Dur 170 B3
Blackhall Mill Gatesd 180 D7
Blackhaugh Border 200 F5
Blackheath Essex 72 D2
Blackheath Gt Lon 51 K4
Blackheath Sandw 98 B6
Blackheath Suffk 107 J8
Blackheath Surrey 36 F2
Black Heddon Nthumb 180 C4
Blackhill Abers 257 K3
Blackhill Abers 269 K5
Blackhill Dur 180 D8
Blackhill of Clackriach Abers 269 G7
Blackhorse Devon 14 A4
Blackjack Lincs 119 H4
Blackland Wilts 46 E5
Black Lane Ends Lancs 149 G7
Blacklaw D & G 186 F4
Blackley Manch 140 C7
Blackley Crematorium Manch 140 C7
Blacklunans P & K 233 H3
Blackmarstone Herefs 80 C7
Blackmill Brdgnd 42 D4
Blackmoor Hants 36 A4
Black Moor Leeds 150 D7
Blackmoor N Som 44 F6
Blackmoorfoot Kirk 141 H5
Blackmore Essex 70 F6
Blackmore End Essex 71 J1
Blackmore End Herts 68 D3
Blackness Falk 210 E3
Blacknest Hants 36 B3
Blacknest W & M 50 B5
Black Notley Essex 71 J3
Blacko Lancs 148 E7
Black Pill Swans 57 H6
Blackpool Bpool 146 F2
Blackpool Devon 8 C5
Blackpool Devon 13 J7
Blackpool Gate Cumb 178 C3
Blackridge W Loth 210 A5

Blackrock Cnwll ... 3 G4
Blackrock Mons ... 61 K4
Blackrod Bolton ... 139 J5
Blacksboat Moray ... 254 D4
Blackshaw D & G ... 176 D5
Blackshaw Head Calder ... 140 E2
Blacksmith's Green Suffk ... 90 D2
Blacksnape Bl w D ... 139 L3
Blackstone W Susx ... 22 C4
Black Street Suffk ... 107 K6
Black Tar Pembks ... 55 G5
Blackthorn Oxon ... 66 F3
Blackthorpe Suffk ... 89 H3
Blacktoft E R Yk ... 143 L3
Blacktop C Aber ... 245 J3
Black Torrington Devon ... 12 B2
Blackwall Derbys ... 115 L2
Blackwall Tunnel Gt Lon ... 51 K3
Blackwater Cnwll ... 4 B5
Blackwater Hants ... 49 K7
Blackwater IoW ... 19 H6
Blackwater Somset ... 30 C7
Blackwaterfoot N Ayrs ... 194 D5
Blackwell Cumb ... 177 L8
Blackwell Darltn ... 169 H8
Blackwell Derbys ... 132 C5
Blackwell Derbys ... 133 J7
Blackwell Warwks ... 82 F6
Blackwell Worcs ... 82 A1
Blackwellsend Green Gloucs ... 63 M2
Blackwood Caerph ... 43 J2
Blackwood D & G ... 176 B2
Blackwood S Lans ... 198 C4
Blackwood Hill Staffs ... 131 H8
Blacon Ches W ... 129 J6
Bladbean Kent ... 41 G6
Bladnoch D & G ... 174 C4
Bladon Oxon ... 66 C4
Bladon Somset ... 30 F6
Blaenannerch Cerdgn ... 75 M2
Blaenau Ffestiniog Gwynd ... 110 D2
Blaenavon Torfn ... 61 L5
Blaen Dyryn Powys ... 78 C7
Blaenffos Pembks ... 75 L5
Blaengarw Brdgnd ... 42 D3
Blaengeuffordd Cerdgn ... 92 E7
Blaengwrach Neath ... 60 C6
Blaengwynfi Neath ... 42 D2
Blaenllechau Rhondd ... 42 F2
Blaenpennal Cerdgn ... 77 H2
Blaenplwyf Cerdgn ... 92 C8
Blaenporth Cerdgn ... 76 A5
Blaenrhondda Rhondd ... 60 D7
Blaenwaun Carmth ... 75 M6
Blaen-y-Coed Carmth ... 58 C3
Blaen-y-cwm Blae G ... 61 H5
Blaenycwm Cerdgn ... 93 H8
Blaen-y-cwm Rhondd ... 60 D7
Blagdon N Som ... 45 J4
Blagdon Somset ... 30 B7
Blagdon Torbay ... 8 C3
Blagdon Hill Somset ... 30 B7
Blagill Cumb ... 167 G1
Blaguegate Lancs ... 138 F6
Blaich Highld ... 239 G8
Blain Highld ... 237 K6
Blaina Blae G ... 61 K5
Blair Atholl P & K ... 232 C2
Blair Drummond Stirlg ... 220 C7
Blairgowrie P & K ... 233 J6
Blairhall Fife ... 210 C2
Blairingone P & K ... 221 H7
Blairlogie Stirlg ... 220 E7
Blairmore Ag & B ... 207 L2
Blairmore Highld ... 276 B4
Blair's Ferry Ag & B ... 206 F5
Blaisdon Gloucs ... 63 K4
Blakebrook Worcs ... 97 J8
Blakedown Worcs ... 97 K7
Blake End Essex ... 71 H3
Blakeley Lane Staffs ... 114 F7
Blakemere Ches W ... 130 A5
Blakemere Herefs ... 79 L7
Blakemore Devon ... 7 M3
Blakenall Heath Wsall ... 98 C3
Blakeney Gloucs ... 63 K5
Blakeney Norfk ... 122 A3
Blakenhall Ches E ... 114 A2
Blakenhall Wolves ... 97 K4
Blakeshall Worcs ... 97 J7
Blakesley Nhants ... 84 C5
Blanchland Nthumb ... 168 B1
Blandford Camp Dorset ... 17 H1
Blandford Forum Dorset ... 17 G1
Blandford St Mary Dorset ... 17 G2
Bland Hill N York ... 150 B5
Blanefield Stirlg ... 208 F3
Blankney Lincs ... 135 L7
Blantyre S Lans ... 209 J7

Blàr a' Chaorainn Highld ... 229 H2
Blargie Highld ... 241 G4
Blarmachfoldach Highld ... 229 H2
Blashford Hants ... 18 A2
Blaston Leics ... 101 H4
Blatherwycke Nhants ... 101 L4
Blawith Cumb ... 156 C5
Blawquhairn D & G ... 184 F6
Blaxhall Suffk ... 91 J4
Blaxton Donc ... 143 H7
Blaydon Gatesd ... 180 F6
Bleadney Somset ... 31 H2
Bleadon N Som ... 44 C7
Bleak Street Somset ... 32 C4
Blean Kent ... 40 F3
Bleasby Lincs ... 136 B3
Bleasby Notts ... 117 J2
Bleasdale Lancs ... 147 L6
Bleatarn Cumb ... 167 G7
Bleathwood Herefs ... 80 D1
Blebocraigs Fife ... 223 G4
Bleddfa Powys ... 79 H2
Bledington Gloucs ... 65 K3
Bledlow Bucks ... 67 J6
Bledlow Ridge Bucks ... 67 J7
Bleet Wilts ... 46 C7
Blegbie E Loth ... 212 B6
Blencarn Cumb ... 166 E4
Blencogo Cumb ... 165 G1
Blendworth Hants ... 35 L8
Blennerhasset Cumb ... 165 G2
Bletchingdon Oxon ... 66 D3
Bletchingley Surrey ... 37 M1
Bletchley M Keyn ... 85 G8
Bletchley Shrops ... 113 K5
Bletherston Pembks ... 55 H3
Bletsoe Bed ... 85 K4
Blewbury Oxon ... 48 D2
Blickling Norfk ... 122 D6
Blidworth Notts ... 134 B8
Blidworth Bottoms Notts ... 117 G1
Blindburn Nthumb ... 189 L4
Blindcrake Cumb ... 164 F4
Blindley Heath Surrey ... 38 A4
Blisland Cnwll ... 10 F8
Blissford Hants ... 33 L8
Bliss Gate Worcs ... 81 G1
Blisworth Nhants ... 84 D4
Blithbury Staffs ... 115 H7
Blitterlees Cumb ... 176 F8
Blockley Gloucs ... 82 E8
Blofield Norfk ... 107 G2
Blofield Heath Norfk ... 107 G1
Blo Norton Norfk ... 105 K7
Bloomfield Border ... 189 G2
Blore Staffs ... 114 A4
Blore Staffs ... 115 J2
Blounce Hants ... 35 L2
Blounts Green Staffs ... 115 H5
Blowick Sefton ... 138 D4
Bloxham Oxon ... 83 K8
Bloxholm Lincs ... 118 E1
Bloxwich Wsall ... 98 C3
Bloxworth Dorset ... 17 G4
Blubberhouses N York ... 149 L5
Blue Anchor Cnwll ... 4 E3
Blue Anchor Somset ... 29 J2
Blue Bell Hill Kent ... 52 F6
Blundellsands Sefton ... 138 C7
Blundeston Suffk ... 107 L4
Blunham C Beds ... 86 C5
Blunsdon St Andrew Swindn ... 47 H1
Bluntington Worcs ... 97 K8
Bluntisham Cambs ... 103 H8
Blunts Cnwll ... 6 C2
Blunts Green Warwks ... 82 D2
Blurton C Stke ... 114 D3
Blyborough Lincs ... 135 J1
Blyford Suffk ... 107 J8
Blymhill Staffs ... 97 H1
Blymhill Lawn Staffs ... 97 J1
Blyth Notts ... 134 C2
Blyth Nthumb ... 181 H3
Blyth Bridge Border ... 199 K4
Blythburgh Suffk ... 107 J8
Blyth Crematorium Nthumb ... 181 H3
Blythe Border ... 201 J3
Blythe Bridge Staffs ... 114 F3
Blythe End Warwks ... 99 G5
Blythe Marsh Staffs ... 114 F3
Blyton Lincs ... 135 G1
Boarhills Fife ... 223 K4
Boarhunt Hants ... 19 K2
Boarley Kent ... 53 G7
Boarsgreave Lancs ... 140 C4
Boarshead E Susx ... 38 E6
Boar's Head Wigan ... 139 H6
Boars Hill Oxon ... 66 D6
Boarstall Bucks ... 66 F4

Boasley Cross Devon ... 12 C4
Boath Highld ... 263 G5
Boat of Garten Highld ... 253 H7
Bobbing Kent ... 53 J6
Bobbington Staffs ... 97 H5
Bobbingworth Essex ... 70 D6
Bocaddon Cnwll ... 5 L3
Bocking Essex ... 71 J2
Bocking Churchstreet Essex ... 71 J2
Bockleton Worcs ... 80 D3
Boconnoc Cnwll ... 5 K3
Boddam Abers ... 257 L3
Boddam Shet ... 281 d8
Boddington Gloucs ... 64 C2
Bodedern IoA ... 124 F4
Bodelwyddan Denbgs ... 127 K4
Bodenham Herefs ... 80 C5
Bodenham Wilts ... 33 L5
Bodenham Moor Herefs ... 80 D5
Bodewryd IoA ... 125 G2
Bodfari Denbgs ... 128 C5
Bodffordd IoA ... 125 G4
Bodfuan Gwynd ... 108 E4
Bodham Norfk ... 122 C3
Bodiam E Susx ... 24 E2
Bodicote Oxon ... 83 K7
Bodieve Cnwll ... 10 D7
Bodinnick Cnwll ... 5 K4
Bodle Street Green E Susx ... 23 L4
Bodmin Cnwll ... 5 H2
Bodney Norfk ... 105 G4
Bodorgan IoA ... 125 G6
Bodsham Kent ... 40 E6
Bodwen Cnwll ... 5 H3
Bodymoor Heath Warwks ... 99 G4
Bogallan Highld ... 251 H2
Bogbrae Abers ... 257 J4
Bogend S Ayrs ... 196 D4
Boggs Holdings E Loth ... 212 A5
Boghall Mdloth ... 211 H6
Boghall W Loth ... 210 C5
Boghead S Lans ... 198 C5
Bogmoor Moray ... 267 G4
Bogmuir Abers ... 235 G1
Bogniebrae Abers ... 255 M3
Bognor Regis W Susx ... 20 F7
Bogroy Highld ... 253 G7
Bogue D & G ... 185 G6
Bohetherick Cnwll ... 6 E1
Bohortha Cnwll ... 3 L4
Bohuntine Highld ... 240 A6
Bojewyan Cnwll ... 2 B4
Bokiddick Cnwll ... 5 H2
Bolam Dur ... 169 G6
Bolam Nthumb ... 180 D2
Bolberry Devon ... 7 K7
Bold Heath St Hel ... 129 M2
Boldmere Birm ... 98 E4
Boldon Colliery S Tyne ... 181 J6
Boldre Hants ... 18 E4
Boldron Dur ... 168 C7
Bole Notts ... 134 F2
Bolehill Derbys ... 132 F8
Bole Hill Derbys ... 133 G5
Bolenowe Cnwll ... 3 H3
Bolham Devon ... 29 G7
Bolham Water Devon ... 29 L8
Bolingey Cnwll ... 4 C4
Bollington Ches E ... 131 J4
Bollington Cross Ches E ... 131 H4
Bollow Gloucs ... 63 L4
Bolney W Susx ... 37 L6
Bolnhurst Bed ... 86 B3
Bolnore W Susx ... 22 E3
Bolshan Angus ... 234 F5
Bolsover Derbys ... 133 J5
Bolster Moor Kirk ... 141 G5
Bolsterstone Sheff ... 141 L8
Boltby N York ... 161 H5
Boltenstone Abers ... 243 M2
Bolter End Bucks ... 67 J8
Bolton Bolton ... 139 L6
Bolton Cumb ... 166 E6
Bolton E Loth ... 212 B5
Bolton E R Yk ... 152 B5
Bolton Nthumb ... 191 G3
Bolton Abbey N York ... 149 K5
Bolton Bridge N York ... 149 K5
Bolton-by-Bowland Lancs ... 148 D6
Boltonfellend Cumb ... 178 B5
Boltongate Cumb ... 165 H3
Bolton-le-Sands Lancs ... 147 J2
Bolton Low Houses Cumb ... 165 H2
Bolton New Houses Cumb ... 165 H2
Bolton-on-Swale N York ... 160 C3
Bolton Percy N York ... 151 H7
Bolton Town End Lancs ... 147 J2
Bolton upon Dearne Barns ... 142 C7
Bolventor Cnwll ... 11 H7

Bomarsund Nthumb ... 181 G2
Bomere Heath Shrops ... 113 G7
Bonar Bridge Highld ... 263 G3
Bonawe Ag & B ... 228 F8
Bonby N Linc ... 144 C5
Boncath Pembks ... 75 L4
Bonchester Bridge Border ... 189 G4
Bonchurch IoW ... 19 K8
Bondleigh Devon ... 12 F2
Bonds Lancs ... 147 J6
Bonehill Devon ... 13 G7
Bonehill Staffs ... 99 G3
Bo'ness Falk ... 210 D3
Boney Hay Staffs ... 98 D2
Bonhill W Duns ... 208 C3
Boningale Shrops ... 97 J3
Bonjedward Border ... 189 H2
Bonkle N Lans ... 209 M7
Bonnington Angus ... 234 F7
Bonnington Kent ... 40 D8
Bonnybank Fife ... 222 F6
Bonnybridge Falk ... 209 L3
Bonnykelly Abers ... 268 F5
Bonnyrigg Mdloth ... 211 J6
Bonnyton Angus ... 233 M7
Bonsall Derbys ... 132 E8
Bonshaw Tower D & G ... 177 H4
Bont Mons ... 62 D3
Bontddu Gwynd ... 110 C7
Bont-Dolgadfan Powys ... 93 J3
Bont-goch Cerdgn ... 92 E6
Bonthorpe Lincs ... 137 J5
Bontnewydd Cerdgn ... 77 H2
Bontnewydd Gwynd ... 125 J7
Bontuchel Denbgs ... 128 C8
Bonvilston V Glam ... 43 G7
Bonwm Denbgs ... 111 L3
Bon-y-maen Swans ... 57 J6
Boode Devon ... 27 J3
Booker Bucks ... 49 K1
Booley Shrops ... 113 J6
Boon Border ... 201 J4
Boon Hill Staffs ... 114 C2
Boorley Green Hants ... 35 G8
Boosbeck R & Cl ... 170 F7
Boose's Green Essex ... 71 K1
Boot Cumb ... 155 M3
Booth Calder ... 141 G2
Boothby Graffoe Lincs ... 135 K7
Boothby Pagnell Lincs ... 118 C5
Boothferry E R Yk ... 143 H3
Booth Green Ches E ... 131 H3
Boothstown Salfd ... 139 L7
Booth Town Calder ... 141 G2
Boothville Nhants ... 84 F2
Bootle Cumb ... 155 K5
Bootle Sefton ... 138 D8
Boots Green Ches W ... 130 E5
Boot Street Suffk ... 90 F5
Booze N York ... 159 H2
Boraston Shrops ... 80 E1
Bordeaux Guern ... 9 k2
Borden Kent ... 53 J6
Borden W Susx ... 36 B6
Border Cumb ... 177 G8
Borders Crematorium Border ... 201 H6
Bordley N York ... 149 G3
Boreham Essex ... 71 J5
Boreham Wilts ... 32 E2
Boreham Street E Susx ... 24 B5
Borehamwood Herts ... 69 G7
Boreland D & G ... 187 J8
Boreraig Highld ... 258 B6
Boreston Shrops ... 96 C2
Borgh W Isls ... 282 g1
Borgh W Isls ... 283 b13
Borgie Highld ... 278 B4
Borgue D & G ... 175 G5
Borgue Highld ... 274 F3
Borley Essex ... 89 G6
Borley Green Essex ... 89 G6
Borley Green Suffk ... 89 K3
Borneskitaig Highld ... 258 F2
Borness D & G ... 175 G6
Boroughbridge N York ... 150 E3
Borough Green Kent ... 38 F2
Borras Head Wrexhm ... 112 E1
Borrowash Derbys ... 116 C4
Borrowby N York ... 160 F5
Borrowby N York ... 171 H7
Borrowstoun Falk ... 210 D3
Borstal Medway ... 52 F5
Borth Cerdgn ... 92 D5
Borthwickbrae Border ... 188 C3
Borthwickshiels Border ... 188 D3
Borth-y-Gest Gwynd ... 109 K4
Borve Highld ... 259 G7
Borve W Isls ... 282 d6
Borve W Isls ... 282 g1

Place	Page	Grid
Borve W Isls	283	b13
Borwick Lancs	147	K1
Borwick Lodge Cumb	156	E3
Borwick Rails Cumb	156	A6
Bosavern Cnwll	2	B5
Bosbury Herefs	80	F6
Boscarne Cnwll	5	H1
Boscastle Cnwll	10	F4
Boscombe Bmouth	17	M4
Boscombe Wilts	33	L3
Boscoppa Cnwll	5	H4
Bosham W Susx	20	C6
Bosham Hoe W Susx	20	D6
Bosherston Pembks	54	F7
Boskednan Cnwll	2	C4
Boskenna Cnwll	2	C6
Bosley Ches E	131	H6
Bosoughan Cnwll	4	E3
Bossall N York	151	M4
Bossiney Cnwll	10	F5
Bossingham Kent	40	F5
Bossington Somset	28	F1
Bostock Green Ches W	130	C6
Boston Lincs	119	K3
Boston Crematorium Lincs	119	K3
Boston Spa Leeds	150	F6
Boswarthan Cnwll	2	C4
Boswinger Cnwll	5	G6
Botallack Cnwll	2	B4
Botany Bay Gt Lon	69	J7
Botcheston Leics	100	B2
Botesdale Suffk	105	L8
Bothal Nthumb	180	F2
Bothampstead W Berk	48	D4
Bothamsall Notts	134	D5
Bothel Cumb	165	G3
Bothenhampton Dorset	15	L4
Bothwell S Lans	209	J7
Botley Bucks	68	B6
Botley Hants	35	G8
Botley Oxon	66	C6
Botolph Claydon Bucks	67	H2
Botolphs W Susx	21	L5
Botolph's Bridge Kent	40	F8
Bottesford Leics	117	L4
Bottesford N Linc	143	M6
Bottisham Cambs	87	L3
Bottomcraig Fife	222	F2
Bottom of Hutton Lancs	138	F2
Bottom o' th' Moor Bolton	139	K5
Bottoms Calder	140	D3
Bottoms Cnwll	2	B6
Botts Green Warwks	99	H5
Botusfleming Cnwll	6	E3
Botwnnog Gwynd	108	D5
Bough Beech Kent	38	D4
Boughrood Powys	79	G7
Boughspring Gloucs	63	H7
Boughton Nhants	84	E2
Boughton Norfk	104	D3
Boughton Notts	134	D6
Boughton Aluph Kent	40	D6
Boughton End C Beds	85	J7
Boughton Green Kent	39	J3
Boughton Malherbe Kent	39	M3
Boughton Monchelsea Kent	39	J3
Boughton Street Kent	40	D3
Boulby R & Cl	171	H7
Boulder Clough Calder	140	F3
Bouldnor IoW	18	F5
Bouldon Shrops	96	C6
Boulmer Nthumb	191	K3
Boulston Pembks	55	G4
Boultham Lincs	135	J6
Bourn Cambs	87	G4
Bourne Lincs	118	E7
Bournebridge Essex	70	D8
Bournebrook Birm	98	D6
Bourne End Bed	85	K3
Bourne End Bucks	49	L2
Bourne End C Beds	85	K3
Bourne End Herts	68	C6
Bournemouth Bmouth	17	L4
Bournemouth Crematorium Bmouth	17	M4
Bournes Green Gloucs	64	C6
Bournes Green Sthend	53	K2
Bournheath Worcs	98	B8
Bournmoor Dur	181	H8
Bournstream Gloucs	63	L8
Bournville Birm	98	b7
Bourton Dorset	32	C5
Bourton N Som	44	D6
Bourton Oxon	47	K2
Bourton Shrops	96	D4
Bourton Wilts	46	F6
Bourton on Dunsmore Warwks	83	K1
Bourton-on-the-Hill Gloucs	65	J1
Bourton-on-the-Water Gloucs	65	H3
Bousd Ag & B	225	H3
Boustead Hill Cumb	177	J7
Bouth Cumb	156	D5
Bouthwaite N York	149	L2
Bouts Worcs	82	B3
Boveney Bucks	50	B3
Boveridge Dorset	33	J7
Bovey Tracey Devon	13	J7
Bovingdon Herts	68	C6
Bovingdon Green Bucks	49	K2
Bovinger Essex	70	D6
Bovington Dorset	16	F5
Bovington Camp Dorset	16	F5
Bow Cumb	177	K7
Bow Devon	8	B3
Bow Devon	13	G2
Bow Gt Lon	51	K2
Bow Ork	275	C6
Bowbank Dur	168	B6
Bow Brickhill M Keyn	85	H8
Bowbridge Gloucs	64	B6
Bowburn Dur	169	J3
Bowcombe IoW	19	H6
Bowd Devon	14	D4
Bowden Border	201	H7
Bowden Devon	8	C5
Bowden Hill Wilts	46	D5
Bowdon Traffd	130	E2
Bower Highld	280	B4
Bower Ashton Bristl	45	H4
Bowerchalke Wilts	33	H6
Bowerhill Wilts	46	C6
Bower Hinton Somset	31	G7
Bower House Tye Suffk	89	K7
Bowermadden Highld	280	B3
Bowers Staffs	114	C4
Bowers Gifford Essex	53	G1
Bowershall Fife	210	E1
Bower's Row Leeds	142	B2
Bowes Dur	168	C7
Bowgreave Lancs	147	K7
Bowhouse D & G	176	D5
Bowithick Cnwll	11	H6
Bowker's Green Lancs	138	E6
Bowland Border	200	F5
Bowland Bridge Cumb	156	F5
Bowley Herefs	80	C5
Bowley Town Herefs	80	C5
Bowlhead Green Surrey	36	D3
Bowling C Brad	141	J2
Bowling W Duns	208	D4
Bowling Bank Wrexhm	112	F2
Bowling Green Worcs	81	J5
Bowmanstead Cumb	156	D3
Bowmore Ag & B	204	D4
Bowness-on-Solway Cumb	177	H6
Bowness-on-Windermere Cumb	156	F3
Bow of Fife Fife	222	E4
Bowriefauld Angus	234	D6
Bowscale Cumb	165	K4
Bowsden Nthumb	202	F5
Bowston Cumb	157	H3
Bowthorpe Norfk	106	D2
Bow Street Cerdgn	92	D6
Bow Street Norfk	105	L4
Box Gloucs	64	B7
Box Wilts	46	B5
Boxbush Gloucs	63	G5
Boxbush Gloucs	63	L4
Box End Bed	85	K5
Boxford Suffk	89	K7
Boxford W Berk	48	B4
Boxgrove W Susx	20	E5
Box Hill Surrey	51	G8
Boxley Kent	53	G7
Boxmoor Herts	68	C6
Box's Shop Cnwll	11	H2
Boxted Essex	72	E1
Boxted Suffk	89	K8
Boxted Suffk	89	G5
Boxted Cross Essex	72	E1
Boxwell Gloucs	64	A8
Boxworth Cambs	87	G2
Boyden End Suffk	88	E4
Boyden Gate Kent	41	H2
Boylestone Derbys	115	K4
Boyndie Abers	268	B3
Boyndlie Abers	269	G4
Boynton E R Yk	153	J2
Boysack Angus	234	F5
Boys Hill Dorset	16	C1
Boythorpe Derbys	133	G5
Boyton Cnwll	11	L4
Boyton Suffk	91	J6
Boyton Wilts	32	F3
Boyton Cross Essex	70	F5
Boyton End Suffk	88	E6
Bozeat Nhants	85	H3
Braaid IoM	154	d6
Brabling Green Suffk	91	G2
Brabourne Kent	40	E7
Brabourne Lees Kent	40	E7
Brabstermire Highld	280	D2
Bracadale Highld	246	E1
Braceborough Lincs	102	B1
Bracebridge Heath Lincs	135	K6
Bracebridge Low Fields Lincs	135	J6
Braceby Lincs	118	D4
Bracewell Lancs	148	F6
Brackenfield Derbys	133	G7
Brackenhirst N Lans	209	K5
Brackenthwaite Cumb	165	J1
Brackenthwaite N York	150	C5
Bracklesham W Susx	20	C7
Brackletter Highld	239	K7
Brackley Nhants	84	B7
Brackley Hatch Nhants	84	C7
Bracknell Br For	49	L5
Braco P & K	220	E5
Bracobrae Moray	267	K5
Bracon Ash Norfk	106	D3
Bracora Highld	237	L2
Bracorina Highld	237	L2
Bradaford Devon	11	M4
Bradbourne Derbys	115	K1
Bradbury Dur	169	J5
Bradden Nhants	84	C5
Braddock Cnwll	5	K2
Bradeley C Stke	114	D1
Bradenham Bucks	67	K7
Bradenstoke Wilts	46	E3
Bradfield Devon	14	B1
Bradfield Essex	73	H1
Bradfield Norfk	122	F5
Bradfield Sheff	132	E1
Bradfield W Berk	48	F4
Bradfield Combust Suffk	89	H4
Bradfield Green Ches E	130	D7
Bradfield Heath Essex	73	H1
Bradfield St Clare Suffk	89	H4
Bradfield St George Suffk	89	H3
Bradford C Brad	141	J1
Bradford Cnwll	11	G7
Bradford Devon	12	A1
Bradford Nthumb	180	C3
Bradford Nthumb	203	J6
Bradford Abbas Dorset	31	K8
Bradford Leigh Wilts	46	B6
Bradford-on-Avon Wilts	46	B6
Bradford-on-Tone Somset	30	B6
Bradford Peverell Dorset	16	C4
Bradiford Devon	27	K4
Brading IoW	19	K6
Bradley Derbys	115	L2
Bradley Hants	35	K3
Bradley Kirk	141	J4
Bradley N York	159	J6
Bradley NE Lin	145	G6
Bradley Staffs	114	D7
Bradley Wolves	98	B4
Bradley Worcs	82	A3
Bradley Wrexhm	112	E1
Bradley Common Ches W	113	H2
Bradley Green Somset	30	C3
Bradley Green Warwks	99	H3
Bradley Green Worcs	82	A3
Bradley in the Moors Staffs	115	H3
Bradley Stoke S Glos	45	J3
Bradmore Notts	117	G5
Bradney Somset	30	E3
Bradninch Devon	14	A2
Bradninch Devon	27	L4
Bradnop Staffs	131	K8
Bradnor Green Herefs	79	K4
Bradpole Dorset	15	L4
Bradshaw Bolton	139	L5
Bradshaw Calder	141	G2
Bradshaw Kirk	141	G5
Bradstone Devon	11	M6
Bradwall Green Ches E	130	E7
Bradwell Derbys	132	C3
Bradwell Devon	27	J4
Bradwell Essex	71	K3
Bradwell M Keyn	85	G7
Bradwell Norfk	107	K3
Bradwell Crematorium Staffs	114	C2
Bradwell-on-Sea Essex	72	E5
Bradwell Waterside Essex	72	E5
Bradworthy Devon	26	D7
Brae Highld	263	H7
Brae Shet	281	d4
Braeface Falk	209	K3
Braehead Angus	235	H5
Braehead D & G	173	K4
Braehead S Lans	198	F3
Braemar Abers	243	G5
Braemore Highld	261	L4
Braemore Highld	274	E2
Brae Roy Lodge Highld	240	B5
Braeside Inver	207	L4
Braes of Coul Angus	233	L4
Braes of Enzie Moray	267	H4
Braeswick Ork	275	e2
Braevallich Ag & B	216	C5
Brafferton Darltn	169	H6
Brafferton N York	150	F2
Brafield-on-the-Green Nhants	84	F3
Bragar W Isls	282	f2
Bragbury End Herts	69	H3
Braidwood S Lans	198	D3
Brailsford Derbys	115	L3
Brailsford Green Derbys	115	L3
Brain's Green Gloucs	63	K5
Braintree Essex	71	J2
Braiseworth Suffk	90	D1
Braishfield Hants	34	C5
Braithwaite C Brad	149	J7
Braithwaite Cumb	165	H6
Braithwell Donc	133	K4
Braken Hill Wakefd	142	C4
Bramber W Susx	21	L5
Brambridge Hants	35	G6
Bramcote Notts	116	E4
Bramcote Warwks	99	L5
Bramcote Crematorium Notts	116	E4
Bramdean Hants	35	J5
Bramerton Norfk	106	F2
Bramfield Herts	69	H4
Bramfield Suffk	107	H8
Bramford Suffk	90	D6
Bramhall Stockp	131	H3
Bramham Leeds	150	F7
Bramhope Leeds	150	C7
Bramley Hants	49	G8
Bramley Leeds	141	K1
Bramley Rothm	133	K1
Bramley Surrey	36	F2
Bramley Corner Hants	48	F7
Bramley Green Hants	49	G7
Bramley Head N York	149	L4
Bramling Kent	41	H4
Brampford Speke Devon	13	L4
Brampton Cambs	86	E1
Brampton Cumb	166	F6
Brampton Cumb	178	C3
Brampton Lincs	135	G4
Brampton Norfk	122	E6
Brampton Rothm	142	C7
Brampton Suffk	107	J7
Brampton Abbotts Herefs	63	J2
Brampton Ash Nhants	101	H6
Brampton Bryan Herefs	79	L7
Brampton-en-le-Morthen Rothm	133	J2
Bramshall Staffs	115	H5
Bramshaw Hants	34	C4
Bramshill Hants	49	H6
Bramshott Hants	36	C4
Bramwell Somset	31	G5
Branault Highld	237	G3
Brancaster Norfk	121	G3
Brancaster Staithe Norfk	121	H3
Brancepeth Dur	169	G3
Branchill Moray	266	B5
Brand End Lincs	119	L3
Branderburgh Moray	266	E2
Brandesburton E R Yk	153	H6
Brandeston Suffk	90	F3
Brand Green Gloucs	63	L2
Brandis Corner Devon	12	A2
Brandiston Norfk	122	C7
Brandon Dur	169	G3
Brandon Lincs	118	B2
Brandon Nthumb	190	F3
Brandon Suffk	104	F6
Brandon Warwks	99	L8
Brandon Bank Norfk	104	C5
Brandon Creek Norfk	104	C5
Brandon Parva Norfk	106	B2
Brandsby N York	151	J1
Brandy Wharf Lincs	144	C8
Brane Cnwll	2	B5
Bran End Essex	71	C8
Branksome Poole	17	L4
Branksome Park Poole	17	L4
Bransbury Hants	34	F2
Bransby Lincs	135	H4
Branscombe Devon	14	E5
Bransford Worcs	81	H5
Bransgore Hants	18	B4
Bransholme C KuH	144	E1
Bransley Shrops	96	E8
Branson's Cross Worcs	82	C1
Branston Leics	117	L5
Branston Lincs	135	L6

Branston – Brock 297

Branston Staffs 115 L7
Branston Booths Lincs 135 L6
Branstone IoW 19 J7
Brant Broughton Lincs 118 B1
Brantham Suffk 90 D8
Branthwaite Cumb 164 E5
Branthwaite Cumb 165 J3
Brantingham E R Yk 144 B2
Branton Donc 143 G7
Branton Nthumb 190 F3
Branton Green N York 150 F3
Branxton Nthumb 202 D5
Brassey Green Ches W 129 M7
Brassington Derbys 115 L1
Brasted Kent 38 D2
Brasted Chart Kent 51 M8
Brathens Abers 244 F4
Bratoft Lincs 137 J6
Brattleby Lincs 135 J3
Bratton Somset 29 G2
Bratton Wilts 46 C8
Bratton Wrekin 96 E1
Bratton Clovelly Devon 12 B4
Bratton Fleming Devon 27 M3
Bratton Seymour Somset 31 L5
Braughing Herts 69 K2
Braughing Friars Herts 70 B2
Braunston Nhants 84 A2
Braunston Rutlnd 101 H2
Braunstone Town Leics 100 C3
Braunton Devon 27 J4
Brawby N York 162 C7
Brawl Highld 278 D3
Braworth N York 161 H1
Bray W & M 49 L3
Braybrooke Nhants 101 G6
Braydon Wilts 46 F1
Braydon Brook Wilts 64 E8
Braydon Side Wilts 46 E2
Brayford Devon 28 B4
Bray's Hill E Susx 24 B4
Bray Shop Cnwll 11 L7
Braystones Cumb 155 H2
Braythorn N York 150 C6
Brayton N York 142 F2
Braywick W & M 49 L3
Braywoodside W & M 49 L4
Brazacott Cnwll 11 K4
Breach Kent 41 G6
Breach Kent 53 H6
Breachwood Green Herts 68 F3
Breaden Heath Shrops 113 G4
Breadsall Derbys 116 B4
Breadstone Gloucs 63 L7
Breadward Herefs 79 K4
Breage Cnwll 3 G5
Breakachy Highld 250 E3
Breakspear Crematorium Gt Lon 50 D1
Brealangwell Lodge Highld 262 F1
Bream Gloucs 63 J6
Breamore Hants 33 L7
Brean Somset 44 C7
Breanais W Isls 282 d4
Brearley Calder 140 F3
Brearton N York 150 D4
Breascleit W Isls 282 f3
Breasclete W Isls 282 f3
Breaston Derbys 116 D5
Brechfa Carmth 58 F3
Brechin Angus 234 F3
Breckles Norfk 105 J4
Brecon Powys 61 G2
Bredbury Stockp 131 H2
Brede E Susx 24 E4
Bredenbury Herefs 80 E4
Bredfield Suffk 91 G4
Bredgar Kent 53 J7
Bredhurst Kent 53 G6
Bredon Worcs 81 L7
Bredon's Hardwick Worcs 81 L8
Bredon's Norton Worcs 81 L7
Bredwardine Herefs 79 L6
Breedon on the Hill Leics 116 C7
Breich W Loth 210 C7
Breightmet Bolton 139 L6
Breighton E R Yk 143 H1
Breinton Herefs 80 B7
Bremhill Wilts 46 E4
Bremridge Devon 28 B5
Brenchley Kent 39 H5
Brendon Devon 11 L1
Brendon Devon 28 D1
Brendon Hill Somset 29 J4
Brenfield Ag & B 206 D3
Brenish W Isls 282 d4
Brenkley N u Ty 180 F4
Brent Cross Gt Lon 51 G2
Brent Eleigh Suffk 89 J5
Brentford Gt Lon 50 F3
Brentingby Leics 117 K7
Brent Knoll Somset 30 E1
Brent Mill Devon 7 K3
Brent Pelham Herts 70 B1
Brentwood Essex 70 E8
Brenzett Kent 25 J2
Brenzett Green Kent 25 J2
Brereton Staffs 115 G8
Brereton Green Ches E 130 F6
Brereton Heath Ches E 130 F6
Brereton Hill Staffs 115 G8
Bressay Shet 281 e6
Bressingham Norfk 106 B7
Bressingham Common Norfk 106 B7
Bretby Derbys 116 A7
Bretby Crematorium Derbys 115 M7
Bretford Warwks 99 L7
Bretforton Worcs 82 C6
Bretherton Lancs 138 F4
Brettabister Shet 281 e5
Brettenham Norfk 105 J6
Brettenham Suffk 89 K4
Bretton Derbys 132 D4
Bretton Flints 129 H7
Brewers End Essex 70 E3
Brewer Street Surrey 51 J8
Brewood Staffs 97 K2
Briantspuddle Dorset 16 F4
Brick End Essex 70 E2
Brickendon Herts 69 J5
Bricket Wood Herts 68 E6
Brick Houses Sheff 132 F3
Brickkiln Green Essex 71 H1
Bricklehampton Worcs 82 A6
Bride IoM 154 f2
Bridekirk Cumb 164 F4
Bridell Pembks 75 L4
Bridestowe Devon 12 C5
Brideswell Abers 255 M4
Bridford Devon 13 J5
Bridge Kent 41 G4
Bridge End Cumb 156 A6
Bridge End Cumb 165 L1
Bridge End Devon 7 K5
Bridge End Dur 168 C3
Bridge End Essex 71 G1
Bridge End Lincs 118 F4
Bridgefoot Cumb 164 E5
Bridge Green Essex 87 K7
Bridgehampton Somset 31 J6
Bridge Hewick N York 150 D2
Bridgehill Dur 180 D8
Bridgehouse Gate N York 149 L3
Bridgemary Hants 19 K3
Bridgemere Ches E 113 M2
Bridgend Abers 255 K4
Bridgend Ag & B 194 B3
Bridgend Ag & B 204 E4
Bridgend Angus 234 E2
Bridgend Brdgnd 42 D5
Bridgend Cerdgn 75 L3
Bridgend Cumb 165 L7
Bridgend D & G 187 G4
Bridgend Devon 7 G5
Bridgend Fife 223 G5
Bridgend Moray 255 H5
Bridgend P & K 221 L2
Bridgend W Loth 210 D4
Bridgend of Lintrathen Angus 233 L4
Bridge of Alford Abers 255 L8
Bridge of Allan Stirlg 220 D7
Bridge of Avon Moray 254 C7
Bridge of Avon Moray 254 D4
Bridge of Balgie P & K 231 G6
Bridge of Brewlands Angus 233 J3
Bridge of Brown Highld 254 C7
Bridge of Cally P & K 233 H5
Bridge of Canny Abers 244 E4
Bridge of Craigisla Angus 233 K4
Bridge of Dee D & G 175 J3
Bridge of Don C Aber 245 L2
Bridge of Dulsie Highld 253 H3
Bridge of Dye Abers 244 E6
Bridge of Earn P & K 221 L3
Bridge of Ericht P & K 230 F4
Bridge of Feugh Abers 244 F4
Bridge of Forss Highld 279 J3
Bridge of Gairn Abers 243 K4
Bridge of Gaur P & K 230 F4
Bridge of Marnoch Abers 267 M6
Bridge of Muchalls Abers 245 K5
Bridge of Orchy Ag & B 230 B7
Bridge of Tilt P & K 232 C2
Bridge of Tynet Moray 267 H4
Bridge of Walls Shet 281 c6
Bridge of Weir Rens 208 C6
Bridge Reeve Devon 28 B8
Bridgerule Devon 11 K2
Bridges Shrops 95 J4
Bridge Sollers Herefs 80 A6
Bridge Street Suffk 89 H5
Bridgetown Cnwll 11 L5
Bridgetown Somset 29 G4
Bridge Trafford Ches W 129 K5
Bridge Yate S Glos 45 K4
Bridgham Norfk 105 J6
Bridgnorth Shrops 97 G5
Bridgwater Somset 30 D3
Bridlington E R Yk 153 K3
Bridport Dorset 15 K4
Bridstow Herefs 63 H2
Brierfield Lancs 148 E8
Brierley Barns 142 B5
Brierley Gloucs 63 J4
Brierley Herefs 80 C4
Brierley Hill Dudley 97 L6
Brierlow Bar Derbys 132 B5
Brierton Hartpl 170 B5
Briery Cumb 165 J6
Brigg N Linc 144 C6
Briggate Norfk 123 G6
Briggswath N York 162 F1
Brigham Cumb 164 E4
Brigham Cumb 165 J6
Brigham E R Yk 153 H5
Brighouse Calder 141 J3
Brighstone IoW 19 G7
Brightgate Derbys 132 E7
Brighthampton Oxon 66 A6
Brightholmlee Sheff 132 F1
Brightley Devon 12 E3
Brightling E Susx 24 C3
Brightlingsea Essex 73 G4
Brighton Br & H 22 D6
Brighton Cnwll 4 E4
Brighton le Sands Sefton 138 C7
Brightons Falk 210 B3
Brightwalton W Berk 48 B3
Brightwalton Green W Berk 48 B3
Brightwalton Holt W Berk 48 B3
Brightwell Suffk 90 F6
Brightwell Baldwin Oxon 67 G8
Brightwell-cum-Sotwell Oxon 48 E1
Brightwell Upperton Oxon 67 G8
Brignall Dur 168 D8
Brig o'Turk Stirlg 219 J6
Brigsley NE Lin 145 H7
Brigsteer Cumb 157 G5
Brigstock Nhants 101 L6
Brill Bucks 67 G4
Brill Cnwll 3 J5
Brilley Herefs 79 J5
Brimfield Herefs 80 C2
Brimfield Cross Herefs 80 C2
Brimington Derbys 133 H5
Brimley Devon 13 J7
Brimpsfield Gloucs 64 D4
Brimpton W Berk 48 E6
Brimpton Common W Berk 48 E6
Brimscombe Gloucs 64 C6
Brimstage Wirral 129 G3
Brincliffe Sheff 132 F3
Brind E R Yk 143 J2
Brindham Somset 31 H3
Brindister Shet 281 c5
Brindle Lancs 139 J3
Brindley Ches E 113 K1
Brineton Staffs 97 H1
Bringhurst Leics 101 J5
Bringsty Common Herefs 81 G4
Brington Cambs 102 B8
Brininghm Norfk 122 A5
Brinkely Notts 117 J1
Brinkhill Lincs 137 G5
Brinkley Cambs 88 C4
Brinklow Warwks 99 L7
Brinkworth Wilts 46 E2
Brinscall Lancs 139 J3
Brinscombe Somset 44 E8
Brinsea N Som 44 F6
Brinsley Notts 116 D2
Brinsop Herefs 80 B6
Brinsworth Rothm 133 H2
Brinton Norfk 122 A4
Brinyan Ork 275 c3
Brisco Cumb 178 A8
Brisley Norfk 121 L7
Brislington Bristl 45 J5
Brissenden Green Kent 40 B7
Bristol Bristl 45 H4
Briston Norfk 122 B5
Brisworthy Devon 7 G2
Britannia Lancs 140 C3
Britford Wilts 33 L5
Brithdir Caerph 61 J6
Brithdir Gwynd 110 E7
British Legion Village Kent 52 F7
Briton Ferry Neath 57 K6
Britwell Salome Oxon 67 G8
Brixham Torbay 8 D4
Brixton Devon 7 G4
Brixton Gt Lon 51 J4
Brixton Deverill Wilts 32 E3
Brixworth Nhants 84 E1
Brize Norton Oxon 65 L5
Broad Alley Worcs 81 K2
Broad Blunsdon Swindn 47 H1
Broadbottom Tamesd 131 K1
Broadbridge W Susx 20 D6
Broadbridge Heath W Susx 37 H4
Broad Campden Gloucs 82 E7
Broad Carr Calder 141 H4
Broad Chalke Wilts 33 H5
Broad Clough Lancs 140 C3
Broadclyst Devon 14 A3
Broadfield Inver 208 B4
Broadfield Pembks 55 K6
Broadford Highld 247 K4
Broad Ford Kent 39 H5
Broadford Bridge W Susx 37 G6
Broadgairhill Border 187 K4
Broadgrass Green Suffk 89 K3
Broad Green Cambs 88 D3
Broad Green Essex 72 C2
Broad Green Worcs 81 H4
Broad Green Worcs 82 A1
Broadhaugh Border 202 D2
Broad Haven Pembks 54 D4
Broadheath Traffd 130 E2
Broadheath Worcs 80 F2
Broadhembury Devon 14 C2
Broadhempston Devon 8 B2
Broad Hill Cambs 104 B8
Broad Hinton Wilts 47 G4
Broadholme Lincs 135 H5
Broadland Row E Susx 24 F3
Broadlay Carmth 56 C3
Broad Layings Hants 48 B6
Broadley Essex 70 B5
Broadley Lancs 140 C4
Broadley Moray 267 H4
Broadley Common Essex 70 B5
Broad Marston Worcs 82 D6
Broadmayne Dorset 16 D5
Broad Meadow Staffs 114 C2
Broadmere Hants 35 J2
Broadmoor Gloucs 63 J4
Broadmoor Pembks 55 J5
Broadnymett Devon 13 G2
Broad Oak Carmth 59 G4
Broad Oak Cumb 155 K4
Broadoak Dorset 15 K3
Broad Oak E Susx 23 K3
Broad Oak E Susx 24 E3
Broadoak Gloucs 63 K4
Broad Oak Hants 49 H8
Broad Oak Herefs 62 F3
Broad Oak Kent 41 G3
Broad Oak St Hel 139 G8
Broadoak Wrexhm 129 J7
Broad Road Suffk 106 F8
Broad's Green Essex 71 G4
Broadstairs Kent 41 L2
Broadstone Mons 63 G6
Broadstone Poole 17 K3
Broadstone Shrops 96 C5
Broad Street E Susx 24 F4
Broad Street Essex 70 E4
Broad Street Kent 39 L2
Broad Street Kent 40 F7
Broad Street Medway 53 G4
Broad Street Wilts 47 G7
Broad Street Green Essex 71 L5
Broad Town Wilts 47 G3
Broadwas Worcs 81 H4
Broadwater Herts 69 H3
Broadwater W Susx 21 K6
Broadwaters Worcs 97 J7
Broadway Carmth 56 B3
Broadway Carmth 56 C3
Broadway Pembks 54 E4
Broadway Somset 30 D7
Broadway Suffk 107 H7
Broadway Worcs 82 C7
Broadwell Gloucs 63 H5
Broadwell Gloucs 65 J2
Broadwell Oxon 65 K6
Broadwell Warwks 83 K2
Broadwey Dorset 16 C6
Broadwindsor Dorset 15 K2
Broadwood Kelly Devon 12 E2
Broadwoodwidger Devon 12 A5
Brobury Herefs 79 L6
Brochel Highld 259 K7
Brochroy Ag & B 216 F1
Brock Lancs 147 K7

Place	County	Page	Grid
Brockamin	Worcs	81	H4
Brockbridge	Hants	35	J7
Brockdish	Norfk	106	E7
Brockencote	Worcs	97	K8
Brockenhurst	Hants	18	D3
Brocketsbrae	S Lans	198	D5
Brockford Green	Suffk	90	D2
Brockford Street	Suffk	90	D2
Brockhall	Nhants	84	C3
Brockham	Surrey	37	J1
Brockhampton	Gloucs	64	D2
Brockhampton	Gloucs	64	F3
Brockhampton	Hants	20	M3
Brockhampton	Herefs	63	H1
Brockhampton Green	Dorset	16	D2
Brockholes	Kirk	141	J5
Brockhurst	Derbys	133	G6
Brockhurst	Warwks	100	A6
Brocklebank	Cumb	165	J2
Brocklesby	Lincs	144	E5
Brockley	N Som	44	F5
Brockley	Suffk	89	G1
Brockley Green	Suffk	88	E6
Brockley Green	Suffk	89	G4
Brockleymoor	Cumb	166	C3
Brockmoor	Dudley	97	K5
Brockscombe	Devon	12	B4
Brock's Green	Hants	48	D6
Brockton	Shrops	95	H3
Brockton	Shrops	95	H6
Brockton	Shrops	96	D4
Brockton	Shrops	97	G3
Brockton	Staffs	114	C5
Brockweir	Gloucs	63	G6
Brockwood Park	Hants	35	K4
Brockworth	Gloucs	64	C4
Brocton	Cnwll	5	G1
Brocton	Staffs	114	F7
Brodick	N Ayrs	195	G4
Brodie	Moray	264	F8
Brodsworth	Donc	142	D6
Brogaig	Highld	259	H3
Brogborough	C Beds	85	J7
Brokenborough	Wilts	46	D1
Broken Cross	Ches E	131	H5
Broken Cross	Ches W	130	D5
Brokerswood	Wilts	46	B8
Bromborough	Wirral	129	H3
Brome	Suffk	106	C8
Brome Street	Suffk	106	C8
Bromeswell	Suffk	91	G5
Bromfield	Cumb	165	G1
Bromfield	Shrops	96	B8
Bromham	Bed	85	K5
Bromham	Wilts	46	D6
Bromley	Barns	141	M7
Bromley	Dudley	97	K5
Bromley	Gt Lon	51	L5
Bromley	Shrops	97	G4
Bromley Common	Gt Lon	51	L5
Bromley Cross	Bolton	139	L5
Bromley Cross	Essex	72	F2
Bromley Green	Kent	40	C8
Bromlow	Shrops	95	H3
Brompton	Medway	53	G5
Brompton	N York	160	E3
Brompton-by-Sawdon	N York	163	G6
Brompton-on-Swale	N York	160	D3
Brompton Ralph	Somset	29	K4
Brompton Regis	Somset	29	G4
Bromsash	Herefs	63	J2
Bromsberrow	Gloucs	81	G8
Bromsberrow Heath	Gloucs	81	G8
Bromsgrove	Worcs	81	M1
Bromstead Heath	Staffs	114	B8
Bromyard	Herefs	80	F4
Bromyard Downs	Herefs	80	F4
Bronaber	Gwynd	110	D5
Bronant	Cerdgn	77	H2
Broncroft	Shrops	96	C6
Brongest	Cerdgn	76	B6
Bronington	Wrexhm	113	H3
Bronllys	Powys	79	G8
Bronwydd	Carmth	58	D4
Bronydd	Powys	79	J6
Bronygarth	Shrops	112	C4
Brook	Carmth	56	A3
Brook	Hants	34	C8
Brook	Hants	34	D5
Brook	IoW	18	F6
Brook	Kent	40	E6
Brook	Surrey	36	D3
Brook	Surrey	37	G2
Brooke	Norfk	106	C4
Brooke	Rutlnd	101	J2
Brookenby	Lincs	145	G8
Brook End	Bed	86	B3
Brook End	C Beds	86	D5
Brook End	Cambs	86	B1
Brook End	M Keyn	85	H6
Brookfield	Rens	208	C6
Brookhampton	Oxon	66	F7
Brookhampton	Somset	31	K5
Brook Hill	Hants	34	C7
Brook House	Denbgs	128	C6
Brookhouse	Lancs	147	K3
Brookhouse	Rothm	133	K2
Brookhouse Green	Ches E	130	F7
Brookhouses	Derbys	131	K2
Brookland	Kent	25	J2
Brooklands	Traffd	130	F2
Brookmans Park	Herts	69	H6
Brooks	Powys	94	E3
Brooksby	Leics	117	H8
Brooks End	Kent	41	J2
Brooks Green	W Susx	37	H6
Brook Street	Essex	70	E8
Brook Street	Kent	40	B8
Brook Street	Suffk	89	G5
Brook Street	W Susx	22	D2
Brookthorpe	Gloucs	64	B4
Brookville	Norfk	104	E4
Brookwood	Surrey	50	B7
Broom	C Beds	86	D6
Broom	Rothm	133	J1
Broom	Warwks	82	C4
Broome	Norfk	107	G5
Broome	Shrops	95	K7
Broome	Worcs	97	K7
Broomedge	Warrtn	130	D3
Broome Park	Nthumb	191	G4
Broomer's Corner	W Susx	21	K3
Broomershill	W Susx	21	H3
Broomfield	Essex	71	H5
Broomfield	Kent	39	L3
Broomfield	Kent	41	G2
Broomfield	Somset	30	B4
Broomfields	Shrops	112	F1
Broomfleet	E R Yk	143	M2
Broom Green	Norfk	121	L6
Broomhall	W & M	50	B5
Broomhaugh	Nthumb	180	B6
Broom Hill	Barns	142	C7
Broom Hill	Dorset	17	K2
Broom Hill	Notts	116	F2
Broomhill	Nthumb	191	K6
Broom Hill	Worcs	97	L8
Broomhill Green	Ches E	113	K2
Broomley	Nthumb	180	C6
Broompark	Dur	169	H2
Broom's Green	Gloucs	81	G8
Broomsthorpe	Norfk	121	J6
Broom Street	Kent	40	D3
Brora	Highld	274	B7
Broseley	Shrops	96	F3
Brotherhouse Bar	Lincs	119	J8
Brotherlee	Dur	167	L3
Brothertoft	Lincs	119	J2
Brotherton	N York	142	D3
Brotton	R & Cl	170	F6
Broubster	Highld	279	J4
Brough	Cumb	167	J7
Brough	Derbys	132	D3
Brough	E R Yk	144	B2
Brough	Highld	280	B2
Brough	Notts	135	G7
Brough	Shet	281	f5
Brough Lodge	Shet	281	f3
Brough Sowerby	Cumb	167	J8
Broughall	Shrops	113	J3
Broughton	Border	199	K6
Broughton	Bucks	67	K4
Broughton	Cambs	102	F7
Broughton	Flints	129	H7
Broughton	Hants	34	C4
Broughton	Lancs	139	G1
Broughton	M Keyn	85	H7
Broughton	N Linc	144	B6
Broughton	N York	149	G5
Broughton	N York	162	D8
Broughton	Nhants	101	H8
Broughton	Oxon	83	K7
Broughton	Salfd	140	B7
Broughton	Staffs	114	B5
Broughton	V Glam	42	D7
Broughton Astley	Leics	100	C5
Broughton Beck	Cumb	156	C6
Broughton Gifford	Wilts	46	C6
Broughton Green	Worcs	81	M3
Broughton Hackett	Worcs	81	L4
Broughton-in-Furness	Cumb	156	B5
Broughton Mains	D & G	174	C6
Broughton Mills	Cumb	156	B5
Broughton Moor	Cumb	164	E4
Broughton Poggs	Oxon	65	K6
Broughton Tower	Cumb	156	B5
Broughty Ferry	C Dund	223	H1
Brough with St Giles	N York	160	B3
Brow End	Cumb	156	C7
Brownber	Cumb	158	B2
Brown Candover	Hants	35	J3
Brown Edge	Lancs	138	D5
Brown Edge	Staffs	114	E1
Brown Heath	Ches W	129	K6
Brownheath	Shrops	113	G5
Brownhill	Abers	256	F4
Brownhills	Fife	223	J4
Brownhills	Wsall	98	D2
Brownieside	Nthumb	191	H2
Browninghill Green	Hants	48	E7
Brown Lees	Staffs	131	G8
Brownlow Heath	Ches E	131	G7
Brownrigg	Cumb	164	D6
Brownrigg	Cumb	177	G8
Brownsea Island	Dorset	17	K5
Brown's Green	Birm	98	D5
Brownshill	Gloucs	64	C6
Brownsover	Warwks	100	B7
Brownston	Devon	7	K4
Brown Street	Suffk	90	C3
Brow-of-the-Hill	Norfk	120	E7
Browston Green	Norfk	107	K3
Broxa	N York	163	G4
Broxbourne	Herts	69	K5
Broxburn	E Loth	212	F3
Broxburn	W Loth	210	E4
Broxfield	Nthumb	191	J3
Broxted	Essex	70	E2
Broxton	Ches W	113	H1
Broyle Side	E Susx	23	G4
Bruan	Highld	280	D8
Bruar	P & K	232	B2
Brucefield	Highld	264	E3
Bruchag	Ag & B	207	J7
Bruera	Ches W	129	K7
Bruern Abbey	Oxon	65	K3
Bruichladdich	Ag & B	204	C4
Bruisyard	Suffk	91	H2
Bruisyard Street	Suffk	91	H2
Brumby	N Linc	143	M6
Brund	Staffs	132	B7
Brundall	Norfk	107	G2
Brundish	Suffk	91	G1
Brundish Street	Suffk	91	G1
Brunery	Highld	237	L6
Brunnion	Cnwll	2	D4
Brunslow	Shrops	95	J6
Brunswick Village	N u Ty	180	F4
Bruntcliffe	Leeds	141	L2
Brunthwaite	C Brad	149	J6
Bruntingthorpe	Leics	100	D5
Brunton	Fife	222	E3
Brunton	Nthumb	191	J1
Brunton	Wilts	47	K7
Brushford	Devon	12	F1
Brushford	Somset	29	G5
Bruton	Somset	31	L4
Bryan's Green	Worcs	81	K2
Bryanston	Dorset	17	G1
Bryant's Bottom	Bucks	67	L7
Brydekirk	D & G	177	G5
Bryher	IoS	10	b2
Brymbo	Wrexhm	112	D1
Brympton	Somset	31	H4
Bryn	Carmth	57	G5
Bryn	Ches W	130	B5
Bryn	Neath	42	B3
Bryn	Shrops	95	H6
Bryn	Wigan	139	H7
Brynamman	Carmth	59	K6
Brynberian	Pembks	75	J5
Brynbryddan	Neath	57	L6
Bryn-bwbach	Gwynd	110	B4
Bryncae	Rhondd	42	F5
Bryncethin	Brdgnd	42	D5
Bryncir	Gwynd	109	H3
Bryn-côch	Neath	57	K5
Bryncroes	Gwynd	108	C5
Bryncrug	Gwynd	92	D3
Bryn Du	IoA	124	F5
Bryn-Eden	Gwynd	110	D5
Bryneglwys	Denbgs	112	A2
Brynfields	Wrexhm	112	D3
Brynford	Flints	128	E5
Bryn Gates	Wigan	139	J7
Bryn Golau	Rhondd	42	F4
Bryngwran	IoA	124	F4
Bryngwyn	Mons	62	D5
Bryngwyn	Powys	79	H5
Bryn-Henllan	Pembks	75	G4
Brynhoffnant	Cerdgn	76	B5
Bryning	Lancs	138	E2
Brynithel	Blae G	61	K6
Brynmawr	Blae G	61	J5
Bryn-mawr	Gwynd	108	D5
Brynmenyn	Brdgnd	42	D5
Brynmill	Swans	57	H6
Brynna	Rhondd	42	F5
Bryn-penarth	Powys	94	D3
Brynrefail	Gwynd	125	K7
Brynrefail	IoA	125	H2
Brynsadler	Rhondd	42	F5
Bryn Saith Marchog	Denbgs	111	L2
Brynsiencyn	IoA	125	H6
Brynteg	IoA	125	J3
Bryn-y-bal	Flints	128	F6
Bryn-y-Maen	Conwy	127	G4
Bryn-yr-Eos	Wrexhm	112	D3
Bualintur	Highld	246	F4
Buarth-draw	Flints	128	E4
Bubbenhall	Warwks	83	J1
Bubwith	E R Yk	151	M8
Buccleuch	Border	188	B3
Buchanan Smithy	Stirlg	208	D1
Buchanhaven	Abers	269	L6
Buchanty	P & K	221	G2
Buchany	Stirlg	220	C6
Buchlyvie	Stirlg	219	J8
Buckabank	Cumb	165	L1
Buckden	Cambs	86	D2
Buckden	N York	159	G7
Buckenham	Norfk	107	G2
Buckerell	Devon	14	D3
Buckfast	Devon	7	L2
Buckfastleigh	Devon	7	L2
Buckhaven	Fife	222	F7
Buckholt	Mons	63	G4
Buckhorn	Devon	11	M3
Buckhorn Weston	Dorset	32	C6
Buckhurst Hill	Essex	69	L8
Buckie	Moray	267	J3
Buckingham	Bucks	84	D8
Buckland	Bucks	67	L4
Buckland	Devon	7	K6
Buckland	Gloucs	82	C8
Buckland	Hants	18	E4
Buckland	Herts	87	G8
Buckland	Kent	41	J4
Buckland	Oxon	65	M7
Buckland	Surrey	37	K1
Buckland Brewer	Devon	27	G6
Buckland Common	Bucks	68	A5
Buckland Dinham	Somset	32	C1
Buckland Filleigh	Devon	12	B1
Buckland in the Moor	Devon	13	G7
Buckland Monachorum	Devon	6	F1
Buckland Newton	Dorset	16	D2
Buckland Ripers	Dorset	16	C6
Buckland St Mary	Somset	30	C8
Buckland-Tout-Saints	Devon	7	L5
Bucklebury	W Berk	48	E5
Bucklers Hard	Hants	18	F4
Bucklesham	Suffk	90	F6
Buckley	Flints	129	G7
Buckley Green	Warwks	82	E2
Bucklow Hill	Ches E	130	E3
Buckminster	Leics	118	A7
Bucknall	C Stke	114	E2
Bucknall	Lincs	136	C6
Bucknell	Oxon	66	E2
Bucknell	Shrops	95	J8
Buckpool	Moray	267	H3
Buck's Cross	Devon	26	F6
Bucks Green	W Susx	37	G4
Bucks Hill	Herts	68	D7
Bucks Horn Oak	Hants	36	B3
Buck's Mills	Devon	26	F6
Buckton	E R Yk	153	K1
Buckton	Herefs	95	J8
Buckton	Nthumb	203	H5
Buckworth	Cambs	102	C8
Budby	Notts	134	C5
Buddileigh	Staffs	114	B2
Bude	Cnwll	11	H2
Budge's Shop	Cnwll	6	C3
Budlake	Devon	14	A3
Budle	Nthumb	203	H4
Budleigh Salterton	Devon	14	C6
Budlett's Common	E Susx	23	H3
Budock Water	Cnwll	3	K5
Buerton	Ches E	113	L3
Bugbrooke	Nhants	84	D4
Bugford	Devon	8	B5
Buglawton	Ches E	131	G7
Bugle	Cnwll	5	G3
Bugley	Dorset	32	C6
Bugthorpe	E R Yk	152	B4
Buildwas	Shrops	96	E2
Builth Road	Powys	78	E4
Builth Wells	Powys	78	E5
Bulbourne	Herts	68	B4
Bulbridge	Wilts	33	J5
Bulby	Lincs	118	D6

Name	Page	Grid
Bulford Wilts	33	L2
Bulford Camp Wilts	33	L2
Bulkeley Ches E	113	J1
Bulkington Warwks	99	K6
Bulkington Wilts	46	D7
Bulkworthy Devon	27	G8
Bullamoor N York	160	F4
Bull Bay IoA	125	G1
Bullbridge Derbys	116	B1
Bullbrook Br For	49	L5
Bullen's Green Herts	69	G6
Bulley Gloucs	63	M3
Bullgill Cumb	164	E3
Bullinghope Herefs	80	C7
Bullington Hants	34	F3
Bullington Lincs	136	A4
Bullockstone Kent	41	G2
Bull's Green Herts	69	H4
Bull's Green Norfk	107	J4
Bulmer Essex	89	G7
Bulmer N York	151	L2
Bulmer Tye Essex	89	G7
Bulphan Thurr	52	D2
Bulstone Devon	14	E4
Bulstrode Herts	68	C6
Bulverhythe E Susx	24	D5
Bulwark Abers	257	G3
Bulwell C Nott	116	F3
Bulwick Nhants	101	L4
Bumble's Green Essex	69	L6
Bunacaimb Highld	237	J3
Bunarkaig Highld	239	K6
Bunbury Ches E	130	A8
Bunbury Heath Ches E	130	A8
Bunchrew Highld	251	K5
Buncton W Susx	21	K4
Bundalloch Highld	248	E6
Bunessan Ag & B	226	D8
Bungay Suffk	107	G5
Bunker's Hill Lincs	119	J1
Bunnahabhain Ag & B	204	F2
Bunny Notts	117	G5
Buntait Highld	250	C5
Buntingford Herts	69	K1
Bunwell Norfk	106	C4
Bunwell Hill Norfk	106	C5
Bupton Derbys	115	L4
Burbage Derbys	131	L5
Burbage Leics	99	L5
Burbage Wilts	47	K6
Burcher Herefs	79	L3
Burchett's Green E Susx	39	G7
Burchett's Green W & M	49	K3
Burcombe Wilts	33	J5
Burcot Oxon	66	E7
Burcot Worcs	82	A1
Burcote Shrops	97	G4
Burcott Bucks	67	K4
Burcott Bucks	67	L2
Burdale N York	152	D3
Bures Essex	89	H8
Burford Oxon	65	K5
Burford Shrops	80	D2
Burg Ag & B	226	D3
Burgate Suffk	106	B8
Burgates Hants	36	A5
Burge End Herts	68	F1
Burgess Hill W Susx	22	E3
Burgh Suffk	90	F5
Burgh by Sands Cumb	177	K7
Burgh Castle Norfk	107	K2
Burghclere Hants	48	C6
Burghead Moray	266	C2
Burghfield W Berk	49	G5
Burghfield Common W Berk	49	G5
Burgh Heath Surrey	51	H7
Burgh Hill E Susx	24	C2
Burghill Herefs	80	B6
Burgh Island Devon	7	J6
Burgh le Marsh Lincs	137	J6
Burgh next Aylsham Norfk	122	E6
Burgh on Bain Lincs	136	D2
Burgh St Margaret Norfk	123	J8
Burgh St Peter Norfk	107	K5
Burghwallis Donc	142	E5
Burham Kent	52	F6
Buriton Hants	20	B3
Burland Ches E	113	K1
Burlawn Cnwll	10	D8
Burleigh Gloucs	64	C6
Burlescombe Devon	29	K7
Burleston Dorset	16	E4
Burlestone Devon	8	B5
Burley Hants	18	C3
Burley Rutlnd	101	J1
Burley Shrops	96	B7
Burleydam Ches E	113	K3
Burley Gate Herefs	80	E6
Burley in Wharfedale C Brad	149	L6

Name	Page	Grid
Burley Lawn Hants	18	C3
Burley Street Hants	18	B3
Burley Wood Head C Brad	149	L7
Burlingham Green Norfk	107	H1
Burlingjobb Powys	79	J4
Burlington Shrops	97	H1
Burlton Shrops	113	G6
Burmarsh Kent	25	L1
Burmington Warwks	83	G7
Burn N York	142	F2
Burnage Manch	131	G1
Burnaston Derbys	115	M5
Burnbanks Cumb	166	C7
Burnbrae N Lans	210	A7
Burnby E R Yk	152	C6
Burn Cross Sheff	142	A8
Burndell W Susx	21	G6
Burnden Bolton	139	L6
Burnedge Rochdl	140	D5
Burneside Cumb	157	H3
Burneston N York	160	D5
Burnett BaNES	45	K6
Burnfoot Border	188	C4
Burnfoot Border	188	F3
Burnfoot D & G	177	K1
Burnfoot D & G	186	E7
Burnfoot D & G	188	C6
Burnfoot P & K	221	H6
Burnham Bucks	50	A3
Burnham N Linc	144	D4
Burnham Deepdale Norfk	121	H3
Burnham Green Herts	69	H4
Burnham Market Norfk	121	H3
Burnham Norton Norfk	121	H3
Burnham-on-Crouch Essex	72	D7
Burnham-on-Sea Somset	30	D1
Burnham Overy Norfk	121	J3
Burnham Overy Staithe Norfk	121	J3
Burnham Thorpe Norfk	121	J3
Burnhaven Abers	257	L3
Burnhead D & G	186	C7
Burnhervie Abers	256	C7
Burnhill Green Staffs	97	H3
Burnhope Dur	169	G1
Burnhouse N Ayrs	196	D1
Burniston N York	163	H4
Burnley Lancs	140	C1
Burnley Crematorium Lancs	140	B2
Burnmouth Border	213	L6
Burn Naze Lancs	147	G2
Burn of Cambus Stirlg	220	C6
Burnopfield Dur	180	E7
Burnrigg Cumb	178	C2
Burnsall N York	149	J3
Burnside Angus	234	C3
Burnside Angus	234	D5
Burnside Fife	222	B5
Burnside Moray	266	D2
Burnside W Loth	210	E4
Burnside of Duntrune Angus	234	C8
Burntcommon Surrey	50	D8
Burntheath Derbys	115	L5
Burnt Heath Essex	72	F2
Burnt Hill W Berk	48	L4
Burnthouse Cnwll	3	K4
Burnt Houses Dur	168	E6
Burntisland Fife	211	H2
Burnt Oak E Susx	23	H2
Burnton E Ayrs	184	D2
Burntwood Staffs	98	D2
Burntwood Green Staffs	98	D2
Burnt Yates N York	150	C4
Burnworthy Somset	30	B7
Burpham Surrey	50	C8
Burpham W Susx	21	H5
Burradon N Tyne	181	G4
Burradon Nthumb	190	D5
Burrafirth Shet	281	f1
Burras Cnwll	3	H4
Burraton Cnwll	6	E2
Burravoe Shet	281	e4
Burrells Cumb	166	F7
Burrelton P & K	233	J7
Burridge Devon	15	H2
Burridge Devon	27	K4
Burridge Hants	19	J2
Burrill N York	160	C5
Burringham N Linc	143	L6
Burrington Devon	27	L7
Burrington Herefs	80	B1
Burrington N Som	44	F7
Burrough End Cambs	88	C4
Burrough Green Cambs	88	C4
Burrough on the Hill Leics	101	J1
Burrow Lancs	157	K7
Burrow Somset	29	G2
Burrow Bridge Somset	30	E5
Burrowhill Surrey	50	B6
Burrows Cross Surrey	37	G2

Name	Page	Grid
Burry Swans	56	E6
Burry Green Swans	56	E6
Burry Port Carmth	56	E5
Burscough Lancs	138	E5
Burscough Bridge Lancs	138	F5
Bursea E R Yk	143	K1
Burshill E R Yk	153	H6
Bursledon Hants	19	H2
Burslem C Stke	114	D2
Burstall Suffk	90	C6
Burstock Dorset	15	K2
Burston Norfk	106	C6
Burston Staffs	114	E5
Burstow Surrey	37	M3
Burstwick E R Yk	145	G2
Burtersett N York	158	F5
Burtholme Cumb	178	D6
Burthorpe Green Suffk	88	F2
Burthwaite Cumb	165	M1
Burthy Cnwll	4	E4
Burtle Hill Somset	30	F2
Burtoft Lincs	119	J4
Burton Ches W	129	H5
Burton Ches W	129	L7
Burton Dorset	16	D4
Burton Dorset	18	B5
Burton Lincs	135	J5
Burton Nthumb	203	K6
Burton Pembks	55	G5
Burton Somset	30	B2
Burton Somset	31	H8
Burton Wilts	32	D4
Burton Wilts	46	B3
Burton Agnes E R Yk	153	H3
Burton Bradstock Dorset	15	L5
Burton Coggles Lincs	118	C6
Burton Dassett Warwks	83	J5
Burton End Essex	70	D2
Burton End Suffk	88	D6
Burton Fleming E R Yk	153	H2
Burton Green Warwks	99	H8
Burton Green Wrexhm	129	H7
Burton Hastings Warwks	99	L5
Burton-in-Kendal Cumb	157	H7
Burton in Lonsdale N York	148	A2
Burton Joyce Notts	117	H3
Burton Latimer Nhants	101	K8
Burton Lazars Leics	117	K8
Burton Leonard N York	150	D3
Burton on the Wolds Leics	117	G7
Burton Overy Leics	100	E4
Burton Pedwardine Lincs	118	F3
Burton Pidsea E R Yk	145	H2
Burton Salmon N York	142	D2
Burton's Green Essex	71	K2
Burton upon Stather N Linc	143	L4
Burton upon Trent Staffs	115	L4
Burton Waters Lincs	135	J5
Burtonwood Warrtn	130	A1
Burwardsley Ches W	129	L8
Burwarton Shrops	96	E6
Burwash E Susx	24	B2
Burwash Common E Susx	23	L3
Burwash Weald E Susx	23	L3
Burwell Cambs	88	B2
Burwell Lincs	137	G4
Burwen IoA	125	G1
Burwick Ork	275	C6
Bury Bury	140	B5
Bury Cambs	102	F6
Bury Somset	29	G5
Bury W Susx	21	G4
Bury End C Beds	86	C8
Bury Green Herts	70	C3
Bury St Edmunds Suffk	89	G2
Burythorpe N York	152	B3
Busby E Rens	208	F7
Busby Stoop N York	160	E6
Buscot Oxon	65	J7
Bush Abers	235	J2
Bush Cnwll	11	J1
Bush Bank Herefs	80	B5
Bushbury Wolves	97	L3
Bushbury Crematorium Wolves	97	L3
Bushby Leics	100	E3
Bushey Herts	68	E8
Bushey Heath Herts	68	F8
Bush Green Norfk	106	E6
Bush Green Suffk	89	H4
Bush Hill Park Gt Lon	69	J7
Bushley Worcs	81	K8
Bushley Green Worcs	81	K8
Bushmead Bed	86	C3
Bushmoor Shrops	95	K6
Bushton Wilts	46	F3
Busk Cumb	166	E2
Buslingthorpe Lincs	135	M3
Bussage Gloucs	64	C6

Name	Page	Grid
Bussex Somset	30	E4
Butcher's Cross E Susx	23	J2
Butcombe N Som	45	G6
Bute Ag & B	207	G5
Butleigh Somset	31	H4
Butleigh Wootton Somset	31	H4
Butler's Cross Bucks	67	K5
Butler's Hill Notts	116	F2
Butlers Marston Warwks	83	H5
Butley Suffk	91	J5
Butley High Corner Suffk	91	J5
Buttercrambe N York	151	M4
Butterdean Border	213	H6
Butterknowle Dur	168	E5
Butterleigh Devon	14	A1
Butterley Derbys	116	C1
Buttermere Cumb	165	G3
Buttermere Wilts	47	M6
Butters Green Staffs	114	C2
Buttershaw C Brad	141	H2
Butterstone P & K	233	G6
Butterton Staffs	114	C3
Butterton Staffs	131	L8
Butterwick Dur	169	K5
Butterwick Lincs	119	L3
Butterwick N York	152	F2
Butterwick N York	162	C7
Butt Green Ches E	113	L1
Buttington Powys	95	G2
Buttonbridge Shrops	97	G7
Buttonoak Shrops	97	G7
Buttsash Hants	19	G2
Buttsbear Cross Cnwll	11	K2
Butt's Green Essex	71	J6
Buxhall Suffk	89	K4
Buxhall Fen Street Suffk	89	K3
Buxted E Susx	23	H3
Buxton Derbys	131	L5
Buxton Norfk	122	E7
Buxton Heath Norfk	122	D7
Bwlch Powys	61	J3
Bwlchgwyn Wrexhm	112	C1
Bwlchllan Cerdgn	77	G3
Bwlchnewydd Carmth	58	C4
Bwlchtocyn Gwynd	108	E6
Bwlch-y-cibau Powys	112	B8
Bwlch-y-Ddar Powys	112	B7
Bwlchyfadfa Cerdgn	76	D5
Bwlch-y-ffridd Powys	94	C4
Bwlch-y-groes Pembks	75	M5
Bwlchymyrdd Swans	57	G5
Bwlch-y-sarnau Powys	94	B8
Byermoor Gatesd	180	F7
Byers Green Dur	169	G4
Byfield Nhants	83	M4
Byfleet Surrey	50	D6
Byford Herefs	79	M6
Bygrave Herts	86	F7
Byker N u Ty	181	G6
Byland Abbey N York	161	J6
Bylaugh Norfk	122	A7
Bylchau Conwy	127	K7
Byley Ches W	130	E6
Bynea Carmth	57	G5
Byrness Nthumb	189	K5
Bystock Devon	14	B6
Bythorn Cambs	102	B8
Byton Herefs	79	L2
Bywell Nthumb	180	C6
Byworth W Susx	36	E6

C

Name	Page	Grid
Cabbacott Devon	27	G6
Cabourne Lincs	144	E7
Cabrach Ag & B	205	H3
Cabrach Moray	255	H6
Cabus Lancs	147	J6
Cackle Street E Susx	23	G2
Cackle Street E Susx	24	C3
Cackle Street E Susx	24	E3
Cadbury Devon	13	L2
Cadbury Barton Devon	28	B7
Cadder E Duns	209	G4
Caddington C Beds	68	D3
Caddonfoot Border	200	F6
Cadeby Donc	142	E7
Cadeby Leics	99	L3
Cadeleigh Devon	13	L1
Cade Street E Susx	23	K3
Cadgwith Cnwll	3	J8
Cadham Fife	222	D6
Cadishead Salfd	130	D1
Cadle Swans	57	H5
Cadley Lancs	139	G2
Cadley Wilts	47	J5
Cadley Wilts	47	K8

Cadmore End Bucks ... 67 J8
Cadnam Hants ... 34 C8
Cadney N Linc ... 144 C7
Cadole Flints ... 128 E7
Cadoxton V Glam ... 43 H7
Cadoxton Juxta-Neath Neath ... 57 L5
Cadwst Denbgs ... 111 K4
Caeathro Gwynd ... 125 J7
Caehopkin Powys ... 59 M6
Caenby Lincs ... 135 K2
Caeo Carmth ... 77 J7
Caerau Brdgnd ... 42 C3
Caerau Cardif ... 43 H6
Cae'r-bont Powys ... 59 M6
Cae'r bryn Carmth ... 59 H6
Caerdeon Gwynd ... 110 C7
Caerfarchell Pembks ... 74 C6
Caergeiliog IoA ... 124 E4
Caergwrle Flints ... 129 G8
Caerhun Conwy ... 126 F5
Caerlanrig Border ... 188 C5
Caerleon Newpt ... 44 D1
Caernarfon Gwynd ... 125 H7
Caerphilly Caerph ... 43 J4
Caersws Powys ... 94 B5
Caerwedros Cerdgn ... 76 C4
Caerwent Mons ... 44 F1
Caerwys Flints ... 128 D5
Caerynwch Gwynd ... 110 E8
Caggle Street Mons ... 62 D4
Caim IoA ... 126 C3
Cairinis W Isls ... 283 c8
Cairnbaan Ag & B ... 206 C1
Cairnbulg Abers ... 269 J3
Cairncross Border ... 213 K6
Cairncurran Inver ... 208 A5
Cairndow Ag & B ... 217 K5
Cairneyhill Fife ... 210 D2
Cairngarroch D & G ... 172 C5
Cairnie Abers ... 255 K3
Cairnorrie Abers ... 256 F3
Cairnryan D & G ... 172 D1
Cairnty Moray ... 267 G5
Caister-on-Sea Norfk ... 107 L1
Caistor Lincs ... 144 E7
Caistor St Edmund Norfk ... 106 E3
Cakebole Worcs ... 81 K1
Cake Street Norfk ... 106 B5
Calais Street Suffk ... 89 K7
Calanais W Isls ... 282 f3
Calbourne IoW ... 19 G6
Calceby Lincs ... 137 G4
Calcot Flints ... 128 E5
Calcot Gloucs ... 65 G5
Calcot W Berk ... 49 G4
Calcot Row W Berk ... 49 G4
Calcots Moray ... 266 E3
Calcott Kent ... 41 G8
Calcott Shrops ... 113 G8
Calcutt N York ... 150 E4
Calcutt Wilts ... 65 G8
Caldbeck Cumb ... 165 K3
Caldbergh N York ... 159 K5
Caldecote Cambs ... 87 G4
Caldecote Cambs ... 102 C5
Caldecote Herts ... 86 E7
Caldecote Nhants ... 84 D5
Caldecote Highfields Cambs ... 87 G3
Caldecott Nhants ... 85 K2
Caldecott Oxon ... 66 D7
Caldecott Rutlnd ... 101 J4
Caldecotte M Keyn ... 85 H8
Calder Cumb ... 155 J2
Calderbank N Lans ... 209 K6
Calder Bridge Cumb ... 155 J2
Calderbrook Rochdl ... 140 E4
Caldercruix N Lans ... 209 L5
Calder Grove Wakefd ... 141 M4
Caldermill S Lans ... 197 J3
Caldermore Rochdl ... 140 D4
Calder Vale Lancs ... 147 K6
Calderwood S Lans ... 209 H7
Caldey Island Pembks ... 55 K7
Caldicot Mons ... 44 F1
Caldmore Wsall ... 98 C4
Caldwell N York ... 168 F8
Caldy Wirral ... 128 F3
Caledfwlch Carmth ... 59 J4
Calenick Cnwll ... 4 D6
Calf of Man IoM ... 154 a8
Calford Green Suffk ... 88 D6
Calfsound Ork ... 275 d2
Calgary Ag & B ... 226 D2
Califer Moray ... 265 H8
California Falk ... 210 B4
California Norfk ... 123 K8
California Cross Devon ... 7 K4
Calke Derbys ... 116 B7
Callakille Highld ... 259 M5

Callander Stirlg ... 219 K5
Callanish W Isls ... 282 f3
Callaughton Shrops ... 96 E4
Callestick Cnwll ... 4 C5
Calligarry Highld ... 247 K7
Callington Cnwll ... 6 D1
Callingwood Staffs ... 115 K6
Callow Herefs ... 80 C8
Callow End Worcs ... 81 J5
Callow Hill Wilts ... 46 F2
Callow Hill Worcs ... 82 B2
Callow Hill Worcs ... 97 G8
Callows Grave Worcs ... 80 D2
Calmore Hants ... 34 D7
Calmsden Gloucs ... 64 F5
Calne Wilts ... 46 E5
Calow Derbys ... 133 H5
Calshot Hants ... 19 H3
Calstock Cnwll ... 6 E1
Calstone Wellington Wilts ... 46 F5
Calthorpe Norfk ... 122 D5
Calthorpe Street Norfk ... 123 H6
Calthwaite Cumb ... 166 B3
Calton N York ... 148 F4
Calton Staffs ... 115 H2
Calveley Ches E ... 130 B7
Calver Derbys ... 132 E5
Calverhall Shrops ... 113 K4
Calver Hill Herefs ... 79 L5
Calverleigh Devon ... 29 G8
Calverley Leeds ... 150 B8
Calver Sough Derbys ... 132 E5
Calvert Bucks ... 67 G2
Calverton M Keyn ... 84 F7
Calverton Notts ... 117 G2
Calvine P & K ... 232 B2
Calvo Cumb ... 176 F8
Calzeat Border ... 199 K6
Cam Gloucs ... 63 M7
Camasachoirce Highld ... 228 B3
Camasine Highld ... 237 L8
Camas Luinie Highld ... 248 F6
Camastianavaig Highld ... 247 G1
Camault Muir Highld ... 250 E4
Camber E Susx ... 25 H3
Camberley Surrey ... 49 L6
Camberwell Gt Lon ... 51 J4
Camblesforth N York ... 143 G3
Cambo Nthumb ... 180 B2
Cambois Nthumb ... 181 H2
Camborne Cnwll ... 3 G3
Cambourne Cambs ... 87 G3
Cambridge Cambs ... 87 J3
Cambridge Gloucs ... 63 L6
Cambridge City Crematorium
    Cambs ... 87 H3
Cambrose Cnwll ... 4 A5
Cambus Clacks ... 220 E8
Cambusavie Platform Highld ... 263 L1
Cambusbarron Stirlg ... 220 D8
Cambuskenneth Stirlg ... 220 D8
Cambuslang S Lans ... 209 H7
Cambus o' May Abers ... 243 M4
Cambuswallace S Lans ... 199 H5
Camden Town Gt Lon ... 51 H2
Cameley BaNES ... 45 J7
Camelford Cnwll ... 10 F6
Camelon Falk ... 209 M3
Camerory Highld ... 253 K5
Camer's Green Worcs ... 81 H8
Camerton BaNES ... 45 K7
Camerton Cumb ... 164 D4
Camghouran P & K ... 231 G4
Camieston Border ... 201 J7
Cammachmore Abers ... 245 K4
Cammeringham Lincs ... 135 J3
Camore Highld ... 263 L2
Campbeltown Ag & B ... 192 E4
Camperdown N Tyne ... 181 G4
Cample D & G ... 186 D7
Campmuir P & K ... 233 K7
Camps W Loth ... 210 E5
Campsall Donc ... 142 E5
Campsea Ash Suffk ... 91 H4
Camps End Cambs ... 88 C6
Campton C Beds ... 86 C7
Camptown Border ... 189 J4
Camrose Pembks ... 54 F3
Camserney P & K ... 232 B5
Camusnagaul Highld ... 239 H8
Camusnagaul Highld ... 261 H2
Camusteel Highld ... 248 A3
Camusterrach Highld ... 248 A3
Canada Hants ... 34 C7
Canal Foot Cumb ... 156 D7
Canaston Bridge Pembks ... 55 H4
Candacraig Abers ... 243 K4
Candlesby Lincs ... 137 H6
Candle Street Suffk ... 105 L8

Candover Green Shrops ... 96 C2
Candy Mill Border ... 199 J5
Cane End Oxon ... 49 G3
Canewdon Essex ... 72 C8
Canford Bottom Dorset ... 17 K3
Canford Cliffs Poole ... 17 L5
Canford Crematorium Bristl ... 45 H3
Canford Heath Poole ... 17 K4
Canford Magna Poole ... 17 K3
Canhams Green Suffk ... 90 C2
Canisbay Highld ... 280 D2
Canklow Rothm ... 133 H2
Canley Covtry ... 99 J7
Canley Crematorium Covtry ... 99 J8
Cann Dorset ... 32 E6
Canna Highld ... 246 B7
Cann Common Dorset ... 32 E6
Cannich Highld ... 250 B5
Cannington Somset ... 30 C3
Canning Town Gt Lon ... 51 L3
Cannock Staffs ... 98 B2
Cannock Wood Staffs ... 98 D1
Cannon Bridge Herefs ... 80 A7
Canon Frome Herefs ... 80 F6
Canon Pyon Herefs ... 80 B5
Canons Ashby Nhants ... 84 B5
Canonstown Cnwll ... 2 E4
Canterbury Kent ... 40 F4
Cantley Norfk ... 107 H3
Cantlop Shrops ... 96 C2
Canton Cardif ... 43 J6
Cantraywood Highld ... 252 E2
Cantsfield Lancs ... 147 M1
Canvey Island Essex ... 53 G2
Canwick Lincs ... 135 K6
Canworthy Water Cnwll ... 11 J4
Caol Highld ... 239 J8
Caolas Scalpaigh W Isls ... 282 f6
Caoles Ag & B ... 224 D5
Caonich Highld ... 239 H5
Capel Kent ... 39 G4
Capel Surrey ... 37 J3
Capel Bangor Cerdgn ... 92 E7
Capel Betws Lleucu Cerdgn ... 77 H4
Capel Coch IoA ... 125 H3
Capel Curig Conwy ... 126 E8
Capel Cynon Cerdgn ... 76 C5
Capel Dewi Carmth ... 58 E5
Capel Dewi Cerdgn ... 76 E6
Capel-Dewi Cerdgn ... 92 D7
Capel Garmon Conwy ... 127 G8
Capel Green Suffk ... 91 J5
Capel Gwyn Carmth ... 58 E4
Capel Gwyn IoA ... 124 F4
Capel Gwynfe Carmth ... 59 K4
Capel Hendre Carmth ... 59 G6
Capel Isaac Carmth ... 59 G3
Capel Iwan Carmth ... 58 B2
Capel le Ferne Kent ... 41 H7
Capelles Guern ... 9 j2
Capel Llanilltern Cardif ... 43 H5
Capel Mawr IoA ... 125 G5
Capel Parc IoA ... 125 H2
Capel St Andrew Suffk ... 91 J5
Capel St Mary Suffk ... 90 C7
Capel Seion Cerdgn ... 92 D7
Capel Trisant Cerdgn ... 92 F8
Capeluchaf Gwynd ... 109 H2
Capelulo Conwy ... 126 E4
Capel-y-ffin Powys ... 61 L1
Capel-y-graig Gwynd ... 125 K6
Capenhurst Ches W ... 129 J5
Capernwray Lancs ... 147 K2
Capheaton Nthumb ... 180 C3
Caplaw E Rens ... 208 D7
Capon's Green Suffk ... 91 G2
Cappercleuch Border ... 187 K2
Capstone Medway ... 53 G6
Capton Devon ... 7 K5
Capton Somset ... 29 K3
Caputh P & K ... 233 G7
Caradon Town Cnwll ... 11 K8
Carbeth Inn Stirlg ... 208 E2
Carbis Cnwll ... 5 G3
Carbis Bay Cnwll ... 2 E3
Carbost Highld ... 246 E2
Carbost Highld ... 259 H3
Carbrook Sheff ... 133 G2
Carbrooke Norfk ... 105 J3
Carburton Notts ... 134 C6
Carclaze Cnwll ... 5 H4
Car Colston Notts ... 117 J3
Carcroft Donc ... 142 E6
Cardenden Fife ... 222 D8
Cardeston Shrops ... 95 J1
Cardewlees Cumb ... 177 K8
Cardhu Moray ... 254 D3
Cardiff Cardif ... 43 J6

Cardiff & Glamorgan
    Crematorium Cardif ... 43 J5
Cardigan Cerdgn ... 75 L3
Cardinal's Green Cambs ... 88 C6
Cardington Bed ... 86 B5
Cardington Shrops ... 96 C4
Cardinham Cnwll ... 5 J1
Cardrain D & G ... 172 E8
Cardrona Border ... 200 C5
Cardross Ag & B ... 208 B3
Cardross Crematorium Ag & B ... 208 B3
Cardryne D & G ... 172 E8
Cardurnock Cumb ... 177 G7
Careby Lincs ... 118 B2
Careston Angus ... 234 E3
Carew Pembks ... 55 H6
Carew Cheriton Pembks ... 55 H6
Carew Newton Pembks ... 55 H6
Carey Herefs ... 63 H1
Carfin N Lans ... 209 K7
Carfraemill Border ... 201 G2
Cargate Green Norfk ... 107 H1
Cargenbridge D & G ... 176 C4
Cargill P & K ... 233 H8
Cargo Cumb ... 177 L7
Cargreen Cnwll ... 6 E2
Cargurrel Cnwll ... 3 M4
Carham Nthumb ... 202 B5
Carhampton Somset ... 29 H2
Carharrack Cnwll ... 3 J3
Carie P & K ... 231 H4
Carinish W Isls ... 283 c8
Carisbrooke IoW ... 19 H6
Cark Cumb ... 156 E7
Carkeel Cnwll ... 6 E3
Carlabhagh W Isls ... 282 e2
Carland Cross Cnwll ... 4 D4
Carlbury Darltn ... 169 G7
Carlby Lincs ... 102 A1
Carlcroft Nthumb ... 190 B4
Carlecotes Barns ... 141 J7
Carleen Cnwll ... 3 G5
Carlesmoor N York ... 160 B7
Carleton Cumb ... 155 J1
Carleton Cumb ... 166 C5
Carleton Cumb ... 178 A8
Carleton Lancs ... 146 F7
Carleton N York ... 149 H6
Carleton Wakefd ... 142 D4
Carleton Crematorium Bpool ... 146 F7
Carleton Forehoe Norfk ... 106 B2
Carleton Rode Norfk ... 106 C5
Carleton St Peter Norfk ... 107 G3
Carlidnack Cnwll ... 3 K5
Carlincraig Abers ... 256 B3
Carlingcott BaNES ... 45 K7
Carlin How R & Cl ... 171 G6
Carlisle Cumb ... 177 L7
Carlisle Crematorium Cumb ... 177 L8
Carloggas Cnwll ... 4 E2
Carlops Border ... 199 K2
Carloway W Isls ... 282 e2
Carlton Barns ... 142 B5
Carlton Bed ... 85 J4
Carlton Cambs ... 88 C4
Carlton Leeds ... 142 A2
Carlton Leics ... 99 L2
Carlton N York ... 143 G3
Carlton N York ... 159 J5
Carlton N York ... 161 K5
Carlton Notts ... 117 G3
Carlton S on T ... 169 K6
Carlton Suffk ... 91 J2
Carlton Colville Suffk ... 107 K5
Carlton Curlieu Leics ... 100 F4
Carlton Green Cambs ... 88 C5
Carlton Husthwaite N York ... 161 H7
Carlton-in-Cleveland N York ... 161 H2
Carlton in Lindrick Notts ... 134 B3
Carlton-le-Moorland Lincs ... 135 H6
Carlton Miniott N York ... 160 F6
Carlton-on-Trent Notts ... 134 F7
Carlton Scroop Lincs ... 118 B3
Carluke S Lans ... 198 D2
Carlyon Bay Cnwll ... 5 H4
Carmacoup S Lans ... 198 C7
Carmarthen Carmth ... 58 D5
Carmel Carmth ... 59 G5
Carmel Flints ... 128 E4
Carmel Gwynd ... 125 J8
Carmichael S Lans ... 198 F5
Carmountside Crematorium
    C Stke ... 114 E2
Carmunnock C Glas ... 209 G7
Carmyle C Glas ... 209 H6
Carmyllie Angus ... 234 E6
Carnaby E R Yk ... 153 J3
Carnbee Fife ... 223 J6
Carnbo P & K ... 221 J6

Carn Brea Cnwll ... 3 H3
Carnbrogie Abers ... 256 F6
Carndu Highld ... 248 E6
Carnduff S Lans ... 197 J2
Carne Cnwll ... 3 K6
Carne Cnwll ... 4 E7
Carne Cnwll ... 4 F3
Carnell E Ayrs ... 196 F4
Carnewas Cnwll ... 4 D1
Carnforth Lancs ... 147 K2
Carn-gorm Highld ... 248 F7
Carnhedryn Pembks ... 74 C6
Carnhell Green Cnwll ... 3 G4
Carnie Abers ... 245 H2
Carnkie Cnwll ... 3 H3
Carnkie Cnwll ... 3 H4
Carnkiet Cnwll ... 4 C4
Carno Powys ... 93 L4
Carnock Fife ... 210 D1
Carnon Downs Cnwll ... 3 K3
Carnousie Abers ... 268 B6
Carnoustie Angus ... 234 E8
Carnsmerry Cnwll ... 5 G3
Carnwath S Lans ... 199 G4
Carnyorth Cnwll ... 2 B4
Carol Green Solhll ... 99 H7
Carpalla Cnwll ... 4 F4
Carperby N York ... 159 H5
Carr Rothm ... 133 K2
Carradale Ag & B ... 194 C3
Carrbridge Highld ... 253 G7
Carrbrook Tamesd ... 140 E7
Carrefour Jersey ... 9 c2
Carreglefn IoA ... 125 G2
Carr Gate Wakefd ... 141 M3
Carrhouse N Linc ... 143 K6
Carrick Ag & B ... 206 E2
Carrick Castle Ag & B ... 217 K8
Carriden Falk ... 210 D3
Carrington Lincs ... 136 F8
Carrington Mdloth ... 211 K7
Carrington Traffd ... 130 E1
Carrog Conwy ... 110 E2
Carrog Denbgs ... 111 L3
Carron Falk ... 210 A3
Carron Moray ... 254 E3
Carronbridge D & G ... 186 C6
Carron Bridge Stirlg ... 209 K2
Carronshore Falk ... 210 A2
Carrow Hill Mons ... 44 E1
Carr Shield Nthumb ... 167 J1
Carrutherstown D & G ... 176 E4
Carruth House Inver ... 208 B6
Carr Vale Derbys ... 133 J5
Carrville Dur ... 169 J2
Carsaig Ag & B ... 227 G8
Carseriggan D & G ... 173 H1
Carsethorn D & G ... 176 C7
Carshalton Gt Lon ... 51 H6
Carsington Derbys ... 115 L1
Carskey Ag & B ... 192 D6
Carsluith D & G ... 174 D4
Carsphairn D & G ... 184 E4
Carstairs S Lans ... 198 F4
Carstairs Junction S Lans ... 198 F4
Carswell Marsh Oxon ... 65 L7
Carter's Clay Hants ... 34 C6
Carters Green Essex ... 70 D5
Carterton Oxon ... 65 L5
Carterway Heads Nthumb ... 180 C8
Carthew Cnwll ... 5 G4
Carthorpe N York ... 160 D6
Cartington Nthumb ... 190 E5
Cartland S Lans ... 198 E4
Cartledge Derbys ... 132 F4
Cartmel Cumb ... 156 E7
Cartmel Fell Cumb ... 156 F5
Carway Carmth ... 56 E3
Carwinley Cumb ... 177 L4
Cashe's Green Gloucs ... 64 B6
Cashmoor Dorset ... 33 G8
Cassington Oxon ... 66 C5
Cassop Colliery Dur ... 169 K3
Castallack Cnwll ... 2 C6
Castel Guern ... 9 j3
Castell Conwy ... 126 F6
Castell-y-bwch Torfn ... 62 B8
Casterton Cumb ... 157 K6
Castle Cnwll ... 5 J3
Castle Acre Norfk ... 121 H8
Castle Ashby Nhants ... 85 G3
Castlebay W Isls ... 283 b13
Castle Bolton N York ... 159 J4
Castle Bromwich Solhll ... 98 F5
Castle Bytham Lincs ... 118 C7
Castlebythe Pembks ... 75 H6
Castle Caereinion Powys ... 94 E2
Castle Camps Cambs ... 88 C6
Castle Carrock Cumb ... 178 D7

Castlecary Falk ... 209 L3
Castle Cary Somset ... 31 L4
Castle Combe Wilts ... 46 B3
Castle Donington Leics ... 116 D6
Castle Douglas D & G ... 175 J2
Castle Eaton Swindn ... 65 H7
Castle Eden Dur ... 169 L3
Castle End C Pete ... 102 C2
Castleford Wakefd ... 142 C3
Castle Frome Herefs ... 80 F6
Castle Gate Cnwll ... 2 D4
Castle Green Cumb ... 157 H4
Castle Green Surrey ... 50 B6
Castle Gresley Derbys ... 115 M7
Castle Hedingham Essex ... 88 F8
Castlehill Border ... 200 B6
Castlehill Highld ... 280 B3
Castle Hill Kent ... 39 H5
Castle Hill Suffk ... 90 D6
Castlehill W Duns ... 208 C4
Castle Kennedy D & G ... 172 D3
Castle Lachlan Ag & B ... 217 G8
Castlemartin Pembks ... 54 E7
Castlemilk C Glas ... 209 G7
Castle Morris Pembks ... 74 E6
Castlemorton Worcs ... 81 H7
Castlemorton Common Worcs ... 81 H7
Castle O'er D & G ... 187 K7
Castle Rising Norfk ... 120 E6
Castleside Dur ... 168 D1
Castle Stuart Highld ... 252 D2
Castlethorpe M Keyn ... 84 F6
Castlethorpe N Linc ... 144 B6
Castleton Border ... 188 C3
Castleton Derbys ... 132 C3
Castleton N York ... 162 B1
Castleton Newpt ... 43 L5
Castleton Rochdl ... 140 C5
Castletown Ches W ... 113 G1
Castletown Dorset ... 16 D1
Castletown Highld ... 280 A3
Castletown IoM ... 154 C8
Castletown Sundld ... 181 J7
Castley N York ... 150 C6
Caston Norfk ... 105 J4
Castor C Pete ... 102 C4
Caswell Bay Swans ... 57 G7
Catacol N Ayrs ... 194 E1
Cat and Fiddle Derbys ... 131 K5
Catbrain S Glos ... 45 H3
Catbrook Mons ... 63 G6
Catch Flints ... 128 F5
Catchall Cnwll ... 2 C5
Catchem's Corner Solhll ... 99 H8
Catchgate Dur ... 180 E8
Catcliffe Rothm ... 133 H2
Catcomb Wilts ... 46 E4
Catcott Somset ... 30 F3
Catcott Burtle Somset ... 30 F2
Caterham Surrey ... 51 J7
Catfield Norfk ... 123 H7
Catfield Common Norfk ... 123 H7
Catford Gt Lon ... 51 K4
Catforth Lancs ... 138 F1
Cathcart C Glas ... 209 G7
Cathedine Powys ... 61 J2
Catherine-de-Barnes Solhll ... 98 F7
Catherine Slack C Brad ... 141 G2
Catherington Hants ... 35 L8
Catherston Leweston Dorset ... 15 J4
Catherton Shrops ... 96 E7
Catisfield Hants ... 19 J2
Catley Herefs ... 80 F6
Catley Lane Head Rochdl ... 140 C4
Catlodge Highld ... 241 H5
Catlow Lancs ... 148 F8
Catlowdy Cumb ... 178 B3
Catmere End Essex ... 87 K7
Catmore W Berk ... 48 C3
Caton Devon ... 13 H8
Caton Lancs ... 147 K3
Caton Green Lancs ... 147 L3
Cator Court Devon ... 13 G7
Catrine E Ayrs ... 197 G6
Cat's Ash Newpt ... 44 D1
Catsfield E Susx ... 24 C4
Catsfield Stream E Susx ... 24 C4
Catsgore Somset ... 31 H5
Catsham Somset ... 31 J4
Catshill Worcs ... 98 B8
Catstree Shrops ... 97 G4
Cattadale Ag & B ... 192 D6
Cattal N York ... 150 F5
Cattawade Suffk ... 90 C8
Catterall Lancs ... 147 K7
Catteralslane Shrops ... 113 J3
Catterick N York ... 160 C3
Catterick Bridge N York ... 160 B3
Catterick Garrison N York ... 160 B3

Catterlen Cumb ... 166 B4
Catterline Abers ... 245 J7
Catterton N York ... 151 H6
Catteshall Surrey ... 36 E2
Catthorpe Leics ... 100 C7
Cattishall Suffk ... 89 H2
Cattistock Dorset ... 16 B3
Catton N York ... 160 E7
Catton Nthumb ... 179 J7
Catwick E R Yk ... 153 J6
Catworth Cambs ... 86 B1
Caudle Green Gloucs ... 64 D5
Caulcott C Beds ... 85 K6
Caulcott Oxon ... 66 D2
Cauldcots Angus ... 235 G6
Cauldhame Stirlg ... 219 L8
Cauldmill Border ... 188 F3
Cauldon Staffs ... 115 H2
Cauldon Lowe Staffs ... 115 H2
Cauldwell Derbys ... 115 L8
Caulkerbush D & G ... 176 B7
Caulside D & G ... 178 B3
Caundle Marsh Dorset ... 31 L8
Caunsall Worcs ... 97 J7
Caunton Notts ... 134 E7
Causeway Hants ... 35 M6
Causeway End Cumb ... 157 G5
Causeway End D & G ... 173 K3
Causeway End Essex ... 71 G3
Causewayend S Lans ... 199 H6
Causewayhead Cumb ... 176 F8
Causewayhead Stirlg ... 220 D8
Causeyend Abers ... 257 H7
Causey Park Nthumb ... 191 H7
Causey Park Bridge Nthumb ... 191 H7
Cavendish Suffk ... 88 F6
Cavenham Suffk ... 88 F1
Caversfield Oxon ... 66 E2
Caversham Readg ... 49 H4
Caverswall Staffs ... 114 F3
Caverton Mill Border ... 202 A7
Cavil E R Yk ... 143 J2
Cawdor Highld ... 252 F2
Cawkwell Lincs ... 136 E4
Cawood N York ... 151 J8
Cawsand Cnwll ... 6 E5
Cawston Norfk ... 122 C6
Cawston Warwks ... 100 A8
Cawthorn N York ... 162 D5
Cawthorne Barns ... 141 L6
Cawton N York ... 161 K7
Caxton Cambs ... 86 F3
Caxton End Cambs ... 87 G4
Caxton Gibbet Cambs ... 86 F3
Caynham Shrops ... 80 D1
Caythorpe Lincs ... 118 B2
Caythorpe Notts ... 117 J2
Cayton N York ... 163 J6
Ceann a Bhaigh W Isls ... 283 b8
Ceannacroc Lodge Highld ... 239 L1
Cearsiadar W Isls ... 282 f4
Ceciliford Mons ... 63 G6
Cefn Newpt ... 44 B1
Cefn Berain Conwy ... 127 K6
Cefn-brith Conwy ... 111 H2
Cefn-bryn-brain Carmth ... 59 K6
Cefn Byrle Powys ... 60 C5
Cefn Canel Powys ... 112 C5
Cefn Coch Powys ... 111 L6
Cefn-coed-y-cymmer Myr Td ... 60 F5
Cefn Cribwr Brdgnd ... 42 C5
Cefn Cross Brdgnd ... 42 C5
Cefn-ddwysarn Gwynd ... 111 J4
Cefn-Einion Shrops ... 95 G6
Cefneithin Carmth ... 59 G6
Cefngorwydd Powys ... 78 B6
Cefn-mawr Wrexhm ... 112 D3
Cefnpennar Rhondd ... 61 G7
Cefn-y-bedd Flints ... 129 H8
Cefn-y-pant Carmth ... 75 L7
Ceint IoA ... 125 J4
Cellan Cerdgn ... 77 H5
Cellardyke Fife ... 223 K6
Cellarhead Staffs ... 114 F2
Celleron Cumb ... 166 C5
Celynen Caerph ... 43 K3
Cemaes IoA ... 124 F1
Cemmaes Powys ... 93 H2
Cemmaes Road Powys ... 93 H3
Cenarth Cerdgn ... 76 A7
Cerbyd Pembks ... 74 D6
Ceres Fife ... 223 G5
Cerne Abbas Dorset ... 16 C2
Cerney Wick Gloucs ... 65 G7
Cerrigceinwen IoA ... 125 G5
Cerrigydrudion Conwy ... 111 J2
Cess Norfk ... 123 J3
Ceunant Gwynd ... 125 J7
Chaceley Gloucs ... 64 B1

Chacewater Cnwll ... 4 B6
Chackmore Bucks ... 84 D8
Chacombe Nhants ... 83 L6
Chadbury Worcs ... 82 B6
Chadderton Oldham ... 140 D6
Chadderton Fold Oldham ... 140 D6
Chaddesden C Derb ... 116 C4
Chaddesley Corbett Worcs ... 97 K8
Chaddlehanger Devon ... 12 B7
Chaddleworth W Berk ... 48 B3
Chadlington Oxon ... 65 M3
Chadshunt Warwks ... 83 H4
Chadwell Leics ... 117 K6
Chadwell Shrops ... 114 B8
Chadwell End Bed ... 86 B2
Chadwell Heath Gt Lon ... 52 A1
Chadwell St Mary Thurr ... 52 E3
Chadwick Worcs ... 81 J2
Chadwick End Solhll ... 82 F1
Chadwick Green St Hel ... 139 G7
Chaffcombe Somset ... 15 H1
Chafford Hundred Thurr ... 52 D3
Chagford Devon ... 13 G5
Chailey E Susx ... 22 F3
Chainbridge Cambs ... 103 J3
Chainhurst Kent ... 39 J4
Chalbury Dorset ... 17 K1
Chalbury Common Dorset ... 17 K2
Chaldon Surrey ... 51 J7
Chale IoW ... 19 H8
Chale Green IoW ... 19 H7
Chalfont Common Bucks ... 68 C8
Chalfont St Giles Bucks ... 68 C8
Chalfont St Peter Bucks ... 50 C1
Chalford Gloucs ... 64 C6
Chalford Oxon ... 67 H7
Chalford Wilts ... 32 E1
Chalgrave C Beds ... 68 C2
Chalgrove Oxon ... 66 F7
Chalk Kent ... 52 E4
Chalk End Essex ... 70 F5
Chalkhouse Green Oxon ... 49 H3
Chalkway Somset ... 15 J1
Chalkwell Kent ... 53 J2
Challaborough Devon ... 7 J6
Challacombe Devon ... 28 B3
Challoch D & G ... 173 K2
Challock Kent ... 40 C5
Chalmington Dorset ... 16 B2
Chalton C Beds ... 68 C2
Chalton C Beds ... 86 C5
Chalton Hants ... 20 B4
Chalvey Slough ... 50 B3
Chalvington E Susx ... 23 H5
Chambers Green Kent ... 40 B6
Chandler's Cross Herts ... 68 D7
Chandlers Cross Worcs ... 81 H7
Chandler's Ford Hants ... 34 F7
Channel's End Bed ... 86 C4
Channel Tunnel Terminal Kent ... 41 G7
Chanterlands Crematorium C KuH ... 144 D2
Chantry Somset ... 32 B2
Chantry Suffk ... 90 D6
Chapel Cumb ... 165 H4
Chapel Fife ... 222 D8
Chapel Allerton Leeds ... 150 D8
Chapel Allerton Somset ... 30 F1
Chapel Amble Cnwll ... 10 D7
Chapel Brampton Nhants ... 84 E2
Chapelbridge Cambs ... 102 F4
Chapel Chorlton Staffs ... 114 C4
Chapel Cross E Susx ... 23 K3
Chapel End Bed ... 86 B4
Chapel End C Beds ... 85 L6
Chapel End Cambs ... 102 C6
Chapel End Warwks ... 99 J5
Chapelend Way Essex ... 88 E7
Chapel-en-le-Frith Derbys ... 131 L3
Chapel Field Bury ... 140 B6
Chapelgate Lincs ... 119 L6
Chapel Green Warwks ... 83 L3
Chapel Green Warwks ... 99 H6
Chapel Haddlesey N York ... 142 F3
Chapelhall N Lans ... 209 K6
Chapel Hill Abers ... 257 K4
Chapel Hill Lincs ... 119 G1
Chapel Hill Mons ... 63 G7
Chapel Hill N York ... 150 D6
Chapelhope Border ... 187 K2
Chapelknowe D & G ... 177 K4
Chapel Lawn Shrops ... 95 H8
Chapel-le-Dale N York ... 158 C7
Chapel Leigh Somset ... 29 L5
Chapel Milton Derbys ... 131 L3
Chapel of Garioch Abers ... 256 C7
Chapel Rossan D & G ... 172 D6
Chapel Row E Susx ... 23 L5
Chapel Row Essex ... 71 J7

Name	Page	Grid
Chapel Row W Berk	48	E5
Chapels Cumb	156	B6
Chapel St Leonards Lincs	137	K5
Chapel Stile Cumb	156	D2
Chapelton Angus	234	F6
Chapelton Devon	27	K5
Chapelton S Lans	197	K1
Chapeltown Bl w D	139	L4
Chapel Town Cnwll	4	E4
Chapeltown Moray	254	E7
Chapeltown Sheff	142	A8
Chapmanslade Wilts	32	D1
Chapmans Well Devon	11	L4
Chapmore End Herts	69	J4
Chappel Essex	72	C2
Charaton Cnwll	6	B1
Chard Somset	15	H1
Chard Junction Somset	15	H2
Chardleigh Green Somset	30	D8
Chardstock Devon	15	G2
Charfield S Glos	63	L8
Chargrove Gloucs	64	D3
Charing Kent	40	B5
Charing Crematorium Kent	40	B5
Charing Heath Kent	40	B5
Charing Hill Kent	40	B5
Charingworth Gloucs	82	E7
Charlbury Oxon	66	A3
Charlcombe BaNES	45	L5
Charlcutt Wilts	46	E4
Charlecote Warwks	83	G4
Charlemont Sandw	98	C4
Charles Devon	28	B4
Charleshill Surrey	36	D2
Charleston Angus	234	B6
Charlestown C Aber	245	L3
Charlestown C Brad	149	L8
Charlestown Calder	140	E2
Charlestown Cnwll	5	H4
Charlestown Derbys	131	L1
Charlestown Dorset	16	C6
Charlestown Fife	210	E2
Charlestown Highld	251	H2
Charlestown Highld	260	C5
Charlestown Salfd	140	B7
Charlestown of Aberlour Moray	254	E3
Charles Tye Suffk	89	L5
Charlesworth Derbys	131	K1
Charlinch Somset	30	C3
Charlottetown Fife	222	E5
Charlton Gt Lon	51	L3
Charlton Hants	34	D2
Charlton Herts	68	F2
Charlton Nhants	83	M8
Charlton Nthumb	179	J2
Charlton Oxon	48	B1
Charlton Somset	30	D5
Charlton Somset	31	K2
Charlton Somset	45	K8
Charlton Surrey	50	D5
Charlton W Susx	20	E4
Charlton Wilts	32	F6
Charlton Wilts	46	D1
Charlton Worcs	81	J1
Charlton Worcs	82	B6
Charlton Wrekin	96	D1
Charlton Abbots Gloucs	64	F2
Charlton Adam Somset	31	J5
Charlton All Saints Wilts	33	L6
Charlton Down Dorset	16	C4
Charlton Hill Shrops	96	D2
Charlton Horethorne Somset	31	L6
Charlton Kings Gloucs	64	D3
Charlton Mackrell Somset	31	H5
Charlton Marshall Dorset	17	H2
Charlton Musgrove Somset	32	B5
Charlton-on-Otmoor Oxon	66	E4
Charlton on the Hill Dorset	17	H2
Charlton St Peter Wilts	47	G7
Charlwood Hants	35	K4
Charlwood Surrey	37	K3
Charminster Dorset	16	C4
Charmouth Dorset	15	H4
Charndon Bucks	67	G2
Charney Bassett Oxon	66	A8
Charnock Green Lancs	139	H4
Charnock Richard Lancs	139	H4
Charnock Richard Crematorium Lancs	139	H4
Charsfield Suffk	90	F4
Chart Corner Kent	39	K3
Charter Alley Hants	48	E7
Charterhall Border	202	B4
Charterhouse Somset	45	G7
Charterhall Stirlg	209	L1
Charterville Allotments Oxon	65	L5
Chartham Kent	40	E4
Chartham Hatch Kent	40	E4
Chart Hill Kent	39	K3
Chartridge Bucks	68	B6
Chart Sutton Kent	39	K3
Chartway Street Kent	39	L3
Charvil Wokham	49	J4
Charwelton Nhants	83	M4
Chase Terrace Staffs	98	D2
Chasetown Staffs	98	D2
Chastleton Oxon	65	K1
Chasty Devon	11	L2
Chatburn Lancs	148	D7
Chatcull Staffs	114	B4
Chatham Caerph	43	K4
Chatham Medway	53	G5
Chatham Green Essex	71	H4
Chathill Nthumb	203	K7
Chatley Worcs	81	J3
Chattenden Medway	53	G4
Chatter End Essex	70	C2
Chatteris Cambs	103	H6
Chatterton Lancs	140	B4
Chattisham Suffk	90	C6
Chatto Border	189	K3
Chatton Nthumb	203	G7
Chaul End C Beds	68	D3
Chawleigh Devon	28	C8
Chawley Oxon	66	C6
Chawston Bed	86	C4
Chawton Hants	35	L3
Chaxhill Gloucs	63	L4
Chazey Heath Oxon	49	G3
Cheadle Staffs	115	G3
Cheadle Stockp	131	G2
Cheadle Heath Stockp	131	G2
Cheadle Hulme Stockp	131	G2
Cheam Gt Lon	51	H6
Cheapside W & M	50	B5
Chearsley Bucks	67	H5
Chebsey Staffs	114	D6
Checkendon Oxon	49	G2
Checkley Ches E	114	A2
Checkley Herefs	80	E7
Checkley Staffs	115	G4
Checkley Green Ches E	114	A2
Chedburgh Suffk	88	F4
Cheddar Somset	44	F8
Cheddington Bucks	68	A4
Cheddleton Staffs	114	F1
Cheddleton Heath Staffs	114	F1
Cheddon Fitzpaine Somset	30	C5
Chedglow Wilts	64	D8
Chedgrave Norfk	107	H3
Chedington Dorset	15	L2
Chediston Suffk	107	G7
Chediston Green Suffk	107	G7
Chedworth Gloucs	64	F5
Chedzoy Somset	30	E3
Cheeseman's Green Kent	40	D7
Cheetham Hill Manch	140	C7
Cheldon Devon	28	C8
Chelford Ches E	130	F5
Chellaston C Derb	116	C5
Chellington Bed	85	J4
Chelmarsh Shrops	97	G5
Chelmick Shrops	95	L5
Chelmondiston Suffk	90	E7
Chelmorton Derbys	132	B5
Chelmsford Essex	71	H5
Chelmsford Crematorium Essex	71	G6
Chelmsley Wood Solhll	98	F6
Chelsea Gt Lon	51	H3
Chelsfield Gt Lon	52	A6
Chelsham Surrey	51	K7
Chelston Somset	29	L6
Chelsworth Suffk	89	K5
Cheltenham Gloucs	64	D3
Cheltenham Crematorium Gloucs	64	E3
Chelveston Nhants	85	K1
Chelvey N Som	44	F5
Chelwood BaNES	45	J6
Chelwood Common E Susx	38	B7
Chelwood Gate E Susx	38	B7
Chelworth Wilts	64	E8
Chelworth Lower Green Wilts	65	G8
Chelworth Upper Green Wilts	65	G8
Cheney Longville Shrops	95	K6
Chenies Bucks	68	C7
Chepstow Mons	63	G8
Chequerbent Bolton	139	K6
Chequers Corner Norfk	103	K2
Cherhill Wilts	46	F5
Cherington Gloucs	64	C7
Cherington Warwks	83	G7
Cheriton Devon	28	C2
Cheriton Hants	35	J5
Cheriton Kent	41	G7
Cheriton Pembks	55	G7
Cheriton Swans	56	E6
Cheriton Bishop Devon	13	H4
Cheriton Fitzpaine Devon	13	K2
Cherrington Wrekin	113	L7
Cherry Burton E R Yk	152	F7
Cherry Hinton Cambs	87	K4
Cherry Orchard Worcs	81	K4
Cherry Willingham Lincs	135	L5
Chertsey Surrey	50	D5
Cheselbourne Dorset	16	E3
Chesham Bucks	68	B6
Chesham Bury	140	B5
Chesham Bois Bucks	68	B7
Cheshunt Herts	69	K6
Chesley Kent	53	J6
Cheslyn Hay Staffs	98	B2
Chessetts Wood Warwks	99	G8
Chessington Gt Lon	50	F6
Chester Ches W	129	J6
Chester Crematorium Ches W	129	J6
Chesterblade Somset	31	L3
Chesterfield Derbys	133	G5
Chesterfield Staffs	98	E2
Chesterfield Crematorium Derbys	133	H5
Chesterhill Mdloth	211	L6
Chester-le-Street Dur	181	G8
Chester Moor Dur	169	H1
Chesters Border	189	G2
Chesters Border	189	H4
Chesterton Cambs	87	K3
Chesterton Cambs	102	C4
Chesterton Gloucs	64	E7
Chesterton Oxon	66	E3
Chesterton Shrops	97	H4
Chesterton Staffs	114	C2
Chesterton Green Warwks	83	H4
Chesterwood Nthumb	179	J6
Chestfield Kent	40	F2
Chestnut Street Kent	53	J6
Cheston Devon	7	K3
Cheswardine Shrops	114	A5
Cheswick Nthumb	203	G4
Cheswick Green Solhll	98	E8
Chetnole Dorset	16	B1
Chettiscombe Devon	29	H7
Chettisham Cambs	103	L6
Chettle Dorset	32	F8
Chetton Shrops	96	F5
Chetwode Bucks	66	F1
Chetwynd Wrekin	114	A7
Chetwynd Aston Wrekin	114	B8
Cheveley Cambs	88	D3
Chevening Kent	52	A7
Cheverton IoW	19	G6
Chevington Suffk	88	F3
Chevithorne Devon	29	H7
Chew Magna BaNES	45	H6
Chew Moor Bolton	139	K6
Chew Stoke BaNES	45	H6
Chewton Keynsham BaNES	45	K5
Chewton Mendip Somset	45	H8
Chichacott Devon	12	E3
Chicheley M Keyn	85	H6
Chichester W Susx	20	E6
Chichester Crematorium W Susx	20	E5
Chickerell Dorset	16	C6
Chickering Suffk	106	E8
Chicklade Wilts	32	F4
Chicksands C Beds	86	C7
Chickward Herefs	79	K4
Chidden Hants	35	K7
Chiddingfold Surrey	36	E4
Chiddingly E Susx	23	J4
Chiddingstone Kent	38	D4
Chiddingstone Causeway Kent	38	E4
Chideock Dorset	15	K4
Chidham W Susx	20	C6
Chidswell Kirk	141	L3
Chieveley W Berk	48	C4
Chignall St James Essex	71	G5
Chignall Smealy Essex	71	G5
Chigwell Essex	70	B8
Chigwell Row Essex	70	C8
Chilbolton Hants	34	E3
Chilcomb Hants	35	G5
Chilcombe Dorset	15	M4
Chilcompton Somset	45	J8
Chilcote Leics	99	H1
Childer Thornton Ches W	129	J4
Child Okeford Dorset	32	D8
Childrey Oxon	48	A2
Child's Ercall Shrops	113	L6
Childswickham Worcs	82	C7
Childwall Lpool	129	K2
Childwick Bury Herts	68	F5
Childwick Green Herts	68	F5
Chilfrome Dorset	16	B3
Chilgrove W Susx	20	D4
Chilham Kent	40	E4
Chilla Devon	12	B2
Chillaton Devon	12	B6
Chillenden Kent	41	J4
Chillerton IoW	19	H6
Chillesford Suffk	91	J5
Chillingham Nthumb	203	H7
Chillington Devon	8	B6
Chillington Somset	30	F8
Chilmark Wilts	33	G4
Chilmington Green Kent	40	C7
Chilson Oxon	65	L3
Chilsworthy Cnwll	12	A8
Chilsworthy Devon	11	L1
Chiltern Green C Beds	68	E3
Chilterns Crematorium Bucks	68	B7
Chilthorne Domer Somset	31	H7
Chilton Bucks	67	G5
Chilton Devon	13	K2
Chilton Dur	169	H5
Chilton Kent	41	H4
Chilton Oxon	48	C2
Chilton Suffk	89	H6
Chilton Candover Hants	35	J3
Chilton Cantelo Somset	31	J6
Chilton Foliat Wilts	47	L5
Chilton Polden Somset	30	E3
Chilton Street Suffk	88	E6
Chilton Trinity Somset	30	D3
Chilwell Notts	116	E4
Chilworth Hants	34	E7
Chilworth Surrey	36	F2
Chimney Oxon	65	M7
Chineham Hants	49	G7
Chingford Gt Lon	69	K8
Chinley Derbys	131	L3
Chinnor Oxon	67	J6
Chipchase Castle Nthumb	179	K4
Chipnall Shrops	114	A5
Chippenham Cambs	88	D1
Chippenham Wilts	46	D4
Chipperfield Herts	68	D6
Chipping Herts	69	K1
Chipping Lancs	147	M7
Chipping Campden Gloucs	82	E7
Chipping Hill Essex	71	K4
Chipping Norton Oxon	65	L2
Chipping Ongar Essex	70	E6
Chipping Sodbury S Glos	45	L3
Chipping Warden Nhants	83	L5
Chipshop Devon	12	B7
Chipstable Somset	29	J5
Chipstead Kent	38	D2
Chipstead Surrey	51	H7
Chirbury Shrops	95	G4
Chirk Wrexhm	112	D4
Chirnside Border	202	D2
Chirnsidebridge Border	202	C2
Chirton Wilts	47	G7
Chisbury Wilts	47	K5
Chiselborough Somset	31	H7
Chiseldon Swindn	47	J3
Chiselhampton Oxon	66	E7
Chisholme Border	188	D4
Chislehurst Gt Lon	51	L5
Chislet Kent	41	H2
Chisley Calder	140	F2
Chiswell Green Herts	68	E6
Chiswick Gt Lon	51	G3
Chiswick End Cambs	87	H6
Chisworth Derbys	131	K2
Chitcombe E Susx	24	E5
Chithurst W Susx	36	C6
Chittering Cambs	87	K1
Chitterne Wilts	33	G2
Chittlehamholt Devon	28	B6
Chittlehampton Devon	27	L5
Chittoe Wilts	46	D5
Chivelstone Devon	8	A7
Chivenor Devon	27	J4
Chiverton Cross Cnwll	4	B5
Chlenry D & G	172	E3
Chobham Surrey	50	B6
Cholderton Wilts	34	B2
Cholesbury Bucks	68	B5
Chollerford Nthumb	179	L5
Chollerton Nthumb	179	L4
Cholmondeston Ches E	130	C7
Cholsey Oxon	48	E2
Cholstrey Herefs	80	B3
Chop Gate N York	161	J3
Choppington Nthumb	181	G2
Chopwell Gatesd	180	D7
Chorley Ches E	113	J4
Chorley Lancs	139	H4
Chorley Shrops	96	F6
Chorley Staffs	98	D1

Chorleywood Herts 68 D7
Chorleywood West Herts 68 C7
Chorlton Ches E. 114 A2
Chorlton-cum-Hardy Manch 130 F1
Chorlton Lane Ches W. 113 G2
Choulton Shrops 95 J5
Chowley Ches W. 129 L8
Chrishall Essex 87 J7
Chrisswell Inver 207 L4
Christchurch Cambs 103 K4
Christchurch Dorset 18 B5
Christchurch Gloucs 63 H4
Christchurch Newpt 44 D1
Christian Malford Wilts 46 D3
Christleton Ches W. 129 K6
Christmas Common Oxon 67 H8
Christmas Pie Surrey 36 D1
Christon N Som 44 D7
Christon Bank Nthumb 191 J2
Christow Devon 13 J5
Christ's Hospital W Susx 37 H5
Chuck Hatch E Susx 38 D6
Chudleigh Devon 13 K6
Chudleigh Knighton Devon 13 K7
Chulmleigh Devon 28 B8
Chunal Derbys 131 L2
Church Lancs 139 L2
Churcham Gloucs 63 M3
Church Aston Wrekin 114 A8
Church Brampton Nhants 84 D2
Church Brough Cumb 167 J7
Church Broughton Derbys 115 K5
Church Cove Cnwll 3 H8
Church Crookham Hants 49 K8
Churchdown Gloucs 64 C3
Church Eaton Staffs 114 C8
Church End Bed 85 L3
Church End Bed 86 C3
Church End Bucks 67 H5
Church End C Beds 68 C3
Church End C Beds 68 C3
Church End C Beds 85 J8
Church End C Beds 85 K8
Church End C Beds 86 D4
Church End C Beds 86 D7
Church End Cambs 102 B8
Church End Cambs 102 E6
Church End Cambs 103 G7
Church End Essex 70 F3
Church End Essex 71 H2
Church End Essex 71 H4
Churchend Essex 72 E8
Church End Gloucs 81 K8
Church End Gt Lon 51 H1
Church End Herts 68 E5
Church End Herts 69 H1
Church End Herts 70 C3
Church End Lincs 119 H1
Church End Lincs 145 L8
Church End Warwks 99 H5
Church End Warwks 99 H5
Church Enstone Oxon 66 A2
Church Fenton N York 151 H8
Churchfield Sandw 98 C5
Churchgate Herts 69 K6
Churchgate Street Essex 70 C5
Church Green Devon 14 E3
Church Gresley Derbys 115 M7
Church Hanborough Oxon 66 B4
Church Hill Staffs 98 C1
Church Houses N York 161 L3
Churchill Devon 15 G2
Churchill Devon 27 L3
Churchill N Som 44 E7
Churchill Oxon 65 L2
Churchill Worcs 81 L4
Churchill Worcs 97 K7
Churchinford Somset 30 B8
Church Knowle Dorset 17 H6
Church Laneham Notts 135 G4
Church Langton Leics 100 F5
Church Lawford Warwks 99 M8
Church Lawton Ches E. 130 F8
Church Leigh Staffs 115 G6
Church Lench Worcs 82 B5
Church Mayfield Staffs 115 J3
Church Minshull Ches E 130 C7
Church Norton W Susx 20 E7
Churchover Warwks 100 B7
Church Preen Shrops 96 C4
Church Pulverbatch Shrops 95 K3
Churchstanton Somset 30 B7
Churchstoke Powys 95 G4
Churchstow Devon 7 K5
Church Stowe Nhants 84 C4
Church Street Essex 88 F6
Church Street Kent 52 F4
Church Street Suffk 107 K6
Church Stretton Shrops 95 L4

Churchthorpe Lincs 145 J8
Churchtown Bpool 146 F7
Churchtown Cnwll 10 F7
Churchtown Derbys 132 E7
Churchtown Devon 28 B2
Churchtown IoM 154 f3
Churchtown Lancs 147 J7
Church Town N Linc 143 K6
Churchtown Sefton 138 D4
Church Village Rhondd 43 G4
Church Warsop Notts 133 L6
Church Wilne Derbys 116 D5
Churnsike Lodge Nthumb 178 F3
Churston Ferrers Torbay 8 D4
Churt Surrey 36 C3
Churton Ches W. 129 K8
Churwell Leeds 141 L2
Chwilog Gwynd 109 H4
Chyandour Cnwll 2 D5
Chyanvounder Cnwll 3 G6
Chyeowling Cnwll 3 K3
Chyvarloe Cnwll 3 G6
Cil Powys 94 E3
Cilcain Flints 128 E6
Cilcennin Cerdgn 76 F3
Cilcewydd Powys 94 F3
Cilfrew Neath 57 L5
Cilfynydd Rhondd 43 H3
Cilgerran Pembks 75 L4
Cilgwyn Carmth 59 K3
Cilgwyn Gwynd 109 J1
Ciliau-Aeron Cerdgn 76 F4
Cilmaengwyn Neath 57 K4
Cilmery Powys 78 D5
Cilrhedyn Pembks 58 A2
Cilsan Carmth 59 H4
Ciltalgarth Gwynd 111 G3
Cilycwm Carmth 77 L7
Cimla Neath 57 L5
Cinderford Gloucs 63 K4
Cinder Hill Wolves 97 L6
Cippenham Slough 50 B3
Cirencester Gloucs 64 F6
Citadilla N York 160 B3
City Gt Lon 51 J3
City V Glam 42 F6
City Dulas IoA 125 H2
City of London Crematorium
    Gt Lon 51 L2
Clabhach Ag & B. 224 F3
Clachaig Ag & B. 207 J3
Clachan Ag & B. 206 B7
Clachan Ag & B. 216 B3
Clachan Ag & B. 228 D6
Clachan Highld 247 H1
Clachan-a-Luib W Isls 283 c8
Clachan Mor Ag & B. 224 C5
Clachan na Luib W Isls 283 c8
Clachan of Campsie E Duns 209 G3
Clachan-Seil Ag & B. 216 B3
Clachnaharry Highld 251 H2
Clachtoll Highld 270 D3
Clackavoid P & K 233 J7
Clackmannan Clacks 210 B1
Clackmannanshire Bridge Fife ... 210 B2
Clackmarras Moray 266 E4
Clacton-on-Sea Essex 73 J4
Cladich Ag & B 217 H3
Cladswell Worcs 82 C3
Claggan Highld 227 K3
Claigan Highld 258 C6
Clandown BaNES 45 K7
Clanfield Hants 35 L7
Clanfield Oxon 65 L6
Clannaborough Devon 13 H2
Clanville Hants 34 D1
Clanville Somset 31 K4
Claonaig Ag & B. 206 D7
Clapgate Dorset 17 K2
Clapgate Herts 70 C2
Clapham Bed 85 L3
Clapham Devon 13 L5
Clapham Gt Lon 51 H4
Clapham N York 148 C2
Clapham W Susx 21 J5
Clapham Green Bed 85 K4
Clap Hill Kent 40 D7
Clappersgate Cumb 156 F2
Clapton Somset 15 J1
Clapton Somset 45 J8
Clapton-in-Gordano N Som 44 F4
Clapton-on-the-Hill Gloucs 65 H3
Clapworthy Devon 28 B6
Clarach Cerdgn 92 D6
Claravale Gatesd 180 E6
Clarbeston Pembks 55 H3
Clarbeston Road Pembks 55 G3
Clarborough Notts 134 E3
Clare Suffk 88 F6

Clarebrand D & G 175 J2
Clarencefield D & G 176 E5
Clarewood Nthumb 180 B5
Clarilaw Border 188 F3
Clark's Green Surrey 37 J3
Clarkston E Rens 208 F7
Clashmore Highld 263 K2
Clashmore Highld 270 D2
Clashnessie Highld 270 E2
Clashnoir Moray 254 E7
Clathy P & K 221 H3
Clathymore P & K 221 H3
Clatt Abers 255 L6
Clatter Powys 94 B4
Clatterford End Essex 70 F4
Clatworthy Somset 29 J4
Claughton Lancs 147 K7
Claughton Lancs 147 L3
Claughton Wirral 129 G2
Clavelshay Somset 30 C4
Claverdon Warwks 82 E2
Claverham N Som 44 F5
Clavering Essex 70 C1
Claverley Shrops 97 H5
Claverton BaNES 46 A6
Claverton Down BaNES 45 M6
Clawdd-coch V Glam 43 G6
Clawdd-newydd Denbgs 111 L1
Clawthorpe Cumb 157 H7
Clawton Devon 11 L3
Claxby Lincs 136 B1
Claxby Lincs 137 H5
Claxton N York 151 L4
Claxton Norfk 107 G3
Claybrooke Magna Leics 100 B5
Clay Common Suffk 107 K7
Clay Coton Nhants 100 D8
Clay Cross Derbys 133 H7
Clay End Herts 69 J2
Claygate D & G 177 L3
Claygate Kent 39 H4
Claygate Surrey 50 F6
Claygate Cross Kent 38 F2
Clayhall Gt Lon 51 L1
Clayhanger Devon 29 J6
Clayhanger Wsall 98 D3
Clayhidon Devon 29 L7
Clayhill E Susx 24 F3
Clayhill Hants 18 D2
Clayhithe Cambs 87 K2
Clayock Highld 279 L4
Claypit Cambs 87 G4
Claypits Gloucs 63 M6
Claypole Lincs 117 M2
Claythorpe Lincs 137 H4
Clayton C Brad 141 H2
Clayton Donc 142 C6
Clayton W Susx 22 D4
Clayton Green Lancs 139 H3
Clayton-le-Moors Lancs 139 M2
Clayton-le-Woods Lancs 139 H3
Clayton West Kirk 141 L5
Clayworth Notts 134 E2
Cleadale Highld 236 F3
Cleadon S Tyne 181 J6
Clearbrook Devon 7 G2
Clearwell Gloucs 63 H5
Clearwell Meend Gloucs 63 H5
Cleasby N York 169 H8
Cleat Ork 275 c6
Cleatlam Dur 168 E7
Cleator Cumb 164 D7
Cleator Moor Cumb 164 D7
Cleckheaton Kirk 141 J3
Cleedownton Shrops 96 D7
Cleehill Shrops 96 D8
Clee St Margaret Shrops 96 D6
Cleestanton Shrops 96 D7
Cleethorpes NE Lin 145 J6
Cleeton St Mary Shrops 96 E7
Cleeve N Som 44 F5
Cleeve Oxon 48 F3
Cleeve Hill Gloucs 64 E2
Cleeve Prior Worcs 82 C5
Cleghornie E Loth 212 D2
Clehonger Herefs 80 B7
Cleish P & K 221 K7
Cleland N Lans 209 L7
Clement's End C Beds 68 C4
Clement Street Kent 52 C5
Clenamacrie Ag & B 216 E2
Clench Common Wilts 47 H6
Clenchwarton Norfk 120 D7
Clenerty Abers 268 D4
Clent Worcs 97 L7
Cleobury Mortimer Shrops 96 F8

Cleobury North Shrops 96 E6
Cleongart Ag & B 192 D2
Clephanton Highld 252 F2
Clerkhill D & G 187 L6
Cleuch-head D & G 185 K3
Clevancy Wilts 46 F4
Clevedon N Som 44 E5
Cleveley Oxon 66 B2
Cleveleys Lancs 146 F7
Cleverton Wilts 46 E2
Clewer Somset 31 G1
Cley next the Sea Norfk 122 A3
Cliburn Cumb 166 E5
Cliddesden Hants 35 K1
Cliff Warwks 99 G4
Cliffe Lancs 139 L1
Cliffe Medway 52 F4
Cliffe N York 143 G2
Cliffe N York 169 G7
Cliff End E Susx 25 G4
Cliffe Woods Medway 52 F4
Clifford Herefs 79 J6
Clifford Leeds 150 F7
Clifford Chambers Warwks 82 E5
Clifford's Mesne Gloucs 63 K2
Cliffsend Kent 41 K2
Clifton Bristl 45 H4
Clifton C Beds 86 D7
Clifton C Nott 116 F4
Clifton C York 151 J5
Clifton Calder 141 J3
Clifton Cumb 166 C5
Clifton Derbys 115 K3
Clifton Devon 27 L3
Clifton Donc 142 E8
Clifton Lancs 138 F2
Clifton N York 150 B6
Clifton Nthumb 180 F2
Clifton Oxon 66 C1
Clifton Salfd 140 A7
Clifton Worcs 81 J6
Clifton Campville Staffs 99 H1
Clifton Hampden Oxon 66 D7
Clifton Reynes M Keyn 85 H5
Clifton upon Dunsmore
    Warwks 100 C8
Clifton upon Teme Worcs 81 G3
Cliftonville Kent 41 L1
Climping W Susx 21 G6
Clink Somset 32 C1
Clint N York 150 C4
Clinterty C Aber 245 J1
Clint Green Norfk 105 L1
Clintmains Border 201 J6
Clipiau Gwynd 93 H1
Clippesby Norfk 123 J8
Clipsham Rutlnd 118 C8
Clipston Nhants 100 F7
Clipston Notts 117 H5
Clipstone C Beds 68 B2
Clipstone Notts 134 B7
Clitheroe Lancs 148 C7
Clive Shrops 113 H6
Clixby Lincs 144 E7
Cloatley Wilts 46 E1
Clocaenog Denbgs 111 L1
Clochan Moray 267 H4
Clock Face St Hel 129 M2
Cloddiau Powys 94 F2
Clodock Herefs 62 C2
Cloford Somset 32 B2
Clola Abers 257 J3
Clophill C Beds 86 B7
Clopton Nhants 102 B7
Clopton Suffk 90 F4
Clopton Corner Suffk 90 F4
Clopton Green Suffk 88 F4
Clopton Green Suffk 89 K3
Clos du Valle Guern 9 k1
Closeburn D & G 186 D7
Closeburnmill D & G. 186 D7
Closeclark IoM 154 c7
Closworth Somset 16 A1
Clothall Herts 69 H1
Clotton Ches W. 129 M6
Cloudesley Bush Warwks 100 A6
Clouds Herefs 80 D7
Clough Oldham 140 E6
Clough Foot Calder 140 D3
Clough Head Calder 141 H4
Cloughton N York 163 H4
Cloughton Newlands N York 163 h3
Clousta Shet 281 d5
Clova Angus 233 M1
Clovelly Devon 26 E6
Clovenfords Border 200 F6
Clovulin Highld 228 F3
Clow Bridge Lancs 140 B2
Clowne Derbys 133 K4

Clows Top Worcs 81 G1
Cloy Wrexhm 112 F3
Cluanie Inn Highld 239 H1
Cluanie Lodge Highld 239 H2
Clubworthy Cnwll 11 K4
Clugston D & G 173 J3
Clun Shrops 95 H7
Clunas Highld 253 G2
Clunbury Shrops 95 J7
Clunderwen Carmth 55 J3
Clune Highld 252 E6
Clunes Highld 239 K6
Clungunford Shrops 95 K7
Clunie P & K 233 H6
Clunton Shrops 95 H7
Cluny Fife 222 D8
Clutton BaNES 45 J7
Clutton Ches W 113 G1
Clutton Hill BaNES 45 J7
Clwt-y-bont Gwynd 125 K7
Clydach Mons 61 K4
Clydach Swans 57 J4
Clydach Vale Rhondd 42 E3
Clydebank W Duns 208 E5
Clydebank Crematorium
   W Duns 208 E4
Clydey Pembks 75 M5
Clyffe Pypard Wilts 47 G3
Clynder Ag & B 207 L2
Clyne Neath 60 B7
Clynnog-fawr Gwynd 109 G2
Clyro Powys 79 H6
Clyst Honiton Devon 14 A4
Clyst Hydon Devon 14 B2
Clyst St George Devon 14 A5
Clyst St Lawrence Devon 14 B3
Clyst St Mary Devon 14 A4
Cnoc W Isls 282 g3
Cnwch Coch Cerdgn 92 E8
Coad's Green Cnwll 11 K7
Coal Aston Derbys 133 G4
Coalbrookvale Blae G 61 K5
Coalburn S Lans 198 D6
Coalburns Gatesd 180 D6
Coaley Gloucs 63 M6
Coalhill Essex 71 J7
Coalmoor Wrekin 96 F2
Coalpit Heath S Glos 45 K3
Coal Pool Wsall 98 C3
Coalport Wrekin 96 F3
Coalsnaughton Clacks 221 G8
Coal Street Suffk 90 F1
Coaltown of Balgonie Fife 222 E7
Coaltown of Wemyss Fife 222 E8
Coalville Leics 99 L1
Coanwood Nthumb 178 F7
Coat Somset 31 G6
Coatbridge N Lans 209 J6
Coatdyke N Lans 209 K6
Coate Swindn 47 J2
Coate Wilts 46 F6
Coates Cambs 102 F4
Coates Gloucs 64 E7
Coates Lincs 135 H3
Coates Notts 135 G3
Coates W Susx 21 G3
Coatham R & Cl 170 E5
Coatham Mundeville Darltn 169 H6
Cobbaton Devon 27 L5
Coberley Gloucs 64 D4
Cobhall Common Herefs 80 B8
Cobham Kent 52 E5
Cobham Surrey 50 E7
Coblers Green Essex 71 G3
Cobley Dorset 33 H6
Cobnash Herefs 80 B3
Cobo Guern 9 j2
Cobridge C Stke 114 D2
Coburby Abers 269 G3
Cock Alley Derbys 133 H5
Cockayne N York 161 K3
Cockayne Hatley C Beds 86 F5
Cock Bank Wrexhm 112 E2
Cock Bevington Warwks 82 C5
Cock Bridge Abers 243 J2
Cockburnspath Border 213 G5
Cock Clarks Essex 71 K6
Cock & End Suffk 88 E4
Cockenzie and Port Seton
   E Loth 211 L4
Cocker Bar Lancs 139 G3
Cocker Brook Lancs 139 L3
Cockerham Lancs 147 J5
Cockermouth Cumb 164 F4
Cockernhoe Herts 68 D4
Cockersdale Leeds 141 K2
Cockett Swans 57 H6
Cockfield Dur 168 E6
Cockfield Suffk 89 H4

Cockfosters Gt Lon 69 H7
Cock Green Essex 71 G3
Cocking W Susx 20 E3
Cocking Causeway W Susx 20 E3
Cockington Torbay 8 D2
Cocklake Somset 31 G1
Cockley Beck Cumb 156 C2
Cockley Cley Norfk 104 F3
Cock Marling E Susx 24 F3
Cockpole Green Wokham 49 J3
Cocks Cnwll 4 C4
Cockshutford Shrops 96 D6
Cockshutt Shrops 113 G5
Cockthorpe Norfk 121 L3
Cockwells Cnwll 2 E4
Cockwood Devon 14 A6
Cockwood Somset 30 B2
Cockyard Derbys 131 L4
Cockyard Herefs 80 A8
Coddenham Suffk 90 D4
Coddington Ches W 129 K8
Coddington Herefs 81 G6
Coddington Notts 117 L1
Codford St Mary Wilts 33 G3
Codford St Peter Wilts 33 G3
Codicote Herts 69 G3
Codmore Hill W Susx 21 H3
Codnor Derbys 116 C2
Codrington S Glos 45 L3
Codsall Staffs 97 K3
Codsall Wood Staffs 97 J2
Coedely Rhondd 42 F4
Coedkernew Newpt 44 B2
Coed Morgan Mons 62 D5
Coedpoeth Wrexhm 112 D1
Coed Talon Flints 129 G7
Coedway Powys 112 E8
Coed-y-Bryn Cerdgn 76 C6
Coed-y-caerau Newpt 44 D1
Coed-y-paen Mons 62 C7
Coed-yr-ynys Powys 61 J3
Coed Ystumgwern Gwynd 109 K6
Coelbren Powys 60 C5
Coffinswell Devon 8 D1
Coffle End Bed 85 K3
Cofton Devon 13 M6
Cofton Hackett Worcs 98 C8
Cogan V Glam 43 J7
Cogenhoe Nhants 84 F3
Cogges Oxon 65 M5
Coggeshall Essex 71 K3
Coggin's Mill E Susx 23 K2
Coignafearn Highld 251 J8
Coilacriech Abers 243 K4
Coilantogle Stirlg 219 K5
Coillore Highld 246 E1
Coity Brdgnd 42 D5
Col W Isls 282 g3
Colaboll Highld 272 E6
Colan Cnwll 4 E3
Colaton Raleigh Devon 14 C5
Colbost Highld 258 C7
Colburn N York 160 B3
Colby Cumb 166 F6
Colby IoM 154 b7
Colby Norfk 122 E5
Colchester Essex 72 E2
Colchester Crematorium
   Essex 72 E3
Cold Ash W Berk 48 D5
Cold Ashby Nhants 100 E8
Cold Ashton S Glos 45 L4
Cold Aston Gloucs 65 H3
Coldbackie Highld 277 K4
Coldbeck Cumb 158 C2
Cold Blow Pembks 55 J4
Cold Brayfield M Keyn 85 H5
Cold Cotes N York 148 C2
Coldean Br & H 22 E5
Coldeast Devon 13 J7
Colden Calder 140 E2
Colden Common Hants 35 G6
Coldfair Green Suffk 91 K3
Coldham Cambs 103 J3
Cold Hanworth Lincs 135 L3
Coldharbour Cnwll 4 B5
Coldharbour Devon 29 J8
Coldharbour Gloucs 63 H6
Cold Harbour Herts 68 F4
Cold Harbour Oxon 48 F3
Coldharbour Surrey 37 H2
Cold Harbour Wilts 32 E2
Cold Hatton Wrekin 113 K7
Cold Hatton Heath Wrekin 113 K7
Cold Hesledon Dur 169 L2
Cold Hiendley Wakefd 142 B5
Cold Higham Nhants 84 C4
Coldingham Border 213 K6

Cold Kirby N York 161 H6
Coldmeece Staffs 114 D5
Cold Newton Leics 100 F3
Cold Northcott Cnwll 11 H5
Cold Norton Essex 71 K7
Cold Overton Leics 101 H2
Coldred Kent 41 J6
Coldridge Devon 13 G1
Coldstream Border 202 C5
Coldwaltham W Susx 21 H3
Coldwell Herefs 80 A8
Coldwells Abers 257 H4
Cold Weston Shrops 96 C6
Cole Somset 31 L4
Colebatch Shrops 95 H6
Colebrook C Plym 7 G3
Colebrook Devon 14 B2
Colebrooke Devon 13 H3
Coleby Lincs 135 K7
Coleby N Linc 143 M4
Cole End Warwks 99 G5
Coleford Devon 13 H2
Coleford Gloucs 63 H5
Coleford Somset 31 L1
Coleford Water Somset 29 L4
Colegate End Norfk 106 D6
Cole Green Herts 69 H5
Cole Green Herts 70 B1
Cole Henley Hants 34 F1
Colehill Dorset 17 K2
Coleman Green Herts 69 G4
Coleman's Hatch E Susx 38 C6
Colemere Shrops 113 G5
Colemore Hants 35 L5
Colemore Green Shrops 97 G4
Colenden P & K 221 K1
Coleorton Leics 116 C8
Colerne Wilts 46 B5
Colesbourne Gloucs 64 E4
Cole's Cross Devon 8 A5
Coles Cross Dorset 15 J2
Colesden Bed 86 C4
Coles Green Suffk 90 C7
Coleshill Bucks 68 B8
Coleshill Oxon 65 K8
Coleshill Warwks 99 G5
Colestocks Devon 14 C3
Coley BaNES 45 H7
Colgate W Susx 37 K4
Colinsburgh Fife 223 H6
Colinton C Edin 211 H5
Colintraive Ag & B 207 G4
Colkirk Norfk 121 K6
Coll Ag & B 225 G4
Coll W Isls 282 g3
Collace P & K 222 C1
Collafirth Shet 281 d3
Collaton Devon 7 L7
Collaton St Mary Torbay 8 C3
College of Roseisle Moray 266 C3
College Town Br For 49 K6
Collessie Fife 222 D4
Colleton Mills Devon 28 B7
Collier Row Gt Lon 52 B1
Collier's End Herts 69 K3
Collier's Green E Susx 24 E3
Colliers Green Kent 39 J5
Collier Street Kent 39 H4
Colliery Row Sundld 169 J1
Collieston Abers 257 J6
Collin D & G 176 D4
Collingbourne Ducis Wilts 47 K8
Collingbourne Kingston Wilts 47 K7
Collingham Leeds 150 E6
Collingham Notts 135 G7
Collington Herefs 80 F3
Collingtree Nhants 84 E4
Collins Green Warrtn 130 A1
Collins Green Worcs 81 G4
Colliston Angus 234 F6
Colliton Devon 14 C2
Collyweston Nhants 101 M3
Colmonell S Ayrs 182 E5
Colmworth Bed 86 C4
Colnabaichin Abers 243 J2
Colnbrook Slough 50 C3
Colne Cambs 103 H8
Colne Lancs 148 F7
Colne Bridge Kirk 141 J4
Colne Edge Lancs 148 F7
Colne Engaine Essex 71 K1
Colney Norfk 106 D2
Colney Heath Herts 69 G6
Colney Street Herts 68 F6
Coln Rogers Gloucs 65 G5
Coln St Aldwyns Gloucs 65 H6
Coln St Dennis Gloucs 65 G5
Colonsay Ag & B 214 D5
Colpy Abers 256 B5

Colquhar Border 200 D5
Colquite Cnwll 10 E8
Colscott Devon 26 F7
Colsterdale N York 159 L6
Colsterworth Lincs 118 B6
Colston Bassett Notts 117 J5
Coltfield Moray 266 C3
Colt Hill Hants 49 H8
Coltishall Norfk 122 F7
Colton Cumb 156 D5
Colton Leeds 142 B1
Colton N York 151 H6
Colton Norfk 106 C2
Colton Staffs 115 G7
Colt's Hill Kent 39 G4
Columbjohn Devon 13 M3
Colva Powys 79 H4
Colvend D & G 175 L4
Colwall Herefs 81 H6
Colwell Nthumb 179 M4
Colwich Staffs 115 G7
Colwick Notts 117 G3
Colwinston V Glam 42 E6
Colworth W Susx 20 F6
Colwyn Bay Conwy 127 G4
Colwyn Bay Crematorium
   Conwy 127 G4
Colyford Devon 14 F4
Colyton Devon 14 F4
Combe Devon 7 L7
Combe Herefs 79 L3
Combe Oxon 66 B4
Combe W Berk 48 A6
Combe Almer Dorset 17 J3
Combe Common Surrey 36 E4
Combe Down BaNES 45 M6
Combe Fishacre Devon 8 C2
Combe Florey Somset 29 L4
Combe Hay BaNES 45 L7
Combeinteignhead Devon 13 L8
Combe Martin Devon 27 K2
Combe Raleigh Devon 14 E2
Comberbach Ches W 130 C4
Comberford Staffs 99 G2
Comberton Cambs 87 H4
Comberton Herefs 80 C2
Combe St Nicholas Somset 30 D8
Combpyne Devon 15 G4
Combridge Staffs 115 H4
Combrook Warwks 83 H5
Combs Derbys 131 L4
Combs Suffk 90 B4
Combs Ford Suffk 90 B4
Combwich Somset 30 C2
Comers Abers 244 F2
Comhampton Worcs 81 J2
Commercial End Cambs 87 L3
Commins Coch Powys 93 H3
Commondale N York 170 F8
Common Edge Bpool 138 C1
Common End Cumb 164 D6
Common Moor Cnwll 6 A1
Common Platt Wilts 47 G2
Commonside Ches W 130 A5
Commonside Derbys 115 L3
Common Side Derbys 133 G4
Commonwood Shrops 113 H6
Commonwood Wrexhm 112 F1
Compass Somset 30 D4
Compstall Stockp 131 J2
Compstonend D & G 175 G4
Compton Devon 8 C2
Compton Hants 34 D5
Compton Hants 34 F5
Compton Staffs 97 J6
Compton Surrey 36 E2
Compton W Berk 48 D3
Compton W Susx 20 C4
Compton Wilts 47 H8
Compton Abbas Dorset 32 E7
Compton Abdale Gloucs 64 D4
Compton Bassett Wilts 46 F4
Compton Beauchamp Oxon 47 K2
Compton Bishop Somset 44 F7
Compton Chamberlayne Wilts 33 H5
Compton Dando BaNES 45 J6
Compton Dundon Somset 31 H4
Compton Durville Somset 30 F7
Compton Greenfield S Glos 45 H3
Compton Martin BaNES 45 G7
Compton Pauncefoot Somset 31 L5
Compton Valence Dorset 16 B4
Comrie Fife 210 D1
Comrie P & K 220 D3
Conaglen House Highld 229 G2
Conchra Highld 248 E6
Concraigie P & K 233 G6
Conder Green Lancs 147 J4
Conderton Worcs 81 M7

Condicote Gloucs	65	H2
Condorrat N Lans	209	K4
Condover Shrops	96	B2
Coney Hill Gloucs	64	B3
Coneyhurst Common W Susx	37	H6
Coneysthorpe N York	151	M2
Coneythorpe N York	150	E4
Coney Weston Suffk	105	J7
Conford Hants	36	B4
Congdon's Shop Cnwll	11	K7
Congerstone Leics	99	K2
Congham Norfk	120	F6
Congleton Ches E	131	G7
Congl-y-wal Gwynd	110	D3
Congresbury N Som	44	E6
Congreve Staffs	97	K1
Conheath D & G	176	C5
Conicavel Moray	253	J1
Coningsby Lincs	136	D8
Conington Cambs	87	G2
Conington Cambs	102	D6
Conisbrough Donc	142	D8
Conisholme Lincs	145	K8
Coniston Cumb	156	D3
Coniston E R Yk	144	F1
Coniston Cold N York	148	F5
Conistone N York	149	H2
Connah's Quay Flints	129	G6
Connel Ag & B	228	E8
Connel Park E Ayrs	197	H8
Connor Downs Cnwll	2	F3
Conon Bridge Highld	250	F1
Cononley N York	149	H6
Consall Staffs	114	F2
Consett Dur	180	D8
Constable Burton N York	159	L4
Constable Lee Lancs	140	B3
Constantine Cnwll	3	J5
Constantine Bay Cnwll	10	B7
Contin Highld	262	D8
Conwy Conwy	126	F4
Conyer Kent	40	C2
Conyer's Green Suffk	89	H2
Cooden E Susx	24	C6
Cookbury Devon	12	A2
Cookbury Wick Devon	11	M2
Cookham W & M	49	L2
Cookham Dean W & M	49	L2
Cookham Rise W & M	49	L2
Cookhill Worcs	82	C3
Cookley Suffk	107	G8
Cookley Worcs	97	J7
Cookley Green Oxon	49	G1
Cookney Abers	245	J5
Cooksbridge E Susx	22	F4
Cooksey Green Worcs	81	L1
Cook's Green Essex	73	J3
Cooks Green Suffk	89	K4
Cookshill Staffs	114	E3
Cooksland Cnwll	5	J1
Cooksmill Green Essex	70	F6
Cookson Green Ches W	130	B5
Coolham W Susx	37	H6
Cooling Medway	53	G4
Cooling Street Medway	52	F4
Coombe Cnwll	3	G3
Coombe Cnwll	3	L3
Coombe Cnwll	4	F4
Coombe Devon	13	J6
Coombe Devon	13	L7
Coombe Devon	14	C4
Coombe Gloucs	63	M8
Coombe Hants	35	K6
Coombe Wilts	33	K1
Coombe Bissett Wilts	33	K5
Coombe Cellars Devon	13	L8
Coombe Cross Hants	35	K6
Coombe Hill Gloucs	64	C2
Coombe Keynes Dorset	17	G6
Coombe Pafford Torbay	8	D2
Coombes W Susx	21	L5
Coombes-Moor Herefs	79	L3
Coombe Street Somset	32	C4
Coombeswood Dudley	98	B6
Coopersale Common Essex	70	C6
Coopersale Street Essex	70	C6
Cooper's Corner Kent	38	D3
Coopers Green E Susx	23	H3
Coopers Green Herts	69	G5
Cooper Street Kent	41	J3
Cooper Turning Bolton	139	J6
Cootham W Susx	21	J4
Copdock Suffk	90	D7
Copford Green Essex	72	D3
Copgrove N York	150	D3
Copister Shet	281	e4
Cople Bed	86	C5
Copley Calder	141	G3
Copley Dur	168	D5

Copley Tamesd	140	E8
Coplow Dale Derbys	132	C4
Copmanthorpe C York	151	J6
Copmere End Staffs	114	C5
Copp Lancs	147	H7
Coppathorne Cnwll	11	H3
Coppenhall Staffs	114	E7
Coppenhall Moss Ches E	130	D8
Copperhouse Cnwll	2	F3
Coppicegate Shrops	97	G7
Coppingford Cambs	102	D7
Coppins Corner Kent	40	B5
Copplestone Devon	13	H2
Coppull Lancs	139	H5
Coppull Moor Lancs	139	H5
Copsale W Susx	37	J6
Copster Green Lancs	139	K1
Copston Magna Warwks	99	M5
Cop Street Kent	41	J3
Copthall Green Essex	70	B7
Copt Heath Solhll	98	F7
Copt Hewick N York	150	D2
Copthorne Cnwll	11	K4
Copthorne W Susx	37	M3
Copt Oak Leics	100	B1
Copy's Green Norfk	121	L4
Copythorne Hants	34	C8
Coram Street Suffk	89	K6
Corbets Tey Gt Lon	52	C2
Corbière Jersey	9	a3
Corbridge Nthumb	180	B6
Corby Nhants	101	K5
Corby Glen Lincs	118	C6
Corby Hill Cumb	178	B7
Cordon N Ayrs	195	G5
Cordwell Derbys	132	F4
Coreley Shrops	96	E8
Cores End Bucks	49	L2
Corfe Somset	30	C7
Corfe Castle Dorset	17	J6
Corfe Mullen Dorset	17	J3
Corfton Shrops	96	B6
Corgarff Abers	243	J2
Corhampton Hants	35	J6
Corks Pond Kent	39	G5
Corley Warwks	99	J6
Corley Ash Warwks	99	J6
Corley Moor Warwks	99	H6
Cormuir Angus	233	L2
Cornard Tye Suffk	89	H7
Corndon Devon	13	G5
Corner Row Lancs	138	E1
Corney Cumb	155	K4
Cornforth Dur	169	J4
Cornhill Abers	267	M4
Cornhill-on-Tweed Nthumb	202	D5
Cornholme Calder	140	D3
Cornish Hall End Essex	88	D7
Cornoigmore Ag & B	224	C6
Cornriggs Dur	167	K2
Cornsay Dur	168	F2
Cornsay Colliery Dur	168	F2
Corntown Highld	262	F8
Corntown V Glam	42	D6
Cornwell Oxon	65	K2
Cornwood Devon	7	H3
Cornworthy Devon	8	B4
Corpach Highld	239	H8
Corpusty Norfk	122	C5
Corrachree Abers	244	B3
Corran Highld	229	G3
Corran Highld	238	D2
Corrany IoM	154	f4
Corrie D & G	177	G3
Corrie N Ayrs	195	G2
Corriecravie N Ayrs	193	J4
Corriegills N Ayrs	195	G4
Corriegour Lodge Hotel		
Highld	239	M5
Corriemoille Highld	262	C7
Corrimony Highld	250	C5
Corringham Lincs	135	H2
Corringham Thurr	52	F2
Corris Gwynd	93	G2
Corris Uchaf Gwynd	92	F2
Corrow Ag & B	217	K7
Corry Highld	247	K4
Corscombe Devon	12	E3
Corscombe Dorset	15	L2
Corse Gloucs	64	A2
Corse Lawn Gloucs	64	B1
Corsham Wilts	46	C5
Corsindae Abers	244	F2
Corsley Wilts	32	D2
Corsley Heath Wilts	32	D2
Corsock D & G	185	J7
Corston BaNES	45	K6
Corston Wilts	46	D2
Corstorphine C Edin	211	G4

Cors-y-Gedol Gwynd	109	L7
Cortachy Angus	234	B3
Corton Suffk	107	L4
Corton Wilts	32	F3
Corton Denham Somset	31	K6
Coruanan Highld	229	H2
Corwen Denbgs	111	L3
Coryates Dorset	16	B5
Coryton Devon	12	B6
Coryton Thurr	52	F2
Cosby Leics	100	C4
Coseley Dudley	97	L4
Cosford Shrops	97	H2
Cosgrove Nhants	84	F6
Cosham C Port	19	L3
Cosheston Pembks	55	G6
Coshieville P & K	231	L5
Cossall Notts	116	E3
Cossall Marsh Notts	116	E3
Cossington Leics	100	D1
Cossington Somset	30	E3
Costessey Norfk	106	D1
Costock Notts	116	F6
Coston Leics	117	M7
Coston Norfk	106	C2
Cote Oxon	65	M6
Cote Somset	30	E2
Cotebrook Ches W	130	B6
Cotehill Cumb	166	B1
Cotes Cumb	157	G5
Cotes Leics	116	F7
Cotes Staffs	114	C4
Cotesbach Leics	100	C7
Cotes Heath Staffs	114	C4
Cotford St Luke Somset	30	A5
Cotgrave Notts	117	H4
Cotham Notts	117	L2
Cothal Abers	256	F8
Cotham Notts	117	L2
Cothelstone Somset	30	B4
Cotherstone Dur	168	C6
Cothill Oxon	66	C7
Cotleigh Devon	14	E2
Cotmanhay Derbys	116	D3
Coton Cambs	87	H3
Coton Nhants	84	D1
Coton Shrops	113	J4
Coton Staffs	98	F2
Coton Staffs	114	C7
Coton Staffs	114	F5
Coton Clanford Staffs	114	D7
Coton Hayes Staffs	114	F5
Coton Hill Shrops	96	B1
Coton in the Clay Staffs	115	K5
Coton in the Elms Derbys	115	L8
Coton Park Derbys	115	M7
Cott Devon	8	B3
Cottam E R Yk	152	F3
Cottam Lancs	139	G1
Cottam Notts	135	G4
Cottenham Cambs	87	J2
Cotterdale N York	158	E4
Cottered Herts	69	J1
Cotteridge Birm	98	D7
Cotterstock Nhants	102	A5
Cottesbrooke Nhants	100	F8
Cottesmore Rutlnd	101	K1
Cottingham E R Yk	144	D1
Cottingham Nhants	101	J5
Cottingley C Brad	149	K8
Cottingley Hall Crematorium		
Leeds	141	L2
Cottisford Oxon	66	E1
Cotton Suffk	90	C2
Cotton End Bed	86	B6
Cotton Tree Lancs	148	F7
Cottown Abers	255	M6
Cottown Abers	256	D8
Cottown of Gight Abers	256	E4
Cotts Devon	6	E2
Cotwall Wrekin	113	K8
Cotwalton Staffs	114	E4
Couch's Mill Cnwll	5	K3
Coughton Herefs	63	H3
Coughton Warwks	82	C3
Coulaghailtro Ag & B	206	A6
Coulags Highld	248	F3
Coulderton Cumb	155	H1
Coull Abers	244	B3
Coulport Ag & B	207	L2
Coulsdon Gt Lon	51	J7
Coulston Wilts	46	D8
Coulter S Lans	199	H6
Coultershaw Bridge W Susx	21	G3
Coultings Somset	30	C3
Coulton N York	161	K7
Coultra Fife	222	F3
Cound Shrops	96	D2
Coundlane Shrops	96	D2
Coundon Dur	169	G5

Coundon Grange Dur	169	G5
Countersett N York	159	G5
Countess Wilts	33	K2
Countess Cross Essex	72	C1
Countess Wear Devon	13	M5
Countesthorpe Leics	100	D4
Counties Crematorium Nhants	84	E4
Countisbury Devon	28	C1
Coupar Angus P & K	233	K7
Coup Green Lancs	139	H2
Coupland Cumb	167	G5
Coupland Nthumb	202	E7
Cour Ag & B	194	C2
Court-at-Street Kent	40	E8
Courteachan Highld	237	K1
Courteenhall Nhants	84	E4
Court Henry Carmth	59	G4
Courtsend Essex	72	F8
Courtway Somset	30	B4
Cousland Mdloth	211	L5
Cousley Wood E Susx	39	G6
Cove Ag & B	207	L3
Cove Border	213	G4
Cove Devon	29	G7
Cove Hants	49	L7
Cove Highld	260	C2
Cove Bay C Aber	245	L3
Cove Bottom Suffk	107	K7
Covehithe Suffk	107	L7
Coven Staffs	97	K2
Coveney Cambs	103	K7
Covenham St Bartholomew		
Lincs	136	F1
Covenham St Mary Lincs	136	F1
Coven Heath Staffs	97	K2
Coventry Covtry	99	J7
Coverack Cnwll	3	K7
Coverack Bridges Cnwll	3	H5
Coverham N York	159	K5
Covington Cambs	85	L1
Covington S Lans	199	G5
Cowan Bridge Lancs	157	K7
Cowbeech E Susx	23	K4
Cowbit Lincs	119	H7
Cowbridge V Glam	42	F6
Cowdale Derbys	132	B5
Cowden Kent	38	C5
Cowdenbeath Fife	211	G1
Cowden Pound Kent	38	C5
Cowden Station Kent	38	D5
Cowers Lane Derbys	116	A2
Cowes IoW	19	H4
Cowesby N York	161	G5
Cowesfield Green Wilts	34	B6
Cowfold W Susx	37	K6
Cowgill Cumb	158	C5
Cow Green Suffk	90	C2
Cowhill S Glos	45	J1
Cowie Stirlg	209	M1
Cowlam E R Yk	152	E3
Cowley Devon	13	L3
Cowley Gloucs	64	D4
Cowley Gt Lon	50	D3
Cowley Oxon	66	D6
Cowling Lancs	139	J4
Cowling N York	149	H7
Cowling N York	160	C5
Cowlinge Suffk	88	E4
Cowmes Kirk	141	J4
Cowpe Lancs	140	C4
Cowpen Nthumb	181	H3
Cowpen Bewley S on T	170	B5
Cowplain Hants	19	M2
Cowshill Dur	167	K3
Cowslip Green N Som	44	F6
Cowthorpe N York	150	F5
Coxall Herefs	95	J8
Coxbank Ches E	113	L3
Coxbench Derbys	116	C3
Coxbridge Somset	31	J3
Cox Common Suffk	107	H7
Coxford Cnwll	11	H3
Coxford Norfk	121	J5
Coxgreen Staffs	97	H6
Coxheath Kent	39	J3
Coxhoe Dur	169	J3
Coxley Somset	31	H2
Coxley Wakefd	141	L4
Coxley Wick Somset	31	H2
Coxpark Cnwll	12	A8
Coxtie Green Essex	70	E7
Coxwold N York	161	H7
Coychurch Brdgnd	42	E6
Coychurch Crematorium		
Brdgnd	42	D5
Coylton S Ayrs	196	E7
Coylumbridge Highld	242	B1
Coytrahen Brdgnd	42	D4
Crabbs Cross Worcs	82	B2

Crab Orchard Dorset	17	L1
Crabtree W Susx	37	K6
Crabtree Green Wrexhm	112	E3
Crackenthorpe Cumb	166	F6
Crackington Haven Cnwll	11	G3
Crackley Staffs	114	C2
Crackley Warwks	99	J8
Crackleybank Shrops	97	G1
Crackpot N York	159	H3
Cracoe N York	149	H4
Craddock Devon	29	K8
Cradle End Herts	70	C3
Cradley Dudley	97	L6
Cradley Herefs	81	G6
Cradley Heath Sandw	97	L6
Cradoc Powys	60	F1
Crafthole Cnwll	6	D4
Crafton Bucks	67	L3
Crag Foot Lancs	157	F6
Craggan Highld	253	K6
Cragg Hill Leeds	150	B8
Cragg Vale Calder	140	F3
Craghead Dur	180	F8
Crai Powys	60	D2
Craibstone Moray	267	K4
Craichie Angus	234	D6
Craig Angus	235	H4
Craig Highld	249	H2
Craigbank E Ayrs	197	H8
Craigburn Border	200	B2
Craigcefnparc Swans	57	J4
Craigcleuch D & G	177	K2
Craigdam Abers	256	F5
Craigdhu Ag & B	216	C6
Craigearn Abers	245	G1
Craigellachie Moray	254	F3
Craigend P & K	221	K3
Craigend Rens	208	D5
Craigendoran Ag & B	208	A3
Craigends Rens	208	C6
Craighlaw D & G	173	H3
Craighouse Ag & B	205	H3
Craigie P & K	233	H6
Craigie S Ayrs	196	F4
Craigiefold Abers	269	G3
Craigley D & G	175	J3
Craig Llangiwg Neath	57	K4
Craiglockhart C Edin	211	H5
Craigmillar C Edin	211	J4
Craignant Shrops	112	C4
Craigneston D & G	185	J5
Craigneuk N Lans	209	K6
Craigneuk N Lans	209	K7
Craignure Ag & B	227	L5
Craigo Angus	235	H3
Craig Penllyn V Glam	42	E6
Craigrothie Fife	222	F5
Craigruie Stirlg	219	H3
Craig's End Essex	88	E7
Craigton Angus	234	D7
Craigton C Aber	245	J3
Craigton E Rens	208	E8
Craigton Crematorium C Glas	208	F6
Craigton of Airlie Angus	233	M5
Craig-y-Duke Neath	57	K4
Craig-y-nos Powys	60	C4
Crail Fife	223	L5
Crailing Border	189	J1
Craiselound N Linc	143	J8
Crakehall N York	160	C5
Crakehill N York	160	F7
Crakemarsh Staffs	115	H4
Crambe N York	151	M3
Cramlington Nthumb	181	G3
Cramond C Edin	211	G4
Cramond Bridge C Edin	211	G4
Crampmoor Hants	34	E6
Cranage Ches E	130	E6
Cranberry Staffs	114	C4
Cranborne Dorset	33	H8
Cranbourne Br For	50	A4
Cranbrook Devon	14	A4
Cranbrook Kent	39	J6
Cranbrook Common Kent	39	K5
Crane Moor Barns	141	M7
Crane's Corner Norfk	105	J1
Cranfield C Beds	85	J6
Cranford Devon	26	F6
Cranford Gt Lon	50	E4
Cranford St Andrew Nhants	101	K7
Cranford St John Nhants	101	K8
Cranham Gloucs	64	C4
Cranham Gt Lon	52	C2
Cranhill Warwks	82	D4
Crank St Hel	139	G7
Cranleigh Surrey	37	G3
Cranmer Green Suffk	89	L1
Cranmore IoW	18	F5
Cranmore Somset	31	L2
Cranoe Leics	101	G4
Cransford Suffk	91	H2
Cranshaws Border	212	F6
Cranstal IoM	154	f2
Cranswick E R Yk	152	F5
Crantock Cnwll	4	C3
Cranwell Lincs	118	D2
Cranwich Norfk	104	F4
Cranworth Norfk	105	K3
Craobh Haven Ag & B	216	B5
Crapstone Devon	6	F1
Crarae Ag & B	216	F7
Crask Inn Highld	272	D3
Crask of Aigas Highld	250	E3
Craster Nthumb	191	K2
Craswall Herefs	79	K8
Crateford Staffs	97	K2
Cratfield Suffk	107	G8
Crathes Abers	245	G4
Crathes Crematorium Abers	245	G4
Crathie Abers	243	J4
Crathie Highld	241	G5
Crathorne N York	161	G1
Craven Arms Shrops	95	K6
Crawcrook Gatesd	180	D6
Crawford Lancs	139	G2
Crawford S Lans	186	E2
Crawfordjohn S Lans	186	C2
Crawley Hants	34	F4
Crawley Oxon	65	M4
Crawley W Susx	37	L4
Crawley Down W Susx	38	A6
Crawleyside Dur	168	C3
Crawshawbooth Lancs	140	B3
Crawton Abers	245	J7
Craxe's Green Essex	72	D3
Cray N York	159	G6
Crayford Gt Lon	52	B4
Crayke N York	151	J2
Craymere Beck Norfk	122	B5
Crays Hill Essex	71	H8
Cray's Pond Oxon	48	F3
Craythorne Staffs	115	L6
Craze Lowman Devon	29	H8
Crazies Hill Wokham	49	J3
Creacombe Devon	28	E7
Creagan Inn Ag & B	228	F6
Creag Ghoraidh W Isls	283	c9
Creagorry W Isls	283	c9
Creaguaineach Lodge Highld	230	B2
Creamore Bank Shrops	113	H5
Creaton Nhants	84	D1
Creca D & G	177	H5
Credenhill Herefs	80	B6
Crediton Devon	13	J3
Creebank D & G	183	J7
Creebridge D & G	173	K2
Creech Dorset	17	H6
Creech Heathfield Somset	30	D5
Creech St Michael Somset	30	C6
Creed Cnwll	4	F5
Creekmoor Poole	17	K4
Creekmouth Gt Lon	51	M3
Creeksea Essex	72	D7
Creeting St Mary Suffk	90	C4
Creeton Lincs	118	D7
Creetown D & G	174	D3
Cregneash IoM	154	b8
Creg ny Baa IoM	154	e5
Cregrina Powys	79	G5
Creich Fife	222	E3
Creigiau Cardif	43	G5
Cremyll Cnwll	6	E5
Cressage Shrops	96	D3
Cressbrook Derbys	132	C5
Cresselly Pembks	55	H5
Cressex Bucks	67	K8
Cressing Essex	71	J3
Cresswell Nthumb	191	K7
Cresswell Pembks	55	H5
Cresswell Staffs	114	F4
Creswell Derbys	133	K5
Creswell Green Staffs	98	D1
Cretingham Suffk	90	F3
Cretshengan Ag & B	206	A5
Crewe Ches E	130	D8
Crewe-by-Farndon Ches W	112	F1
Crewe Crematorium Ches E	130	D8
Crewe Green Ches E	130	E8
Crew Green Powys	112	D8
Crewkerne Somset	15	K1
Crews Hill Station Gt Lon	69	J7
Crewton C Derb	116	C5
Crianlarich Stirlg	218	F2
Cribyn Cerdgn	76	F5
Criccieth Gwynd	109	J4
Crich Derbys	116	B1
Crich Carr Derbys	116	B1
Crichton Mdloth	211	L6
Crick Mons	44	F1
Crick Nhants	84	B1
Crickadarn Powys	78	F6
Cricket St Thomas Somset	15	J1
Crickheath Shrops	112	D7
Crickhowell Powys	61	K3
Cricklade Wilts	65	G8
Cricklewood Gt Lon	51	G2
Cridling Stubbs N York	142	E3
Crieff P & K	220	F3
Criggan Cnwll	5	G3
Criggion Powys	112	D8
Crigglestone Wakefd	141	M4
Crimble Rochdl	140	C5
Crimond Abers	269	K5
Crimplesham Norfk	104	C3
Crimscote Warwks	82	F5
Crinaglack Highld	250	D4
Crinan Ag & B	216	B8
Crindledyke N Lans	209	L7
Cringleford Norfk	106	D2
Cringles C Brad	149	J6
Crinow Pembks	55	K4
Cripplesease Cnwll	2	D4
Cripplestyle Dorset	33	J8
Cripp's Corner E Susx	24	D3
Croachy Highld	251	H6
Croanford Cnwll	10	E8
Crockenhill Kent	52	B5
Crocker End Oxon	49	H2
Crockerhill W Susx	20	F5
Crockernwell Devon	13	H4
Crocker's Ash Herefs	63	G4
Crockerton Wilts	32	E2
Crocketford D & G	185	K8
Crockey Hill C York	151	K6
Crockham Hill Kent	38	C3
Crockhurst Street Kent	39	G4
Crockleford Heath Essex	72	F2
Crock Street Somset	30	D8
Croeserw Neath	42	C3
Croes-goch Pembks	74	D6
Croes-lan Cerdgn	76	C6
Croesor Gwynd	110	B3
Croesyceiliog Carmth	58	D5
Croesyceiliog Torfn	62	C7
Croes-y-mwyalch Torfn	62	C8
Croes-y-pant Mons	62	C6
Croft Leics	100	B4
Croft Lincs	137	J7
Croft Warrtn	130	C1
Croftamie Stirlg	208	E2
Croft Mitchell Cnwll	3	H4
Crofton Cumb	165	J1
Crofton Wakefd	142	B4
Crofton Wilts	47	K6
Croft-on-Tees N York	160	D1
Croftown Highld	261	K3
Crofts Moray	266	F6
Crofts Bank Traffd	139	M8
Crofts of Dipple Moray	267	G4
Crofts of Savoch Abers	269	J4
Crofty Swans	56	F6
Crogen Gwynd	111	K4
Croggan Ag & B	227	K7
Croglin Cumb	166	D1
Croick Highld	262	D2
Cromarty Highld	264	B6
Crombie Fife	210	E2
Cromdale Highld	253	L6
Cromer Herts	69	J2
Cromer Norfk	122	E3
Cromford Derbys	132	F8
Cromhall S Glos	45	K1
Cromhall Common S Glos	45	K1
Cromor W Isls	282	g4
Crompton Fold Oldham	140	E6
Cromwell Notts	134	F7
Cronberry E Ayrs	197	H6
Crondall Hants	36	B1
Cronkbourne IoM	154	e6
Cronk-y-Voddy IoM	154	d5
Cronton Knows	129	L2
Crook Cumb	157	G4
Crook Dur	168	F4
Crookdake Cumb	165	G2
Crooke Wigan	139	H6
Crooked End Gloucs	63	J3
Crookedholm E Ayrs	196	E3
Crooked Soley Wilts	47	L4
Crookes Sheff	132	F2
Crookhall Dur	180	D8
Crookham Nthumb	202	E5
Crookham W Berk	48	D6
Crookham Village Hants	49	J8
Crook Inn Border	199	J7
Crooklands Cumb	157	H6
Crook of Devon P & K	221	J7
Cropper Derbys	115	L4
Cropredy Oxon	83	L6
Cropston Leics	100	C1
Cropthorne Worcs	82	B6
Cropton N York	162	D5
Cropwell Bishop Notts	117	H4
Cropwell Butler Notts	117	J4
Cros W Isls	282	h1
Crosbost W Isls	282	g4
Crosby Cumb	164	E3
Crosby IoM	154	d6
Crosby N Linc	143	H5
Crosby Sefton	138	C8
Crosby Garret Cumb	158	C1
Crosby Ravensworth Cumb	166	E7
Crosby Villa Cumb	164	E3
Croscombe Somset	31	K2
Crosemere Shrops	113	G5
Crosland Edge Kirk	141	H5
Crosland Hill Kirk	141	H5
Cross Somset	44	E8
Crossaig Ag & B	194	C1
Crossapol Ag & B	224	C6
Cross Ash Mons	62	E4
Cross-at-Hand Kent	39	K4
Crossbush W Susx	21	H5
Crosscanonby Cumb	164	E3
Cross Coombe Cnwll	4	E4
Crossdale Street Norfk	122	E4
Cross End Bed	85	L4
Cross End Essex	89	G4
Crossens Sefton	138	D4
Cross Flatts C Brad	149	K7
Crossford Fife	210	E2
Crossford S Lans	198	D4
Crossgate Cnwll	11	L5
Crossgate Lincs	119	H6
Crossgate Staffs	114	E4
Crossgatehall E Loth	211	L3
Crossgates E Ayrs	196	D2
Crossgates Fife	210	F1
Cross Gates Leeds	142	A4
Crossgates N York	163	J6
Crossgates Powys	78	F2
Crossgill Lancs	147	L3
Cross Green Devon	11	M5
Cross Green Leeds	141	M2
Cross Green Staffs	97	K2
Cross Green Suffk	89	G4
Cross Green Suffk	89	H4
Cross Green Suffk	89	K4
Crosshands Carmth	55	L2
Cross Hands Carmth	59	J4
Crosshands E Ayrs	196	F5
Cross Hands Pembks	55	H4
Cross Hill Derbys	116	C2
Crosshill Fife	222	B7
Crosshill S Ayrs	183	J2
Cross Hills N York	149	H6
Crosshouse E Ayrs	196	D3
Cross Houses Shrops	96	C3
Cross Houses Shrops	96	F5
Cross in Hand E Susx	23	J3
Cross Inn Cerdgn	76	D4
Cross Inn Cerdgn	77	G2
Cross Inn Pembks	55	J5
Cross Inn Rhondd	43	G5
Cross Keys Ag & B	208	B2
Crosskeys Caerph	43	K3
Cross Keys Wilts	46	C5
Crosskirk Highld	279	H2
Crosslands Cumb	156	E5
Cross Lane IoW	19	H5
Cross Lane Head Shrops	97	G4
Cross Lanes Cnwll	3	H6
Cross Lanes Cnwll	4	C6
Cross Lanes N York	151	H3
Crosslanes Shrops	112	E7
Cross Lanes Wrexhm	112	C6
Crosslee Rens	208	C6
Crossley Kirk	141	K3
Crossmichael D & G	175	J2
Cross Oak Powys	61	J4
Cross of Jackston Abers	256	D5
Cross o' th' hands Derbys	115	M2
Crosspost W Susx	37	L3
Crossroads Abers	244	D5
Crossroads Abers	245	G5
Cross Roads C Brad	149	J4
Cross Street Suffk	106	E4
Crosston Angus	234	E4
Cross Town Ches E	130	E4
Crossway Mons	62	F3
Crossway Powys	78	E4
Crossway Green Mons	63	G8
Crossway Green Worcs	81	J2
Crossways Dorset	16	E5
Crosswell Pembks	75	J5
Crosthwaite Cumb	156	F4
Croston Lancs	138	F4

Crostwick – Damerham 307

Crostwick Norfk 122 E8
Crostwight Norfk 123 G5
Crouch Kent 38 F2
Crouch Kent 40 D4
Crouch End Gt Lon 51 J1
Croucheston Wilts 33 J6
Crouch Hill Dorset 32 B8
Crough House Green Kent 38 C4
Croughton Nhants 84 A8
Crovie Abers 268 E3
Crow Hants 18 B3
Crowan Cnwll 3 G4
Crowborough E Susx 38 D7
Crowborough Town E Susx 38 D7
Crowcombe Somset 29 L3
Crowdecote Derbys 132 B6
Crowden Derbys 141 G7
Crowden Devon 12 C3
Crowdhill Hants 35 G6
Crowdleham Kent 52 C7
Crow Edge Barns 141 J6
Crowell Oxon 67 H7
Crow End Cambs 87 G4
Crowfield Nhants 84 B7
Crowfield Suffk 90 D4
Crowfield Green Suffk 90 D4
Crowgate Street Norfk 123 G7
Crow Green Essex 70 E7
Crowhill E Loth 213 G4
Crow Hill Herefs 63 J2
Crowhole Derbys 133 G4
Crowhurst E Susx 24 D5
Crowhurst Surrey 38 B4
Crowhurst Lane End Surrey 38 B4
Crowland Lincs 102 E2
Crowland Suffk 89 K1
Crowlas Cnwll 2 E4
Crowle N Linc 143 K5
Crowle Worcs 81 L4
Crowle Green Worcs 81 L4
Crowmarsh Gifford Oxon 48 F1
Crown Corner Suffk 90 F1
Crownhill C Plym 6 F3
Crownhill Crematorium M Keyn 84 F7
Crownpits Surrey 36 E2
Crownthorpe Norfk 106 B3
Crowntown Cnwll 3 G5
Crows-an-Wra Cnwll 2 B5
Crow's Green Essex 71 G2
Crowshill Norfk 105 J2
Crow's Nest Cnwll 6 B1
Crowsnest Shrops 95 J3
Crowthorne Wokham 49 K6
Crowton Ches W 130 B5
Croxall Staffs 99 G1
Croxby Lincs 144 F8
Croxdale Dur 169 H3
Croxden Staffs 115 H4
Croxley Green Herts 68 D7
Croxteth Lpool 138 E8
Croxton Cambs 86 E3
Croxton N Linc 144 E5
Croxton Norfk 105 H6
Croxton Norfk 121 L5
Croxton Staffs 114 B5
Croxtonbank Staffs 114 B5
Croxton Green Ches E 113 J1
Croxton Kerrial Leics 117 L5
Croy Highld 252 E2
Croy N Lans 209 J4
Croyde Devon 27 H3
Croyde Bay Devon 27 G3
Croydon Cambs 87 G5
Croydon Gt Lon 51 J6
Croydon Crematorium Gt Lon 51 J5
Crubenmore Highld 241 J5
Cruckmeole Shrops 95 K2
Cruckton Shrops 95 K1
Cruden Bay Abers 257 K4
Crudgington Wrekin 113 K7
Crudwell Wilts 64 D8
Cruft Devon 12 C3
Crûg Powys 79 H1
Crugmeer Cnwll 10 C7
Crugybar Carmth 77 J7
Crug-y-byddar Powys 94 E7
Crumlin Caerph 43 K2
Crumplehorn Cnwll 5 L4
Crumpsall Manch 140 C7
Crundale Kent 40 E5
Crundale Pembks 54 F3
Crunwear Pembks 55 L5
Cruwys Morchard Devon 28 F8
Crux Easton Hants 48 B7
Cruxton Dorset 16 B3
Crwbin Carmth 58 E6
Cryers Hill Bucks 67 L7
Crymych Pembks 75 L5
Crynant Neath 60 B6
Crystal Palace Gt Lon 51 J5
Cuaig Highld 260 A8
Cuan Ag & B 215 L2
Cubbington Warwks 83 H2
Cubert Cnwll 4 C3
Cubley Barns 141 K7
Cublington Bucks 67 K3
Cublington Herefs 79 M7
Cuckfield W Susx 22 D2
Cucklington Somset 32 C5
Cuckney Notts 133 L5
Cuckoo Bridge Lincs 119 G7
Cuckoo's Corner Hants 35 M3
Cuckoo's Nest Ches W 129 J7
Cuddesdon Oxon 66 F6
Cuddington Bucks 67 H5
Cuddington Ches W 130 B5
Cuddington Heath Ches W 113 G2
Cuddy Hill Lancs 147 J8
Cudham Gt Lon 51 L7
Cudliptown Devon 12 C6
Cudnell Bmouth 17 L3
Cudworth Barns 142 B6
Cudworth Somset 30 F8
Cuerdley Cross Warrtn 130 A2
Cufaude Hants 49 G7
Cuffley Herts 69 J6
Cuil Highld 228 F4
Culbokie Highld 263 G7
Culbone Somset 28 E1
Culburnie Highld 250 E3
Culcabock Highld 251 J3
Culcharry Highld 253 G2
Culcheth Warrtn 130 C1
Culdrain Abers 255 K5
Culduie Highld 248 A4
Culford Suffk 89 G1
Culgaith Cumb 166 E5
Culham Oxon 66 D8
Culkein Highld 270 D2
Culkein Drumbeg Highld 270 F1
Culkerton Gloucs 64 D7
Cullen Moray 267 K3
Cullercoats N Tyne 181 J4
Cullerlie Abers 245 G3
Cullicudden Highld 263 H7
Cullingworth C Brad 149 J8
Cullipool Ag & B 215 L2
Cullivoe Shet 281 e2
Culloden Highld 252 D3
Cullompton Devon 14 B1
Culm Davy Devon 29 L7
Culmington Shrops 96 B7
Culmstock Devon 29 K8
Culnacraig Highld 270 E7
Culnaightrie D & G 175 J5
Culnaknock Highld 259 J4
Culpho Suffk 90 F5
Culrain Highld 263 G1
Culross Fife 210 C2
Culroy S Ayrs 196 C8
Culsalmond Abers 256 B5
Culscadden D & G 174 D5
Culshabbin D & G 173 H4
Culswick Shet 281 c6
Cultercullen Abers 257 G7
Cults C Aber 245 K3
Culverstone Green Kent 52 D6
Culverthorpe Lincs 118 D3
Culworth Nhants 84 A6
Cumbernauld N Lans 209 K4
Cumbernauld Village N Lans 209 K4
Cumberworth Lincs 137 J5
Cumdivock Cumb 165 K1
Cuminestown Abers 268 E6
Cumledge Border 202 B2
Cummersdale Cumb 177 L8
Cummertrees D & G 176 F5
Cummingston Moray 266 C2
Cumnock E Ayrs 197 H7
Cumnor Oxon 66 C6
Cumrew Cumb 178 D8
Cumrue D & G 176 E2
Cumwhinton Cumb 178 B8
Cumwhitton Cumb 178 C8
Cundall N York 150 F1
Cunninghamhead N Ayrs 196 D3
Cunningsburgh Shet 281 e7
Cupar Fife 222 F4
Cupar Muir Fife 222 F4
Curbar Derbys 132 E5
Curbridge Hants 19 J1
Curbridge Oxon 65 M5
Curdridge Hants 35 H8
Curdworth Warwks 98 F5
Curland Somset 30 C7
Curridge W Berk 48 C4
Currie C Edin 211 G5
Curry Mallet Somset 30 E6
Curry Rivel Somset 30 F6
Curteis Corner Kent 39 L5
Curtisden Green Kent 39 J5
Curtisknowle Devon 7 L4
Cury Cnwll 3 H6
Cushnie Abers 244 C1
Cushuish Somset 30 B5
Cusop Herefs 79 J7
Cusworth Donc 142 E7
Cutcloy D & G 174 C7
Cutcombe Somset 29 G3
Cutgate Rochdl 140 C5
Cuthill Highld 263 K2
Cutiau Gwynd 110 B8
Cutler's Green Essex 70 E1
Cutmadoc Cnwll 5 J2
Cutmere Cnwll 6 C3
Cutnall Green Worcs 81 K2
Cutsdean Gloucs 65 G1
Cutsyke Wakefd 142 C3
Cutthorpe Derbys 133 G5
Cuttivett Cnwll 6 D2
Cuxham Oxon 67 G8
Cuxton Medway 52 F5
Cuxwold Lincs 144 F7
Cwm Blae G 61 J6
Cwm Denbgs 128 C4
Cwmafan Neath 57 L6
Cwmaman Rhondd 60 F7
Cwmann Carmth 77 G6
Cwmavon Torfn 62 B6
Cwm-bach Carmth 56 E4
Cwmbach Carmth 75 M7
Cwmbâch Powys 79 G7
Cwmbach Rhondd 60 F6
Cwmbach Llechrhyd Powys 78 E4
Cwmbelan Powys 93 K7
Cwmbran Torfn 62 C8
Cwmbrwyno Cerdgn 92 F7
Cwm Capel Carmth 56 E4
Cwmcarn Caerph 43 K3
Cwmcarvan Mons 62 F5
Cwm-celyn Blae G 61 K5
Cwm-Cewydd Gwynd 93 J1
Cwm-cou Cerdgn 76 B6
Cwm Crawnon Powys 61 J3
Cwmdare Rhondd 60 F6
Cwmdu Carmth 59 H3
Cwmdu Powys 61 J2
Cwmdu Swans 57 H6
Cwmduad Carmth 58 C3
Cwm Dulais Swans 57 H4
Cwmdwr Carmth 59 K2
Cwmfelin Brdgnd 42 C4
Cwmfelin Myr Td 61 H6
Cwmfelin Boeth Carmth 55 L3
Cwmfelinfach Caerph 43 J3
Cwmfelin Mynach Carmth 75 L7
Cwmffrwd Carmth 58 D5
Cwmgiedd Powys 59 L6
Cwmgorse Carmth 57 K3
Cwmgwili Carmth 57 G3
Cwmgwrach Neath 60 C6
Cwmhiraeth Carmth 76 C7
Cwm-Ifor Carmth 59 J4
Cwm Irfon Powys 78 A5
Cwmisfael Carmth 58 F5
Cwm Llinau Powys 93 J2
Cwmllynfell Neath 59 K6
Cwmmawr Carmth 58 F6
Cwm Morgan Carmth 58 B2
Cwmparc Rhondd 42 E3
Cwmpengraig Carmth 58 C2
Cwm Penmachno Conwy 110 E2
Cwmpennar Rhondd 61 G7
Cwmrhos Powys 61 J2
Cwmrhydyceirw Swans 57 J5
Cwmsychbant Cerdgn 76 E6
Cwmtillery Blae G 61 K6
Cwm-twrch Isaf Powys 57 L3
Cwm-twrch Uchaf Powys 59 L6
Cwm-y-glo Carmth 59 G6
Cwm-y-glo Gwynd 125 K7
Cwmyoy Mons 62 C3
Cwmystwyth Cerdgn 93 G8
Cwrt Gwynd 92 E3
Cwrt-newydd Cerdgn 76 E5
Cwrt-y-gollen Powys 61 K4
Cyfronydd Powys 94 E2
Cylibebyll Neath 57 K4
Cymau Flints 129 G8
Cymer Neath 42 C3
Cymmer Rhondd 42 F3
Cynghordy Carmth 77 M7
Cynheidre Carmth 56 E3
Cynonville Neath 42 C3
Cynwyd Denbgs 111 K3
Cynwyl Elfed Carmth 58 C3

D

Daccombe Devon 8 D1
Dacre Cumb 166 B5
Dacre N York 150 B4
Dacre Banks N York 150 B3
Daddry Shield Dur 167 K3
Dadford Bucks 84 C7
Dadlington Leics 99 L4
Dafen Carmth 56 F4
Daffy Green Norfk 105 J2
Dagenham Gt Lon 52 B2
Daglingworth Gloucs 64 E6
Dagnall Bucks 68 C4
Dagworth Suffk 89 L3
Dailly S Ayrs 183 H3
Dainton Devon 8 C2
Dairsie Fife 223 G4
Daisy Hill Bolton 139 K6
Daisy Hill Leeds 141 L2
Dalabrog W Isls 283 b11
Dalavich Ag & B 216 F5
Dalbeattie D & G 175 L3
Dalbury Derbys 115 M5
Dalby IoM 154 b6
Dalby Lincs 137 H5
Dalby N York 151 K2
Dalcapon P & K 232 E4
Dalchalm Highld 274 B6
Dalchreichart Highld 240 A1
Dalchruin P & K 220 C4
Dalcrue P & K 221 J2
Dalderby Lincs 136 E6
Dalditch Devon 14 B6
Daldowie Crematorium C Glas 209 H6
Dale Cumb 166 D2
Dale Derbys 116 D4
Dale Pembks 54 C5
Dale Bottom Cumb 165 J6
Dale End Derbys 132 D7
Dale End N York 149 G6
Dale Hill E Susx 39 H7
Dalehouse N York 171 H7
Dalelia Highld 237 L6
Dalgarven N Ayrs 196 B2
Dalgety Bay Fife 211 G2
Dalgig E Ayrs 197 G8
Dalginross P & K 220 D3
Dalguise P & K 232 E6
Dalhalvaig Highld 278 F5
Dalham Suffk 88 E3
Daliburgh W Isls 283 b11
Dalkeith Mdloth 211 K5
Dallas Moray 266 C5
Dallinghoo Suffk 91 G4
Dallington E Susx 24 B3
Dallington Nhants 84 E3
Dallow N York 150 B2
Dalmally Ag & B 217 K2
Dalmary Stirlg 219 H8
Dalmellington E Ayrs 184 D2
Dalmeny C Edin 210 F3
Dalmore Highld 263 H6
Dalmuir W Duns 208 E5
Dalnabreck Highld 237 K6
Dalnacardoch P & K 231 K1
Dalnahaitnach Highld 252 F7
Dalnaspidal P & K 231 J1
Dalnawillan Lodge Highld 279 H8
Daloist P & K 231 L4
Dalqueich P & K 221 K6
Dalquhairn S Ayrs 183 J4
Dalreavoch Lodge Highld 273 H6
Dalry N Ayrs 196 B1
Dalrymple E Ayrs 196 D8
Dalserf S Lans 198 C3
Dalsmeran Ag & B 192 D5
Dalston Cumb 165 L1
Dalston Gt Lon 51 J2
Dalswinton D & G 176 B2
Dalton Cumb 157 H7
Dalton D & G 176 F4
Dalton Lancs 139 G6
Dalton N York 159 K1
Dalton N York 160 F7
Dalton Nthumb 180 D4
Dalton Rothm 133 J1
Dalton-in-Furness Cumb 156 B7
Dalton-le-Dale Dur 169 L1
Dalton Magna Rothm 133 J1
Dalton-on-Tees N York 160 D1
Dalton Parva Rothm 133 J1
Dalton Piercy Hartpl 170 B4
Dalveich Stirlg 219 K2
Dalwhinnie Highld 241 H6
Dalwood Devon 14 F3
Damask Green Herts 69 H1
Damerham Hants 33 J7

Damgate Norfk	107	H2
Dam Green Norfk	105	L6
Damnaglaur D & G	172	E7
Danaway Kent	53	J6
Danbury Essex	71	J6
Danby N York	162	C1
Danby Bottom N York	162	B2
Danby Wiske N York	160	E3
Dandaleith Moray	254	F3
Danderhall Mdloth	211	J5
Danebridge Ches E	131	J6
Dane End Herts	69	J3
Danegate E Susx	38	E6
Danehill E Susx	22	F2
Dane Hills C Leic	100	C3
Danemoor Green Norfk	105	L2
Danesford Shrops	97	G5
Danesmoor Derbys	133	H7
Dane Street Kent	40	D5
Daniel's Water Kent	40	C7
Danshillock Abers	268	C5
Danskine E Loth	212	C5
Danthorpe E R Yk	145	H1
Danzey Green Warwks	82	D2
Dapple Heath Staffs	115	G6
Darby Green Hants	49	K7
Darcy Lever Bolton	139	L6
Dardy Powys	61	K3
Daren-felen Mons	61	K4
Darenth Kent	52	C5
Daresbury Halton	130	B3
Darfield Barns	142	C6
Darfoulds Notts	133	L4
Dargate Kent	40	E3
Darite Cnwll	6	B1
Darland Medway	53	G6
Darland Wrexhm	129	J8
Darlaston Wsall	98	B4
Darlaston Green Wsall	98	B4
Darley N York	150	B4
Darley Abbey C Derb	116	B4
Darley Bridge Derbys	132	E7
Darley Dale Derbys	132	E7
Darley Green Solhll	98	F8
Darleyhall Herts	68	F3
Darley Head N York	150	B4
Darlingscott Warwks	82	F6
Darlington Darltn	169	H7
Darlington Crematorium		
Darltn	169	H7
Darliston Shrops	113	J5
Darlton Notts	134	F5
Darnford Staffs	98	E2
Darnick Border	201	H6
Darowen Powys	93	H3
Darra Abers	268	D6
Darracott Devon	26	D7
Darracott Devon	27	H3
Darras Hall Nthumb	180	E5
Darrington Wakefd	142	D4
Darsham Suffk	91	K1
Darshill Somset	31	K2
Dartford Kent	52	B4
Dartford Crossing Kent	52	C4
Dartington Devon	8	B2
Dartmeet Devon	12	F7
Dartmouth Devon	8	C4
Darton Barns	141	M5
Darvel E Ayrs	197	H3
Darwell Hole E Susx	24	C3
Darwen Bl w D	139	K3
Datchet W & M	50	C3
Datchworth Herts	69	H3
Datchworth Green Herts	69	H3
Daubhill Bolton	139	L6
Daugh of Kinermony Moray	254	E3
Dauntsey Wilts	46	E3
Dava Highld	253	J4
Davenham Ches W	130	C5
Davenport Stockp	131	H2
Davenport Green Ches E	131	G4
Davenport Green Traffd	130	F2
Daventry Nhants	84	B3
Davidson's Mains C Edin	211	H4
Davidstow Cnwll	11	G5
David Street Kent	52	E6
Davington D & G	187	K5
Davington Hill Kent	40	D3
Daviot Abers	256	D6
Daviot Highld	252	D4
Daviot House Highld	252	D4
Davis's Town E Susx	23	J4
Davoch of Grange Moray	267	K6
Davyhulme Traffd	139	M8
Daw End Wsall	98	C3
Dawesgreen Surrey	37	K2
Dawley Wrekin	96	F2
Dawlish Devon	13	M7
Dawlish Warren Devon	14	A7
Dawn Conwy	127	G5
Daws Green Somset	30	B6
Daws Heath Essex	53	K6
Daw's House Cnwll	11	K6
Dawsmere Lincs	120	A5
Daybrook Notts	116	F3
Day Green Ches E	130	F8
Dayhills Staffs	114	F5
Dayhouse Bank Worcs	98	B7
Daylesford Gloucs	65	K2
Ddol Flints	128	D5
Ddol-Cownwy Powys	111	K8
Deal Kent	41	L5
Dean Cumb	164	E5
Dean Devon	7	L2
Dean Devon	27	L2
Dean Devon	28	C1
Dean Dorset	33	G7
Dean Hants	34	F4
Dean Hants	35	H7
Dean Lancs	140	C3
Dean Oxon	65	M3
Dean Somset	31	L2
Dean Bottom Kent	52	C5
Deanburnhaugh Border	188	C4
Deancombe Devon	7	L2
Dean Court Oxon	66	C6
Deane Bolton	139	K6
Deane Hants	35	H1
Dean End Dorset	33	G7
Dean Head Barns	141	L7
Deanhead Kirk	141	G4
Deanland Dorset	33	G7
Deanlane End W Susx	20	B4
Dean Prior Devon	7	L2
Deanraw Nthumb	179	J6
Dean Row Ches E	131	G3
Deans W Loth	210	D5
Deanscales Cumb	164	E5
Deanshanger Nhants	84	D7
Deanshaugh Moray	267	G6
Deanston Stirlg	220	C6
Dearham Cumb	164	E3
Dearnley Rochdl	140	D4
Debach Suffk	90	F4
Debden Essex	70	C7
Debden Essex	87	L8
Debden Green Essex	70	E1
Debenham Suffk	90	E3
Deblin's Green Worcs	81	J5
Dechmont W Loth	210	D5
Dechmont Road W Loth	210	D5
Deddington Oxon	66	C2
Dedham Essex	90	C8
Dedham Heath Essex	72	F1
Dedworth W & M	50	B4
Deene Nhants	101	L5
Deenethorpe Nhants	101	L5
Deepcar Sheff	141	L8
Deepcut Surrey	49	L7
Deepdale Cumb	158	C5
Deepdale N York	158	F6
Deeping Gate C Pete	102	C2
Deeping St James Lincs	102	D2
Deeping St Nicholas Lincs	119	H8
Deerhurst Gloucs	64	C1
Deerhurst Walton Gloucs	64	C2
Deerton Street Kent	40	E3
Defford Worcs	81	L6
Defynnog Powys	60	D2
Deganwy Conwy	126	F4
Degnish Ag & B	216	B5
Deighton C York	151	K7
Deighton N York	160	E2
Deiniolen Gwynd	125	K7
Delabole Cnwll	10	F6
Delamere Ches W	130	A6
Delfrigs Abers	257	H7
Delley Devon	27	K6
Delliefure Highld	253	L5
Dell Quay W Susx	20	D6
Delly End Oxon	65	M4
Delnabo Moray	254	C8
Delnashaugh Inn Moray	254	D4
Delny Highld	263	K5
Delph Oldham	140	E6
Delves Dur	168	E1
Delvin End Essex	88	F8
Dembleby Lincs	118	D4
Demelza Cnwll	5	G2
Denaby Donc	142	D7
Denaby Main Donc	142	D7
Denbies Surrey	37	H1
Denbigh Denbgs	128	C6
Denbighshire Crematorium		
Denbgs	127	K5
Denbrae Fife	222	F3
Denbury Devon	8	B1
Denby Derbys	116	C2
Denby Bottles Derbys	116	C2
Denby Dale Kirk	141	K6
Denchworth Oxon	48	A1
Dendron Cumb	146	E2
Denel End C Beds	85	K8
Denfield P & K	221	G6
Denford Nhants	101	L8
Dengie Essex	72	E6
Denham Bucks	50	D2
Denham Suffk	88	E3
Denham Suffk	106	D8
Denham End Suffk	88	F3
Denham Green Bucks	50	D1
Denham Green Suffk	106	D8
Denhead Abers	269	J5
Denhead Fife	223	H4
Denhead of Gray C Dund	222	F1
Denholm Border	189	G3
Denholme C Brad	141	G1
Denholme Clough C Brad	141	G1
Denio Gwynd	108	F4
Denmead Hants	19	L1
Denmore C Aber	245	L1
Denne Park W Susx	37	J3
Dennington Suffk	91	G2
Denny Falk	209	L3
Dennyloanhead Falk	209	L3
Den of Lindores Fife	222	D4
Denshaw Oldham	140	E5
Denside Abers	245	H4
Densole Kent	41	G7
Denston Suffk	88	F5
Denstone Staffs	115	H3
Denstroude Kent	40	E3
Dent Cumb	158	B5
Denton Cambs	102	C6
Denton Darltn	169	G7
Denton E Susx	23	G6
Denton Kent	41	G6
Denton Kent	52	E4
Denton Lincs	117	M5
Denton N York	149	L6
Denton Nhants	85	G4
Denton Norfk	106	F5
Denton Oxon	66	E6
Denton Tamesd	131	H1
Denver Norfk	104	C3
Denwick Nthumb	191	J3
Deopham Norfk	105	L3
Deopham Green Norfk	105	L4
Depden Suffk	88	F4
Depden Green Suffk	88	F4
Deptford Gt Lon	51	K3
Deptford Wilts	33	H3
Derby C Derb	116	B4
Derby Devon	27	K4
Derbyhaven IoM	154	C8
Derculich P & K	232	C5
Dereham Norfk	105	K1
Deri Caerph	61	H6
Derril Devon	11	K2
Derringstone Kent	41	G5
Derrington Staffs	114	D7
Derriton Devon	11	L2
Derry Hill Wilts	46	D5
Derrythorpe N Linc	143	L6
Dersingham Norfk	120	F5
Dervaig Ag & B	226	E2
Derwen Denbgs	111	L2
Derwenlas Powys	92	F4
Derwydd Carmth	59	H5
Desborough Nhants	101	H6
Desford Leics	100	B3
Deskford Moray	267	K4
Detchant Nthumb	203	H6
Detling Kent	53	G7
Deuxhill Shrops	96	F6
Devauden Mons	62	F7
Devil's Bridge Cerdgn	92	F8
Devitts Green Warwks	99	H5
Devizes Wilts	46	E6
Devonport C Plym	6	E4
Devonside Clacks	221	G7
Devoran Cnwll	3	K3
Dewarton Mdloth	211	L6
Dewlish Dorset	16	E3
Dewsbury Kirk	141	K3
Dewsbury Moor Kirk	141	K3
Dewsbury Moor Crematorium Kirk	141	K3
Deytheur Powys	112	C8
Dial N Som	45	G5
Dial Green W Susx	36	D5
Dial Post W Susx	21	K3
Dibberford Dorset	15	K2
Dibden Hants	18	F2
Dibden Purlieu Hants	18	F2
Dickens Heath Solhll	98	E8
Dickleburgh Norfk	106	D7
Didbrook Gloucs	64	F1
Didcot Oxon	48	D1
Diddington Cambs	86	C6
Diddlebury Shrops	96	C6
Didley Herefs	62	F1
Didling W Susx	20	B3
Didmarton Gloucs	46	B2
Didsbury Manch	131	G1
Didworthy Devon	7	K2
Digby Lincs	135	M8
Digg Highld	259	H3
Diggle Oldham	140	F6
Digmoor Lancs	139	G6
Digswell Herts	69	H4
Digswell Water Herts	69	H4
Dihewyd Cerdgn	76	E4
Dilham Norfk	123	G6
Dilhorne Staffs	114	F3
Dill Hall Lancs	139	M2
Dillington Cambs	86	C2
Dilston Nthumb	180	A6
Dilton Wilts	32	E1
Dilton Marsh Wilts	32	D1
Dilwyn Herefs	80	A4
Dimple Bolton	139	L4
Dimple Derbys	132	F7
Dinas Carmth	58	A3
Dinas Cnwll	10	C7
Dinas Gwynd	108	D3
Dinas Pembks	75	G4
Dinas Rhondd	42	F3
Dinas Dinlle Gwynd	125	H7
Dinas-Mawddwy Gwynd	111	G8
Dinas Powys V Glam	43	J7
Dinder Somset	31	J2
Dinedor Herefs	80	C7
Dingestow Mons	62	F5
Dingle Lpool	129	J2
Dingleden Kent	39	K7
Dingley Nhants	101	H5
Dingwall Highld	262	F8
Dinmael Conwy	111	J3
Dinnet Abers	244	D4
Dinnington N u Ty	180	F4
Dinnington Rothm	133	K3
Dinnington Somset	30	F8
Dinorwic Gwynd	125	L7
Dinton Bucks	67	J5
Dinton Wilts	33	H4
Dinwoodie D & G	187	H3
Dinworthy Devon	26	E7
Dipford Somset	30	B6
Dipley Hants	49	H7
Dippen Ag & B	194	D3
Dippen N Ayrs	195	G6
Dippenhall Surrey	36	B2
Dippermill Devon	12	B1
Dippertown Devon	12	B5
Dipple Moray	267	G4
Dipple S Ayrs	182	F2
Diptford Devon	7	L3
Dipton Dur	180	E8
Diptonmill Nthumb	179	L6
Dirleton E Loth	212	B2
Dirt Pot Nthumb	167	K2
Discoed Powys	79	K2
Diseworth Leics	116	D6
Dishforth N York	160	E8
Disley Ches E	131	J3
Diss Norfk	106	C7
Disserth Powys	78	E4
Distington Cumb	164	D6
Distington Hall Crematorium		
Cumb	164	D6
Ditchampton Wilts	33	J4
Ditcheat Somset	31	K4
Ditchingham Norfk	107	G5
Ditchling E Susx	22	E4
Ditherington Shrops	113	H8
Ditteridge Wilts	46	B5
Dittisham Devon	8	C4
Ditton Kent	52	F7
Ditton Green Cambs	88	D4
Ditton Priors Shrops	96	E5
Dixton Gloucs	64	E1
Dixton Mons	63	G4
Dizzard Cnwll	11	H3
Dobcross Oldham	140	F6
Dobwalls Cnwll	5	L2
Doccombe Devon	13	H6
Dochgarroch Highld	251	H3
Dockenfield Surrey	36	B3
Docker Lancs	157	J7
Docking Norfk	121	G4
Docklow Herefs	80	D4
Dockray Cumb	165	J1
Dockray Cumb	165	L6
Dodbrooke Devon	7	L6

Doddinghurst Essex 70 E7
Doddington Cambs 103 H5
Doddington Kent 40 B4
Doddington Lincs 135 H5
Doddington Nthumb 202 F6
Doddington Shrops 96 E8
Doddiscombsleigh Devon 13 K5
Dodd's Green Ches E 113 K3
Doddshill Norfk 120 F5
Doddy Cross Cnwll 6 C2
Dodford Nhants 84 B3
Dodford Worcs 97 L8
Dodington S Glos 45 L3
Dodington Somset 30 A3
Dodleston Ches W 129 J7
Dodscott Devon 27 K7
Dodside E Rens 208 E8
Dod's Leigh Staffs 115 G4
Dodworth Barns 141 M6
Dodworth Bottom Barns 141 M7
Dodworth Green Barns 141 M6
Doe Bank Birm 98 E4
Doe Lea Derbys 133 J6
Dogdyke Lincs 136 D8
Dogley Lane Kirk 141 J5
Dogmersfield Hants 49 J8
Dogridge Wilts 47 G2
Dogsthorpe C Pete 102 D3
Dog Village Devon 14 A3
Dolanog Powys 94 C1
Dolau Powys 79 G2
Dolaucothi Carmth 77 J7
Dolbenmaen Gwynd 109 J3
Doley Staffs 114 A5
Dolfach Powys 93 K3
Dol-för Powys 93 H2
Dolfor Powys 94 D6
Dolgarrog Conwy 126 F6
Dolgellau Gwynd 110 D7
Dolgoch Gwynd 92 E3
Dol-gran Carmth 58 D2
Doll Highld 273 L7
Dollar Clacks 221 G7
Dollarfield Clacks 221 G7
Dolley Green Powys 79 K2
Dollwen Cerdgn 92 E7
Dolphin Flints 128 E5
Dolphinholme Lancs 147 K5
Dolphinton S Lans 199 J4
Dolton Devon 27 K8
Dolwen Conwy 127 H5
Dolwyddelan Conwy 110 D1
Dolybont Cerdgn 92 D5
Dolyhir Powys 79 J4
Domgay Powys 112 D7
Donaldson's Lodge Nthumb 202 D5
Doncaster Donc 142 F7
Doncaster Carr Donc 142 F7
Donhead St Andrew Wilts 32 F6
Donhead St Mary Wilts 32 F6
Donibristle Fife 211 J1
Doniford Somset 29 K2
Donington Lincs 119 H4
Donington on Bain Lincs 136 D3
Donington Southing Lincs 119 G5
Donisthorpe Leics 99 J1
Donkey Street Kent 25 L1
Donkey Town Surrey 50 B6
Donnington Gloucs 65 J2
Donnington Herefs 81 G8
Donnington Shrops 96 D2
Donnington W Berk 48 C5
Donnington W Susx 20 D6
Donnington Wrekin 113 M8
Donnington Wood Wrekin 97 G1
Donyatt Somset 30 E8
Doomsday Green W Susx 37 J5
Doonfoot S Ayrs 196 C7
Dorback Lodge Highld 253 L8
Dorchester Dorset 16 D4
Dorchester-on-Thames Oxon 66 E8
Dordon Warwks 99 H3
Dore Sheff 132 F3
Dores Highld 251 G5
Dorking Surrey 37 J1
Dorking Tye Suffk 89 J7
Dormansland Surrey 38 B5
Dormans Park Surrey 38 B5
Dormington Herefs 80 D7
Dormston Worcs 82 A4
Dorn Gloucs 82 F8
Dorney Bucks 50 B3
Dornie Highld 248 D6
Dornoch Highld 264 B2
Dornock D & G 177 H5
Dorrery Highld 279 J5
Dorridge Solhll 98 F8
Dorrington Lincs 118 E1
Dorrington Shrops 96 B3

Dorrington Shrops 114 A3
Dorsington Warwks 82 D5
Dorstone Herefs 79 K7
Dorton Bucks 67 G4
Dosthill Staffs 99 G3
Dothan IoA 124 F5
Dottery Dorset 15 K4
Doublebois Cnwll 5 L2
Doughton Gloucs 46 C1
Douglas IoM 154 e6
Douglas S Lans 198 D7
Douglas and Angus C Dund 234 C8
Douglas Crematorium IoM 154 e6
Douglas Pier Ag & B. 217 K7
Douglastown Angus 234 B6
Douglas Water S Lans 198 E6
Douglas West S Lans 198 D7
Doulting Somset 31 L2
Dounby Ork 275 b4
Doune Highld 272 B7
Doune Stirlg 220 C6
Dounepark S Ayrs 182 F3
Dounie Highld 263 G2
Dousland Devon 7 G1
Dovaston Shrops 112 E7
Dove Green Notts 116 D1
Dove Holes Derbys 131 L4
Dovenby Cumb 164 E4
Dover Kent 41 K7
Dover Wigan 139 J7
Dovercourt Essex 73 K1
Doverdale Worcs 81 K2
Doveridge Derbys 115 J5
Doversgreen Surrey 37 L1
Dowally P & K 232 F5
Dowbridge Lancs 138 E2
Dowdeswell Gloucs 64 E3
Dowlais Myr Td 61 G5
Dowland Devon 12 D1
Dowlish Ford Somset 30 E8
Dowlish Wake Somset 30 E8
Down Ampney Gloucs 65 G7
Downderry Cnwll 6 C4
Downe Gt Lon 51 L6
Downend Gloucs 64 B7
Downend IoW 19 J6
Downend S Glos 45 K3
Downend W Berk 48 C4
Downfield C Dund 223 G1
Downgate Cnwll 11 K8
Downgate Cnwll 11 L8
Downham Essex 71 H7
Downham Gt Lon 51 K4
Downham Lancs 148 D7
Downham Market Norfk 104 C3
Down Hatherley Gloucs 64 C3
Downhead Somset 31 J6
Downhead Somset 32 A2
Downhill Cnwll 4 D1
Downhill P & K 221 K1
Downholland Cross Lancs 138 D6
Downholme N York 159 K3
Downicarey Devon 11 M4
Downies Abers 245 K4
Downing Flints 128 D4
Downley Bucks 67 K8
Down St Mary Devon 13 H2
Downs Crematorium Br & H 22 E6
Downside Somset 31 K2
Downside Somset 31 L1
Downside Surrey 50 E7
Down Thomas Devon 6 F5
Downton Hants 18 D5
Downton Wilts 33 L6
Dowsby Lincs 118 F5
Dowsdale Lincs 102 F2
Doxey Staffs 114 D6
Doxford Nthumb 191 H2
Doynton S Glos 45 L4
Draethen Caerph 43 K4
Draffan S Lans 198 C4
Dragonby N Linc 143 M5
Dragons Green W Susx 37 H6
Drakeholes Notts 134 E2
Drakelow Worcs 97 J7
Drakemyre N Ayrs 196 B1
Drakes Broughton Worcs 81 L5
Drakewalls Cnwll 12 B8
Draughton N York 149 J5
Draughton Nhants 101 G8
Drax N York 143 H3
Drax Hales N York 143 H3
Draycote Warwks 83 K1
Draycot Foliat Swindn 47 J3
Draycott Derbys 116 D5
Draycott Gloucs 82 E8
Draycott Shrops 97 H5
Draycott Somset 31 G1
Draycott Somset 31 J6

Draycott Worcs 81 K5
Draycott in the Clay Staffs 115 J6
Draycott in the Moors Staffs 114 F3
Drayford Devon 28 D8
Drayton C Port 19 L3
Drayton Leics 101 H5
Drayton Lincs 119 H4
Drayton Norfk 106 D1
Drayton Oxon 66 C8
Drayton Oxon 83 K7
Drayton Somset 30 F6
Drayton Worcs 97 K8
Drayton Bassett Staffs 99 G3
Drayton Beauchamp Bucks 67 L5
Drayton Parslow Bucks 67 K2
Drayton St Leonard Oxon 66 E7
Drebley N York 149 J4
Dreemskerry IoM 154 g4
Dreen Hill Pembks 54 F4
Drefach Carmth 58 F6
Drefach Carmth 76 C7
Drefach Cerdgn 76 F6
Drefelin Carmth 76 C7
Dreghorn N Ayrs 196 C3
Drellingore Kent 41 H7
Drem E Loth 212 B3
Dresden C Stke 114 E3
Drewsteignton Devon 13 H4
Driby Lincs 137 G5
Driffield E R Yk 152 F4
Driffield Gloucs 65 G7
Driffield Cross Roads Gloucs 64 F7
Drift Cnwll 2 C5
Drigg Cumb 155 K3
Drighlington Leeds 141 K2
Drimnin Highld 227 G2
Drimpton Dorset 15 K2
Drimsallie Highld 238 F7
Dringhouses C York 151 J6
Drinkstone Suffk 89 J3
Drinkstone Green Suffk 89 J3
Drive End Dorset 16 B1
Driver's End Herts 69 G3
Drointon Staffs 115 G6
Droitwich Spa Worcs 81 K3
Dron P & K 221 L4
Dronfield Derbys 133 G4
Dronfield Woodhouse Derbys 133 G4
Drongan E Ayrs 196 E7
Dronley Angus 234 A8
Droop Dorset 16 E1
Dropping Well Rothm 133 H1
Droxford Hants 35 J7
Droylsden Tamesd 140 D8
Druid Denbgs 111 K3
Druidston Pembks 54 E3
Druimarbin Highld 229 H1
Druimavuic Ag & B. 229 G6
Druimdrishaig Ag & B. 206 A5
Druimindarroch Highld 237 K4
Drum Ag & B 206 E4
Drum P & K. 221 J7
Drumalbin S Lans 198 F5
Drumbeg Highld 270 F2
Drumblade Abers 255 M4
Drumbreddon D & G. 172 D6
Drumbuie Highld 248 B5
Drumburgh Cumb 177 J7
Drumburn D & G 175 L4
Drumchapel C Glas 208 E5
Drumchastle P & K 231 J4
Drumclog S Lans 197 J3
Drumeldrie Fife 223 G6
Drumelzier Border 199 K6
Drumfearn Highld 247 L5
Drumfrennie Abers 244 F4
Drumgley Angus 234 C5
Drumguish Highld 241 L3
Drumin Moray 254 D5
Drumjohn D & G 184 E3
Drumlamford S Ayrs 183 H7
Drumlasie Abers 244 E2
Drumleaning Cumb 177 J8
Drumlemble Ag & B 192 D4
Drumlithie Abers 245 H7
Drummoddie D & G 173 K6
Drummore D & G. 172 E7
Drummuir Moray 255 M5
Drumnadrochit Highld 250 E5
Drumnagorrach Moray 267 L5
Drumpark D & G 185 L7
Drumrunie Lodge Highld 271 G7
Drumshang S Ayrs 195 L8
Drumuie Highld 259 G7
Drumuillie Highld 253 H7
Drumvaich Stirlg 220 B6
Drunzie P & K 221 L5
Druridge Nthumb 191 K7
Drury Flints 129 G6

Drybeck Cumb 166 F7
Drybridge Moray 267 J4
Drybridge N Ayrs 196 D4
Drybrook Gloucs 63 J4
Dryburgh Border 201 J6
Dry Doddington Lincs 117 M2
Dry Drayton Cambs 87 H3
Drymen Stirlg 208 E1
Drymuir Abers 257 G3
Drynoch Highld 246 F2
Dry Sandford Oxon 66 C7
Dryslwyn Carmth 59 G5
Dry Street Essex 52 E2
Dryton Shrops 96 D2
Dubford Abers 268 E3
Dublin Suffk 90 E1
Duchally Highld 271 L4
Duck End Bed 85 L6
Duck End Cambs 86 E2
Duck End Essex 71 G2
Duck End Essex 88 D8
Duckend Green Essex 71 H3
Duckington Ches W 113 H1
Ducklington Oxon 65 M5
Duck's Cross Bed 86 C4
Duddenhoe End Essex 87 J7
Duddingston C Edin 211 J4
Duddington Nhants 101 L3
Duddlestone Somset 30 C6
Duddleswell E Susx 38 C7
Duddlewick Shrops 96 F6
Duddo Nthumb 202 E4
Duddon Ches W 129 L6
Duddon Bridge Cumb 156 B5
Duddon Common Ches W 129 M6
Dudleston Shrops 112 E4
Dudleston Heath Shrops 112 E4
Dudley Dudley 97 L5
Dudley N Tyne 181 G4
Dudley Hill C Brad 141 J2
Dudley Port Sandw 98 B5
Dudnill Shrops 96 E8
Dudsbury Dorset 17 L3
Dudswell Herts 68 B5
Duffield Derbys. 116 B3
Duffryn Neath 42 C3
Dufftown Moray. 255 G4
Duffus Moray 266 D3
Dufton Cumb. 166 F5
Duggleby N York 152 D2
Duirinish Highld 248 B5
Duisdalemore Highld 247 L6
Duisky Highld 239 G8
Dukestown Blae G. 61 J5
Duke Street Suffk. 90 C6
Dukinfield Tamesd 140 E8
Dukinfield Crematorium
Tamesd 140 E8
Dulas IoA 125 H2
Dulcote Somset 31 J2
Dulford Devon 14 C2
Dull P & K. 232 B5
Dullatur N Lans 209 K4
Dullingham Cambs 88 C4
Dullingham Ley Cambs 88 C4
Dulnain Bridge Highld 253 H4
Duloe Bed. 86 D3
Duloe Cnwll 5 M3
Dulverton Somset 29 G5
Dulwich Gt Lon 51 J4
Dumbarton W Duns 208 C4
Dumbleton Gloucs 82 B8
Dumfries D & G 176 C4
Dumgoyne Stirlg 208 E2
Dummer Hants 35 J2
Dumpton Kent 41 L2
Dun Angus 235 G3
Dunalastair P & K. 231 K4
Dunan Ag & B. 207 J5
Dunan Highld 247 J3
Dunan P & K. 230 E4
Dunaverty Ag & B 192 E6
Dunball Somset 30 D3
Dunbar E Loth 212 E3
Dunbeath Highld 275 G2
Dunbeg Ag & B 228 D8
Dunblane Stirlg 220 D7
Dunbog Fife 222 D4
Dunbridge Hants 34 D5
Duncanston Highld 263 G8
Duncanstone Abers 255 L6
Dunchideock Devon 13 K5
Dunchurch Warwks 83 L1
Duncote Nhants 84 C5
Duncow D & G 176 C2
Duncrievie P & K 221 L5
Dunton W Susx 20 F3
Dundee C Dund 223 G1
Dundee Crematorium C Dund 222 F1

Place	Page	Grid
Dundon Somset	31	G4
Dundonald S Ayrs	196	D4
Dundraw Cumb	165	H1
Dundreggan Highld	240	B1
Dundrennan D & G	175	J5
Dundry N Som	45	H5
Dunecht Abers	245	G2
Dunfermline Fife	210	E2
Dunfermline Crematorium Fife	210	F2
Dunfield Gloucs	65	H7
Dunford Bridge Barns	141	J7
Dungate Kent	40	B3
Dungavel S Lans	197	J3
Dunge Wilts	46	C8
Dungworth Sheff	132	E2
Dunham-on-the-Hill Ches W	129	L5
Dunham-on-Trent Notts	135	G5
Dunhampstead Worcs	81	L3
Dunhampton Worcs	81	J2
Dunham Town Traffd	130	E2
Dunham Woodhouses Traffd	130	E2
Dunholme Lincs	135	L4
Dunino Fife	223	J5
Dunipace Falk	209	L2
Dunkeld P & K	232	F6
Dunkerton BaNES	45	L7
Dunkeswell Devon	14	D1
Dunkeswick N York	150	D6
Dunkirk Ches W	129	J5
Dunkirk Kent	40	E3
Dunkirk S Glos	46	A2
Dunkirk Wilts	46	E6
Dunk's Green Kent	38	F3
Dunlappie Angus	234	F2
Dunley Hants	48	C8
Dunley Worcs	81	H2
Dunlop E Ayrs	196	E1
Dunmaglass Highld	251	J3
Dunmere Cnwll	5	H1
Dunmore Falk	210	A1
Dunnet Highld	280	B2
Dunnichen Angus	234	D5
Dunning P & K	221	J4
Dunnington C York	151	L5
Dunnington E R Yk	153	J5
Dunnington Warwks	82	C4
Dunnockshaw Lancs	140	B2
Dunn Street Kent	53	G6
Dunoon Ag & B	207	K4
Dunphail Moray	253	J2
Dunragit D & G	172	E3
Duns Border	202	B2
Dunsa Derbys	132	E5
Dunsby Lincs	118	E6
Dunscar Bolton	139	L5
Dunscore D & G	185	L6
Dunscroft Donc	143	G6
Dunsdale R & Cl	170	E6
Dunsden Green Oxon	49	H3
Dunsdon Devon	11	K1
Dunsfold Surrey	36	F4
Dunsford Devon	13	J5
Dunshalt Fife	222	D5
Dunshillock Abers	269	H6
Dunsill Notts	133	J7
Dunsley N York	171	K8
Dunsley Staffs	97	J6
Dunsmore Bucks	67	L6
Dunsop Bridge Lancs	148	B6
Dunstable C Beds	68	C3
Dunstall Staffs	115	K7
Dunstall Common Worcs	81	K6
Dunstall Green Suffk	88	E3
Dunstan Nthumb	191	K2
Dunstan Steads Nthumb	191	L1
Dunster Somset	29	H2
Duns Tew Oxon	66	C2
Dunston Gatesd	180	F6
Dunston Lincs	135	L6
Dunston Norfk	106	E3
Dunston Staffs	114	E8
Dunstone Devon	7	H4
Dunstone Devon	13	G7
Dunston Heath Staffs	114	E8
Dunsville Donc	143	G6
Dunswell E R Yk	144	D1
Dunsyre S Lans	199	J3
Dunterton Devon	11	M6
Dunthrop Oxon	65	M2
Duntisbourne Abbots Gloucs	64	E5
Duntisbourne Leer Gloucs	64	E5
Duntisbourne Rouse Gloucs	64	E6
Duntish Dorset	16	D2
Duntocher W Duns	208	E4
Dunton Bucks	67	K2
Dunton C Beds	86	E6
Dunton Norfk	121	J5
Dunton Bassett Leics	100	C5
Dunton Green Kent	38	D2
Dunton Wayletts Essex	52	E1
Duntulm Highld	259	G2
Dunure S Ayrs	195	L7
Dunvant Swans	57	G6
Dunvegan Highld	258	C7
Dunwich Suffk	91	L1
Dunwood Staffs	131	J8
Durdar Cumb	177	L8
Durgan Cnwll	3	K5
Durham Dur	169	H2
Durham Crematorium Dur	169	H3
Durisdeer D & G	186	C5
Durisdeermill D & G	186	C5
Durkar Wakefd	141	M4
Durleigh Somset	30	C4
Durley Hants	35	G7
Durley Wilts	47	K6
Durley Street Hants	35	H7
Durlock Kent	41	J2
Durlock Kent	41	J4
Durlow Common Herefs	80	E7
Durn Rochdl	140	E4
Durness Highld	276	F3
Durno Abers	256	C6
Duror Highld	228	F4
Durran Ag & B	216	F5
Durrington W Susx	21	J6
Durrington Wilts	33	K2
Durris Abers	245	G4
Dursley Gloucs	63	M7
Dursley Cross Gloucs	63	K3
Durston Somset	30	D5
Durweston Dorset	17	G1
Duston Nhants	84	D3
Duthil Highld	253	H6
Dutlas Powys	94	F7
Duton Hill Essex	70	F2
Dutson Cnwll	11	L5
Dutton Ches W	130	B4
Duxford Cambs	87	K6
Duxford Oxon	66	A7
Dwygyfylchi Conwy	126	E4
Dwyran IoA	125	H6
Dyce C Aber	245	K1
Dyer's End Essex	88	E7
Dyfatty Carmth	56	E5
Dyffrydan Gwynd	110	D8
Dyffryn Brdgnd	42	C3
Dyffryn Myr Td	61	G2
Dyffryn V Glam	43	H7
Dyffryn Ardudwy Gwynd	109	K7
Dyffryn Castell Cerdgn	93	G7
Dyffryn Cellwen Neath	60	C5
Dyke Lincs	118	E7
Dyke Moray	264	F8
Dykehead Angus	233	K4
Dykehead Angus	234	B3
Dykehead N Lans	210	A7
Dykehead Stirlg	219	K7
Dykelands Abers	235	L2
Dykends Angus	233	K4
Dykeside Abers	256	C3
Dylife Powys	93	J4
Dymchurch Kent	25	L1
Dymock Gloucs	63	K1
Dyrham S Glos	45	L4
Dysart Fife	222	E8
Dyserth Denbgs	128	C4

E

Place	Page	Grid
Eachway Worcs	98	C8
Eachwick Nthumb	180	D4
Eagland Hill Lancs	147	H6
Eagle Lincs	135	H6
Eagle Barnsdale Lincs	135	H6
Eagle Moor Lincs	135	H6
Eaglescliffe S on T	169	L7
Eaglesfield Cumb	164	E5
Eaglesfield D & G	177	H4
Eaglesham E Rens	208	F8
Eagley Bolton	139	L5
Eairy IoM	154	d6
Eakring Notts	134	D7
Ealand N Linc	143	K5
Ealing Gt Lon	50	F3
Eals Nthumb	178	F7
Eamont Bridge Cumb	166	C5
Earby Lancs	148	F6
Earcroft Bl w D	139	K3
Eardington Shrops	97	G5
Eardisland Herefs	80	A4
Eardisley Herefs	79	K5
Eardiston Shrops	112	E6
Eardiston Worcs	80	F2
Earith Cambs	103	H8
Earle Nthumb	202	F7
Earlestown St Hel	130	B1
Earley Wokham	49	H4
Earlham Norfk	106	D2
Earlham Crematorium Norfk	106	E2
Earlish Highld	258	F4
Earls Barton Nhants	85	G3
Earls Colne Essex	71	L1
Earls Common Worcs	81	M3
Earl's Croome Worcs	81	K6
Earlsditton Shrops	96	E8
Earlsdon Covtry	99	J7
Earl's Down E Susx	23	L3
Earlsferry Fife	223	H7
Earlsfield Gt Lon	51	H4
Earlsford Abers	256	E5
Earl's Green Suffk	90	B2
Earlsheaton Kirk	141	L3
Earl Shilton Leics	100	A4
Earl Soham Suffk	90	F3
Earl Sterndale Derbys	132	B6
Earlston Border	201	J5
Earlston E Ayrs	196	D4
Earl Stonham Suffk	90	D3
Earlswood Surrey	37	L1
Earlswood Warwks	98	E8
Earlswood Common Mons	62	F8
Earnley W Susx	20	D7
Earnshaw Bridge Lancs	139	G3
Earsdon N Tyne	181	H4
Earsdon Nthumb	191	J7
Earsham Norfk	107	G5
Earswick C York	151	K4
Eartham W Susx	20	F5
Earthcott S Glos	45	K2
Easby N York	161	J1
Easdale Ag & B	215	L1
Easebourne W Susx	36	D6
Easenhall Warwks	100	A7
Eashing Surrey	36	E2
Easington Bucks	67	G5
Easington Dur	169	L2
Easington E R Yk	145	K4
Easington Nthumb	203	J6
Easington Oxon	67	G7
Easington R & Cl	171	H7
Easington Colliery Dur	169	L2
Easington Lane Sundld	169	K2
Easingwold N York	151	H2
Easole Street Kent	41	H5
Eassie and Nevay Angus	233	M6
East Aberthaw V Glam	42	F8
East Allington Devon	7	M5
East Anstey Devon	28	F5
East Anton Hants	34	E1
East Appleton N York	160	C3
East Ashey IoW	19	K6
East Ashling W Susx	20	D5
East Aston Hants	34	F2
East Ayton N York	163	H5
East Balsdon Cnwll	11	K3
East Bank Blae G	61	K6
East Barkwith Lincs	136	C3
East Barming Kent	39	H3
East Barnby N York	171	J8
East Barnet Gt Lon	69	H8
East Barns E Loth	212	F4
East Barsham Norfk	121	K5
East Beckham Norfk	122	D4
East Bedfont Gt Lon	50	D4
East Bergholt Suffk	90	C8
East Bierley Kirk	141	J2
East Bilney Norfk	121	L7
East Blatchington E Susx	23	H7
East Bloxworth Dorset	17	H4
East Boldon S Tyne	181	J6
East Boldre Hants	18	F4
East Bolton Nthumb	191	G3
Eastbourne Darltn	169	J7
Eastbourne E Susx	23	K7
Eastbourne Crematorium E Susx	23	L6
East Bower Somset	30	D3
East Bradenham Norfk	105	J2
East Brent Somset	44	D8
Eastbridge Suffk	91	K2
East Bridgford Notts	117	J3
East Briscoe Dur	168	B6
Eastbrook V Glam	43	J7
East Buckland Devon	28	B4
East Budleigh Devon	14	C5
Eastburn C Brad	149	J7
Eastburn E R Yk	152	F4
East Burnham Bucks	50	B2
East Burton Dorset	16	F5
Eastbury Herts	68	E8
Eastbury W Berk	47	M3
East Butsfield Dur	168	E2
East Butterwick N Linc	143	L6
Eastby N York	149	J5
East Calder W Loth	210	E5
East Carleton Norfk	106	D3
East Carlton Leeds	150	B7
East Carlton Nhants	101	H5
East Chaldon (Chaldon Herring) Dorset	16	F6
East Challow Oxon	48	A1
East Charleton Devon	7	L6
East Chelborough Dorset	16	A2
East Chiltington E Susx	22	F4
East Chinnock Somset	31	H8
East Chisenbury Wilts	47	H8
East Cholderton Hants	34	C2
Eastchurch Kent	53	L5
East Clandon Surrey	50	D8
East Claydon Bucks	67	H2
East Clevedon N Som	44	E5
East Coker Somset	31	J8
Eastcombe Gloucs	64	C6
Eastcombe Somset	29	L4
East Compton Somset	31	K3
East Cornworthy Devon	8	C4
East Cote Cumb	176	B7
Eastcote Gt Lon	50	E1
Eastcote Nhants	84	D4
Eastcote Solhll	99	G7
Eastcott Cnwll	26	D7
Eastcott Wilts	46	F7
East Cottingwith E R Yk	151	L7
Eastcourt Wilts	47	L8
Eastcourt Wilts	64	E8
East Cowes IoW	19	H4
East Cowick E R Yk	143	G4
East Cowton N York	160	D4
East Cramlington Nthumb	181	G4
East Cranmore Somset	31	L2
East Creech Dorset	17	H6
East Curthwaite Cumb	165	K1
East Dean E Susx	23	J7
East Dean Gloucs	63	K3
East Dean Hants	34	C5
East Dean W Susx	20	E4
East Devon Crematorium Devon	14	B3
Eastdown Devon	8	B5
East Down Devon	27	L3
East Drayton Notts	134	F4
East Dulwich Gt Lon	51	J4
East Dundry N Som	45	H5
East Ella C KuH	144	D2
East End Bed	86	C4
East End C Beds	85	J4
East End E R Yk	145	G2
East End E R Yk	145	H2
East End Essex	70	B5
Eastend Essex	72	D8
East End Hants	18	E4
East End Hants	48	B8
East End Herts	70	C2
East End Kent	39	L6
East End Kent	53	L4
East End M Keyn	85	J4
East End N Som	44	F5
East End Oxon	66	B4
East End Somset	31	L3
East End Suffk	90	C8
Easter Balmoral Abers	243	J5
Easter Compton S Glos	45	H2
Easter Dalziel Highld	252	E2
Eastergate W Susx	20	F6
Easterhouse C Glas	209	J6
Easter Howgate Mdloth	211	H6
Easter Kinkell Highld	263	G8
Easter Moniack Highld	250	F2
Eastern Green Covtry	99	H7
Easter Ord Abers	245	J3
Easter Pitkierie Fife	223	K6
Easter Skeld Shet	281	B6
Easter Softlaw Border	202	B6
Easterton Wilts	46	F8
Eastertown Somset	44	D7
East Everleigh Wilts	47	J7
East Farleigh Kent	39	J3
East Farndon Nhants	101	G6
East Ferry Lincs	143	K1
Eastfield N Lans	210	B6
Eastfield N York	163	J6
East Firsby Lincs	135	K2
East Fortune E Loth	212	C3
East Garforth Leeds	142	C1
East Garston W Berk	47	M4
Eastgate Dur	168	B3
Eastgate Lincs	118	C7
Eastgate Norfk	122	C7
East Ginge Oxon	48	C2
East Goscote Leics	100	E1

East Grafton Wilts 47 K6
East Green Suffk 91 J2
East Grimstead Wilts 34 B5
East Grinstead W Susx 38 B5
East Guldeford E Susx 25 H3
East Haddon Nhants 84 C2
East Hagbourne Oxon 48 D1
East Halton N Linc 144 E4
East Ham Gt Lon 51 L2
Eastham Wirral 129 H4
Eastham Ferry Wirral 129 J3
Easthampstead Park
   Crematorium Br For 49 K5
Easthampton Herefs 80 A3
East Hanney Oxon 66 B8
East Hanningfield Essex 71 J6
East Hardwick Wakefd 142 D4
East Harling Norfk 105 K6
East Harlsey N York 160 F3
East Harnham Wilts 33 K5
East Harptree BaNES 45 H7
East Hartford Nthumb 181 G3
East Harting W Susx 20 C3
East Hatch Wilts 32 F5
East Hatley Cambs 86 F5
East Hauxwell N York 159 L4
East Haven Angus 234 F8
Eastheath Wokham 49 J5
East Heckington Lincs 119 G3
East Hedleyhope Dur 168 F3
East Helmsdale Highld 274 D5
East Hendred Oxon 48 C1
East Heslerton N York 163 G7
East Hewish N Som 44 E6
East Hoathly E Susx 23 H4
East Holme Dorset 17 H5
Easthope Shrops 96 D4
Easthorpe Essex 72 C3
Easthorpe Notts 117 J1
East Horrington Somset 31 J2
East Horsley Surrey 50 E8
East Horton Nthumb 203 G7
East Howe Bmouth 17 L3
East Huntington C York 151 K5
East Huntspill Somset 30 E2
East Hyde C Beds 68 E4
East Ilkerton Devon 28 C2
East Ilsley W Berk 48 D3
Eastington Devon 13 H1
Eastington Gloucs 63 M6
Eastington Gloucs 65 H4
East Keal Lincs 137 G7
East Kennett Wilts 47 G5
East Keswick Leeds 150 D7
East Kilbride S Lans 209 H8
East Kimber Devon 12 C3
East Kirkby Lincs 136 F7
East Knighton Dorset 16 F7
East Knowstone Devon 28 E6
East Knoyle Wilts 32 E5
East Lambrook Somset 31 G7
East Lancashire Crematorium
   Bury 140 A6
Eastlands D & G 185 K8
East Langdon Kent 41 K6
East Langton Leics 100 F5
East Lavant W Susx 20 D5
East Lavington W Susx 20 F4
East Layton N York 159 L1
Eastleach Martin Gloucs 65 J6
Eastleach Turville Gloucs 65 J6
East Leake Notts 116 F6
East Learmouth Nthumb 202 D5
East Leigh Devon 7 K4
East Leigh Devon 7 L3
East Leigh Devon 13 G2
Eastleigh Devon 27 J5
Eastleigh Hants 34 F7
East Lexham Norfk 121 J8
Eastling Kent 40 C4
East Linton E Loth 212 D3
East Liss Hants 36 A5
East Lockinge Oxon 48 B2
East London Crematorium
   Gt Lon 51 L2
East Lound N Linc 143 K7
East Lulworth Dorset 17 G6
East Lutton N York 152 E2
East Lydeard Somset 30 B5
East Lydford Somset 31 J4
East Malling Kent 39 H2
East Malling Heath Kent 39 H2
East Marden W Susx 20 C4
East Markham Notts 134 E5
East Martin Hants 33 J7
East Marton N York 148 F5
East Meon Hants 35 L6
East Mere Devon 29 H7
East Mersea Essex 72 F4

East Molesey Surrey 50 F5
Eastmoor Norfk 104 E3
East Morden Dorset 17 H4
East Morton C Brad 149 K7
East Morton D & G 186 C6
East Ness N York 162 B7
East Newton E R Yk 153 L8
Eastney C Port 19 L4
Eastnor Herefs 81 G7
East Norton Leics 101 G3
Eastoft N Linc 143 K4
East Ogwell Devon 13 J8
Easton Cambs 86 C1
Easton Cumb 177 J7
Easton Devon 13 G5
Easton Dorset 16 D8
Easton Hants 35 G4
Easton Lincs 118 B6
Easton Norfk 106 C1
Easton Somset 31 H2
Easton Suffk 91 G3
Easton W Berk 48 B4
Easton Wilts 46 C5
Easton Grey Wilts 46 C2
Easton-in-Gordano N Som 45 G4
Easton Maudit Nhants 85 H3
Easton-on-the-Hill Nhants 101 M3
Easton Royal Wilts 47 J7
East Orchard Dorset 32 D7
East Ord Nthumb 202 F3
East Panson Devon 11 L4
East Parley Dorset 17 M3
East Peckham Kent 39 G4
East Pennar Pembks 54 F6
East Pennard Somset 31 K3
East Perry Cambs 86 C2
East Portlemouth Devon 7 L7
East Prawle Devon 8 A7
East Preston W Susx 21 J6
East Pulham Dorset 16 D1
East Putford Devon 26 F7
East Quantoxhead Somset 29 L2
East Rainham Medway 53 H5
East Rainton Sundld 169 J1
East Ravendale NE Lin 145 G7
East Raynham Norfk 121 J6
Eastrea Cambs 102 F4
East Riding Crematorium
   E R Yk 152 F2
Eastriggs D & G 177 H5
East Rigton Leeds 150 E7
Eastrington E R Yk 143 K2
East Rolstone N Som 44 E6
Eastrop Swindn 65 J8
East Rounton N York 160 F2
East Rudham Norfk 121 H6
East Runton Norfk 122 D3
East Ruston Norfk 123 G6
Eastry Kent 41 J4
East Saltoun E Loth 212 B5
Eastshaw W Susx 36 C6
East Sheen Gt Lon 51 G4
East Shefford W Berk 48 A4
East Sleekburn Nthumb 181 G2
East Somerton Norfk 123 K7
East Stockwith Lincs 134 F1
East Stoke Dorset 17 G5
East Stoke Notts 117 K2
East Stour Dorset 32 D6
East Stourmouth Kent 41 H3
East Stowford Devon 27 L5
East Stratton Hants 35 H3
East Studdal Kent 41 J5
East Sutton Kent 39 L3
East Taphouse Cnwll 5 L2
East-the-Water Devon 27 H5
East Thirston Nthumb 191 J6
East Tilbury Thurr 52 E3
East Tisted Hants 35 L4
East Torrington Lincs 136 B3
East Tuddenham Norfk 106 B1
East Tytherley Hants 34 C5
East Tytherton Wilts 46 D4
East Village Devon 13 K2
Eastville Bristl 45 J4
Eastville Lincs 137 H8
East Wall Shrops 96 C4
East Walton Norfk 121 G8
East Water Somset 31 J1
East Week Devon 12 F4
Eastwell Leics 117 K6
East Wellow Hants 34 C6
East Wemyss Fife 222 F7
East Whitburn W Loth 210 C6
Eastwick Herts 70 B5
East Wickham Gt Lon 51 M3
East Williamston Pembks 55 J6
East Winch Norfk 120 F8
East Winterslow Wilts 34 B4

East Wittering W Susx 20 C7
East Witton N York 159 L5
Eastwood Notts 116 D2
Eastwood Sthend 53 H1
East Woodburn Nthumb 179 L2
Eastwood End Cambs 103 J5
East Woodhay Hants 48 B6
East Woodlands Somset 32 C2
East Worldham Hants 35 M3
East Wretham Norfk 105 J5
East Youlstone Devon 26 D7
Eathorpe Warwks 83 J2
Eaton Ches E 131 G6
Eaton Ches W 130 B7
Eaton Leics 117 L5
Eaton Norfk 106 E2
Eaton Notts 134 E4
Eaton Oxon 66 C6
Eaton Shrops 95 J5
Eaton Shrops 96 B5
Eaton Bishop Herefs 80 B7
Eaton Bray C Beds 68 B3
Eaton Constantine Shrops 96 D2
Eaton Ford Cambs 86 D3
Eaton Green C Beds 68 B3
Eaton Hastings Oxon 65 K7
Eaton Mascott Shrops 96 C2
Eaton Socon Cambs 86 D3
Eaton upon Tern Shrops 113 L7
Eaves Brow Warrtn 130 C1
Eaves Green Solhll 99 H6
Ebberston N York 162 F6
Ebbesborne Wake Wilts 33 G6
Ebbw Vale Blae G 61 J5
Ebchester Dur 180 D7
Ebdon N Som 44 D6
Ebford Devon 14 A5
Ebley Gloucs 64 B6
Ebnal Ches W 113 H2
Ebnall Herefs 80 B3
Ebrington Gloucs 82 E7
Ebsworthy Devon 12 C4
Ecchinswell Hants 48 D7
Ecclaw Border 213 G5
Ecclefechan D & G 177 G4
Eccles Border 202 B5
Eccles Kent 52 F6
Eccles Salfd 140 A8
Eccles Green Herefs 79 L5
Ecclesall Sheff 132 F3
Ecclesfield Sheff 133 G1
Eccleshall Staffs 114 C5
Eccleshill C Brad 149 M8
Ecclesmachan W Loth 210 E4
Eccles on Sea Norfk 123 H5
Eccles Road Norfk 105 L5
Eccleston Ches W 129 J7
Eccleston Lancs 139 G4
Eccleston St Hel 138 F8
Eccleston Green Lancs 139 G4
Echt Abers 245 G2
Eckford Border 201 L7
Eckington Derbys 133 H4
Eckington Worcs 81 L7
Ecton Nhants 84 F3
Ecton Staffs 132 B8
Edale Derbys 132 B3
Eday Ork 275 d3
Edburton W Susx 22 C5
Edderside Cumb 164 E2
Edderton Highld 263 J3
Eddington Kent 41 G2
Eddlewood S Lans 209 J8
Edenbridge Kent 38 C4
Edenfield Lancs 140 B4
Edenhall Cumb 166 D4
Edenham Lincs 118 E7
Eden Mount Cumb 156 F7
Eden Park Gt Lon 51 K5
Edensor Derbys 132 E5
Edentaggart Ag & B 218 D8
Edenthorpe Donc 143 G6
Edern Gwynd 108 E4
Edgarley Somset 31 H3
Edgbaston Birm 98 D6
Edgcombe Cnwll 3 J4
Edgcott Bucks 67 G3
Edgcott Somset 28 C4
Edge Gloucs 64 B5
Edge Shrops 95 K2
Edgebolton Shrops 113 J7
Edge End Gloucs 63 H4
Edgefield Norfk 122 B5
Edgefield Green Norfk 122 B4
Edgefold Bolton 139 L6
Edge Green Ches W 113 H1
Edgehill Warwks 83 J5
Edgerley Shrops 112 E7

Edgerton Kirk 141 H4
Edgeside Lancs 140 C3
Edgeworth Gloucs 64 D6
Edgeworthy Devon 28 E8
Edginswell Torbay 8 C3
Edgiock Worcs 82 B3
Edgmond Wrekin 114 A7
Edgmond Marsh Wrekin 114 A7
Edgton Shrops 95 J6
Edgware Gt Lon 51 G1
Edgworth Bl w D 139 L4
Edinbane Highld 258 G6
Edinburgh C Edin 211 J4
Edingale Staffs 99 G1
Edingham D & G 175 L2
Edingley Notts 134 D8
Edingthorpe Norfk 123 G5
Edingthorpe Green Norfk 122 F5
Edington Border 202 D2
Edington Nthumb 180 E2
Edington Somset 30 F3
Edington Wilts 46 D8
Edington Burtle Somset 30 F2
Edingworth Somset 44 D8
Edistone Devon 26 D6
Edithmead Somset 30 E1
Edith Weston Rutlnd 101 K2
Edlesborough Bucks 68 B3
Edlingham Nthumb 191 G4
Edlington Lincs 136 D5
Edmond Castle Cumb 178 C7
Edmondsham Dorset 33 J8
Edmondsley Dur 169 G1
Edmondthorpe Leics 117 M8
Edmonton Cnwll 10 D8
Edmonton Gt Lon 69 J8
Edmundbyers Dur 168 C1
Ednam Border 202 A5
Ednaston Derbys 115 L3
Edney Common Essex 71 G6
Edradynate P & K 232 C5
Edrom Border 202 C2
Edstaston Shrops 113 H5
Edstone Warwks 82 E3
Edvin Loach Herefs 80 F3
Edwalton Notts 117 G4
Edwardstone Suffk 89 J6
Edwardsville Myr Td 43 G2
Edwinsford Carmth 59 H2
Edwinstowe Notts 134 C6
Edworth C Beds 86 E7
Edwyn Ralph Herefs 80 F4
Edzell Angus 234 F2
Edzell Woods Abers 234 F2
Efail-fach Neath 57 L6
Efail Isaf Rhondd 43 H5
Efailnewydd Gwynd 108 F4
Efail-Rhyd Powys 112 A6
Efailwen Carmth 75 K7
Efenechtyd Denbgs 128 D8
Effgill D & G 187 L7
Effingham Surrey 50 E8
Efflinch Staffs 115 K8
Efford Devon 13 K2
Efford Crematorium
   C Plym 6 F3
Egbury Hants 48 B8
Egdean W Susx 21 G3
Egerton Bolton 139 L5
Egerton Kent 40 B6
Egerton Forstal Kent 40 A6
Eggborough N York 142 E3
Eggbuckland C Plym 6 F3
Eggesford Devon 28 B8
Eggington C Beds 68 B2
Egginton Derbys 115 M6
Egglescliffe S on T 169 L7
Eggleston Dur 168 C6
Egham Surrey 50 C5
Egham Wick Surrey 50 B5
Egleton Rutlnd 101 J2
Eglingham Nthumb 191 G2
Egloshayle Cnwll 10 D8
Egloskerry Cnwll 11 K5
Eglwysbach Conwy 126 F5
Eglwys-Brewis V Glam 42 F7
Eglwys Cross Wrexhm 113 G3
Eglwys Fach Cerdgn 92 F4
Eglwyswrw Pembks 75 K4
Egmanton Notts 134 E6
Egremont Cumb 164 D8
Egremont Wirral 129 H1
Egton N York 162 E2
Egton Bridge N York 162 D2
Egypt Bucks 50 B2
Egypt Hants 34 F3
Eigg Highld 236 F3
Eight Ash Green Essex 72 D2
Eilanreach Highld 248 C8

Eisteddfa Gurig Cerdgn 93 H6
Elan Village Powys 78 C2
Elberton S Glos 45 J1
Elbridge W Susx 20 F6
Elburton C Plym 7 G4
Elcombe Swindn 47 H3
Elcot W Berk 48 B5
Eldernell Cambs 103 G4
Eldersfield Worcs 64 A1
Elderslie Rens 208 D6
Elder Street Essex 88 B8
Eldon Dur 169 G5
Eldwick C Brad 149 L7
Elerch Cerdgn 92 E6
Elfhill Abers 245 H6
Elford Nthumb 203 K7
Elford Staffs 98 F1
Elgin Moray 266 E4
Elgol Highld 247 H6
Elham Kent 41 G6
Elie Fife 223 J7
Elilaw Nthumb 190 D4
Elim IoA 124 F3
Eling Hants 18 F1
Elkesley Notts 134 D4
Elkstone Gloucs 64 D4
Ella Abers 268 B4
Ellacombe Torbay 8 D2
Elland Calder 141 H4
Elland Lower Edge Calder 141 H3
Ellary Ag & B 206 A4
Ellastone Staffs 115 J3
Ellel Lancs 147 J4
Ellemford Border 212 F7
Ellenabeich Ag & B. 215 L1
Ellenborough Cumb 164 D3
Ellenbrook Salfd 139 L7
Ellenhall Staffs 114 C6
Ellen's Green Surrey 37 G4
Ellerbeck N York 160 F3
Ellerby N York 171 J7
Ellerdine Heath Wrekin 113 K7
Ellerhayes Devon 14 A2
Elleric Ag & B. 229 G5
Ellerker E R Yk 144 A2
Ellers N York 149 H7
Ellerton E R Yk 151 L7
Ellerton N York 160 C3
Ellerton Shrops 113 M6
Ellesborough Bucks 67 K6
Ellesmere Shrops 112 F4
Ellesmere Port Ches W 129 J4
Ellingham Hants 18 A2
Ellingham Norfk 107 H5
Ellingham Nthumb 203 K8
Ellingstring N York 159 M6
Ellington Cambs 86 D1
Ellington Nthumb 191 K7
Ellington Thorpe Cambs 86 D1
Elliots Green Somset 32 D2
Ellisfield Hants 35 K2
Ellishader Highld 259 H3
Ellistown Leics 99 L1
Ellon Abers 257 H5
Ellonby Cumb 166 A4
Ellough Suffk 107 J4
Elloughton E R Yk 144 B2
Ellwood Gloucs 63 H5
Elm Cambs 103 K2
Elmbridge Worcs 81 K2
Elmdon Essex 87 J7
Elmdon Solhll 98 F6
Elmdon Heath Solhll 98 F7
Elmer W Susx 21 G6
Elmers End Gt Lon 51 K5
Elmer's Green Lancs 139 G6
Elmesthorpe Leics 100 A4
Elm Green Essex 71 J6
Elmhurst Staffs 98 E1
Elmley Castle Worcs 82 A7
Elmley Lovett Worcs 81 K1
Elmore Gloucs 64 A4
Elmore Back Gloucs 63 M4
Elm Park Gt Lon 52 B2
Elmscott Devon 26 D6
Elmsett Suffk 90 C6
Elms Green Worcs 81 G2
Elmstead Heath Essex 72 F3
Elmstead Market Essex 72 F2
Elmstead Row Essex 72 F3
Elmsted Kent 40 F6
Elmstone Kent 41 H4
Elmstone Hardwicke Gloucs 64 D2
Elmswell E R Yk 152 F4
Elmswell Suffk 89 K2
Elmton Derbys 133 K5
Elphin Highld 271 H6
Elphinstone E Loth 211 L5
Elrick Abers 245 H2

Elrig D & G 173 J5
Elrington Nthumb 179 K6
Elsdon Nthumb 190 C7
Elsecar Barns 142 B7
Elsenham Essex 70 D2
Elsfield Oxon 66 D5
Elsham N Linc 144 C5
Elsing Norfk 122 B8
Elslack N York 149 G6
Elson Hants 19 K3
Elson Shrops 112 F4
Elsrickle S Lans 199 J4
Elstead Surrey 36 D2
Elsted W Susx 20 D3
Elsthorpe Lincs 118 E6
Elstob Dur 169 J6
Elston Lancs 139 J1
Elston Notts 117 K2
Elston Wilts 33 J2
Elstone Devon 28 B7
Elstow Bed 85 L6
Elstree Herts 68 F4
Elstronwick E R Yk 145 G1
Elswick Lancs 147 H8
Elswick N u Ty 180 F6
Elsworth Cambs 87 G3
Elterwater Cumb 156 D2
Eltham Gt Lon 51 L4
Eltham Crematorium
Gt Lon 51 L4
Eltisley Cambs 86 F3
Elton Bury 140 B5
Elton Cambs 102 B4
Elton Ches W 129 K4
Elton Derbys 132 D7
Elton Gloucs 63 K4
Elton Herefs 80 B1
Elton Notts 117 K4
Elton S on T 169 L7
Elton Green Ches W 129 K5
Eltringham Nthumb 180 C6
Elvanfoot S Lans 186 E3
Elvaston Derbys 116 C5
Elveden Suffk 105 G7
Elvetham Heath Hants 49 K7
Elvingston E Loth 212 A4
Elvington C York 151 L6
Elvington Kent 41 J5
Elwell Devon 28 B4
Elwick Hartpl 170 B4
Elwick Nthumb 203 J5
Elworth Ches E 130 E7
Elworth Somset 29 K4
Ely Cambs 103 L7
Ely Cardif 43 J6
Emberton M Keyn 85 H5
Embleton Cumb 165 G4
Embleton Dur 169 L5
Embleton Nthumb 191 J2
Embo Highld 264 C1
Emborough Somset 31 K1
Embo Street Highld 264 C2
Embsay N York 149 H5
Emery Down Hants 18 D2
Emley Kirk 141 K5
Emley Moor Kirk 141 K5
Emmbrook Wokham 49 J5
Emmer Green Readg 49 H4
Emmett Carr Derbys 133 J4
Emmington Oxon 67 H6
Emneth Norfk 103 K2
Emneth Hungate Norfk 103 K2
Empingham Rutlnd 101 L2
Empshott Hants 35 M4
Empshott Green Hants 35 M5
Emstrey Crematorium
Shrops 96 C1
Emsworth Hants 20 B5
Enborne W Berk 48 B6
Enborne Row W Berk 48 C6
Enchmarsh Shrops 96 B4
Enderby Leics 100 C3
Endmoor Cumb 157 H5
Endon Staffs 114 E1
Endon Bank Staffs 114 E1
Enfield Gt Lon 69 K7
Enfield Crematorium Gt Lon 69 K7
Enfield Lock Gt Lon 69 K7
Enfield Wash Gt Lon 69 K7
Enford Wilts 47 H8
Engine Common S Glos 45 K2
England's Gate Herefs 80 D5
Englefield W Berk 48 F4
Englefield Green Surrey 50 C4
Engleseabrook Ches E 114 B1
English Bicknor Gloucs 63 H4
Englishcombe BaNES 45 L6
English Frankton Shrops 113 G5
Engollan Cnwll 10 B8

Enham-Alamein Hants 34 D1
Enmore Somset 30 C4
Enmore Green Dorset 32 E6
Ennerdale Bridge Cumb 164 E7
Enniscaven Cnwll 4 F3
Enochdhu P & K 233 G3
Ensay Ag & B 226 D3
Ensbury Bmouth 17 L3
Ensdon Shrops 112 F8
Ensis Devon 27 K5
Enson Staffs 114 K6
Enstone Oxon 66 A2
Enterkinfoot D & G 186 C5
Enterpen N York 161 G2
Enville Staffs 97 J6
Eolaigearraidh W Isls 283 b12
Epney Gloucs 63 M5
Epperstone Notts 117 H2
Epping Essex 70 C6
Epping Green Essex 70 B6
Epping Green Herts 69 J5
Epping Upland Essex 70 C6
Eppleby N York 168 F8
Eppleworth E R Yk 144 C2
Epsom Surrey 51 G6
Epwell Oxon 83 H7
Epworth N Linc 143 K7
Epworth Turbary N Linc 143 J7
Erbistock Wrexhm 112 E3
Erdington Birm 98 E5
Eridge Green E Susx 38 E6
Eridge Station E Susx 38 E6
Erines Ag & B 206 D4
Eriska Ag & B 228 D6
Eriswell Suffk 104 E7
Erith Gt Lon 52 B3
Erlestoke Wilts 46 D8
Ermington Devon 7 J4
Erpingham Norfk 122 D5
Erriottwood Kent 40 B3
Errogie Highld 250 F7
Errol P & K 222 D3
Erskine Rens 208 D5
Erskine Bridge Rens 208 D4
Ervie D & G 172 B1
Erwarton Suffk 90 F8
Erwood Powys 78 F6
Eryholme N York 160 D1
Eryrys Denbgs 128 E8
Escalls Cnwll 2 B5
Escomb Dur 168 F4
Escott Somset 29 K3
Escrick N York 151 K7
Esgair Carmth 58 C3
Esgair Cerdgn 77 G2
Esgairgeiliog Powys 93 G2
Esgerdawe Carmth 77 H7
Esgyryn Conwy 126 F4
Esh Dur 169 G2
Esher Surrey 50 E6
Esholt C Brad 150 A7
Eshott Nthumb 191 J6
Eshton N York 149 G4
Esh Winning Dur 169 G2
Eskadale Highld 250 D4
Eskbank Mdloth 211 K5
Eskdale Green Cumb 155 L3
Eskdalemuir D & G 187 K6
Eske E R Yk 153 G7
Eskham Lincs 145 K8
Eskholme Donc 143 G4
Esperley Lane Ends Dur 168 E6
Esprick Lancs 147 H8
Essendine Rutlnd 102 A1
Essendon Herts 69 H5
Essich Highld 251 H4
Essington Staffs 98 B3
Esslemont Abers 257 G6
Eston R & Cl 170 D7
Etal Nthumb 202 E5
Etchilhampton Wilts 46 F7
Etchingham E Susx 24 C2
Etchinghill Kent 41 G7
Etchinghill Staffs 115 G7
Etchingwood E Susx 23 H3
Etling Green Norfk 105 K1
Etloe Gloucs 63 K6
Eton W & M 50 B3
Eton Wick W & M. 50 B3
Etruria C Stke 114 D2
Etteridge Highld 241 J5
Ettersgill Dur 167 K5
Ettiley Heath Ches E 130 E7
Ettingshall Wolves 97 L4
Ettington Warwks 83 G5
Etton C Pete 102 C2
Etton E R Yk 152 F7
Ettrick Border 187 L3
Ettrickbridge Border 188 C1

Ettrickhill Border 187 L3
Etwall Derbys 115 M5
Eudon George Shrops 96 F5
Euston Suffk 105 H2
Euximoor Drove Cambs 103 K4
Euxton Lancs 139 H4
Evancoyd Powys 79 J3
Evanton Highld 263 G6
Evedon Lincs 118 E2
Evelith Shrops 97 G3
Evelix Highld 263 L5
Evenjobb Powys 79 J3
Evenley Nhants 84 B8
Evenlode Gloucs 65 J1
Evenwood Dur 168 F5
Evenwood Gate Dur 168 F5
Evercreech Somset 31 L3
Everingham E R Yk 152 B7
Everleigh Wilts 47 J6
Everley N York 163 H5
Eversholt C Beds 85 K8
Evershot Dorset 16 A2
Eversley Hants 49 J6
Eversley Cross Hants 49 J6
Everthorpe E R Yk 144 A2
Everton C Beds 86 D5
Everton Hants 18 D5
Everton Lpool 129 H1
Everton Notts 134 D2
Evertown D & G. 177 L3
Evesbatch Herefs 80 F5
Evesham Worcs 82 B3
Evington C Leic 100 D3
Ewden Village Sheff 141 L8
Ewell Surrey 51 G6
Ewell Minnis Kent 41 H6
Ewelme Oxon 48 F1
Ewen Gloucs 64 E7
Ewenny V Glam 42 D6
Ewerby Lincs 118 F2
Ewerby Thorpe Lincs 118 F2
Ewhurst Surrey 37 G3
Ewhurst Green E Susx 24 C2
Ewhurst Green Surrey 37 G3
Ewloe Flints 129 G6
Ewloe Green Flints 129 G6
Ewood Bl w D. 139 K3
Ewood Bridge Lancs 140 B4
Eworthy Devon 12 B4
Ewshot Hants 36 B1
Ewyas Harold Herefs 62 D2
Exbourne Devon 12 D1
Exbury Hants 19 G4
Exceat E Susx 23 H7
Exebridge Somset 29 G4
Exelby N York 160 D5
Exeter Devon 13 L4
Exeter & Devon Crematorium
Devon 13 L4
Exford Somset 28 E4
Exfordsgreen Shrops 95 L2
Exhall Warwks 82 D4
Exhall Warwks 99 L6
Exlade Street Oxon 49 G3
Exley Head C Brad 149 J7
Exminster Devon 13 M5
Exmouth Devon 14 A6
Exning Suffk 88 C3
Exted Kent 41 G6
Exton Devon 14 A5
Exton Hants 35 J5
Exton Rutlnd 101 K1
Exton Somset 29 G4
Exwick Devon 13 L4
Eyam Derbys 132 D4
Eydon Nhants 83 M5
Eye C Pete 102 E2
Eye Herefs 80 C2
Eye Suffk 106 D7
Eye Green C Pete 102 E2
Eye Kettleby Leics 117 K8
Eyemouth Border 213 L6
Eyeworth C Beds 86 E6
Eyhorne Street Kent 39 L2
Eyke Suffk 91 H5
Eynesbury Cambs 86 D4
Eynsford Kent 52 B7
Eynsham Oxon 66 B5
Eype Dorset 15 K4
Eyre Highld 259 G7
Eythorne Kent 41 J7
Eyton Herefs 80 B2
Eyton Shrops 95 J4
Eyton Shrops 112 F5
Eyton Shrops 113 G4
Eyton Wrexhm 112 E3
Eyton on Severn Shrops 96 D2
Eyton upon the Weald Moors
Wrekin 113 L8

F

Faccombe Hants 48 A7
Faceby N York 161 H2
Fachwen Powys 111 K8
Facit Lancs 140 D4
Fackley Notts 133 J7
Faddiley Ches E 113 K1
Fadmoor N York 161 L5
Faerdre Swans 57 J4
Fagwyr Swans 57 J4
Faifley W Duns 208 E4
Failand N Som 45 G4
Failford S Ayrs 196 F5
Failsworth Oldham 140 D7
Fairbourne Gwynd 92 D1
Fairburn N York 142 D2
Fairfield Derbys 131 L5
Fairfield Kent 25 H2
Fairfield Worcs 97 L8
Fairfield Park Herts 86 D8
Fairford Gloucs 65 H6
Fairford Gloucs 65 H6
Fairgirth D & G 175 L3
Fair Green Norfk 120 E8
Fairhaven Lancs 138 C2
Fair Isle Shet 281 b8
Fairlands Surrey 50 B8
Fairlie N Ayrs 207 L8
Fairlight E Susx 24 F5
Fairmile Devon 14 C3
Fairmile Surrey 50 E6
Fairnilee Border 200 F6
Fair Oak Hants 35 G7
Fairoak Staffs 114 B5
Fair Oak Green Hants 49 G6
Fairseat Kent 52 D6
Fairstead Essex 71 J4
Fairstead Norfk 120 E7
Fairstead Norfk 122 F6
Fairwarp E Susx 23 G2
Fairwater Cardif 43 J6
Fairy Cross Devon 27 G6
Fakenham Norfk 121 K5
Fakenham Magna Suffk 105 H8
Fala Mdloth 211 M6
Fala Dam Mdloth 211 M6
Falcut Nhants 84 B6
Faldingworth Lincs 135 L3
Faldouët Jersey 9 f2
Falfield S Glos 63 K8
Falkenham Suffk 91 G7
Falkirk Falk 210 A3
Falkirk Crematorium Falk ... 210 A3
Falkland Fife 222 D5
Fallburn S Lans 199 G5
Fallgate Derbys 133 G7
Fallin Stirlg 209 L1
Fallodon Nthumb 191 H2
Fallowfield Manch 131 G1
Fallowfield Nthumb 179 L5
Falls of Blarghour Ag & B ... 216 F4
Falmer E Susx 22 E5
Falmouth Cnwll 3 K4
Falnash Border 188 C5
Falsgrave N York 163 J5
Falstone Nthumb 179 G2
Fanagmore Highld 276 B6
Fancott C Beds 68 C2
Fanellan Highld 250 E3
Fangdale Beck N York 161 L4
Fangfoss E R Yk 152 A5
Fanmore Ag & B 226 E3
Fannich Lodge Highld 261 L6
Fans Border 201 J5
Far Bletchley M Keyn 85 G8
Farcet Cambs 102 D4
Far Cotton Nhants 84 E3
Farden Shrops 96 D8
Fareham Hants 19 K2
Far End Cumb 156 D3
Farewell Staffs 98 D1
Far Forest Worcs 97 G8
Farforth Lincs 136 F4
Far Green Gloucs 63 M7
Faringdon Oxon 65 L8
Farington Lancs 139 G3
Farlam Cumb 178 D7
Farleigh N Som 45 G4
Farleigh Surrey 51 K7
Farleigh Hungerford Somset ... 46 A7
Farleigh Wallop Hants 35 J2
Farlesthorpe Lincs 137 J5
Farleton Cumb 157 H6
Farleton Lancs 147 L2
Farley Derbys 132 F7
Farley Staffs 115 H3
Farley Wilts 34 B5

Farley Green Suffk 88 E4
Farley Green Surrey 37 G2
Farley Hill Wokham 49 H6
Farleys End Gloucs 63 M4
Farlington C Port 19 M3
Farlington N York 151 K2
Farlow Shrops 96 E7
Farmborough BaNES 45 K7
Farmbridge End Essex 70 F5
Farmcote Gloucs 64 F1
Farmcote Shrops 97 H5
Farmers Carmth 77 J6
Farmington Gloucs 65 H4
Farmoor Oxon 66 C5
Far Moor Wigan 139 G7
Farms Common Cnwll 3 H4
Farm Town Leics 116 C8
Farmtown Moray 267 K6
Farnah Green Derbys 116 B2
Farnborough Gt Lon 51 L6
Farnborough Hants 49 L8
Farnborough W Berk 48 B3
Farnborough Warwks 83 K5
Farnborough Park Hants 49 L7
Farncombe Surrey 36 E2
Farndish Bed 85 H3
Farndon Ches W 112 F1
Farndon Notts 117 K1
Farne Islands Nthumb 203 L5
Farnell Angus 235 G4
Farnham Dorset 33 G7
Farnham Essex 70 C2
Farnham N York 150 E4
Farnham Suffk 91 H3
Farnham Surrey 36 B2
Farnham Common Bucks 50 B2
Farnham Green Essex 70 C2
Farnham Royal Bucks 50 B2
Farningham Kent 52 C5
Farnley Leeds 141 L1
Farnley N York 150 B6
Farnley Tyas Kirk 141 J5
Farnsfield Notts 134 C8
Farnworth Bolton 139 L6
Farnworth Halton 129 L2
Far Oakridge Gloucs 64 D6
Farr Highld 241 L3
Farr Highld 251 J5
Farr Highld 278 B4
Farraline Highld 251 G7
Farringdon Devon 14 B4
Farrington Gurney BaNES 45 J7
Far Sawrey Cumb 156 E4
Farsley Leeds 141 K1
Farther Howegreen
    Essex 71 K6
Farthing Green Kent 39 K4
Farthinghoe Nhants 83 M7
Farthingloe Kent 41 J7
Farthingstone Nhants 84 B4
Farthing Street Gt Lon 51 L6
Fartown Kirk 141 J4
Farway Devon 14 E3
Fasnacloich Ag & B 229 G6
Fasnakyle Highld 250 B6
Fassfern Highld 239 G7
Fatfield Sundld 181 H8
Faugh Cumb 178 C7
Fauld Staffs 115 K6
Fauldhouse W Loth 210 B6
Faulkbourne Essex 71 J4
Faulkland Somset 45 L8
Fauls Shrops 113 K5
Faversham Kent 40 D3
Fawdington N York 150 F1
Fawdon N u Ty 180 F5
Fawdon Nthumb 190 E3
Fawfieldhead Staffs 131 L7
Fawkham Green Kent 52 C6
Fawler Oxon 66 A4
Fawley Bucks 49 J2
Fawley Hants 19 G3
Fawley W Berk 48 B3
Fawley Chapel Herefs 63 H1
Fawnog Flints 128 F6
Fawsley Nhants 84 A4
Faxfleet E R Yk 143 L3
Faygate W Susx 37 K4
Fazakerley Lpool 138 D8
Fazeley Staffs 99 G3
Fearby N York 160 B6
Fearn Highld 264 C4
Fearnan P & K 231 K6
Fearnbeg Highld 260 B7
Fearnhead Warrtn 130 C2
Fearnmore Highld 260 A7
Fearnoch Ag & B 206 E3
Featherstone Staffs 97 L2
Featherstone Wakefd 142 C4

Feckenham Worcs 82 B3
Feering Essex 72 C3
Feetham N York 159 H3
Feizor N York 148 D2
Felbridge Surrey 38 B5
Felbrigg Norfk 122 E4
Felcourt Surrey 38 B5
Felden Herts 68 D6
Felindre Carmth 59 G4
Felindre Carmth 59 K3
Felindre Carmth 76 C7
Felindre Cerdgn 77 G4
Felindre Powys 61 J2
Felindre Powys 94 E7
Felindre Swans 57 H4
Felindre Farchog Pembks 75 J4
Felin Fach Cerdgn 76 F4
Felinfach Powys 78 F8
Felinfoel Carmth 56 F4
Felingwm Isaf Carmth 58 F4
Felingwm Uchaf Carmth 58 F4
Felin-newydd Powys 78 F8
Felixkirk N York 161 G5
Felixstowe Suffk 91 G8
Felixstowe Ferry Suffk 91 H7
Felkington Nthumb 202 E4
Felkirk Wakefd 142 B5
Felling Gatesd 181 G6
Fell Lane C Brad 149 J7
Fell Side Cumb 165 J3
Felmersham Bed 85 K4
Felmingham Norfk 122 E5
Felpham W Susx 20 F7
Felsham Suffk 89 J4
Felsted Essex 71 G3
Feltham Gt Lon 50 E4
Felthamhill Surrey 50 E5
Felthorpe Norfk 122 D7
Felton Herefs 80 D5
Felton N Som 45 G6
Felton Nthumb 191 H6
Felton Butler Shrops 112 F8
Feltwell Norfk 104 E5
Fenay Bridge Kirk 141 J4
Fence Lancs 148 E8
Fence Rothm 133 J3
Fence Houses Sundld 169 J1
Fencott Oxon 66 E4
Fendike Corner Lincs 137 H7
Fen Ditton Cambs 87 K3
Fen Drayton Cambs 87 G2
Fen End Lincs 119 H7
Fen End Solhll 99 G8
Fenham Nthumb 203 H5
Feniscliffe Bl w D 139 K2
Feniscowles Bl w D 139 K3
Feniton Devon 14 D3
Fenland Crematorium
    Cambs 103 H4
Fenn Green Shrops 97 H6
Fenn Street Medway 53 G4
Fenny Bentley Derbys 115 K2
Fenny Bridges Devon 14 D3
Fenny Compton Warwks 83 K5
Fenny Drayton Leics 99 K4
Fenny Stratford M Keyn 85 G8
Fenrother Nthumb 191 H7
Fenstanton Cambs 87 G2
Fenstead End Suffk 88 F5
Fen Street Norfk 105 K4
Fen Street Suffk 90 E3
Fenton C Stke 114 D3
Fenton Cambs 103 G7
Fenton Cumb 178 C7
Fenton Lincs 118 A1
Fenton Lincs 135 G4
Fenton Notts 134 F3
Fenton Nthumb 202 F6
Fenton Barns E Loth 212 B3
Fenwick Donc 142 F4
Fenwick E Ayrs 196 F2
Fenwick Nthumb 180 C4
Fenwick Nthumb 203 H5
Feock Cnwll 3 L3
Feolin Ferry Ag & B 205 G3
Fergushill N Ayrs 196 C2
Feriniquarrie Highld 258 B6
Fermain Bay Guern 9 k3
Fern Angus 234 D3
Ferndale Rhondd 42 F2
Ferndown Dorset 17 L3
Ferness Highld 253 J3
Fernham Oxon 65 L8
Fernhill Heath Worcs 81 K3
Fernhurst W Susx 36 D5
Fernie Fife 222 E4
Ferniegair S Lans 209 K8
Fernilea Highld 246 E2
Fernilee Derbys 131 K4

Fernwood Notts 117 L2
Ferrensby N York 150 E4
Ferriby Sluice N Linc 144 B4
Ferrindonald Highld 247 L7
Ferring W Susx 21 J6
Ferrybridge Wakefd 142 D3
Ferryden Angus 235 H4
Ferryhill Dur 169 H4
Ferryhill Station Dur 169 J4
Ferry Point Highld 263 K3
Ferryside Carmth 56 C3
Ferrytown Highld 263 K2
Fersfield Norfk 106 B6
Fersit Highld 240 B7
Feshiebridge Highld 241 M3
Fetcham Surrey 50 F7
Fetlar Shet 281 f3
Fetterangus Abers 269 H6
Fettercairn Abers 235 G1
Fewcott Oxon 66 D2
Fewston N York 150 B5
Ffairfach Carmth 59 H4
Ffair Rhos Cerdgn 77 K2
Ffald-y-Brenin Carmth 77 H6
Ffawyddog Powys 61 K3
Ffestiniog Gwynd 110 D3
Ffordd-las Denbgs 128 D6
Fforest Carmth 57 G4
Fforest Mons 62 B3
Fforest Fach Swans 57 H5
Fforest Göch Neath 57 K4
Ffostrasol Cerdgn 76 C5
Ffrith Flints 129 G8
Ffynnonddewi Cerdgn 76 C4
Ffynnongroyw Flints 128 D3
Ffynnon-Oer Cerdgn 76 F4
Fiag Lodge Highld 272 C2
Fickleshole Surrey 51 K6
Fiddington Gloucs 64 D1
Fiddington Somset 30 B3
Fiddleford Dorset 32 D8
Fiddlers Green Cnwll 4 D4
Fiddlers Hamlet Essex 70 C6
Field Staffs 115 G5
Field Broughton Cumb 156 E6
Field Dalling Norfk 121 M4
Fieldhead Cumb 166 B3
Field Head Leics 100 B2
Fifehead Magdalen Dorset 32 C6
Fifehead Neville Dorset 32 C8
Fifehead St Quintin Dorset 16 E1
Fife Keith Moray 267 H6
Fifield Oxon 65 K3
Fifield W & M 49 L4
Fifield Wilts 33 K1
Figheldean Wilts 33 K2
Filands Wilts 46 D1
Filby Norfk 107 K1
Filey N York 163 L6
Filgrave M Keyn 85 G5
Filkins Oxon 65 K6
Filleigh Devon 28 B5
Filleigh Devon 28 C8
Fillingham Lincs 135 J3
Fillongley Warwks 99 H6
Filmore Hill Hants 35 K5
Filton S Glos 45 J3
Fimber E R Yk 152 D4
Finavon Angus 234 D4
Fincham Norfk 104 D2
Finchampstead Wokham 49 J6
Fincharn Ag & B 216 D6
Finchdean Hants 20 B4
Finchingfield Essex 88 D8
Finchley Gt Lon 51 H1
Findern Derbys 116 A5
Findhorn Moray 265 G7
Findhorn Bridge Highld 252 E6
Findochty Moray 267 J3
Findo Gask P & K 221 H3
Findon Abers 245 L4
Findon W Susx 21 J5
Findon Mains Highld 263 G7
Findrack House Abers 244 D3
Finedon Nhants 85 H1
Fingal Street Suffk 90 F1
Fingask P & K 222 B3
Fingest Bucks 49 J1
Finghall N York 160 B5
Fingland Cumb 177 H7
Fingland D & G 197 L2
Finglesham Kent 41 K4
Fingringhoe Essex 72 F3
Finkle Green Essex 88 D7
Finkle Street Barns 141 M7
Finlarig Stirlg 231 G8
Finmere Oxon 84 C8
Finnart P & K 230 F4
Finningham Suffk 90 C2

Finningley Donc 143 H7
Finsbay W Isls 282 e6
Finstall Worcs 82 A1
Finsthwaite Cumb 156 E5
Finstock Oxon 66 A4
Finstown Ork 275 c4
Fintry Abers 268 D5
Fintry Stirlg 209 G2
Finzean Abers 244 D5
Fionnphort Ag & B 226 B7
Fionnsbhagh W Isls 282 e6
Firbank Cumb 157 K4
Firbeck Rothm 133 L2
Firby N York 152 A3
Firby N York 160 C5
Firgrove Rochdl 140 D5
Firle E Susx 23 G6
Firsby Lincs 137 H7
Firsdown Wilts 34 B4
Fir Tree Dur 168 F4
Fishbourne IoW 19 J5
Fishbourne W Susx 20 D6
Fishburn Dur 169 K4
Fishcross Clacks 220 F8
Fisher W Susx 20 E6
Fisherford Abers 256 B4
Fisherrow E Loth 211 K4
Fisher's Pond Hants 35 G6
Fisher's Row Lancs 147 H6
Fisherstreet W Susx 36 E4
Fisherton Highld 252 D2
Fisherton S Ayrs 196 B3
Fisherton de la Mere Wilts 33 G3
Fisherwick Staffs 98 F2
Fishery Estate W & M 49 L3
Fishguard Pembks 74 F5
Fishlake Donc 143 G5
Fishleigh Devon 12 D2
Fishmere End Lincs 119 J4
Fishnish Pier Ag & B 227 J4
Fishpond Bottom Dorset 15 J3
Fishponds Bristl 45 J4
Fishtoft Lincs 119 K3
Fishtoft Drove Lincs 119 K2
Fishwick Lancs 139 H2
Fiskavaig Highld 246 D2
Fiskerton Lincs 135 L5
Fiskerton Notts 117 K1
Fitling E R Yk 145 H1
Fittleton Wilts 33 K1
Fittleworth W Susx 21 G3
Fitton End Cambs 103 J1
Fitz Shrops 113 G7
Fitzhead Somset 29 L5
Fitzroy Somset 30 B5
Fitzwilliam Wakefd 142 C5
Five Ash Down E Susx 23 H3
Five Ashes E Susx 23 J2
Five Bells Somset 29 K2
Five Bridges Herefs 80 F6
Fivecrosses Ches W 129 M4
Fivehead Somset 30 E6
Fivelanes Cnwll 11 J6
Five Lanes Mons 44 F1
Five Oak Green Kent 39 G4
Five Oaks Jersey 9 e3
Five Oaks W Susx 37 G5
Five Roads Carmth 56 E4
Five Wents Kent 39 K3
Flack's Green Essex 71 J4
Flackwell Heath Bucks 49 L1
Fladbury Worcs 82 A6
Fladdabister Shet 281 e7
Flagg Derbys 132 C6
Flamborough E R Yk 153 K2
Flamstead Herts 68 D4
Flamstead End Herts 69 J6
Flansham W Susx 20 F6
Flanshaw Wakefd 141 M4
Flappit Spring C Brad 149 J8
Flasby N York 149 G4
Flash Staffs 131 K6
Flashader Highld 258 E6
Flaunden Herts 68 C7
Flawborough Notts 117 K3
Flawith N York 151 G3
Flax Bourton N Som 45 G5
Flaxby N York 150 E4
Flaxley Gloucs 63 K4
Flaxmere Ches W 130 A5
Flaxpool Somset 29 L4
Flaxton N York 151 L3
Fleckney Leics 100 E5
Flecknoe Warwks 83 M3
Fledborough Notts 134 F5
Fleet Dorset 16 C6
Fleet Hants 20 B6
Fleet Hants 49 K8
Fleet Lincs 119 L6

Fleetend Hants 19 H3
Fleet Hargate Lincs 119 L6
Fleetwood Lancs 146 F6
Fleggburgh Norfk 107 J1
Flemingston V Glam 42 F7
Flemington S Lans 209 H7
Flempton Suffk 89 G1
Fletchersbridge Cnwll 5 J2
Fletcher's Green Kent 38 E3
Fletchertown Cumb 165 G2
Fletching E Susx 23 G3
Fleur-de-lis Caerph 43 J3
Flexbury Cnwll 11 J1
Flexford Surrey 36 D1
Flimby Cumb 164 D4
Flimwell E Susx 39 H7
Flint Flints 128 F5
Flintham Notts 117 K2
Flint Mountain Flints 128 F5
Flinton E R Yk 153 K8
Flint's Green Solhll 99 H7
Flishinghurst Kent 39 J6
Flitcham Norfk 120 F6
Flitton C Beds 85 L8
Flitwick C Beds 85 K8
Flixborough N Linc 143 L5
Flixborough Stather
   N Linc 143 L5
Flixton N York 163 J6
Flixton Suffk 107 G6
Flixton Traffd 130 E1
Flockton Kirk 141 K5
Flockton Green Kirk 141 K5
Flodden Nthumb 202 E6
Flodigarry Highld 259 H2
Flookburgh Cumb 156 E7
Flordon Norfk 106 D4
Flore Nhants 84 C3
Flotterton Nthumb 190 E6
Flowers Green E Susx 23 L5
Flowton Suffk 90 C6
Flushdyke Wakefd 141 L3
Flushing Cnwll 3 K4
Fluxton Devon 14 C4
Flyford Flavell Worcs 82 A4
Fobbing Thurr 52 F2
Fochabers Moray 267 G4
Fochriw Caerph 61 H6
Fockerby N Linc 143 L4
Foddington Somset 31 J5
Foel Powys 94 B1
Foelgastell Carmth 59 G6
Foel y Dyffryn Brdgnd 42 C3
Foggathorpe E R Yk 152 A8
Fogo Border 202 B3
Fogwatt Moray 266 E5
Foindle Highld 276 B6
Folda Angus 233 J3
Fole Staffs 115 G4
Foleshill Covtry 99 K7
Folke Dorset 31 L8
Folkestone Kent 41 H8
Folkingham Lincs 118 E5
Folkington E Susx 23 J6
Folksworth Cambs 102 C5
Folkton N York 163 J6
Folla Rule Abers 256 C5
Follifoot N York 150 D5
Folly Gate Devon 12 D3
Folly Hill Surrey 36 B1
Fonmon V Glam 43 G8
Fonthill Bishop Wilts 32 F4
Fonthill Gifford Wilts 32 F4
Fontmell Magna Dorset 32 E7
Fontmell Parva Dorset 32 D7
Fontwell W Susx 20 F5
Font-y-gary V Glam 43 G8
Foolow Derbys 132 D4
Foots Cray Gt Lon 52 A5
Forbestown Abers 243 L1
Forcett N York 168 F8
Ford Ag & B 216 D6
Ford Bucks 67 J5
Ford Derbys 133 H4
Ford Devon 7 J5
Ford Devon 8 B6
Ford Devon 27 G6
Ford Gloucs 65 G1
Ford Nthumb 202 E5
Ford Shrops 95 K1
Ford Somset 29 K5
Ford Somset 45 K4
Ford Staffs 115 H1
Ford W Susx 21 G6
Ford Wilts 33 L4
Ford Wilts 46 B4
Forda Devon 12 D4
Fordcombe Kent 38 E5
Fordell Fife 211 G1

Forden Powys 94 F3
Ford End Essex 71 G4
Forder Green Devon 8 B2
Ford Green Lancs 147 J6
Fordham Cambs 88 C1
Fordham Essex 72 D2
Fordham Norfk 104 C3
Fordham Heath Essex 72 D2
Ford Heath Shrops 95 K1
Fordingbridge Hants 33 K8
Fordon E R Yk 163 J7
Fordoun Abers 245 G8
Ford's Green Suffk 90 C2
Fordstreet Essex 72 D2
Ford Street Somset 29 L7
Fordton Devon 13 J3
Fordwells Oxon 65 L4
Fordwich Kent 41 G3
Fordyce Abers 267 L3
Forebridge Staffs 114 E7
Foremark Derbys 116 B6
Forest Guern 9 j4
Forest N York 160 C3
Forest Becks Lancs 148 D5
Forestburn Gate Nthumb 190 F7
Forest Chapel Ches E 131 J5
Forest Gate Gt Lon 51 L2
Forest Green Surrey 37 H3
Forest Hall N Tyne 181 G5
Forest Head Cumb 178 D7
Forest Hill Gt Lon 51 K4
Forest Hill Oxon 66 E5
Forest-in-Teesdale Dur 167 K4
Forest Lane Head N York 150 D4
Forest Mill Clacks 221 G8
Forest of Dean Crematorium
   Gloucs 63 J4
Forest Park Crematorium
   Gt Lon 70 C8
Forest Row E Susx 38 C6
Forest Side IoW 19 H5
Forestside W Susx 20 C4
Forest Town Notts 133 L7
Forfar Angus 234 C5
Forgandenny P & K 221 K3
Forge Powys 93 G3
Forge Hammer Torfn 62 B7
Forge Side Torfn 61 L5
Forgie Moray 267 H5
Forgieside Moray 267 H5
Forgue Abers 256 A3
Forhill Worcs 98 D8
Formby Sefton 138 C6
Forncett End Norfk 106 C4
Forncett St Mary Norfk 106 D4
Forncett St Peter Norfk 106 D5
Fornham All Saints Suffk 89 G2
Fornham St Martin Suffk 89 G2
Fornighty Highld 253 H2
Forres Moray 265 G8
Forsbrook Staffs 114 F3
Forse Highld 275 H1
Forshaw Heath Warwks 98 E8
Forsinard Highld 278 F7
Forston Dorset 16 C3
Fort Augustus Highld 240 C2
Forteviot P & K 221 J4
Forth S Lans 198 F2
Forthampton Gloucs 64 B1
Fort Hommet Guern 9 i2
Forth Road Bridge Fife 210 F3
Fortingall P & K 231 K6
Fort le Marchant Guern 9 k1
Forton Hants 34 F2
Forton Lancs 147 J5
Forton Shrops 113 G8
Forton Somset 15 H1
Forton Staffs 114 B7
Fortrie Abers 256 B3
Fortrose Highld 263 K8
Fortuneswell Dorset 16 D7
Fort William Highld 239 J8
Forty Green Bucks 50 A1
Forty Hill Gt Lon 69 J7
Forward Green Suffk 90 C3
Fosbury Wilts 47 L7
Foscot Oxon 65 K3
Foscote Nhants 84 C6
Fosdyke Lincs 119 K5
Fosdyke Bridge Lincs 119 K5
Foss P & K 231 L4
Fossebridge Gloucs 65 G4
Foss-y-ffin Cerdgn 76 E3
Fosterhouses Donc 143 G5
Foster Street Essex 70 C4
Foston Derbys 115 K5
Foston Leics 100 D4
Foston Lincs 117 M3
Foston N York 151 L3

Foston on the Wolds
   E R Yk 153 H4
Fotherby Lincs 136 F2
Fothergill Cumb 164 D4
Fotheringhay Nhants 102 B5
Foula Shet 281 a7
Foulbridge Cumb 165 M1
Foulby Wakefd 142 B4
Foulden Border 202 E2
Foulden Norfk 104 F4
Foul End Warwks 99 H4
Foul Mile E Susx 23 K4
Foulness Island Essex 53 L1
Foulon Vale Crematorium
   Guern 9 j3
Foulridge Lancs 148 F7
Foulsham Norfk 122 A6
Fountainhall Border 200 F3
Four Ashes Solhll 98 F8
Four Ashes Staffs 97 H6
Four Ashes Staffs 97 L2
Four Ashes Suffk 89 K1
Four Cabots Guern 9 j3
Four Crosses Powys 112 C7
Four Crosses Staffs 98 B2
Four Elms Kent 38 C4
Four Foot Somset 31 J4
Four Forks Somset 30 C3
Four Gates Bolton 139 J6
Four Gotes Cambs 120 A8
Four Lane End Barns 141 L7
Four Lane Ends Ches W 130 A7
Four Lanes Cnwll 3 H3
Fourlanes End Ches E 130 F7
Four Marks Hants 35 K4
Four Mile Bridge IoA 124 E4
Four Oaks Birm 98 E4
Four Oaks E Susx 24 F2
Four Oaks Gloucs 63 K2
Four Oaks Solhll 99 H7
Fourpenny Highld 264 C1
Four Points W Berk 48 E3
Four Roads Carmth 56 E3
Four Shire Stone Warwks 65 K1
Fourstones Nthumb 179 K5
Four Throws Kent 39 J7
Four Wents Kent 38 F3
Fovant Wilts 33 H5
Foveran Abers 257 H7
Fowey Cnwll 5 K4
Fowley Common Warrtn 139 K8
Fowlhall Kent 39 H4
Fowlis Angus 233 M8
Fowlis Wester P & K 221 G2
Fowlmere Cambs 87 J6
Fownhope Herefs 80 D8
Foxbar Rens 208 D6
Foxcombe Devon 12 C5
Fox Corner Surrey 50 B7
Foxcote Gloucs 64 E3
Foxcote Somset 45 L7
Foxdale IoM 154 c6
Foxearth Essex 89 G6
Foxendown Kent 52 E5
Foxfield Cumb 156 B5
Foxham Wilts 46 B5
Fox Hatch Essex 70 E7
Foxhills Hants 18 E1
Foxhole Cnwll 4 F4
Foxholes N York 163 H8
Foxhunt Green E Susx 23 J4
Foxley Nhants 84 C5
Foxley Norfk 122 A7
Foxley Wilts 46 C2
Foxlydiate Worcs 82 B2
Fox Street Essex 72 F2
Foxt Staffs 115 G2
Foxton Cambs 87 H5
Foxton Dur 169 K5
Foxton Leics 100 F5
Foxton N York 160 F3
Foxup N York 158 F7
Foxwist Green Ches W 130 C6
Foxwood Shrops 96 E8
Foy Herefs 63 H2
Foyers Highld 250 E3
Foynesfield Highld 253 G1
Fraddam Cnwll 2 F4
Fraddon Cnwll 4 E5
Fradley Staffs 98 F1
Fradswell Staffs 114 F5
Fraisthorpe E R Yk 153 J3
Framfield E Susx 23 H3
Framingham Earl Norfk 106 F3
Framingham Pigot Norfk 106 F3
Framlingham Suffk 91 G3
Frampton Dorset 16 B4
Frampton Lincs 119 K4
Frampton Cotterell S Glos 45 K3

Frampton Mansell Gloucs............ 64 D6
Frampton-on-Severn
Gloucs 63 L5
Frampton West End Lincs 119 J3
Framsden Suffk 90 E3
Framwellgate Moor Dur 169 H2
Franche Worcs 97 J7
Frandley Ches W 130 C4
Frankaborough Devon 11 M4
Frankby Wirral 128 F2
Frankfort Norfk 122 F6
Franklands Gate Herefs 80 C6
Frankley Worcs 98 C7
Franksbridge Powys 78 F4
Frankton Warwks 83 K1
Frant E Susx 38 F6
Fraserburgh Abers 269 J3
Frating Essex 73 G3
Frating Green Essex 73 G2
Fratton C Port 19 L4
Freathy Cnwll 6 D4
Freckenham Suffk 88 D1
Freckleton Lancs 138 E2
Freebirch Derbys.................. 132 F5
Freeby Leics 117 L7
Freefolk Hants 35 G1
Freehay Staffs 115 G3
Freeland Oxon 66 B4
Freethorpe Norfk 107 H2
Freethorpe Common
Norfk 107 H2
Freiston Lincs 119 L3
Fremington Devon 27 J4
Fremington N York 159 J3
Frenchay S Glos 45 J3
Frenchbeer Devon 12 F5
French Street Kent 51 M8
Frenich P & K 232 B4
Frensham Surrey 36 C3
Freshfield Sefton 138 C6
Freshford Wilts 46 A7
Freshwater IoW 18 E6
Freshwater Bay IoW 18 E6
Freshwater East Pembks 55 G7
Fressingfield Suffk 106 F7
Freston Suffk 90 E7
Freswick Highld 280 E3
Fretherne Gloucs 63 L5
Frettenham Norfk 122 E8
Freuchie Fife 222 D6
Freystrop Pembks 54 F4
Friar Park Sandw 98 C4
Friar's Gate E Susx 38 D6
Friars' Hill N York 162 C5
Friar Waddon Dorset 16 C5
Friday Bridge Cambs 103 K2
Friday Street Suffk 90 F3
Friday Street Suffk 91 H5
Friday Street Suffk 91 J3
Friday Street Surrey 37 H2
Fridaythorpe E R Yk 152 N4
Friden Derbys 132 C7
Friendly Calder 141 G3
Friern Barnet Gt Lon 69 H8
Friesthorpe Lincs 135 M3
Frieston Lincs 118 B2
Frieth Bucks 49 J1
Friezeland Notts 116 D2
Frilford Oxon 66 B7
Frilsham W Berk 48 E4
Frimley Surrey 49 L7
Frimley Green Surrey 49 L7
Frindsbury Medway 52 F5
Fring Norfk 121 G4
Fringford Oxon 66 F1
Frinsted Kent 40 A4
Frinton-on-Sea Essex 73 K3
Friockheim Angus 234 F5
Friog Gwynd 92 D1
Frisby on the Wreake Leics .. 117 J8
Friskney Lincs 137 J8
Friskney Eaudike Lincs 137 J8
Friston E Susx 23 J7
Friston Suffk 91 J3
Fritchley Derbys 116 B1
Fritham Hants 34 B8
Frith Bank Lincs 119 K2
Frith Common Worcs 80 F1
Frithelstock Devon 27 H7
Frithelstock Stone Devon ... 27 H7
Frithend Hants 36 B3
Frithsden Herts 68 C5
Frithville Lincs 119 K2
Frittenden Kent 39 K5
Frittiscombe Devon 8 B6
Fritton Norfk 106 E5
Fritton Norfk 107 K3
Fritwell Oxon 66 D1
Frizinghall C Brad 149 L8

Frizington Cumb 164 D7
Frocester Gloucs 63 M6
Frodesley Shrops 96 C3
Frodsham Ches W 129 M4
Frogden Border 202 B7
Frog End Cambs 87 H6
Frog End Cambs 87 K6
Froggatt Derbys 132 E4
Froghall Staffs 115 G2
Frogham Hants 33 L8
Frogham Kent 41 H5
Frogmore Devon 7 M6
Frognall Lincs 102 D2
Frogpool Cnwll 3 L3
Frog Pool Worcs 81 J2
Frogwell Cnwll 6 C1
Frolesworth Leics 100 B5
Frome Somset 32 C1
Frome St Quintin Dorset 16 B2
Fromes Hill Herefs 80 F6
Fron Denbgs 128 C6
Fron Gwynd 108 F4
Fron Gwynd 109 J1
Fron Powys 94 E4
Fron Powys 94 F3
Froncysyllte Denbgs 112 C3
Fron-goch Gwynd 111 H4
Fron Isaf Wrexhm 112 C3
Frostenden Suffk 107 K7
Frosterley Dur 168 C3
Froxfield C Beds 85 J8
Froxfield Wilts 47 L5
Froxfield Green Hants 35 L5
Fryern Hill Hants 34 F6
Fryerning Essex 70 F7
Fryton N York 162 B7
Fulbeck Lincs 118 B2
Fulbourn Cambs 87 L4
Fulbrook Oxon 65 K4
Fulflood Hants 35 G5
Fulford C York 151 K6
Fulford Somset 30 B5
Fulford Staffs 114 F4
Fulham Gt Lon 51 H4
Fulking W Susx 22 C5
Fullaford Devon 28 B3
Fullarton N Ayrs 196 C3
Fuller's End Essex 70 D2
Fuller's Moor Ches W 113 H1
Fuller Street Essex 71 H4
Fuller Street Kent 38 E2
Fullerton Hants 34 E3
Fulletby Lincs 136 E5
Fullready Warwks 83 G6
Full Sutton E R Yk 152 A5
Fullwood E Ayrs 196 E1
Fulmer Bucks 50 C2
Fulmodeston Norfk 121 M5
Fulnetby Lincs 136 B4
Fulney Lincs 119 J6
Fulstone Kirk 141 J6
Fulstow Lincs 145 J8
Fulwell Oxon 66 A3
Fulwell Sundld 181 J7
Fulwood Lancs 139 H2
Fulwood Notts 133 J8
Fulwood Sheff 132 F3
Fulwood Somset 30 B6
Fundenhall Norfk 106 C4
Funtington W Susx 20 C5
Funtley Hants 19 J2
Funtullich P & K 220 C2
Furley Devon 15 G2
Furnace Ag & B 217 G7
Furnace Carmth 56 F4
Furnace Cerdgn 92 E4
Furnace End Warwks 99 H5
Furner's Green E Susx 22 F2
Furness Vale Derbys 131 K3
Furneux Pelham Herts 70 B2
Further Quarter Kent 39 M5
Furtho Nhants 84 E6
Furzehill Devon 28 C2
Furzehill Dorset 17 K2
Furzehills Lincs 136 E5
Furzeley Corner Hants 19 L2
Furze Platt W & M 49 L3
Furzley Hants 34 C7
Fyfett Somset 30 C7
Fyfield Essex 70 E6
Fyfield Hants 34 C2
Fyfield Oxon 66 B7
Fyfield Wilts 47 H5
Fyfield Wilts 47 H6
Fyfield Bavant Wilts 33 H6
Fylingthorpe N York 163 G2
Fyning W Susx 36 B6
Fyvie Abers 256 D4

G

Gabroc Hill E Ayrs 196 E1
Gaddesby Leics 100 F1
Gaddesden Row Herts 68 D4
Gadfa IoA 125 H2
Gadgirth S Ayrs 196 E6
Gadlas Shrops 112 E4
Gaer Powys 61 J3
Gaerllwyd Mons 62 F7
Gaerwen IoA 125 H5
Gagingwell Oxon 66 B2
Gailes N Ayrs 196 C4
Gailey Staffs 97 K1
Gainford Dur 168 F7
Gainsborough Lincs 135 G2
Gainsford End Essex 88 E8
Gairloch Highld 260 C4
Gairlochy Highld 239 K6
Gairneybridge P & K 221 L7
Gaisgill Cumb 157 K2
Gaitsgill Cumb 165 L1
Galashiels Border 201 G6
Galgate Lancs 147 J6
Galhampton Somset 31 K5
Gallanachbeg Ag & B 216 C2
Gallanachmore Ag & B 216 C2
Gallantry Bank Ches E 113 H1
Gallatown Fife 222 E8
Galley Common Warwks 99 J5
Galleywood Essex 71 H6
Gallovie Highld 240 F5
Gallowfauld Angus 234 C7
Gallowhill P & K 233 J8
Gallows Green Essex 72 D2
Gallows Green Worcs 81 L3
Gallowstree Common Oxon... 49 G3
Galltair Highld 248 C7
Gallt-y-foel Gwynd 125 K7
Gally Hill Hants 49 K8
Gallypot Street E Susx 38 D6
Galmpton Devon 7 K6
Galmpton Torbay 8 D4
Galphay N York 150 C1
Galston E Ayrs 196 F4
Gamballs Green Staffs 131 L6
Gamblesby Cumb 166 E3
Gambles Green Essex 71 J4
Gamelsby Cumb 177 H8
Gamesley Derbys 131 K1
Gamlingay Cambs 86 E5
Gamlingay Cinques Cambs 86 E4
Gamlingay Great Heath
Cambs 86 E5
Gammersgill N York 159 J6
Gamrie Abers 268 E4
Gamston Notts 117 G4
Gamston Notts 134 E4
Ganarew Herefs 63 G4
Ganavan Bay Ag & B 216 D1
Gang Cnwll 6 C1
Ganllwyd Gwynd 110 D6
Gannachy Angus 234 F1
Ganstead E R Yk 144 F1
Ganthorpe N York 151 L2
Ganton N York 163 H7
Ganwick Corner Herts 69 H7
Gappah Devon 13 K7
Garbity Moray 266 F5
Garboldisham Norfk 105 K7
Garbole Highld 252 E7
Garchory Abers 243 J2
Garden City Flints 129 H6
Gardeners Green Wokham 49 K5
Garden of England
Crematorium Kent.......... 53 J5
Gardenstown Abers 268 E3
Garden Village Sheff 141 L8
Garderhouse Shet 281 d6
Gardham E R Yk 152 E7
Gare Hill Somset 32 C3
Garelochhead Ag & B 207 L1
Garford Oxon 66 B7
Garforth Leeds 142 B1
Gargrave N York 149 G5
Gargunnock Stirlg 220 B8
Garizim Conwy 126 D4
Garlic Street Norfk 106 E6
Garlieston D & G 174 D5
Garlinge Kent 41 K2
Garlinge Green Kent 40 F5
Garlogie Abers 245 H2
Garmond Abers 268 E5
Garmouth Moray 267 G3
Garmston Shrops 96 E2
Garnant Carmth 59 J6
Garn-Dolbenmaen Gwynd ... 109 J3
Garnett Bridge Cumb 157 H3

Garnfadryn Gwynd 108 E5
Garnkirk N Lans 209 H5
Garnswllt Swans 57 H3
Garn-yr-erw Torfn 61 K5
Garrabost W Isls 282 h3
Garrallan E Ayrs 197 G7
Garras Cnwll 3 H6
Garreg Gwynd 109 L3
Garrigill Cumb 167 H2
Garriston N York 159 L4
Garroch D & G 184 F6
Garrochtrie D & G 172 D7
Garrochty Ag & B 207 H8
Garros Highld 259 H4
Garsdale Cumb 158 C5
Garsdale Head Cumb 158 D4
Garsdon Wilts 46 D2
Garshall Green Staffs 114 F5
Garsington Oxon 66 E6
Garstang Lancs 147 J6
Garston Herts 68 E7
Garston Lpool 129 J3
Gartachossan Ag & B 204 E4
Gartcosh N Lans 209 J5
Garth Brdgnd 42 C4
Garth Mons 62 D8
Garth Powys 78 C5
Garth Powys 79 J1
Garth Wrexhm 112 C3
Garthamlock C Glas 209 H5
Garthbrengy Powys 78 E8
Gartheli Cerdgn 77 G4
Garthmyl Powys 94 F3
Garthorpe Leics 117 L7
Garthorpe N Linc 143 L4
Garth Row Cumb 157 H3
Garths Cumb 157 H5
Gartly Abers 255 K5
Gartmore Stirlg 219 H7
Gartness N Lans 209 K6
Gartness Stirlg 208 E2
Gartocharn W Duns 208 D2
Garton E R Yk 145 H1
Garton-on-the-Wolds E R Yk.. 152 F4
Gartymore Highld 274 D5
Garva Bridge Highld 240 F4
Garvald E Loth 212 D5
Garvan Highld 238 F8
Garvard Ag & B 214 D6
Garve Highld 262 C7
Garvellachs Ag & B 215 J2
Garvestone Norfk 105 L2
Garvock Inver 207 L5
Garway Herefs 62 F3
Garway Common Herefs 62 F3
Garway Hill Herefs 62 F2
Garyvard W Isls 282 g4
Gasper Wilts 32 C4
Gastard Wilts 46 C5
Gasthorpe Norfk 105 K7
Gaston Green Essex 70 D4
Gatcombe IoW 19 H6
Gatebeck Cumb 157 J5
Gate Burton Lincs 135 G3
Gateford Notts 134 B3
Gateforth N York 142 E2
Gate Helmsley N York 151 L5
Gatehouse Nthumb 179 H1
Gatehouse of Fleet D & G.... 174 F4
Gateley Norfk 121 L6
Gatenby N York 160 D5
Gatesgarth Cumb 165 G7
Gateshaw Border 189 L2
Gateshead Gatesd 181 G6
Gates Heath Ches W 129 L7
Gateside Angus 234 C6
Gateside E Rens 208 E7
Gateside Fife 222 B5
Gateside N Ayrs 208 B8
Gateslack D & G 186 C5
Gathurst Wigan 139 G6
Gatley Stockp 131 G2
Gatton Surrey 51 H8
Gattonside Border 201 H6
Gaufron Powys 78 D2
Gaulby Leics 100 F3
Gauldry Fife 222 F2
Gauldswell P & K 233 K5
Gaulkthorn Lancs 139 M3
Gaultree Norfk 103 K2
Gaunt's Bank Ches E 113 J2
Gaunt's Common Dorset 17 K2
Gaunt's End Essex 70 E2
Gautby Lincs 136 C5
Gavinton Border 202 B3
Gawber Barns 141 M6
Gawcott Bucks 67 G1
Gawsworth Ches E 131 H5

Gawthorpe Wakefd ... 141 L3
Gawthrop Cumb ... 158 B5
Gawthwaite Cumb ... 156 C5
Gay Bowers Essex ... 71 J6
Gaydon Warwks ... 83 J4
Gayhurst M Keyn ... 85 G6
Gayle N York ... 158 F5
Gayles N York ... 159 L1
Gay Street W Susx ... 21 J3
Gayton Nhants ... 84 D4
Gayton Norfk ... 120 F7
Gayton Staffs ... 114 F6
Gayton Wirral ... 129 G4
Gayton le Marsh Lincs ... 137 H3
Gayton Thorpe Norfk ... 121 G7
Gaywood Norfk ... 120 E7
Gazeley Suffk ... 88 E2
Gear Cnwll ... 3 J6
Gearraidh Bhaird W Isls ... 282 g4
Geary Highld ... 258 D4
Gedding Suffk ... 89 J4
Geddington Nhants ... 101 K6
Gedling Notts ... 117 G3
Gedney Lincs ... 119 L6
Gedney Broadgate Lincs ... 119 L7
Gedney Drove End Lincs ... 120 A5
Gedney Dyke Lincs ... 119 L6
Gedney Hill Lincs ... 103 G1
Gee Cross Tamesd ... 131 J1
Geeston Rutlnd ... 101 L3
Geldeston Norfk ... 107 H5
Gelli Rhondd ... 42 E3
Gelli Torfn ... 62 B8
Gellifor Denbgs ... 128 D7
Gelligaer Caerph ... 43 H2
Gelligroes Caerph ... 43 J3
Gelligron Neath ... 57 K4
Gellilydan Gwynd ... 110 C4
Gellinudd Neath ... 57 K4
Gelly Pembks ... 55 J3
Gellyburn P & K ... 233 G7
Gellywen Carmth ... 58 A4
Gelston D & G ... 175 J3
Gelston Lincs ... 118 B3
Gembling E R Yk ... 153 H4
Gentleshaw Staffs ... 98 D1
Georgefield D & G ... 187 L7
George Green Bucks ... 50 C3
Georgeham Devon ... 27 H3
Georgemas Junction Station Highld ... 279 L4
George Nympton Devon ... 28 B6
Georgetown Blae G ... 61 J5
Georgia Cnwll ... 2 D4
Georth Ork ... 275 c3
Gerlan Gwynd ... 126 C6
Germansweek Devon ... 12 B4
Germoe Cnwll ... 2 F5
Gerrans Cnwll ... 3 M4
Gerrards Cross Bucks ... 50 C1
Gerrick R & Cl ... 171 G8
Gestingthorpe Essex ... 89 G7
Geuffordd Powys ... 112 B8
Gib Hill Ches W ... 130 C4
Gibraltar Lincs ... 137 K7
Gibsmere Notts ... 117 J2
Giddeahall Wilts ... 46 B4
Giddy Green Dorset ... 16 F5
Gidea Park Gt Lon ... 52 B1
Gidleigh Devon ... 12 F5
Giffnock E Rens ... 208 F7
Gifford E Loth ... 212 C5
Giffordtown Fife ... 222 E6
Giggleswick N York ... 148 D3
Gigha Ag & B ... 205 L6
Gilberdyke E R Yk ... 143 L2
Gilbert's End Worcs ... 81 J6
Gilbert Street Hants ... 35 K4
Gilchriston E Loth ... 212 B6
Gilcrux Cumb ... 164 F3
Gildersome Leeds ... 141 K2
Gildingwells Rothm ... 133 L3
Gilesgate Moor Dur ... 169 J2
Gileston V Glam ... 42 F8
Gilfach Caerph ... 43 J2
Gilfach Goch Brdgnd ... 42 E4
Gilfachrheda Cerdgn ... 76 D3
Gilgarran Cumb ... 164 D6
Gill Cumb ... 166 B5
Gillamoor N York ... 162 B4
Gillan Cnwll ... 3 K6
Gillen Highld ... 258 D5
Gillesbie D & G ... 187 J7
Gilling East N York ... 161 K7
Gillingham Dorset ... 32 D5
Gillingham Medway ... 53 L6
Gillingham Norfk ... 107 H5
Gilling West N York ... 160 B2
Gillock Highld ... 280 B4

Gillow Heath Staffs ... 131 H7
Gills Highld ... 280 D2
Gill's Green Kent ... 39 J7
Gilmanscleuch Border ... 188 B2
Gilmerton C Edin ... 211 J5
Gilmerton P & K ... 220 F2
Gilmonby Dur ... 168 C8
Gilmorton Leics ... 100 C6
Gilroes Crematorium C Leic ... 100 C2
Gilsland Nthumb ... 178 E5
Gilson Warwks ... 99 G5
Gilstead C Brad ... 149 L7
Gilston Border ... 200 F2
Gilston Herts ... 70 C4
Gilston Park Herts ... 70 B4
Giltbrook Notts ... 116 E2
Gilwern Mons ... 61 L4
Gimingham Norfk ... 122 F4
Ginclough Ches E ... 131 J4
Gingers Green E Susx ... 23 K5
Gipping Suffk ... 90 C3
Gipsey Bridge Lincs ... 119 J2
Girdle Toll N Ayrs ... 196 C3
Girlington C Brad ... 141 H1
Girsby N York ... 160 E1
Girtford C Beds ... 86 D5
Girthon D & G ... 174 F4
Girton Cambs ... 87 J3
Girton Notts ... 135 G6
Girvan S Ayrs ... 182 F3
Gisburn Lancs ... 148 E6
Gisleham Suffk ... 107 K5
Gislingham Suffk ... 90 C1
Gissing Norfk ... 106 C6
Gittisham Devon ... 14 D3
Gladestry Powys ... 79 J4
Gladsmuir E Loth ... 212 A4
Glais Swans ... 57 K5
Glaisdale N York ... 162 D2
Glamis Angus ... 234 B6
Glanaber Gwynd ... 110 B1
Glanafon Pembks ... 54 F3
Glanaman Carmth ... 59 J6
Glandford Norfk ... 122 A3
Glan-Duar Carmth ... 76 F6
Glandwr Pembks ... 75 L6
Glan-Dwyfach Gwynd ... 109 J3
Glandyfi Cerdgn ... 92 F4
Glangrwyney Powys ... 61 K4
Glanllynfi Brdgnd ... 42 C3
Glanmule Powys ... 94 E5
Glanrhyd Pembks ... 75 K4
Glan-rhyd Powys ... 57 L3
Glanton Nthumb ... 190 F3
Glanton Pike Nthumb ... 190 F3
Glanvilles Wootton Dorset ... 16 C1
Glan-y-don Flints ... 128 E4
Glan-y-llyn Rhondd ... 43 H5
Glan-y-nant Powys ... 93 K6
Glan-yr-afon Gwynd ... 111 H3
Glan-yr-afon Gwynd ... 111 K3
Glan-yr-afon IoA ... 126 B4
Glan-yr-afon Swans ... 57 H4
Glapthorn Nhants ... 101 M5
Glapwell Derbys ... 133 J6
Glasbury Powys ... 79 H7
Glascoed Denbgs ... 127 K5
Glascoed Mons ... 62 C6
Glascote Staffs ... 99 G3
Glascwm Powys ... 79 G5
Glasfryn Conwy ... 111 H2
Glasgow C Glas ... 209 G6
Glasinfryn Gwynd ... 125 K6
Glasnacardoch Bay Highld ... 237 K2
Glasnakille Highld ... 247 H6
Glaspwll Powys ... 92 F4
Glassenbury Kent ... 39 J6
Glassford S Lans ... 197 L2
Glass Houghton Wakefd ... 142 C3
Glasshouse Gloucs ... 63 L3
Glasshouse Hill Gloucs ... 63 L3
Glasshouses N York ... 149 L3
Glasson Cumb ... 177 H6
Glasson Lancs ... 147 J4
Glassonby Cumb ... 166 D3
Glasterlaw Angus ... 234 F5
Glaston Rutlnd ... 101 K3
Glastonbury Somset ... 31 H3
Glatton Cambs ... 102 C6
Glazebrook Warrtn ... 130 D1
Glazebury Warrtn ... 139 K8
Glazeley Shrops ... 96 F5
Gleadless Sheff ... 133 G3
Gleadsmoss Ches E ... 130 F6
Gleaston Cumb ... 146 E2
Glebe Highld ... 250 F8
Gledhow Leeds ... 150 D8
Gledpark D & G ... 175 G5

Gledrid Shrops ... 112 D4
Glemsford Suffk ... 89 G5
Glenallachie Moray ... 254 E3
Glenancross Highld ... 237 K2
Glenaros House Ag & B ... 227 G4
Glen Auldyn IoM ... 154 f4
Glenbarr Ag & B ... 192 D1
Glenbarry Abers ... 267 L5
Glenbeg Highld ... 237 H8
Glenbervie Abers ... 245 G7
Glenboig N Lans ... 209 J5
Glenborrodale Highld ... 237 H8
Glenbranter Ag & B ... 217 J7
Glenbreck Border ... 187 G2
Glenbrittle House Highld ... 246 F4
Glenbuck E Ayrs ... 198 B7
Glencally Angus ... 234 A3
Glencaple D & G ... 176 C5
Glencarron Lodge Highld ... 249 H2
Glencarse P & K ... 222 C3
Glen Clunie Lodge Abers ... 242 F7
Glencoe Highld ... 229 H4
Glencothe Border ... 199 J7
Glencraig Fife ... 222 B8
Glencrosh D & G ... 185 J5
Glendale Highld ... 258 B6
Glendaruel Ag & B ... 206 F2
Glendevon P & K ... 221 H6
Glendoe Lodge Highld ... 240 C2
Glendoick P & K ... 222 C3
Glenduckie Fife ... 222 D3
Glenegedale Ag & B ... 204 E6
Glenelg Highld ... 248 C7
Glenerney Moray ... 253 K2
Glenfarg P & K ... 221 L5
Glenfield Leics ... 100 C2
Glenfinnan Highld ... 238 E7
Glenfintaig Lodge Highld ... 239 L6
Glenfoot P & K ... 222 B4
Glenfyne Lodge Ag & B ... 218 B4
Glengarnock N Ayrs ... 208 B8
Glengolly Highld ... 279 K3
Glengorm Castle Ag & B ... 226 E1
Glengrasco Highld ... 259 G7
Glenholm Border ... 199 J6
Glenhoul D & G ... 184 F5
Glenisla Angus ... 233 K3
Glenkin Ag & B ... 207 J3
Glenkindie Abers ... 243 M1
Glenlivet Moray ... 254 D6
Glenlochar D & G ... 175 J2
Glenlomond P & K ... 222 B6
Glenluce D & G ... 172 F3
Glenmassen Ag & B ... 207 H2
Glenmavis N Lans ... 209 K5
Glen Maye IoM ... 154 b6
Glen Mona IoM ... 154 f4
Glenmore Highld ... 259 G8
Glenmore Lodge Highld ... 242 C2
Glen Nevis House Highld ... 229 J1
Glenochil Clacks ... 220 F8
Glen Parva Leics ... 100 C4
Glenquiech Angus ... 234 C3
Glenralloch Ag & B ... 206 D5
Glenridding Cumb ... 165 L7
Glenrothes Fife ... 222 D7
Glenshero Lodge Highld ... 240 F5
Glenstriven Ag & B ... 207 H3
Glentham Lincs ... 135 K2
Glentrool D & G ... 183 J7
Glen Trool Lodge D & G ... 183 K7
Glentruim House Highld ... 241 J4
Glentworth Lincs ... 135 J2
Glenuig Highld ... 237 K5
Glenvarragill Highld ... 259 H8
Glen Vine IoM ... 154 d6
Glenwhilly D & G ... 182 F8
Glespin S Lans ... 198 D7
Glewstone Herefs ... 63 H3
Glinton C Pete ... 102 C2
Glooston Leics ... 101 G4
Glossop Derbys ... 131 L1
Gloster Hill Nthumb ... 191 K5
Gloucester Gloucs ... 64 B3
Gloucester Crematorium Gloucs ... 64 B4
Glusburn N York ... 149 H6
Glutt Lodge Highld ... 274 D1
Gluvian Cnwll ... 4 F2
Glympton Oxon ... 66 B3
Glynarthen Cerdgn ... 76 B5
Glyn Ceiriog Wrexhm ... 112 B4
Glyncorrwg Neath ... 60 C7
Glynde E Susx ... 23 G5
Glyndebourne E Susx ... 23 G5
Glyndyfrdwy Denbgs ... 112 A3
Glynneath Neath ... 60 D5
Glynn Valley Crematorium Cnwll ... 5 J2

Glyntaff Rhondd ... 43 H4
Glyntaff Crematorium Rhondd ... 43 H4
Glyntawe Powys ... 60 C4
Glynteg Carmth ... 76 C7
Gnosall Staffs ... 114 C7
Gnosall Heath Staffs ... 114 C7
Goadby Leics ... 101 G4
Goadby Marwood Leics ... 117 K6
Goatacre Wilts ... 46 F4
Goatham Green E Susx ... 24 E3
Goathill Dorset ... 31 K8
Goathland N York ... 162 E2
Goathurst Somset ... 30 C4
Goathurst Common Kent ... 38 D3
Goat Lees Kent ... 40 D6
Gobowen Shrops ... 112 D5
Godalming Surrey ... 36 E2
Goddard's Corner Suffk ... 91 G2
Goddard's Green Kent ... 39 K6
Goddards Green W Susx ... 22 D3
Godden Green Kent ... 38 E2
Godford Cross Devon ... 14 D2
Godington Oxon ... 66 F2
Godley Tamesd ... 140 E8
Godmanchester Cambs ... 86 E1
Godmanstone Dorset ... 16 C3
Godmersham Kent ... 40 D5
Godney Somset ... 31 H2
Godolphin Cross Cnwll ... 2 F5
Godre'r-graig Neath ... 57 L3
Godshill Hants ... 33 L7
Godshill IoW ... 19 J7
Godstone Staffs ... 115 G5
Godstone Surrey ... 51 K8
Godsworthy Devon ... 12 C7
Godwinscroft Hants ... 18 B4
Goetre Mons ... 62 C6
Goff's Oak Herts ... 69 J6
Gogar C Edin ... 211 G4
Goginan Cerdgn ... 92 E7
Golan Gwynd ... 109 J3
Golant Cnwll ... 5 K4
Golberdon Cnwll ... 11 L8
Golborne Wigan ... 139 J8
Golcar Kirk ... 141 H4
Goldcliff Newpt ... 44 F2
Golden Cross E Susx ... 23 J5
Golden Green Kent ... 39 G4
Golden Grove Carmth ... 59 G5
Goldenhill C Stke ... 114 D7
Golden Hill Pembks ... 55 G6
Golden Pot Hants ... 35 L2
Golden Valley Derbys ... 116 C1
Golders Green Gt Lon ... 51 H2
Golders Green Crematorium Gt Lon ... 51 H1
Goldfinch Bottom W Berk ... 48 D6
Goldhanger Essex ... 72 C5
Gold Hill Cambs ... 103 L5
Gold Hill Dorset ... 32 D8
Golding Shrops ... 96 C3
Goldington Bed ... 86 B5
Goldsborough N York ... 150 E4
Goldsborough N York ... 171 J7
Golds Green Sandw ... 98 C5
Goldsithney Cnwll ... 2 E5
Goldstone Kent ... 41 J3
Goldstone Shrops ... 113 M6
Goldsworth Park Surrey ... 50 C7
Goldthorpe Barns ... 142 C7
Goldworthy Devon ... 27 G6
Golford Kent ... 39 K6
Golford Green Kent ... 39 K6
Gollanfield Highld ... 252 F1
Gollinglith Foot N York ... 159 L6
Golly Wrexhm ... 129 H7
Golsoncott Somset ... 29 J3
Golspie Highld ... 273 K8
Gomeldon Wilts ... 33 L4
Gomersal Kirk ... 141 K3
Gomshall Surrey ... 37 G1
Gonalston Notts ... 117 H2
Gonerby Hill Foot Lincs ... 118 B4
Gonfirth Shet ... 281 d5
Goodameavy Devon ... 7 G2
Good Easter Essex ... 70 F5
Gooderstone Norfk ... 104 F3
Goodleigh Devon ... 27 L4
Goodmanham E R Yk ... 152 D7
Goodmayes Gt Lon ... 51 M2
Goodnestone Kent ... 40 D3
Goodnestone Kent ... 41 H4
Goodrich Herefs ... 63 H3
Goodrington Torbay ... 8 D3
Goodshaw Lancs ... 140 B3
Goodshaw Fold Lancs ... 140 B2
Goodstone Devon ... 13 H8
Goodwick Pembks ... 74 F4

Goodworth Clatford Hants 34   D2
Goodyers End Warwks 99   J6
Goole E R Yk 143   J3
Goole Fields E R Yk 143   J3
Goom's Hill Worcs 82   B4
Goonbell Cnwll 4   B5
Goonhavern Cnwll 4   C4
Goonvrea Cnwll 4   B5
Goosecruives Abers 245   G7
Gooseford Devon 12   F4
Goose Green Essex 73   H2
Goose Green Kent 39   G3
Goose Green Kent 39   L6
Goose Green S Glos 45   K4
Goose Green W Susx 21   J3
Goose Green Wigan 139   H7
Gooseham Cnwll 26   D7
Gooseham Mill Cnwll 26   D7
Goosehill Green Worcs 81   L3
Goose Pool Herefs 80   B7
Goosey Oxon 47   M1
Goosnargh Lancs 147   L8
Goostrey Ches E 130   F5
Gorddinog Conwy 126   D5
Gordon Border 201   K4
Gordon Arms Hotel Border 200   C8
Gordonstown Abers 256   C4
Gordonstown Abers 267   L5
Gore Powys 79   J3
Gorebridge Mdloth 211   K6
Gorefield Cambs 103   J1
Gore Pit Essex 72   C3
Gores Wilts 47   G7
Gore Street Kent 41   J2
Gorey Jersey 9   f3
Goring Oxon 48   F3
Goring-by-Sea W Susx 21   J6
Goring Heath Oxon 49   G3
Gorleston on Sea Norfk 107   L3
Gornal Wood Crematorium
  Dudley 97   K5
Gorrachie Abers 268   D4
Gorran Churchtown Cnwll 5   G6
Gorran Haven Cnwll 5   G6
Gorran High Lanes Cnwll 5   G6
Gorrig Cerdgn 76   D6
Gors Cerdgn 92   D7
Gorsedd Flints 128   E4
Gorse Hill Swindn 47   H2
Gorseinon Swans 57   G5
Gorseybank Derbys 115   M1
Gorsgoch Cerdgn 76   E5
Gorslas Carmth 59   G6
Gorsley Gloucs 63   K2
Gorsley Common Herefs 63   K2
Gorstage Ches W 130   B5
Gorstan Highld 262   C7
Gorstella Ches W 129   H7
Gorst Hill Worcs 97   G8
Gorsty Hill Staffs 115   H6
Gorten Ag & B 227   L6
Gorthleck Highld 250   F7
Gorton Manch 140   C8
Gosbeck Suffk 90   D4
Gosberton Lincs 119   H5
Gosberton Clough Lincs 119   G5
Gosfield Essex 71   J1
Gosford Devon 14   C3
Gosford Oxon 66   D4
Gosforth Cumb 155   J2
Gosforth N u Ty 180   F5
Gosling Street Somset 31   J4
Gosmore Herts 68   F2
Gospel End Staffs 97   K4
Gospel Green W Susx 36   D4
Gosport Hants 19   K4
Gossard's Green C Beds 85   J6
Gossington Gloucs 63   L6
Goswick Nthumb 203   G4
Gotham Notts 116   F5
Gotherington Gloucs 64   D1
Gotton Somset 30   C5
Goudhurst Kent 39   H6
Goulceby Lincs 136   E4
Gourdas Abers 256   D3
Gourdie C Dund 222   F1
Gourdon Abers 235   K1
Gourock Inver 207   L3
Govan C Glas 208   F6
Goveton Devon 7   L5
Govilon Mons 61   L4
Gowdall E R Yk 143   G3
Gower Highld 262   E8
Gowerton Swans 57   G5
Gowkhall Fife 210   E1
Gowthorpe E R Yk 152   A5
Goxhill E R Yk 153   K6
Goxhill N Linc 144   E3
Grabhair W Isls 282   g4

Graby Lincs 118   E5
Grade Cnwll 3   H8
Gradeley Green Ches E 113   K1
Graffham W Susx 20   F3
Grafham Cambs 86   D2
Grafham Surrey 36   F3
Grafton Herefs 80   C7
Grafton N York 150   F3
Grafton Oxon 65   K7
Grafton Shrops 113   G7
Grafton Worcs 80   D3
Grafton Worcs 82   A7
Grafton Flyford Worcs 81   M4
Grafton Regis Nhants 84   E6
Grafton Underwood Nhants 101   K7
Grafty Green Kent 39   L4
Graianrhyd Denbgs 128   F8
Graig Conwy 126   F5
Graig Denbgs 128   C5
Graigfechan Denbgs 112   A1
Grain Medway 53   J4
Grains Bar Oldham 140   E6
Grainsby Lincs 145   H7
Grainthorpe Lincs 145   K8
Grampound Cnwll 4   F5
Grampound Road Cnwll 4   E5
Gramsdal W Isls 283   c9
Gramsdale W Isls 283   c9
Granborough Bucks 67   J2
Granby Notts 117   K4
Grandborough Warwks 83   L2
Grand Chemins Jersey 9   e3
Grandes Rocques Guern 9   j2
Grandtully P & K 232   D5
Grange Cumb 165   H7
Grange Medway 53   G5
Grange P & K 222   D2
Grange Wirral 128   F2
Grange Crossroads Moray 267   K5
Grange Hall Moray 265   H7
Grangehall S Lans 199   G4
Grange Hill Essex 70   C8
Grangemill Derbys 132   E8
Grange Moor Kirk 141   K4
Grangemouth Falk 210   B3
Grange of Lindores Fife 222   D4
Grange-over-Sands Cumb 156   F7
Grangepans Falk 210   D3
Grange Park Nhants 84   E4
Grangetown R & Cl 170   D6
Grangetown Sundld 181   K8
Grange Villa Dur 180   F8
Gransmoor E R Yk 153   H4
Gransmore Green Essex 71   G3
Granston Pembks 74   E5
Grantchester Cambs 87   J4
Grantham Lincs 118   B4
Grantham Crematorium Lincs ... 118   B4
Granton C Edin 211   H4
Grantown-on-Spey Highld 253   K6
Grantsfield Herefs 80   C3
Grantshouse Border 213   H6
Grappenhall Warrtn 130   C2
Grasby Lincs 144   D6
Grasmere Cumb 156   D1
Grasscroft Oldham 140   E6
Grassendale Lpool 129   J3
Grassgarth Cumb 165   K2
Grass Green Essex 88   E7
Grassington N York 149   H3
Grassmoor Derbys 133   H6
Grassthorpe Notts 134   F6
Grateley Hants 34   C3
Gratwich Staffs 115   G5
Graveley Cambs 86   E3
Graveley Herts 69   J2
Gravelly Hill Birm 98   E5
Gravelsbank Shrops 95   H3
Graveney Kent 40   D3
Gravesend Kent 52   E4
Gravir W Isls 282   g4
Grayingham Lincs 144   A8
Grayrigg Cumb 157   J3
Grays Thurr 52   D3
Grayshott Hants 36   C4
Grayson Green Cumb 164   C5
Grayswood Surrey 36   C4
Graythorpe Hartpl 170   C5
Grazeley Wokham 49   G5
Greasbrough Rothm 142   C8
Greasby Wirral 128   F2
Greasley Notts 116   E2
Great Abington Cambs 87   L5
Great Addington Nhants 101   L8
Great Alne Warwks 82   D4
Great Altcar Lancs 138   C6
Great Amwell Herts 69   K4
Great Asby Cumb 166   F8
Great Ashfield Suffk 89   K2

Great Ayton N York 170   D8
Great Baddow Essex 71   H6
Great Badminton S Glos 46   A2
Great Bardfield Essex 71   G1
Great Barford Bed 86   C5
Great Barr Sandw 98   D4
Great Barrington Gloucs 65   J4
Great Barrow Ches W 129   L6
Great Barton Suffk 89   H2
Great Barugh N York 162   C6
Great Bavington Nthumb 180   B3
Great Bealings Suffk 90   F5
Great Bedwyn Wilts 47   K6
Great Bentley Essex 73   J1
Great Billing Nhants 84   F3
Great Bircham Norfk 121   G5
Great Blakenham Suffk 90   D5
Great Blencow Cumb 166   B4
Great Bolas Wrekin 113   L7
Great Bookham Surrey 50   E8
Great Bosullow Cnwll 2   C4
Great Bourton Oxon 83   K6
Great Bowden Leics 101   G5
Great Bradley Suffk 88   D4
Great Braxted Essex 72   B4
Great Bricett Suffk 90   B5
Great Brickhill Bucks 67   L1
Great Bridgeford Staffs 114   D6
Great Brington Nhants 84   C2
Great Bromley Essex 73   G2
Great Broughton Cumb 164   E4
Great Broughton N York 161   J2
Great Budworth Ches W 130   C4
Great Burdon Darltn 169   J7
Great Burstead Essex 71   G8
Great Busby N York 161   H2
Great Canfield Essex 70   E3
Great Carlton Lincs 137   H3
Great Casterton Rutlnd 101   M2
Great Chalfield Wilts 46   B6
Great Chart Kent 40   C7
Great Chatwell Staffs 114   B8
Great Chell C Stke 114   D1
Great Chesterford Essex 87   K6
Great Cheverell Wilts 46   E8
Great Chishill Cambs 87   J7
Great Clacton Essex 73   J4
Great Cliffe Wakefd 141   M4
Great Clifton Cumb 164   D5
Great Coates NE Lin 145   G6
Great Comberton Worcs 81   L6
Great Comp Kent 39   G2
Great Corby Cumb 178   B7
Great Cornard Suffk 89   H7
Great Cowden E R Yk 153   L7
Great Coxwell Oxon 65   K8
Great Cransley Nhants 101   H8
Great Cressingham Norfk 105   J3
Great Crosthwaite Cumb 165   J6
Great Cubley Derbys 115   K4
Great Cumbrae Island N Ayrs ... 207   K7
Great Dalby Leics 117   K3
Great Denham Bed 85   K5
Great Doddington Nhants 85   H2
Great Doward Herefs 63   G4
Great Dunham Norfk 121   J8
Great Dunmow Essex 70   F3
Great Durnford Wilts 33   K3
Great Easton Essex 70   F2
Great Easton Leics 101   J5
Great Eccleston Lancs 147   H7
Great Edstone N York 162   C6
Great Ellingham Norfk 105   L4
Great Elm Somset 32   C1
Great Everdon Nhants 84   B4
Great Eversden Cambs 87   H4
Great Fencote N York 160   D4
Greatfield Wilts 47   G2
Great Finborough Suffk 89   K4
Greatford Lincs 102   B1
Great Fransham Norfk 105   H1
Great Gaddesden Herts 68   C5
Greatgate Staffs 115   G3
Great Gidding Cambs 102   C6
Great Givendale E R Yk 152   B5
Great Glemham Suffk 91   H3
Great Glen Leics 100   E4
Great Gonerby Lincs 118   B4
Great Gransden Cambs 86   F4
Great Green Cambs 86   F6
Great Green Norfk 106   F5
Great Green Suffk 89   J3
Great Green Suffk 89   J4
Great Habton N York 162   D7
Great Hale Lincs 118   F3
Great Hallingbury Essex 70   D3
Greatham Hants 36   A5
Greatham Hartpl 170   C5
Greatham W Susx 21   H4

Great Hampden Bucks 67   K6
Great Harrowden Nhants 85   G1
Great Harwood Lancs 139   L1
Great Haseley Oxon 66   F6
Great Hatfield E R Yk 153   K7
Great Haywood Staffs 114   F7
Great Heck N York 142   F3
Great Henny Essex 89   H7
Great Hinton Wilts 46   C7
Great Hockham Norfk 105   J5
Great Holland Essex 73   J3
Great Hollands Br For 49   L5
Great Horkesley Essex 72   E1
Great Hormead Herts 69   L1
Great Horton C Brad 141   J2
Great Horwood Bucks 67   J1
Great Houghton Barns 142   C6
Great Houghton Nhants 84   F3
Great Hucklow Derbys 132   D4
Great Kelk E R Yk 153   H4
Great Kimble Bucks 67   K6
Great Kingshill Bucks 67   L7
Great Langdale Cumb 156   D2
Great Langton N York 160   D3
Great Leighs Essex 71   H4
Great Limber Lincs 144   E6
Great Linford M Keyn 85   G6
Great Livermere Suffk 89   H1
Great Longstone Derbys 132   D5
Great Lumley Dur 169   J1
Great Lyth Shrops 95   L2
Great Malvern Worcs 81   H6
Great Maplestead Essex 89   G8
Great Marton Bpool 138   C1
Great Massingham Norfk 121   H7
Great Melton Norfk 106   C2
Great Meols Wirral 128   F2
Great Milton Oxon 66   F6
Great Missenden Bucks 67   L6
Great Mitton Lancs 148   C8
Great Mongeham Kent 41   K5
Great Moulton Norfk 106   D5
Great Munden Herts 69   K2
Great Musgrave Cumb 167   H7
Great Ness Shrops 112   F7
Great Notley Essex 71   H3
Great Oak Mons 62   D5
Great Oakley Essex 73   J2
Great Oakley Nhants 101   J6
Great Offley Herts 68   F2
Great Ormside Cumb 167   G7
Great Orton Cumb 177   K7
Great Ouseburn N York 150   F3
Great Oxendon Nhants 100   F6
Great Oxney Green Essex 71   G6
Great Palgrave Norfk 105   G1
Great Park N u Ty 180   F5
Great Parndon Essex 70   B5
Great Pattenden Kent 39   J4
Great Paxton Cambs 86   E2
Great Plumpton Lancs 138   D1
Great Plumstead Norfk 106   F2
Great Ponton Lincs 118   B5
Great Potheridge Devon 27   J7
Great Preston Leeds 142   B2
Great Purston Nhants 83   M7
Great Raveley Cambs 102   E7
Great Rissington Gloucs 65   J4
Great Rollright Oxon 65   L1
Great Rudbaxton Pembks 54   F3
Great Ryburgh Norfk 121   L6
Great Ryle Nthumb 190   E4
Great Ryton Shrops 96   B3
Great Saling Essex 71   G2
Great Salkeld Cumb 166   D3
Great Sampford Essex 88   C8
Great Saredon Staffs 98   B2
Great Saughall Ches W 129   H5
Great Saxham Suffk 88   F3
Great Shefford W Berk 48   A4
Great Shelford Cambs 87   J5
Great Smeaton N York 160   E2
Great Snoring Norfk 121   L4
Great Somerford Wilts 46   D2
Great Soudley Shrops 114   A5
Great Stainton Darltn 169   J6
Great Stambridge Essex 53   J1
Great Staughton Cambs 86   D2
Great Steeping Lincs 137   H6
Great Stoke S Glos 45   J3
Great Stonar Kent 41   K3
Greatstone-on-Sea Kent 25   K3
Great Strickland Cumb 166   D6
Great Stukeley Cambs 102   E8
Great Sturton Lincs 136   D4
Great Sutton Ches W 129   J4
Great Sutton Shrops 96   C6
Great Swinburne Nthumb 179   L4
Great Tew Oxon 66   B1

Great Tey Essex 72 C2
Great Thurlow Suffk 88 D5
Great Torrington Devon ... 27 J7
Great Tosson Nthumb 190 E6
Great Totham Essex 72 B5
Great Totham Essex 72 C4
Great Tows Lincs 136 D2
Great Urswick Cumb 156 C7
Great Wakering Essex 53 K2
Great Waldingfield Suffk ... 89 H6
Great Walsingham Norfk ... 121 L4
Great Waltham Essex 71 G4
Great Warford Ches E 130 F4
Great Warley Essex 52 C1
Great Washbourne Gloucs .. 82 A8
Great Weeke Devon 13 G5
Great Welnetham Suffk 89 H3
Great Wenham Suffk 90 C7
Great Whittington Nthumb .. 180 B5
Great Wigborough Essex ... 72 D4
Great Wilbraham Cambs ... 87 L4
Great Wilne Derbys 116 D5
Great Wishford Wilts 33 J4
Great Witchingham Norfk ... 122 C7
Great Witcombe Gloucs 64 D4
Great Witley Worcs 81 H2
Great Wolford Warwks 82 F8
Greatworth Nhants 84 A6
Great Wratting Suffk 88 D5
Great Wymondley Herts 69 G2
Great Wyrley Staffs 98 C2
Great Wytheford Shrops 113 J7
Great Yarmouth Norfk 107 L2
Great Yarmouth
  Crematorium Norfk 107 K3
Great Yeldham Essex 88 F7
Grebby Lincs 137 H6
Greeba IoM 154 d6
Green Denbgs 128 C6
Green Bank Cumb 156 E6
Greenbottom Cnwll 4 C6
Greenburn W Loth 210 B7
Greencroft Hall Dur 168 F1
Green Cross Surrey 36 C3
Green Down Somset 45 H8
Green End Bed 85 K5
Green End Bed 86 B2
Green End Bed 86 B3
Green End Bed 86 C5
Green End Cambs 87 H4
Green End Cambs 87 K2
Green End Cambs 87 K3
Green End Cambs 102 D6
Green End Cambs 102 E8
Green End Herts 69 H1
Green End Herts 69 J3
Green End Herts 87 G8
Greenend Oxon 65 L3
Green End Warwks 99 H6
Greenfield Ag & B 207 L1
Greenfield C Beds 85 L8
Greenfield Flints 128 E4
Greenfield Highld 239 L3
Greenfield Oldham 140 F7
Greenfield Oxon 49 H1
Greenford Gt Lon 50 F3
Greengairs N Lans 209 L5
Greengates C Brad 150 B8
Greenhalgh Lancs 147 H8
Greenham Somset 29 K6
Greenham W Berk 48 C6
Green Hammerton N York ... 151 G4
Greenhaugh Nthumb 179 J2
Green Head Cumb 165 L1
Greenhead Nthumb 178 F6
Green Heath Staffs 98 C1
Greenheys Salfd 139 L7
Greenhill D & G 176 F3
Greenhill Falk 209 L3
Greenhill Herefs 81 G5
Greenhill Kent 40 F2
Greenhill S Lans 198 F6
Green Hill Wilts 46 F2
Greenhillocks Derbys 116 C2
Greenhithe Kent 52 C4
Greenholm E Ayrs 197 G3
Greenholme Cumb 157 G2
Greenhouse Border 188 F2
Greenhow Hill N York 149 K3
Greenland Highld 280 B3
Greenland Sheff 133 H2
Greenlands Bucks 49 J2
Green Lane Devon 13 H7
Green Lane Worcs 82 C2
Greenlaw Border 201 L4
Greenlea D & G 176 D4
Greenloaning P & K 220 E5
Green Moor Barns 141 L7

Greenmount Bury 140 A5
Green Oak E R Yk 143 K2
Greenock Inver 207 M4
Greenodd Cumb 156 D6
Green Ore Somset 31 J1
Green Quarter Cumb 157 G2
Greensgate Norfk 122 B8
Greenshields S Lans 199 H4
Greenside Gatesd 180 E6
Greenside Kirk 141 J4
Greens Norton Nhants 84 C5
Greenstead Green Essex 71 K2
Greensted Essex 70 D6
Green Street E Susx 24 D5
Green Street Gloucs 64 C4
Green Street Herts 69 G7
Green Street Herts 70 C3
Green Street Worcs 81 K5
Green Street Green Gt Lon .. 51 M6
Green Street Green Kent 52 C5
Greenstreet Green Suffk 90 B5
Green Tye Herts 70 C3
Greenway Gloucs 81 G8
Greenway Somset 30 D6
Greenway V Glam 43 G7
Greenway Worcs 81 G5
Greenwich Gt Lon 51 K3
Greet Gloucs 64 F1
Greete Shrops 80 D1
Greetham Lincs 136 F5
Greetham Rutlnd 118 B8
Greetland Calder 141 G3
Gregson Lane Lancs 139 J2
Greinton Somset 30 F4
Grenaby IoM 154 c7
Grendon Nhants 85 G3
Grendon Warwks 99 H3
Grendon Green Herefs 80 E4
Grendon Underwood Bucks .. 67 G3
Grenofen Devon 12 C8
Grenoside Sheff 133 G1
Grenoside Crematorium Sheff .. 132 F1
Greosabhagh W Isls 282 e6
Gresford Wrexhm 112 E1
Gresham Norfk 122 D4
Greshornish House Hotel
  Highld 258 E6
Gressenhall Norfk 121 L8
Gressenhall Green Norfk 121 L8
Gressingham Lancs 147 L2
Gresty Green Ches E 113 M1
Greta Bridge Dur 168 D8
Gretna D & G 177 K5
Gretna Green D & G 177 K5
Gretton Gloucs 64 E1
Gretton Nhants 101 K4
Gretton Shrops 96 C4
Grewelthorpe N York 160 C7
Grey Friars Suffk 91 L1
Greygarth N York 150 A1
Grey Green N Linc 143 K6
Greylake Somset 30 F4
Greylees Lincs 118 D3
Greyrigg D & G 176 E1
Greys Green Oxon 49 H2
Greysouthen Cumb 164 E5
Greystoke Cumb 166 B4
Greystone Angus 234 E6
Greywell Hants 35 L1
Gribb Dorset 15 J2
Gribthorpe E R Yk 143 J1
Griff Warwks 99 K5
Griffithstown Torfn 62 C7
Griffydam Leics 116 C7
Griggs Green Hants 36 B4
Grimeford Village Lancs 139 J5
Grimesthorpe Sheff 133 G2
Grimethorpe Barns 142 C6
Grimley Worcs 81 J3
Grimmet S Ayrs 183 J1
Grimoldby Lincs 137 G2
Grimpo Shrops 112 E6
Grimsargh Lancs 139 H1
Grimsby NE Lin 145 H5
Grimsby Crematorium NE Lin .. 145 H6
Grimscote Nhants 84 C4
Grimscott Cnwll 11 J1
Grimshader W Isls 282 g4
Grimston E R Yk 145 H1
Grimston Leics 117 J7
Grimston Norfk 120 F7
Grimstone Dorset 16 C4
Grimstone End Suffk 89 J2
Grinacombe Moor Devon 12 A4
Grindale E R Yk 153 J2
Grindle Shrops 97 G3

Grindleford Derbys 132 E4
Grindleton Lancs 148 D6
Grindley Brook Shrops 113 H3
Grindlow Derbys 132 D4
Grindon Nthumb 202 E4
Grindon S on T 169 K5
Grindon Staffs 115 H1
Grindon Hill Nthumb 179 J5
Grindonrigg Nthumb 202 E4
Gringley on the Hill Notts ... 134 E2
Grinsdale Cumb 177 L7
Grinshill Shrops 113 H6
Grinton N York 159 J3
Griomaisiader W Isls 282 g4
Griomsaigh W Isls 283 c9
Grishipoll Ag & B 224 F3
Grisling Common E Susx 23 G3
Gristhorpe N York 163 K6
Griston Norfk 105 J4
Gritley Ork 275 d5
Grittenham Wilts 46 F2
Grittleton Wilts 46 B3
Grizebeck Cumb 156 C5
Grizedale Cumb 156 D4
Groby Leics 100 B2
Groes Conwy 127 K6
Groes-faen Rhondd 43 G5
Groesffordd Gwynd 108 D4
Groesffordd Marli Denbgs ... 127 K5
Groesllwyd Powys 94 F1
Groeslon Gwynd 125 H8
Groeslon Gwynd 125 J7
Groes-Wen Caerph 43 H4
Grogarry W Isls 283 c10
Grogport Ag & B 194 C2
Groigearraidh W Isls 283 c10
Gromford Suffk 91 J3
Gronant Flints 128 C3
Groombridge E Susx 38 E6
Grosebay W Isls 282 e6
Grosmont Mons 62 E2
Grosmont N York 162 E2
Groton Suffk 89 J7
Grotton Oldham 140 E6
Grouville Jersey 9 e3
Grove Bucks 67 M3
Grove Dorset 16 D8
Grove Kent 41 H3
Grove Notts 134 E4
Grove Oxon 48 B1
Grove Pembks 55 G6
Grove Green Kent 39 K2
Grovenhurst Kent 39 H5
Grove Park Gt Lon 51 L4
Grovesend S Glos 45 K1
Grovesend Swans 57 G5
Grubb Street Kent 52 C5
Gruinard Highld 260 F2
Gruinart Ag & B 204 D3
Grula Highld 246 E3
Gruline Ag & B 227 G4
Grumbla Cnwll 2 C5
Grundisburgh Suffk 90 F5
Gruting Shet 281 c6
Grutness Shet 281 d9
Gualachulain Highld 229 J6
Guanockgate Lincs 103 H2
Guardbridge Fife 223 H3
Guarlford Worcs 81 J6
Guay P & K 232 F5
Guernsey Guern 9 j3
Guestling Green E Susx 24 F4
Guestling Thorn E Susx 24 F4
Guestwick Norfk 122 B6
Guide Bridge Tamesd 140 D8
Guide Post Nthumb 181 G2
Guilden Morden Cambs 86 F6
Guilden Sutton Ches W 129 K6
Guildford Surrey 36 F1
Guildford Crematorium Surrey .. 36 E2
Guildstead Kent 53 H6
Guildtown P & K 221 L1
Guilsborough Nhants 84 D1
Guilsfield Powys 94 F1
Guilton Kent 41 J4
Guiltreehill S Ayrs 183 J1
Guineaford Devon 27 K3
Guisborough R & Cl 170 E7
Guiseley Leeds 150 B7
Guist Norfk 121 M6
Guiting Power Gloucs 65 G2
Gullane E Loth 212 B2
Gulling Green Suffk 89 G4
Gulval Cnwll 2 D5
Gulworthy Devon 12 B8
Gumfreston Pembks 55 J6
Gumley Leics 100 F5
Gummow's Shop Cnwll 4 E3
Gunby E R Yk 143 H1

Gunby Lincs 118 B7
Gunby Lincs 137 J6
Gundleton Hants 35 J4
Gun Green Kent 39 J7
Gun Hill E Susx 23 J4
Gun Hill Warwks 99 H5
Gunn Devon 27 L4
Gunnerside N York 159 G3
Gunnerton Nthumb 179 L4
Gunness N Linc 143 L5
Gunnislake Cnwll 12 B8
Gunnista Shet 281 e6
Gunthorpe C Pete 102 D3
Gunthorpe N Linc 143 K8
Gunthorpe Norfk 121 M4
Gunthorpe Notts 117 H3
Gunton Suffk 107 L4
Gunwalloe Cnwll 3 G6
Gupworthy Somset 29 H4
Gurnard IoW 19 H4
Gurnett Ches E 131 H5
Gurney Slade Somset 31 K1
Gurnos Powys 57 L3
Gushmere Kent 40 D4
Gussage All Saints Dorset ... 33 G8
Gussage St Andrew Dorset .. 33 G8
Gussage St Michael Dorset .. 33 G8
Guston Kent 41 K6
Gutcher Shet 281 f2
Guthrie Angus 234 E5
Guyhirn Cambs 103 H3
Guyhirn Gull Cambs 103 H3
Guy's Marsh Dorset 32 D6
Guyzance Nthumb 191 J5
Gwaenysgor Flints 128 C3
Gwalchmai IoA 125 G4
Gwastadnant Gwynd 126 C8
Gwaun-Cae-Gurwen Carmth .. 59 J6
Gwbert on Sea Cerdgn 75 K2
Gwealavellan Cnwll 2 F3
Gweek Cnwll 3 H5
Gwehelog Mons 62 D6
Gwenddwr Powys 78 E6
Gwennap Cnwll 3 J3
Gwent Crematorium Mons ... 62 C7
Gwenter Cnwll 3 J7
Gwernaffield Flints 128 F6
Gwernesney Mons 62 E6
Gwernogle Carmth 58 F2
Gwernymynydd Flints 128 F7
Gwersyllt Wrexhm 112 D1
Gwespyr Flints 128 D3
Gwindra Cnwll 4 F4
Gwinear Cnwll 2 F4
Gwithian Cnwll 2 F3
Gwredog IoA 125 G3
Gwrhay Caerph 61 J7
Gwyddelwern Denbgs 111 L2
Gwyddgrug Carmth 58 E2
Gwynfryn Wrexhm 112 C1
Gwystre Powys 78 E2
Gwytherin Conwy 127 H7
Gyfelia Wrexhm 112 E3
Gyrn-gôch Gwynd 109 G2

H

Habberley Shrops 95 K3
Habberley Worcs 97 H7
Habergham Lancs 140 B1
Habertoft Lincs 137 J6
Habin W Susx 36 B6
Habrough NE Lin 144 F5
Hacconby Lincs 118 E6
Haceby Lincs 118 D4
Hacheston Suffk 91 G3
Hackbridge Gt Lon 51 H5
Hackenthorpe Sheff 133 H3
Hackford Norfk 106 B3
Hackforth N York 160 C4
Hack Green Ches E 113 L2
Hackland Ork 275 c4
Hackleton Nhants 84 F4
Hacklinge Kent 41 K4
Hackman's Gate Worcs 97 K7
Hackness N York 163 H4
Hackness Somset 30 E2
Hackney Gt Lon 51 K2
Hackthorn Lincs 135 K3
Hackthorpe Cumb 166 D6
Hacton Gt Lon 52 C2
Hadden Border 202 B6
Haddenham Bucks 67 H5
Haddenham Cambs 103 J8
Haddington E Loth 212 B4
Haddington Lincs 135 H7
Haddiscoe Norfk 107 J4

Haddo Abers 256 E4
Haddon Cambs 102 C5
Hade Edge Kirk 141 J6
Hadfield Derbys 140 F8
Hadham Cross Herts 70 B3
Hadham Ford Herts 70 B3
Hadleigh Essex 53 H2
Hadleigh Suffk 89 L6
Hadleigh Heath Suffk 89 K7
Hadley Worcs 81 K2
Hadley Wrekin 96 F1
Hadley End Staffs 115 J7
Hadley Wood Gt Lon 69 H7
Hadlow Kent 39 G3
Hadlow Down E Susx 23 J2
Hadnall Shrops 113 H7
Hadstock Essex 88 B6
Hadzor Worcs 81 L3
Haffenden Quarter Kent 39 M5
Hafodunos Conwy 127 H6
Hafod-y-bwch Wrexhm 112 D2
Hafod-y-coed Blae G 61 K7
Hafodyrynys Caerph 61 K7
Haggate Lancs 140 C1
Haggbeck Cumb 178 B4
Haggersta Shet 281 d6
Haggerston Nthumb 203 G4
Haggington Hill Devon 27 K2
Haggs Falk 209 L3
Hagley Herefs 80 D7
Hagley Worcs 97 K7
Hagmore Green Suffk 89 J7
Hagnaby Lincs 136 F7
Hagnaby Lincs 137 J4
Hagworthingham Lincs 136 F6
Haigh Wigan 139 J6
Haighton Green Lancs 139 H1
Haile Cumb 155 J1
Hailes Gloucs 64 F1
Hailey Herts 69 K5
Hailey Oxon 48 F2
Hailey Oxon 65 M4
Hailsham E Susx 23 K5
Hail Weston Cambs 86 D3
Hainault Gt Lon 70 C8
Haine Kent 41 K2
Hainford Norfk 122 E7
Hainton Lincs 136 C3
Hainworth C Brad 149 J8
Haisthorpe E R Yk 153 H3
Hakin Pembks 54 E5
Halam Notts 117 H1
Halbeath Fife 210 F1
Halberton Devon 29 H8
Halcro Highld 280 B4
Hale Cumb 157 H7
Hale Halton 129 L3
Hale Hants 33 L7
Hale Somset 32 C5
Hale Surrey 36 C1
Hale Traffd 130 F2
Hale Bank Halton 129 L3
Halebarns Traffd 130 F3
Hale Green E Susx 23 J4
Hale Nook Lancs 147 G7
Hales Norfk 107 H4
Hales Staffs 113 M5
Halesgate Lincs 119 K6
Hales Green Derbys 115 K3
Halesowen Dudley 98 B6
Hales Place Kent 40 F3
Hale Street Kent 39 G3
Halesville Essex 72 C8
Halesworth Suffk 107 H7
Halewood Knows 129 K3
Halford Devon 13 J7
Halford Shrops 95 K6
Halford Warwks 83 G6
Halfpenny Cumb 157 H5
Halfpenny Green Staffs 97 J3
Halfpenny Houses N York 160 B5
Halfway Carmth 59 J3
Halfway Carmth 59 M2
Halfway Sheff 133 J3
Halfway W Berk 48 B5
Halfway Bridge W Susx 36 D6
Halfway House Shrops 95 H1
Halfway Houses Kent 53 K4
Halifax Calder 141 H3
Halket E Ayrs 208 D8
Halkirk Highld 279 K4
Halkyn Flints 128 F5
Hall E Rens 208 C8
Hallam Fields Derbys 116 D4
Halland E Susx 23 H4
Hallaton Leics 101 H4
Hallatrow BaNES 45 J7
Hallbankgate Cumb 178 D7
Hallbeck Cumb 157 K5

Hall Cliffe Wakefd 141 L4
Hall Cross Lancs 138 E2
Hall Dunnerdale Cumb 156 B3
Hallen S Glos 45 H3
Hall End Bed 85 K6
Hall End C Beds 86 B7
Hallfield Gate Derbys 133 H8
Hallgarth Dur 169 J2
Hall Glen Falk 210 A3
Hall Green Birm 98 E7
Hallin Highld 258 C5
Halling Medway 52 F6
Hallington Lincs 136 F3
Hallington Nthumb 180 B4
Halliwell Bolton 139 L5
Halloughton Notts 117 J1
Hallow Worcs 81 J3
Hallow Heath Worcs 81 J3
Hallsands Devon 8 B7
Hall's Green Essex 69 L5
Hall's Green Herts 69 H2
Hallthwaites Cumb 156 A5
Hallworthy Cnwll 11 H5
Hallyne Border 199 L5
Halmer End Staffs 114 B2
Halmond's Frome Herefs 80 F5
Halmore Gloucs 63 K6
Halnaker W Susx 20 E5
Halsall Lancs 138 D5
Halse Nhants 84 A7
Halse Somset 29 L5
Halsetown Cnwll 2 D3
Halsham E R Yk 145 H2
Halsinger Devon 27 J3
Halstead Essex 71 K1
Halstead Kent 52 A6
Halstead Leics 101 G2
Halstock Dorset 15 M1
Halsway Somset 29 L3
Haltcliff Bridge Cumb 165 L3
Haltemprice Crematorium
   E R Yk 144 C2
Haltham Lincs 136 D7
Haltoft End Lincs 119 L3
Halton Bucks 67 L5
Halton Halton 129 M3
Halton Lancs 147 K3
Halton Leeds 142 A1
Halton Nthumb 180 B5
Halton Wrexhm 112 D3
Halton East N York 149 J5
Halton Fenside Lincs 137 H7
Halton Gill N York 158 F7
Halton Green Lancs 147 K3
Halton Holegate Lincs 137 H6
Halton Lea Gate Nthumb 178 F7
Halton Quay Cnwll 6 E2
Halton Shields Nthumb 180 B5
Halton West N York 148 E5
Haltwhistle Nthumb 179 G6
Halvergate Norfk 107 J2
Halwell Devon 8 A4
Halwill Devon 12 B3
Halwill Junction Devon 12 B3
Ham Devon 14 F2
Ham Gloucs 63 K7
Ham Gloucs 64 E3
Ham Gt Lon 50 F4
Ham Kent 41 K4
Ham Somset 30 D6
Ham Somset 31 L1
Ham Wilts 47 L6
Hambleden Bucks 49 J2
Hambledon Hants 35 K7
Hambledon Surrey 36 E3
Hamble-le-Rice Hants 19 H2
Hambleton Lancs 147 G7
Hambleton N York 142 E2
Hambleton Moss Side Lancs 147 G7
Hambridge Somset 30 F6
Hambrook S Glos 45 J3
Hambrook W Susx 20 C5
Ham Common Dorset 32 D5
Hameringham Lincs 136 F6
Hamerton Cambs 102 C7
Ham Green Herefs 81 H6
Ham Green Kent 25 G2
Ham Green Kent 53 H5
Ham Green N Som 45 G4
Ham Green Worcs 82 B3
Ham Hill Kent 52 F6
Hamilton S Lans 209 J7
Hamlet Dorset 16 B1
Hamlins E Susx 23 K5
Hammerpot W Susx 21 H5
Hammersmith Gt Lon 51 G3
Hammerwich Staffs 98 D2
Hammerwood E Susx 38 C5
Hammond Street Herts 69 J7

Hammoon Dorset 32 D7
Hamnavoe Shet 281 d7
Hampden Park E Susx 23 K6
Hamperden End Essex 70 E1
Hampnett Gloucs 65 G4
Hampole Donc. 142 D5
Hampreston Dorset 17 L3
Hampsfield Cumb 156 F6
Hampson Green Lancs 147 J5
Hampstead Gt Lon 51 H2
Hampstead Norreys W Berk 48 D4
Hampsthwaite N York 150 C4
Hampton C Pete 102 D4
Hampton Devon 15 G3
Hampton Gt Lon 50 F5
Hampton Kent 40 F2
Hampton Shrops 97 G6
Hampton Swindn 47 J8
Hampton Worcs 82 B6
Hampton Bishop Herefs 80 D7
Hampton Fields Gloucs 64 C7
Hampton Green Ches W 113 H2
Hampton Heath Ches W 113 H2
Hampton-in-Arden Solhll 99 G7
Hampton Loade Shrops 97 G6
Hampton Lovett Worcs 81 K2
Hampton Lucy Warwks 83 G4
Hampton Magna Warwks 83 G2
Hampton on the Hill Warwks 82 F2
Hampton Poyle Oxon 66 D4
Hampton Wick Gt Lon 50 F5
Hamptworth Wilts 34 B7
Hamrow Norfk 121 K6
Hamsey E Susx 22 F5
Hamsey Green Surrey 51 K7
Hamstall Ridware Staffs 115 H7
Hamstead Birm 98 D5
Hamstead IoW 18 F5
Hamstead Marshall W Berk 48 B6
Hamsterley Dur 168 E4
Hamsterley Dur 180 D7
Hamstreet Kent 40 C8
Ham Street Somset 31 J4
Hamwood N Som 44 D7
Hamworthy Poole 17 K4
Hanbury Staffs 115 K6
Hanbury Worcs 81 M2
Hanby Lincs 118 D5
Hanchet End Suffk 88 C6
Hanchurch Staffs 114 C3
Handa Island Highld 276 A6
Handale R & Cl 171 G7
Handbridge Ches W 129 K6
Handcross W Susx 37 L5
Handforth Ches E 131 G3
Hand Green Ches W 130 A7
Handley Ches W 129 L8
Handley Derbys 133 G7
Handley Green Essex 71 G6
Handsacre Staffs 115 H8
Handsworth Birm 98 D5
Handsworth Sheff 133 H2
Handy Cross Bucks 49 K1
Hanford C Stke 114 D3
Hanford Dorset 32 D8
Hanging Heaton Kirk 141 L3
Hanging Houghton Nhants 101 G8
Hanging Langford Wilts 33 H3
Hangleton Br & H 22 D6
Hangleton W Susx 21 J6
Hanham S Glos 45 J4
Hankelow Ches E 113 L2
Hankerton Wilts 46 E1
Hankham E Susx 23 K6
Hanley C Stke 114 D2
Hanley Castle Worcs 81 J6
Hanley Child Worcs 80 F2
Hanley Swan Worcs 81 J6
Hanley William Worcs 80 F2
Hanlith N York 148 F3
Hanmer Wrexhm 113 G3
Hannaford Devon 27 L5
Hannah Lincs 137 J4
Hannington Hants 48 D7
Hannington Nhants 84 F1
Hannington Swindn 65 H8
Hannington Wick Swindn 65 H8
Hanscombe End C Beds 86 C8
Hanslope M Keyn 84 F6
Hanwell Gt Lon 50 F3
Hanwell Oxon 83 K6
Hanwood Shrops 95 K2
Hanworth Gt Lon 50 E5
Hanworth Norfk 122 D4
Happendon S Lans 198 E6
Happisburgh Norfk 123 H5
Happisburgh Common Norfk 123 H5

Hapsford Ches W 129 L5
Hapton Lancs 140 B2
Hapton Norfk 106 D4
Harberton Devon 8 A3
Harbertonford Devon 8 A4
Harbledown Kent 40 F4
Harborne Birm 98 C6
Harborough Magna Warwks 100 B7
Harbottle Nthumb 190 C5
Harbourneford Devon 7 K2
Harbours Hill Worcs 81 M2
Harbridge Hants 18 A2
Harbridge Green Hants 33 K8
Harbury Warwks 83 J3
Harby Leics 117 K6
Harby Notts 135 H5
Harcombe Devon 13 K6
Harcombe Devon 14 D4
Harcombe Bottom Devon 15 H3
Harden C Brad 149 K8
Harden Wsall 98 C3
Hardendale Cumb 166 D7
Hardenhuish Wilts 46 C4
Hardgate Abers 245 H3
Hardgate D & G 175 K2
Hardgate N York 150 C3
Hardgate W Duns 208 E4
Hardham W Susx 21 H3
Hardhorn Lancs 147 G8
Hardingham Norfk 105 L3
Hardingstone Nhants 84 E4
Hardington Somset 45 L8
Hardington Mandeville
   Somset 31 H8
Hardington Marsh Somset 15 L1
Hardington Moor Somset 31 H8
Hardisworthy Devon 26 D6
Hardley Hants 19 G3
Hardley Street Norfk 107 H3
Hardmead M Keyn 85 H5
Hardraw N York 158 F4
Hardsough Lancs 140 B4
Hardstoft Derbys 133 J7
Hardway Hants 19 K3
Hardway Somset 32 B4
Hardwick Bucks 67 K3
Hardwick Cambs 87 H3
Hardwick Nhants 85 G1
Hardwick Norfk 106 E5
Hardwick Oxon 66 A6
Hardwick Oxon 66 E1
Hardwick Rothm 133 K3
Hardwick Wsall 98 D4
Hardwicke Gloucs 64 A4
Hardwicke Gloucs 64 C2
Hardy's Green Essex 72 D3
Harebeating E Susx 23 K5
Hareby Lincs 136 F6
Hare Croft C Brad 149 K8
Harefield Gt Lon 50 D1
Hare Green Essex 73 G2
Hare Hatch Wokham 49 J3
Harehill Derbys 115 K4
Harehills Leeds 141 M1
Harehope Nthumb 191 G2
Harelaw Border 188 F2
Harelaw D & G 178 B3
Harelaw Dur 180 E8
Hareplain Kent 39 L5
Haresceugh Cumb 166 E2
Harescombe Gloucs 64 B5
Haresfield Gloucs 64 A5
Harestock Hants 34 F4
Hare Street Essex 70 B5
Hare Street Essex 70 D7
Hare Street Herts 69 K1
Harewood Leeds 150 D6
Harewood End Herefs 63 G2
Harford Devon 7 J3
Hargate Norfk 106 C5
Hargatewall Derbys 132 B4
Hargrave Ches W 129 L7
Hargrave Nhants 85 K1
Hargrave Suffk 88 F3
Harker Cumb 177 L6
Harkstead Suffk 90 E8
Harlaston Staffs 99 G1
Harlaxton Lincs 118 A5
Harlech Gwynd 109 K5
Harlescott Shrops 113 H8
Harlesden Gt Lon 51 G2
Harlesthorpe Derbys 133 K4
Harleston Devon 8 B6
Harleston Norfk 106 E6
Harleston Suffk 89 L3
Harlestone Nhants 84 D2
Harle Syke Lancs 140 C1
Harley Rothm 142 B8
Harley Shrops 96 D3

Harlington C Beds......68 D1
Harlington Donc......142 D7
Harlington Gt Lon......50 E3
Harlosh Highld......258 D8
Harlow Essex......70 C5
Harlow Hill Nthumb......180 C5
Harlthorpe E R Yk......152 A8
Harlton Cambs......87 H5
Harlyn Cnwll......10 B7
Harman's Cross Dorset......17 J6
Harmby N York......159 L5
Harmer Green Herts......69 H4
Harmer Hill Shrops......113 H7
Harmondsworth Gt Lon......50 D3
Harmston Lincs......135 K7
Harnage Shrops......96 D3
Harnham Nthumb......180 C3
Harnhill Gloucs......64 F7
Harold Hill Gt Lon......70 D8
Haroldston West Pembks......54 D4
Haroldswick Shet......281 f1
Harold Wood Gt Lon......52 C1
Harome N York......161 L6
Harpenden Herts......68 E4
Harpford Devon......14 C4
Harpham E R Yk......153 H3
Harpley Norfk......121 H6
Harpley Worcs......80 F3
Harpole Nhants......84 D3
Harpsdale Highld......279 K5
Harpsden Oxon......49 J3
Harpswell Lincs......135 J2
Harpurhey Manch......140 C7
Harpur Hill Derbys......131 L5
Harraby Cumb......177 M7
Harracott Devon......27 K5
Harrapool Highld......247 K4
Harrietfield P & K......221 H1
Harrietsham Kent......39 L3
Harringay Gt Lon......51 J1
Harrington Cumb......164 C5
Harrington Lincs......137 G5
Harrington Nhants......101 G7
Harringworth Nhants......101 K4
Harris W Isls......282 e6
Harriseahead Staffs......131 G8
Harriston Cumb......165 G2
Harrogate N York......150 D5
Harrogate Crematorium
   N York......150 D5
Harrold Bed......85 J4
Harrop Dale Oldham......140 F6
Harrow Gt Lon......50 F1
Harrowbarrow Cnwll......12 A8
Harrowden Bed......86 B5
Harrowgate Village Darltn......169 H7
Harrow Green Suffk......89 H4
Harrow on the Hill Gt Lon......50 F2
Harrow Weald Gt Lon......50 F1
Harston Cambs......87 J5
Harston Leics......117 L5
Harswell E R Yk......152 C7
Hart Hartpl......170 B4
Hartburn Nthumb......180 D2
Hartburn S on T......169 L7
Hartest Suffk......89 G5
Hartfield E Susx......38 D6
Hartford Cambs......86 E1
Hartford Ches W......130 C5
Hartford Somset......29 C4
Hartfordbridge Hants......49 J7
Hartford End Essex......71 G3
Hartforth N York......159 L2
Hartgrove Dorset......32 D7
Harthill Ches W......129 L8
Harthill N Lans......210 B6
Harthill Rothm......133 K3
Hartington Derbys......132 C7
Hartington Nthumb......180 B1
Hartland Devon......26 D6
Hartland Quay Devon......26 C6
Hartlebury Worcs......81 J1
Hartlepool Hartpl......170 C4
Hartlepool Crematorium
   Hartpl......170 C4
Hartley Cumb......158 D1
Hartley Kent......39 J6
Hartley Kent......52 D5
Hartley Nthumb......181 H4
Hartley Green Kent......52 D5
Hartley Green Staffs......114 F6
Hartley Wespall Hants......49 G7
Hartley Wintney Hants......49 J7
Hartlip Kent......53 H6
Hartoft End N York......162 C4
Harton N York......151 L3
Harton S Tyne......181 J6
Harton Shrops......96 B5
Hartpury Gloucs......64 A2

Hartshead Kirk......141 J3
Hartshill C Stke......114 D2
Hartshill Warwks......99 J4
Hartshorne Derbys......116 B7
Hartside Nthumb......190 D3
Hartsop Cumb......165 L8
Hart Station Hartpl......170 B3
Hartswell Somset......29 K5
Hartwell Nhants......84 F5
Hartwith N York......150 B3
Hartwood N Lans......209 M7
Hartwoodmyres Border......188 D1
Harvel Kent......52 E6
Harvington Worcs......82 C5
Harvington Worcs......97 K8
Harwell Notts......134 D2
Harwell Oxon......48 C1
Harwich Essex......73 K1
Harwood Bolton......139 L5
Harwood Dur......167 J4
Harwood Dale N York......163 H3
Harwood Lee Bolton......139 L5
Harwood Park Crematorium
   Herts......69 H3
Harworth Notts......134 C2
Hasbury Dudley......98 B6
Hascombe Surrey......36 F3
Haselbech Nhants......100 F7
Haselbury Plucknett Somset......31 G8
Haseley Warwks......82 F2
Haseley Green Warwks......82 F1
Haseley Knob Warwks......82 F1
Haselor Warwks......82 D4
Hasfield Gloucs......64 B2
Hasguard Pembks......54 D5
Hasholme E R Yk......143 L1
Haskayne Lancs......138 D6
Hasketon Suffk......90 F5
Hasland Derbys......133 H5
Haslemere Surrey......36 D4
Haslingden Lancs......140 B3
Haslingfield Cambs......87 H5
Haslington Ches E......130 E8
Hassall Ches E......130 E8
Hassall Green Ches E......130 F7
Hassell Street Kent......40 E6
Hassingham Norfk......107 H2
Hassness Cumb......165 G7
Hassocks W Susx......22 D4
Hassop Derbys......132 D5
Haste Hill Surrey......36 D4
Haster Highld......280 D6
Hasthorpe Lincs......137 J5
Hastingleigh Kent......40 E6
Hastings E Susx......24 E5
Hastings Somset......30 D7
Hastings Crematorium E Susx......24 E5
Hastingwood Essex......70 C5
Hastoe Herts......68 A5
Haswell Dur......169 K2
Haswell Plough Dur......169 K2
Hatch C Beds......86 D5
Hatch Beauchamp Somset......30 D6
Hatch End Bed......86 B3
Hatch End Gt Lon......50 E1
Hatchet Gate Hants......18 F3
Hatching Green Herts......68 E4
Hatchmere Ches W......130 A5
Hatcliffe NE Lin......145 G7
Hatfield Donc......143 G6
Hatfield Herefs......80 E3
Hatfield Herts......69 G5
Hatfield Worcs......81 K5
Hatfield Broad Oak Essex......70 E4
Hatfield Heath Essex......70 D4
Hatfield Peverel Essex......71 J5
Hatfield Woodhouse Donc......143 H6
Hatford Oxon......65 M8
Hatherden Hants......34 D1
Hatherleigh Devon......12 D2
Hathern Leics......116 E7
Hatherop Gloucs......65 H6
Hathersage Derbys......132 E3
Hathersage Booths Derbys......132 E3
Hatherton Ches E......113 L2
Hatherton Staffs......98 B1
Hatley St George Cambs......86 F5
Hatt Cnwll......6 D2
Hattersley Tamesd......131 K1
Hattingley Hants......35 K3
Hatton Abers......257 K4
Hatton Angus......234 C6
Hatton Derbys......115 L5
Hatton Gt Lon......50 E4
Hatton Lincs......136 C4
Hatton Shrops......95 L5
Hatton Warrtn......130 B3
Hatton Warwks......82 F2
Hatton Heath Ches W......129 K7

Hatton of Fintray Abers......256 F8
Haugh E Ayrs......196 F6
Haugh Lincs......137 H4
Haugh Rochdl......140 D5
Haugham Lincs......136 F3
Haughhead E Duns......209 G3
Haugh Head Nthumb......202 F7
Haughley Suffk......89 L3
Haughley Green Suffk......89 L2
Haugh of Glass Moray......255 H4
Haugh of Urr D & G......175 K2
Haughs of Kinnaird Angus......235 G4
Haughton Ches E......130 B8
Haughton Notts......134 D5
Haughton Powys......112 D7
Haughton Shrops......96 F4
Haughton Shrops......97 G2
Haughton Shrops......112 F6
Haughton Shrops......113 J8
Haughton Staffs......114 D7
Haughton Green Tamesd......131 J1
Haughton le Skerne Darltn......169 J7
Haultwick Herts......69 J3
Haunton Staffs......99 G1
Hautes Croix Jersey......9 d1
Hauxton Cambs......87 J5
Havannah Ches E......131 G6
Havant Hants......20 B5
Havant Crematorium Hants......20 B5
Haven Herefs......79 M4
Haven Bank Lincs......119 H1
Haven Side E R Yk......144 F2
Havenstreet IoW......19 J5
Havercroft Wakefd......142 B5
Haverfordwest Pembks......54 F4
Haverhill Suffk......88 D6
Haverigg Cumb......155 L7
Havering-atte-Bower Gt Lon......70 D8
Haversham M Keyn......84 F6
Haverthwaite Cumb......156 E6
Haverton Hill S on T......170 C6
Havyat N Som......44 F6
Havyatt Somset......31 H3
Hawarden Flints......129 H6
Hawbridge Worcs......81 L5
Hawbush Green Essex......71 J3
Hawcoat Cumb......146 D2
Hawen Cerdgn......76 C6
Hawes N York......158 F5
Hawe's Green Norfk......106 F4
Hawford Worcs......81 J3
Hawick Border......188 E3
Hawkchurch Devon......15 H3
Hawkedon Suffk......88 F4
Hawkenbury Kent......39 K4
Hawkeridge Wilts......46 B8
Hawkerland Devon......14 C5
Hawker's Cove Cnwll......10 C7
Hawkesbury S Glos......45 M2
Hawkesbury Warwks......99 K6
Hawkesbury Upton S Glos......45 M2
Hawkes End Covtry......99 J6
Hawk Green Stockp......131 J2
Hawkhill Nthumb......191 J4
Hawkhurst Kent......39 J7
Hawkhurst Common E Susx......23 J4
Hawkinge Kent......41 H7
Hawkinge Crematorium Kent......41 G7
Hawkley Hants......35 M5
Hawkley Wigan......139 H7
Hawkridge Somset......28 F5
Hawksdale Cumb......165 L1
Hawkshaw Bury......139 M5
Hawkshead Cumb......156 E3
Hawkshead Hill Cumb......156 D3
Hawksland S Lans......198 D5
Hawkspur Green Essex......71 G1
Hawkstone Shrops......113 J5
Hawkswick N York......149 G5
Hawksworth Leeds......149 L7
Hawksworth Notts......117 K3
Hawkwell Essex......53 J1
Hawkwell Nthumb......180 C4
Hawley Hants......49 L7
Hawley Kent......52 C4
Hawling Gloucs......64 F3
Hawnby N York......161 J5
Haworth C Brad......149 J8
Hawridge Bucks......68 B6
Hawstead Suffk......89 G3
Hawstead Green Suffk......89 H3
Hawthorn Dur......169 L2
Hawthorn Hants......35 K4
Hawthorn Rhondd......43 H4
Hawthorn Hill Br For......49 L4
Hawthorn Hill Lincs......136 D8
Hawthorpe Lincs......118 D6
Hawton Notts......117 L1
Haxby C York......151 K4

Haxby Gates C York......151 K4
Haxey N Linc......143 J7
Haxey Carr N Linc......143 J7
Haxted Surrey......38 C4
Haxton Wilts......33 K1
Hay Cnwll......4 F4
Hay Cnwll......10 D8
Haycombe Crematorium
   BaNES......45 L6
Haydock St Hel......139 H8
Haydon BaNES......45 K8
Haydon Dorset......31 L7
Haydon Somset......30 C6
Haydon Bridge Nthumb......179 J6
Haydon Wick Swindn......47 H2
Haye Cnwll......11 L8
Hayes Gt Lon......50 E3
Hayes Gt Lon......51 L5
Hayes End Gt Lon......50 D3
Hayfield Ag & B......217 H2
Hayfield Derbys......131 L2
Haygate Wrekin......96 E1
Hay Green Norfk......120 C7
Hayhillock Angus......234 E7
Hayle Cnwll......2 E4
Hayley Green Dudley......98 B6
Hayling Island Hants......20 B6
Haymoor Green Ches E......113 L2
Hayne Devon......13 H5
Hayne Devon......29 G7
Haynes (Church End) C Beds......86 B7
Haynes (Northwood End)
   C Beds......86 B6
Haynes (Silver End) C Beds......86 B6
Haynes (West End) C Beds......85 L7
Hay-on-Wye Powys......79 J6
Hayscastle Pembks......74 E7
Hayscastle Cross Pembks......74 E7
Haysden Kent......38 F4
Hay Street Herts......69 K2
Hayton Cumb......164 F2
Hayton Cumb......178 C7
Hayton E R Yk......152 C6
Hayton Notts......134 E3
Hayton's Bent Shrops......96 C7
Haytor Vale Devon......13 H7
Haytown Devon......26 F7
Haywards Heath W Susx......22 E2
Haywood Donc......142 F5
Haywood Herefs......80 B8
Haywood Oaks Notts......134 C8
Hazards Green E Susx......24 C5
Hazelbank S Lans......198 D4
Hazelbury Bryan Dorset......16 E1
Hazeleigh Essex......71 K6
Hazeley Hants......49 H7
Hazelford Notts......117 J2
Hazel Grove Stockp......131 H2
Hazelhurst Tamesd......140 E7
Hazelslade Staffs......98 C1
Hazel Street Kent......39 H5
Hazel Stub Suffk......88 D6
Hazelton Walls Fife......222 E3
Hazelwood Derbys......116 B2
Hazlemere Bucks......67 L8
Hazlerigg N u Ty......180 F4
Hazles Staffs......114 F2
Hazleton Gloucs......65 G3
Heacham Norfk......120 E4
Headbourne Worthy Hants......35 G4
Headbrook Herefs......79 K4
Headcorn Kent......39 L4
Headingley Leeds......150 C8
Headington Oxon......66 D5
Headlam Dur......168 F7
Headlesscross N Lans......210 B7
Headless Cross Worcs......82 B2
Headley Hants......36 B4
Headley Hants......48 D6
Headley Surrey......51 G8
Headley Down Hants......36 B4
Headley Heath Worcs......98 D8
Headon Devon......11 M2
Headon Notts......134 E4
Heads Nook Cumb......178 C7
Heage Derbys......116 B2
Healaugh N York......151 L6
Healaugh N York......159 H3
Heald Green Stockp......131 G3
Heale Devon......28 A2
Heale Somset......30 C6
Heale Somset......30 F5
Healey N York......160 B6
Healey Nthumb......180 B7
Healey Rochdl......140 D4
Healey Wakefd......141 L4
Healeyfield Dur......168 D1
Healing NE Lin......145 G5
Heamoor Cnwll......2 D5

Heanor Derbys	116	D2
Heanton Punchardon Devon	27	J4
Heapham Lincs	135	H2
Hearn Hants	36	B3
Heart of England Crematorium Warwks	99	K5
Hearts Delight Kent	53	J6
Heasley Mill Devon	28	C4
Heast Highld	247	K5
Heath Derbys	133	J6
Heath Wakefd	142	A4
Heath and Reach C Beds	68	A2
Heath Common W Susx	21	J4
Heathcote Derbys	132	C7
Heathcote Shrops	113	L6
Heath End Bucks	67	L7
Heath End Hants	48	B6
Heath End Leics	116	B7
Heath End Warwks	82	F3
Heather Leics	99	K1
Heathfield Cambs	87	J6
Heathfield Devon	13	J7
Heathfield E Susx	23	K3
Heathfield N York	149	L3
Heathfield Somset	29	L5
Heathfield Village Oxon	66	D4
Heath Green Worcs	82	C1
Heath Hall D & G	176	C3
Heath Hayes & Wimblebury Staffs	98	C2
Heath Hill Shrops	97	H1
Heath House Somset	30	F2
Heathstock Devon	14	F2
Heathton Shrops	97	H5
Heath Town Wolves	97	L3
Heathwaite N York	161	G2
Heatley Staffs	115	H6
Heatley Warrtn	130	D2
Heaton Bolton	139	L6
Heaton C Brad	149	L8
Heaton Lancs	147	J4
Heaton N u Ty	181	G5
Heaton Staffs	131	J7
Heaton Chapel Stockp	131	H1
Heaton Mersey Stockp	131	G2
Heaton Norris Stockp	131	H2
Heaton's Bridge Lancs	138	E5
Heaverham Kent	52	C7
Heaviley Stockp	131	H2
Heavitree Devon	13	L4
Hebburn S Tyne	181	H6
Hebden N York	149	J3
Hebden Bridge Calder	140	F2
Hebden Green Ches W	130	C6
Hebing End Herts	69	J3
Hebron Carmth	75	L6
Hebron IoA	125	H3
Hebron Nthumb	191	J8
Heckfield Hants	49	H6
Heckfield Green Suffk	106	D8
Heckfordbridge Essex	72	D3
Heckington Lincs	118	F3
Heckmondwike Kirk	141	K3
Heddington Wilts	46	E5
Heddon-on-the-Wall Nthumb	180	D5
Hedenham Norfk	107	G5
Hedge End Hants	19	H1
Hedgerley Bucks	50	B2
Hedgerley Green Bucks	50	B2
Hedging Somset	30	D5
Hedley on the Hill Nthumb	180	C7
Hednesford Staffs	98	C1
Hedon E R Yk	145	F2
Hedsor Bucks	49	L2
Heeley Sheff	133	G3
Hegdon Hill Herefs	80	D4
Heglibister Shet	281	d6
Heighington Darltn	169	H6
Heighington Lincs	135	L6
Heightington Worcs	81	H1
Heiton Border	201	L7
Hele Devon	13	H8
Hele Devon	14	A2
Hele Devon	27	J2
Hele Somset	30	B6
Helebridge Cnwll	11	J2
Hele Lane Devon	28	D8
Helensburgh Ag & B	208	A3
Helenton S Ayrs	196	D5
Helford Cnwll	3	J6
Helford Passage Cnwll	3	J5
Helhoughton Norfk	121	J6
Helions Bumpstead Essex	88	C7
Hellaby Rothm	133	K1
Helland Cnwll	10	F8
Hellandbridge Cnwll	10	F8
Hell Corner W Berk	48	A6
Hellescott Cnwll	11	K5
Hellesdon Norfk	106	E1
Hellesveor Cnwll	2	D3
Hellidon Nhants	83	M4
Hellifield N York	148	E4
Hellingly E Susx	23	K5
Hellington Norfk	107	G3
Helm Nthumb	191	H7
Helmdon Nhants	84	B6
Helme Kirk	141	H5
Helmingham Suffk	90	E4
Helmington Row Dur	168	F4
Helmsdale Highld	274	D5
Helmshore Lancs	140	B3
Helmsley N York	161	K6
Helperby N York	150	F2
Helperthorpe N York	152	E2
Helpringham Lincs	118	F3
Helpston C Pete	102	C2
Helsby Ches W	129	L4
Helsey Lincs	137	K5
Helston Cnwll	3	G5
Helstone Cnwll	10	F6
Helton Cumb	166	C6
Helwith N York	159	K2
Helwith Bridge N York	148	D2
Hemblington Norfk	107	G1
Hembridge Somset	31	K3
Hemel Hempstead Herts	68	D5
Hemerdon Devon	7	H3
Hemingbrough N York	143	H2
Hemingby Lincs	136	D5
Hemingfield Barns	142	B7
Hemingford Abbots Cambs	86	F1
Hemingford Grey Cambs	86	F1
Hemingstone Suffk	90	D4
Hemington Leics	116	D6
Hemington Nhants	102	B6
Hemington Somset	45	L8
Hemley Suffk	91	G6
Hemlington Middsb	170	C7
Hempholme E R Yk	153	H5
Hempnall Norfk	106	E4
Hempnall Green Norfk	106	E5
Hempriggs Moray	266	B3
Hempstead Essex	88	C7
Hempstead Medway	53	G6
Hempstead Norfk	122	C4
Hempstead Norfk	123	H6
Hempsted Gloucs	64	B4
Hempton Norfk	121	K5
Hempton Oxon	66	C1
Hemsby Norfk	123	K8
Hemswell Lincs	135	J2
Hemswell Cliff Lincs	135	J2
Hemsworth Wakefd	142	C5
Hemyock Devon	29	L8
Henbury Bristl	45	H3
Henbury Ches E	131	H5
Hendham Devon	7	L5
Hendomen Powys	94	F4
Hendon Gt Lon	51	G1
Hendon Sundld	181	K7
Hendon Crematorium Gt Lon	51	G1
Hendra Cnwll	3	J4
Hendra Cnwll	10	E7
Hendre Brdgnd	42	E5
Hendre Flints	128	E6
Hendre Mons	62	F4
Hendy Carmth	57	G4
Heneglwys IoA	125	G4
Henfield W Susx	22	C4
Henford Devon	11	M4
Henghurst Kent	40	B8
Hengoed Caerph	43	J3
Hengoed Powys	79	J4
Hengoed Shrops	112	D5
Hengrave Suffk	89	G2
Henham Essex	70	E2
Heniarth Powys	94	D2
Henlade Somset	30	C6
Henley Dorset	16	D2
Henley Gloucs	64	C4
Henley Shrops	95	L5
Henley Shrops	96	C8
Henley Somset	30	F4
Henley Suffk	90	E5
Henley W Susx	36	D5
Henley Green Covtry	99	K7
Henley-in-Arden Warwks	82	E2
Henley-on-Thames Oxon	49	J2
Henley Park Surrey	50	B8
Henley's Down E Susx	24	D5
Henley Street Kent	52	E5
Henllan Cerdgn	76	C7
Henllan Denbgs	127	L6
Henllan Amgoed Carmth	55	L3
Henllys Torfn	44	B1
Henlow C Beds	86	D7
Hennock Devon	13	J6
Henny Street Essex	89	H7
Henryd Conwy	126	F5
Henry's Moat (Castell Hendre) Pembks	75	H6
Hensall N York	142	F3
Henshaw Nthumb	179	H6
Hensingham Cumb	164	C7
Henstead Suffk	107	K6
Hensting Hants	35	G6
Henstridge Somset	32	B7
Henstridge Ash Somset	32	B6
Henstridge Marsh Somset	32	B6
Henton Oxon	67	J6
Henton Somset	31	H2
Henwick Worcs	81	J4
Henwood Cnwll	11	K7
Henwood Oxon	66	C6
Heol-las Swans	57	J5
Heol Senni Powys	60	D2
Heol-y-Cyw Brdgnd	42	E5
Hepburn Nthumb	190	F1
Hepple Nthumb	190	E6
Hepscott Nthumb	180	F2
Heptonstall Calder	140	E2
Hepworth Kirk	141	J6
Hepworth Suffk	105	K8
Herbrandston Pembks	54	E5
Hereford Herefs	80	C7
Hereford Crematorium Herefs	80	C7
Hereson Kent	41	L2
Heribusta Highld	258	F3
Heriot Border	200	E2
Hermiston C Edin	211	G5
Hermitage Border	188	E7
Hermitage Dorset	16	C1
Hermitage W Berk	48	D4
Hermitage W Susx	20	B5
Hermit Hill Barns	141	M7
Hermon Carmth	58	C3
Hermon IoA	125	G6
Hermon Pembks	75	L6
Herne Kent	41	G2
Herne Bay Kent	41	G2
Herne Common Kent	41	G2
Herne Hill Gt Lon	51	J4
Herne Pound Kent	39	G3
Herner Devon	27	K5
Hernhill Kent	40	E3
Herodsfoot Cnwll	5	L3
Heronden Kent	41	J4
Herongate Essex	52	D1
Heronsford S Ayrs	182	E6
Heronsgate Herts	68	C8
Herriard Hants	35	K2
Herringfleet Suffk	107	K4
Herring's Green Bed	86	B6
Herringswell Suffk	88	E1
Herringthorpe Rothm	133	J1
Herrington Sundld	181	J8
Hersden Kent	41	G3
Hersham Cnwll	11	J1
Hersham Surrey	50	E6
Herstmonceux E Susx	23	L5
Herston Dorset	17	K6
Herston Ork	275	c6
Hertford Herts	69	J4
Hertford Heath Herts	69	K5
Hertingfordbury Herts	69	J5
Hesketh Bank Lancs	138	F3
Hesketh Lane Lancs	147	M7
Hesket Newmarket Cumb	165	K3
Heskin Green Lancs	139	G4
Hesleden Dur	170	B3
Hesleden N York	158	F7
Hesley Donc	134	C1
Hesleyside Nthumb	179	J2
Heslington C York	151	K5
Hessay C York	151	H5
Hessenford Cnwll	6	C3
Hessett Suffk	89	J3
Hessle E R Yk	144	C3
Hessle Wakefd	142	C4
Hest Bank Lancs	147	J3
Hestley Green Suffk	90	D2
Heston Gt Lon	50	E3
Hestwall Ork	275	b4
Heswall Wirral	129	G3
Hethe Oxon	66	E1
Hethersett Norfk	106	C2
Hethersgill Cumb	178	B5
Hetherside Cumb	178	B5
Hetherson Green Ches W	113	H2
Hethpool Nthumb	202	D7
Hett Dur	169	H3
Hetton N York	149	G6
Hetton-le-Hole Sundld	169	K1
Hetton Steads Nthumb	203	G6
Heugh Nthumb	180	D4
Heughhead Abers	243	L1
Heugh Head Border	213	J6
Heveningham Suffk	91	H1
Hever Kent	38	D4
Heversham Cumb	157	H6
Hevingham Norfk	122	D7
Hewas Water Cnwll	4	F5
Hewelsfield Gloucs	63	H6
Hewenden C Brad	149	K8
Hewish N Som	44	E6
Hewish Somset	15	K1
Hewood Dorset	15	H2
Hexham Nthumb	179	L6
Hextable Kent	52	B5
Hexthorpe Donc	142	F7
Hexton Herts	68	E1
Hexworthy Cnwll	11	L6
Hexworthy Devon	12	F8
Hey Lancs	148	F7
Heybridge Essex	70	F7
Heybridge Essex	71	L5
Heybridge Basin Essex	72	C5
Heybrook Bay Devon	6	F5
Heydon Cambs	87	J7
Heydon Norfk	122	C6
Heydour Lincs	118	D4
Heyhead Manch	131	G3
Hey Houses Lancs	138	D2
Heylipoll Ag & B	224	B6
Heylor Shet	281	d4
Heyrod Tamesd	140	E7
Heysham Lancs	147	H4
Heyshaw N York	149	L3
Heyshott W Susx	20	E3
Heyside Oldham	140	D6
Heytesbury Wilts	32	F2
Heythrop Oxon	65	M2
Heywood Rochdl	140	C5
Heywood Wilts	46	C8
Hibaldstow N Linc	144	B7
Hickleton Donc	142	D6
Hickling Norfk	123	J6
Hickling Notts	117	J6
Hickling Green Norfk	123	H6
Hickling Heath Norfk	123	H7
Hickling Pastures Notts	117	H6
Hickmans Green Kent	40	E4
Hicks Forstal Kent	41	G3
Hickstead W Susx	22	D3
Hidcote Bartrim Gloucs	82	E6
Hidcote Boyce Gloucs	82	E6
High Ackworth Wakefd	142	C4
Higham Barns	141	M6
Higham Derbys	133	H7
Higham Kent	38	F4
Higham Kent	52	F5
Higham Lancs	148	E8
Higham Suffk	88	E2
Higham Suffk	89	L8
Higham Dykes Nthumb	180	D4
Higham Ferrers Nhants	85	J2
Higham Gobion C Beds	86	C8
Higham Hill Gt Lon	51	K1
Higham on the Hill Leics	99	K4
Highampton Devon	12	C2
Highams Park Gt Lon	69	K8
High Angerton Nthumb	180	D2
High Ardwell D & G	172	D5
High Auldgirth D & G	176	B1
High Bankhill Cumb	166	D2
High Beach Essex	69	L7
High Bentham N York	148	B2
High Bewaldeth Cumb	165	H4
High Bickington Devon	27	L6
High Biggins Cumb	157	K7
High Birkwith N York	158	D7
High Blantyre S Lans	209	H7
High Bonnybridge Falk	209	L3
High Borrans Cumb	156	F3
High Bradley N York	149	H6
High Bray Devon	28	B4
Highbridge Hants	34	F6
Highbridge Somset	30	D2
Highbrook W Susx	38	A7
High Brooms Kent	38	F5
High Bullen Devon	27	J6
Highburton Kirk	141	J5
Highbury Gt Lon	51	J2
Highbury Somset	31	M1
High Buston Nthumb	191	J4
High Callerton Nthumb	180	E5
High Casterton Cumb	157	K7
High Catton E R Yk	151	M5
Highclere Hants	48	B7
Highcliffe Dorset	18	C5
High Close Dur	168	F7
High Cogges Oxon	66	A5
High Common Norfk	105	K2
High Coniscliffe Darltn	169	G7
High Crosby Cumb	178	B6
High Cross Cnwll	3	J5

High Cross E Ayrs.................. 196 D2
High Cross Hants.................. 35 L5
High Cross Herts.................. 69 K3
Highcross Lancs.................. 147 G8
High Cross W Susx.................. 22 C4
High Cross Warwks.................. 82 E2
High Drummore D & G.................. 172 E1
High Dubmire Sundld.................. 169 J1
High Easter Essex.................. 70 F4
High Eggborough N York.................. 142 F3
High Ellington N York.................. 160 B6
Higher Alham Somset.................. 31 L3
Higher Ansty Dorset.................. 16 E2
Higher Ballam Lancs.................. 138 D2
Higher Bartle Lancs.................. 139 G1
Higher Berry End C Beds.................. 85 J8
Higher Bockhampton Dorset.................. 16 D4
Higher Brixham Torbay.................. 8 D4
Higher Burrowton Devon.................. 14 B3
Higher Burwardsley Ches W.................. 129 M8
High Ercall Wrekin.................. 113 K8
Higher Chillington Somset.................. 15 J1
Higher Clovelly Devon.................. 26 E6
Highercombe Somset.................. 28 F5
Higher Coombe Dorset.................. 15 M4
Higher Disley Ches E.................. 131 J3
Higher Folds Wigan.................. 139 K7
Higherford Lancs.................. 148 F7
Higher Gabwell Devon.................. 8 D1
Higher Halstock Leigh Dorset.................. 15 L1
Higher Harpers Lancs.................. 148 E8
Higher Heysham Lancs.................. 147 H4
Higher Hurdsfield Ches E.................. 131 J5
Higher Irlam Salfd.................. 130 E1
Higher Kingcombe Dorset.................. 15 M3
Higher Kinnerton Flints.................. 129 H7
Higher Marston Ches W.................. 130 C4
Higher Muddiford Devon.................. 27 K3
Higher Nyland Dorset.................. 32 B6
Higher Ogden Rochdl.................. 140 E5
Higher Pentire Cnwll.................. 3 G6
Higher Penwortham Lancs.................. 139 G2
Higher Prestacott Devon.................. 11 M3
Higher Studfold N York.................. 148 E2
Higher Town Cnwll.................. 4 C6
Higher Town Cnwll.................. 5 G3
Higher Town IoS.................. 10 C2
Higher Tregantle Cnwll.................. 6 D4
Higher Walton Lancs.................. 139 H2
Higher Walton Warrtn.................. 130 B3
Higher Wambrook Somset.................. 15 G1
Higher Waterston Dorset.................. 16 D3
Higher Whatcombe Dorset.................. 17 G2
Higher Wheelton Lancs.................. 139 J3
Higher Whitley Ches W.................. 130 B4
Higher Wincham Ches W.................. 130 D4
Higher Wraxhall Dorset.................. 16 A2
Higher Wych Ches W.................. 113 H3
High Etherley Dur.................. 168 F5
High Ferry Lincs.................. 119 K2
Highfield E R Yk.................. 151 M8
Highfield Gatesd.................. 180 E7
Highfield N Ayrs.................. 196 C1
Highfields Donc.................. 142 E6
High Flats Kirk.................. 141 K6
High Garrett Essex.................. 71 J2
Highgate E Susx.................. 38 C6
Highgate Gt Lon.................. 51 H2
Highgate Kent.................. 39 J7
High Grange Dur.................. 168 F4
High Grantley N York.................. 150 B2
High Green Cumb.................. 156 F2
High Green Kirk.................. 141 K5
High Green Norfk.................. 106 C2
High Green Norfk.................. 106 D5
High Green Sheff.................. 142 A8
High Green Shrops.................. 96 F6
High Green Suffk.................. 89 G3
High Green Worcs.................. 81 K6
Highgreen Manor Nthumb.................. 189 L7
High Halden Kent.................. 40 A7
High Halstow Medway.................. 53 G4
High Ham Somset.................. 30 F4
High Harrington Cumb.................. 164 D5
High Harrogate N York.................. 150 D5
High Haswell Dur.................. 169 K2
High Hatton Shrops.................. 113 K6
High Hauxley Nthumb.................. 191 K5
High Hawsker N York.................. 163 G1
High Hesket Cumb.................. 166 B2
High Hoyland Barns.................. 141 L5
High Hunsley E R Yk.................. 144 B1
High Hurstwood E Susx.................. 23 H2
High Hutton N York.................. 152 A2
High Ireby Cumb.................. 165 H3
High Kelling Norfk.................. 122 C3
High Kilburn N York.................. 161 H6
High Killerby N York.................. 163 J6
High Knipe Cumb.................. 166 C6

High Lands Dur.................. 168 E5
Highlane Ches E.................. 131 H6
Highlane Derbys.................. 133 H3
High Lane Stockp.................. 131 J3
High Lanes Cnwll.................. 2 F4
High Laver Essex.................. 70 D5
Highlaws Cumb.................. 164 F1
Highleadon Gloucs.................. 63 M2
High Legh Ches E.................. 130 D3
Highleigh W Susx.................. 20 D7
High Leven S on T.................. 170 B8
Highley Shrops.................. 97 G6
High Littleton BaNES.................. 45 J7
High Lorton Cumb.................. 165 G5
High Marishes N York.................. 162 E7
High Marnham Notts.................. 134 F5
High Melton Donc.................. 142 D7
High Mickley Nthumb.................. 180 C6
Highmoor Cumb.................. 165 J1
Highmoor Oxon.................. 49 H2
Highmoor Cross Oxon.................. 49 H2
Highmoor Hill Mons.................. 44 F1
High Moorsley Sundld.................. 169 J2
Highnam Gloucs.................. 64 A3
Highnam Green Gloucs.................. 64 A3
High Newport Sundld.................. 181 J8
High Newton Cumb.................. 156 F6
High Nibthwaite Cumb.................. 156 D5
High Offley Staffs.................. 114 B6
High Ongar Essex.................. 70 E6
High Onn Staffs.................. 114 C8
High Park Corner Essex.................. 72 F3
High Pennyvenie E Ayrs.................. 184 D2
High Post Wilts.................. 33 K4
Highridge N Som.................. 45 H5
High Roding Essex.................. 70 F4
High Row Cumb.................. 165 K3
High Row Cumb.................. 165 L6
High Salter Lancs.................. 147 M3
High Salvington W Susx.................. 21 K5
High Scales Cumb.................. 165 G2
High Seaton Cumb.................. 164 D4
High Shaw N York.................. 158 F4
High Side Cumb.................. 165 H4
High Spen Gatesd.................. 180 E7
Highstead Kent.................. 41 G2
Highsted Kent.................. 40 B3
High Stoop Dur.................. 168 E3
High Street Cnwll.................. 5 G4
High Street Kent.................. 39 J7
Highstreet Kent.................. 40 E3
High Street Suffk.................. 91 J1
High Street Suffk.................. 91 K4
Highstreet Green Essex.................. 88 F8
Highstreet Green Surrey.................. 36 E4
Hightae D & G.................. 176 E3
Highter's Heath Birm.................. 98 E7
High Throston Hartpl.................. 170 C4
Hightown Ches E.................. 131 G7
Hightown Hants.................. 18 B3
Hightown Sefton.................. 138 C7
High Town Staffs.................. 98 C1
Hightown Green Suffk.................. 89 K4
High Toynton Lincs.................. 136 E5
High Trewhitt Nthumb.................. 190 E5
High Urpeth Dur.................. 181 G8
High Valleyfield Fife.................. 210 D2
High Warden Nthumb.................. 179 L5
Highway Herefs.................. 80 B5
Highway Wilts.................. 46 F4
Highweek Devon.................. 13 K8
High Westwood Dur.................. 180 D7
Highwood Essex.................. 70 F6
Highwood Staffs.................. 115 H5
Highwood Hill Gt Lon.................. 69 G8
High Woolaston Gloucs.................. 63 H7
High Worsall N York.................. 160 F1
Highworth Swindn.................. 65 J8
High Wray Cumb.................. 156 E3
High Wych Herts.................. 70 C4
High Wycombe Bucks.................. 67 L8
Hilborough Norfk.................. 105 G3
Hilcote Derbys.................. 133 J8
Hilcott Wilts.................. 47 G7
Hildenborough Kent.................. 38 E4
Hilden Park Kent.................. 38 F4
Hildersham Cambs.................. 87 L5
Hilderstone Staffs.................. 114 E4
Hilderthorpe E R Yk.................. 153 J3
Hilfield Dorset.................. 16 C2
Hilgay Norfk.................. 104 C4
Hill S Glos.................. 63 J8
Hill Warwks.................. 83 K2
Hillam N York.................. 142 D2
Hillbeck Cumb.................. 167 H7
Hillborough Kent.................. 41 G2
Hill Brow Hants.................. 36 B5
Hillbutts Dorset.................. 17 K2
Hill Chorlton Staffs.................. 114 B4

Hillclifflane Derbys.................. 115 M2
Hill Common Norfk.................. 123 H7
Hill Common Somset.................. 29 L5
Hill Deverill Wilts.................. 32 E3
Hilldyke Lincs.................. 119 K2
Hill End Dur.................. 168 C3
Hillend Fife.................. 210 F2
Hill End Fife.................. 221 J8
Hill End Gloucs.................. 81 K7
Hillend Mdloth.................. 211 H5
Hillend N Lans.................. 209 L5
Hillend Swans.................. 56 D6
Hillersland Gloucs.................. 63 H4
Hillerton Devon.................. 13 G1
Hillesden Bucks.................. 67 G1
Hillesley Gloucs.................. 45 M1
Hillfarrance Somset.................. 29 L6
Hill Green Kent.................. 53 H6
Hillgrove W Susx.................. 36 D5
Hillhampton Herefs.................. 80 D6
Hillhead Abers.................. 255 M4
Hillhead Devon.................. 8 D4
Hill Head Hants.................. 19 J3
Hillhead S Lans.................. 199 G5
Hillhead of Cocklaw Abers.................. 257 K3
Hilliard's Cross Staffs.................. 98 F1
Hilliclay Highld.................. 279 L3
Hillingdon Gt Lon.................. 50 D2
Hillington C Glas.................. 208 E6
Hillington Norfk.................. 120 F6
Hillis Corner IoW.................. 19 H5
Hillmorton Warwks.................. 100 C8
Hillock Vale Lancs.................. 140 A2
Hill of Beath Fife.................. 210 F1
Hill of Fearn Highld.................. 264 C4
Hillowton D & G.................. 175 J2
Hillpool Worcs.................. 97 K8
Hillpound Hants.................. 35 J7
Hill Ridware Staffs.................. 115 H8
Hillside Abers.................. 245 K4
Hillside Angus.................. 235 H3
Hillside Devon.................. 7 K3
Hill Side Kirk.................. 141 J4
Hill Side Worcs.................. 81 H3
Hills Town Derbys.................. 133 J5
Hillstreet Hants.................. 34 D7
Hillswick Shet.................. 281 c4
Hill Top Dur.................. 168 C6
Hill Top Hants.................. 18 F3
Hill Top Kirk.................. 141 G5
Hill Top Rothm.................. 133 H1
Hill Top Sandw.................. 98 C5
Hill Top Wakefd.................. 142 A4
Hillwell Shet.................. 281 c8
Hilmarton Wilts.................. 46 E4
Hilperton Wilts.................. 46 C7
Hilperton Marsh Wilts.................. 46 C7
Hilsea C Port.................. 19 L3
Hilston E R Yk.................. 145 H1
Hiltingbury Hants.................. 34 F6
Hilton Border.................. 202 D3
Hilton Cambs.................. 86 F2
Hilton Cumb.................. 167 G6
Hilton Derbys.................. 115 L5
Hilton Dorset.................. 16 E2
Hilton Dur.................. 168 F6
Hilton Highld.................. 264 D4
Hilton S on T.................. 170 B8
Hilton Shrops.................. 97 H4
Himbleton Worcs.................. 81 L3
Himley Staffs.................. 97 K5
Hincaster Cumb.................. 157 H5
Hinchley Wood Surrey.................. 50 F6
Hinckley Leics.................. 99 L4
Hinderclay Suffk.................. 105 L8
Hinderwell N York.................. 171 J7
Hindford Shrops.................. 112 E5
Hindhead Surrey.................. 36 C4
Hindhead Tunnel Surrey.................. 36 D4
Hindle Fold Lancs.................. 139 L1
Hindley Nthumb.................. 180 C7
Hindley Wigan.................. 139 J6
Hindley Green Wigan.................. 139 J7
Hindlip Worcs.................. 81 K3
Hindolveston Norfk.................. 122 A5
Hindon Wilts.................. 32 F4
Hindringham Norfk.................. 121 L4
Hingham Norfk.................. 105 L3
Hinksford Staffs.................. 97 J5
Hinstock Shrops.................. 113 M6
Hintlesham Suffk.................. 90 C6
Hinton Gloucs.................. 63 K6
Hinton Hants.................. 18 C4
Hinton Herefs.................. 79 L7
Hinton S Glos.................. 45 L4
Hinton Shrops.................. 95 K2
Hinton Shrops.................. 96 E7
Hinton Admiral Hants.................. 18 C4
Hinton Ampner Hants.................. 35 J5

Hinton Blewett BaNES.................. 45 H...
Hinton Charterhouse BaNES.................. 45 M...
Hinton Green Worcs.................. 82 B...
Hinton-in-the-Hedges Nhants.................. 84 A...
Hinton Marsh Hants.................. 35 J...
Hinton Martell Dorset.................. 17 K...
Hinton on the Green Worcs.................. 82 B...
Hinton Parva Swindn.................. 47 L...
Hinton St George Somset.................. 30 F...
Hinton St Mary Dorset.................. 32 C...
Hinton Waldrist Oxon.................. 66 A...
Hints Shrops.................. 96 F...
Hints Staffs.................. 98 F...
Hinwick Bed.................. 85 J...
Hinxhill Kent.................. 40 D...
Hinxton Cambs.................. 87 K...
Hinxworth Herts.................. 86 F...
Hipperholme Calder.................. 141 H...
Hipsburn Nthumb.................. 191 K...
Hipswell N York.................. 160 B...
Hirn Abers.................. 245 G...
Hirnant Powys.................. 111 K...
Hirst Nthumb.................. 181 G...
Hirst Courtney N York.................. 142 F...
Hirwaen Denbgs.................. 128 D...
Hirwaun Rhondd.................. 60 E...
Hiscott Devon.................. 27 K...
Histon Cambs.................. 87 J...
Hitcham Suffk.................. 89 K...
Hitcham Causeway Suffk.................. 89 K...
Hitcham Street Suffk.................. 89 K...
Hitchin Herts.................. 68 F...
Hither Green Gt Lon.................. 51 K...
Hittisleigh Devon.................. 13 K...
Hive E R Yk.................. 143 K...
Hixon Staffs.................. 114 F...
Hoaden Kent.................. 41 J...
Hoar Cross Staffs.................. 115 J...
Hoarwithy Herefs.................. 63 G...
Hoath Kent.................. 41 G...
Hoathly Kent.................. 39 G...
Hobarris Shrops.................. 95 H...
Hobbles Green Suffk.................. 88 D...
Hobbs Cross Essex.................. 70 C...
Hobbs Cross Essex.................. 70 C...
Hobkirk Border.................. 189 ...
Hobland Hall Norfk.................. 107 K...
Hobsick Notts.................. 116 ...
Hobson Dur.................. 180 E...
Hoby Leics.................. 117 H...
Hoccombe Somset.................. 29 K...
Hockering Norfk.................. 106 B...
Hockerton Notts.................. 134 ...
Hockley Ches E.................. 131 J...
Hockley Covtry.................. 99 H...
Hockley Essex.................. 71 K...
Hockley Staffs.................. 99 G...
Hockley Heath Solhll.................. 82 E...
Hockliffe C Beds.................. 68 K...
Hockwold cum Wilton Norfk.................. 104 E...
Hockworthy Devon.................. 29 J...
Hoddesdon Herts.................. 69 K...
Hoddlesden Bl w D.................. 139 L...
Hoddom Cross D & G.................. 177 G...
Hoddom Mains D & G.................. 177 G...
Hodgehill Ches E.................. 131 G...
Hodgeston Pembks.................. 55 H...
Hodnet Shrops.................. 113 K...
Hodsock Notts.................. 134 C...
Hodsoll Street Kent.................. 52 D...
Hodson Swindn.................. 47 H...
Hodthorpe Derbys.................. 133 L...
Hoe Hants.................. 35 H...
Hoe Norfk.................. 121 M...
Hoe Benham W Berk.................. 48 B...
Hoe Gate Hants.................. 35 K...
Hoff Cumb.................. 166 F...
Hogben's Hill Kent.................. 40 D...
Hoggards Green Suffk.................. 89 H...
Hoggeston Bucks.................. 67 K...
Hoggrill's End Warwks.................. 99 G...
Hog Hill E Susx.................. 25 G...
Hoghton Lancs.................. 139 J...
Hoghton Bottoms Lancs.................. 139 J...
Hognaston Derbys.................. 115 K...
Hogsthorpe Lincs.................. 137 K...
Holbeach Lincs.................. 119 K...
Holbeach Bank Lincs.................. 119 K...
Holbeach Clough Lincs.................. 119 K...
Holbeach Drove Lincs.................. 103 G...
Holbeach Hurn Lincs.................. 119 K...
Holbeach St Johns Lincs.................. 119 K...
Holbeach St Mark's Lincs.................. 119 K...
Holbeach St Matthew Lincs.................. 119 K...
Holbeck Notts.................. 133 L...
Holbeck Woodhouse Notts.................. 133 L...
Holberrow Green Worcs.................. 82 B...
Holbeton Devon.................. 7 J...
Holborn Gt Lon.................. 51 J...

Holborough Kent 52 F6
Holbrook Derbys 116 B3
Holbrook Sheff 133 J3
Holbrook Suffk 90 E7
Holbrook Moor Derbys 116 B3
Holbrooks Covtry 99 J6
Holburn Nthumb 203 G6
Holbury Hants 19 G3
Holcombe Devon 13 M7
Holcombe Somset 31 L1
Holcombe Rogus Devon 29 J7
Holcot Nhants 84 F1
Holden Lancs 148 D6
Holdenby Nhants 84 D2
Holden Gate Calder 140 D3
Holder's Green Essex 70 F1
Holdgate Shrops 96 D5
Holdingham Lincs 118 E2
Holditch Dorset 15 H2
Holdsworth Calder 141 G2
Holehouse Derbys 131 K1
Hole-in-the-Wall Herefs 63 J2
Holemoor Devon 12 A2
Hole Street W Susx 21 K4
Holford Somset 29 L3
Holgate C York 151 J5
Holker Cumb 156 E7
Holkham Norfk 121 K3
Hollacombe Devon 11 M2
Holland Fen Lincs 119 H2
Holland Lees Lancs 139 G6
Holland-on-Sea Essex 73 J4
Hollandstoun Ork 275 f1
Hollee D & G 177 J5
Hollesley Suffk 91 H6
Hollicombe Torbay 8 D2
Hollingbourne Kent 39 L2
Hollingbury Br & H 22 D5
Hollingdon Bucks 67 L2
Hollingthorpe Leeds 142 B2
Hollington Derbys 115 L4
Hollington Staffs 115 G4
Hollingworth Tamesd 140 F8
Hollinlane Ches E 131 G3
Hollins Bury 140 B6
Hollins Derbys 132 F5
Hollins Staffs 114 F2
Hollinsclough Staffs 131 L6
Hollins End Sheff 133 H3
Hollins Green Warrtn 130 D2
Hollins Lane Lancs 147 K5
Hollinswood Wrekin 96 F2
Hollinwood Shrops 113 H4
Hollingrove E Susx 24 C3
Hollocombe Devon 27 L8
Holloway Derbys 132 F8
Holloway Gt Lon 51 J2
Holloway Wilts 32 E5
Hollowell Nhants 84 D1
Hollowmoor Heath Ches W 129 L6
Hollows D & G 177 L3
Hollybush Caerph 61 J6
Hollybush E Ayrs 196 D7
Hollybush Herefs 81 H7
Holly End Norfk 103 K2
Holly Green Worcs 81 K7
Hollyhurst Ches E 113 J3
Hollym E R Yk 145 J3
Hollywood Worcs 98 D7
Holmbridge Kirk 141 H6
Holmbury St Mary Surrey 37 H2
Holmbush Cnwll 5 H4
Holmcroft Staffs 114 E6
Holme Cambs 102 D6
Holme Cumb 157 H7
Holme Kirk 141 H6
Holme N Linc 144 A6
Holme N York 160 E6
Holme Notts 134 F7
Holme Chapel Lancs 140 C2
Holme Green N York 151 J7
Holme Hale Norfk 105 H2
Holme Lacy Herefs 80 D8
Holme Marsh Herefs 79 L4
Holme next the Sea Norfk 120 F3
Holme on the Wolds E R Yk 152 E6
Holme Pierrepont Notts 117 G4
Holmer Herefs 80 C6
Holmer Green Bucks 67 L7
Holme St Cuthbert Cumb 164 F1
Holmes Chapel Ches E 130 E6
Holmesfield Derbys 132 F4
Holmeswood Lancs 138 E4
Holmethorpe Surrey 51 H8
Holme upon Spalding Moor
  E R Yk 152 B8
Holmewood Derbys 133 H6
Holmfield Calder 141 G2

Holmfirth Kirk 141 H6
Holmhead E Ayrs 197 H7
Holmpton E R Yk 145 K3
Holmrook Cumb 155 K3
Holmsford Bridge
  Crematorium N Ayrs 196 D3
Holmshurst E Susx 23 L2
Holmside Dur 169 G1
Holmwrangle Cumb 166 C1
Holne Devon 7 K1
Holnest Dorset 16 C1
Holnicote Somset 29 G2
Holsworthy Devon 11 L2
Holsworthy Beacon Devon 11 L1
Holt Dorset 17 K2
Holt Norfk 122 B4
Holt Wilts 46 B6
Holt Worcs 81 J3
Holt Wrexhm 112 F1
Holtby C York 151 L5
Holt End Worcs 82 C1
Holt Fleet Worcs 81 J3
Holt Green Lancs 138 E6
Holt Heath Dorset 17 L2
Holt Heath Worcs 81 J3
Holton Oxon 66 F5
Holton Somset 31 L5
Holton Suffk 107 H7
Holton cum Beckering
  Lincs 136 B3
Holton Heath Dorset 17 J4
Holton Hill E Susx 24 B2
Holton le Clay Lincs 145 H7
Holton le Moor Lincs 144 D8
Holton St Mary Suffk 90 C7
Holt Street Kent 41 H5
Holtye E Susx 38 C5
Holway Flints 128 E4
Holwell Dorset 32 B8
Holwell Herts 86 D8
Holwell Leics 117 J6
Holwell Oxon 65 K5
Holwick Dur 167 L5
Holworth Dorset 16 E6
Holybourne Hants 35 M3
Holy Cross Worcs 97 L7
Holyfield Essex 69 K6
Holyhead IoA 124 D3
Holy Island IoA 124 D3
Holy Island Nthumb 203 J4
Holy Island Nthumb 203 J5
Holymoorside Derbys 133 G6
Holyport W & M 49 L3
Holystone Nthumb 190 D5
Holytown N Lans 209 K6
Holytown Crematorium
  N Lans 209 K6
Holywell C Beds 68 C4
Holywell Cambs 87 G1
Holywell Cnwll 4 C3
Holywell Dorset 16 B2
Holywell Flints 128 E4
Holywell Nthumb 181 H4
Holywell Warwks 82 E2
Holywell Green Calder 141 G4
Holywell Lake Somset 29 K6
Holywell Row Suffk 104 E7
Holywood D & G 176 B3
Holywood Village D & G 176 C3
Homer Shrops 96 E3
Homer Green Sefton 138 D7
Homersfield Suffk 106 F6
Homescales Cumb 157 J5
Hom Green Herefs 63 H3
Homington Wilts 33 K5
Honeyborough Pembks 54 F5
Honeybourne Worcs 82 D6
Honeychurch Devon 12 E2
Honey Hill Kent 40 F3
Honeystreet Wilts 47 G6
Honey Tye Suffk 89 J8
Honiley Warwks 82 F1
Honing Norfk 123 G6
Honingham Norfk 106 C1
Honington Lincs 118 B3
Honington Suffk 105 H8
Honington Warwks 83 G6
Honiton Devon 14 E3
Honley Kirk 141 H5
Honnington Wrekin 114 A8
Honor Oak Crematorium
  Gt Lon 51 K4
Hoo Kent 41 J2
Hoobrook Worcs 97 J8
Hood Green Barns 141 M7
Hood Hill Rothm 142 B8
Hooe C Plym 6 F4
Hooe E Susx 24 C5
Hoo End Herts 68 F3

Hoo Green Ches E 130 D3
Hoohill Bpool 146 F8
Hook Cambs 103 J3
Hook Devon 15 G2
Hook E R Yk 143 J3
Hook Gt Lon 50 F6
Hook Hants 19 H3
Hook Hants 49 H8
Hook Pembks 55 G4
Hook Wilts 47 G2
Hookagate Shrops 95 L2
Hook Bank Worcs 81 J7
Hooke Dorset 15 M3
Hook End Essex 70 E7
Hookgate Staffs 114 A4
Hook Green Kent 39 G6
Hook Green Kent 52 D5
Hook Norton Oxon 83 H8
Hook Street Gloucs 63 K7
Hook Street Wilts 47 G2
Hookway Devon 13 K3
Hookwood Surrey 37 L2
Hooley Surrey 51 H7
Hooley Bridge Rochdl 140 C5
Hoo Meavy Devon 7 G2
Hoo St Werburgh Medway 53 G4
Hooton Ches W 129 J4
Hooton Levitt Rothm 133 K2
Hooton Pagnell Donc 142 D6
Hooton Roberts Rothm 142 D8
Hopcrofts Holt Oxon 66 C2
Hope Derbys 132 C3
Hope Devon 7 K6
Hope Flints 129 G7
Hope Powys 95 G2
Hope Shrops 95 H3
Hope Staffs 132 B8
Hope Bagot Shrops 96 D8
Hope Bowdler Shrops 95 L5
Hope End Green Essex 70 E3
Hopehouse Border 187 L3
Hopeman Moray 266 C2
Hope Mansell Herefs 63 J3
Hopesay Shrops 95 J6
Hopetown Wakefd 142 B3
Hope under Dinmore Herefs 80 C5
Hopgrove C York 151 K5
Hopperton N York 150 F4
Hop Pole Lincs 102 D1
Hopsford Warwks 99 L6
Hopstone Shrops 97 H4
Hopton Derbys 115 L1
Hopton Shrops 112 F7
Hopton Staffs 114 E6
Hopton Suffk 105 K7
Hopton Cangeford Shrops 96 C7
Hopton Castle Shrops 95 J7
Hoptonheath Shrops 95 J7
Hopton on Sea Norfk 107 L3
Hopton Wafers Shrops 96 E8
Hopwas Staffs 98 F3
Hopwood Rochdl 140 C6
Hopwood Worcs 98 C8
Horam E Susx 23 K4
Horbling Lincs 118 F4
Horbury Wakefd 141 L4
Horcott Gloucs 65 H7
Horden Dur 170 B3
Horderley Shrops 95 K6
Hordle Hants 18 D4
Hordley Shrops 112 F5
Horeb Carmth 56 F4
Horeb Cerdgn 76 D6
Horfield Bristl 45 H4
Horham Suffk 90 F1
Horkesley Heath Essex 72 E1
Horkstow N Linc 144 B4
Horley Oxon 83 K6
Horley Surrey 37 L2
Hornblotton Green Somset 31 K4
Hornby Lancs 147 L2
Hornby N York 160 B4
Hornby N York 160 E2
Horncastle Lincs 136 E6
Hornchurch Gt Lon 52 B2
Horncliffe Nthumb 202 E3
Horndean Border 202 E3
Horndean Hants 35 L8
Horndon Devon 12 C6
Horndon on the Hill Thurr 52 E2
Horne Surrey 38 A4
Horner Somset 28 F2
Horne Row Essex 71 J6
Horners Green Suffk 89 K7
Horney Common E Susx 23 G2
Horn Hill Bucks 68 C8
Horning Norfk 123 G8
Horninghold Leics 101 H4
Horninglow Staffs 115 L6

Horningsea Cambs 87 K3
Horningsham Wilts 32 D3
Horningtoft Norfk 121 K6
Horningtops Cnwll 6 B3
Hornsbury Somset 30 E8
Hornsby Cumb 166 C1
Hornsbygate Cumb 166 C1
Horns Cross Devon 27 G6
Horns Cross E Susx 24 E3
Hornsea E R Yk 153 K6
Hornsey Gt Lon 51 J1
Horn's Green Gt Lon 51 M7
Horn Street Kent 41 G8
Hornton Oxon 83 J6
Horpit Swindn 47 J2
Horra Shet 281 e3
Horrabridge Devon 7 G1
Horringer Suffk 89 G3
Horringford IoW 19 J6
Horrocks Fold Bolton 139 L5
Horrocksford Lancs 148 C7
Horsacott Devon 27 J4
Horsebridge Devon 12 A7
Horsebridge E Susx 23 K5
Horsebridge Hants 34 D5
Horsebridge Shrops 95 J2
Horsebridge Staffs 114 F1
Horsebrook Staffs 97 K1
Horsecastle N Som 44 E5
Horsedown Cnwll 3 G4
Horsehay Wrekin 96 F2
Horseheath Cambs 88 C5
Horsehouse N York 159 J6
Horsell Surrey 50 C7
Horseman's Green Wrexhm 113 G3
Horsenden Bucks 67 J7
Horsey Norfk 123 J7
Horsey Somset 30 D3
Horsey Corner Norfk 123 J6
Horsford Norfk 122 D8
Horsforth Leeds 150 B8
Horsham W Susx 37 J5
Horsham Worcs 81 G4
Horsham St Faith Norfk 122 D8
Horsington Lincs 136 C6
Horsington Somset 32 B6
Horsley Derbys 116 C3
Horsley Gloucs 64 B7
Horsley Nthumb 180 D5
Horsley Nthumb 190 B6
Horsley Cross Essex 73 H2
Horsleycross Street Essex 73 G1
Horsley-Gate Derbys 132 F4
Horsleyhill Border 188 F2
Horsley's Green Bucks 67 J8
Horsley Woodhouse Derbys 116 C3
Horsmonden Kent 39 H5
Horspath Oxon 66 E6
Horstead Norfk 122 F7
Horsted Keynes W Susx 22 F2
Horton Bucks 68 J3
Horton Dorset 17 K1
Horton Lancs 148 E6
Horton Nhants 84 F4
Horton S Glos 45 M2
Horton Shrops 113 H5
Horton Somset 30 D7
Horton Staffs 131 J8
Horton Surrey 51 G6
Horton Swans 56 E7
Horton W & M 50 C4
Horton Wilts 46 F6
Horton Wrekin 113 L8
Horton Cross Somset 30 E7
Horton-cum-Studley Oxon 66 F4
Horton Green Ches W 113 G2
Horton Heath Hants 35 G7
Horton-in-Ribblesdale
  N York 148 D2
Horton Kirby Kent 52 C5
Horwich Bolton 139 J4
Horwich End Derbys 131 K3
Horwood Devon 27 J5
Hoscar Lancs 138 F5
Hoscote Border 188 C4
Hose Leics 117 J5
Hosey Hill Kent 51 M8
Hosh P & K 220 E3
Hoswick Shet 281 e8
Hotham E R Yk 143 M1
Hothfield Kent 40 C6
Hoton Leics 116 F7
Hott Nthumb 179 H2
Hough Ches E 113 M1
Hough Ches E 131 G4
Hougham Lincs 118 A3
Hough End Leeds 141 K1
Hough Green Halton 129 L2
Hough-on-the-Hill Lincs 118 B2

Houghton Cambs 86 F1
Houghton Cumb 177 L7
Houghton Hants 34 D4
Houghton Nthumb 180 D5
Houghton Pembks 55 G5
Houghton W Susx 21 H4
Houghton Conquest C Beds 85 L7
Houghton Gate Dur 181 H8
Houghton Green E Susx 25 G3
Houghton Green Warrtn 130 C1
Houghton le Side Darltn 169 G6
Houghton-le-Spring Sundld 169 J1
Houghton on the Hill Leics 100 E3
Houghton Regis C Beds 68 C2
Houghton St Giles Norfk 121 K4
Hound Green Hants 49 H7
Houndslow Border 201 K4
Houndsmoor Somset 29 L5
Houndwood Border 213 J6
Hounslow Gt Lon 50 F4
Househill Highld 253 G1
Houses Hill Kirk 141 K4
Housieside Abers 257 G6
Houston Rens 208 C5
Houstry Highld 275 G1
Houton Ork 275 b5
Hove Br & H 22 D6
Hove Edge Calder 141 H3
Hoveringham Notts 117 J2
Hoveton Norfk 122 F7
Hovingham N York 161 L7
Howbrook Barns 141 M8
How Caple Herefs 63 J1
Howden E R Yk 143 J2
Howden-le-Wear Dur 168 F4
Howe Highld 280 D4
Howe IoM 154 b8
Howe N York 160 E6
Howe Norfk 106 F3
Howe Bridge Wigan 139 K7
Howe Bridge Crematorium Wigan 139 K7
Howe Green Essex 71 H6
Howegreen Essex 71 K6
Howell Lincs 118 F2
How End C Beds 85 K7
Howe of Teuchar Abers 268 E6
Howes D & G 177 G5
Howe Street Essex 71 G4
Howe Street Essex 88 D8
Howey Powys 78 E3
Howgate Cumb 164 C6
Howgate Mdloth 211 H7
Howgill Lancs 148 E6
Howick Nthumb 191 K3
Howle Wrekin 113 M6
Howle Hill Herefs 63 J3
Howlett End Essex 88 B8
Howley Somset 15 G1
How Mill Cumb 178 C7
Howmore W Isls 283 b10
Hownam Border 189 L2
Howrigg Cumb 165 K1
Howsham N Linc 144 D6
Howsham N York 151 M3
Howtel Nthumb 202 D6
Howt Green Kent 53 J6
Howton Herefs 62 E1
Howtown Cumb 166 B6
How Wood Herts 68 F6
Howwood Rens 208 C7
Hoxa Ork 275 c6
Hoxne Suffk 106 D7
Hoy Ork 275 b5
Hoylake Wirral 128 F2
Hoyland Common Barns 142 B7
Hoyland Nether Barns 142 B7
Hoyland Swaine Barns 141 L6
Hoyle W Susx 20 E3
Hoyle Mill Barns 142 A6
Hubberholme N York 159 G7
Hubberston Pembks 54 E5
Hubbert's Bridge Lincs 119 J3
Huby N York 150 C6
Huby N York 151 J3
Huccaby Devon 12 F8
Hucclecote Gloucs 64 C4
Hucking Kent 53 H7
Hucknall Notts 116 F2
Huddersfield Kirk 141 H4
Huddersfield Crematorium Kirk 141 J4
Huddington Worcs 81 L4
Hudnall Herts 68 C4
Hudswell N York 159 L3
Huggate E R Yk 152 D5
Hugglescote Leics 99 L1
Hughenden Valley Bucks 67 L7
Hughley Shrops 96 D4

Hugh Town IoS 10 C3
Huish Devon 27 J8
Huish Wilts 47 H6
Huish Champflower Somset 29 J5
Huish Episcopi Somset 31 G5
Huisinis W Isls 282 d5
Hulcote C Beds 85 J7
Hulcote Nhants 84 D5
Hulcott Bucks 67 K4
Hulham Devon 14 B6
Hulland Derbys 115 L2
Hulland Ward Derbys 115 L2
Hullavington Wilts 46 C3
Hull Bridge E R Yk 153 G7
Hullbridge Essex 71 K8
Hull, Kingston upon C KuH 144 D2
Hulme Manch 140 C8
Hulme Staffs 114 E4
Hulme Warrtn 130 B2
Hulme End Staffs 132 B7
Hulme Walfield Ches E 131 G6
Hulse Heath Ches E 130 B3
Hulton Lane Ends Bolton 139 K6
Hulverstone IoW 18 F6
Hulver Street Norfk 105 J1
Hulver Street Suffk 107 K6
Humber Devon 13 L7
Humber Herefs 80 C4
Humber Bridge N Linc 144 C3
Humberston NE Lin 145 J6
Humberstone C Leic 100 E2
Humberton N York 150 F2
Humbie E Loth 212 A6
Humbleton E R Yk 145 G1
Humbleton Nthumb 202 F7
Humby Lincs 118 D5
Hume Border 201 L5
Humshaugh Nthumb 179 L4
Huna Highld 280 E2
Huncoat Lancs 140 A2
Huncote Leics 100 B4
Hundalee Border 189 H3
Hundall Derbys 133 H4
Hunderthwaite Dur 168 C6
Hundleby Lincs 137 G6
Hundle Houses Lincs 119 H1
Hundleton Pembks 54 F6
Hundon Suffk 88 E5
Hundred End Lancs 138 E3
Hundred House Powys 78 F4
Hungarton Leics 100 F2
Hungerford Hants 33 L8
Hungerford Somset 29 J3
Hungerford W Berk 47 M5
Hungerford Newtown W Berk 47 M4
Hunger Hill Bolton 139 K6
Hunger Hill Lancs 139 G5
Hungerstone Herefs 80 B8
Hungerton Lincs 118 A5
Hungryhatton Shrops 113 L6
Hunmanby N York 163 K7
Hunningham Warwks 83 J2
Hunnington Worcs 98 B7
Hunsbury Hill Nhants 84 E4
Hunsdon Herts 69 L4
Hunsingore N York 150 F5
Hunslet Leeds 141 M2
Hunsonby Cumb 166 D4
Hunstanton Norfk 120 E3
Hunstanworth Dur 168 B1
Hunsterson Ches E 113 M2
Hunston Suffk 89 K2
Hunston W Susx 20 D6
Hunston Green Suffk 89 K2
Hunstrete BaNES 45 K4
Hunsworth Kirk 141 J2
Hunt End Worcs 82 B2
Hunter's Inn Devon 28 B1
Hunter's Quay Ag & B 207 K3
Huntham Somset 30 E5
Hunthill Lodge Angus 234 D1
Huntingdon Cambs 86 E1
Huntingfield Suffk 107 G8
Huntingford Dorset 32 D5
Huntington C York 151 K4
Huntington Ches W 129 K6
Huntington E Loth 212 B4
Huntington Herefs 79 J4
Huntington Herefs 80 B6
Huntington Staffs 98 B1
Huntley Gloucs 63 L3
Huntly Abers 255 L4
Hunton Hants 35 J3
Hunton Kent 39 H3
Hunton N York 160 B4
Hunton Bridge Herts 68 D7
Hunt's Corner Norfk 105 L5

Huntscott Somset 29 G2
Hunt's Cross Lpool 129 K3
Hunts Green Bucks 67 L6
Hunts Green Warwks 98 F4
Huntsham Devon 29 H6
Huntshaw Devon 27 J6
Huntshaw Cross Devon 27 J6
Huntspill Somset 30 D2
Huntstile Somset 30 C4
Huntworth Somset 30 D4
Hunwick Dur 168 F4
Hunworth Norfk 122 D4
Hurcott Somset 30 F7
Hurdcott Wilts 33 L4
Hurdsfield Ches E 131 H5
Hurley W & M 49 K2
Hurley Warwks 99 H4
Hurley Bottom W & M 49 K2
Hurley Common Warwks 99 H4
Hurlford E Ayrs 196 E4
Hurlston Green Lancs 138 E5
Hurn Dorset 18 A4
Hurn's End Lincs 119 M2
Hursley Hants 34 F6
Hurst Dorset 16 F4
Hurst N York 159 J2
Hurst Somset 31 G7
Hurst Wokham 49 J4
Hurstbourne Priors Hants 34 F2
Hurstbourne Tarrant Hants 48 A8
Hurst Green E Susx 24 D2
Hurst Green Essex 73 G4
Hurst Green Lancs 148 B8
Hurst Green Surrey 38 B3
Hurst Hill Dudley 97 L4
Hurstley Herefs 79 L5
Hurstpierpoint W Susx 22 E4
Hurst Wickham W Susx 22 D4
Hurstwood Lancs 140 C2
Hurtiso Ork 275 d5
Hurtmore Surrey 36 E2
Hurworth Burn Dur 169 L4
Hurworth-on-Tees Darltn 169 J8
Hurworth Place Darltn 160 D1
Hury Dur 168 B6
Husbands Bosworth Leics 100 E6
Husborne Crawley C Beds 85 J8
Husthwaite N York 161 H7
Hutcherleigh Devon 8 A5
Hutcliffe Wood Crematorium Sheff 133 G3
Hut Green N York 142 F3
Huthwaite Notts 133 J7
Huttoft Lincs 137 K4
Hutton Border 202 E2
Hutton Cumb 166 B5
Hutton E R Yk 152 F5
Hutton Essex 70 E4
Hutton Lancs 139 G2
Hutton N Som 44 D7
Hutton Bonville N York 160 E3
Hutton Buscel N York 163 H6
Hutton Conyers N York 160 D7
Hutton Cranswick E R Yk 153 G5
Hutton End Cumb 166 B3
Hutton Hang N York 159 L5
Hutton Henry Dur 169 L3
Hutton-le-Hole N York 162 B4
Hutton Lowcross R & Cl 170 E7
Hutton Magna Dur 168 E8
Hutton Mulgrave N York 162 E1
Hutton Roof Cumb 157 J7
Hutton Roof Cumb 165 L4
Hutton Rudby N York 161 G2
Hutton Sessay N York 161 G7
Hutton Wandesley N York 151 H5
Huxham Devon 13 M3
Huxham Green Somset 31 K4
Huxley Ches W 129 L7
Huyton Knows 129 K2
Hycemoor Cumb 155 K5
Hyde Gloucs 64 C6
Hyde Hants 33 L8
Hyde Tamesd 131 J1
Hyde End Wokham 49 H5
Hyde Heath Bucks 68 B7
Hyde Lea Staffs 114 E7
Hydestile Surrey 36 E3
Hykeham Moor Lincs 135 J6
Hyndford Bridge S Lans 198 F5
Hynish Ag & B 224 C7
Hyssington Powys 95 H4
Hystfield Gloucs 63 K7
Hythe Essex 72 E2
Hythe Hants 19 G2
Hythe Kent 41 G8
Hythe Somset 44 F8
Hythe End W & M 50 C4
Hyton Cumb 155 K5

I

Ibberton Dorset 16 F
Ible Derbys 132 E
Ibsley Hants 18 A
Ibstock Leics 99 L
Ibstone Bucks 67 L
Ibthorpe Hants 48 A
Iburndale N York 162 F
Ibworth Hants 48 F
Icelton N Som 44 D
Ichrachan Ag & B 217 G
Ickburgh Norfk 105 G
Ickenham Gt Lon 50 D
Ickford Bucks 66 F
Ickham Kent 41 H
Ickleford Herts 68 F
Icklesham E Susx 24 F
Ickleton Cambs 87 K
Icklingham Suffk 88 F
Ickornshaw N York 149 C
Ickwell Green C Beds 86 C
Icomb Gloucs 65 J
Idbury Oxon 65 K
Iddesleigh Devon 12 L
Ide Devon 13 L
Ideford Devon 13 K
Ide Hill Kent 38 D
Iden E Susx 25 G
Iden Green Kent 39 G
Iden Green Kent 39 K
Idle C Brad 149 M8
Idless Cnwll 4 D
Idlicote Warwks 83 G
Idmiston Wilts 33 L
Idole Carmth 58 D
Idridgehay Derbys 115 M2
Idrigill Highld 258 F
Idstone Oxon 47 K
Iffley Oxon 66 D
Ifield W Susx 37 K
Ifold W Susx 36 F
Iford Bmouth 18 A
Iford E Susx 22 F
Ifton Mons 44 D
Ifton Heath Shrops 112 E
Ightfield Shrops 113 K
Ightham Kent 38 D
Iken Suffk 91 J
Ilam Staffs 115 J
Ilchester Somset 31 H
Ilderton Nthumb 190 E
Ilford Gt Lon 51 L
Ilford Somset 30 E
Ilfracombe Devon 27 J
Ilkeston Derbys 116 D
Ilketshall St Andrew Suffk 107 H
Ilketshall St John Suffk 107 H
Ilketshall St Lawrence Suffk 107 H
Ilketshall St Margaret Suffk 107 G
Ilkley C Brad 149 K
Illand Cnwll 11 K
Illey Dudley 98 B7
Illidge Green Ches E 130 F
Illingworth Calder 141 G
Illogan Cnwll 3 H
Illston on the Hill Leics 100 F
Ilmer Bucks 67 J
Ilmington Warwks 82 F
Ilminster Somset 30 E
Ilsington Devon 13 H
Ilsington Dorset 16 E
Ilston Swans 57 G
Ilton N York 160 B
Ilton Somset 30 E
Imachar N Ayrs 194 D
Immingham NE Lin 144 F
Immingham Dock NE Lin 145 G
Impington Cambs 87 J
Ince Ches W 129 K
Ince Blundell Sefton 138 C
Ince-in-Makerfield Wigan 139 J
Inchbae Lodge Hotel Highld 262 C
Inchbare Angus 234 E
Inchberry Moray 266 F
Incheril Highld 261 G
Inchinnan Rens 208 C
Inchlaggan Highld 239 K
Inchmichael P & K 222 D
Inchnacardoch Hotel Highld 240 C
Inchnadamph Highld 271 H
Inchture P & K 222 D
Inchvuilt Highld 249 L
Inchyra P & K 222 C
Indian Queens Cnwll 4 E
Ingate Place Suffk 107 J
Ingatestone Essex 70 F
Ingbirchworth Barns 141 K6

ngerthorpe N York.......... 150 C3
ngestre Staffs.......... 114 F6
ngham Lincs.......... 135 L2
ngham Norfk.......... 123 H6
ngham Suffk.......... 89 G1
ngham Corner Norfk.......... 123 H6
ngleborough Norfk.......... 120 B8
ngleby Derbys.......... 116 B6
ngleby Arncliffe N York.......... 161 G3
ngleby Barwick S on T.......... 170 B7
ngleby Cross N York.......... 161 G3
ngleby Greenhow N York.......... 161 J2
ngleigh Green Devon.......... 12 E1
nglesbatch BaNES.......... 45 L6
nglesham Swindn.......... 65 J7
ngleton D & G.......... 176 C6
ngleton Dur.......... 168 F6
ngleton N York.......... 158 B8
nglewhite Lancs.......... 147 L7
ngmanthorpe N York.......... 150 F5
ngoe Nthumb.......... 180 C4
ngol Lancs.......... 139 G1
ngoldisthorpe Norfk.......... 120 F5
ngoldmells Lincs.......... 137 K6
ngoldsby Lincs.......... 118 D5
ngram Nthumb.......... 190 E3
ngrave Essex.......... 52 D1
ngrow C Brad.......... 149 J7
ngs Cumb.......... 157 G3
ngst S Glos.......... 45 H2
ngthorpe Rutlnd.......... 101 M2
ngworth Norfk.......... 122 D5
nkberrow Worcs.......... 82 B4
nkerman Dur.......... 168 E3
nkhorn Abers.......... 257 G4
nkpen W Berk.......... 48 A6
nkstack Highld.......... 280 C2
nmarsh Wilts.......... 46 D6
nnellan Ag & B.......... 207 J5
nnerleithen Border.......... 200 D6
nnerleven Fife.......... 222 F7
nnermessan D & G.......... 172 D2
nnerwick E Loth.......... 212 F4
nnesmill Moray.......... 266 F3
nnsworth Gloucs.......... 64 B3
nsch Abers.......... 256 A6
nsh Highld.......... 241 L3
nskip Lancs.......... 147 J8
nskip Moss Side Lancs.......... 147 J8
nstow Devon.......... 27 H5
nsworke Cnwll.......... 6 G4
ntake Sheff.......... 133 H3
nver Abers.......... 243 H5
nver Highld.......... 264 D3
nver P & K.......... 232 F7
nverailort Highld.......... 238 B7
nveralligin Highld.......... 260 D8
nverallochy Abers.......... 269 J3
nveran Highld.......... 272 E8
nveraray Ag & B.......... 217 H5
nverarish Highld.......... 247 H2
nverarity Angus.......... 234 C6
nverarnan Stirlg.......... 218 D3
nverasdale Highld.......... 260 C3
nverbeg Ag & B.......... 218 E7
nverbervie Abers.......... 235 K1
nverboyndie Abers.......... 268 B3
nvercreran House Hotel
  Ag & B.......... 229 G6
nverdruie Highld.......... 242 B1
nveresk E Loth.......... 211 K5
nveresragan Ag & B.......... 228 F8
nverey Abers.......... 242 E5
nverfarigaig Highld.......... 250 F7
nverfolla Ag & B.......... 228 E6
nvergarry Highld.......... 240 A3
nvergeldie P & K.......... 232 C2
nvergloy Highld.......... 239 L6
nvergordon Highld.......... 263 J6
nvergowrie P & K.......... 222 F7
nverguseran Highld.......... 238 B2
nverhadden P & K.......... 231 J4
nverherive Hotel Stirlg.......... 218 E2
nverie Highld.......... 238 B3
nverinan Ag & B.......... 216 F4
nverinate Highld.......... 248 E7
nverkeilor Angus.......... 235 G5
nverkeithing Fife.......... 210 F2
nverkeithny Abers.......... 268 A6
nverkip Inver.......... 207 K4
nverkirkaig Highld.......... 270 C4
nverlael Highld.......... 261 K3
nverlair Highld.......... 240 B7
nverliever Lodge Ag & B.......... 216 D6
nverlochy Ag & B.......... 217 K2
nvermark Angus.......... 244 A7
nvermoriston Highld.......... 250 D8
nvernaver Highld.......... 278 B4
nverness Highld.......... 251 H3

Inverness Crematorium
  Highld.......... 251 H3
Invernoaden Ag & B.......... 217 J7
Inveroran Hotel Ag & B.......... 229 M7
Inverquharity Angus.......... 234 B4
Inverquhomery Abers.......... 257 J2
Inverroy Highld.......... 239 M7
Inversanda Highld.......... 228 E3
Invershiel Highld.......... 248 F7
Invershin Highld.......... 272 E8
Invershore Highld.......... 275 H1
Inversnaid Hotel Stirlg.......... 218 D5
Inveruglas Ag & B.......... 218 D5
Inveruglass Highld.......... 241 L3
Inverurie Abers.......... 256 D7
Inwardleigh Devon.......... 12 D3
Inworth Essex.......... 72 C3
Iona Ag & B.......... 226 B7
Iping W Susx.......... 36 C6
iPort Logistics Park Donc.......... 142 F8
Ipplepen Devon.......... 8 B2
Ipsden Oxon.......... 48 F2
Ipstones Staffs.......... 115 G2
Ipswich Suffk.......... 90 E6
Ipswich Crematorium Suffk.......... 90 E6
Irby Wirral.......... 128 F3
Irby in the Marsh Lincs.......... 137 J7
Irby upon Humber NE Lin.......... 145 G6
Irchester Nhants.......... 85 H2
Ireby Cumb.......... 165 H3
Ireby Lancs.......... 157 L7
Ireland C Beds.......... 86 C7
Ireleth Cumb.......... 156 B7
Ireshopeburn Dur.......... 167 K3
Ireton Wood Derbys.......... 115 M4
Irlam Salfd.......... 130 E1
Irnham Lincs.......... 118 D6
Iron Acton S Glos.......... 45 K2
Iron Bridge Cambs.......... 103 K4
Ironbridge Wrekin.......... 96 F3
Iron Cross Warwks.......... 82 C5
Ironmacannie D & G.......... 185 G7
Irons Bottom Surrey.......... 37 K2
Ironville Derbys.......... 116 D1
Irstead Norfk.......... 123 H7
Irthington Cumb.......... 178 C6
Irthlingborough Nhants.......... 85 J1
Irton N York.......... 163 H6
Irvine N Ayrs.......... 196 C3
Isauld Highld.......... 279 G3
Isbister Shet.......... 281 d3
Isbister Shet.......... 281 f5
Isfield E Susx.......... 23 G4
Isham Nhants.......... 101 J8
Isington Hants.......... 36 A2
Islandpool Worcs.......... 97 K7
Islay Ag & B.......... 204 E1
Isle Abbotts Somset.......... 30 E6
Isle Brewers Somset.......... 30 E6
Isleham Cambs.......... 104 C8
Isle of Dogs Gt Lon.......... 51 K3
Isle of Lewis W Isls.......... 282 f3
Isle of Man IoM.......... 154 e5
Isle of Mull Ag & B.......... 227 H5
Isle of Sheppey Kent.......... 40 C2
Isle of Skye Highld.......... 246 F1
Isle of Walney Cumb.......... 146 D3
Isle of Whithorn D & G.......... 174 D7
Isle of Wight IoW.......... 19 J6
Isle of Wight Crematorium
  IoW.......... 19 J5
Isleornsay Highld.......... 247 L6
Isles of Scilly IoS.......... 10 C2
Islesteps D & G.......... 176 C4
Islet Village Guern.......... 9 k2
Isleworth Gt Lon.......... 50 F4
Isley Walton Leics.......... 116 C6
Islibhig W Isls.......... 282 d3
Islington Gt Lon.......... 51 J2
Islington Crematorium Gt Lon.......... 51 H1
Islip Nhants.......... 101 L7
Islip Oxon.......... 66 D4
Isliviq W Isls.......... 282 d3
Isombridge Wrekin.......... 96 E1
Istead Rise Kent.......... 52 D5
Itchen Abbas Hants.......... 35 H4
Itchen Stoke Hants.......... 35 H4
Itchingfield W Susx.......... 37 H5
Itchington S Glos.......... 45 K2
Itteringham Norfk.......... 122 C5
Itton Devon.......... 12 F3
Itton Mons.......... 62 F8
Itton Common Mons.......... 62 F7
Ivegill Cumb.......... 165 M2
Ivelet N York.......... 159 G3
Iver Bucks.......... 50 D3
Iver Heath Bucks.......... 50 C2
Iveston Dur.......... 168 E1

Ivinghoe Bucks.......... 68 B4
Ivinghoe Aston Bucks.......... 68 B3
Ivington Herefs.......... 80 B4
Ivington Green Herefs.......... 80 B4
Ivybridge Devon.......... 7 J4
Ivychurch Kent.......... 25 J2
Ivy Cross Dorset.......... 32 E6
Ivy Hatch Kent.......... 38 F3
Ivy Todd Norfk.......... 105 H2
Iwade Kent.......... 40 A2
Iwerne Courtney Dorset.......... 32 E8
Iwerne Minster Dorset.......... 32 E8
Ixworth Suffk.......... 89 J1
Ixworth Thorpe Suffk.......... 89 J1

J

Jack Green Lancs.......... 139 J3
Jack Hill N York.......... 150 B5
Jack-in-the-Green Devon.......... 14 B3
Jack's Bush Hants.......... 34 C3
Jacksdale Notts.......... 116 D1
Jackson Bridge Kirk.......... 141 J6
Jackton S Lans.......... 209 G8
Jacobstow Cnwll.......... 11 H3
Jacobstowe Devon.......... 12 E2
Jacobs Well Surrey.......... 50 C8
Jameston Pembks.......... 55 H7
Jamestown Highld.......... 262 E8
Jamestown W Duns.......... 208 C3
Janetstown Highld.......... 275 G2
Janetstown Highld.......... 280 D6
Jardine Hall D & G.......... 176 E1
Jarrow S Tyne.......... 181 H6
Jarvis Brook E Susx.......... 38 E7
Jasper's Green Essex.......... 71 H2
Jawcraig Falk.......... 209 M4
Jaywick Essex.......... 73 H4
Jealott's Hill Br For.......... 49 L4
Jeater Houses N York.......... 160 F4
Jedburgh Border.......... 189 H2
Jeffreyston Pembks.......... 55 J5
Jemimaville Highld.......... 263 K7
Jerbourg Guern.......... 9 k4
Jersey Jersey.......... 9 d2
Jersey Crematorium Jersey.......... 9 d3
Jersey Marine Neath.......... 57 K6
Jerusalem Lincs.......... 135 J5
Jesmond N u Ty.......... 181 G5
Jevington E Susx.......... 23 J7
Jingle Street Mons.......... 62 F5
Jockey End Herts.......... 68 D4
Jodrell Bank Ches E.......... 130 F5
Johnby Cumb.......... 166 B4
John o' Groats Highld.......... 280 E2
Johns Cross E Susx.......... 24 D3
Johnshaven Abers.......... 235 K2
Johnson Street Norfk.......... 123 H8
Johnston Pembks.......... 54 F5
Johnstone D & G.......... 187 K6
Johnstone Rens.......... 208 D6
Johnstonebridge D & G.......... 187 G7
Johnstown Carmth.......... 58 D5
Johnstown Wrexhm.......... 112 D2
Joppa C Edin.......... 211 K4
Joppa Cerdgn.......... 77 G2
Joppa S Ayrs.......... 196 E7
Jordans Bucks.......... 50 B1
Jordanston Pembks.......... 74 F5
Jordanthorpe Sheff.......... 133 G3
Joyden's Wood Kent.......... 52 B4
Jubilee Corner Kent.......... 39 L4
Jump Barns.......... 142 B7
Jumper's Town E Susx.......... 38 C6
Juniper Nthumb.......... 179 L7
Juniper Green C Edin.......... 211 G5
Jura Ag & B.......... 215 G7
Jurby IoM.......... 154 e3
Jurston Devon.......... 13 G5

K

Kaber Cumb.......... 167 J8
Kaimend S Lans.......... 199 G4
Kames Ag & B.......... 206 F5
Kames E Ayrs.......... 197 K5
Kea Cnwll.......... 4 C6
Keadby N Linc.......... 143 L5
Keal Cotes Lincs.......... 137 G2
Kearby Town End N York.......... 150 E6
Kearsley Bolton.......... 139 M6
Kearsley Nthumb.......... 180 B4
Kearsney Kent.......... 41 J6
Kearstwick Cumb.......... 157 K6
Kearton N York.......... 159 H3

Keasden N York.......... 148 C3
Keaton Devon.......... 7 J4
Keckwick Halton.......... 130 B3
Keddington Lincs.......... 136 F2
Keddington Corner Lincs.......... 137 G2
Kedington Suffk.......... 88 E6
Kedleston Derbys.......... 116 A3
Keelby Lincs.......... 144 F5
Keele Staffs.......... 114 C3
Keele University Staffs.......... 114 C3
Keeley Green Bed.......... 85 K6
Keelham C Brad.......... 141 G1
Keeres Green Essex.......... 70 F4
Keeston Pembks.......... 54 E3
Keevil Wilts.......... 46 D7
Kegworth Leics.......... 116 E6
Kehelland Cnwll.......... 3 G3
Keig Abers.......... 256 A7
Keighley C Brad.......... 149 J7
Keighley Crematorium C Brad.......... 149 J8
Keilarsbrae Clacks.......... 220 F8
Keillour P & K.......... 221 L2
Keiloch Abers.......... 243 G5
Keils Ag & B.......... 205 H3
Keinton Mandeville Somset.......... 31 J5
Keir Mill D & G.......... 186 C7
Keirsleywell Row Nthumb.......... 179 H8
Keisby Lincs.......... 118 D6
Keisley Cumb.......... 167 G6
Keiss Highld.......... 280 D4
Keith Moray.......... 267 J6
Keithick P & K.......... 233 J7
Keithock Angus.......... 234 F3
Keithtown Highld.......... 262 F8
Kelbrook Lancs.......... 148 F7
Kelby Lincs.......... 118 D3
Keld Cumb.......... 166 D7
Keld N York.......... 158 F3
Keld Head N York.......... 162 D5
Keldholme N York.......... 162 C5
Kelfield N Linc.......... 143 L7
Kelfield N York.......... 151 J8
Kelham Notts.......... 134 F8
Kelhead D & G.......... 176 F5
Kellacott Devon.......... 12 A5
Kellamergh Lancs.......... 138 E2
Kellas Angus.......... 234 C8
Kellas Moray.......... 266 D5
Kellaton Devon.......... 8 B7
Kelleth Cumb.......... 157 L2
Kelling Norfk.......... 122 B3
Kellington N York.......... 142 E3
Kelloe Dur.......... 169 K3
Kelloholm D & G.......... 185 J1
Kells Cumb.......... 164 C7
Kelly Devon.......... 11 M6
Kelly Bray Cnwll.......... 11 L8
Kelmarsh Nhants.......... 101 G7
Kelmscott Oxon.......... 65 K7
Kelsale Suffk.......... 91 J2
Kelsall Ches W.......... 129 M6
Kelshall Herts.......... 87 G7
Kelsick Cumb.......... 165 G1
Kelso Border.......... 201 M6
Kelstedge Derbys.......... 133 G7
Kelstern Lincs.......... 136 D2
Kelsterton Flints.......... 129 G5
Kelston BaNES.......... 45 K5
Keltneyburn P & K.......... 231 L5
Kelton D & G.......... 176 C5
Kelty Fife.......... 221 L8
Kelvedon Essex.......... 72 C3
Kelvedon Hatch Essex.......... 70 E7
Kelynack Cnwll.......... 2 B5
Kemacott Devon.......... 28 B2
Kemback Fife.......... 223 G4
Kemberton Shrops.......... 97 G3
Kemble Gloucs.......... 64 E7
Kemble Wick Gloucs.......... 64 E7
Kemerton Worcs.......... 81 L7
Kemeys Commander Mons.......... 62 D6
Kemnay Abers.......... 256 D8
Kempe's Corner Kent.......... 40 D6
Kempley Gloucs.......... 63 K1
Kempley Green Gloucs.......... 63 K1
Kempsey Worcs.......... 81 J5
Kempsford Gloucs.......... 65 H7
Kemps Green Warwks.......... 82 D1
Kempshott Hants.......... 35 J1
Kempston Bed.......... 85 K5
Kempston Hardwick Bed.......... 85 K6
Kempton Shrops.......... 95 J6
Kemp Town Br & H.......... 22 E6
Kemsing Kent.......... 52 C7
Kemsley Kent.......... 40 B2
Kemsley Street Kent.......... 53 H6
Kenardington Kent.......... 25 H1
Kenchester Herefs.......... 80 B6
Kencot Oxon.......... 65 K6

Kendal Cumb 157 H4
Kenderchurch Herefs 62 E2
Kendleshire S Glos 45 K3
Kenfig Brdgnd 42 B5
Kenfig Hill Brdgnd 42 C5
Kenilworth Warwks 83 G1
Kenley Gt Lon 51 J7
Kenley Shrops 96 D3
Kenmore Highld 260 B8
Kenmore P & K 231 L6
Kenn Devon 13 L5
Kenn N Som 44 E5
Kennacraig Ag & B 206 C6
Kennards House Cnwll 11 L4
Kenneggy Cnwll 2 F5
Kennerleigh Devon 13 J1
Kennessee Green Sefton 138 D7
Kennet Clacks 210 B1
Kennethmont Abers 255 L6
Kennett Cambs 88 D2
Kennford Devon 13 L5
Kenninghall Norfk 105 L6
Kennington Kent 40 D6
Kennington Oxon 66 D6
Kennoway Fife 222 F6
Kenny Somset 30 D7
Kenny Hill Suffk 104 D7
Kennythorpe N York 152 B3
Kenovay Ag & B 224 C6
Kensaleyre Highld 259 G6
Kensington Gt Lon 51 H3
Kensworth Common C Beds 68 C3
Kentallen Highld 228 F4
Kent and Sussex
    Crematorium Kent 38 F6
Kentchurch Herefs 62 E2
Kentford Suffk 88 E2
Kent Green Ches E 131 G8
Kentisbeare Devon 14 C1
Kentisbury Devon 27 L2
Kentisbury Ford Devon 27 L2
Kentish Town Gt Lon 51 H2
Kentmere Cumb 157 G2
Kenton Devon 13 M6
Kenton Gt Lon 50 F1
Kenton N u Ty 180 F5
Kenton Suffk 90 E2
Kenton Bankfoot N u Ty 180 F5
Kentra Highld 237 J6
Kents Bank Cumb 156 F7
Kent's Green Gloucs 63 L2
Kent's Oak Hants 34 D6
Kent Street E Susx 24 E4
Kent Street Kent 39 G2
Kenwick Shrops 112 F5
Kenwyn Cnwll 4 D5
Kenyon Warrtn 139 J8
Keoldale Highld 276 F3
Keppoch Highld 248 E6
Kepwick N York 161 G4
Keresley Covtry 99 J6
Kermincham Ches E 130 F6
Kernborough Devon 8 B6
Kerne Bridge Herefs 63 H3
Kerrera Ag & B 216 C2
Kerridge Ches E 131 J4
Kerridge-end Ches E 131 J4
Kerris Cnwll 2 C5
Kerry Powys 94 K5
Kerrycroy Ag & B 207 J6
Kersall Notts 134 E7
Kersbrook Devon 14 C6
Kerscott Devon 27 L5
Kersey Suffk 89 K6
Kersey Tye Suffk 89 K6
Kersey Upland Suffk 89 K6
Kershader W Isls 282 f4
Kershopefoot Cumb 178 B2
Kersoe Worcs 82 A7
Kerswell Devon 14 C2
Kerswell Green Worcs 81 K6
Kerthen Wood Cnwll 2 F4
Kesgrave Suffk 90 F6
Kessingland Suffk 107 L6
Kessingland Beach Suffk 107 L6
Kestle Cnwll 5 G5
Kestle Mill Cnwll 4 D3
Keston Gt Lon 51 L6
Keswick Cumb 165 J6
Keswick Norfk 106 E2
Ketsby Lincs 137 G4
Kettering Nhants 101 J7
Kettering Crematorium
    Nhants 101 J7
Ketteringham Norfk 106 D2
Kettins P & K 233 K7
Kettlebaston Suffk 89 K5
Kettlebridge Fife 222 E5
Kettlebrook Staffs 99 G3

Kettleburgh Suffk 91 G3
Kettle Green Herts 69 L3
Kettleholm D & G 176 F3
Kettleness N York 171 J7
Kettleshulme Ches E 131 K4
Kettlesing N York 150 B4
Kettlesing Bottom N York 150 B4
Kettlestone Norfk 121 L5
Kettlethorpe Lincs 135 G4
Kettletoft Ork 275 e2
Kettlewell N York 149 H4
Ketton Rutlnd 101 L3
Kew Gt Lon 50 F4
Kewstoke N Som 44 C6
Kexbrough Barns 141 M6
Kexby C York 151 L5
Kexby Lincs 135 H3
Key Green Ches E 131 H7
Key Green N York 162 D2
Keyham Leics 100 E2
Keyhaven Hants 18 D5
Keyingham E R Yk 145 H3
Keymer W Susx 22 D4
Keynsham BaNES 45 K5
Keysoe Bed 86 B3
Keysoe Row Bed 86 B3
Keyston Cambs 102 A8
Key Street Kent 53 J6
Keyworth Notts 117 G5
Kibbear Somset 30 B6
Kibblesworth Gatesd 181 G7
Kibworth Beauchamp Leics 100 F4
Kibworth Harcourt Leics 100 F4
Kidbrooke Gt Lon 51 L4
Kidburngill Cumb 164 E6
Kiddemore Green Staffs 97 J2
Kidderminster Worcs 97 J8
Kiddington Oxon 66 B3
Kidlington Oxon 66 D4
Kidmore End Oxon 49 G3
Kidsdale D & G 174 C7
Kidsgrove Staffs 131 G8
Kidstones N York 159 G6
Kidwelly Carmth 56 D3
Kiel Crofts Ag & B 228 D7
Kielder Nthumb 189 H7
Kiells Ag & B 204 F3
Kilbarchan Rens 208 C6
Kilbeg Highld 247 K7
Kilberry Ag & B 206 A6
Kilbirnie N Ayrs 208 A8
Kilbride Ag & B 207 G5
Kilbride Ag & B 215 L8
Kilbuiack Moray 266 B4
Kilburn Derbys 116 C2
Kilburn Gt Lon 51 H2
Kilburn N York 161 H6
Kilby Leics 100 D4
Kilchamaig Ag & B 206 C6
Kilchattan Ag & B 207 H8
Kilchattan Ag & B 214 D5
Kilcheran Ag & B 228 C7
Kilchoan Highld 236 F7
Kilchoman Ag & B 204 B4
Kilchrenan Ag & B 217 G3
Kilconquhar Fife 223 H6
Kilcot Gloucs 63 K2
Kilcoy Highld 251 G2
Kilcreggan Ag & B 207 L3
Kildale N York 161 K1
Kildalloig Ag & B 192 F4
Kildary Highld 263 K5
Kildavaig Ag & B 206 F6
Kildavanan Ag & B 207 G5
Kildonan Highld 274 B4
Kildonan N Ayrs 195 G6
Kildonan Lodge Highld 274 B4
Kildonnan Highld 236 F3
Kildrochet House D & G 172 D4
Kildrummy Abers 255 J8
Kildwick N York 149 H6
Kilfinan Ag & B 206 E3
Kilfinnan Highld 239 M4
Kilford Denbgs 128 C6
Kilgetty Pembks 55 K5
Kilgrammie S Ayrs 183 G3
Kilgwrrwg Common Mons 62 F7
Kilham E R Yk 153 G3
Kilham Nthumb 202 D6
Kilkenneth Ag & B 224 B6
Kilkenzie Ag & B 192 D3
Kilkerran Ag & B 192 E4
Kilkhampton Cnwll 26 D8
Killamarsh Derbys 133 J3
Killay Swans 57 H6
Killearn Stirlg 208 E2
Killen Highld 263 J8
Killerby Darltn 169 G6

Killerton Devon 14 A3
Killichonan P & K 231 G4
Killiechonate Highld 239 L7
Killiechronan Ag & B 227 G4
Killiecrankie P & K 232 D3
Killilan Highld 248 F5
Killimster Highld 280 D5
Killin Stirlg 231 G8
Killinghall N York 150 C4
Killington Cumb 157 K5
Killington Devon 28 B2
Killingworth N Tyne 181 G5
Killiow Cnwll 4 C6
Killochyett Border 200 F4
Kilmacolm Inver 208 B5
Kilmahog Stirlg 219 K5
Kilmahumaig Ag & B 216 B8
Kilmaluag Highld 259 G2
Kilmany Fife 222 F3
Kilmarnock E Ayrs 196 E3
Kilmartin Ag & B 216 C7
Kilmaurs E Ayrs 196 E3
Kilmelford Ag & B 216 C4
Kilmersdon Somset 45 K8
Kilmeston Hants 35 J5
Kilmichael Ag & B 192 E4
Kilmichael Glassary Ag & B 216 D8
Kilmichael of Inverlussa
    Ag & B 206 B2
Kilmington Devon 15 G3
Kilmington Wilts 32 C3
Kilmington Common Wilts 32 C4
Kilmington Street Wilts 32 C4
Kilmorack Highld 250 E3
Kilmore Ag & B 216 D2
Kilmore Highld 247 K7
Kilmory Ag & B 205 M2
Kilmory Highld 237 G6
Kilmory N Ayrs 193 K4
Kilmuir Highld 251 J2
Kilmuir Highld 258 D7
Kilmuir Highld 258 F3
Kilmuir Highld 263 K5
Kilmun Ag & B 207 K3
Kilnave Ag & B 204 D2
Kilncadzow S Lans 198 E3
Kilndown Kent 39 H6
Kiln Green Wokham 49 K3
Kilnhill Cumb 165 H4
Kilnhouses Ches W 130 C6
Kilnhurst Rothm 142 C8
Kilninver Ag & B 216 C3
Kiln Pit Hill Nthumb 180 C7
Kilnsea E R Yk 145 L4
Kilnsey N York 149 H2
Kilnwick E R Yk 152 F6
Kilnwick Percy E R Yk 152 C6
Kiloran Ag & B 214 D5
Kilpatrick N Ayrs 194 D5
Kilpeck Herefs 62 F1
Kilpin E R Yk 143 K2
Kilpin Pike E R Yk 143 J2
Kilrenny Fife 223 K6
Kilsby Nhants 84 A1
Kilspindie P & K 222 C2
Kilstay D & G 172 E7
Kilsyth N Lans 209 J3
Kiltarlity Highld 250 E3
Kilton R & Cl 171 G7
Kilton Thorpe R & Cl 171 G7
Kilvaxter Highld 258 F3
Kilve Somset 29 L2
Kilvington Notts 117 L3
Kilwinning N Ayrs 196 B2
Kimberley Norfk 106 B3
Kimberley Notts 116 E3
Kimberworth Rothm 133 H1
Kimblesworth Dur 169 H1
Kimble Wick Bucks 67 J5
Kimbolton Cambs 86 B2
Kimbolton Herefs 80 C3
Kimcote Leics 100 D6
Kimmeridge Dorset 17 H6
Kimmerston Nthumb 202 E6
Kimpton Hants 34 C2
Kimpton Herts 68 F3
Kimworthy Devon 26 E8
Kinbrace Highld 273 L2
Kinbuck Stirlg 220 D6
Kincaple Fife 223 H3
Kincardine Fife 210 B2
Kincardine Highld 263 G2
Kincardine Bridge Fife 210 B2
Kincardine O'Neil Abers 244 D4
Kinclaven P & K 233 H7
Kincorth C Aber 245 L3
Kincorth House Moray 265 G7
Kincraig Highld 241 M2
Kincraigie P & K 232 E5

Kindallachan P & K 232 E5
Kinerarach Ag & B 205 L5
Kineton Gloucs 65 G2
Kineton Warwks 83 H5
Kinfauns P & K 222 B3
Kingarth Ag & B 207 H7
Kingcausie Abers 245 J3
Kingcoed Mons 62 D7
Kingerby Lincs 135 L1
Kingford Devon 11 K2
Kingham Oxon 65 K2
Kingholm Quay D & G 176 D4
Kinghorn Fife 211 J2
Kinglassie Fife 222 C7
Kingoldrum Angus 233 M4
Kingoodie P & K 222 F1
King's Acre Herefs 80 B7
Kingsand Cnwll 6 E5
Kingsash Bucks 67 L6
Kingsbarns Fife 223 K5
Kingsbridge Devon 7 L6
Kingsbridge Somset 29 H3
Kings Bridge Swans 57 H3
King's Bromley Staffs 115 J8
Kingsburgh Highld 258 F5
Kingsbury Gt Lon 51 G1
Kingsbury Warwks 99 G4
Kingsbury Episcopi Somset 31 H2
King's Caple Herefs 63 H2
Kingsclere Hants 48 D5
King's Cliffe Nhants 101 M4
Kings Clipstone Notts 134 C6
Kingscote Gloucs 64 B7
Kingscott Devon 27 K7
King's Coughton Warwks 82 C3
Kingscross N Ayrs 195 G5
Kingsdon Somset 31 H5
Kingsdown Kent 41 L5
Kingsdown Swindn 47 H1
Kingsdown Wilts 46 A5
Kingsdown Crematorium
    Swindn 47 H1
Kingseat Fife 210 F1
Kingsey Bucks 67 H6
Kingsfold W Susx 37 J4
Kingsford C Aber 245 J2
Kingsford E Ayrs 196 E2
Kingsford Worcs 97 J7
Kingsgate Kent 41 L1
Kings Green Gloucs 81 H8
Kingshall Street Suffk 89 J3
Kingsheanton Devon 27 K3
King's Heath Birm 98 D7
Kings Hill Kent 39 H7
King's Hill Wsall 98 C4
Kings House Hotel Highld 229 L4
Kingshouse Hotel Stirlg 219 J3
Kingshurst Solhll 98 F5
Kingside Hill Cumb 177 G8
Kingskerswell Devon 8 C1
Kingskettle Fife 222 E5
Kingsland Dorset 15 K3
Kingsland Herefs 80 B3
Kingsland IoA 124 D3
Kings Langley Herts 68 D6
Kingsley Ches W 130 A5
Kingsley Hants 36 B3
Kingsley Staffs 115 G1
Kingsley Green W Susx 36 B5
Kingsley Park Nhants 84 E1
Kingslow Shrops 97 H4
King's Lynn Norfk 120 D7
Kings Meaburn Cumb 166 C5
Kingsmead Hants 35 J4
King's Mills Guern 9 i3
King's Moss St Hel 139 G7
Kingsmuir Angus 234 D5
Kings Muir Border 200 B5
Kingsmuir Fife 223 J5
Kings Newnham Warwks 99 M7
King's Newton Derbys 116 C5
Kingsnorth Kent 40 C7
King's Norton Birm 98 D7
King's Norton Leics 100 E4
Kings Nympton Devon 28 B7
King's Pyon Herefs 80 B5
Kings Ripton Cambs 102 F7
King's Somborne Hants 34 D4
King's Stag Dorset 32 B7
King's Stanley Gloucs 64 A7
King's Sutton Nhants 83 L7
Kingstanding Birm 98 D5
Kingsteignton Devon 13 K7
King Sterndale Derbys 132 F7
Kingsthorne Herefs 63 G2
Kingsthorpe Nhants 84 E2
Kingston Cambs 87 G2
Kingston Cnwll 11 L4
Kingston Devon 7 J5

ngston Devon....................14 C5
ngston Dorset...................16 E1
ngston Dorset...................17 J6
ngston E Loth..................212 C3
ngston Hants....................18 A3
ngston IoW......................19 H7
ngston Kent.....................41 G5
ngston W Susx...................21 J6
ngston Bagpuize Oxon............66 B7
ngston Blount Oxon..............67 H7
ngston Deverill Wilts...........32 D3
ngstone Herefs..................80 A8
ngstone Somset..................30 E8
ngstone Staffs.................115 H5
ngstone Winslow Oxon............47 K2
ngston Lisle Oxon...............47 L2
ngston near Lewes E Susx........22 F5
ngston on Soar Notts...........116 E6
ngston on Spey Moray...........267 G3
ngston Russell Dorset...........16 A4
ngston St Mary Somset...........30 B5
ngston Seymour N Som............44 E5
ngston Stert Oxon...............67 H7
ngston upon Hull C KuH.........144 D2
ngston upon Thames Gt Lon.......50 F5
ngston upon Thames
  Crematorium Gt Lon............51 G5
ngstown Cumb...................177 L7
ng's Walden Herts...............68 F2
ngswear Devon....................8 C4
ngswells C Aber................245 J2
ngsweston Bristl................45 G3
ngswinford Dudley...............97 K5
ngswood Bucks...................67 G3
ngswood Gloucs..................63 L8
ngswood Kent....................39 L3
ngswood Powys...................94 F3
ngswood S Glos..................45 J4
ngswood Somset..................29 K3
ngswood Surrey..................51 H7
ngswood Warwks..................82 E1
ngswood Brook Warwks............82 E1
ngswood Common Herefs...........79 K4
ngswood Common Staffs...........97 J3
ngs Worthy Hants................35 G4
ngthorpe Lincs.................136 B6
ngton Herefs....................79 K4
ngton S Glos....................45 J1
ngton Worcs.....................82 A4
ngton Langley Wilts.............46 D3
ngton Magna Dorset..............32 C6
ngton St Michael Wilts..........46 C3
ngussie Highld.................241 K3
nharrachie Abers...............257 G5
nharvie D & G..................176 B5
nkell Bridge P & K.............221 G4
nknockie Abers.................257 J3
nleith C Edin..................211 G5
nlet Shrops.....................97 G7
nloch Highld...................246 E8
nloch Highld...................271 K1
nloch Highld...................277 J5
nloch P & K....................233 H6
nlochard Stirlg................219 G6
nlochbervie Highld.............276 C5
nlocheil Highld................238 F7
nlochewe Highld................261 G7
nloch Hourn Highld.............238 F2
nlochlaggan Highld.............240 F5
nlochleven Highld..............229 K3
nlochmoidart Highld............237 K6
nlochnanuagh Highld............237 L4
nloch Rannoch P & K............231 J4
nloss Moray....................265 H7
nmel Bay Conwy.................127 K4
nmuck Abers....................256 E7
nmundy Abers...................256 F8
nnabus Ag & B..................204 D7
nnadie Abers...................257 H3
nnaird P & K...................232 E4
nneff Abers....................245 J8
nnelhead D & G.................186 F6
nnell Angus....................234 F5
nnerley Shrops.................112 E7
nnersley Herefs.................79 L5
nnersley Worcs..................81 K6
nnerton Powys...................79 J3
nnerton Shrops..................95 J4
nnerton Green Flints...........129 H7
nnesswood P & K................222 B6
ninvie Dur.....................168 D6
nnordy Angus...................234 B4
noulton Notts..................117 H5
nross P & K....................221 K6
nrossie P & K..................222 C1
sbourne Green Herts.............68 E4
sey Heath Ches E...............113 L3
sham Herefs.....................79 L2

Kinsham Worcs...................81 L8
Kinsley Wakefd.................142 C5
Kinson Bmouth...................17 L3
Kintbury W Berk.................48 A5
Kintessack Moray...............264 F7
Kintillo P & K.................221 L4
Kinton Herefs...................95 K8
Kinton Shrops..................112 E7
Kintore Abers..................256 E8
Kintour Ag & B.................205 G6
Kintra Ag & B..................204 D6
Kintra Ag & B..................226 C7
Kintraw Ag & B.................216 C6
Kinveachy Highld...............253 G7
Kinver Staffs...................97 J6
Kiplin N York..................160 C3
Kippax Leeds...................142 C2
Kippen Stirlg..................219 L8
Kippford D & G.................175 L4
Kipping's Cross Kent............39 G5
Kirbister Ork..................275 C5
Kirby Bedon Norfk..............106 F2
Kirby Bellars Leics............117 J7
Kirby Cane Norfk...............107 H5
Kirby Corner Covtry.............99 J8
Kirby Cross Essex...............73 J3
Kirby Fields Leics.............100 B3
Kirby Grindalythe N York.......152 D2
Kirby Hill N York..............150 E2
Kirby Hill N York..............159 L2
Kirby Knowle N York............161 G5
Kirby-le-Soken Essex............73 J3
Kirby Misperton N York.........162 D6
Kirby Muxloe Leics.............100 B3
Kirby Sigston N York...........160 F4
Kirby Underdale E R Yk.........152 B4
Kirby Wiske N York.............160 E5
Kirdford W Susx.................36 F5
Kirk Highld....................280 C4
Kirkabister Shet...............281 e7
Kirkandrews D & G..............174 F5
Kirkandrews upon Eden
  Cumb.........................177 K7
Kirkbampton Cumb...............177 J7
Kirkbean D & G.................176 C7
Kirk Bramwith Donc.............143 G5
Kirkbride Cumb.................177 H7
Kirkbridge N York..............160 C4
Kirkbuddo Angus................234 D6
Kirkburn Border................200 C5
Kirkburn E R Yk................152 F5
Kirkburton Kirk................141 K5
Kirkby Knows...................138 E7
Kirkby Lincs...................135 L1
Kirkby N York..................161 H2
Kirkby Fleetham N York.........160 D4
Kirkby Green Lincs.............136 A8
Kirkby-in-Ashfield Notts.......133 K8
Kirkby-in-Furness Cumb.........156 B6
Kirkby la Thorpe Lincs.........118 E2
Kirkby Lonsdale Cumb...........157 K7
Kirkby Malham N York...........148 F4
Kirkby Mallory Leics...........99 M3
Kirkby Malzeard N York.........160 C7
Kirkby Mills N York............162 C5
Kirkbymoorside N York..........162 B5
Kirkby on Bain Lincs...........136 D7
Kirkby Overblow N York.........150 D6
Kirkby Stephen Cumb............158 D1
Kirkby Thore Cumb..............166 E5
Kirkby Underwood Lincs.........118 E6
Kirkby Wharf N York............151 H7
Kirkby Woodhouse Notts.........116 E1
Kirkcaldy Fife.................211 J1
Kirkcaldy Crematorium Fife.....222 D8
Kirkcambeck Cumb...............178 C5
Kirkchrist D & G...............175 G4
Kirkcolm D & G.................172 C1
Kirkconnel D & G...............197 L8
Kirkconnell D & G..............176 C5
Kirkcowan D & G................173 J3
Kirkcudbright D & G............175 H5
Kirkdale Lpool.................129 H1
Kirk Deighton N York...........150 F5
Kirk Ella E R Yk...............144 C2
Kirkfieldbank S Lans...........198 E4
Kirkgunzeon D & G..............175 L2
Kirk Hallam Derbys.............116 D3
Kirkham Lancs..................138 E1
Kirkham N York.................151 M3
Kirkhamgate Wakefd.............141 L3
Kirk Hammerton N York..........151 G5
Kirkharle Nthumb...............180 B2
Kirkhaugh Nthumb...............167 G1
Kirkheaton Kirk................141 J4
Kirkheaton Nthumb..............180 B3
Kirkhill Highld................250 F3
Kirkhope S Lans................186 E5
Kirkhouse Cumb.................178 D7

Kirkhouse Green Donc...........143 G5
Kirkibost Highld...............247 H5
Kirkinch P & K.................233 L6
Kirkinner D & G................174 C4
Kirkintilloch E Duns...........209 H4
Kirk Ireton Derbys.............115 M2
Kirkland Cumb..................164 E7
Kirkland Cumb..................166 F4
Kirkland D & G.................185 K5
Kirkland D & G.................186 F8
Kirkland D & G.................197 L8
Kirkland Guards Cumb...........165 G3
Kirk Langley Derbys............115 M4
Kirkleatham R & Cl.............170 E6
Kirkleatham Crematorium
  R & Cl.......................170 E6
Kirklevington S on T...........160 F1
Kirkley Suffk..................107 L5
Kirklington N York.............160 D6
Kirklington Notts..............134 D8
Kirklinton Cumb................178 B5
Kirkliston C Edin..............210 F4
Kirkmabreck D & G..............174 D4
Kirkmaiden D & G...............172 E7
Kirk Merrington Dur............169 H4
Kirk Michael IoM...............154 d4
Kirkmichael P & K..............233 G3
Kirkmichael S Ayrs.............183 J1
Kirkmuirhill S Lans............198 C4
Kirknewton Nthumb..............202 E7
Kirknewton W Loth..............210 F5
Kirkney Abers..................255 K5
Kirk of Shotts N Lans..........209 M6
Kirkoswald Cumb................166 D3
Kirkoswald S Ayrs..............183 G2
Kirkpatrick D & G..............186 D8
Kirkpatrick Durham D & G.......175 K1
Kirkpatrick-Fleming D & G......177 J5
Kirk Sandall Donc..............142 F6
Kirksanton Cumb................155 L6
Kirk Smeaton N York............142 E4
Kirkstall Leeds................150 C8
Kirkstead Lincs................136 C7
Kirkstile Abers................255 L5
Kirkstile D & G................188 C8
Kirkstone Pass Inn Cumb........156 F1
Kirkstyle Highld...............280 D2
Kirkthorpe Wakefd..............142 B3
Kirkton Abers..................256 B6
Kirkton D & G..................176 C3
Kirkton Fife...................222 F2
Kirkton Highld.................248 C6
Kirkton Highld.................248 E3
Kirkton P & K..................221 G3
Kirkton Manor Border...........200 B5
Kirkton of Airlie Angus........233 M5
Kirkton of Auchterhouse
  Angus........................234 A7
Kirkton of Barevan Highld......252 F2
Kirkton of Collace P & K.......222 C1
Kirkton of Glenbuchat Abers....255 H8
Kirkton of Logie Buchan
  Abers........................257 H6
Kirkton of Maryculter Abers....245 J4
Kirkton of Menmuir Angus.......234 E3
Kirkton of Monikie Angus.......234 D7
Kirkton of Rayne Abers.........256 C5
Kirkton of Skene Abers.........245 H2
Kirkton of Strathmartine
  Angus........................234 B8
Kirkton of Tealing Angus.......234 B7
Kirkton of Tough Abers.........244 D1
Kirktown Abers.................269 J3
Kirktown Abers.................269 K6
Kirktown of Alvah Abers........268 B4
Kirktown of Bourtie Abers......256 E6
Kirktown of Fetteresso Abers...245 J6
Kirktown of Mortlach Moray.....255 G4
Kirktown of Slains Abers.......257 J6
Kirkurd Border.................199 K4
Kirkwall Ork...................275 C4
Kirkwhelpington Nthumb.........180 B2
Kirk Yetholm Border............202 C7
Kirmington N Linc..............144 E5
Kirmond le Mire Lincs..........136 C1
Kirn Ag & B....................207 K3
Kirriemuir Angus...............234 B4
Kirstead Green Norfk...........106 F4
Kirtlebridge D & G.............177 H4
Kirtling Cambs..................88 D4
Kirtling Green Cambs............88 D4
Kirtlington Oxon................66 D3
Kirtomy Highld.................278 C3
Kirton Lincs...................119 J4
Kirton Notts...................134 D6
Kirton Suffk....................91 G7
Kirton End Lincs...............119 J3
Kirtonhill W Duns..............208 C4
Kirton Holme Lincs.............119 J3

Kirton in Lindsey N Linc.......144 A8
Kirwaugh D & G.................173 K4
Kishorn Highld.................248 D4
Kislingbury Nhants..............84 D3
Kitebrook Warwks................65 K1
Kite Green Warwks...............82 E2
Kites Hardwick Warwks...........83 L2
Kitleigh Cnwll..................11 J3
Kitt Green Wigan...............139 H6
Kittisford Somset...............29 K6
Kittle Swans....................57 G7
Kitt's Green Birm...............98 F6
Kittybrewster C Aber...........245 K2
Kitwood Hants...................35 K4
Kivernoll Herefs................62 F1
Kiveton Park Rothm.............133 K3
Knaith Lincs...................135 G3
Knaith Park Lincs..............135 G3
Knap Corner Dorset..............32 D6
Knaphill Surrey.................50 B7
Knapp Somset....................30 D5
Knapp Hill Hants................34 E6
Knapthorpe Notts...............134 E7
Knapton C York.................151 J5
Knapton N York.................162 F7
Knapton Norfk..................122 F5
Knapton Green Herefs............80 B5
Knapwell Cambs..................87 G3
Knaresborough N York...........150 E4
Knarsdale Nthumb...............178 F8
Knaven Abers...................257 G3
Knayton N York.................160 F5
Knebworth Herts.................69 H3
Knedlington E R Yk.............143 J2
Kneesall Notts.................134 D6
Kneeton Notts..................117 J2
Knelston Swans..................56 E7
Knenhall Staffs................114 E4
Knettishall Suffk..............105 K7
Knightacott Devon...............28 B3
Knightcote Warwks...............83 J4
Knightley Staffs...............114 C6
Knightley Dale Staffs..........114 C6
Knighton C Leic................100 D3
Knighton Devon...................7 G5
Knighton Dorset.................31 K8
Knighton Poole.................17 L3
Knighton Powys..................79 K1
Knighton Somset.................30 B2
Knighton Staffs................114 A3
Knighton Staffs................114 B6
Knighton Wilts..................47 L4
Knighton on Teme Worcs.........80 E1
Knightsbridge Gloucs...........64 C2
Knightsmill Cnwll...............10 F6
Knightwick Worcs................81 G4
Knill Herefs....................79 K3
Knipton Leics..................117 L5
Knitsley Dur...................168 E1
Kniveton Derbys................115 K2
Knock Cumb.....................166 F5
Knock Highld...................247 L6
Knock Moray....................267 L5
Knock W Isls...................282 g3
Knockally Highld...............274 F2
Knockan Highld.................271 H6
Knockando Moray................254 D3
Knockbain Highld...............250 F3
Knockbain Highld...............263 H8
Knock Castle N Ayrs............207 K6
Knockdee Highld................279 L4
Knockdow Ag & B................207 J5
Knockdown Wilts.................46 B1
Knockeen S Ayrs................183 H4
Knockenkelly N Ayrs............195 G5
Knockentiber E Ayrs............196 D3
Knockhall Kent..................52 C4
Knockholt Kent..................51 M7
Knockholt Pound Kent...........52 A7
Knockin Shrops.................112 E7
Knockinlaw E Ayrs..............196 E3
Knockmill Kent..................52 C6
Knocknain D & G................172 B2
Knockrome Ag & B...............205 J2
Knocksharry IoM................154 c5
Knocksheen D & G...............184 F6
Knockvennie Smithy D & G.......175 J1
Knodishall Suffk................91 K3
Knodishall Common Suffk.........91 K3
Knole Somset....................31 G6
Knole Park S Glos...............45 H2
Knolls Green Ches E............130 F4
Knolton Wrexhm.................112 F4
Knook Wilts.....................32 F3
Knossington Leics..............101 K2
Knott End-on-Sea Lancs.........147 G6
Knotting Bed....................85 K3
Knotting Green Bed..............85 K3
Knottingley Wakefd.............142 D3

Knotty Ash Lpool 129 J1
Knotty Green Bucks 68 B8
Knowbury Shrops 96 D8
Knowe D & G 183 H8
Knowehead D & G 184 F5
Knoweside S Ayrs 195 L8
Knowle Bristl 45 J5
Knowle Devon 13 H2
Knowle Devon 14 B1
Knowle Devon 14 B6
Knowle Devon 27 J3
Knowle Shrops 96 D8
Knowle Solhll 98 F8
Knowle Somset 29 H2
Knowle Cross Devon 14 B3
Knowlefield Cumb 177 L7
Knowle Green Lancs 148 A8
Knowle Hill Surrey 50 C5
Knowle St Giles Somset 30 E8
Knowle Village Hants 19 J2
Knowle Wood Calder 140 D3
Knowl Green Essex 88 F7
Knowl Hill W & M 49 K3
Knowlton Dorset 17 K1
Knowlton Kent 41 J4
Knowsley Knows 138 E8
Knowstone Devon 28 E6
Knox N York 150 C4
Knox Bridge Kent 39 K5
Knucklas Powys 95 G8
Knuston Nhants 85 H2
Knutsford Ches E 130 E4
Knutton Staffs 114 C2
Krumlin Calder 141 G4
Kuggar Cnwll 3 J7
Kyleakin Highld 248 B6
Kyle of Lochalsh Highld 248 B6
Kylerhea Highld 248 C7
Kylesku Highld 271 H1
Kylesmorar Highld 238 C5
Kyles Scalpay W Isls 282 f6
Kylestrome Highld 271 H1
Kynaston Herefs 80 E8
Kynaston Shrops 112 E7
Kynnersley Wrekin 113 L8
Kyre Green Worcs 80 E3
Kyre Park Worcs 80 E3
Kyrewood Worcs 80 E2
Kyrle Somset 29 J6

L

La Bellieuse Guern 9 j3
Lacasaigh W Isls 282 f4
Lacasdal W Isls 282 g3
Laceby NE Lin 145 G6
Lacey Green Bucks 67 K7
Lach Dennis Ches W 130 D5
Lackenby R & Cl 170 D6
Lackford Suffk 88 F1
Lackford Green Suffk 88 F1
Lacock Wilts 46 C5
Ladbroke Warwks 83 K3
Ladderedge Staffs 114 F1
Laddingford Kent 39 H4
Lade Bank Lincs 119 L1
Ladock Cnwll 4 E5
Lady Ork 275 e2
Ladybank Fife 222 E5
Ladycross Cnwll 11 L5
Ladygill S Lans 198 F7
Lady Hall Cumb 156 B5
Ladykirk Border 202 D3
Ladyridge Herefs 63 H1
Lady's Green Suffk 88 E3
Ladywood Birm 98 D6
Ladywood Worcs 81 K3
La Fontenelle Guern 9 k1
La Fosse Guern 9 j4
Lag D & G 185 L5
Laga Highld 237 J8
Lagavulin Ag & B 204 F7
Lagg N Ayrs 193 K4
Laggan Highld 240 A4
Laggan Highld 241 G5
Lagganlia Highld 241 M3
La Greve Guern 9 k2
La Grève de Lecq Jersey 9 b1
La Hougue Bie Jersey 9 e3
La Houguette Guern 9 h3
Laid Highld 277 G4
Laide Highld 260 E2
Laig Highld 236 F3
Laigh Clunch E Ayrs 196 F2
Laigh Fenwick E Ayrs 196 F3
Laigh Glenmuir E Ayrs 197 J7
Laighstonehall S Lans 209 J8

Laindon Essex 52 E1
Lairg Highld 272 E6
Laisterdyke C Brad 141 J1
Laithes Cumb 166 B4
Lake Devon 12 C5
Lake Devon 27 K4
Lake IoW 19 K7
Lake Wilts 33 K3
Lakenheath Suffk 104 E6
Lakesend Norfk 103 L4
Lakeside Cumb 156 E5
Laleham Surrey 50 D5
Laleston Brdgnd 42 C5
Lamanva Cnwll 3 J5
Lamarsh Essex 89 H8
Lamas Norfk 122 E7
Lambden Border 202 A4
Lamberhurst Kent 39 H6
Lamberhurst Down Kent 39 G6
Lamberton Border 213 L7
Lambeth Gt Lon 51 J3
Lambeth Crematorium Gt Lon .. 51 H4
Lambfair Green Suffk 88 E4
Lambley Notts 117 H2
Lambley Nthumb 178 F7
Lambourn W Berk 47 L3
Lambourne End Essex 70 C8
Lambourn Woodlands W Berk .. 47 L4
Lamb Roe Lancs 148 C8
Lambs Green W Susx 37 K3
Lambston Pembks 54 E3
Lamellion Cnwll 6 A2
Lamerton Devon 12 B7
Lamesley Gatesd 181 G7
Lamington S Lans 199 G7
Lamlash N Ayrs 195 G5
Lamonby Cumb 165 L3
Lamorick Cnwll 5 H2
Lamorna Cnwll 2 C6
Lamorran Cnwll 4 E6
Lampen Cnwll 5 L2
Lampeter Cerdgn 77 G5
Lampeter Velfrey Pembks 55 K4
Lamphey Pembks 55 G6
Lamplugh Cumb 164 E6
Lamport Nhants 101 G8
Lamyatt Somset 31 L4
Lana Devon 11 K1
Lana Devon 11 L3
Lanark S Lans 198 E4
Lancaster Lancs 147 J3
Lancaster & Morecambe
    Crematorium Lancs 147 J3
Lancaut Gloucs 63 G7
Lanchester Dur 168 F1
Lancing W Susx 21 L6
L'Ancresse Guern 9 k1
Landbeach Cambs 87 K2
Landcross Devon 27 H6
Landerberry Abers 245 G3
Landford Wilts 34 B7
Land-hallow Highld 275 G2
Landican Crematorium Wirral .. 129 G3
Landimore Swans 56 E6
Landkey Devon 27 L4
Landore Swans 57 J5
Landrake Cnwll 6 D3
Landscove Devon 7 M2
Land's End Cnwll 2 A6
Landshipping Pembks 55 G4
Landue Cnwll 11 L6
Landulph Cnwll 6 E3
Landwade Suffk 88 C2
Lane Cnwll 4 D3
Laneast Cnwll 11 J6
Lane Bottom Lancs 140 C1
Lane End Bucks 49 K1
Lane End Cnwll 5 H1
Lane End Hants 35 H5
Lane End Kent 52 C4
Lane End Lancs 148 F6
Lane End Warrtn 130 D2
Lane End Wilts 32 D2
Lane Ends Derbys 115 L4
Lane Ends Lancs 140 B2
Lane Ends N York 149 H7
Lane Green Staffs 97 K3
Laneham Notts 134 F4
Lanehead Dur 167 J2
Lane Head Dur 168 E8
Lanehead Nthumb 179 H2
Lane Head Wigan 139 J8
Lane Head Wsall 98 B3
Lane Heads Lancs 147 H7
Laneshaw Bridge Lancs 149 G7
Lane Side Lancs 140 B3
Langaford Devon 12 A3
Langaller Somset 30 C5

Langar Notts 117 J4
Langbank Rens 208 C4
Langbar N York 149 K5
Langbaurgh N York 170 D8
Langcliffe N York 148 E3
Langdale End N York 163 G4
Langdon Cnwll 11 K5
Langdon Beck Dur 167 K4
Langdown Hants 19 G2
Langdyke Fife 222 E6
Langenhoe Essex 72 E3
Langford C Beds 86 D7
Langford Devon 14 B2
Langford Essex 71 K5
Langford N Som 44 F6
Langford Notts 135 G7
Langford Oxon 65 K6
Langford Budville Somset 29 K6
Langham Dorset 32 C5
Langham Essex 72 F1
Langham Norfk 121 M3
Langham Rutlnd 101 J1
Langham Suffk 89 K1
Langho Lancs 139 L1
Langholm D & G 177 L2
Langland Swans 57 H7
Langlee Border 201 G6
Langley Ches E 131 J5
Langley Derbys 116 D2
Langley Gloucs 64 E2
Langley Hants 19 G3
Langley Herts 69 G3
Langley Kent 39 K3
Langley Nthumb 179 J6
Langley Oxon 65 L4
Langley Rochdl 140 C6
Langley Slough 50 C3
Langley Somset 29 K5
Langley W Susx 36 B5
Langley Warwks 82 E3
Langley Burrell Wilts 46 D4
Langley Castle Nthumb 179 J6
Langley Common Derbys 115 M4
Langley Green Derbys 115 M4
Langley Green Essex 72 C3
Langley Green Warwks 82 E3
Langley Lower Green Essex 87 J8
Langley Marsh Somset 29 K5
Langley Mill Derbys 116 D2
Langley Moor Dur 169 H3
Langley Park Dur 169 G2
Langley Street Norfk 107 H3
Langley Upper Green Essex ... 87 J8
Langney E Susx 23 L6
Langold Notts 134 B2
Langore Cnwll 11 K5
Langport Somset 30 F5
Langrick Lincs 119 J2
Langridge BaNES 45 L5
Langridgeford Devon 27 K6
Langrigg Cumb 165 G2
Langrish Hants 35 L6
Langsett Barns 141 K7
Langside P & K 220 D4
Langstone Hants 20 B6
Langstone Newpt 44 D1
Langthorne N York 160 C4
Langthorpe N York 150 E2
Langthwaite N York 159 H2
Langtoft E R Yk 152 F3
Langtoft Lincs 102 C1
Langton Dur 168 F6
Langton Lincs 136 D6
Langton Lincs 137 G5
Langton N York 152 B2
Langton by Wragby Lincs 136 C4
Langton Green Kent 38 E5
Langton Green Suffk 106 C8
Langton Herring Dorset 16 B6
Langton Long Blandford
    Dorset 17 H2
Langton Matravers Dorset 17 K6
Langtree Devon 27 H7
Langtree Week Devon 27 H7
Langwathby Cumb 166 D4
Langwell House Highld 274 F3
Langwith Derbys 133 K5
Langwith Junction Derbys ... 133 K6
Langworth Lincs 135 L4
Lanivet Cnwll 5 H2
Lanjeth Cnwll 5 G4
Lank Cnwll 10 F7
Lanlivery Cnwll 5 J3
Lanner Cnwll 3 J3
Lanoy Cnwll 11 K7
Lanreath Cnwll 5 L3
Lansallos Cnwll 5 K4
Lanteglos Cnwll 10 F6
Lanteglos Highway Cnwll 5 K4

Lanton Border 189 G7
Lanton Nthumb 202 E4
La Passee Guern 9 j1
Lapford Devon 13 G2
Laphroaig Ag & B 204 F7
Lapley Staffs 97 K1
La Pulente Jersey 9 a3
Lapworth Warwks 82 E8
Larachbeg Highld 227 K2
Larbert Falk 209 M8
Larbreck Lancs 147 H7
Largie Abers 256 C7
Largiemore Ag & B 206 F2
Largoward Fife 223 G5
Largs N Ayrs 207 K7
Largybeg N Ayrs 195 G6
Largymore N Ayrs 195 G6
Larkbeare Devon 14 C3
Larkfield Inver 207 L5
Larkfield Kent 52 F7
Larkhall S Lans 198 C4
Larkhill Wilts 33 K2
Larling Norfk 105 L4
La Rocque Jersey 9 e4
La Rousaillerie Guern 9 j2
Lartington Dur 168 C7
Lasborough Gloucs 64 E8
Lasham Hants 35 J3
Lashbrook Devon 12 A3
Lashbrook Devon 12 B1
Lashenden Kent 39 J4
Lask Edge Staffs 131 H8
Lassodie Fife 221 G8
Lasswade Mdloth 211 J7
Lastingham N York 162 C6
Latcham Somset 31 G2
Latchford Herts 69 K3
Latchford Oxon 67 G6
Latchford Warrtn 130 B1
Latchingdon Essex 72 E6
Latchley Cnwll 12 A8
Lately Common Warrtn 139 L7
Lathbury M Keyn 85 J6
Latheron Highld 275 H5
Latheronwheel Highld 275 H5
Lathones Fife 223 H5
Latimer Bucks 68 E7
Latteridge S Glos 45 K2
Lattiford Somset 32 B5
Latton Wilts 65 G7
Lauder Border 201 J3
Laugharne Carmth 56 C4
Laughterton Lincs 135 G4
Laughton E Susx 23 H6
Laughton Leics 100 E5
Laughton Lincs 118 D3
Laughton Lincs 143 J7
Laughton-en-le-Morthen
    Rothm 133 K2
Launcells Cnwll 11 J2
Launcells Cross Cnwll 11 J2
Launceston Cnwll 11 L7
Launton Oxon 66 E3
Laurencekirk Abers 235 K2
Laurieston D & G 175 G3
Laurieston Falk 210 C4
Lavendon M Keyn 85 J4
Lavenham Suffk 89 J5
Lavernock V Glam 43 J7
Laversdale Cumb 178 C6
Laverstock Wilts 33 K4
Laverstoke Hants 35 G1
Laverton Gloucs 82 B8
Laverton N York 160 B8
Laverton Somset 45 L8
La Villette Guern 9 i3
Lavister Wrexhm 129 K8
Law S Lans 209 M7
Lawers P & K 231 J8
Lawford Essex 73 H1
Lawford Somset 29 K4
Law Hill S Lans 209 M7
Lawhitton Cnwll 11 L7
Lawkland N York 148 E2
Lawkland Green N York 148 E2
Lawley Wrekin 96 F2
Lawnhead Staffs 114 D6
Lawns Wood Crematorium
    Leeds 150 F7
Lawrenny Pembks 55 H5
Lawshall Suffk 89 H4
Lawshall Green Suffk 89 H4
Lawton Herefs 80 C3
Laxay W Isls 282 f4
Laxdale W Isls 282 g3
Laxey IoM 154 e5
Laxfield Suffk 91 G1
Laxford Bridge Highld 276 D4
Laxo Shet 281 e4
Laxton E R Yk 143 J2

Laxton Nhants 101 L4
Laxton Notts 134 E6
Laycock C Brad 149 J7
Layer Breton Essex 72 D3
Layer-de-la-Haye Essex 72 D3
Layer Marney Essex 72 C4
Layham Suffk 89 L7
Layland's Green W Berk 48 A5
Laymore Dorset 15 J2
Layter's Green Bucks 50 C1
Laytham E R Yk 152 A7
Laythes Cumb 177 H7
Lazenby R & Cl 170 D6
Lazonby Cumb 166 D3
Lea Derbys 132 F8
Lea Herefs 63 K3
Lea Lincs 135 G2
Lea Shrops 95 J5
Lea Shrops 95 K2
Lea Wilts 46 D2
Leachkin Highld 251 H3
Leadburn Border 200 B2
Leadenham Lincs 118 B1
Leaden Roding Essex 70 E4
Leadgate Dur 180 D8
Leadgate Nthumb 180 D7
Leadhills S Lans 186 C3
Leadingcross Green Kent 39 M3
Leadmill Derbys 132 E4
Leafield Oxon 65 L4
Leagrave Luton 68 D2
Leahead Ches W 130 D6
Lea Heath Staffs 115 G6
Leake N York 160 F4
Leake Common Side Lincs 119 L1
Lealholm N York 162 D1
Lealholm Side N York 162 D1
Lealt Highld 259 H4
Leam Derbys 132 E4
Lea Marston Warwks 99 G5
Leamington Hastings Warwks 83 K2
Leamington Spa Warwks 83 H2
Leamside Dur 169 J1
Leap Cross E Susx 23 K5
Leasgill Cumb 157 H6
Leasingham Lincs 118 E2
Leasingthorne Dur 169 H4
Leatherhead Surrey 50 F7
Leathley N York 150 B6
Leaton Shrops 113 G7
Leaton Wrekin 96 E1
Lea Town Lancs 138 F2
Leaveland Kent 40 C4
Leavenheath Suffk 89 J7
Leavening N York 152 B3
Leaves Green Gt Lon 51 L6
Lea Yeat Cumb 158 D5
Lebberston N York 163 K6
Le Bigard Guern 9 i4
Le Bourg Guern 9 j4
Le Bourg Jersey 9 f4
Lechlade on Thames Gloucs 65 J7
Leck Lancs 157 K7
Leckbuie P & K 231 K7
Leckford Hants 34 E3
Leckhampstead Bucks 84 D7
Leckhampstead W Berk 48 B4
Leckhampstead Thicket
  W Berk 48 B4
Leckhampton Gloucs 64 D3
Leckmelm Highld 261 K2
Leckwith V Glam 43 J6
Leconfield E R Yk 152 F7
Ledaig Ag & B 228 G4
Ledburn Bucks 67 L3
Ledbury Herefs 81 G7
Leddington Gloucs 80 F8
Ledgemoor Herefs 80 A5
Ledicot Herefs 80 A3
Ledmore Junction Highld 271 H5
Ledsham Ches W 129 H5
Ledsham Leeds 142 C2
Ledston Leeds 142 C2
Ledstone Devon 7 L5
Ledston Luck Leeds 142 C2
Ledwell Oxon 66 B2
Lee Devon 27 H2
Lee Gt Lon 51 K4
Lee Hants 34 D7
Lee Shrops 112 F5
Leebotwood Shrops 96 B4
Lee Brockhurst Shrops 113 J6
Leece Cumb 146 E2
Lee Chapel Essex 52 E2
Lee Clump Bucks 67 M6
Lee Common Bucks 67 M6
Leeds Kent 39 K3
Leeds Leeds 141 L1

Leedstown Cnwll 2 F4
Lee Green Ches E 130 C7
Leek Staffs 131 K8
Leek Wootton Warwks 83 G2
Lee Mill Devon 7 H4
Leeming C Brad 141 G1
Leeming N York 160 D5
Leeming Bar N York 160 D4
Lee Moor Devon 7 H3
Lee-on-the-Solent Hants 19 J3
Lees C Brad 149 J8
Lees Derbys 115 L4
Lees Oldham 140 E6
Lees Green Derbys 115 L4
Leesthorpe Leics 101 H1
Lee Street Surrey 37 L2
Leeswood Flints 129 G7
Leetown P & K 222 C3
Leftwich Ches W 130 C5
Legar Powys 61 K4
Legbourne Lincs 137 G2
Legburthwaite Cumb 165 K6
Legerwood Border 201 J4
Le Gron Guern 9 i3
Legsby Lincs 136 B3
Le Haguais Jersey 9 e4
Le Hocq Jersey 9 e4
Leicester C Leic 100 D3
Leicester Forest East Leics 100 B3
Leigh Devon 28 C8
Leigh Dorset 16 B1
Leigh Gloucs 64 C2
Leigh Kent 38 E4
Leigh Shrops 95 H3
Leigh Surrey 37 K2
Leigh Wigan 139 K7
Leigh Wilts 64 F8
Leigh Worcs 81 H4
Leigh Beck Essex 53 H2
Leigh Delamere Wilts 46 C3
Leigh Green Kent 40 A8
Leigh Knoweglass S Lans 197 J1
Leighland Chapel Somset 29 J4
Leigh-on-Sea Sthend 53 H2
Leigh Park Dorset 17 K3
Leigh Park Hants 20 B5
Leigh Sinton Worcs 81 H5
Leighswood Wsall 98 D3
Leighterton Gloucs 46 B1
Leighton N York 159 L6
Leighton Powys 94 F2
Leighton Shrops 96 E2
Leighton Somset 32 B2
Leighton Bromswold Cambs 102 C8
Leighton Buzzard C Beds 68 A2
Leigh upon Mendip Somset 31 M2
Leigh Woods N Som 45 H4
Leinthall Earls Herefs 80 B2
Leinthall Starkes Herefs 80 A1
Leintwardine Herefs 95 K8
Leire Leics 100 B5
Leiston Suffk 91 K3
Leith C Edin 211 J4
Leitholm Border 202 B4
Lelant Cnwll 2 E4
Lelley E R Yk 145 G1
Lem Hill Worcs 97 G8
Lempitlaw Border 202 B6
Lemreway W Isls 282 g5
Lemsford Herts 69 G4
Lenchwick Worcs 82 B6
Lendalfoot S Ayrs 182 E5
Lendrick Stirlg 219 J6
Lendrum Terrace Abers 257 L3
Lenham Kent 40 A4
Lenham Heath Kent 40 B5
Lenie Highld 250 F6
Lennel Border 202 C5
Lennox Plunton D & G 174 F4
Lennoxtown E Duns 209 G3
Lent Bucks 50 A3
Lenton C Nott 116 F4
Lenton Lincs 118 D5
Lenwade Norfk 122 B7
Lenzie E Duns 209 H4
Leochel-Cushnie Abers 244 C2
Leomansley Staffs 98 D2
Leominster Herefs 80 C3
Leonard Stanley Gloucs 64 A6
Leoville Jersey 9 b1
Lepe Hants 19 G4
Lephin Highld 258 B6
Leppington N York 152 A4
Lepton Kirk 141 K5
Lerags Ag & B 216 C2
L'Erée Guern 9 h3
Lerryn Cnwll 5 K3
Lerwick Shet 281 e6
Les Arquêts Guern 9 h3

Lesbury Nthumb 191 J4
Les Hubits Guern 9 k3
Leslie Abers 255 M6
Leslie Fife 222 D6
Les Lohiers Guern 9 i3
Lesmahagow S Lans 198 D5
Les Murchez Guern 9 i4
Lesnewth Cnwll 11 G4
Les Nicolles Guern 9 j4
Les Quartiers Guern 9 j2
Les Quennevais Jersey 9 b3
Les Sages Guern 9 i3
Lessingham Norfk 123 H6
Lessonhall Cumb 165 H1
Lestowder Cnwll 3 K6
Les Villets Guern 9 i4
Leswalt D & G 172 C2
L'Etacq Jersey 9 a2
Letchmore Heath Herts 68 F7
Letchworth Garden City Herts 86 E8
Letcombe Bassett Oxon 48 A2
Letcombe Regis Oxon 48 A2
Letham Angus 234 E5
Letham Border 189 J4
Letham Falk 210 B2
Letham Fife 222 E4
Letham Grange Angus 235 G6
Lethendy P & K 233 H7
Lethenty Abers 255 M7
Lethenty Abers 256 E4
Letheringham Suffk 91 G4
Letheringsett Norfk 122 B4
Lettaford Devon 13 G6
Letterewe Highld 260 F5
Letterfearn Highld 248 D7
Letterfinlay Lodge Hotel
  Highld 239 L5
Lettermorar Highld 237 L3
Letters Highld 261 K2
Lettershaw S Lans 186 D2
Letterston Pembks 74 F6
Lettoch Highld 253 K7
Lettoch Highld 254 B5
Letton Herefs 79 L1
Letton Herefs 79 L6
Lett's Green Kent 51 M7
Letty Green Herts 69 H5
Letwell Rothm 133 L2
Leuchars Fife 223 H3
Leumrabhagh W Isls 282 g5
Leurbost W Isls 282 g4
Levalsa Meor Cnwll 5 G5
Levedale Staffs 114 D8
Leven E R Yk 153 H6
Leven Fife 222 F7
Levens Cumb 157 G5
Levens Green Herts 69 K3
Levenshulme Manch 131 G1
Levenwick Shet 281 d8
Leverburgh W Isls 282 d6
Leverington Cambs 103 J1
Leverstock Green Herts 68 D5
Leverton Lincs 119 L2
Le Villocq Guern 9 j2
Levington Suffk 90 F7
Levisham N York 162 E4
Lew Oxon 65 L6
Lewannick Cnwll 11 K6
Lewdown Devon 12 B5
Lewes E Susx 22 F5
Leweston Pembks 54 F2
Lewisham Gt Lon 51 K4
Lewisham Crematorium
  Gt Lon 51 L4
Lewiston Highld 250 F6
Lewistown Brdgnd 42 E4
Lewis Wych Herefs 79 L4
Lewknor Oxon 67 H7
Leworthy Devon 11 L2
Leworthy Devon 28 B3
Lewson Street Kent 40 C3
Lewth Lancs 147 J3
Lewtrenchard Devon 12 B5
Lexden Essex 72 D2
Lexworthy Somset 30 C4
Ley Cnwll 5 K2
Leybourne Kent 52 E7
Leyburn N York 159 K4
Leycett Staffs 114 B2
Leygreen Herts 68 F2
Ley Hill Bucks 68 C6
Leyland Lancs 139 H3
Leyland Green St Hel 139 H7
Leylodge Abers 245 G1
Leys Abers 269 J5
Leys P & K 233 K7
Leysdown-on-Sea Kent 53 M5
Leysmill Angus 234 F6

Leys of Cossans Angus 234 B5
Leysters Herefs 80 D2
Leyton Gt Lon 51 K2
Leytonstone Gt Lon 51 K2
Lezant Cnwll 11 L6
Lezerea Cnwll 3 H4
Lhanbryde Moray 266 F4
Libanus Powys 60 F2
Libberton S Lans 199 G4
Liberton C Edin 211 J5
Lichfield Staffs 98 E2
Lichfield & District
  Crematorium Staffs 98 F1
Lickey Worcs 98 C8
Lickey End Worcs 81 M1
Lickey Rock Worcs 98 B8
Lickfold W Susx 36 D5
Liddaton Green Devon 12 B6
Liddesdale Highld 228 B3
Liddington Swindn 47 J3
Lidgate Derbys 132 F4
Lidgate Suffk 88 E4
Lidget Donc 143 G7
Lidgett Notts 134 C6
Lidham Hill E Susx 24 F4
Lidlington C Beds 85 K7
Lidsey W Susx 20 F6
Lidsing Kent 53 G6
Liff Angus 222 E1
Lifford Birm 98 D7
Lifton Devon 11 M5
Liftondown Devon 11 M5
Lighthorne Warwks 83 H4
Lighthorne Heath Warwks 83 H4
Lightwater Surrey 50 B6
Lightwood C Stke 114 E3
Lightwood Green Ches E 113 L3
Lightwood Green Wrexhm 112 F3
Lilbourne Nhants 100 C8
Lilburn Tower Nthumb 190 E1
Lilleshall Wrekin 114 A8
Lilley Herts 68 E2
Lilley W Berk 48 C3
Lilliesleaf Border 201 H8
Lillingstone Dayrell Bucks 84 D7
Lillingstone Lovell Bucks 84 D7
Lillington Dorset 31 K8
Lilliput Poole 17 K5
Lilstock Somset 29 L2
Lilyhurst Shrops 97 G1
Limbrick Lancs 139 J4
Limbury Luton 68 D2
Limebrook Herefs 79 L2
Limefield Bury 140 B5
Limekilnburn S Lans 197 K1
Limekilns Fife 210 E2
Limerigg Falk 209 M5
Limerstone IoW 19 G7
Limestone Brae Nthumb 167 J1
Lime Street Worcs 64 A1
Limington Somset 31 J6
Limmerhaugh E Ayrs 197 J5
Limpenhoe Norfk 107 H3
Limpley Stoke Wilts 45 M6
Limpsfield Surrey 51 L8
Limpsfield Chart Surrey 51 L8
Linby Notts 116 F1
Linchmere W Susx 36 C5
Lincluden D & G 176 C3
Lincoln Lincs 135 K5
Lincoln Crematorium Lincs 135 K5
Lincomb Worcs 81 J2
Lincombe Devon 7 L6
Lincombe Devon 27 J2
Lindale Cumb 156 F6
Lindal in Furness Cumb 156 C7
Lindfield W Susx 22 E2
Lindford Hants 36 B4
Lindley Kirk 141 H4
Lindley N York 150 B6
Lindores Fife 222 D4
Lindow End Ches E 130 F4
Lindridge Worcs 80 F2
Lindsell Essex 70 F2
Lindsey Suffk 89 K6
Lindsey Tye Suffk 89 K6
Liney Somset 30 L4
Linford Hants 18 B2
Linford Thurr 52 E3
Lingbob C Brad 149 K8
Lingdale R & Cl 170 F7
Lingen Herefs 79 L2
Lingfield Surrey 38 B4
Lingwood Norfk 107 G2
Linicro Highld 258 F3
Linkend Worcs 64 B1
Linkenholt Hants 48 A7
Linkhill Kent 24 E2
Linkinhorne Cnwll 11 L7

Place	County	Page	Grid
Linktown	Fife	211	J1
Linkwood	Moray	266	E4
Linley	Shrops	95	J5
Linley Green	Herefs	80	F4
Linleygreen	Shrops	96	F4
Linlithgow	W Loth	210	C4
Linn Crematorium	E Rens	209	G7
Linshiels	Nthumb	190	C5
Linsidemore	Highld	272	D8
Linslade	C Beds	67	M2
Linstead Parva	Suffk	107	G7
Linstock	Cumb	178	A7
Linthurst	Worcs	82	B1
Linthwaite	Kirk	141	H5
Lintlaw	Border	213	H7
Lintmill	Moray	267	K3
Linton	Border	202	B7
Linton	Cambs	88	B6
Linton	Derbys	115	M8
Linton	Herefs	63	K2
Linton	Kent	39	J3
Linton	Leeds	150	E6
Linton	N York	149	H3
Linton	Nthumb	191	M4
Linton Heath	Derbys	115	M8
Linton Hill	Herefs	63	K2
Linton-on-Ouse	N York	151	G4
Linwood	Hants	18	B2
Linwood	Lincs	136	B2
Linwood	Rens	208	D6
Lionacleit	W Isls	283	c9
Lional	W Isls	282	h1
Lions Green	E Susx	23	J4
Liphook	Hants	36	C4
Lipley	Shrops	114	A5
Liscard	Wirral	129	G1
Liscombe	Somset	28	F4
Liskeard	Cnwll	6	D2
Lismore	Ag & B	228	C7
Liss	Hants	36	A5
Lissett	E R Yk	153	J4
Liss Forest	Hants	36	A5
Lissington	Lincs	136	B3
Liston	Essex	89	G6
Lisvane	Cardif	43	J5
Liswerry	Newpt	44	D2
Litcham	Norfk	121	J8
Litchard	Brdgnd	42	D5
Litchborough	Nhants	84	C4
Litchfield	Hants	48	C8
Litherland	Sefton	138	D8
Litlington	Cambs	87	G6
Litlington	E Susx	23	J7
Little Abington	Cambs	87	L5
Little Addington	Nhants	101	L8
Little Airies	D & G	173	K5
Little Almshoe	Herts	69	G2
Little Alne	Warwks	82	D3
Little Altcar	Sefton	138	C6
Little Amwell	Herts	69	K5
Little Asby	Cumb	158	B1
Little Aston	Staffs	98	E3
Little Atherfield	IoW	19	G7
Little Ayton	N York	170	D8
Little Baddow	Essex	71	J5
Little Badminton	S Glos	46	A2
Little Bampton	Cumb	177	J7
Little Bardfield	Essex	71	G1
Little Barford	Bed	86	D4
Little Barningham	Norfk	122	C5
Little Barrington	Gloucs	65	J4
Little Barrow	Ches W	129	L5
Little Barugh	N York	162	D6
Little Bavington	Nthumb	180	B3
Little Bealings	Suffk	90	F5
Littlebeck	N York	162	F6
Little Bedwyn	Wilts	47	L5
Little Bentley	Essex	73	G2
Little Berkhamsted	Herts	69	H5
Little Billing	Nhants	84	F3
Little Billington	C Beds	68	B3
Little Birch	Herefs	63	G1
Little Bispham	Bpool	146	F7
Little Blakenham	Suffk	90	C5
Little Blencow	Cumb	166	B4
Little Bloxwich	Wsall	98	C3
Little Bognor	W Susx	21	G3
Little Bolehill	Derbys	116	A1
Little Bollington	Ches E	130	E2
Little Bookham	Surrey	50	E8
Littleborough	Devon	28	E8
Littleborough	Notts	135	G3
Littleborough	Rochdl	140	E4
Littlebourne	Kent	41	G4
Little Bourton	Oxon	83	K6
Little Bowden	Leics	101	G6
Little Bradley	Suffk	88	D5
Little Brampton	Herefs	79	K3
Little Brampton	Shrops	95	J7
Little Braxted	Essex	71	K4
Little Brechin	Angus	234	F3
Littlebredy	Dorset	16	B5
Little Brickhill	M Keyn	67	L1
Little Bridgeford	Staffs	114	D6
Little Brington	Nhants	84	C3
Little Bromley	Essex	73	G2
Little Broughton	Cumb	164	E4
Little Budworth	Ches W	130	B6
Littleburn	Highld	251	H1
Little Burstead	Essex	71	G8
Littlebury	Essex	87	L7
Littlebury Green	Essex	87	K7
Little Bytham	Lincs	118	D7
Little Canfield	Essex	70	E3
Little Carlton	Lincs	137	G3
Little Carlton	Notts	134	F8
Little Casterton	Rutlnd	101	M2
Little Catwick	E R Yk	153	H6
Little Catworth	Cambs	86	B1
Little Cawthorpe	Lincs	137	G3
Little Chalfont	Bucks	68	C7
Little Chart	Kent	40	B6
Little Chesterford	Essex	87	L7
Little Cheveney	Kent	39	H4
Little Cheverell	Wilts	46	E8
Little Chishill	Cambs	87	J7
Little Clacton	Essex	73	H3
Little Clanfield	Oxon	65	K6
Little Clifton	Cumb	164	E5
Little Coates	NE Lin	145	H6
Little Comberton	Worcs	81	M6
Little Common	E Susx	24	C5
Little Comp	Kent	39	G2
Little Compton	Warwks	65	K1
Little Cornard	Suffk	89	H7
Littlecott	Wilts	47	H8
Little Cowarne	Herefs	80	E5
Little Coxwell	Oxon	65	L8
Little Crakehall	N York	160	C4
Little Cransley	Nhants	101	H8
Little Cressingham	Norfk	105	H3
Little Crosby	Sefton	138	C7
Little Crosthwaite	Cumb	165	H5
Little Cubley	Derbys	115	J4
Little Dalby	Leics	117	K8
Littledean	Gloucs	63	K4
Little Dewchurch	Herefs	63	G1
Little Ditton	Cambs	88	D3
Little Doward	Herefs	63	G4
Littledown	Hants	47	M7
Little Downham	Cambs	103	L6
Little Driffield	E R Yk	152	F4
Little Dunham	Norfk	105	H1
Little Dunkeld	P & K	232	F7
Little Dunmow	Essex	71	G3
Little Durnford	Wilts	33	K4
Little Easton	Essex	70	F2
Little Eaton	Derbys	116	B3
Little Ellingham	Norfk	105	K3
Little Elm	Somset	32	B2
Little Everdon	Nhants	84	B4
Little Eversden	Cambs	87	H4
Little Faringdon	Oxon	65	J6
Little Fencote	N York	160	D4
Little Fenton	N York	142	E1
Little Fransham	Norfk	105	H1
Little Gaddesden	Herts	68	C4
Little Garway	Herefs	62	F2
Little Gidding	Cambs	102	C7
Little Glemham	Suffk	91	H4
Little Gorsley	Herefs	63	K2
Little Gransden	Cambs	86	F4
Little Green	Notts	117	J3
Little Green	Somset	32	B1
Little Grimsby	Lincs	136	F2
Little Gringley	Notts	134	E3
Little Habton	N York	162	C7
Little Hadham	Herts	70	B3
Little Hale	Lincs	118	F3
Little Hallam	Derbys	116	D3
Little Hallingbury	Essex	70	D4
Littleham	Devon	14	B6
Littleham	Devon	27	H6
Little Hampden	Bucks	67	L6
Littlehampton	W Susx	21	H6
Little Hanford	Dorset	32	D8
Little Harrowden	Nhants	85	G1
Little Haseley	Oxon	66	F7
Little Hatfield	E R Yk	153	J7
Little Hautbois	Norfk	122	E7
Little Haven	Pembks	54	D4
Littlehaven	W Susx	37	J4
Little Hay	Staffs	98	E3
Little Hayfield	Derbys	131	K2
Little Haywood	Staffs	115	G7
Little Heath	Staffs	114	D8
Little Heath	W Berk	49	G4
Littlehempston	Devon	8	B2
Little Hereford	Herefs	80	D2
Little Horkesley	Essex	72	D1
Little Hormead	Herts	69	L2
Little Horsted	E Susx	23	G4
Little Horton	C Brad	141	J2
Little Horton	Wilts	46	F6
Little Horwood	Bucks	67	J1
Little Houghton	Barns	142	C6
Little Houghton	Nhants	84	F3
Littlehoughton	Nthumb	191	J3
Little Hucklow	Derbys	132	C4
Little Hulton	Salfd	139	L7
Little Hungerford	W Berk	48	D4
Little Hutton	N York	161	G7
Little Irchester	Nhants	85	H2
Little Kelk	E R Yk	153	H4
Little Keyford	Somset	32	C2
Little Kimble	Bucks	67	K5
Little Kineton	Warwks	83	H5
Little Kingshill	Bucks	67	L7
Little Knox	D & G	175	K3
Little Langdale	Cumb	156	D2
Little Langford	Wilts	33	H4
Little Laver	Essex	70	E5
Little Leigh	Ches W	130	B4
Little Leighs	Essex	71	H4
Little Lever	Bolton	139	M6
Little Linford	M Keyn	85	G6
Little Load	Somset	31	G6
Little London	Bucks	66	F4
Little London	Cambs	103	J4
Little London	E Susx	23	J3
Little London	Essex	70	C1
Little London	Essex	88	D8
Little London	Gloucs	63	L3
Little London	Hants	34	E1
Little London	Hants	48	F7
Little London	Leeds	150	B7
Little London	Lincs	119	H7
Little London	Lincs	119	M6
Little London	Lincs	136	F5
Little London	Norfk	120	C7
Little London	Powys	94	C5
Little Longstone	Derbys	132	D5
Little Madeley	Staffs	114	B3
Little Malvern	Worcs	81	H7
Little Mancot	Flints	129	H6
Little Maplestead	Essex	89	G8
Little Marcle	Herefs	80	F7
Little Marland	Devon	27	J8
Little Marlow	Bucks	49	L2
Little Massingham	Norfk	121	H6
Little Melton	Norfk	106	D2
Littlemill	Abers	243	K4
Littlemill	Highld	253	H2
Little Mill	Mons	62	C6
Little Milton	Oxon	66	F7
Little Missenden	Bucks	68	A7
Little Mongeham	Kent	41	K5
Littlemoor	Derbys	133	G7
Little Moor	Somset	30	D4
Littlemore	Oxon	66	D6
Little Musgrave	Cumb	167	H8
Little Ness	Shrops	112	F7
Little Neston	Ches W	129	G4
Little Newcastle	Pembks	75	G6
Little Newsham	Dur	168	E7
Little Norton	Somset	31	G7
Little Oakley	Essex	73	J1
Little Oakley	Nhants	101	K6
Little Odell	Bed	85	J4
Little Offley	Herts	68	E2
Little Ormside	Cumb	167	G3
Little Orton	Cumb	177	K7
Little Ouse	Cambs	104	C5
Little Ouseburn	N York	150	F4
Littleover	C Derb	116	B5
Little Oxendon	Nhants	100	F6
Little Packington	Warwks	99	G6
Little Pattenden	Kent	39	J4
Little Paxton	Cambs	86	D3
Little Petherick	Cnwll	10	C8
Little Plumpton	Lancs	138	D1
Little Plumstead	Norfk	107	G1
Little Ponton	Lincs	118	B5
Littleport	Cambs	104	B6
Littleport Bridge	Cambs	104	B6
Little Posbrook	Hants	19	J3
Little Potheridge	Devon	27	J8
Little Preston	Leeds	142	B2
Little Preston	Nhants	84	B4
Littler	Ches W	130	C6
Little Raveley	Cambs	102	E7
Little Reedness	E R Yk	143	K3
Little Ribston	N York	150	E5
Little Rissington	Gloucs	65	J3
Little Rollright	Oxon	65	L1
Little Rowsley	Derbys	132	E6
Little Ryburgh	Norfk	121	L6
Little Ryle	Nthumb	190	E6
Little Ryton	Shrops	96	B3
Little Salkeld	Cumb	166	D3
Little Sampford	Essex	88	C3
Little Sandhurst	Br For	49	K6
Little Saredon	Staffs	97	L2
Little Saughall	Ches W	129	J6
Little Saxham	Suffk	88	F3
Little Scatwell	Highld	262	C8
Little Shelford	Cambs	87	J5
Little Shrewley	Warwks	82	F2
Little Silver	Devon	13	L1
Little Singleton	Lancs	147	G7
Little Skipwith	N York	151	K8
Little Smeaton	N York	142	E4
Little Snoring	Norfk	121	L5
Little Sodbury	S Glos	45	M2
Little Sodbury End	S Glos	45	L2
Little Somborne	Hants	34	E4
Little Somerford	Wilts	46	D2
Little Soudley	Shrops	114	A6
Little Stainforth	N York	148	E2
Little Stainton	Darltn	169	K6
Little Stanion	Nhants	101	K6
Little Stanney	Ches W	129	J5
Little Staughton	Bed	86	B3
Little Steeping	Lincs	137	H7
Little Stoke	Staffs	114	E5
Little Stonham	Suffk	90	D3
Little Stretton	Leics	100	E3
Little Stretton	Shrops	95	K5
Little Strickland	Cumb	166	D6
Little Stukeley	Cambs	102	E8
Little Sugnall	Staffs	114	C5
Little Sutton	Ches W	129	J4
Little Sutton	Shrops	96	C6
Little Swinburne	Nthumb	179	M3
Little Sypland	D & G	175	H4
Little Tew	Oxon	66	A2
Little Tey	Essex	72	C2
Little Thetford	Cambs	103	L8
Little Thirkleby	N York	161	G7
Little Thornage	Norfk	122	B4
Little Thornton	Lancs	147	G2
Little Thorpe	Dur	169	L2
Littlethorpe	Leics	100	C4
Littlethorpe	N York	150	D2
Little Thurlow	Suffk	88	D5
Little Thurlow Green	Suffk	88	D5
Little Thurrock	Thurr	52	D3
Littleton	Angus	233	M5
Littleton	BaNES	45	H6
Littleton	Ches W	129	K6
Littleton	D & G	175	G4
Littleton	Dorset	17	H2
Littleton	Hants	34	F4
Littleton	Somset	31	H5
Littleton	Surrey	36	E2
Littleton	Surrey	50	D5
Littleton Drew	Wilts	46	B3
Littleton-on-Severn	S Glos	45	H1
Littleton Pannell	Wilts	46	E8
Little Torrington	Devon	27	J7
Little Totham	Essex	72	C5
Little Town	Cumb	165	H6
Littletown	Dur	169	J2
Little Town	Lancs	148	B8
Little Town	Warrtn	130	C1
Little Twycross	Leics	99	J2
Little Urswick	Cumb	156	C7
Little Wakering	Essex	53	K1
Little Walden	Essex	87	L7
Little Waldingfield	Suffk	89	J6
Little Walsingham	Norfk	121	K4
Little Waltham	Essex	71	H4
Little Warley	Essex	52	D1
Little Washbourne	Gloucs	82	A8
Little Weighton	E R Yk	144	B1
Little Welnetham	Suffk	89	H3
Little Welton	Lincs	136	F2
Little Wenham	Suffk	90	C7
Little Wenlock	Wrekin	96	E2
Little Weston	Somset	31	K5
Little Whitefield	IoW	19	K5
Little Whittingham Green	Suffk	106	F8
Little Whittington	Nthumb	180	B5
Littlewick Green	W & M	49	K5
Little Wilbraham	Cambs	87	L3
Littlewindsor	Dorset	15	K2
Little Witcombe	Gloucs	64	C4
Little Witley	Worcs	81	H3
Little Wittenham	Oxon	66	E8
Little Wolford	Warwks	83	G8
Littlewood	Staffs	98	C2
Little Woodcote	Gt Lon	51	H6
Littleworth	Bucks	67	L3

Littleworth Oxon 65 L7
Littleworth Staffs 98 C1
Littleworth Staffs 114 E7
Littleworth W Susx 21 L3
Littleworth Worcs 81 K5
Littleworth Worcs 82 B3
Littleworth Common Bucks 50 B2
Little Wratting Suffk 88 D5
Little Wymington Bed 85 J2
Little Wymondley Herts 69 G2
Little Wyrley Staffs 98 C2
Little Wytheford Shrops 113 J7
Little Yeldham Essex 88 F7
Littley Green Essex 71 G4
Litton Derbys 132 C4
Litton N York 158 F7
Litton Somset 45 H8
Litton Cheney Dorset 15 M4
Liurbost W Isls 282 g4
Liverpool Lpool 129 H2
Liversedge Kirk 141 J3
Liverton Devon 13 J7
Liverton R & Cl 171 G7
Liverton Mines R & Cl 171 G7
Liverton Street Kent 39 L3
Livingston W Loth 210 E5
Livingston Village W Loth 210 D5
Lixwm Flints 128 E5
Lizard Cnwll 3 H8
Llaingoch IoA 124 D3
Llaithddu Powys 94 C7
Llan Powys 93 J3
Llanaber Gwynd 109 L7
Llanaelhaearn Gwynd 109 G3
Llanafan Cerdgn 77 J1
Llanafan-Fawr Powys 78 D4
Llanafan-fechan Powys 78 D5
Llanallgo IoA 125 J3
Llanarmon Gwynd 109 G4
Llanarmon Dyffryn Ceiriog
  Wrexhm 112 A5
Llanarmon-yn-Ial Denbgs 128 E8
Llanarth Cerdgn 76 D4
Llanarth Mons 62 D5
Llanarthne Carmth 58 F5
Llanasa Flints 128 D3
Llanbabo IoA 124 F2
Llanbadarn Fawr Cerdgn 92 D7
Llanbadarn Fynydd Powys 94 D7
Llanbadarn-y-garreg Powys 78 F5
Llanbadoc Mons 62 D7
Llanbadrig IoA 124 F1
Llanbeder Newpt 44 D1
Llanbedr Gwynd 109 K6
Llanbedr Powys 61 K3
Llanbedr Powys 79 G6
Llanbedr-Dyffryn-Clwyd
  Denbgs 128 D7
Llanbedrgoch IoA 125 J4
Llanbedrog Gwynd 108 F5
Llanbedr-y-Cennin Conwy 126 E6
Llanberis Gwynd 125 K7
Llanbethêry V Glam 43 G7
Llanbister Powys 94 D8
Llanblethian V Glam 42 F7
Llanboidy Carmth 55 L2
Llanbradach Caerph 43 J4
Llanbrynmair Powys 93 K3
Llancadle V Glam 42 F8
Llancarfan V Glam 43 G7
Llancayo Mons 62 D6
Llancloudy Herefs 63 G3
Llancynfelyn Cerdgn 92 E5
Llandaff Cardif 43 J6
Llandanwg Gwynd 109 K6
Llandarcy Neath 57 K6
Llandawke Carmth 58 A6
Llanddaniel Fab IoA 125 J5
Llanddarog Carmth 58 F5
Llanddeiniol Cerdgn 77 G1
Llanddeiniolen Gwynd 125 K6
Llandderfel Gwynd 111 J4
Llanddeusant Carmth 59 L4
Llanddeusant IoA 124 F3
Llanddew Powys 61 G1
Llanddewi Swans 56 E7
Llanddewi Brefi Cerdgn 77 J4
Llanddewi'r Cwm Powys 78 E5
Llanddewi Rhydderch Mons 62 D4
Llanddewi Velfrey Pembks 55 K3
Llanddewi Ystradenni Powys 78 F2
Llanddoget Conwy 126 F7
Llanddona IoA 125 K4
Llanddowror Carmth 55 M4
Llanddulas Conwy 127 H4
Llanddwywe Gwynd 109 K7
Llanddyfnan IoA 125 J4
Llandecwyn Gwynd 110 B4
Llandefaelog Powys 60 F1

Llandefaelog-Tre'r-Graig
  Powys 61 H1
Llandefalle Powys 78 F8
Llandegfan IoA 125 K5
Llandegla Denbgs 112 H1
Llandegley Powys 79 G3
Llandegveth Mons 62 C8
Llandegwning Gwynd 108 D5
Llandeilo Carmth 59 H4
Llandeilo Graban Powys 78 F6
Llandeilo'r Fan Powys 78 B8
Llandeloy Pembks 74 D6
Llandenny Mons 62 E6
Llandevaud Newpt 44 E1
Llandevenny Mons 44 E2
Llandinabo Herefs 63 G4
Llandinam Powys 94 B5
Llandissilio Pembks 55 J3
Llandogo Mons 63 G6
Llandough V Glam 42 F7
Llandough V Glam 43 J7
Llandovery Carmth 59 L2
Llandow V Glam 42 E7
Llandre Carmth 77 J6
Llandre Cerdgn 92 D6
Llandre Isaf Pembks 75 K6
Llandrillo Denbgs 111 K4
Llandrillo-yn-Rhos Conwy 127 G4
Llandrindod Wells Powys 78 E3
Llandrinio Powys 112 D8
Llandudno Conwy 126 F3
Llandudno Junction Conwy 126 F4
Llandulas Powys 78 B7
Llandwrog Gwynd 125 H8
Llandybie Carmth 59 H6
Llandyfaelog Carmth 58 D6
Llandyfan Carmth 59 H5
Llandyfriog Cerdgn 76 B7
Llandyfrydog IoA 125 H3
Llandygai Gwynd 126 B5
Llandygwydd Cerdgn 75 M3
Llandynan Denbgs 112 B3
Llandyrnog Denbgs 128 D6
Llandyssil Powys 94 F4
Llandysul Cerdgn 76 D7
Llanedeyrn Cardif 43 K5
Llanedi Carmth 57 G3
Llaneglwys Powys 78 E7
Llanegryn Gwynd 92 D3
Llanegwad Carmth 58 F4
Llaneilian IoA 125 H1
Llanelian-yn-Rhôs Conwy 127 G4
Llanelidan Denbgs 111 L2
Llanelieu Powys 79 H8
Llanellen Mons 62 C5
Llanelli Carmth 56 F5
Llanelli Crematorium Carmth 56 F4
Llanelltyd Gwynd 110 D7
Llanelly Mons 61 K4
Llanelwedd Powys 78 E5
Llanenddwyn Gwynd 109 L6
Llanengan Gwynd 108 E6
Llanerch Gwynd 111 G8
Llanerch Powys 95 H4
Llanerchymedd IoA 125 G3
Llanerfyl Powys 94 B2
Llanfachraeth Carmth 58 E3
Llanfachreth Gwynd 110 E7
Llanfaelog IoA 124 F5
Llanfaelrhys Gwynd 108 C6
Llanfaenor Mons 62 E4
Llanfaes IoA 126 B4
Llanfaes Powys 61 G2
Llanfaethlu IoA 124 E2
Llanfair Gwynd 109 K5
Llanfair Caereinion Powys 94 D2
Llanfair Clydogau Cerdgn 77 H5
Llanfair Dyffryn Clwyd
  Denbgs 128 D8
Llanfairfechan Conwy 126 D5
Llanfair Kilgeddin Mons 62 D5
Llanfair-Nant-Gwyn Pembks 75 K5
Llanfairpwllgwyngyll IoA 125 J5
Llanfair Talhaiarn Conwy 127 J5
Llanfair Waterdine Shrops 94 F8
Llanfairynghornwy IoA 124 E2
Llanfair-yn-Neubwll IoA 124 E4
Llanfallteg Carmth 55 K3
Llanfallteg West Carmth 55 K3
Llanfarian Cerdgn 92 D7
Llanfechain Powys 112 B7
Llanfechell IoA 124 F2
Llanferres Denbgs 128 E7
Llanfflewyn IoA 124 F2
Llanfigael IoA 124 F3
Llanfihangel-ar-arth Carmth 76 E7
Llanfihangel Glyn Myfyr
  Conwy 111 J2
Llanfihangel Nant Bran Powys 78 C8

Llanfihangel-nant-Melan
  Powys 79 H4
Llanfihangel Rhydithon
  Powys 79 G2
Llanfihangel Rogiet Mons 44 F2
Llanfihangel Tal-y-llyn Powys 61 H2
Llanfihangel-uwch-Gwili
  Carmth 58 E4
Llanfihangel-y-Creuddyn
  Cerdgn 92 E8
Llanfihangel-yng-Ngwynfa
  Powys 111 L8
Llanfihangel yn Nhowyn IoA 124 E4
Llanfihangel-y-pennant
  Gwynd 92 E2
Llanfihangel-y-pennant
  Gwynd 109 J3
Llanfihangel-y-traethau
  Gwynd 109 L4
Llanfilo Powys 78 F8
Llanfoist Mons 62 B4
Llanfor Gwynd 111 H4
Llanfrechfa Torfn 62 C8
Llanfrothen Gwynd 110 B3
Llanfrynach Powys 61 G2
Llanfwrog Denbgs 128 D8
Llanfwrog IoA 124 E3
Llanfyllin Powys 112 A7
Llanfynydd Carmth 59 G3
Llanfynydd Flints 129 G8
Llanfyrnach Pembks 75 L6
Llangadfan Powys 94 B1
Llangadog Carmth 56 D3
Llangadog Carmth 59 K3
Llangadwaladr IoA 125 G6
Llangadwaladr Powys 112 B5
Llangaffo IoA 125 H6
Llangain Carmth 58 C5
Llangammarch Wells Powys 78 C6
Llangan V Glam 42 E6
Llangarron Herefs 63 G3
Llangasty-Talyllyn Powys 61 H2
Llangathen Carmth 59 G4
Llangattock Powys 61 K3
Llangattock Lingoed Mons 62 D3
Llangattock-Vibon-Avel Mons 62 F4
Llangedwyn Powys 112 B6
Llangefni IoA 125 H4
Llangeinor Brdgnd 42 D4
Llangeitho Cerdgn 77 H3
Llangeler Carmth 76 C7
Llangelynin Gwynd 92 C2
Llangendeirne Carmth 58 E6
Llangennech Carmth 57 G4
Llangennith Swans 56 D6
Llangenny Powys 61 K3
Llangernyw Conwy 127 H6
Llangian Gwynd 108 E5
Llangiwg Neath 57 K4
Llangloffan Pembks 74 E5
Llanglydwen Carmth 75 L6
Llangoed IoA 126 C4
Llangoedmor Cerdgn 75 L3
Llangollen Denbgs 112 B3
Llangolman Pembks 75 J6
Llangors Powys 61 H2
Llangovan Mons 62 E7
Llangower Gwynd 111 G5
Llangrannog Cerdgn 76 B4
Llangristiolus IoA 125 H5
Llangrove Herefs 63 G4
Llangua Mons 62 E2
Llangunllo Powys 79 H1
Llangunnor Carmth 58 D5
Llangurig Powys 93 K7
Llangwm Conwy 111 J3
Llangwm Mons 62 E7
Llangwm Pembks 55 G5
Llangwnnadl Gwynd 108 C5
Llangwyfan Denbgs 128 D6
Llangwyllog IoA 125 H4
Llangwyryfon Cerdgn 77 H1
Llangybi Cerdgn 77 H4
Llangybi Gwynd 109 G3
Llangybi Mons 62 D7
Llangyfelach Swans 57 H5
Llangynhafal Denbgs 128 D7
Llangynidr Powys 61 J3
Llangynin Carmth 55 M3
Llangynllo Cerdgn 76 C6
Llangynog Carmth 58 C6
Llangynog Powys 111 K6
Llangynwyd Brdgnd 42 C4
Llanhamlach Powys 61 H2
Llanharan Rhondd 42 F5
Llanharry Rhondd 42 F5
Llanhennock Mons 62 D8
Llanhilleth Blae G 61 K7
Llanidan IoA 125 J6

Llanidloes Powys 93 L6
Llaniestyn Gwynd 108 D5
Llanigon Powys 79 H7
Llanilar Cerdgn 92 D8
Llanilid Rhondd 42 E5
Llanina Cerdgn 76 D3
Llanio Cerdgn 77 H4
Llanishen Cardif 43 J5
Llanishen Mons 62 F6
Llanllechid Gwynd 126 C6
Llanlleonfel Powys 78 C5
Llanllowell Mons 62 D7
Llanllugan Powys 94 C3
Llanllwch Carmth 58 C5
Llanllwchaiarn Powys 94 D5
Llanllwni Carmth 76 E7
Llanllyfni Gwynd 109 H1
Llanmadoc Swans 56 D6
Llanmaes V Glam 42 E7
Llanmartin Newpt 44 E1
Llanmerewig Powys 94 E5
Llanmihangel V Glam 42 E7
Llanmiloe Carmth 55 M5
Llanmorlais Swans 56 F6
Llannefydd Conwy 127 K5
Llannon Carmth 56 F3
Llannor Gwynd 108 F4
Llanon Cerdgn 76 F2
Llanover Mons 62 C5
Llanpumsaint Carmth 58 D3
Llanrhaeadr-ym-Mochnant
  Powys 111 M6
Llanrhian Pembks 74 D6
Llanrhidian Swans 56 F6
Llanrhos Conwy 126 F4
Llanrhychwyn Conwy 126 F7
Llanrhyddlad IoA 124 F2
Llanrhystud Cerdgn 76 F1
Llanrothal Herefs 62 F3
Llanrug Gwynd 125 J7
Llanrumney Cardif 43 K5
Llanrwst Conwy 126 F7
Llansadurnen Carmth 56 A3
Llansadwrn Carmth 59 J3
Llansadwrn IoA 125 K4
Llansaint Carmth 56 C3
Llansamlet Swans 57 J5
Llansanffraid Glan Conwy
  Conwy 126 F4
Llansannan Conwy 127 J6
Llansannor V Glam 42 F6
Llansantffraed Powys 61 H2
Llansantffraed-Cwmdeuddwr
  Powys 78 D2
Llansantffraed-in-Elvel Powys 78 F4
Llansantffraid Cerdgn 76 F2
Llansantffraid-ym-Mechain
  Powys 112 C7
Llansawel Carmth 59 H2
Llansilin Powys 112 B6
Llansoy Mons 62 E6
Llanspyddid Powys 60 F2
Llanstadwell Pembks 54 F6
Llansteffan Carmth 56 C3
Llanstephan Powys 78 F6
Llantarnam Torfn 62 C8
Llanteg Pembks 55 L5
Llanthewy Skirrid Mons 62 D4
Llanthony Mons 62 B2
Llantilio-Crossenny Mons 62 E4
Llantilio Pertholey Mons 62 C4
Llantood Pembks 75 K4
Llantrisant IoA 124 F3
Llantrisant Mons 62 D7
Llantrisant Rhondd 43 G5
Llantrithyd V Glam 43 G7
Llantwit Fardre Rhondd 43 G4
Llantwit Major V Glam 42 E7
Llantysilio Denbgs 112 B3
Llanuwchllyn Gwynd 111 G5
Llanvaches Newpt 44 E1
Llanvair Discoed Mons 62 F8
Llanvapley Mons 62 D4
Llanvetherine Mons 62 D4
Llanveynoe Herefs 62 C1
Llanvihangel Crucorney Mons 62 C3
Llanvihangel Gobion Mons 62 D5
Llanvihangel-Ystern-Llewern
  Mons 62 E4
Llanwarne Herefs 63 G2
Llanwddyn Powys 111 K7
Llanwenarth Mons 62 B4
Llanwenog Cerdgn 76 F6
Llanwern Newpt 44 D2
Llanwinio Carmth 58 A4
Llanwnda Gwynd 125 H8
Llanwnda Pembks 74 F4
Llanwnnen Cerdgn 76 F6
Llanwnog Powys 94 B4

Llanwonno Rhondd 42 F3
Llanwrda Carmth 59 K3
Llanwrin Powys 93 G3
Llanwrthwl Powys 78 D3
Llanwrtyd Powys 78 B5
Llanwrtyd Wells Powys 78 B6
Llanwyddelan Powys 94 C3
Llanyblodwel Shrops 112 C7
Llanybri Carmth 58 B6
Llanybydder Carmth 76 F6
Llanycefn Pembks 55 J2
Llanychaer Pembks 75 G5
Llanycrwys Carmth 77 H6
Llanymawddwy Gwynd 111 G7
Llanymynech Powys 112 C7
Llanynghenedl IoA 124 E3
Llanynys Denbgs 128 C7
Llan-y-pwll Wrexhm 112 F1
Llanyre Powys 78 E3
Llanystumdwy Gwynd 109 H4
Llanywern Powys 61 H2
Llawhaden Pembks 55 H3
Llawnt Shrops 112 C5
Llawryglyn Powys 93 K5
Llay Wrexhm 129 H8
Llechcynfarwy IoA 125 G3
Llechfaen Powys 61 G2
Llechrhyd Caerph 61 H5
Llechryd Cerdgn 75 L3
Llechylched IoA 124 F4
Lledrod Cerdgn 77 H1
Llidiardau Gwynd 111 G4
Llidiartnenog Carmth 77 G7
Llidiart-y-parc Denbgs 111 M3
Llithfaen Gwynd 108 F3
Lloc Flints 128 D4
Llowes Powys 79 H7
Llwydcoed Rhondd 60 F6
Llwydcoed Crematorium
     Rhondd 60 F6
Llwydiarth Powys 111 K8
Llwyn Denbgs 128 C6
Llwyncelyn Cerdgn 76 E3
Llwyndafydd Cerdgn 76 C4
Llwynderw Powys 94 F3
Llwyn-drain Pembks 58 A2
Llwyn-du Mons 62 C4
Llwyndyrys Gwynd 108 F3
Llwyngwril Gwynd 92 D2
Llwynhendy Carmth 56 F5
Llwynmawr Wrexhm 112 C4
Llwyn-on Myr Td 60 F5
Llwyn-y-brain Carmth 55 L4
Llwyn-y-groes Cerdgn 77 G4
Llwynypia Rhondd 42 F3
Llynclys Shrops 112 D6
Llynfaes IoA 125 G4
Llyn-y-pandy Flints 128 E6
Llysfaen Conwy 127 H4
Llyswen Cerdgn 76 E3
Llyswen Powys 79 G7
Llysworney V Glam 42 E6
Llys-y-frân Pembks 55 H2
Llywel Powys 60 C1
Load Brook Sheff 132 E2
Loan Falk 210 C4
Loanend Nthumb 202 E3
Loanhead Mdloth 211 J6
Loaningfoot D & G 176 C7
Loans S Ayrs 196 C4
Lobb Devon 27 H3
Lobhillcross Devon 12 B5
Lochailort Highld 238 B7
Lochaline Highld 227 K3
Lochans D & G 172 D3
Lochanbriggs D & G 176 C3
Lochavich Ag & B 216 E4
Lochawe Ag & B 217 J2
Loch Baghasdail W Isls 283 c11
Lochboisdale W Isls 283 c11
Lochbuie Ag & B 227 H7
Lochcarron Highld 248 E4
Lochdar W Isls 283 b9
Lochdon Ag & B 227 L6
Lochdonhead Ag & B. 227 L5
Lochead Ag & B 206 B3
Lochearnhead Stirlg 219 K2
Lochee C Dund 222 F1
Locheilside Station Highld. 239 G7
Lochend Highld 251 G4
Locheport W Isls 283 c8
Loch Euphoirt W Isls 283 c8
Lochfoot D & G 176 B4
Lochgair Ag & B 206 E1
Lochgelly Fife 222 C8
Lochgilphead Ag & B 206 D2
Lochgoilhead Ag & B 217 K7
Lochieheads Fife 222 D4
Lochill Moray 266 F3

Lochindorb Lodge Highld 253 J4
Lochinver Highld 270 E4
Lochluichart Highld 262 B7
Lochmaben D & G 176 E2
Lochmaddy W Isls 283 d8
Loch Maree Hotel Highld 260 E6
Loch nam Madadh W Isls 283 d8
Lochore Fife 222 B7
Lochranza N Ayrs 194 E1
Lochside Abers 235 J3
Lochside D & G 176 C3
Lochside Highld 252 F1
Lochslin Highld 264 C4
Lochton S Ayrs 183 G7
Lochty Angus 234 E3
Lochty Fife 223 J5
Lochuisge Highld 228 B4
Lochwinnoch Rens 208 B7
Lochwood D & G 187 G6
Lockengate Cnwll 5 H3
Lockerbie D & G 176 F3
Lockeridge Wilts 47 H5
Lockerley Hants 34 C5
Locking N Som 44 D7
Locking Stumps Warrtn 130 C1
Lockington E R Yk 152 F6
Lockington Leics 116 D6
Lockleywood Shrops 113 M6
Locksbottom Gt Lon 51 L6
Locksgreen IoW 19 G5
Locks Heath Hants 19 H2
Lockton N York 162 E5
Loddington Leics 101 H3
Loddington Nhants 101 H7
Loddiswell Devon 7 L5
Loddon Norfk 107 G4
Lode Cambs 87 L3
Lode Heath Solhll 98 F7
Loders Dorset 15 L4
Lodge Hill Crematorium Birm 98 C7
Lodsworth W Susx 36 D6
Lofthouse Leeds 142 A3
Lofthouse N York 159 K8
Lofthouse Gate Wakefd 142 A3
Loftus R & Cl 171 G7
Logan E Ayrs 197 H6
Loganbeck Cumb 156 A4
Loganlea W Loth 210 C6
Loggerheads Staffs 114 A4
Logie Angus 235 H3
Logie Fife 223 G3
Logie Moray 253 K2
Logie Coldstone Abers 243 M3
Logie Newton Abers 256 B4
Logie Pert Angus 235 G3
Logierait P & K 232 E5
Logierieve Abers 257 G6
Login Carmth 55 K2
Lolworth Cambs 87 H2
Lonbain Highld 259 M6
Londesborough E R Yk 152 C6
London Gt Lon 51 J3
London Apprentice Cnwll 5 G5
London Beach Kent 39 M6
London Colney Herts 68 F6
Londonderry N York 160 D5
London End Nhants 85 H2
Londonthorpe Lincs 118 C4
Londubh Highld 260 D4
Lonemore Highld 260 C4
Long Ashton N Som 45 H5
Long Bank Worcs 97 H8
Long Bennington Lincs 117 L3
Longbenton N Tyne 181 G5
Longborough Gloucs 65 J1
Long Bredy Dorset 16 A4
Longbridge Birm 98 C7
Longbridge Warwks 83 G3
Longbridge Deverill Wilts 32 E3
Long Buckby Nhants 84 C2
Longburgh Cumb 177 J7
Longburton Dorset 31 L8
Long Cause Devon 8 B3
Long Clawson Leics 117 J6
Longcliffe Derbys 132 D8
Longcombe Devon 8 C3
Long Common Hants 35 G7
Long Compton Staffs 114 D7
Long Compton Warwks 83 G8
Longcot Oxon 47 K1
Long Crendon Bucks 67 G5
Long Crichel Dorset 17 J1
Longcroft Cumb 177 H7
Longcross Surrey 50 C6
Longden Shrops 95 K2
Longden Common Shrops 95 K2
Long Ditton Surrey 50 F5
Longdon Staffs 115 H8
Longdon Worcs 81 J7

Longdon Green Staffs 98 D1
Longdon Heath Worcs 81 J7
Longdon upon Tern Wrekin 113 K8
Longdown Devon 13 K4
Longdowns Cnwll 3 J4
Long Drax N York 143 H2
Long Duckmanton Derbys 133 J5
Long Eaton Derbys 116 E5
Longfield Kent 52 D5
Longford Covtry 99 K6
Longford Derbys 115 L4
Longford Gloucs 64 B3
Longford Gt Lon 50 D4
Longford Kent 38 D2
Longford Shrops 113 L5
Longford Wrekin 114 A7
Longforgan P & K 222 E1
Longformacus Border 212 F7
Longframlington Nthumb 191 G6
Long Green Ches W 129 L5
Long Green Worcs 81 J8
Longham Dorset 17 L3
Longham Norfk 121 L8
Long Hanborough Oxon 66 B4
Longhaven Abers 257 L4
Long Hedges Lincs 119 K2
Longhirst Nthumb 191 J8
Longhope Gloucs 63 K3
Longhope Ork 275 b6
Longhorsley Nthumb 191 H7
Longhoughton Nthumb 191 J3
Long Itchington Warwks 83 K2
Longlands Cumb 165 J3
Longlane Derbys 115 L4
Long Lawford Warwks 100 A8
Longlevens Gloucs 64 B3
Longley Calder 141 G3
Longley Kirk 141 J6
Longley Green Worcs 81 G5
Longleys P & K 233 L6
Long Load Somset 31 G6
Longmanhill Abers 268 D4
Long Marston Herts 67 L4
Long Marston N York 151 H5
Long Marston Warwks 82 E5
Long Meadowend Shrops 95 K7
Long Melford Suffk 89 H6
Longmoor Camp Hants 36 B4
Longmorn Moray 266 E4
Longmoss Ches E 131 H5
Long Newnton Gloucs 64 C8
Longnewton Border 201 J7
Long Newton E Loth 212 B6
Longnewton S on T 169 K7
Longney Gloucs 63 M4
Longniddry E Loth 212 A4
Longnor Shrops 96 B3
Longnor Staffs 132 B6
Longparish Hants 34 F2
Longpark Cumb 178 A6
Long Preston N York 148 E4
Longridge Lancs 147 M8
Longridge Staffs 114 E8
Longridge W Loth 210 C6
Longriggend N Lans 209 L5
Long Riston E R Yk 153 H7
Longrock Cnwll 2 D5
Longsdon Staffs 114 F1
Longshaw Wigan 139 G7
Longside Abers 269 J6
Long Sight Oldham 140 D6
Longslow Shrops 113 L4
Longstanton Cambs 87 H2
Longstock Hants 34 D3
Longstone Pembks 55 K5
Longstowe Cambs 86 F4
Long Stratton Norfk 106 D5
Long Street M Keyn 84 F5
Longstreet Wilts 47 H8
Long Sutton Hants 35 M2
Long Sutton Lincs 119 M7
Long Sutton Somset 31 G6
Longthorpe C Pete 102 D4
Long Thurlow Suffk 89 K2
Longthwaite Cumb 166 B6
Longton C Stke 114 E3
Longton Lancs 138 F3
Longtown Cumb 177 L5
Longtown Herefs 62 C1
Longueville Jersey 9 e3
Longville in the Dale Shrops 96 C4
Long Waste Wrekin 113 K8
Long Whatton Leics 116 D6
Longwick Bucks 67 J6
Long Wittenham Oxon 66 E8
Longwitton Nthumb 180 C1
Longwood D & G 175 H3
Longwood Shrops 96 D2

Longworth Oxon 66 A7
Longyester E Loth 212 C6
Lôn-las Swans 57 K5
Lonmay Abers 269 J4
Lonmore Highld 258 D7
Looe Cnwll 6 B4
Loose Kent 39 J3
Loosebeare Devon 13 G2
Loosegate Lincs 119 K6
Loosley Row Bucks 67 K7
Lootcherbrae Abers 268 A5
Lopcombe Corner Wilts 34 B4
Lopen Somset 30 F8
Loppington Shrops 113 L6
Lorbottle Nthumb 190 E5
Lordington W Susx 20 C5
Lordsbridge Norfk 104 B1
Lordshill C Sotn 34 E7
Lords Wood Medway 53 G6
Lornty P & K 233 J6
Loscoe Derbys 116 C2
Loscombe Dorset 15 L3
Lossiemouth Moray 266 E2
Lostford Shrops 113 K5
Lostock Gralam Ches W 130 D5
Lostock Green Ches W 130 D5
Lostock Hall Lancs 139 H3
Lostock Hall Fold Bolton 139 K6
Lostock Junction Bolton 139 K6
Lostwithiel Cnwll 5 J3
Lothbeg Highld 274 C6
Lothersdale N York 149 G6
Lothmore Highld 274 C6
Loudwater Bucks 49 L1
Loughborough Leics 116 F7
Loughborough Crematorium
     Leics 116 F7
Loughor Swans 57 G5
Loughton Essex 70 B7
Loughton M Keyn 85 G7
Loughton Shrops 96 E6
Lound Lincs 118 E7
Lound Notts 134 D2
Lound Suffk 107 K4
Lounston Devon 13 J7
Lount Leics 116 C7
Louth Lincs 136 E1
Love Clough Lancs 140 B2
Lovedean Hants 19 M1
Lover Wilts 34 B6
Loversall Donc 142 F8
Loves Green Essex 70 F6
Lovesome Hill N York 160 E3
Loveston Pembks 55 J5
Lovington Somset 31 K5
Low Ackworth Wakefd 142 C4
Low Angerton Nthumb 180 D2
Lowbands Gloucs 63 M1
Low Barbeth D & G 172 C2
Low Barlings Lincs 136 A5
Low Bell End N York 162 C5
Low Bentham N York 148 A2
Low Biggins Cumb 157 K7
Low Borrowbridge Cumb 157 K2
Low Bradfield Sheff 132 E2
Low Bradley N York 149 H6
Low Braithwaite Cumb 166 A2
Low Burnham N Linc 143 K7
Low Buston Nthumb 191 J5
Lowca Cumb 164 C6
Low Catton E R Yk 151 L5
Low Coniscliffe Darltn 169 H7
Low Crosby Cumb 178 B7
Lowdham Notts 117 H2
Low Dinsdale Darltn 169 K8
Lowe Shrops 113 H5
Lowe Hill Staffs 131 K8
Low Ellington N York 160 B6
Lower Aisholt Somset 30 B4
Lower Ansty Dorset 16 E2
Lower Apperley Gloucs 64 B2
Lower Arncott Oxon 66 F3
Lower Ashton Devon 13 K6
Lower Assendon Oxon 49 H2
Lower Ballam Lancs 138 D2
Lower Bartle Lancs 139 G1
Lower Basildon W Berk 48 F3
Lower Bearwood Herefs 79 M4
Lower Beeding W Susx 37 K5
Lower Benefield Nhants 101 L5
Lower Bentley Worcs 82 A2
Lower Beobridge Shrops 97 H5
Lower Birchwood Derbys 116 C1
Lower Boddington Nhants 83 L5
Lower Boscaswell Cnwll 2 B4
Lower Bourne Surrey 36 C2
Lower Brailes Warwks 83 H7
Lower Breakish Highld 247 L4
Lower Bredbury Stockp 131 H2

Lower Broadheath Worcs 81 J4
Lower Broxwood Herefs 79 L4
Lower Buckenhill Herefs 80 E8
Lower Bullingham Herefs 80 C7
Lower Burgate Hants 33 K7
Lower Burrowton Devon 14 B3
Lower Burton Herefs 80 A4
Lower Caldecote C Beds 86 D6
Lower Cam Gloucs 63 L7
Lower Canada N Som 44 D7
Lower Catesby Nhants 83 M3
Lower Chapel Powys 78 E8
Lower Chicksgrove Wilts 33 G5
Lower Chute Wilts 47 L8
Lower Clapton Gt Lon 51 K2
Lower Clent Worcs 97 L7
Lower Common Hants 49 J6
Lower Creedy Devon 13 K2
Lower Crossings Derbys 131 L4
Lower Cumberworth Kirk 141 K6
Lower Darwen Bl w D 139 K4
Lower Dean Bed 85 L2
Lower Denby Kirk 141 K6
Lower Diabaig Highld 260 C7
Lower Dicker E Susx 23 J5
Lower Dinchope Shrops 95 L6
Lower Down Shrops 95 H6
Lower Dunsforth N York 150 F3
Lower Egleton Herefs 80 E6
Lower Elkstone Staffs 131 L8
Lower Ellastone Staffs 115 J3
Lower End Bucks 67 G5
Lower End M Keyn 85 H7
Lower End Nhants 84 F3
Lower End Nhants 85 H3
Lower Everleigh Wilts 47 J8
Lower Exbury Hants 19 G4
Lower Eythorne Kent 41 J5
Lower Failand N Som 45 G4
Lower Farringdon Hants 35 L4
Lower Feltham Gt Lon 50 E4
Lower Fittleworth W Susx 21 G3
Lower Foxdale IoM 154 c6
Lower Frankton Shrops 112 E5
Lower Freystrop Pembks 54 F4
Lower Froyle Hants 36 A2
Lower Gabwell Devon 8 D1
Lower Gledfield Highld 263 G2
Lower Godney Somset 31 G2
Lower Gornal Dudley 97 L5
Lower Gravenhurst C Beds 86 C8
Lower Green Herts 86 D8
Lower Green Herts 87 J8
Lower Green Kent 38 C5
Lower Green Kent 39 G5
Lower Green Norfk 121 L4
Lower Green Staffs 97 K2
Lower Green Suffk 88 E2
Lower Hacheston Suffk 91 H4
Lower Halliford Surrey 50 E5
Lower Halstock Leigh Dorset 15 M1
Lower Halstow Kent 53 J5
Lower Hamworthy Poole 17 K4
Lower Hardres Kent 40 F5
Lower Harpton Herefs 79 K3
Lower Hartlip Kent 53 H6
Lower Hartshay Derbys 116 C1
Lower Hartwell Bucks 67 J4
Lower Hatton Staffs 114 C4
Lower Hawthwaite Cumb 156 B5
Lower Hergest Herefs 79 K4
Lower Heyford Oxon 66 C2
Lower Heysham Lancs 147 H4
Lower Higham Kent 52 F4
Lower Holbrook Suffk 90 E8
Lower Hordley Shrops 112 F5
Lower Horncroft W Susx 21 G3
Lowerhouse Lancs 140 B1
Lower Houses Kirk 141 J5
Lower Howsell Worcs 81 H5
Lower Irlam Salfd 130 D1
Lower Kilburn Derbys 116 C3
Lower Kilcott Gloucs 46 A1
Lower Killeyan Ag & B 204 D7
Lower Kingcombe Dorset 16 A3
Lower Kingswood Surrey 51 H8
Lower Kinnerton Ches W 129 H7
Lower Langford N Som 44 F6
Lower Largo Fife 223 G6
Lower Leigh Staffs 115 G4
Lower Lemington Gloucs 82 F8
Lower Llanfadog Powys 78 C2
Lower Lovacott Devon 27 J5
Lower Loxhore Devon 27 L3
Lower Lybrook Gloucs 63 H4
Lower Lye Herefs 79 M2
Lower Machen Newpt 43 K4
Lower Maes-coed Herefs 62 D1
Lower Mannington Dorset 17 L2

Lower Marston Somset 32 C2
Lower Meend Gloucs 63 H6
Lower Merridge Somset 30 B4
Lower Middleton Cheney
    Nhants 83 L7
Lower Milton Somset 31 J2
Lower Moor Worcs 82 A6
Lower Morton S Glos 63 J8
Lower Nazeing Essex 69 K6
Lower Norton Warwks 82 F3
Lower Nyland Dorset 32 C6
Lower Penarth V Glam 43 J7
Lower Penn Staffs 97 K4
Lower Pennington Hants 18 E5
Lower Penwortham Lancs 139 K4
Lower Peover Ches E 130 E5
Lower Place Rochdl 140 D5
Lower Pollicott Bucks 67 H4
Lower Quinton Warwks 82 E6
Lower Rainham Medway 53 H5
Lower Raydon Suffk 90 B7
Lower Roadwater Somset 29 C3
Lower Salter Lancs 147 M3
Lower Seagry Wilts 46 D3
Lower Sheering Essex 70 C4
Lower Shelton C Beds 85 K6
Lower Shiplake Oxon 49 J3
Lower Shuckburgh Warwks 83 L3
Lower Slaughter Gloucs 65 H4
Lower Soothill Kirk 141 L3
Lower Soudley Gloucs 63 K5
Lower Standen Kent 41 H7
Lower Stanton St Quintin
    Wilts 46 D3
Lower Stoke Medway 53 H4
Lower Stone Gloucs 63 K8
Lower Stonnall Staffs 98 D3
Lower Stow Bedon Norfk 105 K4
Lower Street Dorset 17 G3
Lower Street E Susx 24 C5
Lower Street Norfk 122 F4
Lower Street Suffk 88 F5
Lower Street Suffk 90 D5
Lower Stretton Warrtn 130 C3
Lower Stroud Dorset 15 K3
Lower Sundon C Beds 68 D2
Lower Swanwick Hants 19 H2
Lower Swell Gloucs 65 H2
Lower Tadmarton Oxon 83 J7
Lower Tale Devon 14 C2
Lower Tean Staffs 115 G4
Lower Thurlton Norfk 107 J3
Lower Town Cnwll 3 G5
Lower Town Devon 13 G4
Lower Town Herefs 80 E6
Lower Town Pembks 74 F5
Lower Trebullett Cnwll 11 L7
Lower Treluswell Cnwll 3 K4
Lower Tysoe Warwks 83 H6
Lower Ufford Suffk 91 G5
Lower Upcott Devon 13 K6
Lower Upham Hants 35 H1
Lower Upnor Medway 53 G5
Lower Vexford Somset 29 L4
Lower Walton Warrtn 130 B3
Lower Waterston Dorset 16 E4
Lower Weare Somset 44 E8
Lower Weedon Nhants 84 C3
Lower Welson Herefs 79 K5
Lower Westmancote Worcs 81 L7
Lower Whatcombe Dorset 17 G2
Lower Whatley Somset 32 B2
Lower Whitley Ches W 130 B4
Lower Wick Gloucs 63 L7
Lower Wick Worcs 81 J5
Lower Wield Hants 35 K3
Lower Willingham E Susx 23 K6
Lower Withington Ches E 130 F5
Lower Woodend Bucks 49 K2
Lower Woodford Wilts 33 K4
Lower Wraxhall Dorset 16 A2
Lower Wyche Worcs 81 H6
Lower Wyke C Brad 141 J3
Lowesby Leics 100 F2
Lowestoft Suffk 107 L5
Loweswater Cumb 164 F6
Low Fell Gatesd 181 G7
Lowfield Heath W Susx 37 L3
Low Gartachorrans Stirlg 208 D2
Low Gate Nthumb 179 L6
Low Gettbridge Cumb 178 C7
Lowgill Cumb 157 K3
Lowgill Lancs 148 A3
Low Grantley N York 150 B2
Low Green N York 150 B4
Low Habberley Worcs 97 H7
Low Ham Somset 30 F5
Low Harrogate N York 150 C5
Low Hawsker N York 163 G1

Low Hesket Cumb 166 B2
Low Hutton N York 152 A2
Lowick Cumb 156 D5
Lowick Nhants 101 L7
Lowick Nthumb 203 G5
Lowick Bridge Cumb 156 D5
Lowick Green Cumb 156 D5
Low Knipe Cumb 166 C6
Low Laithe N York 150 B3
Low Langton Lincs 136 C4
Low Leighton Derbys 131 K3
Low Lorton Cumb 164 F5
Low Marishes N York 162 E7
Low Marnham Notts 134 F6
Low Middleton Nthumb 203 H6
Low Mill N York 161 L4
Low Moor C Brad 141 J2
Low Moorsley Sundld 169 J2
Low Moresby Cumb 164 C6
Low Newton Cumb 156 F6
Low Row Cumb 165 G2
Low Row Cumb 165 K3
Low Row Cumb 178 D6
Low Row N York 159 H3
Low Salchrie D & G 172 C2
Low Santon N Linc 144 B5
Lowsonford Warwks 82 E2
Low Street Norfk 123 G6
Low Street Thurr 52 E3
Low Tharston Norfk 106 D4
Lowther Cumb 166 C6
Lowther Castle Cumb 166 C6
Lowthorpe E R Yk 153 H4
Lowton Devon 12 F2
Lowton Somset 30 B7
Lowton Wigan 139 J8
Lowton Common Wigan 139 J8
Lowton St Mary's Wigan 139 J8
Low Torry Fife 210 D2
Low Toynton Lincs 136 E5
Low Valley Barns 142 B7
Low Wood Cumb 156 A6
Low Worsall N York 160 F1
Low Wray Cumb 156 E2
Loxbeare Devon 29 G7
Loxhill Surrey 36 F3
Loxhore Devon 27 L3
Loxhore Cott Devon 27 L3
Loxley Warwks 83 G4
Loxley Green Staffs 115 H5
Loxter Herefs 81 G7
Loxton N Som 44 D7
Loxwood W Susx 36 F4
Loyal Lodge Highld 277 L7
Lubenham Leics 100 F6
Lucasgate Lincs 119 M2
Lucas Green Surrey 50 B7
Luccombe Somset 29 G2
Luccombe Village IoW 19 K7
Lucker Nthumb 203 J7
Luckett Cnwll 11 M7
Lucking Street Essex 89 G8
Luckington Wilts 46 B2
Lucklawhill Fife 223 G3
Lucknam Wilts 46 B4
Luckwell Bridge Somset 28 F3
Lucton Herefs 80 B2
Lucy Cross N York 169 G8
Ludag W Isls 283 c12
Ludborough Lincs 145 H8
Ludbrook Devon 7 J4
Ludchurch Pembks 55 K4
Luddenden Calder 141 G3
Luddenden Foot Calder 140 F3
Luddenham Court Kent 40 C3
Luddesdown Kent 52 E5
Luddington N Linc 143 L4
Luddington Warwks 82 E5
Luddington in the Brook
    Nhants 102 C6
Ludford Lincs 136 D2
Ludford Shrops 96 C8
Ludgershall Bucks 67 G4
Ludgershall Wilts 34 B1
Ludgvan Cnwll 2 D4
Ludham Norfk 123 H7
Ludlow Shrops 96 C8
Ludney Somset 30 F8
Ludwell Wilts 32 F6
Ludworth Dur 169 K2
Luffenhall Herts 69 J1
Luffincott Devon 11 L4
Luffness E Loth 212 B3
Lugar E Ayrs 197 H6
Luggate Burn E Loth 212 D4
Luggiebank N Lans 209 K4

Lugton E Ayrs 208 C8
Lugwardine Herefs 80 D7
Luib Highld 247 J3
Luing Ag & B 215 L2
Lulham Herefs 80 A7
Lullington Derbys 99 H1
Lullington E Susx 23 J6
Lullington Somset 45 M8
Lulsgate Bottom N Som 45 G6
Lulsley Worcs 81 G4
Lulworth Camp Dorset 16 F6
Lumb Calder 140 F3
Lumb Lancs 140 C3
Lumbutts Calder 140 E3
Lumby N York 142 D2
Lumloch E Duns 209 H5
Lumphanan Abers 244 D3
Lumphinnans Fife 222 B8
Lumsden Abers 255 K7
Lunan Angus 235 H5
Lunanhead Angus 234 D5
Luncarty P & K 221 K1
Lund E R Yk 152 E6
Lund N York 143 G1
Lundie Angus 233 L8
Lundin Links Fife 223 G6
Lundin Mill Fife 223 G6
Lundy Devon 26 B2
Lundy Green Norfk 106 E5
Lunga Ag & B 215 K3
Lunna Shet 281 e4
Lunsford Kent 52 F7
Lunsford's Cross E Susx 24 C5
Lunt Sefton 138 D7
Luntley Herefs 79 M4
Luppitt Devon 14 E1
Lupridge Devon 7 L2
Lupset Wakefd 141 M4
Lupton Cumb 157 J6
Lurgashall W Susx 36 D5
Lurley Devon 29 G7
Lusby Lincs 136 F6
Luscombe Devon 8 B3
Luson Devon 7 H5
Luss Ag & B 218 E8
Lussagiven Ag & B 215 J7
Lusta Highld 258 D5
Lustleigh Devon 13 H6
Luston Herefs 80 B3
Luthermuir Abers 235 G2
Luthrie Fife 222 E3
Lutley Dudley 97 L6
Luton Devon 13 L7
Luton Devon 14 C2
Luton Luton 68 E3
Luton Medway 53 G5
Lutterworth Leics 100 C6
Lutton Devon 7 H3
Lutton Devon 7 K3
Lutton Lincs 119 M6
Lutton Nhants 102 C6
Luxborough Somset 29 H3
Luxulyan Cnwll 5 H3
Luzley Tamesd 140 E7
Lybster Highld 275 H1
Lydbury North Shrops 95 J6
Lydcott Devon 28 B4
Lydd Kent 25 K3
Lydden Kent 41 H6
Lydden Kent 41 K2
Lyddington Rutlnd 101 J4
Lydeard St Lawrence Somset 29 L4
Lyde Green Hants 49 H7
Lydford Devon 12 C5
Lydford on Fosse Somset 31 J5
Lydgate Calder 140 D3
Lydgate Rochdl 140 E4
Lydham Shrops 95 H5
Lydiard Green Wilts 47 G2
Lydiard Millicent Wilts 47 G2
Lydiard Tregoze Swindn 47 G2
Lydiate Sefton 138 D7
Lydiate Ash Worcs 98 B8
Lydlinch Dorset 32 B8
Lydney Gloucs 63 J6
Lydstep Pembks 55 J7
Lye Dudley 97 L6
Lye Cross N Som 44 F6
Lye Green Bucks 68 B6
Lye Green E Susx 38 D6
Lye Green Warwks 82 E2
Lye Head Worcs 97 G8
Lye's Green Wilts 32 D2
Lyford Oxon 66 B8
Lymbridge Green Kent 40 F6
Lyme Regis Dorset 15 H4
Lyminge Kent 40 F7
Lymington Hants 18 E4
Lyminster W Susx 21 H6

Lymm Warrtn 130 D2
Lympne Kent 40 F8
Lympsham Somset 44 C8
Lynbridge Devon 28 C1
Lynchat Highld 241 L3
Lynch Green Norfk 106 C2
Lyndhurst Hants 18 D2
Lyndon Rutlnd 101 K3
Lyndon Green Birm 98 F6
Lyne Border 199 L5
Lyne Surrey 50 C5
Lyneal Shrops 113 G5
Lyne Down Herefs 63 J1
Lyneham Devon 13 K6
Lyneham Oxon 65 K3
Lyneham Wilts 46 F3
Lyneholmford Cumb 178 C4
Lynemouth Nthumb 191 K7
Lyne of Skene Abers 245 G2
Lynesack Dur 168 E5
Lyness Ork 275 b6
Lyng Norfk 122 B7
Lyng Somset 30 E5
Lynmouth Devon 28 C1
Lynn Staffs 98 D3
Lynn Wrekin 114 B8
Lynsted Kent 40 B3
Lynstone Cnwll 11 H2
Lynton Devon 28 C1
Lyon's Gate Dorset 16 C2
Lyonshall Herefs 79 L4
Lytchett Matravers Dorset ... 17 J3
Lytchett Minster Dorset ... 17 J4
Lyth Highld 280 C4
Lytham Lancs 138 D2
Lytham St Anne's Lancs 138 D2
Lythbank Shrops 95 L2
Lythe N York 171 K8
Lythmore Highld 279 J3

M

Mabe Burnthouse Cnwll 3 J4
Mablethorpe Lincs 137 J3
Macclesfield Ches E 131 H5
Macclesfield Crematorium
    Ches E 131 H5
Macduff Abers 268 C3
Macharioch Ag & B 192 E6
Machen Caerph 43 K4
Machrie N Ayrs 194 D4
Machrihanish Ag & B 192 D4
Machrins Ag & B 214 D5
Machynlleth Powys 93 G3
Machynys Carmth 56 F5
Mackworth Derbys 116 A4
Macmerry E Loth 211 M4
Maddaford Devon 12 D4
Madderty P & K 221 G3
Maddington Wilts 33 J2
Maddiston Falk 210 B4
Madehurst W Susx 21 G5
Madeley Staffs 114 B3
Madeley Wrekin 96 F3
Madeley Heath Staffs 114 B2
Madford Devon 29 L8
Madingley Cambs 87 H3
Madley Herefs 80 A7
Madresfield Worcs 81 J5
Madron Cnwll 2 C5
Maenaddwyn IoA 125 H3
Maenan Conwy 126 F6
Maenclochog Pembks 75 J6
Maendy V Glam 42 F6
Maenporth Cnwll 3 K5
Maentwrog Gwynd 110 C3
Maen-y-groes Cerdgn 76 C3
Maer Cnwll 11 H1
Maer Staffs 114 B4
Maerdy Carmth 59 J3
Maerdy Rhondd 42 E2
Maesbrook Shrops 112 D7
Maesbury Shrops 112 D6
Maesbury Marsh Shrops ... 112 D6
Maes-glas Newpt 44 C3
Maesgwynne Carmth 55 L2
Maeshafn Denbgs 128 E7
Maesllyn Cerdgn 76 C6
Maesmynis Powys 78 D6
Maesmynis Powys 78 E5
Maesteg Brdgnd 42 C3
Maesybont Carmth 59 G5
Maesycwmmer Caerph 43 J3
Magdalen Laver Essex 70 D5
Maggieknockater Moray ... 254 F3
Maggots End Essex 70 C2

Magham Down E Susx 23 K5
Maghull Sefton 138 D7
Magna Park Leics 100 B6
Magor Mons 44 E2
Maidenbower W Susx 37 L4
Maiden Bradley Wilts 32 D3
Maidencombe Torbay 8 D1
Maidenhayne Devon 15 G3
Maiden Head N Som 45 H5
Maidenhead W & M 49 L3
Maiden Law Dur 168 F1
Maiden Newton Dorset 16 B3
Maidens S Ayrs 182 F1
Maidenwell Lincs 136 F4
Maiden Wells Pembks 55 G7
Maidford Nhants 84 B5
Maids Moreton Bucks 84 D8
Maidstone Kent 39 J2
Maidwell Nhants 101 G8
Mail Shet 281 e6
Maindee Newpt 44 C1
Mainland Ork 275 c4
Mainland Shet 281 d6
Mainsforth Dur 169 J4
Mains of Balhall Angus 234 D3
Mains of Balnakettle Abers ... 244 E8
Mains of Dalvey Highld 254 B5
Mains of Haulkerton Abers ... 235 H1
Mains of Lesmoir Abers 255 J6
Mains of Melgunds Angus ... 234 E4
Mainsriddle D & G 176 B7
Mainstone Shrops 95 G6
Maisemore Gloucs 64 A3
Major's Green Worcs 98 E7
Makeney Derbys 116 B3
Malborough Devon 7 K7
Malcoff Derbys 131 L3
Malden Rushett Gt Lon 50 F6
Maldon Essex 71 K5
Malham N York 148 F3
Maligar Highld 259 H4
Mallaig Highld 237 K1
Mallaigvaig Highld 237 K1
Malleny Mills C Edin 211 G6
Mallows Green Essex 70 C2
Malltraeth IoA 125 G6
Mallwyd Gwynd 93 J1
Malmesbury Wilts 46 D2
Malmsmead Devon 28 D1
Malpas Ches W 113 H2
Malpas Cnwll 4 D6
Malpas Newpt 44 C1
Malshanger Hants 48 E8
Malswick Gloucs 63 L2
Maltby Lincs 136 F3
Maltby Rothm 133 K1
Maltby S on T 170 B8
Maltby le Marsh Lincs 137 J3
Malting Green Essex 72 E3
Maltman's Hill Kent 40 A6
Malton N York 152 B2
Malvern Worcs 81 H6
Malvern Link Worcs 81 H5
Malvern Wells Worcs 81 H6
Mamble Worcs 80 F1
Mamhilad Mons 62 C6
Manaccan Cnwll 3 J6
Manafon Powys 94 D3
Manais W Isls 282 e6
Manaton Devon 13 H6
Manby Lincs 137 G2
Mancetter Warwks 99 J4
Manchester Manch 140 C8
Manchester Crematorium
    Manch 131 G1
Mancot Flints 129 H6
Mandally Highld 240 A3
Manea Cambs 103 K5
Maney Birm 98 E4
Manfield N York 169 G8
Mangerton Dorset 15 L3
Mangotsfield S Glos 45 K4
Mangrove Green Herts 68 E2
Manhay Cnwll 3 H5
Manish W Isls 282 e6
Mankinholes Calder 140 E3
Manley Ches W 129 L5
Manmoel Caerph 61 J6
Mannel Ag & B 224 C7
Manningford Bohune Wilts ... 47 H7
Manningford Bruce Wilts ... 47 H7
Manningham C Brad 141 J1
Manning's Heath W Susx ... 37 K5
Mannington Dorset 17 L2
Manningtree Essex 73 G1
Mannofield C Aber 245 K3
Manorbier Pembks 55 H7
Manorbier Newton Pembks ... 55 H6

Manordeilo Carmth 59 J4
Manorhill Border 201 K6
Manorowen Pembks 74 F5
Manor Park Gt Lon 51 L2
Manor Park Crematorium
    Gt Lon 51 L2
Mansell Gamage Herefs ... 79 M6
Mansell Lacy Herefs 80 A7
Mansergh Cumb 157 K6
Mansfield E Ayrs 197 J8
Mansfield Notts 133 K7
Mansfield & District
    Crematorium Notts 133 K7
Mansfield Woodhouse Notts ... 133 K7
Mansriggs Cumb 156 D6
Manston Dorset 32 D7
Manston Kent 41 K2
Manston Leeds 142 B1
Manswood Dorset 17 J1
Manthorpe Lincs 118 B4
Manthorpe Lincs 118 E8
Manton N Linc 144 A7
Manton Notts 134 C4
Manton Rutlnd 101 J3
Manton Wilts 47 H5
Manuden Essex 70 C2
Manwood Green Essex 70 E4
Maperton Somset 31 L5
Maplebeck Notts 134 E7
Maple Cross Herts 68 C8
Mapledurham Oxon 49 G4
Mapledurwell Hants 49 G8
Maplehurst W Susx 37 J6
Maplescombe Kent 52 C6
Mapleton Derbys 115 K2
Mapleton Kent 38 C3
Mapperley Derbys 116 D3
Mapperley Park C Nott 117 G3
Mapperton Dorset 15 L3
Mappleborough Green
    Warwks 82 C2
Mappleton E R Yk 153 K7
Mapplewell Barns 141 M5
Mappowder Dorset 16 E2
Marazanvose Cnwll 4 C5
Marazion Cnwll 2 E5
Marbury Ches E 113 J2
March Cambs 103 J4
March S Lans 186 E3
Marcham Oxon 66 C7
Marchamley Shrops 113 K5
Marchamley Wood Shrops ... 113 K5
Marchington Staffs 115 J5
Marchington Woodlands
    Staffs 115 J6
Marchros Gwynd 108 E6
Marchwiel Wrexhm 112 E2
Marchwood Hants 18 F2
Marcross V Glam 42 D7
Marden Herefs 80 C6
Marden Kent 39 J4
Marden Wilts 47 G7
Marden Ash Essex 70 E6
Marden Beech Kent 39 J5
Mardens Hill E Susx 38 D7
Marden Thorn Kent 39 J5
Mardlebury Herts 69 H3
Mardy Mons 62 C4
Marefield Leics 101 G2
Mareham le Fen Lincs 136 E7
Mareham on the Hill Lincs ... 136 E6
Marehay Derbys 116 C2
Marehill W Susx 21 H3
Maresfield E Susx 23 G2
Marfleet C KuH 144 E2
Marford Wrexhm 129 H8
Margam Neath 57 L7
Margam Crematorium Neath ... 42 B4
Margaret Marsh Dorset 32 D7
Margaret Roding Essex 70 F5
Margaretting Essex 71 G6
Margaretting Tye Essex 71 G7
Margate Kent 41 K1
Margnaheglish N Ayrs 195 G4
Margrie D & G 174 F5
Margrove Park R & Cl 170 F7
Marham Norfk 104 E2
Marhamchurch Cnwll 11 J2
Marholm C Pete 102 C3
Marian-glas IoA 125 J3
Mariansleigh Devon 28 C6
Marine Town Kent 53 K4
Marionburgh Abers 244 F2
Marishader Highld 259 H4
Maristow Devon 6 F2
Marjoriebanks D & G 176 E2
Mark Somset 30 F1
Markbeech Kent 38 D5
Markby Lincs 137 J4

Mark Causeway Somset 30 E2
Mark Cross E Susx 38 F7
Markeaton C Derb 116 B4
Markeaton Crematorium
    C Derb 116 B4
Market Bosworth Leics 99 L3
Market Deeping Lincs 102 C2
Market Drayton Shrops 113 L5
Market Harborough Leics ... 100 F6
Market Lavington Wilts 46 E8
Market Overton Rutlnd 118 A8
Market Rasen Lincs 136 B2
Market Stainton Lincs 136 D4
Market Warsop Notts 133 L6
Market Weighton E R Yk ... 152 D7
Market Weston Suffk 105 K7
Markfield Leics 100 B2
Markham Caerph 61 J6
Markham Moor Notts 134 E5
Markinch Fife 222 E6
Markington N York 150 C3
Markle E Loth 212 C3
Marksbury BaNES 45 K6
Mark's Corner IoW 19 H5
Marks Tey Essex 72 C2
Markwell Cnwll 6 D3
Markyate Herts 68 C4
Marlborough Wilts 47 J5
Marlbrook Herefs 80 C4
Marlbrook Worcs 98 B8
Marlcliff Warwks 82 C5
Marldon Devon 8 C2
Marle Green E Susx 23 K4
Marlesford Suffk 91 H3
Marley Kent 41 G5
Marley Kent 41 K4
Marley Green Ches E 113 J2
Marley Hill Gatesd 180 F7
Marlingford Norfk 106 C2
Marloes Pembks 54 C5
Marlow Bucks 49 K2
Marlow Herefs 95 K8
Marlow Bottom Bucks 49 K1
Marlpit Hill Kent 38 C4
Marlpits E Susx 24 C4
Marlpits E Susx 38 C7
Marlpool Derbys 116 D3
Marnhull Dorset 32 C7
Marple Stockp 131 J2
Marple Bridge Stockp 131 J2
Marr Donc 142 E6
Marrick N York 159 K3
Marros Carmth 55 L5
Marsden Kirk 141 G5
Marsden S Tyne 181 K6
Marsden Height Lancs 148 F5
Marsett N York 158 F5
Marsh Bucks 67 K5
Marsh C Brad 149 J3
Marsh Devon 30 C8
Marshall's Heath Herts 68 F4
Marshalswick Herts 68 F5
Marsham Norfk 122 D6
Marsh Baldon Oxon 66 E7
Marsh Benham W Berk 48 B5
Marshborough Kent 41 J4
Marshbrook Shrops 95 K5
Marshchapel Lincs 145 K7
Marsh Farm Luton 68 D2
Marshfield Newpt 43 L5
Marshfield S Glos 45 M4
Marshgate Cnwll 11 G4
Marsh Gibbon Bucks 66 F3
Marsh Green Devon 14 B4
Marsh Green Kent 38 C4
Marsh Green Wrekin 113 K8
Marshland St James Norfk ... 103 L2
Marsh Lane Derbys 133 H4
Marsh Lane Gloucs 63 H5
Marshside Sefton 138 D4
Marsh Street Somset 29 H2
Marshwood Dorset 15 J3
Marske N York 159 K3
Marske-by-the-Sea R & Cl ... 170 E6
Marsland Green Wigan 139 K7
Marston Ches W 130 D5
Marston Herefs 79 L4
Marston Lincs 118 A3
Marston Oxon 66 D5
Marston Staffs 97 J1
Marston Staffs 114 E6
Marston Warwks 99 G4
Marston Wilts 46 E8
Marston Green Solhll 98 F6
Marston Jabbet Warwks ... 99 K5
Marston Magna Somset ... 31 K6
Marston Meysey Wilts 65 H7
Marston Montgomery Derbys ... 115 J4
Marston Moretaine C Beds ... 85 K7

Marston on Dove Derbys 115 L5
Marston St Lawrence Nhants 83 M6
Marston Stannett Herefs 80 D4
Marston Trussell Nhants 100 F6
Marstow Herefs 63 H3
Marsworth Bucks 68 A4
Marten Wilts 47 L7
Marthall Ches E 130 F4
Martham Norfk 123 J7
Martin Hants 33 J7
Martin Kent 41 K6
Martin Lincs 136 B7
Martin Lincs 136 D6
Martindale Cumb 166 B6
Martin Dales Lincs 136 C7
Martin Drove End Hants 33 H6
Martinhoe Devon 28 B1
Martin Hussingtree Worcs 81 K3
Martinscroft Warrtn 130 C2
Martinstown Dorset 16 C5
Martlesham Suffk 90 F6
Martlesham Heath Suffk 90 F6
Martletwy Pembks 55 H5
Martley Worcs 81 H3
Martock Somset 31 G7
Marton Ches E 131 G6
Marton Ches W 130 C6
Marton Cumb 156 C7
Marton E R Yk 153 J7
Marton E R Yk 153 K2
Marton Lincs 135 G3
Marton Middsb 170 C7
Marton N York 150 F3
Marton N York 162 C6
Marton Shrops 95 G3
Marton Warwks 83 J2
Marton-le-Moor N York 150 F2
Martyr's Green Surrey 50 E7
Martyr Worthy Hants 35 G4
Marwick Ork 275 b3
Marwood Devon 27 K3
Marybank Highld 250 E1
Maryburgh Highld 262 F8
Marygold Border 213 H7
Maryhill C Glas 208 F5
Maryhill Crematorium C Glas 208 F5
Marykirk Abers 235 H2
Maryland Mons 63 G6
Marylebone Gt Lon 51 H3
Marylebone Wigan 139 H6
Marypark Moray 254 D4
Maryport Cumb 164 D3
Maryport D & G 172 E7
Marystow Devon 12 B6
Mary Tavy Devon 12 C6
Maryton Angus 235 H4
Marywell Abers 244 D4
Marywell Abers 245 L4
Marywell Angus 235 G6
Masham N York 160 B6
Mashbury Essex 71 G5
Mason N u Ty 180 F4
Masongill N York 157 L7
Masonhill Crematorium S Ayrs 196 D7
Mastin Moor Derbys 133 J4
Matching Essex 70 D5
Matching Green Essex 70 D5
Matching Tye Essex 70 D5
Matfen Nthumb 180 C4
Matfield Kent 39 G5
Mathern Mons 45 G1
Mathon Herefs 81 G6
Mathry Pembks 74 E6
Matlask Norfk 122 C4
Matlock Derbys 132 F7
Matlock Bank Derbys 132 F7
Matlock Bath Derbys 132 F8
Matlock Dale Derbys 132 F7
Matson Gloucs 64 B4
Matterdale End Cumb 165 L6
Mattersey Notts 134 D2
Mattersey Thorpe Notts 134 D2
Mattingley Hants 49 H7
Mattishall Norfk 105 L1
Mattishall Burgh Norfk 105 L1
Mauchline E Ayrs 196 F5
Maud Abers 269 G6
Maufant Jersey 9 e2
Maugersbury Gloucs 65 J2
Maughold IoM 154 g4
Mauld Highld 250 C4
Maulden C Beds 85 L7
Maulds Meaburn Cumb 166 E7
Maunby N York 160 E5
Maund Bryan Herefs 80 D5
Maundown Somset 29 J5
Mautby Norfk 107 K1
Mavesyn Ridware Staffs 115 H8
Mavis Enderby Lincs 137 G6

Mawbray Cumb 164 E1
Mawdesley Lancs 139 G5
Mawdlam Brdgnd 42 B5
Mawgan Cnwll 3 H6
Mawgan Porth Cnwll 4 D2
Maw Green Ches E 130 D8
Mawla Cnwll 4 A5
Mawnan Cnwll 3 K5
Mawnan Smith Cnwll 3 K5
Mawsley Nhants 101 H8
Mawthorpe Lincs 137 J5
Maxey C Pete 102 C2
Maxstoke Warwks 99 G6
Maxted Street Kent 40 F6
Maxton Border 201 J7
Maxton Kent 41 J7
Maxwell Town D & G 176 C4
Maxworthy Cnwll 11 J4
Mayals Swans 57 H6
May Bank Staffs 114 D2
Maybole S Ayrs 183 H1
Maybury Surrey 50 C7
Mayes Green Surrey 37 H3
Mayfield E Susx 23 K2
Mayfield Mdloth 211 K6
Mayfield Staffs 115 J2
Mayford Surrey 50 C7
May Hill Gloucs 63 L3
Mayland Essex 72 D6
Maylandsea Essex 72 C6
Maynard's Green E Susx 23 K3
Maypole Birm 98 D7
Maypole Kent 41 G2
Maypole Mons 62 F4
Maypole Green Norfk 107 J4
Maypole Green Suffk 89 J3
Maypole Green Suffk 91 G2
May's Green Oxon 49 H3
May's Green Surrey 50 E7
Mead Devon 26 C7
Meadgate BaNES 45 K7
Meadle Bucks 67 K6
Meadowfield Dur 169 H3
Meadowtown Shrops 95 H3
Meadwell Devon 12 A6
Meaford Staffs 114 D4
Meal Bank Cumb 157 H4
Mealrigg Cumb 164 F2
Mealsgate Cumb 165 H2
Meanwood Leeds 150 C8
Mearbeck N York 148 E4
Meare Somset 31 G3
Meare Green Somset 30 D6
Meare Green Somset 30 E5
Mearns E Rens 208 F7
Mears Ashby Nhants 85 G2
Measham Leics 99 J1
Meathop Cumb 156 F6
Meaux E R Yk 153 H7
Meavy Devon 7 G2
Medbourne Leics 101 H5
Meddon Devon 26 D7
Meden Vale Notts 134 B5
Medlam Lincs 136 F8
Medlar Lancs 147 H8
Medmenham Bucks 49 K2
Medomsley Dur 180 D7
Medstead Hants 35 K3
Medway Crematorium Kent 53 G6
Meerbrook Staffs 131 K7
Meer Common Herefs 79 L5
Meesden Herts 70 B1
Meeson Wrekin 113 L7
Meeth Devon 12 D1
Meeting Green Suffk 88 E4
Meeting House Hill Norfk 122 F6
Meidrim Carmth 58 B5
Meifod Powys 94 E1
Meigle P & K 233 L6
Meikle Carco D & G 186 A3
Meikle Earnock S Lans 209 J8
Meikle Kilmory Ag & B 207 G6
Meikle Obney P & K 232 F7
Meikleour P & K 233 J7
Meikle Wartle Abers 256 C5
Meinciau Carmth 56 E3
Meir C Stke 114 E3
Meir Heath Staffs 114 E3
Melbourn Cambs 87 H6
Melbourne Derbys 116 C6
Melbourne E R Yk 152 A7
Melbur Cnwll 4 F4
Melbury Devon 26 F7
Melbury Abbas Dorset 32 E6
Melbury Bubb Dorset 16 B2
Melbury Osmond Dorset 16 A1
Melbury Sampford Dorset 16 A2
Melchbourne Bed 85 K2
Melcombe Bingham Dorset 16 E2

Meldon Devon 12 D4
Meldon Nthumb 180 D2
Meldon Park Nthumb 180 D2
Meldreth Cambs 87 H6
Meldrum Stirlg 220 C7
Melfort Ag & B 216 C4
Meliden Denbgs 128 C3
Melinau Pembks 55 K4
Melin-byrhedyn Powys 93 H4
Melincourt Neath 60 B6
Melin-y-coed Conwy 127 G7
Melin-y-ddol Powys 94 D2
Melin-y-wig Denbgs 111 K2
Melkinthorpe Cumb 166 D5
Melkridge Nthumb 179 G6
Melksham Wilts 46 C6
Mellangoose Cnwll 3 H5
Mell Green W Berk 48 C3
Mellguards Cumb 166 B2
Melling Lancs 147 M2
Melling Sefton 138 E7
Melling Mount Sefton 138 E7
Mellis Suffk 106 B8
Mellon Charles Highld 260 D2
Mellon Udrigle Highld 260 E1
Mellor Lancs 139 K2
Mellor Stockp 131 K2
Mellor Brook Lancs 139 J2
Mells Somset 32 B1
Mells Suffk 107 H8
Melmerby Cumb 166 E3
Melmerby N York 159 K5
Melmerby N York 160 E7
Melness Highld 277 K4
Melon Green Suffk 89 G4
Melplash Dorset 15 L3
Melrose Border 201 H6
Melsetter Ork 275 b6
Melsonby N York 160 B1
Meltham Kirk 141 H5
Meltham Mills Kirk 141 H5
Melton E R Yk 144 B2
Melton Suffk 91 G5
Meltonby E R Yk 152 B5
Melton Constable Norfk 122 A5
Melton Mowbray Leics 117 K7
Melton Ross N Linc 144 D5
Melvaig Highld 260 B3
Melverley Shrops 112 E8
Melverley Green Shrops 112 E7
Melvich Highld 278 E3
Membury Devon 15 G2
Memsie Abers 269 H4
Memus Angus 234 C4
Menabilly Cnwll 5 J4
Menagissey Cnwll 4 B5
Menai Bridge IoA 125 K5
Mendham Suffk 106 F6
Mendip Crematorium Somset 31 K2
Mendlesham Suffk 90 D2
Mendlesham Green Suffk 90 C3
Menheniot Cnwll 6 B2
Menithwood Worcs 81 G2
Menna Cnwll 4 E4
Mennock D & G 185 K2
Menston C Brad 149 L7
Menstrie Clacks 220 E7
Menthorpe N York 143 H1
Mentmore Bucks 67 M3
Meoble Highld 238 C6
Meole Brace Shrops 96 B1
Meonstoke Hants 35 J7
Meopham Kent 52 D5
Meopham Green Kent 52 D6
Meopham Station Kent 52 D5
Mepal Cambs 103 J7
Meppershall C Beds 86 C8
Merbach Herefs 79 K6
Mere Ches E 130 E3
Mere Wilts 32 D4
Mere Brow Lancs 138 E4
Mereclough Lancs 140 C2
Mere Green Birm 98 E4
Mere Green Worcs 81 L3
Mere Heath Ches W 130 C5
Meresborough Medway 53 H6
Mereworth Kent 39 G3
Meriden Solhll 99 G7
Merkadale Highld 246 E2
Merley Poole 17 K3
Merlin's Bridge Pembks 54 F4
Merrington Shrops 113 G7
Merrion Pembks 54 F7
Merriott Somset 31 G8
Merrivale Devon 12 D7
Merrow Surrey 36 F1
Merry Field Hill Dorset 17 K3
Merry Hill Herts 68 E5
Merryhill Wolves 97 K4

Merry Lees Leics 100 A2
Merrymeet Cnwll 6 B2
Mersea Island Essex 72 F4
Mersey Crossing Halton 129 L3
Mersham Kent 40 D7
Merstham Surrey 51 H8
Merston W Susx 20 E6
Merstone IoW 19 J6
Merther Cnwll 4 D6
Merthyr Carmth 58 C5
Merthyr Cynog Powys 78 D7
Merthyr Dyfan V Glam 43 H7
Merthyr Mawr Brdgnd 42 D6
Merthyr Tydfil Myr Td 61 G6
Merthyr Vale Myr Td 61 G7
Merton Devon 27 J8
Merton Gt Lon 51 H5
Merton Norfk 105 H4
Merton Oxon 66 E3
Meshaw Devon 28 D7
Messing Essex 72 C3
Messingham N Linc 143 M6
Metfield Suffk 106 F7
Metherell Cnwll 6 E1
Metheringham Lincs 135 L7
Methil Fife 222 F7
Methilhill Fife 222 F7
Methley Leeds 142 B2
Methley Junction Leeds 142 B3
Methlick Abers 256 F4
Methven P & K 221 J2
Methwold Norfk 104 E4
Methwold Hythe Norfk 104 E4
Mettingham Suffk 107 H5
Metton Norfk 122 D4
Mevagissey Cnwll 5 G6
Mexborough Donc 142 D7
Mey Highld 280 C2
Meysey Hampton Gloucs 65 G7
Miabhig W Isls 282 e3
Miavaig W Isls 282 e3
Michaelchurch Herefs 63 G2
Michaelchurch Escley Herefs 79 K8
Michaelchurch-on-Arrow
   Powys 79 J5
Michaelstone-y-Fedw Newpt 43 K5
Michaelston-le-Pit V Glam 43 J7
Michaelstow Cnwll 10 F6
Michelcombe Devon 7 K1
Micheldever Hants 35 G3
Micheldever Station Hants 35 G2
Michelmersh Hants 34 D5
Mickfield Suffk 90 D3
Micklebring Donc 133 K1
Mickleby N York 171 J8
Micklefield Leeds 142 C1
Micklefield Green Herts 68 D7
Mickleham Surrey 50 F8
Mickleover C Derb 116 A5
Micklethwaite C Brad 149 K7
Micklethwaite Cumb 165 J1
Mickleton Dur 168 B6
Mickleton Gloucs 82 E6
Mickletown Leeds 142 B2
Mickle Trafford Ches W 129 K5
Mickley Derbys 132 F4
Mickley N York 160 C7
Mickley Green Suffk 89 G4
Mickley Square Nthumb 180 C6
Mid Ardlaw Abers 269 H3
Midbea Ork 275 c2
Mid Beltie Abers 244 E3
Mid Bockhampton Dorset 18 B4
Mid Calder W Loth 210 E5
Mid Clyth Highld 280 C8
Mid Culbeuchly Abers 268 B4
Middle Assendon Oxon 49 H2
Middle Aston Oxon 66 C2
Middle Barton Oxon 66 B2
Middlebie D & G 177 H4
Middlebridge P & K 232 C2
Middle Chinnock Somset 31 G8
Middle Claydon Bucks 67 H2
Middlecliffe Barns 142 C6
Middlecott Devon 13 G5
Middle Duntisbourne Gloucs 64 E6
Middleham N York 159 L5
Middle Handley Derbys 133 H4
Middle Harling Norfk 105 K6
Middlehill Cnwll 6 B1
Middlehill Wilts 46 B5
Middlehope Shrops 96 B5
Middle Kames Ag & B 206 E1
Middle Littleton Worcs 82 C6
Middle Madeley Staffs 114 B3
Middle Maes-coed Herefs 79 L8
Middlemarsh Dorset 16 C1
Middle Mayfield Staffs 115 J3

Middle Mill Pembks.... 74 C7
Middlemore Devon.... 12 C8
Middle Quarter Kent.... 40 A7
Middle Rasen Lincs.... 136 A2
Middle Rocombe Devon.... 8 D1
Middle Salter Lancs.... 147 M3
Middlesbrough Middsb.... 170 C6
Middlesceugh Cumb.... 165 L2
Middleshaw Cumb.... 157 J5
Middlesmoor N York.... 159 K7
Middle Stoford Somset.... 30 B6
Middle Stoke Medway.... 53 H4
Middlestone Dur.... 169 H4
Middlestone Moor Dur.... 169 H4
Middle Stoughton Somset.... 30 F1
Middlestown Wakefd.... 141 L4
Middle Street Gloucs.... 63 M6
Middle Taphouse Cnwll.... 5 K2
Middlethird Border.... 201 L4
Middleton Ag & B.... 224 B6
Middleton Cumb.... 157 K5
Middleton Derbys.... 132 D7
Middleton Derbys.... 132 E8
Middleton Essex.... 89 H7
Middleton Hants.... 34 F2
Middleton Herefs.... 80 D1
Middleton Lancs.... 147 H4
Middleton Leeds.... 141 M2
Middleton N York.... 149 L6
Middleton N York.... 162 D5
Middleton Nhants.... 101 J5
Middleton Norfk.... 120 E8
Middleton Nthumb.... 180 C2
Middleton Nthumb.... 203 H6
Middleton P & K.... 221 L6
Middleton Rochdl.... 140 C6
Middleton Shrops.... 96 C7
Middleton Shrops.... 112 D5
Middleton Suffk.... 91 K2
Middleton Swans.... 56 D7
Middleton Warwks.... 98 F4
Middleton Cheney Nhants.... 83 L7
Middleton Crematorium
   Rochdl.... 140 C6
Middleton Green Staffs.... 114 F4
Middleton Hall Nthumb.... 202 F8
Middleton-in-Teesdale Dur.... 168 B5
Middleton Moor Suffk.... 91 J2
Middleton One Row Darltn.... 169 K8
Middleton-on-Leven N York.... 161 G1
Middleton-on-Sea W Susx.... 20 F6
Middleton on the Hill Herefs.... 80 C2
Middleton on the Wolds
   E R Yk.... 152 E6
Middleton Park C Aber.... 245 K1
Middleton Priors Shrops.... 96 E5
Middleton Quernhow N York.... 160 E7
Middleton St George Darltn.... 169 K8
Middleton Scriven Shrops.... 96 F6
Middleton Stoney Oxon.... 66 D2
Middleton Tyas N York.... 160 B2
Middletown Cumb.... 155 H1
Middle Town IoS.... 10 b3
Middletown N Som.... 44 F4
Middletown Powys.... 95 H1
Middle Tysoe Warwks.... 83 H6
Middle Wallop Hants.... 34 C3
Middlewich Ches E.... 130 D6
Middle Winterslow Wilts.... 34 B4
Middlewood Cnwll.... 11 K7
Middlewood Herefs.... 79 K6
Middlewood Green Suffk.... 90 C3
Middleyard E Ayrs.... 197 G4
Middle Yard Gloucs.... 64 B6
Middlezoy Somset.... 30 E4
Middridge Dur.... 169 H5
Midford BaNES.... 45 M6
Midge Hall Lancs.... 139 G3
Midgeholme Cumb.... 178 E7
Midgham W Berk.... 48 E5
Midgley Calder.... 140 F3
Midgley Wakefd.... 141 L5
Mid Holmwood Surrey.... 37 J2
Midhopestones Sheff.... 141 K7
Midhurst W Susx.... 36 C6
Mid Lavant W Susx.... 20 D5
Midlem Border.... 201 H7
Mid Mains Highld.... 250 D4
Midney Somset.... 31 H5
Midsomer Norton BaNES.... 45 K8
Midtown Highld.... 277 K4
Midville Lincs.... 137 G8
Mid Warwickshire
   Crematorium Warwks.... 83 G3
Midway Ches E.... 131 H3
Mid Yell Shet.... 281 e3
Migvie Abers.... 244 A2

Milborne Port Somset.... 31 L7
Milborne St Andrew Dorset.... 16 F3
Milborne Wick Somset.... 31 L6
Milbourne Nthumb.... 180 D4
Milbourne Wilts.... 46 D2
Milburn Cumb.... 166 F5
Milbury Heath S Glos.... 45 K1
Milby N York.... 150 F2
Milcombe Oxon.... 83 K8
Milden Suffk.... 89 J6
Mildenhall Suffk.... 104 E8
Mildenhall Wilts.... 47 J5
Milebrook Powys.... 79 K1
Milebush Kent.... 39 J4
Mile Elm Wilts.... 46 E5
Mile End Essex.... 72 E2
Mile End Gloucs.... 63 H5
Mile End Suffk.... 107 G5
Mileham Norfk.... 121 K7
Mile Oak Br & H.... 22 C5
Mile Oak Kent.... 39 H4
Mile Oak Staffs.... 98 F3
Miles Hope Herefs.... 80 D2
Milesmark Fife.... 210 E1
Miles Platting Manch.... 140 C7
Mile Town Kent.... 53 K4
Milfield Nthumb.... 202 E6
Milford Derbys.... 116 B3
Milford Devon.... 26 D6
Milford Powys.... 94 D5
Milford Staffs.... 114 F7
Milford Surrey.... 36 E2
Milford Haven Pembks.... 54 E5
Milford on Sea Hants.... 18 D5
Milkwall Gloucs.... 63 H5
Millais Jersey.... 9 a1
Milland W Susx.... 36 B5
Milland Marsh W Susx.... 36 C5
Mill Bank Calder.... 140 F3
Millbeck Cumb.... 165 H5
Millbreck Abers.... 257 J3
Millbridge Surrey.... 36 C2
Millbrook C Beds.... 85 K7
Millbrook C Sotn.... 34 E8
Millbrook Cnwll.... 6 E4
Millbrook Jersey.... 9 c3
Millbrook Tamesd.... 140 E7
Mill Brow Stockp.... 131 J2
Millbuie Abers.... 245 H2
Millbuie Highld.... 250 F1
Millcombe Devon.... 8 B5
Mill Common Norfk.... 107 G3
Mill Common Suffk.... 107 H7
Millcorner E Susx.... 24 E3
Millcraig Highld.... 263 H5
Mill Cross Devon.... 7 L3
Milldale Staffs.... 115 J1
Mill End Bucks.... 49 J2
Mill End Cambs.... 103 G7
Millend Gloucs.... 63 L7
Mill End Herts.... 87 G8
Millerhill Mdloth.... 211 K5
Miller's Dale Derbys.... 132 C5
Millers Green Derbys.... 115 M1
Miller's Green Essex.... 70 E5
Millerston C Glas.... 209 H5
Millgate Lancs.... 140 D4
Mill Green Cambs.... 88 C6
Mill Green Essex.... 70 F6
Mill Green Herts.... 69 G5
Mill Green Lincs.... 119 H6
Mill Green Norfk.... 106 C6
Millgreen Shrops.... 113 L6
Mill Green Staffs.... 98 D3
Mill Green Staffs.... 115 H7
Mill Green Suffk.... 89 J6
Mill Green Suffk.... 89 K4
Mill Green Suffk.... 90 D3
Mill Green Suffk.... 91 H3
Millhalf Herefs.... 79 K5
Millhayes Devon.... 14 F2
Millhead Lancs.... 147 K2
Millheugh S Lans.... 198 B3
Mill Hill E Susx.... 23 L6
Mill Hill Gt Lon.... 69 G8
Millhouse Ag & B.... 206 F5
Millhouse Cumb.... 165 K3
Millhousebridge D & G.... 176 F2
Millhouse Green Barns.... 141 K7
Millhouses Barns.... 142 C6
Millhouses Sheff.... 133 G3
Milliken Park Rens.... 208 C6
Millin Cross Pembks.... 55 G4
Millington E R Yk.... 152 C5
Millmeece Staffs.... 114 C5
Millness Cumb.... 157 H6
Mill of Drummond P & K.... 220 E4
Mill of Haldane W Duns.... 208 C3
Millom Cumb.... 155 M6

Millook Cnwll.... 11 H3
Millpool Cnwll.... 2 F5
Millpool Cnwll.... 11 G8
Millport N Ayrs.... 207 K8
Mill Side Cumb.... 157 G6
Mill Street Kent.... 39 H2
Mill Street Norfk.... 122 B7
Mill Street Suffk.... 90 C1
Millthorpe Derbys.... 132 F4
Millthrop Cumb.... 157 L4
Milltimber C Aber.... 245 J2
Milltown Abers.... 243 J2
Milltown Abers.... 255 J8
Milltown Cnwll.... 5 J3
Milltown D & G.... 177 K4
Milltown Derbys.... 133 G7
Milltown Devon.... 27 K3
Milltown of Auchindoun
   Moray.... 255 G4
Milltown of Campfield Abers.... 244 E3
Milltown of Edinvillie Moray.... 254 F4
Milltown of Learney Abers.... 244 E3
Milnathort P & K.... 221 L6
Milngavie E Duns.... 208 F4
Milnrow Rochdl.... 140 D5
Milnthorpe Cumb.... 157 H6
Milnthorpe Wakefd.... 142 A4
Milovaig Highld.... 258 B6
Milson Shrops.... 80 E1
Milstead Kent.... 40 A3
Milston Wilts.... 33 L2
Milthorpe Lincs.... 118 F5
Milthorpe Nhants.... 84 B6
Milton C Stke.... 114 E2
Milton Cambs.... 87 K3
Milton Cumb.... 166 D5
Milton D & G.... 172 F4
Milton D & G.... 175 L1
Milton Derbys.... 116 A6
Milton Highld.... 248 A3
Milton Highld.... 250 E5
Milton Highld.... 251 G2
Milton Highld.... 263 K5
Milton Highld.... 280 D6
Milton Inver.... 208 B5
Milton Kent.... 52 E4
Milton Moray.... 254 D7
Milton Moray.... 267 K4
Milton N Som.... 44 D6
Milton Newpt.... 44 D1
Milton Notts.... 134 E5
Milton Oxon.... 66 C8
Milton Oxon.... 83 K8
Milton P & K.... 233 G3
Milton Pembks.... 55 H6
Milton Somset.... 31 G6
Milton Stirlg.... 219 H7
Milton W Duns.... 208 D4
Milton Abbas Dorset.... 16 F2
Milton Abbot Devon.... 12 A6
Milton Bridge Mdloth.... 211 H6
Milton Bryan C Beds.... 68 B1
Milton Clevedon Somset.... 31 L3
Milton Combe Devon.... 6 F2
Milton Common Oxon.... 67 G6
Milton Damerel Devon.... 27 G8
Milton End Gloucs.... 63 L5
Milton End Gloucs.... 65 H7
Milton Ernest Bed.... 85 K4
Milton Green Ches W.... 129 K7
Milton Hill Oxon.... 48 C1
Milton Keynes M Keyn.... 85 G7
Milton Lilbourne Wilts.... 47 J7
Milton Malsor Nhants.... 84 E4
Milton Morenish P & K.... 231 H8
Milton of Auchinhove Abers.... 244 C3
Milton of Balgonie Fife.... 222 E7
Milton of Buchanan Stirlg.... 208 D1
Milton of Campsie E Duns.... 209 H4
Milton of Leys Highld.... 251 J3
Milton of Murtle C Aber.... 245 J3
Milton of Tullich Abers.... 243 L4
Milton on Stour Dorset.... 32 D5
Milton Regis Kent.... 40 A2
Milton Street E Susx.... 23 J6
Milton-under-Wychwood
   Oxon.... 65 K3
Milverton Somset.... 29 L5
Milverton Warwks.... 83 H2
Milwich Staffs.... 114 F5
Milwr Flints.... 128 E5
Minard Ag & B.... 216 F7
Minchington Dorset.... 33 G7
Minchinhampton Gloucs.... 64 C7
Mindrum Nthumb.... 202 D6
Minehead Somset.... 29 H2
Minera Wrexhm.... 112 C1
Minety Wilts.... 46 F1
Minffordd Gwynd.... 109 L4

Mingarrypark Highld.... 237 K6
Miningsby Lincs.... 136 F6
Minions Cnwll.... 11 J8
Minishant S Ayrs.... 196 C6
Minllyn Gwynd.... 111 G8
Minnigaff D & G.... 173 K2
Minnonie Abers.... 268 C4
Minshull Vernon Ches E.... 130 D7
Minskip N York.... 150 E3
Minstead Hants.... 18 D2
Minsted W Susx.... 20 D3
Minster Kent.... 41 L2
Minster Kent.... 53 L4
Minsterley Shrops.... 95 J2
Minster Lovell Oxon.... 65 L5
Minsterworth Gloucs.... 63 M4
Minterne Magna Dorset.... 16 C2
Minterne Parva Dorset.... 16 C2
Minting Lincs.... 136 C5
Mintlaw Abers.... 269 J6
Mintlyn Crematorium Norfk.... 120 E7
Minto Border.... 188 F2
Minton Shrops.... 95 K5
Minwear Pembks.... 55 H4
Minworth Birm.... 98 F5
Mirehouse Cumb.... 164 C7
Mireland Highld.... 280 D4
Mirfield Kirk.... 141 K4
Miserden Gloucs.... 64 D5
Miskin Rhondd.... 43 G2
Miskin Rhondd.... 43 G5
Misson Notts.... 134 D1
Misterton Leics.... 100 C5
Misterton Notts.... 134 F1
Misterton Somset.... 15 K1
Mistley Essex.... 73 C1
Mistley Heath Essex.... 73 H1
Mitcham Gt Lon.... 51 H5
Mitcheldean Gloucs.... 63 K3
Mitchell Cnwll.... 4 D4
Mitchellslacks D & G.... 186 E7
Mitchel Troy Mons.... 62 F5
Mitford Nthumb.... 180 E2
Mithian Cnwll.... 4 B5
Mitton Staffs.... 114 D8
Mixbury Oxon.... 84 B8
Mixenden Calder.... 141 G2
Moats Tye Suffk.... 90 B4
Mobberley Ches E.... 130 F4
Mobberley Staffs.... 115 G3
Moccas Herefs.... 79 L6
Mochdre Conwy.... 127 G4
Mochdre Powys.... 94 C5
Mochrum D & G.... 173 J5
Mockbeggar Hants.... 18 B2
Mockbeggar Kent.... 39 H4
Mockerkin Cumb.... 164 E6
Modbury Devon.... 7 J4
Moddershall Staffs.... 114 E4
Moelfre IoA.... 125 J2
Moelfre Powys.... 112 B6
Moel Tryfan Gwynd.... 125 J8
Moffat D & G.... 187 G5
Mogador Surrey.... 51 H8
Moggerhanger C Beds.... 86 C5
Moira Leics.... 116 A8
Molash Kent.... 40 D5
Mol-chlach Highld.... 246 F6
Mold Flints.... 128 F2
Moldgreen Kirk.... 141 J4
Molehill Green Essex.... 70 E2
Molehill Green Essex.... 71 H3
Molescroft E R Yk.... 152 F7
Molesden Nthumb.... 180 E2
Molesworth Cambs.... 102 B8
Molland Devon.... 28 E5
Mollington Ches W.... 129 J5
Mollington Oxon.... 83 K5
Mollinsburn N Lans.... 209 J5
Monachty Cerdgn.... 76 F3
Mondynes Abers.... 245 G7
Monewden Suffk.... 90 F3
Moneydie P & K.... 221 J1
Moneyrow Green W & M.... 49 L3
Moniaive D & G.... 185 J1
Monifieth Angus.... 223 J1
Monikie Angus.... 234 D7
Monimail Fife.... 222 E4
Monington Pembks.... 75 K3
Monk Bretton Barns.... 142 B6
Monken Hadley Gt Lon.... 69 H7
Monk Fryston N York.... 142 D2
Monkhide Herefs.... 80 E6
Monkhill Cumb.... 177 K7
Monkhopton Shrops.... 96 E5
Monkland Herefs.... 80 B4
Monkleigh Devon.... 27 H6
Monknash V Glam.... 42 D7
Monkokehampton Devon.... 12 E2

Monkseaton – Mutterton 337

Monkseaton N Tyne 181 J4
Monks Eleigh Suffk 89 K5
Monk's Gate W Susx 37 K5
Monks Heath Ches E 131 G5
Monk Sherborne Hants 48 F7
Monks Horton Kent 40 E7
Monksilver Somset 29 K3
Monks Kirby Warwks 100 A6
Monk Soham Suffk 90 F2
Monkspath Solhll 98 E8
Monks Risborough Bucks 67 K6
Monksthorpe Lincs 137 H6
Monk Street Essex 70 F2
Monkswood Mons 62 D6
Monkton Devon 14 E2
Monkton Kent 41 J2
Monkton S Ayrs 196 D5
Monkton S Tyne 181 H6
Monkton V Glam 42 D7
Monkton Combe BaNES 45 M6
Monkton Deverill Wilts 32 E3
Monkton Farleigh Wilts 46 A6
Monkton Heathfield Somset 30 C5
Monkton Up Wimborne Dorset 33 H8
Monkton Wyld Dorset 15 H3
Monkwearmouth Sundld 181 K7
Monkwood Hants 35 K5
Monmore Green Wolves 97 L4
Monmouth Mons 63 G4
Monnington on Wye Herefs 79 L6
Monreith D & G 173 J6
Montacute Somset 31 H7
Montcliffe Bolton 139 K5
Montford Shrops 112 F8
Montford Bridge Shrops 113 G8
Montgarrie Abers 255 L8
Montgomery Powys 94 F4
Monton Salfd 140 A7
Montrose Angus 235 H4
Mont Saint Guern 9 i3
Monxton Hants 34 C2
Monyash Derbys 132 C6
Monymusk Abers 256 C8
Monzie P & K 220 F2
Moodiesburn N Lans 209 J5
Moonzie Fife 222 F4
Moor Allerton Leeds 150 D8
Moorbath Dorset 15 K4
Moorby Lincs 136 E6
Moorcot Herefs 79 L4
Moor Crichel Dorset 17 K1
Moordown Bmouth 17 L4
Moore Halton 130 B3
Moor End C Beds 68 B3
Moor End Calder 141 G2
Moor End Devon 12 F1
Moorend Gloucs 63 L6
Moor End Lancs 147 G6
Moor End N York 151 J8
Moorends Donc 143 H4
Moorgreen Hants 35 G7
Moor Green Herts 69 J2
Moorgreen Notts 116 E2
Moorhall Derbys 132 F5
Moorhampton Herefs 79 M6
Moorhead C Brad 149 L8
Moor Head Leeds 141 K2
Moorhouse Cumb 177 H8
Moorhouse Cumb 177 K7
Moorhouse Donc 142 D5
Moorhouse Notts 134 E6
Moorhouse Bank Surrey 51 L8
Moorland Somset 30 E4
Moorlinch Somset 30 F3
Moor Monkton N York 151 H4
Moor Row Cumb 164 D7
Moor Row Cumb 165 H1
Moorsholm R & Cl 170 F7
Moorside Dorset 32 D7
Moor Side Lancs 138 E1
Moor Side Lancs 147 K8
Moorside Leeds 150 C8
Moor Side Lincs 136 E8
Moorside Oldham 140 E6
Moorstock Kent 40 E7
Moor Street Birm 98 C6
Moor Street Medway 53 H6
Moorswater Cnwll 5 M2
Moorthorpe Wakefd 142 C5
Moortown Devon 12 C7
Moortown Hants 18 A3
Moortown IoW 19 G7
Moortown Leeds 150 D7
Moortown Lincs 144 D7
Moortown Wrekin 113 K7
Morangie Highld 263 K3
Morar Highld 237 K2
Moray Crematorium Moray 267 H4
Morborne Cambs 102 C5
Morchard Bishop Devon 13 H1
Morcombelake Dorset 15 J4
Morcott Rutlnd 101 K3
Morda Shrops 112 D6
Morden Dorset 17 H3
Morden Gt Lon 51 H5
Mordiford Herefs 80 D7
Mordon Dur 169 J5
More Shrops 95 H5
Morebath Devon 29 G6
Morebattle Border 189 K1
Morecambe Lancs 147 H3
Moredon Swindn 47 H2
Morefield Highld 261 J1
Morehall Kent 41 G7
Moreleigh Devon 7 L4
Morenish P & K 231 H8
Moresby Parks Cumb 164 C6
Morestead Hants 35 G6
Moreton Dorset 16 F5
Moreton Essex 70 D5
Moreton Herefs 80 C2
Moreton Oxon 67 G6
Moreton Staffs 114 B8
Moreton Staffs 115 J5
Moreton Wirral 129 G2
Moreton Corbet Shrops 113 J6
Moretonhampstead Devon 13 H5
Moreton-in-Marsh Gloucs 65 J1
Moreton Jeffries Herefs 80 E5
Moretonmill Shrops 113 J7
Moreton Morrell Warwks 83 H4
Moreton on Lugg Herefs 80 C6
Moreton Paddox Warwks 83 H4
Moreton Pinkney Nhants 84 B5
Moreton Say Shrops 113 K4
Moreton Valence Gloucs 63 M5
Morfa Cerdgn 76 B4
Morfa Bychan Gwynd 109 K4
Morfa Dinlle Gwynd 125 H8
Morfa Glas Neath 60 C6
Morfa Nefyn Gwynd 108 E3
Morganstown Cardif 43 H5
Morgan's Vale Wilts 33 L6
Morham E Loth 212 C5
Moriah Cerdgn 92 D7
Morland Cumb 166 E6
Morley Ches E 130 F3
Morley Derbys 116 C3
Morley Dur 168 E5
Morley Leeds 141 L2
Morley Green Ches E 130 F3
Morley St Botolph Norfk 106 B3
Mornick Cnwll 11 L8
Morningside C Edin 211 H5
Morningside N Lans 209 L7
Morningthorpe Norfk 106 E5
Morpeth Nthumb 180 F2
Morphie Abers 235 H3
Morrey Staffs 115 J7
Morridge Side Staffs 115 G1
Morriston Swans 57 J5
Morston Norfk 121 M3
Mortehoe Devon 27 H2
Morthen Rothm 133 J2
Mortimer W Berk 49 G6
Mortimer Common W Berk 49 G6
Mortimer's Cross Herefs 80 A3
Mortimer West End Hants 48 F6
Mortlake Gt Lon 51 G4
Mortlake Crematorium Gt Lon 51 G4
Morton Cumb 166 B3
Morton Cumb 177 L7
Morton Derbys 133 H7
Morton IoW 19 K6
Morton Lincs 118 E6
Morton Lincs 134 F1
Morton Notts 117 J1
Morton Shrops 112 D6
Morton Hall Lincs 135 H7
Mortonhall Crematorium C Edin 211 J5
Morton-on-Swale N York 160 D4
Morton on the Hill Norfk 122 C8
Morton Tinmouth Dur 168 F6
Morvah Cnwll 2 B4
Morval Cnwll 6 B3
Morvich Highld 248 F7
Morville Shrops 96 F4
Morville Heath Shrops 96 F4
Morwenstow Cnwll 26 C7
Mosborough Sheff 133 H3
Moscow E Ayrs 196 F3
Mose Shrops 97 G5
Mosedale Cumb 165 K4
Moseley Birm 98 D6
Moseley Wolves 97 L4
Moseley Worcs 81 J3
Moses Gate Bolton 139 L6
Moss Ag & B 224 B6
Moss Donc 142 F5
Moss Wrexhm 112 D1
Mossat Abers 255 K7
Mossbank Shet 281 e4
Moss Bank St Hel 139 G8
Mossbay Cumb 164 C5
Mossblown S Ayrs 196 D6
Mossbrow Traffd 130 D2
Mossburnford Border 189 H3
Mossdale D & G 175 G1
Mossdale E Ayrs 184 D2
Moss Edge Lancs 147 H7
Moss End Ches E 130 D4
Mossend N Lans 209 K7
Mosser Mains Cumb 164 F5
Mossley Ches E 131 H7
Mossley Tamesd 140 E7
Mosspaul Hotel Border 188 C6
Moss Side Cumb 177 G8
Moss-side Highld 253 G1
Moss Side Lancs 138 D2
Moss Side Sefton 138 D7
Mosstodloch Moray 267 G4
Mossyard D & G 174 E4
Mossy Lea Lancs 139 G5
Mosterton Dorset 15 K2
Moston Manch 140 C7
Moston Shrops 113 J6
Moston Green Ches E 130 E7
Mostyn Flints 128 E4
Motcombe Dorset 32 E6
Mothecombe Devon 7 H5
Motherby Cumb 166 A5
Motherwell N Lans 209 K7
Motspur Park Gt Lon 51 G5
Mottingham Gt Lon 51 L4
Mottisfont Hants 34 D5
Mottistone IoW 18 F7
Mottram in Longdendale Tamesd 140 F8
Mottram St Andrew Ches E 131 G4
Mouilpied Guern 9 j3
Mouldsworth Ches W 129 L5
Moulin P & K 232 D3
Moulsecoomb Br & H 22 E6
Moulsford Oxon 48 E2
Moulsoe M Keyn 85 H7
Moultavie Highld 263 H5
Moulton Ches W 130 C5
Moulton Lincs 119 J6
Moulton N York 160 C2
Moulton Nhants 84 F2
Moulton Suffk 88 D2
Moulton V Glam 43 G7
Moulton Chapel Lincs 119 J7
Moulton St Mary Norfk 107 H2
Moulton Seas End Lincs 119 K6
Mount Cnwll 4 C4
Mount Cnwll 5 K1
Mount Kirk 141 H4
Mountain C Brad 141 G2
Mountain Ash Rhondd 61 G7
Mountain Cross Border 199 K4
Mountain Street Kent 40 E5
Mount Ambrose Cnwll 4 B6
Mount Bures Essex 89 H8
Mountfield E Susx 24 D3
Mountgerald House Highld 263 G7
Mount Hawke Cnwll 4 B5
Mount Hermon Cnwll 3 H7
Mountjoy Cnwll 4 E3
Mount Lothian Mdloth 200 C2
Mountnessing Essex 70 F7
Mounton Mons 63 G8
Mount Pleasant Ches E 131 G8
Mount Pleasant Derbys 115 M8
Mount Pleasant Derbys 116 B2
Mount Pleasant Dur 169 H4
Mount Pleasant E R Yk 153 L7
Mount Pleasant E Susx 23 G4
Mount Pleasant Norfk 105 K4
Mount Pleasant Suffk 88 E5
Mount Pleasant Worcs 82 B2
Mountsett Crematorium Dur 180 E7
Mountsorrel Leics 116 F8
Mount Sorrel Wilts 33 H6
Mount Tabor Calder 141 G2
Mousehole Cnwll 2 D5
Mouswald D & G 176 E4
Mow Cop Ches E 131 G8
Mowhaugh Border 189 L2
Mowmacre Hill C Leic 100 D2
Mowsley Leics 100 E5
Moy Highld 240 D7
Moy Highld 252 E5
Moyle Highld 248 D7
Moylegrove Pembks 75 J3
Muasdale Ag & B 205 L8
Muchalls Abers 245 K5
Much Birch Herefs 63 G1
Much Cowarne Herefs 80 E6
Much Dewchurch Herefs 62 F1
Muchelney Somset 30 F6
Muchelney Ham Somset 31 G6
Much Hadham Herts 70 B3
Much Hoole Lancs 138 F3
Much Hoole Town Lancs 138 F3
Muchlarnick Cnwll 5 L3
Much Marcle Herefs 80 F8
Much Wenlock Shrops 96 E3
Muck Highld 236 E4
Mucking Thurr 52 E3
Muckingford Thurr 52 E3
Muckleford Dorset 16 C4
Mucklestone Staffs 114 A4
Muckley Shrops 96 E4
Muckton Lincs 137 G3
Muddiford Devon 27 K3
Muddles Green E Susx 23 J4
Mudeford Dorset 18 B5
Mudford Somset 31 J7
Mudford Sock Somset 31 J7
Mudgley Somset 31 G2
Mud Row Kent 53 M4
Mugdock Stirlg 208 F4
Mugeary Highld 246 F1
Mugginton Derbys 115 M3
Muggintonlane End Derbys 115 M3
Muggleswick Dur 168 D1
Muirden Abers 268 C5
Muirdrum Angus 234 E7
Muiresk Abers 268 C6
Muirhead Angus 233 M8
Muirhead Fife 222 D6
Muirhead N Lans 209 J5
Muirkirk E Ayrs 197 K5
Muirmill Stirlg 209 J2
Muir of Fowlis Abers 244 C1
Muir of Miltonduff Moray 266 D4
Muir of Ord Highld 250 F2
Muirshearlich Highld 239 J7
Muirtack Abers 257 J4
Muirton P & K 221 G5
Muirton Mains Highld 250 E1
Muirton of Ardblair P & K 233 J6
Muker N York 158 F3
Mulbarton Norfk 106 D3
Mulben Moray 267 G6
Mulfra Cnwll 2 C4
Mull Ag & B 227 H5
Mullacott Cross Devon 27 J2
Mullion Cnwll 3 H7
Mullion Cove Cnwll 3 H7
Mumby Lincs 137 K5
Munderfield Row Herefs 80 F5
Munderfield Stocks Herefs 80 F5
Mundesley Norfk 123 G4
Mundford Norfk 104 F4
Mundham Norfk 107 G4
Mundon Hill Essex 72 C6
Mundy Bois Kent 40 B6
Mungrisdale Cumb 165 L4
Munlochy Highld 251 H1
Munnoch N Ayrs 195 L1
Munsley Herefs 80 F7
Munslow Shrops 96 C6
Murchington Devon 13 G5
Murcot Worcs 82 C7
Murcott Oxon 66 E4
Murcott Wilts 46 D1
Murkle Highld 279 L3
Murlaggan Highld 239 G5
Murrell Green Hants 49 H7
Murroes Angus 234 C8
Murrow Cambs 103 H2
Mursley Bucks 67 K2
Murston Kent 40 B2
Murthill Angus 234 C4
Murthly P & K 233 G7
Murton C York 151 K5
Murton Cumb 167 G6
Murton Dur 169 K1
Murton N Tyne 181 H5
Murton Nthumb 202 F3
Murton Swans 57 G7
Musbury Devon 15 G4
Muscoates N York 162 B6
Musselburgh E Loth 211 K4
Muston Leics 117 L4
Muston N York 163 K6
Mustow Green Worcs 97 K8
Muswell Hill Gt Lon 51 H1
Mutehill D & G 175 H5
Mutford Suffk 107 K5
Muthill P & K 220 F4
Mutterton Devon 14 B2

Muxton Wrekin 114 A8
Mybster Highld 279 L5
Myddfai Carmth 59 L3
Myddle Shrops 113 G6
Mydroilyn Cerdgn 76 E4
Myerscough Lancs 147 K7
Mylor Cnwll 3 L4
Mylor Bridge Cnwll 3 K4
Mynachlog ddu Pembks 75 K6
Myndd-llan Flints 128 D5
Myndtown Shrops 95 J5
Mynydd-bach Mons 62 F8
Mynydd-Bach Swans 57 J5
Mynydd Buch Cerdgn 92 F8
Mynyddgarreg Carmth 56 D3
Mynydd Isa Flints 128 F7
Mynydd Llandygai Gwynd 126 B6
Mynytho Gwynd 108 E5
Myrebird Abers 245 G4
Myredykes Border 189 G6
Mytchett Surrey 49 L7
Mytholm Calder 140 E2
Mytholmroyd Calder 140 F3
Mythop Lancs 138 D1
Myton-on-Swale N York 150 F3

N

Naast Highld 260 C3
Nab's Head Lancs 139 J2
Na Buirgh W Isls 282 d6
Naburn C York 151 J6
Nab Wood Crematorium C Brad 149 L8
Naccolt Kent 40 D6
Nackington Kent 40 F4
Nacton Suffk 90 F7
Nafferton E R Yk 153 G4
Nag's Head Gloucs 64 C7
Nailbridge Gloucs 63 J4
Nailsbourne Somset 30 B5
Nailsea N Som 44 F5
Nailstone Leics 99 L2
Nailsworth Gloucs 64 B7
Nairn Highld 264 D8
Nalderswood Surrey 37 K2
Nancegollan Cnwll 3 G4
Nancledra Cnwll 2 D4
Nanhoron Gwynd 108 E5
Nannerch Flints 128 E5
Nanpantan Leics 116 E8
Nanpean Cnwll 4 F4
Nanquidno Cnwll 2 B5
Nanstallon Cnwll 5 H2
Nant-ddu Powys 60 F4
Nanternis Cerdgn 76 C4
Nantgaredig Carmth 58 F4
Nantgarw Rhondd 43 H4
Nant-glas Powys 78 D2
Nantglyn Denbgs 127 K7
Nantgwyn Powys 93 L8
Nant Gwynant Gwynd 110 B2
Nantlle Gwynd 109 J1
Nantmawr Shrops 112 C6
Nantmel Powys 78 E2
Nantmor Gwynd 109 L2
Nant Peris Gwynd 126 B7
Nantwich Ches E 113 L1
Nant-y-Bwch Blae G 61 H5
Nant-y-caws Carmth 58 E5
Nant-y-derry Mons 62 C6
Nantyffyllon Brdgnd 42 C3
Nantyglo Blae G 61 K5
Nant-y-gollen Shrops 112 C5
Nant-y-moel Brdgnd 42 D3
Nant-y-pandy Conwy 126 D5
Naphill Bucks 67 K7
Napleton Worcs 81 K5
Nappa N York 148 E5
Napton on the Hill Warwks 83 L3
Narberth Pembks 55 J4
Narborough Leics 100 C4
Narborough Norfk 104 E1
Narkurs Cnwll 6 C4
Nasareth Gwynd 109 H2
Naseby Nhants 100 F7
Nash Bucks 84 F8
Nash Ct Lon 51 L6
Nash Herefs 79 K3
Nash Newpt 44 D2
Nash Shrops 80 E1
Nash End Worcs 97 H7
Nash Lee Bucks 67 K5
Nash's Green Hants 35 K2
Nash Street Kent 52 D5
Nassington Nhants 102 B4
Nastend Gloucs 64 A6

Nasty Herts 69 K2
Nateby Cumb 158 D1
Nateby Lancs 147 J7
Natland Cumb 157 H5
Naughton Suffk 89 L5
Naunton Gloucs 65 G2
Naunton Worcs 81 K7
Naunton Beauchamp Worcs 81 M5
Navenby Lincs 135 K8
Navestock Essex 70 D7
Navestock Side Essex 70 E7
Navidale House Hotel Highld 274 D5
Navity Highld 264 B7
Nawton N York 161 L5
Nayland Suffk 89 K8
Nazeing Essex 69 L6
Nazeing Gate Essex 69 L6
Neacroft Hants 18 B4
Neal's Green Warwks 99 J6
Neap Shet 281 e5
Near Cotton Staffs 115 H2
Near Sawrey Cumb 156 E3
Neasden Gt Lon 51 G2
Neasham Darltn 169 J8
Neath Neath 57 L5
Neatham Hants 35 M3
Neatishead Norfk 123 G7
Nebo Cerdgn 77 G2
Nebo Conwy 127 G8
Nebo Gwynd 109 H2
Nebo IoA 125 H2
Necton Norfk 105 H2
Nedd Highld 270 F2
Nedderton Nthumb 180 F2
Nedging Suffk 89 K5
Nedging Tye Suffk 89 L5
Needham Norfk 106 E7
Needham Market Suffk 90 C4
Needham Street Suffk 88 E2
Needingworth Cambs 87 G1
Neen Savage Shrops 96 F7
Neen Sollars Shrops 80 F1
Neenton Shrops 96 E6
Nefyn Gwynd 108 E3
Neilston E Rens 208 E7
Nelson Caerph 43 H3
Nelson Lancs 148 F8
Nemphlar S Lans 198 E4
Nempnett Thrubwell BaNES 45 G7
Nenthall Cumb 167 H2
Nenthead Cumb 167 H2
Nenthorn Border 201 L5
Neopardy Devon 13 J3
Nep Town W Susx 22 B4
Nercwys Flints 128 F7
Nereabolls Ag & B 204 C5
Nerston S Lans 209 H7
Nesbit Nthumb 202 F6
Nesfield N York 149 K6
Ness Ches W 129 G4
Nesscliffe Shrops 112 F7
Neston Ches W 129 G4
Neston Wilts 46 B5
Netchwood Shrops 96 E5
Nether Alderley Ches E 131 G4
Netheravon Wilts 33 K1
Nether Blainslie Border 201 H4
Netherbrae Abers 268 E4
Nether Broughton Leics 117 J6
Netherburn S Lans 198 C4
Netherbury Dorset 15 L3
Netherby Cumb 177 L4
Netherby N York 150 D6
Nether Cerne Dorset 16 C3
Nethercleuch D & G 176 F2
Nether Compton Dorset 31 K7
Nethercote Warwks 83 M2
Nethercott Devon 11 J3
Nethercott Devon 27 H3
Nether Crimond Abers 256 E7
Nether Dallachy Moray 267 G3
Netherend Gloucs 63 H7
Nether Exe Devon 13 L3
Netherfield E Susx 24 C3
Netherfield Leics 117 G8
Netherfield Notts 117 G3
Nether Fingland S Lans 186 D4
Nethergate N Linc 143 J7
Nethergate Norfk 122 B5
Netherhampton Wilts 33 K5
Nether Handley Derbys 133 H4
Nether Handwick Angus 234 B7
Nether Haugh Rothm 142 C8
Netherhay Dorset 15 J2
Nether Headon Notts 134 E4
Nether Heage Derbys 116 B2
Nether Heyford Nhants 84 C3
Nether Howcleugh S Lans 186 F4
Nether Kellet Lancs 147 K2

Nether Kinmundy Abers 257 K3
Netherland Green Staffs 115 H5
Nether Langwith Notts 133 K5
Netherlaw D & G 175 J2
Netherley Abers 245 J5
Nethermill D & G 176 D1
Nethermuir Abers 257 G3
Netherne-on-the-Hill Surrey 51 J7
Netheroyd Hill Kirk 141 H4
Nether Padley Derbys 132 E4
Netherplace E Rens 208 E7
Nether Poppleton C York 151 J5
Nether Row Cumb 165 K3
Netherseal Derbys 99 H1
Nether Silton N York 161 L6
Nether Skyborry Shrops 95 G8
Nether Stowey Somset 30 B3
Nether Street Essex 70 E5
Netherstreet Wilts 46 E6
Netherthong Kirk 141 H6
Netherthorpe Derbys 133 J5
Netherton Angus 234 E4
Netherton Devon 13 L8
Netherton Dudley 97 L5
Netherton Hants 48 A7
Netherton Herefs 63 G2
Netherton Kirk 141 H5
Netherton N Lans 209 K8
Netherton Nthumb 190 E4
Netherton Oxon 66 B3
Netherton P & K 233 H5
Netherton Sefton 138 D7
Netherton Shrops 97 G6
Netherton Stirlg 208 F3
Netherton Wakefd 141 L4
Netherton Worcs 82 A7
Nethertown Cumb 155 H1
Nethertown Highld 280 E1
Nethertown Lancs 148 C8
Nethertown Staffs 115 J8
Netherurd Border 199 J4
Nether Wallop Hants 34 C4
Nether Wasdale Cumb 155 L2
Nether Welton Cumb 165 K2
Nether Westcote Gloucs 65 J3
Nether Whitacre Warwks 99 G5
Nether Whitecleuch S Lans 186 B2
Nether Winchendon Bucks 67 H4
Netherwitton Nthumb 191 G8
Nethy Bridge Highld 253 J7
Netley Hants 19 G2
Netley Marsh Hants 34 D8
Nettlebed Oxon 49 G2
Nettlebridge Somset 31 L1
Nettlecombe Dorset 15 L3
Nettlecombe IoW 19 J8
Nettleden Herts 68 C5
Nettleham Lincs 135 K4
Nettlestead Kent 39 H3
Nettlestead Green Kent 39 H3
Nettlestone IoW 19 L5
Nettlesworth Dur 169 H1
Nettleton Lincs 144 E7
Nettleton Wilts 46 B3
Nettleton Shrub Wilts 46 B3
Netton Devon 7 G3
Netton Wilts 33 K3
Neuadd Carmth 59 K4
Neuadd-ddu Powys 93 K8
Nevendon Essex 53 G1
Nevern Pembks 75 J4
Nevill Holt Leics 101 H4
New Abbey D & G 176 C5
New Aberdour Abers 268 F3
New Addington Gt Lon 51 K6
Newall Leeds 150 B6
New Alresford Hants 35 J4
New Alyth P & K 233 K6
Newark C Pete 102 E3
Newark Ork 275 f2
Newark-on-Trent Notts 117 L1
New Arram E R Yk 153 G7
Newarthill N Lans 209 L7
New Ash Green Kent 52 D6
New Balderton Notts 117 L1
Newbarn Kent 40 F7
New Barn Kent 52 D5
New Barnet Gt Lon 69 H7
New Barton Nhants 85 G2
Newbattle Mdloth 211 K6
New Bewick Nthumb 190 F2
Newbie D & G 177 G6
Newbiggin Cumb 146 E2
Newbiggin Cumb 155 K4
Newbiggin Cumb 166 B5
Newbiggin Cumb 166 D1
Newbiggin Cumb 166 E5
Newbiggin Dur 167 L5
Newbiggin Dur 168 F1

Newbiggin N York 159 G4
Newbiggin N York 159 H5
Newbiggin-by-the-Sea Nthumb 181 H1
Newbigging Angus 233 L7
Newbigging Angus 234 C7
Newbigging Angus 234 D8
Newbigging S Lans 199 H4
Newbiggin-on-Lune Cumb 158 C2
New Bilton Warwks 100 B8
Newbold Derbys 133 G5
Newbold Leics 116 C7
Newbold on Avon Warwks 100 B7
Newbold on Stour Warwks 82 F6
Newbold Pacey Warwks 83 G4
Newbold Revel Warwks 99 M3
Newbold Verdon Leics 99 L3
New Bolingbroke Lincs 136 F8
Newborough C Pete 102 D2
Newborough IoA 125 G6
Newborough Staffs 115 J6
Newbottle Nhants 83 M7
Newbottle Sundld 181 H4
New Boultham Lincs 135 K5
Newbourne Suffk 91 G6
New Bradwell M Keyn 84 F7
New Brampton Derbys 133 G5
New Brancepeth Dur 169 G2
Newbridge C Edin 210 F4
Newbridge Caerph 43 K2
Newbridge Cerdgn 76 F3
Newbridge Cnwll 2 C5
Newbridge Cnwll 4 C5
Newbridge D & G 176 C3
Newbridge Hants 34 C7
Newbridge IoW 18 F6
New Bridge N York 162 D5
Newbridge Oxon 66 B4
Newbridge Wrexhm 112 D3
Newbridge Green Worcs 81 J7
Newbridge-on-Usk Mons 62 D4
Newbridge-on-Wye Powys 78 E4
New Brighton Flints 128 F6
New Brighton Wirral 129 G1
New Brinsley Notts 116 D2
New Brotton R & Cl 171 G6
Newbrough Nthumb 179 K5
New Broughton Wrexhm 112 D1
New Buckenham Norfk 106 C4
Newbuildings Devon 13 J2
Newburgh Abers 257 J6
Newburgh Abers 269 H4
Newburgh Fife 222 C3
Newburgh Lancs 138 F5
Newburgh Priory N York 161 J7
Newburn N u Ty 180 E6
New Bury Bolton 139 L6
Newbury Somset 32 B1
Newbury W Berk 48 C5
Newbury Wilts 32 D3
Newbury Park Gt Lon 51 L1
Newby Cumb 166 E6
Newby Lancs 148 E6
Newby N York 148 C2
Newby N York 163 J4
Newby N York 170 C8
Newby Bridge Cumb 156 E6
Newby Cross Cumb 177 L8
Newby East Cumb 178 B7
Newby Head Cumb 166 E6
New Byth Abers 268 E5
Newby West Cumb 177 L8
Newby Wiske N York 160 E5
Newcastle Mons 62 F4
Newcastle Shrops 95 G7
Newcastle Emlyn Carmth 76 B7
Newcastleton Border 178 C2
Newcastle-under-Lyme Staffs 114 D2
Newcastle upon Tyne N u Ty 181 G6
Newchapel Pembks 75 L4
Newchapel Staffs 131 G8
Newchapel Surrey 38 A5
Newchurch Blae G 61 J5
Newchurch Herefs 79 L5
Newchurch IoW 19 J6
Newchurch Kent 25 K1
Newchurch Mons 62 F7
Newchurch Powys 79 H5
Newchurch Staffs 115 J7
Newchurch in Pendle Lancs 148 E7
New Costessey Norfk 106 D2
New Cowper Cumb 164 F2
Newcraighall C Edin 211 K4
New Crofton Wakefd 142 B4
New Cross Cerdgn 92 D8
New Cross Gt Lon 51 K4
New Cross Somset 30 F7
New Cumnock E Ayrs 197 J8
New Cut E Susx 24 E4

New Deer Abers 268 F6
New Delaval Nthumb 181 H3
New Delph Oldham 140 F6
New Denham Bucks 50 D2
Newdigate Surrey 37 J3
New Duston Nhants 84 D3
New Earswick C York 151 K5
New Eastwood Notts 116 D2
New Edlington Donc 142 E7
New Elgin Moray 266 E4
New Ellerby E R Yk 153 J7
Newell Green Br For 49 L5
New Eltham Gt Lon 51 L4
New End Worcs 82 C3
Newenden Kent 24 F2
New England C Pete 102 D3
New England Essex 88 E6
Newent Gloucs 63 L2
New Farnley Leeds 141 L2
New Ferry Wirral 129 H3
Newfield Dur 169 G4
Newfield Dur 181 G8
Newfield Highld 264 B4
New Fletton C Pete 102 D4
Newfound Hants 48 E8
New Fryston Wakefd 142 C2
Newgale Pembks 54 D2
New Galloway D & G 185 G7
Newgate Norfk 122 A3
Newgate Street Herts 69 J6
New Gilston Fife 223 G5
New Grimsby IoS 10 b2
Newhall Ches E 113 K2
Newhall Derbys 115 M7
Newham Nthumb 203 K7
New Hartley Nthumb 181 H3
Newhaven C Edin 211 H4
Newhaven Derbys 132 C7
Newhaven E Susx 23 G7
New Haw Surrey 50 D6
New Hedges Pembks 55 K6
New Herrington Sundld 181 H8
Newhey Rochdl 140 E5
New Holkham Norfk 121 J4
New Holland N Linc 144 D3
Newholm N York 171 K8
New Houghton Derbys 133 K6
New Houghton Norfk 121 H6
Newhouse N Lans 209 L6
New Houses N York 158 D7
New Houses Wigan 139 H7
New Hutton Cumb 157 J4
New Hythe Kent 52 F7
Newick E Susx 22 F3
Newingreen Kent 40 F8
Newington Kent 41 G7
Newington Kent 53 J6
Newington Oxon 66 F7
Newington Shrops 95 K6
Newington Bagpath Gloucs 64 B8
New Inn Carmth 58 E2
New Inn Torfn 62 C7
New Invention Shrops 95 H8
New Lakenham Norfk 106 E2
New Lanark S Lans 198 E4
Newland C KuH 144 D2
Newland Cumb 156 D6
Newland E R Yk 143 K2
Newland Gloucs 63 H5
Newland N York 143 H3
Newland Oxon 66 A5
Newland Somset 28 E3
Newland Worcs 81 H5
Newlandrig Mdloth 211 L6
Newlands Border 188 E7
Newlands Cumb 165 K3
Newlands Nthumb 180 D7
Newlands of Dundurcas
  Moray 266 F6
New Lane Lancs 138 E5
New Lane End Warrtn 130 C1
New Langholm D & G 177 K2
New Leake Lincs 137 G8
New Leeds Abers 269 H5
New Lodge Barns 142 A6
New Longton Lancs 139 G3
New Luce D & G 172 F2
Newlyn Cnwll 2 D5
Newmachar Abers 256 F7
Newmains N Lans 209 L7
New Malden Gt Lon 51 G5
Newman's End Essex 70 D4
Newman's Green Suffk 89 H6
Newmarket Suffk 88 C3
Newmarket W Isls 282 g3
New Marske R & Cl 170 E6
New Marston Oxon 66 D5
New Marton Shrops 112 E4
New Mill Abers 245 H7

Newmill Border 188 D4
New Mill Cnwll 2 D4
New Mill Herts 68 A4
Newmill Kirk 141 J6
Newmill Moray 267 J5
Newmillerdam Wakefd 141 M4
Newmill of Inshewan Angus 234 C3
Newmills C Edin 211 G5
New Mills Cnwll 4 E4
New Mills Derbys 131 K3
New Mills Fife 210 D2
Newmills Mons 63 L6
New Mills Powys 94 D3
Newmiln P & K 221 L1
Newmilns E Ayrs 197 G3
New Milton Hants 18 C4
New Mistley Essex 73 H1
New Moat Pembks 75 H7
Newnes Shrops 112 F5
Newney Green Essex 71 G5
Newnham Hants 49 H8
Newnham Herts 86 E7
Newnham Kent 40 B4
Newnham Nhants 84 B3
Newnham Worcs 80 E2
Newnham on Severn Gloucs 63 K5
New Ollerton Notts 134 D6
New Oscott Birm 98 E4
New Pitsligo Abers 268 F5
New Polzeath Cnwll 10 C6
Newport Cnwll 11 L5
Newport Dorset 17 G4
Newport E R Yk 143 L2
Newport Essex 87 L8
Newport Gloucs 63 K7
Newport Highld 274 F3
Newport IoW 19 H6
Newport Newpt 44 C1
Newport Norfk 123 K8
Newport Pembks 75 H4
Newport Wrekin 114 A7
Newport-on-Tay Fife 223 G2
Newport Pagnell M Keyn 85 G6
Newpound Common W Susx 37 G5
New Prestwick S Ayrs 196 C6
New Quay Cerdgn 76 D3
Newquay Cnwll 4 D3
New Quay Essex 72 F2
New Rackheath Norfk 106 F1
New Radnor Powys 79 H3
New Rent Cumb 166 B3
New Ridley Nthumb 180 C7
New Road Side N York 149 H7
New Romney Kent 25 K2
New Rossington Donc 143 G6
New Row Cerdgn 92 F8
New Row Lancs 148 A8
New Sauchie Clacks 220 F8
Newsbank Ches E 131 G6
Newseat Abers 256 C5
Newsham Lancs 147 K8
Newsham N York 160 B4
Newsham N York 168 E8
Newsham Nthumb 181 H3
New Sharlston Wakefd 142 B4
Newsholme E R Yk 143 H2
Newsholme Lancs 148 E5
New Shoreston Nthumb 203 K6
New Silksworth Sundld 181 J8
New Skelton R & Cl 170 F7
Newsome Kirk 141 J5
New Somerby Lincs 118 B4
New Southgate Crematorium
  Gt Lon 69 H8
New Springs Wigan 139 J6
Newstead Border 201 H6
Newstead Notts 116 E1
Newstead Nthumb 203 J7
New Stevenston N Lans 209 K7
Newthorpe N York 142 D1
Newthorpe Notts 116 E2
New Thundersley Essex 53 G1
Newtimber W Susx 22 D4
Newtoft Lincs 135 L2
Newton Ag & B 217 G7
Newton Border 189 G2
Newton Brdgnd 42 C6
Newton C Beds 86 E6
Newton Cambs 87 J5
Newton Cambs 119 M8
Newton Cardif 43 K6
Newton Ches W 129 J6
Newton Ches W 129 L7
Newton Ches W 129 M4
Newton Cumb 146 D2
Newton Derbys 133 J7
Newton Herefs 79 L1

Newton Herefs 79 L8
Newton Herefs 80 C4
Newton Highld 251 G2
Newton Highld 252 D2
Newton Highld 263 L6
Newton Highld 280 D6
Newton Lancs 147 G8
Newton Lancs 157 J7
Newton Lincs 118 D4
Newton Mdloth 211 K5
Newton Moray 266 C3
Newton Moray 267 K5
Newton N York 152 D1
Newton Nhants 101 J6
Newton Norfk 121 H8
Newton Notts 117 J3
Newton Nthumb 180 C6
Newton Nthumb 190 D5
Newton S Lans 198 F6
Newton S Lans 209 H6
Newton Sandw 98 C4
Newton Shrops 112 F4
Newton Somset 29 K4
Newton Staffs 115 G6
Newton Suffk 89 J7
Newton W Loth 210 E3
Newton Warwks 100 C7
Newton Wilts 34 B6
Newton Abbot Devon 13 K8
Newton Arlosh Cumb 177 G2
Newton Aycliffe Dur 169 H5
Newton Bewley Hartpl 170 B5
Newton Blossomville M Keyn 85 H5
Newton Bromswold Nhants 85 K4
Newton Burgoland Leics 99 K2
Newton-by-the-Sea Nthumb 203 L8
Newton by Toft Lincs 135 L2
Newton Ferrers Devon 7 G5
Newton Ferry W Isls 282 C7
Newton Flotman Norfk 106 E4
Newtongrange Mdloth 211 K6
Newton Green Mons 45 G1
Newton Harcourt Leics 100 E4
Newton Heath Manch 140 C7
Newtonhill Abers 245 K5
Newton Hill Wakefd 141 M3
Newton-in-Bowland Lancs 148 B5
Newton Kyme N York 151 G6
Newton-le-Willows N York 160 B4
Newton-le-Willows St Hel 139 H8
Newtonloan Mdloth 211 K6
Newton Longville Bucks 67 K1
Newton Mearns E Rens 208 F7
Newtonmill Angus 234 F3
Newtonmore Highld 241 J4
Newton Morrell N York 160 C1
Newton Mountain Pembks 55 G5
Newton Mulgrave N York 171 H7
Newton of Balcanquhal P & K ... 222 B3
Newton of Balcormo Fife 223 J6
Newton-on-Ouse N York 151 H4
Newton-on-Rawcliffe N York 162 E4
Newton on the Hill Shrops 113 H7
Newton-on-the-Moor
  Nthumb 191 H5
Newton on Trent Lincs 135 G6
Newton Poppleford Devon 14 C5
Newton Purcell Oxon 66 F1
Newton Regis Warwks 99 H2
Newton Reigny Cumb 166 B4
Newton St Cyres Devon 13 K3
Newton St Faith Norfk 122 E8
Newton St Loe BaNES 45 L6
Newton St Petrock Devon 27 G4
Newton Solney Derbys 115 M6
Newton Stacey Hants 34 E3
Newton Stewart D & G 173 K2
Newton Tony Wilts 34 B3
Newton Tracey Devon 27 J5
Newton under Roseberry
  R & Cl 170 D8
Newton Underwood Nthumb 180 E2
Newton upon Derwent E R Yk ... 151 M6
Newton Valence Hants 35 L4
Newton Wamphray D & G 187 H7
Newton with Scales Lancs 138 F2
Newtown Blae G 61 J5
Newtown Ches W 129 M4
Newtown Cnwll 2 F5
Newtown Cnwll 11 K7
Newtown Cumb 164 E1
Newtown Cumb 166 C6
Newtown Cumb 177 L6
Newtown Cumb 178 C6
Newtown D & G 185 J1
Newtown Derbys 131 K3
Newtown Devon 14 C3
Newtown Devon 28 D6
Newtown Dorset 15 L2

New Town Dorset 17 K1
New Town Dorset 32 F7
New Town Dorset 33 G7
New Town E Susx 23 H3
Newtown Gloucs 63 K6
Newtown Hants 18 D2
Newtown Hants 35 J8
Newtown Hants 48 C6
Newtown Herefs 80 B4
Newtown Herefs 80 C8
Newtown Herefs 80 E6
Newtown Herefs 81 D7
Newtown Highld 240 B3
Newtown IoW 19 G5
Newtown Lancs 139 G4
New Town Nhants 101 L7
Newtown Nthumb 190 E6
Newtown Nthumb 202 F6
Newtown Nthumb 203 G8
Newtown Poole 17 K4
Newtown Powys 94 D5
Newtown Rhondd 61 G7
Newtown Shrops 112 F7
Newtown Shrops 113 H5
Newtown Somset 30 C8
Newtown Staffs 98 C3
Newtown Staffs 131 H7
Newtown Wigan 139 H6
Newtown Wilts 32 F5
New Town Wilts 47 L4
Newtown Wilts 47 L6
Newtown Worcs 81 K4
Newtown Worcs 98 B7
Newtown-in-St Martin Cnwll 3 J6
Newtown Linford Leics 100 B2
Newtown of Beltrees Rens 208 C7
Newtown St Boswells Border 201 J6
Newtown Unthank Leics 100 B3
New Tredegar Caerph 61 J6
New Trows S Lans 198 D5
New Tupton Derbys 133 H6
Newtyle Angus 233 L7
New Walsoken Cambs 103 K2
New Waltham NE Lin 145 H6
New Whittington Derbys 133 H4
New Winton E Loth 211 M5
New Yatt Oxon 66 A4
Newyears Green Gt Lon 50 D1
Newyork Ag & B 216 F5
New York Lincs 136 D8
New York N Tyne 181 H5
New York N York 150 B3
Nextend Herefs 79 L4
Neyland Pembks 54 F6
Niarbyl IoM 154 b6
Nibley Gloucs 63 K5
Nibley S Glos 45 K3
Nibley Green Gloucs 63 L7
Nicholashayne Devon 29 K7
Nicholaston Swans 56 F7
Nickies Hill Cumb 178 D5
Nidd N York 150 D4
Nigg C Aber 245 L3
Nigg Highld 264 C5
Nigg Ferry Highld 264 B6
Nimlet BaNES 45 L5
Ninebanks Nthumb 179 H8
Nine Elms Swindn 47 G2
Nine Wells Pembks 74 C7
Ninfield E Susx 24 C5
Ningwood IoW 18 F6
Nisbet Border 201 L8
Nisbet Hill Border 202 B3
Niton IoW 19 H8
Nitshill C Glas 208 E7
Noah's Ark Kent 52 C7
Noak Bridge Essex 52 E1
Noak Hill Gt Lon 70 D8
Noblethorpe Barns 141 L6
Nobold Shrops 95 L2
Nobottle Nhants 84 C3
Nocton Lincs 135 L6
Nogdam End Norfk 107 H3
Noke Oxon 66 E4
Nolton Pembks 54 E3
Nolton Haven Pembks 54 D3
No Man's Heath Ches W 113 H2
No Man's Heath Warwks 99 H2
No Man's Land Cnwll 6 B3
Nomansland Devon 28 E8
Nomansland Wilts 34 B7
Noneley Shrops 113 H6
Nonington Kent 41 H5
Nook Cumb 157 H6
Nook Cumb 178 B3
Norbiton Gt Lon 51 G5
Norbreck Bpool 146 F7
Norbridge Herefs 81 G6
Norbury Ches E 113 J2

Norbury Derbys 115 J3
Norbury Gt Lon 51 J5
Norbury Shrops 95 J5
Norbury Staffs 114 B6
Norbury Common Ches E ... 113 J2
Norbury Junction Staffs ... 114 B7
Norchard Worcs 81 J2
Norcott Brook Ches W 130 B4
Norcross Lancs 146 F7
Nordelph Norfk 103 L3
Norden Rochdl 140 C5
Nordley Shrops 96 F4
Norham Nthumb 202 D4
Norland Town Calder 141 G3
Norley Ches W 130 B5
Norleywood Hants 18 E4
Norlington E Susx 23 G4
Normanby Lincs 135 K2
Normanby N Linc 143 M4
Normanby N York 162 C6
Normanby R & Cl 170 D7
Normanby le Wold Lincs ... 136 B1
Norman Cross Cambs 102 D5
Normandy Surrey 50 B8
Normans Bay E Susx 24 C6
Norman's Green Devon 14 C2
Normanton C Derb 116 B5
Normanton Leics 117 L3
Normanton Notts 134 E8
Normanton Rutlnd 101 K2
Normanton Wakefd 142 B3
Normanton Wilts 33 K3
Normanton le Heath Leics ... 99 K1
Normanton on Cliffe Lincs ... 118 B2
Normanton on Soar Notts ... 116 E7
Normanton on the Wolds
　Notts 117 G5
Normanton on Trent Notts ... 134 F6
Normoss Lancs 147 G8
Norney Surrey 36 D2
Norrington Common Wilts ... 46 C6
Norris Green Cnwll 6 E1
Norris Green Lpool 129 J1
Norris Hill Leics 116 B8
Norristhorpe Kirk 141 K3
Northacre Norfk 105 J4
Northall Bucks 68 B3
Northallerton N York 160 E4
Northall Green Norfk 121 M8
Northam C Sotn 19 G1
Northam Devon 27 H5
Northampton Nhants 84 E4
Northampton Worcs 81 J2
North Anston Rothm 133 K3
North Ascot Br For 49 M5
North Aston Oxon 66 C1
Northaw Herts 69 H6
Northay Somset 30 D8
North Baddesley Hants 34 E6
North Ballachulish Highld ... 229 G3
North Barrow Somset 31 K5
North Barsham Norfk 121 K4
North Benfleet Essex 53 G1
North Berwick E Loth 212 C2
North Bitchburn Dur 168 F4
North Blyth Nthumb 181 H2
North Boarhunt Hants 19 K2
North Bockhampton Dorset ... 18 B4
Northborough C Pete 102 C2
Northbourne Kent 41 K5
North Bovey Devon 13 H6
North Bradley Wilts 46 B7
North Brentor Devon 12 C6
North Brewham Somset 32 B3
North Bridge Surrey 36 E3
Northbridge Street E Susx ... 24 D2
Northbrook Hants 35 G3
Northbrook Oxon 66 D3
North Brook End Cambs ... 86 F6
North Buckland Devon 27 H3
North Burlingham Norfk ... 107 H2
North Cadbury Somset 31 K5
North Carlton Lincs 135 J4
North Carlton Notts 134 B3
North Cave E R Yk 143 M1
North Cerney Gloucs 64 E5
North Chailey E Susx 22 F3
Northchapel W Susx 36 E5
North Charford Hants 33 L7
North Charlton Nthumb ... 191 H2
North Cheam Gt Lon 51 G6
North Cheriton Somset 31 M5
North Chideock Dorset 15 K4
Northchurch Herts 68 B5
North Cliffe E R Yk 152 D8
North Clifton Notts 135 G5
North Close Dur 169 H4
North Cockerington Lincs ... 137 G2
North Connel Ag & B 228 E8

North Cornelly Brdgnd 42 B5
North Corner Cnwll 3 K7
North Cotes Lincs 145 J7
Northcott Devon 11 L4
Northcott Devon 14 D1
Northcott Devon 29 K8
North Country Cnwll 4 A6
Northcourt Oxon 66 D7
North Cove Suffk 107 K5
North Cowton N York 160 D2
North Crawley M Keyn 85 H6
North Cray Gt Lon 52 A4
North Creake Norfk 121 J4
North Curry Somset 30 D6
North Dalton E R Yk 152 E5
North Deighton N York 150 E5
North Devon Crematorium
　Devon 27 K4
Northdown Kent 41 L1
North Duffield N York 151 L8
North Duntulm Highld 259 G2
North East Surrey
　Crematorium Gt Lon 51 G5
Northedge Derbys 133 G6
North Elham Kent 41 G6
North Elkington Lincs 136 E2
North Elmham Norfk 121 L7
North Elmsall Wakefd 142 D5
Northend Bucks 67 H8
North End C Port 19 L3
North End Cumb 177 K7
North End Dorset 32 D5
North End E R Yk 145 H2
North End E R Yk 153 K7
North End Essex 71 G3
North End Hants 33 J7
North End Hants 35 J5
North End Leics 116 F8
North End Lincs 119 H3
North End Lincs 137 H2
North End Lincs 144 D7
North End Lincs 145 J7
North End N Linc 144 E3
North End N Som 44 E5
North End Nhants 85 J2
North End Norfk 105 K5
North End Nthumb 191 G6
North End Sefton 138 C6
North End W Susx 21 G6
North End W Susx 21 J5
Northend Warwks 83 J5
Northenden Manch 131 G2
Northend Woods Bucks ... 49 L1
North Erradale Highld 260 B4
North Evington C Leic 100 D3
North Fambridge Essex ... 71 K7
North Featherstone
　Wakefd 142 C3
North Ferriby E R Yk 144 B3
Northfield Birm 98 C7
Northfield C Aber 245 K2
Northfield E R Yk 144 C2
Northfields Lincs 102 A2
Northfleet Kent 52 D4
North Frodingham E R Yk ... 153 H5
North Gorley Hants 33 L8
North Green Norfk 106 E5
North Green Suffk 91 G3
North Green Suffk 91 J2
North Greetwell Lincs 135 K5
North Grimston N York ... 152 C2
North Halling Medway 52 F6
North Haven Shet 281 b8
North Hayling Hants 20 B6
North Hazelrigg Nthumb ... 203 G6
North Heasley Devon 28 C4
North Heath W Susx 37 G6
North Hele Devon 29 J6
North Hertfordshire
　Memorial Park &
　Crematorium Herts 86 D8
North Hill Cnwll 11 K7
North Hillingdon Gt Lon ... 50 D2
North Hinksey Village Oxon ... 66 D6
North Holmwood Surrey ... 37 J2
North Huish Devon 7 K3
North Hykeham Lincs 135 J6
Northiam E Susx 24 E3
Northill C Beds 86 C6
Northington Gloucs 63 L5
Northington Hants 35 H3
North Kelsey Lincs 144 D1
North Kessock Highld 251 H2
North Killingholme N Linc ... 144 F4
North Kilvington N York ... 160 F5
North Kilworth Leics 100 D1
North Kingston Hants 18 B3
North Kyme Lincs 118 F1
North Lancing W Susx 21 L5

North Landing E R Yk 153 L2
Northlands Lincs 119 K1
Northleach Gloucs 65 G4
North Lee Bucks 67 K5
North Lees N York 160 D7
Northleigh Devon 14 E3
Northleigh Devon 27 L4
North Leigh Kent 40 F6
North Leigh Oxon 66 A4
North Leverton with
　Habblesthorpe Notts ... 134 F3
Northlew Devon 12 C3
North Littleton Worcs 82 C5
Northload Bridge Somset ... 31 H3
North Lopham Norfk 105 L6
North Luffenham Rutlnd ... 101 K3
North Marden W Susx 20 C4
North Marston Bucks 67 J3
North Middleton Mdloth ... 211 K7
North Middleton Nthumb ... 190 E1
North Millbrex Abers 256 E3
North Milmain D & G 172 D4
North Molton Devon 28 C5
Northmoor Oxon 66 B6
North Moreton Oxon 48 E1
Northmuir Angus 234 B4
North Mundham W Susx ... 20 E6
North Muskham Notts 134 F7
North Newbald E R Yk 152 E5
North Newington Oxon ... 83 K7
North Newnton Wilts 47 H7
North Newton Somset 30 D4
Northney Hants 20 B6
North Nibley Gloucs 63 L7
North Oakley Hants 48 D8
North Ockendon Gt Lon ... 52 C2
Northolt Gt Lon 50 E2
Northop Flints 128 F6
Northop Hall Flints 129 G6
North Ormesby Middsb ... 170 C6
North Ormsby Lincs 136 E1
Northorpe Kirk 141 K3
Northorpe Lincs 118 E8
Northorpe Lincs 119 G4
Northorpe Lincs 143 M8
North Otterington N York ... 160 E5
Northover Somset 31 H3
Northover Somset 31 H6
North Owersby Lincs 135 L1
Northowram Calder 141 H2
North Perrott Somset 15 L1
North Petherton Somset ... 30 D4
North Petherwin Cnwll 11 K5
North Pickenham Norfk ... 105 H2
North Piddle Worcs 81 M4
North Poorton Dorset 15 M3
Northport Dorset 17 H5
North Poulner Hants 18 B2
North Queensferry Fife ... 210 F3
North Radworthy Devon ... 28 C4
North Rauceby Lincs 118 D2
Northrepps Norfk 122 K4
North Reston Lincs 137 G3
North Rigton N York 150 C6
North Ripley Hants 18 B4
North Rode Ches E 131 H6
North Ronaldsay Ork 275 f1
North Row Cumb 165 H4
North Runcton Norfk 120 E8
North Scale Cumb 146 D2
North Scarle Lincs 135 G6
North Seaton Nthumb 181 H2
North Seaton Colliery
　Nthumb 181 H2
North Shian Ag & B 228 E6
North Shields N Tyne 181 J5
North Shoebury Sthend ... 53 K2
North Shore Bpool 146 F8
North Side C Pete 102 F3
North Side Cumb 164 C5
North Skelton R & Cl 170 F7
North Somercotes Lincs ... 145 L8
North Stainley N York 160 D7
North Stainmore Cumb ... 167 J7
North Stifford Thurr 52 D3
North Stoke BaNES 45 L5
North Stoke Oxon 48 F2
North Stoke W Susx 21 H5
Northstowe Cambs 87 H3
North Street Cambs 88 B5
North Street Hants 33 K7
North Street Hants 35 K5
North Street Kent 40 D4
North Street Medway 53 H4
North Street W Berk 48 F4
North Sunderland Nthumb ... 203 K6
North Tamerton Cnwll 11 K3
North Tawton Devon 12 F2
North Third Stirlg 209 K1

North Thoresby Lincs 145 H8
North Togston Nthumb ... 191 K5
Northton W Isls 282 d6
North Town Devon 12 C1
North Town Somset 31 J2
North Town W & M 49 L3
North Tuddenham Norfk ... 122 A8
North Uist W Isls 283 b8
North Walbottle N u Ty ... 180 E5
North Walsham Norfk 122 F5
North Waltham Hants 35 H2
North Warnborough Hants ... 35 M1
Northway Somset 29 L5
North Weald Bassett Essex ... 70 D6
North Wheatley Notts 134 F3
North Whilborough Devon ... 8 C2
Northwich Ches W 130 C5
North Wick BaNES 45 H6
Northwick S Glos 45 K7
Northwick Somset 30 E1
Northwick Worcs 81 J4
North Widcombe BaNES ... 45 H7
North Willingham Lincs ... 136 C2
North Wingfield Derbys ... 133 H6
North Witham Lincs 118 B7
Northwold Norfk 104 E4
Northwood C Stke 114 E2
Northwood Derbys 132 E6
Northwood Gt Lon 50 E1
Northwood IoW 19 G5
Northwood Shrops 113 G5
Northwood Green Gloucs ... 63 L4
North Wootton Dorset 31 L7
North Wootton Norfk 120 E6
North Wootton Somset ... 31 J3
North Wraxall Wilts 46 B4
North Wroughton Swindn ... 47 H3
Norton Donc 142 E5
Norton E Susx 23 G7
Norton Gloucs 64 B2
Norton Halton 130 A3
Norton Herts 86 E8
Norton IoW 18 E6
Norton Mons 62 F3
Norton N Som 44 D6
Norton Nhants 84 B3
Norton Notts 133 L5
Norton Powys 79 K2
Norton S on T 170 B6
Norton Sheff 133 G3
Norton Shrops 95 L7
Norton Shrops 96 B2
Norton Shrops 96 E6
Norton Shrops 97 G3
Norton Suffk 89 J2
Norton Swans 57 H7
Norton W Susx 20 F5
Norton Wilts 46 C2
Norton Worcs 81 K5
Norton Worcs 82 B3
Norton Bavant Wilts 32 F2
Norton Bridge Staffs 114 D5
Norton Canes Staffs 98 C2
Norton Canon Herefs 79 M6
Norton Corner Norfk 122 B6
Norton Disney Lincs 135 H7
Norton Ferris Wilts 32 C4
Norton Fitzwarren Somset ... 30 B5
Norton Green IoW 18 E6
Norton Hawkfield BaNES ... 45 H6
Norton Heath Essex 70 F6
Norton in Hales Shrops ... 113 M4
Norton in the Moors C Stke ... 114 D1
Norton-Juxta-Twycross
　Leics 99 J2
Norton-le-Clay N York 150 F2
Norton Lindsey Warwks ... 82 F3
Norton Little Green Suffk ... 89 K2
Norton Malreward BaNES ... 45 J6
Norton Mandeville Essex ... 70 E6
Norton-on-Derwent N York ... 152 B2
Norton St Philip Somset ... 45 M7
Norton Subcourse Norfk ... 107 H4
Norton sub Hamdon Somset ... 31 G7
Norton Wood Herefs 79 L5
Norwell Notts 134 F7
Norwell Woodhouse Notts ... 134 E7
Norwich Norfk 106 E2
Norwich (St Faith)
　Crematorium Norfk 122 E8
Norwick Shet 281 f1
Norwood Clacks 220 F8
Norwood Derbys 133 J3
Norwood Kent 25 K1
Norwood End Essex 70 E5
Norwood Green Calder ... 141 H2
Norwood Green Gt Lon ... 50 E3
Norwood Hill Surrey 37 K2
Norwoodside Cambs 103 H4

Noseley Leics 101 G4
Noss Mayo Devon 7 G5
Nosterfield N York 160 C6
Nosterfield End Cambs 88 C6
Nostie Highld 248 D6
Notgrove Gloucs 65 G3
Nottage Brdgnd 42 B6
Notter Cnwll 6 D3
Nottingham C Nott 116 F4
Nottington Dorset 16 C6
Notton Wakefd 142 A5
Notton Wilts 46 C5
Nounsley Essex 71 J5
Noutard's Green Worcs 81 J2
Nowton Suffk 89 H3
Nox Shrops 95 K1
Nuffield Oxon 49 G2
Nunburnholme E R Yk 152 C6
Nuncargate Notts 116 E1
Nunclose Cumb 166 C2
Nuneaton Warwks 99 K5
Nuneham Courtenay Oxon 66 E7
Nunhead Gt Lon 51 K4
Nunkeeling E R Yk 153 J6
Nun Monkton N York 151 H4
Nunney Somset 32 B2
Nunney Catch Somset 32 B2
Nunnington Herefs 80 D6
Nunnington N York 161 L6
Nunsthorpe NE Lin 145 H6
Nunthorpe C York 151 J6
Nunthorpe Middsb 170 C7
Nunthorpe Village Middsb 170 D8
Nunton Wilts 33 K5
Nunwick N York 160 D7
Nunwick Nthumb 179 K4
Nupdown S Glos 63 J7
Nup End Bucks 67 L3
Nupend Gloucs 64 A5
Nuptown Br For 49 L4
Nursling Hants 34 E7
Nursted Hants 36 A6
Nursteed Wilts 46 F6
Nurton Staffs 97 J3
Nutbourne W Susx 20 C6
Nutbourne W Susx 21 J3
Nutfield Surrey 37 M1
Nuthall Notts 116 E3
Nuthampstead Herts 87 H8
Nuthurst W Susx 37 J5
Nutley E Susx 23 G2
Nutley Hants 35 J2
Nuttall Bury 140 B4
Nutwell Donc 143 G7
Nybster Highld 280 E3
Nyetimber W Susx 20 E7
Nyewood W Susx 36 B6
Nymet Rowland Devon 13 G1
Nymet Tracey Devon 13 G3
Nympsfield Gloucs 64 A7
Nynehead Somset 29 L6
Nythe Somset 30 F4
Nyton W Susx 20 F5

O

Oadby Leics 100 D3
Oad Street Kent 53 J6
Oakall Green Worcs 81 J3
Oakamoor Staffs 115 G3
Oakbank W Loth 210 E5
Oak Cross Devon 12 D3
Oakdale Caerph 43 J2
Oake Somset 29 L6
Oaken Staffs 97 J3
Oakenclough Lancs 147 K6
Oakengates Wrekin 96 F1
Oakenholt Flints 129 G3
Oakenshaw Dur 169 H4
Oakenshaw Kirk 141 J2
Oakerthorpe Derbys 133 H8
Oakford Cerdgn 76 E4
Oakford Devon 29 G6
Oakfordbridge Devon 29 G6
Oakgrove Ches E 131 H6
Oakham Rutlnd 101 J2
Oakhanger Ches E 114 B1
Oakhanger Hants 36 A4
Oakhill Somset 31 K2
Oakhurst Kent 38 E3
Oakington Cambs 87 H2
Oaklands Powys 78 E5
Oakle Street Gloucs 63 M4
Oakley Bed 85 K4
Oakley Bucks 66 F4
Oakley Fife 210 D1
Oakley Hants 35 H1

Oakley Oxon 67 H7
Oakley Poole 17 K3
Oakley Suffk 106 D7
Oakley Green W & M 50 A4
Oakley Park Powys 93 L6
Oakridge Lynch Gloucs 64 C6
Oaks Lancs 139 K1
Oaks Shrops 95 K2
Oaksey Wilts 64 E8
Oaks Green Derbys 115 J5
Oakshaw Ford Cumb 178 C4
Oakshott Hants 35 M5
Oakthorpe Leics 99 J1
Oak Tree Darltn 169 K8
Oakwood C Derb 116 C4
Oakwood Nthumb 179 L5
Oakworth C Brad 149 J8
Oare Kent 40 C3
Oare Somset 28 D2
Oare Wilts 47 H6
Oasby Lincs 118 D4
Oath Somset 30 F5
Oathlaw Angus 234 D4
Oatlands Park Surrey 50 E6
Oban Ag & B 216 D1
Obley Shrops 95 H7
Obney P & K 232 F8
Oborne Dorset 31 L7
Obthorpe Lincs 118 E8
Occold Suffk 90 D1
Occumster Highld 275 J1
Ochiltree E Ayrs 196 F6
Ockbrook Derbys 116 C4
Ocker Hill Sandw 98 B4
Ockeridge Worcs 81 H3
Ockham Surrey 50 D7
Ockle Highld 237 G6
Ockley Surrey 37 H3
Ocle Pychard Herefs 80 E6
Octon E R Yk 153 G2
Odcombe Somset 31 H7
Odd Down BaNES 45 L6
Oddendale Cumb 166 E8
Oddingley Worcs 81 L3
Oddington Gloucs 65 J2
Oddington Oxon 66 E4
Odell Bed 85 J4
Odham Devon 12 C2
Odiham Hants 49 H8
Odsal C Brad 141 J2
Odsey Cambs 86 F7
Odstock Wilts 33 K5
Odstone Leics 99 K2
Offchurch Warwks 83 J2
Offenham Worcs 82 C6
Offerton Stockp 131 H2
Offerton Sundld 181 J7
Offham E Susx 22 F5
Offham Kent 39 G2
Offham W Susx 21 H5
Offleymarsh Staffs 114 B5
Offord Cluny Cambs 86 E2
Offord D'Arcy Cambs 86 E2
Offton Suffk 90 C5
Offwell Devon 14 E3
Ogbourne Maizey Wilts 47 J4
Ogbourne St Andrew Wilts 47 J4
Ogbourne St George Wilts 47 J4
Ogden Calder 141 G2
Ogle Nthumb 180 E3
Oglet Lpool 129 K3
Ogmore V Glam 42 D6
Ogmore-by-Sea V Glam 42 C6
Ogmore Vale Brdgnd 42 E4
Ogwen Bank Gwynd 126 C6
Okeford Fitzpaine Dorset 32 D8
Okehampton Devon 12 E4
Oker Side Derbys 132 E7
Okewood Hill Surrey 37 H3
Olchard Devon 13 K7
Old Nhants 84 F1
Old Aberdeen C Aber 245 L2
Old Alresford Hants 35 J4
Oldany Highld 270 D2
Old Auchenbrack D & G 185 J3
Old Basford C Nott 116 F3
Old Basing Hants 49 G8
Old Beetley Norfk 121 L7
Oldberrow Warwks 82 D2
Old Bewick Nthumb 190 F2
Old Bolingbroke Lincs 136 F6
Old Bramhope Leeds 150 B7
Old Brampton Derbys 133 G5
Old Bridge of Urr D & G 175 J1
Old Buckenham Norfk 106 B5
Old Burghclere Hants 48 C7
Oldbury Kent 38 F2
Oldbury Sandw 98 C5
Oldbury Shrops 97 G5

Oldbury Warwks 99 J4
Oldbury Naite S Glos 63 J8
Oldbury-on-Severn S Glos 63 J8
Oldbury on the Hill Gloucs 46 B1
Old Byland N York 161 J5
Old Cantley Donc 143 G7
Old Cassop Dur 169 J3
Old Castle Brdgnd 42 D6
Oldcastle Mons 62 C2
Oldcastle Heath Ches W 113 G2
Old Catton Norfk 106 E1
Old Churchstoke Powys 95 G4
Old Clee NE Lin 145 H6
Old Cleeve Somset 29 J3
Old Colwyn Conwy 127 H4
Oldcotes Notts 134 B2
Old Dailly S Ayrs 183 G3
Old Dalby Leics 117 H6
Old Dam Derbys 132 B4
Old Deer Abers 269 H6
Old Ditch Somset 31 H1
Old Edlington Donc 142 E8
Old Eldon Dur 169 H5
Old Ellerby E R Yk 153 J8
Old Felixstowe Suffk 91 H8
Oldfield C Brad 149 H8
Oldfield Worcs 81 J2
Old Fletton C Pete 102 D4
Oldford Somset 32 C1
Old Forge Herefs 63 H3
Old Furnace Herefs 62 F2
Old Glossop Derbys 131 L1
Old Goole E R Yk 143 J3
Old Grimsby IoS 10 b2
Old Hall Green Herts 69 K3
Oldhall Green Suffk 89 H4
Old Hall Street Norfk 122 F5
Oldham Oldham 140 D6

Oldham Crematorium
Oldham 140 D7
Oldhamstocks E Loth 213 G5
Old Harlow Essex 70 C5
Old Heath Essex 72 E3
Old Hunstanton Norfk 120 F3
Old Hurst Cambs 102 F7
Old Hutton Cumb 157 J5
Old Kea Cnwll 4 D6
Old Kilpatrick W Duns 208 D4
Old Knebworth Herts 69 G3
Old Lakenham Norfk 106 E2
Oldland S Glos 45 K4
Old Langho Lancs 148 B8
Old Laxey IoM 154 f5
Old Leake Lincs 119 L2
Old Malton N York 152 B1
Oldmeldrum Abers 256 E6
Oldmill Cnwll 11 M7
Old Milverton Warwks 83 G2
Oldmixon N Som 44 C7
Old Newton Suffk 90 B3
Old Oxted Surrey 51 K8
Old Portlethen Abers 245 L4
Old Quarrington Dur 169 J3
Old Radford C Nott 116 F3
Old Radnor Powys 79 J3
Old Rayne Abers 256 B6
Old Romney Kent 25 J2
Old Shoreham W Susx 22 B6
Oldshoremore Highld 276 C4
Old Soar Kent 38 F3
Old Sodbury S Glos 45 L3
Old Somerby Lincs 118 C5
Oldstead N York 161 H6
Old Stratford Nhants 84 E7
Old Struan P & K 232 B2
Old Swarland Nthumb 191 H6
Old Swinford Dudley 97 K6
Old Tebay Cumb 157 K2
Old Thirsk N York 160 F6
Old Town Calder 140 F2
Old Town Cumb 157 J6
Old Town Cumb 166 B2
Old Town E Susx 23 K7
Old Town IoS 10 C3
Old Trafford Traffd 140 B8
Old Tupton Derbys 133 H6
Oldwalls Swans 56 E6
Old Warden C Beds 86 C6
Oldways End Somset 28 F6
Old Weston Cambs 102 B7
Old Wick Highld 280 E6
Old Windsor W & M 50 C4
Old Wives Lees Kent 40 E4
Old Woking Surrey 50 C7
Old Wolverton M Keyn 84 F7
Old Woodhall Lincs 136 D6
Old Woods Shrops 113 G7
Olgrinmore Highld 279 K5

Olive Green Staffs 115 J7
Oliver's Battery Hants 34 F5
Ollaberry Shet 281 d4
Ollach Highld 247 H1
Ollerton Ches E 130 F4
Ollerton Notts 134 D6
Ollerton Shrops 113 L6
Olmarch Cerdgn 77 H4
Olmstead Green Cambs 88 C7
Olney M Keyn 85 H5
Olrig House Highld 279 L3
Olton Solhll 98 E7
Olveston S Glos 45 J2
Ombersley Worcs 81 J3
Ompton Notts 134 D6
Once Brewed Nthumb 179 H5
Onchan IoM 154 e6
Onecote Staffs 131 L8
Onehouse Suffk 89 K3
Onen Mons 62 E4
Ongar Street Herefs 79 M2
Onibury Shrops 95 L7
Onich Highld 229 G3
Onllwyn Neath 60 C5
Onneley Staffs 114 B3
Onslow Green Essex 71 G3
Onslow Village Surrey 36 E1
Onston Ches W 130 B5
Openwoodgate Derbys 116 B2
Opinan Highld 260 B5
Orbliston Moray 266 F5
Orbost Highld 258 D7
Orby Lincs 137 J6
Orchard Portman Somset 30 C6
Orcheston Wilts 33 J2
Orcop Herefs 62 F2
Orcop Hill Herefs 62 F2
Ord Abers 268 A4
Ordhead Abers 244 E2
Ordie Abers 244 A3
Ordiequish Moray 267 G5
Ordley Nthumb 179 L7
Ordsall Notts 134 D4
Ore E Susx 24 F5
Oreleton Common Herefs 80 B2
Oreton Shrops 96 E7
Orford Suffk 91 K5
Orford Warrtn 130 B2
Organford Dorset 17 H4
Orgreave Staffs 115 J8
Orkney Islands Ork 275 c4
Orlestone Kent 40 C8
Orleton Herefs 80 C2
Orleton Worcs 81 G2
Orlingbury Nhants 85 G1
Ormathwaite Cumb 165 J5
Ormesby R & Cl 170 C7
Ormesby St Margaret
Norfk 123 K8
Ormesby St Michael Norfk 123 K8
Ormiscaig Highld 260 D2
Ormiston E Loth 211 M5
Ormsaigmore Highld 236 D7
Ormsary Ag & B 206 A4
Ormskirk Lancs 138 E6
Ornsby Hill Dur 168 F1
Oronsay Ag & B 214 C6
Orphir Ork 275 b5
Orpington Gt Lon 51 M5
Orrell Sefton 138 D8
Orrell Wigan 139 G7
Orrell Post Wigan 139 G6
Orrisdale IoM 154 d4
Orroland D & G 175 J5
Orsett Thurr 52 D3
Orsett Heath Thurr 52 D3
Orslow Staffs 114 C8
Orston Notts 117 K3
Orthwaite Cumb 165 H4
Ortner Lancs 147 K5
Orton Cumb 157 K1
Orton Nhants 101 H7
Orton Staffs 97 K4
Orton Longueville C Pete 102 C4
Orton-on-the-Hill Leics 99 J3
Orton Rigg Cumb 177 K8
Orton Waterville C Pete 102 C4
Orwell Cambs 87 H5
Osbaldeston Lancs 139 K2
Osbaldeston Green Lancs 139 K1
Osbaldwick C York 151 K5
Osbaston Leics 99 L3
Osbaston Shrops 112 D7
Osborne IoW 19 H5
Osbournby Lincs 118 E4
Oscroft Ches W 129 L6
Ose Highld 258 E8
Osgathorpe Leics 116 D7
Osgodby Lincs 135 M1

Osgodby N York............143 G1
Osgodby N York............163 J5
Oskaig Highld............247 H1
Oskamull Ag & B............226 E4
Osmaston Derbys............115 K3
Osmington Dorset............16 D6
Osmington Mills Dorset............16 D6
Osmondthorpe Leeds............142 A1
Osmotherley N York............161 G3
Osney Oxon............66 D6
Ospringe Kent............40 C3
Ossett Wakefd............141 L4
Ossington Notts............134 E6
Ostend Essex............72 D7
Osterley Gt Lon............50 F3
Oswaldkirk N York............161 K6
Oswaldtwistle Lancs............139 L2
Oswestry Shrops............112 D5
Otford Kent............52 B7
Otham Kent............39 K3
Otham Hole Kent............39 K3
Othery Somset............30 F4
Otley Leeds............150 B6
Otley Suffk............90 E4
Otley Green Suffk............90 F4
Otterbourne Hants............34 F6
Otterburn N York............148 F4
Otterburn Nthumb............190 C7
Otter Ferry Ag & B............206 E2
Otterham Cnwll............11 H4
Otterhampton Somset............30 C2
Otterham Quay Kent............53 H5
Otterham Station Cnwll............11 G5
Otternish W Isls............282 C7
Ottershaw Surrey............50 C6
Otterswick Shet............281 e3
Otterton Devon............14 C5
Otterwood Hants............18 F3
Ottery St Mary Devon............14 C3
Ottinge Kent............41 G6
Ottringham E R Yk............145 H3
Oughterby Cumb............177 J7
Oughtershaw N York............158 F6
Oughterside Cumb............164 F3
Oughtibridge Sheff............132 F1
Oughtrington Warrtn............130 D2
Oulston N York............161 J7
Oulton Cumb............177 H8
Oulton Leeds............142 B2
Oulton Norfk............122 C6
Oulton Staffs............114 B7
Oulton Staffs............114 E4
Oulton Suffk............107 L4
Oulton Broad Suffk............107 L5
Oulton Street Norfk............122 C6
Oundle Nhants............102 A5
Ounsdale Staffs............97 K5
Ousby Cumb............166 E4
Ousden Suffk............88 E3
Ousefleet E R Yk............143 L3
Ouston Dur............181 G8
Outchester Nthumb............203 J6
Out Elmstead Kent............41 G5
Outgate Cumb............156 E3
Outhgill Cumb............158 D2
Outhill Warwks............82 D2
Outlands Staffs............114 B5
Outlane Kirk............141 G4
Out Newton E R Yk............145 K3
Out Rawcliffe Lancs............147 H7
Outwell Norfk............103 K3
Outwick Hants............33 K7
Outwood Surrey............37 M2
Outwood Wakefd............142 A3
Outwood Gate Bury............140 B6
Outwoods Leics............116 C7
Outwoods Staffs............114 B7
Ouzlewell Green Leeds............142 A3
Ovenden Calder............141 G2
Over Cambs............87 H1
Over Ches W............130 C6
Over Gloucs............64 A3
Over S Glos............45 H2
Over Burrows Derbys............115 L4
Overbury Worcs............81 M7
Overcombe Dorset............16 D6
Over Compton Dorset............31 K7
Overdale Crematorium
Bolton............139 K6
Over End Cambs............102 B5
Overgreen Derbys............132 F5
Over Green Warwks............98 F4
Over Haddon Derbys............132 D6
Over Kellet Lancs............147 K2
Over Kiddington Oxon............66 B3
Overleigh Somset............31 G4
Overley Staffs............115 J8
Over Monnow Mons............63 G4
Over Norton Oxon............65 L2

Over Peover Ches E............130 F5
Overpool Ches W............129 J4
Overscaig Hotel Highld............272 B3
Overseal Derbys............115 M8
Over Silton N York............161 G4
Oversland Kent............40 D4
Oversley Green Warwks............82 C4
Overstone Nhants............84 F2
Over Stowey Somset............30 B3
Overstrand Norfk............122 E3
Over Stratton Somset............31 G7
Overstreet Wilts............33 J3
Over Tabley Ches E............130 E4
Overthorpe Nhants............83 L7
Overton C Aber............245 J1
Overton Ches W............129 M4
Overton Hants............35 G5
Overton Lancs............147 H4
Overton N York............151 J5
Overton Shrops............80 C1
Overton Swans............56 E7
Overton Wakefd............141 L4
Overton Wrexhm............112 E3
Overton Bridge Wrexhm............112 E3
Overton Green Ches E............130 F7
Overtown Lancs............157 K7
Overtown N Lans............209 L8
Overtown Swindn............47 H3
Overtown Wakefd............142 A4
Over Wallop Hants............34 C3
Over Whitacre Warwks............99 H5
Over Woodhouse Derbys............133 J3
Over Worton Oxon............66 B1
Overy Oxon............66 E8
Oving Bucks............67 J3
Oving W Susx............20 E6
Ovingdean Br & H............22 E6
Ovingham Nthumb............180 D6
Ovington Dur............168 D7
Ovington Essex............88 F6
Ovington Hants............35 H4
Ovington Norfk............105 J3
Ovington Nthumb............180 C6
Ower Hants............19 H3
Ower Hants............34 D7
Owermoigne Dorset............16 E5
Owlbury Shrops............95 H5
Owlerton Sheff............133 G2
Owl's Green Suffk............91 G1
Owlsmoor Br For............49 K6
Owlswick Bucks............67 J6
Owmby Lincs............135 K2
Owmby Lincs............144 D6
Owslebury Hants............35 G6
Owston Donc............142 E5
Owston Leics............101 G2
Owston Ferry N Linc............143 K7
Owstwick E R Yk............145 H1
Owthorne E R Yk............145 J2
Owthorpe Notts............117 H5
Owton Manor Hartpl............170 C5
Oxborough Norfk............104 E3
Oxbridge Dorset............15 L3
Oxcombe Lincs............136 F4
Oxcroft Derbys............133 J5
Oxen End Essex............71 G1
Oxenholme Cumb............157 H5
Oxenhope C Brad............140 F1
Oxen Park Cumb............156 D5
Oxenpill Somset............31 G3
Oxenton Gloucs............64 D1
Oxenwood Wilts............47 L7
Oxford Oxon............66 D6
Oxford Crematorium Oxon............66 E5
Oxhey Herts............68 E8
Oxhill Dur............180 F8
Oxhill Warwks............83 H6
Oxley Wolves............97 K3
Oxley Green Essex............72 C4
Oxley's Green E Susx............24 C3
Oxlode Cambs............103 K6
Oxnam Border............189 J3
Oxnead Norfk............122 E6
Oxshott Surrey............50 F6
Oxshott Heath Surrey............50 E6
Oxspring Barns............141 J3
Oxted Surrey............51 K8
Oxton Border............201 G2
Oxton N York............151 H7
Oxton Notts............117 G3
Oxton Wirral............129 G2
Oxwich Swans............56 F7
Oxwich Green Swans............56 F7
Oxwick Norfk............121 K6
Oykel Bridge Hotel Highld............271 L7
Oyne Abers............256 B6
Oystermouth Swans............57 H7
Ozleworth Gloucs............64 A8

| **P** |
Pabail W Isls............282 h3
Packers Hill Dorset............16 D1
Packington Leics............116 B8
Packmoor C Stke............114 D1
Packmores Warwks............83 G2
Padanaram Angus............234 D5
Padbury Bucks............67 H1
Paddington Gt Lon............51 H3
Paddington Warrtn............130 C2
Paddlesworth Kent............41 G1
Paddlesworth Kent............52 E6
Paddock Wood Kent............39 G4
Paddolgreen Shrops............113 H5
Padfield Derbys............140 F8
Padgate Warrtn............130 C2
Padhams Green Essex............70 F7
Padiham Lancs............140 B1
Padside N York............149 L4
Padstow Cnwll............10 C7
Padworth W Berk............48 F5
Page Bank Dur............169 G6
Pagham W Susx............20 E7
Paglesham Essex............72 D8
Paignton Torbay............8 C3
Pailton Warwks............100 A7
Paine's Cross E Susx............23 K3
Painleyhill Staffs............115 G5
Painscastle Powys............79 G6
Painshawfield Nthumb............180 C6
Painsthorpe E R Yk............152 B4
Painswick Gloucs............64 C5
Painter's Forstal Kent............40 C3
Paisley Rens............208 E6
Paisley Woodside
Crematorium Rens............208 D6
Pakefield Suffk............107 L5
Pakenham Suffk............89 J2
Pale Gwynd............111 J4
Pale Green Essex............88 D6
Palestine Hants............34 B3
Paley Street W & M............49 L4
Palfrey Wsall............98 C4
Palgrave Suffk............106 C7
Pallington Dorset............16 F4
Palmersbridge Cnwll............11 H7
Palmers Green Gt Lon............69 J8
Palmerston E Ayrs............196 F7
Palmerstown V Glam............43 H7
Palnackie D & G............175 K3
Palnure D & G............174 C2
Palterton Derbys............133 J6
Pamber End Hants............48 F7
Pamber Green Hants............48 F7
Pamber Heath Hants............48 F6
Pamington Gloucs............81 L8
Pamphill Dorset............17 K3
Pampisford Cambs............87 K5
Panborough Somset............31 G2
Panbride Angus............234 E8
Pancrasweek Devon............11 K2
Pancross V Glam............43 G7
Pandy Caerph............43 J4
Pandy Gwynd............92 D3
Pandy Gwynd............111 G5
Pandy Mons............62 C3
Pandy Powys............93 K3
Pandy Wrexhm............112 B4
Pandy'r Capel Denbgs............111 L2
Pandy Tudur Conwy............127 G6
Panfield Essex............71 H2
Pangbourne W Berk............48 F4
Pangdean W Susx............22 D5
Panks Bridge Herefs............80 D5
Pannal N York............150 D5
Pannal Ash N York............150 C5
Pannanich Wells Hotel Abers............243 L4
Pant Shrops............112 D7
Pantasaph Flints............128 E4
Panteg Pembks............74 F5
Pant Glas Gwynd............109 H2
Pantglas Powys............93 G4
Pant-Gwyn Carmth............59 G4
Pant-lasau Swans............57 J5
Pant Mawr Powys............93 J7
Panton Lincs............136 C4
Pant-pastynog Denbgs............128 B7
Pantperthog Gwynd............93 G3
Pant-y-dwr Powys............93 L8
Pant-y-ffridd Powys............94 E3
Pantyffynnon Carmth............57 H3
Pantygaseg Torfn............61 L7
Pant-y-gog Brdgnd............42 D3
Pantymenyn Carmth............75 K7
Pant-y-mwyn Flints............128 E6

Panxworth Norfk............107 G1
Papcastle Cumb............164 F4
Papigoe Highld............280 E6
Papple E Loth............212 D4
Papplewick Notts............116 F1
Papworth Everard Cambs............86 B8
Papworth St Agnes Cambs............86 F2
Par Cnwll............5 H4
Paramour Street Kent............41 J3
Parbold Lancs............139 G5
Parbrook Somset............31 J4
Parbrook W Susx............37 G6
Parc Gwynd............111 G5
Parc Gwyn Crematorium
Pembks............55 K4
Parcllyn Cerdgn............75 M2
Parc Seymour Newpt............44 E1
Pardshaw Cumb............164 E5
Parham Suffk............91 G3
Park D & G............186 D7
Park Nthumb............178 F5
Park Bottom Cnwll............3 H3
Park Bridge Tamesd............140 E7
Park Corner E Susx............38 E6
Park Corner Oxon............49 G5
Park Corner W & M............49 K2
Park Crematorium Hants............36 C1
Park Crematorium Lancs............138 D2
Park End Bed............85 K4
Parkend Gloucs............63 J5
Park End Nthumb............179 K4
Parkers Green Kent............38 F4
Parkeston Essex............73 K1
Parkeston Quay Essex............90 F8
Park Farm Kent............40 D7
Parkgate Ches W............129 G4
Parkgate Cumb............165 H1
Parkgate D & G............176 D1
Parkgate E Susx............24 C4
Parkgate Essex............71 G1
Park Gate Hants............19 J2
Parkgate Kent............39 L6
Parkgate Kent............52 B6
Park Gate Leeds............150 A7
Parkgate Surrey............37 K2
Park Gate Worcs............81 L1
Park Green Essex............70 C5
Park Green Suffk............90 D2
Parkgrove Crematorium
Angus............234 F5
Parkhall W Duns............208 E4
Parkham Devon............27 G6
Parkham Ash Devon............26 F6
Park Head Derbys............116 B1
Park Hill Gloucs............63 H7
Parkhouse Mons............63 G6
Parkmill Swans............57 G7
Park Royal Gt Lon............51 G3
Parkside Dur............169 L1
Parkside N Lans............209 L7
Parkside Wrexhm............129 J3
Parkstone Poole............17 K4
Park Street Herts............68 F6
Park Street W Susx............37 H4
Parkway Herefs............81 G8
Park Wood Crematorium
Calder............141 H3
Parley Green Dorset............17 M3
Parmoor Bucks............49 J1
Parndon Wood Crematorium
Essex............70 C5
Parracombe Devon............28 B2
Parrog Pembks............75 H4
Parsonby Cumb............164 F3
Parson Cross Sheff............133 G1
Parson Drove Cambs............103 J3
Parson's Heath Essex............72 F2
Parson's Hill Derbys............116 A6
Partick C Glas............208 F5
Partington Traffd............130 D2
Partney Lincs............137 H6
Parton Cumb............164 C6
Partridge Green W Susx............22 B3
Partrishow Powys............62 B3
Parwich Derbys............115 K1
Paslow Wood Common Essex............70 C6
Passenham Nhants............84 F7
Passfield Hants............36 B4
Passingford Bridge Essex............70 D7
Paston C Pete............102 D3
Paston Norfk............123 G4
Pasturefields Staffs............114 F6
Patchacott Devon............12 B5
Patcham Br & H............22 D5
Patchetts Green Herts............68 F7
Patching W Susx............21 J5
Patchole Devon............27 J2
Patchway S Glos............45 J3
Pateley Bridge N York............149 L3

Paternoster Heath Essex... 72 D4
Pathe Somset... 30 F5
Pathhead Fife... 222 E8
Pathhead Mdloth... 211 L6
Pathlow Warwks... 82 E3
Path of Condie P & K... 221 K5
Patmore Heath Herts... 70 B2
Patna E Ayrs... 183 K1
Patney Wilts... 47 G7
Patrick IoM... 154 C5
Patrick Brompton N York... 160 B4
Patricroft Salfd... 139 M8
Patrington E R Yk... 145 J3
Patrington Haven E R Yk... 145 J3
Patrixbourne Kent... 41 G4
Patterdale Cumb... 165 L1
Pattingham Staffs... 97 J4
Pattishall Nhants... 84 C4
Pattiswick Green Essex... 71 K2
Patton Shrops... 96 D4
Patton Bridge Cumb... 157 J3
Paul Cnwll... 2 D5
Paulerspury Nhants... 84 D6
Paull E R Yk... 144 F3
Paul's Dene Wilts... 33 K4
Paulton BaNES... 45 K7
Paunton Herefs... 80 F5
Pauperhaugh Nthumb... 191 G6
Pave Lane Wrekin... 114 B8
Pavenham Bed... 85 K4
Pawlett Somset... 30 D2
Pawston Nthumb... 202 C6
Paxford Gloucs... 82 E7
Paxton Border... 202 E3
Payden Street Kent... 40 B4
Payhembury Devon... 14 C2
Paynter's Lane End Cnwll... 3 H2
Paythorne Lancs... 148 E5
Paytoe Herefs... 80 A1
Peacehaven E Susx... 22 F7
Peak Dale Derbys... 132 B4
Peak Forest Derbys... 132 B4
Peak Hill Lincs... 119 J8
Peakirk C Pete... 102 D2
Pearson's Green Kent... 39 H4
Peartree Green Herefs... 80 E8
Peasedown St John BaNES... 45 K7
Peasehill Derbys... 116 C2
Peaseland Green Norfk... 122 B8
Peasemore W Berk... 48 C3
Peasenhall Suffk... 91 H2
Pease Pottage W Susx... 37 L4
Peaslake Surrey... 37 G2
Peasley Cross St Hel... 129 M1
Peasmarsh E Susx... 25 G3
Peasmarsh Somset... 30 E8
Peasmarsh Surrey... 36 E2
Peathill Abers... 269 G3
Peat Inn Fife... 223 H5
Peatling Magna Leics... 100 D5
Peatling Parva Leics... 100 D5
Peaton Shrops... 96 C6
Pebmarsh Essex... 89 G8
Pebworth Worcs... 82 D6
Pecket Well Calder... 140 F2
Peckforton Ches E... 129 M8
Peckham Gt Lon... 51 J4
Peckleton Leics... 100 A3
Pedairffordd Powys... 111 M6
Pedlinge Kent... 40 F8
Pedmore Dudley... 97 K7
Pedwell Somset... 30 F4
Peebles Border... 200 B5
Peel IoM... 154 C5
Peel Lancs... 138 D2
Peel Common Hants... 19 K3
Peel Green Crematorium Salfd... 139 M8
Peene Kent... 41 G7
Peening Quarter Kent... 39 M7
Peggs Green Leics... 116 C7
Pegsdon C Beds... 68 E1
Pegswood Nthumb... 180 F2
Pegwell Kent... 41 K3
Peinchorran Highld... 247 H2
Peinlich Highld... 259 G5
Pelcomb Pembks... 54 F3
Pelcomb Bridge Pembks... 54 F3
Pelcomb Cross Pembks... 54 F3
Peldon Essex... 72 E4
Pell Green E Susx... 39 G6
Pelsall Wsall... 98 C3
Pelsall Wood Wsall... 98 C3
Pelton Dur... 181 G8
Pelton Fell Dur... 181 G8
Pelutho Cumb... 164 F1
Pelynt Cnwll... 5 L4
Pemberton Carmth... 56 F5
Pemberton Wigan... 139 H7
Pembles Cross Kent... 39 M4

Pembrey Carmth... 56 D4
Pembridge Herefs... 79 M4
Pembroke Pembks... 55 G6
Pembroke Dock Pembks... 54 F6
Pembury Kent... 39 G5
Pen-allt Herefs... 63 H1
Penallt Mons... 63 G5
Penally Pembks... 55 J7
Penare Cnwll... 5 G6
Penarth V Glam... 43 J7
Penblewin Pembks... 55 J4
Pen-bont Rhydybeddau
    Cerdgn... 92 E6
Penbryn Cerdgn... 76 B5
Pencader Carmth... 58 E2
Pencaenewydd Gwynd... 109 G3
Pencaitland E Loth... 212 A5
Pencarnisiog IoA... 124 F5
Pencarreg Carmth... 76 F6
Pencarrow Cnwll... 10 F6
Pencelli Powys... 61 H2
Penclawdd Swans... 57 G5
Pencoed Brdgnd... 42 E5
Pencombe Herefs... 80 E5
Pencoyd Herefs... 63 G2
Pencraig Herefs... 63 H3
Pencraig Powys... 111 K6
Pendeen Cnwll... 2 B4
Penderyn Rhondd... 60 E5
Pendine Carmth... 55 L5
Pendlebury Salfd... 140 B7
Pendleton Lancs... 148 D7
Pendock Worcs... 81 H8
Pendoggett Cnwll... 10 E6
Pendomer Somset... 31 H4
Pendoylan V Glam... 43 G6
Pendre Brdgnd... 42 D5
Penegoes Powys... 93 G3
Penelewey Cnwll... 3 K3
Pen-ffordd Pembks... 55 J2
Pengam Caerph... 43 J2
Pengam Cardif... 43 K6
Penge Gt Lon... 51 K5
Pengelly Cnwll... 10 F6
Pengorffwysfa IoA... 125 H1
Pengover Green Cnwll... 6 B2
Pen-groes-oped Mons... 62 C5
Pengwern Denbgs... 127 K4
Penhale Cnwll... 3 H7
Penhale Cnwll... 4 E3
Penhale Cnwll... 5 J3
Penhale Cnwll... 6 E4
Penhallow Cnwll... 4 C4
Penhalurick Cnwll... 3 H3
Penhalvean Cnwll... 3 H3
Penhill Swindn... 47 H1
Penhow Newpt... 44 E1
Penhurst E Susx... 24 C4
Peniarth Gwynd... 92 D2
Penicuik Mdloth... 211 H1
Peniel Carmth... 58 D4
Peniel Denbgs... 127 L7
Penifiler Highld... 259 H8
Peninver Ag & B... 192 F3
Penisarwaun Gwynd... 125 K7
Penistone Barns... 141 K7
Penjerrick Cnwll... 3 K5
Penketh Warrtn... 130 A2
Penkill S Ayrs... 183 G3
Penkridge Staffs... 97 L1
Penlean Cnwll... 11 H3
Penleigh Wilts... 32 E1
Penley Wrexhm... 112 F3
Penllergaer Swans... 57 H5
Pen-llyn IoA... 124 F3
Penllyn V Glam... 42 E6
Pen-lôn IoA... 125 G6
Penmachno Conwy... 110 E2
Penmaen Caerph... 43 J2
Penmaen Swans... 56 F7
Penmaenan Conwy... 126 E4
Penmaenmawr Conwy... 126 E4
Penmaenpool Gwynd... 110 C7
Penmark V Glam... 43 G7
Penmon IoA... 126 C3
Penmorfa Gwynd... 109 K3
Penmount Crematorium
    Cnwll... 4 D5
Penmynydd IoA... 125 J5
Penn Bucks... 67 M8
Penn Wolves... 97 K4
Pennal Gwynd... 92 F3
Pennan Abers... 268 F3
Pennant Cerdgn... 76 F3
Pennant Denbgs... 111 K5
Pennant Powys... 93 J4
Pennant-Melangell Powys... 111 K6
Pennard Swans... 57 G7
Pennerley Shrops... 95 J3

Pennicott Devon... 13 K2
Pennington Cumb... 156 C7
Pennington Hants... 18 D4
Pennington Green Wigan... 139 J6
Pennorth Powys... 61 H2
Penn Street Bucks... 68 A7
Pennsylvania S Glos... 45 L4
Penny Bridge Cumb... 156 D6
Pennycross Ag & B... 226 F7
Pennygate Norfk... 123 G7
Pennyghael Ag & B... 227 G7
Pennyglen S Ayrs... 183 H1
Penny Green Derbys... 133 L4
Penny Hill Lincs... 119 K6
Pennymoor Devon... 28 F8
Pennywell Sundld... 181 J7
Penparc Cerdgn... 75 L3
Penparcau Cerdgn... 92 D7
Penpedairheol Caerph... 43 J2
Penpedairheol Mons... 62 C6
Penperlleni Mons... 62 C6
Penpethy Cnwll... 10 F5
Penpillick Cnwll... 5 J4
Penpol Cnwll... 3 K3
Penpoll Cnwll... 5 K4
Penponds Cnwll... 3 G3
Penpont Cnwll... 10 F7
Penpont D & G... 186 C7
Penpont Powys... 60 E2
Penquit Devon... 7 J4
Penrest Cnwll... 11 L7
Penrherber Carmth... 76 B4
Pen-rhiw Pembks... 75 M4
Penrhiwceiber Rhondd... 43 G2
Pen Rhiwfawr Neath... 57 K3
Penrhiwllan Cerdgn... 76 C6
Penrhiw-pal Cerdgn... 76 C6
Penrhos Gwynd... 108 F5
Penrhos IoA... 124 D3
Penrhos Mons... 62 E5
Penrhos Powys... 59 L6
Penrhos garnedd Gwynd... 125 K5
Penrhyn Bay Conwy... 127 G3
Penrhyncoch Cerdgn... 92 D6
Penrhyn-coch Cerdgn... 92 E6
Penrhyndeudraeth Gwynd... 109 L4
Penrhyn-side Conwy... 126 F3
Penrice Swans... 56 F7
Penrioch N Ayrs... 194 D2
Penrith Cumb... 166 C4
Penrose Cnwll... 10 B8
Penruddock Cumb... 166 A5
Penryn Cnwll... 3 K4
Pensarn Conwy... 127 J4
Pensax Worcs... 81 G2
Pensby Wirral... 129 G3
Penselwood Somset... 32 C4
Pensford BaNES... 45 J6
Pensham Worcs... 81 L6
Penshaw Sundld... 181 H8
Penshurst Kent... 38 E4
Penshurst Station Kent... 38 E4
Pensilva Cnwll... 11 K8
Pensnett Dudley... 97 K5
Penstone Devon... 13 H3
Penstrowed Powys... 94 C5
Pentewan Cnwll... 5 G5
Pentir Gwynd... 125 K6
Pentire Cnwll... 4 C3
Pentlepoir Pembks... 55 J5
Pentlow Essex... 89 G6
Pentlow Street Essex... 89 G6
Pentney Norfk... 120 F8
Pentonbridge Cumb... 178 B3
Penton Grafton Hants... 34 D2
Penton Mewsey Hants... 34 D2
Pentraeth IoA... 125 J4
Pentre Denbgs... 128 C7
Pentre Flints... 129 H6
Pentre Mons... 62 C6
Pentre Mons... 62 E7
Pentre Powys... 94 C6
Pentre Powys... 94 E5
Pentre Powys... 95 J3
Pentre Rhondd... 42 E2
Pentre Shrops... 112 E7
Pentre Wrexhm... 112 D3
Pentre bâch Cerdgn... 77 G6
Pentre Bach Flints... 128 F4
Pentrebach Myr Td... 61 G6
Pentre-bach Powys... 78 B8
Pentrebeirdd Powys... 94 E1
Pentre Berw IoA... 125 H5
Pentrebychan Crematorium
    Wrexhm... 112 D2
Pentre-cagel Carmth... 76 C7
Pentrecelyn Denbgs... 112 A1
Pentre-celyn Powys... 93 J2

Pentre-chwyth Swans... 57 J6
Pentre-clawdd Shrops... 112 D5
Pentre-cwrt Carmth... 76 D7
Pentredwr Denbgs... 112 B2
Pentrefelin Gwynd... 109 J4
Pentrefelin IoA... 125 H1
Pentre Ffwrndan Flints... 128 F3
Pentrefoelas Conwy... 111 G1
Pentregalar Pembks... 75 L6
Pentregat Cerdgn... 76 C5
Pentre-Gwenlais Carmth... 59 H5
Pentre Gwynfryn Gwynd... 109 L6
Pentre Halkyn Flints... 128 E5
Pentre Hodrey Shrops... 95 H5
Pentre Isaf Conwy... 127 K5
Pentre Llanrhaeadr Denbgs... 128 C7
Pentre Llifior Powys... 94 E4
Pentre-llwyn-llwyd Powys... 78 C4
Pentre-llyn Cerdgn... 92 D8
Pentre-llyn-cymmer Conwy... 111 J1
Pentre-Maw Powys... 93 J3
Pentre Meyrick V Glam... 42 E6
Pentre-piod Torfn... 62 B6
Pentre-poeth Newpt... 44 B2
Pentre'rbryn Cerdgn... 76 D4
Pentre'r-felin Cerdgn... 77 H5
Pentre'r Felin Conwy... 126 F6
Pentre'r-felin Powys... 60 D1
Pentre Saron Denbgs... 127 L7
Pentre-tafarn-y-fedw Conwy... 126 F7
Pentre ty gwyn Carmth... 59 M2
Pentrich Derbys... 116 C1
Pentridge Dorset... 33 H7
Pen-twyn Caerph... 61 K7
Pen-twyn Mons... 63 G5
Pen-twyn Torfn... 61 L6
Pentwynmaur Caerph... 43 K2
Pentyrch Cardif... 43 H5
Penwithick Cnwll... 5 H4
Penwood Hants... 48 C6
Penwyllt Powys... 60 C4
Penybanc Carmth... 59 H4
Penybont Powys... 78 F2
Pen-y-bont Powys... 112 B6
Pen-y-bont-fawr Powys... 111 L6
Pen-y-bryn Pembks... 75 L4
Pen-y-cae Powys... 60 C4
Penycae Wrexhm... 112 D3
Pen-y-cae-mawr Mons... 62 E8
Penycaerau Gwynd... 108 C6
Pen-y-cefn Flints... 128 D4
Pen-y-clawdd Mons... 62 F5
Pen-y-coedcae Rhondd... 43 G4
Penycwn Pembks... 54 D2
Pen-y-fai Brdgnd... 42 D5
Pen-y-felin Flints... 128 D5
Penyffordd Flints... 129 G7
Penyffridd Gwynd... 125 J8
Pen-y-garn Cerdgn... 92 D6
Pen-y-Garnedd Powys... 111 L6
Pen-y-genffordd Powys... 61 J1
Pen-y-graig Gwynd... 108 C5
Penygraig Rhondd... 42 F3
Penygroes Carmth... 59 G6
Penygroes Gwynd... 109 H1
Pen-y-Gwryd Gwynd... 126 D8
Pen-y-lan V Glam... 42 F6
Pen-y-Mynydd Carmth... 56 E4
Penymynydd Flints... 129 G7
Pen-y-pass Gwynd... 126 C8
Pen-yr-Heol Mons... 62 E5
Pen-yr-Heolgerrig Myr Td... 60 F6
Penysarn IoA... 125 H2
Pen-y-stryt Denbgs... 112 B1
Penywaun Rhondd... 60 E6
Penzance Cnwll... 2 D5
Peopleton Worcs... 81 L5
Peover Heath Ches E... 130 F5
Peper Harow Surrey... 36 D2
Peplow Shrops... 113 K6
Pepper's Green Essex... 70 F5
Pepperstock C Beds... 68 D3
Perceton N Ayrs... 196 C3
Percyhorner Abers... 269 H3
Perelle Guern... 9 i3
Perham Down Wilts... 34 B1
Periton Somset... 29 G2
Perivale Gt Lon... 50 F2
Perkins Village Devon... 14 B4
Perkinsville Dur... 181 G8
Perlethorpe Notts... 134 C5
Perranarworthal Cnwll... 3 K3
Perranporth Cnwll... 4 B4
Perranuthnoe Cnwll... 2 E5
Perranwell Cnwll... 3 K3
Perranwell Cnwll... 4 C4
Perran Wharf Cnwll... 3 K3
Perranzabuloe Cnwll... 4 C4
Perrott's Brook Gloucs... 64 E6

Place	Page	Grid
Perry Birm	98	D5
Perry Barr Birm	98	D5
Perry Barr Crematorium Birm	98	D5
Perry Green Essex	71	K3
Perry Green Herts	70	B4
Perry Green Wilts	46	E1
Perrystone Hill Herefs	63	J1
Perry Street Somset	15	H2
Pershall Staffs	114	C5
Pershore Worcs	81	L6
Pertenhall Bed	86	B2
Perth P & K	221	K3
Perth Crematorium P & K	221	K2
Perthy Shrops	112	E5
Perton Herefs	80	E7
Perton Staffs	97	J3
Pertwood Wilts	32	E4
Peterborough C Pete	102	D4
Peterborough Crematorium C Pete	102	D3
Peterchurch Herefs	79	L7
Peterculter C Aber	245	J3
Peterhead Abers	257	L2
Peterlee Dur	169	L2
Petersfield Hants	35	M6
Peter's Green Herts	68	F3
Petersham Gt Lon	50	F4
Peters Marland Devon	27	H8
Peterstone Wentlooge Newpt	43	L4
Peterston-super-Ely V Glam	43	G6
Peterstow Herefs	63	H2
Peters Village Kent	52	F6
Peter Tavy Devon	12	C7
Petham Kent	40	F5
Petherwin Gate Cnwll	11	K5
Petrockstow Devon	12	C1
Petsoe End M Keyn	85	H5
Pet Street Kent	40	E6
Pett E Susx	24	F4
Pettaugh Suffk	90	E3
Pett Bottom Kent	40	F5
Petterden Angus	234	C7
Pettinain S Lans	198	F4
Pettistree Suffk	91	G4
Petton Devon	29	H6
Petton Shrops	113	G6
Petts Wood Gt Lon	51	M5
Pettycur Fife	211	J2
Petty France S Glos	46	A2
Pettymuk Abers	257	G7
Petworth W Susx	36	E6
Pevensey E Susx	23	L6
Pevensey Bay E Susx	24	B6
Pewsey Wilts	47	H7
Pheasant's Hill Bucks	49	J2
Phepson Worcs	81	L3
Philadelphia Sundld	181	H8
Philham Devon	26	D6
Philiphaugh Border	200	F7
Phillack Cnwll	2	F3
Philleigh Cnwll	3	L3
Philpot End Essex	70	F3
Philpstoun W Loth	210	E4
Phocle Green Herefs	63	J2
Phoenix Green Hants	49	J7
Phones Highld	241	J5
Pibsbury Somset	31	G5
Pica Cumb	164	D6
Piccadilly Warwks	99	G5
Piccotts End Herts	68	D5
Pickburn Donc	142	E6
Pickering N York	162	D6
Picket Piece Hants	34	E2
Picket Post Hants	18	B2
Picket Twenty Hants	34	E2
Pickford Covtry	99	H7
Pickford Green Covtry	99	H7
Pickhill N York	160	E6
Picklescott Shrops	95	K3
Pickmere Ches E	130	D4
Pickney Somset	30	B5
Pickstock Wrekin	114	A6
Pickup Bank Bl w D	139	L3
Pickwell Devon	27	H3
Pickwell Leics	101	G1
Pickwick Wilts	46	B5
Pickworth Lincs	118	D5
Pickworth Rutlnd	101	L1
Picton Ches W	129	K5
Picton Flints	128	D3
Picton N York	160	F1
Piddinghoe E Susx	23	L6
Piddington Bucks	67	K8
Piddington Nhants	84	F4
Piddington Oxon	66	F4
Piddlehinton Dorset	16	D3
Piddletrenthide Dorset	16	D3
Pidley Cambs	103	G7
Piercebridge Darltn	169	G7
Pierowall Ork	275	C1
Piff's Elm Gloucs	64	C2
Pigdon Nthumb	180	E1
Pigeon Green Warwks	82	F3
Pig Oak Dorset	17	K2
Pig Street Herefs	79	L5
Pikehall Derbys	132	D7
Pilford Dorset	17	K2
Pilgrims Hatch Essex	70	E7
Pilham Lincs	135	H1
Pill N Som	45	G4
Pillaton Cnwll	6	D2
Pillatonmill Cnwll	6	D2
Pillerton Hersey Warwks	83	G5
Pillerton Priors Warwks	83	G5
Pilleth Powys	79	J2
Pilley Barns	142	A7
Pilley Hants	18	E4
Pilley Bailey Hants	18	E4
Pillgwenlly Newpt	44	C2
Pillhead Devon	27	H5
Pilling Lancs	147	H6
Pilling Lane Lancs	147	G6
Pilning S Glos	45	H2
Pilot Inn Kent	25	K4
Pilsbury Derbys	132	B7
Pilsdon Dorset	15	J3
Pilsgate C Pete	102	B2
Pilsley Derbys	132	E5
Pilsley Derbys	133	H7
Pilson Green Norfk	107	H1
Piltdown E Susx	23	G3
Pilton Devon	27	K4
Pilton Nhants	101	M6
Pilton Rutlnd	101	K3
Pilton Somset	31	K3
Pilton Green Swans	56	E7
Pimbo Lancs	139	G7
Pimlico Herts	68	E6
Pimlico Lancs	148	C7
Pimlico Nhants	84	B7
Pimperne Dorset	17	H1
Pinchbeck Lincs	119	H6
Pinchbeck Bars Lincs	119	G6
Pincheon Green Donc	143	G4
Pinchinthorpe R & Cl	170	D7
Pincock Lancs	139	H4
Pinfold Lancs	138	E5
Pinford End Suffk	89	G3
Pinged Carmth	56	D4
Pingewood W Berk	49	G5
Pin Green Herts	69	H2
Pinhoe Devon	13	M4
Pinkett's Booth Covtry	99	H7
Pinkney Wilts	46	B3
Pinkneys Green W & M	49	L3
Pinley Covtry	99	K7
Pinley Green Warwks	82	F2
Pin Mill Suffk	90	E7
Pinminnoch S Ayrs	182	F4
Pinmore S Ayrs	182	F4
Pinn Devon	14	C5
Pinner Gt Lon	50	E1
Pinner Green Gt Lon	50	E1
Pinsley Green Ches E	113	K2
Pinvin Worcs	81	M5
Pinwherry S Ayrs	182	F5
Pinxton Derbys	133	J8
Pipe and Lyde Herefs	80	C5
Pipe Aston Herefs	80	B1
Pipe Gate Shrops	114	A3
Pipehill Staffs	98	E2
Piperhill Highld	253	G2
Pipers Pool Cnwll	11	J6
Pipewell Nhants	101	J6
Pippacott Devon	27	J3
Pippin Street Lancs	139	H3
Pipton Powys	79	G7
Pirbright Surrey	50	B7
Pirbright Camp Surrey	50	B7
Pirnie Border	201	K7
Pirnmill N Ayrs	194	D2
Pirton Herts	68	F1
Pirton Worcs	81	K5
Pisgah Cerdgn	92	E7
Pishill Oxon	49	H1
Pistyll Gwynd	108	E3
Pitagowan P & K	232	B2
Pitblae Abers	269	H3
Pitcairngreen P & K	221	J2
Pitcalnie Highld	264	C5
Pitcaple Abers	256	C6
Pitcarity Angus	233	M2
Pitchcombe Gloucs	64	B5
Pitchcott Bucks	67	J3
Pitcher Row Lincs	119	J5
Pitchford Shrops	96	C3
Pitch Green Bucks	67	J6
Pitch Place Surrey	36	C3
Pitch Place Surrey	50	B8
Pitchroy Moray	254	D4
Pitcombe Somset	31	L4
Pitcot V Glam	42	D6
Pitcox E Loth	212	E4
Pitfichie Abers	256	C3
Pitglassie Abers	256	C3
Pitgrudy Highld	264	B2
Pitlessie Fife	222	E5
Pitlochry P & K	232	D4
Pitmachie Abers	256	B6
Pitmain Highld	241	K3
Pitmedden Abers	256	F6
Pitminster Somset	30	B7
Pitmuies Angus	234	E5
Pitmunie Abers	256	B8
Pitney Somset	31	G5
Pitroddie P & K	222	C2
Pitscottie Fife	223	G4
Pitsea Essex	52	F1
Pitses Oldham	140	E7
Pitsford Nhants	84	E2
Pitstone Bucks	68	B4
Pitt Devon	29	J7
Pitt Hants	34	F5
Pittarrow Abers	245	G8
Pitt Court Gloucs	63	L7
Pittenweem Fife	223	K6
Pitteuchar Fife	222	D7
Pittington Dur	169	J2
Pittodrie House Hotel Abers	256	C6
Pitton Wilts	34	B4
Pitt's Wood Kent	38	F3
Pittulie Abers	269	H3
Pityme Cnwll	10	C7
Pity Me Dur	169	H2
Pivington Kent	40	B6
Pixey Green Suffk	106	E8
Pixham Surrey	37	J1
Plains N Lans	209	L5
Plain Street Cnwll	10	D6
Plaish Shrops	96	C4
Plaistow Gt Lon	51	L2
Plaistow W Susx	36	F5
Plaitford Hants	34	C7
Plank Lane Wigan	139	J7
Plas Cymyran IoA	124	E4
Plastow Green Hants	48	D6
Platt Bridge Wigan	139	J7
Platt Lane Shrops	113	H4
Platts Heath Kent	39	L3
Plawsworth Dur	169	H1
Plaxtol Kent	38	F3
Playden E Susx	25	G3
Playford Suffk	90	F5
Play Hatch Oxon	49	H4
Playing Place Cnwll	4	C6
Playley Green Gloucs	63	M1
Plealey Shrops	95	K2
Plean Stirlg	209	M2
Pleasance Fife	222	C4
Pleasington Bl w D	139	J2
Pleasington Crematorium Bl w D	139	K2
Pleasley Derbys	133	K6
Pleasleyhill Notts	133	K6
Pleck Dorset	32	B8
Pledgdon Green Essex	70	E2
Pledwick Wakefd	142	A4
Pleinheaume Guern	9	j2
Plemont Jersey	9	a1
Plemstall Ches W	129	K5
Plenmeller Nthumb	179	G6
Pleshey Essex	71	G4
Plockton Highld	248	C5
Plowden Shrops	95	J6
Plox Green Shrops	95	J3
Pluckley Kent	40	B6
Pluckley Station Kent	40	B6
Pluckley Thorne Kent	40	B6
Plucks Gutter Kent	41	J3
Plumbland Cumb	164	F3
Plumgarths Cumb	157	G4
Plumley Ches E	130	E5
Plumpton Cumb	156	D7
Plumpton Cumb	166	C3
Plumpton E Susx	22	E4
Plumpton Nhants	84	B5
Plumpton End Nhants	84	D6
Plumpton Green E Susx	22	E4
Plumpton Head Cumb	166	C4
Plumstead Gt Lon	51	L3
Plumstead Norfk	122	C4
Plumstead Green Norfk	122	C4
Plumtree Notts	117	G5
Plumtree Green Kent	39	K4
Plungar Leics	117	K5
Plurenden Kent	40	B7
Plush Dorset	16	D2
Plusha Cnwll	11	J6
Plushabridge Cnwll	11	K8
Plwmp Cerdgn	76	C6
Plymouth C Plym	6	F4
Plympton C Plym	7	G4
Plymstock C Plym	7	G4
Plymtree Devon	14	B2
Pockley N York	161	K5
Pocklington E R Yk	152	B6
Pode Hole Lincs	119	H7
Podimore Somset	31	J6
Podington Bed	85	J3
Podmore Staffs	114	B4
Point Clear Essex	73	G4
Pointon Lincs	118	F5
Pokesdown Bmouth	18	A5
Polbain Highld	270	C6
Polbathic Cnwll	6	C3
Polbeth W Loth	210	D6
Polbrock Cnwll	5	G1
Polebrook Nhants	102	B6
Pole Elm Worcs	81	J5
Polegate E Susx	23	K6
Pole Moor Kirk	141	G4
Polesworth Warwks	99	H3
Polgigga Cnwll	2	B8
Polglass Highld	270	D6
Polgooth Cnwll	5	G5
Polgown D & G	185	H2
Poling W Susx	21	H6
Poling Corner W Susx	21	H5
Polkerris Cnwll	5	J4
Pollard Street Norfk	123	G5
Pollington E R Yk	142	F4
Polloch Highld	228	B2
Pollokshaws C Glas	208	F6
Pollokshields C Glas	208	F6
Polmassick Cnwll	5	G5
Polmear Cnwll	5	J4
Polmont Falk	210	B3
Polnish Highld	237	L4
Polperro Cnwll	5	L4
Polruan Cnwll	5	K5
Polsham Somset	31	H2
Polstead Suffk	89	K7
Polstead Heath Suffk	89	K7
Poltalloch Ag & B	216	C7
Poltescoe Cnwll	3	J7
Poltimore Devon	13	M3
Polton Mdloth	211	J6
Polwarth Border	202	A4
Polyphant Cnwll	11	J6
Polzeath Cnwll	10	C6
Pomathorn Mdloth	211	H7
Pomeroy Derbys	132	B6
Ponde Powys	78	F7
Pondersbridge Cambs	102	F5
Ponders End Gt Lon	69	K7
Ponsanooth Cnwll	3	J4
Ponsonby Cumb	155	J2
Ponsongath Cnwll	3	J7
Ponsworthy Devon	13	M3
Pontac Jersey	9	e4
Pontamman Carmth	59	H6
Pontantwn Carmth	58	E6
Pontardawe Neath	57	K4
Pontarddulais Swans	57	G4
Pont-ar-gothi Carmth	58	F4
Pont-ar-Hydfer Powys	60	C2
Pont-ar-llechau Carmth	59	K2
Pontarsais Carmth	58	E3
Pontblyddyn Flints	129	G7
Pont Cyfyng Conwy	126	F6
Pont Dolgarrog Conwy	126	F6
Pontdolgoch Powys	94	B5
Pont-Ebbw Newpt	44	C2
Pontefract Wakefd	142	C6
Pontefract Crematorium Wakefd	142	C6
Ponteland Nthumb	180	E4
Ponterwyd Cerdgn	93	G6
Pontesbury Shrops	95	K2
Pontesbury Hill Shrops	95	K2
Pontesford Shrops	95	K2
Pontfadog Wrexhm	112	D4
Pontfaen Pembks	75	H5
Pont-faen Powys	75	D8
Pontgarreg Cerdgn	76	C6
Pontgarreg Pembks	75	H5
Ponthenry Carmth	56	E3
Ponthir Torfn	62	C7
Ponthirwaun Cerdgn	76	A5
Pontllanfraith Caerph	43	J3
Pontlliw Swans	57	H5
Pontlottyn Caerph	61	H7
Pontlyfni Gwynd	109	H1
Pont Morlais Carmth	56	F4
Pontnêddféchan Neath	60	D6
Pontnewydd Torfn	62	B7

Pontnewynydd Torfn 62 B6
Pont Pen-y-benglog Gwynd 126 C7
Pontrhydfendigaid Cerdgn 77 K2
Pont Rhyd-sarn Gwynd 111 G6
Pont Rhyd-y-cyff Brdgnd 42 C4
Pont-rhyd-y-fen Neath 42 B3
Pontrhydygroes Cerdgn 77 K1
Pontrhydyrun Torfn 62 C7
Pontrilas Herefs 62 E2
Pont Robert Powys 94 D1
Pont-rug Gwynd 125 J7
Ponts Green E Susx 24 B4
Pontshaen Cerdgn 76 D6
Pontshill Herefs 63 J3
Pontsticill Myr Td 61 G5
Pont Walby Neath 60 D6
Pontwelly Carmth 76 D7
Pontyates Carmth 56 E3
Pontyberem Carmth 58 F6
Pont-y-blew Wrexhm 112 D4
Pontybodkin Flints 129 G6
Pontyclun Rhondd 42 F5
Pontycymer Brdgnd 42 D3
Pontyglasier Pembks 75 K5
Pontygwaith Rhondd 42 F3
Pontygynon Pembks 75 K5
Pont-y-pant Conwy 110 E1
Pontypool Torfn 62 B7
Pontypool Road Torfn 62 C7
Pontypridd Rhondd 43 G4
Pont-yr-hafod Pembks 74 E7
Pont-yr-Rhyl Brdgnd 42 D4
Pontywaun Caerph 43 K3
Pool Cnwll 3 H3
Pool IoS 10 b2
Pool Leeds 150 C6
Poole Poole 17 K4
Poole Crematorium Poole 17 K3
Poole Keynes Gloucs 64 E8
Poolewe Highld 260 D4
Pooley Bridge Cumb 166 B6
Pooley Street Norfk 105 L7
Poolfold Staffs 131 H7
Pool Head Herefs 80 D5
Poolhill Gloucs 63 L1
Pool of Muckhart Clacks 221 H7
Pool Quay Powys 95 G1
Pool Street Essex 88 F7
Pooting's Kent 38 C3
Popham Hants 35 H2
Poplar Gt Lon 51 K3
Poplar Street Suffk 91 K2
Porchfield IoW 19 G5
Poringland Norfk 106 F3
Porkellis Cnwll 3 H4
Porlock Somset 28 F2
Porlock Weir Somset 28 F1
Portachoillan Ag & B 206 B7
Port-an-Eorna Highld 248 B5
Port Appin Ag & B 228 D6
Port Askaig Ag & B 205 G3
Portavadie Ag & B 206 E5
Port Bannatyne Ag & B 207 H5
Portbury N Som 45 G4
Port Carlisle Cumb 177 H6
Port Charlotte Ag & B 204 C4
Portchester Hants 19 K3
Portchester Crematorium
   Hants 19 K2
Port Clarence S on T 170 C6
Port Driseach Ag & B 206 F4
Port Ellen Ag & B 204 E7
Port Elphinstone Abers 256 D7
Portencalzie D & G 182 C8
Portencross N Ayrs 195 K1
Port Erin IoM 154 b8
Portesham Dorset 16 B5
Portessie Moray 267 J3
Port e Vullen IoM 154 g4
Port Eynon Swans 56 E7
Portfield Gate Pembks 54 F4
Portgate Devon 12 A5
Port Gaverne Cnwll 10 D6
Port Glasgow Inver 208 B4
Portgordon Moray 267 H3
Portgower Highld 274 D5
Porth Cnwll 4 D2
Porth Rhondd 42 F3
Porthallow Cnwll 3 K6
Porthallow Cnwll 5 L4
Porthcawl Brdgnd 42 B6
Porthcothan Cnwll 10 B8
Porthcurno Cnwll 2 B6
Porthdinllaen Gwynd 108 D3
Port Henderson Highld 260 B5
Porthgain Pembks 74 D5
Porthgwarra Cnwll 2 B6
Porthill Staffs 114 D2
Porthkea Cnwll 4 D6

Porthkerry V Glam 43 G8
Porthleven Cnwll 3 G6
Porthmadog Gwynd 109 K4
Porthmeor Cnwll 2 C4
Porth Navas Cnwll 3 J5
Portholland Cnwll 4 F6
Porthoustock Cnwll 3 K6
Porthpean Cnwll 5 H5
Porthtowan Cnwll 4 A5
Porthwgan Wrexhm 112 F2
Porthyrhyd Carmth 58 F5
Porth-y-Waen Shrops 112 C6
Portincaple Ag & B 218 C8
Portinfer Jersey 9 a1
Portington E R Yk 143 K2
Portinnisherrich Ag & B 216 F5
Portinscale Cumb 165 H6
Port Isaac Cnwll 10 D6
Portishead N Som 44 F4
Portknockie Moray 267 K3
Portlethen Abers 245 K1
Portling D & G 175 L4
Portloe Cnwll 4 F7
Port Logan D & G 172 D6
Portlooe Cnwll 6 A4
Portmahomack Highld 264 E3
Portmellon Cnwll 5 G6
Port Mor Highld 236 E4
Portmore Hants 18 E4
Port Mulgrave N York 171 J7
Portnacroish Ag & B 228 E6
Portnaguran W Isls 282 h3
Portnahaven Ag & B 204 B6
Portnalong Highld 246 D2
Port nan Giuran W Isls 282 h3
Port nan Long W Isls 282 c7
Port Nis W Isls 282 h1
Portobello C Edin 211 J4
Portobello Gatesd 181 G7
Portobello Wolves 98 B4
Port of Menteith Stirlg 219 J7
Port of Ness W Isls 282 h1
Porton Wilts 33 L4
Portontown Devon 12 A7
Portpatrick D & G 172 B4
Port Quin Cnwll 10 D6
Port Ramsay Ag & B 228 D6
Portreath Cnwll 3 G2
Portree Highld 259 H7
Port St Mary IoM 154 b8
Portscatho Cnwll 3 M4
Portsea C Port 19 L4
Portskerra Highld 278 E3
Portskewett Mons 45 G1
Portslade Br & H 22 C6
Portslade-by-Sea Br & H 22 C6
Portslogan D & G 172 B3
Portsmouth C Port 19 L4
Portsmouth Calder 140 D3
Port Soderick IoM 154 d7
Port Solent C Port 19 L3
Portsonachan Hotel Ag & B 217 G3
Portsoy Abers 267 M3
Port Sunlight Wirral 129 H3
Portswood C Sotn 34 F8
Port Talbot Neath 57 L7
Port Tennant Swans 57 J6
Portuairk Highld 236 E7
Portway Herefs 80 B6
Portway Herefs 80 C8
Portway Sandw 98 B6
Portway Worcs 82 C1
Port Wemyss Ag & B 204 B6
Port William D & G 173 J6
Portwrinkle Cnwll 6 D4
Portyerrock D & G 174 D7
Posbury Devon 13 J3
Posenhall Shrops 96 E3
Poslingford Suffk 88 F5
Posso Border 199 L6
Postbridge Devon 12 F6
Postcombe Oxon 67 H7
Post Green Dorset 17 J4
Postling Kent 40 F7
Postwick Norfk 106 F2
Potarch Abers 244 D4
Potsgrove C Beds 68 B1
Potten End Herts 68 C5
Potten Street Kent 41 H2
Potter Brompton N York 163 H7
Pottergate Street Norfk 106 D5
Potterhanworth Lincs 135 L6
Potterhanworth Booths Lincs 135 M6
Potter Heigham Norfk 123 J7
Potterne Wilts 46 E7
Potterne Wick Wilts 46 E7
Potter Row Bucks 67 L6
Potters Bar Herts 69 H6
Potters Brook Lancs 147 J5

Potter's Cross Staffs 97 J6
Potters Crouch Herts 68 E6
Potter's Forstal Kent 39 M4
Potters Green Covtry 99 K7
Potter's Green E Susx 23 H3
Potter's Green Herts 69 K3
Pottersheath Herts 69 G3
Potters Marston Leics 100 B4
Potter Somersal Derbys 115 J4
Potterspury Nhants 84 E6
Potter Street Essex 70 C5
Potterton Abers 257 H8
Potterton Leeds 150 F8
Potthorpe Norfk 121 L7
Pottle Street Wilts 32 D3
Potto N York 161 G2
Potton C Beds 86 E5
Pott Row Norfk 120 F7
Pott's Green Essex 72 C3
Pott Shrigley Ches E 131 J4
Poughill Cnwll 11 J1
Poughill Devon 13 K1
Poulner Hants 18 B2
Poulshot Wilts 46 E7
Poulton Gloucs 65 G7
Poulton Wirral 129 G5
Poulton-le-Fylde Lancs 147 G7
Poulton Priory Gloucs 65 G7
Pound Bank Worcs 97 G6
Poundbury Dorset 16 C4
Poundffald Swans 57 G6
Poundgate E Susx 38 D7
Pound Green E Susx 23 H3
Pound Green Suffk 88 E4
Pound Green Worcs 97 G7
Pound Hill W Susx 37 L3
Poundon Bucks 66 F2
Poundsbridge Kent 38 E5
Poundsgate Devon 13 G8
Poundstock Cnwll 11 J3
Pound Street Hants 48 C6
Pounsley E Susx 23 J3
Pouton D & G 174 C5
Pouy Street Suffk 91 H3
Povey Cross Surrey 37 L3
Powburn Nthumb 190 F3
Powderham Devon 13 M5
Powerstock Dorset 15 L3
Powfoot D & G 176 F5
Pow Green Herefs 81 G6
Powhill Cumb 177 H1
Powick Worcs 81 J5
Powmill P & K 221 J7
Poxwell Dorset 16 E6
Poyle Slough 50 C5
Poynings W Susx 22 C5
Poyntington Dorset 31 L6
Poynton Ches E 131 J3
Poynton Wrekin 113 J8
Poynton Green Wrekin 113 J7
Poyston Cross Pembks 55 G3
Poystreet Green Suffk 89 K4
Praa Sands Cnwll 2 F5
Pratt's Bottom Gt Lon 52 A6
Praze-an-Beeble Cnwll 3 G4
Predannack Wollas Cnwll 3 H7
Prees Shrops 113 J5
Preesall Lancs 147 G6
Prees Green Shrops 113 J5
Preesgweene Shrops 112 D4
Prees Heath Shrops 113 J4
Prees Higher Heath Shrops 113 J4
Prees Lower Heath Shrops 113 J5
Prendwick Nthumb 190 E4
Pren-gwyn Cerdgn 76 D6
Prenteg Gwynd 109 K3
Prenton Wirral 129 G2
Prescot Knows 129 L1
Prescott Devon 29 K8
Prescott Shrops 96 F7
Prescott Shrops 112 F7
Presnerb Angus 233 J2
Pressen Nthumb 202 C6
Prestatyn Denbgs 128 C3
Prestbury Ches E 131 H4
Prestbury Gloucs 64 E2
Presteigne Powys 79 K2
Prestleigh Somset 31 K7
Prestolee Bolton 139 M6
Preston Border 213 H7
Preston Br & H 22 D6
Preston Devon 13 K7
Preston Dorset 16 D6
Preston E R Yk 144 F2
Preston Gloucs 64 F7
Preston Herts 68 F3
Preston Kent 40 D3
Preston Kent 41 H3
Preston Lancs 139 G2

Preston Nthumb 203 K8
Preston Rutlnd 101 J3
Preston Shrops 96 C1
Preston Somset 29 K4
Preston Torbay 8 D3
Preston Wilts 46 F3
Preston Wilts 47 K4
Preston Bagot Warwks 82 E2
Preston Bissett Bucks 67 G1
Preston Bowyer Somset 29 L5
Preston Brockhurst Shrops 113 J6
Preston Brook Halton 130 B4
Preston Candover Hants 35 J3
Preston Capes Nhants 84 B4
Preston Crematorium Lancs 139 H1
Preston Crowmarsh Oxon 48 F1
Preston Deanery Nhants 84 F4
Preston Green Warwks 82 E2
Preston Gubbals Shrops 113 H7
Preston Montford Shrops 113 G8
Preston on Stour Warwks 82 F5
Preston on Tees S on T 169 L7
Preston on the Hill Halton 130 B3
Preston on Wye Herefs 79 M7
Prestonpans E Loth 211 L4
Preston Patrick Cumb 157 H6
Preston Plucknett Somset 31 H7
Preston St Mary Suffk 89 J5
Preston Street Kent 41 H3
Preston-under-Scar N York 159 K4
Preston upon the Weald
   Moors Wrekin 113 L8
Preston Wynne Herefs 80 D6
Prestwich Bury 140 B6
Prestwick Nthumb 180 E4
Prestwick S Ayrs 196 C6
Prestwood Bucks 67 L7
Prestwood Staffs 97 K6
Price Town Brdgnd 42 E3
Prickwillow Cambs 104 B7
Priddy Somset 31 H1
Priestacott Devon 12 B1
Priestcliffe Derbys 132 C5
Priestcliffe Ditch Derbys 132 C5
Priest Hutton Lancs 157 H7
Priestland E Ayrs 197 H3
Priestley Green Calder 141 H3
Priest Weston Shrops 95 H4
Priestwood Green Kent 52 E6
Primethorpe Leics 100 B5
Primrose Green Norfk 122 B8
Primrosehill Border 213 H7
Primrose Hill Cambs 103 H5
Primrose Hill Derbys 133 J8
Primrose Hill Dudley 97 L6
Primrose Hill Lancs 138 E6
Primsidemill Border 202 C7
Princes Gate Pembks 55 K4
Princes Risborough Bucks 67 K6
Princethorpe Warwks 83 J1
Princetown Devon 12 E7
Prinsted W Susx 20 C5
Prion Denbgs 128 C7
Prior Rigg Cumb 178 B5
Priors Halton Shrops 96 B8
Priors Hardwick Warwks 83 L1
Priorslee Wrekin 97 G1
Priors Marston Warwks 83 L4
Priors Norton Gloucs 64 C2
Priory Wood Herefs 79 J6
Prisk V Glam 42 F6
Pristow Green Norfk 106 C5
Prittlewell Sthend 53 J2
Privett Hants 35 L5
Prixford Devon 27 K3
Probus Cnwll 4 E5
Prora E Loth 212 B3
Prospect Cumb 164 F3
Prospidnick Cnwll 3 G5
Protstonhill Abers 268 E3
Prudhoe Nthumb 180 D6
Prussia Cove Cnwll 2 E5
Publow BaNES 45 J6
Puckeridge Herts 69 K2
Puckington Somset 30 E7
Pucklechurch S Glos 45 K4
Puckrup Gloucs 81 K7
Puddinglake Ches W 130 E5
Puddington Ches W 129 H5
Puddington Devon 28 E8
Puddledock Norfk 105 L5
Puddletown Dorset 16 E4
Pudleston Herefs 80 D3
Pudsey Leeds 141 K1
Pulborough W Susx 21 H5
Puleston Wrekin 114 A7
Pulford Ches W 129 J7
Pulham Dorset 16 D1

Pulham Market Norfk 106 D6
Pulham St Mary Norfk 106 E6
Pullens Green S Glos 63 J8
Pulloxhill C Beds 85 L8
Pulverbatch Shrops 95 K3
Pumpherston W Loth 210 E5
Pumsaint Carmth 77 J7
Puncheston Pembks 75 G6
Puncknowle Dorset 15 M5
Punnett's Town E Susx 23 K3
Purbrook Hants 19 M2
Purfleet Thurr 52 C3
Puriton Somset 30 D3
Purleigh Essex 71 K6
Purley Gt Lon 51 J6
Purley W Berk 49 G4
Purlogue Shrops 95 G7
Purlpit Wilts 46 C5
Purls Bridge Cambs 103 K6
Purse Caundle Dorset 32 B7
Purshull Green Worcs 81 K1
Purslow Shrops 95 J7
Purston Jaglin Wakefd 142 C4
Purtington Somset 15 J1
Purton Gloucs 63 K6
Purton Gloucs 63 K6
Purton Wilts 47 G2
Purton Stoke Wilts 47 G1
Pury End Nhants 84 D6
Pusey Oxon 65 M7
Putley Herefs 80 E7
Putley Green Herefs 80 F7
Putloe Gloucs 64 A5
Putney Gt Lon 51 G4
Putney Vale Crematorium
  Gt Lon 51 G4
Putsborough Devon 27 H3
Puttenham Herts 67 L4
Puttenham Surrey 36 D2
Puttock End Essex 89 G7
Putton Dorset 16 C6
Puxley Nhants 84 E6
Puxton N Som 44 E6
Pwll Carmth 56 E4
Pwllcrochan Pembks 54 F6
Pwll-du Mons 61 L5
Pwll-glâs Denbgs 111 M1
Pwllgloyw Powys 78 E8
Pwllheli Gwynd 108 F4
Pwllmeyric Mons 63 G8
Pwll Trap Carmth 58 A5
Pwll-y-glaw Neath 42 B3
Pydew Conwy 126 F4
Pye Bridge Derbys 116 D1
Pyecombe W Susx 22 D4
Pye Corner Newpt 44 D2
Pye Green Staffs 114 F8
Pyle Brdgnd 42 B5
Pyleigh Somset 29 L5
Pylle Somset 31 K3
Pymoor Cambs 103 K6
Pymore Dorset 15 L4
Pyrford Surrey 50 D7
Pyrton Oxon 67 G7
Pytchley Nhants 101 J8
Pyworthy Devon 11 K2

Q

Quabbs Shrops 94 F7
Quadring Lincs 119 H5
Quadring Eaudike Lincs 119 H5
Quainton Bucks 67 H3
Quaker's Yard Myr Td 43 H3
Quaking Houses Dur 180 F8
Quarff Shet 281 e7
Quarley Hants 34 C2
Quarndon Derbys 116 B3
Quarr Hill IoW 19 K5
Quarrier's Village Inver 208 B5
Quarrington Lincs 118 E3
Quarrington Hill Dur 169 J3
Quarrybank Ches W 130 A6
Quarry Bank Dudley 97 L6
Quarrywood Moray 266 D3
Quarter N Ayrs 207 K6
Quarter S Lans 197 L1
Quatford Shrops 97 G5
Quatt Shrops 97 G5
Quebec Dur 168 F2
Quedgeley Gloucs 64 A4
Queen Adelaide Cambs 104 B7
Queenborough Kent 53 K4
Queen Camel Somset 31 K6
Queen Charlton BaNES 45 J5
Queen Dart Devon 28 E7
Queenhill Worcs 81 K7

Queen Oak Dorset 32 C4
Queen's Bower IoW 19 J6
Queensbury C Brad 141 H2
Queensferry Flints 129 H6
Queensferry Crossing Fife 210 F3
Queen's Head Shrops 112 E6
Queenslie C Glas 209 H6
Queen's Park Bed 85 L5
Queen's Park Nhants 84 E3
Queen Street Kent 39 H4
Queen Street Wilts 46 F2
Queenzieburn N Lans 209 J3
Quendon Essex 70 D1
Queniborough Leics 100 E1
Quenington Gloucs 65 H6
Quernmore Lancs 147 K4
Queslett Birm 98 D4
Quethiock Cnwll 6 C7
Quick's Green W Berk 48 E4
Quidenham Norfk 105 L6
Quidhampton Hants 35 G1
Quidhampton Wilts 33 K5
Quina Brook Shrops 113 H5
Quinbury End Nhants 84 B5
Quinton Dudley 98 C6
Quinton Nhants 84 E4
Quinton Green Nhants 84 F4
Quintrell Downs Cnwll 4 D3
Quixhall Staffs 115 H3
Quixwood Border 213 H6
Quoditch Devon 12 A3
Quoig P & K 220 E3
Quorn Leics 116 F2
Quothquan S Lans 199 G5
Quoyburray Ork 275 d5
Quoyloo Ork 275 b4

R

Raasay Highld 259 K8
Rabbit's Cross Kent 39 K4
Rableyheath Herts 69 G3
Raby Cumb 177 G8
Raby Wirral 129 H4
Rachan Mill Border 199 K6
Rachub Gwynd 126 C6
Rackenford Devon 28 E7
Rackham W Susx 21 H4
Rackheath Norfk 122 F8
Racks D & G 176 D4
Rackwick Ork 275 a5
Radbourne Derbys 115 M4
Radcliffe Bury 140 B6
Radcliffe Nthumb 191 K5
Radcliffe on Trent Notts 117 H4
Radclive Bucks 84 D8
Radcot Oxon 65 L7
Raddery Highld 263 J7
Raddington Somset 29 J5
Radernie Fife 223 H5
Radford Covtry 99 J7
Radford Semele Warwks 83 H2
Radlet Somset 30 B3
Radlett Herts 68 F7
Radley Devon 28 C6
Radley Oxon 66 D7
Radley W Berk 48 A5
Radley Green Essex 70 F6
Radmore Green Ches E 130 B8
Radnage Bucks 67 J7
Radstock BaNES 45 K8
Radstone Nhants 84 B7
Radway Warwks 83 J5
Radwell Bed 85 K4
Radwell Herts 86 E8
Radwinter Essex 88 C7
Radwinter End Essex 88 C7
Radyr Cardif 43 H5
RAF College (Cranwell) Lincs ...118 D2
Rafford Moray 265 H8
Ragdale Leics 117 H7
Ragdon Shrops 95 L5
Raginnis Cnwll 2 D6
Raglan Mons 62 E5
Ragnall Notts 134 F5
Raigbeg Highld 252 F6
Rainbow Hill Worcs 81 K4
Rainford St Hel 138 F7
Rainham Gt Lon 52 B3
Rainham Medway 53 H6
Rainhill St Hel 129 L2
Rainhill Stoops St Hel 129 L2
Rainow Ches E 131 J4
Rainsbrook Crematorium
  Warwks 83 M1
Rainsough Bury 140 B7
Rainton N York 160 E7

Rainworth Notts 134 B8
Raisbeck Cumb 157 K1
Raise Cumb 167 G2
Raisthorpe N York 152 C3
Rait P & K 222 C2
Raithby Lincs 136 F3
Raithby Lincs 137 G5
Raithwaite N York 171 K8
Rake Hants 36 B5
Rakewood Rochdl 140 E5
Ralia Highld 241 G1
Ram Carmth 77 G6
Ramasaig Highld 258 B7
Rame Cnwll 3 J4
Rame Cnwll 6 E5
Ram Hill S Glos 45 K3
Ram Lane Kent 40 C6
Rampisham Dorset 16 A2
Rampside Cumb 146 E3
Rampton Cambs 87 J2
Rampton Notts 134 F4
Ramsbottom Bury 140 B4
Ramsbury Wilts 47 K4
Ramscraigs Highld 274 F3
Ramsdean Hants 35 L2
Ramsdell Hants 48 E7
Ramsden Oxon 65 M4
Ramsden Worcs 81 L6
Ramsden Bellhouse Essex 71 H8
Ramsden Heath Essex 71 H7
Ramsey Cambs 102 F6
Ramsey Essex 73 J1
Ramsey IoM 154 f3
Ramsey Forty Foot Cambs 102 F6
Ramsey Heights Cambs 102 E6
Ramsey Island Essex 72 D6
Ramsey Island Pembks 74 A7
Ramsey Mereside Cambs 102 F5
Ramsey St Mary's Cambs 102 E6
Ramsgate Kent 41 L2
Ramsgill N York 149 K2
Ramshaw Dur 168 B1
Ramshaw Dur 168 F5
Ramsholt Suffk 91 H7
Ramshope Nthumb 189 K5
Ramshorn Staffs 115 H3
Ramsley Devon 12 F4
Ramsnest Common Surrey 36 E4
Ranby Lincs 136 D4
Ranby Notts 134 C3
Rand Lincs 136 B4
Randalls Park Crematorium
  Surrey 50 F7
Randwick Gloucs 64 B5
Ranfurly Rens 208 C6
Rangemore Staffs 115 K7
Rangeworthy S Glos 45 K2
Rankinston E Ayrs 196 E8
Ranksborough Rutlnd 101 H1
Rank's Green Essex 71 H3
Rannoch Station P & K 230 D4
Ranscombe Somset 29 G2
Ranskill Notts 134 C2
Ranton Staffs 114 D6
Ranton Green Staffs 114 D7
Ranworth Norfk 123 G8
Raploch Stirlg 220 D8
Rapness Ork 275 d2
Rapps Somset 30 E7
Rascarrel D & G 175 K5
Rashfield Ag & B 207 J2
Rashwood Worcs 81 L2
Raskelf N York 151 G2
Rassau Blae G 61 J5
Rastrick Calder 141 H3
Ratagan Highld 248 E7
Ratby Leics 100 B2
Ratcliffe Culey Leics 99 J3
Ratcliffe on Soar Notts 116 E6
Ratcliffe on the Wreake Leics ..117 G8
Ratfyn Wilts 33 L2
Rathen Abers 269 J4
Rathillet Fife 222 F3
Rathmell N York 148 D3
Ratho C Edin 210 F5
Ratho Station C Edin 210 F4
Rathven Moray 267 J3
Ratlake Hants 34 E6
Ratley Warwks 83 J5
Ratling Kent 41 H4
Ratlinghope Shrops 95 K4
Rattar Highld 280 C2
Ratten Row Cumb 165 K3
Ratten Row Cumb 165 L1
Ratten Row Lancs 147 H7
Rattery Devon 7 L3
Rattlesden Suffk 89 K3
Ratton Village E Susx 23 K7
Rattray P & K 233 J6

Raughton Cumb 165 L1
Raughton Head Cumb 165 L2
Raunds Nhants 85 K1
Ravenfield Rothm 133 C4
Ravenglass Cumb 155 K3
Ravenhills Green Worcs 81 G4
Raveningham Norfk 107 H4
Ravenscar N York 163 H2
Ravenscraig N Lans 209 K7
Ravensdale IoM 154 e4
Ravensden Bed 86 B4
Ravenseat N York 158 C2
Ravenshead Notts 133 L8
Ravensmoor Ches E 113 K2
Ravensthorpe Kirk 141 K4
Ravensthorpe Nhants 84 C1
Ravenstone Leics 99 L1
Ravenstone M Keyn 85 G5
Ravenstonedale Cumb 158 C2
Ravenstruther S Lans 198 F4
Ravensworth N York 159 L1
Raw N York 163 G2
Rawcliffe C York 151 J5
Rawcliffe E R Yk 143 H3
Rawcliffe Bridge E R Yk 143 H3
Rawdon Leeds 150 B4
Rawdon Crematorium Leeds.... 150 B4
Rawling Street Kent 40 B3
Rawmarsh Rothm 142 C3
Rawnsley Staffs 98 C1
Rawreth Essex 71 J8
Rawridge Devon 14 E2
Rawtenstall Lancs 140 B3
Raydon Suffk 90 B7
Raylees Nthumb 190 C7
Rayleigh Essex 53 H1
Raymond's Hill Devon 15 H3
Rayne Essex 71 H3
Raynes Park Gt Lon 51 G5
Reach Cambs 88 B2
Read Lancs 140 A1
Reading Readg 49 H4
Reading Crematorium Readg.... 49 H4
Reading Street Kent 25 G1
Reading Street Kent 41 L2
Reagill Cumb 166 E7
Realwa Cnwll 2 F4
Rearquhar Highld 263 K3
Rearsby Leics 117 H8
Rease Heath Ches E 113 L1
Reay Highld 279 G3
Reculver Kent 41 J6
Red Ball Devon 29 K7
Redberth Pembks 55 J6
Redbourn Herts 68 E4
Redbourne N Linc 144 B7
Redbrook Gloucs 63 G5
Redbrook Wrexhm 113 H3
Redbrook Street Kent 40 B8
Redburn Highld 253 H2
Redburn Nthumb 179 H6
Redcar R & Cl 170 C4
Redcastle D & G 175 K2
Redcastle Highld 251 G2
Red Dial Cumb 165 H2
Redding Falk 210 B3
Reddingmuirhead Falk 210 B3
Reddish Stockp 131 H1
Redditch Worcs 82 B2
Redditch Crematorium Worcs ... 82 B2
Rede Suffk 88 F4
Redenhall Norfk 106 F6
Redenham Hants 34 C1
Redesmouth Nthumb 179 K3
Redford Abers 235 J2
Redford Angus 234 E6
Redford W Susx 36 C5
Redfordgreen Border 188 C3
Redgate Rhondd 42 F4
Redgorton P & K 221 K2
Redgrave Suffk 105 L7
Redhill Abers 245 H3
Red Hill Bmouth 17 L3
Redhill Herts 86 F8
Redhill N Som 45 G4
Redhill Surrey 37 L1
Red Hill Warwks 82 D4
Redisham Suffk 107 H6
Redland Bristl 45 H4
Redland Ork 275 c3
Redlingfield Suffk 90 E1
Redlingfield Green Suffk 90 E1
Red Lodge Suffk 88 D1
Redlynch Somset 32 B4
Redlynch Wilts 33 L6
Redmain Cumb 164 F4
Redmarley Worcs 81 H2
Redmarley D'Abitot Gloucs 63 L1

Redmarshall S on T........169 K6
Redmile Leics........117 L4
Redmire N York........159 J4
Redmyre Abers........245 G8
Rednal Birm........98 C8
Rednal Shrops........112 E6
Redpath Border........201 J6
Redpoint Highld........260 B6
Red Post Cnwll........11 K2
Red Rock Wigan........139 H6
Red Roses Carmth........55 L4
Red Row Nthumb........191 K6
Redruth Cnwll........4 A6
Redstocks Wilts........46 D6
Redstone P & K........233 J8
Redstone Cross Pembks........55 J4
Red Street Staffs........114 C1
Redvales Bury........140 B6
Red Wharf Bay IoA........125 J3
Redwick Newpt........44 E2
Redwick S Glos........45 H2
Redworth Darltn........169 G6
Reed Herts........87 H8
Reedham Norfk........107 J3
Reedness E R Yk........143 K3
Reeds Beck Lincs........136 D6
Reeds Holme Lancs........140 B3
Reepham Lincs........135 L5
Reepham Norfk........122 B7
Reeth N York........159 J3
Reeves Green Solhll........99 H7
Regaby IoM........154 f3
Regil N Som........45 G6
Reiff Highld........270 C5
Reigate Surrey........37 L1
Reighton N York........163 L7
Reisque Abers........256 F7
Reiss Highld........280 D5
Rejerrah Cnwll........4 C4
Releath Cnwll........3 G4
Relubbus Cnwll........2 F4
Relugas Moray........253 J2
Remenham Wokham........49 J2
Remenham Hill Wokham........49 J2
Rempstone Notts........116 F6
Rendcomb Gloucs........64 C8
Rendham Suffk........91 H2
Rendlesham Suffk........91 H4
Renfrew Rens........208 E5
Renhold Bed........86 B5
Renishaw Derbys........133 J4
Rennington Nthumb........191 J3
Renton W Duns........208 C3
Renwick Cumb........166 E2
Repps Norfk........123 J8
Repton Derbys........116 A6
Resaurie Highld........251 J3
Rescassa Cnwll........5 G6
Rescorla Cnwll........5 G5
Resipole Highld........237 L7
Reskadinnick Cnwll........3 G3
Resolis Highld........263 J6
Resolven Neath........60 C6
Rest and be thankful Ag & B........218 C5
Reston Border........213 J6
Restronguet Cnwll........3 K4
Reswallie Angus........234 D5
Reterth Cnwll........4 F2
Retford Notts........134 D3
Retire Cnwll........5 G2
Rettendon Essex........71 J7
Retyn Cnwll........4 E3
Revesby Lincs........136 E7
Rew Devon........7 K7
Rew Devon........13 H8
Rewe Devon........13 M3
Rew Street IoW........19 H5
Rexon Devon........12 A5
Reydon Suffk........107 K7
Reymerston Norfk........105 L2
Reynalton Pembks........55 J5
Reynoldston Swans........56 E6
Rezare Cnwll........11 L7
Rhadyr Mons........62 D6
Rhandirmwyn Carmth........77 L6
Rhayader Powys........78 D2
Rheindown Highld........250 F2
Rhes-y-cae Flints........128 E5
Rhewl Denbgs........112 B3
Rhewl Denbgs........128 D7
Rhewl-fawr Flints........128 D3
Rhewl Mostyn Flints........128 D4
Rhicarn Highld........270 E3
Rhiconich Highld........276 D5
Rhicullen Highld........263 J5
Rhigos Rhondd........60 D6
Rhireavach Highld........261 G1
Rhives Highld........273 K7
Rhiwbina Cardif........43 J5

Rhiwbryfdir Gwynd........110 D2
Rhiwderyn Newpt........43 L4
Rhiwen Gwynd........125 K7
Rhiwinder Rhondd........42 F4
Rhiwlas Gwynd........111 H4
Rhiwlas Gwynd........125 K6
Rhiwlas Powys........112 B5
Rhiwsaeson Rhondd........43 G5
Rhode Somset........30 C4
Rhoden Green Kent........39 H4
Rhodesia Notts........133 L4
Rhodes Minnis Kent........40 F6
Rhodiad-y-brenin Pembks........74 C6
Rhonehouse D & G........175 J3
Rhoose V Glam........43 G8
Rhos Carmth........58 C2
Rhos Denbgs........128 D2
Rhos Neath........57 K4
Rhosbeirio IoA........125 G2
Rhoscefnhir IoA........125 J4
Rhoscolyn IoA........124 D4
Rhoscrowther Pembks........54 E6
Rhosesmor Flints........128 F6
Rhos-fawr Gwynd........109 G4
Rhosgadfan Gwynd........125 J8
Rhosgoch IoA........125 G2
Rhosgoch Powys........79 H5
Rhos Haminiog Cerdgn........76 F2
Rhoshill Pembks........75 L4
Rhoshirwaun Gwynd........108 C5
Rhoslan Gwynd........109 H3
Rhoslefain Gwynd........92 C2
Rhosllanerchrugog Wrexhm........112 D2
Rhôs Lligwy IoA........125 J2
Rhosmaen Carmth........59 H4
Rhosmeirch IoA........125 H4
Rhosneigr IoA........124 E5
Rhosnesni Wrexhm........112 E2
Rhôs-on-Sea Conwy........127 G4
Rhosrobin Wrexhm........112 E1
Rhossili Swans........56 D7
Rhostryfan Gwynd........125 J8
Rhostyllen Wrexhm........112 D2
Rhosybol IoA........125 G2
Rhos y-brithdir Powys........111 M7
Rhosygadfa Shrops........112 D3
Rhos-y-garth Cerdgn........77 H1
Rhos-y-gwaliau Gwynd........111 H4
Rhos-y-llan Gwynd........108 D4
Rhosymedre Wrexhm........112 D3
Rhos-y-meirch Powys........79 K1
Rhu Ag & B........207 M2
Rhuallt Denbgs........128 C5
Rhubodach Ag & B........207 G4
Rhuddall Heath Ches W........130 A7
Rhuddlan Cerdgn........76 F6
Rhuddlan Denbgs........127 L4
Rhulen Powys........79 G5
Rhunahaorine Ag & B........205 M6
Rhyd Gwynd........110 B3
Rhydargaeau Carmth........58 D4
Rhydcymerau Carmth........77 G7
Rhydd Worcs........81 J6
Rhyd-Ddu Gwynd........109 K1
Rhydding Neath........57 K5
Rhydgaled Conwy........127 K6
Rhydlanfair Conwy........110 F1
Rhydlewis Cerdgn........76 C5
Rhydlios Gwynd........108 C5
Rhyd-lydan Conwy........111 G2
Rhydowen Cerdgn........76 E6
Rhydrosser Cerdgn........77 G2
Rhydspence Herefs........79 J5
Rhydtalog Flints........128 F8
Rhyd-uchaf Gwynd........111 G4
Rhyd-y-clafdy Gwynd........108 E4
Rhydycroesau Shrops........112 C5
Rhydyfelin Cerdgn........92 D7
Rhydyfelin Rhondd........43 H4
Rhyd-y-foel Conwy........127 H4
Rhydyfro Neath........57 K4
Rhyd-y-groes Gwynd........125 K6
Rhydymain Gwynd........110 F7
Rhyd-y-meirch Mons........62 C5
Rhydymwyn Flints........128 E6
Rhyd-y-pennau Cerdgn........92 D6
Rhyd-yr-onnen Gwynd........92 D3
Rhyd-y-sarn Gwynd........110 C3
Rhyl Denbgs........127 K3
Rhymney Caerph........61 H5
Rhynd P & K........222 B3
Rhynie Abers........255 K6
Rhynie Highld........264 C4
Ribbesford Worcs........97 H8
Ribbleton Lancs........139 H2
Ribby Lancs........138 E2
Ribchester Lancs........139 K1
Riber Derbys........132 F7
Riby Lincs........144 F6

Riccall N York........151 K8
Riccarton Border........188 F7
Riccarton E Ayrs........196 E4
Richards Castle Herefs........80 C1
Richings Park Bucks........50 C3
Richmond Gt Lon........50 F4
Richmond N York........159 M2
Richmond Sheff........133 H3
Richmond Fort Guern........9 i2
Rich's Holford Somset........29 L4
Rickerscote Staffs........114 E7
Rickford N Som........44 F7
Rickham Devon........7 L7
Rickinghall Suffk........105 L8
Rickling Essex........70 D1
Rickling Green Essex........70 D1
Rickmansworth Herts........68 D8
Riddell Border........188 E1
Riddings Derbys........116 C1
Riddlecombe Devon........27 L8
Riddlesden C Brad........149 K7
Ridge BaNES........45 H7
Ridge Dorset........17 H5
Ridge Herts........69 G7
Ridge Wilts........33 G4
Ridgebourne Powys........78 E3
Ridge Green Surrey........37 L1
Ridge Lane Warwks........99 J4
Ridge Row Kent........41 G6
Ridgeway Derbys........133 H3
Ridgeway Worcs........82 B3
Ridgeway Cross Herefs........81 G5
Ridgewell Essex........88 E7
Ridgewood E Susx........23 H3
Ridgmont C Beds........85 J8
Riding Mill Nthumb........180 B6
Ridley Kent........52 D6
Ridley Nthumb........179 H6
Ridley Green Ches E........113 J1
Ridlington Norfk........123 G5
Ridlington Rutlnd........101 J3
Ridlington Street Norfk........123 G5
Ridsdale Nthumb........179 L2
Rievaulx N York........161 J5
Rigg D & G........177 J5
Riggend N Lans........209 K5
Righoul Highld........253 G2
Rigmadon Park Cumb........157 K5
Rigsby Lincs........137 H4
Rigside S Lans........198 E6
Riley Green Lancs........139 J3
Rileyhill Staffs........115 J8
Rilla Mill Cnwll........11 K7
Rillaton Cnwll........11 K7
Rillington N York........162 E7
Rimington Lancs........148 D6
Rimpton Somset........31 K6
Rimswell E R Yk........145 J2
Rinaston Pembks........75 G7
Rindleford Shrops........97 G4
Ringford D & G........175 H3
Ringinglow Sheff........132 F3
Ringland Norfk........106 C1
Ringles Cross E Susx........23 H3
Ringlestone Kent........39 L2
Ringley Bolton........139 M6
Ringmer E Susx........23 G5
Ringmore Devon........7 J5
Ringmore Devon........13 L8
Ring o'Bells Lancs........138 F5
Ringorm Moray........254 E3
Ring's End Cambs........103 H3
Ringsfield Suffk........107 H5
Ringsfield Corner Suffk........107 H6
Ringshall Herts........68 C4
Ringshall Suffk........90 B5
Ringshall Stocks Suffk........90 B5
Ringstead Nhants........101 L8
Ringstead Norfk........120 F3
Ringwood Hants........18 A3
Ringwould Kent........41 K5
Rinmore Abers........255 H8
Rinsey Cnwll........2 F5
Rinsey Croft Cnwll........2 F5
Ripe E Susx........23 H5
Ripley Derbys........116 C2
Ripley Hants........18 B4
Ripley N York........150 C4
Ripley Surrey........50 D7
Riplingham E R Yk........144 B2
Riplington Hants........35 K4
Ripon N York........150 D2
Rippingale Lincs........118 E6
Ripple Kent........41 K5
Ripple Worcs........81 K7
Ripponden Calder........140 F4
Risabus Ag & B........204 D7
Risbury Herefs........80 D4
Risby N Linc........144 A5

Risby Suffk........88 F2
Risca Caerph........43 K3
Rise E R Yk........153 J7
Riseden E Susx........38 F7
Riseden Kent........39 H6
Risegate Lincs........119 H5
Riseholme Lincs........135 K5
Risehow Cumb........164 D4
Riseley Bed........85 L3
Riseley Wokham........49 H6
Rishangles Suffk........90 E2
Rishton Lancs........139 L2
Rishworth Calder........140 F4
Rising Bridge Lancs........140 A3
Risley Derbys........116 D4
Risley Warrtn........130 C1
Risplith N York........150 B2
Rivar Wilts........47 L6
Rivenhall End Essex........71 K4
River Kent........41 J6
River W Susx........36 D6
River Bank Cambs........87 L2
Riverford Highld........250 F1
Riverhead Kent........38 D2
Rivers Corner Dorset........32 C8
Rivington Lancs........139 J5
Roachill Devon........28 E6
Roade Nhants........84 E5
Road Green Norfk........106 F4
Roadhead Cumb........178 C4
Roadmeetings S Lans........198 E3
Roadside E Ayrs........197 H7
Roadside Highld........279 L4
Roadwater Somset........29 J3
Roag Highld........258 D7
Roa Island Cumb........146 D3
Roan of Craigoch S Ayrs........183 H2
Roast Green Essex........87 J8
Roath Cardif........43 K6
Roberton Border........188 D3
Roberton S Lans........198 F7
Robertsbridge E Susx........24 D3
Roberttown Kirk........141 J3
Robeston Wathen Pembks........55 J4
Robgill Tower D & G........177 H4
Robin Hill Staffs........131 H8
Robin Hood Lancs........139 G5
Robin Hood Leeds........141 M2
Robin Hood Crematorium
  Solhll........98 E7
Robinhood End Essex........88 E7
Robin Hood's Bay N York........163 G2
Roborough Devon........6 F2
Roborough Devon........27 K7
Roby Knows........129 K2
Roby Mill Lancs........139 G6
Rocester Staffs........115 J4
Roch Pembks........54 E3
Rochdale Rochdl........140 D5
Rochdale Crematorium
  Rochdl........140 C5
Roche Cnwll........5 G3
Rochester Medway........52 F5
Rochester Nthumb........189 M6
Rochford Essex........53 J1
Rochford Worcs........80 E2
Roch Gate Pembks........54 E3
Rock Cnwll........10 C7
Rock Neath........57 L6
Rock Nthumb........191 J2
Rock W Susx........21 K4
Rock Worcs........81 G1
Rockbeare Devon........14 B4
Rockbourne Hants........33 K7
Rockcliffe Cumb........177 K6
Rockcliffe D & G........175 L4
Rockcliffe Cross Cumb........177 K6
Rock End Staffs........131 H8
Rockend Torbay........8 D2
Rock Ferry Wirral........129 H2
Rockfield Highld........264 E3
Rockfield Mons........62 F4
Rockford Devon........28 D1
Rockford Hants........18 B2
Rockgreen Shrops........96 C8
Rockhampton S Glos........63 K8
Rockhead Cnwll........10 F5
Rockhill Shrops........95 G7
Rock Hill Worcs........81 L1
Rockingham Nhants........101 J5
Rockland All Saints Norfk........105 K4
Rockland St Mary Norfk........107 G3
Rockland St Peter Norfk........105 K4
Rockley Notts........134 E5
Rockley Wilts........47 H4
Rockliffe Lancs........140 C3
Rockville Ag & B........207 L1
Rockwell End Bucks........49 J1
Rockwell Green Somset........29 L6

348 Rodborough – Ryebank

Rodborough Gloucs 64 B6
Rodbourne Swindn 47 H2
Rodbourne Wilts 46 D2
Rodd Herefs 79 K3
Roddam Nthumb 190 E2
Rodden Dorset 16 B5
Roddymoor Dur 168 F3
Rode Somset 46 A8
Rode Heath Ches E 130 F8
Rode Heath Ches E 131 G6
Rodel W Isls 282 d7
Roden Wrekin 113 J8
Rodhuish Somset 29 J3
Rodington Wrekin 113 K8
Rodington Heath Wrekin 113 K8
Rodley Gloucs 63 L5
Rodley Leeds 150 B8
Rodmarton Gloucs 64 D7
Rodmell E Susx 22 F6
Rodmersham Kent 40 B3
Rodmersham Green Kent 40 B3
Rodney Stoke Somset 31 H1
Rodsley Derbys 115 K3
Rodway Somset 30 C3
Roecliffe N York 150 E3
Roe Cross Tamesd 140 E8
Roe Green Herts 69 G5
Roe Green Herts 87 G8
Roe Green Salfd 139 L7
Roehampton Gt Lon 51 G4
Roffey W Susx 37 J4
Rogart Highld 273 H7
Rogate W Susx 36 B6
Roger Ground Cumb 156 E3
Rogerstone Newpt 44 B2
Roghadal W Isls 282 d7
Rogiet Mons 44 F2
Roke Oxon 66 F8
Roker Sundld 181 K7
Rollesby Norfk 123 J8
Rolleston Leics 100 F3
Rolleston Notts 117 K1
Rolleston on Dove Staffs 115 L6
Rolston E R Yk 153 K6
Rolstone N Som 44 D6
Rolvenden Kent 39 L7
Rolvenden Layne Kent 39 L7
Romaldkirk Dur 168 C6
Romanby N York 160 E4
Romanno Bridge Border 199 K3
Romansleigh Devon 28 C6
Romden Castle Kent 40 A7
Romesdal Highld 258 F6
Romford Dorset 17 L1
Romford Gt Lon 52 B1
Romiley Stockp 131 J2
Romney Street Kent 52 C6
Romsey Cambs 87 K4
Romsey Hants 34 D6
Romsley Shrops 97 H6
Romsley Worcs 98 B7
Rona Highld 259 L5
Ronachan Ag & B 206 B8
Rood Ashton Wilts 46 C7
Rookhope Dur 167 L2
Rookley IoW 19 H6
Rookley Green IoW 19 H7
Rooks Bridge Somset 44 D8
Rooks Nest Somset 29 K4
Rookwith N York 160 B5
Roos E R Yk 145 H2
Roose Cumb 146 D2
Roosebeck Cumb 146 E2
Roothams Green Bed 86 B4
Ropley Hants 35 K4
Ropley Dean Hants 35 K4
Ropley Soke Hants 35 K4
Ropsley Lincs 118 C5
Rora Abers 269 K6
Rorrington Shrops 95 H3
Rosarie Moray 267 H6
Rose Cnwll 4 C4
Roseacre Lancs 147 H8
Rose Ash Devon 28 D6
Rosebank S Lans 198 D3
Rosebush Pembks 75 J6
Rosecare Cnwll 11 H3
Rosecliston Cnwll 4 D3
Rosedale Abbey N York 162 C3
Rose Green Essex 72 C2
Rose Green Suffk 89 J7
Rose Green Suffk 89 K6
Rose Green W Susx 20 E7
Rosehall Highld 272 C7
Rosehearty Abers 269 G3
Rose Hill E Susx 23 G4
Rose Hill Lancs 140 B2
Rosehill Shrops 113 G8
Rose Hill Crematorium Donc 142 F7
Roseisle Moray 266 C3
Roselands E Susx 23 K7
Rosemarket Pembks 54 F5
Rosemarkie Highld 263 K8
Rosemary Lane Devon 29 L7
Rosemount P & K 233 J6
Rosenannon Cnwll 4 F2
Rosenithon Cnwll 3 K6
Roser's Cross E Susx 23 J3
Rosevean Cnwll 5 H3
Rosevine Cnwll 3 M4
Rosewarne Cnwll 2 F4
Rosewell Mdloth 211 J6
Roseworth S on T 169 L6
Roseworthy Cnwll 3 G3
Rosgill Cumb 166 D7
Roskestal Cnwll 2 B6
Roskhill Highld 258 D7
Roskorwell Cnwll 3 K6
Rosley Cumb 165 K2
Roslin Mdloth 211 J6
Rosliston Derbys 115 L8
Rosneath Ag & B 207 L2
Ross D & G 175 G6
Ross Nthumb 203 J5
Rossett Wrexhm 129 J8
Rossett Green N York 150 D5
Rossington Donc 143 G8
Rossland Rens 208 D5
Ross-on-Wye Herefs 63 J2
Roster Highld 280 C8
Rostherne Ches E 130 E3
Rosthwaite Cumb 165 H7
Roston Derbys 115 J3
Rosudgeon Cnwll 2 E5
Rosyth Fife 210 F2
Rothbury Nthumb 190 F6
Rotherby Leics 117 H8
Rotherfield E Susx 38 E7
Rotherfield Greys Oxon 49 H3
Rotherfield Peppard Oxon 49 H3
Rotherham Rothm 133 H1
Rotherham Crematorium Rothm 133 J1
Rothersthorpe Nhants 84 D4
Rotherwick Hants 49 H7
Rothes Moray 266 F6
Rothesay Ag & B 207 H6
Rothiebrisbane Abers 256 D4
Rothiemay Moray 267 L6
Rothiemurchus Lodge Highld 242 C2
Rothienorman Abers 256 C4
Rothley Leics 100 D1
Rothley Nthumb 180 C1
Rothmaise Abers 256 B5
Rothwell Leeds 142 A2
Rothwell Lincs 144 F7
Rothwell Nhants 101 H7
Rotsea E R Yk 153 G5
Rottal Lodge Angus 234 B2
Rottingdean Br & H 22 F6
Rottington Cumb 164 C8
Roucan D & G 176 D3
Roucan Loch Crematorium D & G 176 D3
Roud IoW 19 H7
Rougham Norfk 121 H7
Rougham Suffk 89 H3
Rough Close Staffs 114 E4
Rough Common Kent 40 F3
Roughlee Lancs 148 E7
Roughpark Abers 243 K1
Roughton Lincs 136 D6
Roughton Norfk 122 E4
Roughton Shrops 97 G4
Roughway Kent 38 F3
Roundbush Essex 72 B6
Round Bush Herts 68 F7
Roundbush Green Essex 70 E4
Round Green Luton 68 E3
Roundham Somset 15 K1
Roundhay Leeds 150 D8
Rounds Green Sandw 98 C5
Round Street Kent 52 E5
Roundstreet Common W Susx 37 G5
Roundswell Devon 27 K4
Roundway Wilts 46 E6
Roundyhill Angus 234 B5
Rousay Ork 275 c3
Rousdon Devon 15 G4
Rousham Oxon 66 C2
Rous Lench Worcs 82 B4
Routenburn N Ayrs 207 K6
Routh E R Yk 153 H7
Rout's Green Bucks 67 J7
Row Cnwll 10 F7
Row Cumb 157 G5
Row Cumb 166 E4
Rowanburn D & G 177 L3
Rowardennan Stirlg 218 E7
Rowarth Derbys 131 K2
Row Ash Hants 35 H8
Rowberrow Somset 44 F7
Rowborough IoW 19 G6
Rowde Wilts 46 E6
Rowden Devon 12 F3
Rowen Conwy 126 E5
Rowfield Derbys 115 K2
Rowfoot Nthumb 178 F6
Rowford Somset 30 C5
Row Green Essex 71 H3
Rowhedge Essex 72 F3
Rowhook W Susx 37 H4
Rowington Warwks 82 F2
Rowland Derbys 132 D5
Rowland's Castle Hants 20 B5
Rowlands Gill Gatesd 180 E7
Rowledge Surrey 36 B2
Rowley Dur 168 E1
Rowley E R Yk 144 B1
Rowley Shrops 95 H2
Rowley Hill Kirk 141 J5
Rowley Regis Sandw 98 B6
Rowley Regis Crematorium Sandw 98 B6
Rowlstone Herefs 62 D2
Rowly Surrey 37 G3
Rowner Hants 19 K3
Rowney Green Worcs 82 B1
Rownhams Hants 34 E7
Rowrah Cumb 164 E7
Rowsham Bucks 67 K3
Rowsley Derbys 132 E6
Rows of Trees Ches E 131 G4
Rowstock Oxon 48 C1
Rowston Lincs 136 A8
Rowthorne Derbys 133 J6
Rowton Ches W 129 K6
Rowton Shrops 95 J1
Rowton Shrops 95 K7
Rowton Wrekin 113 K7
Row Town Surrey 50 D6
Roxburgh Border 201 L7
Roxby N Linc 144 A4
Roxby N York 171 H7
Roxton Bed 86 C4
Roxwell Essex 70 F5
Royal Leamington Spa Warwks 83 H2
Royal Oak Darltn 169 G6
Royal Oak Lancs 138 E7
Royal's Green Ches E 113 K3
Royal Sutton Coldfield Birm 98 E4
Royal Tunbridge Wells Kent 38 F5
Royal Wootton Bassett Wilts 46 F3
Roy Bridge Highld 239 M7
Roydhouse Kirk 141 K5
Roydon Essex 69 L5
Roydon Norfk 106 C7
Roydon Norfk 120 F7
Roydon Hamlet Essex 69 L5
Royston Barns 142 B5
Royston Herts 87 G7
Royton Oldham 140 D6
Rozel Jersey 9 e2
Ruabon Wrexhm 112 D3
Ruaig Ag & B 224 D5
Ruan High Lanes Cnwll 4 E6
Ruan Lanihorne Cnwll 4 E6
Ruan Major Cnwll 3 H7
Ruan Minor Cnwll 3 J8
Ruardean Gloucs 63 J3
Ruardean Hill Gloucs 63 J4
Ruardean Woodside Gloucs 63 J4
Rubery Birm 98 C7
Rubha Ban W Isls 283 c12
Ruckcroft Cumb 166 C2
Ruckhall Herefs 80 B7
Ruckinge Kent 40 D8
Ruckland Lincs 136 F4
Ruckley Shrops 96 C3
Rudby N York 161 G1
Rudchester Nthumb 180 D5
Ruddington Notts 116 F5
Ruddle Gloucs 63 K5
Ruddlemoor Cnwll 5 G4
Rudford Gloucs 63 M3
Rudge Somset 46 B8
Rudgeway S Glos 45 J2
Rudgwick W Susx 37 G4
Rudhall Herefs 63 J2
Rudheath Ches W 130 D5
Rudheath Woods Ches E 130 E5
Rudley Green Essex 71 K6
Rudloe Wilts 46 B5
Rudry Caerph 43 K4
Rudston E R Yk 153 H2
Rudyard Staffs 131 J8
Ruecastle Border 189 G2
Rufford Lancs 138 F4
Rufforth C York 151 H5
Rug Denbgs 111 K3
Rugby Warwks 100 B8
Rugeley Staffs 115 G7
Ruishton Somset 30 C6
Ruislip Gt Lon 50 E2
Rùm Highld 236 D1
Rumbach Moray 267 H5
Rumbling Bridge P & K 221 J7
Rumburgh Suffk 107 G7
Rumby Hill Dur 168 F4
Rumford Cnwll 10 B8
Rumford Falk 210 B4
Rumney Cardif 43 K6
Rumwell Somset 30 B6
Runcorn Halton 129 L3
Runcton W Susx 20 E6
Runcton Holme Norfk 104 C2
Runfold Surrey 36 C2
Runhall Norfk 105 L2
Runham Norfk 107 J1
Runham Norfk 107 L2
Runnington Somset 29 L6
Runsell Green Essex 71 J6
Runshaw Moor Lancs 139 G4
Runswick N York 171 J7
Runtaleave Angus 233 L2
Runwell Essex 71 J8
Ruscombe Wokham 49 J4
Rushall Herefs 80 E8
Rushall Norfk 106 D6
Rushall Wilts 47 H7
Rushall Wsall 98 C3
Rushbrooke Suffk 89 H3
Rushbury Shrops 96 C5
Rushden Herts 69 J1
Rushden Nhants 85 J2
Rushenden Kent 53 K5
Rusher's Cross E Susx 38 F7
Rushford Devon 12 B7
Rushford Norfk 105 J7
Rush Green Essex 73 H4
Rush Green Gt Lon 52 B2
Rush Green Herts 69 G2
Rush Green Warrtn 130 D2
Rushlake Green E Susx 23 L3
Rushmere Suffk 107 K6
Rushmere St Andrew Suffk 90 E6
Rushmoor Surrey 36 C3
Rushock Herefs 79 K3
Rushock Worcs 81 K1
Rusholme Manch 131 G1
Rushton Ches W 130 B7
Rushton Nhants 101 J6
Rushton Shrops 96 D2
Rushton Spencer Staffs 131 J7
Rushwick Worcs 81 J4
Rushyford Dur 169 H5
Ruskie Stirlg 219 K7
Ruskington Lincs 118 E1
Rusland Cross Cumb 156 E5
Rusper W Susx 37 K3
Ruspidge Gloucs 63 K5
Russell Green Essex 71 H4
Russell's Water Oxon 49 H1
Russel's Green Suffk 90 F1
Russ Hill Surrey 37 K3
Rusthall Kent 38 E5
Rustington W Susx 21 H6
Ruston N York 163 G6
Ruston Parva E R Yk 153 G3
Ruswarp N York 162 F1
Ruthall Shrops 96 D5
Rutherford Border 201 K7
Rutherglen S Lans 209 G6
Ruthernbridge Cnwll 5 G2
Ruthin Denbgs 128 D8
Ruthrieston C Aber 245 K3
Ruthven Abers 267 K6
Ruthven Angus 233 L5
Ruthven Highld 241 K4
Ruthven Highld 252 F5
Ruthvoes Cnwll 4 F3
Ruthwaite Cumb 165 H3
Ruthwell D & G 176 E5
Ruxley Corner Gt Lon 52 A5
Ruxton Green Herefs 63 G3
Ruyton-XI-Towns Shrops 112 F7
Ryal Nthumb 180 B4
Ryall Dorset 15 J4
Ryall Worcs 81 K7
Ryarsh Kent 52 E7
Rycote Oxon 67 G6
Rydal Cumb 156 E2
Ryde IoW 19 K5
Rye E Susx 25 G3
Ryebank Shrops 113 H5

Ryeford Herefs ... 63 J3
Rye Foreign E Susx ... 25 G3
Rye Harbour E Susx ... 25 H3
Ryehill E R Yk ... 145 G3
Ryeish Green Wokham ... 49 H5
Rye Street Worcs ... 81 H8
Ryhall Rutlnd ... 102 A1
Ryhill Wakefd ... 142 B5
Ryhope Sundld ... 181 K8
Rylah Derbys ... 133 J6
Ryland Lincs ... 135 K4
Rylands Notts ... 116 F4
Rylstone N York ... 149 H4
Ryme Intrinseca Dorset ... 31 J8
Ryther N York ... 151 J7
Ryton Gatesd ... 180 E6
Ryton N York ... 162 D7
Ryton Shrops ... 97 G3
Ryton Warwks ... 99 L6
Ryton-on-Dunsmore Warwks ... 99 K8
Ryton Woodside Gatesd ... 180 E6

S

Sabden Lancs ... 148 D8
Sabine's Green Essex ... 70 E7
Sacombe Herts ... 69 J3
Sacombe Green Herts ... 69 J3
Sacriston Dur ... 169 G1
Sadberge Darltn ... 169 J7
Saddell Ag & B ... 194 B4
Saddington Leics ... 100 E5
Saddle Bow Norfk ... 120 D8
Saddlescombe W Susx ... 22 D5
Sadgill Cumb ... 157 G2
Saffron Walden Essex ... 87 L7
Sageston Pembks ... 55 H6
Saham Hills Norfk ... 105 H3
Saham Toney Norfk ... 105 H3
Saighton Ches W ... 129 K7
St Abbs Border ... 213 K5
St Agnes Border ... 212 F6
St Agnes Cnwll ... 4 B5
St Agnes IoS ... 10 b3
St Albans Herts ... 68 F5
St Allen Cnwll ... 4 D5
St Andrew Guern ... 9 j3
St Andrews Fife ... 223 J4
St Andrew's Major V Glam ... 43 H7
St Andrews Well Dorset ... 15 L4
St Anne's Lancs ... 138 C2
St Ann's D & G ... 187 G7
St Ann's Chapel Cnwll ... 12 A8
St Ann's Chapel Devon ... 7 J5
St Anthony Cnwll ... 3 K6
St Anthony's Hill E Susx ... 23 L7
St Arvans Mons ... 63 G7
St Asaph Denbgs ... 128 B5
St Athan V Glam ... 42 F8
St Aubin Jersey ... 9 c3
St Austell Cnwll ... 5 G4
St Bees Cumb ... 164 C8
St Blazey Cnwll ... 5 H4
St Blazey Gate Cnwll ... 5 H4
St Boswells Border ... 201 J7
St Brelade Jersey ... 9 b3
St Brelade's Bay Jersey ... 9 b3
St Breock Cnwll ... 10 D8
St Breward Cnwll ... 10 F7
St Briavels Gloucs ... 63 H6
St Brides Pembks ... 54 C5
St Bride's Major V Glam ... 42 D6
St Brides Netherwent Mons ... 44 E1
St Brides-super-Ely V Glam ... 43 H6
St Brides Wentlooge Newpt ... 44 C3
St Budeaux C Plym ... 6 E3
Saintbury Gloucs ... 82 D7
St Buryan Cnwll ... 2 C6
St Catherine BaNES ... 45 M5
St Catherines Ag & B ... 217 J5
St Chloe Gloucs ... 64 B6
St Clears Carmth ... 58 A5
St Cleer Cnwll ... 6 A1
St Clement Cnwll ... 4 D6
St Clement Jersey ... 9 e4
St Clether Cnwll ... 11 H5
St Colmac Ag & B ... 207 G5
St Columb Major Cnwll ... 4 E2
St Columb Minor Cnwll ... 4 D2
St Columb Road Cnwll ... 4 E3
St Combs Abers ... 269 K4
St Cross South Elmham Suffk ... 106 F6
St Cyrus Abers ... 235 J2
St David's P & K ... 221 G3
St Davids Pembks ... 74 B7
St Day Cnwll ... 4 B6
St Decumans Somset ... 29 K2

St Dennis Cnwll ... 4 F3
St Devereux Herefs ... 62 E1
St Dogmaels Pembks ... 75 K3
St Dogwells Pembks ... 75 G6
St Dominick Cnwll ... 6 D1
St Donats V Glam ... 42 E8
St Edith's Marsh Wilts ... 46 E6
St Endellion Cnwll ... 10 D6
St Enoder Cnwll ... 4 E3
St Erme Cnwll ... 4 D5
St Erney Cnwll ... 6 D3
St Erth Cnwll ... 2 E4
St Erth Praze Cnwll ... 2 F4
St Ervan Cnwll ... 10 B8
St Eval Cnwll ... 4 E1
St Ewe Cnwll ... 5 G5
St Fagans Cardif ... 43 H6
St Fergus Abers ... 269 K6
St Fillans P & K ... 220 B2
St Florence Pembks ... 55 J6
St Gennys Cnwll ... 11 G3
St George Conwy ... 127 K4
St Georges N Som ... 44 D6
St George's V Glam ... 43 H6
St George's Hill Surrey ... 50 D6
St Germans Cnwll ... 6 D3
St Giles in the Wood Devon ... 27 J7
St Giles-on-the-Heath Devon ... 11 L4
St Gluvia's Cnwll ... 3 K4
St Harmon Powys ... 78 D1
St Helen Auckland Dur ... 168 F5
St Helens Cumb ... 164 D4
St Helen's E Susx ... 24 E5
St Helens IoW ... 19 L6
St Helens St Hel ... 139 G8
St Helens Crematorium St Hel ... 139 G8
St Helier Gt Lon ... 51 H5
St Helier Jersey ... 9 d3
St Hilary Cnwll ... 2 E5
St Hilary V Glam ... 42 F7
Saint Hill Devon ... 14 C1
Saint Hill W Susx ... 38 B6
St Illtyd Blae G ... 61 K6
St Ippollitts Herts ... 69 G2
St Ishmael's Pembks ... 54 D5
St Issey Cnwll ... 10 C8
St Ive Cnwll ... 6 C2
St Ive Cross Cnwll ... 6 C2
St Ives Cambs ... 87 G1
St Ives Cnwll ... 2 E5
St Ives Dorset ... 17 M2
St James Norfk ... 122 F7
St James's End Nhants ... 84 E3
St James South Elmham Suffk ... 107 G7
St Jidgey Cnwll ... 4 F1
St John Cnwll ... 6 E4
St John Jersey ... 9 c1
St Johns Dur ... 168 D4
St John's IoM ... 154 c5
St John's Kent ... 38 E2
St Johns Surrey ... 50 C7
St Johns Worcs ... 81 J4
St John's Chapel Devon ... 27 J5
St John's Chapel Dur ... 167 K3
St John's Fen End Norfk ... 103 L1
St John's Highway Norfk ... 120 L8
St John's Kirk S Lans ... 199 G6
St John's Town of Dalry D & G ... 184 F6
St John's Wood Gt Lon ... 51 H2
St Jude's IoM ... 154 e3
St Just Cnwll ... 2 B5
St Just-in-Roseland Cnwll ... 3 L4
St Katherines Abers ... 256 D5
St Keverne Cnwll ... 3 K6
St Kew Cnwll ... 10 E7
St Kew Highway Cnwll ... 10 E7
St Keyne Cnwll ... 6 A3
St Lawrence Cnwll ... 5 H2
St Lawrence Essex ... 72 D6
St Lawrence IoW ... 19 J8
St Lawrence Jersey ... 9 c2
St Lawrence Kent ... 41 K2
St Leonards Bucks ... 67 M5
St Leonards Dorset ... 17 M2
St Leonards E Susx ... 24 E5
St Leonard's Street Kent ... 39 H2
St Levan Cnwll ... 2 B6
St Lythans V Glam ... 43 H7
St Mabyn Cnwll ... 10 E7
St Madoes P & K ... 222 C3
St Margarets Herefs ... 79 L8
St Margarets Herts ... 69 K5
St Margaret's at Cliffe Kent ... 41 K6
St Margaret's Hope Ork ... 275 c6
St Margaret South Elmham Suffk ... 107 G6
St Marks IoM ... 154 d7
St Martin Cnwll ... 3 J6
St Martin Cnwll ... 6 B4

St Martin Guern ... 9 j3
St Martin Jersey ... 9 e2
St Martin's IoS ... 10 c1
St Martin's P & K ... 221 L1
St Martin's Shrops ... 112 D4
St Martin's Moor Shrops ... 112 D4
St Mary Jersey ... 9 c2
St Mary Bourne Hants ... 34 F1
St Marychurch Torbay ... 8 D2
St Mary Church V Glam ... 42 F7
St Mary Cray Gt Lon ... 52 A5
St Mary Hill V Glam ... 42 E6
St Mary in the Marsh Kent ... 25 K2
St Marylebone Crematorium Gt Lon ... 51 H1
St Mary's IoS ... 10 c3
St Mary's Ork ... 275 d5
St Mary's Bay Kent ... 25 K2
St Mary's Grove N Som ... 44 F5
St Mary's Hoo Medway ... 53 H4
St Mary's Platt Kent ... 39 G2
St Maughans Mons ... 62 F4
St Maughans Green Mons ... 62 F4
St Mawes Cnwll ... 3 L4
St Mawgan Cnwll ... 4 E2
St Mellion Cnwll ... 6 D2
St Mellons Cardif ... 43 K5
St Merryn Cnwll ... 10 B7
St Mewan Cnwll ... 5 G4
St Michael Caerhays Cnwll ... 4 F6
St Michael Church Somset ... 30 D5
St Michael Penkevil Cnwll ... 4 D6
St Michaels Kent ... 39 M6
St Michaels Worcs ... 80 D2
St Michael's on Wyre Lancs ... 147 J7
St Michael South Elmham Suffk ... 107 G6
St Minver Cnwll ... 10 D7
St Monans Fife ... 223 L2
St Neot Cnwll ... 5 L1
St Neots Cambs ... 86 D3
St Newlyn East Cnwll ... 4 D3
St Nicholas Pembks ... 74 E5
St Nicholas V Glam ... 43 H6
St Nicholas-at-Wade Kent ... 41 J2
St Ninians Stirlg ... 209 L1
St Olaves Norfk ... 107 J3
St Osyth Essex ... 73 H4
St Ouen Jersey ... 9 b2
St Owens Cross Herefs ... 63 G2
St Paul's Cray Gt Lon ... 52 A5
St Paul's Walden Herts ... 69 G3
St Peter Jersey ... 9 b2
St Peter Port Guern ... 9 k3
St Peter's Guern ... 9 i3
St Peter's Kent ... 41 L2
St Peter's Cambs ... 86 E1
St Petrox Pembks ... 55 G7
St Pinnock Cnwll ... 5 L2
St Quivox S Ayrs ... 196 D6
St Ruan Cnwll ... 3 J8
St Sampson Guern ... 9 k2
St Saviour Guern ... 9 i3
St Saviour Jersey ... 9 d3
St Stephen Cnwll ... 4 F4
St Stephens Cnwll ... 6 E3
St Stephens Cnwll ... 11 L5
St Teath Cnwll ... 10 F6
St Tudy Cnwll ... 10 F7
St Twynnells Pembks ... 54 F7
St Veep Cnwll ... 5 K4
St Vigeans Angus ... 235 G6
St Wenn Cnwll ... 5 G2
St Weonards Herefs ... 63 G2
St y-Nyll V Glam ... 43 H6
Salcombe Devon ... 7 L7
Salcombe Regis Devon ... 14 D5
Salcott-cum-Virley Essex ... 72 D4
Sale Traffd ... 130 F2
Saleby Lincs ... 137 J4
Sale Green Worcs ... 81 L4
Salehurst E Susx ... 24 D2
Salem Carmth ... 59 H4
Salem Cerdgn ... 92 E6
Salen Ag & B ... 227 H4
Salen Highld ... 237 K7
Salesbury Lancs ... 139 K1
Salford C Beds ... 85 H7
Salford Oxon ... 65 L2
Salford Salfd ... 140 B8
Salford Priors Warwks ... 82 C5
Salfords Surrey ... 37 L2
Salhouse Norfk ... 123 G8
Saline Fife ... 221 J8
Salisbury Wilts ... 33 K5
Salisbury Crematorium Wilts ... 33 K4
Salkeld Dykes Cumb ... 166 D3
Salle Norfk ... 122 C6

Salmonby Lincs ... 136 F5
Salperton Gloucs ... 65 G3
Salph End Bed ... 86 B5
Salsburgh N Lans ... 209 L6
Salt Staffs ... 114 F6
Salta Cumb ... 164 E2
Saltaire C Brad ... 149 L8
Saltash Cnwll ... 6 E3
Saltburn Highld ... 263 K6
Saltburn-by-the-Sea R & Cl ... 170 F6
Saltby Leics ... 117 M6
Salt Coates Cumb ... 177 G8
Saltcoats Cumb ... 155 K3
Saltcoats N Ayrs ... 195 L3
Saltcotes Lancs ... 138 D2
Saltdean Br & H ... 22 F6
Salterbeck Cumb ... 164 C5
Salterforth Lancs ... 148 F6
Salterswall Ches W ... 130 C6
Salterton Wilts ... 33 K4
Saltfleet Lincs ... 137 H1
Saltfleetby All Saints Lincs ... 137 H2
Saltfleetby St Clement Lincs ... 137 J1
Saltfleetby St Peter Lincs ... 137 H2
Saltford BaNES ... 45 K5
Salthouse Norfk ... 122 B3
Saltley Birm ... 98 E5
Saltmarsh Newpt ... 44 D2
Saltmarshe E R Yk ... 143 K3
Saltney Flints ... 129 J6
Salton N York ... 162 C6
Saltrens Devon ... 27 H6
Saltwell Crematorium Gatesd ... 181 G6
Saltwick Nthumb ... 180 E3
Saltwood Kent ... 40 F8
Salvington W Susx ... 21 K6
Salwarpe Worcs ... 81 K3
Salway Ash Dorset ... 15 K3
Sambourne Warwks ... 82 C3
Sambrook Wrekin ... 113 M6
Samlesbury Lancs ... 139 H2
Samlesbury Bottoms Lancs ... 139 J2
Sampford Arundel Somset ... 29 K7
Sampford Brett Somset ... 29 K5
Sampford Courtenay Devon ... 12 F2
Sampford Moor Somset ... 29 K7
Sampford Peverell Devon ... 29 J5
Sampford Spiney Devon ... 12 D8
Samsonlane Ork ... 275 e3
Samson's Corner Essex ... 73 G3
Samuelston E Loth ... 212 B5
Sanaigmore Ag & B ... 204 C2
Sancreed Cnwll ... 2 C5
Sancton E R Yk ... 152 D7
Sand Somset ... 31 G2
Sandaig Highld ... 247 M8
Sandale Cumb ... 165 H3
Sandal Magna Wakefd ... 142 A4
Sandavore Highld ... 236 F4
Sanday Ork ... 275 e2
Sandbach Ches E ... 130 E7
Sandbank Ag & B ... 207 K3
Sandbanks Poole ... 17 K5
Sandend Abers ... 267 L3
Sanderstead Gt Lon ... 51 J6
Sandford Cumb ... 167 G7
Sandford Devon ... 13 J2
Sandford Dorset ... 17 H5
Sandford Hants ... 18 B3
Sandford IoW ... 19 J7
Sandford N Som ... 44 E7
Sandford S Lans ... 197 L2
Sandford Shrops ... 112 E6
Sandford Shrops ... 113 J5
Sandford-on-Thames Oxon ... 66 D6
Sandford Orcas Dorset ... 31 K6
Sandford St Martin Oxon ... 66 B2
Sandgate Kent ... 41 G8
Sandhaven Abers ... 269 H3
Sandhead D & G ... 172 D6
Sandhill Rothm ... 142 C8
Sandhills Dorset ... 16 B3
Sandhills Dorset ... 31 L8
Sand Hills Leeds ... 150 E7
Sandhills Oxon ... 66 E5
Sandhills Surrey ... 36 D3
Sandhoe Nthumb ... 180 A5
Sand Hole E R Yk ... 152 B8
Sandholme E R Yk ... 143 L2
Sandholme Lincs ... 119 K4
Sandhurst Br For ... 49 K6
Sandhurst Gloucs ... 64 B2
Sandhurst Kent ... 39 K7
Sandhurst Cross Kent ... 24 L3
Sand Hutton N York ... 151 L4
Sandhutton N York ... 160 E6
Sandiacre Derbys ... 116 E4
Sandilands Lincs ... 137 K3

Place	Page	Grid
Sandiway Ches W	130	B5
Sandleheath Hants	33	K7
Sandleigh Oxon	66	C6
Sandley Dorset	32	C6
Sandling Kent	53	G7
Sandlow Green Ches E	130	F6
Sandness Shet	281	c5
Sandon Essex	71	H6
Sandon Herts	87	G8
Sandon Staffs	114	E5
Sandon Bank Staffs	114	E6
Sandown IoW	19	K6
Sandplace Cnwll	6	A3
Sandridge Herts	68	F5
Sandridge Wilts	46	D6
Sandringham Norfk	120	F5
Sands Bucks	67	K8
Sandsend N York	171	K8
Sand Side Cumb	156	B6
Sandside Cumb	157	G6
Sandtoft N Linc	143	J6
Sandway Kent	39	M3
Sandwell Valley Crematorium Sandw	98	C5
Sandwich Kent	41	K4
Sandwick Cumb	166	A6
Sandwick Shet	281	e8
Sandwick W Isls	282	g3
Sandwith Cumb	164	C7
Sandwith Newtown Cumb	164	C7
Sandy C Beds	86	D5
Sandy Bank Lincs	136	E8
Sandycroft Flints	129	H6
Sandy Cross E Susx	23	K3
Sandy Cross Herefs	80	F4
Sandyford D & G	187	J7
Sandygate Devon	13	K7
Sandygate IoM	154	e3
Sandy Haven Pembks	54	D5
Sandyhills D & G	175	M4
Sandylands Lancs	147	H3
Sandy Lane C Brad	149	K8
Sandylane Staffs	113	M4
Sandylane Swans	57	G7
Sandy Lane Wilts	46	D5
Sandy Lane Wrexhm	112	F3
Sandy Park Devon	13	G5
Sandysike Cumb	177	L5
Sandyway Herefs	63	G2
Sangobeg Highld	277	L3
Sangomore Highld	276	F3
Sankey Bridges Warrtn	130	B2
Sankyn's Green Worcs	81	H2
Sanna Bay Highld	236	E6
Sanndabhaig W Isls	282	g3
Sannox N Ayrs	195	G2
Sanquhar D & G	185	K1
Santon Cumb	155	K2
Santon IoM	154	d7
Santon Bridge Cumb	155	K2
Santon Downham Suffk	105	G6
Sapcote Leics	100	B5
Sapey Common Herefs	81	G2
Sapiston Suffk	105	J8
Sapley Cambs	102	E8
Sapperton Derbys	115	K4
Sapperton Gloucs	64	D6
Sapperton Lincs	118	D5
Saracen's Head Lincs	119	K6
Sarclet Highld	280	D7
Sarisbury Hants	19	H2
Sarn Brdgnd	42	D5
Sarn Gwynd	108	D5
Sarn Powys	93	L4
Sarn Powys	94	F5
Sarnau Carmth	58	B5
Sarnau Cerdgn	76	B5
Sarnau Gwynd	111	J4
Sarnau Powys	78	E8
Sarnau Powys	112	C8
Sarn Bach Gwynd	108	E6
Sarnesfield Herefs	79	L5
Sarn-wen Powys	112	D7
Saron Carmth	59	H6
Saron Carmth	76	C7
Saron Gwynd	125	H7
Saron Gwynd	125	J6
Sarratt Herts	68	D7
Sarre Kent	41	H2
Sarsden Oxon	65	L3
Sarson Hants	34	C2
Satley Dur	168	E2
Satmar Kent	41	H7
Satron N York	159	G3
Satterleigh Devon	28	B6
Satterthwaite Cumb	156	D4
Satwell Oxon	49	H2
Sauchen Abers	244	F1
Saucher P & K	233	J8
Sauchieburn Abers	235	G2
Saul Gloucs	63	L5
Saundby Notts	134	F2
Saundersfoot Pembks	55	K6
Saunderton Bucks	67	J6
Saunderton Station Bucks	67	K7
Saunton Devon	27	H3
Sausthorpe Lincs	137	G6
Saverley Green Staffs	114	F4
Savile Town Kirk	141	K4
Sawbridge Warwks	83	L2
Sawbridgeworth Herts	70	C4
Sawdon N York	163	G5
Sawley Derbys	116	D5
Sawley Lancs	148	D6
Sawley N York	150	C2
Sawston Cambs	87	K5
Sawtry Cambs	102	D6
Saxby Leics	117	L7
Saxby Lincs	135	K3
Saxby All Saints N Linc	144	C4
Saxelbye Leics	117	J7
Saxham Street Suffk	90	C3
Saxilby Lincs	135	H4
Saxlingham Norfk	122	H4
Saxlingham Green Norfk	106	E4
Saxlingham Nethergate Norfk	106	E4
Saxlingham Thorpe Norfk	106	E4
Saxmundham Suffk	91	J3
Saxon Street Cambs	88	D3
Saxondale Notts	117	H3
Saxtead Suffk	91	J2
Saxtead Green Suffk	90	F2
Saxtead Little Green Suffk	90	F2
Saxthorpe Norfk	122	C5
Saxton N York	151	L8
Sayers Common W Susx	22	D4
Scackleton N York	161	L8
Scaftworth Notts	134	D2
Scagglethorpe N York	152	C1
Scalasaig Ag & B	214	D5
Scalby E R Yk	143	L2
Scalby N York	163	H4
Scald End Bed	85	L4
Scaldwell Nhants	84	E1
Scaleby Cumb	178	B6
Scalebyhill Cumb	178	B6
Scale Houses Cumb	166	E2
Scales Cumb	146	E2
Scales Cumb	165	K5
Scalesceugh Cumb	166	B1
Scalford Leics	117	K6
Scaling N York	171	H7
Scaling Dam R & Cl	171	H8
Scalloway Shet	281	d7
Scalpay Highld	247	J2
Scamblesby Lincs	136	E4
Scammonden Kirk	141	G4
Scamodale Highld	228	C1
Scampston N York	162	F7
Scampton Lincs	135	J4
Scaniport Highld	251	H4
Scapegoat Hill Kirk	141	G4
Scarba Ag & B	215	K3
Scarborough N York	163	J5
Scarcewater Cnwll	4	F4
Scarcliffe Derbys	133	K6
Scarcroft Leeds	150	E7
Scarfskerry Highld	280	C2
Scargill Dur	168	D8
Scarinish Ag & B	224	D6
Scarisbrick Lancs	138	D5
Scarness Cumb	165	H4
Scarning Norfk	105	J1
Scarrington Notts	117	J3
Scarth Hill Lancs	138	E6
Scarthingwell N York	151	G8
Scartho NE Lin	145	H6
Scaur D & G	175	L4
Scawby N Linc	144	B6
Scawsby Donc	142	E6
Scawthorpe Donc	142	E6
Scawton N York	161	J6
Scayne's Hill W Susx	22	F3
Scethrog Powys	61	H2
Scholar Green Ches E	131	G8
Scholemoor Crematorium C Brad	141	H1
Scholes Kirk	141	J3
Scholes Kirk	141	J6
Scholes Leeds	150	E8
Scholes Rothm	142	B8
Scholes Wigan	139	J6
School Aycliffe Dur	169	H6
School Green C Brad	141	H1
School Green Ches W	130	C6
Schoolgreen Wokham	49	H5
School House Dorset	15	J2
Scissett Kirk	141	L5
Scleddau Pembks	74	F5
Scofton Notts	134	C4
Scole Norfk	106	C7
Scone P & K	221	L2
Sconser Highld	247	H2
Scoonie Fife	222	F6
Scopwick Lincs	135	M8
Scoraig Highld	261	G1
Scorborough E R Yk	152	F6
Scorrier Cnwll	4	B6
Scorriton Devon	7	K1
Scorton Lancs	147	K6
Scorton N York	160	C3
Sco Ruston Norfk	122	F7
Scotby Cumb	178	B7
Scotch Corner N York	160	B2
Scotforth Lancs	147	K4
Scot Hay Staffs	114	B2
Scothern Lincs	135	L4
Scotland Lincs	118	C5
Scotland Gate Nthumb	181	G2
Scotlandwell P & K	222	C7
Scot Lane End Bolton	139	J6
Scotscalder Station Highld	279	K5
Scotsdike Cumb	177	L4
Scot's Gap Nthumb	180	C2
Scotsmill Abers	255	L7
Scotstoun C Glas	208	F5
Scotswood N u Ty	180	F6
Scotter Lincs	143	M7
Scotterthorpe Lincs	143	L7
Scottlethorpe Lincs	118	D7
Scotton Lincs	143	M7
Scotton N York	150	D4
Scotton N York	160	B3
Scottow Norfk	122	F6
Scott Willoughby Lincs	118	D4
Scoulton Norfk	105	K3
Scounslow Green Staffs	115	H5
Scourie Highld	276	B7
Scourie More Highld	276	A7
Scousburgh Shet	281	d8
Scouthead Oldham	140	E6
Scrabster Highld	279	K2
Scraesburgh Border	189	J3
Scrafield Lincs	136	F6
Scrainwood Nthumb	190	D4
Scrane End Lincs	119	L3
Scraptoft Leics	100	E2
Scratby Norfk	123	K8
Scrayingham N York	151	M4
Scrays E Susx	24	D3
Scredington Lincs	118	E3
Scremby Lincs	137	H6
Scremerston Nthumb	202	F3
Screveton Notts	117	J3
Scrivelsby Lincs	136	E6
Scriven N York	150	E4
Scrooby Notts	134	C2
Scropton Derbys	115	K5
Scrub Hill Lincs	136	D8
Scruton N York	160	D4
Scuggate Cumb	178	B4
Scullomie Highld	277	L4
Sculthorpe Norfk	121	K5
Scunthorpe N Linc	143	M5
Scurlage Swans	56	E7
Sea Somset	30	E8
Seaborough Dorset	15	K2
Seabridge Staffs	114	C3
Seabrook Kent	41	G8
Seaburn Sundld	181	K6
Seacombe Wirral	129	H2
Seacroft Leeds	150	E8
Seacroft Lincs	137	L7
Seadyke Lincs	119	K4
Seafield Highld	259	H8
Seafield W Loth	210	D6
Seafield Crematorium C Edin	211	J4
Seaford E Susx	23	H7
Seaforth Sefton	138	C8
Seagrave Leics	117	G8
Seagry Heath Wilts	46	D3
Seaham Dur	169	L1
Seahouses Nthumb	203	L6
Seal Kent	38	E2
Sealand Flints	129	H6
Seale Surrey	36	D1
Seamer N York	163	J6
Seamer N York	170	C8
Seamill N Ayrs	195	K2
Sea Palling Norfk	123	J6
Searby Lincs	144	D6
Seasalter Kent	40	E2
Seascale Cumb	155	J2
Seathwaite Cumb	156	B3
Seathwaite Cumb	165	H8
Seatle Cumb	156	E6
Seatoller Cumb	165	H7
Seaton Cnwll	6	C4
Seaton Cumb	164	D4
Seaton Devon	14	K1
Seaton Dur	169	L1
Seaton E R Yk	153	J6
Seaton Kent	41	H4
Seaton Nthumb	181	H3
Seaton Rutlnd	101	K4
Seaton Burn N Tyne	181	G4
Seaton Carew Hartpl	170	C5
Seaton Delaval Nthumb	181	H4
Seaton Ross E R Yk	152	B7
Seaton Sluice Nthumb	181	H5
Seatown Dorset	15	K4
Seave Green N York	161	J4
Seaview IoW	19	L5
Seaville Cumb	177	G8
Seavington St Mary Somset	30	E7
Seavington St Michael Somset	30	F7
Sebastopol Torfn	62	C7
Sebergham Cumb	165	K2
Seckington Warwks	99	H3
Second Severn Crossing Mons	45	G2
Sedbergh Cumb	157	L4
Sedbury Gloucs	63	H5
Sedbusk N York	158	F4
Sedgeberrow Worcs	82	B7
Sedgebrook Lincs	117	M4
Sedge Fen Suffk	104	D3
Sedgefield Dur	169	K5
Sedgeford Norfk	120	F4
Sedgehill Wilts	32	E5
Sedgemoor Crematorium Somset	30	D2
Sedgley Dudley	97	L4
Sedgley Park Bury	140	B7
Sedgwick Cumb	157	H5
Sedlescombe E Susx	24	E4
Sedrup Bucks	67	J5
Seed Kent	40	E4
Seend Wilts	46	D6
Seend Cleeve Wilts	46	D6
Seer Green Bucks	68	B8
Seething Norfk	107	J2
Sefton Sefton	138	D7
Seghill Nthumb	181	G4
Seighford Staffs	114	C6
Seion Gwynd	125	K6
Seisdon Staffs	97	J4
Selattyn Shrops	112	C5
Selborne Hants	35	M4
Selby N York	142	F1
Selham W Susx	20	F3
Selhurst Gt Lon	51	J5
Selkirk Border	201	L4
Sellack Herefs	63	H2
Sellafield Station Cumb	155	J2
Sellafirth Shet	281	e4
Sellan Cnwll	2	C5
Sellick's Green Somset	30	B7
Sellindge Kent	40	E7
Selling Kent	40	F4
Sells Green Wilts	46	D6
Selly Oak Birm	98	D7
Selmeston E Susx	23	H6
Selsdon Gt Lon	51	K6
Selsey Gloucs	64	B6
Selsey W Susx	20	D8
Selsfield Common W Susx	38	A6
Selside Cumb	157	H3
Selside N York	158	D7
Selsted Kent	41	H6
Selston Notts	116	D2
Selworthy Somset	29	G2
Semer Suffk	89	K6
Semington Wilts	46	C6
Semley Wilts	32	E5
Sempringham Lincs	118	F5
Send Surrey	50	C7
Send Marsh Surrey	50	D7
Senghenydd Caerph	43	H3
Sennen Cnwll	2	B6
Sennen Cove Cnwll	2	B6
Sennybridge Powys	60	D2
Serlby Notts	134	C2
Sessay N York	161	G7
Setchey Norfk	104	C1
Setley Hants	18	D5
Seton Mains E Loth	211	M4
Settle N York	148	E3
Settrington N York	152	C2
Seven Ash Somset	29	L4
Sevenhampton Gloucs	64	F3
Sevenhampton Swindn	47	J1
Seven Hills Crematorium Suffk	90	F3
Seven Kings Gt Lon	51	M2
Sevenoaks Kent	38	E2
Sevenoaks Weald Kent	38	E3
Seven Sisters Neath	60	B5

Seven Springs Gloucs 64 D4
Seven Star Green Essex 72 D2
Severn Beach S Glos 45 G2
Severn Bridge S Glos 45 H1
Severn Stoke Worcs 81 K6
Sevick End Bed 86 B4
Sevington Kent 40 D7
Sewards End Essex 88 B7
Sewardstonebury Essex 69 K7
Sewell C Beds 68 C3
Sewerby E R Yk 153 K2
Seworgan Cnwll 3 H5
Sewstern Leics 118 A7
Sexhow N York 161 G2
Sezincote Gloucs 65 H1
Sgiogarstaigh W Isls 282 h1
Shabbington Bucks 67 G5
Shackerley Shrops 97 J2
Shackerstone Leics 99 K2
Shacklecross Derbys 116 C5
Shackleford Surrey 36 D2
Shade Calder 140 D3
Shader W Isls 282 g1
Shadforth Dur 169 J3
Shadingfield Suffk 107 J6
Shadoxhurst Kent 40 C7
Shadwell Leeds 150 D7
Shadwell Norfk 105 J6
Shaftenhoe End Herts 87 H7
Shaftesbury Dorset 32 E6
Shaftholme Donc 142 F6
Shafton Barns 142 B5
Shafton Two Gates Barns 142 B5
Shakerley Wigan 139 K7
Shalbourne Wilts 47 L6
Shalcombe IoW 18 F6
Shalden Hants 35 L3
Shalden Green Hants 35 L2
Shaldon Devon 13 L8
Shalfleet IoW 18 F6
Shalford Essex 71 H1
Shalford Surrey 36 F2
Shalford Green Essex 71 H2
Shallowford Staffs 114 D5
Shalmsford Street Kent 40 E4
Shalstone Bucks 84 C7
Shamley Green Surrey 36 F2
Shandford Angus 234 D3
Shandon Ag & B 207 L2
Shandwick Highld 264 D5
Shangton Leics 100 F4
Shankhouse Nthumb 181 G3
Shanklin IoW 19 K7
Shap Cumb 166 D7
Shapinsay Ork 275 d4
Shapwick Dorset 17 H2
Shapwick Somset 30 F3
Shard End Birm 98 F5
Shardlow Derbys 116 D5
Shareshill Staffs 97 L2
Sharlston Wakefd 142 B4
Sharlston Common Wakefd 142 B4
Sharman's Cross Solhll 98 E7
Sharnal Street Medway 53 G4
Sharnbrook Bed 85 K3
Sharneyford Lancs 140 C3
Sharnford Leics 100 B5
Sharnhill Green Dorset 16 D2
Sharoe Green Lancs 139 G1
Sharow N York 150 D2
Sharpenhoe C Beds 68 D1
Sharperton Nthumb 190 D5
Sharp Green Norfk 123 H7
Sharpness Gloucs 63 K6
Sharpthorne W Susx 38 B6
Sharptor Cnwll 11 J8
Sharpway Gate Worcs 81 L2
Sharrington Norfk 122 A4
Shatterford Worcs 97 H7
Shatterling Kent 41 J4
Shatton Derbys 132 D3
Shaugh Prior Devon 7 G2
Shave Cross Dorset 15 J3
Shavington Ches E 113 M1
Shaw C Brad 140 F1
Shaw Oldham 140 D6
Shaw Swindn 47 G2
Shaw W Berk 48 C5
Shaw Wilts 46 C6
Shawbirch Wrekin 113 L8
Shawbost W Isls 282 f2
Shawbury Shrops 113 J7
Shawclough Rochdl 140 D5
Shaw Common Gloucs 63 K2
Shawdon Hill Nthumb 190 F3
Shawell Leics 100 C7
Shawford Hants 34 F6
Shawforth Lancs 140 D4
Shaw Green Herts 69 J1

Shaw Green Lancs 139 G4
Shaw Green N York 150 C5
Shawhead D & G 185 L7
Shaw Mills N York 150 C3
Shawsburn S Lans 198 C3
Shear Cross Wilts 32 E3
Shearington D & G 176 D5
Shearsby Leics 100 D5
Shearston Somset 30 D5
Shebbear Devon 12 B1
Shebdon Staffs 114 B6
Shebster Highld 279 H3
Sheddens E Rens 208 F7
Shedfield Hants 35 H8
Sheen Staffs 132 B7
Sheepbridge Derbys 133 G5
Sheep Hill Dur 180 E7
Sheepridge Kirk 141 J4
Sheepscar Leeds 141 M1
Sheepscombe Gloucs 64 C5
Sheepstor Devon 7 G1
Sheepwash Devon 12 C2
Sheepwash Nthumb 181 G2
Sheepway N Som 45 G4
Sheepy Magna Leics 99 J3
Sheepy Parva Leics 99 J3
Sheering Essex 70 D4
Sheerness Kent 53 K4
Sheerwater Surrey 50 D6
Sheet Hants 36 A6
Sheffield Cnwll 2 D5
Sheffield Sheff 133 G2
Sheffield Bottom W Berk 49 G5
Sheffield City Road
    Crematorium Sheff 133 G3
Sheffield Green E Susx 22 F2
Shefford C Beds 86 C7
Shefford Woodlands W Berk 48 A4
Sheigra Highld 276 B4
Sheinton Shrops 96 E3
Shelderton Shrops 95 K7
Sheldon Birm 98 F6
Sheldon Derbys 132 C6
Sheldon Devon 14 D1
Sheldwich Kent 40 D4
Sheldwich Lees Kent 40 D4
Shelf Calder 141 H2
Shelfanger Norfk 106 C6
Shelfield Warwks 82 D3
Shelfield Wsall 98 C3
Shelfield Green Warwks 82 D3
Shelford Notts 117 H3
Shelford Warwks 99 L5
Shellacres Nthumb 202 D4
Shelley Essex 70 E6
Shelley Kirk 141 K5
Shelley Suffk 89 L7
Shelley Far Bank Kirk 141 K5
Shellingford Oxon 65 L8
Shellow Bowells Essex 70 F5
Shelsley Beauchamp Worcs 81 G3
Shelsley Walsh Worcs 81 G3
Shelton Bed 85 K2
Shelton Norfk 106 E5
Shelton Notts 117 K3
Shelton Shrops 95 L1
Shelton Green Norfk 106 E5
Shelton Lock C Derb 116 C5
Shelton Under Harley Staffs 114 C4
Shelve Shrops 95 H4
Shelwick Herefs 80 C6
Shenfield Essex 70 F8
Shenington Oxon 83 J6
Shenley Herts 68 F7
Shenley Brook End M Keyn 85 G8
Shenleybury Herts 68 F6
Shenley Church End M Keyn 85 G7
Shenmore Herefs 79 M7
Shennanton D & G 173 J2
Shenstone Staffs 98 E3
Shenstone Worcs 97 J8
Shenstone Woodend Staffs 98 E3
Shenton Leics 99 K3
Shenval Moray 254 E6
Shepeau Stow Lincs 102 F1
Shephall Herts 69 H2
Shepherd's Bush Gt Lon 51 G3
Shepherd's Green Oxon 49 H2
Shepherds Patch Gloucs 63 L6
Shepherdswell Kent 41 H5
Shepley Kirk 141 K5
Shepperdine S Glos 63 J8
Shepperton Surrey 50 D5
Shepperton Green Surrey 50 D5
Shepreth Cambs 87 H5
Shepshed Leics 116 E7
Shepton Beauchamp Somset 30 F7
Shepton Mallet Somset 31 K2
Shepton Montague Somset 31 L4

Shepway Kent 39 J3
Sheraton Dur 170 B4
Sherborne Dorset 31 L7
Sherborne Gloucs 65 H4
Sherborne Somset 45 H7
Sherborne St John Hants 48 F7
Sherbourne Warwks 83 G3
Sherburn Dur 169 J2
Sherburn N York 163 G7
Sherburn Hill Dur 169 J2
Sherburn in Elmet N York 142 D1
Shere Surrey 37 G1
Shereford Norfk 121 K5
Sherfield English Hants 34 C6
Sherfield on Loddon Hants 49 G7
Sherfin Lancs 140 B3
Sherford Devon 8 A6
Sherford Dorset 17 H4
Sheriffhales Shrops 97 G1
Sheriff Hutton N York 151 K3
Sheringham Norfk 122 D3
Sherington M Keyn 85 H6
Shermanbury W Susx 22 B3
Shernborne Norfk 120 F5
Sherrington Wilts 33 G3
Sherston Wilts 46 B2
Sherwood C Nott 116 F3
Sherwood Forest
    Crematorium Notts 134 D6
Shetland Islands Shet 281 d6
Shettleston C Glas 209 H6
Shevington Wigan 139 H6
Shevington Moor Wigan 139 H5
Shevington Vale Wigan 139 G6
Sheviock Cnwll 6 D4
Shibden Head C Brad 141 H2
Shide IoW 19 H6
Shidlaw Nthumb 202 C5
Shiel Bridge Highld 248 F7
Shieldaig Highld 248 C1
Shieldhill D & G 176 D2
Shieldhill Falk 210 B4
Shieldhill House Hotel S Lans 199 G5
Shields N Lans 209 K7
Shielfoot Highld 237 J6
Shielhill Angus 234 C4
Shielhill Inver 207 L4
Shifford Oxon 66 A6
Shifnal Shrops 97 G2
Shilbottle Nthumb 191 J4
Shildon Dur 169 G5
Shillford E Rens 208 D7
Shillingford Devon 29 H6
Shillingford Oxon 66 E8
Shillingford Abbot Devon 13 L5
Shillingford St George
    Devon 13 L5
Shillingstone Dorset 32 D8
Shillington C Beds 86 C8
Shillmoor Nthumb 190 B4
Shilton Oxon 65 K5
Shilton Warwks 99 L6
Shimpling Norfk 106 D6
Shimpling Suffk 89 H5
Shimpling Street Suffk 89 H4
Shincliffe Dur 169 H2
Shiney Row Sundld 181 H8
Shinfield Wokham 49 H5
Shingay Cambs 86 F5
Shingle Street Suffk 91 J6
Shinnersbridge Devon 8 B2
Shinness Highld 272 D5
Shipbourne Kent 38 F2
Shipdham Norfk 105 J2
Shipham Somset 44 E7
Shiphay Torbay 8 D2
Shiplake Oxon 49 J3
Shiplake Row Oxon 49 H3
Shiplate N Som 44 D7
Shipley C Brad 149 L3
Shipley Derbys 116 D3
Shipley Shrops 97 H4
Shipley W Susx 37 H6
Shipley Bridge Surrey 37 M3
Shipley Hatch Kent 40 D7
Shipmeadow Suffk 107 H5
Shippea Hill Station Cambs 104 C6
Shippon Oxon 66 C7
Shipston-on-Stour Warwks 83 G7
Shipton Bucks 67 J2
Shipton Gloucs 64 F3
Shipton N York 151 H4
Shipton Shrops 96 D5
Shipton Bellinger Hants 34 B2
Shipton Gorge Dorset 15 L4
Shipton Green W Susx 20 C6
Shipton Moyne Gloucs 46 C1
Shipton-on-Cherwell Oxon 66 C4
Shiptonthorpe E R Yk 152 C7

Shipton-under-Wychwood
    Oxon 65 L3
Shirburn Oxon 67 G7
Shirdley Hill Lancs 138 D5
Shire Cumb 166 E4
Shirebrook Derbys 133 K6
Shiregreen Sheff 133 G1
Shirehampton Bristl 45 G4
Shiremoor N Tyne 181 H4
Shirenewton Mons 62 F8
Shire Oak Wsall 98 D3
Shireoaks Notts 133 L3
Shirkoak Kent 40 B8
Shirland Derbys 133 H8
Shirlett Shrops 96 E4
Shirley C Sotn 34 E8
Shirley Derbys 115 L3
Shirley Gt Lon 51 K6
Shirley Solhll 98 E7
Shirl Heath Herefs 80 A3
Shirrell Heath Hants 35 H8
Shirvan Ag & B 206 D2
Shirwell Devon 27 L3
Shiskine N Ayrs 194 E5
Shittlehope Dur 168 C3
Shobdon Herefs 79 M3
Shobley Hants 18 B2
Shobrooke Devon 13 K2
Shoby Leics 117 H7
Shocklach Ches W 113 G2
Shocklach Green Ches W 113 G2
Shoeburyness Sthend 53 K2
Sholden Kent 41 K5
Sholing C Sotn 19 G2
Shoot Hill Shrops 95 K1
Shop Cnwll 10 B7
Shop Cnwll 26 D7
Shopwyke W Susx 20 E6
Shore Rochdl 140 D4
Shoreditch Gt Lon 51 J2
Shoreditch Somset 30 C6
Shoreham Kent 52 B6
Shoreham-by-Sea W Susx 22 C6
Shoreswood Nthumb 202 E4
Shorley Hants 35 J5
Shorncote Gloucs 64 F7
Shorne Kent 52 E5
Shorta Cross Cnwll 6 B3
Shortbridge E Susx 23 G3
Shortfield Common Surrey 36 C2
Shortgate E Susx 23 H4
Short Heath Birm 98 E5
Shortheath Hants 36 A4
Short Heath Wsall 98 B3
Shortlanesend Cnwll 4 C5
Shortlees E Ayrs 196 E4
Shortstown Bed 86 B6
Shorwell IoW 19 G7
Shoscombe BaNES 45 L7
Shotesham Norfk 106 E4
Shotgate Essex 71 J8
Shotley Suffk 90 F8
Shotley Bridge Dur 180 D8
Shotleyfield Nthumb 180 C8
Shotley Gate Suffk 90 F8
Shotley Street Suffk 90 F8
Shottenden Kent 40 D4
Shottermill Surrey 36 C4
Shottery Warwks 82 E4
Shotteswell Warwks 83 K6
Shottisham Suffk 91 H6
Shottle Derbys 116 A2
Shottlegate Derbys 116 A2
Shotton Dur 169 K5
Shotton Dur 169 L3
Shotton Flints 129 H6
Shotton Nthumb 180 F3
Shotton Nthumb 202 C7
Shotton Colliery Dur 169 K3
Shotts N Lans 210 A7
Shotwick Ches W 129 H5
Shougle Moray 266 D5
Shouldham Norfk 104 D2
Shouldham Thorpe Norfk 104 D2
Shoulton Worcs 81 J3
Shover's Green E Susx 39 G7
Shraleybrook Staffs 114 B2
Shrawardine Shrops 112 F8
Shrawley Worcs 81 J2
Shreding Green Bucks 50 C3
Shrewley Warwks 82 F2
Shrewsbury Shrops 96 B1
Shrewton Wilts 33 J2
Shripney W Susx 20 F6
Shrivenham Oxon 47 K1
Shropham Norfk 105 K5
Shroton Dorset 32 E8
Shrub End Essex 72 E2
Shucknall Herefs 80 D6

Shudy Camps Cambs...... 88 C6
Shuna Ag & B...... 216 B5
Shurdington Gloucs...... 64 D3
Shurlock Row W & M...... 49 K4
Shurnock Worcs...... 82 B3
Shurrery Highld...... 279 J4
Shurrery Lodge Highld...... 279 J5
Shurton Somset...... 30 B2
Shustoke Warwks...... 99 G5
Shute Devon...... 13 L3
Shute Devon...... 14 F3
Shutford Oxon...... 83 J7
Shut Heath Staffs...... 114 D7
Shuthonger Gloucs...... 81 K8
Shutlanger Nhants...... 84 E5
Shutterton Devon...... 13 M6
Shutt Green Staffs...... 97 K2
Shuttington Warwks...... 99 H2
Shuttlewood Derbys...... 133 J5
Shuttleworth Bury...... 140 B4
Siabost W Isls...... 282 f2
Siadar W Isls...... 282 g1
Sibbertoft Nhants...... 100 E6
Sibdon Carwood Shrops...... 95 K6
Sibford Ferris Oxon...... 83 H7
Sibford Gower Oxon...... 83 H7
Sible Hedingham Essex...... 88 F8
Sibley's Green Essex...... 70 F2
Siblyback Cnwll...... 11 J8
Sibsey Lincs...... 119 K2
Sibsey Fenside Lincs...... 119 K1
Sibson Cambs...... 102 B4
Sibson Leics...... 99 K3
Sibster Highld...... 280 D5
Sibthorpe Notts...... 117 K2
Sibthorpe Notts...... 134 E5
Sibton Suffk...... 91 J2
Sicklesmere Suffk...... 89 H3
Sicklinghall N York...... 150 E6
Sidbrook Somset...... 30 C5
Sidbury Devon...... 14 D4
Sidbury Shrops...... 96 F6
Sid Cop Barns...... 142 B6
Sidcot N Som...... 44 E7
Sidcup Gt Lon...... 51 M4
Siddick Cumb...... 164 D4
Siddington Ches E...... 131 G5
Siddington Gloucs...... 64 F7
Sidemoor Worcs...... 81 L1
Sidestrand Norfk...... 122 F3
Sidford Devon...... 14 D4
Sidlesham W Susx...... 20 D7
Sidlesham Common W Susx...... 20 D6
Sidley E Susx...... 24 D5
Sidmouth Devon...... 14 D5
Siefton Shrops...... 96 B6
Sigford Devon...... 13 H7
Sigglesthorne E R Yk...... 153 J6
Sigingstone V Glam...... 42 E7
Signet Oxon...... 65 K5
Silchester Hants...... 48 F6
Sileby Leics...... 117 G8
Silecroft Cumb...... 155 L6
Silfield Norfk...... 106 C3
Silian Cerdgn...... 77 G5
Silkstead Hants...... 34 F6
Silkstone Barns...... 141 L6
Silkstone Common Barns...... 141 L6
Silk Willoughby Lincs...... 118 E3
Silloth Cumb...... 176 F8
Silpho N York...... 163 H4
Silsden C Brad...... 149 J6
Silsoe C Beds...... 86 B8
Silton Dorset...... 32 C5
Silverburn Mdloth...... 211 G7
Silverdale Lancs...... 157 G7
Silverdale Staffs...... 114 C2
Silver End Essex...... 71 K3
Silverford Abers...... 268 D3
Silvergate Norfk...... 122 D6
Silverlace Green Suffk...... 91 H3
Silverley's Green Suffk...... 106 F8
Silverstone Nhants...... 84 C6
Silver Street Kent...... 53 J7
Silver Street Somset...... 31 J4
Silverton Devon...... 13 M2
Silverwell Cnwll...... 4 B5
Silvington Shrops...... 96 E7
Simister Bury...... 140 C6
Simmondley Derbys...... 131 K1
Simonburn Nthumb...... 179 K4
Simonsbath Somset...... 28 D3
Simonsburrow Devon...... 29 L7
Simonstone Lancs...... 140 A1
Simonstone N York...... 158 F4
Simprim Border...... 202 C4
Simpson M Keyn...... 85 H8
Simpson Cross Pembks...... 54 E3
Sinclair's Hill Border...... 202 C3

Sinclairston E Ayrs...... 196 F7
Sinderby N York...... 160 E6
Sinderhope Nthumb...... 179 K8
Sinderland Green Traffd...... 130 E2
Sindlesham Wokham...... 49 J5
Sinfin C Derb...... 116 B5
Singleborough Bucks...... 67 J1
Single Street Gt Lon...... 51 L7
Singleton Kent...... 40 C7
Singleton Lancs...... 147 G8
Singleton W Susx...... 20 E4
Singlewell Kent...... 52 E5
Sinkhurst Green Kent...... 39 K5
Sinnarhard Abers...... 244 B1
Sinnington N York...... 162 C5
Sinope Leics...... 116 C8
Sinton Worcs...... 81 J3
Sinton Worcs...... 81 J3
Sinton Green Worcs...... 81 J3
Sipson Gt Lon...... 50 D3
Sirhowy Blae G...... 61 J5
Sissinghurst Kent...... 39 K6
Siston S Glos...... 45 K4
Sitcott Devon...... 11 L4
Sithney Cnwll...... 3 G5
Sithney Common Cnwll...... 3 G5
Sithney Green Cnwll...... 3 G5
Sittingbourne Kent...... 40 B3
Six Ashes Shrops...... 97 H5
Six Bells Blae G...... 61 K6
Sixhills Lincs...... 136 C2
Six Mile Bottom Cambs...... 88 B4
Sixmile Cottages Kent...... 40 F6
Sixpenny Handley Dorset...... 33 G7
Six Rues Jersey...... 9 c2
Sizewell Suffk...... 91 L3
Skaill Ork...... 275 d5
Skares E Ayrs...... 197 G7
Skateraw Abers...... 245 K5
Skateraw E Loth...... 213 G4
Skeabost Highld...... 259 G7
Skeeby N York...... 160 B2
Skeffington Leics...... 101 G3
Skeffling E R Yk...... 145 K4
Skegby Notts...... 133 K7
Skegby Notts...... 134 F5
Skegness Lincs...... 137 L7
Skelbo Highld...... 264 B1
Skelbo Street Highld...... 264 B1
Skelbrooke Donc...... 142 D5
Skeldyke Lincs...... 119 K4
Skellingthorpe Lincs...... 135 J5
Skellorn Green Ches E...... 131 H3
Skellow Donc...... 142 D5
Skelmanthorpe Kirk...... 141 K5
Skelmersdale Lancs...... 138 F6
Skelmorlie N Ayrs...... 207 K5
Skelpick Highld...... 278 B5
Skelston D & G...... 185 K6
Skelton C York...... 151 J4
Skelton Cumb...... 166 B4
Skelton E R Yk...... 143 J3
Skelton N York...... 159 K3
Skelton R & Cl...... 170 F7
Skelton on Ure N York...... 150 E2
Skelwith Bridge Cumb...... 156 E2
Skendleby Lincs...... 137 H5
Skene House Abers...... 245 G2
Skenfrith Mons...... 62 F3
Skerne E R Yk...... 153 G5
Skerray Highld...... 277 L4
Skerricha Highld...... 276 C6
Skerton Lancs...... 147 J3
Sketchley Leics...... 99 L5
Sketty Swans...... 57 H6
Skewen Neath...... 57 K5
Skewsby N York...... 151 K2
Skeyton Norfk...... 122 E6
Skeyton Corner Norfk...... 122 E6
Skiall Highld...... 279 H3
Skidbrooke Lincs...... 137 H1
Skidbrooke North End Lincs...... 137 H1
Skidby E R Yk...... 144 C1
Skigersta W Isls...... 282 h1
Skilgate Somset...... 29 H5
Skillington Lincs...... 118 A6
Skinburness Cumb...... 176 F7
Skinflats Falk...... 210 B2
Skinidin Highld...... 258 C7
Skinners Green W Berk...... 48 C6
Skinningrove R & Cl...... 171 G6
Skipness Ag & B...... 206 E7
Skipper's Bridge D & G...... 177 L2
Skiprigg Cumb...... 165 L2
Skipsea E R Yk...... 153 J5
Skipsea Brough E R Yk...... 153 J5
Skipton N York...... 149 H5
Skipton-on-Swale N York...... 160 E6
Skipwith N York...... 151 L8

Skirlaugh E R Yk...... 153 J7
Skirling Border...... 199 J5
Skirmett Bucks...... 49 J1
Skirpenbeck E R Yk...... 152 A4
Skirwith Cumb...... 166 E4
Skirwith N York...... 158 C7
Skirza Highld...... 280 E3
Skitby Cumb...... 178 B5
Skittle Green Bucks...... 67 J6
Skokholm Island Pembks...... 54 B6
Skomer Island Pembks...... 54 B5
Skulamus Highld...... 247 L4
Skyborry Green Shrops...... 95 G8
Skye Green Essex...... 72 C3
Skye of Curr Highld...... 253 J6
Skyreholme N York...... 149 J4
Slack Calder...... 140 E2
Slackcote Oldham...... 140 E6
Slack Head Cumb...... 157 G6
Slackholme End Lincs...... 137 K5
Slacks of Cairnbanno Abers...... 256 F3
Slad Gloucs...... 64 C5
Slade Devon...... 14 D1
Slade Devon...... 27 J2
Slade Devon...... 28 E5
Slade End Oxon...... 48 E1
Slade Green Gt Lon...... 52 B4
Slade Heath Staffs...... 97 L2
Slade Hooton Rothm...... 133 K2
Sladesbridge Cnwll...... 10 E8
Slades Green Worcs...... 81 J8
Slaggyford Nthumb...... 178 F8
Slaidburn Lancs...... 148 C5
Slaithwaite Kirk...... 141 G5
Slaley Derbys...... 132 E8
Slaley Nthumb...... 180 A7
Slamannan Falk...... 209 M4
Slapton Bucks...... 68 B3
Slapton Devon...... 8 A6
Slapton Nhants...... 84 C6
Slattocks Rochdl...... 140 D6
Slaugham W Susx...... 37 L5
Slaughterford Wilts...... 46 B4
Slawston Leics...... 101 G4
Sleaford Hants...... 36 B3
Sleaford Lincs...... 118 E2
Sleagill Cumb...... 166 E6
Sleap Shrops...... 113 H6
Sleapford Wrekin...... 113 L8
Sleapshyde Herts...... 69 G5
Sleasdairidh Highld...... 272 F1
Slebech Pembks...... 55 H4
Sledge Green Worcs...... 81 J8
Sledmere E R Yk...... 152 E3
Sleetbeck Cumb...... 178 C3
Sleight Dorset...... 17 J3
Sleightholme Dur...... 168 B8
Sleights N York...... 162 F1
Slepe Dorset...... 17 H4
Slickly Highld...... 280 C3
Sliddery N Ayrs...... 193 J4
Sligachan Highld...... 247 G3
Sligrachan Ag & B...... 207 K1
Slimbridge Gloucs...... 63 L6
Slindon Staffs...... 114 C5
Slindon W Susx...... 20 F5
Slinfold W Susx...... 37 H4
Sling Gwynd...... 126 B6
Slingsby N York...... 162 B7
Slip End C Beds...... 68 D3
Slip End Herts...... 86 F7
Slipton Nhants...... 101 L7
Slitting Mill Staffs...... 115 G8
Slockavullin Ag & B...... 216 C7
Sloley Norfk...... 122 F6
Sloncombe Devon...... 13 H5
Sloothby Lincs...... 137 J5
Slough Slough...... 50 C3
Slough Crematorium Bucks...... 50 B3
Slough Green Somset...... 30 C7
Slough Green W Susx...... 37 L5
Slumbay Highld...... 248 E4
Slyfield Green Surrey...... 50 C8
Slyne Lancs...... 147 J3
Smailholm Border...... 201 K6
Smallbridge Rochdl...... 140 D5
Smallbrook Devon...... 13 K3
Smallbrook Gloucs...... 63 H7
Smallburgh Norfk...... 123 G6
Smalldale Derbys...... 132 B4
Smalldale Derbys...... 132 C3
Small Dole W Susx...... 22 C5
Smalley Derbys...... 116 C3
Smalley Common Derbys...... 116 C3
Smalley Green Derbys...... 116 C3
Smallfield Surrey...... 37 M2
Small Heath Birm...... 98 E6
Small Hythe Kent...... 25 G1
Smallridge Devon...... 15 G2

Smallthorne C Stke...... 114 D2
Smallways N York...... 168 E8
Smallwood Ches E...... 130 F7
Small Wood Hey Lancs...... 147 H6
Smallworth Norfk...... 105 K7
Smannell Hants...... 34 E1
Smardale Cumb...... 158 C1
Smarden Kent...... 39 L5
Smarden Bell Kent...... 39 L5
Smart's Hill Kent...... 38 E5
Smeafield Nthumb...... 203 H5
Smearisary Highld...... 237 J5
Smeatharpe Devon...... 30 B8
Smeeth Kent...... 40 E7
Smeeton Westerby Leics...... 100 E5
Smelthouses N York...... 150 B3
Smerral Highld...... 275 G2
Smestow Staffs...... 97 J5
Smethwick Sandw...... 98 C6
Smethwick Green Ches E...... 130 F7
Smisby Derbys...... 116 B7
Smitheclose IoW...... 19 G5
Smith End Green Worcs...... 81 H5
Smithfield Cumb...... 178 B6
Smith Green Lancs...... 147 J5
Smithies Barns...... 142 A6
Smithincott Devon...... 29 J8
Smith's End Herts...... 87 H7
Smith's Green Essex...... 70 E2
Smith's Green Essex...... 88 D7
Smithstown Highld...... 260 C4
Smithton Highld...... 252 D3
Smithy Bridge Rochdl...... 140 D5
Smithy Green Ches E...... 130 E5
Smithy Green Stockp...... 131 G3
Smithy Houses Derbys...... 116 C2
Smockington Leics...... 99 M5
Smoo Highld...... 277 G3
Smythe's Green Essex...... 72 D3
Snade D & G...... 185 L5
Snailbeach Shrops...... 95 J3
Snailwell Cambs...... 88 C2
Snainton N York...... 163 G6
Snaith E R Yk...... 143 G2
Snake Pass Inn Derbys...... 132 B2
Snape N York...... 160 C6
Snape Suffk...... 91 J3
Snape Green Lancs...... 138 D5
Snape Street Suffk...... 91 J4
Snaresbrook Gt Lon...... 51 L1
Snarestone Leics...... 99 K2
Snarford Lincs...... 135 L3
Snargate Kent...... 25 J2
Snave Kent...... 25 J1
Sneachill Worcs...... 81 L4
Snead Powys...... 95 H5
Sneath Common Norfk...... 106 D5
Sneaton N York...... 162 F1
Sneatonthorpe N York...... 162 F2
Snelland Lincs...... 135 M4
Snelson Ches E...... 130 F5
Snelston Derbys...... 115 J3
Snetterton Norfk...... 105 K5
Snettisham Norfk...... 120 F4
Snibston Leics...... 116 C8
Snig's End Gloucs...... 64 A1
Snitter Nthumb...... 190 E5
Snitterby Lincs...... 135 K1
Snitterfield Warwks...... 82 F3
Snitterton Derbys...... 132 E7
Snitton Shrops...... 96 D8
Snoadhill Kent...... 40 B6
Snodhill Herefs...... 79 K7
Snodland Kent...... 52 F6
Snoll Hatch Kent...... 39 G4
Snowden Hill Barns...... 141 L7
Snowdon Gwynd...... 41 H5
Snow End Herts...... 69 L1
Snowshill Gloucs...... 82 C8
Snow Street Norfk...... 106 D6
Soake Hants...... 19 L2
Soar Cardif...... 43 H5
Soar Devon...... 7 K7
Soar Powys...... 60 E1
Soay Highld...... 246 F6
Soberton Hants...... 35 J7
Soberton Heath Hants...... 35 J8
Sockbridge Cumb...... 166 C5
Sockburn Darltn...... 160 E1
Sodom Denbgs...... 128 C5
Sodylt Bank Shrops...... 112 D3
Soham Cambs...... 104 B8
Soham Cotes Cambs...... 104 B8
Solas W Isls...... 282 c7
Solbury Pembks...... 54 E4
Soldon Devon...... 26 E8
Soldon Cross Devon...... 26 E8
Soldridge Hants...... 35 K4
Sole Street Kent...... 40 E5

Sole Street Kent 52 E5
Solihull Solhll 98 F7
Sollers Dilwyn Herefs 80 A4
Sollers Hope Herefs 80 E8
Sollom Lancs 138 F4
Solva Pembks 74 C7
Solwaybank D & G 177 J3
Somerby Leics 101 G1
Somerby Lincs 144 D6
Somercotes Derbys 116 C1
Somerford Dorset 18 B5
Somerford Keynes Gloucs 64 E8
Somerley W Susx 20 D7
Somerleyton Suffk 107 K4
Somersal Herbert Derbys 115 J4
Somersby Lincs 136 F5
Somersham Cambs 103 C3
Somersham Suffk 90 C5
Somerton Oxon 66 D2
Somerton Somset 31 H5
Somerton Suffk 89 G4
Somerwood Shrops 113 J8
Sompting W Susx 21 K6
Sompting Abbotts W Susx 21 K5
Sonning Wokham 49 J4
Sonning Common Oxon 49 H3
Sonning Eye Oxon 49 H4
Sontley Wrexhm 112 E2
Sopley Hants 18 B4
Sopwell Herts 68 F6
Sopworth Wilts 46 B2
Sorbie D & G 174 C5
Sordale Highld 279 L4
Sorisdale Ag & B 225 H3
Sorn E Ayrs 197 G5
Sortat Highld 280 C4
Sotby Lincs 136 D4
Sots Hole Lincs 136 B6
Sotterley Suffk 107 J6
Soughton Flints 128 F6
Soulbury Bucks 67 L2
Soulby Cumb 166 B5
Soulby Cumb 167 H8
Souldern Oxon 66 D1
Souldrop Bed 85 J3
Sound Ches E 113 K2
Sound Muir Moray 267 G5
Soundwell S Glos 45 J4
Sourton Devon 12 D4
Soutergate Cumb 156 B6
South Acre Norfk 121 H8
South Alkham Kent 41 H7
Southall Gt Lon 50 E3
South Allington Devon 8 B7
South Alloa Falk 210 A1
Southam Gloucs 64 E2
Southam Warwks 83 K3
South Ambersham W Susx 20 F3
Southampton C Sotn 19 G1
Southampton Crematorium
   Hants 34 F7
South Anston Rothm 133 K3
South Ascot W & M 50 A5
South Ashford Kent 40 C7
South Baddesley Hants 18 E4
South Ballachulish Highld 229 G4
South Bank C York 151 J5
South Bank R & Cl 170 C6
South Barrow Somset 31 K5
South Beddington Gt Lon 51 H6
South Beer Cnwll 11 K4
South Benfleet Essex 53 G2
South Bockhampton Dorset 18 B4
Southborough Gt Lon 51 L5
Southborough Kent 38 F5
Southbourne Bmouth 18 A5
Southbourne W Susx 20 C5
South Bowood Dorset 15 K3
South Bramwith Donc 143 G5
South Brent Devon 7 K3
South Brewham Somset 32 B4
South Bristol Crematorium
   Bristl 45 H5
South Broomhill Nthumb 191 K6
Southburgh Norfk 105 K2
South Burlingham Norfk 107 H2
Southburn E R Yk 152 F5
South Cadbury Somset 31 K5
South Carlton Lincs 135 J4
South Carlton Notts 134 B3
South Cave E R Yk 144 A2
South Cerney Gloucs 64 F7
South Chailey E Susx 22 F4
South Chard Somset 15 H2
South Charlton Nthumb 191 H2
South Cheriton Somset 32 B6
South Church Dur 169 G5
Southchurch Sthend 53 J2
South Cleatlam Dur 168 E7

South Cliffe E R Yk 152 D8
South Clifton Notts 135 G5
South Cockerington Lincs 137 G2
South Cornelly Brdgnd 42 B5
Southcott Cnwll 11 H3
Southcott Devon 12 D4
Southcott Devon 13 H6
Southcott Devon 27 H7
Southcott Wilts 47 H7
Southcourt Bucks 67 K5
South Cove Suffk 107 K7
South Creake Norfk 121 J4
South Crosland Kirk 141 H5
South Croxton Leics 100 F3
South Dalton E R Yk 152 E6
South Darenth Kent 52 C5
South Dell W Isls 282 g1
South Duffield N York 143 H1
South Earlswood Surrey 37 L1
Southease E Susx 23 G6
South Elkington Lincs 136 E2
South Elmsall Wakefd 142 D5
Southend Ag & B 192 E6
South End E R Yk 145 K4
South End Hants 33 J7
South End Herefs 81 G6
South End N Linc 144 E4
South End Norfk 105 K5
Southend Wilts 47 J4
Southend Crematorium
   Sthend 53 J2
Southend-on-Sea Sthend 53 J2
Southernby Cumb 165 L3
Southernden Kent 39 L4
Southerndown V Glam 42 D7
Southerness D & G 176 C7
South Erradale Highld 260 B5
Southerton Devon 14 C4
Southery Norfk 104 C4
South Essex Crematorium
   Gt Lon 52 C2
South Fambridge Essex 72 B8
South Fawley W Berk 48 A3
South Ferriby N Linc 144 B4
South Field E R Yk 144 C3
Southfield Falk 209 M4
Southfleet Kent 52 D5
Southford IoW 19 J7
Southgate Gt Lon 69 J8
Southgate Norfk 120 E5
Southgate Norfk 121 J4
Southgate Norfk 122 C6
Southgate Swans 57 G7
South Godstone Surrey 38 A4
South Gorley Hants 18 B2
South Gosforth N u Ty 181 G5
South Green Essex 71 G8
South Green Essex 72 F3
South Green Kent 53 J7
South Green Norfk 105 L1
South Green Suffk 106 D8
South Gyle C Edin 211 G4
South Hanningfield Essex 71 H7
South Harting W Susx 20 C3
South Hayling Hants 20 B6
South Hazelrigg Nthumb 203 G6
South Heath Bucks 67 M6
South Heighton E Susx 23 G6
South Hetton Dur 169 K2
South Hiendley Wakefd 142 B5
South Hill Cnwll 11 L8
South Hill Somset 31 G6
South Hinksey Oxon 66 D6
South Hole Devon 26 C6
South Holmwood Surrey 37 J2
South Hornchurch Gt Lon 52 B2
South Horrington Somset 31 J2
South Huish Devon 7 K6
South Hykeham Lincs 135 J4
South Hylton Sundld 181 J7
Southill C Beds 86 C6
Southington Hants 35 G1
South Kelsey Lincs 144 D8
South Kessock Highld 251 H2
South Killingholme N Linc 144 F4
South Kilvington N York 160 F6
South Kilworth Leics 100 D7
South Kirkby Wakefd 142 C5
South Knighton Devon 13 J8
South Kyme Lincs 119 G2
South Lanarkshire
   Crematorium S Lans 209 H7
South Leicestershire
   Crematorium Leics 100 D4
Southleigh Devon 14 E4
South Leigh Oxon 66 B5
South Leverton Notts 134 F3
South Lincolnshire
   Crematorium Lincs 119 H6

South Littleton Worcs 82 C6
South London Crematorium
   Gt Lon 51 H5
South Lopham Norfk 105 L7
South Luffenham Rutlnd 101 K3
South Lynn Norfk 120 D7
South Malling E Susx 23 G5
South Marston Swindn 47 J2
South Merstham Surrey 51 H8
South Middleton Nthumb 190 E2
South Milford N York 142 D2
South Milton Devon 7 K6
South Mimms Herts 69 G6
Southminster Essex 72 D7
South Molton Devon 28 C5
South Moor Dur 180 F8
Southmoor Oxon 66 B7
South Moreton Oxon 48 E1
Southmuir Angus 234 B5
South Mundham W Susx 20 E6
South Muskham Notts 134 F8
South Newbald E R Yk 152 D8
South Newington Oxon 83 J8
South Newton Wilts 33 J4
South Normanton Derbys 133 J8
South Norwood Gt Lon 51 J5
South Nutfield Surrey 37 M1
South Ockendon Thurr 52 D2
Southoe Cambs 86 D2
South Ormsby Lincs 137 G4
Southorpe C Pete 102 B3
South Ossett Wakefd 141 L4
South Otterington N York 160 E5
Southover Dorset 16 B4
Southover E Susx 24 B2
South Owersby Lincs 135 L1
Southowram Calder 141 H3
South Oxfordshire
   Crematorium Oxon 66 B8
South Park Surrey 37 K1
South Perrott Dorset 15 L1
South Petherton Somset 31 G7
South Petherwin Cnwll 11 K6
South Pickenham Norfk 105 G3
South Pill Cnwll 6 E3
South Pool Devon 7 M6
South Poorton Dorset 15 M3
Southport Sefton 138 D4
Southport Crematorium Lancs 138 D5
South Queensferry C Edin 210 F3
South Radworthy Devon 28 C4
South Rauceby Lincs 118 D2
South Raynham Norfk 121 J6
South Reddish Stockp 131 H1
Southrepps Norfk 122 E4
South Reston Lincs 137 G3
Southrey Lincs 136 B6
South Ronaldsay Ork 275 c6
Southrop Gloucs 65 J6
Southrope Hants 35 J2
South Runcton Norfk 104 C2
South Scarle Notts 135 G7
Southsea C Port 19 L4
Southsea Wrexhm 112 H1
South Shian Ag & B 228 E7
South Shields S Tyne 181 J5
South Shields Crematorium
   S Tyne 181 J6
South Shore Bpool 138 C1
Southside Dur 168 E5
South Somercotes Lincs 137 H1
South Stainley N York 150 D3
South Stifford Thurr 52 D3
South Stoke BaNES 45 L6
South Stoke Oxon 48 F2
South Stoke W Susx 21 H5
South Stour Kent 40 D7
South Street Kent 40 D4
South Street Kent 40 F7
South Street Kent 52 D6
South Tarbrax S Lans 199 H3
South Tawton Devon 12 F4
South Tehidy Cnwll 3 G3
South Thoresby Lincs 137 G4
South Thorpe Dur 168 E7
South Town Hants 35 J4
Southtown Norfk 107 L2
Southtown Somset 30 D7
South Uist W Isls 283 c10
Southwaite Cumb 166 B2
South Walsham Norfk 107 H1
Southwark Gt Lon 51 J3
South Warnborough Hants 35 L2
Southwater W Susx 37 J3
Southwater Street W Susx 37 H5
Southway Somset 31 H2
South Weald Essex 70 E8
Southwell Dorset 16 D8

Southwell Notts 117 J1
South West Middlesex
   Crematorium Gt Lon 50 E4
South Weston Oxon 67 H7
South Wheatley Cnwll 11 J4
South Wheatley Notts 134 F3
Southwick Hants 19 L2
Southwick Nhants 101 M5
Southwick Somset 30 E2
Southwick Sundld 181 J7
Southwick W Susx 22 C6
Southwick Wilts 46 B7
South Widcombe BaNES 45 H7
South Wigston Leics 100 D4
South Willesborough Kent 40 D7
South Willingham Lincs 136 C3
South Wingate Dur 169 L4
South Wingfield Derbys 133 G8
South Witham Lincs 118 B7
Southwold Suffk 107 K8
South Wonston Hants 34 F4
Southwood Norfk 107 H2
Southwood Somset 31 J4
South Woodham Ferrers
   Essex 71 K7
South Wootton Norfk 120 E7
South Wraxall Wilts 46 B6
South Zeal Devon 12 F4
Sovereign Harbour E Susx 23 L6
Sowerby Calder 141 G3
Sowerby N York 160 F6
Sowerby Bridge Calder 141 G3
Sowerby Row Cumb 165 L3
Sower Carr Lancs 147 G7
Sowerhill Somset 28 F6
Sowhill Torfn 62 B7
Sowley Green Suffk 88 D5
Sowood Calder 141 G4
Sowton Devon 6 F2
Sowton Devon 14 A4
Soyland Town Calder 140 F4
Spa Common Norfk 122 F5
Spain's End Essex 88 D7
Spalding Lincs 119 H7
Spaldington E R Yk 143 J1
Spaldwick Cambs 86 C1
Spalford Notts 135 G6
Spanby Lincs 118 E4
Spanish Green Hants 49 G7
Sparham Norfk 122 B7
Sparhamill Norfk 122 B7
Spark Bridge Cumb 156 D5
Sparket Cumb 166 B5
Sparkford Somset 31 K5
Sparkhill Birm 98 E6
Sparkwell Devon 7 H3
Sparrow Green Norfk 121 L8
Sparrowpit Derbys 132 B4
Sparrows Green E Susx 39 G6
Sparsholt Hants 34 F4
Sparsholt Oxon 47 M2
Spartylea Nthumb 167 K1
Spath Staffs 115 H4
Spaunton N York 162 C5
Spaxton Somset 30 C3
Spean Bridge Highld 239 L7
Spear Hill W Susx 21 K3
Spearywell Hants 34 D5
Speen Bucks 67 K7
Speen W Berk 48 C5
Speeton N York 163 L7
Speke Lpool 129 K3
Speldhurst Kent 38 E5
Spellbrook Herts 70 C4
Spelmonden Kent 39 H6
Spelsbury Oxon 65 M3
Spen Kirk 141 K3
Spencers Wood Wokham 49 H5
Spen Green Ches E 130 F7
Spennithorne N York 159 L5
Spennymoor Dur 169 H4
Spernall Warwks 82 C3
Spetchley Worcs 81 K4
Spetisbury Dorset 17 H2
Spexhall Suffk 107 H7
Spey Bay Moray 267 G3
Speybridge Highld 253 K6
Speyview Moray 254 E3
Spilsby Lincs 137 G6
Spindlestone Nthumb 203 J6
Spinkhill Derbys 133 J4
Spinningdale Highld 263 J2
Spion Kop Notts 133 L6
Spirthill Wilts 46 E4
Spital Wirral 129 H3
Spital Hill Donc 134 C1
Spital in the Street Lincs 135 K2
Spithurst E Susx 23 G4
Spittal E Loth 212 A4

Spittal E R Yk............... 152 B5
Spittal Highld............... 279 L5
Spittal Nthumb............... 202 F3
Spittal Pembks............... 55 G2
Spittalfield P & K............... 233 H7
Spittal of Glenmuick Abers......... 243 K6
Spittal of Glenshee P & K......... 233 H2
Spittal-on-Rule Border............... 189 G2
Spixworth Norfk............... 122 E8
Splatt Cnwll............... 10 C7
Splatt Cnwll............... 11 J5
Splatt Devon............... 12 E2
Splayne's Green E Susx............... 23 G2
Splottlands Cardif............... 43 K6
Spofforth N York............... 150 E5
Spondon C Derb............... 116 C4
Spon Green Flints............... 129 G7
Spooner Row Norfk............... 106 B4
Sporle Norfk............... 105 G1
Spott E Loth............... 212 E4
Spottiswoode Border............... 201 J3
Spratton Nhants............... 84 D1
Spreakley Surrey............... 36 B3
Spreyton Devon............... 13 G3
Spriddlestone Devon............... 7 G4
Spridlington Lincs............... 135 K3
Springburn C Glas............... 209 G5
Springfield D & G............... 177 K5
Springfield Essex............... 71 H5
Springfield Fife............... 222 F5
Springhill Staffs............... 98 B3
Springhill Staffs............... 98 D2
Springholm D & G............... 175 K1
Springside N Ayrs............... 196 D3
Springthorpe Lincs............... 135 H2
Spring Vale Barns............... 141 L7
Springwell Sundld............... 181 G7
Springwood Crematorium
  Lpool............... 129 K3
Sproatley E R Yk............... 145 F1
Sproston Green Ches W............... 130 E6
Sprotbrough Donc............... 142 E7
Sproughton Suffk............... 90 D6
Sprouston Border............... 202 B6
Sprowston Norfk............... 106 E1
Sproxton Leics............... 117 M6
Sproxton N York............... 161 K6
Spunhill Shrops............... 112 F5
Spurstow Ches E............... 130 A8
Spyway Dorset............... 15 M4
Square & Compass Pembks............... 74 D6
Stableford Shrops............... 97 G4
Stableford Staffs............... 114 C4
Stacey Bank Sheff............... 132 F2
Stackhouse N York............... 148 E3
Stackpole Pembks............... 55 G7
Stackpole Elidor Pembks............... 55 G7
Stacksford Norfk............... 105 L5
Stacksteads Lancs............... 140 C3
Staddiscombe C Plym............... 7 G4
Staddlethorpe E R Yk............... 143 L2
Staden Derbys............... 131 L5
Stadhampton Oxon............... 66 F7
Stadhlaigearraidh W Isls............... 283 b10
Staffield Cumb............... 166 D2
Staffin Highld............... 259 H3
Stafford Staffs............... 114 E7
Stafford Crematorium Staffs............... 114 E6
Stagsden Bed............... 85 J5
Stainborough Barns............... 141 M7
Stainburn Cumb............... 164 D5
Stainburn N York............... 150 C6
Stainby Lincs............... 118 B7
Staincross Barns............... 141 M5
Staindrop Dur............... 168 E6
Staines-upon-Thames Surrey............... 50 D5
Stainfield Lincs............... 118 E6
Stainfield Lincs............... 136 B5
Stainforth Donc............... 143 G5
Stainforth N York............... 148 E2
Staining Lancs............... 147 G8
Stainland Calder............... 141 G4
Stainsacre N York............... 163 G1
Stainsby Derbys............... 133 J6
Stainton Cumb............... 157 H5
Stainton Cumb............... 166 C5
Stainton Cumb............... 177 L7
Stainton Donc............... 133 L1
Stainton Dur............... 168 D7
Stainton Middsb............... 170 B7
Stainton N York............... 159 K3
Stainton by Langworth Lincs............... 135 L4
Staintondale N York............... 163 H3
Stainton le Vale Lincs............... 136 C1
Stainton with Adgarley Cumb............... 146 E1
Stair Cumb............... 165 H6
Stair E Ayrs............... 196 E6
Stairfoot Barns............... 142 B6
Stairhaven D & G............... 172 F4

Staithes N York............... 171 H7
Stakeford Nthumb............... 181 G2
Stake Pool Lancs............... 147 H6
Stakes Hants............... 19 M2
Stalbridge Dorset............... 32 B7
Stalbridge Weston Dorset............... 32 B7
Stalham Norfk............... 123 H6
Stalham Green Norfk............... 123 H6
Stalisfield Green Kent............... 40 B5
Stalland Common Norfk............... 105 L4
Stallen Dorset............... 31 K7
Stallingborough NE Lin............... 145 G5
Stalling Busk N York............... 159 G5
Stallington Staffs............... 114 E4
Stalmine Lancs............... 147 G6
Stalmine Moss Side Lancs............... 147 G6
Stalybridge Tamesd............... 140 F4
Stambourne Essex............... 88 E7
Stambourne Green Essex............... 88 D7
Stamford Lincs............... 102 A2
Stamford Nthumb............... 191 J2
Stamford Bridge Ches W............... 129 L6
Stamford Bridge E R Yk............... 151 M5
Stamfordham Nthumb............... 180 C4
Stamford Hill Gt Lon............... 51 J2
Stanah Lancs............... 147 G7
Stanborough Herts............... 69 G5
Stanbridge C Beds............... 68 B2
Stanbridge Dorset............... 17 K2
Stanbury C Brad............... 149 H8
Stand Bury............... 140 B6
Stand N Lans............... 209 K5
Standburn Falk............... 210 B4
Standeford Staffs............... 97 K2
Standen Kent............... 39 L5
Standen Street Kent............... 39 K7
Standerwick Somset............... 32 D1
Standford Hants............... 36 B4
Standingstone Cumb............... 164 D4
Standish Gloucs............... 64 A5
Standish Wigan............... 139 H5
Standish Lower Ground Wigan............... 139 H6
Standlake Oxon............... 66 B6
Standon Hants............... 34 F5
Standon Herts............... 69 K3
Standon Staffs............... 114 C4
Standon Green End Herts............... 69 K3
Standwell Green Suffk............... 90 D1
Stane N Lans............... 210 A7
Stanfield Norfk............... 121 K7
Stanford C Beds............... 86 D7
Stanford Kent............... 40 F7
Stanford Shrops............... 95 H1
Stanford Bishop Herefs............... 80 F5
Stanford Bridge Worcs............... 81 G2
Stanford Bridge Wrekin............... 113 M6
Stanford Dingley W Berk............... 48 E4
Stanford in the Vale Oxon............... 65 M8
Stanford le Hope Thurr............... 52 E3
Stanford on Avon Nhants............... 100 D7
Stanford on Soar Notts............... 116 F7
Stanford on Teme Worcs............... 81 G2
Stanford Rivers Essex............... 70 D7
Stanfree Derbys............... 133 J5
Stanghow R & Cl............... 170 F7
Stanground C Pete............... 102 D4
Stanhill Lancs............... 139 L2
Stanhoe Norfk............... 121 H4
Stanhope Border............... 199 K7
Stanhope Dur............... 168 C3
Stanhope Kent............... 40 C7
Stanhope Bretby Derbys............... 115 M7
Stanion Nhants............... 101 K6
Stanklin Worcs............... 97 J8
Stanley Derbys............... 116 C3
Stanley Dur............... 180 F8
Stanley Notts............... 133 J7
Stanley P & K............... 221 K1
Stanley Shrops............... 97 G6
Stanley Staffs............... 114 E1
Stanley Wakefd............... 142 A3
Stanley Common Derbys............... 116 C3
Stanley Crook Dur............... 168 F3
Stanley Ferry Wakefd............... 142 A3
Stanley Gate Lancs............... 138 F6
Stanley Moor Staffs............... 114 E1
Stanley Pontlarge Gloucs............... 64 C2
Stanmer Br & H.............. 22 E5
Stanmore Gt Lon............... 68 F8
Stanmore Hants............... 34 F5
Stanmore W Berk............... 48 C3
Stannersburn Nthumb............... 179 G2
Stanningfield Suffk............... 89 H4
Stanningley Leeds............... 141 K1
Stannington Nthumb............... 180 F3
Stannington Sheff............... 132 F2
Stannington Station Nthumb............... 180 F3
Stansbatch Herefs............... 79 L3
Stansfield Suffk............... 88 F5

Stanshope Staffs............... 115 J1
Stanstead Suffk............... 89 G5
Stanstead Abbotts Herts............... 69 K5
Stansted Kent............... 52 D6
Stansted Mountfitchet Essex............... 70 D2
Stanton Derbys............... 115 M7
Stanton Gloucs............... 82 C8
Stanton Mons............... 62 C3
Stanton Nthumb............... 191 G8
Stanton Staffs............... 115 J2
Stanton Suffk............... 105 K8
Stanton by Bridge Derbys............... 116 B6
Stanton by Dale Derbys............... 116 D4
Stanton Drew BaNES............... 45 H6
Stanton Fitzwarren Swindn............... 47 J1
Stanton Harcourt Oxon............... 66 B6
Stanton Hill Notts............... 133 J7
Stanton in Peak Derbys............... 132 E6
Stanton Lacy Shrops............... 96 B7
Stanton Lees Derbys............... 132 E7
Stanton Long Shrops............... 96 B5
Stanton-on-the-Wolds Notts............... 117 G5
Stanton Prior BaNES............... 45 K6
Stanton St Bernard Wilts............... 47 G6
Stanton St John Oxon............... 66 E5
Stanton St Quintin Wilts............... 46 C3
Stanton Street Suffk............... 89 J2
Stanton under Bardon Leics............... 100 A1
Stanton upon Hine Heath
  Shrops............... 113 J6
Stanton Wick BaNES............... 45 J6
Stantway Gloucs............... 63 L4
Stanwardine in the Field
  Shrops............... 112 F6
Stanwardine in the Wood
  Shrops............... 113 G6
Stanway Essex............... 72 D2
Stanway Gloucs............... 64 F1
Stanway Green Essex............... 72 D2
Stanway Green Suffk............... 90 F1
Stanwell Surrey............... 50 D4
Stanwell Moor Surrey............... 50 D4
Stanwick Nhants............... 85 J1
Stanwick St John N York............... 168 F8
Stanwix Cumb............... 177 L7
Staoinebrig W Isls............... 283 b10
Stape N York............... 162 D4
Stapehill Dorset............... 17 L3
Stapeley Ches E............... 113 L2
Stapenhill Staffs............... 115 L7
Staple Kent............... 41 J4
Staple Cross Devon............... 29 J6
Staplecross E Susx............... 24 E3
Staplefield W Susx............... 37 L5
Staple Fitzpaine Somset............... 30 C7
Stapleford Cambs............... 87 K5
Stapleford Herts............... 69 J4
Stapleford Leics............... 117 L7
Stapleford Lincs............... 135 H8
Stapleford Notts............... 116 E4
Stapleford Wilts............... 33 J3
Stapleford Abbotts Essex............... 70 D8
Stapleford Tawney Essex............... 70 D7
Staplegrove Somset............... 30 B5
Staplehay Somset............... 30 B6
Staple Hill Worcs............... 98 B8
Staplehurst Kent............... 39 K5
Staplers IoW............... 19 H6
Stapleton Cumb............... 178 C4
Stapleton Herefs............... 79 L2
Stapleton Leics............... 99 L4
Stapleton N York............... 169 H8
Stapleton Shrops............... 95 L3
Stapleton Somset............... 31 G6
Stapley Somset............... 30 B8
Staploe Bed............... 86 C3
Staplow Herefs............... 80 F7
Star Fife............... 222 F6
Star IoA............... 125 J5
Star Pembks............... 75 M5
Star Somset............... 44 E7
Starbeck N York............... 150 D4
Starbotton N York............... 159 G7
Starcross Devon............... 14 A6
Stareton Warwks............... 83 H1
Starkholmes Derbys............... 132 F7
Starlings Green Essex............... 70 C1
Starr's Green E Susx............... 24 D4
Starston Norfk............... 106 E6
Start Devon............... 8 B6
Startforth Dur............... 168 D7
Startley Wilts............... 46 D3
Statenborough Kent............... 41 J4
Statham Warrtn............... 130 D2
Stathe Somset............... 30 E5
Stathern Leics............... 117 K5
Station Town Dur............... 169 L3
Staughton Green Cambs............... 86 C2

Staughton Highway Cambs............... 86 C2
Staunton Gloucs............... 63 H4
Staunton Gloucs............... 64 A1
Staunton in the Vale Notts............... 117 L3
Staunton on Arrow Herefs............... 79 L3
Staunton on Wye Herefs............... 79 L6
Staveley Cumb............... 156 E5
Staveley Cumb............... 157 G3
Staveley Derbys............... 133 H5
Staveley N York............... 150 E5
Staverton Devon............... 8 B2
Staverton Gloucs............... 64 C2
Staverton Nhants............... 83 M3
Staverton Wilts............... 46 A4
Staverton Bridge Gloucs............... 64 C3
Stawell Somset............... 30 E3
Stawley Somset............... 29 J7
Staxigoe Highld............... 280 E5
Staxton N York............... 163 J6
Staylittle Cerdgn............... 92 E5
Staylittle Powys............... 93 J5
Staynall Lancs............... 147 G7
Staythorpe Notts............... 117 K1
Stead C Brad............... 149 L6
Stean N York............... 159 K8
Stearsby N York............... 151 K2
Steart Somset............... 30 C2
Stebbing Essex............... 71 G2
Stebbing Green Essex............... 71 G2
Stechford Birm............... 98 E6
Stede Quarter Kent............... 39 L5
Stedham W Susx............... 36 C6
Steel Nthumb............... 179 L7
Steel Cross E Susx............... 38 E7
Steelend Fife............... 210 F1
Steele Road Border............... 188 F7
Steel Green Cumb............... 155 L6
Steel Heath Shrops............... 113 J4
Steen's Bridge Herefs............... 80 C4
Steep Hants............... 35 M6
Steephill IoW............... 19 J8
Steep Lane Calder............... 140 F3
Steeple Dorset............... 17 L5
Steeple Essex............... 72 D6
Steeple Ashton Wilts............... 46 C7
Steeple Aston Oxon............... 66 C2
Steeple Barton Oxon............... 66 C2
Steeple Bumpstead Essex............... 88 D7
Steeple Claydon Bucks............... 67 H2
Steeple Gidding Cambs............... 102 C7
Steeple Langford Wilts............... 33 H3
Steeple Morden Cambs............... 86 F6
Steep Marsh Hants............... 35 M5
Steeton C Brad............... 149 H7
Stein Highld............... 258 D5
Stella Gatesd............... 180 E6
Stelling Minnis Kent............... 40 F6
Stembridge Somset............... 30 F6
Stenalees Cnwll............... 5 G3
Stenhouse D & G............... 185 K4
Stenhousemuir Falk............... 210 B2
Stenigot Lincs............... 136 D3
Stenscholl Highld............... 259 H3
Stenson Fields Derbys............... 116 B5
Stenton E Loth............... 212 E4
Steornabhagh W Isls............... 282 g3
Stepaside Pembks............... 55 K5
Stepford D & G............... 185 L4
Stepney Gt Lon............... 51 K3
Stepping Hill Stockp............... 131 H2
Steppingley C Beds............... 85 K8
Stepps N Lans............... 209 H5
Sternfield Suffk............... 91 J3
Stert Wilts............... 46 F7
Stetchworth Cambs............... 88 C3
Stevenage Herts............... 69 G2
Steven's Crouch E Susx............... 24 C4
Stevenston N Ayrs............... 196 B3
Steventon Hants............... 35 H1
Steventon Oxon............... 48 C1
Steventon End Essex............... 88 B6
Stevington Bed............... 85 K4
Stewartby Bed............... 85 K6
Stewartfield S Lans............... 209 E4
Stewarton Ag & B............... 192 E4
Stewarton E Ayrs............... 196 E2
Stewkley Bucks............... 67 K3
Stewley Somset............... 30 C7
Stewton Lincs............... 137 L3
Steyne Cross IoW............... 19 L6
Steyning W Susx............... 21 L4
Steynton Pembks............... 54 E5
Stibb Cnwll............... 26 C8
Stibbard Norfk............... 121 L6
Stibb Cross Devon............... 27 G7
Stibb Green Wilts............... 47 J6
Stibbington Cambs............... 102 B4
Stichill Border............... 201 L5
Sticker Cnwll............... 4 G5

Stickford Lincs 136 F7
Sticklepath Devon 12 F4
Sticklepath Somset 29 J4
Stickling Green Essex 87 K8
Stickney Lincs 136 F8
Stiffkey Norfk 121 L3
Stifford Clays Thurr 52 D3
Stifford's Bridge Herefs 81 G5
Stiff Street Kent 53 J6
Stile Bridge Kent 39 J4
Stileway Somset 31 G3
Stilligarry W Isls 283 b10
Stillingfleet N York 151 J7
Stillington N York 151 J2
Stillington S on T 169 K6
Stilton Cambs 102 D5
Stinchcombe Gloucs 63 L7
Stinsford Dorset 16 D4
Stiperstones Shrops 95 J3
Stirchley Birm 98 D7
Stirchley Wrekin 96 F2
Stirling Abers 257 L3
Stirling Stirlg 220 D8
Stirtloe Cambs 86 D2
Stirton N York 149 H5
Stisted Essex 71 J2
Stitchcombe Wilts 47 K5
Stithians Cnwll 3 J4
Stivichall Covtry 99 J8
Stixwould Lincs 136 C6
Stoak Ches W 129 K5
Stobo Border 199 L5
Stoborough Dorset 17 H5
Stoborough Green Dorset 17 H5
Stobs Castle Border 188 E4
Stobswood Nthumb 191 J7
Stock Essex 71 G7
Stock N Som 44 F6
Stockbridge Hants 34 D4
Stockbriggs S Lans 198 C6
Stockbury Kent 53 H6
Stockcross W Berk 48 B5
Stockdalewath Cumb 165 L2
Stocker's Hill Kent 40 C5
Stockerston Leics 101 H4
Stock Green Worcs 82 A3
Stocking Herefs 63 J1
Stockingford Warwks 99 J5
Stocking Pelham Herts 70 C1
Stockland Devon 14 F2
Stockland Bristol Somset 30 C2
Stockland Green Kent 38 E5
Stockleigh English Devon 13 K2
Stockleigh Pomeroy Devon 13 K2
Stockley Wilts 46 E5
Stockley Hill Herefs 79 L7
Stocklinch Somset 30 F7
Stockmoor Herefs 79 M4
Stockport Stockp 131 H2
Stockport Crematorium
  Stockp 131 H2
Stocksbridge Sheff 141 L8
Stocksfield Nthumb 180 C6
Stockton Herefs 80 C3
Stockton Norfk 107 H4
Stockton Shrops 95 G3
Stockton Shrops 97 G3
Stockton Warwks 83 K3
Stockton Wilts 33 G3
Stockton Wrekin 114 B8
Stockton Brook Staffs 114 E1
Stockton Heath Warrtn 130 B3
Stockton-on-Tees S on T 170 B6
Stockton on Teme Worcs 81 G2
Stockton on the Forest C York 151 L4
Stockwell Gloucs 64 D4
Stockwell End Wolves 97 K3
Stockwell Heath Staffs 115 G7
Stockwood Bristl 45 J5
Stockwood Dorset 16 B1
Stock Wood Worcs 82 B3
Stodday Lancs 147 J4
Stodmarsh Kent 41 H3
Stody Norfk 122 B4
Stoer Highld 270 D2
Stoford Somset 31 J8
Stoford Wilts 33 J4
Stogumber Somset 29 K3
Stogursey Somset 30 B2
Stoke Covtry 99 K7
Stoke Devon 26 D6
Stoke Hants 20 B6
Stoke Hants 48 B8
Stoke Medway 53 H4
Stoke Abbott Dorset 15 K3
Stoke Albany Nhants 101 H5
Stoke Ash Suffk 90 D1
Stoke Bardolph Notts 117 H3
Stoke Bliss Worcs 80 F3

Stoke Bruerne Nhants 84 E5
Stoke-by-Clare Suffk 88 E6
Stoke-by-Nayland Suffk 89 K7
Stoke Canon Devon 13 L3
Stoke Charity Hants 35 G3
Stoke Climsland Cnwll 11 L2
Stoke Cross Herefs 80 E5
Stoke D'Abernon Surrey 50 E7
Stoke Doyle Nhants 102 A6
Stoke Dry Rutlnd 101 J2
Stoke Edith Herefs 80 E7
Stoke End Warwks 98 F4
Stoke Farthing Wilts 33 H5
Stoke Ferry Norfk 104 D3
Stoke Fleming Devon 8 C5
Stokeford Dorset 17 G5
Stoke Gabriel Devon 8 C3
Stoke Gifford S Glos 45 J3
Stoke Golding Leics 99 L4
Stoke Goldington M Keyn 85 G5
Stoke Green Bucks 50 B3
Stokeham Notts 134 F4
Stoke Hammond Bucks 67 L1
Stoke Heath Shrops 113 L5
Stoke Heath Worcs 81 L2
Stoke Holy Cross Norfk 106 E3
Stokeinteignhead Devon 13 L8
Stoke Lacy Herefs 80 E5
Stoke Lyne Oxon 66 E2
Stoke Mandeville Bucks 67 K5
Stokenchurch Bucks 67 J7
Stoke Newington Gt Lon 51 J2
Stokenham Devon 8 B6
Stoke-on-Trent C Stke 114 D2
Stoke Orchard Gloucs 64 D2
Stoke Poges Bucks 50 B2
Stoke Pound Worcs 81 M2
Stoke Prior Herefs 80 C4
Stoke Prior Worcs 81 L2
Stoke Rivers Devon 27 L4
Stoke Rochford Lincs 118 B6
Stoke Row Oxon 49 G2
Stoke St Gregory Somset 30 E5
Stoke St Mary Somset 30 C6
Stoke St Michael Somset 31 L2
Stoke St Milborough Shrops 96 D7
Stokesay Shrops 95 K7
Stokesby Norfk 107 J1
Stokesley N York 161 H1
Stoke sub Hamdon Somset 31 G7
Stoke Talmage Oxon 67 G7
Stoke Trister Somset 32 B5
Stoke upon Tern Shrops 113 L6
Stoke-upon-Trent C Stke 114 D2
Stoke Wake Dorset 16 E1
Stoke Wharf Worcs 81 L2
Stolford Somset 30 C2
Stondon Massey Essex 70 E7
Stone Bucks 67 J4
Stone Gloucs 63 K8
Stone Kent 52 C4
Stone Rothm 133 L2
Stone Somset 31 J4
Stone Staffs 114 E5
Stone Worcs 97 J8
Stonea Cambs 103 J5
Stone Allerton Somset 30 F1
Ston Easton Somset 45 J3
Stonebridge N Som 44 D7
Stonebridge Norfk 105 J5
Stonebridge Warwks 99 G6
Stone Bridge Corner C Pete 102 F3
Stonebroom Derbys 133 H7
Stone Chair Calder 141 H2
Stone Cross E Susx 23 K6
Stone Cross E Susx 38 D7
Stone Cross E Susx 39 G7
Stone Cross Kent 38 E5
Stone Cross Kent 40 D7
Stone Cross Kent 41 K4
Stonecross Green Suffk 89 G4
Stonecrouch Kent 39 H6
Stone-edge-Batch N Som 44 F4
Stoneferry C KuH 144 E2
Stonefield Castle Hotel Ag & B 206 D5
Stonegate E Susx 39 G7
Stonegate N York 162 D1
Stonegrave N York 161 L7
Stonehall Worcs 81 K5
Stonehaugh Nthumb 179 J4
Stonehaven Abers 245 J6
Stone Hill Donc 143 H6
Stonehouse C Plym 6 F4
Stone House Cumb 158 D5
Stonehouse Gloucs 64 A6
Stonehouse Nthumb 179 G7
Stonehouse S Lans 198 C4
Stone in Oxney Kent 25 H2
Stoneleigh Warwks 83 H1

Stoneley Green Ches E 113 K1
Stonely Cambs 86 C2
Stoner Hill Hants 35 M5
Stonesby Leics 117 L6
Stonesfield Oxon 66 B4
Stones Green Essex 73 H2
Stone Street Kent 38 F2
Stone Street Suffk 89 K6
Stone Street Suffk 89 K7
Stone Street Suffk 107 H7
Stonestreet Green Kent 40 E2
Stonethwaite Cumb 165 J7
Stonewells Moray 266 F3
Stonewood Kent 52 D4
Stoneybridge W Isls 283 b10
Stoneybridge Worcs 97 L8
Stoneyburn W Loth 210 C6
Stoney Cross Hants 18 D1
Stoneygate C Leic 100 D3
Stoneyhills Essex 72 D7
Stoneykirk D & G 172 D4
Stoney Middleton Derbys 132 E4
Stoney Stanton Leics 100 B4
Stoney Stoke Somset 32 B4
Stoney Stratton Somset 31 L3
Stoney Stretton Shrops 95 J2
Stoneywood C Aber 245 K1
Stoneywood Falk 209 L2
Stonham Aspal Suffk 90 D3
Stonnall Staffs 98 D3
Stonor Oxon 49 H1
Stonton Wyville Leics 101 G4
Stony Cross Herefs 80 D2
Stony Cross Herefs 81 G5
Stonyford Hants 34 D7
Stony Houghton Derbys 133 H4
Stony Stratford M Keyn 84 F7
Stonywell Staffs 98 D1
Stoodleigh Devon 28 B4
Stoodleigh Devon 29 G7
Stopham W Susx 21 H3
Stopsley Luton 68 E2
Stoptide Cnwll 10 C7
Storeton Wirral 129 G3
Storeyard Green Herefs 81 G6
Storey Arms Powys 60 E3
Stornoway W Isls 282 g3
Storridge Herefs 81 H5
Storrington W Susx 21 J4
Storth Cumb 157 G6
Storwood E R Yk 151 M7
Stotfield Moray 266 E2
Stotfold C Beds 86 E7
Stottesdon Shrops 96 F6
Stoughton Leics 100 E3
Stoughton Surrey 50 C8
Stoughton W Susx 20 C4
Stoulton Worcs 81 L5
Stourbridge Dudley 97 K6
Stourbridge Crematorium
  Dudley 97 K6
Stourpaine Dorset 17 G1
Stourport-on-Severn Worcs 81 J1
Stour Provost Dorset 32 C6
Stour Row Dorset 32 D6
Stourton Leeds 141 M2
Stourton Staffs 97 K6
Stourton Warwks 83 G7
Stourton Wilts 32 C4
Stourton Caundle Dorset 32 B7
Stout Somset 31 G4
Stove Shet 281 e6
Stoven Suffk 107 J7
Stow Border 200 F4
Stow Lincs 135 H3
Stow Bardolph Norfk 104 D2
Stow Bedon Norfk 105 J4
Stowbridge Norfk 104 B2
Stow-cum-Quy Cambs 87 L3
Stowe Gloucs 63 H5
Stowe Shrops 95 H8
Stowe by Chartley Staffs 114 F6
Stowehill Nhants 84 C3
Stowell Somset 31 L6
Stowey BaNES 45 H7
Stowford Devon 12 B3
Stowford Devon 12 B3
Stowford Devon 14 D5
Stowford Devon 28 B3
Stowlangtoft Suffk 89 J2
Stow Longa Cambs 86 C1
Stow Maries Essex 71 K7
Stowmarket Suffk 90 B3
Stow-on-the-Wold Gloucs 65 J2
Stowting Kent 40 F7
Stowting Common Kent 40 F6
Stowupland Suffk 90 C3
Straanruie Highld 253 J8
Strachan Abers 244 F5

Strachur Ag & B 217 H6
Stradbroke Suffk 106 E8
Stradbrook Wilts 46 D8
Stradishall Suffk 88 E5
Stradsett Norfk 104 D2
Stragglethorpe Lincs 118 B1
Stragglethorpe Notts 117 H4
Straight Soley Wilts 47 L4
Straiton Mdloth 211 J5
Straiton S Ayrs 183 K2
Straloch Abers 256 F7
Straloch P & K 232 F3
Stramshall Staffs 115 H4
Strang IoM 154 e6
Strangeways Salfd 140 B7
Strangford Herefs 63 H2
Stranraer D & G 172 C3
Strata Florida Cerdgn 77 K2
Stratfield Mortimer W Berk 49 G6
Stratfield Saye Hants 49 G6
Stratfield Turgis Hants 49 G7
Stratford C Beds 86 D5
Stratford Gt Lon 51 K2
Stratford St Andrew Suffk 91 H3
Stratford St Mary Suffk 90 B8
Stratford sub Castle Wilts 33 K4
Stratford Tony Wilts 33 J5
Stratford-upon-Avon Warwks 82 F4
Strath Highld 260 C4
Strathan Highld 270 E4
Strathan Highld 277 K3
Strathaven S Lans 197 K2
Strathblane Stirlg 208 F3
Strathcanaird Highld 270 F7
Strathcarron Highld 248 F3
Strathcoil Ag & B 227 K6
Strathdon Abers 243 K1
Strathkinness Fife 223 H4
Strathloanhead W Loth 210 B4
Strathmashie House Highld 241 G5
Strathmiglo Fife 222 C5
Strathpeffer Highld 262 E8
Strathtay P & K 232 D4
Strathwhillan N Ayrs 195 G4
Strathy Highld 278 E3
Strathy Inn Highld 278 E3
Strathyre Stirlg 219 J4
Stratton Cnwll 11 J1
Stratton Dorset 16 C4
Stratton Gloucs 64 E6
Stratton Audley Oxon 66 F2
Stratton-on-the-Fosse
  Somset 31 L1
Stratton St Margaret Swindn 47 H2
Stratton St Michael Norfk 106 D4
Stratton Strawless Norfk 122 E7
Stream Somset 29 K3
Streat E Susx 22 E4
Streatham Gt Lon 51 J4
Streatley C Beds 68 D2
Streatley W Berk 48 E3
Street Devon 14 E5
Street Lancs 147 K5
Street N York 162 C2
Street Somset 31 H3
Street Ashton Warwks 99 M7
Street Dinas Shrops 112 E4
Street End E Susx 23 K3
Street End Kent 40 F4
Street End W Susx 20 D7
Street Gate Gatesd 180 F7
Streethay Staffs 98 F1
Street Houses N York 151 H6
Streetlam N York 160 D3
Street Lane Derbys 116 C2
Streetly Wsall 98 D4
Streetly Crematorium Wsall 98 D4
Streetly End Cambs 88 C5
Street on the Fosse Somset 31 K3
Strefford Shrops 95 K6
Strelitz P & K 233 J8
Strelley Notts 116 E3
Strensall C York 151 K4
Strensham Worcs 81 L7
Stretcholt Somset 30 D2
Strete Devon 8 C5
Stretford Herefs 80 B4
Stretford Herefs 80 C4
Stretford Traffd 130 F1
Strethall Essex 87 K7
Stretham Cambs 103 K8
Strettington W Susx 20 E5
Stretton Ches W 113 G1
Stretton Derbys 133 H7
Stretton Rutlnd 118 C4
Stretton Staffs 97 K1
Stretton Staffs 115 L6
Stretton Warrtn 130 C3
Stretton en le Field Leics 99 J1

Stretton Grandison Herefs 80 E6
Stretton-on-Dunsmore Warwks 83 J1
Stretton on Fosse Warwks 82 F7
Stretton on Sugwas Herefs 80 B6
Stretton under Fosse Warwks 99 M7
Stretton Westwood Shrops 96 D4
Strichen Abers 269 H5
Strines Stockp 131 J2
Stringston Somset 30 B2
Strixton Nhants 85 H3
Stroat Gloucs 63 H7
Stroma Highld 280 E1
Stromeferry Highld 248 D5
Stromness Ork 275 b4
Stronachlachar Stirlg 218 F5
Stronafian Ag & B 207 G3
Stronchrubie Highld 271 H4
Strone Ag & B 207 K3
Strone Highld 239 J7
Strone Highld 250 F6
Stronenaba Highld 239 L6
Stronmilchan Ag & B 217 J2
Stronsay Ork 275 e3
Strontian Highld 228 C3
Strood Kent 39 L7
Strood Medway 52 F5
Strood Green Surrey 37 J1
Strood Green W Susx 36 F6
Stroud Gloucs 64 B6
Stroud Hants 35 L6
Stroude Surrey 50 C5
Stroud Green Essex 53 J1
Stroud Green Gloucs 64 A5
Stroxton Lincs 118 B5
Struan Highld 246 D1
Struan P & K 232 B2
Strubby Lincs 137 H3
Strumpshaw Norfk 107 G2
Strutherhill S Lans 198 C3
Struthers Fife 222 F5
Struy Highld 250 C4
Stryd-y-Facsen IoA 124 F3
Stryt-issa Wrexhm 112 D2
Stuartfield Abers 257 H3
Stubbers Green Wsall 98 D3
Stubbington Hants 19 J3
Stubbins Lancs 140 B4
Stubbs Green Norfk 106 E4
Stubhampton Dorset 32 F8
Stubley Derbys 133 G4
Stubshaw Cross Wigan 139 H7
Stubton Lincs 118 A2
Stuckton Hants 33 L8
Studfold N York 148 E2
Stud Green W & M 49 L3
Studham C Beds 68 C4
Studholme Cumb 177 H7
Studland Dorset 17 K6
Studley Warwks 82 C2
Studley Wilts 46 D4
Studley Common Warwks 82 C2
Studley Roger N York 150 C2
Studley Royal N York 150 C2
Stuntney Cambs 103 L7
Stunts Green E Susx 23 K4
Sturbridge Staffs 114 C5
Sturgate Lincs 135 H2
Sturmer Essex 88 D6
Sturminster Common Dorset 32 C8
Sturminster Marshall Dorset 17 J3
Sturminster Newton Dorset 32 C8
Sturry Kent 41 G3
Sturton N Linc 144 B7
Sturton by Stow Lincs 135 H4
Sturton le Steeple Notts 134 F3
Stuston Suffk 106 G3
Stutton N York 151 G7
Stutton Suffk 90 D8
Styal Ches E 131 G3
Stydd Lancs 148 A8
Stynie Moray 267 G4
Styrrup Notts 134 C2
Succoth Ag & B 218 D6
Suckley Worcs 81 G5
Suckley Green Worcs 81 G4
Sudborough Nhants 101 L7
Sudbourne Suffk 91 J4
Sudbrook Lincs 118 C3
Sudbrook Mons 45 G2
Sudbrooke Lincs 135 L4
Sudbury Derbys 115 K5
Sudbury Gt Lon 50 F2
Sudbury Suffk 89 H7
Sudden Rochdl 140 C5
Sudgrove Gloucs 64 D5

Suffield N York 163 H4
Suffield Norfk 122 E5
Sugdon Wrekin 113 K8
Sugnall Staffs 114 B5
Sugwas Pool Herefs 80 B6
Suisnish Highld 247 J5
Sulby IoM 154 e3
Sulgrave Nhants 84 A6
Sulham W Berk 48 F4
Sulhamstead W Berk 48 F5
Sulhamstead Abbots W Berk 48 F5
Sulhamstead Bannister W Berk 48 F5
Sullington W Susx 21 J4
Sullom Shet 281 d4
Sullom Voe Shet 281 d4
Sully V Glam 43 J8
Summerbridge N York 150 B3
Summercourt Cnwll 4 E4
Summerfield Norfk 121 G4
Summerfield Worcs 97 J8
Summer Heath Bucks 49 H1
Summerhill Pembks 55 K5
Summerhill Staffs 98 D2
Summer Hill Wrexhm 112 D1
Summerhouse Darltn 169 G6
Summerlands Cumb 157 H5
Summerley Derbys 133 G4
Summersdale W Susx 20 D5
Summerseat Bury 140 B5
Summertown Oxon 66 D5
Summit Oldham 140 D6
Summit Rochdl 140 E4
Sunbiggin Cumb 157 L1
Sunbury-on-Thames Surrey 50 E5
Sundaywell D & G 185 K6
Sunderland Ag & B 204 C3
Sunderland Cumb 165 G4
Sunderland Lancs 147 H4
Sunderland Sundld 181 K7
Sunderland Bridge Dur 169 H3
Sunderland Crematorium Sundld 181 J7
Sundhope Border 200 D8
Sundon Park Luton 68 D2
Sundridge Kent 38 D2
Sunk Island E R Yk 145 H4
Sunningdale W & M 50 B5
Sunninghill W & M 50 B5
Sunningwell Oxon 66 D7
Sunniside Dur 168 F3
Sunniside Gatesd 180 F7
Sunny Brow Dur 169 G4
Sunnyhill C Derb 116 B5
Sunnyhurst Bl w D 139 K3
Sunnylaw Stirlg 220 D7
Sunnymead Oxon 66 D5
Sunton Wilts 47 K8
Surbiton Gt Lon 50 F5
Surfleet Lincs 119 H6
Surfleet Seas End Lincs 119 J6
Surlingham Norfk 107 G2
Surrex Essex 72 C3
Surrey & Sussex Crematorium W Susx 37 L3
Sustead Norfk 122 D4
Susworth Lincs 143 L7
Sutcombe Devon 26 F8
Sutcombemill Devon 26 F8
Suton Norfk 106 B4
Sutterby Lincs 137 G5
Sutterton Lincs 119 J4
Sutton C Beds 86 E5
Sutton C Pete 102 B4
Sutton Cambs 103 J7
Sutton Devon 7 K6
Sutton Devon 13 G2
Sutton Donc 142 E5
Sutton E Susx 23 H7
Sutton Gt Lon 51 H6
Sutton Kent 41 K5
Sutton N York 142 D3
Sutton Norfk 123 H6
Sutton Notts 117 K4
Sutton Oxon 66 B6
Sutton Pembks 54 E4
Sutton Shrops 96 C1
Sutton Shrops 97 G6
Sutton Shrops 112 E6
Sutton Shrops 113 L5
Sutton St Hel 129 M1
Sutton Staffs 114 B7
Sutton Suffk 91 G6
Sutton W Susx 21 G4
Sutton Abinger Surrey 37 J2
Sutton-at-Hone Kent 52 C5
Sutton Bassett Nhants 101 G5
Sutton Benger Wilts 46 D3
Sutton Bingham Somset 31 J8

Sutton Bonington Notts 116 E6
Sutton Bridge Lincs 120 B7
Sutton Cheney Leics 99 L3
Sutton Coldfield Birm 98 E4
Sutton Coldfield Crematorium Birm 98 F4
Sutton Courtenay Oxon 66 D8
Sutton Crosses Lincs 119 M7
Sutton cum Lound Notts 134 D3
Sutton Fields Notts 116 E6
Sutton Green Surrey 50 C8
Sutton Green Wrexhm 112 F2
Sutton Howgrave N York 160 D6
Sutton-in-Ashfield Notts 133 K7
Sutton-in-Craven N York 149 H7
Sutton in the Elms Leics 100 B4
Sutton Lane Ends Ches E 131 H5
Sutton Maddock Shrops 97 G3
Sutton Mallet Somset 30 E3
Sutton Mandeville Wilts 33 G5
Sutton Manor St Hel 129 L2
Sutton Marsh Herefs 80 D6
Sutton Montis Somset 31 K6
Sutton-on-Hull C KuH 144 E1
Sutton on Sea Lincs 137 K3
Sutton-on-the-Forest N York 151 J3
Sutton on the Hill Derbys 115 L5
Sutton on Trent Notts 134 F6
Sutton Poyntz Dorset 16 D6
Sutton St Edmund Lincs 103 H1
Sutton St James Lincs 119 L7
Sutton St Nicholas Herefs 80 C6
Sutton Scotney Hants 34 F3
Sutton Street Kent 39 K2
Sutton-under-Brailes Warwks 83 G7
Sutton-under-Whitestonecliffe N York 161 G6
Sutton upon Derwent E R Yk 151 L6
Sutton Valence Kent 39 K3
Sutton Veny Wilts 32 E3
Sutton Waldron Dorset 32 E7
Sutton Weaver Ches W 130 A4
Sutton Wick BaNES 45 H7
Sutton Wick Oxon 66 C8
Swaby Lincs 137 G4
Swadlincote Derbys 116 A7
Swaffham Norfk 105 G2
Swaffham Bulbeck Cambs 87 L3
Swaffham Prior Cambs 88 B2
Swafield Norfk 122 F5
Swainby N York 161 G2
Swainshill Herefs 80 B7
Swainsthorpe Norfk 106 E3
Swainswick BaNES 45 M5
Swalcliffe Oxon 83 J7
Swalecliffe Kent 40 F2
Swallow Lincs 144 F7
Swallow Beck Lincs 135 J6
Swallowcliffe Wilts 33 G5
Swallowfield Wokham 49 H6
Swallownest Rothm 133 J3
Swallows Cross Essex 70 F7
Swampton Hants 34 E1
Swanage Dorset 17 K6
Swanbourne Bucks 67 K2
Swanbridge V Glam 43 J8
Swancote Shrops 97 G4
Swan Green Ches W 130 E5
Swanland E R Yk 144 C2
Swanley Kent 52 B5
Swanley Village Kent 52 B5
Swanmore Hants 35 J7
Swannington Leics 116 C8
Swannington Norfk 122 C7
Swanpool Lincs 135 J6
Swanscombe Kent 52 D4
Swansea Swans 57 J6
Swansea Crematorium Swans 57 J5
Swan Street Essex 72 C2
Swanton Abbot Norfk 122 F6
Swanton Morley Norfk 121 M8
Swanton Novers Norfk 121 M5
Swanton Street Kent 53 J7
Swan Valley Nhants 84 D4
Swan Village Sandw 98 C5
Swanwick Derbys 116 C1
Swanwick Hants 19 H2
Swarby Lincs 118 D3
Swardeston Norfk 106 D3
Swarkestone Derbys 116 B6
Swarland Nthumb 191 H5
Swarraton Hants 35 H3
Swartha C Brad 149 J6
Swarthmoor Cumb 156 C7
Swaton Lincs 118 F4
Swavesey Cambs 87 G2

Sway Hants 18 D4
Swayfield Lincs 118 C7
Swaythling C Sotn 34 F7
Sweet Green Worcs 80 F3
Sweetham Devon 13 K3
Sweethaws E Susx 38 C7
Sweetlands Corner Kent 39 K4
Sweets Cnwll 11 G3
Sweetshouse Cnwll 5 J3
Swefling Suffk 91 H3
Swepstone Leics 99 K1
Swerford Oxon 66 A1
Swettenham Ches E 130 F6
Swffryd Blae G 61 K7
Swift's Green Kent 39 L4
Swilland Suffk 90 E4
Swillbrook Lancs 138 F1
Swillington Leeds 142 B2
Swimbridge Devon 27 L5
Swimbridge Newland Devon 27 L5
Swinbrook Oxon 65 L4
Swincliffe Kirk 141 K2
Swincliffe N York 150 C4
Swincombe Devon 28 B3
Swinden N York 148 E5
Swinderby Lincs 135 H7
Swindon Gloucs 64 D2
Swindon Nthumb 190 D6
Swindon Staffs 97 J5
Swindon Swindn 47 H2
Swine E R Yk 153 J4
Swinefleet E R Yk 143 J3
Swineford S Glos 45 K5
Swineshead Bed 85 L2
Swineshead Lincs 119 H3
Swineshead Bridge Lincs 119 H3
Swiney Highld 275 H1
Swinford Leics 100 C7
Swinford Oxon 66 C5
Swingfield Minnis Kent 41 G6
Swingfield Street Kent 41 H6
Swingleton Green Suffk 89 K6
Swinhoe Nthumb 203 K7
Swinhope Lincs 145 G8
Swinithwaite N York 159 J5
Swinmore Common Herefs 80 F7
Swinscoe Staffs 115 J2
Swinside Cumb 165 H6
Swinstead Lincs 118 D7
Swinthorpe Lincs 135 L4
Swinton Border 202 C4
Swinton N York 160 B6
Swinton N York 162 D8
Swinton Rothm 142 C7
Swinton Salfd 140 A7
Swithland Leics 100 C1
Swordale Highld 263 G6
Swordland Highld 238 B5
Swordly Highld 278 C4
Sworton Heath Ches E 130 D3
Swyddffynnon Cerdgn 77 G3
Swyncombe Oxon 49 G1
Swynnerton Staffs 114 D4
Swyre Dorset 15 M5
Sycharth Powys 112 C4
Sychnant Powys 93 L7
Sychtyn Powys 94 B2
Sydallt Wrexhm 129 H8
Syde Gloucs 64 D5
Sydenham Gt Lon 51 K4
Sydenham Oxon 67 H6
Sydenham Damerel Devon 12 A7
Sydenhurst Surrey 36 E4
Syderstone Norfk 121 H5
Sydling St Nicholas Dorset 16 C3
Sydmonton Hants 48 C7
Sydnal Lane Shrops 97 H2
Syerston Notts 117 K2
Syke Rochdl 140 D4
Sykehouse Donc 143 H4
Syleham Suffk 106 E7
Sylen Carmth 56 F3
Symbister Shet 281 e5
Symington S Ayrs 196 D5
Symington S Lans 199 G6
Symondsbury Dorset 15 K4
Symonds Yat (East) Herefs 63 H4
Symonds Yat (West) Herefs 63 H4
Sympson Green C Brad 150 A8
Synderford Dorset 15 J2
Synod Inn Cerdgn 76 D4
Syre Highld 278 B7
Syreford Gloucs 64 E3
Syresham Nhants 84 C7
Syston Leics 100 D1
Syston Lincs 118 B3
Sytchampton Worcs 81 J2
Sywell Nhants 84 F2

T

Tabley Hill Ches E 130 E4
Tackley Oxon 66 C3
Tacolneston Norfk 106 C4
Tadcaster N York 151 G7
Taddington Derbys 132 C5
Taddington Gloucs 65 G1
Taddiport Devon 27 H7
Tadley Hants 48 F6
Tadlow Cambs 86 F5
Tadmarton Oxon 83 J7
Tadwick BaNES 45 L5
Tadworth Surrey 51 G7
Tafarnaubach Blae G 61 H5
Tafarn-y-bwlch Pembks 75 J5
Tafarn-y-Gelyn Denbgs 128 E7
Taff's Well Rhondd 43 H5
Tafolwern Powys 93 J3
Taibach Neath 57 L7
Tain Highld 263 L3
Tain Highld 280 B3
Tai'n Lôn Gwynd 109 H2
Tairbeart W Isls 282 e5
Tai'r Bull Powys 60 F2
Takeley Essex 70 E3
Takeley Street Essex 70 E3
Talachddu Powys 78 F8
Talacre Flints 128 D3
Talaton Devon 14 C3
Talbenny Pembks 54 D4
Talbot Green Rhondd 43 G5
Talbot Village Bmouth 17 L4
Taleford Devon 14 C3
Talerddig Powys 93 K3
Talgarreg Cerdgn 76 D5
Talgarth Powys 79 G8
Talisker Highld 246 D3
Talke Staffs 114 C1
Talke Pits Staffs 114 C1
Talkin Cumb 178 D7
Talladale Highld 260 E6
Talla Linnfoots Border 187 H2
Tallaminnock S Ayrs 183 K3
Tallarn Green Wrexhm 113 G3
Tallentire Cumb 164 F4
Talley Carmth 59 H2
Tallington Lincs 102 B2
Tallwrn Wrexhm 112 D2
Talmine Highld 277 K4
Talog Carmth 58 B4
Talsarn Cerdgn 77 G4
Talsarnau Gwynd 109 L4
Talskiddy Cnwll 4 E2
Talwrn IoA 125 J4
Talwrn Wrexhm 112 F2
Tal-y-bont Cerdgn 92 E5
Tal-y-Bont Conwy 126 F6
Tal-y-bont Gwynd 109 L7
Tal-y-bont Gwynd 126 C5
Talybont-on-Usk Powys 61 H3
Tal-y-Cafn Conwy 126 F5
Tal-y-coed Mons 62 E4
Tal-y-garn Rhondd 42 F5
Tal-y-llyn Gwynd 92 F2
Talysarn Gwynd 109 J1
Tal-y-Waun Torfn 61 L6
Talywern Powys 93 H3
Tamer Lane End Wigan 139 J7
Tamerton Foliot C Plym 6 F3
Tamworth Staffs 99 G3
Tamworth Green Lincs 119 L3
Tancred N York 151 G4
Tancredston Pembks 74 E7
Tandridge Surrey 38 B3
Tanfield Dur 180 F7
Tanfield Lea Dur 180 F8
Tangiers Pembks 54 F3
Tangley Hants 47 L8
Tangmere W Susx 20 E5
Tangusdale W Isls 283 b13
Tan Hill N York 158 F1
Tankerness Ork 275 d4
Tankersley Barns 142 A7
Tankerton Kent 40 F2
Tannach Highld 280 D6
Tannachie Abers 245 H6
Tannadice Angus 234 D4
Tanner's Green Worcs 98 D8
Tannington Suffk 90 F2
Tannochside N Lans 209 J6
Tansley Derbys 132 F7
Tansor Nhants 102 B5
Tantobie Dur 180 E7
Tanton N York 170 C8
Tanwood Worcs 97 K8
Tanworth in Arden Warwks 82 D1
Tan-y-Bwlch Gwynd 110 C3

Tan-y-fron Conwy 127 J6
Tan-y-fron Wrexhm 112 D1
Tan-y-grisiau Gwynd 110 C3
Tan-y-groes Cerdgn 76 B5
Taobh Tuath W Isls 282 d6
Taplow Bucks 49 M3
Tarbert Ag & B 205 L6
Tarbert Ag & B 206 B5
Tarbert W Isls 282 e5
Tarbet Ag & B 218 D6
Tarbet Highld 238 C5
Tarbet Highld 276 B6
Tarbock Green Knows 129 K2
Tarbolton S Ayrs 196 E5
Tarbrax S Lans 199 H2
Tardebigge Worcs 82 B2
Tarfside Angus 244 B7
Tarland Abers 244 B3
Tarleton Lancs 138 F4
Tarlscough Lancs 138 E5
Tarlton Gloucs 64 D7
Tarnock Somset 44 D8
Tarns Cumb 164 F1
Tarnside Cumb 156 F4
Tarporley Ches W 130 A7
Tarr Somset 28 F4
Tarrant Crawford Dorset 17 H2
Tarrant Gunville Dorset 32 F8
Tarrant Hinton Dorset 32 F8
Tarrant Keyneston Dorset 17 H2
Tarrant Launceston Dorset 17 J1
Tarrant Monkton Dorset 17 J1
Tarrant Rawston Dorset 17 H1
Tarrant Rushton Dorset 17 H2
Tarring Neville E Susx 23 G6
Tarrington Herefs 80 E7
Tarskavaig Highld 247 J6
Tarves Abers 256 F5
Tarvin Ches W 129 L6
Tarvin Sands Ches W 129 L6
Tasburgh Norfk 106 D4
Tasley Shrops 96 F4
Taston Oxon 65 M3
Tatenhill Staffs 115 K7
Tathall End M Keyn 84 F6
Tatham Lancs 147 M2
Tathwell Lincs 136 F3
Tatsfield Surrey 51 L7
Tattenhall Ches W 129 L7
Tatterford Norfk 121 J6
Tattersett Norfk 121 J5
Tattershall Lincs 136 D8
Tattershall Bridge Lincs 136 C8
Tattershall Thorpe Lincs 136 D7
Tattingstone Suffk 90 D7
Tattingstone White Horse
   Suffk 90 D7
Tatworth Somset 15 H2
Tauchers Moray 267 H6
Taunton Somset 30 C6
Taunton Deane Crematorium
   Somset 30 B6
Taverham Norfk 122 D8
Taverners Green Essex 70 E3
Tavernspite Pembks 55 L4
Tavistock Devon 12 C7
Taw Green Devon 12 F3
Tawstock Devon 27 K5
Taxal Derbys 131 K4
Tay Bridge C Dund 223 G1
Taychreggan Hotel Ag & B 217 G3
Tayinloan Ag & B 205 M7
Taynton Gloucs 63 L3
Taynton Oxon 65 K4
Taynuilt Ag & B 216 F1
Tayport Fife 223 H2
Tayvallich Ag & B 215 L7
Tealby Lincs 136 C2
Tealing Angus 234 B7
Team Valley Gatesd 181 G7
Teangue Highld 247 K6
Teanord Highld 263 G7
Tebay Cumb 157 K2
Tebworth C Beds 68 C2
Tedburn St Mary Devon 13 J4
Teddington Gloucs 81 M8
Teddington Gt Lon 50 F5
Tedstone Delamere Herefs 80 F3
Tedstone Wafer Herefs 80 F3
Teesport R & Cl 170 D6
Teesside Crematorium Middsb 170 C7
Teesside Park S on T 170 B7
Teeton Nhants 84 D1
Teffont Evias Wilts 33 G4
Teffont Magna Wilts 33 G4
Tegryn Pembks 75 L5
Teigh Rutlnd 117 M8
Teigncombe Devon 12 F5
Teigngrace Devon 13 K7

Teignmouth Devon 13 L8
Teindside Border 188 D4
Telford Wrekin 96 F2
Telford Crematorium Wrekin 97 G1
Tellisford Somset 46 A7
Telscombe E Susx 22 F6
Telscombe Cliffs E Susx 22 F7
Tempar P & K 231 J4
Templand D & G 176 E2
Temple Cnwll 11 G7
Temple Mdloth 211 K7
Temple Balsall Solhll 99 G8
Temple Bar Cerdgn 76 F4
Temple Cloud BaNES 45 J7
Templecombe Somset 32 B6
Temple End Suffk 88 D5
Temple Ewell Kent 41 J6
Temple Grafton Warwks 82 D4
Temple Guiting Gloucs 65 G2
Temple Herdewyke Warwks 83 J5
Temple Hirst N York 142 F3
Temple Normanton Derbys 133 H6
Temple of Fiddes Abers 245 H7
Temple Sowerby Cumb 166 E5
Templeton Devon 28 F8
Templeton Pembks 55 J4
Templetown Dur 168 E1
Tempsford C Beds 86 D4
Tenbury Wells Worcs 80 E2
Tenby Pembks 55 K6
Tendring Essex 73 H2
Tendring Green Essex 73 H2
Tendring Heath Essex 73 H2
Ten Mile Bank Norfk 104 B4
Tenpenny Heath Essex 73 G3
Tenterden Kent 39 M6
Terling Essex 71 J4
Tern Wrekin 113 K8
Ternhill Shrops 113 L5
Terregles D & G 176 B3
Terrington N York 151 L2
Terrington St Clement Norfk 120 C7
Terrington St John Norfk 104 A1
Terry's Green Warwks 98 E8
Teston Kent 39 H3
Testwood Hants 34 D7
Tetbury Gloucs 64 C8
Tetbury Upton Gloucs 64 C8
Tetchill Shrops 112 F5
Tetcott Devon 11 L3
Tetford Lincs 136 F5
Tetney Lincs 145 J7
Tetney Lock Lincs 145 J7
Tetsworth Oxon 67 G6
Tettenhall Wolves 97 K3
Tettenhall Wood Wolves 97 K3
Teversal Notts 133 J7
Teversham Cambs 87 K3
Teviothead Border 188 C5
Tewin Herts 69 H4
Tewin Wood Herts 69 H4
Tewkesbury Gloucs 81 K8
Teynham Kent 40 B3
Thackley C Brad 149 M8
Thackthwaite Cumb 164 F6
Thackthwaite Cumb 166 A5
Thainstone Abers 256 D8
Thakeham W Susx 21 J3
Thame Oxon 67 H6
Thames Ditton Surrey 50 F5
Thamesmead Gt Lon 52 A3
Thamesport Medway 53 J4
Thanet Crematorium Kent 41 K2
Thanington Kent 40 F4
Thankerton S Lans 199 G5
Tharston Norfk 106 D4
Thatcham W Berk 48 D5
Thatto Heath St Hel 129 L1
Thaxted Essex 70 F1
Theakston N York 160 D5
Thealby N Linc 143 M4
Theale Somset 31 G2
Theale W Berk 48 F5
Thearne E R Yk 153 G8
The Bank Ches E 131 G8
The Bank Shrops 96 E3
The Beeches Gloucs 64 F6
The Beeches Gloucs 64 F6
Theberton Suffk 91 K2
The Blythe Staffs 115 G6
The Bog Shrops 95 J4
The Bourne Worcs 82 A4
The Braes Highld 247 J2
The Bratch Staffs 97 K4
The Broad Herefs 80 C3
The Brunt E Loth 212 F4
The Bungalow IoM 154 e5
The Burf Worcs 81 J2
The Butts Gloucs 64 C4
The Camp Gloucs 64 C5

The Chequer Wrexhm 113 H3
The City Bed 86 C3
The City Bucks 67 J7
The Common Oxon 65 L2
The Common Wilts 34 B4
The Common Wilts 46 F2
The Corner Kent 39 H5
The Cronk IoM 154 d3
Theddingworth Leics 100 E6
Theddlethorpe All Saints Lincs 137 J2
Theddlethorpe St Helen Lincs 137 J2
The Den N Ayrs 196 C1
The Forge Herefs 79 L3
The Forstal Kent 40 D7
The Fouralls Shrops 113 L5
The Green Cumb 156 A5
The Green Essex 71 J3
The Green N York 162 D2
The Green Wilts 32 E4
The Grove Worcs 81 K7
The Haven W Susx 37 G5
The Haw Gloucs 64 B2
The Headland Hartpl 170 C4
The Hill Cumb 156 A6
The Holt Wokham 49 K3
The Hundred Herefs 80 C2
Thelbridge Cross Devon 28 D8
The Leacon Kent 40 C8
The Lee Bucks 67 L6
The Lhen IoM 154 e2
Thelnetham Suffk 105 L7
The Lochs Moray 266 F4
Thelveton Norfk 106 D7
Thelwall Warrtn 130 C2
The Marsh Powys 95 H4
Themelthorpe Norfk 122 B6
The Middles Dur 180 F8
The Moor Kent 39 J7
The Mumbles Swans 57 H7
The Murray S Lans 209 H8
The Mythe Gloucs 81 K8
The Narth Mons 63 G6
The Neuk Abers 245 G4
Thenford Nhants 83 M7
Theobald's Green Wilts 46 F5
The Quarry Gloucs 63 L7
The Quarter Kent 39 M4
The Reddings Gloucs 64 C3
Therfield Herts 87 G7
The Rhôs Powys 61 J1
The Ross P & K 220 D3
The Sands Surrey 36 C2
The Shoe Wilts 46 A4
The Smithies Shrops 96 F4
The Spring Warwks 83 G1
The Square Torfn 62 B7
The Stair Kent 38 F4
The Stocks Kent 25 G2
The Straits Hants 36 A3
The Strand Wilts 46 D7
Thetford Norfk 105 H6
Thethwaite Cumb 165 L2
The Towans Cnwll 2 E3
The Vauld Herefs 80 C5
The Wyke Shrops 97 G2
Theydon Bois Essex 70 C7
Theydon Mount Essex 70 C7
Thicket Priory N York 151 L7
Thickwood Wilts 46 B4
Thimbleby Lincs 136 D5
Thimbleby N York 161 G3
Thingwall Wirral 129 G3
Thirkleby N York 161 G6
Thirlby N York 161 G6
Thirlestane Border 201 H4
Thirn N York 160 B5
Thirsk N York 160 F6
Thirtleby E R Yk 144 F1
Thistleton Lancs 147 H8
Thistleton Rutlnd 118 B7
Thistley Green Suffk 104 D8
Thixendale N York 152 C4
Thockrington Nthumb 179 M3
Tholomas Drove Cambs 103 H2
Tholthorpe N York 151 L2
Thomas Chapel Pembks 55 J5
Thomas Close Cumb 166 B3
Thomastown Abers 255 L4
Thomas Town Warwks 82 C3
Thompson Norfk 105 J4
Thong Kent 52 E5
Thongsbridge Kirk 141 H5
Thoralby N York 159 H5
Thoresby Notts 134 C5
Thoresthorpe Lincs 137 J4
Thoresway Lincs 144 F8
Thorganby Lincs 145 G8
Thorganby N York 151 L7
Thorgill N York 162 C3

Thorington Suffk.... 107 J8
Thorington Street Suffk 89 K8
Thorlby N York.... 149 H5
Thorley Herts.... 70 C3
Thorley IoW.... 18 F6
Thorley Houses Herts.... 70 C3
Thorley Street IoW.... 18 F6
Thormanby N York.... 161 H7
Thornaby-on-Tees S on T.... 170 B7
Thornage Norfk.... 122 B4
Thornborough Bucks.... 84 E8
Thornborough N York.... 160 D6
Thornbury C Brad.... 141 J1
Thornbury Devon.... 12 A1
Thornbury Herefs.... 80 E3
Thornbury S Glos.... 45 J1
Thornby Cumb.... 177 J8
Thornby Nhants.... 100 E8
Thorncliff Staffs.... 131 K7
Thorncliffe Crematorium Cumb.... 146 D2
Thorncombe Dorset.... 15 J2
Thorncombe Street Surrey.... 36 F3
Thorncott Green C Beds.... 86 C5
Thorncross IoW.... 19 G7
Thorndon Suffk.... 90 D1
Thorndon Cross Devon.... 12 D4
Thorne Donc.... 143 H5
Thorne Coffin Somset.... 31 H7
Thornecroft Devon.... 7 M2
Thornehillhead Devon.... 27 G7
Thorner Leeds.... 150 E7
Thornes Staffs.... 98 D3
Thornes Wakefd.... 141 M4
Thorne St Margaret Somset.... 29 K6
Thorney Bucks.... 50 D3
Thorney C Pete.... 102 F3
Thorney Notts.... 135 G5
Thorney Somset.... 30 F6
Thorney Hill Hants.... 18 B4
Thorney Island W Susx.... 20 C6
Thorney Toll Cambs.... 103 G3
Thornfalcon Somset.... 30 D6
Thornford Dorset.... 31 K8
Thorngrafton Nthumb.... 179 H6
Thorngrove Somset.... 30 E4
Thorngumbald E R Yk.... 145 G3
Thornham Norfk.... 121 G3
Thornham Magna Suffk.... 90 C1
Thornham Parva Suffk.... 90 D1
Thornhaugh C Pete.... 102 B3
Thornhill C Sotn.... 19 G1
Thornhill Caerph.... 43 J5
Thornhill Cumb.... 155 H1
Thornhill D & G.... 186 C7
Thornhill Derbys.... 132 D3
Thornhill Kirk.... 141 L4
Thornhill Stirlg.... 219 L7
Thornhill Lees Kirk.... 141 K4
Thornhills Calder.... 141 J3
Thornholme E R Yk.... 153 H3
Thornicombe Dorset.... 17 G2
Thornington Nthumb.... 202 D6
Thornley Dur.... 168 E3
Thornley Dur.... 169 K3
Thornley Gate Nthumb.... 179 J7
Thornliebank E Rens.... 208 F7
Thorns Suffk.... 88 E4
Thornsett Derbys.... 131 K2
Thorns Green Ches E.... 130 F3
Thornthwaite Cumb.... 165 H5
Thornthwaite N York.... 149 L4
Thornton Angus.... 234 B6
Thornton Bucks.... 84 E8
Thornton C Brad.... 141 H1
Thornton E R Yk.... 152 A6
Thornton Fife.... 222 E7
Thornton Lancs.... 146 F7
Thornton Leics.... 100 A2
Thornton Lincs.... 136 D6
Thornton Middsb.... 170 B7
Thornton Nthumb.... 202 E4
Thornton Pembks.... 54 E5
Thornton Sefton.... 138 D7
Thornton Curtis N Linc.... 144 D4
Thornton Garden of Rest Crematorium Sefton.... 138 D7
Thorntonhall S Lans.... 209 G8
Thornton Heath Gt Lon.... 51 J5
Thornton Hough Wirral.... 129 G3
Thornton-in-Craven N York.... 148 F6
Thornton in Lonsdale N York.... 158 B8
Thornton-le-Beans N York.... 160 F4
Thornton-le-Clay N York.... 151 L3
Thornton-le-Dale N York.... 162 E6
Thornton le Moor Lincs.... 144 D8
Thornton-le-Moor N York.... 160 F5
Thornton-le-Moors Ches W.... 129 K5
Thornton-le-Street N York.... 160 F5

Thorntonloch E Loth.... 213 G4
Thornton Rust N York.... 159 G5
Thornton Steward N York.... 160 A5
Thornton Watlass N York.... 160 C5
Thornwood Common Essex.... 70 C6
Thornydykes Border.... 201 J3
Thornythwaite Cumb.... 165 L6
Thoroton Notts.... 117 K3
Thorp Arch Leeds.... 150 F6
Thorpe Derbys.... 115 J2
Thorpe E R Yk.... 152 F6
Thorpe Lincs.... 137 J3
Thorpe N York.... 149 H3
Thorpe Norfk.... 107 J4
Thorpe Notts.... 117 K2
Thorpe Surrey.... 50 C5
Thorpe Abbotts Norfk.... 106 D7
Thorpe Acre Leics.... 116 E7
Thorpe Arnold Leics.... 117 K7
Thorpe Audlin Wakefd.... 142 D4
Thorpe Bassett N York.... 162 F8
Thorpe Bay Sthend.... 53 K2
Thorpe by Water Rutlnd.... 101 K4
Thorpe Common Rothm.... 133 G1
Thorpe Constantine Staffs.... 99 H2
Thorpe End Norfk.... 107 F1
Thorpe Green Essex.... 73 H3
Thorpe Green Lancs.... 139 H3
Thorpe Green Suffk.... 89 J4
Thorpe Hesley Rothm.... 142 B8
Thorpe in Balne Donc.... 142 F5
Thorpe Langton Leics.... 101 G5
Thorpe Larches Dur.... 169 K5
Thorpe Lea Surrey.... 50 C5
Thorpe le Fallows Lincs.... 135 H4
Thorpe-le-Soken Essex.... 73 J3
Thorpe le Street E R Yk.... 152 C7
Thorpe Malsor Nhants.... 101 H7
Thorpe Mandeville Nhants.... 83 M6
Thorpe Market Norfk.... 122 E4
Thorpe Marriot Norfk.... 122 D8
Thorpe Morieux Suffk.... 89 J4
Thorpeness Suffk.... 91 L3
Thorpe on the Hill Leeds.... 141 M2
Thorpe on the Hill Lincs.... 135 H6
Thorpe St Andrew Norfk.... 106 F2
Thorpe St Peter Lincs.... 137 J7
Thorpe Salvin Rothm.... 133 K3
Thorpe Satchville Leics.... 100 F1
Thorpe Thewles S on T.... 169 L6
Thorpe Tilney Lincs.... 136 B8
Thorpe Underwood N York.... 151 G4
Thorpe Underwood Nhants.... 101 H7
Thorpe Waterville Nhants.... 102 A7
Thorpe Willoughby N York.... 142 F2
Thorpland Norfk.... 104 C2
Thorrington Essex.... 73 G3
Thorverton Devon.... 13 L2
Thrales End C Beds.... 68 E4
Thrandeston Suffk.... 106 C8
Thrapston Nhants.... 101 M7
Threapland Cumb.... 165 G3
Threapland N York.... 149 H4
Threapwood Ches W.... 113 G3
Threapwood Staffs.... 115 G3
Threapwood Head Staffs.... 115 G3
Threave S Ayrs.... 183 J2
Three Ashes Herefs.... 63 G3
Three Bridges W Susx.... 37 L3
Three Burrows Cnwll.... 4 B5
Three Chimneys Kent.... 39 K5
Three Cocks Powys.... 79 G7
Three Counties Crematorium Essex.... 71 J2
Three Crosses Swans.... 57 G6
Three Cups Corner E Susx.... 23 L3
Three Gates Worcs.... 80 F3
Threehammer Common Norfk.... 123 G7
Three Hammers Cnwll.... 11 J5
Three Holes Norfk.... 103 K3
Threekingham Lincs.... 118 E4
Three Leg Cross E Susx.... 39 H7
Three Legged Cross Dorset.... 17 L2
Three Mile Cross Wokham.... 49 H5
Threemilestone Cnwll.... 4 C6
Three Miletown W Loth.... 210 E4
Three Oaks E Susx.... 24 F4
Threlkeld Cumb.... 165 K5
Threshers Bush Essex.... 70 D5
Threshfield N York.... 149 H3
Thrigby Norfk.... 107 J1
Thringarth Dur.... 167 L6
Thringstone Leics.... 116 D8
Thrintoft N York.... 160 D4
Thriplow Cambs.... 87 J6
Throapham Rothm.... 133 K2
Throckenhalt Lincs.... 103 G2
Throcking Herts.... 69 J1
Throckley N u Ty.... 180 E5

Throckmorton Worcs.... 82 A5
Throop Bmouth.... 17 M3
Throop Dorset.... 16 F4
Throphill Nthumb.... 180 D2
Thropton Nthumb.... 190 E5
Throsk Stirlg.... 209 M1
Througham Gloucs.... 64 D5
Throughgate D & G.... 185 L6
Throwleigh Devon.... 12 F4
Throwley Kent.... 40 C4
Throwley Forstal Kent.... 40 C4
Thrumpton Notts.... 116 E5
Thrumpton Notts.... 134 D4
Thrumster Highld.... 280 D7
Thrunscoe NE Lin.... 145 J6
Thrunton Nthumb.... 190 F4
Thrup Oxon.... 65 L7
Thrupp Gloucs.... 64 B6
Thrupp Oxon.... 66 C4
Thrushelton Devon.... 12 B5
Thrussington Leics.... 117 H8
Thruxton Hants.... 34 C2
Thruxton Herefs.... 80 B8
Thrybergh Rothm.... 142 D8
Thulston Derbys.... 116 C5
Thundersley Essex.... 53 C1
Thurcaston Leics.... 100 C1
Thurcroft Rothm.... 133 K2
Thurdon Cnwll.... 11 G2
Thurgarton Norfk.... 122 D4
Thurgarton Notts.... 117 J2
Thurgoland Barns.... 141 L7
Thurlaston Leics.... 100 B4
Thurlaston Warwks.... 83 L1
Thurlbear Somset.... 30 C6
Thurlby Lincs.... 118 F8
Thurlby Lincs.... 135 H7
Thurlby Lincs.... 137 J4
Thurleigh Bed.... 85 L3
Thurlestone Devon.... 7 K6
Thurloxton Somset.... 30 C5
Thurlstone Barns.... 141 K7
Thurlton Norfk.... 107 J4
Thurlwood Ches E.... 130 F8
Thurmaston Leics.... 100 D2
Thurnby Leics.... 100 E3
Thurne Norfk.... 123 H8
Thurnham Kent.... 53 H7
Thurning Nhants.... 102 B6
Thurning Norfk.... 122 B5
Thurnscoe Barns.... 142 C6
Thursby Cumb.... 165 K1
Thursden Lancs.... 140 D1
Thursford Norfk.... 121 L5
Thursley Surrey.... 36 D3
Thurso Highld.... 279 K3
Thurstaston Wirral.... 128 F3
Thurston Suffk.... 89 J2
Thurston Clough Oldham.... 140 E6
Thurstonfield Cumb.... 177 K7
Thurstonland Kirk.... 141 J5
Thurston Planch Suffk.... 89 J2
Thurton Norfk.... 107 G3
Thurvaston Derbys.... 115 L4
Thuxton Norfk.... 105 L2
Thwaite N York.... 158 F3
Thwaite Suffk.... 90 D2
Thwaite Head Cumb.... 156 E4
Thwaites C Brad.... 149 K7
Thwaite St Mary Norfk.... 107 G4
Thwaites Brow C Brad.... 149 K7
Thwing E R Yk.... 153 G2
Tibbermore P & K.... 221 J3
Tibbers D & G.... 186 C6
Tibberton Gloucs.... 63 M3
Tibberton Worcs.... 81 L4
Tibberton Wrekin.... 113 L7
Tibbie Shiels Inn Border.... 187 K2
Tibenham Norfk.... 106 C5
Tibshelf Derbys.... 133 J7
Tibthorpe E R Yk.... 152 E5
Ticehurst E Susx.... 39 H7
Tichborne Hants.... 35 H5
Tickencote Rutlnd.... 101 L2
Tickenham N Som.... 44 F4
Tickford End M Keyn.... 85 H6
Tickhill Donc.... 134 B1
Ticklerton Shrops.... 96 B5
Ticknall Derbys.... 116 B6
Tickton E R Yk.... 153 G7
Tidbury Green Solhll.... 98 E8
Tidcombe Wilts.... 47 L7
Tiddington Oxon.... 67 G6
Tiddington Warwks.... 82 F4
Tiddleywink Wilts.... 46 C4
Tidebrook E Susx.... 38 F7
Tideford Cnwll.... 6 C3
Tideford Cross Cnwll.... 6 C3
Tidenham Gloucs.... 63 H7

Tideswell Derbys.... 132 C4
Tidmarsh W Berk.... 48 F4
Tidmington Warwks.... 83 G7
Tidpit Hants.... 33 J7
Tidworth Wilts.... 34 B1
Tiers Cross Pembks.... 54 E5
Tiffield Nhants.... 84 D3
Tigerton Angus.... 234 E3
Tigh a Ghearraidh W Isls.... 282 b7
Tigharry W Isls.... 282 b7
Tighnabruaich Ag & B.... 206 F4
Tigley Devon.... 7 L3
Tilbrook Cambs.... 86 B2
Tilbury Thurr.... 52 D4
Tilbury Dock Thurr.... 52 D4
Tilbury Green Essex.... 88 E7
Tilbury Juxta Clare Essex.... 88 F7
Tile Cross Birm.... 98 F6
Tile Hill Covtry.... 99 H7
Tilehouse Green Solhll.... 98 F8
Tilehurst Readg.... 49 G4
Tilford Surrey.... 36 C2
Tilgate W Susx.... 37 L4
Tilgate Forest Row W Susx.... 37 L4
Tilham Street Somset.... 31 J4
Tillers Green Gloucs.... 80 F8
Tillicoultry Clacks.... 221 G7
Tillietudlem S Lans.... 198 D4
Tillingham Essex.... 72 E6
Tillington Herefs.... 80 B6
Tillington W Susx.... 36 E6
Tillington Common Herefs.... 80 B6
Tillybirloch Abers.... 244 F2
Tillyfourie Abers.... 244 E1
Tillygreig Abers.... 256 F7
Tillyrie P & K.... 221 K6
Tilmanstone Kent.... 41 J5
Tilney All Saints Norfk.... 120 C7
Tilney High End Norfk.... 120 C8
Tilney St Lawrence Norfk.... 120 C8
Tilshead Wilts.... 33 H1
Tilstock Shrops.... 113 J4
Tilston Ches W.... 113 G1
Tilstone Bank Ches W.... 130 A7
Tilstone Fearnall Ches W.... 130 A7
Tilsworth C Beds.... 68 B2
Tilton on the Hill Leics.... 101 G2
Tiltups End Gloucs.... 64 D7
Tilty Essex.... 70 E2
Timberland Lincs.... 136 B7
Timbersbrook Ches E.... 131 H7
Timberscombe Somset.... 29 G2
Timble N York.... 149 M5
Timewell Devon.... 29 H5
Timpanheck D & G.... 177 K4
Timperley Traffd.... 130 F2
Timsbury BaNES.... 45 K7
Timsbury Hants.... 34 D6
Timsgarry W Isls.... 282 d3
Timsgearraidh W Isls.... 282 d3
Timworth Suffk.... 89 H2
Timworth Green Suffk.... 89 H2
Tincleton Dorset.... 16 E4
Tindale Cumb.... 178 E7
Tingewick Bucks.... 84 C8
Tingley Leeds.... 141 L3
Tingrith C Beds.... 68 C1
Tingwall Ork.... 275 c3
Tinhay Devon.... 12 A5
Tinker's Hill Hants.... 34 E2
Tinkersley Derbys.... 132 E6
Tinsley Sheff.... 133 H2
Tinsley Green W Susx.... 37 L3
Tintagel Cnwll.... 10 D5
Tintern Parva Mons.... 63 G7
Tintinhull Somset.... 31 H7
Tintwistle Derbys.... 140 F8
Tinwald D & G.... 176 D3
Tinwell Rutlnd.... 101 M2
Tippacott Devon.... 28 D2
Tipp's End Norfk.... 103 K4
Tiptoe Hants.... 18 C4
Tipton Sandw.... 98 B5
Tipton Green Sandw.... 98 B5
Tipton St John Devon.... 14 C4
Tiptree Essex.... 72 C4
Tiptree Heath Essex.... 72 C4
Tirabad Powys.... 78 B7
Tiree Ag & B.... 224 C6
Tiretigan Ag & B.... 206 A6
Tirley Gloucs.... 64 B2
Tiroran Ag & B.... 226 F6
Tirphil Caerph.... 61 H6
Tirril Cumb.... 166 C5
Tir-y-fron Flints.... 129 G7
Tisbury Wilts.... 32 F5
Tisman's Common W Susx.... 37 G4
Tissington Derbys.... 115 K1
Titchberry Devon.... 26 D5

Titchfield Hants 19 J3
Titchfield Common Hants 19 J2
Titchmarsh Nhants 102 A7
Titchwell Norfk 121 G3
Tithby Notts 117 J4
Titley Herefs 79 L3
Titmore Green Herts 69 G2
Titsey Surrey 51 L7
Titson Cnwll 11 J2
Tittensor Staffs 114 D4
Tittleshall Norfk 121 K7
Titton Worcs 81 J1
Tiverton Ches W 130 A7
Tiverton Devon 29 G8
Tivetshall St Margaret Norfk 106 D6
Tivetshall St Mary Norfk 106 D6
Tivington Somset 29 G2
Tivy Dale Barns 141 L6
Tixall Staffs 114 F7
Tixover Rutlnd 101 L3
Toab Shet 281 d9
Toadhole Derbys 133 H8
Toadmoor Derbys 116 B1
Tobermory Ag & B 226 F1
Toberonochy Ag & B 215 L3
Tobha Mor W Isls 283 b10
Tocher Abers 256 C5
Tochieneal Moray 267 K3
Tockenham Wilts 46 F3
Tockenham Wick Wilts 46 F3
Tocketts R & Cl 170 E7
Tockholes Bl w D 139 K3
Tockington S Glos 45 J2
Tockwith N York 151 G5
Todber Dorset 32 D7
Todburn Nthumb 191 G7
Toddington C Beds 68 C2
Toddington Gloucs 82 B8
Todds Green Herts 69 G2
Todenham Gloucs 82 F8
Todhills Angus 234 C7
Todhills Cumb 177 L6
Todhills Dur 169 G4
Todmorden Calder 140 E3
Todwick Rothm 133 K3
Toft Cambs 87 G4
Toft Ches E 130 E4
Toft Lincs 118 E8
Toft Shet 281 e4
Toft Warwks 83 L1
Toft Hill Dur 168 F5
Toft Hill Lincs 136 D7
Toft Monks Norfk 107 J4
Toft next Newton Lincs 135 L2
Toftrees Norfk 121 K6
Toftwood Norfk 105 K1
Togston Nthumb 191 J6
Tokavaig Highld 247 J6
Tokers Green Oxon 49 H3
Tolastadh W Isls 282 h2
Toldish Cnwll 4 F3
Toll W Isls 282 g3
Tolland Somset 29 K4
Tollard Farnham Dorset 32 F7
Tollard Royal Wilts 32 F7
Toll Bar Donc 142 E6
Tollbar End Covtry 99 K8
Toller Fratrum Dorset 16 B3
Toller Porcorum Dorset 16 A3
Tollerton N York 151 H3
Tollerton Notts 117 G4
Toller Whelme Dorset 15 L2
Tollesbury Essex 72 D5
Tolleshunt D'Arcy Essex 72 D5
Tolleshunt Knights Essex 72 D4
Tolleshunt Major Essex 72 C5
Tollingham E R Yk 152 C8
Tolpuddle Dorset 16 F4
Tolsta W Isls 282 h2
Tolworth Gt Lon 51 G5
Tomatin Highld 252 E6
Tomchrasky Highld 239 M1
Tomdoun Highld 239 K3
Tomich Highld 250 B6
Tomich Highld 250 F2
Tomich Highld 263 J5
Tomich Highld 272 F7
Tomintoul Moray 254 D7
Tomlow Warwks 83 K3
Tomnacross Highld 250 F3
Tomnavoulin Moray 254 D6
Tompkin Staffs 114 E1
Ton Mons 62 C6
Ton Mons 62 D7
Tonbridge Kent 38 F4
Tondu Brdgnd 42 D5
Tonedale Somset 29 L6
Ton fanau Gwynd 92 C3
Tong C Brad 141 K2

Tong Kent 40 C4
Tong Shrops 97 H2
Tonga W Isls 282 g3
Tonge Leics 116 C7
Tong Green Kent 40 C4
Tongham Surrey 36 C1
Tongland D & G 175 H4
Tong Norton Shrops 97 H2
Tongue Highld 277 K5
Tongue End Lincs 118 F7
Tongwynlais Cardif 43 H5
Tonmawr Neath 42 B2
Tonna Neath 57 L5
Ton-teg Rhondd 43 H4
Tonwell Herts 69 J4
Tonypandy Rhondd 42 F3
Tonyrefail Rhondd 42 F4
Toot Baldon Oxon 66 E7
Toot Hill Essex 70 D6
Toothill Hants 34 E7
Toothill Swindn 47 G2
Tooting Gt Lon 51 H5
Tooting Bec Gt Lon 51 H4
Topcliffe N York 160 F7
Topcroft Norfk 106 F5
Topcroft Street Norfk 106 F5
Top End Bed 85 L3
Topham Donc 143 G4
Top of Hebers Rochdl 140 C6
Toppesfield Essex 88 E7
Toprow Norfk 106 D4
Topsham Devon 13 M5
Top-y-rhos Flints 128 F7
Torbeg N Ayrs 194 D5
Torboll Highld 273 H8
Torbreck Highld 251 H3
Torbryan Devon 8 B2
Torcastle Highld 239 J7
Torcross Devon 8 B6
Tore Highld 251 G1
Torfrey Cnwll 5 J4
Torinturk Ag & B 206 C6
Torksey Lincs 135 G4
Tormarton S Glos 45 M3
Tormore N Ayrs 194 D4
Tornagrain Highld 252 E2
Tornaveen Abers 244 D2
Torness Highld 251 G6
Toronto Dur 169 G4
Torpenhow Cumb 165 G3
Torphichen W Loth 210 C4
Torphins Abers 244 E3
Torpoint Cnwll 6 E4
Torquay Torbay 8 D2
Torquay Crematorium Torbay 8 D2
Torquhan Border 200 F3
Torr Devon 7 H4
Torran Highld 259 K6
Torrance E Duns 209 G4
Torranyard N Ayrs 196 D2
Torre Somset 29 J3
Torridon Highld 260 E8
Torridon House Highld 260 D8
Torrin Highld 247 J4
Torrisdale Ag & B 194 B4
Torrisdale Highld 278 B4
Torrish Highld 274 C4
Torrisholme Lancs 147 J3
Torrobull Highld 272 E7
Torry C Aber 245 L3
Torryburn Fife 210 D2
Torteval Guern 9 h4
Torthorwald D & G 176 D3
Tortington W Susx 21 G6
Torton Worcs 81 J1
Tortworth S Glos 63 L8
Torvaig Highld 259 H7
Torver Cumb 156 C4
Torwood Falk 209 M2
Torwoodlee Border 201 G5
Torworth Notts 134 D2
Tosberry Devon 26 D6
Toscaig Highld 247 L1
Toseland Cambs 86 E3
Tosside Lancs 148 D4
Tostock Suffk 89 J3
Totaig Highld 258 B6
Tote Highld 259 G6
Tote Highld 259 J4
Tote Hill W Susx 36 C6
Totford Hants 35 H3
Tothill Lincs 137 H3
Totland IoW 18 E6
Totley Sheff 132 F4
Totley Brook Sheff 132 F4
Totnes Devon 8 B3
Toton Notts 116 B4
Totronald Ag & B 224 F4
Totscore Highld 258 F3

Tottenham Gt Lon 51 J1
Tottenhill Norfk 104 C1
Totteridge Gt Lon 69 H8
Totternhoe C Beds 68 C3
Tottington Bury 140 A5
Tottleworth Lancs 139 L2
Totton Hants 34 D8
Touchen End W & M 49 L4
Toulston N York 151 G7
Toulton Somset 30 B4
Toulvaddie Highld 264 D4
Tovil Kent 39 J3
Towan Cnwll 5 G5
Towan Cnwll 10 B7
Toward Ag & B 207 J5
Toward Quay Ag & B 207 J5
Towcester Nhants 84 D5
Towednack Cnwll 2 D3
Towersey Oxon 67 H6
Towie Abers 244 A1
Tow Law Dur 168 E3
Town End Cambs 103 J4
Town End Cumb 156 E1
Town End Cumb 156 F6
Town End Cumb 166 E5
Townend W Duns 208 C4
Towngate Cumb 166 C1
Towngate Lincs 102 C1
Town Green Lancs 138 E6
Town Green Norfk 107 G5
Townhead Barns 141 J7
Town Head Cumb 156 F2
Townhead Cumb 164 E8
Townhead Cumb 166 E4
Town Head N York 148 E4
Townhead D & G 176 D1
Townhead of Greenlaw D & G 175 J2
Townhill Fife 210 F1
Town Kelloe Dur 169 K3
Townlake Devon 12 A7
Town Lane Wigan 139 K7
Town Littleworth E Susx 22 F4
Town of Lowton Wigan 139 J8
Town Row E Susx 38 C7
Towns End Hants 48 E7
Townsend Somset 30 E7
Townshend Cnwll 2 F4
Town Street Suffk 104 F6
Townwell S Glos 45 K1
Town Yetholm Border 202 C7
Towthorpe C York 151 K4
Towthorpe E R Yk 152 D3
Towton N York 151 G7
Towyn Conwy 127 K4
Toxteth Lpool 129 H2
Toynton All Saints Lincs 137 G7
Toynton Fen Side Lincs 137 G7
Toynton St Peter Lincs 137 G7
Toy's Hill Kent 38 D3
Trabboch E Ayrs 196 E6
Trabbochburn E Ayrs 196 F6
Traboe Cnwll 3 J6
Tracebridge Somset 29 K6
Tradespark Highld 264 D8
Trafford Park Traffd 140 B8
Trallong Powys 60 E1
Tranent E Loth 211 L4
Tranmere Wirral 129 H2
Trantelbeg Highld 278 F5
Trantlemore Highld 278 F5
Tranwell Nthumb 180 F2
Trap Carmth 59 J5
Traprain E Loth 212 D4
Trap's Green Warwks 82 D1
Trapshill W Berk 48 A6
Traquair Border 200 D6
Trash Green W Berk 49 G5
Trawden Lancs 148 F8
Trawscoed Cerdgn 77 J1
Trawsfynydd Gwynd 110 D4
Trealaw Rhondd 42 F3
Treales Lancs 138 F1
Trearddur Bay IoA 124 D4
Treaslane Highld 258 F6
Treator Cnwll 10 C7
Tre Aubrey V Glam 43 G7
Trebanog Rhondd 42 F4
Trebanos Neath 57 H4
Trebartha Cnwll 11 K7
Trebarwith Cnwll 10 E5
Trebeath Cnwll 11 J5
Trebetherick Cnwll 10 C7
Treborough Somset 29 H4
Trebudannon Cnwll 4 E3
Trebullett Cnwll 11 L7
Treburgett Cnwll 10 E6
Treburley Cnwll 11 L7
Treburrick Cnwll 10 B8
Trebyan Cnwll 5 J2

Trecastle Powys 60 C1
Trecogo Cnwll 11 K6
Trecott Devon 12 F3
Trecwn Pembks 74 F5
Trecynon Rhondd 60 F6
Tredaule Cnwll 11 J6
Tredavoe Cnwll 2 C5
Tredegar Blae G 61 G3
Tredethy Cnwll 10 F8
Tredington Gloucs 64 C1
Tredington Warwks 83 G6
Tredinnick Cnwll 5 H3
Tredinnick Cnwll 5 K2
Tredinnick Cnwll 5 M3
Tredinnick Cnwll 6 B3
Tredinnick Cnwll 10 C8
Tredomen Powys 61 H1
Tredrissi Pembks 75 J4
Tredrizzick Cnwll 10 D7
Tredunnock Mons 62 D8
Tredustan Powys 61 H1
Treen Cnwll 2 B6
Treen Cnwll 2 C3
Treesmill Cnwll 5 J4
Treeton Rothm 133 J2
Trefasser Pembks 74 E4
Trefdraeth IoA 125 G5
Trefecca Powys 61 J1
Trefeglwys Powys 93 L5
Trefenter Cerdgn 77 H2
Treffgarne Pembks 54 F2
Treffgarne Owen Pembks 74 E7
Trefforest Rhondd 43 G4
Treffynnon Pembks 74 D6
Trefil Blae G 61 H4
Trefilan Cerdgn 77 G4
Trefin Pembks 74 D5
Treflach Wood Shrops 112 C6
Trefnannau Powys 112 C8
Trefnant Denbgs 128 C5
Trefonen Shrops 112 C6
Trefor Gwynd 108 F2
Trefor IoA 124 F4
Trefrew Cnwll 10 F5
Trefriw Conwy 126 F7
Tregadillett Cnwll 11 K6
Tre-gagle Mons 63 G5
Tregaian IoA 125 H4
Tregare Mons 62 E5
Tregarne Cnwll 3 K6
Tregaron Cerdgn 77 J3
Tregarth Gwynd 126 B6
Tregaswith Cnwll 4 E2
Tregatta Cnwll 10 F5
Tregawne Cnwll 5 G2
Tregeare Cnwll 11 J5
Tregeiriog Wrexhm 112 B5
Tregele IoA 124 F1
Tregellist Cnwll 10 E7
Tregenna Cnwll 4 E6
Tregeseal Cnwll 2 B5
Tregew Cnwll 3 K4
Tre-Gibbon Rhondd 60 F6
Tregidden Cnwll 3 J6
Tregiskey Cnwll 5 G5
Treglemais Pembks 74 D6
Tregole Cnwll 11 H3
Tregolls Cnwll 3 J4
Tregonce Cnwll 10 C7
Tregonetha Cnwll 4 F2
Tregony Cnwll 4 F6
Tregoodwell Cnwll 11 G6
Tregorrick Cnwll 5 G4
Tregoss Cnwll 4 F3
Tregoyd Powys 79 H7
Tregrehan Mills Cnwll 5 H4
Tre-groes Cerdgn 76 D6
Tregullon Cnwll 5 H2
Tregunna Cnwll 10 D7
Tregunnon Cnwll 11 J6
Tregurrian Cnwll 4 D2
Tregynon Powys 94 D4
Tre-gynwr Carmth 58 D5
Trehafod Rhondd 43 G3
Trehan Cnwll 6 D3
Treharris Myr Td 43 H2
Treharrock Cnwll 10 E6
Trehemborne Cnwll 10 B7
Treherbert Carmth 77 G6
Treherbert Rhondd 42 E2
Trehunist Cnwll 6 C2
Trekenner Cnwll 11 L7
Treknow Cnwll 10 E5
Trelan Cnwll 3 J7
Trelash Cnwll 11 H4
Trelassick Cnwll 4 E4
Trelawne Cnwll 5 L4
Trelawnyd Flints 128 C4
Treleague Cnwll 3 K6

Place	Area	Page	Grid
Treleaver Cnwll		3	K7
Trelech Carmth		58	A3
Trelech a'r Betws Carmth		58	B3
Treleddyd-fawr Pembks		74	B6
Trelew Cnwll		3	K4
Trelewis Myr Td		43	H2
Treligga Cnwll		10	E5
Trelights Cnwll		10	D6
Trelill Cnwll		10	E7
Trelinnoe Cnwll		11	K6
Trelion Cnwll		4	F4
Trelissick Cnwll		3	L3
Trellech Mons		63	G6
Trelleck Grange Mons		62	F6
Trelogan Flints		128	D4
Trelow Cnwll		4	F1
Trelowarren Cnwll		3	J6
Trelowia Cnwll		6	B3
Treluggan Cnwll		3	M3
Trelystan Powys		95	G3
Tremadog Gwynd		109	K3
Tremail Cnwll		11	H5
Tremain Cerdgn		75	M3
Tremaine Cnwll		11	J5
Tremar Cnwll		6	B1
Trematon Cnwll		6	D3
Trembraze Cnwll		6	B2
Tremeirchion Denbgs		128	C5
Tremethick Cross Cnwll		2	C6
Tremore Cnwll		5	G2
Tre-Mostyn Flints		128	D4
Trenance Cnwll		3	K6
Trenance Cnwll		4	D1
Trenance Cnwll		10	C8
Trenarren Cnwll		5	H5
Trench Wrekin		96	F1
Trench Green Oxon		49	G3
Trendeal Cnwll		4	E4
Trendrine Cnwll		2	D3
Treneague Cnwll		10	D8
Trenear Cnwll		3	H5
Treneglos Cnwll		11	H5
Trenerth Cnwll		2	F4
Trenewan Cnwll		5	K4
Trenewth Cnwll		10	F7
Trengune Cnwll		11	H4
Treninnick Cnwll		4	D3
Trenowah Cnwll		4	C3
Trenoweth Cnwll		3	J4
Trent Dorset		31	K7
Trentham C Stke		114	D3
Trentishoe Devon		28	A1
Trentlock Derbys		116	E5
Trent Port Lincs		135	G3
Trent Vale C Stke		114	D3
Trenwheal Cnwll		3	G4
Treoes V Glam		42	E6
Treorchy Rhondd		42	E2
Trequite Cnwll		10	E7
Tre'r-ddol Cerdgn		92	E5
Trerhyngyll V Glam		42	F6
Trerulefoot Cnwll		6	C3
Tresaith Cerdgn		76	A5
Tresawle Cnwll		4	E5
Tresco IoS		10	b2
Trescott Staffs		97	J4
Trescowe Cnwll		2	F5
Tresean Cnwll		4	C3
Tresham Gloucs		46	A1
Treshnish Isles Ag & B		225	H7
Tresillian Cnwll		4	E5
Tresinney Cnwll		10	F6
Treskinnick Cross Cnwll		11	H3
Tresmeer Cnwll		11	J5
Tresparrett Cnwll		11	G4
Tressait P & K		232	B3
Tresta Shet		281	d6
Tresta Shet		281	f3
Treswell Notts		134	F4
Treswithian Cnwll		3	G3
Treswithian Downs Crematorium Cnwll		3	G3
Tre Taliesin Cerdgn		92	E5
Trethevey Cnwll		10	F5
Trethewey Cnwll		2	B6
Trethomas Caerph		43	J4
Trethosa Cnwll		4	F4
Trethurgy Cnwll		5	H4
Tretio Pembks		74	C6
Tretire Herefs		63	G2
Tretower Powys		61	J3
Treuddyn Flints		128	F8
Trevadlock Cnwll		11	K6
Trevalga Cnwll		10	F4
Trevalyn Wrexhm		129	J8
Trevanger Cnwll		10	D7
Trevanson Cnwll		10	D8
Trevarrack Cnwll		2	D5
Trevarren Cnwll		4	E3
Trevarrian Cnwll		4	D2
Trevarrick Cnwll		5	G6
Trevarth Cnwll		3	J3
Trevaughan Carmth		55	L4
Tre-Vaughan Carmth		58	D4
Treveal Cnwll		2	D3
Treveal Cnwll		4	C3
Treveighan Cnwll		10	F6
Trevellas Downs Cnwll		4	B4
Trevelmond Cnwll		5	L2
Trevemper Cnwll		4	D3
Treveor Cnwll		5	G6
Treverbyn Cnwll		4	E5
Treverbyn Cnwll		5	G3
Treverva Cnwll		3	J5
Trevescan Cnwll		2	B6
Trevethin Torfn		62	B6
Trevia Cnwll		10	F6
Trevigro Cnwll		6	C1
Trevilla Cnwll		3	L3
Trevilson Cnwll		4	D4
Treviscoe Cnwll		4	F4
Treviskey Cnwll		4	F6
Trevithick Cnwll		4	E2
Trevithick Cnwll		4	F6
Trevoll Cnwll		4	D3
Trevone Cnwll		10	B7
Trevor Wrexhm		112	C3
Trevorgans Cnwll		2	B6
Trevorrick Cnwll		10	C7
Trevose Cnwll		10	B7
Trew Cnwll		3	G5
Trewalder Cnwll		10	F6
Trewalkin Powys		61	J1
Trewarmett Cnwll		10	F5
Trewassa Cnwll		11	G5
Trewavas Cnwll		2	F5
Treween Cnwll		11	J6
Trewellard Cnwll		2	B4
Trewen Cnwll		11	J6
Trewennack Cnwll		3	H5
Trewent Pembks		55	G7
Trewern Powys		95	G1
Trewetha Cnwll		10	E6
Trewethern Cnwll		10	E7
Trewidland Cnwll		6	B3
Trewillis Cnwll		3	K7
Trewint Cnwll		6	B2
Trewint Cnwll		11	J6
Trewithian Cnwll		3	M4
Trewoodloe Cnwll		11	L8
Trewoon Cnwll		3	H7
Trewoon Cnwll		5	G4
Treworga Cnwll		4	E6
Treworgan Cnwll		4	D5
Treworlas Cnwll		4	E7
Treworld Cnwll		11	G4
Treworthal Cnwll		3	M3
Tre-wyn Mons		62	C3
Treyarnon Cnwll		10	B7
Treyford W Susx		20	D3
Trickett's Cross Dorset		17	L2
Triermain Cumb		178	E5
Triffleton Pembks		75	G7
Trillacott Cnwll		11	K4
Trimdon Dur		169	K4
Trimdon Colliery Dur		169	K4
Trimdon Grange Dur		169	K3
Trimingham Norfk		122	F4
Trimley Lower Street Suffk		91	G7
Trimley St Martin Suffk		91	G7
Trimley St Mary Suffk		91	G7
Trimpley Worcs		97	H1
Trimsaran Carmth		56	E4
Trims Green Herts		70	C4
Trimstone Devon		27	J2
Trinafour P & K		231	K3
Trinant Caerph		61	K7
Tring Herts		68	A5
Tringford Herts		67	M4
Tring Wharf Herts		68	A4
Trinity Angus		234	F3
Trinity Jersey		9	d2
Trinity Gask P & K		221	G3
Triscombe Somset		29	L4
Trislaig Highld		239	H8
Trispen Cnwll		4	D5
Tritlington Nthumb		191	J7
Troan Cnwll		4	E3
Trochry P & K		232	E7
Troedrhiwfuwch Caerph		61	H6
Troedyraur Cerdgn		76	B6
Troedyrhiw Myr Td		61	G6
Trofarth Conwy		127	G5
Trois Bois Jersey		9	c2
Troon Cnwll		3	G3
Troon S Ayrs		196	C5
Trossachs Pier Stirlg		219	H5
Troston Suffk		89	H1
Troswell Cnwll		11	J4
Trotshill Worcs		81	K4
Trottiscliffe Kent		52	D7
Trotton W Susx		36	B6
Troughend Nthumb		190	B7
Trough Gate Lancs		140	D3
Troutbeck Cumb		156	F2
Troutbeck Cumb		165	L5
Troutbeck Bridge Cumb		156	F3
Troway Derbys		133	H4
Trowbridge Wilts		46	B2
Trowell Notts		116	E3
Trowle Common Wilts		46	B7
Trowley Bottom Herts		68	D4
Trowse Newton Norfk		106	E2
Troy Leeds		150	C8
Trudoxhill Somset		32	C2
Trull Somset		30	B6
Trumfleet Donc		142	F5
Trumpan Highld		258	C4
Trumpet Herefs		80	F7
Trumpington Cambs		87	J4
Trumpsgreen Surrey		50	C5
Trunch Norfk		122	F4
Trunnah Lancs		147	G7
Truro Cnwll		4	D6
Truscott Cnwll		11	K5
Trusham Devon		13	K6
Trusley Derbys		115	L4
Trusthorpe Lincs		137	K3
Trysull Staffs		97	J4
Tubney Oxon		66	B7
Tuckenhay Devon		8	B4
Tuckhill Shrops		97	H5
Tuckingmill Cnwll		3	G3
Tuckingmill Wilts		32	F5
Tuckton Bmouth		18	A5
Tucoyse Cnwll		4	F5
Tuddenham Suffk		88	E1
Tuddenham Suffk		90	E5
Tudeley Kent		38	F4
Tudhoe Dur		169	H3
Tudorville Herefs		63	H3
Tudweiliog Gwynd		108	D4
Tuesley Surrey		36	E3
Tuffley Gloucs		64	B4
Tufton Hants		34	F2
Tufton Pembks		75	H6
Tugby Leics		101	G3
Tugford Shrops		96	D6
Tughall Nthumb		203	K7
Tullibody Clacks		220	E8
Tullich Highld		251	H6
Tullich Highld		264	D4
Tulliemet P & K		232	F5
Tulloch Abers		256	E5
Tulloch Station Highld		240	B7
Tullochgorm Ag & B		216	F8
Tullymurdoch P & K		233	J5
Tullynessle Abers		255	L7
Tulse Hill Gt Lon		51	J4
Tumble Carmth		58	F6
Tumbler's Green Essex		71	K2
Tumby Lincs		136	D7
Tumby Woodside Lincs		136	E8
Tummel Bridge P & K		231	L4
Tunbridge Wells Kent		38	F5
Tundergarth D & G		177	G3
Tungate Norfk		122	F5
Tunley BaNES		45	K7
Tunstall C Stke		114	D1
Tunstall E R Yk		145	J2
Tunstall Kent		40	A3
Tunstall Lancs		157	K8
Tunstall N York		160	B3
Tunstall Norfk		107	J2
Tunstall Staffs		114	B6
Tunstall Suffk		91	H4
Tunstall Sundld		181	J8
Tunstead Derbys		132	B5
Tunstead Norfk		122	F7
Tunstead Milton Derbys		131	K4
Tunworth Hants		35	K1
Tupsley Herefs		80	C7
Turgis Green Hants		49	G7
Turkdean Gloucs		65	G4
Tur Langton Leics		100	F4
Turleigh Wilts		46	A6
Turleygreen Shrops		97	H6
Turn Lancs		140	B4
Turnastone Herefs		79	L7
Turnberry S Ayrs		182	F2
Turnchapel C Plym		6	F4
Turnditch Derbys		116	A2
Turner Green Lancs		139	J2
Turner's Green E Susx		23	L3
Turner's Green Warwks		82	E2
Turner's Hill W Susx		38	A6
Turners Puddle Dorset		16	F4
Turnford Herts		69	K6
Turnhouse C Edin		211	G4
Turnworth Dorset		16	F1
Turriff Abers		268	C5
Turton Bottoms Bl w D		139	L4
Turves Cambs		103	G4
Turvey Bed		85	J5
Turville Bucks		49	J1
Turville Heath Bucks		49	H1
Turweston Bucks		84	B7
Tushielaw Inn Border		187	L3
Tutbury Staffs		115	L6
Tutnall Worcs		82	A1
Tutshill Gloucs		63	G8
Tuttington Norfk		122	E6
Tutwell Cnwll		11	M7
Tuxford Notts		134	E5
Twatt Ork		275	b3
Twatt Shet		281	b6
Twechar E Duns		209	J4
Tweedbank Border		201	H6
Tweedmouth Nthumb		202	F3
Tweedsmuir Border		187	G1
Twelveheads Cnwll		4	B6
Twelve Oaks E Susx		24	C3
Twemlow Green Ches E		130	F6
Twenty Lincs		118	F7
Twerton BaNES		45	L6
Twickenham Gt Lon		50	F4
Twigworth Gloucs		64	B3
Twineham W Susx		22	C3
Twineham Green W Susx		22	C3
Twinhoe BaNES		45	L7
Twinstead Essex		89	H7
Twitchen Devon		28	D5
Twitchen Shrops		95	J7
Twitham Kent		41	H4
Two Bridges Devon		12	E7
Two Dales Derbys		132	E7
Two Gates Staffs		99	G3
Two Mile Oak Cross Devon		8	C1
Two Pots Devon		27	J2
Two Waters Herts		68	D6
Twycross Leics		99	J2
Twyford Bucks		67	G2
Twyford Hants		35	G6
Twyford Leics		100	F2
Twyford Lincs		118	B6
Twyford Norfk		121	M6
Twyford Wokham		49	J4
Twyford Common Herefs		80	C8
Twyn-carno Caerph		61	H7
Twynholm D & G		175	G4
Twyning Green Gloucs		81	L7
Twynllanan Carmth		59	L4
Twyn-yr-Odyn V Glam		43	H7
Twyn-y-Sheriff Mons		62	E6
Twywell Nhants		101	L7
Tyberton Herefs		79	M7
Tyburn Birm		98	E5
Tycroes Carmth		57	H3
Ty Croes IoA		124	F5
Tycrwyn Powys		111	L7
Tydd Gote Lincs		120	A7
Tydd St Giles Cambs		119	M8
Tydd St Mary Lincs		119	M7
Tye Hants		20	B6
Tye Green Essex		70	D2
Tye Green Essex		71	J3
Tye Green Essex		88	B8
Tyersal C Brad		141	J1
Tyldesley Wigan		139	K7
Tyler Hill Kent		40	F3
Tylers Green Bucks		67	L8
Tyler's Green Essex		70	D6
Tylers Green Surrey		51	K8
Tylorstown Rhondd		42	F3
Tylwch Powys		93	L7
Ty-nant Conwy		111	J3
Ty-nant Gwynd		111	H6
Tyndrum Stirlg		218	C2
Ty'n-dwr Denbgs		112	C3
Tyneham Dorset		17	G6
Tynemouth S Tyne		181	J5
Tynemouth Crematorium N Tyne		181	J5
Tyne Tunnel S Tyne		181	H5
Tynewydd Rhondd		60	E7
Tyningham E Loth		212	D3
Tynron D & G		185	K4
Ty'n-y-bryn Rhondd		42	F4
Ty'n-y-coedcae Caerph		43	K3
Tynygongl IoA		125	J3
Tynygraig Cerdgn		77	J1
Ty'n-y-Groes Conwy		126	F5
Tyn-y-nant Rhondd		43	G6
Tyringham M Keyn		85	G6
Tyseley Birm		98	E6
Tythegston Brdgnd		42	C6

Place	County	Page	Grid
Tytherington	Ches E	131	H4
Tytherington	S Glos	45	K1
Tytherington	Somset	32	C2
Tytherington	Wilts	32	F3
Tytherleigh	Devon	15	H2
Tytherton Lucas	Wilts	46	D4
Tyttenhanger	Herts	68	F6
Tywardreath	Cnwll	5	J4
Tywardreath Highway	Cnwll	5	J4
Tywyn	Conwy	126	F4
Tywyn	Gwynd	92	C3

U

Place	County	Page	Grid
Ubbeston Green	Suffk	91	H1
Ubley	BaNES	45	G7
Uckerby	N York	160	C2
Uckfield	E Susx	23	H3
Uckinghall	Worcs	81	K7
Uckington	Gloucs	64	C2
Uckington	Shrops	96	D2
Uddingston	S Lans	209	J6
Uddington	S Lans	198	E6
Udimore	E Susx	24	F3
Udny Green	Abers	256	F6
Udny Station	Abers	257	G6
Uffcott	Wilts	47	H3
Uffculme	Devon	29	K8
Uffington	Lincs	102	B2
Uffington	Oxon	47	L1
Uffington	Shrops	96	C1
Ufford	C Pete	102	B3
Ufford	Suffk	91	G5
Ufton	Warwks	83	J3
Ufton Nervet	W Berk	48	F5
Ugadale	Ag & B	194	B5
Ugborough	Devon	7	K4
Uggeshall	Suffk	107	J7
Ugglebarnby	N York	162	F1
Ughill	Sheff	132	E2
Ugley	Essex	70	D2
Ugley Green	Essex	70	D2
Ugthorpe	N York	171	J8
Uibhist A Deas	W Isls	283	c10
Uibhist A Tuath	W Isls	283	b8
Uig	Ag & B	224	F4
Uig	Highld	258	B6
Uig	Highld	258	F4
Uig	W Isls	282	d3
Uigshader	Highld	259	G7
Uisken	Ag & B	226	D8
Ulbster	Highld	280	D7
Ulcat Row	Cumb	165	L6
Ulceby	Lincs	137	H5
Ulceby	N Linc	144	E5
Ulceby Skitter	N Linc	144	E5
Ulcombe	Kent	39	L4
Uldale	Cumb	165	H3
Uley	Gloucs	63	M7
Ulgham	Nthumb	191	J7
Ullapool	Highld	261	J1
Ullenhall	Warwks	82	D2
Ullenwood	Gloucs	64	D4
Ulleskelf	N York	151	H7
Ullesthorpe	Leics	100	B6
Ulley	Rothm	133	J2
Ullingswick	Herefs	80	E5
Ullinish Lodge Hotel	Highld	246	D1
Ullock	Cumb	164	E6
Ulpha	Cumb	156	B4
Ulpha	Cumb	157	G6
Ulrome	E R Yk	153	J4
Ulsta	Shet	281	e4
Ulting Wick	Essex	71	K5
Ulva	Ag & B	226	D4
Ulverley Green	Solhll	98	E7
Ulverston	Cumb	156	C7
Ulwell	Dorset	17	K6
Ulzieside	D & G	185	J1
Umberleigh	Devon	27	L6
Unapool	Highld	271	H2
Underbarrow	Cumb	157	G4
Under Burnmouth	Border	178	B2
Undercliffe	C Brad	141	J1
Underdale	Shrops	96	B1
Underling Green	Kent	39	J4
Underriver	Kent	38	E3
Underwood	Notts	116	D2
Undley	Suffk	104	D7
Undy	Mons	44	E2
Union Mills	IoM	154	e6
Union Street	E Susx	39	H7
Unst	Shet	281	f2
Unstone	Derbys	133	G4
Unstone Green	Derbys	133	G4
Unthank	Cumb	165	L1
Unthank	Cumb	166	B3
Unthank	Cumb	166	E3
Unthank	Derbys	132	F4
Unthank	Nthumb	202	F3
Upavon	Wilts	47	H7
Up Cerne	Dorset	16	C2
Upchurch	Kent	53	H5
Upcott	Devon	28	D5
Upcott	Herefs	79	K5
Upend	Cambs	88	D3
Up Exe	Devon	13	L2
Upgate	Norfk	122	C7
Upgate Street	Norfk	106	B5
Upgate Street	Norfk	106	F5
Uphall	Dorset	16	A2
Uphall	W Loth	210	E5
Upham	Devon	13	K1
Upham	Hants	35	H6
Uphampton	Herefs	79	M3
Uphampton	Worcs	81	J2
Uphill	N Som	44	C7
Up Holland	Lancs	139	G6
Uplawmoor	E Rens	208	D8
Upleadon	Gloucs	63	L2
Upleatham	R & Cl	170	E6
Uplees	Kent	40	C2
Uploders	Dorset	15	L4
Uplowman	Devon	29	J7
Uplyme	Devon	15	H4
Up Marden	W Susx	20	C4
Up Mudford	Somset	31	J7
Up Nately	Hants	49	G8
Upottery	Devon	14	E1
Upper Affcot	Shrops	95	K6
Upper Ardchronie	Highld	263	G2
Upper Arley	Worcs	97	H3
Upper Arncott	Oxon	66	F4
Upper Astrop	Nhants	83	L7
Upper Basildon	W Berk	48	F4
Upper Batley	Kirk	141	K3
Upper Beeding	W Susx	22	B5
Upper Benefield	Nhants	101	L5
Upper Bentley	Worcs	82	B2
Upper Bighouse	Highld	278	F5
Upper Birchwood	Derbys	133	J8
Upper Boat	Rhondd	43	H4
Upper Boddington	Nhants	83	L5
Upper Borth	Cerdgn	92	D5
Upper Brailes	Warwks	83	G7
Upper Breakish	Highld	247	L4
Upper Breinton	Herefs	80	B7
Upper Broadheath	Worcs	81	J4
Upper Broughton	Notts	117	J6
Upper Bucklebury	W Berk	48	D5
Upper Burgate	Hants	33	K7
Upper Bush	Medway	52	E5
Upperby	Cumb	177	L8
Upper Caldecote	C Beds	86	D6
Upper Canada	N Som	44	D7
Upper Canterton	Hants	18	D1
Upper Catesby	Nhants	83	M3
Upper Catshill	Worcs	98	B8
Upper Chapel	Powys	78	D7
Upper Cheddon	Somset	30	C5
Upper Chicksgrove	Wilts	33	G5
Upper Chute	Wilts	47	L8
Upper Clapton	Gt Lon	51	K2
Upper Clatford	Hants	34	D2
Upper Coberley	Gloucs	64	E4
Upper Cotton	Staffs	115	G2
Upper Cound	Shrops	96	C2
Upper Cudworth	Barns	142	B6
Upper Cumberworth	Kirk	141	K6
Upper Dallachy	Moray	267	G4
Upper Deal	Kent	41	K5
Upper Dean	Bed	85	L2
Upper Denby	Kirk	141	K6
Upper Denton	Cumb	178	E5
Upper Dicker	E Susx	23	J5
Upper Dinchope	Shrops	95	L6
Upper Dounreay	Highld	279	H3
Upper Dovercourt	Essex	73	K1
Upper Drumbane	Stirlg	219	L6
Upper Dunsforth	N York	150	F3
Upper Eashing	Surrey	36	E2
Upper Eathie	Highld	263	K7
Upper Egleton	Herefs	80	E6
Upper Elkstone	Staffs	131	L7
Upper Ellastone	Staffs	115	J3
Upper End	Derbys	132	B4
Upper Enham	Hants	34	E1
Upper Farmcote	Shrops	97	H5
Upper Farringdon	Hants	35	L4
Upper Framilode	Gloucs	63	L5
Upper Froyle	Hants	35	M2
Upperglen	Highld	258	E6
Upper Godney	Somset	31	H2
Upper Gravenhurst	C Beds	86	C8
Upper Green	Mons	62	D3
Upper Green	Suffk	88	E2
Upper Green	W Berk	48	A6
Upper Grove Common	Herefs	63	H2
Upper Hackney	Derbys	132	F7
Upper Hale	Surrey	36	B1
Upper Halliford	Surrey	50	E5
Upper Halling	Medway	52	E6
Upper Hambleton	Rutlnd	101	K2
Upper Harbledown	Kent	40	F4
Upper Hardres Court	Kent	40	F5
Upper Hardwick	Herefs	79	M4
Upper Hartfield	E Susx	38	C6
Upper Hartshay	Derbys	116	C2
Upper Hatherley	Gloucs	64	D3
Upper Hatton	Staffs	114	C4
Upper Haugh	Rothm	142	C8
Upper Hayton	Shrops	96	C7
Upper Heaton	Kirk	141	J4
Upper Helmsley	N York	151	L4
Upper Hergest	Herefs	79	J4
Upper Heyford	Nhants	84	C3
Upper Heyford	Oxon	66	D2
Upper Hill	Herefs	80	B4
Upper Hockenden	Kent	52	B5
Upper Hopton	Kirk	141	K4
Upper Howsell	Worcs	81	H5
Upper Hulme	Staffs	131	K7
Upper Ifold	Surrey	36	F4
Upper Inglesham	Swindn	65	J7
Upper Kilcott	Gloucs	46	A1
Upper Killay	Swans	57	G6
Upper Kinchrackine	Ag & B	217	J2
Upper Knockando	Moray	254	D3
Upper Lambourn	W Berk	47	L3
Upper Landywood	Staffs	98	C2
Upper Langford	N Som	44	F7
Upper Langwith	Derbys	133	K5
Upper Largo	Fife	223	G6
Upper Leigh	Staffs	115	G4
Upper Littleton	N Som	45	H6
Upper Lochton	Abers	244	F5
Upper Longdon	Staffs	115	H8
Upper & Lower Stondon	C Beds	86	D8
Upper Ludstone	Shrops	97	H4
Upper Lybster	Highld	275	H1
Upper Lydbrook	Gloucs	63	J4
Upper Lyde	Herefs	80	C6
Upper Lye	Herefs	79	M2
Upper Maes-coed	Herefs	79	L8
Upper Midhope	Sheff	141	K7
Uppermill	Oldham	140	F6
Upper Milton	Worcs	81	J1
Upper Minety	Wilts	46	E1
Upper Moor	Worcs	82	A5
Upper Moor Side	Leeds	141	K2
Upper Mulben	Moray	267	G6
Upper Netchwood	Shrops	96	E5
Upper Nobut	Staffs	115	G4
Upper Norwood	W Susx	20	F3
Upper Padley	Derbys	132	E4
Upper Pennington	Hants	18	D4
Upper Pollicott	Bucks	67	H4
Upper Poppleton	C York	151	J5
Upper Quinton	Warwks	82	E6
Upper Ratley	Hants	34	D6
Upper Rissington	Gloucs	65	J3
Upper Rochford	Worcs	80	E2
Upper Ruscoe	D & G	174	E3
Upper Sapey	Herefs	80	F3
Upper Saxondale	Notts	117	H4
Upper Seagry	Wilts	46	D3
Upper Shelton	C Beds	85	K6
Upper Sheringham	Norfk	122	C3
Upper Skelmorlie	N Ayrs	207	K5
Upper Slaughter	Gloucs	65	H3
Upper Soudley	Gloucs	63	K5
Upper Spond	Herefs	79	K4
Upper Standen	Kent	41	H7
Upper Staple	Bed	86	C3
Upper Stoke	Norfk	106	E3
Upper Stowe	Nhants	84	C4
Upper Street	Hants	33	K7
Upper Street	Norfk	106	D7
Upper Street	Norfk	123	G7
Upper Street	Norfk	123	G8
Upper Street	Suffk	90	C5
Upper Street	Suffk	90	D8
Upper Strensham	Worcs	81	K7
Upper Sundon	C Beds	68	D2
Upper Swell	Gloucs	65	H2
Upper Tankersley	Barns	142	A7
Upper Tasburgh	Norfk	106	E4
Upper Tean	Staffs	115	G4
Upperthong	Kirk	141	H6
Upperthorpe	Derbys	133	J4
Upperthorpe	N Linc	143	J7
Upper Threapwood	Ches W	113	G3
Upperton	W Susx	36	E6
Upper Town	Derbys	115	L1
Uppertown	Derbys	132	F6
Upper Town	Dur	168	D3
Upper Town	Herefs	80	D5
Uppertown	Highld	280	D1
Upper Town	N Som	45	G6
Upper Town	Suffk	89	J7
Upper Tumble	Carmth	59	G6
Upper Tysoe	Warwks	83	H6
Upper Ufford	Suffk	91	G5
Upperup	Gloucs	64	F7
Upper Upham	Wilts	47	J3
Upper Upnor	Medway	53	G5
Upper Victoria	Angus	234	E8
Upper Vobster	Somset	32	B1
Upper Wardington	Oxon	83	L6
Upper Weald	M Keyn	84	F7
Upper Weedon	Nhants	84	B3
Upper Welland	Worcs	81	H7
Upper Wellingham	E Susx	23	G4
Upper Weston	BaNES	45	L5
Upper Weybread	Suffk	106	E7
Upper Wick	Worcs	81	J5
Upper Wield	Hants	35	K3
Upper Winchendon	Bucks	67	H4
Upperwood	Derbys	132	F8
Upper Woodford	Wilts	33	K3
Upper Wootton	Hants	48	E7
Upper Wraxall	Wilts	46	A4
Upper Wyche	Worcs	81	H6
Uppincott	Devon	13	L2
Uppingham	Rutlnd	101	J3
Uppington	Dorset	17	K2
Uppington	Shrops	96	D2
Upsall	N York	161	G5
Upsettlington	Border	202	D4
Upshire	Essex	69	L7
Up Somborne	Hants	34	E4
Upstreet	Kent	41	H3
Up Sydling	Dorset	16	B2
Upthorpe	Suffk	89	K1
Upton	Bucks	67	J5
Upton	C Pete	102	C3
Upton	Cambs	102	D7
Upton	Ches W	129	J6
Upton	Cnwll	11	H2
Upton	Cnwll	11	K8
Upton	Cumb	165	K3
Upton	Devon	7	K6
Upton	Devon	14	C2
Upton	Dorset	16	E6
Upton	Dorset	17	J4
Upton	E R Yk	153	J5
Upton	Halton	129	L2
Upton	Hants	34	E7
Upton	Hants	47	M7
Upton	Leics	99	K3
Upton	Lincs	135	H2
Upton	Nhants	84	D3
Upton	Norfk	107	H1
Upton	Notts	117	J1
Upton	Notts	134	E4
Upton	Oxon	48	D2
Upton	Oxon	65	K4
Upton	Pembks	55	G6
Upton	R & Cl	171	G6
Upton	Slough	50	B3
Upton	Somset	29	H5
Upton	Somset	31	G5
Upton	Wakefd	142	D5
Upton	Warwks	82	D4
Upton	Wilts	32	E4
Upton	Wirral	129	G2
Upton Bishop	Herefs	63	K2
Upton Cheyney	S Glos	45	K5
Upton Cressett	Shrops	96	E5
Upton Crews	Herefs	63	J2
Upton Cross	Cnwll	11	K8
Upton End	C Beds	86	C8
Upton Grey	Hants	35	L1
Upton Heath	Ches W	129	J5
Upton Hellions	Devon	13	K2
Upton Lovell	Wilts	32	F3
Upton Magna	Shrops	96	C1
Upton Noble	Somset	32	B3
Upton Pyne	Devon	13	L3
Upton St Leonards	Gloucs	64	B4
Upton Scudamore	Wilts	32	E1
Upton Snodsbury	Worcs	81	L4
Upton Towans	Cnwll	2	F3
Upton-upon-Severn	Worcs	81	K7
Upton Warren	Worcs	81	L2
Upwaltham	W Susx	20	F4
Upware	Cambs	87	L1
Upwell	Norfk	103	K3
Upwey	Dorset	16	C5
Upwick Green	Herts	70	C2
Upwood	Cambs	102	E6

Urchfont Wilts 46 F7
Urdimarsh Herefs 80 C5
Ure Bank N York 150 D1
Urlay Nook S on T 169 L7
Urmston Traffd 130 E1
Urpeth Dur 181 G7
Urquhart Moray 266 F4
Urra N York 161 J2
Urray Highld 250 E1
Usan Angus 235 H4
Ushaw Moor Dur 169 G2
Usk Mons 62 D7
Usselby Lincs 136 A1
Usworth Sundld 181 H7
Utkinton Ches W 130 A6
Utley C Brad 149 J7
Uton Devon 13 J3
Utterby Lincs 136 F1
Uttoxeter Staffs 115 H5
Uwchmynydd Gwynd 108 B6
Uxbridge Gt Lon 50 D2
Uyeasound Shet 281 f2
Uzmaston Pembks 54 F4

V

Vale Guern 9 k2
Vale Crematorium Luton 68 E2
Vale of Glamorgan
   Crematorium V Glam 43 H7
Valley IoA 124 E4
Valley End Surrey 50 B6
Valley Truckle Cnwll 10 F6
Valtos Highld 259 J4
Valtos W Isls 282 e3
Vange Essex 52 F2
Varteg Torfn 61 L6
Vatsetter Shet 281 e4
Vatten Highld 258 D7
Vaynor Myr Td 61 G5
Vazon Bay Guern 9 i2
Veensgarth Shet 281 e6
Velindre Powys 79 H7
Vellow Somset 29 K3
Velly Devon 26 E6
Venngreen Devon 26 F8
Vennington Shrops 95 H2
Venn Ottery Devon 14 C4
Venny Tedburn Devon 13 J3
Venterdon Cnwll 11 L7
Ventnor IoW 19 J8
Venton Devon 7 H3
Vernham Dean Hants 47 M7
Vernham Street Hants 47 M7
Vernolds Common Shrops 95 L7
Verwood Dorset 17 L1
Veryan Cnwll 4 E7
Veryan Green Cnwll 4 F6
Vicarage Devon 14 E5
Vickerstown Cumb 146 C2
Victoria Barns 141 J6
Victoria Blae G 61 J5
Victoria Cnwll 5 G3
Vidlin Shet 281 e5
Viewfield Moray 266 F3
Viewpark N Lans 209 J6
Vigo Kent 52 D6
Village de Putron Guern 9 k3
Ville la Bas Jersey 9 a1
Villiaze Guern 9 i3
Vinehall Street E Susx 24 D3
Vines Cross E Susx 23 K4
Vinters Park Crematorium
   Kent 39 K2
Virginia Water Surrey 50 C5
Virginstow Devon 11 M4
Vobster Somset 32 B1
Voe Shet 281 d5
Vowchurch Herefs 79 L7
Vulcan Village St Hel 130 B1

W

Waberthwaite Cumb 155 K4
Wackerfield Dur 168 F6
Wacton Norfk 106 D5
Wadborough Worcs 81 K5
Waddesdon Bucks 67 H4
Waddeton Devon 8 C3
Waddicar Sefton 138 E7
Waddingham Lincs 144 B8
Waddington Lancs 148 C7
Waddington Lincs 135 K6
Waddon Devon 13 K6
Waddon Dorset 16 B5

Wadebridge Cnwll 10 D8
Wadeford Somset 30 D8
Wadenhoe Nhants 101 M6
Wadesmill Herts 69 K4
Wadhurst E Susx 39 G7
Wadshelf Derbys 132 F5
Wadswick Wilts 46 B5
Wadworth Donc 142 F8
Waen Denbgs 127 K7
Waen Denbgs 128 D6
Waen Powys 112 C7
Waen Fach Powys 112 B8
Waen-pentir Gwynd 125 K6
Waen-wen Gwynd 125 K6
Wagbeach Shrops 95 J3
Wainfelin Torfn 62 B6
Wainfleet All Saints Lincs 137 J7
Wainfleet Bank Lincs 137 J7
Wainfleet St Mary Lincs 137 J8
Wainford Norfk 107 G5
Wainhouse Corner Cnwll 11 H3
Wainscott Medway 52 F5
Wain's Hill N Som 44 E5
Wainstalls Calder 141 G2
Waitby Cumb 158 C1
Waithe Lincs 145 H7
Wakefield Wakefd 142 A4
Wakefield Crematorium
   Wakefd 141 M4
Wake Green Birm 98 E6
Wakerley Nhants 101 L3
Wakes Colne Essex 72 C2
Walberswick Suffk 107 K8
Walberton W Susx 21 G5
Walbottle N u Ty 180 E5
Walbutt D & G 175 J1
Walby Cumb 178 B6
Walcombe Somset 31 J2
Walcot Lincs 118 E4
Walcot N Linc 143 M3
Walcot Shrops 95 J6
Walcot Shrops 96 D1
Walcot Swindn 47 H2
Walcot Warwks 82 D4
Walcote Leics 100 C6
Walcot Green Norfk 106 C7
Walcott Lincs 136 B8
Walcott Norfk 123 G5
Walden N York 159 H6
Walden Head N York 159 H6
Walden Stubbs N York 142 E4
Walderslade Medway 53 G6
Walderton W Susx 20 C5
Walditch Dorset 15 L4
Waldley Derbys 115 J4
Waldridge Dur 169 H1
Waldringfield Suffk 91 G6
Waldron E Susx 23 J3
Wales Rothm 133 J3
Wales Somset 31 K6
Walesby Lincs 136 B1
Walesby Notts 134 D5
Walford Herefs 63 H3
Walford Herefs 79 M1
Walford Shrops 113 G7
Walford Staffs 114 C5
Walford Heath Shrops 113 G7
Walgherton Ches E 113 M2
Walgrave Nhants 84 F1
Walhampton Hants 18 E4
Walkden Salfd 139 L7
Walker N u Ty 181 H6
Walkerburn Border 200 D5
Walker Fold Lancs 148 B7
Walkeringham Notts 134 F1
Walkerith Lincs 134 F1
Walkern Herts 69 H2
Walker's Green Herefs 80 C5
Walker's Heath Birm 98 D7
Walkerton Fife 222 C7
Walkford Dorset 18 C5
Walkhampton Devon 7 G1
Walkington E R Yk 152 F8
Walkley Sheff 133 G2
Walk Mill Lancs 140 C2
Walkwood Worcs 82 B2
Wall Nthumb 179 L5
Wall Staffs 98 E2
Wallacetown S Ayrs 183 H2
Wallacetown S Ayrs 196 C6
Wallands Park E Susx 22 F5
Wallasey Wirral 129 G1
Wallasey (Kingsway) Tunnel
   Wirral 129 H2
Wall End Cumb 156 B6
Wall End Herefs 80 B4
Wallend Medway 53 J4
Waller's Green Herefs 80 F7
Wallhead Cumb 178 B6

Wall Heath Dudley 97 K5
Wall Houses Nthumb 180 C5
Wallingford Oxon 48 F7
Wallington Gt Lon 51 H6
Wallington Hants 19 K2
Wallington Herts 86 F8
Wallington Heath Wsall 98 C3
Wallis Pembks 75 G7
Wallisdown Poole 17 L4
Walliswood Surrey 37 H3
Walls Shet 281 c6
Wallsend N Tyne 181 H5
Wallthwaite Cumb 165 K5
Wall under Haywood Shrops 96 C5
Wallyford E Loth 211 L4
Walmer Kent 41 L5
Walmer Bridge Lancs 138 F2
Walmersley Bury 140 B5
Walmestone Kent 41 H3
Walmley Birm 98 F5
Walmley Ash Birm 98 F5
Walmsgate Lincs 137 G4
Walpole Somset 30 D3
Walpole Suffk 107 H8
Walpole Cross Keys Norfk 120 B7
Walpole Highway Norfk 120 B8
Walpole St Andrew Norfk 120 B8
Walpole St Peter Norfk 120 B8
Walrow Somset 30 E2
Walsall Wsall 98 C4
Walsall Wood Wsall 98 D3
Walsden Calder 140 D3
Walsgrave on Sowe Covtry 99 K7
Walsham le Willows Suffk 89 K1
Walshaw Bury 140 A5
Walshford N York 150 F5
Walsoken Norfk 103 K1
Walston S Lans 199 H4
Walsworth Herts 69 G1
Walter's Ash Bucks 67 K7
Walters Green Kent 38 D5
Walterston V Glam 43 G7
Walterstone Herefs 62 D2
Waltham Kent 40 E5
Waltham NE Lin 145 H7
Waltham Abbey Essex 69 K7
Waltham Chase Hants 35 H7
Waltham Cross Herts 69 K7
Waltham on the Wolds Leics 117 L6
Waltham St Lawrence W & M 49 K4
Waltham's Cross Essex 71 G1
Walthamstow Gt Lon 51 K1
Walton C Pete 102 D3
Walton Cumb 178 C6
Walton Derbys 133 G6
Walton Leeds 150 F6
Walton Leics 100 D6
Walton M Keyn 85 H7
Walton Powys 79 J3
Walton Shrops 95 L7
Walton Somset 31 G4
Walton Staffs 114 C6
Walton Staffs 114 D6
Walton Suffk 91 G8
Walton W Susx 20 D6
Walton Wakefd 142 A4
Walton Warwks 83 G4
Walton Wrekin 113 K7
Walton Cardiff Gloucs 64 C1
Walton East Pembks 55 H2
Walton Elm Dorset 32 C7
Walton Grounds Nhants 83 L8
Walton Highway Norfk 103 K1
Walton-in-Gordano N Som 44 E4
Walton Lea Crematorium
   Warrtn 130 B3
Walton-le-Dale Lancs 139 H2
Walton-on-Thames Surrey 50 E5
Walton-on-the-Hill Staffs 114 F7
Walton on the Hill Surrey 51 G7
Walton-on-the-Naze Essex 73 K3
Walton on the Wolds Leics 117 G7
Walton-on-Trent Derbys 115 L7
Walton Park N Som 44 E4
Walton West Pembks 54 D4
Waltonwrays Crematorium
   N York 149 H5
Walwen Flints 128 D4
Walwen Flints 128 E4
Walwen Flints 128 E5
Walwick Nthumb 179 L5
Walworth Darltn 169 G7
Walworth Gt Lon 51 J3
Walworth Gate Darltn 169 G6
Walwyn's Castle Pembks 54 E4
Wambrook Somset 15 G1
Wampool Cumb 177 H7
Wanborough Surrey 36 D1
Wanborough Swindn 47 J2

Wandon End Herts 68 E3
Wandsworth Gt Lon 51 H4
Wangford Suffk 107 J7
Wanlip Leics 100 D1
Wanlockhead D & G 186 C4
Wannock E Susx 23 K6
Wansford C Pete 102 B3
Wansford E R Yk 153 G4
Wanshurst Green Kent 39 J4
Wanstead Gt Lon 51 L1
Wanstrow Somset 32 B3
Wanswell Gloucs 63 K6
Wantage Oxon 48 B1
Wants Green Worcs 81 H4
Wapley S Glos 45 L3
Wappenbury Warwks 83 J2
Wappenham Nhants 84 C6
Warbleton E Susx 23 K4
Warborough Oxon 66 F8
Warboys Cambs 102 F7
Warbreck Bpool 146 F2
Warbstow Cnwll 11 H4
Warburton Traffd 130 D2
Warcop Cumb 167 H7
Warden Kent 53 M5
Warden Nthumb 179 L5
Ward End Birm 98 E5
Warden Street C Beds 86 C6
Ward Green Suffk 90 B2
Ward Green Cross Lancs 148 A8
Wardhedges C Beds 85 L8
Wardington Oxon 83 L6
Wardle Ches E 130 B8
Wardle Rochdl 140 D4
Wardley Gatesd 181 H6
Wardley Rutlnd 101 H3
Wardley Salfd 140 A7
Wardlow Derbys 132 D5
Wardsend Ches E 131 J3
Wardy Hill Cambs 103 K7
Ware Herts 69 K4
Wareham Dorset 17 H5
Warehorne Kent 25 J1
Warenford Nthumb 203 J7
Waren Mill Nthumb 203 J6
Warenton Nthumb 203 J6
Wareside Herts 69 K4
Waresley Cambs 86 E4
Waresley Worcs 81 J1
Ware Street Kent 39 K2
Warfield Br For 49 L4
Warfleet Devon 8 C5
Wargate Lincs 119 H5
Wargrave Wokham 49 J3
Warham Herefs 80 B7
Warham Norfk 121 L3
Wark Nthumb 179 K3
Wark Nthumb 202 C5
Warkleigh Devon 27 M6
Warkton Nhants 101 K7
Warkworth Nhants 83 L1
Warkworth Nthumb 191 K5
Warlaby N York 160 E4
Warland Calder 140 E4
Warleggan Cnwll 5 K1
Warleigh BaNES 46 A6
Warley Town Calder 141 G3
Warlingham Surrey 51 K7
Warmbrook Derbys 115 M1
Warmfield Wakefd 142 B4
Warmingham Ches E 130 D7
Warmington Nhants 102 B5
Warmington Warwks 83 K5
Warminster Wilts 32 E2
Warmley S Glos 45 K4
Warmsworth Donc 142 F7
Warmwell Dorset 16 E5
Warndon Worcs 81 K4
Warnford Hants 35 J6
Warnham W Susx 37 J4
Warnham Court W Susx 37 J4
Warningcamp W Susx 21 H5
Warninglid W Susx 37 K5
Warren Ches E 131 H5
Warren Pembks 54 F7
Warrenby R & Cl 170 D5
Warrenhill S Lans 198 F5
Warren Row W & M 49 K3
Warren's Green Herts 69 H2
Warren Street Kent 40 B5
Warrington M Keyn 85 H4
Warrington Warrtn 130 B2
Warriston C Edin 211 H4
Warriston Crematorium
   C Edin 211 H4
Warsash Hants 19 H2
Warslow Staffs 132 B7
Warsop Vale Notts 133 L6
Warter E R Yk 152 D5

Warthermaske N York 160 B6
Warthill N York 151 L5
Wartling E Susx 24 B5
Wartnaby Leics 117 J7
Warton Lancs 138 E2
Warton Lancs 147 K2
Warton Nthumb 190 E5
Warton Warwks 99 H3
Warwick Warwks 83 G2
Warwick Bridge Cumb 178 B7
Warwick-on-Eden Cumb 178 B7
Warwicksland Cumb 178 B3
Wasbister Ork 275 c3
Wasdale Head Cumb 156 B1
Wash Derbys 131 L3
Washall Green Herts 70 C1
Washaway Cnwll 5 H1
Washbourne Devon 8 B4
Washbrook Somset 30 F1
Washbrook Suffk 90 D6
Washfield Devon 29 G7
Washfold N York 159 J2
Washford Somset 29 J3
Washford Pyne Devon 28 E8
Washingborough Lincs 135 L5
Washington Sundld 181 H7
Washington W Susx 21 J4
Washwood Heath Birm 98 E5
Wasing W Berk 48 E6
Waskerley Dur 168 D2
Wasperton Warwks 83 G3
Wasps Nest Lincs 135 M6
Wass N York 161 J6
Watchet Somset 29 K2
Watchfield Oxon 47 K1
Watchfield Somset 30 E2
Watchgate Cumb 157 H3
Watchill Cumb 165 G2
Watcombe Torbay 8 D2
Watendlath Cumb 165 H2
Water Devon 13 H6
Water Lancs 140 C3
Waterbeach Cambs 87 K2
Waterbeach W Susx 20 E5
Waterbeck D & G 177 H3
Waterden Norfk 121 J4
Water Eaton Oxon 66 D5
Water Eaton Staffs 97 K1
Water End Bed 86 C5
Water End Bed 86 C5
Water End C Beds 85 L7
Waterend Cumb 164 F6
Water End E R Yk 152 B8
Water End Essex 88 B7
Water End Herts 68 D5
Water End Herts 69 G6
Waterfall Staffs 115 H1
Waterfoot Ag & B 194 C3
Waterfoot E Rens 208 F7
Waterford Herts 69 J4
Water Fryston Wakefd 142 D2
Watergate Cnwll 11 G6
Waterhead Cumb 156 E2
Waterheads Border 200 B3
Waterhouses Dur 168 F3
Waterhouses Staffs 115 H2
Wateringbury Kent 39 H3
Waterlane Gloucs 64 D6
Waterloo Cnwll 10 F8
Waterloo Derbys 133 H7
Waterloo Herefs 79 L5
Waterloo Highld 247 K4
Waterloo N Lans 209 L8
Waterloo Norfk 122 E7
Waterloo P & K 233 G7
Waterloo Pembks 55 G6
Waterloo Sefton 138 C8
Waterloo Cross Devon 29 J8
Waterloo Port Gwynd 125 J6
Waterlooville Hants 19 M2
Watermead Bucks 67 K4
Watermillock Cumb 166 B6
Water Newton Cambs 102 C4
Water Orton Warwks 98 F5
Waterperry Oxon 66 F6
Waterrow Somset 29 J6
Watersfield W Susx 21 G4
Waterside Bl w D 139 L3
Waterside Bucks 68 B7
Waterside Cumb 165 H2
Waterside Donc 143 H5
Waterside E Ayrs 184 C1
Waterside E Ayrs 196 F2
Waterside E Duns 209 H4
Water's Nook Bolton 139 K6
Waterstein Highld 258 A7
Waterstock Oxon 66 F6
Waterston Pembks 54 F5
Water Stratford Bucks 84 C8

Water Street Neath 42 B5
Waters Upton Wrekin 113 K7
Water Yeat Cumb 156 D5
Watford Herts 68 E7
Watford Nhants 84 B2
Wath N York 149 L2
Wath N York 160 D3
Wath upon Dearne Rothm 142 C7
Watlington Norfk 104 C1
Watlington Oxon 67 G8
Watnall Notts 116 E2
Watten Highld 280 B5
Wattisfield Suffk 105 K8
Wattisham Suffk 89 K5
Watton Dorset 15 K4
Watton E R Yk 152 F6
Watton Norfk 105 J3
Watton-at-Stone Herts 69 J3
Watton Green Norfk 105 J3
Wattons Green Essex 70 D8
Wattston N Lans 209 K5
Wattstown Rhondd 42 F3
Wattsville Caerph 43 K3
Wauldby E R Yk 144 B2
Waulkmill Abers 244 E5
Waunarlwydd Swans 57 H6
Waunfawr Cerdgn 92 D7
Waunfawr Gwynd 125 J7
Waungron Swans 57 G4
Waunlwyd Blae G 61 J5
Wavendon M Keyn 85 H7
Waveney Crematorium Suffk 107 J6
Waverbridge Cumb 165 H1
Waverton Ches W 129 K7
Waverton Cumb 165 H1
Wawne E R Yk 153 H8
Waxham Norfk 123 J6
Waxholme E R Yk 145 J2
Way Kent 41 K2
Waye Devon 13 H8
Wayford Somset 15 J1
Waytown Dorset 15 L3
Way Village Devon 28 F8
Way Wick N Som 44 D6
Weacombe Somset 29 K3
Weald Oxon 65 L6
Wealdstone Gt Lon 50 F1
Weardley Leeds 150 D7
Weare Somset 44 E8
Weare Giffard Devon 27 H6
Wearhead Dur 167 K3
Wearne Somset 30 F5
Wear Valley Crematorium Dur .. 169 H4
Weasdale Cumb 158 D3
Weasenham All Saints Norfk 121 J7
Weasenham St Peter Norfk 121 J7
Weaste Salfd 140 B8
Weatheroak Hill Worcs 98 D8
Weaverham Ches W 130 B5
Weaverslake Staffs 115 J7
Weaverthorpe N York 152 E2
Webbington Somset 44 D7
Webb's Heath S Glos 45 K4
Webheath Worcs 82 B2
Webton Herefs 80 A7
Wedderlairs Abers 256 F5
Wedding Hall Fold N York 149 G6
Weddington Kent 41 J3
Weddington Warwks 99 K5
Wedhampton Wilts 46 F7
Wedmore Somset 31 G1
Wednesbury Sandw 98 C4
Wednesfield Wolves 97 L3
Weecar Notts 135 G6
Weedon Bucks 67 K3
Weedon Bec Nhants 84 C3
Weedon Lois Nhants 84 B6
Weeford Staffs 98 F3
Week Devon 8 A2
Week Devon 27 K5
Week Devon 28 C7
Weeke Devon 13 H2
Weeke Hants 34 F5
Weekley Nhants 101 K1
Week St Mary Cnwll 11 J3
Weel E R Yk 153 G7
Weeley Essex 73 H3
Weeley Crematorium Essex 73 H3
Weeley Heath Essex 73 H3
Weem P & K 232 B5
Weeping Cross Staffs 114 E7
Weethley Warwks 82 C4
Weeting Norfk 104 F5
Weeton E R Yk 145 K4
Weeton Lancs 138 D1
Weeton N York 150 C6
Weetwood Leeds 150 C8
Weir Lancs 140 C3
Weirbrook Shrops 112 E6

Weir Quay Devon 6 E2
Weisdale Shet 281 d5
Welborne Norfk 106 B2
Welbourn Lincs 118 C1
Welburn N York 151 M2
Welbury N York 160 F2
Welby Lincs 118 C4
Welches Dam Cambs 103 K6
Welcombe Devon 26 D7
Weldon Nhants 101 K5
Weldon Bridge Nthumb 191 L6
Welford Nhants 100 E7
Welford W Berk 48 B4
Welford-on-Avon Warwks 82 D5
Welham Leics 101 G5
Welham Notts 134 E3
Welham Bridge E R Yk 143 K1
Welham Green Herts 69 G6
Well Hants 36 A2
Well Lincs 137 H5
Well N York 160 C6
Welland Worcs 81 H7
Wellbank Angus 234 D7
Well End Bucks 49 L1
Well End Herts 69 G7
Wellesbourne Warwks 83 G4
Wellesbourne Mountford
    Warwks 83 G4
Well Head Herts 68 F2
Well Hill Kent 52 B6
Wellhouse W Berk 48 D4
Welling Gt Lon 51 M4
Wellingborough Nhants 85 H2
Wellingham Norfk 121 J7
Wellingore Lincs 135 K8
Wellington Cumb 155 K2
Wellington Herefs 80 C5
Wellington Somset 29 L6
Wellington Wrekin 96 E1
Wellington Heath Herefs 81 G7
Wellington Marsh Herefs 80 C6
Wellow BaNES 45 L7
Wellow IoW 18 F6
Wellow Notts 134 D6
Wellpond Green Herts 69 L3
Wells Somset 31 J2
Wellsborough Leics 99 K3
Wells Green Ches E 113 M1
Wells Head C Brad 141 G1
Wells-next-the-Sea Norfk 121 K3
Wellstye Green Essex 70 F3
Well Town Devon 13 L1
Welltree P & K 221 G3
Wellwood Fife 210 E1
Welney Norfk 103 L4
Welshampton Shrops 113 G4
Welsh Bicknor Herefs 63 H4
Welsh End Shrops 113 H4
Welsh Frankton Shrops 112 E5
Welsh Hook Pembks 74 F6
Welsh Newton Herefs 63 G3
Welshpool Powys 94 F2
Welsh St Donats V Glam 42 F6
Welton Cumb 165 K2
Welton E R Yk 144 B2
Welton Lincs 135 K4
Welton Nhants 84 B2
Welton le Marsh Lincs 137 J6
Welton le Wold Lincs 136 E2
Welwick E R Yk 145 J3
Welwyn Herts 69 G4
Welwyn Garden City Herts 69 G4
Wem Shrops 113 H6
Wembdon Somset 30 D3
Wembley Gt Lon 50 F2
Wembury Devon 7 G5
Wembworthy Devon 12 F1
Wemyss Bay Inver 207 K5
Wenallt Cerdgn 77 J1
Wendens Ambo Essex 87 K8
Wendlebury Oxon 66 E3
Wendling Norfk 105 J1
Wendover Bucks 67 L5
Wendron Cnwll 3 H5
Wendy Cambs 87 G5
Wenfordbridge Cnwll 10 F7
Wenhaston Suffk 107 J8
Wennington Cambs 102 E7
Wennington Gt Lon 52 B3
Wennington Lancs 147 M2
Wensley Derbys 132 E7
Wensley N York 159 K5
Wentbridge Wakefd 142 D4
Wentnor Shrops 95 J5
Wentworth Cambs 103 K7
Wentworth Rothm 142 B8
Wenvoe V Glam 43 H7
Weobley Herefs 79 M5
Weobley Marsh Herefs 80 A5

Wepham W Susx 21 H5
Wereham Norfk 104 D3
Wergs Wolves 97 K3
Wern Gwynd 109 K4
Wern Powys 61 H3
Wern Powys 95 G1
Wern Shrops 112 D4
Werneth Low Tamesd 131 J1
Wernffrwd Swans 56 F6
Wern-y-gaer Flints 128 F6
Werrington C Pete 102 D3
Werrington Cnwll 11 L5
Werrington Staffs 114 E2
Wervin Ches W 129 K5
Wesham Lancs 138 E1
Wessex Vale Crematorium
    Hants 35 G7
Wessington Derbys 133 G8
West Aberthaw V Glam 42 F8
West Acre Norfk 121 G8
West Allerdean Nthumb 202 F4
West Alvington Devon 7 L6
West Amesbury Wilts 33 K3
West Anstey Devon 28 E5
West Appleton N York 160 B4
West Ashby Lincs 136 E5
West Ashling W Susx 20 D5
West Ashton Wilts 46 C7
West Auckland Dur 168 F5
West Ayton N York 163 H5
West Bagborough Somset 30 A4
West Bank Blae G 61 K6
West Bank Halton 129 L3
West Barkwith Lincs 136 C4
West Barnby N York 171 J8
West Barns E Loth 212 E3
West Barsham Norfk 121 K5
West Bay Dorset 15 K4
West Beckham Norfk 122 C4
West Bedfont Surrey 50 D4
Westbere Kent 41 G3
West Bergholt Essex 72 D2
West Berkshire Crematorium
    W Berk 48 D5
West Bexington Dorset 15 M5
West Bilney Norfk 120 F8
West Blatchington Br & H 22 D6
West Boldon S Tyne 181 J6
Westborough Lincs 117 M3
Westbourne Bmouth 17 L4
Westbourne W Susx 20 B5
West Bourton Dorset 32 C5
West Bowling C Brad 141 J2
West Brabourne Kent 40 E6
West Bradenham Norfk 105 J2
West Bradford Lancs 148 C7
West Bradley Somset 31 J3
West Bretton Wakefd 141 L5
West Bridgford Notts 117 G4
West Briscoe Dur 168 B6
West Bromwich Sandw 98 C5
Westbrook Kent 41 K1
Westbrook W Berk 48 B4
Westbrook Wilts 46 D5
West Buckland Devon 28 B4
West Buckland Somset 30 B6
West Burrafirth Shet 281 c5
West Burton N York 159 H5
West Burton W Susx 21 G4
Westbury Bucks 84 B8
Westbury Shrops 95 J2
Westbury Wilts 46 C8
Westbury Leigh Wilts 32 E1
Westbury on Severn Gloucs 63 L4
Westbury-on-Trym Bristl 45 H3
Westbury-sub-Mendip Somset 31 H1
West Butsfield Dur 168 E2
West Butterwick N Linc 143 L6
Westby Lancs 138 D2
West Byfleet Surrey 50 D6
West Cairngaan D & G 172 E8
West Caister Norfk 107 K1
West Calder W Loth 210 D6
West Camel Somset 31 J6
West Chaldon Dorset 16 E6
West Challow Oxon 48 A1
West Charleton Devon 7 L6
West Chelborough Dorset 15 M2
West Chevington Nthumb 191 J6
West Chiltington W Susx 21 J3
West Chinnock Somset 31 G8
West Chisenbury Wilts 47 H8
West Clandon Surrey 50 D8
West Cliffe Kent 41 K6
Westcliff-on-Sea Sthend 53 J2
West Coker Somset 31 H8
West Combe Devon 7 L2
Westcombe Somset 31 L3
West Compton Somset 31 K2

West Compton Abbas Dorset 16 A4
Westcote Gloucs 65 J3
Westcote Barton Oxon 66 B2
Westcott Bucks 67 H4
Westcott Devon 14 B2
Westcott Surrey 37 H1
West Cottingwith N York 151 L7
Westcourt Wilts 47 J6
West Cowick E R Yk 143 G3
West Cross Swans 57 H7
West Curry Cnwll 11 K4
West Curthwaite Cumb 165 K1
Westdean E Susx 23 J7
West Dean W Susx 20 E4
West Dean Wilts 34 B5
West Deeping Lincs 102 C2
West Derby Lpool 129 J1
West Dereham Norfk 104 D3
West Ditchburn Nthumb 191 G2
West Down Devon 27 J3
Westdown Camp Wilts 33 H2
Westdowns Cnwll 10 F6
West Drayton Gt Lon 50 D3
West Drayton Notts 134 E5
West Dunnet Highld 280 B2
Wested Kent 52 B5
West Ella E R Yk 144 C2
West End Bed 85 J4
West End Br For 49 L5
West End Caerph 43 K3
West End Cambs 87 G2
West End Cumb 177 K7
West End E R Yk 144 A2
West End E R Yk 144 F2
West End E R Yk 145 H2
Westend Gloucs 64 A5
West End Hants 34 F7
West End Hants 35 K4
West End Herts 69 H5
West End Herts 69 J6
West End Lancs 139 L2
West End Leeds 150 B8
West End Lincs 145 K8
West End N Som 44 F5
West End N York 151 H7
West End Norfk 105 H2
West End Norfk 107 K1
West End Oxon 48 E2
West End S Glos 45 L1
West End Somset 31 L4
West End Surrey 50 B6
West End Surrey 50 E6
West End W & M 49 K4
West End W Susx 22 B4
West End Wilts 32 F6
West End Wilts 33 G6
West End Wilts 46 E3
West End Green Hants 49 G6
Westend Town Nthumb 179 H6
Westenhanger Kent 40 F7
Wester Aberchalder Highld 250 F7
Westerdale Highld 279 K6
Westerdale N York 161 L2
Westerfield Suffk 90 E5
Westergate W Susx 20 F6
Westerham Kent 51 L8
Westerhope N u Ty 180 F5
Westerland Devon 8 C2
Westerleigh S Glos 45 K3
Westerleigh Crematorium
    S Glos 45 L3
Western Isles W Isls 282 e6
Wester Ochiltree W Loth 210 D4
Wester Pitkierie Fife 223 K6
Westerton W Susx 20 E5
Westerton of Rossie Angus 235 G4
Westerwick Shet 281 c6
West Ewell Surrey 51 G6
West Farleigh Kent 39 H3
West Farndon Nhants 83 M5
West Felton Shrops 112 E6
Westfield BaNES 45 K8
Westfield Cumb 164 C5
Westfield E Susx 24 E4
Westfield Highld 279 J3
Westfield N Lans 209 J4
Westfield Norfk 105 K2
Westfield W Loth 210 B4
Westfields Dorset 16 D2
Westfields Herefs 80 C7
Westfields of Rattray P & K 233 J6
Westfield Sole Kent 53 G6
West Flotmanby N York 163 K6
Westford Somset 29 L6
Westgate Dur 167 L3
Westgate N Linc 143 K6
Westgate Norfk 121 L3
Westgate Hill C Brad 141 K2
Westgate-on-Sea Kent 41 K1

Westgate Street Norfk 122 D7
West Ginge Oxon 48 C2
West Grafton Wilts 47 K7
West Green Hants 49 H7
West Grimstead Wilts 33 L5
West Grinstead W Susx 37 J6
West Haddlesey N York 142 F2
West Haddon Nhants 84 C1
West Hagbourne Oxon 48 D2
West Hagley Worcs 97 K7
Westhall Suffk 107 J7
West Hallam Derbys 116 D3
West Hallam Common Derbys 116 C3
West Halton N Linc 144 A4
Westham Dorset 16 C6
Westham E Susx 23 L6
West Ham Gt Lon 51 K2
Westham Somset 30 F2
Westhampnett W Susx 20 E5
West Handley Derbys 133 H4
West Hanney Oxon 66 B8
West Hanningfield Essex 71 H1
West Harnham Wilts 33 K5
West Harptree BaNES 45 H7
West Harting W Susx 20 C3
West Hatch Somset 30 D6
West Hatch Wilts 32 F5
West Haven Angus 234 E8
Westhay Somset 31 G2
Westhead Lancs 138 F6
West Head Norfk 104 B2
West Heath Birm 98 C7
West Heath Hants 48 E7
West Helmsdale Highld 274 D5
West Hendred Oxon 48 C1
West Hertfordshire
    Crematorium Herts 68 E6
West Heslerton N York 163 G7
West Hewish N Som 44 D6
Westhide Herefs 80 D6
Westhill Abers 245 J2
West Hill Devon 14 C4
West Hoathly W Susx 38 A6
West Holme Dorset 17 G5
Westholme Somset 31 J3
Westhope Herefs 80 B5
Westhope Shrops 95 L6
West Horndon Essex 52 D1
Westhorp Nhants 83 L5
Westhorpe Lincs 119 H5
Westhorpe Suffk 90 B2
West Horrington Somset 31 J2
West Horsley Surrey 50 D8
West Horton Nthumb 203 G7
West Hougham Kent 41 H7
Westhoughton Bolton 139 K6
Westhouse N York 157 L7
Westhouses Derbys 133 H8
West Howe Bmouth 17 L3
West Howetown Somset 29 G4
Westhumble Surrey 50 F8
West Huntingtower P & K 221 K2
West Huntspill Somset 30 D2
West Hyde C Beds 68 E4
West Hyde Herts 50 C1
West Hythe Kent 40 F8
West Ilkerton Devon 28 C2
West Ilsley W Berk 48 C3
West Itchenor W Susx 20 C6
West Keal Lincs 137 G7
West Kennett Wilts 47 G5
West Kilbride N Ayrs 195 K1
West Kingsdown Kent 52 C6
West Kington Wilts 46 A3
West Kirby Wirral 128 F2
West Knapton N York 162 F7
West Knighton Dorset 16 D5
West Knoyle Wilts 32 E4
West Kyloe Nthumb 203 G5
Westlake Devon 7 J4
West Lambrook Somset 30 F7
West Lancashire
    Crematorium Lancs 138 E5
Westland Green Herts 70 B3
West Langdon Kent 41 K6
West Lavington W Susx 20 E3
West Lavington Wilts 46 E8
West Layton N York 168 F8
West Leake Notts 116 E6
West Learmouth Nthumb 202 C5
West Lees N York 161 G2
West Leigh Devon 13 G2
Westleigh Devon 27 H5
Westleigh Devon 29 J7
West Leigh Somset 29 L5
Westleton Suffk 91 K2
West Lexham Norfk 121 J8
Westley Shrops 95 J2
Westley Suffk 89 G2

Westley Waterless Cambs 88 C4
West Lilling N York 151 K3
Westlington Bucks 67 J5
West Linton Border 199 K3
Westlinton Cumb 177 L6
West Littleton S Glos 45 M4
West Lockinge Oxon 48 B2
West London Crematorium
    Gt Lon 51 G3
West Lothian Crematorium
    W Loth 210 D5
West Lulworth Dorset 16 F6
West Lutton N York 152 E2
West Lydford Somset 31 J4
West Lyn Devon 28 C1
West Lyng Somset 30 D5
West Lynn Norfk 120 D7
West Malling Kent 52 E7
West Malvern Worcs 81 H6
West Marden W Susx 20 C4
West Markham Notts 134 E5
Westmarsh Kent 41 J3
West Marsh NE Lin 145 H5
West Marton N York 148 F5
West Melbury Dorset 32 E6
West Melton Rothm 142 C7
West Meon Hants 35 K6
West Meon Hut Hants 35 K5
West Meon Woodlands Hants 35 K5
West Mersea Essex 72 E4
Westmeston E Susx 22 E4
Westmill Herts 69 J4
Westmill Herts 69 K2
West Mickley Nthumb 180 C6
West Milton Dorset 15 L3
Westminster Gt Lon 51 J3
West Molesey Surrey 50 E5
West Monkton Somset 30 C5
West Moors Dorset 17 L2
West Morden Dorset 17 H3
West Morriston Border 201 J5
West Morton C Brad 149 K7
West Mudford Somset 31 J6
Westmuir Angus 234 A5
West Ness N York 162 B6
West Newbiggin Darltn 169 K7
Westnewton Cumb 164 F2
West Newton E R Yk 153 K8
West Newton Norfk 120 F6
West Newton Somset 30 D5
West Norwood Gt Lon 51 J4
West Norwood Crematorium
    Gt Lon 51 J4
Westoe S Tyne 181 J5
West Ogwell Devon 13 J8
Weston BaNES 45 L5
Weston Ches E 114 A1
Weston Devon 14 D3
Weston Devon 14 E5
Weston Dorset 16 D8
Weston Halton 129 L3
Weston Hants 35 M6
Weston Herefs 79 L4
Weston Herts 69 H1
Weston Lincs 119 J6
Weston N York 149 M6
Weston Nhants 84 B6
Weston Notts 134 F6
Weston Shrops 95 M6
Weston Shrops 96 D5
Weston Shrops 112 D6
Weston Staffs 114 F6
Weston W Berk 48 B4
Weston Beggard Herefs 80 D7
Westonbirt Gloucs 46 B1
Weston by Welland Nhants 101 G5
Weston Colley Hants 35 G3
Weston Colville Cambs 88 C4
Weston Corbett Hants 35 L2
Weston Coyney C Stke 114 E3
Weston Favell Nhants 84 F3
Weston Green Cambs 88 C5
Weston Heath Shrops 97 H1
Weston Hills Lincs 119 J7
Weston in Arden Warwks 99 K6
Westoning C Beds 85 K8
Weston-in-Gordano N Som 44 F4
Westoning Woodend C Beds 68 C1
Weston Jones Staffs 114 B6
Weston Longville Norfk 122 C8
Weston Lullingfields Shrops 112 F6
Weston Mill Crematorium
    C Plym 6 F3
Weston-on-Avon Warwks 82 E5
Weston-on-the-Green Oxon 66 D3
Weston Patrick Hants 35 L2
Weston Rhyn Shrops 112 D4
Weston-sub-Edge Gloucs 82 D7
Weston-super-Mare N Som 44 C6

Weston-super-Mare
    Crematorium N Som 44 D6
Weston Turville Bucks 67 K5
Weston-under-Lizard Staffs 97 H1
Weston under Penyard Herefs 63 J3
Weston-under-Redcastle
    Shrops 113 J5
Weston under Wetherley
    Warwks 83 J1
Weston Underwood Derbys 115 M3
Weston Underwood M Keyn 85 G5
Weston-upon-Trent Derbys 116 C6
Westonzoyland Somset 30 E4
West Orchard Dorset 32 D7
West Overton Wilts 47 H5
Westow N York 152 A3
West Panson Devon 11 L4
West Park Abers 245 H4
West Parley Dorset 17 L3
West Peckham Kent 39 G3
West Peeke Devon 11 L4
West Pelton Dur 180 F8
West Pennard Somset 31 J3
West Pentire Cnwll 4 C3
West Perry Cambs 86 C2
West Pinchbeck Lincs 119 G6
West Porlock Somset 28 F2
Westport Somset 30 F6
West Pulham Dorset 16 D1
West Putford Devon 26 F3
West Quantoxhead Somset 29 K3
Westquarter Falk 210 B3
Westra V Glam 43 J7
West Raddon Devon 13 L2
West Rainton Dur 169 J1
West Rasen Lincs 135 L2
West Ravendale NE Lin 145 G7
Westray Ork 275 C2
West Raynham Norfk 121 J6
West Retford Notts 134 D3
Westridge Green W Berk 48 E3
Westrigg W Loth 210 B5
West Road Crematorium
    N u Ty 180 F6
Westrop Swindn 65 J8
West Rounton N York 160 F2
West Row Suffk 104 D8
West Rudham Norfk 121 H6
West Runton Norfk 122 D3
Westruther Border 201 K3
Westry Cambs 103 H4
West Saltoun E Loth 212 A5
West Sandford Devon 13 J2
West Sandwick Shet 281 e3
West Scrafton N York 159 K6
West Sleekburn Nthumb 181 G2
West Somerton Norfk 123 K7
West Stafford Dorset 16 D5
West Stockwith Notts 134 F1
West Stoke W Susx 20 D5
West Stonesdale N York 158 F2
West Stoughton Somset 30 F1
West Stour Dorset 32 C6
West Stourmouth Kent 41 H3
West Stow Suffk 89 G1
West Stowell Wilts 47 H6
West Stratton Hants 35 H3
West Street Kent 40 A4
West Street Kent 41 H4
West Street Medway 52 F4
West Street Suffk 89 K1
West Suffolk Crematorium
    Suffk 89 G2
West Tanfield N York 160 C7
West Taphouse Cnwll 5 K2
West Tarbert Ag & B 206 D5
West Tarring W Susx 21 J6
West Thirston Nthumb 191 H6
West Thorney W Susx 20 C6
Westthorpe Derbys 133 J4
West Thorpe Notts 117 G6
West Thurrock Thurr 52 C3
West Tilbury Thurr 52 E3
West Tisted Hants 35 K5
West Torrington Lincs 136 B3
West Town BaNES 45 G6
West Town Hants 20 B7
West Town Herefs 80 B3
West Town N Som 44 F5
West Town Somset 31 J4
West Town Somset 32 B3
West Tytherley Hants 34 C5
West Walton Norfk 103 K1
Westward Cumb 165 J2
Westward Ho! Devon 27 G5
Westwell Kent 40 C5
Westwell Oxon 65 J5
Westwell Leacon Kent 40 C5
West Wellow Hants 34 C7

Place	County	Page	Grid
West Wembury	Devon	7	G5
West Wemyss	Fife	222	E8
Westwick	Cambs	87	J2
Westwick	Dur	168	D7
West Wick	N Som	44	D6
Westwick	Norfk	122	F6
West Wickham	Cambs	88	C5
West Wickham	Gt Lon	51	K5
West Williamston	Pembks	55	H5
West Wiltshire Crematorium	Wilts	46	C7
West Winch	Norfk	120	E8
West Winterslow	Wilts	34	B4
West Wittering	W Susx	20	C7
West Witton	N York	159	J5
Westwood	Devon	14	B3
Westwood	Kent	41	K2
Westwood	Kent	52	D5
Westwood	Notts	116	D1
Westwood	Nthumb	179	H6
Westwood	Wilts	46	A7
West Woodburn	Nthumb	179	K2
West Woodhay	W Berk	48	B6
Westwood Heath	Covtry	99	H8
West Woodlands	Somset	32	C2
Westwoodside	N Linc	143	J7
West Worldham	Hants	35	M3
West Worthing	W Susx	21	K6
West Wratting	Cambs	88	C5
West Wycombe	Bucks	67	K8
West Wylam	Nthumb	180	D6
West Yatton	Wilts	46	B4
West Yoke	Kent	52	D5
West Youlstone	Cnwll	26	D7
Wetham Green	Kent	53	H5
Wetheral	Cumb	178	B7
Wetherby	Leeds	150	F6
Wetherden	Suffk	89	K3
Wetheringsett	Suffk	90	D2
Wethersfield	Essex	71	H1
Wetherup Street	Suffk	90	D2
Wetley Rocks	Staffs	114	F2
Wettenhall	Ches E	130	C7
Wetton	Staffs	132	B8
Wetwang	E R Yk	152	E4
Wetwood	Staffs	114	B5
Wexcombe	Wilts	47	K7
Wexham	Slough	50	C3
Wexham Street	Bucks	50	C2
Weybourne	Norfk	122	C3
Weybourne	Surrey	36	C1
Weybread	Suffk	106	E7
Weybread Street	Suffk	106	E7
Weybridge	Surrey	50	D6
Weycroft	Devon	15	G3
Weydale	Highld	279	L3
Weyhill	Hants	34	D2
Weymouth	Dorset	16	C6
Weymouth Crematorium	Dorset	16	C6
Whaddon	Bucks	84	F8
Whaddon	Cambs	87	G6
Whaddon	Gloucs	64	B4
Whaddon	Gt Lon	51	J6
Whaddon	Wilts	33	L5
Whaddon	Wilts	46	C6
Whale	Cumb	166	C6
Whaley	Derbys	133	K5
Whaley Bridge	Derbys	131	K3
Whaley Thorns	Derbys	133	K5
Whaligoe	Highld	280	D8
Whalley	Lancs	148	C8
Whalley Banks	Lancs	139	L1
Whalsay	Shet	281	f5
Whalton	Nthumb	180	D3
Whaplode	Lincs	119	K6
Whaplode Drove	Lincs	103	G1
Wharf	Warwks	83	K5
Wharfe	N York	148	D2
Wharles	Lancs	147	J8
Wharley End	C Beds	85	J6
Wharncliffe Side	Sheff	132	F1
Wharram-le-Street	N York	152	C3
Wharton	Ches W	130	C6
Wharton	Herefs	80	C4
Whashton	N York	159	L2
Whasset	Cumb	157	H6
Whatcote	Warwks	83	G6
Whateley	Warwks	99	G3
Whatfield	Suffk	89	L6
Whatley	Somset	15	H1
Whatley	Somset	32	B2
Whatley's End	S Glos	45	K3
Whatlington	E Susx	24	D4
Whatsole Street	Kent	40	F6
Whatstandwell	Derbys	116	B1
Whatton	Notts	117	K4
Whauphill	D & G	173	K5
Whaw	N York	159	H2
Wheal Rose	Cnwll	4	B6
Wheatacre	Norfk	107	J4
Wheatfield	Oxon	67	G7
Wheathampstead	Herts	68	F4
Wheathill	Shrops	96	E7
Wheathill	Somset	31	J5
Wheatley	Calder	141	G3
Wheatley	Hants	36	A3
Wheatley	Oxon	66	E6
Wheatley Hill	Dur	169	K3
Wheatley Hills	Donc	142	F6
Wheatley Lane	Lancs	148	E8
Wheaton Aston	Staffs	97	J1
Wheatsheaf	Wrexhm	112	D1
Wheddon Cross	Somset	29	G3
Wheelbarrow Town	Kent	40	F6
Wheeler End	Bucks	67	K8
Wheeler's Green	Wokham	49	J4
Wheeler's Street	Kent	39	L4
Wheelerstreet	Surrey	36	E3
Wheelock	Ches E	130	E7
Wheelock Heath	Ches E	130	E8
Wheelton	Lancs	139	J3
Wheldale	Wakefd	142	C3
Wheldrake	C York	151	L6
Whelford	Gloucs	65	H7
Whelpley Hill	Bucks	68	C6
Whelpo	Cumb	165	J3
Whelston	Flints	128	F4
Whempstead	Herts	69	J3
Whenby	N York	151	K2
Whepstead	Suffk	89	G4
Wherstead	Suffk	90	E7
Wherwell	Hants	34	E3
Wheston	Derbys	132	C4
Whetsted	Kent	39	G4
Whetstone	Gt Lon	69	H8
Whetstone	Leics	100	C4
Wheyrigg	Cumb	165	G1
Whicham	Cumb	155	L6
Whichford	Warwks	83	H8
Whickham	Gatesd	180	F6
Whiddon	Devon	12	B3
Whiddon Down	Devon	13	G4
Whigstreet	Angus	234	D6
Whilton	Nhants	84	C2
Whimble	Devon	11	L2
Whimple	Devon	14	B3
Whimpwell Green	Norfk	123	H5
Whinburgh	Norfk	105	K2
Whin Lane End	Lancs	147	H7
Whinnie Liggate	D & G	175	H4
Whinnow	Cumb	177	J8
Whinnyfold	Abers	257	K5
Whinny Hill	S on T	169	K7
Whippingham	IoW	19	H5
Whipsnade	C Beds	68	C3
Whipton	Devon	13	M4
Whirlow	Sheff	132	F3
Whisby	Lincs	135	H6
Whissendine	Rutlnd	117	L8
Whissonsett	Norfk	121	K7
Whistlefield	Ag & B	218	C8
Whistlefield Inn	Ag & B	217	J8
Whistley Green	Wokham	49	J4
Whiston	Knows	129	L2
Whiston	Nhants	85	G3
Whiston	Rothm	133	J2
Whiston	Staffs	114	D8
Whiston	Staffs	115	G2
Whiston Cross	Shrops	97	H3
Whiston Eaves	Staffs	115	G2
Whitacre Fields	Warwks	99	H5
Whitbeck	Cumb	155	K5
Whitbourne	Herefs	81	G4
Whitburn	S Tyne	181	K6
Whitburn	W Loth	210	C6
Whitby	Ches W	129	J4
Whitby	N York	171	K8
Whitbyheath	Ches W	129	J5
Whitchester	Border	212	F7
Whitchurch	BaNES	45	J5
Whitchurch	Bucks	67	J3
Whitchurch	Cardif	43	J5
Whitchurch	Devon	12	C8
Whitchurch	Hants	34	F1
Whitchurch	Herefs	63	H4
Whitchurch	Oxon	48	F3
Whitchurch	Pembks	74	C7
Whitchurch	Shrops	113	J3
Whitchurch Canonicorum	Dorset	15	J3
Whitchurch Hill	Oxon	48	F3
Whitcombe	Dorset	16	D5
Whitcot	Shrops	95	J5
Whitcott Keysett	Shrops	95	G6
Whiteacre	Kent	40	E5
Whiteacre Heath	Warwks	99	G5
Whiteash Green	Essex	71	J1
White Ball	Somset	29	K7
Whitebridge	Highld	250	E8
Whitebrook	Mons	63	G6
Whitebushes	Surrey	37	L1
Whitecairns	Abers	257	G8
Whitechapel	Gt Lon	51	J3
White Chapel	Lancs	147	L7
Whitechurch	Pembks	75	K5
Whitecliffe	Gloucs	63	H5
White Colne	Essex	72	C1
White Coppice	Lancs	139	J4
Whitecraig	E Loth	211	K5
Whitecroft	Gloucs	63	J6
Whitecrook	D & G	172	F3
Whitecross	Cnwll	2	E4
White Cross	Cnwll	3	H6
Whitecross	Cnwll	10	D8
Whitecross	Falk	210	C4
White End	Worcs	81	H8
Whiteface	Highld	263	J2
Whitefarland	N Ayrs	194	D3
Whitefaulds	S Ayrs	183	H1
Whitefield	Bury	140	B6
Whitefield	Devon	28	C4
Whitefield	Somset	29	K5
Whitefield Lane End	Knows	129	K2
Whiteford	Abers	256	C6
Whitegate	Ches W	130	C6
Whitehall	Hants	49	H8
Whitehall	Ork	275	e3
Whitehall	W Susx	37	H6
Whitehaven	Cumb	164	C7
Whitehill	Kent	40	C3
Whitehill	Leics	99	L1
Whitehill and Bordon	Hants	36	A4
Whitehills	Abers	268	B3
Whitehouse	Abers	256	A8
Whitehouse	Ag & B	206	C6
Whitehouse Common	Birm	98	E4
Whitekirk	E Loth	212	D3
White Kirkley	Dur	168	C3
White Lackington	Dorset	16	D3
Whitelackington	Somset	30	F7
White Ladies Aston	Worcs	81	L4
Whiteleaf	Bucks	67	K6
White-le-Head	Dur	180	E7
Whiteley	Hants	19	J2
Whiteley Bank	IoW	19	J7
Whiteley Green	Ches E	131	H4
Whiteley Village	Surrey	50	E6
Whitemans Green	W Susx	22	D2
White Mill	Carmth	58	E4
Whitemire	Moray	253	J1
Whitemoor	C Nott	116	F3
Whitemoor	Cnwll	5	G3
Whitemoor	Derbys	116	B2
Whitemoor	Staffs	131	H7
Whiteness	Shet	281	d6
White Notley	Essex	71	J3
Whiteoak Green	Oxon	65	M4
White Ox Mead	BaNES	45	L7
Whiteparish	Wilts	34	B6
White Pit	Lincs	137	G4
Whiterashes	Abers	256	F7
White Roding	Essex	70	E4
Whiterow	Highld	280	E6
Whiterow	Moray	265	G8
Whiteshill	Gloucs	64	B5
Whitesmith	E Susx	23	J4
White Stake	Lancs	139	G3
Whitestaunton	Somset	30	D8
Whitestone	Devon	13	K4
White Stone	Herefs	80	D6
Whitestone Cross	Devon	13	L4
Whitestreet Green	Suffk	89	K7
Whitewall Corner	N York	152	B2
White Waltham	W & M	49	K3
Whiteway	BaNES	45	L6
Whiteway	Gloucs	64	C5
Whitewell	Lancs	148	B5
Whiteworks	Devon	12	E8
Whitfield	C Dund	234	C8
Whitfield	Kent	41	J6
Whitfield	Nhants	84	B7
Whitfield	Nthumb	179	H7
Whitfield	S Glos	63	K8
Whitfield Hall	Nthumb	179	H7
Whitford	Devon	14	F3
Whitford	Flints	128	D4
Whitgift	E R Yk	143	K3
Whitgreave	Staffs	114	D6
Whithorn	D & G	174	C6
Whiting Bay	N Ayrs	195	G6
Whitkirk	Leeds	142	B1
Whitland	Carmth	55	L3
Whitlaw	Border	188	E4
Whitletts	S Ayrs	196	D6
Whitley	N York	142	E4
Whitley	Readg	49	H5
Whitley	Sheff	133	G1
Whitley	Wilts	46	C5
Whitley Bay	N Tyne	181	J4
Whitley Bay Crematorium	N Tyne	181	J4
Whitley Chapel	Nthumb	179	L7
Whitley Heath	Staffs	114	C6
Whitley Lower	Kirk	141	K4
Whitley Row	Kent	38	D3
Whitlock's End	Solhll	98	E8
Whitminster	Gloucs	63	M5
Whitmore	Dorset	17	L1
Whitmore	Staffs	114	C3
Whitnage	Devon	29	J7
Whitnash	Warwks	83	H3
Whitney-on-Wye	Herefs	79	J5
Whitrigg	Cumb	165	G3
Whitrigg	Cumb	177	H7
Whitrigglees	Cumb	177	H7
Whitsbury	Hants	33	K7
Whitsome	Border	202	D3
Whitson	Newpt	44	D2
Whitstable	Kent	40	E2
Whitstone	Cnwll	11	K3
Whittingham	Nthumb	190	F4
Whittingslow	Shrops	95	K5
Whittington	Derbys	133	H4
Whittington	Gloucs	64	E3
Whittington	Lancs	157	K7
Whittington	Norfk	104	E3
Whittington	Shrops	112	E5
Whittington	Staffs	97	J6
Whittington	Staffs	98	F2
Whittington	Warwks	99	J4
Whittington	Worcs	81	K4
Whittington Moor	Derbys	133	G5
Whittlebury	Nhants	84	D6
Whittle-le-Woods	Lancs	139	H3
Whittlesey	Cambs	102	F4
Whittlesford	Cambs	87	K5
Whittlestone Head	Bl w D	139	L4
Whitton	N Linc	143	M3
Whitton	Nthumb	190	F6
Whitton	Powys	79	J2
Whitton	S on T	169	K6
Whitton	Shrops	80	D1
Whitton	Suffk	90	D5
Whittonditch	Wilts	47	L4
Whittonstall	Nthumb	180	C7
Whitway	Hants	48	C7
Whitwell	Derbys	133	K4
Whitwell	Herts	68	F3
Whitwell	IoW	19	J8
Whitwell	N York	160	D3
Whitwell	Rutlnd	101	K2
Whitwell-on-the-Hill	N York	151	M3
Whitwell Street	Norfk	122	B7
Whitwick	Leics	116	D8
Whitwood	Wakefd	142	B4
Whitworth	Lancs	140	D4
Whixall	Shrops	113	H4
Whixley	N York	150	F4
Whorlton	Dur	168	E7
Whorlton	N York	161	G2
Whyle	Herefs	80	D3
Whyteleafe	Surrey	51	J7
Wibdon	Gloucs	63	H7
Wibsey	C Brad	141	J2
Wibtoft	Warwks	100	B6
Wichenford	Worcs	81	H3
Wichling	Kent	40	B4
Wick	Bmouth	18	B5
Wick	Devon	14	E2
Wick	Highld	280	E6
Wick	S Glos	45	K4
Wick	Somset	30	B2
Wick	Somset	30	F5
Wick	V Glam	42	D7
Wick	W Susx	21	H6
Wick	Wilts	33	L6
Wick	Worcs	81	M6
Wicken	Cambs	88	B1
Wicken	Nhants	84	E7
Wicken Bonhunt	Essex	87	K8
Wickenby	Lincs	136	A3
Wick End	Bed	85	K5
Wicken Green Village	Norfk	121	J5
Wickersley	Rothm	133	J2
Wicker Street Green	Suffk	89	K6
Wickford	Essex	71	H8
Wickham	Hants	19	K2
Wickham	W Berk	48	B5
Wickham Bishops	Essex	71	K5
Wickhambreaux	Kent	41	H3
Wickhambrook	Suffk	88	E4
Wickhamford	Worcs	82	C7
Wickham Green	Suffk	90	C2
Wickham Green	W Berk	48	B4
Wickham Heath	W Berk	48	B5

Wickham Market Suffk 91 G4
Wickhampton Norfk 107 J2
Wickham St Paul Essex 89 G7
Wickham Skeith Suffk 90 C2
Wickham Street Suffk 88 F4
Wickham Street Suffk 90 C1
Wickhurst Green W Susx 37 H5
Wicklewood Norfk 106 B3
Wickmere Norfk 122 D5
Wick St Lawrence N Som 44 D6
Wickstreet E Susx 23 J5
Wickwar S Glos 45 L1
Widdington Essex 70 D1
Widdop Calder 140 D1
Widdrington Nthumb 191 K7
Widdrington Station Nthumb 191 J7
Widecombe in the Moor
    Devon 13 G7
Widegates Cnwll 6 B3
Widemouth Bay Cnwll 11 H2
Wide Open N Tyne 181 G4
Widford Essex 71 G6
Widford Herts 70 B4
Widham Wilts 47 G1
Widley Hants 19 M2
Widmer End Bucks 67 L7
Widmerpool Notts 117 G6
Widmore Gt Lon 51 L5
Widnes Halton 129 L3
Widnes Crematorium Halton ... 129 L2
Widworthy Devon 14 F3
Wigan Wigan 139 H6
Wigan Crematorium Wigan ... 139 H7
Wigborough Somset 31 G7
Wiggaton Devon 14 C4
Wiggenhall St Germans Norfk ... 120 D8
Wiggenhall St Mary Magdalen
    Norfk 104 B1
Wiggenhall St Mary the
    Virgin Norfk 104 B1
Wiggenhall St Peter Norfk ... 104 C1
Wiggens Green Essex 88 D6
Wiggenstall Staffs 132 B7
Wiggington Shrops 112 E4
Wigginton C York 151 J4
Wigginton Herts 68 B5
Wigginton Oxon 83 J8
Wigginton Staffs 99 G2
Wigginton Bottom Herts ... 68 B5
Wigglesworth N York 148 E4
Wiggonby Cumb 177 J8
Wiggonholt W Susx 21 H3
Wighill N York 151 G6
Wighton Norfk 121 L3
Wightwick Wolves 97 K4
Wigley Derbys 132 F5
Wigley Hants 34 D7
Wigmore Herefs 80 A2
Wigmore Medway 53 G6
Wigsley Notts 135 G5
Wigsthorpe Nhants 102 A6
Wigston Leics 100 D4
Wigston Fields Leics 100 D3
Wigston Parva Leics 100 A5
Wigthorpe Notts 134 B3
Wigtoft Lincs 119 J4
Wigton Cumb 165 H1
Wigtown D & G 174 C4
Wigtwizzle Sheff 141 L8
Wike Leeds 150 D7
Wilbarston Nhants 101 H5
Wilberfoss E R Yk 151 M5
Wilburton Cambs 103 K8
Wilby Nhants 85 G2
Wilby Norfk 105 L5
Wilby Suffk 90 F1
Wilcot Wilts 47 H6
Wilcott Shrops 112 F7
Wilcrick Newpt 44 E2
Wilday Green Derbys 132 F5
Wildboarclough Ches E 131 K6
Wilden Bed 86 B4
Wilden Worcs 81 J1
Wilde Street Suffk 104 D7
Wildhern Hants 34 D1
Wildhill Herts 69 H5
Wildmanbridge S Lans 209 L8
Wildmoor Hants 49 G7
Wildmoor Worcs 98 B8
Wildsworth Lincs 143 K8
Wilford C Nott 116 F4
Wilford Hill Crematorium
    Notts 116 F4
Wilkesley Ches E 113 K3
Wilkhaven Highld 264 E3
Wilkieston W Loth 210 F5
Wilkin's Green Herts 69 G5
Wilksby Lincs 136 E7
Willand Devon 29 J8

Willards Hill E Susx 24 C2
Willaston Ches E 113 L1
Willaston Ches W 129 H4
Willen M Keyn 85 G7
Willenhall Covtry 99 K8
Willenhall Wsall 98 B4
Willerby E R Yk 144 C2
Willerby N York 163 H6
Willersey Gloucs 82 D7
Willersley Herefs 79 K6
Willesborough Kent 40 D7
Willesborough Lees Kent ... 40 D7
Willesden Gt Lon 51 G2
Willesleigh Devon 27 L4
Willesley Wilts 46 B1
Willett Somset 29 K4
Willey Shrops 96 F3
Willey Warwks 100 B6
Willey Green Surrey 50 B8
Williamscot Oxon 83 L6
Williamstown Rhondd 42 F4
Willian Herts 69 G1
Willicote Warwks 82 E5
Willingale Essex 70 E5
Willingdon E Susx 23 K6
Willingham Cambs 87 H1
Willingham by Stow Lincs ... 135 H3
Willingham Green Cambs ... 88 C4
Willington Bed 86 C5
Willington Derbys 116 A6
Willington Dur 169 G4
Willington Kent 39 K3
Willington N Tyne 181 H5
Willington Warwks 83 G7
Willington Corner Ches W ... 129 M6
Willitoft E R Yk 143 J1
Williton Somset 29 K3
Willoughby Lincs 137 J5
Willoughby Warwks 83 M2
Willoughby Hills Lincs 119 K2
Willoughby-on-the-Wolds
    Notts 117 H6
Willoughby Waterleys Leics ... 100 C5
Willoughton Lincs 135 J1
Willow Green Ches W 130 B4
Willows Green Essex 71 H3
Willsbridge S Glos 45 K5
Willsworthy Devon 12 D6
Willtown Somset 30 F6
Wilmcote Warwks 82 E4
Wilmington BaNES 45 K6
Wilmington Devon 14 F3
Wilmington E Susx 23 J6
Wilmington Kent 52 B4
Wilmslow Ches E 131 G3
Wilnecote Staffs 99 G3
Wilpshire Lancs 139 K1
Wilsden C Brad 149 K8
Wilsford Lincs 118 D3
Wilsford Wilts 33 K3
Wilsford Wilts 47 G7
Wilsham Devon 28 D1
Wilshaw Kirk 141 H6
Wilsill N York 150 A3
Wilsley Green Kent 39 K6
Wilsley Pound Kent 39 K6
Wilson Herefs 63 H2
Wilson Leics 116 C6
Wilsontown S Lans 198 F2
Wilstead Bed 85 L6
Wilsthorpe Lincs 102 B1
Wilstone Herts 67 L4
Wilstone Green Herts 67 M4
Wilton Cumb 164 D8
Wilton Herefs 63 H2
Wilton N York 162 F6
Wilton R & Cl 170 D6
Wilton Wilts 33 J4
Wilton Wilts 47 K6
Wilton Dean Border 188 E3
Wimbish Essex 88 B7
Wimbish Green Essex 88 C8
Wimbledon Gt Lon 51 G5
Wimblington Cambs 103 J5
Wimboldsley Ches W 130 D7
Wimborne Minster Dorset... 17 K3
Wimborne St Giles Dorset ... 33 H8
Wimbotsham Norfk 104 C2
Wimpole Cambs 87 G5
Wimpstone Warwks 82 F5
Wincanton Somset 32 B5
Winceby Lincs 136 F6
Wincham Ches W 130 C4
Winchburgh W Loth 210 E4
Winchcombe Gloucs 64 D7
Winchelsea E Susx 25 G4
Winchelsea Beach E Susx ... 25 G4
Winchester Hants 35 G5
Winchet Hill Kent 39 J5

Winchfield Hants............ 49 J8
Winchmore Hill Bucks 68 B8
Winchmore Hill Gt Lon 69 J8
Wincle Ches E 131 J6
Wincobank Sheff 133 G1
Winder Cumb 164 D7
Windermere Cumb 156 F3
Winderton Warwks 83 H7
Windhill Highld 250 F2
Windlehurst Stockp 131 J3
Windlesham Surrey 50 A6
Windmill Cnwll 10 B7
Windmill Derbys 132 C4
Windmill Hill E Susx 23 L5
Windmill Hill Somset 30 D7
Windrush Gloucs 65 J4
Windsole Abers 267 L4
Windsor W & M 50 B4
Windsoredge Gloucs 64 B7
Windsor Green Suffk 89 H4
Windygates Fife 222 F7
Windyharbour Ches E 131 G5
Windy Hill Wrexhm 129 G8
Wineham W Susx 22 C3
Winestead E R Yk 145 J3
Winewall Lancs 148 F7
Winfarthing Norfk 106 C6
Winford IoW 19 J6
Winford N Som 45 G6
Winforton Herefs 79 K6
Winfrith Newburgh Dorset ... 16 F5
Wing Bucks 67 L3
Wing Rutlnd 101 K3
Wingate Dur 169 L3
Wingates Bolton 139 K6
Wingates Nthumb 191 G7
Wingerworth Derbys 133 G6
Wingfield C Beds 68 C2
Wingfield Suffk 106 E7
Wingfield Wilts 46 B7
Wingfield Green Suffk 106 E7
Wingham Kent 41 H4
Wingland Lincs 120 B6
Wingmore Kent 41 G6
Wingrave Bucks 67 L3
Winkburn Notts 134 E7
Winkfield Br For 49 L4
Winkfield Row Br For 49 L5
Winkhill Staffs 115 H1
Winkhurst Green Kent 38 D3
Winkleigh Devon 12 F1
Winksley N York 150 C2
Winkton Dorset 18 B4
Winlaton Gatesd 180 E6
Winlaton Mill Gatesd 180 E6
Winless Highld 280 D5
Winllan Powys 112 C7
Winmarleigh Lancs 147 J6
Winnall Hants 35 G5
Winnersh Wokham 49 J5
Winnington Ches W 130 C5
Winscales Cumb 164 D5
Winscombe N Som 44 E7
Winsford Ches W 130 C6
Winsford Somset 28 F4
Winsham Devon 27 J3
Winsham Somset 15 J2
Winshill Staffs 115 M7
Winshwen Swans 57 J5
Winskill Cumb 166 D4
Winslade Hants 35 K1
Winsley Wilts 46 A6
Winslow Bucks 67 J2
Winson Gloucs 65 G5
Winsor Hants 34 D8
Winster Cumb 156 F4
Winster Derbys 132 E7
Winston Dur 168 F7
Winston Suffk 90 E3
Winstone Gloucs 64 D5
Winswell Devon 27 J8
Winterborne Came Dorset ... 16 D5
Winterborne Clenston Dorset ... 17 G2
Winterborne Herringston
    Dorset 16 D5
Winterborne Houghton
    Dorset 16 F2
Winterborne Kingston Dorset... 17 G3
Winterborne Monkton Dorset... 16 C5
Winterborne Stickland Dorset ... 16 F2
Winterborne Tomson Dorset ... 17 G3
Winterborne Whitechurch
    Dorset 17 G3
Winterborne Zelston Dorset ... 17 H3
Winterbourne S Glos 45 J3
Winterbourne W Berk 48 C4
Winterbourne Abbas Dorset ... 16 B4
Winterbourne Bassett Wilts ... 47 G4
Winterbourne Dauntsey Wilts ... 33 L4

Winterbourne Earls Wilts 33 L4
Winterbourne Gunner Wilts 33 L4
Winterbourne Monkton Wilts... 47 G4
Winterbourne Steepleton
    Dorset 16 B4
Winterbourne Stoke Wilts 33 J3
Winterbrook Oxon 48 F1
Winterburn N York 149 G4
Winteringham N Linc 144 A3
Winterley Ches E 130 E8
Wintersett Wakefd 142 B4
Winterslow Wilts 34 A4
Winterton N Linc 144 A4
Winterton-on-Sea Norfk ... 123 K7
Winthorpe Lincs 137 K6
Winthorpe Notts 135 G8
Winton Bmouth 17 L4
Winton Cumb 167 H8
Winton E Susx 23 H6
Winton N York 160 F3
Wintringham N York 162 F8
Winwick Cambs 102 B7
Winwick Nhants 100 D8
Winwick Warrtn 130 B5
Wirksworth Derbys 115 M1
Wirswall Ches E 113 J3
Wisbech Cambs 103 J2
Wisbech St Mary Cambs ... 103 J2
Wisborough Green W Susx ... 37 G5
Wiseman's Bridge Pembks ... 55 K5
Wiseton Notts 134 E2
Wishanger Gloucs 64 D5
Wishaw N Lans 209 L7
Wishaw Warwks 98 F4
Wisley Surrey 50 D7
Wispington Lincs 136 D5
Wissenden Kent 40 B7
Wissett Suffk 107 H7
Wissington Norfk 104 D4
Wissington Suffk 89 J8
Wistanstow Shrops 95 K6
Wistanswick Shrops 113 L5
Wistaston Ches E 113 L1
Wistaston Green Ches E ... 130 D8
Wisterfield Ches E 131 G5
Wiston Pembks 55 H3
Wiston S Lans 198 F6
Wiston W Susx 21 K4
Wistow Cambs 102 F7
Wistow Leics 100 E4
Wistow N York 142 F1
Wiswell Lancs 148 C8
Witcham Cambs 103 J7
Witchampton Dorset 17 J2
Witchford Cambs 103 K7
Witcombe Somset 31 G6
Witham Essex 71 K4
Witham Friary Somset 32 B3
Witham on the Hill Lincs 118 D8
Witham St Hughs Lincs 135 H7
Withcall Lincs 136 E3
Withdean Br & H 22 D5
Witherenden Hill E Susx 23 L2
Witheridge Devon 28 D8
Witherley Leics 99 J4
Withern Lincs 137 H3
Withernsea E R Yk 145 J2
Withernwick E R Yk 153 M7
Withersdale Street Suffk 106 F7
Withersfield Suffk 88 D5
Witherslack Cumb 156 F5
Withiel Cnwll 5 G2
Withiel Florey Somset 29 H4
Withielgoose Cnwll 5 G2
Withington Gloucs 64 F4
Withington Herefs 80 D6
Withington Manch 131 G1
Withington Shrops 96 D1
Withington Staffs 115 G5
Withington Green Ches E ... 130 F5
Withington Marsh Herefs ... 80 D6
Withleigh Devon 28 F8
Withnell Lancs 139 J2
Withybed Green Worcs 82 B1
Withybrook Warwks 99 L6
Withycombe Somset 29 J3
Withyham E Susx 38 D6
Withy Mills BaNES 45 K7
Withypool Somset 28 E4
Withywood Bristl 45 H5
Witley Surrey 36 E3
Witnesham Suffk 90 E5
Witney Oxon 65 M5
Wittering C Pete 102 B3
Wittersham Kent 25 G2
Witton Birm 98 D5
Witton Norfk 107 G2
Witton Norfk 123 G8
Witton Gilbert Dur 169 G2

Place	County	Page	Grid
Witton Green	Norfk	107	J3
Witton le Wear	Dur	168	F4
Witton Park	Dur	168	F4
Wiveliscombe	Somset	29	K5
Wivelrod	Hants	35	K3
Wivelsfield	E Susx	22	E3
Wivelsfield Green	E Susx	22	E3
Wivelsfield Station	W Susx	22	E3
Wivenhoe	Essex	72	F3
Wivenhoe Cross	Essex	72	F2
Wiveton	Norfk	122	A3
Wix	Essex	73	H2
Wixams	Bed	85	L6
Wixford	Warwks	82	C4
Wix Green	Essex	73	H2
Wixhill	Shrops	113	J6
Wixoe	Suffk	88	E6
Woburn	C Beds	85	J8
Woburn Sands	M Keyn	85	H8
Wokefield Park	W Berk	49	G6
Woking	Surrey	50	C7
Woking Crematorium	Surrey	50	B7
Wokingham	Wokham	49	K5
Wolborough	Devon	13	K8
Woldingham	Surrey	51	K7
Wold Newton	E R Yk	163	J8
Wold Newton	NE Lin	145	G8
Wolfclyde	S Lans	199	H6
Wolferlow	Herefs	80	F3
Wolferton	Norfk	120	E6
Wolfhampcote	Warwks	83	M2
Wolfhill	P & K	233	H8
Wolf Hills	Nthumb	179	G7
Wolf's Castle	Pembks	74	F6
Wolfsdale	Pembks	54	F3
Wollaston	Dudley	97	K6
Wollaston	Nhants	85	H3
Wollaston	Shrops	95	H1
Wollaton	C Nott	116	E4
Wolleigh	Devon	13	J6
Wollerton	Shrops	113	K5
Wollescote	Dudley	97	L6
Wolseley Bridge	Staffs	115	G7
Wolsingham	Dur	168	D3
Wolstanton	Staffs	114	D2
Wolstenholme	Rochdl	140	C5
Wolston	Warwks	99	L8
Wolsty	Cumb	176	E8
Wolvercote	Oxon	66	D5
Wolverhampton	Wolves	97	K4
Wolverley	Shrops	113	G5
Wolverley	Worcs	97	J7
Wolverton	Hants	48	E7
Wolverton	Kent	41	H6
Wolverton	M Keyn	84	F7
Wolverton	Warwks	82	F3
Wolverton	Wilts	32	C4
Wolverton Common	Hants	48	E7
Wolvesnewton	Mons	62	F7
Wolvey	Warwks	99	L6
Wolvey Heath	Warwks	99	L5
Wolviston	S on T	170	B5
Wombleton	N York	161	L6
Wombourne	Staffs	97	K5
Wombwell	Barns	142	B7
Womenswold	Kent	41	H5
Womersley	N York	142	E4
Wonastow	Mons	62	F5
Wonersh	Surrey	36	F2
Wonford	Devon	13	L4
Wonson	Devon	12	F5
Wonston	Dorset	16	E1
Wonston	Hants	35	G3
Wooburn	Bucks	49	M2
Wooburn Green	Bucks	49	M1
Wooburn Moor	Bucks	49	M1
Woodacott	Devon	11	M1
Woodale	N York	159	J6
Woodall	Rothm	133	J3
Woodbank	Ches W	129	H5
Woodbastwick	Norfk	123	G8
Woodbeck	Notts	134	F4
Wood Bevington	Warwks	82	C4
Woodborough	Notts	117	G2
Woodborough	Wilts	47	G7
Woodbridge	Devon	14	E4
Woodbridge	Dorset	32	E7
Woodbridge	Suffk	91	G5
Wood Burcote	Nhants	84	D6
Woodbury	Devon	14	B5
Woodbury Salterton	Devon	14	B5
Woodchester	Gloucs	64	B6
Woodchurch	Kent	40	B8
Woodchurch	Wirral	129	G2
Woodcombe	Somset	29	G2
Woodcote	Gt Lon	51	J6
Woodcote	Oxon	48	F3
Woodcote	Wrekin	114	B8
Woodcote Green	Worcs	81	L1
Woodcott	Hants	48	B7
Woodcroft	Gloucs	63	G7
Woodcutts	Dorset	33	G7
Wood Dalling	Norfk	122	B6
Woodditton	Cambs	88	D3
Woodeaton	Oxon	66	D5
Wood Eaton	Staffs	114	C7
Wooden	Pembks	55	J6
Wood End	Bed	85	K6
Wood End	Bed	86	B2
Wood End	C Beds	85	J7
Wood End	Cambs	103	H8
Wood End	Gt Lon	50	E3
Wood End	Herts	69	J2
Woodend	Highld	228	B3
Woodend	Nhants	84	B5
Woodend	Staffs	115	K6
Woodend	W Loth	210	B5
Woodend	W Susx	20	D5
Wood End	Warwks	82	D1
Wood End	Warwks	99	H4
Wood End	Warwks	99	J6
Wood End	Wolves	97	L3
Wood Enderby	Lincs	136	E6
Woodend Green	Essex	70	E2
Woodfalls	Wilts	33	L6
Woodford	Cnwll	26	C8
Woodford	Devon	8	B5
Woodford	Gloucs	63	K7
Woodford	Gt Lon	69	L8
Woodford	Nhants	101	L8
Woodford	Stockp	131	H3
Woodford Bridge	Gt Lon	51	L1
Woodford Green	Gt Lon	69	L8
Woodford Halse	Nhants	84	A5
Woodford Wells	Gt Lon	69	L8
Woodgate	Birm	98	C6
Woodgate	Devon	29	K7
Woodgate	Norfk	121	K8
Woodgate	Norfk	121	M8
Woodgate	W Susx	20	F6
Woodgate	Worcs	81	M2
Wood Green	Gt Lon	51	J1
Woodgreen	Hants	33	L7
Woodgreen	Oxon	66	A5
Woodhall	N York	159	H4
Woodhall	Leeds	141	K1
Woodhall Spa	Lincs	136	C7
Woodham	Bucks	67	H3
Woodham	Dur	169	H5
Woodham	Surrey	50	D6
Woodham Ferrers	Essex	71	J7
Woodham Mortimer	Essex	71	K6
Woodham Walter	Essex	71	K5
Wood Hayes	Wolves	97	L3
Woodhead	Abers	256	E4
Woodhill	Shrops	97	G6
Woodhill	Somset	30	E5
Woodhorn	Nthumb	181	H1
Woodhorn Demesne	Nthumb	181	H1
Woodhouse	Leeds	141	L1
Woodhouse	Leics	116	F8
Woodhouse	Sheff	133	H3
Woodhouse	Wakefd	142	B3
Woodhouse Eaves	Leics	116	F8
Woodhouse Green	Staffs	131	H7
Woodhouselee	Mdloth	211	H6
Woodhouselees	D & G	177	L4
Woodhouse Mill	Sheff	133	H3
Woodhouses	Cumb	177	K8
Woodhouses	Oldham	140	D7
Woodhouses	Staffs	98	D2
Woodhouses	Staffs	115	J7
Woodhuish	Devon	8	D4
Woodhurst	Cambs	103	G8
Woodingdean	Br & H.	22	E6
Woodkirk	Leeds	141	L3
Woodland	Abers	256	F7
Woodland	Devon	7	J4
Woodland	Devon	8	B1
Woodland	Dur	168	D5
Woodland	Kent	40	F7
Woodland	S Ayrs	182	F4
Woodland Head	Devon	13	H3
Woodlands	Abers	245	H4
Woodlands	Donc	142	E6
Woodlands	Dorset	17	L1
Woodlands	Hants	18	E1
Woodlands	Kent	52	C6
Woodlands	N York	150	D5
Woodlands	Somset	29	L3
Woodlands (Coleshill) Crematorium	Warwks	98	F5
Woodlands Park	W & M	49	L3
Woodlands St Mary	W Berk	47	M4
Woodlands (Scarborough) Crematorium	N York	163	J5
Woodlands (Scunthorpe) Crematorium	N Linc	143	M5
Woodland Street	Somset	31	J3
Woodland View	Sheff	132	F2
Wood Lane	Shrops	112	F5
Wood Lane	Staffs	114	C2
Woodleigh	Devon	7	L5
Woodlesford	Leeds	142	B2
Woodley	Stockp	131	J1
Woodley	Wokham	49	J4
Woodmancote	Gloucs	63	M7
Woodmancote	Gloucs	64	E2
Woodmancote	Gloucs	64	E5
Woodmancote	W Susx	20	C5
Woodmancote	W Susx	22	C4
Woodmancote	Worcs	81	L6
Woodmancott	Hants	35	H2
Woodmansey	E R Yk	153	G8
Woodmansgreen	W Susx	36	C5
Woodmansterne	Surrey	51	H7
Woodmanton	Devon	14	B5
Woodmarsh	Wilts	46	B7
Woodmill	Staffs	115	J7
Woodminton	Wilts	33	H6
Woodnesborough	Kent	41	J4
Woodnewton	Nhants	102	A4
Woodnook	Notts	116	D1
Wood Norton	Norfk	121	M6
Woodplumpton	Lancs	139	G1
Woodrising	Norfk	105	K3
Wood Row	Leeds	142	B2
Woodrow	Worcs	97	K8
Wood's Corner	E Susx	24	B3
Woods Eaves	Herefs	79	K5
Woodseaves	Shrops	113	M5
Woodseaves	Staffs	114	B6
Woodsend	Wilts	47	J4
Woodsetts	Rothm	133	L3
Woodsford	Dorset	16	E4
Wood's Green	E Susx	39	G6
Woodside	Br For	50	B5
Woodside	Cumb	164	D4
Woodside	Essex	70	C6
Woodside	Fife	223	G5
Woodside	Gt Lon	51	J5
Woodside	Hants	18	E5
Woodside	Herts	69	H5
Woodside	P & K	233	J7
Woodside Crematorium	Inver	207	M4
Woodside Green	Kent	40	B4
Woodstock	Oxon	66	C4
Woodstock	Pembks	75	H7
Woodston	C Pete	102	D4
Wood Street	Norfk	123	H7
Wood Street Village	Surrey	36	E1
Woodthorpe	Derbys	133	J5
Woodthorpe	Leics	116	F8
Woodthorpe	Lincs	137	H4
Woodton	Norfk	106	F4
Woodtown	Devon	27	G6
Woodvale	Sefton	138	C5
Woodvale Crematorium	Br & H	22	E6
Woodville	Derbys	116	A7
Woodwall Green	Staffs	114	B5
Wood Walton	Cambs	102	E7
Woodyates	Dorset	33	H7
Woody Bay	Devon	28	B1
Woofferton	Shrops	80	C2
Wookey	Somset	31	H2
Wookey Hole	Somset	31	H2
Wool	Dorset	17	G5
Woolacombe	Devon	27	H2
Woolage Green	Kent	41	H5
Woolage Village	Kent	41	H5
Woolaston	Gloucs	63	H7
Woolaston Common	Gloucs	63	H6
Woolavington	Somset	30	E3
Woolbeding	W Susx	36	C6
Woolbrook	Devon	14	D5
Woolcotts	Somset	29	H4
Wooldale	Kirk	141	L6
Wooler	Nthumb	202	F7
Woolfardisworthy	Devon	13	J1
Woolfardisworthy	Devon	26	F6
Woolfold	Bury	140	B5
Woolfords	S Lans	199	G2
Woolhampton	W Berk	48	E5
Woolhope	Herefs	80	E8
Woolland	Dorset	16	E1
Woollard	BaNES	45	J6
Woollensbrook	Herts	69	K5
Woolley	BaNES	45	L5
Woolley	Cambs	102	C8
Woolley	Cnwll	26	D7
Woolley	Derbys	133	G7
Woolley	Wakefd	141	M5
Woolley Bridge	Derbys	131	K1
Woolley Green	W & M	49	K3
Woolmere Green	Worcs	81	M3
Woolmer Green	Herts	69	H3
Woolmerston	Somset	30	D4
Woolminstone	Somset	15	J1
Woolpack	Kent	39	L6
Woolpit	Suffk	89	K3
Woolpit Green	Suffk	89	K3
Woolscott	Warwks	83	L2
Woolsgrove	Devon	13	J2
Woolsington	N u Ty	180	F5
Woolstaston	Shrops	95	L4
Woolsthorpe	Lincs	117	L5
Woolsthorpe-by-Colsterworth	Lincs	118	B6
Woolston	C Sotn	19	G2
Woolston	Devon	7	L5
Woolston	Devon	7	L6
Woolston	Shrops	95	K6
Woolston	Shrops	112	D6
Woolston	Somset	29	K3
Woolston	Somset	31	L5
Woolston	Warrtn	130	C2
Woolstone	Gloucs	64	D1
Woolstone	M Keyn	85	G7
Woolstone	Oxon	47	L2
Woolston Green	Devon	8	A2
Woolton	Lpool	129	K2
Woolton Hill	Hants	48	B6
Woolverstone	Suffk	90	E7
Woolverton	Somset	46	A8
Woolwich	Gt Lon	51	L3
Woonton	Herefs	79	L5
Woonton	Herefs	80	D3
Wooperton	Nthumb	190	F2
Woore	Shrops	114	A3
Wootten Green	Suffk	90	F1
Wootton	Bed	85	K6
Wootton	Hants	18	C4
Wootton	Herefs	79	L5
Wootton	IoW	19	J5
Wootton	Kent	41	H6
Wootton	N Linc	144	D4
Wootton	Nhants	84	E4
Wootton	Oxon	66	B3
Wootton	Oxon	66	C6
Wootton	Shrops	112	D6
Wootton	Staffs	114	C6
Wootton	Staffs	115	H3
Wootton Bassett	Wilts	46	F3
Wootton Bridge	IoW	19	J5
Wootton Broadmead	Bed	85	K6
Wootton Common	IoW	19	J5
Wootton Courtenay	Somset	29	G2
Wootton Fitzpaine	Dorset	15	J3
Wootton Rivers	Wilts	47	J6
Wootton St Lawrence	Hants	48	E8
Wootton Wawen	Warwks	82	E3
Worcester	Worcs	81	K4
Worcester Crematorium	Worcs	81	K4
Worcester Park	Gt Lon	51	G6
Wordsley	Dudley	97	K6
Worfield	Shrops	97	G4
Worgret	Dorset	17	H5
Workhouse End	Bed	86	B5
Workhouse Green	Suffk	89	H7
Workington	Cumb	164	D5
Worksop	Notts	134	B4
Worlaby	Lincs	136	F4
Worlaby	N Linc	144	C5
Worlds End	Bucks	67	L5
Worlds End	Hants	19	L1
World's End	W Berk	48	C3
Worlds End	W Susx	22	E3
Worle	N Som	44	D6
Worleston	Ches E	130	C8
Worlingham	Suffk	107	J5
Worlington	Devon	28	D8
Worlington	Suffk	104	D8
Worlingworth	Suffk	90	F2
Wormald Green	N York	150	D3
Wormbridge	Herefs	62	E1
Wormegay	Norfk	104	D3
Wormelow Tump	Herefs	62	F1
Wormhill	Derbys	132	C5
Wormhill	Herefs	80	A7
Wormingford	Essex	72	D1
Worminghall	Bucks	66	F5
Wormington	Gloucs	82	B7
Worminster	Somset	31	J2
Wormit	Fife	223	G2
Wormleighton	Warwks	83	K4
Wormley	Herts	69	K6
Wormley	Surrey	36	E3
Wormleybury	Herts	69	K6
Wormley Hill	Donc	143	G4
Wormshill	Kent	39	M2
Wormsley	Herefs	80	A5
Worplesdon	Surrey	50	B8
Worrall	Sheff	132	F1
Worrall Hill	Gloucs	63	J4

Worsbrough Barns.................. 142 A7
Worsbrough Bridge Barns.......... 142 A7
Worsbrough Dale Barns............ 142 B7
Worsley Salfd..................... 139 M7
Worstead Norfk................... 122 F6
Worsthorne Lancs................. 140 C1
Worston Devon...................... 7 H4
Worston Lancs.................... 148 D7
Worth Kent........................ 41 K4
Worth Somset...................... 31 H2
Worth W Susx...................... 37 L4
Wortham Suffk.................... 106 B7
Worthen Shrops.................... 95 H2
Worthenbury Wrexhm............... 112 F2
Worthing Norfk................... 121 M7
Worthing W Susx................... 21 K6
Worthing Crematorium
    W Susx......................... 21 J5
Worthington Leics................ 116 C7
Worth Matravers Dorset............ 17 J7
Worthybrook Mons.................. 62 F5
Worting Hants..................... 48 F8
Wortley Barns.................... 141 M7
Wortley Leeds.................... 141 L1
Worton N York.................... 159 G5
Worton Wilts...................... 46 E7
Wortwell Norfk................... 106 F6
Wotherton Shrops.................. 95 G3
Wothorpe C Pete.................. 101 M2
Wotter Devon....................... 7 H3
Wotton Surrey..................... 37 H2
Wotton-under-Edge Gloucs.......... 63 M8
Wotton Underwood Bucks............ 67 G4
Woughton on the Green
    M Keyn......................... 85 G7
Wouldham Kent..................... 52 F6
Woundale Shrops................... 97 H5
Wrabness Essex.................... 73 J1
Wrafton Devon..................... 27 J4
Wragby Lincs..................... 136 B4
Wragby Wakefd.................... 142 C4
Wramplingham Norfk............... 106 C2
Wrangaton Devon.................... 7 K3
Wrangbrook Wakefd................ 142 D5
Wrangle Lincs.................... 119 M2
Wrangle Common Lincs............. 119 M1
Wrangle Lowgate Lincs............ 119 M1
Wrangway Somset................... 29 L7
Wrantage Somset................... 30 D6
Wrawby N Linc.................... 144 C6
Wraxall N Som..................... 44 F4
Wraxall Somset.................... 31 K4
Wray Lancs....................... 147 M2
Wray Castle Cumb................. 156 E3
Wraysbury W & M................... 50 C4
Wrayton Lancs.................... 147 M2
Wrea Green Lancs................. 138 E2
Wreaks End Cumb.................. 156 B5
Wreay Cumb....................... 166 B1
Wreay Cumb....................... 166 B6
Wrecclesham Surrey................ 36 B2
Wrekenton Gatesd................. 181 G7
Wrelton N York................... 162 D5
Wrenbury Ches E.................. 113 K2
Wrench Green N York.............. 163 H5
Wreningham Norfk................. 106 D4
Wrentham Suffk................... 107 K6
Wrenthorpe Wakefd................ 141 M3
Wrentnall Shrops.................. 95 K3
Wressle E R Yk................... 143 H2
Wressle N Linc................... 144 B6
Wrestlingworth C Beds............. 86 E5
Wretton Norfk.................... 104 D3
Wrexham Wrexhm................... 112 E2
Wrexham Industrial Estate
    Wrexhm........................ 112 F2
Wribbenhall Worcs................. 97 H8
Wrickton Shrops................... 96 E6
Wrightington Bar Lancs........... 139 G5
Wright's Green Essex.............. 70 D4
Wrinehill Staffs................. 114 B2
Wrington N Som.................... 44 F6
Writhlington BaNES................ 45 K8
Writtle Essex..................... 71 G6
Wrockwardine Wrekin............... 96 E1
Wroot N Linc..................... 143 H7
Wrose C Brad..................... 149 L8
Wrotham Kent...................... 52 D7
Wrotham Heath Kent................ 52 D7
Wrottesley Staffs................. 97 J3
Wroughton Swindn.................. 47 H3
Wroxall IoW....................... 19 J7
Wroxall Warwks.................... 82 F1
Wroxeter Shrops................... 96 D2
Wroxham Norfk.................... 122 H8
Wroxton Oxon...................... 83 K7
Wyaston Derbys................... 115 K3
Wyatt's Green Essex............... 70 F7
Wyberton East Lincs.............. 119 K3

Wyberton West Lincs.............. 119 J3
Wyboston Bed...................... 86 D4
Wybunbury Ches E................. 113 M2
Wychbold Worcs.................... 81 L2
Wych Cross E Susx................. 38 C7
Wychnor Staffs................... 115 K8
Wyck Hants........................ 35 M3
Wyck Rissington Gloucs............ 65 J3
Wycliffe Dur..................... 168 E7
Wycoller Lancs................... 149 G8
Wycomb Leics..................... 117 K6
Wycombe Marsh Bucks............... 67 L8
Wyddial Herts..................... 69 K1
Wye Kent.......................... 40 D6
Wyesham Mons...................... 63 G5
Wyfordby Leics................... 117 L7
Wyke C Brad...................... 141 J2
Wyke Devon........................ 13 K3
Wyke Devon........................ 15 G3
Wyke Dorset....................... 32 D5
Wyke Shrops....................... 96 E3
Wyke Surrey....................... 50 A8
Wyke Champflower Somset........... 31 L4
Wykeham N York................... 163 H6
Wyken Covtry...................... 99 K7
Wyken Shrops...................... 97 H4
Wyke Regis Dorset................. 16 C7
Wykey Shrops..................... 112 F6
Wykin Leics....................... 99 L4
Wylam Nthumb..................... 180 D6
Wylde Green Birm.................. 98 E4
Wylye Wilts....................... 33 H3
Wymeswold Leics.................. 117 G6
Wymington Bed..................... 85 J2
Wymondham Leics.................. 117 M7
Wymondham Norfk.................. 106 C3
Wyndham Brdgnd.................... 42 E3
Wynford Eagle Dorset.............. 16 B3
Wynyard Park S on T.............. 169 L5
Wynyard Village S on T........... 169 L5
Wyre Forest Crematorium
    Worcs......................... 97 J8
Wyre Piddle Worcs................. 81 M5
Wysall Notts..................... 117 G6
Wyson Herefs...................... 80 C2
Wythall Worcs..................... 98 D8
Wytham Oxon....................... 66 C5
Wythburn Cumb.................... 165 K7
Wythenshawe Manch................ 131 G2
Wythop Mill Cumb................. 165 G5
Wyton Cambs....................... 86 F1
Wyton E R Yk..................... 144 F1
Wyverstone Suffk.................. 90 B2
Wyverstone Street Suffk........... 89 L2
Wyville Lincs.................... 118 A5

Y

Yaddlethorpe N Linc.............. 143 M6
Yafford IoW....................... 19 G7
Yafforth N York.................. 160 E4
Yalberton Torbay................... 8 C3
Yalding Kent...................... 39 H3
Yanwath Cumb..................... 166 C5
Yanworth Gloucs................... 65 G4
Yapham E R Yk.................... 152 B5
Yapton W Susx..................... 21 G6
Yarborough N Som.................. 44 D7
Yarbridge IoW..................... 19 K6
Yarburgh Lincs................... 136 F1
Yarcombe Devon.................... 14 F1
Yard Devon........................ 28 D6
Yardley Birm...................... 98 E6
Yardley Crematorium Birm.......... 98 E6
Yardley Gobion Nhants............. 84 E6
Yardley Hastings Nhants........... 85 G4
Yardley Wood Birm................. 98 E7
Yardro Powys...................... 79 J3
Yarford Somset.................... 30 B5
Yarkhill Herefs................... 80 E6
Yarley Somset..................... 31 H2
Yarlington Somset................. 31 L5
Yarm S on T...................... 169 L8
Yarmouth IoW...................... 18 E5
Yarnacott Devon................... 27 L6
Yarnbrook Wilts................... 46 C7
Yarner Devon...................... 13 H7
Yarnfield Staffs................. 114 D5
Yarnscombe Devon.................. 27 K6
Yarnton Oxon...................... 66 C5
Yarpole Herefs.................... 80 B2
Yarrow Border.................... 200 D7
Yarrow Somset..................... 30 L2
Yarrow Feus Border............... 200 D7
Yarrowford Border................ 200 E7
Yarsop Herefs..................... 80 A6
Yarwell Nhants................... 102 B4

Yate S Glos....................... 45 L3
Yateley Hants..................... 49 K6
Yatesbury Wilts................... 46 F4
Yattendon W Berk.................. 48 E4
Yatton Herefs..................... 80 A2
Yatton N Som...................... 44 E6
Yatton Keynell Wilts.............. 46 C4
Yaverland IoW..................... 19 K6
Yawl Devon........................ 15 H4
Yawthorpe Lincs.................. 135 H1
Yaxham Norfk..................... 105 K1
Yaxley Cambs..................... 102 D5
Yaxley Suffk..................... 106 C8
Yazor Herefs...................... 79 M6
Yeading Gt Lon.................... 50 E3
Yeadon Leeds..................... 150 B7
Yealand Conyers Lancs............ 157 H7
Yealand Redmayne Lancs........... 157 H7
Yealand Storrs Lancs............. 157 H7
Yealmbridge Devon.................. 7 H4
Yealmpton Devon.................... 7 H4
Yearby R & Cl.................... 170 E6
Yearngill Cumb................... 164 F2
Yearsley N York.................. 161 J7
Yeaton Shrops.................... 113 G7
Yeaveley Derbys.................. 115 K3
Yeavering Nthumb................. 202 E7
Yedingham N York................. 162 F6
Yelford Oxon...................... 66 A6
Yell Shet........................ 281 e3
Yelland Devon..................... 27 J4
Yelling Cambs..................... 86 F3
Yelvertoft Nhants................ 100 D8
Yelverton Devon.................... 7 G1
Yelverton Norfk.................. 106 F3
Yenston Somset.................... 32 B6
Yeoford Devon..................... 13 H3
Yeolmbridge Cnwll................. 11 L5
Yeo Mill Devon.................... 28 E5
Yeo Vale Devon.................... 27 G6
Yeovil Somset..................... 31 J7
Yeovil Crematorium Somset......... 31 H7
Yeovil Marsh Somset............... 31 J7
Yeovilton Somset.................. 31 J6
Yerbeston Pembks.................. 55 H5
Yesnaby Ork...................... 275 b4
Yetlington Nthumb................ 190 E4
Yetminster Dorset................. 31 K8
Yetson Devon....................... 8 B4
Yettington Devon.................. 14 B5
Yetts o'Muckhart Clacks.......... 221 H6
Yews Green C Brad................ 141 H2
Yew Tree Sandw.................... 98 C4
Y Felinheli Gwynd................ 125 J6
Y Ferwig Cerdgn................... 75 L2
Y Ffor Gwynd..................... 109 G4
Y Gyffylliog Denbgs.............. 128 C8
Yielden Bed....................... 85 K2
Yieldingtree Worcs................ 97 K7
Yieldshields S Lans.............. 198 E3
Yiewsley Gt Lon................... 50 D3
Y Maerdy Conwy................... 111 K3
Y Nant Wrexhm.................... 112 D2
Ynysboeth Rhondd.................. 43 G3
Ynysddu Caerph.................... 43 J3
Ynysforgan Swans.................. 57 J5
Ynyshir Rhondd.................... 42 F3
Ynyslas Cerdgn.................... 92 D5
Ynysmaerdy Rhondd................. 42 F5
Ynysmeudwy Neath.................. 57 K4
Ynystawe Swans.................... 57 J5
Ynyswen Powys..................... 60 C4
Ynyswen Rhondd.................... 42 E2
Ynysybwl Rhondd................... 43 G3
Ynysymaengwyn Gwynd............... 92 D3
Yockenthwaite N York............. 158 F6
Yockleton Shrops.................. 95 K2
Yokefleet E R Yk................. 143 K3
Yoker C Glas..................... 208 E5
York C York...................... 151 J5
York Lancs....................... 139 L1
York City Crematorium C York 151 J6
Yorkletts Kent.................... 40 E3
Yorkley Gloucs.................... 63 J5
York Town Surrey.................. 49 L7
Yorton Heath Shrops.............. 113 H7
Youlgreave Derbys................ 132 D6
Youlthorpe E R Yk................ 152 B5
Youlton N York................... 151 G3
Youngsbury Herts.................. 69 K3
Young's End Essex................. 71 H3
Yoxall Staffs.................... 115 J7
Yoxford Suffk..................... 91 J2
Y Rhiw Gwynd..................... 108 D6
Ysbyty Cynfyn Cerdgn.............. 93 G7
Ysbyty Ifan Conwy................ 110 F2
Ysbyty Ystwyth Cerdgn............. 77 K1
Ysceifiog Flints................. 128 D5
Ysgubor-y-Coed Cerdgn............. 92 E4

Ystalyfera Neath.................. 57 L3
Ystrad Rhondd..................... 42 F3
Ystrad Aeron Cerdgn............... 76 F4
Ystradfellte Powys................ 60 D4
Ystrad Ffin Carmth................ 77 L6
Ystradgynlais Powys............... 60 B5
Ystrad Meurig Cerdgn.............. 77 K2
Ystrad Mynach Caerph.............. 43 J3
Ystradowen V Glam................. 42 F6
Ystumtuen Cerdgn.................. 92 F7
Ythanbank Abers.................. 257 G5
Ythanwells Abers................. 256 B4
Ythsie Abers..................... 256 F5

Z

Zeal Monachorum Devon............. 13 G2
Zeals Wilts....................... 32 C4
Zelah Cnwll........................ 4 C4
Zennor Cnwll....................... 2 C3
Zoar Cnwll......................... 3 J7
Zouch Notts...................... 116 E6

Map pages north

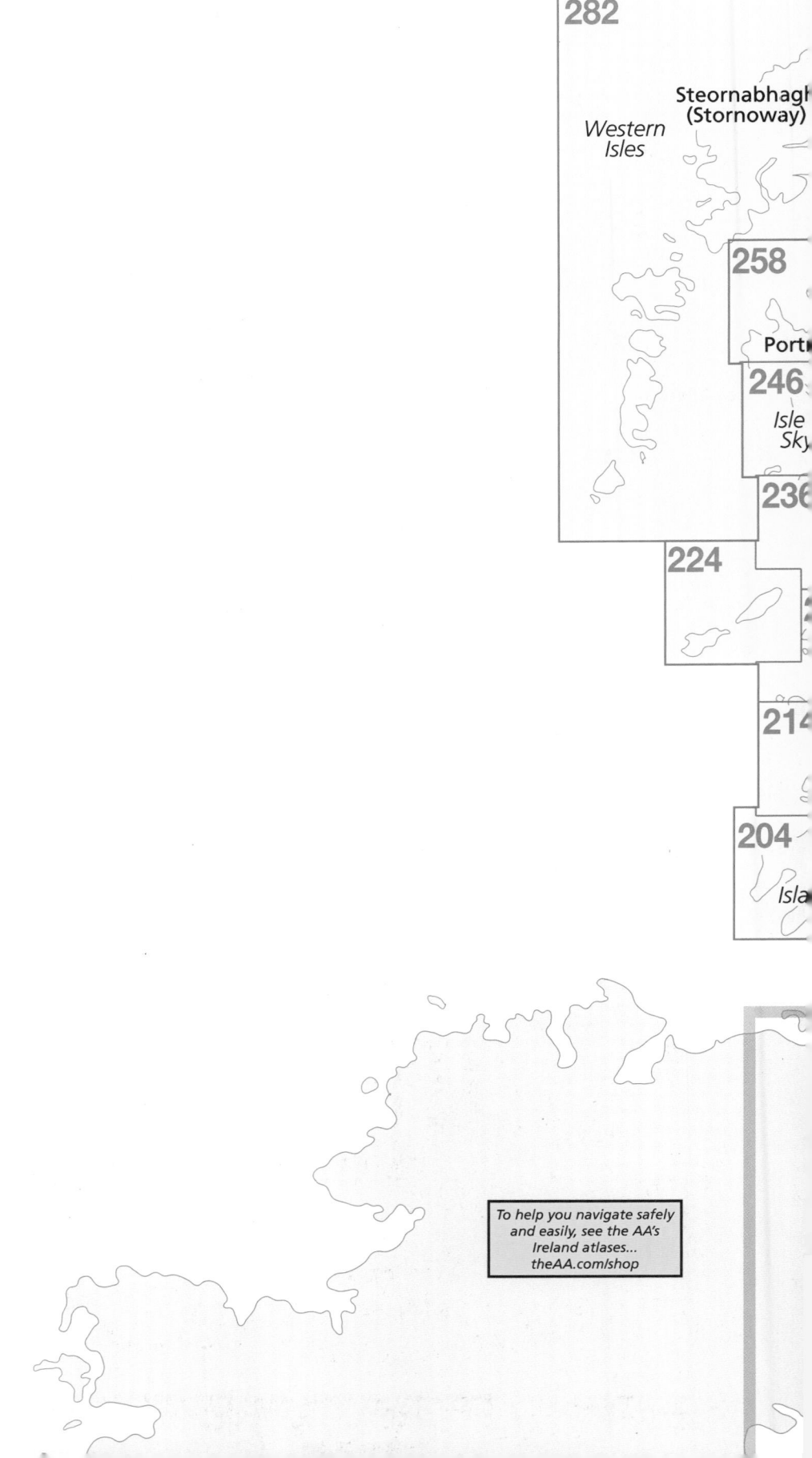

282

Steornabhagh
(Stornoway)

Western
Isles

258

Port

246

Isle
Sky

236

224

214

204

Isla

To help you navigate safely
and easily, see the AA's
Ireland atlases...
theAA.com/shop